rctic Ocean

FINLAND

Helsinki ■

■ Tallinn

EST.

Riga ■

LAT.

LITH.

Vilnius ■

■ Minsk

BELARUS

■ Warsaw

AND

OVAKIA

ratislava

■ Budapest

NGARY

eb

ROMANIA

A

■ Belgrade

NIA

OSLAVIA

■ Sofia

Skopje ■

BULGARIA

rana ■ ■ FYROM.

ALB.

GREECE

Athens ■

Crete

CYPRUS

rranean Sea

LIBYA

R U S S I A

■ Moscow

■ Kiev

UKRAINE

Dnieper R.

MOLDOVA

■ Chisinau

■ Bucharest

Don R.

Volga R.

KAZAKHSTAN

Caspian Sea

Black Sea

GEORGIA

Tbilisi ■

ARM.

Yerevan ■

Baku ■

AZER.

■ Ankara

TURKEY

Tigris R.

Euphrates

Teheran ■

CYPRUS

LEB.

Beirut ■

SYRIA

Damascus ■

Baghdad ■

IRAN

ISR.

Jerusalem ■

■ Amman

JOR.

IRAQ

R.

Cairo ■

Kuwait ■

KUWAIT

SAUDI

ARABIA

EGYPT

Nile R.

QATAR

www.wadsworth.com

wadsworth.com is the World Wide Web site for Wadsworth Publishing Company and is your direct source to dozens of online resources.

At *wadsworth.com* you can find out about supplements, demonstration software, and student resources. You can also send e-mail to many of our authors and preview new publications and exciting new technologies.

wadsworth.com
Changing the way the world learns®

WESTERN CIVILIZATION

A Brief History

JACKSON J. SPIELVOGEL

The Pennsylvania State University

West/Wadsworth
I(T)P® An International Thomson Publishing Company

Belmont, CA • Albany, NY • Boston • Cincinnati • Johannesburg • London
Madrid • Melbourne • Mexico City • New York • Pacific Grove, CA • Scottsdale, AZ • Singapore • Tokyo • Toronto

History Editor: Clark Baxter
Senior Development Editor: Sharon Adams Poore
Editorial Assistant: Melissa Gleason
Marketing Manager: Jay Hu
Print Buyer: Barbara Britton
Permissions Manager: Susan Walters
Production: Lori Harvey, Carlisle Publishers Services
Designer: Diane Beasley
Copy Editor: Lorretta Palagi
Maps: GeoSystems
Cover Design: Diane Beasley
Cover Image: The Middle Ages was an era of technological advances. This illustration from a medieval manuscript shows a mechanical clock, one of the more inventive creations of the Middle Ages. Bibliotheque Nationale, Paris.
Compositor: Carlisle Communications, Ltd.
Printer: World Color/Taunton

Printed in the United States of America
3 4 5 6 7 8 9 10

For more information, contact Wadsworth Publishing Company, 10 Davis Drive, Belmont, CA 94002, or electronically at http://www.wadsworth.com

International Thomson Publishing Europe
Berkshire House
168-173 High Holborn
London, WC1V 7AA, United Kingdom

Nelson ITP, Australia
102 Dodds Street
South Melbourne
Victoria 3205 Australia

Nelson Canada
1120 Birchmount Road
Scarborough, Ontario
Canada M1K 5G4

International Thomson Publishing Southern Africa
Building 18, Constantia Square
138 Sixteenth Road, P.O. Box 2459
Halfway House, 1685 South Africa

International Thomson Editores
Seneca, 53
Colonia Polanco
11560 México D.F. México

International Thomson Publishing Asia
60 Albert Street
#15-01 Albert Complex
Singapore 189969

International Thomson Publishing Japan
Hirakawa-cho Kyowa Building, 3F
2-2-1 Hirakawa-cho, Chiyoda-ku
Tokyo 102 Japan

Library of Congress Cataloging-in-Publication Data
Spielvogel, Jackson J., 1939–
    Western civilization : a brief history / Jackson J. Spielvogel.
      p.   cm.
    Includes bibliographical references and index.
    ISBN 0-534-56061-X (alk. paper)
    1. Civilization, Western—History. I. Title.
CB245.S63   1999
909'.09821—dc21   98–39741

About the Author

Jackson J. Spielvogel is associate professor of history at The Pennsylvania State University. He received his Ph.D. from The Ohio State University, where he specialized in Reformation history under Harold J. Grimm. His articles and reviews have appeared in such journals as Moreana, Journal of General Education, Catholic Historical Review, Archiv für Reformationsgeschichte, *and* American Historical Review. *He has also contributed chapters or articles to* The Social History of the Reformation, The Holy Roman Empire: A Dictionary Handbook, Simon Wiesenthal Center Annual of Holocaust Studies, *and* Utopian Studies. *His work has been supported by fellowships from the Fulbright Foundation and the Foundation for Reformation Research. At Penn State, he helped inaugurate the Western civilization courses as well as a popular course on Nazi Germany. His book* Hitler and Nazi Germany *was published in 1987 (third edition, 1996). He is the co-author (with William Duiker) of* World History, *published in January 1994. Professor Spielvogel has won three major university-wide teaching awards. During the year 1988–1989, he held the Penn State Teaching Fellowship, the university's most prestigious teaching award. In 1996, he won the Dean Arthur Ray Warnock Award for Outstanding Faculty Member.*

◆

*To Diane,
whose love and support made it all possible*

Contents

CHAPTER 16

✦✦✦✦✦✦✦✦✦✦

Response to Crisis: State Building and the Search for Order in the Seventeenth Century 326

CHAPTER 17

✦✦✦✦✦✦✦✦✦✦

Toward a New Heaven and a New Earth: The Scientific Revolution and the Emergence of Modern Science 348

CHAPTER 18

✦✦✦✦✦✦✦✦✦✦

The Eighteenth Century: An Age of Enlightenment 366

CHAPTER 23

✦✦✦✦✦✦✦✦✦✦

An Age of Nationalism and Realism, 1850–1871   468

CHAPTER 24

✦✦✦✦✦✦✦✦✦✦

Mass Society in an "Age of Progress," 1871–1894   490

CHAPTER 25

✦✦✦✦✦✦✦✦✦✦

An Age of Modernity and Anxiety, 1894–1914   512

CHAPTER 26
◆◆◆◆◆◆◆◆◆◆◆

The Beginning of the Twentieth-Century Crisis: War and Revolution   536

CHAPTER 27
◆◆◆◆◆◆◆◆◆◆◆

The Futile Search for a New Stability: Europe Between the Wars, 1919–1939   558

CHAPTER 28
◆◆◆◆◆◆◆◆◆◆◆

The Deepening of the European Crisis: World War II   580

CHAPTER 29

Cold War and a New Western World, 1945–1970   604

CHAPTER 30

The Contemporary Western World (Since 1970)   628

Documents

We are grateful to the authors and publishers acknowledged here for their permission to reprint copyrighted material. We have made every reasonable effort to identify copyright owners of materials in the boxed documents. If any information is found to be incomplete, we will gladly make whatever additional acknowledgements might be necessary.

Maps

Chronologies

Preface

We are often reminded how important it is to understand today's world if we are to deal with our growing number of challenges. And yet that understanding will be incomplete if we in the Western world do not comprehend the meaning of Western civilization and the role Western civilization has played in the world. For all of our modern progress, we still greatly reflect our religious traditions, our political systems and theories, our economic and social structures, and our cultural heritage. I have written this brief history of Western civilization to assist a new generation of students in learning more about the past that has helped create them and the world in which they live.

I began this project with two primary goals. First, I wanted to write a well-balanced work in which the political, economic, social, religious, intellectual, cultural, and military aspects of Western civilization would be integrated into a chronologically ordered synthesis. Second, I wanted to avoid the approach that is quite common in other brief histories of Western civilization—an approach that makes them collections of facts with little continuity from section to section. Instead, I sought to keep the story in history. Narrative history effectively transmits the knowledge of the past and is the form that best enables students to remember and understand the past. At the same time, I have not overlooked the need for the kind of historical analysis that makes students aware that historians often disagree in their interpretations of the past.

To enliven the past and let readers see for themselves the materials that historians use to create their pictures of the past, I have included in each chapter primary sources (boxed documents) that are keyed to the discussion in the text. The documents include examples of the religious, artistic, intellectual, social, economic, and political aspects of Western life. Such varied sources as a Roman banquet menu, advice from a Carolingian mother to her son, marriage negotiations in Renaissance Italy, the diary of a German soldier at Stalingrad, and a debate in the Reformation era all reveal in a vivid fashion what Western civilization meant to the individual men and women who shaped it by their activities.

Each chapter has a lengthy introduction and conclusion to help maintain the continuity of the narrative and to provide a synthesis of important themes. Anecdotes in the chapter introductions convey more dramatically the major theme or themes of each chapter. Detailed chronologies reinforce the events discussed in the text while timelines at the beginning of each chapter enable students to see at a glance the major developments of an era. An annotated bibliography at the end of each chapter reviews the most recent literature on each period and also gives references to some of the older, "classic" works in each field. Extensive maps and illustrations serve to deepen the reader's understanding of the text. To facilitate understanding of cultural movements, illustrations of artistic works discussed in the text are placed next to the discussions.

Because courses in Western civilization at American and Canadian colleges and universities follow different chronological divisions, a one-volume edition and a two-volume edition of this text are being made available to fit the needs of instructors. Teaching and learning ancillaries include the following:

For Instructors: Instructor's Manual/Test Bank—contains chapter outlines, suggested lecture topics, discussion questions for the primary documents, map and art discussion questions. Suggested films, music, and readings are included to spice up lectures. Examination questions include essay, identification, multiple choice, and true/false questions. By Kevin Robbins, Indiana University-Purdue University Indianapolis, available in one volume only.

Thomson World Class Testing Tools—is a fully-integrated suite of test creation, delivery and classroom management tools. The package includes: World Class Test, Test Online, and World Class Manager software.

Western Civilization Map Acetates—this extensive four color acetate package includes maps from the text and from other sources and includes map commentary prepared by James Harrison, Siena College. The acetates and commentary are packaged in a three ring binder.

Western Civilization Powerpoint—contains all the four color maps from the map acetate package, described above.

Color Map Slides—approximately 100 full color slides feature all the texts maps as well as images from other sources. Commentary is also provided.

Sights and Sounds of History Videodisk—contains short, focused video clips, photos, artwork, animations, music and dramatic readings that bring history to life. Video segments averaging four minutes in length are available on VHS. These segments make excellent lecture launchers.

Western Civilization Video Library—ask your local sales representative for details and qualifications.

For Students: **Study Guide**—prepared by James Baker, Western Kentucky University, contains chapter outlines, chapter summaries, and seven different types of exercises for each chapter. The exercises include: words to identify, words to match with their definitions, multiple choice questions, sentences to complete, chronological arrangements, questions for critical thought, and analysis of primary source documents. Map exercises appear at the end of many chapters. Available in volumes I and II that correspond with volumes I and II of the text.

Study Tips—prepared by James Baker, Western Kentucky University, contains brief chapter outlines, key terms, questions for critical thought and questions on primary documents for each chapter. Available in volumes I and II that correspond with volumes I and II of the text.

Document Exercises Workbook—prepared by Donna Van Raaphorst, Cuyahoga Community College, is a two-volume collection of exercises based around primary sources, teaching students how to use documents and historiographic methods.

Map Exercise Workbook—prepared by Cynthia Kosso, Northern Arizona University, is a two-volume workbook, each featuring over 20 map exercises. The exercises are designed to help students understand the relationship between places and people through time. All map exercises incorporate three parts: an introduction, a locations section where students are asked to correctly place a city, site, or boundary, and a question section.

Western Civilization Canadian Supplement—prepared by Maryann Farkus, Dawson College, Montreal, is a 30 page supplement for students that discusses Canadian history and culture in the context of Western civilization. Material is linked to chapters of Spielvogel.

Journey of Civilization CD-Rom: This exciting Windows CD-Rom takes the student on 18 interactive journeys through history. Enhanced with Quicktime movies, animations, sound clips, maps, and more, the journeys allow students to engage in history as active participants rather than as readers of past events.

Archer, Documents of Western Civilization, Volume I: To 1715

Archer, Documents of Western Civilization, Volume II: Since 1300

For Both: **Internet Guide for History**—prepared by Daniel Kurland and John Soares. Section One introduces students to the internet including tips for searching on the Web. Section Two introduces students to how history research can be done and lists URL sites by topic.

Web Page

Acknowledgments

I would like to thank the many teachers and students who have used the first three editions of my *Western Civilization*. I am gratified by their enthusiastic response to a textbook that was intended to put the story back in history and capture the imagination of the reader. I especially thank the many teachers and students who made the effort to contact me personally to share their enthusiasm. I continue to be grateful to the many historians who reviewed the three editions of *Western Civilization*, but I also want to thank the following who made suggestions for this new brief history of Western Civilization:

Dieter Buse, Laurentian University
Don R. Fisher, Albuquerque Technical-Vocational Community College
Stephen C. Govedich, Yavapai College
Robert E. Herzstein, University of South Carolina
Daniel W. Hollis, III, Jacksonville State University
Paul W. Knoll, University of Southern California
Clayton Lehmann, University of South Dakota
Chris Oldstone-Moore, Augustana College
Matthew Redinger, Montana State University-Billings
Fiona Stoertz, Trent University

The editors at Wadsworth Publishing Company have been both helpful and congenial at all times. Hal Humphrey guided the overall production of the book with much insight. I especially with to thank Clark Baxter, whose clever wit, wisdom, gentle prodding, and good friendship have added much depth to our working relationship. Sharon Adams Poore thoughtfully guided the preparation of outstanding teaching and learning ancillaries. Lori Harvey, of Carlisle Publishers Services, was cooperative and competent in the production of the book.

Above all, I thank my family for their support. The gifts of love, laughter, and patience from my daughters Jennifer and Kathryn, my sons Eric and Christian, and my daughters-in-law Liz and Michelle were invaluable. My wife and best friend Diane contributed editorial assistance, wise counsel, humor, and the loving support that made it possible to complete yet another writing project. I could not have written the book without her.

Introduction to Students of Western Civilization

Civilization, as historians define it, first emerged between 5,000 and 6,000 years ago when people began to live in organized communities with distinct political, military, economic, and social structures. Religious, intellectual, and artistic activities also assumed important roles in these early societies. The focus of this book is on Western civilization, a civilization that for most of its history has been identified with the continent of Europe. Its origins, however, go back to the Mediterranean basin, including lands in North Africa, and the Near East as well as Europe itself. Moreover, the spread of Europeans abroad led to the development of offshoots of Western civilization in other parts of the world.

Because civilized life includes all the deeds and experiences of people organized in communities, the history of a civilization must encompass a series of studies. An examination of Western civilization requires us to study the political, economic, social, military, cultural, intellectual, and religious aspects that make up the life of that civilization and show how they are interrelated. In so doing, we need also at times to focus on some of the unique features of Western civilization. Certainly, science played a crucial role in the development of modern Western civilization. Although such societies as those of the Greeks, the Romans, and medieval Europeans were based largely on a belief in the existence of a spiritual order, Western civilization experienced a dramatic departure to a natural or material view of the universe in the seventeenth-century Scientific Revolution. Science and technology have been important in the growth of a modern and largely secular Western civilization, although antecedents to scientific development also existed in Greek, Islamic, and medieval thought and practice.

Many historians have also viewed the concept of political liberty, the fundamental value of every individual, and the creation of a rational outlook, based on a system of log-ical, analytical thought, as unique aspects of Western civilization. Of course, Western civilization has also witnessed the frightening negation of liberty, individualism, and reason. Racism, violence, world wars, totalitarianism—these, too, must form part of the story. Finally, regardless of our concentration on Western civilization and its characteristics, we need to take into account that other civilizations have influenced Western civilization and it, in turn, has affected the development of other civilizations.

In our examination of Western civilization, we need also to be aware of the dating of time. In recording the past, historians try to determine the exact time when events occurred. World War II in Europe, for example, began on September 1, 1939, when Hitler sent German troops into Poland, and ended on May 7, 1945, when Germany surrendered. By using dates, historians can place events in order and try to determine the development of patterns over periods of time.

If someone asked you when you were born, you would reply with a number, such as 1980. In the United States, we would all accept that number without question because it is part of the dating system followed in the Western world (Europe and the Western Hemisphere). In this system, events are dated by counting backward or forward from the birth of Christ (assumed to be the year 1). An event that took place 400 years before the birth of Christ would be dated 400 B.C. (before Christ). Dates after the birth of Christ are labeled A.D. These letters stand for the Latin words *anno Domini*, which mean "in the year of the lord." Thus, an event that took place 250 years after the birth of Christ is written A.D. 250, or in the year of the lord 250. It can also be written as 250, just as you would not give your birth year as A.D. 1980, but simply 1980.

Historians also make use of other terms to refer to time. A decade is 10 years; a century is 100 years; and a millennium is 1,000 years. The phrase fourth century B.C. refers to the fourth period of 100 years counting backward from 1, the assumed date of the birth of Christ. Since the first century B.C. would be the years 100 B.C. to 1 B.C., the fourth century B.C. would be the years 400 B.C. to 301 B.C. We could say, then, that an event in 350 B.C. took place in the fourth century B.C.

The phrase fourth century A.D. refers to the fourth period of 100 years after the birth of Christ. Since the first period of 100 years would be the years 1 to 100, the fourth period or fourth century would be the years 301 to 400. We could say, then, for example, that an event in 350 took place in the fourth century. Likewise, the first millennium B.C. refers to the years 1000 B.C. to 1 B.C.; the second millennium A.D. refers to the years 1001 to 2000.

Some historians now prefer to use the abbreviations B.C.E. ("before the common era") and C.E. ("common era") instead of B.C. and A.D. This is especially true of world historians who prefer to use symbols that are not so Western or Christian oriented. The dates, of course, remain the same. Thus, 1950 B.C.E. and 1950 B.C. would be the same year. In keeping with current usage by many historians of Western civilization, this book will use the terms B.C. and A.D.

The dating of events can also vary from people to people. Most people in the Western world use the Western calendar, also known as the Gregorian calendar after Pope Gregory XIII who refined it in 1582. The Hebrew calendar, on the other hand, uses a different system in which the year 1 is the equivalent of the Western year 3760 B.C., considered by Jews to be the date of the creation of the world. Thus, the Western year 2000 will be the year 5760 on the Jewish calendar. The Islamic calendar begins year 1 on the day Muhammad fled Mecca, which is the year 622 on the Western calendar.

WESTERN CIVILIZATION

A Brief History

The Ancient Near East: The First Civilizations

In 1849, a daring young Englishman made a hazardous journey into the deserts and swamps of southern Iraq. Moving south down the banks of the Euphrates River while braving high winds and temperatures that reached 120 degrees Fahrenheit, William Loftus led a small expedition in search of the roots of civilization. As he said, "From our childhood we have been led to regard this place as the cradle of the human race."

Guided by native Arabs into the southernmost reaches of Iraq, Loftus and his small group of explorers were soon overwhelmed by what they saw. He wrote, "I know of nothing more exciting or impressive than the first sight of one of these great piles, looming in solitary grandeur from the surrounding plains and marshes." One of these piles, known to the natives as the mound of Warka, contained the ruins of Uruk, one of the first cities in the world and part of the world's first civilization.

Southern Iraq, known to ancient peoples as Mesopotamia, was one of the four areas in the world where civilization began. In the fertile valleys of the Tigris and Euphrates, the Nile, the Indus, and the Yellow River, in Mesopotamia, Egypt, India, and China, intensive agriculture became capable of supporting large groups of people. In these regions the first civilizations were born. The beginnings of Western civilization can be traced back to the ancient Near East, where people in Mesopotamia and Egypt developed organized societies and created the ideas and institutions that we associate with civilization. The later Greeks and Romans, who played such a crucial role in the development of Western civilization, were themselves nourished and influenced by these older societies in the Near East. It is appropriate, therefore, to begin our story of Western civilization in the ancient Near East with the early civilizations of Mesopotamia and Egypt. Before considering them, however, we must briefly examine humankind's prehistory and observe how human beings made the shift from hunting and gathering to agricultural communities and ultimately to cities and civilization.

Emergence of Sumerian city-states

Babylonian Kingdom

Emergence of
Egyptian civilization

Egypt—Old Kingdom

Egypt—Middle Kingdom

Egypt—New Kingdom

Beginning of cuneiform

Code of Hammurabi

Great Pyramid

Akhenaten's religious upheaval

The First Humans

Historians rely primarily on documents to create their pictures of the past, but no written records exist for the prehistory of humankind. In their absence, the story of early humanity depends on archaeological and, more recently, biological information, which anthropologists and archaeologists use to formulate theories about our early past.

The earliest humanlike creatures—known as hominids—lived in Africa as long as three to four million years ago. Known as Australopithecines, they flourished in East and South Africa and were the first hominids to make simple stone tools.

A second stage in early human development occurred around 1.5 million years ago when *Homo erectus* ("upright human being") emerged. *Homo erectus* made use of larger and more varied tools and was the first hominid to leave Africa and to move into both Europe and Asia.

Around 250,000 years ago, a third—and crucial—stage in human development began with the emergence of *Homo sapiens* ("wise human being"). By 100,000 B.C., two groups of *Homo sapiens* had developed. One type was the Neanderthal, whose remains were first found in the Neander valley in Germany. Neanderthal remains have since been found in both Europe and the Middle East and have been dated to between 100,000 and 30,000 B.C. Neanderthals relied on a variety of stone tools and were the first early people to bury their dead.

The first anatomically modern humans, known as *Homo sapiens sapiens* ("wise, wise human being") appeared in Africa between 200,000 and 150,000 years ago. Recent evidence indicates that they began to spread outside Africa around 100,000 years ago. Map 1.1 on p. 4 shows probable dates for different movements, although many of these are still controversial. By 30,000 B.C., *Homo sapiens sapiens* had replaced the Neanderthals, who had largely become extinct, and by 10,000 B.C., members of the *Homo sapiens sapiens* species could be found throughout the world. By that time, it was the only human species left. All humans today, be they Europeans, Australian aborigines, or Africans, belong to the same subspecies of human being.

The Hunter-Gatherers of the Old Stone Age

One of the basic distinguishing features of the human species is the ability to make tools. The earliest tools were made of stone, and the term *Paleolithic* (Greek for "old stone") Age is used to designate this early period of human history (c. 2,500,000–10,000 B.C.).

For hundreds of thousands of years, humans relied on hunting and gathering for their daily food. Paleolithic peoples had a close relationship with the world around them, and over a period of time, they came to know which animals to hunt and which plants to eat. They did not know how to grow crops or raise animals, however. They gathered wild nuts, berries, fruits, and a variety of wild grains and green plants. Around the world, they hunted and consumed different animals, including buffalo, horses, bison, wild goats, and reindeer. In coastal areas, fish provided a rich source of food.

The hunting of animals and the gathering of wild plants no doubt led to certain patterns of living. Archaeologists and anthropologists have speculated that Paleolithic people lived in small bands of twenty or thirty people. They were nomadic (they moved from place to place) since they had no choice but to follow animal to the camps, but they played an important role in acquiring food by gathering berries, nuts, and grains. Men hunted the wild animals, an activity that took them far from camp. Because both men and women played important roles in providing for the band's survival, scientists have argued that a rough equality existed between men and women. Indeed, some speculate that both men and women made the decisions that affected the activities of the Paleolithic band.

These groups of Paleolithic peoples, especially those who lived in cold climates, found shelter in caves. Over time, they created new types of shelter as well. Perhaps the most common was a simple structure of wood poles or sticks covered with animal hides. The systematic use of fire, which archaeologists believe began around 500,000 years ago, made it possible for the caves and human-made structures to have a source of light and heat. Fire also enabled early humans to cook their food, making it better tasting, longer lasting, and, in the case of some plants, such as wild grain, easier to chew and digest.

The making of tools and the use of fire—two important technological innovations of Paleolithic peoples—remind us how crucial the ability to adapt was to human survival. But Paleolithic peoples did more than just survive. The cave paintings of large animals found in south-

migrations and vegetation cycles. Hunting depended on careful observation of animal behavior patterns and required a group effort to achieve any real degree of success. Over the years, tools became more refined and more useful. The invention of the spear, and later the bow and arrow, made hunting considerably easier. Harpoons and fishhooks made of bone increased the catch of fish.

Both men and women were responsible for finding food—the chief work of Paleolithic people. Since women bore and raised the children, they generally stayed close

Map 1.1 The Spread of *Homo Sapiens Sapiens*.

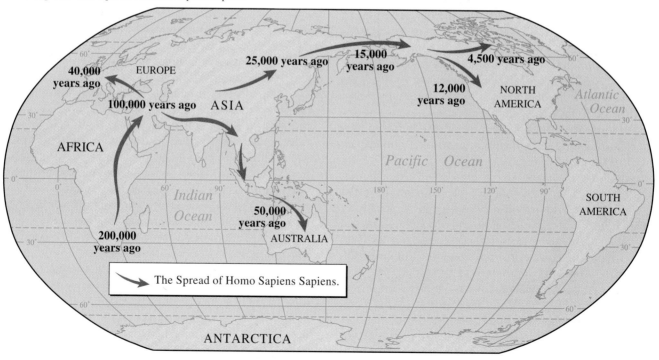

western France and northern Spain bear witness to the cultural activity of Paleolithic peoples. A cave discovered in southern France in 1994 contains more than 300 paintings of lions, oxen, owls, panthers, and other animals. Most of these are animals that Paleolithic people did not hunt, which suggests that they were painted for religious or even decorative purposes.

The Agricultural Revolution, c. 10,000–4000 B.C.

The end of the last ice age around 10,000 B.C. was followed by what is called the Neolithic Revolution; that is, the revolution that occurred in the New Stone Age (the word *Neolithic* is Greek for "new stone"). The name New Stone Age is misleading, however. Although Neolithic peoples made a new type of polished stone axe, this was not the major change that occurred after 10,000 B.C.

The real change was the shift from hunting animals and gathering plants for sustenance to producing food by systematic agriculture. The planting of grains and vegetables provided a regular supply of food while the taming of animals, such as sheep, goats, cattle, and pigs, added a steady source of meat, milk, and fibers such as wool for clothing. Larger animals could also be used as beasts of burden. The growing of crops and the taming of food-producing animals created a new relationship between humans and nature. Historians like to speak of this as an agricultural revolution. Revolutionary change is dramatic and requires great effort, but the ability to acquire food on a regular basis gave humans greater control over their environment. It also enabled them to give up their nomadic ways of life and begin to live in settled communities.

Systematic agriculture probably developed independently between 8000 and 7000 B.C. in four different areas of the world. In each of these areas, different plants were cultivated: wheat, barley, and lentils in the Near East, rice and millet in southern Asia, millet and yams in western Africa, and beans, potatoes, and corn in the middle Americas. In the Near East as elsewhere, the Neolithic agricultural revolution needed a favorable environment. The upland areas above the Fertile Crescent (present-day northern Iraq and southern Turkey) were initially more conducive to systematic farming than the river valleys. This region received the necessary rainfall and was the home of two wild plant (barley, wheat) and four wild animal (pigs, cows, goats, sheep) species that humans eventually domesticated for their use.

The growing of crops on a regular basis gave rise to more permanent settlements, which historians refer to as

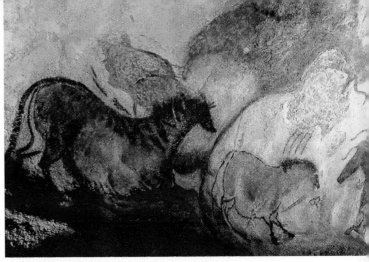

✦ **Paleolithic Cave Painting.** Cave paintings of large animals provide good examples of the cultural creativity of Paleolithic peoples. This scene is part of a large underground chamber found accidentally in 1940 at Lascaux, France, by some boys looking for their dog. This work is dated around 15,000 B.C.

Neolithic farming villages or towns. One of the oldest and most extensive agricultural villages was Çatal Hüyük, located in modern-day Turkey. Its walls enclosed thirty-two acres, and its population probably reached 6,000 inhabitants during its high point from 6700 to 5700 B.C. People lived in simple mudbrick houses that were built so close to one another that there were few streets. To get to their homes, people had to walk along the rooftops and then enter the house through a hole in the roof.

Archaeologists have discovered twelve cultivated products in Çatal Hüyük, including fruits, nuts, and three kinds of wheat. Artisans made weapons and jewelry that were traded with neighboring people. Religious shrines housing figures of gods and goddesses have been found at Çatal Hüyük, as have a number of female statuettes. Molded with noticeably large breasts and buttocks, these "earth-mothers" perhaps symbolically represented the fertility of both "our mother" earth and human mothers. Both the shrines and the statues point to the growing role of religion in the lives of these Neolithic peoples.

The Neolithic agricultural revolution had far-reaching consequences. Once people settled in villages or towns, they built houses for protection and other structures for the storage of goods. As organized communities stored food and accumulated material goods, they began to engage in trade. People also began to specialize in certain crafts, and a division of labor developed. Pottery was made from clay and baked in a fire to make it hard. The pots were used for cooking and to store grains. Woven baskets were also used for storage. Stone tools became refined as flint blades were used to make sickles and hoes for use in the fields. In the course of the Neolithic Age, many of the food plants still in use today began to be cultivated. Moreover, vegetable fibers from such plants as flax and cotton were used to make thread that was woven into cloth.

The change to systematic agriculture in the Neolithic Age also had consequences for the relationship between men and women. Men assumed the primary responsibility for working in the fields and herding animals, jobs that kept them away from the home. Women remained behind, caring for the children, weaving clothes, and performing other tasks that required much labor in one place. In time, as work outside the home was increasingly perceived as more important than work done at home, men came to play the more dominant role in society, a basic pattern that would persist until our own times.

Other patterns set in the Neolithic Age also proved to be enduring elements of human history. Fixed dwellings, domesticated animals, regular farming, a division of labor, men holding power, all of these are part of the human story. For all of our scientific and technological progress, human survival still depends on the growing and storing of food, an accomplishment of people in the Neolithic Age. The Neolithic Revolution was truly a turning point in human history.

Between 4000 and 3000 B.C., significant technical developments began to transform the Neolithic towns. The invention of writing enabled records to be kept, and the use of metals marked a new level of human control over the environment and its resources. Already before 4000 B.C., craftspeople had discovered that metal-bearing rocks could be heated to liquefy metals, which could then be cast in molds to produce tools and weapons that were more useful than stone instruments. Although copper was the first metal to be utilized in producing tools, after 4000 B.C., craftspeople in western Asia discovered that a combination of copper and tin created bronze, a much harder and more durable metal than copper. Its widespread use has led historians to speak of a Bronze Age from around 3000 to 1200 B.C., after which bronze was increasingly replaced by iron.

At first, Neolithic settlements were hardly more than villages. But as their inhabitants mastered the art of farming, they gradually began to give birth to more complex human societies. As wealth increased, such societies began to develop armies and to build walled cities. By the beginning of the Bronze Age, the concentration of larger numbers of people in the river valleys of Mesopotamia and Egypt was leading to a whole new pattern for human life.

The Emergence of Civilization

As we have seen, early human beings formed small groups that developed a simple culture that enabled them to survive. As human societies grew and developed greater complexity, a new form of human existence—called civilization—came into being. A civilization is a complex culture in which large numbers of human beings share a number of common elements. Historians have identified a number of basic characteristics of civilization. These include (1) an urban revolution: cities became the focal points for political, economic, social, cultural, and religious development; (2) a distinct religious structure: the gods were deemed crucial to the community's success, and professional priestly classes, as stewards of the gods' property, regulated relations with the gods; (3) new political and military structures: an organized government bureaucracy arose to meet the administrative demands of the growing population while armies were organized to gain land and power; (4) a new social structure based on economic power: while kings and an upper class of priests, political leaders, and warriors dominated, there also existed a large group of free men (farmers, artisans, craftspeople) and at the very bottom, socially, a class of slaves; (5) the development of writing: kings, priests, merchants, and artisans used writing to keep records; (6) new forms of significant artistic and intellectual activity: monumental architectural structures, usually religious, occupied a prominent place in urban environments; and (7) the development of more complexity in a material sense: capital was accumulated and metals smelted to produce a variety of material objects.

Why early civilizations developed remains difficult to explain. A theory of challenge and response maintains that challenges forced human beings to make efforts that resulted in the rise of civilization. Some scholars have argued that material forces, such as the growth of food surpluses, made possible the specialization of labor and development of large communities with bureaucratic organization. But some areas were not naturally conducive to agriculture. Abundant food could only be produced with a massive human effort to carefully manage the water, an effort that created the need for organization and led to civilized cities. Some historians have argued that nonmaterial forces, primarily religious, provided the sense of unity and purpose that made such organized activities possible. Finally, some scholars doubt that we are capable of ever discovering the actual causes of early civilization.

Civilization in Mesopotamia

The Greeks spoke of the valley between the Tigris and Euphrates Rivers as Mesopotamia, the land "between the rivers." The region receives little rain, but the soil of the plain of southern Mesopotamia was enlarged and enriched over the years by layers of silt deposited by the two rivers. In late spring, the Tigris and Euphrates overflow their banks and deposit their fertile silt, but since this flooding depends on the melting of snows in the upland mountains where the rivers begin, it is irregular and sometimes catastrophic. In such circumstances, farming could be accomplished only with human intervention in the form of irrigation and drainage ditches. A complex system was required to control the flow of the rivers and produce the crops. Large-scale irrigation made possible the expansion of agriculture in this region, and the abundant food provided the material base for the emergence of civilization in Mesopotamia.

The City-States of Ancient Mesopotamia

The creators of the first Mesopotamian civilization were the Sumerians, a people whose origins remain unclear. By 3000 B.C., they had established a number of independent cities in southern Mesopotamia, including Eridu, Ur, Uruk, Umma, and Lagash. As cities expanded in size, they came to exercise political and economic control over the surrounding countryside, forming city-states. These city-states were the basic units of Sumerian civilization.

Sumerian cities were surrounded by walls. Uruk, for example, occupied an area of approximately 1000 acres encircled by a wall six miles long with defense towers located every thirty to thirty-five feet along the wall. City dwellings, built of sun-dried bricks, included both the small flats of peasants and the larger dwellings of the civic and priestly officials. Although Mesopotamia had little stone or wood for building purposes, it did have plenty of mud. Mudbricks, easily shaped by hand, were left to bake in the hot sun until they were hard enough to use for building. People in Mesopotamia were remarkably inventive with mudbricks, inventing the arch and the dome and constructing some of the largest brick buildings in the world. Mudbricks are still used in rural areas of the Middle East today.

The most prominent building in a Sumerian city was the temple, which was dedicated to the chief god or goddess of the city and often built atop a massive stepped tower called a ziggurat. The Sumerians believed that gods and goddesses owned the cities, and much wealth was used

✦ **The "Royal Standard" of Ur.** This series of panels is from the "Royal Standard" of Ur, a box dating from c. 2700 B.C. and discovered in a stone tomb from the royal cemetery of the Sumerian city-state of Ur. These scenes from the box depict the activities of the king and his court after a military victory. In the top panel, the king and his court drink wine while at the right a musician plays a bull-headed harp. The middle panel shows bulls, rams, and fish being brought to the banquet hall. The bottom panel shows booty from the king's victory.

to build temples as well as elaborate houses for the priests and priestesses who served the gods. Priests and priestesses, who supervised the temples and their property, had great power. The temples owned much of the city land and livestock and served not only as the physical center of the city, but also its economic and political center. In fact, historians believe that in the early stages of the city-states, priests and priestesses played an important role in ruling. The Sumerians believed that the gods ruled the cities, making the state a theocracy (government by a divine authority). Eventually, however, ruling power passed into the hands of worldly figures known as kings.

Sumerians viewed kingship as divine in origin; they believed kings derived their power from the gods and were the agents of the gods. Regardless of their origins, kings had power—they led armies, initiated legislation, supervised the building of public works, provided courts, and organized workers for the irrigation projects on which Mesopotamian agriculture depended. The army, the government bureaucracy, and the priests and priestesses all aided the kings in their rule. Befitting their power, Sumerian kings lived in large palaces with their wives and children.

The economy of the Sumerian city-states was primarily agricultural, but commerce and industry became important as well. The people of Mesopotamia produced woolen textiles, pottery, and the metalwork for which they were especially well known. Foreign trade, which was primarily a royal monopoly, could be extensive. Royal officials imported luxury items, such as copper and tin, aromatic woods, and fruit trees, in exchange for dried fish, wool, barley, wheat, and the metal goods produced by Mesopotamian craftspeople. Traders traveled by land to the eastern Mediterranean in the west and by sea to India in the east. The invention of the wheel around 3000 B.C. led to carts with wheels that made the transport of goods easier.

Sumerian city-states contained three major social groups—nobles, commoners, and slaves. Nobles included royal and priestly officials and their families. Commoners included the nobles' clients who worked for the palace and temple estates and other free citizens who worked as farmers, merchants, fishermen, scribes, and craftspeople. Probably 90 percent or more of the population were farmers. They could exchange their crops for the goods of the artisans in free town markets. Slaves belonged to palace officials, who used them mostly in building projects; temple officials, who used mostly female slaves to weave cloth and grind grain; and rich landowners, who used them for farming and domestic work.

Empires in Ancient Mesopotamia

As the number of Sumerian city-states grew and the states expanded, new conflicts arose as city-state fought city-state for control of land and water. The fortunes of various city-states rose and fell over the centuries. The constant wars, with their burning and sacking of cities, left many Sumerians in deep despair, as is evident in the words of this Sumerian poem from the city of Ur: "Ur is

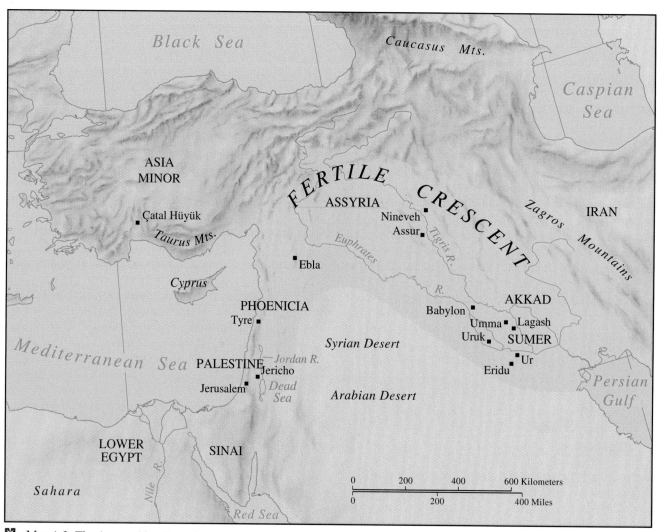

✵ Map 1.2 The Ancient Near East.

destroyed, bitter is its lament. The country's blood now fills its holes like hot bronze in a mould. Bodies dissolve like fat in the sun. Our temple is destroyed, the gods have abandoned us, like migrating birds. Smoke lies on our city like a shroud."

Located on the flat land of Mesopotamia, the Sumerian city-states were also open to invasion. To the north of the Sumerian city-states were the Akkadians. We call them a Semitic people because of the type of language they spoke (see Table 1.1). Around 2340 B.C., Sargon, leader of the Akkadians, overran the Sumerian city-states and established an empire that included most of Mesopotamia as well as lands westward to the Mediterranean. But the Akkadian empire eventually disintegrated, and its end by 2100 B.C. brought a return to the system of warring city-states until Ur-Nammu of Ur succeeded in reunifying most of Mesopotamia. But this final flowering of Sumerian culture collapsed with the coming of the Amorites. Under Hammurabi, the Amorites or Old Babylonians, a large group of Semitic-speaking seminomads, created a new empire.

Hammurabi (1792–1750 B.C.) employed a well-disciplined army of foot soldiers who carried axes, spears, and copper or bronze daggers. He learned to divide his opponents and subdue them one by one. Using such methods, he gained control of Sumer and Akkad and reunified Mesopotamia almost to the old borders created by Sargon of Akkad. After his conquests, he called himself "the sun of Babylon, the king who has made the four quarters of the world subservient," and established a new capital at Babylon, north of Akkad.

Hammurabi, the man of war, was also a man of peace. He followed in the footsteps of previous conquerors by assimilating Mesopotamian culture with the result that Sumerian ways continued to exist despite the end of the Sumerians as a political entity. A collection of his letters,

Chief Events in Mesopotamian History

Early development of Sumerian city-states	c. 3000–2340 B.C.
The Akkadian empire	c. 2340–2100 B.C.
The dynasty of Ur-Nammu	c. 2112–2000 B.C.
Hammurabi's reign	1792–1750 B.C.

found by archaeologists, reveals that he took a strong interest in state affairs. He built temples, defensive walls, and irrigation canals; encouraged trade; and brought about an economic revival. After his death, however, a series of weak kings were unable to keep Hammurabi's empire united, and it finally fell to new invaders.

THE CODE OF HAMMURABI

Hammurabi is best remembered for his law code, a collection of 282 laws. For centuries, laws had regulated people's relationships with one another in the lands of Mesopotamia, but only fragments of these earlier codes survive. Hammurabi's collection provides considerable insight into almost every aspect of everyday life there and provides us a priceless glimpse of the values of this early society (see the box on p. 10).

The Code of Hammurabi reveals a society with a system of strict justice. Penalties for criminal offenses were severe and varied according to the social class of the victim. A crime against a member of the upper class (a noble) was punished more severely than the same offense against a member of the lower class. Moreover, the principle of retaliation ("an eye for an eye, tooth for a tooth") was fundamental to this system of justice. It was applied in cases where members of the upper class committed crimes against their social equals. For crimes against members of the lower classes, a money payment was made instead.

Hammurabi's code took seriously the responsibilities of public officials. The governor of an area and city officials were expected to catch burglars. If they failed to do so, the officials in the district where the crime was committed had to replace the lost property. If murderers were not found, the officials had to pay a fine to the relatives of the murdered person. Soldiers were likewise expected to fulfill their duties for the order and maintenance of the state. If a soldier hired a substitute to fight for him, he was

❖ **Table 1.1   Some Semitic Languages**

Assyrian
Akkadian
Aramaic
Babylonian
Canaanitic
Phoenician
Syriac
Arabic
Hebrew

Note: Languages in italic type are no longer spoken.

The Code of Hammurabi

Hammurabi's code is the most complete, although not the earliest, Mesopotamian law code. It was inscribed on a stone stele topped by a bas-relief picturing Hammurabi receiving the inspiration for the law code from the sun god Shamash, who was also the god of justice. The law code emphasizes the principle of retribution ("an eye for an eye") and punishments that vary according to social status. Punishments could be severe. Marriage and family affairs also play a large role in the code. The following examples illustrate these concerns.

The Code of Hammurabi

25. If fire broke out in a free man's house and a free man, who went to extinguish it, cast his eye on the goods of the owner of the house and has appropriated the goods of the owner of the house, that free man shall be thrown into that fire.

129. If the wife of a free man has been caught while lying with another man, they shall bind them and throw them into the water. If the husband of the woman wishes to spare his wife, then the king in turn may spare his subject.

131. If a free man's wife was accused by her husband, but she was not caught while lying with another man, she shall make affirmation by god and return to her house.

196. If a free man has destroyed the eye of a member of the aristocracy, they shall destroy his eye.

198. If he has destroyed the eye of a commoner or broken the bone of a commoner, he shall pay one mina of silver.

199. If he has destroyed the eye of a free man's slave or broken the bone of a free man's slave, he shall pay one-half his value.

209. If a free man struck another free man's daughter and has caused her to have a miscarriage, he shall pay ten shekels of silver for her fetus.

210. If that woman has died, they shall put his daughter to death.

211. If by a blow he has caused a commoner's daughter to have a miscarriage, he shall pay five shekels of silver.

212. If that woman has died, he shall pay one-half mina of silver.

213. If he struck a free man's female slave and has caused her to have a miscarriage, he shall pay two shekels of silver.

214. If that female slave has died, he shall pay one-third mina of silver.

put to death, and the substitute was given control of his estate.

The law code also furthered the proper performance of work with what virtually amounted to consumer protection laws. Builders were held responsible for the buildings they constructed. If a house collapsed and caused the death of the owner, the builder was put to death. If the collapse caused the death of the son of the owner, the son of the builder was put to death. If goods were destroyed by the collapse, they had to be replaced and the house itself reconstructed at the builder's expense.

The number of laws in Hammurabi's code dedicated to land tenure and commerce reveals the importance of agriculture and trade in the Mesopotamian economy. Laws concerning land use and irrigation were especially strict, an indication of the danger of declining crop yields if the land were used incompetently. Commercial activity was also carefully regulated. Rates of interest on loans were watched closely. If the lender raised the interest rate after a loan was made, he lost the entire amount of the loan. The Code of Hammurabi even specified the precise wages of laborers and artisans, such as brickmakers and jewelers.

The largest number of laws in the Code of Hammurabi focused on marriage and the family. Parents arranged marriages for their children. After marriage, the parties involved signed a marriage contract; without it, no one was considered legally married. The husband provided a bridal payment, and the woman's parents were responsible for a dowry to the new husband.

As in many patriarchal societies, women possessed far fewer privileges and rights in marriage than men. A woman's place was in the home, and failure to fulfill her expected duties was grounds for divorce. If she was not able to bear children, her husband could divorce her, but he did have to return the dowry to the woman's family. If his wife tried to leave home to engage in business, thus neglecting her house, her husband could divorce her and did not have to repay the dowry. Furthermore, a wife who was a "gadabout, . . . neglecting her house [and] humiliating her husband," could be drowned. We do know that in practice not all women remained at home. Some worked in business and were especially prominent in the running of taverns.

Women were guaranteed some rights, however. If a woman was divorced without good reason, she received the dowry back. A woman could seek divorce and get her dowry back if her husband was unable to show that she had done anything wrong. In theory, a wife was guaranteed use of her husband's property in the event of his death. The mother could also decide which of her sons would receive an inheritance.

Sexual relations were strictly regulated as well. Husbands, but not wives, were permitted sexual activity outside marriage. A wife caught committing adultery was pitched into the river, although her husband could ask the king to pardon her. Incest was strictly forbidden. If a father committed incestuous relations with his daughter, he would be banished. Incest between a son and mother resulted in both being burned.

Fathers ruled their children as well as their wives. Obedience was duly expected: "If a son has struck his father, they shall cut off his hand." If a son committed a serious enough offense, his father could disinherit him, although fathers were not permitted to disinherit their sons arbitrarily.

The Culture of Mesopotamia

A spiritual worldview was of fundamental importance to Mesopotamian culture. To the peoples of Mesopotamia, the gods were living realities who affected all aspects of life. It was crucial, therefore, that the correct hierarchies be observed. Leaders could prepare armies for war, but success really depended on a favorable relationship with the gods. This helps to explain the importance of the priestly class and is the reason why even the kings took great care to dedicate offerings and monuments to the gods.

THE IMPORTANCE OF RELIGION

The Mesopotamians viewed their city-states as earthly copies of a divine model and order. Each city-state was sacred since it was linked to a god or goddess. Hence, Nippur, the earliest center of Sumerian religion, was dedi-

◆ **Stele of Hammurabi (Code of Hammurabi, King of Babylonia).** Although the Sumerians compiled earlier law codes, Hammurabi's code was the most famous in early Mesopotamian history. The code recognized three social classes in Babylonia (nobles, freemen, and slaves) and included laws dealing with marriage and divorce, job performance, punishments for crime, and even sexual relations. The upper section of the stele depicts Hammurabi standing in front of the seated sun god Shamash who orders the king to record the law. The lower section contains the actual code.

cated to Enlil, the god of wind. Moreover, located at the heart of each city-state was a temple complex. Occupying several acres, this sacred area consisted of a ziggurat with a temple at the top dedicated to the god or goddess who owned the city. The temple complex was the true center of the community. The main god or goddess dwelt there symbolically in the form of a statue, and the ceremony of dedication included a ritual that linked the statue to the god or goddess and thus supposedly harnessed the power of the deity for the city's benefit. Considerable wealth was poured into the construction of temples and other buildings used for the residences of priests and priestesses who helped the gods. Although the gods literally owned the city, the temple complex used only part of the land and rented out the remainder. Essentially, the temples dominated individual and commercial life, an indication of the close relationship between Mesopotamian religion and culture.

The physical environment had an obvious impact on the Mesopotamian view of the universe. Ferocious floods, heavy downpours, scorching winds, and oppressive humidity were all part of the Mesopotamian climate. These conditions and the resulting famines easily convinced Mesopotamians that this world was controlled by supernatural forces and that the days of human beings "are numbered; whatever he may do, he is but wind," as the *Epic of Gilgamesh* put it. In the presence of nature, Mesopotamians could easily feel helpless, as this poem relates:

> *The rampant flood which no man can oppose,*
> *Which shakes the heavens and causes earth to tremble,*
> *In an appalling blanket folds mother and child,*
> *Beats down the canebrake's full luxuriant greenery,*
> *And drowns the harvest in its time of ripeness.*[1]

The Mesopotamians discerned cosmic rhythms in the universe and accepted its order, but perceived that it was not completely safe because of the presence of willful, powerful cosmic powers that they identified with gods and goddesses.

With its numerous gods and goddesses animating all aspects of the universe, Mesopotamian religion was polytheistic in nature. The four most important deities were An, Enlil, Enki, and Ninhursaga. An was the god of the sky and hence the most important force in the universe. Since his basic essence was authority, he was also viewed as the source or active principle of all authority, including the earthly power of rulers and fathers alike. Enlil, god of wind, was considered the second greatest power of the visible universe. In charge of the wind and thus an expression of the legitimate use of force, Enlil became the symbol of the proper use of force on earth as well. Enki was god of the earth. Since the earth was the source of life-giving waters, Enki was also god of rivers, wells, and canals. More generally, he represented the waters of creativity and was responsible for inventions and crafts. Ninhursaga began as a goddess associated with soil, mountains, and vegetation. Eventually, however, she was worshiped as a mother goddess, a "mother of all children," who manifested her power by giving birth to kings and conferring the royal insignia of officialdom on them.

Human beings' relationship with their gods was based on subservience since, according to Sumerian myth, human beings were created to do the manual labor the gods were unwilling to do for themselves. Moreover, humans were insecure because they could never be sure of the gods' actions. But humans did make attempts to circumvent or relieve their anxiety by discovering the intentions of the gods; these efforts gave rise to the development of the arts of divination.

Divination took a variety of forms. A common form, at least for kings and priests who could afford it, involved killing animals, such as sheep or goats, and examining their livers or other organs. Supposedly, features seen in the organs of the sacrificed animals foretold events to come. Thus, one handbook states that if the animal organ has shape x, then the outcome of the military campaign will be y. Private individuals relied on cheaper divinatory techniques. These included interpreting patterns of smoke from burning incense or the pattern formed when oil was poured into water. The Mesopotamian arts of divination arose out of the desire to discover the purposes of the gods: If people could decipher the signs that foretold events, the events would be predictable and humans could act wisely.

THE CULTIVATION OF NEW ARTS AND SCIENCES

The realization of writing's great potential was another aspect of Mesopotamian culture. The oldest Mesopotamian texts date to around 3000 B.C. and were written by the Sumerians, who used a cuneiform ("wedge-shaped") system of writing. Using a reed stylus, they made wedge-shaped impressions on clay tablets, which were then baked or dried in the sun. Once dried, these tablets were virtually indestructible, and the several hundred thousand that have been discovered have provided a valuable source of information for modern scholars. Sumerian writing evolved from pictures of concrete objects to simplified and stylized signs, leading eventually to a phonetic system that made possible the written expression of abstract ideas.

Mesopotamian peoples used writing primarily for record keeping. The most common cuneiform tablets record transactions of daily life: tallies of cattle kept by herdsmen for their owners, lists of taxes, and wage payments, accounts, contracts, and court decisions affecting business life. There are also monumental texts, documents that were intended to last forever, such as inscriptions etched in stone on statues and royal buildings.

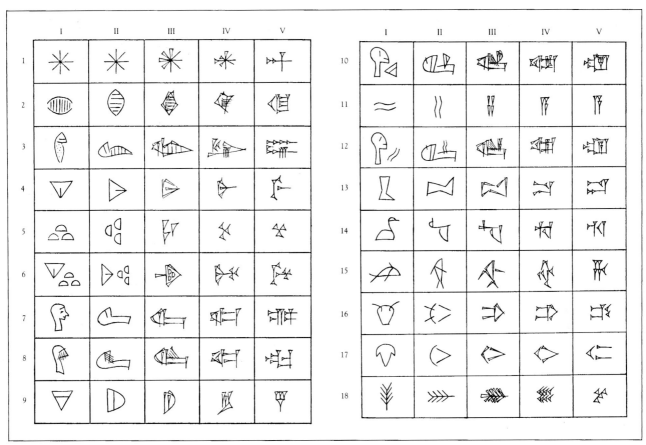

♦ **The Development of the Cuneiform System of Writing.** This table shows the evolution of eighteen representative signs from c. 3000 B.C. to 600 B.C. Examples: No. 1 is a picture of a star. The sign for star also meant heaven, sky, or god. No. 11 is a picture of a stream of water. The sign for water was also used for the word "in" since the Sumerian words for "water" and "in" sounded alike. No. 12 combines a picture of a head emphasizing the mouth with the sign for water. The compound sign represents a Sumerian word meaning to eat.

Still another category of cuneiform inscriptions includes the large body of texts produced for teaching purposes. Schools for scribes were in operation by 2500 B.C. They were necessary because much time was needed to master the cuneiform system of writing. The primary goal of scribal education was to produce professionally trained scribes for careers in the temples and palaces, the military, and government. Pupils were male and primarily from wealthy families. Gradually, the schools became centers for culture because Mesopotamian literature was used for instructional purposes.

Writing was important because it enabled a society to keep records and maintain knowledge of previous practices and events. Writing also made it possible for people to communicate ideas in new ways, which is especially evident in Mesopotamian literary works. The most famous piece of Mesopotamian literature was *The Epic of Gilgamesh*, an epic poem that records the exploits of a legendary king of Uruk. Gilgamesh—wise, strong and perfect in body, part man, part god—befriends a hairy beast named Enkidu. Together, they set off in pursuit of heroic deeds. When Enkidu dies, Gilgamesh experiences the pain of mortality and enters upon a search for the secret of immortality. But his efforts fail (see the box on p. 14) and Gilgamesh remains mortal. The desire for immortality, one of humankind's great searches, ends in complete frustration. "Everlasting life," as this Mesopotamian epic makes clear, is only for the gods.

Peoples in Mesopotamia also made outstanding achievements in mathematics and astronomy. In math, the Sumerians devised a number system based on 60, using combinations of 6 and 10 for practical solutions.

➤ *The Great Flood* ➤

*T*he great epic poem of Mesopotamian literature, The Epic of Gilgamesh, *includes an account by Utnapishtim (a Mesopotamian version of the later biblical Noah), who had built a ship and survived the flood unleashed by the gods to destroy humankind. This selection recounts how the god Ea advised Utnapishtim to build a boat and how he came to land his boat at the end of the flood. In this section, Utnapishtim is telling his story to Gilgamesh.*

The Epic of Gilgamesh

"In those days the world teemed, the people multiplied, the world bellowed like a wild bull, and the great god was aroused by the clamor. Enlil heard the clamor and he said to the gods in council, 'The uproar of mankind is intolerable and sleep is no longer possible by reason of the babel.' So the gods agreed to exterminate mankind. Enlil did this, but Ea [Sumerian Enki, god of the waters] because of his oath warned me in a dream . . . . 'tear down your house and build a boat, abandon possessions and look for life, despise worldly goods and save your soul alive. Tear down your house, I say, and build a boat. . . . then take up into the boat the seed of all living creatures. . . .' [Utnapishtim did as he was told and then the destruction came.]

"For six days and six nights the winds blew, torrent and tempest and flood overwhelmed the world, tempest and flood raged together like warring hosts. When the seventh day dawned the storm from the south subsided, the sea grew calm, the flood was stilled; I looked at the face of the world and there was silence, all mankind was turned to clay. The surface of the sea stretched as flat as a rooftop; I opened a hatch and the light fell on my face. Then I bowed low, I sat down and I wept, the tears streamed down my face, for on every side was the waste of water. I looked for land in vain, but fourteen leagues distant there appeared a mountain, and there the boat grounded; on the mountain of Nisir the boat held fast, she held fast and did not budge. . . . When the seventh day dawned I loosed a dove and let her go. She flew away, but finding no resting-place she returned. Then I loosed a swallow, and she flew away but finding no resting-place she returned. I loosed a raven, she saw that the waters had retreated, she ate, she flew around, she cawed, and she did not come back. Then I threw everything open to the four winds, I made a sacrifice and poured out a libation on the mountain top."

Geometry was used to measure fields and erect buildings. In astronomy, the Sumerians made use of units of 60 and charted the heavenly constellations. Their calendar was based on twelve lunar months and was brought into harmony with the solar year by adding an extra month from time to time.

*E*gyptian Civilization: "The Gift of the Nile"

Although contemporaneous with Mesopotamia, civilization in Egypt evolved along somewhat different lines. Of central importance to the development of Egyptian civilization was the Nile River. That the Egyptian people recognized its significance is apparent in this Hymn to the Nile (also see the box on p. 15): "The bringer of food, rich in provisions, creator of all good, lord of majesty, sweet of fragrance. . . . He who . . . fills the magazines, makes the granaries wide, and gives things to the poor. He who

makes every beloved tree to grow. . . ."[2] Egypt, like Mesopotamia, was a river valley civilization.

The Nile is a unique river, beginning in the heart of Africa and coursing northward for thousands of miles. It is the longest river in the world. The Nile was responsible for creating an area several miles wide on both banks of the river that was fertile and capable of producing abundant harvests. The "miracle" of the Nile was its annual flooding. The river rose in the summer from rains in central Africa, crested in Egypt in September and October, and left a deposit of silt that created an area of rich soil. The Egyptians called this fertile land the "Black Land," because it was dark in color from the silt and lush crops that grew on it. Beyond these narrow strips of fertile fields lay the deserts (the "Red Land").

Unlike the floods of Mesopotamia's rivers, the flooding of the Nile was gradual and usually predictable, and the river itself was seen as life enhancing, not life threatening. Although a system of organized irrigation was still necessary, the small villages along the Nile could make the

≋ Significance of the Nile River and the Pharaoh ≋

Two of the most important sources of life for the ancient Egyptians were the Nile River and the pharaoh. Egyptians perceived that the Nile River made possible the abundant food that was a major source of their well-being. This *Hymn to the Nile*, probably from the nineteenth and twentieth dynasties in the New Kingdom, expresses the gratitude Egyptians felt for the Nile.

Hymn to the Nile

Hail to you, O Nile, that issues from the earth and comes to keep Egypt alive! . . .

He that waters the meadows which Re created, in order to keep every kid alive.

He that makes to drink the desert and the place distant from water: that is his dew coming down from heaven. . . .

The lord of fishes, he who makes the marsh-birds to go up-stream. . . .

He who makes barley and brings emmer into being, that he may make the temples festive.

If he is sluggish, then nostrils are stopped up, and every-body is poor. . . .

When he rises, then the land is in jubilation, then every belly is in joy, every backbone takes on laughter, and every tooth is exposed.

The bringer of good, rich in provisions, creater of all good, lord of majesty, sweet of fragrance. . . .

He who makes every beloved tree to grow, without lack of them.

The Egyptian king, or pharaoh, was viewed as a god and the absolute ruler of Egypt. His significance and the gratitude of the Egyptian people for his existence are evident in this hymn from the reign of Sesotris III (c. 1880–1840 B.C.).

Hymn to the Pharaoh

He has come unto us that he may carry away Upper Egypt; the double diadem [crown of Upper and Lower Egypt] has rested on his head.

He has come unto us and has united the Two Lands; he has mingled the reed with the bee [symbols of Lower and Upper Egypt].

He has come unto us and has brought the Black Land under his sway; he has apportioned to himself the Red Land.

He has come unto us and has taken the Two Lands under his protection; he has given peace to the Two Riverbanks.

He has come unto us and has made Egypt to live; he has banished its suffering.

He has come unto us and has made the people to live; he has caused the throat of the subjects to breathe. . . .

He has come unto us and has done battle for his bound-aries; he has delivered them that were robbed.

effort without the massive state intervention that was required in Mesopotamia. Egyptian civilization, consequently, tended to remain more rural with many small population centers congregated along a narrow band on both sides of the Nile. About 100 miles before it empties into the Mediterranean, the river splits into two major branches, forming the delta, a triangular-shaped territory called Lower Egypt to distinguish it from Upper Egypt, the land upstream to the south. Egypt's important cities developed at the tip of the delta. Even today, most of Egypt's people are crowded along the banks of the Nile River.

The surpluses of food that Egyptian farmers grew in the fertile Nile valley made Egypt prosperous. But the Nile also served a unifying factor in Egyptian history. In ancient times, the Nile was the fastest way to travel through the land, making both transportation and communication easier. Winds from the north pushed sailboats south, and the current of the Nile carried them north. Often when they headed downstream (or north), people used long poles or paddles to propel their boats forward.

Unlike Mesopotamia, which was subject to constant invasion, Egypt was blessed by natural barriers that fostered isolation, protected it from invasion, and gave it a sense of security. These barriers included the deserts to the west and east, the cataracts (rapids) on the southern part of the Nile, which made defense relatively easy, and the Mediterranean Sea to the north. These barriers, however, did not prevent the development of trade.

In essence, Egyptian geography and topography played important roles in the early history of the country. The

Map 1.3 Ancient Egypt.

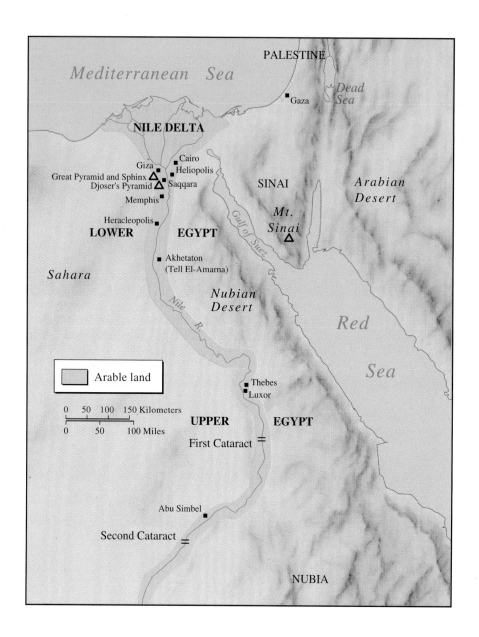

The Old and Middle Kingdoms

regularity of the Nile floods and the relative isolation of the Egyptians created a sense of security that was accompanied by a feeling of changelessness. Egyptian civilization was characterized by a remarkable degree of continuity over thousands of years. It was certainly no accident that Egyptians believed in cyclical rather than linear progress. Just as the sun passed through its daily cycle and the Nile its annual overflow, Egyptian kings reaffirmed the basic, unchanging principles of justice at the beginning of each new cycle of rule.

The basic framework for the study of Egyptian history was provided by Manetho, an Egyptian priest and historian who lived in the early third century B.C. He divided Egyptian history into thirty-one dynasties of kings. Using Manetho and other king lists, modern historians have divided Egyptian history into three major periods known as the Old Kingdom, Middle Kingdom, and New Kingdom. These were periods of long-term stability characterized by strong monarchical authority, competent bureaucracy, freedom from invasion, much construction of temples and pyramids, and considerable intellectual and cultural activity. But between the periods of stability were times of political chaos known as the Intermediate periods, which were characterized by weak political structures and rivalry for leadership, invasions, a decline in building activity, and a restructuring of society.

According to the Egyptians' own tradition, their land consisted initially of numerous populated areas ruled by tribal chieftains. Around 3100 B.C., the first Egyptian royal dynasty, under a king called Menes, united both Upper and Lower Egypt into a single kingdom. Henceforth, the king would be called "King of Upper and King of Lower Egypt," and the royal crown would be a double diadem, signifying the unification of all Egypt. Just as the Nile served to unite Upper and Lower Egypt physically, kingship served to unite the two areas politically.

The Old Kingdom encompassed the third through sixth dynasties of Egyptian kings, lasting from around 2700 to 2200 B.C. It was an age of prosperity and splendor, made visible in the construction of the greatest and largest pyramids in Egypt's history. The capital of the Old Kingdom was located at Memphis, south of the delta.

Kingship was a divine institution in ancient Egypt and formed part of a universal cosmic scheme (see the box on p. 15): "What is the king of Upper and Lower Egypt? He is a god by whose dealings one lives, the father and mother of all men, alone by himself, without an equal."[3] In obeying their king, subjects helped to maintain the cosmic order. A breakdown in royal power could only mean that citizens were offending divinity and weakening the universal structure. Among the various titles of Egyptian kings, that of pharaoh (originally meaning "great house" or "palace") eventually came to be the most common.

Although they possessed absolute power, Egyptian kings were not supposed to rule arbitrarily, but according to set principles. The chief principle was called *Ma'at*, a spiritual precept that conveyed the idea of truth and justice, but especially right order and harmony. To ancient Egyptians, this fundamental order and harmony had existed throughout the universe since the beginning of time. Pharaohs were the divine instruments who maintained it and were themselves subject to it.

Although theoretically absolute in their power, in practice Egyptian kings did not rule alone. Initially, members of the king's family performed administrative tasks, but by the fourth dynasty a bureaucracy with regular procedures had developed. Especially important was the office of vizier, "steward of the whole land." Directly responsible to the king, the vizier was in charge of the bureaucracy with its numerous departments, such as police, justice, river

♦ **Pair Statue of King Menkaure and His Queen.** The period designated as the Old Kingdom began approximately four centuries after Egypt's unification (c. 3100 B.C.) and lasted until approximately 2200 B.C. During this period, Egypt's greatest and largest pyramids were constructed. The kings (eventually called "pharaohs") were regarded as gods, divine instruments who maintained the fundamental order and harmony of the universe and wielded absolute power. This statue depicts King Menkaure and his queen (Dynasty IV).

transport, and public works. Agriculture and the treasury were the two most important departments. Agriculture was, of course, the backbone of Egyptian prosperity, and the treasury collected the taxes that were paid in kind. A careful assessment of land and tenants was undertaken to provide the tax base. For administrative purposes, Egypt was divided into provinces or nomes, as they were later called by the Greeks—twenty-two in Upper and twenty in Lower Egypt. A governor, called by the Greeks a nomarch, was head of each nome and was responsible to the king and vizier. Nomarchs, however, tended to build up large holdings of land and power within their nomes, creating a potential rivalry with the pharaohs.

Despite the theory of divine order, the Old Kingdom eventually collapsed, ushering in a period of chaos. Finally, a new royal dynasty managed to pacify all Egypt and inaugurated the Middle Kingdom, a new period of stability lasting from c. 2050 to 1652 B.C. Several factors contributed to its vitality. The nome structure was reorganized. The boundaries of each nome were now settled precisely, and the obligations of the nomes to the state were clearly delineated. Nomarchs were confirmed as hereditary officeholders but with the understanding that their duties must be performed faithfully. These included the collection of taxes for the state and the recruitment of labor forces for royal projects, such as stone quarrying.

The Middle Kingdom was characterized by a new concern on the part of the pharaohs for the people. In the Old Kingdom, the pharaoh had been viewed as an inaccessible god-king. Now he was portrayed as the shepherd of his people with the responsibility to build public works and provide for the public welfare. As one pharaoh expressed it: "He [a particular god] created me as one who should do that which he had done, and to carry out that which he commanded should be done. He appointed me herdsman of this land, for he knew who would keep it in order for him."[4]

Society and Economy in Ancient Egypt

Egyptian society had a simple structure in the Old and Middle Kingdoms; basically, it was organized along hierarchical lines with the god-king at the top. The king was surrounded by an upper class of nobles and priests who participated in the elaborate rituals of life that surrounded the pharaoh. This ruling class ran the government and managed its own landed estates, which provided much of its wealth.

Below the upper classes were merchants and artisans. Within Egypt, merchants engaged in active trade up and down the Nile as well as in town and village markets. Some merchants also engaged in international trade; they were sent by the king to Crete and Syria where they obtained wood and other products. Expeditions traveled into Nubia for ivory and down the Red Sea to Punt for incense and spices. Egyptian artisans displayed unusually high standards of craftsmanship and physical beauty and produced an incredible variety of goods: stone dishes; beautifully painted boxes made of clay; wooden furniture; gold, silver, and copper tools and containers; paper and rope made of papyrus; and linen clothes.

By far, the largest number of people in Egypt simply worked the land. In theory, the king owned all the land, but granted out portions of it to his subjects. Large sections were in the possession of nobles and the temple complexes. Most of the lower classes were serfs or common people bound to the land who cultivated the estates. They paid taxes in the form of crops to the king, nobles, and priests, lived in small villages or towns, and provided military service and forced labor for building projects.

The Culture of Egypt

Egypt produced a culture that dazzled and overawed its later conquerors. The Egyptians' technical achievements alone, especially visible in the construction of the pyramids, demonstrated a measure of skill unique to the world of that time. To the Egyptians, all of these achievements were part of a cosmic order suffused with the presence of the divine.

SPIRITUAL LIFE IN EGYPTIAN SOCIETY

The Egyptians had no word for religion, because it was an inseparable element of the entire world order to which Egyptian society belonged. The Egyptians possessed a remarkable number of gods associated with heavenly bodies and natural forces. Two groups, sun gods and land gods, came to have special prominence, hardly unusual in view of the importance of the sun, the river, and the fertile land along its banks to Egypt's well-being. The sun was the source of life and hence worthy of worship. A sun cult developed, and the sun god took on different forms and names, depending on his specific function. He was worshipped as Atum in human form and as Re, who had a human body but the head of a falcon. The pharaoh took the title of "Son of Re," because he was regarded as the earthly embodiment of Re. Eventually, Re became associated with Amon, an air god of Thebes, as Amon-Re.

River and land deities included Osiris and Isis with their child Horus, who was related to the Nile and to the sun as well. Osiris became especially important as a symbol of resurrection. A famous Egyptian myth told of the struggle between Osiris, who brought civilization to Egypt, and his evil brother Seth, who killed him, cut his body into fourteen parts, and tossed them into the Nile River. Osiris's faithful wife Isis found the pieces and, with help from other gods, restored Osiris to life. As a symbol of resurrection and judge of the dead, Osiris took on an important role for the Egyptians. By identifying with Osiris, one could hope to gain new life, just as Osiris had done. The dead, embalmed and mummified, were placed in tombs (in the case of kings, in pyramidal tombs), given the name of Osiris, and, by a process of magical identification, became Osiris. Like Osiris, they would then be reborn. The flood of the Nile and the new life it brought to Egypt were symbolized by Isis gathering all of Osiris's parts together and were celebrated each spring in the festival of the new land.

Later Egyptian spiritual practice began to emphasize morality by stressing Osiris's role as judge of the dead. The dead were asked to give an account of their earthly deeds to show whether they deserved a reward. Other means were also employed to gain immortality. Magical incantations, preserved in the *Book of the Dead*, were used to ensure a favorable journey to a happy afterlife. Specific instructions explained what to do when confronted by the judge of the dead. These instructions had two aspects. The negative confession gave a detailed list of what one had not done:

I have not committed evil against men.
I have not mistreated cattle.
I have not blasphemed a god. . . .
I have not done violence to a poor man. . . .
I have not defamed a slave to his superior.
I have not made anyone sick.
I have not made anyone weep.
I have not killed. . . .
I have not caused anyone suffering. . . .
I have not had sexual relations with a boy.
I have not defiled myself. . . .[5]

Later the supplicant made a speech listing his good actions: "I have done that which men said and that with which gods are content. . . . I have given bread to the hungry, water to the thirsty, clothing to the naked, and a ferry-boat to him who was marooned. I have provided divine offerings for the gods and mortuary offerings for the dead."[6] At first the Osiris cult was reserved for the very wealthy who could afford to take expensive measures to preserve the body after death. During the Middle Kingdom, however, the cult became "democratized"—extended to all Egyptians who aspired to an afterlife.

THE PYRAMIDS

One of the great achievements of Egyptian civilization, the building of pyramids, occurred in the time of the Old Kingdom. Pyramids were not built in isolation but as part of a larger complex dedicated to the dead, in effect, a city of the dead. The area included a large pyramid for the king's burial, smaller pyramids for his family, and mastabas, rectangular structures with flat roofs as tombs for the pharaoh's noble officials. The tombs were well prepared for their residents. The rooms were furnished and stocked with numerous supplies, including chairs, boats, chests, weapons, games, dishes, and a variety of food. The Egyptians believed that human beings had two bodies, a physical one and a spiritual one, which they called the *ka*. If the physical body was properly preserved (that is, mummified) and the tomb furnished with all the various objects of regular life, the *ka* could return and continue its life despite the death of the physical body.

To preserve the physical body after death, the Egyptians practiced mummification, a process of slowly drying a dead body to prevent it from rotting. Special workshops, run by priests, performed this procedure, primarily for the wealthy families who could afford it. Workers first removed the liver, lungs, stomach, and intestines and placed them in four special jars. The priests also removed the brain by extracting it through the nose. They then covered the corpse with a natural salt that absorbed the body's water. Later, they filled the body with spices and wrapped it with layers of linen soaked in resin. At the end of the process, which took about seventy days, a lifelike mask was placed over the head and shoulders of the mummy, which was then sealed in a case and placed in its tomb in a pyramid.

The largest and most magnificent of all the pyramids was built under King Khufu. Constructed at Giza around 2540 B.C., this famous Great Pyramid covers thirteen acres, measures 756 feet at each side of its base, and stands 481 feet high. Its four sides are almost precisely oriented to the four points of the compass. The interior included a grand gallery to the burial chamber, which was built of granite with a lidless sarcophagus for the pharaoh's body. The Great Pyramid still stands as a visible symbol of the power of Egyptian kings and the spiritual conviction that underlay Egyptian society. No pyramid built later ever matched its size or splendor. But an Egyptian pyramid was not only the king's tomb; it was also an important symbol of royal power. It could be seen for miles away as a visible reminder of the glory and might of the ruler who was a living god on earth.

ART AND WRITING

Commissioned by kings or nobles for use in temples and tombs, Egyptian art was largely functional. Wall paintings and statues of gods and kings in temples served a strictly spiritual purpose. They were an integral part of the performance of ritual, which was thought necessary to

◆ **The Great Pyramid of Giza.**
The three pyramids at Giza, across the Nile River from Cairo, are the most famous in Egypt. Pyramids served as tombs for both the king and his immediate family. The largest of the three pyramids at Giza is the Great Pyramid of Khufu.

preserve the cosmic order and hence the well-being of Egypt. Likewise, the mural scenes and sculptured figures found in the tombs had a specific function. They were supposed to aid the journey of the deceased into the afterworld.

Egyptian art was also formulaic. Artists and sculptors were expected to observe a strict canon of proportions that determined both form and presentation. This canon gave Egyptian art a distinctive appearance for thousands of years. Especially characteristic was the convention of combining the profile, semiprofile, and frontal views of the human body in relief work and painting in order to represent each part of the body accurately. The result was an art that was highly stylized, yet still allowed distinctive features to be displayed.

Writing in Egypt emerged during the first two dynasties. The Greeks later labeled Egyptian writing hieroglyphics, meaning "priest-carvings" or "sacred writings." Hieroglyphs were sacred characters used as picture signs that depicted objects and had a sacred value at the same time. Although hieroglyphs were later simplified into two scripts for writing purposes, they never developed into an alphabet. Egyptian hieroglyphs were initially carved in stone, but later the two simplified scripts were written on papyrus, a paper made from the papyrus reed that grew along the Nile. Most of the ancient Egyptian literature that has come down to us was written on papyrus rolls and wooden tablets.

Chaos and a New Order: The New Kingdom

The Middle Kingdom came to an end in the midst of another period of instability. An incursion into the delta region by a people known as the Hyksos initiated this second age of chaos. The Hyksos, a Semitic-speaking people, infiltrated Egypt in the seventeenth century B.C. and came to dominate much of Egypt. However, the presence of the Hyksos was not entirely negative for Egypt. They introduced Egypt to Bronze Age technology by teaching the Egyptians how to make bronze for use in new agricultural tools and weapons. More significantly, the Hyksos introduced new aspects of warfare to Egypt, including the horse-drawn war chariot, a heavier sword, and the compound bow. Eventually, a new line of pharaohs—the eighteenth dynasty—made use of the new weapons to throw off Hyksos domination, reunite Egypt, establish the New Kingdom (c. 1567–1085 B.C.), and launch the Egyptians along a new militaristic and imperialistic path. During the period of the New Kingdom, Egypt became the most powerful state in the Middle East. The Egyptians occupied Palestine and Syria, but permitted the local native princes to rule under Egyptian control. Egyptian armies also moved westward into Libya.

The eighteenth dynasty was not without its own troubles, however. Amenhotep IV (c. 1364–1347 B.C.) introduced the worship of Aton, god of the sun disk, as the chief god and pursued his worship with great enthusiasm. Changing his own name to Akhenaten ("It is well with Aton"), the pharaoh closed the temples of other gods and especially endeavored to lessen the power of Amon-Re and his priesthood at Thebes. Akhenaten strove to reduce their influence by replacing Thebes as the capital of Egypt with Akhetaton ("dedicated to Aton"), a new city located near modern Tell-el-Amarna, 200 miles north of Thebes.

Akhenaten's attempt at religious change proved to be a failure. It was too much to ask Egyptians to give up their traditional ways and beliefs, especially since they saw the destruction of the old gods as subversive of the very cosmic order on which Egypt's survival and continuing prosperity depended. Moreover, the priests at Thebes were unalterably opposed to the changes, which diminished their influence and power. At the same time, Akhenaten's preoccupation with religion caused him to ignore foreign affairs and led to the loss of both Syria and Palestine. Akhenaten's changes were soon undone after his death by those who influenced his successor, the boy-pharaoh Tutankhamon (1347–1338 B.C.). Tutankhamon returned the government to Thebes and restored the old gods. The Aton experiment had failed to take hold, and the eighteenth dynasty itself came to an end in 1333.

The nineteenth dynasty managed to restore Egyptian power one more time. Under Rameses II (c. 1279–1213 B.C.), the Egyptians regained control of Palestine but were unable to reestablish the borders of their earlier empire. New invasions in the thirteenth century by the "Sea Peoples," as Egyptians called them, destroyed Egyptian power in Palestine and drove the Egyptians back within their old frontiers. The days of Egyptian empire were ended, and the New Kingdom itself expired with the end of the twentieth dynasty in 1085. For the next 1,000 years, despite periodical revivals of strength, Egypt was dominated by Libyans, Nubians, Persians, and finally Macedonians after the conquest of Alexander the Great (see Chapter 4). In the first century B.C., Egypt became a province in Rome's mighty empire.

Daily Life in Ancient Egypt: Family and Marriage

Ancient Egyptians had a very positive attitude toward daily life on earth and followed the advice of the wisdom literature, which suggested that people marry young and

CHRONOLOGY

The Egyptians

Thinite Period or Early Dynastic (dynasties 1–2)	c. 3100–2700 B.C.
Old Kingdom (dynasties 3–6)	c. 2700–2200 B.C.
First Intermediate Period (dynasties 7–10)	c. 2200–2050 B.C.
Middle Kingdom (dynasties 11–12)	c. 2050–1652 B.C.
Second Intermediate Period (dynasties 13–17)	c. 1652–1567 B.C.
New Kingdom (dynasties 18–20)	c. 1567–1085 B.C.
Post-empire (dynasties 21–31)	1085–30 B.C.

establish a home and family. Monogamy was the general rule, although a husband was allowed to keep additional wives if his first wife was childless. Pharaohs, of course, were entitled to harems. The queen was acknowledged, however, as the Great Wife with a status higher than that of the other wives. The husband was master in the house, but wives were very much respected and in charge of the household and education of the children. From a book of wise sayings came this advice:

> If you are a man of standing, you should found your household and love your wife at home as is fitting. Fill her belly; clothe her back. Ointment is the prescription for her body. Make her heart glad as long as you live. She is a profitable field for her lord. You should not contend with her at law, and keep her far from gaining control. . . . Let her heart be soothed through what may accrue to you; it means keeping her long in your house.[7]

Women's property and inheritance remained in their hands, even in marriage. Although most careers and public offices were closed to women, some did operate businesses. Peasant women worked long hours in the fields and at numerous domestic tasks. Upper-class women could function as priestesses, and some queens even became pharaohs in their own right. The most famous was Hatshepsut in the New Kingdom. Since pharaohs were almost always male, Hatshepsut's official statues show her clothed and bearded like a king. She was addressed as "His Majesty."

◆ **A Hunting Scene.** A favorite pastime of the Egyptian upper classes was hunting waterfowl in the stands of papyrus that grew along the riverbanks. This tomb painting shows a wealthy Egyptian with members of his family hunting geese with throwsticks.

Marriages were arranged by parents. The primary concerns were family and property, and clearly the chief purpose of marriage was to produce children, especially sons (see the box on p. 23). From the New Kingdom came this piece of wisdom: "Take to yourself a wife while you are [still] a youth, that she may produce a son for you."[8] Only sons could carry on the family name. Daughters were not slighted, however. Numerous tomb paintings show the close and affectionate relationship parents had with both sons and daughters. Although marriages were arranged, some of the surviving love poems from ancient Egypt would indicate an element of romance in some marriages. Marriages could and did end in divorce, which was allowed, apparently with compensation for the wife. Adultery, however, was strictly prohibited with stiff punishments, especially for women, who could have their noses cut off or be burned at the stake.

Conclusion

The foundation stones for the building of Western civilization were laid by the Mesopotamians and Egyptians.

They developed cities and struggled with the problems of organized states. They developed writing to keep records and created literature. They constructed monumental architecture to please their gods, symbolize their power, and preserve their culture for all time. They developed new political, military, social, and religious structures to deal with the basic problems of human existence and organization. These first literate civilizations left detailed records that allow us to view how they grappled with three of the fundamental problems that humans have pondered: the nature of human relationships, the nature of the universe, and the role of divine forces in that cosmos. Although later peoples in Western civilization would provide different answers from those of the Mesopotamians and Egyptians, it was they who first posed the questions, gave answers, and wrote them down. Human memory begins with these two civilizations.

By the middle of the second millennium B.C., much of the creative impulse of the Mesopotamian and Egyptian civilizations was beginning to wane. The invasion of the Sea Peoples around 1200 B.C. ushered in a whole new pattern of petty states and new kingdoms that would lead to the largest empires the ancient Near East had seen.

➤ A Father's Advice ➤

Upper-class Egyptians enjoyed compiling collections of wise sayings to provide guidance for leading an upright and successful life. This excerpt is taken from "The Instruction of the Vizier Ptah-hotep" and dates from around 2450 B.C. The vizier was the pharaoh's chief official. In this selection, Ptah-hotep advises his son on how to be a successful official.

The Instruction of the Vizier Ptah-hotep

Then he said to his son:

Let not your heart be puffed-up because of your knowledge; be not confident because you are a wise man. Take counsel with the ignorant as well as the wise. The full limits of skill cannot be attained, and there is no skilled man equipped to his full advantage. Good speech is more hidden than the emerald, but it may be found with maidservants at the grindstones. . . .

If you are a leader commanding the affairs of the multitude, seek out for yourself every beneficial deed, until it may be that your own affairs are without wrong. Justice is great, and its appropriateness is lasting; it has been disturbed since the time of him who made it, whereas there is punishment for him who passes over its laws. It is the right path before him who knows nothing. Wrongdoing has never brought its undertaking into port. It may be that it is fraud that gains riches, but the strength of justice is that it lasts . . . .

If you are a man of intimacy, whom one great man sends to another, be thoroughly reliable when he sends you. Carry out the errand for him as he has spoken. Do not be reserved about what is said to you, and beware of any act of forgetfulness. Grasp hold of truth, and do not exceed it. Mere gratification is by no means to be repeated. Struggle against making words worse, thus making one great man hostile to another through vulgar speech. . . .

If you are a man of standing and found a household and produce a son who is pleasing to god, if he is correct and inclines toward your ways and listens to your instruction, while his manners in your house are fitting, and if he takes care of your property as it should be, seek out for him every useful action. He is your son, . . . you should not cut your heart off from him.

But a man's seed often creates enmity. If he goes astray and transgresses your plans and does not carry out your instruction, so that his manners in your household are wretched, and he rebels against all that you say, while his mouth runs on in the most wretched talk, quite apart from his experience, while he possesses nothing, you should cast him off: he is not your son at all. He was not really born to you. Thus you enslave him entirely according to his own speech. He is one whom god has condemned in the very womb. . . .

NOTES

1. Quoted in Thorkild Jacobsen, "Mesopotamia," in Henri Frankfort et al., *Before Philosophy* (Baltimore, 1949), p. 139.
2. James B. Pritchard, *Ancient Near Eastern Texts*, 3d ed. (Princeton, N.J., 1969), p. 372.
3. Quoted in Milton Covensky, *The Ancient Near Eastern Tradition* (New York, 1966), p. 51.
4. Quoted in B. G. Trigger, B. J. Kemp, D. O'Connor, and A. B. Lloyd, *Ancient Egypt: A Social History* (Cambridge, 1983), p. 74.
5. Pritchard, *Ancient Near Eastern Texts*, p. 34.
6. Ibid., p. 36.
7. Ibid., p. 413.
8. Ibid., p. 420.

SUGGESTIONS FOR FURTHER READING

For a beautifully illustrated introduction to the ancient world, see *Past Worlds: The Times Atlas of Archaeology* (Maplewood, N.J., 1988), written by an international group of scholars. A similar kind of guide with more elaborate historical discussions is provided by A. Cotterell, ed., *The Penguin Encyclopedia of Ancient Civilization* (London, 1980). A detailed history of the ancient world with chapters written by different specialists is available in the twelve volumes of *The Cambridge Ancient History*, now in its third edition. Less detailed but sound surveys can be found in C. G. Starr, *A History of the Ancient World*, 4th ed. (New York, 1991); and L. De Blois and R. J. van der Spek, *An Introduction to the Ancient World*, trans. Susan Mellor (London, 1997). The following works are of considerable value in examining the prehistory of humankind: M. N. Cohen, *The Food Crisis in Prehistory: Overpopulation and the Origins of Agriculture* (New Haven, Conn., 1977); R. Leakey, *The Making of Mankind* (London, 1981); P. Mellars and C. Stringer, *The Human Revolution* (Edinburgh, 1989); D. O. Henry, *From Foraging to Agriculture* (Philadelphia, 1989); C. Renfrew, *Before Civilization: The Radiocarbon Revolution and Prehistoric Europe* (London, 1973); and C. Redman, *The Rise of Civilization* (San Francisco, 1978). For a specialized study of the role of women in early human society, see F. Dahlberg, ed., *Woman the Gatherer* (New Haven, Conn., 1981).

A fascinating introduction to the world of ancient Near Eastern studies can be found in W. D. Jones, *Venus and Sothis: How the Ancient Near East Was Rediscovered* (Chicago, 1982). A very competent general survey primarily of the political history of Mesopotamia and Egypt is W. W. Hallo and W. K. Simpson, *The Ancient Near East: A History* (New York, 1971). Also valuable are A. Kuhrt, *The Ancient Near East, c. 3000–330 B.C.*, 2 vols. (London, 1996); A. B. Knapp, *The History and Culture of Ancient Western Asia and Egypt* (Chicago, 1987); W. von Soden, *The Ancient Orient: An Introduction to the Study of the Ancient Near East* (Grand Rapids, Mich., 1994); and H. J. Nissen, *The Early History of the Ancient Near East, 9000–2000 B.C.* (Chicago, 1988). H. W. F. Saggs, *Babylonians* (Norman, Okla., 1995) provides an overview of the peoples of ancient Mesopotamia. The fundamental collection of translated documents

from the ancient Near East is J. B. Pritchard, *Ancient Near Eastern Texts*, 3d ed. with supplement (Princeton, N.J., 1969). For a good translation of *The Epic of Gilgamesh*, see the edition by N. K. Sandars (London, 1972).

General works on ancient Mesopotamia include J. N. Postgate, *Early Mesopotamia. Society and Economy at the Dawn of History* (London, 1992); S. Lloyd, *The Archaeology of Mesopotamia*, rev. ed. (London, 1984); and G. Roux, *Ancient Iraq* (Harmondsworth, 1966). A beautifully illustrated survey can be found in M. Roaf, *Cultural Atlas of Mesopotamia and the Ancient Near East* (New York, 1996). The world of the Sumerians has been well described in S. N. Kramer, *The Sumerians* (Chicago, 1963) and *History Begins at Sumer* (New York, 1959). See also the recent summary of the historical and archaeological evidence by H. Crawford, *Sumer and the Sumerians* (Cambridge, 1991). The fundamental work on the spiritual perspective of ancient Mesopotamia is T. Jacobsen, *The Treasures of Darkness: A History of Mesopotamian Religion* (New Haven, Conn., 1976). On art, see P. Amiet, *Art of the Ancient Near East* (New York, 1980).

For a good introduction to ancient Egypt, see the beautifully illustrated works by J. Baines and J. Málek, *The Cultural Atlas of the World: Ancient Egypt* (Alexandria, Va., 1991); and D. P. Silverman, ed. *Ancient Egypt* (New York, 1997). Other general surveys include C. Hobson, *The World of the Pharaohs* (New York, 1987); N. Grimal, *A History of Ancient Egypt*, trans. Ian Shaw (Oxford, 1992); and C. Aldred, *The Egyptians* (London, 1984). For an interesting introduction to Egyptian history, see B. J. Kemp, *Ancient Egypt* (London, 1989). A new approach is attempted in B. G. Trigger, B. J. Kemp, D. O'Connor, and A. B. Lloyd, *Ancient Egypt: A Social History* (Cambridge, 1983). On Akhenaten and his religious changes, see D. Redford, *Akhenaten: The Heretic King* (Princeton, N.J., 1984). Egyptian religion is covered in H. Frankfort, *Ancient Egyptian Religion* (New York, 1948), a brief but superb study; and E. Hornung, *Conceptions of God in Ancient Egypt: The One and the Many* (Ithaca, N.Y., 1982). On culture in general, see J. A. Wilson, *The Culture of Ancient Egypt* (Chicago, 1956). The leading authority on the pyramids is I. E. S. Edwards, *The Pyramids of Egypt*, rev. ed. (Harmondsworth, 1976). On art, see H. Schäfer, *The*

Principles of Egyptian Art (Oxford, 1974). An important new study on women is G. Robins, *Women in Ancient Egypt* (Cambridge, Mass., 1993). Daily life in ancient Egypt can be examined in P. Montet, *Everyday Life in* *Egypt in the Days of Ramses the Great,* trans. A. R. Maxwell-Hyslop (New York, 1974); and T. G. H. James, *Pharaoh's People: Scenes from Life in Imperial Egypt* (London, 1984).

CHAPTER 2

The Ancient Near East: Empires and Peoples

Around 971 B.C., Solomon came to the throne of Israel, a small state in western Asia. He was lacking in military prowess, but excelled in many other ways. Through trade and a series of foreign alliances, he became a well-known figure in the ancient Near East. But he was especially famed for another of his qualities. When confronted with two women who each claimed that the child before them was her natural child, Solomon ordered his servant to cut the child in half and give half to each woman. The first woman objected: "Please, my lord, give her the living baby! Don't kill him!" The second woman replied, "Neither I nor you shall have him. Cut him in two!" Then Solomon rendered his judgement: "Give the living baby to the first woman. Do not kill him; she is his mother." According to the biblical account, "when all Israel heard the verdict the king had given, they held the king in awe, because they saw that he had wisdom from God to administer justice." Outside Israel, too, the fame of Solomon spread far. But how was the king of such a small nation able to achieve such renown? And how was such a small nation able to survive for as long as it did in a Near East dominated by mighty empires?

The weakening of Egypt around 1200 B.C. temporarily left no dominant powers in the Near East, allowing a patchwork of petty kingdoms and city-states to emerge, especially in the area of Syria and Palestine. One of these small states, the Hebrew nation, has played a role in Western civilization completely disproportionate to its size. The Hebrews played a minor part in the politics of the ancient Near East, but their spiritual heritage—in the form of the Judaeo-Christian view of life—is one of the basic pillars of Western civilization.

The small states did not last, however. Ever since the first city-states had arisen in the Near East around 3000 B.C., there had been an ongoing movement toward the creation of larger territorial states with more sophisticated systems of control. This process reached a high point in the first millennium B.C. with the appearance of empires that embraced the entire Near East.

Creation of monarchy in Israel

Assyria destroys northern kingdom of Israel

Chaldeans destroy Jerusalem   Return of Hebrew exiles to Jerusalem

Height of Assyrian Empire   Height of Neo-Babylonian Empire

Assyrian Empire destroyed   Conquests of Cyrus   Reign of Darius

Golden Age
of Hebrew   Zoroastrianism
Prophecy   Hanging Gardens of Babylon

Between 1000 and 500 B.C., the Assyrians, Chaldeans, and Persians all created empires that encompassed either large areas or all of the ancient Near East. Each had impressive and grandiose capital cities that emphasized the power and wealth of its rulers. Each brought peace and order for a period of time by employing new administrative techniques. Each eventually fell to other conquerors. In the long run, these large empires had less impact on Western civilization than the Hebrew people. In human history, the power of ideas is often more significant than the power of empires.

On the Fringes of Civilization

Our story of the beginnings of Western civilization has been dominated so far by Mesopotamia and Egypt. But significant developments were also taking place on the fringes of these civilizations. Farming had spread into the Balkan peninsula of Europe by 6500 B.C., and by 4000 B.C., it was well established in southern France, central Europe, and the coastal regions of the Mediterranean. Although migrating farmers from the Near East may have brought some farming techniques into Europe, historians now believe that the Neolithic peoples of Europe domesticated animals and began to farm largely on their own.

One outstanding feature of late Neolithic Europe was the building of megalithic structures. *Megalith* is Greek for "large stone." Radiocarbon dating, a technique that allows scientists to determine the age of objects, shows that the first megalithic structures were built around 4000

B.C., more than 1,000 years before the great pyramids were built in Egypt. Between 3200 and 1500 B.C., standing stones that were placed in circles or lined up in rows were erected throughout the British Isles and northwestern France. Other megalithic constructions have been found as far north as Scandinavia and as far south as the islands of Corsica, Sardinia, and Malta. Some archaeologists have demonstrated that the stone circles were used as observatories to detect not only such simple astronomical phenomena as midwinter and midsummer sunrises, but also such sophisticated observations as the major and minor standstills of the moon.

By far, the most famous of these megalithic constructions is Stonehenge in England. Stonehenge consists of a series of concentric rings of standing stones. Its construction sometime between 2100 and 1900 B.C. was no small accomplishment. The eighty bluestones used at Stonehenge, for example, weigh four tons each and were transported to the site from their original source 135 miles away. Like other megalithic structures, Stonehenge indicates a remarkable awareness of astronomy on the part of its builders, as well as an impressive coordination of workers.

The Impact of the Indo-Europeans

For many historians, both the details of construction and the purpose of the megalithic structures of Europe remain a mystery. Also puzzling is the role of Indo-European people. The phrase *Indo-European* refers to people who used a language derived from a single parent tongue. Indo-European languages include Greek, Latin, Persian, Sanskrit, and the Germanic languages (see Table 2.1). It has been suggested that the original Indo-European-speaking peoples were based somewhere in the steppe region north of the Black Sea or in southwestern Asia, in modern Iran or Afghanistan. Although there had been earlier migrations, around 2000 B.C. they began major nomadic movements into Europe (including present-day Italy and Greece), India, and western Asia. One group of Indo-Europeans who moved into Asia Minor and Anatolia (modern Turkey) around 1750 B.C. coalesced with the native peoples to form the Hittite kingdom with its capital at Hattusha (Bogazköy in modern Turkey).

Between 1600 and 1200 B.C., the Hittites created their own empire in western Asia and even threatened the power of the Egyptians. The Hittites were the first of the Indo-European peoples to make use of iron, enabling them to construct weapons that were stronger and cheaper to make because of the widespread availability of iron ore. But around 1200 B.C., new waves of invading

◆ **Table 2.1**   *Some Indo-European Languages*

Subfamily	Languages
Indo–Iranian	*Sanskrit;* Persian
Balto–Slavic	Russian, Serbo-Croatian, Czech, Polish, Lithuanian
Hellenic	Greek
Italic	*Latin,* romance languages (French, Italian, Spanish, Portuguese, Romanian)
Celtic	Irish, Gaelic
Germanic	Swedish, Danish, Norwegian, German, Dutch, English

Note: Languages in italic type are no longer spoken.

◆ **Stonehenge.** The Bronze Age in northwestern Europe is known for its "megaliths," or large standing stones. Between 3200 and 1500 B.C., standing stones that were placed in circles or lined up in rows were erected throughout the British Isles and northwestern France. By far, the most famous of these megalithic constructions is Stonehenge in England.

Indo-European peoples known only as the Sea Peoples destroyed the Hittite empire. The destruction of the Hittite kingdom and the weakening of Egypt around 1200 B.C. temporarily left no dominant powers in western Asia, allowing a patchwork of petty kingdoms and city-states to emerge, especially in the area of Syria and Palestine. The Hebrews were one of these peoples.

The Hebrews: "The Children of Israel"

The Hebrews were a Semitic-speaking people who had a tradition concerning their origins and history that was eventually written down as part of the Hebrew Bible, known to Christians as the Old Testament. The Hebrews' own tradition states that they were descendants of the patriarch Abraham who had migrated from Mesopotamia to the land of Palestine, where they became identified as the "Children of Israel." This migration of a Semitic people, a common occurrence in the ancient Near East, probably took place around 1800 B.C.

The Hebrews were a nomadic people, organized along tribal lines, who followed a lifestyle based on grazing flocks and herds rather than farming. According to tradition, because of drought the Hebrews migrated to Egypt where they lived peacefully until a pharaoh enslaved them. Thereafter, they remained in bondage until Moses led his people out of Egypt in the well-known "exodus." Some historians believe this would have occurred in the first half of the thirteenth century B.C. The Hebrews then wandered for many years in the desert until they entered Palestine (possibly around 1220 B.C.), where they became involved in a lengthy conflict with the Philistines, a people who had settled in the coastal area of Palestine a southern kingdom of Judah, consisting of two tribes with its capital at Jerusalem. By the end of the ninth century, the independence of the kingdom of Israel was increasingly threatened by the rising power of the Assyrians. In 722 B.C., the Assyrians destroyed Samaria, overran the kingdom of Israel, and deported many Hebrews to other parts of the Assyrian empire. These dispersed Hebrews (the "ten lost tribes") merged with neighboring peoples and gradually lost their identity.

The southern kingdom of Judah was also forced to pay tribute to Assyria but managed to retain its independence as Assyrian power declined. A new enemy, however, appeared on the horizon. The Chaldeans brought the final destruction of Assyria, conquered the kingdom of Judah, and completely destroyed Jerusalem in 586 B.C. Many upper-class Hebrews were deported to Babylonia; the memory of their exile is still evoked in the stirring words of Psalm 137:

but were beginning to move into the inland areas. Around 1000 B.C., under the pressure of the ongoing struggle with the Philistines, the Hebrews embarked on the establishment of a monarchy.

The creation of a monarchy was not an easy task because many Hebrews were still accustomed to tribal life and tribal organization. By the time of King Solomon (c. 971–931 B.C.), however, the Hebrews had established control over all of Palestine and made Jerusalem into the capital of a united kingdom. The formerly nomadic Hebrews had become a settled community based on farming and urban life, and centralized political organization had replaced the independent ways of the twelve Hebrew tribes. Solomon did even more to strengthen royal power. He expanded the political and military establishments and was especially active in extending the trading activities of the Hebrews. Solomon is best known for his building projects, of which the most famous was the Temple in the city of Jerusalem. The Hebrews viewed the Temple as the symbolic center of their religion, and hence of the Hebrew kingdom itself. The Temple now housed the Ark of the Covenant, the holy chest containing the sacred relics of the Hebrew religion and, symbolically, the throne of the invisible God of Israel. Under Solomon, ancient Israel was at the height of its power, but his efforts to centralize royal power along the lines of Mesopotamian despotism led to dissatisfaction among his subjects, who believed that his actions threatened the old Hebrew tribal ties.

After Solomon's death, tension between the northern and southern Hebrew tribes led to the establishment of two separate kingdoms—a kingdom of Israel, composed of the ten northern tribes with its capital at Samaria, and

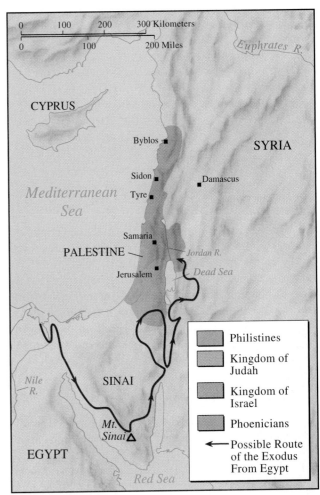

Map 2.1 Palestine in the First Millenium B.C.

♦ **The King of Israel Pays Tribute to the King of Assyria.**
By the end of the ninth century B.C., the kingdom of Israel had
been forced to pay tribute to the Assyrian Empire. The Assyrians
overran the kingdom in 722 B.C. and destroyed the capital city of
Samaria. In this scene from a black obelisk, Jehu, king of Israel, is
shown paying tribute to the king of Assyria.

> *By the rivers of Babylon, we sat and wept when we*
> *   remembered Zion. . . .*
> *How can we sing the songs of the Lord while in a foreign*
> *   land?*
> *If I forget you, O Jerusalem, may my right hand forget its*
> *   skill.*
> *May my tongue cling to the roof of my mouth if I do not*
> *   remember you,*
> *if I do not consider Jerusalem my highest joy.*[1]

But the Babylonian captivity of the Hebrew people did
not last. A new set of conquerors, the Persians, destroyed
the Chaldean kingdom and allowed the Hebrews to return to Jerusalem and rebuild their city and temple. The
revived kingdom of Judah remained under Persian control until the conquests of Alexander the Great in the
fourth century B.C. The people of Judah survived, eventually becoming known as the Jews and giving their name
to Judaism, the religion of Yahweh, the Jewish god.

The Spiritual Dimensions of Israel

The spiritual perspective of the Hebrews evolved over a
period of time. Early Hebrews probably worshiped many
gods, including nature spirits dwelling in trees and rocks.
Yahweh first appears as the god of one Hebrew tribe—the
Midian. By the time they had returned to Palestine from
their captivity in Egypt, many Hebrews had made a com-

mitment to Yahweh as their only god. But it was not until after the Babylonian captivity of the Jews (the sixth
century B.C.) that pure monotheism, or the belief that
there is only one God for all peoples, became standard.

"I AM THE LORD YOUR GOD": RULER OF THE WORLD

According to the Hebrew conception, there is but one
God, whom the Hebrews called YHWH, which by convention is written Yahweh. God is the creator of the
world and everything in it. Indeed, Yahweh means "he
causes to be." To the Hebrews, the gods of all other peoples were simply idols. The Hebrew God ruled the world;
he was subject to nothing. All peoples were his servants,
whether they knew it or not. This God was also tran-
scendent. He had created nature, but was not in nature.
The stars, moon, rivers, wind, and other natural phenomena were not divinities or suffused with divinity, but
God's handiwork. All of God's creations could be admired
for their awesome beauty, but not worshiped as god.

This omnipotent creator of the universe was not removed from the life he had created, however, but was a
just and good God who expected goodness from his people. If they did not obey his will, they would be punished.
But he was also a God of mercy and love: "The Lord is gracious and compassionate, slow to anger and rich in love.
The Lord is good to all; he has compassion on all he has
made."[2]

Each person was important in the Hebrew spiritual
perspective. Possessed of moral freedom, he or she had the
ability to choose between good and evil. But an important condition was attached to this freedom. People could
not simply establish their own ethical standards. Through
Moses and other holy men, God had made known his
commandments, his ideals of behavior. If people chose to
ignore the good, then suffering and evil would follow.
Each individual ultimately bore responsibility for his or
her decisions. Despite the powerful dimensions of God as
creator and sustainer of the universe, the Hebrew message
also emphasized that each person could have a personal
relationship with this powerful being. As the psalmist
sang: "My help comes from the Lord, the Maker of
heaven and earth. He will not let your foot slip—he who
watches over you will not slumber."[3]

"YOU ONLY HAVE I CHOSEN:" COVENANT LAW, AND PROPHETS

The Hebrew conception of God was closely related to
three aspects of the Hebrew religious tradition that have
special significance: the covenant, law, and the prophets.

The Hebrews believed that during the exodus from Egypt, when Moses led his people out of bondage into the promised land, a special event occurred that determined the Hebrew experience for all time. According to tradition, God entered into a covenant or contract with the tribes of Israel who believed that Yahweh had spoken to them through Moses (see the box on p. 32). The Hebrews promised to obey Yahweh and follow his law. In return, Yahweh promised to take special care of his chosen people, "a peculiar treasure unto me above all people."

This covenant between Yahweh and his chosen people could be fulfilled, however, only by Hebrew obedience to the law of God. Law became a crucial element of the Hebrew world and had a number of different dimensions. In some instances, it set forth specific requirements, such as payments for offenses. Most important, since the major characteristic of God was his goodness, ethical concerns stood at the center of the law. Sometimes these took the form of specific standards of moral behavior: "You shall not murder. You shall not commit adultery. You shall not steal."[4] But these concerns were also expressed in decrees that regulated the economic, social, and political life of the community since God's laws of morality applied to all areas of life. These laws made no class distinctions and emphasized the protection of the poor, widows, orphans, and slaves.

The Hebrews believed that certain religious leaders or "holy men," called prophets, were sent by God to serve as his voice to his people. In the ninth century B.C., the prophets were particularly vociferous about the tendency of the Hebrews to accept other gods, chiefly the fertility and earth gods of other peoples in Palestine. They warned of the terrible retribution that God would exact from the Hebrews if they did not keep the covenant to remain faithful to him alone and just in their dealings with one another.

The golden age of prophecy began in the mid-eighth century and continued during the time when the Hebrews were threatened by Assyrian and Chaldean conquerors. These "men of God" went through the land

✦ **A Representation of the Ark of the Covenant.** The most famous project carried out under King Solomon was the building of the Temple of Jerusalem. Within the Temple the Israelites placed the Ark of the Covenant, the holy chest that contained the sacred relics of the Hebrew faith. The Ark was also considered to be the throne of the invisible God on earth. This representation of the Ark, believed to be one of the earliest, is from a second-century A.D. synagogue at Capernaum.

⋙ The Covenant and the Law: The Book of Exodus ⋘

During the Exodus from Egypt, the Hebrews supposedly made their covenant with Yahweh. They agreed to obey their God and follow his law. In return, Yahweh promised to take special care of his chosen people. This selection from the Book of Exodus describes the making of the covenant and God's commandments to the Hebrews.

Exodus 19: 1–8

In the third month after the Israelites left Egypt—on the very day—they came to the Desert of Sinai. After they set out from Rephidim, they entered the desert of Sinai, and Israel camped there in the desert in front of the mountain. Then Moses went up to God, and the Lord, called to him from the mountain, and said, "This is what you are to say to the house of Jacob and what you are to tell the people of Israel: 'You yourselves have seen what I did to Egypt, and how I carried you on eagles's wings and brought you to myself. Now if you obey me fully and keep my covenant, then out of all nations you will be my treasured possession. Although the whole earth is mine, you will be for me a kingdom of priests and a holy nation.' These are the words you are to speak to the Israelites." So Moses went back and summoned the elders of the people and set before them all the words the Lord had commanded him to speak. The people all responded together, "We will do everything the Lord has said." So Moses brought their answer back to the Lord.

Exodus 20: 1–17

And God spoke all these words, "I am the lord your God, who brought you out of Egypt, out of the land of slavery. You shall have no other gods before me. You shall not make for yourself an idol in the form of anything in heaven above or on the earth beneath or in the waters below. You shall not bow down to them or worship them; for I, the Lord your God, am a jealous God, punishing the children for the sin of the fathers to the third and fourth generation of those who hate, but showing love to a thousand generations of those who love me and keep my commandments. You shall not misuse the name of the Lord your God, for the Lord will not hold anyone guiltless who misuse his name. Remember the Sabbath day by keeping it holy. Six days you shall labor and do all your work, but the seventh day is a Sabbath to the Lord you God. On it you shall not do any work, neither you, nor your son or daughter, nor your manservant or maidservant, nor you animals, nor the alien within your gates. For in six days the Lord made the heavens and the earth, the sea, and all that is in them, but he rested on the seventh day. Therefore the Lord blessed the Sabbath day and made it holy. Honor your father and your mother, so that you may live long in the land the Lord your God is giving you. You shall not murder. You shall not commit adultery. You shall not steal. You shall not give false testimony against your neighbor. You shall not covet your neighbor's house. You shall not covet your neighbor's wife, or his manservant or maidservant, his ox or donkey, or anything that belongs to your neighbor.

warning the Hebrews that they had failed to keep God's commandments and would be punished for breaking the covenant: "I will punish you for all your iniquities." Amos prophesied the fall of the northern kingdom of Israel to Assyria; twenty years later Isaiah said the kingdom of Judah too would fall (see the box on p. 33).

Out of the words of the prophets came new concepts that enriched the Hebrew tradition, including a notion of universalism and a yearning for social justice. Although Hebrew religious practices gave Jews a sense of separateness from other peoples, the prophets transcended this by embracing a concern for all humanity. All nations would someday come to the God of Israel: "all the earth shall worship you." A universal community of all people under God would someday be established by Israel's effort. This vision encompassed the elimination of war and the establishment of peace for all the nations of the world. In the words of the prophet Isaiah: "He will judge between the nations and will settle disputes for many people. They will beat their swords into plowshares and their spears into pruning hooks. Nation will not take up sword against nation, nor will they train for war anymore."[5]

The prophets also cried out against social injustice. They condemned the rich for causing the poor to suffer, denounced luxuries as worthless, and threatened Israel with prophecies of dire punishments for these sins. God's

The Hebrew Prophets: Micah, Isaiah, and Amos

The Hebrew prophets warned the Hebrew people that they must obey God's commandments or face being punished for breaking their covenant with God. These selections from the prophets Micah, Isaiah, and Amos make clear that God's punishment would fall upon the Hebrews for their sins. Even the Assyrians, as Isaiah indicated, would be used as God's instrument to punish them.

Micah 6: 9–16

Listen! The Lord is calling to the city—and to fear your name is wisdom—"Heed the rod and the One who appointed it. Am I still to forget, O wicked house, your ill-gotten treasures. . .? Shall I acquit a man with dishonest scales, with a bag of false weights? Her rich men are violent; her people are liars and their tongues speak deceitfully. Therefore, I have begun to destroy you, to ruin you because of your sins. You will eat but not be satisfied; your stomach will still be empty. You will store up but save nothing, because what you save I will give to the sword. You will plant but not harvest: you will press olives but not use the oil on yourselves, you will crush grapes but not drink the wine. . . .Therefore I will give you over to ruin and your people to derision; you will bear the scorn of the nations.

Isaiah 10: 1–6

Woe to those who make unjust laws, to those who issue oppressive decrees, to deprive the poor of their rights and withhold justice from the oppressed of my people, making their prey and robbing the fatherless. What will you do on the day of reckoning, when disaster comes from afar? To whom will you run for help? Where will you leave your riches? Nothing will remain but to cringe among the captives or fall among the slain. Yet for all this, his anger is not turned away, his hand is still upraised. "Woe to the Assyrian, the rod of my anger, in whose hand is the club of my wrath! I send him against a godless nation, I dispatch him against a people who anger me, to seize loot and snatch plunder, and to trample them down like mud in the streets."

Amos 3: 1–2

Hear this word the Lord has spoken against you, O people of Israel—against the whole family I brought up out of Egypt: "You only have I chosen of all the families of the earth; therefore, I will punish you for all your sins."

command was to live justly, share with one's neighbors, care for the poor and the unfortunate, and act with compassion. When God's command was not followed, the social fabric of the community was threatened. These proclamations by Israel's prophets became a source for Western ideals of social justice, even if they have never been very perfectly realized.

UNIQUENESS OF THE HEBREW RELIGION

The Hebrew religion was unique compared to the religions of other people in western Asia and Egypt. The Hebrews' belief that there is only one God for all peoples (a true monotheism) most dramatically separated them from all the others. But the Hebrews also differed in other significant ways. In virtually every religion in ancient Mesopotamia and Egypt, priests alone (and occasionally rulers) had access to the gods and their desires. In the Hebrew tradition, God's wishes, although communicated to the people through a series of special holy men, had all

been written down. No Jewish spiritual leader could claim that he alone knew God's will. It was accessible to anyone who could read Hebrew. Judaism was a religion initially of the spoken word and eventually of the written word. Finally, although the Hebrew prophets eventually developed a sense of universalism, the demands of the Hebrew religion (the need to obey their God) encouraged a separation between Jews and their non-Jewish neighbors. Unlike most other peoples of the Near East, Jews could not simply be amalgamated into a community by accepting the gods of their conquerors and their neighbors. To remain faithful to the demands of their God, they might even have to refuse loyalty to political leaders.

The Neighbors of the Hebrews

The Hebrews were not the only people who settled in the area of Palestine. The Philistines, who invaded from the sea, established five towns on the coastal plain of Palestine. They settled down as farmers and eventually entered into conflict with the Hebrews. Although the Philistines were newcomers to the area, the Phoenicians had resided there for some time, but now found themselves with a new independence. A Semitic-speaking people, the Phoenicians resided along the Mediterranean coast on a narrow band of land 120 miles long. They had rebuilt their major cities after destruction by the Sea Peoples. Their newfound political independence helped the Phoenicians expand the trade that was already the foundation of their prosperity. In fact, the Phoenician city of Byblos had been the principal distribution center for Egyptian papyrus outside Egypt (the Greek work for book, *biblos*, is derived from the name Byblos).

The chief cities of Phoenicia—Byblos, Tyre, and Sidon—were ports on the eastern Mediterranean, but they also served as distribution centers for the lands to the east in Mesopotamia. The Phoenicians themselves produced a number of goods for foreign markets, including purple dye, glass, wine, and lumber from the famous cedars of Lebanon. In addition, the Phoenicians improved their ships and became the great international sea traders of the ancient Near East. They charted new routes, not only in the Mediterranean, but also in the Atlantic Ocean where they reached Britain and sailed south along the west coast of Africa. The Phoenicians established a number of colonies in the western Mediterranean, including settlements in southern Spain, Sicily, and Sardinia. Carthage, the Phoenicians' most famous colony, was located on the north African coast.

Culturally, the Phoenicians are best known as transmitters. Instead of using pictographs or signs to represent whole words and syllables as the Mesopotamians and Egyptians did, the Phoenicians simplified their writing by using twenty-two different signs to represent the sounds of their speech. These twenty-two characters or letters could be used to spell out all the words in the Phoenician language. Although the Phoenicians were not the only people to invent an alphabet, theirs would have special significance because it was eventually passed on to the Greeks. From the Greek alphabet was derived the Roman alphabet that we still use today. The Phoenicians achieved much while independent, but they ultimately fell subject to the Assyrians, Chaldeans, and Persians.

The Assyrian Empire

The existence of independent states in Palestine was only possible because of the power vacuum existing in the ancient Near East after the destruction of the Hittite kingdom and the weakening of the Egyptian empire. But this condition did not last; new empires soon arose and came to dominate vast stretches of the ancient Near East. The first of these empires emerged in Assyria, an area whose location on the upper Tigris River brought it into both cultural and political contact with Mesopotamia.

Although close to Mesopotamia, Assyria, with its hills and adequate, if not ample, rainfall, had a different terrain and climate. The Assyrians were a Semitic-speaking people who exploited the use of iron weapons to establish an empire by 700 B.C. that included Mesopotamia, parts of the Iranian plateau, sections of Asia Minor, Syria, Palestine, and Egypt down to Thebes. Ashurbanipal (669–626 B.C.) was one of the strongest Assyrian rulers, but it was already becoming apparent during his reign that the Assyrian Empire was greatly overextended. Internal strife intensified as powerful Assyrian nobles gained control of vast territories and waged their own private military campaigns. Moreover, subject peoples, such as the Babylonians, greatly resented Assyrian rule and rebelled against it. Soon after Ashurbanipal's reign, the Assyrian Empire began to disintegrate rapidly. The capital city of Nineveh fell to a coalition of Chaldeans and Medes in 612 B.C., and in 605 B.C., the rest of the empire was finally divided between the coalition powers.

At its height, the Assyrian Empire was ruled by kings whose power was considered absolute. Under their leadership, the Assyrian Empire became well organized. By eliminating governorships held by nobles on a hereditary basis and instituting a new hierarchy of local officials directly responsible to the king, the Assyrian kings gained greater control over the resources of the empire. The Assyrians also developed an efficient system of communication to administer their empire more effectively. A network of posting stages was established throughout the empire that used relays of horses (mules or donkeys in mountainous terrain) to carry messages. The system was so effective that a provincial governor anywhere in the empire (except Egypt) could send a question and receive an answer from the king in his palace within a week.

The ability of the Assyrians to conquer and maintain an empire was due to a combination of factors. Over many years of practice, the Assyrians developed effective military leaders and fighters. They were able to enlist and deploy troops numbering in the hundreds of thousands, although most campaigns were not conducted on such a large scale. In 845 B.C., an Assyrian army of 120,000 men crossed the Euphrates on a campaign. Size alone was not decisive, however. The Assyrian army was extremely well organized and disciplined. It included a standing army of infantrymen as its core, accompanied by cavalrymen and horse-drawn war chariots that were used as mobile platforms for shooting arrows. Moreover, the Assyrians had the advantage of having the first large armies equipped with iron weapons. The Hittites had been the first to develop iron metallurgy, but iron came to be used extensively only after new methods for hardening it became common after 1000 B.C.

Another factor in the army's success was its ability to use different kinds of military tactics (see the box on p. 36). The Assyrian army was capable of waging guerrilla warfare in the mountains and set battles on open ground as well as laying siege to cities. The Assyrians were especially renowned for their siege warfare. They would hammer a city's walls with heavy, wheeled siege towers and armored battering rams, while sappers dug tunnels to undermine the walls' foundations and cause them to collapse. The besieging Assyrian armies learned to cut off supplies so effectively that if a city did not fall to them, the inhabitants could be starved into submission.

A final factor in the effectiveness of the Assyrian military machine was its ability to create a climate of terror as an instrument of warfare. The Assyrians became famous for their terror tactics, although some historians believe that their policies were no worse than those of other conquerors. As a matter of regular policy, the Assyrians laid waste the land in which they were fighting, smashing dams, looting and destroying towns, setting crops on fire, and cutting down trees, particularly fruit trees. The Assyrians were especially known for committing atrocities on their captives. King Ashurnasirpal recorded this account of his treatment of prisoners:

> 3000 of their combat troops I felled with weapons. . . . Many of the captives taken from them I burned in a fire. Many I took alive; from some of these I cut off their hands to the wrist, from others I cut off their noses, ears and fingers; I put out the eyes of many of the soldiers. . . . I burned their young men and women to death.

After conquering another city, the same king wrote: "I fixed up a pile of corpses in front of the city's gate. I flayed the nobles, as many as had rebelled, and spread their skins out on the piles. . . . I flayed many within my land and spread their skins out on the walls."[6] (Obviously, not a king to play games with!) Note that this policy of extreme

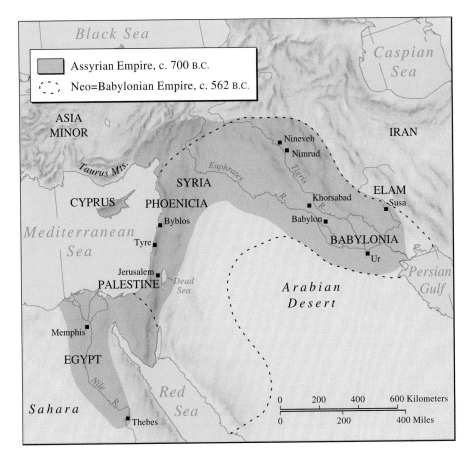

Map 2.2 The Assyrian and Neo-Babylonian Empires.

The Assyrian Military Machine

The Assyrians won a reputation for having a mighty military machine. They were able to use a variety of military tactics and were successful whether they were employing guerrilla warfare, fighting set battles, or laying siege to cities. In these three selections, Assyrian kings describe their military conquests.

King Sennacherib (704–681 B.C.) Describes a Battle with the Elamites in 691

At the command of the god Ashur, the great Lord, I rushed upon the enemy like the approach of a hurricane. . . . I put them to rout and turned them back. I transfixed the troops of the enemy with javelins and arrows. . . . I cut their throats like sheep. . . . My prancing steeds, trained to harness, plunged into their welling blood as into a river; the wheels of my battle chariot were bespattered with blood and filth. I filled the plain with the corpses of their warriors like herbage. . . . As to the sheikhs of the Chaldeans, panic from my onslaught overwhelmed them like a demon. They abandoned their tents and fled for their lives, crushing the corpses of their troop as they went. . . . In their terror they passed scalding urine and voided their excrement into their chariots.

King Sennacherib Describes His Siege of Jerusalem (701 B.C.)

As to Hezekiah, the Jew, he did not submit to my yoke, I laid siege to forty-six of his strong cities, walled forts and to the countless small villages in their vicinity, and conquered them by means of well-stamped earth-ramps, and battering-rams brought thus near to the walls combined with the attack by foot soldiers, using mines, breeches as well as sapper work. I drove out of them 200,150 people, young and old, male and female, horses, mules, donkeys, camels, big and small cattle beyond counting, and considered them booty. Himself I made a prisoner in Jerusalem, his royal residence, like a bird in a cage. I surrounded him with earthwork in order to molest those who were leaving his city's gate.

King Ashurbanipal (669–626 B.C.) Describes His Treatment of Conquered Babylon

I tore out the tongues of those whose slanderous mouths had uttered blasphemies against my god Ashur and had plotted against me, his god-fearing prince; I defeated them completely. The others, I smashed alive with the very same statues of protective deities with which they had smashed my own grandfather Sennacherib—now finally as a belated burial sacrifice for his soul. I fed their corpses, cut into small pieces, to dogs, pigs, . . . vultures, the birds of the sky and also the fish of the ocean. After I had performed this and thus made quiet again the hearts of the great gods, my lords, I removed the corpses of those whom the pestilence had felled, whose leftovers after the dogs and pigs had fed on them were obstructing the streets, filling the places of Babylon, and of those who had lost their lives through the terrible famine.

cruelty to prisoners was not used against all enemies, but was primarily reserved for those who were already part of the empire and then rebelled against Assyrian rule.

Assyrian Society and Culture

Unlike the Hebrews, the Assyrians were not fearful of mixing with other peoples. In fact, the Assyrian policy of deporting many prisoners of newly conquered territories to Assyria created a polyglot society in which ethnic differences were not very important. It has been estimated that over a period of three centuries between four and five million people were deported to Assyria, resulting in a population that was very racially and linguistically mixed. What gave identity to the Assyrians themselves was their language, although even that was akin to that of their southern neighbors in Babylonia who also spoke a Semitic language. Religion was also a cohesive force. Assyria was literally "the land of Ashur," a reference to its chief god. The king, as the human representative of the god Ashur, provided a final unifying focus.

Agriculture formed the principal basis of Assyrian life. Assyria was a land of farming villages with relatively few significant cities, especially in comparison to Mesopotamia. Unlike Mesopotamia, where farming required the minute organization of large numbers of people to control irrigation, Assyrian farms received sufficient moisture from regular rainfall.

Trade was second to agriculture in economic importance. For internal trade, metals, such as gold, silver, copper, and bronze, were used as a medium of exchange. Various agricultural products also served as a form of payment

◆ **King Ashurbanipal's Lion Hunt.** This relief, sculptured on alabaster as a decoration for the northern palace in Nineveh, depicts King Ashurbanipal engaged in a lion hunt. The relief sculpture, one of the best known forms of Assyrian art, ironically reached its high point under Ashurbanipal at the same time that the Assyrian Empire began to disintegrate.

or exchange. Because of their geographical location, the Assyrians served as middlemen and participated in an international trade in which they imported timber, wine, and precious metals and stones while exporting textiles produced in palaces, temples, and private villas.

The culture of the Assyrian Empire was essentially hybrid in nature. The Assyrians assimilated much of Mesopotamian civilization and saw themselves as guardians of Sumerian and Babylonian culture. Ashurbanipal, for example, established a large library at Nineveh that included the available works of Mesopotamian history. Assyrian kings also tried to maintain old traditions when they rebuilt damaged temples by constructing the new buildings on the original foundations, not in new locations. Assyrian religion reflected this assimilation of other cultures as well. Although the Assyrians had their own national god Ashur as their chief deity, virtually all of their remaining gods and goddesses were Mesopotamian.

Among the best known objects of Assyrian art are the relief sculptures found in the royal palaces in three of the Assyrian capital cities, Nimrud, Nineveh, and Khorsabad. These reliefs, which were begun in the ninth century and reached their high point in the reign of Ashurbanipal in the seventh century, depicted two different kinds of subject matter: ritual or ceremonial scenes revolving around the person of the king and scenes of hunting and war. The latter show realistic action scenes of the king and his warriors engaged in battle or hunting animals, especially lions. These pictures depict a strongly masculine world where discipline, brute force, and toughness are the enduring values, indeed, the very values of the Assyrian military monarchy.

The Persian Empire

The Chaldeans, a Semitic-speaking people, had gained ascendancy in Babylonia by the seventh century and came to form the chief resistance to Assyrian control of Mesopotamia. After the collapse of the Assyrian Empire, the Chaldeans, under their king Nebuchadnezzar II (605–562 B.C.), regained for Babylonia a position as the leading power in the ancient Near East.

Nebuchadnezzar rebuilt Babylon as the center of his empire, giving it a reputation as one of the great cities of the ancient world. Babylon was surrounded by great walls, eight miles in length, encircled by a moat filled by the Euphrates River. The city was adorned with temples and palaces; most famous of all were the Hanging Gardens, known as one of the Seven Wonders of the ancient world. These were supposedly built to satisfy Nebuchadnezzar's wife, a princess from the land of Media, who missed the mountains of her homeland. A series of terraces led to a plateau, an artificial mountain, at the top of which grew the lush gardens irrigated by water piped to the top. From a distance the gardens appeared to be suspended in air. But the splendor of the Neo-Babylonian Empire proved to be short-lived when Babylon fell to the Persians in 539 B.C.

The Persians were an Indo-European-speaking people who lived in southwestern Iran and fell subject to the

CHRONOLOGY

The Empires

The Assyrians	
Height of power	700 B.C.
Ashurbanipal	669–626 B.C.
Capture of Nineveh	612 B.C.
Assyrian Empire destroyed	605 B.C.
The Chaldeans	
Ascendancy in Babylonia	600s B.C.
Height of Neo-Babylonian Empire under King Nebuchadnezzar II	605–562 B.C.
Fall of Babylon	539 B.C.
The Persians	
Unification under Achaemenid dynasty	600s B.C.
Persian control over Medes	550 B.C.
Conquests of Cyrus the Great	559–530 B.C.
Cambyses and conquest of Egypt	530–522 B.C.
Reign of Dairus	521–486 B.C.

ethnically related Medes. Primarily nomadic, the Persians were organized in tribes or clans led by petty kings assisted by a group of warriors who formed a class of nobles. At the beginning of the seventh century, the Persians became unified under the Achaemenid dynasty, based in Persis in southern Iran. One of the dynasty's members, Cyrus (559–530 B.C.), created a powerful Persian state that rearranged the political map of the ancient Near East.

In 550 B.C., Cyrus established Persian control over the Medes, making Media the first Persian satrapy or province. Three years later, Cyrus defeated the prosperous Lydian kingdom in western Asia Minor, and Lydia became another Persian satrapy. Cyrus's forces then went on to conquer the Greek city-states that had been established on the Ionian coast. Cyrus then turned eastward, subduing the eastern part of the Iranian plateau, Sogdia, and even western India. His eastern frontiers secured, Cyrus entered Mesopotamia in 539 and captured Babylon. His treatment of Babylonia showed remarkable restraint and wisdom. Babylonia was made into a Persian province under a Persian satrap, but many government officials were kept in their positions. Cyrus took the title "King of All, Great King, Mighty King, King of Babylon,

King of the Land of Sumer and Akkad, King of the Four Rims (of the Earth), the Son of Cambyses the Great King, King of Anshan,"[7] and insisted that he stood in the ancient, unbroken line of Babylonian kings. By appealing to the vanity of the Babylonians, he won their loyalty. Cyrus also issued an edict permitting the Jews, who had been brought to Babylon in the sixth century B.C., to return to Jerusalem with their sacred temple objects and to rebuild their Temple as well.

To his contemporaries, Cyrus the Great was deserving of his epithet. The Greek historian Herodotus recounted that the Persians viewed him as a "father," a ruler who was "gentle, and procured them all manner of goods."[8] Certainly, Cyrus must have been an unusual ruler for his time, a man who demonstrated considerable wisdom and compassion in the conquest and organization of his empire. Cyrus attempted—successfully—to obtain the favor of the priesthoods in his conquered lands by restoring temples and permitting a wide degree of religious toleration. He won approval by using not only Persians, but also native peoples as government officials in their own states. Unlike the Assyrian rulers of an earlier empire, he had a reputation for mercy. Medes, Babylonians, Hebrews, all accepted him as their legitimate ruler. Indeed, the Hebrews regarded him as the anointed one of God: "I am the Lord who says of Cyrus, 'He is my shepherd and will accomplish all that I please;' he will say of Jerusalem, 'Let it be rebuilt;' and of the temple, 'Let its foundations be laid.' This is what the Lord says to his anointed, to Cyrus, whose right hand I take hold of to subdue nations before him."[9] Cyrus had a genuine respect for ancient civilizations—in building his palaces, he made use of Assyrian, Babylonian, Egyptian, and Lydian practices. Indeed, Cyrus had a sense that he was creating a "world empire" that included peoples who had ancient and venerable traditions and institutions.

Cyrus's successors extended the territory of the Persian Empire. His son Cambyses (530–522 B.C.) undertook a successful invasion of Egypt and made it into a satrapy with Memphis as its capital. Darius (521–486 B.C.) added a new Persian province in western India that extended to the Indus River and moved into Europe proper, conquering Thrace and making the Macedonian king a vassal. A revolt of the Ionian Greek cities in 499 B.C. resulted in temporary freedom for these communities in western Asia Minor. Aid from the Greek mainland, most notably from Athens, encouraged the Ionians to invade Lydia and burn Sardis, center of the Lydian satrap. This event led to Darius's involvement with the mainland Greeks. After reestablishing control of the Ionian Greek cities, Darius undertook an invasion of the Greek mainland,

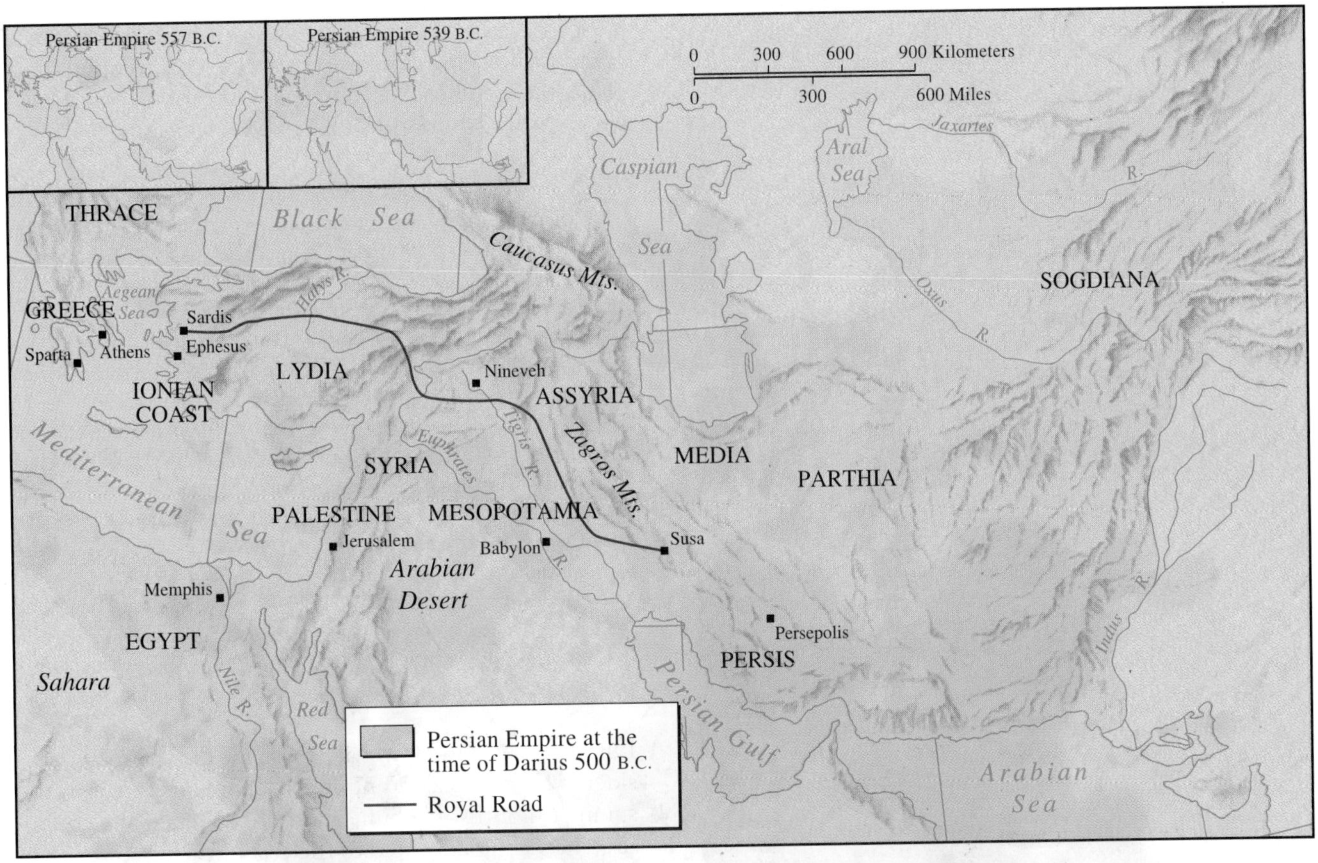

Map 2.3 The Persian Empire at the Time of Darius.

which culminated in the famous Athenian victory in the Battle of Marathon in 490 B.C. (see Chapter 3).

Governing the Empire

By the reign of Darius, the Persians had created the largest empire the world had yet seen. It included not only all the old centers of power in the Near East, Egypt, Mesopotamia, and Assyria, but also extended into Thrace and Asia Minor in the west and into India in the east. For administrative purposes, the empire had been divided into approximately twenty provinces called satrapies. Each province was ruled by a governor or satrap, literally a "protector of the Kingdom." Although Darius had not introduced the system of satrapies, he did see that it was organized more rationally. He created a sensible system for calculating the tribute that each satrapy owed to the central government and gave satraps specific civil and military duties. They collected tributes, were responsible for justice and security, raised military levies for the royal army, and normally commanded the military forces within their satrapies. In terms of real power, the satraps were miniature kings with courts imitative of the Great King's.

From the time of Darius on, satraps were men of Persian descent. The major satrapies were given to princes of the royal family, and their position became essentially hereditary. The minor satrapies were placed in the hands of Persian nobles. Their offices, too, tended to pass from father to son. The hereditary nature of the governors' offices made it necessary to provide some checks to their power. Consequently, royal officials at the satrapal courts acted as spies for the Great King.

An efficient system of communication was crucial to sustaining the Persian Empire. Well-maintained roads facilitated the rapid transit of military and government personnel. One in particular, the so-called Royal Road, stretched from Sardis, the center of Lydia in Asia Minor, to Susa, the chief capital of the Persian Empire. Like the Assyrians, the Persians established staging posts equipped with fresh horses for the king's messengers.

◆ **Darius, the Great King.** Darius ruled the Persian Empire from 521 to 486 B.C. He is shown here on his throne in Persepolis, a new capital city that he built. In his right hand, Darius holds the royal staff. In his left hand, he grasps a lotus blossom with two buds, a symbol of royalty.

palaces. Darius in particular was a palace builder on a grand scale. His description of the construction of a palace in the chief Persian capital of Susa demonstrated what a truly international empire Persia was:

> This is the . . . palace which at Susa I built. From afar its ornamentation was brought. . . . The cedar timber was brought from a mountain named Lebanon; the Assyrians brought it to Babylon, and from Babylon the Carians and Ionians brought it to Susa. Teakwood was brought from Gandara and from Carmania. The gold which was used here was brought from Sardis and from Bactria. The stone—lapis lazuli and carnelian—was brought from Sogdiana. . . . The silver and copper were brought from Egypt. The ornamentation with which the wall was adorned was brought from Ionia. The ivory was brought from Ethiopia, from India, and from Arachosia. The stone pillars were brought from . . . Elam. The artisans who dressed the stone were Ionians and Sardians. The goldsmiths who wrought the gold were Medes and Egyptians. . . . Those who worked the baked brick (with figures) were Babylonians. The men who adorned the wall were Medes and Egyptians. At Susa here a splendid work was ordered; very splendid did it turn out.[10]

But Darius was unhappy with Susa. He did not really consider it his homeland, and it was oppressively hot in the summer months. He built another residence at Persepolis, a new capital located to the east of the old one and at a higher elevation.

The policies of Darius also tended to widen the gap between the king and his subjects. As the Great King himself said of all his subjects: "what was said to them by me, night and day it was done."[11] Over a period of time, the Great Kings in their greed came to hoard immense quantities of gold and silver in the various treasuries located in the capital cities. Both their hoarding of wealth and their later overtaxation of their subjects are seen as crucial factors in the ultimate weakening of the Persian Empire (see the box on p. 41).

In its heyday, however, the empire stood supreme, and much of its power depended on the military. By the time of Darius, the Persian monarchs had created a standing army of professional soldiers. This army was truly international in character, composed of contingents from the various peoples who made up the empire. At its core was a cavalry force of 10,000 and an elite infantry force of 10,000 Medes and Persians known as the Immortals because they were never allowed to fall below 10,000 in number. When one was killed, he was immediately replaced. The Persians made effective use of their cavalry, especially for operating behind enemy lines and breaking up lines of communication.

In this vast administrative system, the Persian king occupied an exalted position. Although not considered to be a god in the manner of an Egyptian pharaoh, he was nevertheless the elect one or regent of the Persian god Ahuramazda (see the next section, "Persian Religion"). All subjects were the king's servants, and he was the source of all justice, possessing the power of life and death over everyone. Persian kings were largely secluded and not easily accessible. They resided in a series of splendid

≋ A Dinner of the Persian King ≋

The Persian kings lived in luxury as a result of their conquests and ability to levy taxes from their conquered subjects. In this selection we read a description of how a Persian king dined with his numerous guests.

Athenaeus, *The Deipnosophists*, IV: 145–46

Heracleides of Cumae, author of the *Persian History* writes in the second book of the work entitled *Equipment*: "All who attend upon the Persian kings when they dine first bathe themselves and then serve in white clothes, and spend nearly half the day on preparations for the dinner. Of those who are invited to eat with the king, some dine outdoors, in full sight of anyone who wishes to look on; others dine indoors in the king's company. Yet even these do not eat in his presence, for there are two rooms opposite each other, in one of which the king has his meal, in the other the invited guests. The king can see them through the curtain at the door, but they cannot see him. Sometimes, however, on the occasion of a public holiday, all dine in a single room with the king, in the great hall. And whenever the king commands a symposium [drinking-bout following the dinner] which he does often, he has about a dozen companions at the drinking. When they have finished dinner, that is the king by himself, the guests in the other room, these fellow-drinkers are summoned by one of the eunuchs; and entering they drink with him, though even they do not have the same wine; moreover, they sit on the floor, while he reclines on a couch supported by feet of gold, and they depart after having drunk to excess. In most cases the king breakfasts and dines alone, but sometimes his wife and some of his sons dine with him. And throughout the dinner his concubines sing and play the lyre; one of them is the soloist, the others sing in chorus. And so, Heracleides continues, the 'king's dinner,' as it is called, will appear prodigal to one who merely hears about it, but when one examines it carefully it will be found to have been got up with economy and even with parsimony; and the same is true of the dinners among other Persians in high station. For one thousand animals are slaughtered daily for the king; these comprise horses, camels, oxen, asses, deer, and most of the small animals; many birds are also consumed, including Arabian ostriches—and the creature is large—geese, and cocks. And of all these only moderate portions are served to each of the king's guests, and each of them may carry home whatever he leaves untouched at the meal. But the greater part of these meats and other foods are taken out into the courtyard for the body-guard and light-armed troopers maintained by the king; there they divide all the half-eaten remnants of meat and bread and share them in equal portions. . . ."

Persian Religion

Of all the Persians' cultural contributions, the most original was their religion. The popular religion of the Iranians before the advent of Zoroastrianism in the sixth century focused on the worship of the powers of nature, such as the sun, moon, fire, and winds. Mithra was an especially popular god of light and war who came to be viewed as a sun god. The people worshiped and sacrificed to these powers of nature with the aid of priests, known as Magi.

Zoroaster was a semilegendary figure who, according to Persian tradition, was born in 660 B.C. After a period of wandering and solitude, he experienced revelations that caused him to be revered as a prophet of the "true religion." It is difficult to know what Zoroaster's original teachings were since the sacred book of Zoroastrianism, the *Zend Avesta*, was not written down until the third century A.D. Scholars believe, however, that the earliest section of the *Zend Avesta*, known as the *Yasna*, consisting of seventeen hymns or gathas, contains the actual writings of Zoroaster. This enables us to piece together his message.

That spiritual message was grounded in a monotheistic framework. Although Ahuramazda was not a new god to the Iranians, to Zoroaster he was the only god and the religion he preached was the only perfect one. Ahuramazda (the "Wise Lord") was the supreme deity who brought all things into being:

This I ask of You, O Ahuramazda; answer me well:
Who at the Creation was the first father of Justice?—
Who assigned their path to the sun and the stars?—
Who decreed the waxing and waning of the moon, if it was not You?— . . .
Who has fixed the earth below, and the heaven above with its clouds that it might not be moved?—

*Who has appointed the waters and the green things upon the
    earth?—*
*Who has harnessed to the wind and the clouds their
    steeds?— . . .*
Thus do I strive to recognize in You, O Wise One,
Together with the Holy Spirit, the Creator of all things.[12]

According to Zoroaster, Ahuramazda also possessed abstract qualities or states that all humans should aspire to, such as Good Thought, Right, and Piety. Although Ahuramazda was supreme, he was not unopposed. Right is opposed by the Lie, Truth by Falsehood, Life by Death. At the beginning of the world, the good spirit of Ahuramazda was opposed by the evil spirit (in later Zoroastrianism, the evil spirit is identified with Ahriman). Although it appears that Zoroaster saw it as simply natural that where there is good, there will be evil, later followers had a tendency to make these abstractions concrete and overemphasize the reality of an evil spirit. Humans also played a role in this cosmic struggle between good and evil. Ahuramazda, the creator, gave all humans free will and the power to choose between right and wrong. The good person chooses the right way of Ahuramazda. Zoroaster taught that there would be an end to the struggle between good and evil. Ahuramazda would eventually triumph, and at the last judgment at the end of the world, the final separation of good and evil would occur. Zoroaster also provided for individual judgment as well. Each soul faced a final evaluation of its actions. If a person had performed good deeds, he or she would achieve paradise, the "House of Song" or the "Kingdom of Good Thought"; if evil deeds, then the soul would be thrown into an abyss, the "House of Worst Thought," where it would experience future ages of darkness, torment, and misery.

The spread of Zoroastrianism was due to its acceptance by the Great Kings of Persia. The inscriptions of Darius make clear that he believed Ahuramazda was the only god. Although Darius himself may have been a monotheist, as the kings and Magi or priests of Persia propagated Zoroaster's teachings on Ahuramazda, dramatic changes occurred. Zoroastrianism lost its monotheistic emphasis, and the old nature worship resurfaced. Hence, Persian religion returned to polytheism with Ahuramazda becoming only the chief of a number of gods of light. Mithra, the sun god, became a helper of Ahuramazda and later, in Roman times, the source of another religion. Persian kings were also very tolerant of other religions, and gods and goddesses of those religions tended to make their way into the Persian pantheon. Moreover, as frequently happens to the ideas of founders of religions, Zoroaster's teachings

acquired concrete forms that he had never originally intended. The struggle between good and evil was taken beyond the abstractions of Zoroaster into a strong ethical dualism. The spirit of evil became an actual being who had to be warded off by the use of spells and incantations. Descriptions of the last judgment came to be filled with minute physical details. Some historians believe that Zoroastrianism, with its emphasis on good and evil, a final judgment, and individual judgment of souls, had an impact on Christianity, a religion that eventually surpassed it in significance.

Conclusion

Around 1200 B.C., the decline of the Hittites and Egyptians had created a power vacuum that allowed a number of small states to emerge and flourish temporarily. All of them were eventually overshadowed by the rise of the great empires of the Assyrians, Chaldeans, and Persians. The Assyrian Empire was the first to unite almost all of the ancient Near East. Even larger, however, was the empire of the Great Kings of Persia. Although it owed much to the administrative organization created by the Assyrians, the Persian Empire had its own peculiar strengths. Persian rule was tolerant as well as efficient. Conquered peoples were allowed to keep their own religions, customs, and methods of doing business. The many years of peace that the Persian Empire brought to the Near East facilitated trade and the general well-being of its peoples. It is no wonder that many peoples expressed their gratitude for being subjects of the Great Kings of Persia.

The Hebrews were one of these peoples. They created no empire and were dominated by the Assyrians, Chaldeans, and Persians. Nevertheless, they left a spiritual legacy that influenced much of the later development of Western civilization. The evolution of Hebrew monotheism created in Judaism one of the world's greatest religions; it influenced the development of both Christianity and Islam. When we speak of the Judaeo-Christian heritage of Western civilization, we refer not only to the concept of monotheism, but also to ideas of law, morality, and social justice that have been important parts of Western culture.

On the western fringes of the Persian Empire, another relatively small group of people, the Greeks, were creating cultural and political ideals that would also have an important impact on Western civilization. It is to the Greeks that we must now turn.

NOTES

1. Psalms 137: 1, 4–6.
2. Psalms 145: 8–9.
3. Psalms 121: 2–3.
4. Exodus 20: 13–15.
5. Isaiah 2: 4.
6. Quoted in H. W. F. Saggs, *The Might That Was Assyria* (London, 1984), pp. 261–262.
7. Quoted in J. M. Cook, *The Persian Empire* (New York, 1983), p. 32.
8. Herodotus, *The Persian Wars*, trans. George Rawlinson (New York, 1942), p. 257.
9. Isaiah, 44: 28; 45: 1.
10. Quoted in A. T. Olmstead, *History of the Persian Empire* (Chicago, 1948), p. 168.
11. Quoted in Cook, *The Persian Empire*, p. 76.
12. Yasna 44: 3–4, 7, as quoted in A. C. Bouquet, *Sacred Books of the World* (Harmondsworth, 1954), pp. 111–112.

SUGGESTIONS FOR FURTHER READING

On the Sea Peoples, see the standard work by N. Sandars, *The Sea Peoples: Warriors of the Ancient Mediterranean* (London, 1978). A good introductory survey on the Hittites can be found in O. R. Gurney, *The Hittites*, 2d ed. (Harmondsworth, 1981).

An enormous amount of literature on ancient Israel exists. Two good studies on the archaeological aspects are Y. Aharoni, *The Archaeology of the Land of Israel* (Philadelphia, 1982); and W. F. Albright, *The Archaeology of Palestine* (Harmondsworth, 1949). For historical narratives, see especially J. Bright, *A History of Israel*, 3d ed. (Philadelphia, 1981), a fundamental study; J. M. Miller and J. H. Hayes, *A History of Ancient Israel and Judah* (Philadelphia, 1986); the well-done survey by M. Grant, *The History of Ancient Israel* (New York, 1984); and H. Shanks, *Ancient Israel: A Short History from Abraham to the Roman Destruction of the Temple* (Englewood Cliffs, N.J., 1988). For a new perspective, see N. P. Lemche, *Ancient Israel: A New History of Israelite Society* (Sheffield, 1988). A brief summary of Hebrew history and thought can be found in J. H. Hexter, *The Judaeo-Christian Tradition* (New York, 1966).

For general studies on the religion of the Hebrews, see Y. Kaufmann, *The Religion of Israel* (Chicago, 1960); and H. Ringgren, *Israelite Religion* (London, 1966). The role of the prophets is examined in J. Lindblom, *Prophecy in Ancient Israel* (Oxford, 1962); and R. B. Y. Scott, *The Relevance of the Prophets* (New York, 1968).

For a good account of the Phoenician domestic and overseas expansion, see D. Harden, *The Phoenicians*, rev. ed. (Harmondsworth, 1980). On the development of the alphabet, see D. Direnger, *The Alphabet* (London, 1975).

A detailed account of Assyrian political, economic, social, military, and cultural history is H. W. F. Saggs, *The Might That Was Assyria* (London, 1984). A. T. Olmstead, *History of Assyria* (Chicago, 1975) is a basic survey of the Assyrian Empire. Information from the Assyrians themselves can be found in A. Grayson, *Assyrian and Babylonian Chronicles* (New York, 1975). The Neo-Babylonian Empire can be examined in J. Oates, *Babylon* (London, 1979); and H. W. F. Saggs, *Babylonians* (Norman, Okla., 1995).

The classic work on the Persian Empire is A. T. Olmstead, *History of the Persian Empire* (Chicago, 1948), but the work by J. M. Cook, *The Persian Empire* (New York, 1983), provides new material and fresh interpretations. Also of value are B. Dicks, *The Ancient Persians* (Newton Abbott, 1979); and R. Frye, *The Heritage of Persia* (Cleveland, 1963). On the history of Zoroastrianism, see especially R. C. Zaehner, *The Dawn and Twilight of Zoroastrianism: Their Religious Beliefs and Practices* (London, 1979).

The Civilization of the Greeks

In 431 B.C., war erupted in Greece as two very different Greek city-states—Athens and Sparta—fought for domination of the Greek world. The people of Athens felt secure behind their walls and in the first winter of the war held a public funeral to honor those who had died in battle. On the day of the ceremony, the citizens of Athens joined in a procession, with the relatives of the dead wailing for their loved ones. As was the custom in Athens, one leading citizen was asked to address the crowd, and on this day it was Pericles who spoke to the people. He talked about the greatness of Athens and reminded the Athenians of the strength of their political system: "Our constitution," he said, "is called a democracy because power is in the hands not of a minority but of the whole people. When it is a question of settling private disputes, everyone is equal before the law. Just as our political life is free and open, so is our day-to-day life in our relations with each other. . . . Here each individual is interested not only in his own affairs but in the affairs of the state as well."

In this famous Funeral Oration, Pericles gave voice to the ideal of democracy and the importance of the individual. It was the Greeks who created the intellectual foundations of our Western heritage. They asked some basic questions about human life that still dominate our own intellectual pursuits: What is the nature of the universe? What is the purpose of human existence? What is our relationship to divine forces? What constitutes a community? What constitutes a state? What is true education? What are the true sources of law? What is truth itself and how do we realize it? The Greeks not only gave answers to these questions, they proceeded to create a system of logical, analytical thought in order to examine them. This rational outlook has remained an important feature of Western civilization.

The story of ancient Greek civilization is a remarkable one that begins with the first arrival of the Greeks around 1900 B.C. By the eighth century B.C., the characteristic institution of ancient Greek life, the polis or city-state, had emerged. Greek civilization flourished

Mycenaean Greece •

Age of Greek Expansion • • • • • • • • • •

Dark Age • • • • • • • • • • • • • • • • • • •

Classical Age • • • • • • • • • •

Reforms • • • • •
in Sparta • Cleisthenes' reforms

Battle of •   • • Great
Marathon   Peloponnesian War

Homer • •

Parthenon • • • Plato and
Aristotle

Greek drama (Aeschylus, Sophocles, Euripides) • • • • • • •

and reached its height in the classical era of the fifth century B.C., which has come to be closely identified with the achievements of Athenian democracy.

Early Greece

Geography played an important role in the evolution of Greek history. Compared to the landmasses of Mesopotamia and Egypt, Greece occupied a small area. It was a mountainous peninsula that encompassed only 45,000 square miles of territory, about the size of the state of Louisiana. The mountains and the sea played especially significant roles in the development of Greek history. Much of Greece consists of small plains and river valleys surrounded by mountain ranges 8,000 to 10,000 feet high. The mountainous terrain had the effect of isolating Greeks from one another. Consequently, Greek communities tended to follow their own separate paths and develop their own way of life. Over a period of time, these communities became attached to their independence and were only too willing to fight one another to gain advantage. No doubt the small size of these independent Greek communities fostered participation in political affairs and unique cultural expressions, but the rivalry among these communities also led to the internecine warfare that ultimately devastated Greek society.

The sea also influenced the evolution of Greek society. Greece had a long seacoast, dotted by bays and inlets that provided numerous harbors. The Greeks also inhabited a number of islands to the west, south, and particularly the east of the Greek mainland. It is no accident that the Greeks became seafarers who sailed out into the Aegean and the Mediterranean Seas first to make contact with the outside world and later to establish colonies that would spread Greek civilization throughout the Mediterranean world.

Greek topography helped to determine the major territories into which Greece was ultimately divided. South of the Gulf of Corinth was the Peloponnesus, virtually an island as seen on a map. Consisting mostly of hills, mountains, and small valleys, the Peloponnesus was the location of Sparta, as well as the site of Olympia where the famous athletic games were held. Northeast of the Peloponnesus was the Attic peninsula (or Attica), the home of Athens, hemmed in by mountains to the north and west and surrounded by the sea to the south and east. Northwest of Attica was Boeotia in central Greece with its chief city of Thebes. To the north of Boeotia was Thessaly, which contained the largest plains and became a great producer of grain and horses. To the north of Thessaly lay Macedonia, which was not of much importance in Greek history until 338 B.C. when the Macedonian king Philip II conquered the Greeks.

Minoan Crete

By 2800 B.C., a Bronze Age civilization that used metals, especially bronze, in the construction of weapons had been established in the area of the Aegean Sea. The early Bronze Age settlements on the Greek mainland, created by non-Greek-speaking peoples, were overshadowed by another Bronze Age civilization on the large island of Crete, southeast of the Greek mainland.

The civilization of Minoan Crete was first discovered by the English archaeologist Arthur Evans, who named it Minoan after Minos, the legendary king of Crete. Evans's excavations on Crete at the beginning of the twentieth century led to the discovery of an enormous palace complex at Knossus near modern Heracleion. The remains revealed a rich and prosperous culture with Knossus as the probable center of a far-ranging "sea empire," probably largely commercial in nature. Because Evans found few military fortifications for the defense of Knossus itself, he assumed that Minoan Crete had a strong navy. We do know from archaeological remains that the people of Minoan Crete were accustomed to sea travel and had made contact with the more advanced civilization of Egypt. Egyptian products have been found in Crete and Cretan products in Egypt.

The Minoan civilization reached its height between 2000 and 1450 B.C. The palace at Knossus, the royal seat of the kings, demonstrates the obvious prosperity and power of this civilization. It was an elaborate structure built around a central courtyard and included numerous private living rooms for the royal family and workshops for making decorated vases, small sculptures, and jewelry. Even bathrooms, with elaborate drains, formed part of the complex. The rooms were decorated with frescoes in bright colors showing sporting events and naturalistic scenes that have led some to assume that the Cretans had a great love of nature. Storerooms in the palace held enormous jars of oil, wine, and grain, presumably paid as taxes to the king.

The centers of Minoan civilization on Crete suffered a sudden and catastrophic collapse around 1450 B.C. The cause of this destruction has been vigorously debated. Some historians believe that a tsunami triggered by a powerful volcanic eruption on the island of Thera was responsible for the devastation. Most historians, however, maintain that the destruction was the result of invasion and pillage by mainland Greeks known as the Mycenaeans.

The First Greek State: The Mycenaeans

The term *Mycenaean* is derived from Mycenae, a remarkable fortified site first excavated by the amateur German archaeologist Heinrich Schliemann. Mycenae was one center in a Mycenaean Greek civilization that flourished between 1600 and 1100 B.C. The Mycenaean Greeks were part of the Indo-European family of peoples (see Chapter 2) who spread from their original location into southern and western Europe, India, and Iran. One group

♦ **The Minoan Sport of Bull Leaping.** Minoan bull games were held on festival days in the great palaces on the island of Crete. As seen in this fresco from the east wing of the palace at Knossus, women and men acrobats (the man in red) somersaulted over the back of the bull. Another person waited behind the bull to catch the leapers.

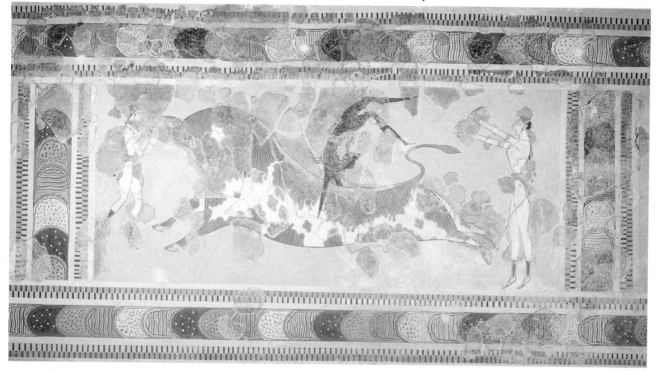

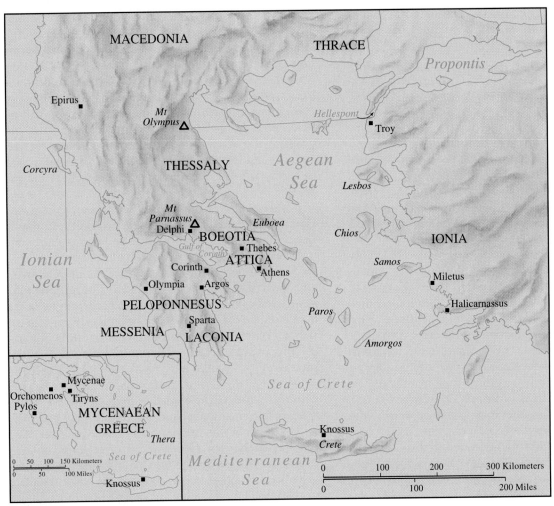

Map 3.1 Classical Greece.

entered the territory of Greece from the north around 1900 B.C. and managed to gain control of the Greek mainland and develop a civilization.

Mycenaean civilization, which reached its high point between 1400 and 1200 B.C., consisted of a number of powerful monarchies that resided in fortified palace complexes. Like Mycenae, they were built on hills and surrounded by gigantic stone walls. These various centers of power probably formed a loose confederacy of independent states with Mycenae being the strongest. Next in importance to the kings in these states were the army commanders, priests, and the bureaucrats who kept careful records. The free citizenry included peasants, soldiers, and artisans, and the lowest rung of the social ladder consisted of serfs and slaves.

The Mycenaeans were, above all, a warrior people who prided themselves on their heroic deeds in battle. Some scholars believe that the Mycenaeans, led by Mycenae itself, spread outward militarily, conquering Crete and making it part of the Mycenaean world. The most famous of all their supposed military adventures has come down to us in the epic poetry of Homer (see the section, "Homer," below). Did the Mycenaean Greeks, led by Agamemnon, king of Mycenae, sack the city of Troy on the northwestern coast of Asia Minor around 1250 B.C.? Since the excavations of Heinrich Schliemann, begun in 1870, scholars have debated this question. Many believe that Homer's account does have a basis in fact.

By the late thirteenth century B.C., Mycenaean Greece was showing signs of serious trouble. Mycenae itself was torched around 1190 B.C., reinhabited, and finally abandoned around 1125 B.C. Other Mycenaean centers show similar patterns of destruction as new waves of Greek-speaking invaders moved into Greece from the north. By 1100 B.C., the Mycenaean culture was coming to an end, and the Greek world was entering a new period of considerable insecurity.

The Greeks in a Dark Age (c. 1100–c. 750 B.C.)

After the collapse of Mycenaean civilization, Greece entered a difficult period in which the population declined and food production dropped. Because of the difficult conditions and our lack of knowledge about the period, historians call it a Dark Age. Not until 850 B.C. was farming revived. At the same time, some new developments provided the basis for a revived Greece.

During the Dark Age, large numbers of Greeks left the mainland and migrated across the Aegean Sea to various islands, and especially to the western shores of Asia Minor, a strip of territory that came to be called Ionia. Based on their dialect, the Greeks who resided there were called Ionians. Two other major groups of Greeks settled in established parts of Greece. The Aeolian Greeks, located in northern and central Greece, colonized the large island of Lesbos and the adjacent territory of the mainland. The Dorians established themselves in southwestern Greece, especially in the Peloponnesus, as well as on some of the islands in the south Aegean Sea, including Crete.

Other important activities occurred in this Dark Age as well. Greece saw a revival of some trade and some economic activity besides agriculture. Iron came into use for the construction of weapons. And at some point in the eighth century B.C., the Greeks adopted the Phoenician alphabet to give themselves a new system of writing. Near the very end of this so-called Dark Age appeared the work of Homer, who has come to be viewed as one of the truly great poets of all time.

Homer

The *Iliad* and the *Odyssey*, the first great epic poems of early Greece, were based on stories that had been passed on from generation to generation. It is generally assumed that early in the eighth century B.C., Homer made use of these oral traditions to compose the *Iliad*, his epic of the Trojan war. The war was caused by an act of Paris, a prince of Troy. By kidnapping Helen, wife of the king of the Greek state of Sparta, he outraged all the Greeks. Under the leadership of the Spartan king's brother, Agamemnon of Mycenae, the Greeks attacked Troy. Ten years later, the Greeks finally won and sacked the city.

But the *Iliad* is not so much the story of the war itself as it is the tale of the Greek hero Achilles and how the "wrath of Achilles" led to disaster. As is true of all great literature, the *Iliad* abounds in universal lessons. Underlying them all is the clear message, as one commentator has observed, that "men will still come and go like the generations of leaves in the forest; that he will still be weak, and the gods strong and incalculable; that the quality of a man matters more than his achievement; that violence and recklessness will still lead to disaster, and that this will fall on the innocent as well as on the guilty."[1]

Although the *Odyssey* has long been considered Homer's other masterpiece, some scholars believe that it was composed later than the *Iliad* and was probably not the work of Homer. The *Odyssey* is an epic romance that recounts the journeys of one of the Greek heroes, Odysseus, after the fall of Troy and his ultimate return to his wife. But there is a larger vision here as well: the testing of the heroic stature of Odysseus until, by both cunning and patience, he prevails. In the course of this testing, the underlying moral message is "that virtue is a better policy than vice."[2]

Although the *Iliad* and the *Odyssey* supposedly deal with the heroes of the Mycenaean age of the thirteenth century B.C., many scholars believe that they really describe the social conditions of the Dark Age. According to the Homeric view, Greece was a society based on agriculture in which a landed warrior-aristocracy controlled much wealth and exercised considerable power. Homer's world reflects the values of aristocratic heroes.

This, of course, explains the importance of Homer to later generations of Greeks. Homer did not so much record history: He made it. The Greeks regarded the *Iliad* and the *Odyssey* as authentic history and as the works of one poet, Homer. These masterpieces gave the Greeks an ideal past with a cast of heroes and came to be used as standard texts for the education of generations of Greek males. As one Athenian stated, "My father was anxious to see me develop into a good man . . . and as a means to this end he compelled me to memorize all of Homer."[3] The values Homer taught were essentially the aristocratic values of courage and honor (see the box on p. 49). A hero strives for excellence, which the Greeks called *arete*. In the warrior-aristocratic world of Homer, *arete* is won in struggle or contest. Through his willingness to fight, the hero protects his family and friends, preserves his own honor and that of his family, and earns his reputation. Homer gave to later generations of Greek males a model of heroism and honor. But in time, as a new world of city-

The Iliad and the Odyssey, which the Greeks believed were both written by Homer, were used as basic texts for the education of Greeks for hundreds of years in antiquity. This passage from the Iliad, describing a conversation between Hector, prince of Troy, and his wife Andromache, illustrates the Greek ideal of gaining honor through combat. At the end of the passage, Homer also reveals the Greek attitude toward women.

Homer, *Iliad*

Hector looked at his son and smiled, but said nothing. Andromache, bursting into tears, went up to him and put her hand in his. "Hector," she said, "you are possessed. This bravery of yours will be your end. You do not think of your little boy or your unhappy wife, whom you will make a widow soon. Some day the Achaeans [Greeks] are bound to kill you in a massed attack. And when I lose you I might as well be dead.... I have no father, no mother, now.... I had seven brothers too at home. In one day all of them went down to Hades' House. The great Achilles of the swift feet killed them all...."

"So you, Hector, are father and mother and brother to me, as well as my beloved husband. Have pity on me now; stay here on the tower; and do not make your boy an orphan and your wife a widow...."

"All that, my dear," said the great Hector of the glittering helmet, "is surely my concern. But if I hid my self like a coward and refused to fight, I could never face the Trojans and the Trojan ladies in their trailing gowns.

Besides, it would go against the grain, for I have trained myself always, like a good soldier, to take my place in the front line and win glory for my father and myself...."

As he finished, glorious Hector held out his arms to take his boy. But the child shrank back with a cry to the bosom of his girdled nurse, alarmed by his father's appearance. He was frightened by the bronze of the helmet and the horsehair plume that he saw nodding grimly down at him. His father and his lady mother had to laugh. But noble Hector quickly took his helmet off and put the dazzling thing on the ground. Then he kissed his son, dandled him in his arms, and prayed to Zeus and the other gods: "Zeus; and you other gods, grant that this boy of mind may be, like me, preeminent in Troy; as strong and brave as I; a mighty king of Ilium. May people say, when he comes back from battle, 'Here is a better man than his father.' Let him bring home the blood stained armor of the enemy he has killed, and make his mother happy."

Hector handed the boy to his wife, who took him to her fragrant breast. She was smiling through her tears, and when her husband saw this he was moved. He stroked her with his hand and said: "My dear, I beg you not to be too much distressed. No one is going to send me down to Hades before my proper time. But Fate is a thing that no man born of woman, coward or hero, can escape. Go home now, and attend to your own work, the loom and the spindle, and see that the maid servants get on with theirs. War is men's business; and this war is the business of every man in Ilium, myself above all."

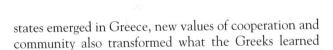

states emerged in Greece, new values of cooperation and community also transformed what the Greeks learned from Homer.

The World of the Greek City-States (c. 750–c. 500 B.C.)

In the eighth century B.C., Greek civilization burst forth with new energies. Two major developments stand out in this era: the evolution of the *polis* as the central institution in Greek life and the Greeks' colonization of the Mediterranean and Black Seas.

The Polis

The Greek *polis* (plural *poleis*) developed slowly during the Dark Age and by the eighth century B.C. had emerged as a truly unique and fundamental institution in Greek society. In a physical sense, the *polis* encompassed a town or city or even a village and its surrounding countryside. But the town or city or village served as the focus or central point where the citizens of the *polis* could assemble for political, social, and religious activities. In some *poleis*, this central meeting point was a hill, like the Acropolis at Athens, which could serve as a place of refuge during an attack and later in some sites came to be the religious center on which temples and public monuments were erected. Below the acropolis would be an *agora*, an open place that served both as a place where citizens could assemble and as a market. Citizens resided in town and country alike, but the town remained the center of political activity.

Poleis varied greatly in size, from a few square miles to a few hundred square miles. The larger ones were the product of consolidation. The territory of Attica, for example, had once had twelve *poleis*, but eventually became a single *polis* (Athens) through a process of amalgamation. Athens's population grew to over 300,000 by the fifth century B.C., with an adult male citizen body of about 43,000. Most *poleis* were much smaller, consisting of only a few hundred to several thousand people.

The *polis* was, above all, a community of citizens who shared a common identity and common goals. As a community, the *polis* consisted of citizens with political rights (adult males), citizens with no political rights (women and children), and noncitizens (slaves and resident aliens). All citizens of a *polis* possessed fundamental rights, but these rights were coupled with responsibilities. The Greek philosopher Aristotle argued that the citizen did not just belong to himself; "we must rather regard every citizen as belonging to the state." The unity of citizens was important and often meant that states would take an active role in directing the patterns of life. However, the loyalty that citizens had to their *poleis* also had a negative side. *Poleis* distrusted one another, and the division of Greece into fiercely patriotic sovereign units helped to bring about its ruin.

As the *polis* developed, so too did a new military system. In earlier times, wars in Greece had been fought by aristocratic cavalry soldiers—nobles on horseback. These aristocrats, who were large landowners, also dominated the political life of their *poleis*. But by the end of the eighth century and beginning of the seventh century B.C., a new military order came into being that was based on hoplites, heavily armed infantrymen who wore bronze or leather helmets, breastplates, and greaves (shin guards). Each carried a round shield, short sword, and a

◆   **The Hoplite Forces.** The Greek hoplites were infantrymen equipped with large round shields and long thrusting spears. In battle they advanced in tight phalanx formation and were dangerous opponents as long as this formation remained unbroken. This vase painting of the seventh century B.C. shows two groups of hoplite warriors engaged in battle. The piper on the left is leading another line of soldiers preparing to enter the fray.

thrusting spear about nine feet long. Hoplites advanced into battle as a unit, forming a phalanx (a rectangular formation) in tight order, usually eight ranks deep. As long as the hoplites kept their order, were not outflanked, and did not break, they either secured victory or, at the very least, suffered no harm. The phalanx was easily routed, however, if its order broke.

The hoplite force had political as well as military repercussions. The aristocratic cavalry was now outdated. Since each hoplite provided his own armor, men of property, both aristocrats and small farmers, made up the new phalanx. Those who could become hoplites and fight for the state could also challenge aristocratic control.

Colonization and the Rise of Tyrants

Between 750 and 550 B.C., large numbers of Greeks left their homeland to settle in distant lands. Poverty and land hunger created by the growing gulf between rich and poor, overpopulation, and the development of trade were all factors that led to the establishment of colonies. Some Greek colonies were simply trading posts or centers for the transshipment of goods to Greece. Most were larger settlements that included good agricultural land taken from the native populations found in those areas. Each colony was founded as a *polis* and was usually independent of the mother *polis* (hence the word *metropolis*) that had established it.

In the western Mediterranean, new Greek settlements were established along the coastline of southern Italy, southern France, eastern Spain, and northern Africa west of Egypt. To the north, the Greeks set up colonies in Thrace, where they sought good farmland to grow grains. Greeks also settled along the shores of the Black Sea and secured the approaches to it with cities on the Hellespont and Bosphorus, most noticeably Byzantium, site of the later Constantinople (Istanbul). By establishing these settlements, the Greeks spread their culture throughout the Mediterranean basin. Colonization also led to increased trade and industry. The Greeks on the mainland sent their pottery, wine, and olive oil to these areas; in return, they received grains and metals from the west and fish, timber, wheat, metals, and slaves from the Black Sea region. In many *poleis*, the expansion of trade and industry created a new group of rich men who desired political privileges commensurate with their wealth, but found them impossible to gain because of the power of the ruling aristocrats.

The desires of these new groups opened the door to the rise of tyrants in the seventh and sixth centuries B.C. They were not necessarily oppressive or wicked as our word *tyrant* connotes. Greek tyrants were rulers who seized power by force and who were not subject to the law. Many tyrants were actually aristocrats who opposed the control of the ruling aristocratic faction in their cities. Support for the tyrants, however, came from the new rich who made their money in trade and industry as well as from poor peasants who were in debt to landholding aristocrats. Both groups were opposed to the domination of political power by aristocratic oligarchies.

Tyrants usually achieved power by a local coup d'etat and maintained it by using mercenary soldiers. Once in power, they built new marketplaces, temples, and walls, that not only glorified the city but also enhanced their own popularity. Tyrants also favored the interests of merchants and traders. Despite these achievements, however, tyrants fell out of favor by the end of the sixth century B.C. Its very nature as a system outside the law seemed contradictory to the ideal of law in a Greek community. Although tyranny did not last, it played a significant role in the evolution of Greek history by ending the rule of narrow aristocratic oligarchies. The end of tyranny opened the door to new and more people in government. Although this trend culminated in the development of democracy in some communities, in other states expanded oligarchies of one kind or another managed to remain in power. Greek states exhibited considerable variety in their governmental structures; this can perhaps best be seen by examining the two most famous and most powerful Greek city-states, Sparta and Athens.

Sparta

Located in the southeastern Peloponnesus, Sparta, like other Greek states, was faced with the need for more land. Rather than solving this problem by colonization, Sparta looked for land nearby and, beginning around 740 B.C., undertook the conquest of neighboring Messenia despite its larger size and population. After its conquest, Sparta subjected the Messenians, although greatly outnumbered by them (seven to one), to serfdom. Known as helots, they were bound to the land for Sparta's benefit. Initially, this imperialistic venture had little apparent effect on Sparta. But in the seventh century, the Messenians revolted. Although Sparta succeeded in quelling the revolt, the struggle was so long and hard that the Spartans made a conscious decision to create a military state so that they could dominate Messenia for ages to come.

After 600 B.C., the Spartans transformed their state into a military camp (see the box on p. 53). The lives of Spartans were now rigidly organized. At birth, each child was examined by state officials who decided whether it was fit to live. Those judged unfit were exposed to die. Boys were taken from their mothers at the age of seven and put

CHRONOLOGY

◆◆◆◆◆◆◆◆◆◆◆◆◆◆◆◆◆◆◆◆◆◆◆◆◆◆◆◆◆◆◆

Sparta and Athens

Sparta

Conquest of Messenia	c. 740–710 B.C.
Messenian revolt	c. 650–625 B.C.
Beginning of Peloponnesian League	c. 560–550 B.C.

Athens

Solon's reforms	594 B.C.
Tyranny of Pisistratus	c. 560–556 and 546–527 B.C.
End of tyranny	510 B.C.
Cleisthenes's reforms	c. 508–501 B.C.

The Spartan government was headed by two kings who led the Spartan army on its campaigns. A group of five men, known as the ephors, were elected each year and were responsible for the education of youth and the conduct of all citizens. A council of elders, composed of the two kings and twenty-eight citizens over the age of sixty, decided on the issues that would be presented to an assembly. This assembly of all male citizens did not debate, but only voted on the issues put before it by the council of elders.

To make their new military state secure, the Spartans deliberately turned their backs on the outside world. Foreigners, who might bring in new ideas, were discouraged from visiting Sparta. Nor were Spartans, except for military reasons, encouraged to travel abroad where they might pick up new ideas that might prove dangerous to the stability of the state. Likewise, Spartan citizens were discouraged from studying philosophy, literature, or the arts—subjects that might encourage new thoughts. The art of war and ruling was the Spartan ideal. All other arts were frowned on.

In the sixth century, Sparta used its military might and the fear it inspired to gain greater control of the Peloponnesus by organizing an alliance of almost all the Peloponnesian states. Sparta's strength enabled it to dominate this Peloponnesian League and determine its policies. By 500 B.C., the Spartans had organized a powerful military state that maintained order and stability in the Peloponnesus. Raised from early childhood to believe that total loyalty to the Spartan state was the basic reason for existence, the Spartans viewed their strength as justification for their militaristic ideals and regimented society.

Athens

By 700 B.C., Athens had established a unified *polis* on the peninsula of Attica. Although early Athens had been ruled by a monarchy, by the seventh century B.C., it had fallen under the control of its aristocrats. They possessed the best land and controlled political and religious life by means of a council of nobles, assisted by a board of nine archons. Although there was an assembly of full citizens, it possessed few powers.

Near the end of the seventh century B.C., Athens faced political turmoil because of serious economic problems. Many Athenian farmers found themselves sold into slavery when they were unable to repay the loans they had borrowed from their aristocratic neighbors, pledging themselves as collateral. Over and over, there were cries to cancel the debts and give land to the poor. Athens seemed on the verge of civil war.

under control of the state. They lived in military-like barracks, where they were subjected to harsh discipline to make them tough and given an education that stressed military training and obedience to authority. At twenty, Spartan males were enrolled in the army for regular military service. Although allowed to marry, they continued to live in the barracks and ate all their meals in public dining halls with their fellow soldiers. Meals were simple; the famous Spartan black broth consisted of a piece of pork boiled in blood, salt, and vinegar, causing a visitor who ate in a public mess to remark that he now understood why Spartans were not afraid to die. At thirty, Spartan males were allowed to vote in the assembly and live at home, but they stayed in the army until the age of sixty.

While their husbands remained in military barracks until age thirty, Spartan women lived at home. Because of this separation, Spartan women had greater freedom of movement and greater power in the household than was common for women elsewhere in Greece. They were encouraged to exercise and remain fit to bear and raise healthy children. Like the men, Spartan women engaged in athletic exercises in the nude. Many Spartan women upheld the strict Spartan values, expecting their husbands and sons to be brave in war. The story is told that as a Spartan mother was burying her son, an old woman came up to her and said, "You poor woman, what a misfortune." "No," replied the other, "because I bore him so that he might die for Sparta and that is what has happened, as I wished."[4] Another Spartan woman, as she was handing her son his shield, told him to come back carrying his shield or being carried on it.

The Lycurgan Reforms

To maintain control over the conquered Messenians, the Spartans instituted the reforms that created their military state. These reforms are associated with the name of the law giver Lycurgus, although historians are not sure of his historicity. In this account of Lycurgus, the ancient Greek historian Plutarch discusses the effect of these reforms on the treatment and education of boys.

Plutarch, *Lycurgus*

Lycurgus was of another mind; he would not have masters brought out of the market for his young Spartans, . . . nor was it lawful, indeed, for the father himself to breed up the children after his own fancy; but as soon as they were seven years old they were to be enrolled in certain companies and classes, where they all lived under the same order and discipline, doing their exercises and taking their play together. Of these, he who showed the most conduct and courage was made captain; they had their eyes always upon him, obeyed his orders, and underwent patiently whatsoever punishment he inflicted; so that the whole course of their education was one continued exercise of a ready and perfect obedience. The old men, too, were spectators of their performances, and often raised quarrels and disputes among them, to have a good opportunity of finding out their different characters, and of seeing which would be valiant, which a coward, when they should come to more dangerous encounters. Reading and writing they gave them just enough to serve their turn; their chief care was to make them good subjects, and to reach them to endure pain and conquer in battle. To this end, as they grew in years, their discipline was proportionately increased; their heads were close-clipped, they were accustomed to go barefoot, and for the most part to play naked.

After they were twelve years old, they were no longer allowed to wear any undergarments, they had one coat to serve them a year; their bodies were hard and dry, with but little acquaintance of baths and unguents; these human indulgences they were allowed only on some few particular days in the year. They lodged together in little bands upon beds made of the rushes which grew by the banks of the river Eurotas, which they were to break off with their hands with a knife; if it were winter, they mingled some thistledown with their rushes, which it was thought had the property of giving warmth. But the time they were come to this age there was not any of the more hopeful boys who had not a lover to bear him company. The old men, too, had an eye upon them, coming often to the grounds to hear and see them contend either in wit or strength with one another, and this as seriously . . . as if they were their fathers, their tutors, or their magistrates; so that there scarcely was any time or place without some one present to put them in mind of their duty, and punish them if they had neglected it.

[Spartan boys were also encouraged to steal their food.] They stole, too, all other meat they could lay their hands on, looking out and watching all opportunities, when people were asleep or more careless than usual. If they were caught, they were not only punished with whipping, but hunger, too, being reduced to their ordinary allowance, which was but very slender, and so contrived on purpose, that they might set about to help themselves, and be forced to exercise their energy and address. This was the principle design of their hard fare.

The ruling Athenian aristocrats responded to this crisis by choosing Solon, a reform-minded aristocrat, as sole archon in 594 B.C. and giving him full power to make changes. Solon canceled all current land debts, outlawed new loans based on humans as collateral, and freed people who had fallen into slavery for debts. He refused, however, to carry out the redistribution of the land and hence failed to deal with the basic cause of the economic crisis.

Like his economic reforms, Solon's political measures were also a compromise. Though by no means eliminating the power of the aristocracy, they opened the door to the participation of new people, especially the nonaristocratic wealthy, in the government. But Solon's reforms, though popular, did not truly solve Athens' problems. Aristocratic factions continued to vie for power, and the poorer peasants resented Solon's failure to institute land redistribution. Internal strife finally led to the very institution Solon had hoped to avoid—tyranny. Pisistratus, an aristocrat, seized power in 560 B.C. Pursuing a foreign policy that aided Athenian trade, Pisistratus remained popular with the merchants. But the Athenians rebelled against his son and ended the tyranny in 510 B.C. Although the aristocrats

The Persian Wars

Rebellion of Greek cities in Asia Minor	499–494 B.C.
Battle of Marathon	490 B.C.
Xerxes invades Greece	480–479 B.C.
Battles of Thermopylae and Salamis	480 B.C.
Battle of Plataea	479 B.C.

attempted to reestablish an aristocratic oligarchy, Cleisthenes, another aristocratic reformer, opposed this plan and, with the backing of the Athenian people, gained the upper hand in 508 B.C. The reforms of Cleisthenes now established the basis for Athenian democracy.

A major aim of Cleisthenes's reforms was to weaken the power of traditional localities and regions, which had provided the foundation for aristocratic strength. He enrolled all citizens in ten new tribes, each of which contained inhabitants located in the country districts of Attica, the coastal areas, and Athens. The ten tribes thus contained a cross section of the population and reflected all of Attica, a move that diminished local interests and increased loyalty to the *polis*. Each of the ten tribes chose fifty members by lot each year for a new council of 500, which was responsible for the administration of both foreign and financial affairs and prepared the business that would be handled by the assembly. This assembly of all male citizens had final authority in the passing of laws after free and open debate; thus, Cleisthenes's reforms strengthened the central role of the assembly of citizens in the Athenian political system.

The reforms of Cleisthenes created the foundations for Athenian democracy. More changes would come in the fifth century when the Athenians themselves would begin to use the word *democracy* to describe their system (our word *democracy* comes from the Greek words *demos* [people] and *kratia* [power]). By 500 B.C., Athens was more united than it had been and was on the verge of playing a more important role in Greek affairs.

The High Point of Greek Civilization: Classical Greece

Classical Greece is the name given to the period of Greek history from around 500 B.C. to the conquest of Greece by the Macedonian king Philip II in 338 B.C. It was a period of brilliant achievement, much of it associated with the flowering of democracy in Athens under the leadership of Pericles. Many of the lasting contributions of the Greeks occurred during this period. The age began with a mighty confrontation between the Greek states and the mammoth Persian Empire.

The Challenge of Persia

As Greek civilization grew and expanded throughout the Mediterranean, it was inevitable that it would come into contact with the Persian Empire to the east. The Ionian Greek cities in western Asia Minor had already fallen subject to the Persian Empire by the mid-sixth century B.C. An unsuccessful revolt by the Ionian cities in 499 B.C.—assisted by the Athenian navy—led the Persian ruler Darius to seek revenge by attacking the mainland Greeks in 490 B.C. The Persians landed an army on the plain of Marathon, only twenty-six miles from Athens. There a mostly Athenian army, though clearly outnumbered, went on the attack and defeated the Persians decisively. Although a minor defeat to the Persians, the Battle of Marathon was of great importance to the Athenians, who had proved that the Persians could be beaten.

Xerxes, the new Persian monarch after the death of Darius in 486 B.C., vowed revenge and renewed the invasion of Greece. In preparation for the attack, some of the Greek states formed a defensive league under Spartan leadership, while the Athenians pursued a new military policy by developing a navy. By the time of the Persian invasion in 480 B.C., the Athenians had produced a fleet of about 200 vessels.

Xerxes led a massive invasion force into Greece: close to 150,000 troops, almost 700 naval ships, and hundreds of supply ships to keep their large army fed. The Greeks decided to fight a delaying action at the pass of Thermopylae along the main road into central Greece, probably to give the Greek fleet of 300 ships the chance to fight the Persian fleet. The Greeks knew that the Persian army was dependent on the fleet for supplies. A Greek force numbering close to 9,000, under the leadership of a Spartan king and his contingent of 300 Spartans, managed to hold the Persian army for two days until a Greek traitor told the Persians of a mountain path that enabled them to outflank the Greek force. Although some of the Greeks retreated when they became aware of the Persian movement, the Spartans fought to the last man.

The Athenians, now threatened by the onslaught of the Persian forces, abandoned their city. While the Persians sacked and burned Athens, the Greek fleet remained offshore near the island of Salamis and challenged the Persian navy to fight. Although the Greeks were outnumbered, they managed to outmaneuver the Persian fleet and utterly defeated it. A few months later, early in 479 B.C., the Greeks formed the largest Greek army seen up to that time and decisively defeated the Persian army at Plataea, northwest of Attica. The Greeks had won the war and were now free to pursue their own destiny.

The Growth of an Athenian Empire in the Age of Pericles

After the defeat of the Persians, Athens stepped in to provide new leadership against the Persians by forming a confederation called the Delian League. Organized in the winter of 478–477 B.C., the Delian League was dominated by the Athenians from the beginning. Its main headquarters was the island of Delos, but its chief officials, including the treasurers and commanders of the fleet, were Athenian. Under the leadership of the Athenians, the Delian League pursued the attack against the Persian Empire. Virtually all of the Greek states in the Aegean were liberated from Persian control. Arguing that the Persian threat was now over, some members of the Delian League wished to withdraw. But the Athenians forced them to remain in the league and to pay tribute. "No secession" became Athenian policy. The Delian League was rapidly becoming the nucleus of an Athenian Empire.

At home, Athenians favored the new imperial policy, especially after 461 B.C., when a political faction, led by a young aristocrat named Pericles, triumphed. Under Pericles, who was a dominant figure in Athenian politics until 429 B.C., Athens embarked on a policy of expanding democracy at home while severing its ties with Sparta and expanding its new empire abroad. This period of Athenian and Greek history, which historians have subsequently labeled the age of Pericles, witnessed the height of Athenian power and the culmination of its brilliance as a civilization.

In the age of Pericles, the Athenians became deeply attached to their democratic system. The sovereignty of the people was embodied in the assembly, which consisted of all male citizens over eighteen years of age. In the 440s, that was probably a group of about 43,000. Not all attended, however, and the number present at the meetings, which were held every ten days on a hillside east of the Acropolis, seldom reached 6,000. The assembly passed all laws and made final decisions on war and foreign policy. Pericles expanded the Athenians' involvement in their democracy (see the box on p. 56) by making lower-class citizens eligible for public offices formerly closed to them and introducing state pay for officerholders, including those who served on large Athenian juries. Poor citizens could now afford to participate in public affairs.

A large body of city magistrates, usually chosen by lot without regard to class, handled routine administrative tasks. The overall directors of policy, a board of ten officials known as generals, were elected by public vote and were usually wealthy aristocrats, even though the people were free to select otherwise. The generals could be reelected, enabling individual leaders to play an important political role. Pericles, for example, was elected to the generalship thirty times between 461 and 429 B.C. But all public officials were subject to scrutiny and could be deposed from office if they lost the people's confidence. The Athenians had also devised the practice of ostracism to protect themselves against overly ambitious politicians. Members of the assembly could write on a broken pottery fragment (*ostrakon*) the name of a person they most disliked or considered most harmful to the polis. A person who received a majority (if at least 6,000 votes were cast) was exiled for ten years.

The Athenian pursuit of democracy at home was coupled with increasing imperialism abroad as Athenian policies converted the voluntary allies of the Delian League into the involuntary subjects of an Athenian naval empire. Citing the threat of the Persian fleet in the Aegean, the Athenians moved the treasury of the league from the island of Delos to Athens itself in 454 B.C. Members were, in effect, charged a fee (tribute) for the Athenian claim of protection. Pericles also used the money in the league treasury, without the approval of its members, to build new temples in Athens, an arrogant reminder that the Delian League had become the Athenian Empire. But Athenian imperialism alarmed the other Greek states, and soon all Greece was confronted with a new war.

The Great Peloponnesian War and the Decline of the Greek States

During the forty years after the defeat of the Persians, the Greek world divided into two major camps: Sparta and its supporters and the Athenian Empire. In his classic *History of the Peloponnesian War*, the great Greek historian Thucydides pointed out that the fundamental, long-range cause of the Peloponnesian War was the fear that Sparta and its allies had of the growing Athenian Empire. Then, too, Athens and Sparta had built two very different kinds of societies, and neither state was able to tolerate the other's system. A series of disputes finally led to the outbreak of war in 431 B.C.

Athenian Democracy: The Funeral Oration of Pericles

In his History of the Peloponnesian War, the Greek historian Thucydides presented his reconstruction of the eulogy given by Pericles in the winter of 431/430 B.C. to honor the Athenians killed in the first campaigns of the Great Peloponnesian War. It is a magnificent, idealized description of the Athenian democracy at its height.

Thucydides, *History of the Peloponnesian War*

Our constitution is called a democracy because power is in the hands not of a minority but of the whole people. When it is a question of settling private disputes, everyone is equal before the law; when it is a question of putting one person before another in positions of public responsibility, what counts is not membership of a particular class, but the actual ability which the man possesses. No one, so long as he has it in him to be of service to the state, is kept in political obscurity because of poverty. And, just as our political life is free and open, so is our day-to-day life in our relations with each other. We do not get into a state with our next-door neighbor if he enjoys himself in his own way, nor do we give him the kind of black looks which, though they do no real harm, still do hurt people's feelings. We are free and tolerant in our private lives; but in public affairs we keep to the law. This is because it commands our deep respect.

We give our obedience to those whom we put in positions of authority, and we obey the laws themselves, especially those which are for the protection of the oppressed, and those unwritten laws which it is an acknowledged shame to break. . . . Here each individual is interested not only in his own affairs but in the affairs of the state as well: even those who are mostly occupied with their own business are extremely well-informed on general politics—this is a peculiarity of ours: we do not say that a man who takes no interest in politics is a man who minds his own business; we say that he has no business here at all. We Athenians, in our own persons, take our decisions on polity or submit them to proper discussions: for we do not think that there is an incompatibility between words and deeds; the worst thing is to rush into action before the consequences have been properly debated. . . . Taking everything together then, I declare that our city is an education to Greece, and I declare that in my opinion each single one of our citizens, in all the manifold aspects of life, is able to show himself the rightful lord and owner of his own person and do this, moreover, with exceptional grace and exceptional versatility. And to show that this is no empty boasting for the present occasion, but real tangible fact, you have only to consider the power which our city possesses and which has been won by those very qualities which I have mentioned.

At the beginning of the war, both sides believed they had winning strategies. The Athenians planned to remain behind the protective walls of Athens while the overseas empire and the navy kept them supplied. Pericles knew perfectly well that the Spartans and their allies could beat the Athenians in pitched battles, which was the chief aim of the Spartan strategy. The Spartans and their allies surrounded Athens, hoping that the Athenians would send out their army to fight beyond the walls. But Pericles was convinced that Athens was secure behind its walls and retaliated by sending out naval excursions to ravage the seacoast of the Peloponnesus.

In the second year of the war, however, plague devastated the crowded city of Athens and wiped out possibly one-third of the Athenian population. Pericles himself died the following year (429 B.C.), a severe loss to Athens. Despite the losses from the plague, the Athenians fought on in a struggle that dragged on for another twenty-seven years. A crushing blow came in 405 B.C., when the Athenian fleet was destroyed at Aegospotami on the Hellespont. Athens was besieged and surrendered in 404 B.C. Its walls were torn down, the navy disbanded, and the Athenian Empire destroyed. The great war was finally over.

The Great Peloponnesian War weakened the major Greek states and certainly destroyed any possibility of cooperation among the Greek states. The next seventy years of Greek history are a sorry tale of efforts by Sparta, Athens, and Thebes, a new Greek power, to dominate Greek affairs. In continuing their petty wars, the Greeks remained oblivious to the growing power of Macedonia to their north and demonstrated convincingly that the genius of the Greeks did not lie in politics. Culture, however, was quite a different story.

The Culture of Classical Greece

Classical Greece saw a period of remarkable intellectual and cultural growth throughout the Greek world. Historians agree, however, that Periclean Athens was the most important center of classical Greek culture. Indeed, the eighteenth-century French philosopher and writer Voltaire listed the Athens of Pericles as one of four happy ages "when the arts were brought to perfection and which, marking an era of the greatness of the human mind, are an example to posterity."[5]

THE WRITING OF HISTORY

History as we know it, as the systematic analysis of past events, was a Greek creation. Herodotus (c. 484–c. 425 B.C.), an Ionian Greek from Asia Minor, was the author of *History of the Persian Wars*, a work commonly regarded as the first real history in Western civilization. The Greek word *historia* (from which we derive our word *history*) means "research" or "investigation," and it is in the opening line of Herodotus's *History* that we find the first recorded use of the word:

> These are the researches [*historia*] of Herodotus of Halicarnassus, which he publishes, in the hope of thereby preserving from decay the remembrance of what men have done, and of preventing the great and wonderful actions of the Greeks and the Barbarians from losing their due meed of glory; and withal to put on record what were their ground of feud.[6]

The central theme of Herodotus's work is the conflict between the Greeks and the Persians, which he viewed as a struggle between Greek freedom and Persian despotism. Herodotus traveled widely for his information and was dependent for his sources on what we today would call oral history. Although he was a master storyteller and sometimes included considerable fanciful material, Herodotus was also capable of exhibiting a critical attitude toward the materials he used. Regardless of its weaknesses, Herodotus's *History* is an important source of information on the Persians and certainly our chief source on the Persian Wars themselves.

Thucydides (c. 460–c. 400 B.C.) was, by far, the better historian; in fact, historians consider him the greatest historian of the ancient world. Thucydides was an Athenian and a participant in the Peloponnesian War. He had been elected a general, but a defeat in battle led the fickle Athenian assembly to send him into exile, which gave him the opportunity to write his *History of the Peloponnesian War*.

Unlike Herodotus, Thucydides was not concerned with divine forces or gods as causal factors in history. He saw war and politics in purely rational terms, as the activities of human beings. He examined the causes of the Peloponnesian War in a clear and objective fashion, placing much emphasis on the accuracy of his facts. As he stated:

> And with regard to my factual reporting of the events of the war I have made it a principle not to write down the first story that came my way, and not even to be guided by my own general impressions; either I was present myself at the events which I have described or else I heard of them from eye-witnesses whose reports I have checked with as much thoroughness as possible.[7]

Thucydides also provided remarkable insight into the human condition. He believed that human nature was a constant: "It will be enough for me, however, if these words of mine are judged useful by those who want to understand clearly the events which happened in the past and which (human nature being what it is) will, at some time or other and in much the same ways, be repeated in the future."[8] He was not so naive as to believe in an exact repetition of events, but felt that political situations recur in similar fashion and that the study of history is of great value in understanding the present.

GREEK DRAMA

Drama, as we know it, was created by the Greeks and was clearly intended to do more than entertain. It was used to educate citizens and was supported by the state for that reason. Plays were presented in outdoor theaters as part of a religious festival. The form of Greek plays remained rather stable. Three male actors who wore masks acted all the parts. A chorus (also male) spoke the important lines that explained what was going on. Action was very limited, because the emphasis was on the story and its meaning. Content was generally based on myths or legends that the audience already knew.

The first Greek dramas were tragedies, plays based on the suffering of a hero and usually ending in disaster. Aeschylus (525–456 B.C.) is the first tragedian whose plays are known to us. Although he wrote ninety tragedies, only seven have survived. As was customary in Greek tragedy, his plots were simple. The entire drama focused on a single tragic event and its meaning. Greek tragedies were supposed to be presented in a trilogy (a set of three plays) built around a common theme. The only complete trilogy we possess, called the *Oresteia*, was written by Aeschylus. The theme of this trilogy is derived from Homer. Agamemnon, the king of Mycenae, returns a hero from the defeat of Troy. His wife Clytemnestra revenges the sacrificial death of her daughter Iphigenia by murdering Agamemnon, who had been responsible for Iphigenia's death. In the second play of the trilogy, Agamemnon's son Orestes avenges his father by killing his mother. Orestes is now pursued by the avenging furies who torment him for killing his mother. Evil acts breed evil acts and suffering is one's lot, suggests Aeschylus. But Orestes is put on trial and acquitted by Athena, the patron goddess of Athens. Personal vendetta has been eliminated and law has prevailed. Reason has triumphed over the forces of evil.

Another great Athenian playwright was Sophocles (c. 496–406 B.C.), whose most famous play was *Oedipus the King*. The oracle of Apollo foretells how a man (Oedipus) will kill his own father and marry his mother. Despite all attempts at prevention, the tragic events occur. Although it appears that Oedipus suffered the fate determined by the gods, Oedipus also accepts that he himself as a free man must bear responsibility for his actions: "It was Apollo, friends, Apollo, that brought this bitter bitterness, my sorrows to completion. But the hand that struck me was none but my own."[9]

The third outstanding Athenian tragedian, Euripides (c. 485–406 B.C.), tried to create more realistic characters. His plots also became more complex with a greater interest in real-life situations. Perhaps the greatest of all his plays was *The Bacchae*, which dealt with the introduction of the hysterical rites associated with Dionysus, god of wine. Euripides is often seen as a skeptic, who questioned traditional moral and religious values. Euripides was also critical of the traditional view that war was glorious. He portrayed war as brutal and barbaric and expressed deep compassion for the women and children who suffered from it.

Greek tragedies dealt with universal themes still relevant to our day. They probed such problems as the nature of good and evil, the conflict between spiritual values and the demands of the state or family, the rights of the individual, the nature of divine forces, and the nature of human beings. Over and over again, the tragic lesson was repeated: Humans were free and yet could operate only within limitations imposed by the gods. The real task was to cultivate the balance and moderation that led to awareness of one's true position. But the pride in human accomplishment and independence is real. As the chorus chants in Sophocles's *Antigone:* "Is there anything more wonderful on earth, our marvelous planet, than the miracle of man?"[10]

Greek comedy developed later than tragedy. We first see comedies organized at the festival of Dionysus in Athens in 488/487 B.C. The plays of Aristophanes (c. 450–c. 385 B.C.), who used both grotesque masks and obscene jokes to entertain the Athenian audience, are examples of Old Comedy, which was used to attack or savagely satirize both politicians and intellectuals. In *The Clouds,* for example, Aristophanes characterized the philosopher Socrates as the operator of a thought factory where people could learn deceitful ways to handle other people. Later plays gave up the element of personal attack and featured contemporary issues. Of special importance to Aristophanes was his opposition to the Peloponnesian War. *Lysistrata*, performed in 411 B.C., at a time when Athens was in serious danger of losing the war, had a comic but effective message against the war (see the box on p. 59).

THE ARTS: THE CLASSICAL IDEAL

The arts of the Western world have been largely dominated by the artistic standards established by the Greeks of the classical period. Classical Greek art did not aim at experimentation for experiment's sake, but was concerned with expressing eternally true ideals. The subject matter of this art was the human being, but presented as an object of great beauty. The classic style, based on the ideals of reason, moderation, balance, and harmony in all things, was meant to civilize the emotions.

In architecture the most important form was the temple dedicated to a god or goddess. Because Greek religious ceremonies were held at altars in the open air, temples were not used to enclose the faithful, as modern churches are. At the center of Greek temples were walled rooms that housed the statues of deities and treasuries in which gifts to the gods and goddesses were safeguarded. These central rooms were surrounded by a screen of columns that make Greek temples open structures rather than closed ones. The columns were originally made of wood, but changed to limestone in the seventh century and to marble in the fifth century B.C.

The Greeks used different shapes and sizes in the columns of their temples. The Doric order, which evolved first in the Dorian Peloponnesus, consisted of thick, fluted columns with simple capitals resting directly on a platform without a base. Above the capitals was a fairly

Athenian Comedy: Sex as an Antiwar Instrument

Greek comedy became a regular feature of the dramatic presentations at the festival of Dionysus in Athens beginning in 488/487 B.C. Aristophanes used his comedies to present political messages, and especially to express his antiwar sentiments. The plot of Lysistrata centers on a sex strike by wives in order to get their husbands to end the Peloponnesian War. In this scene from the play, Lysistrata (whose name means "she who dissolves the armies") has the women take a special oath. The oath involves a bowl of wine offered as a libation to the gods.

Aristophanes, Lysistrata

LYSISTRATA: Lampito: all of you women: come, touch the bowl, and repeat after me: *I will have nothing to do with my husband or my lover*

KALONIKE: I will have nothing to do with my husband or my lover

LYSISTRATA: *Though he come to me in pitiable condition*

KALONIKE: Though he come to me in pitiable condition (Oh, Lysistrata! This is killing me!)

LYSISTRATA: *I will stay in my house untouchable*

KALONIKE: I will stay in my house untouchable

LYSISTRATA: *In my thinnest saffron silk*

KALONIKE: In my thinnest saffron silk

LYSISTRATA: *And make him long for me.*

KALONIKE: And make him long for me.

LYSISTRATA: *I will not give myself*

KALONIKE: I will not give myself

LYSISTRATA: *And if he constrains me*

KALONIKE: And if he constrains me

LYSISTRATA: *I will be as cold as ice and never move*

KALONIKE: I will be as cold as ice and never move

LYSISTRATA: *I will not lift my slippers toward the ceiling*

KALONIKE: I will not lift my slippers toward the ceiling

LYSISTRATA: *Or crouch on all fours like the lioness in the carving*

KALONIKE: Or crouch on all fours like the lioness in the carving

LYSISTRATA: *And if I keep this oath let me drink from this bowl*

KALONIKE: And if I keep this oath let me drink from this bowl

LYSISTRATA: *If not, let my own bowl be filled with water.*

KALONIKE: If not, let my own bowl be filled with water.

LYSISTRATA: You have all sworn?

MYRRHINE: We have.

complex entablature. The Greeks considered the Doric order grave, dignified, and masculine. The Ionic style was first developed in western Asia Minor and consisted of slender columns with a more elaborate base and volute or spiral-shaped capitals. The Greeks characterized the Ionic order as slender, elegant, and feminine in principle. Corinthian columns, with their more detailed capitals modeled after acanthus leaves, came later, near the end of the fifth century B.C.

Some of the finest examples of Greek classical architecture were built in fifth-century Athens. The most famous building, regarded as the greatest example of the classical Greek temple, is the Parthenon, built between 447 and 432 B.C. The master builders Ictinus and Callicrates directed the construction of this temple consecrated to Athena, the patron goddess of Athens. We could say, however, that the Parthenon, an expression of Athenian enthusiasm, was also dedicated to the glory of Athens and the Athenians. The Parthenon typifies the principles of classical architecture: the search for calmness, clarity, and freedom from superfluous detail. The individual parts of the temple were constructed in accordance with certain mathematical ratios also found in natural phenomena. The architects' concern with these laws of proportion is paralleled by the attempt of Greek philosophers to understand the general laws underlying nature.

Greek sculpture also developed a classic style that differed significantly from the artificial stiffness of the figures of an earlier period. Statues of the male nude, the favorite subject of Greek sculptors, now exhibited more relaxed attitudes; their faces were self-assured; their bodies flexible and smooth-muscled. Although the figures possessed natural features that made them lifelike, Greek sculptors sought to achieve not realism, but a standard of ideal beauty. Polyclitus, a fifth-century sculptor, authored a treatise (now lost) on a canon of proportions that he illustrated in a work known as the *Doryphoros*. His theory maintained that the use of ideal proportions, based on mathematical ratios found in nature, could produce an

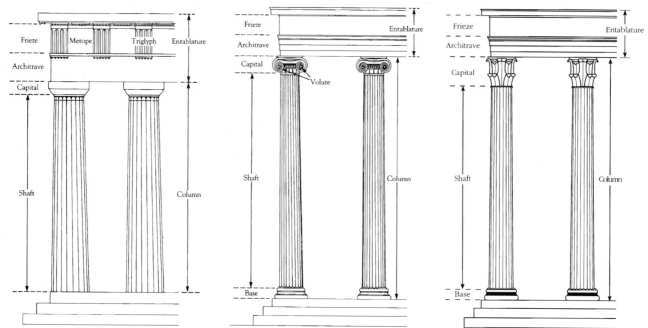

◆ **Doric, Ionic, and Corinthian Orders.** The illustration depicts the Doric, Ionic, and Corinthian orders of columns. The size and shape of a column constituted one of the most important aspects of Greek temple architecture. The Doric order, with plain capitals and no base, developed first in the Dorian Peloponnesus and was rather simple in comparison to the slender Ionic column, which had an elaborate base and spiral-shaped capitals, and the Corinthian column, which featured leaf-shaped capitals.

◆ **The Parthenon.** The arts in classical Greece were designed to express the eternal ideals of reason, moderation, balance, and harmony. In architecture, the most important form was the temple, and the classical example of this kind of architecture is the Parthenon, built between 447 and 432 B.C. The Parthenon, located on the Acropolis, was dedicated to Athena, the patron goddess of the city, but it also served as a shining example of the power and wealth of the Athenian Empire.

ideal human form, beautiful in its perfected and refined features. This search for ideal beauty was the dominant feature of the classical standard in sculpture.

THE GREEK LOVE OF WISDOM

Philosophy is a Greek word that originally meant "love of wisdom." Early Greek philosophers were concerned with the development of critical or rational thought about the nature of the universe and the place of divine forces in it. The Sophists, however, were a group of philosophical teachers in fifth-century Athens who rejected such speculation as foolish; they argued that understanding the universe was beyond the reach of the human mind. It was more important for individuals to improve themselves, so the only worthwhile object of study was human behavior. The Sophists were wandering scholars who sold their services as professional teachers to the young men of Greece, especially those of Athens. The Sophists stressed the importance of rhetoric (the art of persuasive speaking) in winning debates and swaying an audience, a skill that was especially valuable in democratic Athens. To the Sophists, there was no absolute right or wrong—what was right for one individual might be wrong for another. True wisdom consisted of being able to perceive and pursue one's own good. Because of these ideas, many people viewed the Sophists as harmful to society and especially dangerous to the values of young people.

One of the critics of the Sophists was Socrates (469–399 B.C.). Because he left no writings, we know about him only from his pupils, especially his most famous one, Plato. By occupation, Socrates was a stonemason, but his true love was philosophy. He taught a number of pupils, but not for pay, because he believed that the goal of education was only to improve the individual. He made use of a teaching method that is still known by his name. The "Socratic method" utilizes a question-and-answer technique to lead pupils to see things for themselves by using their own reason. Socrates believed that all real knowledge is within each person; only critical examination was needed to call it forth. This was the real task of philosophy since "the unexamined life is not worth living."

Socrates's questioning of authority and public demonstration of others' lack of knowledge led him into trouble. Athens had had a tradition of free thought and inquiry, but its defeat in the Peloponnesian War had created an environment intolerant of open debate and soul-searching. Socrates was accused and convicted of corrupting the youth of Athens by his teaching. An Athenian jury sentenced him to death.

One of Socrates's disciples was Plato (c. 429–347 B.C.), considered by many the greatest philosopher of Western civilization. Unlike his master Socrates, who wrote nothing, Plato wrote a great deal. In his dialogues, he used Socrates as his chief philosophical debater. Plato's philosophical thought focused on the essence of reality and was centered in the concept of Ideas or ideal Forms. According to Plato, a higher world of eternal, unchanging Ideas or Forms has always existed. To know these Forms is to know truth. These ideal Forms constitute reality and can only be apprehended by a trained mind, which, of course, is the goal of philosophy. The objects that we perceive with our senses are simply reflections of the ideal Forms. Hence, they are shadows while reality is found in the Forms themselves.

Plato's ideas of government were set out in his dialogue entitled *The Republic*. Based on his experience in Athens, Plato had come to distrust the workings of democracy. It was obvious to him that individuals could not attain an ethical life unless they lived in a just and rational state. Plato's search for the just state led him to construct an ideal state. *The Republic* is often considered the first major work of utopian literature. In his ideal state, the population was divided into three basic groups. At the top was an upper class, a ruling elite, the famous philosopher-kings: "Unless either philosophers become kings in their countries or those who are now called kings and rulers

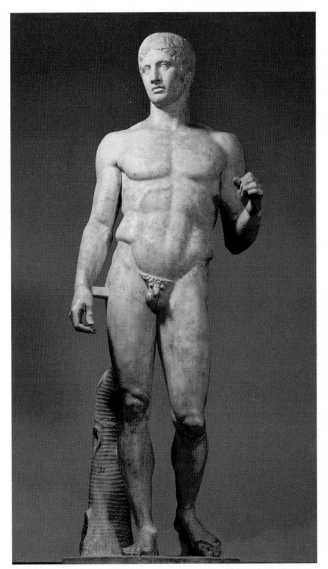

♦ **Doryphoros.** This statue, known as the *Doryphoros*, or spear-carrier, is by the fifth-century sculptor Polyclitus, who believed it illustrated the ideal proportions of the human figure. Classical Greek sculpture moved away from the stiffness of earlier statues, but retained the young male nude as the favorite subject matter. The statues became more lifelike, with relaxed poses and flexible, smooth-muscled bodies. The aim of sculpture, however, was not simply realism, but rather the expression of ideal beauty.

come to be sufficiently inspired with a genuine desire for wisdom; unless, that is to say, political power and philosophy meet together . . . there can be no rest from troubles . . . for states, nor yet, as I believe, for all mankind."[11] The second group were those who showed courage; they would be the warriors who protected the society. All the rest made up the masses, essentially people driven, not by wisdom or courage, but by desire. They would be the producers of society—the artisans, tradesmen, and farmers.

In Plato's ideal state, each group fulfilled its assigned role, creating a society that functioned harmoniously. The needs of the community, rather than the happiness of the individual, were Plato's concern, and he focused on the need for the guardians or rulers, above all, to be removed from any concerns for wealth or prestige so that they could strive for what was best for the community. To rid the guardians of these desires, Plato urged that they live together, forgoing both private property and family life. Plato believed that women, too, could be rulers; in this, he departed radically from the actual practices of the Greek states.

Plato established a school at Athens known as the Academy. One of his pupils, who studied there for twenty years, was Aristotle (384–322 B.C.), who later became a tutor to Alexander the Great. Aristotle differed significantly from his teacher in that he did not accept Plato's theory of ideal Forms. Like Plato, Aristotle believed in universal principles or forms, but he believed that form and matter were inseparable. By examining individual objects, we can perceive their form and arrive at universal principles, but they do not exist as a separate higher world of reality beyond material things, but are a part of things themselves. Aristotle's interests, then, lay in analyzing and classifying things based on thorough research and investigation. His interests were wide ranging, and he wrote treatises on an enormous number of subjects: ethics, logic, politics, poetry, astronomy, geology, biology, and physics.

Like Plato, Aristotle wished for an effective form of government that would ratonally direct human affairs. Unlike Plato, he did not seek an ideal state based on the embodiment of an ideal Form of justice, but tried to find the best form of government by a rational examination of existing governments. For his *Politics*, Aristotle examined the constitutions of 158 states and arrived at general categories for organizing governments. He identified three good forms of government: monarchy, aristocracy, and constitutional government. But based on his examination, he warned that monarchy can easily turn into tyranny, aristocracy into oligarchy, and constitutional government into radical democracy or anarchy. He favored constitutional government as the best form for most people.

Greek Religion

Greek religion was intricately connected to every aspect of daily life; it was both social and practical. Public festivals, which originated from religious practices, served specific functions: Boys were prepared to be warriors, girls to be mothers. Since religion was related to every aspect of life, citizens had to have a proper attitude to the gods. Religion was a civic cult necessary for the well-being of the state. Temples dedicated to a god or goddess were the major buildings in Greek society. Proper ritual rather than belief formed the crucial part of Greek religion. It had no official body of priests enunciating dogma and controlling religious matters. Although there were priests and priestesses to care for certain religious shrines, most religious ceremonies were led by civilians serving as priests, and priesthoods were civic offices.

The work of Homer gave an account of the gods that provided Greek religion with a definite structure. Over a period of time, most Greeks came to accept a common religion based on twelve chief gods and goddesses who were thought to live on Mount Olympus, the highest mountain in Greece. Among the twelve were Zeus, the chief deity and father of the gods; Athena, goddess of wisdom and crafts; Apollo, god of the sun and poetry; Aphrodite, goddess of love; and Poseidon, brother of Zeus and god of the seas and earthquakes.

The twelve Olympian gods were common to all Greeks, who thus shared a basic polytheistic religion. Each *polis* usually singled out one of the twelve Olympians as a guardian deity of its community. Athena was the patron goddess of Athens, for example. But each *polis* also had its own local deities who remained important to the community as a whole, and each family had patron gods as well. Because it was desirable to have the gods look favorably on one's activities, ritual assumed enormous proportions in Greek religion. Prayers were often combined with gifts to the gods based on the principle, "I give so that you [the gods] will give [in return]." Ritual also meant sacrifices, whether of animals or food. Animals were burned on an altar in front of a temple or a small altar in front of a home.

Festivals also developed as a way to honor the gods and goddesses. Some of these (the Panhellenic celebrations) were important to all Greeks and were held at special locations, such as those dedicated to the worship of Zeus at Olympia or to Apollo at Delphi. Numerous events were held in honor of the gods at the great festivals, including athletic competitions to which all Greeks were invited. The first such games were held at the Olympic festival in 776 B.C. and then held every four years thereafter to honor Zeus. Initially the Olympic contests consisted of foot races and wrestling, but later, boxing, javelin throwing, and various other contests were added.

The Greeks also had a great desire to know the will of the gods. To do so, they made use of the oracle, a sacred shrine dedicated to a god or goddess who revealed the future. The most famous was the oracle of Apollo at Delphi, located on the side of Mount Parnassus, overlooking the Gulf of Corinth. At Delphi, a priestess listened to questions while in a state of ecstasy that was believed to be induced by Apollo. Her responses were interpreted by the priests and given in verse form to the person asking questions. Representatives of states and individuals traveled to Delphi to consult the oracle of Apollo. States might inquire whether they should undertake a military expedition; individuals might raise such questions as, "Heracleidas asks the god whether he will have offspring from the wife he has now." Responses were often enigmatic and at times even politically motivated. Croesus, the king of Lydia in Asia Minor who was known for his incredible wealth, sent messengers to the oracle at Delphi, asking "whether he shall go to war with the Persians." The oracle replied that if Croesus attacked the Persians, he would destroy a mighty empire. Overjoyed to hear these words, Croesus made war on the Persians but was crushed by his enemy. A mighty empire—that of Croesus—was destroyed.

Daily Life in Classical Athens

The Greek city-state was, above all, a male community: Only adult male citizens took part in public life. In Athens, this meant the exclusion of women, slaves, and foreign residents, or roughly, 85 percent of the total population in Attica. There were probably 150,000 citizens in Athens, of whom about 43,000 were adult males who exercised political power. Resident foreigners, who numbered about 35,000, received the protection of the laws, but were also subject to some of the responsibilities of citizens, namely, military service and the funding of festivals. The remaining social group, the slaves, numbered around 100,000.

Slavery was a common institution in the ancient world. Economic needs dictated the desirability of owning at least one slave, although the very poor in Athens did not own any. The really wealthy might own large numbers, but those who did usually employed them in industry. Most often, slaves in Athens performed domestic tasks, such as being cooks and maids, or worked in the fields. Few peasants could afford more than one or two. Other slaves worked as unskilled and skilled labor. Those slaves who worked in public construction were paid the same as citizens. In many ways, as some historians have argued, although Athens was a slave-owning society, the economy was not dependent on the use of slaves. Slavery in most instances was a substitute for wage labor, which was frowned on by most freedom-loving Athenians.

The Athenian economy was largely agricultural, but highly diversified as well. Athenian farmers grew grains, vegetables, and fruit trees for local consumption, cultivated vines and olive trees for wine and olive oil, which were exportable products, and grazed sheep and goats for wool and milk products. Given the size of its population and the lack of abundant fertile land, Athens had to import between 50 and 80 percent of its grain, a staple in the Athenian diet. Trade was thus highly important to the Athenian economy. The building of the port at Piraeus and the Long Walls (a series of defensive walls four and one-half miles long connecting Athens and Piraeus) created the physical conditions that made Athens the leading trade center in the fifth-century Greek world.

Artisans were more important to the Athenian economy than their relatively small numbers might suggest. Athens was the chief producer of high-quality painted pottery in the fifth century. Other crafts had moved beyond the small workshop into the factory through the use of slave labor. The shield factory of Lysias, for example, employed 120 slaves. Public works projects also provided considerable jobs for Athenians. The building program of Pericles, financed from the Delian League treasury, made possible the hiring of both skilled and unskilled labor.

The Athenian lifestyle was basically simple. Athenian houses were furnished with necessities bought from craftsmen, such as beds, couches, tables, chests, pottery, stools, baskets, and cooking utensils. Wives and slaves made clothes and blankets at home. The Athenian diet was rather plain and relied on such basic foods as barley, wheat, millet, lentils, grapes, figs, olives, almonds, bread made at home, vegetables, eggs, fish, cheese, and chicken. Olive oil was widely used, not only for eating, but for lighting lamps, and rubbing on the body after washing and exercise. Although country houses kept animals, they were used for reasons other than their flesh: oxen for ploughing, sheep for wool, and goats for milk and cheese.

The family was an important institution in ancient Athens. It was composed of husband, wife, and children (a nuclear family), although other dependent relatives and slaves were regarded as part of the family economic unit. The family's primary social function was to produce new citizens. Strict laws of the fifth century had stipulated that a citizen must be the offspring of a legally acknowledged marriage between two Athenian citizens whose parents were also citizens.

Women were citizens who could participate in most religious cults and festivals, but were otherwise excluded from public life. They could not own property beyond personal items and always had a male guardian. The function of the Athenian woman as wife was very clear. Her

❧ Household Management and the Role of the Athenian Wife ❧

*I*n *fifth-century Athens, a woman's place was in the home. She had two major responsibilities: the bearing and raising of children and the management of the household. In his dialogue on estate management, Xenophon relates the instructions of an Attican gentleman to his new wife.*

Xenophon, *Oeconomicus*

[Ischomachus addresses his new wife] For it seems to me, dear, that the gods with great discernment have coupled together male and female, as they are called, chiefly in order that they may form a perfect partnership in mutual service. For, in the first place that the various species of living creatures may not fail, they are joined in wedlock for the production of children. Secondly, offspring to support them in old age is provided by this union, to human beings, at any rate. Thirdly, human beings live not in the open air, like beasts, but obviously need shelter. Nevertheless, those who mean to win stores to fill the covered place, have need of someone to work at the open-air occupations; since ploughing, sowing, planting and grazing are all such open-air employments; and these supply the needful food.... For he

made the man's body and mind more capable of enduring cold and heat, and journeys and campaigns; and therefore imposed on him the outdoor tasks. To the woman, since he had made her body less capable of such endurance, I take it that God has assigned the indoor tasks. And knowing that he had created in the woman and had imposed on her the nourishment of the infants, he meted out to her a larger portion of affection for newborn babes than to the man....

Your duty will be to remain indoors and send out those servants whose work is outside, and superintend those who are to work indoors, and to receive the incomings, and distribute so much of them as must be spent, and watch over so much as is to be kept in store, and take care that the sum laid by for a year be not spent in a month. And when wool is brought to you, you must see that cloaks are made for those that want them. You must see too that the dry corn is in good condition for making food. One of the duties that fall to you, how-ever, will perhaps seem rather thankless: you will have to see that any servant who is ill is cared for.

foremost obligation was to bear children, especially male children who would preserve the family line. The marriage formula that Athenians used put it succinctly: "I give this woman for the procreation of legitimate children." Secondly, a wife was to take care of her family and her house, either doing the household work herself or supervising the slaves who did the actual work (see the box above).

Women were kept under strict control. Since they were married at fourteen or fifteen, they were taught about their responsibilities at an early age. Although many managed to learn to read and play musical instruments, they were often cut off from any formal education. And women were expected to remain at home out of sight unless they attended funerals or festivals. If they left the house, they were to be accompanied.

Male homosexuality was also a prominent feature of Athenian life. The Greek homosexual ideal was a relationship between a mature man and a young male. It is most likely that this was an aristocratic ideal and not one

practiced by the common people. Although the relationship was frequently physical, the Greeks also viewed it as educational. The older male (the "lover") won the love of his "beloved" by his value as a teacher and by the devotion he demonstrated in training his charge. In a sense, this love relationship was seen as a way of initiating young males into the male world of political and military dominance. The Greeks did not feel that the coexistence of homosexual and heterosexual predilections created any special problems for individuals or their society.

Conclusion

The civilization of the ancient Greeks was the fountainhead of Western culture. Socrates, Plato, and Aristotle established the foundations of Western philosophy. Herodotus and Thucydides created the discipline of history. Our literary forms are largely derived from Greek poetry and drama. Greek notions of harmony, proportion, and beauty have remained the touchstones for all subsequent Western art. A rational method of inquiry, so important to modern science, was conceived in ancient Greece. Many political terms are Greek in origin, and so too are our concepts of the rights and duties of citizenship, especially as they were conceived in Athens, the first great democracy the world had seen. Especially during their classical period, the Greeks raised and debated the fundamental questions about the purpose of human existence, the structure of human society, and the nature of the universe that have concerned Western thinkers ever since.

All of these achievements came from a group of small city-states in ancient Greece. And yet Greek civilization also contains an element of tragedy. For all of their brilliant accomplishments, the Greeks were unable to rise above the divisions and rivalries that caused them to fight each other and undermine their own civilization. Of course, their contributions to Western civilization have outlived their political struggles, but in studying the Greeks and seeing what went wrong, we can come to appreciate one of the remaining challenges of Western civilization.

✦ **Women in the Loom Room.** In Athens, women were considered to be citizens and could participate in religious cults and festivals, but they had no rights and were barred from any political activity. Women were thought to belong in the house, caring for the children and the needs of the household. A principal activity of Greek women was the making of clothes. This vase shows two women working on a warp-weighted loom.

NOTES

1. H. D. F. Kitto, *The Greeks* (Harmondsworth, 1951), p. 64.
2. Homer, *Odyssey*, trans. E. V. Rieu (Harmondsworth, 1946), p. 337.
3. Xenophon, *Symposium*, trans. O. J. Todd (Cambridge, Mass., 1968), III, 5.
4. These words from Plutarch are quoted in E. Fantham, H. P. Foley, N. B. Kampen, S. B. Pomeroy, and H. A. Shapiro, *Women in the Classical World* (New York, 1994), p. 64.
5. Voltaire, *The Age of Louis XIV*, trans. Martyn Pollack (London, 1926), p. 1.

6. Herodotus, *The Persian Wars*, trans. George Rawlinson (New York, 1942), p. 3.
7. Thucydides, *The Peloponnesian Wars*, trans. Rex Warner (Harmondsworth, 1954), p. 24.
8. Ibid.
9. Sophocles, *Oedipus the King*, trans. David Grene (Chicago, 1959), pp. 68–69.
10. Sophocles, *Antigone*, trans. Don Taylor (London, 1986), p. 146.
11. Plato, *The Republic*, trans. F. M. Cornford (New York, 1945), pp. 178–179.

SUGGESTIONS FOR FURTHER READING

The standard one-volume reference work for Greek history remains J. B. Bury and R. Meiggs, *A History of Greece to the Death of Alexander the Great*, 4th ed. (New York, 1975). Other good, general introductions to Greek history include *The Oxford History of the Classical World*, ed. J. Boardman, J. Griffin, and O. Murray (Oxford, 1986), pp. 19–314; N. G. L. Hammond, *A History of Greece to 322 B.C.*, 3d ed. (Oxford, 1986); and two brief works, T. R. Martin, *Ancient Greece* (New Haven, Conn., 1996); and R. Sowerby, *The Greeks* (London, 1995).

Early Greek history is examined in O. Murray, *Early Greece* (London, 1980); M. I. Finley, *Early Greece: The Bronze and Archaic Ages*, 2d ed. (New York, 1982); L. W. Taylor, *The Mycenaeans*, rev. ed. (London, 1983); and J. T. Hooker, *Mycenaean Greece* (New York, 1976). For Dark Age Greece, see A. M. Snodgrass, *The Dark Age of Greece* (Edinburgh, 1971). For good introductions to Homer and the Homeric problem, see J. Griffin, *Homer* (Oxford, 1980); and D. Page, *History and the Homeric Iliad* (Berkeley, 1959). On Homer and his world, see the modern classic by M. I. Finley, *The World of Odysseus*, 2d ed. (New York, 1979).

General works on Greek history from 750 to 500 B.C. include A. M. Snodgrass, *Archaic Greece* (London, 1980); W. G. Forrest, *The Emergence of Greek Democracy* (London, 1966); and M. Grant, *The Rise of the Greeks* (London, 1987). Economic and social history of the period is covered in C. Starr, *The Economic and Social Growth of Early Greece, 800–500 B.C.* (Oxford, 1977). On colonization, see J. Boardman, *The Greeks Overseas*, rev. ed. (Baltimore, 1980). The best work on tyranny is A. Andrewes, *The Greek Tyrants* (New York, 1963). The best histories of Sparta are W. Forrest, *A History of Sparta, 950–121 B.C.*, 2d ed. (London, 1980); and P. A. Cartledge, *Sparta and Laconia: A Regional History, 1300–362 B.C.* (London, 1979). On early Athens, see the still valuable A. Jones, *Athenian Democracy* (London, 1957); and R. Osborne, *Demos* (New York, 1985). The Persian Wars are examined in A. Burn, *Persia and the Greeks: The Defense of the West*, rev. ed. (Stanford, 1984).

A general history of classical Greece can be found in S. Hornblower, *The Greek World, 479–323 B.C.* (London, 1983); and J. K. Davies, *Democracy and Classical Greece* (London, 1978). Economic aspects are examined in R. Hopper, *Trade and Industry in Classical Greece* (London, 1979). Valuable works on Athens include R. Garner, *Law and Society in Classical Athens* (New York, 1987); and D. Kagan, *Pericles of Athens and the Birth of Democracy* (New York, 1991). On the development of the Athenian empire, see R. Meiggs, *The Athenian Empire* (Oxford, 1975); and the recent work by M. F. McGregor, *The Athenians and Their Empire* (Vancouver, 1987). The best way to examine the Great Peloponnesian War is to read the work of Thucydides, *History of the Peloponnesian War*, trans. Rex Warner (Harmondsworth, 1954). A detailed study has been done in the four books by D. Kagan, *Outbreak of the Peloponnesian War* (Ithaca, N.Y., 1969); *The Archidamian War* (Ithaca, N.Y., 1974); *The Peace of Nicias and the Sicilian Expedition* (Ithaca, N.Y., 1981); and *The Fall of the Athenian Empire* (Ithaca, N.Y., 1987).

For a comprehensive history of Greek art, see M. Robertson, *A History of Greek Art*, 2 vols. (Cambridge, 1975). A good, brief study is J. Boardman, *Greek Art* (London, 1985). On sculpture, see G. M. A. Richter, *Sculpture and Sculptors of the Greeks* (Oxford, 1971). A basic survey of architecture is H. W. Lawrence, *Greek Architecture*, rev. ed. (Harmondsworth, 1983). On Greek drama, see the general work by A. Dihle, *A History of Greek Literature* (London, 1994). For sound studies of Greek history writing, see J. A. S. Evans, *Herodotus* (Boston, Mass., 1982); and K. Dover, *Thucydides* (Oxford, 1973). On Greek philosophy, a detailed study is available in W. K. C. Guthrie, *A History of Greek Philosophy*, 6 vols. (Cambridge, 1962–81). Individual works include J. Barnes, *Aristotle*

(Oxford, 1982); J. Findlay, *Plato and Platonism* (New York, 1978); and A. Taylor, *Socrates* (New York, 1933).

A short, general study of Greek religion is W. Guthrie, *The Greeks and Their Gods* (Boston, 1965). Other works of value are W. Burkert, *Greek Religion,* trans. J. Raffan (Cambridge, Mass., 1985); and H. W. Parke, *Greek Oracles* (London, 1967). E. R. Dodds, *The Greeks and the Irrational* (Berkeley, 1951), examines the role of the supernatural in Greek life.

For a general account of daily life in classical Athens, see T. B. L. Webster, *Everyday Life in Classical Athens* (London, 1969). On the family and women, see W. K. Lacey, *The Family in Classical Greece* (London, 1968); S. B. Pomeroy, *Goddesses, Whores, Wives, and Slaves* (New York, 1975), the best general book on women; and E. Fantham, H. P. Foley, N. B. Kampen, S. B. Pomeroy, and H. A. Shapiro, *Women in the Classical World* (New York, 1994). On slavery, see M. I. Finley, ed., *Slavery in Classical Antiquity* (Cambridge, 1960); and Y. Garlan, *Slavery in Ancient Greece* (Ithaca, N.Y., 1988). On homosexuality, see K. J. Dover, *Greek Homosexuality* (London, 1978).

CHAPTER 4

The Hellenistic World

In 334 B.C., Alexander the Great led an army of Greeks and Macedonians into western Asia to launch his attack on the Persian Empire. Years of campaigning resulted in the complete defeat of the Persians, and in 327 B.C. Alexander and his troops pushed east into India. But two more years of fighting in an exotic and difficult terrain exhausted his troops, who rebelled and refused to go on. Reluctantly, Alexander turned back, leading his men across the arid lands of southern Iran. Conditions in the desert were appalling; the blazing sun and lack of water led to thousands of deaths. At one point, when a group of his soldiers found a little water, they scooped it up in a helmet and gave it to Alexander. Then, according to Arrian, an ancient Greek historian, Alexander, "with a word of thanks for the gift, took the helmet and, in full view of his troops, poured the water on the ground. So extraordinary was the effect of this action that the water wasted by Alexander was as good as a drink for every man in the army." Ever the great military leader, Alexander had found yet another way to inspire his troops.

Alexander the Great was the son of King Philip II of Macedonia, who in 338 B.C. had defeated the Greeks and established his control over the Greek peninsula. After Philip's death, Alexander became king and led the Macedonians and Greeks on a spectacular conquest of the Persian Empire and opened the door to the spread of Greek culture throughout the ancient Near East. Greek settlers poured into the lands of the ancient Near East as bureaucrats, traders, soldiers, and scholars. Alexander's triumph created a new series of kingdoms that blended the achievements of the eastern world with the cultural outlook and attitudes of the Greeks. We use the term Hellenistic to designate this new order. The Hellenistic world was the world of Greek and non-Greek easterners, and it resulted, in its own way, in a remarkable series of accomplishments that are sometimes underestimated. They form the story of this chapter.

Philip II conquers Greece   The Hellenistic monarchies

Conquests of Alexander the Great   Roman conquests in the east

Death of Alexander   Seleucids gain control of Judaea

Battle of Ipsus   Uprising of Judas Maccabaeus

Philosophy (Epicurus and Zeno)   Writing of history (Polybius)

Poetry

(Theocritus)   Science (Archimedes)

The Rise of Macedonia and the Conquests of Alexander

While the Greek city-states continued to fight each other, to their north a new and ultimately powerful kingdom was emerging in its own right. Although a Greek-speaking people, the Macedonians were viewed as barbarians by their southern neighbors, the Greeks. The Macedonians were mostly rural folk and were organized in tribes, not city-states. Not until the end of the fifth century B.C. did Macedonia emerge as an important kingdom. When Philip II (359–336 B.C.) came to the throne, he built an efficient army and turned Macedonia into the chief power of the Greek world. He was soon drawn into the interstate conflicts of the Greeks.

The Greeks had mixed reactions to Philip's growing strength. Some viewed Philip as a savior who would rescue the Greeks from themselves by uniting them. Many Athenians, however, especially the orator Demosthenes, portrayed Philip as ruthless, deceitful, treacherous, and barbaric and called on the Athenians to undertake a struggle against him. In a speech to the Athenian assembly, Demosthenes exclaimed: "he [Philip] is not only no Greek, nor related to the Greeks, but not even a barbarian from any place that can be named with honor, but a pestilent knave from Macedonia, from where it was never yet possible to buy a decent slave."

Demosthenes's repeated calls for action, combined with Philip's rapid expansion, finally spurred Athens into action. Allied with a number of other Greek states, Athens fought the Macedonians at the Battle of Chaeronea, near Thebes, in 338 B.C. The Macedonian army crushed the Greeks, and Philip was now free to consolidate his control over the Greek peninsula. The independent Greek *polis*, long the basic political unit of the Greek world, came to an end as Philip formed a league of the Greek states. Although Philip allowed the Greek city-states autonomy in domestic affairs, he retained the general direction of their foreign affairs. Many Greeks still objected to being subject to the less civilized master from the north, but Philip insisted that the Greek states end their bitter rivalries and cooperate with him in a war against Persia. Before Philip could undertake his invasion of Asia, however, he was assassinated, leaving the task to his son Alexander.

Alexander the Great

Alexander was only twenty when he became king of Macedonia. The illustrious conqueror was, in many ways, prepared for kingship by his father, who had taken Alexander along on military campaigns, and indeed, had given him control of the cavalry at the important battle of Chaeronea. After his father's assassination, Alexander moved quickly to assert his authority, securing the Macedonian frontiers and smothering a rebellion in Greece. He then turned to his father's dream, the invasion of the Persian Empire.

There is no doubt that Alexander was taking a chance in attacking the Persian Empire. Although weakened in some respects, it was still a strong state. Alexander's fleet was inferior to that of the Persians, and his finances were shaky at best. In the spring of 334 B.C., Alexander entered Asia Minor with an army of some 37,000 men. About half were Macedonians, the rest Greeks and other allies. The cavalry, which would play an important role as a striking force, numbered about 5,000. The army was accompanied by architects, engineers, historians, and scientists, a clear

♦ **Bust of Alexander the Great.** This bust of Alexander the Great is a Roman copy of the head of the statue, possibly by Lysippus. Although he aspired to be another Achilles, the tragic hero of Homer's *Iliad*, Alexander also sought more divine honors. He claimed to be descended from Heracles, a Greek hero worshipped as a god, and as pharaoh of Egypt, he gained recognition as a living deity.

indication of Alexander's grand vision and positive expectations at the beginning of his campaign.

His first confrontation with the Persians, at the battle at the Granicus River in 334 B.C., almost cost him his life, but resulted in a major victory. By spring of 333 B.C., the entire western half of Asia Minor was in Alexander's hands, and the Ionian Greek cities of western Asia Minor had been "liberated" from the Persian oppressor. Meanwhile, the Persian king Darius III mobilized his forces to stop Alexander's army. Although the Persian troops outnumbered Alexander's, the battle of Issus was fought on a narrow field that canceled the advantage of superior numbers and resulted in another Macedonian success. The Persian cause was certainly not helped when Darius made a spectacular exit from the battlefield before it was even clear who would be victorious. After his victory at

Issus in 333 B.C., Alexander turned south and by the winter of 332, Syria, Palestine, and Egypt were under his domination. He took the traditional title of pharaoh of Egypt and founded the first of a series of cities named after him (Alexandria) as the Greek administrative capital of Egypt. It became (and remains today) one of Egypt's and the Mediterranean world's most important cities.

In 331 B.C., Alexander renewed his offensive, moved into the territory of the ancient Mesopotamian kingdoms, and fought the decisive battle with the Persians at Gaugamela, not far from Babylon. At Gaugamela, Alexander's men were clearly outnumbered by the Persian forces, which had established the battle site on a broad, open plain where their war chariots could maneuver to best advantage. Alexander was able to break through the center of the Persian line with his heavy cavalry, followed by the infantry. The battle turned into a rout, although Darius managed to escape.

After his victory, Alexander entered Babylon and then proceeded to the Persian capitals at Susa and Persepolis where he acquired the Persian treasuries and took possession of vast quantities of gold and silver (see the box on p. 72). By 330, Alexander was again on the march, pursuing Darius. After Darius was killed by one of his own men, Alexander took the title and office of the Great King of the Persians. But he was not content to rest with the spoils of the Persian Empire. During the next three years he moved east and northeast, as far as modern Pakistan. By summer 327 B.C., he had entered India. But two more years of fighting in an exotic and difficult terrain exhausted his troops, who mutinied and refused to go on. Reluctantly, Alexander surrendered to their demands and agreed to return, leading his troops through southern Iran across the Gedrosian Desert, where they suffered heavy losses from appalling desert conditions. Alexander and the remnant of his army went to Susa and then Babylon, where he planned still more campaigns. But in June 323 B.C., weakened from wounds, fever, and probably excessive alcohol, he died at the young age of thirty-two.

THE LEGACY OF ALEXANDER

Alexander is one of the most puzzling great figures in history. Historians relying on the same sources give vastly different pictures of him. Some portray him as an idealistic visionary and others as a ruthless Machiavellian. No doubt, he was a great military leader—a master of strategy and tactics, fighting in every kind of terrain and facing every kind of opponent. Alexander was a brave and even reckless fighter who was quite willing to lead his men into battle and risk his own life. His

◆ **Alexander and Darius at the Battle of Issus.** This late Hellenistic mosaic from Pompeii depicts the battle between Alexander and Darius III, king of Persia, at Issus in 333 B.C.

Alexander landed his forces in western Asia Minor in 334 B.C. to begin his Persian campaign and first met Darius at Issus where the narrow field made the greater numbers of the Persians useless.

✖ **Map 4.1** The Conquests of Alexander the Great.

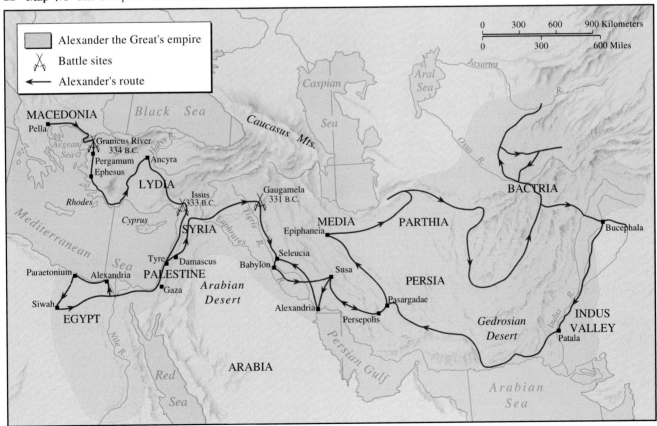

The Destruction of the Persian Palace at Persepolis

After Alexander's decisive victory at Gaugamela, he advanced into Persia where he captured the chief Persian cities. At Persepolis, he burned the Persian grand palace to the ground. The ancient historians Arrian and Diodorus of Sicily gave different explanations of this act: One argues that it was a deliberate act of revenge for the Persian invasion of Greece in the fifth century, the other that the burning resulted from a wild drinking party. Modern historians do not agree on which version is more plausible. Arrian was a Greek-speaking Roman senator of the second century A.D. Diodorus of Sicily lived in the first century B.C.

Arrian, *The Life of Alexander the Great*

Thence he marched to Persepolis with such rapidity that the garrison had no time to plunder the city's treasure before his arrival. He also captured the treasure of Cyrus the First at Pasargadae. . . . He burnt the palace of the Persian kings, though this act was against the advice of Parmenio, who urged him to spare it for various reasons, chiefly because it was hardly wise to destroy what was now his own property, and because the Asians would, in his opinion, be less willing to support him if he seemed bent merely upon passing through their country as a conqueror rather than upon ruling it securely as a king. Alexander's answer was that he wished to punish the Persians for their invasion of Greece; his present act was retribution for the destruction of Athens, the burning of the temples, and all the other crimes they had committed against the Greeks.

Diodorus of Sicily, *Library of History*

Alexander held games in honor of his victories. He performed costly sacrifices to the gods and entertained his friends bountifully. While they were feasting and the drinking was far advanced, as they began to be drunken a madness took possession of the minds of the intoxicated guests. At this point one of the women present, Thaïs by name and Attic by origin, said that for Alexander it would be the finest of all his feats in Asia if he joined them in a triumphal procession, set fire to the palaces, and permitted women's hands in a minute to extinguish the famed accomplishments of the Persians. This was said to men who were still young and giddy with wine, and so, as would be expected someone shouted out to form the procession and light torches, and urged all to take vengeance for the destruction of the Greek temples. Others took up the cry and said that this was a deed worthy of Alexander alone. When the king had caught fire at their words, all leaped up from their couches and passed the word along to form a victory procession in honor of Dionysus [god of wine and religious ecstasy].

Promptly many torches were gathered. Female musicians were present at the banquet, so the king led them all out for the procession to the sound of voices and flutes and pipes, Thaïs the courtesan leading the whole performance. She was the first, after the king, to hurl her blazing torch into the palace. As the others all did the same, immediately the entire palace area was consumed, so great was the conflagration. It was most remarkable that the impious act of Xerxes, king of the Persians, against the acropolis at Athens should have been repaid in kind after many years by one woman, a citizen of the land which had suffered it, and in sport.

example inspired his troops to follow him into unknown lands and difficult situations. We know that he sought to imitate Achilles, the warrior-hero of Homer's *Iliad*, who was an ideal still important in Greek culture. Alexander kept a copy of the *Iliad*—and a dagger—under his pillow. He also claimed to be descended from Heracles, the Greek hero who came to be worshiped as a god. No doubt, Alexander aspired to divine honors; as pharaoh of Egypt, he became a living god according to Egyptian tradition and at one point even sent instructions to the Greek cities to "vote him a god."

Regardless of his ideals, motives, or views about himself, one fact stands out: Alexander truly created a new age, the Hellenistic era. The word *Hellenistic* is derived from a Greek word meaning "to imitate Greeks." It is an appropriate way, then, to describe an age that saw the extension of the Greek language and ideas to the non-Greek world of the Near East. Alexander's destruction of the Persian monarchy had extended Greco-Macedonian rule over an enormous area. It created opportunities for Greek engineers, intellectuals, merchants, soldiers, and administrators. While the Greeks on the mainland might remain committed to the ideals of their city-states, those who followed Alexander and his successors participated in a new political unity based on the principle of monarchy. Alexander had transformed his army from a Macedonian force into an international one, owing loyalty only to himself. His successors used force to establish military monarchies that dominated the Hellenistic world after his death. Autocratic power, based on military strength and pretensions of divine rule, became a regular feature of those Hellenistic monarchies and was part of Alexander's political legacy to the Hellenistic world. His vision of empire no doubt inspired the Romans, who were, of course, the real heirs of Alexander's legacy.

But Alexander also left a cultural legacy. As a result of his conquests, Greek language, art, architecture, and literature spread throughout the Near East. The urban centers of the Hellenistic age, many founded by Alexander and his successors, became springboards for the diffusion of Greek culture. Alexander had established a number of cities and military colonies named Alexandria to guard strategic points and supervise wide areas. Most of the settlers were Greek mercenaries. It has been estimated that, in the course of his campaigns, Alexander summoned some 60,000 to 65,000 additional mercenaries from Greece, at least 36,000 of whom took residence in the garrisons and new cities. While the Greeks spread their culture in the East, they were also inevitably influenced by eastern ways. Thus, Alexander's legacy created one of the basic characteristics of the Hellenistic world: the clash and fusion of different cultures.

The World of the Hellenistic Kingdoms

The united empire that Alexander created by his conquests disintegrated soon after his death. All too soon, the most important Macedonian generals were engaged in a struggle for power. By 300 B.C., any hope of unity was dead, and eventually four Hellenistic kingdoms emerged as the successors to Alexander: Macedonia under the Antigonid dynasty, Syria and the east under the Seleucids, the Attalid kingdom of Pergamum in western Asia Minor, and Egypt under the Ptolemies. All were eventually conquered by the Romans.

The Hellenistic monarchies created a semblance of stability for several centuries, even though Hellenistic kings refused to accept the new status quo and periodically engaged in wars to alter it. At the same time, an underlying strain always existed between the new Greco-Macedonian ruling class and the native populations. Together these factors created a certain degree of tension

CHRONOLOGY

The Rise of Macedonia and the Conquests of Alexander

Reign of Philip II	359–336 B.C.
Battle of Chaeronea; Philip II conquers Greece	338 B.C.
Reign of Alexander the Great	336–323 B.C.
Alexander invades Asia; battle of Granicus River	334 B.C.
Battle of Issus	333 B.C.
Battle of Gaugamela	331 B.C.
Fall of Persepolis, the Persian capital	330 B.C.
Alexander enters India	327 B.C.
Death of Alexander	323 B.C.

that was never truly ended until the vibrant Roman state to the west stepped in and imposed a new order.

The Hellenistic kingdoms shared a common political system that represented a break with their Greek past. To the Greeks, monarchy was an institution for barbarians, associated in their minds with people like the Persians. Although they retained democratic forms of government in their cities, at the same time the Greeks of the Hellenistic world were forced to accept monarchy as a new fact of political life.

Although Alexander the Great apparently had planned to fuse Greeks and easterners—he used Persians as administrators, encouraged his soldiers to marry easterners, and did so himself—Hellenistic monarchs relied primarily on Greeks and Macedonians to form the new ruling class. It has been estimated that in the Seleucid kingdom, for example, only 2.5 percent of the people in authority were non-Greek and most of them were commanders of local military units. Those who did advance to important administrative posts had learned Greek (all government business was transacted in Greek) and had become hellenized in a cultural sense. The policy of excluding non-Greeks from leadership positions, it should be added, was not due to the incompetence of the natives, but to the determination of the Greek ruling class to maintain its privileged position. It was the Greco-Macedonian ruling class that provided the only unity in the Hellenistic world.

Cities played an especially important role in the Hellenistic kingdoms. Throughout his conquests, Alexander had founded a series of new cities and military settlements,

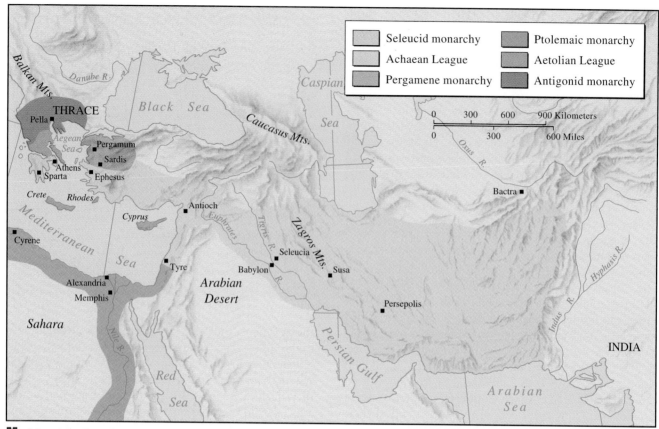

Map 4.2 The World of the Hellenistic Kingdoms.

and Hellenistic kings did likewise. The new population centers varied considerably in size and importance. Military settlements were meant to maintain order and might consist of only a few hundred men who were strongly dependent on the king. But there were also new independent cities with thousands of inhabitants. Alexandria in Egypt was the largest city in the Mediterranean region by the first century B.C.

Hellenistic rulers encouraged this massive spread of Greek colonists to the Near East because of their intrinsic value to the new monarchies. Greeks (and Macedonians) provided not only a recruiting ground for the army, but also a pool of civilian administrators and workers who would contribute to economic development. Even architects, engineers, dramatists, and actors were in demand in the new Greek cities. Many Greeks and Macedonians were quick to see the advantages of moving to the new urban centers and gladly sought their fortunes in the Near East. Greeks of all backgrounds joined the exodus, at least until around 250 B.C. when the outpouring began to slow significantly.

Within the Hellenistic cities, the culture was primarily Greek. The political institutions of the cities were modeled after those of the Greek *polis*. Greeks of the classical period would easily have recognized the councils, assemblies, and codes of law. The physical layout of the new cities was also modeled after those of the Greek homeland. Using the traditional rectilinear grid, cities were laid out with temples, altars, and stone theaters.

Many of the new urban centers were completely dominated by Greeks while the native populations remained cut off from all civic institutions. The Greeks commissioned purely Greek sculpture, read literature of the classical period, and had separate law courts for themselves. Complaints from resentful natives have been recorded. An Egyptian camel-driver, for example, complained bitterly that he was not paid regularly because he did "not know how to behave like a Greek." Not only was it difficult for easterners to enter the ranks of the ruling class, but those who did so had to become thoroughly hellenized. This often required alienation from one's own culture and led to humiliating experiences.

The Greeks' belief in their own cultural superiority provided an easy rationalization for their political dominance of the eastern cities. But Greek control of the new cities of the Near East was also necessary because the kings frequently used the cities as instruments of government, enabling them to rule considerable territory without an extensive bureaucracy. At the same time, for security reasons, the Greeks needed the support of the kings. After all, the Hellenistic cities were islands of Greek culture in a sea of non-Greeks. The relationship between rulers and cities, therefore, was a symbiotic one that bore serious consequences for the cities.

In their political system, religious practices, and city architecture, the Greeks tried to recreate the *poleis* of their homeland in their new cities. But it was no longer possible to do so. The new cities were not autonomous entities and soon found themselves dependent on the power of the Hellenistic monarchies. Although the kings did not rule the cities directly, they restricted their freedom in other ways. Cities knew they could not conduct an independent foreign policy and did not try to do so. The kings also demanded tribute, which could be a heavy burden.

The Greek cities of the Hellenistic era were the chief agents for the spread of Hellenic culture in the Near East, as far, in fact, as modern Afghanistan and India. These Greek cities were also remarkably vibrant despite their subordination to the Hellenistic monarchies and persisted in being a focal point for the loyalty of their citizens.

Economic and Social Trends in the Hellenistic World

Agriculture was still of primary importance to both the native populations and the new Greek cities of the Hellenistic world. The Greek cities continued their old agrarian patterns. A well-defined citizen body owned land and worked it with the assistance of slaves. But their farms were isolated units in a vast area of land ultimately owned by the king or assigned to large estate owners and worked by native peasants dwelling in villages. Overall, then, neither agricultural patterns nor methods of production underwent significant changes.

Few new products or manufacturing methods were introduced during the Hellenistic era, but the centers of manufacturing shifted significantly. Industry spread from Greece to the east—especially to Asia Minor, Rhodes, and Egypt. New textile centers were set up at Pergamum, while glass and silver crafts were developed in Syria. And busiest of all the cities in manufacturing was Alexandria

✦ **A Gaul and His Wife: Monument to the Victory of a Hellenistic King.** After the death of Alexander, the empire he had created collapsed, and four Hellenistic kingdoms arose in its place. Warfare continued to be of importance to these kingdoms, because it was through warfare that they were created, maintained, and expanded. They did not just fight among themselves, however; they also faced foreign enemies, such as the Gauls, who first entered the Hellenistic world in 279 B.C. This statue of a Gaulish chieftain and his wife was part of a larger monument erected to commemorate the victory of Attalus I of Pergamum over the Gauls, a victory that gave Pergamum control over much of Asia Minor.

in Egypt, center of the production of parchment, textiles, linens, oil, metalwork, and glass.

Commerce experienced considerable expansion in the Hellenistic era. Indeed, trading contacts linked much of the Hellenistic world together. The decline in the number of political barriers encouraged more commercial

≋ A New Autonomy for Women ≋

There were noticeable gains for upper-class women in Hellenistic society. But even in the lives of ordinary women, a new assertiveness came to the fore despite the continuing domination of society by men. The first selection is taken from the letter of a wife to her husband, complaining about his failure to return home. In the second selection, a father complains that his daughter has abandoned him, contrary to Egyptian law providing that children who have been properly raised should support their parents.

Letter from Isias to Hephaistion, 168 B.C.

If you are well and other things are going right, it would accord with the prayer that I make continually to the gods. I myself and the child and all the household are in good health and think of you always. When I received your letter from Horos, in which you announce that you are in detention in the Serapeum at Memphis, for the news that you are well I straightway thanked the gods, but about your not coming home, when all the others who had been secluded there have come, I am ill-pleased, because after having piloted myself and your child through such bad times and been driven to every extremity owing to the price of wheat, I thought that now at least, with you at home, I should enjoy some respite, whereas you have not even thought of coming home nor given any regard to our circumstances, remembering how I was in want of everything while you were still here, not to mention this long lapse of time and these critical days, during which you have sent us nothing. As, moreover, Horos who delivered the let-ter has brought news of your having been released from detention, I am thoroughly ill-pleased. Notwithstanding, as your mother also is annoyed, for her sake as well as for mine please return to the city, if nothing more pressing holds you back. You will do me a favor by taking care of your bodily health. Farewell.

Letter from Ktesikles to King Ptolemy, 220 B.C.

I am wronged by Dionysios and by Nike my daughter. For though I raised her, my own daughter, and educated her and brought her to maturity, when I was stricken with bodily ill-health and was losing my eyesight, she was not minded to furnish me with any of the necessities of life. When I sought to obtain justice from her in Alexandria, she begged my pardon, and in the eighteenth year she swore me a written royal oath to give me each month twenty drachmas, which she was to earn by her own bodily labor. . . . But now corrupted by Dionysios, who is a comic actor, she does not do for me anything of what was in the written oath, despising my weakness and ill-health. I beg you, therefore, O King, not to allow me to be wronged by my daughter and by Dionysios the actor who corrupted her, but to order Diophanes the strategus [a provincial administrator] to summon them and hear us out; and if I am speaking the truth, let Diophanes deal with her corrupter as seems good to him and compel my daughter Nike to do justice to me. If this is done I shall no longer be wronged but by fleeing to you, O King, I shall obtain justice.

---

traffic. Although Hellenistic monarchs still fought wars, the conquests of Alexander and the policies of his successors made possible greater trade between east and west. An incredible variety of products were traded: gold and silver from Spain; salt from Asia Minor; timber from Macedonia; ebony, gems, ivory, and spices from India; frankincense (used on altars) from Arabia; slaves from Thrace, Syria, and Asia Minor; fine wines from Syria and western Asia Minor; olive oil from Athens; and numerous exquisite foodstuffs, such as the famous prunes of Damascus. The greatest trade, however, was in the basic staple of life—grain.

One of the more noticeable features of social life in the Hellenistic world was the emergence of new opportu-nities for women—at least, for upper-class women—especially in the economic area. Documents show increasing numbers of women involved in managing slaves, selling property, and making loans. Even then, legal contracts in which women were involved had to include their official male guardians, although in numerous instances these men no longer played an important function but were only listed to satisfy legal requirements. Only in Sparta were women free to control their own economic affairs. Many Spartan women were noticeably wealthy; females owned 40 percent of Spartan land.

Spartan women, however, were an exception, especially on the Greek mainland. Women in Athens, for example, still remained highly restricted and supervised.

Although a few philosophers welcomed female participation in men's affairs, many philosophers rejected equality between men and women and asserted that the traditional roles of wives and mothers were most satisfying for women.

But the opinions of philosophers did not prevent upper-class women from making gains in areas other than the economic sphere (see the box on p. 76). New possibilities for females arose when women in some areas of the Hellenistic world were allowed to pursue education in the traditional fields of literature, music, and even athletics. Education, then, provided new opportunities for women: Female poets appeared again in the third century, and there are instances of women involved in both scholarly and artistic activities.

The creation of the Hellenistic monarchies, which represented a considerable departure from the world of the *polis*, also gave new scope to the role played by the monarchs' wives, the Hellenistic queens. In Macedonia, a pattern of alliances between mothers and sons provided openings for women to take an active role in politics, especially in political intrigue. In Egypt, opportunities for royal women were even greater because the Ptolemaic rulers reverted to an Egyptian custom of kings marrying their own sisters. Of the first eight Ptolemaic rulers, four wed their sisters. Ptolemy II and his sister-wife Arsinoë II were both worshiped as gods in their lifetimes. Arsinoë played an energetic role in government and was involved in the expansion of the Egyptian navy. She was also the first Egyptian queen whose portrait appeared on coins with her husband. Hellenistic queens also showed an intense interest in culture. They wrote poems, collected art, and corresponded with intellectuals.

Culture in the Hellenistic World

Although the Hellenistic kingdoms encompassed vast areas and many diverse peoples, the Greeks provided a sense of unity as a result of the diffusion of Greek culture throughout the Hellenistic world. The Hellenistic era was a period of considerable cultural accomplishment in many areas—literature, art, science, and philosophy. Although these achievements occurred throughout the Hellenistic world, certain centers, especially the great Hellenistic cities of Alexandria and Pergamum, stood out. In both cities, cultural developments were encouraged by the rulers themselves. Rich Hellenistic kings had considerable resources with which to patronize culture.

The Ptolemies in Egypt made Alexandria an especially important cultural center. The library became the largest

✦ **Portrait of Queen Arsinoë II.** Arsinoë II, sister and wife of King Ptolemy II, played an active role in Egyptian political affairs. This statue from around 270–240 B.C. shows the queen in the traditional style of a pharaoh.

in ancient times with more than 500,000 scrolls. The museum (literally, "temple of the Muses") created a favorable environment for scholarly research. Alexandria became home to poets, writers, philosophers, and scientists—scholars of all kinds.

New Directions in Literature and Art

The Hellenistic age produced an enormous quantity of literature, most of which has not survived. Hellenistic monarchs, who held literary talent in high esteem, subsidized writers on a grand scale. The Ptolemaic rulers of Egypt were particularly lavish. The combination of their largess and a famous library drew a host of scholars and authors to Alexandria, including a circle of poets. Theocritus (c. 315–250 B.C.), originally a native of the island of Sicily, wrote "little poems" or idylls dealing with erotic subjects, lovers' complaints, and, above all, pastoral themes expressing his love of nature and his appreciation of nature's beauties. In writing short poems, Theocritus was following the advice of Greek literary scholars who argued that Homer could never be superseded and urged writers to stick to well-composed, short poems instead.

In the Hellenistic era, Athens remained the theatrical center of the Greek world. While little remained of tragedy, a New Comedy developed, which completely rejected political themes and sought only to entertain and amuse. The Athenian playwright Menander (c. 342–291 B.C.) was perhaps the best representative of New Comedy. Plots were simple: Typically, a hero falls in love with a not-really-so-bad prostitute who turns out eventually to be the long-lost daughter of a rich neighbor. The hero marries her and they live happily ever after.

The Hellenistic period saw a great outpouring of historical and biographical literature. The chief historian of the Hellenistic age was Polybius (c. 203–c. 120 B.C.), a Greek who lived for some years in Rome. He is regarded by many historians as second only to Thucydides among Greek historians. His major work consisted of forty books narrating the history of the "inhabited Mediterranean world" from 221 to 146 B.C. Only the first five books are extant although long extracts from the rest of the books survive. His history focuses on the growth of Rome from a city-state to a vast empire. It is apparent that Polybius understood the significance of the Romans' achievement. He followed Thucydides in seeking rational motives for historical events. He also approached his sources critically and used firsthand accounts.

In addition to being patrons of literary talent, the Hellenistic monarchs were eager to spend their money to beautify and adorn the cities within their states. The founding of new cities and the rebuilding of old ones provided numerous opportunities for Greek architects and sculptors. Hellenistic architects laid out their new cities on the rectilinear grid model first used by Hippodamus of Miletus in the fifth century B.C. The buildings of the Greek homeland—gymnasia, baths, theaters, and, of course, temples—lined the streets of these cities. Most noticeable in the construction of temples was the use of the more ornate Corinthian order, which became especially popular during the Hellenistic age.

Sculptors were patronized by Hellenistic kings and rich citizens. Thousands of statues, many paid for by the people honored, were erected in towns and cities all over the Hellenistic world. Hellenistic sculptors traveled throughout this world, attracted by the material rewards offered by wealthy patrons. As a result, although distinct styles developed in Alexandria, Rhodes, and Pergamum, Hellenistic sculpture was characterized by a considerable degree of uniformity. While maintaining the technical skill of the classical period, Hellenistic sculptors moved away from the idealism of fifth-century classicism to a more emotional and realistic art, seen in numerous statues of old women, drunks, and little children at play.

A Golden Age of Science

The Hellenistic era witnessed a more conscious separation of science from philosophy. In classical Greece, what we would call the physical and life sciences had been divisions of philosophical inquiry. Nevertheless, the Greeks, by the time of Aristotle, had already established an important principle of scientific investigation, empirical research, or systematic observation as the basis for generalization. In the Hellenistic age, the sciences tended to be studied in their own right. Although Athens remained the philosophical center, Alexandria and Pergamum, the two leading cultural centers of the Hellenistic world, played a significant role in the development of Hellenistic science.

One of the traditional areas of Greek science was astronomy, and two Alexandrian scholars continued this exploration. Aristarchus of Samos (c. 310–230 B.C.) developed a heliocentric view of the universe; that is, that the sun and the fixed stars remained stationary while the earth rotates around the sun in a circular orbit. This view was not widely accepted, and most scholars clung to the earlier geocentric view of the Greeks, which held that the earth was at the center of the universe. Another astronomer—Eratosthenes (c. 275–194 B.C.)—determined that the earth was round and calculated the earth's circumference at 24,675 miles, an estimate that was within 200 miles of the actual figure.

A third Alexandrian scholar was Euclid, who lived around 300 B.C. He established a school in Alexandria but is primarily known for his work entitled the *Elements*. This was a systematic organization of the fundamental elements of geometry as they had already been worked out; it became the standard textbook of plane geometry and was used up to modern times.

By far the most famous of the scientists of the Hellenistic period, Archimedes (287–212 B.C.) of Syracuse came from the western Mediterranean region. Archimedes was especially important for his work on the geometry of spheres and cylinders, for establishing the value of the mathematical constant pi, and for creating the science of hydrostatics. Archimedes was also a practical inventor. He may have devised the so-called Archimedean screw used to pump water out of mines and to lift irrigation water as well as a compound pulley for transporting heavy weights. During the Roman siege of his native city of Syracuse, he constructed a number of devices to thwart the attackers. According to Plutarch's account, the Romans became so frightened "that if they did but see a little rope or a piece of wood from the wall, instantly crying out, that there it was again, Archimedes was about to let fly some engine at them, they turned their backs and fled."[1] Archimedes's accomplishments inspired a wealth of semilegendary stories. Supposedly, he discovered specific gravity by observing the water he displaced in his bath and became so excited by his realization that he jumped out of the water and ran home naked, shouting "Eureka" ("I have found it"). He is said to have emphasized the importance of levers by proclaiming to the King of Syracuse: "Give me a lever and a place to stand on and I will move the earth." The king was so impressed that he encouraged Archimedes to lower his sights and build defensive weapons instead.

Philosophy: New Schools of Thought

While Alexandria and Pergamum became the renowned cultural centers of the Hellenistic world, Athens remained the prime center for philosophy. After Alexander the Great, the home of Socrates, Plato, and Aristotle continued to attract the most illustrious philosophers from the Greek world who chose to establish their schools there. New schools of philosophical thought (the Epicureans and Stoics) reinforced Athens's reputation as a philosophical center.

Epicurus (341–270 B.C.), the founder of Epicureanism, established a school in Athens near the end of the fourth century B.C. Epicurus's famous belief in a doctrine of "pleasure" began with his view of the world. Though he did not deny the existence of the gods, he did not believe they played any active role in the world. The universe ran on its own. This left human beings free to follow self-interest as a basic motivating force. Happiness was the goal of life, and the means to achieve it was the pursuit of

◆ **Old Market Woman.** Greek architects and sculptors were highly valued throughout the Hellenistic world, as kings undertook projects to beautify the cities of their kingdoms. The sculptors of this period no longer tried to capture ideal beauty in their sculpture, a quest that characterized Greek classicism, but moved toward a more emotional and realistic art. This statue of an old market woman is typical of this new trend in art.

pleasure, the only true good. But the pursuit of pleasure was not meant in a physical, hedonistic sense:

> When, therefore, we maintain that pleasure is the end, we do not mean the pleasures of profligates and those that consist in sensuality, as is supposed by some who are either ignorant or disagree with us or do not understand, but freedom from pain in the body and from trouble in the mind. For it is not continuous drinkings and revellings, nor the satisfaction of lusts, nor the enjoyment of fish and other luxuries of the wealthy table, which produce a pleasant life, but sober reasoning, searching out the motives for all choice and avoidance, and banishing mere opinions, to which are due the greatest disturbance of the spirit.

Pleasure was not satisfying one's desire in an active, gluttonous fashion, but freedom from emotional turmoil, freedom from worry, the freedom that came from a mind at rest. To achieve this passive pleasure, one had to free oneself from public activity: "We must release ourselves from the prison of affairs and politics." They were too strenuous to give peace of mind. But this was not a renunciation of all social life, for to Epicurus, a life could only be complete when it was centered on the basic ideal of friendship: "Of all the things which wisdom acquires to produce the blessedness of the complete life, far the greatest is the possession of friendship."[2] Epicurus's own life in Athens was an embodiment of his teachings. He and his family created their own private community where they could pursue their ideal of true happiness.

Epicureanism was eventually overshadowed by another school of thought known as Stoicism, which became the most popular philosophy of the Hellenistic world and later flourished in the Roman Empire as well. It was the product of a teacher named Zeno (335–263 B.C.), who came to Athens and began to teach in a public colonnade known as the Painted Portico (the *Stoa Poikile*—hence Stoicism). Like Epicureanism, Stoicism was concerned with how individuals find happiness. But Stoics took a radically different approach to the problem. To them, happiness, the supreme good, could be found only in virtue, which meant essentially living in harmony with the will of God: "And this very thing constitutes the virtue of the happy man and the smooth current of life, when all actions promote the harmony of the spirit dwelling in the individual man with the will of him who orders the universe."[3] One achieved happiness by choosing to follow the will of God through the free exercise of one's own will. To the Stoics, the will of God was the same thing as the will of nature because nature was simply a manifestation or expression of God. "Living according to nature," therefore, meant following the will of God or the natural laws that God established to run the universe.

Virtuous living, then, was living in accordance with the laws of nature or submitting to the will of God (see the box on p. 81). This led to the acceptance of whatever one received in life since God's will for us was by its very nature good. By accepting God's law, people mastered themselves and gained inner peace. Life's problems could not disturb such individuals, and they could bear whatever life offered (hence our word *stoic*). The Stoics did not believe that it was difficult to know the will of God. This knowledge could be derived through the senses, or what the Stoics called the "perception conveying direct apprehension." Sense perceptions of overwhelming strength had to be a revelation of God's standards.

Unlike Epicureans, Stoics did not believe in the need to separate oneself from the world and politics. Public service was regarded as noble. The real Stoic was a good citizen and could even be a good government official. Because Stoics believed that a divine principle was present throughout the universe, each human being also contained a divine spark. This led to a belief in the oneness of humanity. The world constituted a single society of equal human beings. Although they were not equal in the outer world, because each contained the divine spark, all were free to follow God's will (what was best for each individual). All persons then, even slaves, though unfree in body, were equal at the level of the soul.

Epicureanism and especially Stoicism appealed to large numbers of people in the Hellenistic world. Both of these philosophies focused primarily on the problem of human happiness. Their popularity would suggest a fundamental change in the character of the Greek lifestyle. In the classical Greek world, the happiness of individuals and the meaning of life were closely associated with the life of the *polis*. One found fulfillment within the community. In the Hellenistic kingdoms, although the *polis* continued to exist, the sense that one could find satisfaction and fulfillment through life in the *polis* had weakened. Not only did individuals seek new philosophies that offered personal happiness, but in the cosmopolitan world of the Hellenistic states with their mixtures of peoples, a new openness to thoughts of universality could also emerge. For some people, Stoicism embodied this larger sense of community. The appeal of new philosophies in the Hellenistic era can also be explained by the apparent decline in certain aspects of traditional religion, which we can see by examining the status of Hellenistic religion.

Religion in the Hellenistic World

When the Greeks spread throughout the Hellenistic kingdoms, they took their gods with them. Although the construction of temples may have been less important than in classical times, there were still many demonstrations of a lively religious faith. But over a period of time, there was a noticeable decline in the vitality of the traditional Greek Olympian religion. Much of Greek religion had always revolved around ritual, but the civic cults based on the traditional gods no longer seemed sufficient to satisfy peoples' emotional needs.

The decline in traditional Greek religion left Greeks receptive to the numerous religious cults of the eastern world. The Greeks were always tolerant of other existing religious institutions. Hence in the Hellenistic cities of the Near East, the traditional civic cults of their own gods

The Stoic Ideal of Harmony with God

The Stoic Cleanthes (331–232 B.C.) succeeded Zeno as head of this school of philosophy. One historian of Hellenistic civilization has called this work by Cleanthes the greatest religious hymn in Greek literature. Certainly, it demonstrates that Stoicism, unlike Epicureanism, did have an underlying spiritual foundation. This poem has been compared to the great psalms of the Hebrews.

Cleanthes, *Hymn to Zeus*

Nothing occurs on the earth apart from you, O God, nor in the heavenly regions nor on the sea, except what bad men do in their folly;

but you know to make the odd even, and to harmonize what is dissonant; to you the alien is akin.

And so you have wrought together into one all things that are good and bad,

So that there arises one eternal logos [rationale] of all things,

Which all bad mortals shun and ignore,

Unhappy wretches, ever seeking the possession of good things

They neither see nor hear the universal law of God,

By obeying which they might enjoy a happy life.

and foreign cults existed side by side. Alexandria had cults of the traditional Greek gods, Egyptian deities, such as Isis and Horus, the Babylonian Astarte, and the Syrian Atargatis. The strongest appeal of eastern religions to Greeks, however, came from the mystery religions. What was the source of their attraction?

The normal forms of religious worship in Hellenistic communities had lost some of their appeal. The practices of traditional, ritualized Greek religion in the civic cults seemed increasingly meaningless. For many people, the search for personal meaning remained unfulfilled, and they sought alternatives. Among educated Greeks, the philosophies of Epicureanism and especially Stoicism offered help. Another source of solace came in the form of mystery religions.

Mystery cults, with their secret initiations and promises of individual salvation, were not new to the Greek world. But the Greeks of the Hellenistic era were also strongly influenced by eastern mystery cults, such as those of Egypt, which offered a distinct advantage over the Greek mystery religions. The latter had usually been connected to specific locations (such as Eleusis), which meant that a would-be initiate had to undertake a pilgrimage in order to participate in the rites. In contrast, the eastern mystery religions were readily available since temples to their gods and goddesses were located throughout the Greek cities of the east.

All of the mystery religions were based on the same fundamental premises. Individuals could pursue a path to salvation and achieve eternal life by being initiated into a union with a savior god or goddess who had died and risen again. The ritual of initiation, by which the seeker identified with the god or goddess, was, no doubt, a highly emotional experience.

The Egyptian cult of Isis was one of the most popular of the mystery religions. The cult of Isis was very ancient, but became truly universal in Hellenistic times. Isis was the goddess of women, marriage, and children, as one of her hymns states: "I am she whom women call goddess. I ordained that women should be loved by men: I brought wife and husband together, and invented the marriage contract. I ordained that women should bear children. . . ."[4] Isis was also portrayed as the giver of civilization who had brought laws and letters to all humankind. The cult of Isis offered a precious commodity to its initiates—the promise of eternal life. In many ways, the mystery religions of the Hellenistic era helped to pave the way for the coming and the success of Christianity.

THE JEWS IN THE HELLENISTIC WORLD

In observing the similarities among their gods and goddesses, Greeks and easterners tended to assume they were the same beings with different names, giving rise to a process of syncretism. But a special position was occupied in the Hellenistic world by the Hebrews, whose monotheistic religion was exclusive and did not permit this kind of fusion of spiritual beings.

The Hebrew kingdom of Judaea was ruled by the Ptolemies until it fell under the control of the Seleucids by 200 B.C. In the reign of the Seleucid king Antiochus IV (175–163 B.C.), conflict erupted in Judaea. Hellenistic monarchs were generally tolerant of all religions, but problems with Rome prompted Antiochus to try to

♦ **The Cult of Isis.** The cult of Isis was one of the most popular mystery religions in the Hellenistic world. This fresco from Herculaneum in Italy depicts a religious ceremony in front of the temple of Isis. At the top, a priest holds a golden vessel while below him another priest leads the worshipers with a staff. A third priest fans the flames at the altar.

impose more cultural and religious unity throughout his kingdom. When he sent troops to Jerusalem and seized the Temple, he sparked a Jewish uprising led by Judas Maccabaeus (164 B.C.). The rebels succeeded in recapturing the Temple, a joyous event that has been celebrated every year since in the Jewish holiday of Hanukkah, the Festival of Light. Although the conflict in Judaea continued, the Seleucids ultimately made concessions and allowed the Jews considerable freedom.

But since the Diaspora (see Chapter 2), large numbers of Jews no longer lived in Judaea. There was a large Jewish population in Egypt, particularly in Alexandria, as well as Jewish settlements throughout the cities of Asia Minor and Syria. In each city, Jews generally set up a synagogue and formed a private association for worship as other foreigners did. But some city authorities also allowed the Jews to form a political corporation that gave them greater rights than other resident aliens. Most importantly, they gained the privilege to live by their own laws and their own judicial system. The Jews were not really interested in citizenship in the cities in which they resided since full citizenship meant worship of the city's gods, an anathema to Jews who believed only in Yahweh.

Conclusion

Although historians used to view the Hellenistic era as a period of stagnation after the brilliant Greek civilization of the fifth century B.C., our survey of the Hellenistic world has shown the weakness of that position. The Hellenistic period was, in its own way, a vibrant one. New cities arose and flourished. New philosophical ideas captured the minds of many. Significant achievements occurred in art, literature, and science. Greek culture spread throughout the Near East and made an impact wherever it was carried. In some areas of the Hellenistic world, queens played an active role in political life, and many upper-class women found new avenues for expressing themselves.

But serious problems remained. Hellenistic kings continued to engage in inconclusive wars. Much of the formal culture was the special preserve of the Greek conquerors whose attitude of superiority kept them largely separated from the native masses of the Hellenistic kingdoms. Although the Hellenistic world achieved a degree of political stability, by the late third century B.C. signs of decline were beginning to multiply. Some of the more farsighted perhaps realized the danger presented to the Hellenistic world by the growing power of Rome. The Romans would ultimately inherit Alexander's empire, and we must now turn to them and try to understand what made them such successful conquerors.

NOTES

1. Plutarch, *Life of Marcellus*, trans. John Dryden (New York, n.d.), p. 378.
2. *Epicurus: The Extant Remains*, trans. Cyril Bailey (Oxford, 1926), pp. (in order of quotations) 89–91, 115, 101.
3. Diogenes Laertius, *Life of Zeno*, Vol. 2, trans. R. D. Hicks (London, 1925), p. 195.
4. Quoted in W. W. Tarn, *Hellenistic Civilization* (London, 1930), p. 324.

SUGGESTIONS FOR FURTHER READING

For a general introduction to the Hellenistic era, see J. Boardman, J. Griffin, and O. Murray, eds., *The Oxford History of the Classical World* (Oxford, 1986), pp. 315–85. A brief, but excellent guide to recent trends in scholarship on the Hellenistic era can be found in C. Starr, *Past and Future in Ancient History* (Lanham, Md., 1987), pp. 19–32. The best general survey is F. W. Walbank, *The Hellenistic World* (Cambridge, Mass., 1993). Other studies include C. B. Welles, *Alexander and the Hellenistic World* (Toronto, 1970); W. W. Tarn and G. T. Griffith, *Hellenistic Civilization*, 3d ed. (London, 1952); M. Grant, *From Alexander to Cleopatra: The Hellenistic World* (London, 1982); and P. Green, *Alexander to Actium: The Historic Evolution of the Hellenistic Age* (Berkeley, 1990).

For a good introduction to the early history of Macedonia, see E. N. Borza, *In the Shadow of Olympus: The Emergence of Macedon* (Princeton, N.J., 1990); and R. M. Errington, *A History of Macedonia* (Berkeley, 1990). Philip of Macedon is covered well in G. L. Cawkwell, *Philip of Macedon* (London, 1978). There are considerable differences of opinion on Alexander the Great. Good biographies include R. L. Fox, *Alexander the Great* (London, 1973); J. R. Hamilton, *Alexander the Great* (London, 1973); N. G. L. Hammond, *Alexander the Great* (London, 1981); and P. Green, *Alexander of Macedon* (Berkeley, 1991).

Studies on the various Hellenistic monarchies include N. G. L. Hammond and F. W. Walbank, *A History of Macedonia*, vol. 3, 336–167 B.C. (Oxford, 1988); H. I. Bell, *Egypt from Alexander the Great to the Arab Conquest* (Oxford, 1948); R. E. Allen, *The Attalid Kingdom* (Oxford, 1983); and S. Sherwin-White and A. Kuhrt, *From Samarkhand to Sardis: A New Approach to the Seleucid Empire* (London, 1993).

A good survey of Hellenistic cities can be found in A. H. M. Jones, *The Greek City from Alexander to Justinian* (Oxford, 1940). Alexandria is covered in P. M. Fraser, *Ptolemaic Alexandria* (Oxford, 1972). On economic and social trends, see M. I. Finley, *The Ancient Economy*, 2d ed. (London, 1985); and the classic and still indispensable M. I. Rostovtzeff, *Social and Economic History of the Hellenistic World*, 3 vols., 2d ed. (Oxford, 1953).

Hellenistic women are examined in two works by S. B. Pomeroy, *Goddesses, Whores, Wives, and Slaves* (New York, 1975), pp. 120–48, and *Women in Hellenistic Egypt* (New York, 1984).

For a general introduction to Hellenistic culture, see J. Onians, *Art and Thought in the Hellenistic Age* (London, 1979). On art, see J. J. Pollitt, *Art in the Hellenistic Age* (New York, 1986). The best general survey of Hellenistic philosophy is A. A. Long, *Hellenistic Philosophy: Stoics, Epicureans, Skeptics*, 2d ed. (London, 1986). A superb work on Hellenistic science is G. E. R. Lloyd, *Greek Science after Aristotle* (London, 1973). A good survey of Hellenistic literature is A. Lesky, *A History of Greek Literature* (London, 1966), pp. 642–806.

On various facets of Hellenistic religion, see L. Martin, *Hellenistic Religions: An Introduction* (New York, 1987); and R. E. Witt, *Isis in the Graeco-Roman World* (London, 1971).

On the entry of Rome into the Hellenistic world, see the basic work by E. S. Gruen, *The Hellenistic World and the Coming of Rome*, 2 vols. (Berkeley, 1984).

The Roman Republic

Early Roman history is filled with legendary stories that tell of the heroes who made Rome great. One of the best known is the story of Horatius at the bridge. Threatened by attack from the neighboring Etruscans, Roman farmers abandoned their fields and moved into the city, where they would be protected by the walls. One weak point in the Roman defenses, however, was a wooden bridge over the Tiber River. Horatius was on guard at the bridge when a sudden assault by the Etruscans caused many Roman troops to throw down their weapons and flee. Horatius urged them to make a stand at the bridge to protect Rome; when they hesitated, as a last resort he told them to destroy the bridge behind him while he held the Etruscans back. Astonished at the sight of a single defender, the confused Etruscans threw their spears at Horatius, who caught them on his shield and barred the way. By the time the Etruscans had regrouped and were about to overwhelm the lone defender, the Roman soldiers brought down the bridge. When Horatius heard the bridge crash into the river behind him, he dove fully armed into the water and swam safely to the other side through a hail of arrows. Rome had been saved by the courageous act of a Roman who knew his duty and was determined to carry it out. Courage, duty, determination—these qualities would also serve the many Romans who believed that it was their mission to rule nations and peoples.

In the first millennium B.C., a group of Latin-speaking people established a small community on the plain of Latium on the Italian peninsula. This community, called Rome, was merely one of numerous Latin-speaking communities in Latium, and the Latin speakers, in turn, constituted just some of the many peoples in Italy. Roman history is basically the story of the Romans' conquest of the plain of Latium, then Italy, and finally the entire Mediterranean world. Why were the Romans able to do this? Scholars do not really know all the answers. The Romans made the right decisions at the right time, which is to say, the Romans were a people distinguished by a high degree of political wisdom.

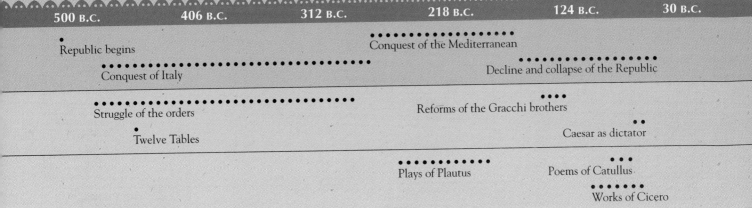

Republic begins

Conquest of the Mediterranean

Conquest of Italy

Decline and collapse of the Republic

Struggle of the orders

Reforms of the Gracchi brothers

Twelve Tables

Caesar as dictator

Plays of Plautus

Poems of Catullus

Works of Cicero

The Romans were also a practical people. Unlike the Greeks, who reserved their citizenship for small, select groups, the Romans often offered their citizenship to the peoples they conquered, thus laying the groundwork for a strong, integrated empire. The Romans also did not hesitate to borrow ideas and culture from the Greeks. Roman strength lay in government, law, and engineering. The Romans knew how to govern people, establish legal structures, and construct the roads that took them to the ends of the known world. Throughout their empire, they carried their law, their political institutions, their engineering skills, and their Latin language. And even after the Romans were gone, those same gifts continued to play an important role in the civilizations that came after them.

The Emergence of Rome

Italy is a peninsula extending about 750 miles from north to south. It is not very wide, however, averaging about 120 miles across. The Apennines traverse the peninsula from north to south, forming a ridge down the middle that divides west from east. Nevertheless, Italy has some fairly large fertile plains ideal for farming. Most important were the Po valley in the north, probably the most fertile agricultural area; the plain of Latium, on which Rome was located; and Campania to the south of Latium. East of the Italian peninsula is the Adriatic Sea and to the west the Tyrrhenian Sea with the nearby large islands of Corsica

and Sardinia. Sicily lies just west of the toe of the boot-shaped Italian peninsula.

Geography had an impact on Roman history. Although the Apennines bisected Italy, they were less rugged than the mountain ranges of Greece and did not divide the peninsula into many small isolated communities. Italy also possessed considerably more productive farmland than Greece, enabling it to support a large population. Rome's location was favorable from a geographical point of view. Located eighteen miles inland on the Tiber River, Rome had access to the sea and was yet far enough inland to be safe from pirates. Built on the famous seven hills, it was easily defended. Situated where the Tiber could be readily forded, Rome became a natural crossing point for north–south traffic in western Italy. All in all, Rome had a good central location in Italy from which to expand.

Moreover, the Italian peninsula juts into the Mediterranean, making it an important crossroads between the western and eastern Mediterranean. Once Rome had unified Italy, involvement in Mediterranean affairs was natural. And after the Romans had conquered their Mediterranean empire, governing it was made considerably easier by Italy's central location.

The Greeks and Etruscans

We know little about the Indo-European peoples who moved into Italy during the second half of the second millennium B.C. By the first millennium B.C., other peoples had also settled in Italy—the two most notable being the Greeks and the Etruscans. The Greeks arrived on the Italian peninsula in large numbers during the age of Greek colonization (750–550 B.C.; see Chapter 3). Initially, the Greeks settled in southern Italy and then crept around the coast and up the peninsula as far as Brindisi (Brundisium). They also occupied the eastern two-thirds of Sicily. Ultimately, the Greeks had considerable influence on Rome. They cultivated the olive and the vine, passed on their alphabetic system of writing, and provided artistic and cultural models through their sculpture, architecture, and literature. Indeed, many historians view Roman culture as a continuation of Greek culture. While Greek influence initially touched Rome indirectly through the Etruscans, the Roman conquest of southern Italy and Sicily brought them into direct contact with Greeks.

The initial development of Rome, however, was influenced most by a people known as the Etruscans, who were

✿ **Map 5.1** Ancient Italy and the City of Rome (inset).

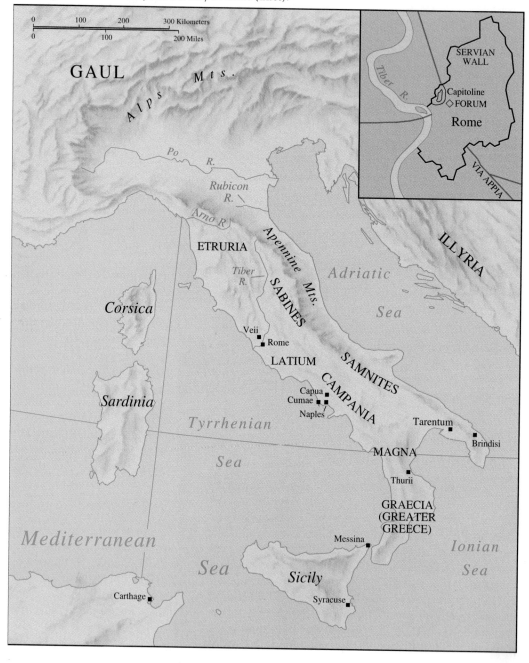

✦ **Etruscan Married Couple.** This sculpture, dating from 550 B.C., depicts a wealthy Etruscan married couple reclining on a couch. The Etruscans greatly influenced the early development of Rome and had an impact on Roman religion, Roman sporting events, and military institutions.

located north of Rome in Etruria. The origins of the Etruscans are not clear, but after 650 B.C., they expanded in Italy and became the dominant cultural and economic force in a number of areas. To the north, they moved into north-central Italy, including the Po valley. To the south, according to Roman tradition and archaeological evidence, they controlled Rome and possibly all of Latium. From Latium they moved south and came into direct conflict with Greek colonists in southern Italy. In the sixth century B.C., the Etruscans were at the height of their power. But by 480 B.C., Etruscan power had begun to decline, and by 400 B.C., the Etruscans were limited to Etruria itself. Later, they were invaded by the Gauls and then conquered by the Romans. But by then the Etruscans had already made an impact. By transforming villages into towns and cities, they brought urbanization to northern and central Italy (the Greeks brought urbanization to southern Italy). Rome was, of course, the Etruscans' most famous product.

Early Rome

According to Roman legend, Rome was founded by the twin brothers, Romulus and Remus, in 753 B.C., and archaeologists have found that by the eighth century B.C. there was a settlement consisting of huts on the tops of Rome's hills. The early Romans, basically a pastoral people, spoke Latin, which, like Greek, belongs to the Indo-European family of languages (see the table in Chapter

2). The Roman historical tradition also maintained that early Rome (753–509 B.C.) had been under the control of seven kings and that two of the last three had been Etruscans. Some historians believe that the king list may have some historical accuracy. What is certain is that Rome did fall under the influence of the Etruscans for about 100 years during the period of the kings.

By the beginning of the sixth century, under Etruscan influence, Rome began to change from a pastoral community to an actual city. The Etruscans were responsible for an outstanding building program. They constructed the first roadbed of the chief street through Rome—the Sacred Way—before 575 B.C. and oversaw the development of temples, markets, shops, streets, and houses. By 509 B.C., the date when the monarchy supposedly was overthrown and a republican form of government was established, a new Rome had emerged, essentially as a result of the fusion of Etruscan and native Roman elements.

The Roman Republic (c. 509–264 B.C.)

The transition from a monarchy to a republican government was not an easy one. Rome felt threatened by enemies from every direction and, in the process of meeting these threats, embarked on a course of military expansion that led to the conquest of the entire Italian peninsula (see later section on "The Roman Conquest of Italy"). During this period of expansion in Italy, the Roman Republic developed political institutions that were, in many ways, determined by the social divisions that existed within the community.

The Roman State

In politics and law, as in conquest, the Romans took a practical approach. They did not concern themselves with the construction of an ideal government, but instead fashioned political institutions in response to problems as they arose. Hence it is important to remember that the political institutions we will discuss evolved over a period of centuries.

The chief executive officers of the Roman Republic were the consuls and praetors. Two consuls, chosen annually, administered the government and led the Roman army into battle. They possessed *imperium*, or "the right to command." In 366 B.C., a new office, that of the praetor, was created. The praetor also possessed *imperium* and could govern Rome when the consuls were away from the city and could also lead armies. The praetor's primary function, however, was the execution of justice. He was

◆ **Lictors with Fasces.** Pictured are lictors bearing the *fasces,* an axe surrounded by a bundle of rods tied with a red thong, an insignia borrowed from the Etruscan kings. The *fasces* was a symbol of the power to rule, and the consuls, the chief executives of the Roman Republic, were always preceded by twelve lictors bearing the *fasces.*

in charge of the civil law as it applied to Roman citizens. In 242 B.C., reflecting Rome's growth, another praetor was added to judge cases in which one or both people were noncitizens.

As Rome expanded into the Mediterranean, additional praetors were established to govern the newly conquered provinces (two in 227, two more in 197 B.C.). But as the number of provinces continued to grow, the Romans devised a new system in which ex-consuls and ex-praetors who had served their one-year terms were given the title of proconsul and propraetor and sent out as provincial governors. This demonstrates once again the Romans' practical solution to an immediate problem. It was reasonable to assume that officials with governmental experience would make good provincial administrators, although this was not always true in practice due to the opportunities for financial corruption in the provinces.

The Roman state also had administrative officials with specialized duties. Quaestors were assigned to assist consuls and praetors in the administration of financial affairs. Aediles supervised the public games and watched over the grain supply of the city, a major problem for a rapidly

growing urban community that relied on imported grain to feed its population.

The Roman senate held an especially important position in the Roman Republic. The senate or council of elders was a select group of about 300 men who served for life. The senate was not a legislative body and could only advise the magistrates. This advice of the senate was not taken lightly, however, and by the third century B.C. it had virtually the force of law. No doubt the prestige of the senate's members furthered this development. But it also helped that the senate met continuously, while the chief magistrates changed annually and the popular assemblies operated slowly and met only periodically.

The Roman Republic possessed a number of popular assemblies. By far the most important was the centuriate assembly, essentially the Roman army functioning in its political role. Organized by classes based on wealth, it was structured in such a way that the wealthiest citizens always had a majority. The centuriate assembly elected the chief magistrates and passed laws. Another assembly, the council of the plebs, came into being in 471 B.C. as a result of the struggle of the orders.

THE STRUGGLE OF THE ORDERS: SOCIAL DIVISIONS IN THE ROMAN REPUBLIC

The most noticeable element in the social organization of early Rome was the division between two groups—the patricians and the plebeians. The patrician class in Rome consisted of those families who were descended from the original senators appointed during the period of the kings. Their initial emergence was probably due to their wealth as great landowners. Thus, patricians constituted an aristocratic governing class. Only they could be consuls, other magistrates, and senators. Through their patronage of large numbers of dependent clients, they could control the centuriate assembly and many other facets of Roman life. The plebeians constituted the considerably larger group of "independent, unprivileged, poorer and vulnerable men" as well as nonpatrician large landowners, less wealthy landholders, craftspeople, merchants, and small farmers. Although they were citizens, they did not possess the same rights as the patricians. Both patricians and plebeians could vote, but only the patricians could be elected to governmental offices. Both had the right to make legal contracts and marriages, but intermarriage between patricians and plebeians was forbidden. At the beginning of the fifth century B.C., the plebeians began a struggle to seek both political and social equality with the patricians.

The first success of the plebeians came in 494 B.C., when they withdrew physically from the state. The patricians, who by themselves could not defend Rome, were forced to compromise. Two new officials known as tribunes of the plebs were instituted (later raised to five and then ten in number). These tribunes were given the power to protect plebeians against arrest by patrician magistrates. Moreover, after a new popular assembly for plebeians only, called the council of the plebs, was created in 471 B.C., the tribunes became responsible for convoking it and placing proposals before it. If adopted, these measures became *plebiscita* ("it is the opinion of the plebs"), but they were binding only on the plebeians, not the patricians. Nevertheless, the council of the plebs gave the plebeians considerable political leverage. After 445 B.C., when a law allowed patricians and plebeians to intermarry, the division between the two groups became less important. In the fourth century B.C., the consulship was opened to the plebeians. The climax of the struggle between the orders came in 287 B.C. with passage of a law that stipulated that all *plebiscita* passed by the council of the plebs had the force of law and were binding on the entire community, including patricians.

The struggle between the orders, then, had a significant impact on the development of the Roman constitution. Plebeians could hold the highest offices of state, they could intermarry with the patricians, and they could pass laws binding on the entire Roman community. Although the struggle had been long, the Romans had handled it by compromise, not violent revolution. Theoretically, by 287 B.C., all Roman citizens were equal under the law, and all could strive for political office. But in reality, as a result of the right of intermarriage, a select number of patrician and plebeian families formed a new senatorial aristocracy that came to dominate the political offices. The Roman Republic had not become a democracy.

The Roman Conquest of Italy

At the beginning of the Republic, Rome was surrounded by enemies, including the Etruscans to the north, and the Sabines, Volscians, and Aequi to the east and south. The Latin communities on the plain of Latium posed an even more immediate threat. If we are to believe Livy, one of the chief ancient sources for the history of the early Roman Republic, Rome was engaged in almost continuous warfare with the Volscians, Sabines, Aequi, and others for the next 100 years.

In his account of these years, the historian Livy provided a detailed narrative of Roman efforts. Many of Livy's stories were legendary in character and indeed were modeled after events in Greek history. But Livy, writing

CHRONOLOGY

The Roman Conquest of Italy

Sack of Rome by the Gauls	387 B.C.
Latin revolt	340–338 B.C.
Creation of the Roman confederation	338 B.C.
Samnite Wars	343–290 B.C.
Defeat of Greek states in southern Italy	281–267 B.C.

in the first century B.C., used such stories to teach Romans the moral values and virtues that had made Rome great. These included tenacity, duty, courage, and especially discipline (see the box on p. 90). Indeed, Livy recounted stories of military leaders who executed their own sons for leaving their place in battle, a serious offense, since the success of the hoplite infantry depended on maintaining a precise order. These stories had little basis in fact, but like the story of George Washington and the cherry tree in American history, they provided mythical images to reinforce Roman patriotism.

The early successes of the Romans against their neighbors seemed to be in vain when, in 387 B.C., the Celts, known to the Romans as the Gauls, a people from north of the Alps who had previously moved into northern Italy, defeated the Romans in a battle outside Rome. The Gauls conquered Rome and sacked large parts of the city. Rome was left in shambles. But Roman tenacity won out. The Romans rebuilt the city and with new determination began again.

In 340 B.C. Rome crushed the Latin states in Latium and inaugurated a new system that ultimately became the basis for organizing the entire Italian peninsula: the Roman confederation, formed in 338 B.C. Under this system, Rome established treaties with the defeated members of the Latin states whereby these communities were related to Rome in one of three ways. The first category included only five or six privileged states in which all the citizens were given full Roman citizenship. A second category of communities acquired municipal status, which entitled their citizens to make legal contracts and intermarry with Romans, but not to vote or hold office in Rome. The remaining communities were made allies and bound to Rome by special treaties specifying their relations with Rome. All three categories of states retained considerable autonomy over their domestic affairs, but were required to provide soldiers for Rome. In the Roman confederation, Rome created a system that could be

❧ *Cincinnatus Saves Rome: A Roman Morality Tale* ❧

There is perhaps no better account of how the virtues of duty and simplicity enabled good Roman citizens to prevail during the travails of the fifth century B.C. than Livy's account of Cincinnatus. He was chosen dictator, supposedly in 457 B.C., to defend Rome against the attacks of the Aequi. The position of dictator was a temporary expedient used only in emergencies; the consuls would resign, and a leader with unlimited power would be appointed for a limited period (usually six months). In this account, Cincinnatus did his duty, defeated the Aequi, and returned to his simple farm in just fifteen days.

Livy, *The Early History of Rome*

The city was thrown into a state of turmoil, and the general alarm was as great as if Rome herself were surrounded. Nautius was sent for, but it was quickly decided that he was not the man to inspire full confidence; the situation evidently called for a dictator, and, with no dissenting voice, Lucius Quinctius Cincinnatus was named for the post.

Now I would solicit the particular attention of those numerous people who imagine that money is everything in this world, and that rank and ability are inseparable from wealth: let them observe that Cincinnatus, the one man in whom Rome reposed all her hope of survival, was at that moment working a little three-acre farm . . . west of the Tiber, just opposite the spot where the shipyards are today. A mission from the city found him at work on his land—digging a ditch, maybe, or ploughing. Greetings were exchanged, and

he was asked—with a prayer for divine blessing on himself and his country—to put on his toga and hear the Senate's instructions. This naturally surprised him, and, asking if all were well, he told his wife Racilia to run to their cottage and fetch his toga. The toga was brought, and wiping the grimy sweat from his hands and face he put it on; at once the envoys from the city saluted him, with congratulations, as Dictator, invited him to enter Rome, and informed him of the terrible danger of Municius's army. A state vessel was waiting for him on the river, and on the city bank he was welcomed by his three sons who had come to meet him, then by other kinsmen and friends, and finally by nearly the whole body of senators. Closely attended by all these people and preceded by his lictors he was then escorted to his residence through streets lined with great crowds of common folk who, be it said, were by no means so pleased to see the new Dictator, as they thought his power excessive and dreaded the way in which he was likely to use it.

[Cincinnatus proceeds to raise an army, march out, and defeat the Aequi.]

In Rome the Senate was convened by Quintus Fabius the City Prefect, and a decree was passed inviting Cincinnatus to enter in triumph with his troops. The chariot he rode in was preceded by the enemy commanders and the military standards, and followed by his army loaded with its spoils. . . . Cincinnatus finally resigned after holding office for fifteen days, having originally accepted it for a period of six months.

as it eventually was, to the rest of Italy. Moreover, the Romans did not regard the status of the conquered states as permanent. Loyal allies could improve their status and even hope to become Roman citizens. Thus, the Romans had found a way to give conquered states a stake in Rome's success.

Between 343 and 290 B.C., the Romans waged a fierce struggle with the Samnites, a hill people from the central Apennines, some of whom had settled in Campania, south of Rome. Rome was victorious and incorporated Campania and the Samnite states of central Italy into an expanded Roman confederation as Italian allies. These communities agreed to provide military aid (cavalry and infantry soldiers) to Rome and to allow Rome to control their foreign policy. Otherwise, they were free to govern themselves and maintain their own laws and political institutions.

The conquest of the Samnites gave Rome considerable control over a large part of Italy and also brought it into direct contact with the Greek communities of southern Italy. Soon the Romans were involved in hostilities with some of these Greek cities and by 267 B.C. had completed their conquest of southern Italy and added the Greek states to the Roman confederation. Their relationship to Rome was the same as the Italian allies, except that the Greeks were required to furnish naval assistance—warships and sailors—instead of infantry and cavalry. After crushing the remaining Etruscan states to the north in 264 B.C., Rome had conquered all of Italy, except the extreme north.

The Romans' conquest of Italy can hardly be said to be the result of a direct policy of expansion. Much of it was opportunistic. The Romans did not hesitate to act once they felt their security threatened. And surrounded by potential enemies, Rome in a sense never felt secure. Yet once embarked on a course of expansion, the Romans pursued consistent policies that help to explain their success. The Romans were superb diplomats who excelled at making the correct diplomatic decisions. Although firm and even cruel when necessary—rebellions were crushed without mercy—they were also shrewd in extending their citizenship and allowing autonomy in domestic affairs. In addition, the Romans were not only good soldiers, but persistent ones. The loss of an army or a fleet did not cause them to quit, but spurred them on to build new armies and new fleets. Finally, the Romans had a practical sense of strategy. As they conquered, they settled Romans and Latins in new communities outside Latium. By 264 B.C., the Romans had established colonies—fortified towns—at all strategic locations. By building roads to these settlements and connecting them, the Romans assured themselves of an impressive military and communications network that enabled them to rule effectively and efficiently. By insisting on military service from the allies in the Roman confederation, Rome essentially mobilized the entire military manpower of all Italy for its wars.

The Roman Conquest of the Mediterranean (264–133 B.C.)

After their conquest of the Italian peninsula, the Romans found themselves face to face with a formidable Mediterranean power—Carthage. Founded around 800 B.C. by Phoenicians from Tyre, Carthage in North Africa was located in a favorable position for commanding Mediterranean trade routes and had become an important commercial center. It had become politically and militarily strong as well. By the third century B.C., the Carthaginian empire included the coast of northern Africa, southern Spain, Sardinia, Corsica, and western Sicily. With its monopoly of western Mediterranean trade, Carthage was the largest and richest state in the area. The presence of Carthaginians in Sicily made the Romans apprehensive about Carthaginian encroachment on the Italian coast. In 264 B.C., mutual suspicions drove the two powers into a lengthy struggle for control of the western Mediterranean.

The Struggle with Carthage

The First Punic War (264–241 B.C.) (the Latin word for Phoenician was *punicus*) began when the Romans decided to intervene in a struggle between two Sicilian cities by sending an army to Sicily. The Carthaginians,

CHRONOLOGY

The Roman Conquest of the Mediterranean

The First Punic War	264–241 B.C.
The Second Punic War	218–201 B.C.
Battle of Cannae	216 B.C.
Rome completes seizure of Spain	206 B.C.
Battle of Zama	202 B.C.
The Third Punic War	149–146 B.C.
Macedonia made a Roman province	148 B.C.
Destruction of Carthage	146 B.C.
Kingdom of Pergamum deeded to Rome	133 B.C.

who considered Sicily within their own sphere of influence, considered this just cause for war. In going to war, both sides determined on the conquest of Sicily. The Romans realized that the war would be long and drawn out if they could not supplement land operations with a navy and promptly developed a substantial naval fleet. The Carthaginians, on the other hand, had difficulty finding enough mercenaries to continue the fight. After a long struggle in which both sides lost battles in northern Africa and Sicily, a Roman fleet defeated the Carthaginian navy off Sicily, and the war quickly came to an end. In 241 B.C., Carthage gave up all rights to Sicily and had to pay an indemnity.

After the war, Carthage made an unexpected recovery and extended its domains in Spain to compensate for the territory lost to Rome. The Carthaginians proceeded to organize a formidable land army in the event of a second war with Rome, because they realized that defeating Rome on land was essential to victory. When the Romans encouraged one of Carthage's Spanish allies to revolt against Carthage, Hannibal, the greatest of the Carthaginian generals, struck back, beginning the Second Punic War (218–201 B.C.).

This time the Carthaginians decided to bring the war home to the Romans by fighting them in their own backyard. Hannibal went into Spain, moved east, and crossed the Alps with an army of 30,000 to 40,000 men and 6,000 horses and elephants. The Alps took a toll on the Carthaginian army; most of the elephants did not survive the trip. The remaining army, however, posed a real

◆ **A Roman Legionary.** The Roman legionaries, with their legendary courage and tenacity, made possible the creation of the Roman Empire. This picture shows a bronze figure of a Roman legionary in full dress at the height of the empire in the second century A.D. The soldier's cuirass is constructed of overlapping metal bands.

threat. At Cannae in 216 B.C., the Romans lost an army of almost 40,000 men. Rome seemed on the brink of disaster but refused to give up, raised yet another army, and gradually recovered. Although Hannibal remained free to roam in Italy, he had neither the men nor the equipment to lay siege to the major cities, including Rome itself. The Romans began to reconquer some of the Italian cities that had rebelled against Roman rule after Hannibal's successes. More important, the Romans pursued a strategy that aimed at undermining the Carthaginian empire in Spain. By 206 B.C., the Romans had pushed the Carthaginians out of Spain.

The Romans then took the war directly to Carthage. Late in 204 B.C. a Roman army under Publius Cornelius Scipio, later known as Scipio Africanus, moved from Sicily into north Africa and forced the Carthaginians to recall Hannibal from Italy. At the Battle of Zama in 202 B.C., the Romans decisively defeated Hannibal's forces, and the war was over. By terms of the peace treaty signed in 201 B.C., Carthage lost Spain, agreed to pay an indemnity, and promised not to go to war without Rome's permission. Spain, like Sicily, Corsica, and Sardinia earlier, was made into a Roman province. Rome had become the dominant power in the western Mediterranean.

But some Romans wanted even more. A number of prominent Romans, especially the conservative politician Cato, advocated the complete destruction of Carthage. Cato ended every speech he made to the senate with the words, "And I think Carthage must be destroyed." When the Carthaginians technically broke their peace treaty with Rome by going to war against one of Rome's north African allies who had been encroaching on Carthage's home territory, the Romans declared war. Roman forces undertook their third and last war with Carthage (149–146 B.C.). This time, Carthage was no match for the Romans, who in 146 B.C. seized this opportunity to carry out the final destruction of Carthage (see the box on p. 93). The territory of Carthage was made a Roman province called Africa.

The Eastern Mediterranean

During the Punic Wars, Rome had become acutely aware of the Hellenistic states of the eastern Mediterranean when the king of Macedonia made an alliance with Hannibal after the Roman defeat at Cannae. But Rome was preoccupied with the Carthaginians, and it was not until after the defeat of Carthage that Rome became involved in the world of Hellenistic politics as an advocate of the freedom of the Greek states. This support of the Greeks brought the Romans into conflict with both Macedonia and the kingdom of the Seleucids. Roman military victories and diplomatic negotiations rearranged the territorial boundaries of the Hellenistic kingdoms and brought the Greek states their freedom in 196 B.C. For fifty years, the Romans tried to be a power broker in the affairs of the Greeks without direct control of their lands. When they failed, the Romans changed their policy.

In 148 B.C., Macedonia was made a Roman province, and when some of the Greek states rose in revolt against Rome's restrictive policies, Rome acted decisively. The city of Corinth, leader of the revolt, was destroyed in 146 B.C. to teach the Greeks a lesson, and Greece was

The Destruction of Carthage

The Romans used a technical breach of Carthage's peace treaty with Rome as a pretext to undertake a third and final war with Carthage (149–146 B.C.). Although Carthage posed no real threat to Rome's security, the Romans still remembered the traumatic experiences of the Second Punic War when Hannibal had ravaged much of their homeland. The hardliners gained the upper hand in the senate and called for the complete destruction of Carthage. The city was razed, the survivors sold into slavery, and the land turned into a province. In this passage, the historian Appian of Alexandria describes the final destruction of Carthage by the Romans under the command of Scipio Aemilianus.

Appian, *Roman History*

Then came new scenes of horror. The fire spread and carried everything down, and the soldiers did not wait to destroy the buildings little by little, but pulled them all down together. So the crashing grew louder, and many fell with the stones into the midst dead. Others were seen still living, especially old men, women, and young children who had hidden in the inmost nooks of the houses, some of them wounded, some more or less burned, and uttering horrible cries. Still others, thrust out and falling from such a height with the stones, timbers, and fire, were torn asunder into all kinds of horrible shapes, crushed, and mangled. Nor was this the end of their miseries, for the street cleaners, who were removing the rubbish with axes, mattocks, and boathooks, and making the roads passable, tossed with these instruments the dead and the living together into holes in the ground, sweeping them along like sticks and stones or turning them over with their iron tools, and man was used for filling up a ditch. Some were thrown in head foremost, while their legs, sticking out of the ground, writhed a long time. Others fell with their feet downward and their heads above the ground. Horses ran over them, crushing their faces and skulls, not purposely on the part of the riders, but in their headlong haste. Nor did the street cleaners either do these things on purpose; but the press of war, the glory of approaching victory, the rush of the soldiery, the confused noise of heralds and trumpeters all round, the tribunes and centurions changing guard and marching the cohorts here and there—all together made everybody frantic and heedless of the spectacle before their eyes.

Six days and nights were consumed in this kind of turmoil, the soldiers being changed so that they might not be worn out with toil, slaughter, lack of sleep, and these horrid sights. . . .

Scipio, beholding this city, which had flourished 700 years from its foundation and had ruled over so many lands, islands, and seas, as rich in arms and fleets, elephants, and money as the mightiest empires, but far surpassing them in hardihood and high spirit . . . now come to its end in total destruction—Scipio, beholding this spectacle, is said to have shed tears and publicly lamented the fortune of the enemy. After meditating by himself a long time and reflecting on the inevitable fall of cities, nations, and empires, as well as of individuals, upon the fate of Troy, that once proud city, upon the fate of the Assyrian, the Median, and afterwards of the great Persian empire, and most recently of all, of the splendid empire of Macedon, either voluntarily or otherwise the words of the poet [Homer, *Iliad*] escaped his lips:

The day shall come in which our sacred Troy
And Priam, and the people over whom
Spear-bearing Priam rules, shall perish all.

Being asked by Polybius in familiar conversation (for Polybius had been his tutor) what he meant by using these words, Polybius says that he did not hesitate frankly to name his own country, for whose fate he feared when he considered the mutability of human affairs. And Polybius wrote this down just as he heard it.

placed under the control of the Roman governor of Macedonia. Thirteen years later, in 133 B.C., the king of Pergamum deeded his kingdom to Rome, giving Rome its first province in Asia. Rome was now master of the Mediterranean Sea.

The Nature of Roman Imperialism

Rome's empire was built in three stages: the conquest of Italy, the conflict with Carthage and expansion into the western Mediterranean, and the involvement with and domination of the Hellenistic kingdoms in the eastern

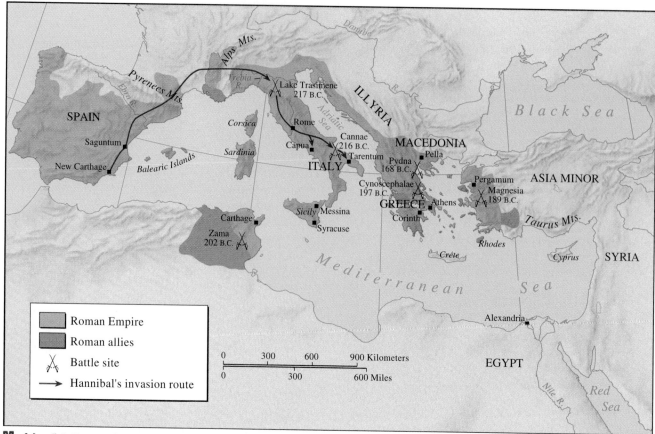

✠ **Map 5.2** Roman Conquests in the Mediterranean (264–133 B.C.).

Mediterranean. The Romans did not possess a master plan for the creation of an empire. Much of their expansion was opportunistic; once involved in a situation that threatened their security, the Romans did not hesitate to act. And the more they expanded, the more threats to their security appeared on the horizon, involving them in yet more conflicts. Indeed, the Romans liked to portray themselves as declaring war only for defensive reasons or to protect allies. That is only part of the story, however. It is likely, as some historians have recently suggested, that at some point a group of Roman aristocratic leaders emerged who favored expansion both for the glory it offered and for the economic benefits it provided. Certainly, by the second century B.C., aristocratic senators perceived new opportunities for lucrative foreign commands, enormous spoils of war, and an abundant supply of slave labor for their growing landed estates. By that same time, the destruction of Corinth and Carthage indicate Roman imperialism had become more arrogant and brutal as well. Rome's foreign success also had enormous repercussions for the internal development of the Roman Republic.

Society and Culture in the Roman World

One of the most noticeable characteristics of Roman culture and society is the impact of the Greeks. The Romans had experienced Greek influence early on through the Greek cities in southern Italy. By the end of the third century B.C., however, Greek civilization played an ever-increasing role in Roman culture. Greek ambassadors, merchants, and artists traveled to Rome and spread Greek thought and practices. After their conquest of the Hellenistic kingdoms, Roman military commanders shipped Greek manuscripts and artworks back to Rome. Multitudes of educated Greek slaves were used in Roman households. Virtually every area of Roman life, from literature and philosophy to religion and education, was affected by Greek models. Rich Romans hired Greek tutors and sent their sons to Athens to study. As the Roman poet Horace said, "captive Greece took captive her rude conqueror." Greek thought captivated the less sophisticated Roman minds, and the Romans became willing transmitters of Greek culture—not, however, without some resistance from Romans who had nothing but contempt for Greek politics and who feared the end of old Roman values. Even those who favored Greek culture blamed the Greeks for Rome's new vices, including luxury and homosexual practices.

Roman Religion

Every aspect of Roman society was permeated with religion. The official state religion focused on the worship of a pantheon of gods and goddesses, including Jupiter, Juno, Minerva, and Mars. As Rome developed and came into contact with other peoples and gods, the community simply adopted new deities. Hence, the Greek Hermes became the Roman Mercury. By the end of the third century B.C., a rather complete amalgamation of Greek and Roman religion had occurred.

Roman religion focused on the worship of the gods for a very practical reason—human beings were thought to be totally dependent on them. Not morality, but the exact performance of ritual was crucial to establishing a right relationship with the gods. What was true for individuals was also valid for the state. It also had to observe correct ritual in order to receive its reward. Accurate performance of ritual was performed by a college of priests or pontiffs, who thus bore responsibility for maintaining the right relationship between the state and the gods. If the rituals were performed correctly, then the Romans would obtain the "peace of the gods." No doubt, the Roman success in creating an empire was a visible confirmation of divine favor. As Cicero, the first-century politician and writer claimed, "We have overcome all the nations of the world, because we have realized that the world is directed and governed by the gods."

Just as the state had an official cult, so too did families. Because the family was regarded as a small state within the state, it had its own household cults, which included Janus, the spirit of the doorway, and Vesta, goddess of the hearth. Here, too, proper ritual was important, and it was the responsibility of the *paterfamilias* as head of the family to ensure that religious obligations were properly fulfilled.

Religious festivals were an important part of Roman religious practice. There were two kinds: public festivals ordained and paid for by the state and private festivals celebrated by individuals and families. By the mid-second century B.C., six public festivals were celebrated annually, each lasting several days. The practice of holding games also grew out of religious festivals. The games were inaugurated in honor of Jupiter Optimus Maximus (best and greatest), the patron deity of Rome, but had become an-

nual events by 366 B.C. In the late Republic, both the number of games and the number of days they lasted were increased. Originally, the games consisted of chariot racing in the Circus Maximus; later, animal hunts and theatrical performances were added. In the empire, gladiatorial contests would become the primary focus.

The Growth of Slavery

Slavery was a common institution throughout the ancient world, but no people possessed more slaves or relied so much on slave labor as the Romans eventually did.

◆ **Temple of Portunus.** The Romans considered the proper worship of the gods an important element of their success. Typical of Roman religious architecture was the small urban temple located in the midst of a crowded commercial center. Pictured here is a rectangular temple built in Rome in the late second or early first century B.C. and dedicated to Portunus, the god of harbors. The temple was located in the cattle market close to the Tiber River.

Before the third century B.C., a small Roman farmer might possess one or two slaves who would help farm his few acres and perform domestic chores. These slaves would most likely be from Italy and be regarded as part of the family household. Only the very rich would have large numbers of slaves.

The Roman conquest of the Mediterranean brought a drastic change in the use of slaves. Large numbers of foreign slaves were brought back to Italy. During the Republic, then, the chief source of slaves was from capture in war, followed by piracy. Of course, the children of slaves also became slaves. While some Roman generals brought back slaves to be sold to benefit the public treasury, ambitious generals of the first century, such as Pompey and Caesar, made personal fortunes by treating slaves captured by their armies as private property.

Slaves were used in many ways in Roman society. The rich, of course, owned the most and the best. In the late Republic it became a badge of prestige to be attended by many slaves. Greeks were in much demand as tutors, musicians, doctors, and artists. Roman businessmen would employ them as shop assistants or craftspeople. Slaves were also used as farm laborers; in fact, huge gangs of

◆ **A Roman Lady.** Roman women, especially those of the upper class, developed comparatively more freedom than women in classical Athens despite the persistent male belief that women required guardianship. This mural decoration was found in the remains of a villa destroyed by the eruption of Mount Vesuvius.

slaves living in pitiful conditions worked the large landed estates known as *latifundia*. Cato the Elder argued that it was cheaper to work slaves to death and then replace them than to treat them well. Many slaves of all nationalities were used as menial household workers, such as cooks, valets, waiters, cleaners, and gardeners. Roads, aqueducts, and other public facilities were constructed by contractors utilizing slave labor. The total number of slaves is difficult to judge—estimates vary from two to four free men to every slave.

It is also difficult to generalize about the treatment of Roman slaves. There are numerous instances of humane treatment by masters and situations where slaves even protected their owners from danger out of gratitude and esteem. But slaves were also subject to severe punishments, torture, abuse, and hard labor that drove some to run away or even revolt against their owners. The Republic had stringent laws against aiding a runaway slave. The murder of a master by a slave might mean the execution of all the other household slaves. Near the end of the second century B.C., large-scale slave revolts occurred in Sicily where enormous gangs of slaves were subjected to horrible working conditions on large landed estates. Slaves were branded, beaten, fed inadequately, worked in chains, and housed at night in underground prisons. It took three years (from 135 to 132 B.C.) to crush a revolt of 70,000 slaves, and the great revolt on Sicily (104–101 B.C.) involved most of the island and took a Roman army of 17,000 men to suppress it. The most famous revolt on the Italian peninsula occurred in 73 B.C. Led by Spartacus, a slave who had been a Thracian gladiator, the revolt broke out in southern Italy and involved 70,000 slaves. Spartacus managed to defeat several Roman armies before he was finally trapped and killed in southern Italy in 71 B.C. Six thousand of his followers were crucified, the traditional form of execution for slaves.

The Roman Family

At the heart of the Roman social structure stood the family, headed by the *paterfamilias*—the dominant male. The household also included the wife, sons with their wives and children, unmarried daughters, and slaves. A family was virtually a small state within the state, and the power of the *paterfamilias* was parallel to that of the state magistrates over the citizens. Like the Greeks, Roman males believed that the weakness of the female sex necessitated male guardians (see the box on p. 97). The *paterfamilias* exercised that authority; on his death, sons or nearest male relatives assumed the role of guardians. By the late Republic, however, although the rights of male guardians

❧ Cato the Elder on Women ❧

During the Second Punic War, the Romans enacted the Oppian Law, which limited the amount of gold women could possess and restricted their dress and use of carriages. In 195 B.C., an attempt to repeal the law was made, and women demonstrated in the streets on behalf of the effort. According to the Roman historian Livy, the conservative Roman official Cato the Elder spoke against repeal and against the women favoring it. Although the words are probably not Cato's own, they do reflect a traditional male Roman attitude toward women.

Livy, *The History of Rome*

"If each of us, citizens, had determined to assert his rights and dignity as a husband with respect to his own spouse, we should have less trouble with the sex as a whole; as it is, our liberty, destroyed at home by female violence, even here in the Forum is crushed and trodden underfoot, and because we have not kept them individually under control, we dread them collectively. . . . But from no class is there not the greatest danger if you permit them meetings and gatherings and secret consultations. . . .

"Our ancestors permitted no women to conduct even personal business without a guardian to intervene in her behalf; they wished them to be under the control of fathers, brothers, husbands; we (Heaven help us!) allow them now even to interfere in public affairs, yes, and to visit the Forum and our informal and formal sessions. What else are they doing now on the streets and at the corners except urging the bill of the tribunes and voting for the repeal of the law? Give loose rein to their uncontrollable nature and to this untamed creature and expect that they will themselves set bounds to their license; unless you act, this is the least of the things enjoined upon women by custom or law and to which they submit with a feeling of injustice. It is complete liberty or rather, if we wish to speak the truth, complete license that they desire.

"If they win in this, what will they not attempt? Review all the laws with which your forefathers restrained their license and made them subject to their husbands; even with all these bonds you can scarcely control them. What of this? If you suffer them to seize these bonds one by one and wrench themselves free and finally to be placed on a parity with their husbands, do you think you will be able to endure them? The moment they begin to be your equals, they will be your superiors. . . .

"Now they publicly address other women's husbands, and, what is more serious, they beg for law and votes, and from various men they get what they ask. In matters affecting yourself, your property, your children, you, Sir, can be importuned; once the law has ceased to set a limit to your wife's expenditures you will never set it yourself. Do not think, citizens, that the situation which existed before the law was passed will ever return. . . ."

remained legally in effect, upper-class women found numerous ways to circumvent the power of their guardians.

Fathers arranged the marriages of daughters, although there are instances of mothers and daughters having influence on the choice. In the Republic, women married *cum manu*, "with legal control" passing from father to husband. By the mid-first century B.C., the dominant practice had changed to *sine manu*, "without legal control," which meant that married daughters officially remained within the father's legal power. Since the fathers of most married women were dead, not being in the "legal control" of a husband made possible independent property rights that forceful women could translate into considerable power within the household and outside it. Traditionally, Roman marriages were intended to be for life, but divorce was introduced in the third century and became relatively easy to obtain since either party could initiate it and no one needed to prove the breakdown of the marriage. Divorce became especially prevalent in the first century B.C.—a period of political turmoil—when marriages were used to cement political alliances.

Some parents in upper-class families provided education for their daughters. Some had private tutors and others may have gone to primary schools. But, at the age when boys were entering secondary schools, girls were pushed into marriage. The legal minimum age was twelve, although fourteen was a more common age in practice. Although some Roman doctors warned that early pregnancies could be dangerous for young girls, early marriages persisted due to the desire to benefit from dowries as soon as possible and the reality of early mortality. A good example is Tullia, Cicero's beloved daughter. She was married at sixteen, widowed at twenty-two, remarried one year later, divorced at twenty-eight, remarried at twenty-nine, and divorced at thirty-three. She died at thirty-four, not unusual for females in Roman society.

The Evolution of Roman Law

One of Rome's chief gifts to the Mediterranean world of its day and to succeeding generations was its development of law. The Twelve Tables of 450 B.C. were the first codification of Roman law, and, although inappropriate for later times, were never officially abrogated and were still memorized by schoolboys in the first century B.C. Civil law derived from the Twelve Tables proved inadequate for later Roman needs, however, and gave way to corrections and additions by the praetors. On taking office, a praetor issued an edict listing his guidelines for dealing with different kinds of legal cases. The praetors were knowledgeable in law, but they also relied on Roman jurists—amateur legal experts—for advice in preparing their edicts. The interpretations of the jurists, often embodied in the edicts of the praetors, created a body of legal principles.

In 242 B.C., the Romans appointed a second praetor who was responsible for examining suits between a Roman and a non-Roman as well as between two non-Romans. The Romans found that although some of their rules of law could be used in these cases, special rules were often needed. These rules gave rise to a body of law known as the law of nations, defined by the Romans as "that part of the law which we apply both to ourselves and to foreigners." But the influence of Greek philosophy, primarily Stoicism, led Romans in the late Republic to develop the idea of the law of nature—or universal divine law derived from right reason. The Romans came to view their law of nations as derived from or identical to this law of nature, thus giving Roman jurists a philosophical justification for systematizing Roman law according to basic principles.

The Development of Literature and Art

The Romans produced little literature before the third century B.C., and the Latin literature that emerged in that century was strongly influenced by Greek models. The demand for plays at public festivals eventually led to a growing number of native playwrights. One of the best-known was Plautus (c. 254–184 B.C.), who used plots from Greek New Comedy (see Chapter 4) for his own plays. The actors wore Greek costumes and Greek masks and portrayed the same basic stock characters: the lecherous old men, the skillful slaves, the prostitutes, and the

young men in love. Plautus wrote for the masses and became a very popular playwright in Rome.

In the last century of the Republic, the Romans began to produce a new poetry, less dependent on epic themes and more inclined to personal expressions. Latin poets were now able to use various Greek forms to express their own feelings about people, social and political life, and love. The finest example of this can be seen in the work of Catullus (c. 87–54 B.C.), Rome's "best lyric poet" and one of the greatest in world literature.

Catullus became a master at adapting and refining Greek forms of poetry to express his emotions. He wrote a variety of poems on, among other things, political figures, social customs, the use of language, the death of his brother, and the travails of love. Catullus became infatuated with Clodia, the promiscuous sister of a tribune and wife of a provincial governor, and addressed a number of poems to her (he called her Lesbia), describing his passionate love and hatred for her (Clodia had many other lovers besides Catullus):

> Lesbia for ever on me rails;
> To talk of me, she never fails.
> Now, hang me, but for all her art
> I find that I have gained her heart.
> My proof is this: I plainly see
> The case is just the same with me;
> I curse her every hour sincerely,
> Yet, hang me, but I love her dearly.[2]

The ability of Catullus to express in simple fashion his intense feelings and curiosity about himself and his world had a noticeable impact on later Latin poets.

The development of Roman prose was greatly aided by the practice of oratory. Romans had great respect for oratory since the ability to persuade people in public debate meant success in politics. Oratory was brought to perfection in a literary fashion by Cicero (106–43 B.C.), the best exemplar of the literary and intellectual interests of the senatorial elite of the late Republic and, indeed, the greatest prose writer of that period. For Cicero, oratory was not simply skillful speaking. An orator was a statesman, a man who achieved his highest goal by pursuing an active life in public affairs.

Later, when the turmoil of the late Republic forced him into semiretirement politically, Cicero became more interested in the writing of philosophical treatises. He was not an original thinker, but served a most valuable purpose for Roman society by popularizing and making understandable the works of Greek philosophers. In his philosophical works, Cicero, more than anyone else, transmitted the classical intellectual heritage to the Western world. Cicero's original contributions came in the field of politics. His works *On the Laws* and *On the Republic* provided fresh insights into political thought. His emphasis on the need to pursue an active life to benefit and improve humankind would greatly influence the later Italian Renaissance.

The Romans were also dependent on the Greeks for artistic inspiration. During the third and second centuries B.C., they adopted many features of the Hellenistic style of art. The Romans developed a taste for Greek statues, which they placed not only in public buildings, but in their private houses. Once demand outstripped the supply of original works, reproductions of Greek statues became fashionable. The Romans' own portrait sculpture was characterized by an intense realism that included even unpleasant physical details. Wall paintings and frescoes in the houses of the rich realistically depicted landscapes, portraits, and scenes from mythological stories.

The Romans excelled in architecture, a highly practical art. Although they continued to utilize Greek styles and made use of colonnades, rectangular structures, and post and lintel construction, the Romans were also innovative. They made considerable use of curvilinear forms: the arch, vault, and dome. The Romans were also the first people in antiquity to develop the use of concrete on a massive scale. By combining concrete and curvilinear forms, they were able to construct massive buildings—public baths and amphitheaters, the most famous of which was the Coliseum in Rome, capable of seating 50,000 spectators. These large buildings were made possible by Roman engineering skills. These same skills were put to use in constructing roads (the Romans built a network of 50,000 miles of roads throughout their empire), aqueducts (in Rome, almost a dozen aqueducts kept a population of one million supplied with water), and bridges.

The Decline and Fall of the Roman Republic (133–31 B.C.)

By the mid-second century B.C., Roman domination of the Mediterranean Sea was well established. Yet the process of creating an empire had weakened and threatened the internal stability of Rome. This internal instability characterizes the period of Roman history from 133 until 31 B.C., when the armies of Octavian defeated Mark Antony and stood supreme over the Roman world. By that time, the constitution of the Roman Republic was in shambles.

By the second century B.C., the senate had become the effective governing body of the Roman state. It comprised some 300 men, drawn primarily from the landed aristocracy; they remained senators for life and held the chief magistracies of the Republic. During the wars of the third and second centuries, the senate came to exercise enormous power. It directed the wars and took control of both foreign and domestic policy, including financial affairs.

Moreover, the magistracies and senate were increasingly controlled by a relatively select circle of wealthy and powerful families—both patrician and plebeian—called the *nobiles* ("nobles"). In the 100 years from 233 to 133 B.C., 80 percent of the consuls came from twenty-six families; moreover, 50 percent came from only ten families. Hence, the *nobiles* constituted a governing oligarchy that managed, through its landed wealth, system of patronage, and intimidation, to maintain its hold over the magistracies and senate and thus guide the destiny of Rome while running the state in its own interests.

By the end of the second century B.C., two types of aristocratic leaders called the *optimates* ("the best men") and the *populares* ("favoring the people") became prominent. *Optimates* and *populares* were terms of political rhetoric that were used by individuals within the aristocracy against fellow aristocratic rivals to distinguish one set of tactics from another. The *optimates* controlled the senate and wished to maintain their oligarchical privileges, while the *populares* were usually other ambitious aristocrats who used the peoples' assemblies as instruments to break the domination of the *optimates*. The conflicts between these two types of aristocratic leaders and their supporters engulfed the first century in political turmoil.

Of course, the aristocrats formed only a tiny minority of the Roman people. The backbone of the Roman state and army had traditionally been the small farmers. But economic changes that began in the period of the Punic Wars increasingly undermined the position of that group. Their lands had been severely damaged during the Second Punic War when Hannibal invaded Italy. Moreover, in order to win the wars, Rome had to increase the term of military service from two to six years. When they returned home, many farmers found their farms so deteriorated that they chose to sell out instead of remaining on the land. By this time, capitalistic agriculture was also increasing rapidly. Landed aristocrats had been able to develop large estates (called *latifundia*) by taking over state-owned land and by buying out small peasant owners. These large estates relied on slave and tenant labor and frequently concentrated on cash crops, such as grapes for wine, olives, and sheep for wool, which small farmers could not afford to do. Thus, the rise of *latifundia* contributed to the decline in the number of small citizen

The Decline and Fall of the Republic

Reforms of Tiberius Gracchus	133 B.C.
Reforms of Gaius Gracchus	123–122 B.C.
Marius: First consulship	107 B.C.
Marius: Consecutive consulships	104–100 B.C.
Sulla seizes Rome	82 B.C.
Sulla as dictator	82–79 B.C.
Pompey's command in Spain	77–71 B.C.
Campaign of Crassus against Spartacus	73–71 B.C.
First Triumvirate (Caesar, Pompey, Crassus)	60 B.C.
Caesar in Gaul	59–49 B.C.
Crassus killed by Parthians	53 B.C.
Caesar crosses the Rubicon	49 B.C.
End of civil war	45 B.C.
Caesar as dictator	47–44 B.C.
Octavian defeats Antony at Actium	31 B.C.

farmers. Because the latter group traditionally provided the foundation of the Roman army, the number of men available for military service declined. Moreover, many of these small farmers drifted to the cities, especially Rome, forming a large class of day laborers who possessed no property. This new urban proletariat was a highly unstable mass with the potential for much trouble in depressed times.

In 133 B.C., Tiberius Gracchus, himself a member of the aristocracy and a new tribune, came to believe that the underlying cause of Rome's problems was the decline of the small farmer. Consequently, Tiberius bypassed the senate, where he knew his rivals would oppose his proposal, and had the council of the plebs pass a land-reform bill that authorized the government to reclaim public land held by large landowners and to distribute it to landless Romans. Many senators, themselves large landowners whose estates included large tracts of public land, were furious, and a group of senators took the law into their own hands and assassinated Tiberius.

The efforts of Tiberius Gracchus were continued by his brother Gaius, elected tribune for both 123 and 122 B.C. Gaius, too, pushed for the distribution of land to displaced farmers. But he broadened his reform program with measures that would benefit the equestrian order, a rising group of wealthy people who wanted a share in the political power held by the ruling aristocracy. Many senators, hostile to Gaius's reforms and fearful of his growing popularity, instigated mob action that resulted in the death of the reformer and many of his friends in 121 B.C. The attempts of the Gracchi brothers to bring reforms had opened the door to more instability and further violence.

A New Role for the Roman Army: Marius and Sulla

In the closing years of the second century B.C., a series of military disasters gave rise to a fresh outburst of popular anger against the old leaders of the senate. Military defeats in northern Africa under a senatorial-appointed general encouraged Marius—a "new man" from the equestrian order—to run for the consulship on a "win the war" campaign slogan. Marius won and became a consul for 107 B.C. Marius then took command of the army in Africa and brought the war to a successful conclusion. He was then called on to defeat the Celts who threatened an invasion of Italy. Marius was made consul for five years, from 104 to 100 B.C., raised a new army, and decisively defeated the Celts, leaving him in a position of personal ascendancy in Rome.

In raising a new army, Marius initiated military reforms that proved to have drastic consequences. The Roman army had traditionally been a conscript army of small landholders. Marius recruited volunteers from both the urban and rural proletariat who possessed no property. These volunteers swore an oath of loyalty to the general, not the senate, and thus inaugurated a professional-type army that might no longer be subject to the state. Moreover, to recruit these men, a general would promise them land, so that generals had to play politics in order to get legislation passed that would provide the land for their veterans. Marius left a powerful legacy. He had created a new system of military recruitment that placed much power in the hands of the individual generals.

Lucius Cornelius Sulla was the next general to take advantage of the new military system. The senate had placed him in charge of a war in Asia Minor, but when the council of the plebs tried to transfer command of this war to Marius, a civil war ensued. Sulla won and seized Rome itself in 82 B.C. He forced the senate to grant him the title of dictator to "reconstitute the Republic." After conducting a reign of terror to wipe out all opposition, Sulla revised the constitution to restore power to the hands of the senate and eliminated most of the powers of the popular assemblies and the tribunes of the plebs. In 79 B.C., believing that he had created a firm foundation for the traditional Republic governed by a powerful senate, he retired. But his real legacy was quite different from what he had intended. His example of using an army to seize power would prove most attractive to ambitious men.

The Collapse of the Republic

For the next fifty years, Roman history would be characterized by two important features: the jostling for power by a number of powerful individuals and the civil wars generated by their conflicts. Three powerful individuals came to hold enormous military and political power—Crassus, Pompey, and Julius Caesar. Crassus, who was known as the richest man in Rome, had successfully put down a major slave rebellion led by Spartacus. Pompey had returned from a successful military command in Spain in 71 B.C. and had been hailed as a military hero. Julius Caesar had been a spokesman for the *populares* from the beginning of his political career and had a military command in Spain. In 60 B.C., Caesar joined with Crassus and Pompey to form a coalition that historians called the First Triumvirate.

Though others had made political deals before, the combined wealth and power of these three men was enormous, enabling them to dominate the political scene and achieve their basic aims: Pompey received lands for his veterans and a command in Spain; Crassus was given a command in Syria; and Caesar was granted a special military command in Gaul (modern France). When Crassus was killed in battle in 53 B.C., his death left two powerful men with armies in direct competition. Caesar had used his time in Gaul wisely. He had conquered all of Gaul and gained fame, wealth, and military experience as well as an army of seasoned veterans who were loyal to him. When leading senators fastened on Pompey as the least harmful to their cause and voted for Caesar to lay down his command and return as a private citizen to Rome, Caesar refused. He chose to keep his army and moved into Italy by illegally crossing the Rubicon, the river that formed the southern boundary of his province. ("Crossing the Rubicon" is a phrase used today to mean being unable to turn back.) Caesar marched on Rome, starting a civil war between his forces and those of Pompey and his allies. The defeat of Pompey's forces left Caesar in complete control of the Roman government.

Caesar had officially been made dictator in 47 B.C., and in 44 B.C., he was made dictator for life. Although his ultimate intentions are a matter of speculation, he did institute a number of reforms designed to solve problems that ambitious senators like himself had previously exploited. In this way he hoped to ensure his continued control unchallenged. He increased the senate to 900 members by filling it with many of his supporters and granted citizenship to a number of people in the provinces who had helped him. He also reformed the calendar by introducing the Egyptian solar year of 365 days (with later changes in 1582, it became the basis of our current calendar). He planned much more in the way of building projects and military adventures in the east, but in 44 B.C., a group of leading senators who resented his domination assassinated him in the belief that they had struck a blow for republican liberty (see the box on p. 103). In truth, they had set the stage for another civil war that delivered the death blow to the Republic.

Within a few years after Caesar's death, two men had divided the Roman world between them—Octavian, Caesar's heir and grandnephew, taking the west, and Antony, Caesar's ally and assistant, the east. But the empire of the Romans, large as it was, was still too small for two masters, and Octavian and Antony eventually came into conflict. Antony allied himself with the Egyptian queen Cleopatra VII, with whom, like Caesar before him, he fell deeply in love. Octavian began a propaganda campaign, accusing Antony of catering to Cleopatra and giving away Roman territory to this "whore of the east." Finally, at the Battle of Actium in Greece in 31 B.C.,

◆ **Caesar.** Conqueror of Gaul and member of the First Triumvirate, Julius Caesar is perhaps the best known figure of the late Republic. Caesar became dictator of Rome in 47 B.C. and, after his victories in the civil war, was made dictator for life. Some members of the senate who resented his power assassinated him in 44 B.C. Pictured is a marble copy of a bust of Caesar.

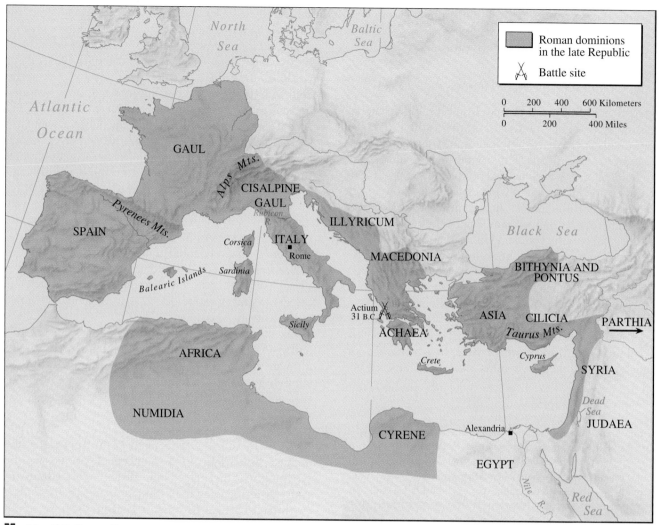

※ Map 5.3 Roman Dominions in the Late Republic, 31 B.C.

Octavian's forces smashed the army and navy of Antony and Cleopatra. Both fled to Egypt where, according to the account of the Roman historian Florus, they committed suicide a year later:

> Antony was the first to commit suicide, by the sword. Cleopatra threw herself at Octavian's feet, and tried her best to attract his gaze: in vain, for his self-control was impervious to her beauty. It was not her life she was after, for that had already been granted, but a portion of her kingdom. When she realized this was hopeless and that she had been earmarked to feature in Octavian's triumph in Rome, she took advantage of her guard's carelessness to get herself into the mausoleum, as the royal tomb is called. Once there, she put on the royal robes which she was accustomed to wear, and lay down in a richly perfumed coffin beside her Antony. Then she applied poisonous snakes to her veins and slipped into death as though into a sleep.[3]

Octavian, at the age of thirty-two, stood supreme over the Roman world. The civil wars were ended. And so was the Republic.

Conclusion

In the eighth and seventh centuries B.C., the pastoral community of Rome emerged as an actual city. Between 509 and 264 B.C., the expansion of this city led to the union of almost all of Italy under Rome's control. Even more dramatically, between 264 and 133 B.C., Rome expanded to the west and east and became master of the Mediterranean Sea.

After 133 B.C., however, Rome's republican institutions proved inadequate for the task of ruling an empire. In the breakdown that ensued, ambitious individuals saw

≱ The Assassination of Julius Caesar ≰

When it quickly became apparent that Julius Caesar had no intention of restoring the Republic as they conceived it, about sixty senators, many of them his friends or pardoned enemies, formed a conspiracy to assassinate the dictator. It was led by Gaius Cassius and Marcus Brutus, who naively imagined that this act would restore the traditional Republic. The conspirators set the Ides of March (March 15) 44 B.C., as the date for the assassination. Caesar was in the midst of preparations for a campaign in the eastern part of the empire. Although warned about a plot against his life, he chose to disregard it. This account of Caesar's death is taken from his biography by the Greek writer Plutarch.

Plutarch, *Life of Caesar*

Fate, however, is to all appearance more unavoidable than unexpected. For many strange prodigies and apparitions are said to have been observed shortly before this event. . . . One finds it also related by many that a soothsayer bade him [Caesar] prepare for some great danger on the Ides of March. When this day was come, Caesar, as he went to the senate, met this soothsayer, and said to him mockingly, "The Ides of March are come," who answered him calmly, "Yes, they are come, but they are not past. . . ."

All these things might happen by chance. But the place which was destined for the scene of this murder, in which the senate met that day, was the same in which Pompey's statue stood, and was one of the edifices which Pompey had raised and dedicated with his theater to the use of the public, plainly showing that there was something of a supernatural influence which guided the action and ordered it to that particular place. Cassius, just before the act, is said to have looked toward Pompey's statue, and silently implored his assistance. . . . When Caesar entered, the senate stood up to show their respect to him, and of Brutus's confederates, some came about his chair and stood behind it, others met him, pretending to add their petitions to those of Tillius Cimber, in behalf of his brother, who was in exile; and they followed him with their joint applications till he came to his seat. When he sat down, he refused to comply with their requests, and upon their urging him further began to reproach them severely for their demand, when Tillius, laying hold of his robe with both his hands, pulled it down from his neck, which was the signal for the assault. Casca gave him the first cut in the neck, which was not mortal nor dangerous, as coming from one who at the beginning of such a bold action was probably very much disturbed; Caesar immediately turned about, and laid his hand upon the dagger and kept hold of it. And both of them at the same time cried out, he that received the blow, in Latin, "Vile Casca, what does this mean?" and he that gave it, in Greek to his brother, "Brother, help!" Upon this first onset, those who were not privy to the design were astonished, and their horror and amazement at what they saw were so great that they dared not fly nor assist Caesar, nor so much as speak a word. But those who came prepared for the business enclosed him on every side, with their naked daggers in their hands. Which way soever he turned he met with blows, and saw their swords leveled at his face and eyes, and was encompassed like a wild beast in the toils on every side. For it had been agreed they should each of them make a thrust at him, and flesh themselves with his blood: for which reason Brutus also gave him one stab in the groin. Some say that he fought and resisted all the rest, shifting his body to avoid the blows, and calling out for help, but that when he saw Brutus's sword drawn, he covered his face with his robe and submitted, letting himself fall, whether it were by chance or that he was pushed in that direction by his murderers, at the foot of the pedestal on which Pompey's statue stood, and which was thus wetted with his blood. So that Pompey himself seemed to have presided, as it were, over the revenge done upon his adversary, who lay here at his feet, and breathed out his soul through his multitude of wounds, for they say he received three-and-twenty. And the conspirators themselves were many of them wounded by each other while they all leveled their blows at the same person.

opportunities for power unparalleled in Roman history and succumbed to the temptations. After a series of bloody civil wars, peace was finally achieved when Octavian defeated Antony and Cleopatra. Octavian's real task was at hand: to create a new system of government that seemed to preserve the Republic while establishing the basis for a new order that would rule the empire in an orderly fashion. Octavian proved equal to the task of establishing a Roman imperial state.

NOTES

1. Quoted in Chester Starr, *Past and Future in Ancient History* (Lanham, Md., 1987), pp. 38–39.
2. Michael Grant, ed., *Roman Readings* (Harmondsworth, 1958), p. 86.
3. Florus, *Epitome of Roman History*, trans. E. S. Forster (Cambridge, Mass., 1961), IV, ii, 149–151.

SUGGESTIONS FOR FURTHER READING

For a general account of the Roman Republic, see J. Boardman, J. Griffin, and O. Murray, eds., *The Oxford History of the Classical World* (Oxford, 1986), pp. 384–523. A brief, but excellent guide to recent trends in scholarship on the Roman Republic can be found in C. Starr, *Past and Future in Ancient History* (Lanham, Md., 1987), pp. 33–45. A standard one-volume reference is M. Cary and H. H. Scullard, *A History of Rome down to the Reign of Constantine*, 3d ed. (New York, 1975). Good surveys of Roman history include M. H. Crawford, *The Roman Republic*, 2nd ed. (Cambridge, Mass., 1993); H. H. Scullard, *History of the Roman World 753–146 B.C.*, 4th ed. (London, 1978), and *From the Gracchi to Nero*, 4th ed. (London, 1976); and A. Kamm, *The Romans* (London, 1995). For a beautifully illustrated survey, see J. F. Drinkwater and A. Drummond, *The World of the Romans* (New York, 1993). A good collection of source materials in translation is contained in N. Lewis and M. Reinhold, eds., *Roman Civilization*, vol. 1 (New York, 1951). The history of early Rome is well covered in M. Pallottino, *A History of Earliest Italy* (London, 1991); and T. J. Cornell, *The Beginnings of Rome: Italy and Rome from the Bronze Age to the Punic Wars (c. 1000–264 B.C.)* (London, 1995). Good works on the Etruscans include M. Pallot-

tino, *The Etruscans*, rev. ed. (Bloomington, Ind., 1975); and M. Grant, *The Etruscans* (New York, 1980).

A general work, heavily political, on Rome's impact on Italy is E. T. Salmon, *The Making of Roman Italy* (London, 1983). Other aspects of the impact of Roman expansion on Italy are examined in P. A. Brunt, *Italian Manpower* (Oxford, 1971).

Aspects of the Roman political structure can be studied in A. N. Sherwin-White, *The Roman Citizenship*, 2d ed. (Oxford, 1973). On Roman military practices, see F. Adcock, *The Roman Art of War under the Republic*, rev. ed. (Cambridge, Mass., 1963). Changes in Rome's economic life can be examined in K. Hopkins, *Conquerors and Slaves* (Cambridge, 1978). On the Roman social structure, see G. Alfoeldy, *The Social History of Rome* (London, 1985).

A general account of Rome's expansion in the Mediterranean world is provided by R. M. Errington, *The Dawn of Empire: Rome's Rise to World Power* (Ithaca, N.Y., 1971). The best work on Carthage is B. H. Warmington, *Carthage*, rev. ed. (London, 1969). On one aspect of Rome's struggle with Carthage, see detailed study by J. Lazenby, *Hannibal's War: A Military History of the Second Punic War* (Warminster, 1978). Especially important works on Roman expansion and imperialism include W. V.

Harris, *War and Imperialism in Republican Rome* (Oxford, 1979); and E. Badian, *Roman Imperialism in the Late Republic* (Oxford, 1968). On Roman expansion in the eastern Mediterranean, see the work by A. N. Sherwin-White, *Roman Foreign Policy in the Greek East* (London, 1984).

Roman religion can be examined in J. Liebeschuetz, *Continuity and Change in Roman Religion* (Oxford, 1979); and H. H. Scullard, *Festivals and Ceremonies of the Roman Republic* (Ithaca, N.Y., 1981). For a general study of daily life in Rome, see F. Dupont, *Daily Life in Ancient Rome* (Oxford, 1994). Roman women are examined in J. Balsdon, *Roman Women*, rev. ed. (London, 1974); S. Pomeroy, *Goddesses, Whores, Wives, and Slaves: Women in Classical Antiquity* (New York, 1976), pp. 149–89; J. F. Gardner, *Women in Roman Law and Society* (Bloomington, Ind., 1986); and S. Dixon, *The Roman Mother* (Norman, Okla., 1988). On various aspects of Roman law, see H. F. Jolowicz and B. Nicholas, *Historical Introduction to Roman Law* (Cambridge, 1972). On slavery and its consequences, see K. R. Bradley, *Slavery and Rebellion in the Roman World, 140 B.C.–70 B.C.* (Bloomington, Ind., 1989). For a brief and readable survey of Latin literature, see R. M. Ogilvie, *Roman Literature and Society* (Harmondsworth, 1980). On Roman art and architecture, see A. Boethius, *Etruscan and Early Roman Architecture* (Harmondsworth, 1978); and G. Richter, *Ancient Italy* (Ann Arbor, 1955).

An excellent account of basic problems in the history of the late Republic can be found in M. Beard and M. H. Crawford, *Rome in the Late Republic* (London, 1985). The classic work on the fall of the Republic is R. Syme, *The Roman Revolution* (Oxford, 1960). A more recent work is D. Shotter, *The Fall of the Roman Republic* (London, 1994). Numerous biographies provide many details on the politics of the period. Especially worthwhile are A.H. Bernstein, *Tiberius Sempronius Gracchus: Tradition and Apostasy* (Ithaca, N.Y., 1978); D. Stockton, *The Gracchi* (Oxford, 1979); C. Meier, *Caesar* (London, 1995); R. Seager, *Pompey: A Political Biography* (Berkeley, 1980); A. Ward, *Marcus Crassus and the Late Roman Republic* (Columbia, Mo., 1977); and D. Stockton, *Cicero: A Political Biography* (London, 1971).

CHAPTER

6

The Roman Empire

With the victories of Octavian, peace finally settled on the Roman world. Although occasional civil conflict still arose, the new imperial state constructed by Octavian experienced a period of remarkable stability for the next 200 years. The Romans imposed their peace on the largest empire established in antiquity. Indeed, Rome's writers proclaimed that "by heaven's will my Rome shall be capital of the world."[1] To the Romans, their divine mission was clearly to rule nations and peoples. Hadrian, an emperor during the second century A.D., was but one of many Roman rulers who believed in Rome's mission. He was a strong and intelligent ruler who took his responsibilities quite seriously. Between 121 and 132, he visited all of the provinces in the empire. According to his Roman biographer, Aelius Spartianus, "hardly any emperor ever traveled with such speed over so much territory." When he arrived in a province, Hadrian dealt firsthand with any problems and bestowed many favors on the local population. He also worked to establish the boundaries of the provinces and provide for their defense. New fortifications, such as the eighty-mile-long Hadrian's Wall across northern Britain, were built to defend the borders. Hadrian insisted on rigid discipline for frontier armies and demanded that the soldiers be kept in training, "just as if war were imminent." He also tried to lead by personal example; according to his biographer, he spent time with the troops and "cheerfully ate out of doors such camp food as bacon, cheese, and vinegar." Moreover, he "would walk as much as twenty miles fully armed."

By the third century A.D., however, Rome's ability to rule nations and people began to weaken as the Roman Empire began to experience renewed civil war, economic chaos, and invasions. Although order was reestablished by the end of the third and beginning of the fourth centuries, Rome's decline was halted only temporarily. In the meantime, the growth of Christianity, one of the remarkable success stories of Western civilization, led to the emergence of a vibrant and powerful institution that picked up the pieces left by Rome's collapse and provided the core for a new medieval civilization.

The Age of Augustus   Five "good emperors"

The Julio-Claudian rulers   The restored empire   Fall of Rome

Jesus of Nazareth   Roman citizenship to all free inhabitants of empire

Constantine legalizes Christianity   Christianity becomes state religion

The silver age of Latin literature   The building of Constantinople

Augustan poets (Virgil, Horace)   The Pantheon

The Age of Augustus (31 B.C.–A.D. 14)

In 27 B.C., Octavian proclaimed the "restoration of the Republic." He understood that only traditional republican forms would satisfy the senatorial aristocracy. At the same time, Octavian was aware that the Republic could not be fully restored and managed to arrive at a compromise that worked at least during his lifetime. In 27 B.C., the senate awarded him the title of Augustus—"the revered one." He preferred the title *princeps*, meaning chief citizen or first among equals. The system of rule that Augustus established is sometimes called the principate, conveying the idea of a constitutional monarch as co-ruler with the senate. But while Augustus worked to maintain this appearance, in reality, power was heavily weighted in favor of the *princeps*.

The New Order

In the new constitutional order that Augustus created, the basic governmental structure consisted of a *princeps* (Augustus) and an aristocratic senate. Augustus retained the senate as the chief deliberative body of the Roman state. Its decrees, screened in advance by the *princeps*, now had the effect of law. The title of *princeps* carried no power in itself, but Augustus held the office of consul each year until 23 B.C., when he assumed the power of a tribune, which enabled him to propose laws and veto any item of public business. By observing proper legal forms for his power, Augustus proved to be highly popular. As the Roman historian Tacitus commented, "Indeed, he attracted everybody's goodwill by the enjoyable gift of peace. . . . Opposition did not exist."[2] No doubt, the ending of the civil wars had greatly bolstered Augustus's popularity (see the box on p. 109). At the same time, his continuing control of the army, while making possible the Roman peace, was a crucial source of his power.

Augustus was especially eager to stabilize the military and administrative structures of the Roman Empire. The peace of the empire depended on the army and so did the security of the *princeps*. While primarily responsible for guarding the frontiers of the empire, the army was also used to maintain domestic order within the provinces. Augustus maintained a standing army of twenty-eight legions or about 150,000 men. Roman legionaries were recruited only from the citizenry and, under Augustus, largely from Italy. Augustus also maintained a large contingent of auxiliary forces—around 130,000—enlisted from the subject peoples. Augustus was also responsible for establishing the praetorian guard. Although nominally a military reserve, these "nine cohorts of elite troops," roughly 9,000 men, had the important task of guarding the person of the *princeps*. Eventually the praetorian guard would play a weighty role in making and deposing emperors.

The role of the *princeps* as military commander gave rise to a title by which this ruler eventually came to be known. When victorious, a military commander was acclaimed by his troops as *imperator*. Augustus was so acclaimed on a number of occasions. *Imperator* is our word *emperor*. Although this title was applied to Augustus and his successors, Augustus himself preferred to use the title of *princeps*.

Augustus inaugurated a new system for governing the provinces. Under the Republic, the senate had appointed the provincial governors. Now, certain provinces were allotted to the *princeps*, who assigned deputies known as legates to govern them. These legates were from the senatorial class and held office as long as the emperor chose. The senate continued to designate the governors of the

✦ **Augustus.** Octavian, Caesar's adopted son, emerged victorious from the civil conflict that rocked the Republic after Caesar's assassination. Augustus operated through a number of legal formalities to ensure that control of the Roman state rested firmly in his hands. This marble statue from Prima Porta depicts the *princeps* Augustus.

sacred in A.D. 9 in the Teutoburg Forest by a coalition of German tribes. The defeat severely dampened Augustus's enthusiasm for continued expansion in central Europe. Thereafter, the Romans were content to use the Rhine as the frontier between the Roman province of Gaul and the German tribes to the east. In fact, Augustus's difficulties had convinced him that "the empire should not be extended beyond its present frontiers."[3] His defeats in Germany taught Augustus that Rome's power was not unlimited. They also left him devastated; for months he beat his head against a door, shouting "Varus, give me back my legions."

Augustan Society

Roman society in the Early Empire was characterized by a system of social stratification, inherited from the Republic, in which Roman citizens were divided into three basic classes: the senatorial, equestrian, and lower classes. Although each class had its own functions and opportunities, the system was not completely rigid. There were possibilities for mobility from one group to another.

Augustus had accepted the senatorial order as a ruling class for the empire. Senators filled the chief magistracies of the Roman government, held the most important military posts, and governed the provinces. One needed to possess property worth 1,000,000 sesterces (an unskilled laborer in Rome received 3 sesterces a day; a Roman legionary 900 sesterces a year in pay) to belong to the senatorial order. The equestrian order was expanded under Augustus and given a share of power in the new imperial state. The equestrian order was open to all Roman citizens of good standing who possessed property valued at 400,000 sesterces. They, too, could now hold military and governmental offices, but the positions open to them were less important than those of the senators.

Those citizens not of the senatorial or equestrian orders belonged to the lower classes, who made up the overwhelming majority of the free citizens. The diminution of the power of the Roman assemblies ended whatever political power they may have possessed earlier in the Republic. Many of these people were provided with free grain and public spectacles to keep them from creating disturbances. Nevertheless, by gaining wealth and serving as lower officers in the Roman legions, it was sometimes possible for them to advance to the equestrian order.

Augustus's belief that Roman morals had been corrupted during the late Republic led him to initiate social legislation to arrest the decline. He thought that increased luxury had undermined traditional Roman frugality and simplicity and caused a decline in morals, evidenced by

remaining provinces, but the authority of Augustus enabled him to overrule the senatorial governors and establish a uniform imperial policy.

Augustus also stabilized the frontiers of the Roman Empire. He conquered the central and maritime Alps and then expanded Roman control of the Balkan peninsula up to the Danube River. His attempt to conquer Germany failed when three Roman legions under Varus were mas-

⇒ *The Achievements of Augustus* ⇐

This excerpt is taken from a text written by Augustus and inscribed on a bronze tablet at Rome. Copies of the text were displayed in stone in many provincial capitals. Called "the most famous ancient inscription," the Res Gestae of Augustus summarizes his accomplishments in three major areas: his offices, his private expenditures on behalf of the state, and his exploits in war and peace. While factual in approach, it is a highly subjective account.

Augustus, *Res Gestae*

Below is a copy of the accomplishments of the deified Augustus by which he brought the whole world under the empire of the Roman people, and of the moneys expended by him on the state and the Roman people, as inscribed on two bronze pillars set up in Rome.

1. At the age of nineteen, on my own initiative and at my own expense, I raised an army by means of which I liberated the Republic, which was oppressed by the tyranny of a faction [Mark Antony and his supporters]. . . .

2. Those who assassinated my father [Julius Caesar, his adoptive father] I drove into exile, avenging their crime by due process of law; and afterwards when they waged war against the state, I conquered them twice on the battlefield.

3. I waged many wars throughout the whole world by land and by sea, both civil and foreign, and when victorious I spared all citizens who sought pardon. . . .

5. The dictatorship offered to me . . . by the people and the senate, both in my absence and in my presence, I refused to accept. . . .

9. The senate decreed that vows for my health should be offered up every fifth year by the consuls and priests. In fulfillment of these vows, games were often celebrated during my lifetime, sometimes by the four most distinguished colleges of priests, sometimes by the consuls. Moreover, the whole citizen body, with one accord, both individually and as members of municipalities, prayed continuously for my health at all the shrines. . . .

17. Four times I came to the assistance of the treasury with my own money, transferring to those in charge of the treasury 150,000,000 sesterces. And in the consulship of Marcus Lepidus and Lucius Arruntius I transferred out of my own patrimony 170,000,000 sesterces to the soldiers' bonus fund, which was established on my advice for the purpose of providing bonuses for soldiers who had completed twenty or more years of service. . . .

20. I repaired the Capitol and the theater of Pompey with enormous expenditures on both works, without having my name inscribed on them. I repaired the conduits of the aqueducts which were falling into ruin in many places because of age, and I doubled the capacity of the aqueduct called Marcia by admitting a new spring into its conduit. . . .

22. I gave a gladiatorial show three times in my own name, and five times in the names of my sons or grandsons; at these shows about 10,000 fought. . . .

25. I brought peace to the sea by suppressing the pirates. In that war I turned over to their masters for punishment nearly 30,000 slaves who had run away from their owners and taken up arms against the state. . . .

26. I extended the frontiers of all the provinces of the Roman people on whose boundaries were peoples not subject to our empire. . . .

27. I added Egypt to the empire of the Roman people. . . .

28. I established colonies of soldiers in Africa, Sicily, Macedonia, in both Spanish provinces, in Achaea, Asia, Syria, Narbonese Gaul, and Pisidia. Italy, moreover, has twenty-eight colonies established by me, which in my lifetime have grown to be famous and populous. . . .

35. When I held my thirteenth consulship, the senate, the equestrian order, and the entire Roman people gave me the title of "father of the country" and decreed that this title should be inscribed in the vestibule of my house, in the Julian senate house, and in the Augustan Forum on the pedestal of the chariot which was set up in my honor by decree of the senate. At the time I wrote this document I was in my seventy-six year.

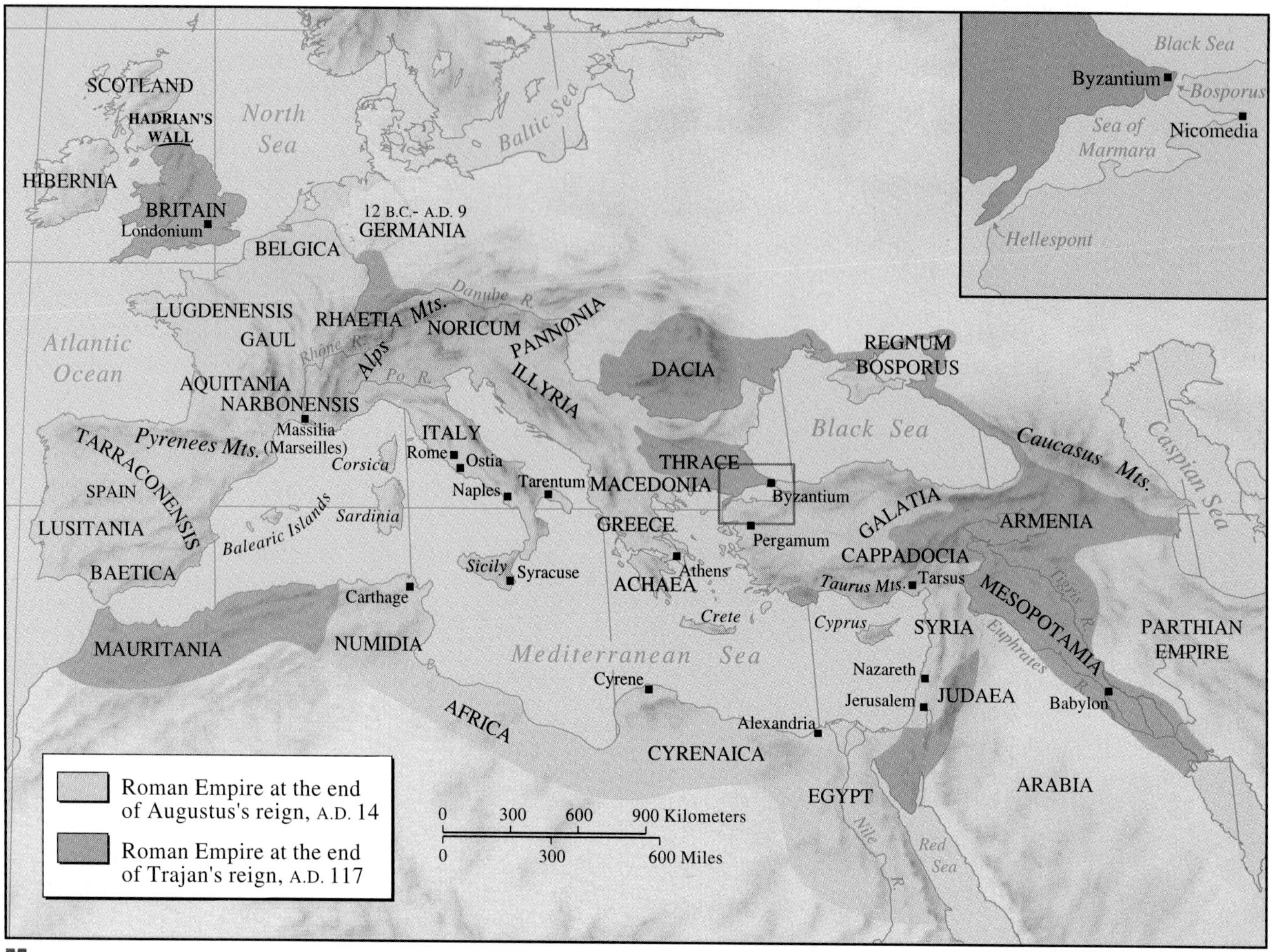

Map 6.1 The Roman Empire from 14 to 117 (Augustus to Trajan).

easy divorce, a falling birthrate among the upper classes, and lax behavior manifested in hedonistic parties and the love affairs of prominent Romans with fashionable women and elegant boys.

Through his new social legislation, Augustus hoped to restore respectability to the upper classes and reverse the declining birthrate as well. Expenditures for feasts were limited, and other laws made adultery a criminal offense. In fact, Augustus's own daughter Julia was exiled for adultery. Augustus also revised the tax laws to penalize bachelors, widowers, and married persons who had fewer than three children.

The Augustan Age was a lengthy one. Augustus died in A.D. 14 after dominating the Roman world for forty-five years. He had created a new order while placating the old by restoring and maintaining traditional values, a fitting combination for a leader whose favorite maxim was "make haste slowly." By the time of his death, his new order was so well established that few agitated for an alternative. Indeed, as the Roman historian Tacitus pointed out, "Actium had been won before the younger men were born. Even most of the older generation had come into a world of civil wars. Practically no one had ever seen truly Republican government. . . . Political equality was a thing of the past; all eyes watched for imperial commands."[4] The Republic was now only a memory and, given its last century of warfare, an unpleasant one at that. The new order was here to stay.

The Early Empire (14–180)

There was no serious opposition to Augustus's choice of his stepson Tiberius as his successor. By designating a family member as *princeps*, Augustus established the Julio-Claudian dynasty; the next four successors of Augustus

♦ **The Emperor Hadrian.** The rule of the five good emperors brought a period of peace and prosperity to the Early Empire. All five treated the ruling classes with respect and implemented beneficial domestic policies. Hadrian was the third of the five good emperors.

were related either to his own family or that of his wife Livia.

Several major tendencies emerged during the reigns of the Julio-Claudians (14–68). In general, more and more of the responsibilities that Augustus had given to the senate tended to be taken over by the emperors, who also instituted an imperial bureaucracy, staffed by talented freedmen, to run the government on a daily basis. As the Julio-Claudian successors of Augustus acted more openly as real rulers rather than "first citizens of the state," the opportunity for arbitrary and corrupt acts also increased. Nero (54–68) freely eliminated people he wanted out of the way, including his own mother, whom he had mur-

dered. Without troops, the senators proved unable to oppose these excesses. However, Nero's extravagances did provoke a revolt of the Roman legions. Abandoned by the guards, Nero chose to commit suicide by stabbing himself in the throat after uttering his final words, "What an artist the world is losing in me." A new civil war erupted in 69, known as the year of the four emperors. The significance of the year 69 was summed up precisely by Tacitus when he stated that "a well-hidden secret of the principate had been revealed: it was possible, it seemed, for an emperor to be chosen outside Rome."[5]

The Five "Good Emperors" (96–180)

At the beginning of the second century, however, a series of five so-called good emperors created a period of peace and prosperity that lasted for almost 100 years. These rulers treated the ruling classes with respect, cooperated with the senate, ended arbitrary executions, maintained peace throughout the empire, and supported domestic policies generally beneficial to the empire. Though absolute monarchs, they were known for their tolerance and diplomacy. By adopting capable men as their successors, the first four good emperors reduced the chances of succession problems.

Under the five good emperors, the powers of the emperor continued to be extended at the expense of the senate. Increasingly, imperial officials appointed and directed by the emperor took over the running of the government. The good emperors also extended the scope of imperial administration to areas previously untouched by the imperial government. Trajan (98–117) established a program that provided state funds to assist poor parents in raising and educating their children.

The good emperors were widely praised by their subjects for their extensive building programs. Trajan and Hadrian (117–138) were especially active in constructing public works—aqueducts, bridges, roads, and harbor facilities—throughout the provinces and in Rome. Trajan built a new forum in Rome to provide a setting for his celebrated victory column. Hadrian's Pantheon, a temple of "all the gods," is one of the grandest ancient buildings surviving in Rome.

The Roman Empire at Its Height: Frontiers and Provinces

Although Trajan broke with Augustus's policy of defensive imperialism by extending Roman rule into Dacia (modern Romania), Mesopotamia, and the Sinai peninsula, his conquests represent the high-water mark of

Rulers of the Early Empire

Augustus	31 B.C.–A.D. 14
Julio-Claudian dynasty	14–68
Nero	54–68
Flavian dynasty	69–96
Five good emperors	96–180
Trajan	98–117
Hadrian	117–138

Roman expansion. His successors recognized that the empire was overextended and pursued a policy of retrenchment. Hadrian withdrew Roman forces from much of Mesopotamia. Although he retained Dacia and Arabia, he went on the defensive in his frontier policy by reinforcing the fortifications along a line connecting the Rhine and Danube Rivers and by building a defensive wall eighty miles long across northern Britain to keep the Scots out of Roman Britain. By the end of the second century, the vulnerability of the empire had become apparent. Frontiers were stabilized, and the Roman forces were established in permanent bases behind the frontiers. But when one frontier was attacked, troops had to be drawn from other frontiers, leaving them vulnerable to attack. The empire lacked a real strategic reserve, and in the next century its weakness would be ever more apparent.

At its height in the second century, the Roman Empire was one of the greatest states the world had seen. It covered about three and a half million square miles and had a population that has been estimated at more than fifty million. While the emperors and the imperial administration provided a degree of unity, considerable leeway was given to local customs, and the privileges of Roman citizenship were extended to many people throughout the empire. In 212, the emperor Caracalla completed the process by giving Roman citizenship to every free inhabitant of the empire. Latin was the language of the western part of the empire while Greek was used in the east. Although Roman culture spread to all parts of the Empire, there were limits to romanization because local languages persisted and many of the empire's residents spoke neither Latin nor Greek.

The administration and cultural life of the Roman Empire depended greatly on cities and towns. A provincial governor's staff was not large, so local city officials were expected to act as Roman agents in carrying out many government functions, especially those related to taxes. Most towns and cities were not large by modern standards. The largest was Rome, but there were also some large cities in the east: Alexandria in Egypt numbered over 300,000 inhabitants, Ephesus in Asia Minor had 200,000, Antioch in Syria around 150,000. In the west, cities were usually small, with only a few thousand inhabitants. Cities were important in the spread of Roman culture, law, and the Latin language. They were also uniform in physical appearance with similar temples, markets, amphitheaters, and other public buildings.

Magistrates and town councillors chosen from the ranks of the wealthy upper classes directed municipal administration. These municipal offices were unsalaried, but were nevertheless desired by wealthy citizens because they received prestige and power at the local level as well as Roman citizenship. Roman municipal policy effectively tied the upper classes to Roman rule and ensured that these classes would retain control over the rest of the population.

The process of romanization in the provinces was reflected in significant changes in the governing classes of the empire. In the course of the first century, there was a noticeable decline in the number of senators from Italian families. By the end of the second century, Italian senators made up less than 50 percent of the total. Increasingly, the Roman senate was being recruited from wealthy provincial equestrian families. The provinces also provided many of the legionaries for the Roman army and, beginning with Trajan, supplied many of the emperors.

Prosperity in the Early Empire

The Early Empire was a period of considerable prosperity. Internal peace resulted in unprecedented levels of trade. Merchants from all over the empire came to the chief Italian ports of Puteoli on the Bay of Naples and Ostia at the mouth of the Tiber. Trade extended beyond the Roman boundaries and included even silk goods from China. The importation of large quantities of grain to feed the people of Rome and an incredible quantity of luxury items for the wealthy upper classes in the west led to a steady drainage of gold and silver coins from Italy and the west to the eastern part of the empire.

Increased trade helped to stimulate manufacturing. The cities of the east still produced the items made in Hellenistic times. The first two centuries of the empire also witnessed the high point of industrial development in Italy. Some industries became concentrated in certain areas, such as bronze work in Capua and pottery in Arretium in Etruria. Other industries, such as brickmaking,

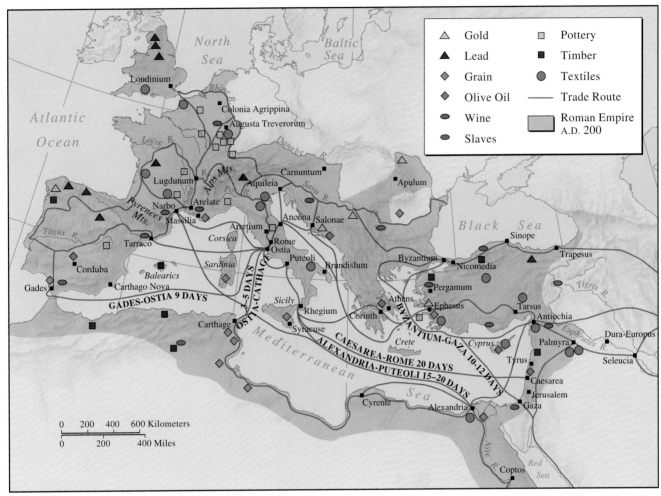

Map 6.2 Trade Routes and Products in the Roman Empire, c. 200.

◆ **The Shipping of Grain.** Trade was an important ingredient in the prosperity of the Early Empire. This tomb painting from Ostia, the port of Rome at the mouth of the Tiber, shows workers loading grain onto the *Isis Giminiana*, a small merchant ship, for shipment upriver to Rome. The captain of the ship stands by the rudder. Next to him is Abascantus, the ship's owner.

Menu from a Roman Banquet

Wealthy Roman homes contained a formal dining room, scene of the dinner parties that were the chief feature of Roman social life. The banquet usually consisted of three courses: appetizers, main course, and dessert. As this menu from a cookbook by Apicius illustrates, each course included an enormous variety of exotic foods. Banquets lasted an entire evening and were accompanied by entertainment provided by acrobats, musicians, dancers, and even poets. Naturally, the diet of lower-class Romans was considerably simpler, consisting of the traditional staples of bread, olives, and grapes. Poorer Romans ate little meat.

A Sample Banquet Menu

Appetizers
Jellyfish and eggs
Sow's udders stuffed with salted sea urchins
Patina of brains cooked with milk and eggs
Boiled tree fungi with peppered fish-fat sauce
Sea urchins with spices, honey, oil and egg sauce

Main Course
Fallow deer roasted with onion sauce and rue
Jericho dates, raisins, oil, and honey
Boiled ostrich with sweet sauce
Turtle dove boiled in its feathers
Roast parrot
Dormice stuffed with pork and pine kernels
Ham boiled with figs and bay leaves, rubbed with
honey, baked in pastry crust
Flamingo boiled with dates

Dessert
Fricassee of roses with pastry
Stoned dates stuffed with nuts and pine kernels,
fried in honey
Hot African sweet-wine cakes with honey

were pursued in rural areas on large landed estates. Much production remained small scale and was done by individual craftsmen, usually freedmen or slaves. In the course of the first century, Italian centers of industry began to experience increasing competition from the provinces.

Despite the extensive trade and commerce, agriculture remained the chief occupation of most people and the underlying basis of Roman prosperity. While the large landed estates called *latifundia* still dominated agriculture, especially in southern and central Italy, small peasant farms persisted, particularly in Etruria and the Po valley. Although large estates concentrating on sheep and cattle raising used slaves, the lands of some *latifundia* were worked by free tenant farmers who paid rent in labor, produce, or sometimes cash.

In considering the prosperity of the Roman world, it is important to remember the enormous gulf between rich and poor (see the box above). The development of towns and cities, so important to the creation of any civilization, is based in large degree on the agricultural surpluses of the countryside. In ancient times, the margin of surplus produced by each farmer was relatively small. Therefore, the upper classes and urban populations had to be supported by the labor of a large number of agricultural producers who never found it easy to produce much more than for

themselves. In lean years, when there were no surpluses, the townspeople often took what they wanted, leaving little for the peasants.

Roman Culture and Society in the Early Empire

From a cultural point of view, the Augustan Age is closely tied to the late Republic. Some of the great literary talents of the Augustan Age matured during the final phases of the Republic. Traditionally, Roman aristocrats had provided financial support for artists and poets in order to gain prestige and enhance their own reputations. Augustus continued this tradition. He perceived the publicity value of literature and art and became the most important patron of the arts during his principate. The literary accomplishments of the Augustan Age caused the period to be called the "golden age" of Latin literature.

The Golden and Silver Ages of Latin Literature

The most distinguished poet of the Augustan Age was Virgil (70–19 B.C.). The son of a small landholder in northern Italy, he proved to be only the first of a series of literary figures in the Augustan Age who welcomed the rule of Augustus. Virgil's masterpiece was the epic poem, the *Aeneid*, clearly meant to rival the work of Homer and fulfill an earlier promise made to Augustus to write a great work in his honor. The connection between Troy and Rome is made explicitly. Aeneas, the son of Anchises of Troy, survives the destruction of Troy and eventually settles in Latium; hence, Roman civilization is linked to Greek history. The character of Aeneas is portrayed in terms that remind us of the ideal Roman—his virtues are duty, piety, and faithfulness. Virgil's overall purpose was to show that Aeneas had fulfilled his mission to establish the Romans in Italy and thereby start Rome on its divine mission to rule the world.

> Let others fashion from bronze more lifelike, breathing
>   images—
> For so they shall—and evoke living faces from marble;
> Others excel as orators, others track with their instruments
> The planets circling in heaven and predict when stars will
>   appear.
> But, Romans, never forget that government is your medium!
> Be this your art:—to practise men in the habit of peace,
> Generosity to the conquered, and firmness against
>   aggressors.[6]

As Virgil expressed it, ruling was Rome's gift.

Another prominent Augustan poet was Horace (65–8 B.C.), a friend of Virgil's. Horace was a very sophisticated writer whose overriding concern seems to have been to point out to his contemporaries the "follies and vices of his age." In the *Satires*, a medley of poems on a variety of subjects, Horace is revealed as a detached observer of human weaknesses. He directed his attacks against movements, not living people, and took on such subjects as sexual immorality, greed, and job dissatisfaction ("How does it happen, Maecenas, that no man alone is content with his lot?"[7]). Horace mostly laughs at the weaknesses of humankind and calls for forbearance: "Supposing my friend has got liquored and wetted my couch, . . . is he for such a lapse to be deemed less dear as a friend, or because when hungry he snatched up before me a chicken from my side of the dish?"[8] In his final work, the *Epistles*, Horace used another Greek form—the imaginary letter in verse—to provide a portrait of his friends and society and those things he held most dear: a simple life, good friends, and his beloved countryside.

Ovid (43 B.C–A.D. 18) was the last of the great poets of the golden age. He belonged to a youthful, privileged social group in Rome that liked to ridicule old Roman values. In keeping with the spirit of this group, Ovid wrote a frivolous series of love poems known as the *Amores*. Intended to entertain and shock, they achieved their goal. Ovid's most popular work was the *Metamorphoses*, a series of fifteen complex mythological tales involving transformations of shapes, such as the change of chaos into order. A storehouse of mythological information, the *Metamorphoses* inspired many painters, sculptors, and writers, including Shakespeare.

Another of Ovid's works was *The Art of Love*. This was essentially a takeoff on didactic poems. Whereas authors of earlier didactic poems had written guides to farming, hunting, or some such subject, Ovid's work was a handbook on the seduction of women (see the box on p. 116). *The Art of Love* appeared to applaud the loose sexual morals of the Roman upper classes at a time when Augustus was trying to clean up the sexual scene in upper-class Rome. Augustus was not pleased. Ovid chose to ignore the wishes of Augustus and paid a price for it. In A.D. 8, he was implicated in a sexual scandal, possibly involving the emperor's daughter Julia, and was banished to a small town on the coast of the Black Sea where he died in exile.

The most famous Latin prose work of the golden age was written by the historian Livy (59 B.C.–A.D. 17). Livy's masterpiece was the *History of Rome* from the foundation of the city to 9 B.C. Only 35 of the original 142 books have survived, although we do possess brief summaries of the whole work from other authors. Livy perceived history in terms of moral lessons. He stated in the preface that

> The study of history is the best medicine for a sick mind; for in history you have a record of the infinite variety of human experience plainly set out for all to see; and in that record you can find for yourself and your country both examples and warnings: fine things to take as models, base things, rotten through and through, to avoid.[9]

For Livy, human character was the determining factor in history.

Livy's history celebrated Rome's greatness. He built scene upon scene that not only revealed the character of the chief figures but also demonstrated the virtues that had made Rome great. Of course, he had serious weaknesses as an historian. He was not always concerned about the factual accuracy of his stories. But he did tell a good story, and his work became the standard history of Rome for a long time.

In the history of Latin literature, the century and a half after Augustus is often labeled the "silver age" to indicate that the literary efforts of the period, while good, were not equal to the high standards of the Augustan "golden age."

⇒ Ovid and the Art of Love ⇐

Ovid has been called the last great poet of the Augustan golden age of literature. One of his most famous works was The Art of Love, *a guidebook for the seduction of women. Unfortunately for Ovid, the work appeared at a time when Augustus was anxious to improve the morals of the Roman upper class. Augustus considered the poem offensive, and Ovid soon found himself in exile.*

Ovid, *The Art of Love*

Now I'll teach you how to captivate and hold the woman of your choice. This is the most important part of all my lessons. Lovers of every land, lend an attentive ear to my discourse; let goodwill warm your hearts, for I am going to fulfill the promises I made you.

First of all, be quite sure that there isn't a woman who cannot be won, and make up your mind that you will win her. Only you must prepare the ground. Sooner would the birds cease their song in the springtime, or the grasshopper be silent in the summer. . . . than a woman resist the tender wooing of a youthful lover. . . .

Now the first thing you have to do is to get on good terms with the fair one's maid. She can make things easy for you. Find out whether she is fully in her mistress's confidence, and if she knows all about her secret dissipations. Leave no stone unturned to win her over. Once you have her on your side, the rest is easy. . . .

In the first place, it's best to send her a letter, just to pave the way. In it you should tell her how you dote on her; pay her beauty compliments and say all the nice things lovers always say. . . . Even the gods are moved by the voice of entreaty. And promise, promise, promise. Promises will cost you nothing. Everyone's a millionaire where promises are concerned. . . .

If she refuses your letter and sends it back unread, don't give up; hope for the best and try again. . . .

Don't let your hair stick up in tufts on your head; see that your hair and your beard are decently trimmed. See also that your nails are clean and nicely filed; don't have any hair growing out of your nostrils; take care that your breath is sweet, and don't go about reeking like a billy-goat. All other toilet refinements leave to the women or to perverts. . . .

When you find yourself at a feast where the wine is flowing freely, and where a woman shares the same couch with you, pray to that god whose mysteries are celebrated during the night, that the wine may not overcloud your brain. 'Tis then you may easily hold converse with your mistress in hidden words whereof she will easily divine the meaning. . . .

By subtle flatteries you may be able to steal into her heart, even as the river insensibly overflows the banks which fringe it. Never cease to sing the praises of her face, her hair, her taper fingers and her dainty foot. . . .

Tears too, are a mighty useful resource in the matter of love. They would melt a diamond. Make a point, therefore, of letting your mistress see your face all wet with tears. Howbeit, if you can't manage to squeeze out any tears—and they won't always flow just when you want them to—put your finger in your eyes.

The popularity of rhetorical training encouraged the use of clever literary expressions at the expense of original content. A good example of this trend can be found in the works of Seneca.

Educated in Rome, Seneca (c. 4 B.C.–A.D. 65) became strongly attached to the philosophy of Stoicism. He was a prolific writer, producing nine tragedies, 124 philosophical letters, seven books of *Natural Questions*, and a number of philosophical dialogues. In letters written to a young friend, he expressed the basic tenets of Stoicism: living according to nature, accepting events dispassionately as part of the divine plan, and a universal love for all humanity. Thus, "The first thing philosophy promises us is the feeling of fellowship, of belonging to mankind and being members of a community. . . . Philosophy calls for simple living, not for doing penance, and the simple way of life need not be a crude one."[10] Viewed in retrospect, Seneca displays some glaring inconsistencies. While preaching the virtues of simplicity, he amassed a fortune and was ruthless at times in protecting it. His letters show humanity, benevolence, and fortitude, but his sentiments are often undermined by an attempt to be clever with words.

The greatest historian of the silver age was Tacitus (c. 56–120). His main works included the *Annals* and *Histories*, which presented a narrative account of Roman history from the reign of Tiberius through the assassination of Domitian (14–96). Tacitus believed that history had a moral purpose: "It seems to me a historian's foremost duty to ensure that merit is recorded, and to confront evil deeds and words with the fear of posterity's denunciations."[11] As a member of the senatorial class, Tacitus was disgusted with the abuses of power perpetrated by the emperors. Forced to be silent in the reign of Domitian, he was determined that the "evil deeds" of wicked men would not be forgotten. Many historians believe he went too far in projecting back into his account of the past the evils of his own day. His work *Germania* is especially important as a source of information about the early Germans. But it too is colored by Tacitus's attempt to show the Germans as noble savages in comparison to the decadent Romans.

Roman Law

The Early Empire experienced great progress in the study and codification of the law. The second and early third centuries A.D. witnessed the "classical age of Roman law," a period in which a number of great jurists classified and compiled basic legal principles that have proved invaluable to the Western world. Most jurists emphasized the emperor as the source of law: "What has pleased the emperor has the force of law."

In the "classical age of Roman law," the identification of the law of nations with natural law led to a concept of natural rights. According to the jurist Ulpian (d. 228), natural rights implied that all men are born equal and should therefore be equal before the law. In practice, however, such a principle was not applied, particularly in the third and later centuries. The Romans did, however, establish standards of justice, applicable to all people, that included principles that we would immediately recognize. A person was regarded as innocent until proven otherwise. People accused of wrongdoing were allowed to defend themselves before a judge. A judge, in turn, was expected to weigh evidence carefully before arriving at a decision. These principles lived on in Western civilization long after the fall of the Roman Empire.

The Upper-Class Roman Family

By the second century A.D., significant changes were occurring in the Roman family. The foundations of the authority of the *paterfamilias* over his family, which had already begun to weaken in the late Republic, were further undermined. The *paterfamilias* no longer had absolute authority over his children; he could no longer sell his children into slavery or have them put to death. Moreover, the husband's absolute authority over his wife also disappeared, a practice that had begun in the late Republic. In the Early Empire, the idea of male guardianship contin-

ued to weaken significantly, and by the late second century, guardianships had become a formality.

Upper-class Roman women in the Early Empire had considerable freedom and independence. They had acquired the right to own, inherit, and dispose of property. Upper-class women could attend races, the theater, and events in the amphitheater, although in the latter two places they were forced to sit in separate female sections. Moreover, ladies of rank were still accompanied by maids and companions when they went out. Some women operated businesses, such as shipping firms. Women could still not participate in politics, but the Early Empire saw a number of important women who influenced politics through their husbands, including Livia, the wife of Augustus; Agrippina, the mother of Nero; and Plotina, the wife of Trajan.

Imperial Rome

At the center of the colossal Roman Empire was the ancient city of Rome. Truly a capital city, Rome had the largest population of any city in the empire. It is estimated that its population was close to one million by the time of Augustus. For anyone with ambitions, Rome was the place to be. A magnet to many people, Rome was extremely cosmopolitan. Nationalities from all over the empire resided there with entire sections inhabited by specific groups, such as Greeks and Syrians.

Rome was, no doubt, an overcrowded and noisy city. Because of the congestion, cart and wagon traffic was banned from the streets during the day. The noise from the resulting vehicular movement at night often made sleep difficult. Evening pedestrian travel was dangerous. Although Augustus had organized a police force, lone travelers could be assaulted, robbed, and soaked by filth thrown out of the upper-story windows of Rome's massive apartment buildings.

An enormous gulf existed between rich and poor in the city of Rome. While the rich had comfortable villas, the poor lived in apartment blocks called *insulae*, which might be six stories high. Constructed of concrete, they were often poorly built and not infrequently collapsed. The use of wooden beams in the floors and movable stoves, torches, candles, and lamps within the rooms for heat and light made the danger of fire a constant companion. Once started, fires were extremely difficult to put out. The famous conflagration of 64, which Nero was unjustly accused of starting, devastated a good part of the city. Besides the hazards of collapse and fire, living conditions were also poor. High rents forced entire families into one room. The absence of plumbing, central heating, and open fireplaces made life so uncomfortable that poorer Romans spent most of their time outdoors in the streets.

Fortunately for these people, Rome boasted public buildings unequaled anywhere in the empire. Its temples, fora, markets, baths, theaters, triumphal arches, governmental buildings, and amphitheaters gave parts of the city an appearance of grandeur and magnificence (see the box on p. 119).

Though the center of a great empire, Rome was also a great parasite. Beginning with Augustus, the emperors accepted responsibility for providing food for the urban populace, with about 200,000 people receiving free grain. Even with the free grain, conditions were grim for the poor. Early in the second century A.D., a Roman doctor claimed that rickets was common among children in the city.

In addition to food, entertainment was also provided on a grand scale for the inhabitants of Rome. The poet Juvenal said of the Roman masses: "But nowadays, with no vote to sell, their motto is 'Couldn't care less.' Time was when their plebiscite elected generals, heads of state, commanders of legions: but now they've pulled in their horns, there's only two things that concern them: Bread and Circuses."[12] Public spectacles were provided by the emperor and other state officials as part of the great festivals—most of them religious in origin—celebrated by the state. More than 100 days a year were given over to these public holidays. The festivals included three major types of entertainment. At the Circus Maximus, horse and chariot races attracted hundreds of thousands, while dramatic and other performances were held in theaters. But the most famous of all the public spectacles were the gladiatorial shows.

The Gladiatorial Shows

The gladiatorial shows were an integral part of Roman society. They took place in amphitheaters, with the first permanent one having been constructed at Rome in 29 B.C. Perhaps the most famous was the Flavian amphitheater, called the Colosseum, constructed at Rome to seat 50,000 spectators. Amphitheaters were not limited to the city of Rome but were constructed throughout the empire. They varied greatly in size with capacities ranging from a few thousand to tens of thousands. Considerable resources and ingenuity went into building them, especially in the arrangements for moving wild beasts efficiently into the arena. In most cities and towns, amphitheaters came to be the biggest buildings, rivaled only by the circuses for races and the public baths. Where a society invests its money gives one an idea of its priorities. Since the amphitheater was the primary location for the gladiatorial games, it is fair to say that public slaughter was an important part of Roman culture.

✳ **Map 6.3** Imperial Rome.

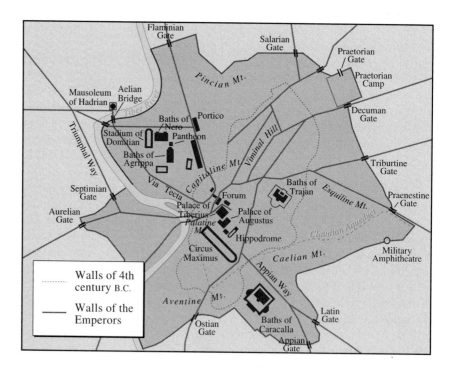

➤ The Public Baths of the Roman Empire ➤

The public baths in Rome and other cities played an important role in urban life. Introduced to Rome in the second century B.C. as a result of Greek influence, the number of public baths grew at a rapid pace in the Early Empire as the emperors contributed funds for their construction. The public baths were especially noisy near the end of the afternoon when Romans stopped in after work to use the baths before dinner. The following description is by Lucian, a traveling lecturer who lived in the second century and wrote satirical dialogues in Greek. This selection is taken from Hippias, or the Bath.

Lucian, *Hippias, or the Bath*

The building suits the magnitude of the site, accords well with the accepted idea of such an establishment, and shows regard for the principles of lighting. The entrance is high, with a flight of broad steps of which the tread is greater than the pitch, to make them easy to ascend. On entering, one is received into a public hall of good size, with ample accommodations for servants and attendants. On the left are the lounging rooms, also of just the right sort for a bath, attractive, brightly lighted retreats. Then, besides them, a hall, larger than need be for the purposes of a bath, but necessary for the reception of richer persons. Next, capacious locker rooms to undress in, on each side, with a very high and brilliantly lighted hall between them, in which are three swimming pools of cold water; it is finished in Laconian marble, and has two statues of white marble in the ancient style. . . .

On leaving this hall, you come into another which is slightly warmed instead of meeting you at once with fierce heat; it is oblong, and has an apse on each side. Next to it, on the right, is a very bright hall, nicely fitted up for massage. . . . Then near this is another hall, the most beautiful in the world, in which one can stand or sit with comfort, linger without danger, and stroll about with profit. It also is radiant with Phrygian marble clear to the roof. Next comes the hot corridor, faced with Numidian marble. The hall beyond it is very beautiful, full of abundant light and aglow with color like that of purple hangings. It contains three hot tubs.

When you have bathed you need not go back through the same rooms, but can go directly to the cold room through a slightly warmed chamber. Everywhere there is copious illumination and full indoor daylight. . . . Why should I go on to tell you of the exercising floor and the cloak rooms? . . . Moreover, it is beautiful with all other marks of thoughtfulness—with two toilets, many exits, and two devices for telling time, a water clock that makes a bellowing sound and a sundial.

Gladiatorial games were held from dawn to dusk. Contests to the death between trained fighters formed the central focus of these games. Most gladiators were slaves or condemned criminals, although some free men lured by the hope of popularity and patronage by wealthy fans participated voluntarily. They were trained for combat in special gladiatorial schools.

Gladiatorial games included other forms of entertainment as well. Criminals of all ages and both sexes were sent into the arena without weapons to face certain death from wild animals who would tear them to pieces. Numerous kinds of animal contests were also staged: wild beasts against each other, such as bears against buffaloes; staged hunts with men shooting safely from behind iron bars; and gladiators in the arena with bulls, tigers, and lions. Reportedly, 5,000 beasts were killed in one day of games when the Emperor Titus inaugurated the Colosseum in A.D. 80. Enormous resources were invested in the capture and shipment of wild animals for slaughter, while whole species were hunted to extinction in parts of the empire.

These bloodthirsty spectacles were highly popular with the Roman people. The Roman historian Tacitus said, "Few indeed are to be found who talk of any other subjects in their homes, and whenever we enter a classroom, what else is the conversation of the youths."[13] But the gladiatorial games served a purpose beyond mere entertainment. The aristocratic statesman Pliny argued that the contests inspired a contempt for pain and death, because even slaves and criminals displayed a love of praise and desire for victory in the arena. Most importantly, the gladiatorial games, as well as the other forms of public entertainment, fulfilled both a political and social need. Certainly, the games served to divert the idle masses from any political unrest. It was said of the Emperor Trajan that he understood that although the distribution of grain and money satisfied the individual, spectacles were necessary for the "contentment of the masses."

Religion in the Roman World: The Rise of Christianity

The rise of Christianity marks a fundamental break with the dominant values of the Greco-Roman world. Christian views of God, human beings, and the world were quite different from those of the Greeks and Romans. Nevertheless, Christianity also had much in common with its contemporary religions. Consequently, to understand the rise of Christianity, we must first examine both the religious environment of the Roman world and the Jewish background from which Christianity emerged.

The Religious World of the Romans

Augustus had taken a number of steps to revive the Roman state religion, which had declined during the turmoil of the late Republic. The official state religion focused on the worship of a pantheon of gods and goddesses. Observance of proper ritual by state priests theoretically established the proper relationship between Romans and the gods and guaranteed security, peace, and prosperity. The polytheistic Romans were extremely tolerant of other religions. The Romans allowed the worship of native gods and goddesses throughout their provinces and even adopted some of the local gods. In addition, the imperial cult of Roma and Augustus was developed to bolster support for the emperors. After Augustus, those dead emperors deified by the Roman senate were included in the official imperial cult.

The desire for a more emotional spiritual experience led many people to the mystery religions of the Hellenistic east, which flooded into the western Roman world during the Early Empire. The mystery religions offered secret teachings that supposedly brought special benefits. They promised their followers advantages unavailable through Roman religion: an entry into a higher world of reality and the promise of a future life superior to the present one. They also featured elaborate rituals with deep emotional appeal. By participating in their ceremonies and performing their rites, an adherent could achieve communion with spiritual beings and undergo purification that opened the door to life after death.

Although many mystery cults competed for the attention of the Roman world, perhaps the most important was Mithraism. Mithras was the chief agent of Ahuramazda, the supreme god of light in Persian Zoroastrianism (see Chapter 2). In the Roman world, Mithras came to be identified with the sun god and was known by his Roman title of the Unconquered Sun. Mithraism had spread rapidly in Rome and the western provinces by the second century A.D. and was especially favored by soldiers who viewed Mithras as their patron deity. Mithraists paid homage to the sun on the first day of the week (Sunday), commemorated the sun's birthday around December 25, and celebrated ceremonial meals. All of these practices had parallels in Christianity.

◆ **The Gladiatorial Games.** Although some gladiators were free men enticed by the possibility of rewards, most were condemned criminals, slaves, or prisoners of war who were trained in special schools. A great gladiator could win his freedom through the games. The more bizarre an event, the more popular it was with the spectators. The fresco pictured here shows a captured tribesman exposed to a wild beast while gladiators are fighting with animals.

The Jewish Background

In Hellenistic times, the Jewish people had been granted considerable independence by their Seleucid rulers (see Chapter 4). Roman involvement with the Jews began in 63 B.C., and by A.D. 6, Judaea (which embraced the lands of the old Hebrew kingdom of Judah) had been made a province and placed under the direction of a Roman procurator. But unrest continued, augmented by divisions among the Jews themselves. The Sadducees favored a rigid adherence to Hebrew law, rejected the possibility of personal immortality, and favored cooperation with the Romans. The Pharisees took a more liberal approach to Jewish law, believed in an afterlife, and wanted to liberate Judaea from Roman control. The Essenes were a Jewish sect that lived in a religious community near the Dead Sea. As revealed in the Dead Sea Scrolls, a collection of documents first discovered in 1947, the Essenes, like many other Jews, awaited a Messiah who would save Israel from oppression, usher in the kingdom of God, and establish a true paradise on earth. A fourth group, the Zealots, were militant extremists who advocated the violent overthrow of Roman rule. A Jewish revolt in 66 was crushed by the Romans four years later. The Jewish temple in Jerusalem was destroyed, and Roman power once more stood supreme in Judaea.

The Rise of Christianity

In the midst of the confusion and conflict in Judaea, Jesus of Nazareth (c. 6 B.C.–A.D. 29) began his public preaching. Jesus grew up in Galilee, an important center of the militant Zealots. Jesus's message was basically simple. He reassured his fellow Jews that he did not plan to undermine their traditional religion: "Do not think that I have come to abolish the Law or the Prophets; I have not come to abolish them but to fulfill them."[14] According to Jesus, what was important was not strict adherence to the letter of the law and attention to rules and prohibitions, but the transformation of the inner person: "So in everything, do to others what you would have them do to you, for this sums up the Law and the Prophets."[15] God's command was a simple one—to love God and one another: "Love the Lord your God with all your heart and with all your soul and with all your mind and with all your strength. The second is this: Love your neighbor as yourself."[16] In the Sermon on the Mount (see the box on p. 122), Jesus presented the ethical concepts—humility, charity, and brotherly love—that would form the basis for the value system of medieval Western civilization. As we have seen, these were not the values of classical Greco-Roman civilization.

✦ **Christ and His Apostles.** Pictured is a fresco from a Roman catacomb depicting Christ and the apostles. Under the leadership of individuals such as Paul of Tarsus, Christianity grew from a small sect within Judaism to a powerful religious force within the empire. Christianity eventually became the official state religion.

While some people welcomed Jesus as the Messiah who would save Israel from oppression and establish God's kingdom on earth, Jesus spoke of a heavenly kingdom, not an earthly one: "My kingdom is not of this world."[17] Consequently, he disappointed the radicals. At the same time, conservative religious leaders believed Jesus was undermining respect for traditional Jewish religion. To the Roman authorities of Palestine and their local allies, the Nazarene was a potential revolutionary who might transform Jewish expectations of a messianic kingdom into a revolt against Rome. Therefore, Jesus found himself denounced on many sides and was given over to the Roman authorities. The procurator Pontius Pilate ordered his crucifixion. But that did not solve the problem. A few loyal followers of Jesus spread the story that Jesus had overcome death and had been resurrected. He was then hailed as the "the anointed one" or the Messiah who would return and usher in the kingdom of God on earth.

Christianity began, then, as a religious movement within Judaism and was viewed that way by Roman authorities for many decades. Although tradition holds that one of Christ's disciples, Peter, founded the Christian church at Rome, the most important figure in early Christianity after Christ was Paul of Tarsus (c. 5–c. 67). Paul reached out to non-Jews and transformed Christianity from a Jewish sect into a broader religious movement.

⮞ Christian Ideals: The Sermon on the Mount ⮜

Christianity was simply one of many religions competing for attention in the Roman Empire during the first and second centuries. The rise of Christianity marked a fundamental break with the value system of the upper-class elites who dominated the world of classical antiquity. As these excerpts from the Sermon on the Mount in the Gospel of Matthew illustrate, Christians emphasized humility, charity, brotherly love, and a belief in the inner being and a spiritual kingdom superior to this material world. These values and principles were not those of classical Greco-Roman civilization as exemplified in the words and deeds of its leaders.

The Gospel according to Matthew

Now when he saw the crowds, he went up on a mountainside and sat down. His disciples came to him, and he began to teach them saying:

Blessed are the poor in spirit: for theirs is the kingdom of heaven.

Blessed are those who mourn: for they will be comforted.

Blessed are the meek: for they will inherit the earth.

Blessed are those who hunger and thirst for righteousness: for they will be filled.

Blessed are the merciful: for they will be shown mercy.

Blessed are the pure in heart: for they will see God.

Blessed are the peacemakers: for they will be called sons of God.

Blessed are those who are persecuted because of righteousness for theirs is the kingdom of heaven. . . .

You have heard that it was said, 'Eye for eye, and tooth for tooth.' But I tell you, Do not resist an evil person. If someone strikes you on the right cheek, turn to him the other also. . . .

You have heard that it was said, 'Love your neighbor, and hate your enemy.' But I tell you, Love your enemies and pray for those who persecute you. . . .

Do not store up for yourselves treasures on earth, where moth and rust destroy, and where thieves break in and steal. But store up for yourselves treasures in heaven, where moth and rust do not destroy, and where thieves do not break in and steal. For where your treasure is, there you heart will be also. . . .

No one can serve two masters. Either he will hate the one and love the other, or he will be devoted to the one and despise the other. You cannot serve both God and Money.

Therefore I tell you, do not worry about your life, what you will eat or drink; or about your body, what you will wear. Is not life more important than food, and the body more important than clothes? Look at the birds of the air; they do not sow or reap to store away in barns, and yet your heavenly Father feeds them. Are you not much more valuable than they? . . . So do not worry, saying, What shall we eat? or What shall we drink? or What shall we wear? For the pagans run after all these things, and your heavenly Father knows that you need them. But seek first his kingdom and his righteousness, and all these things will be given to you as well.

Called the "second founder of Christianity," Paul was a Jewish Roman citizen who had been strongly influenced by Hellenistic Greek culture. He believed that the message of Christ should be preached not only to Jews but to Gentiles (non-Jews) as well. Paul was responsible for founding Christian communities throughout Asia Minor and along the shores of the Aegean.

It was Paul who provided a universal foundation for the spread of Christ's ideas. He taught that Christ was, in effect, a savior-God, the son of God, who had come to earth to save all humans who were basically sinners as a result of Adam's original sin of disobedience against God. By his death, Christ had atoned for the sins of all humans and made it possible for all men and women to experience a new beginning with the potential for individual salvation. By accepting Christ as their Savior, they too could be saved.

At first, Christianity spread slowly. Although the teachings of early Christianity were mostly disseminated by the preaching of convinced Christians, written materials also appeared. Paul had written a series of letters or epistles outlining Christian beliefs for different Christian communities. Some of Christ's disciples may also have preserved some of the sayings of the master in writing and would have passed on personal memories that became the basis of the written gospels—the "good news" concerning Christ—which attempted to provide a record of Christ's life and teachings and formed the core of the New Testament. Although Jerusalem was the first center of Christianity, its destruction by the Romans in A.D. 70 left individual Christian churches with considerable independence. By 100, Christian churches had been established in most of the major cities of the east and in some places in the western part of the empire. Many early Christians came from the ranks of Hellenized Jews and the Greek-speaking populations of the east. But in the second and third centuries, an increasing number of followers came from Latin-speaking people. A Latin translation of the Greek New Testament that appeared soon after 200 aided this process.

Although some of the fundamental values of Christianity differed markedly from those of the Greco-Roman world, the Romans initially did not pay much attention to the Christians, whom they regarded at first as simply another sect of Judaism. The structure of the Roman Empire itself aided the growth of Christianity. Christian missionaries, including some of Christ's original twelve disciples or apostles, used Roman roads to travel throughout the Empire spreading their "good news."

As time passed, however, the Roman attitude toward Christianity began to change. The Romans were tolerant of other religions except when they threatened public order or public morals. Many Romans came to view Christians as harmful to the order of the Roman state. Because Christians held their meetings in secret and seemed to be connected to Christian groups in other areas, the government could view them as potentially dangerous to the state.

Some Romans felt that Christians were overly exclusive and hence harmful to the community and public order. The Christians did not recognize other gods and therefore abstained from public festivals honoring these divinities. Finally, Christians refused to participate in the worship of the state gods and imperial cult. Since the Romans regarded these as important to the state, the Christians' refusal undermined the security of the state and hence constituted an act of treason, punishable by death. But to the Christians, who believed there was only one real god, the worship of state gods and the emperors was idolatry and would endanger their own salvation.

Roman persecution of Christians in the first and second centuries was never systematic, but only sporadic and local. Persecution began during the reign of Nero. After the fire that destroyed much of Rome, the emperor used the Christians as scapegoats, accusing them of arson and hatred of the human race and subjecting them to cruel deaths in Rome. In the second century, Christians were largely ignored as harmless. By the end of the reigns of the five good emperors, Christians still represented a small minority, but one of considerable strength.

The Decline and Fall of the Roman Empire

In the course of the third century, the Roman Empire came near to collapse. After a series of civil wars, Septimius Severus (193–211), who was born in North Africa and spoke Latin with an accent, used his legions to seize power. Septimius Severus's deathbed admonition to his sons "to pay the soldiers, and ignore everyone else" set the tone for the new dynasty he established. The Severan rulers (193–235) began to create a military monarchy. The army was expanded, soldiers' pay was increased, and military officers were appointed to important government positions.

Military monarchy was followed by military anarchy. For a period of almost fifty years, from 235 to 284, the Roman Empire was mired in the chaos of continual civil war, as contenders for the imperial throne found that bribing soldiers was the primary way to become emperor. In these almost fifty years, there were twenty-two emperors, only two of whom did not meet a violent death. At the same time, the empire was beset by a series of invasions, no doubt exacerbated by the civil wars. In the east, the Sassanid Persians made inroads into Roman territory. A fitting symbol of Rome's decline was the capture of the Roman emperor Valerian (253–260) by the Persians and his death in captivity, an event previously unheard of in Roman history. Germanic tribes also poured into the empire. The Goths overran the Balkans and moved into Greece and Asia Minor. The Franks advanced into Gaul and Spain. It was not until the reign of Aurelian (270–275) that most of the boundaries were restored.

Invasions, civil wars, and plague came close to causing an economic collapse of the Roman Empire in the third century. The population declined drastically, possibly by as much as one-third. There was a noticeable decline in trade and small industry. The labor shortage created by plague affected both military recruiting and the economy. Farm production deteriorated significantly. Fields were ravaged by Germanic tribes, but even more often by the defending Roman armies. Many farmers complained that Roman commanders and their soldiers were confiscating produce and livestock. Provincial governors seemed powerless to stop these depredations, and some even joined in the extortion. The monetary system began to show signs of collapse as a result of debased coinage and the beginnings of serious inflation.

Armies were needed more than ever, but financial strains made it difficult to enlist and pay the necessary soldiers. Whereas in the second century the Roman army

Chief Events and Rulers of the Late Empire

Military monarchy (Severan dynasty)	193–235
Septimius Severus	193–211
Caracalla	211–217
Military anarchy	235–284
Valerian	253–260
Aurelian	270–275
Diocletian	284–305
Constantine	306–337
Edict of Milan	313
Visigoths sack Rome	410
Vandals sack Rome	455
Romulus Augustulus is deposed	476

had been recruited from among the inhabitants of frontier provinces, by the mid-third century, the state had to rely on hiring Germans to fight under Roman commanders. These soldiers had no understanding of Roman traditions and no real attachment to either the empire or the emperors.

The Reforms of Diocletian and Constantine

At the end of the third and beginning of the fourth centuries, the Roman Empire gained a new lease on life through the efforts of two strong emperors, Diocletian and Constantine, who restored order and stability. The Roman Empire was virtually transformed into a new state: the so-called Late Empire, which included a new governmental structure, a rigid economic and social system, and a new state religion—Christianity.

Believing that the empire had grown too large for a single ruler, Diocletian (284–305) divided it into four administrative units. Despite the appearance of four-man rule, however, Diocletian's military seniority enabled him to claim a higher status and hold the ultimate authority. Constantine (306–337) continued and even expanded the autocratic policies of Diocletian. Both rulers greatly strengthened and enlarged the administrative bureaucracies of the Roman Empire. Henceforth, civil and military bureaucracies were sharply separated. Each contained a hierarchy of officials who exercised control at the various levels. The emperor presided over both hierarchies of of-

ficials and served as the only link between them. New titles of nobility—such as *illustres* ("illustrious ones") and *illustrissimi* ("the most illustrious ones")—were instituted to dignify the holders of positions in the civil and military bureaucracies.

Additional military reforms were also inaugurated. The army was enlarged to 500,000 men, including barbarian units. Mobile units were established that could be quickly moved to support frontier troops where the borders were threatened. Although larger, the army was less competent, being made up of Germans and Yugoslavs with less training than the traditional legions.

Constantine was especially interested in building programs despite the strain they placed on the budget. His biggest project was the construction of a new capital city in the east on the site of the Greek city of Byzantium on the shores of the Bosporus. Eventually renamed Constantinople (modern Istanbul), it was developed for defensive reasons: It had an excellent strategic location. Calling it his "New Rome," Constantine endowed the city with a forum, large palaces, and a vast amphitheater.

The political and military reforms of Diocletian and Constantine greatly enlarged two institutions—the army

◆ **The Emperor Constantine.** Constantine played an important role in restoring order and stability to the Roman Empire at the beginning of the fourth century. This marble head of Constantine, which is eight feet, six inches high, was part of an enormous seated statue of the emperor in Rome. Constantine used these awe-inspiring statues throughout the empire to build support for imperial policies.

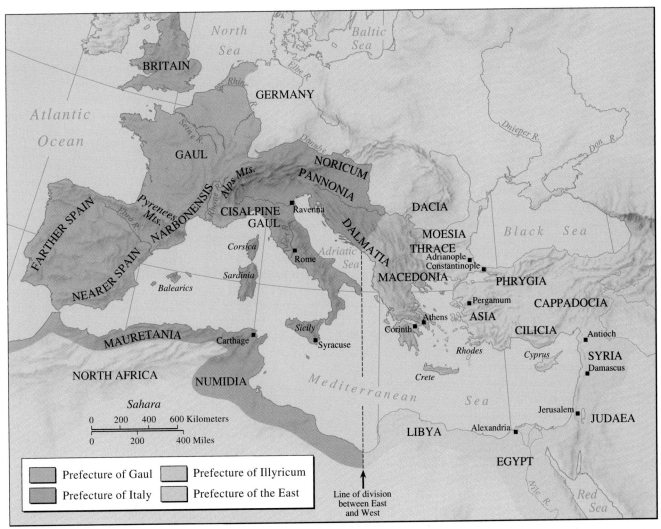

Map 6.4 Divisions of the Restored Roman Empire, c. 300.

and civil service—that drained most of the public funds. Though more revenues were needed to pay for the army and bureaucracy, the population was not growing, so the tax base could not be expanded. Diocletian and Constantine devised new economic and social policies to deal with these financial burdens, but like their political policies, they were all based on coercion and loss of individual freedom. To fight inflation, Diocletian resorted to issuing a price edict in 301 that established maximum wages and prices for the entire empire, but despite severe penalties, it was unenforceable and failed to work.

Coercion also came to form the underlying basis for numerous occupations in the Late Roman Empire. To ensure the tax base and keep the empire going despite the shortage of labor, the emperors issued edicts that forced people to remain in their designated vocations. Hence,

basic jobs, such as bakers and shippers, became hereditary. Free tenant farmers continued to decline and soon found themselves bound to the land by large landowners who took advantage of depressed agricultural conditions to enlarge their landed estates.

In general, the economic and social policies of Diocletian and Constantine were based on an unprecedented degree of control and coercion. Though temporarily successful, such authoritarian policies in the long run stifled the very vitality the Late Empire needed to revive its sagging fortunes.

The Growth of Christianity

The sporadic persecution of Christians by the Romans in the first and second centuries had done nothing to stop the growth of Christianity. It had, in fact, served to strengthen Christianity as an institution in the second and third centuries by causing it to shed the loose structure of the first century and move toward a more centralized organization of its various church communities. Crucial to this change was the emerging role of the bishops, who began to assume more control over church communities. The Christian church was creating a well-defined hierarchical structure in which the bishops and clergy were salaried officers separate from the laity or regular church members.

Christianity grew slowly in the first century, took root in the second, and had spread widely by the third. Why was Christianity able to attract so many followers? Certainly, the Christian message had much to offer the Roman world. The promise of salvation, made possible by Christ's death and resurrection, made a resounding impact on a world full of suffering and injustice. Christianity seemed to imbue life with a meaning and purpose beyond the simple material things of everyday reality. Secondly, Christianity was not entirely unfamiliar. It could be viewed as simply another eastern mystery religion, offering immortality as the result of the sacrificial death of a savior-God. At the same time, it offered advantages that the other mystery religions lacked. Christ had been a human figure, not a mythological one, such as Mithras. Moreover, Christianity had universal appeal. Unlike Mithraism, it was not restricted to men. Furthermore, it did not require a painful or expensive initiation rite as other mystery religions did. Initiation was accomplished simply by baptism—a purification by water—by which one entered into a personal relationship with Christ. In addition, Christianity gave new meaning to life and offered what the Roman state religions could not—a personal relationship with God and connection to higher worlds.

Finally, Christianity fulfilled the human need to belong. Christians formed communities bound to one another in which people could express their love by helping each other and offering assistance to the poor, sick, widows, and orphans. Christianity satisfied the need to belong in a way that the huge, impersonal, and remote Roman Empire could never do.

Christianity proved attractive to all classes. The promise of eternal life was for all—rich, poor, aristocrats, slaves, men, and women. As Paul stated in his Epistle to the Colossians: "And [you] have put on the new self, which is being renewed in knowledge in the image of its Creator. Here there is no Greek nor Jew, circumcised or uncircumcised, barbarian, Scythian, slave or free, but Christ is all, and is in all."[18] Although it did not call for

revolution or social upheaval, Christianity emphasized a sense of spiritual equality for all people.

As the Christian church became more organized, some emperors in the third century responded with more systematic persecutions, but their schemes failed to work. The last great persecution was by Diocletian at the beginning of the fourth century. But even he had to admit what had become apparent in the course of the third century—Christianity had become too strong to be eradicated by force.

In the fourth century, Christianity prospered as never before after the Emperor Constantine became the first Christian emperor. According to the traditional story, before a crucial battle, he saw a vision of a Christian cross with the writing, "In this sign you will conquer." Having won the battle, the story goes, Constantine was convinced of the power of the Christian God. Although he was not baptized until the end of his life, in 313 he issued the famous Edict of Milan officially tolerating the existence of Christianity. Under Theodosius "the Great" (378–395), it was made the official religion of the Roman Empire. Christianity had triumphed.

The Fall of the Western Roman Empire

The restored empire of Diocletian and Constantine limped along for more than a century. After Constantine, the empire continued to divide into western and eastern parts. The west came under increasing pressure from invading barbarian forces. The major breakthrough into the Roman Empire came in the second half of the fourth century. Ferocious warriors from Asia, known as Huns, moved into eastern Europe and put pressure on the Germanic Visigoths who in turn moved south and west, crossed the Danube into Roman territory, and settled down as Roman allies. But the Visigoths soon revolted, and the Roman attempt to stop them at Adrianople in 378 led to a crushing defeat.

Increasing numbers of barbarians now crossed the frontiers. In 410, the Visigoths under Alaric sacked Rome. Vandals poured into southern Spain and Africa, Visigoths into Spain and Gaul. The Vandals crossed into Italy from North Africa and sacked Rome in 455. Twenty-one years later, the western emperor Romulus Augustulus (475–476) was deposed, and a series of German kingdoms replaced the Roman Empire in the west while an Eastern Roman Empire continued with its center at Constantinople.

The end of the Roman Empire has given rise to numerous theories that purport to explain the "decline and fall of the Roman Empire." These include the following:

Christianity's emphasis on a spiritual kingdom undermined Roman military virtues and patriotism; traditional Roman values declined as non-Italians gained prominence in the empire; lead poisoning through leaden water pipes and cups caused a mental decline; plague decimated the population; Rome failed to advance technologically because of slavery; and Rome was unable to achieve a workable political system. There may be an element of truth in each of these theories, but each of them has also been challenged. History is an intricate web of relationships, causes, and effects. No single explanation will ever suffice to explain historical events. One thing is clear. Weakened by a shortage of soldiers, the Roman army in the west was simply not able to fend off the hordes of people invading Italy and Gaul. In contrast, the Eastern Roman Empire, which would survive for another 1,000 years, remained largely free of invasion.

Conclusion

After a century of internal upheaval, Augustus established a new order that began the Roman Empire, which experienced a lengthy period of peace and prosperity between 14 and 180. During this Pax Romana, trade flourished and the provinces were governed efficiently. In the course of the third century, however, the Roman Empire came near to collapse due to invasions, civil wars, and economic decline. Although the emperors Diocletian and Constantine brought new life to the so-called Late Empire, their efforts merely shored up the empire temporarily. In the course of the fifth century, the empire divided into western and eastern parts, and in 476, the Roman Empire in the west came to an end with the ouster of Emperor Romulus Augustulus.

The Roman Empire was the largest empire in antiquity. Using their practical skills, the Romans made achievements in language, law, engineering, and government that were bequeathed to the future. The Romance languages of today (French, Italian, Spanish, Portuguese, and Romanian) are based on Latin. Western practices of impartial justice and trial by jury owe much to Roman law. As great builders, the Romans left monuments to their skills throughout Europe, some of which, such as aqueducts and roads, are still in use today. Aspects of Roman administrative practices survived in the Western world for centuries. The Romans also preserved the intellectual heritage of the ancient world.

While we are justified in praising the empire, it is also important to remember its other side: the enormous gulf between rich and poor, the dependence on enslaved or otherwise subject human beings, the bloodthirsty spectacles in the amphitheaters, and the use of institutionalized terror to maintain the order for which the empire is so often praised. As the British chieftain Calgacus is supposed to have said, "To robbery, slaughter, plunder, they [the Romans] give the lying name of empire; they make a solitude and call it peace."[19] In its last 200 years, as Christianity spread, a slow transformation of the Roman world took place. The Germanic invasions greatly accelerated this process, and while many aspects of the Roman world would continue, a new civilization was emerging that would carry on yet another stage in the development of Western civilization.

NOTES

1. Livy, *The Early History of Rome*, trans. Aubrey de Sélincourt (Harmondsworth, 1960), p. 35.
2. Tacitus, *The Annals of Imperial Rome*, trans. Michael Grant (Harmondsworth, 1956), p. 30.
3. Ibid., p. 37.
4. Ibid., p. 31.
5. Tacitus, *The Histories*, trans. Kenneth Wellesley (Harmondsworth, 1964), p. 23.
6. Virgil, *The Aeneid*, trans. C. Day Lewis (Garden City, N.Y., 1952), p. 154.
7. Horace, *Satires*, in *The Complete Works of Horace*, trans. Lord Dunsany and Michael Oakley (London, 1961), 1.1, p. 139.
8. Ibid., 1.3, p. 151.
9. Livy, *The Early History of Rome*, p. 18.
10. Seneca, *Letters from a Stoic*, trans. Robin Campbell (Harmondsworth, 1969), Letter 5.
11. Tacitus, *The Annals of Imperial Rome*, p. 147.
12. Juvenal, *The Sixteen Satires*, trans. Peter Green (Harmondsworth, 1967), Satire 10, p. 207.
13. Tacitus, *A Dialogue on Oratory*, in *The Complete Works of Tacitus*, trans. Alfred Church and William Brodribb (New York, 1942), 29, p. 758.
14. Matthew 5: 17.
15. Matthew 7: 12.
16. Mark 12: 30–31.

17. John 18: 36.
18. Colossians 3: 10–11.

19. Tacitus, *The Life of Cnaeus Julius Agricola*, in *The Complete Works of Tacitus*, p. 695.

SUGGESTIONS FOR FURTHER READING

For a general account of the Roman Empire, see J. Boardman, J. Griffin, and O. Murray, eds., *The Oxford History of the Classical World* (Oxford, 1986), pp. 531–828. A brief and reliable guide to recent trends in scholarship on the Roman Empire can be found in C. Starr, *Past and Future in Ancient History* (Lanham, Md., 1987), pp. 45–57. Good surveys of the Early Empire include P. Garnsey and R. P. Saller, *The Roman Empire: Economy, Society and Culture* (London, 1987); C. Wells, *The Roman Empire* (Stanford, 1984); J. Wacher, *The Roman Empire* (London, 1987); and F. Millar, *Roman Empire and Its Neighbors*, 2nd ed. (London, 1981). An excellent collection of source materials in translation can be found in N. Lewis and M. Reinhold, ed., *Roman Civilization*, vol. 2 (New York, 1955).

Studies of Roman emperors of the first and second centuries include D. Shotter, *Augustus Caesar* (London, 1991); M. Griffin, *Nero: The End of a Dynsaty* (London, 1984); and M. Hammond, *The Antonine Monarchy* (Rome, 1959). For brief biographies of all the Roman emperors, see M. Grant, *The Roman Emperors* (New York, 1985). A fundamental work on Roman government and the role of the emperor is F. Millar, *The Emperor in the Roman World* (London, 1977).

There are many specialized studies on various aspects of the administrative, economic, and social conditions in the Early Empire. On the growth of cities in Italy and the spread of Roman citizenship outside Italy, see A. N. Sherwin White, *The Roman Citizenship*, 2d ed. (Oxford, 1973). A detailed examination of economic matters is T. Frank, *An Economic Survey of Ancient Rome*, vols. 2–5 (Baltimore, 1933–40). See also M. I Rostovtzeff, *Social and Economic History of the Roman Empire*, 2d ed., 2 vols. (Oxford, 1957); and R. Duncan-Jones, *The Economy of the Roman Empire* (New York, 1982).

The Roman army is examined in G. Webster, *The Imperial Army of the First and Second Centuries* A.D., 2d ed. (London, 1979); L. Keppie, *The Making of the Roman Army* (London, 1984); and J. B. Campbell, *The Emperor and the Roman Army* (Oxford, 1984). On the provinces and Roman foreign policy, see E. M. Luttwak, *The Grand Strategy of the Roman Empire from the First Century* A.D. *to*

the Third (Baltimore, 1976); and B. Isaac, *The Limits of Empire: The Roman Empire in the East* (Oxford, 1990).

A good survey of Roman literature can be found in R. M. Ogilvie, *Roman Literature and Society* (Harmondsworth, 1980). More specialized studies include G. Williams, *Change and Decline: Roman Literature in the Early Empire* (Berkeley, 1978); R. O. Lyne, *The Latin Love Poets from Catullus to Horace* (Oxford, 1980); D. A. West and A. J. Woodman, *Poetry and Politics in the Age of Augustus* (New York, 1984); and M. L. W. Laistner, *The Greater Roman Historians* (Berkeley, 1947).

A brief survey of Roman art can be found in J. M. C. Toynbee, *Art of the Romans* (London and New York, 1965). D. E. Strong, *Roman Art* (Harmondsworth, 1976), presents a more detailed account. Architecture is covered in the standard work by J. B. Ward-Perkins, *Roman Imperial Architecture* (Harmondsworth, 1981).

Various aspects of Roman society are covered in J. P. V. D. Balsdon, *Life and Leisure in Ancient Rome* (London, 1969). See also the essay by P. Veyne on "The Roman Empire" in P. Veyne, ed., *A History of Private Life*, vol. 1 (Cambridge, Mass., 1987). Also useful on urban life is J. E. Stambaugh, *The Ancient Roman City* (Baltimore, 1988). Studies on Roman women include J. P. V. D. Baldson, *Roman Women: Their History and Habits* (London, 1969); and S. B. Pomeroy, *Goddesses, Whores, Wives and Slaves: Women in Classical Antiquity* (New York, 1975), pp. 149–226. On Roman law, see J. Crook, *Law and Life of Rome* (London, 1967). On the gladiators, see T. Wiedemann, *Emperors and Gladiators* (New York, 1992).

An introduction to the problems relating to the religious history of the imperial period is E. R. Dodds, *Pagan and Christian in an Age of Anxiety* (Cambridge, 1965). Useful works on early Christianity include W. A. Meeks, *The First Urban Christians* (New Haven, 1983); W. H. C. Frend, *The Rise of Christianity* (Philadelphia, 1984); and R. MacMullen, *Christianizing the Roman Empire* (New Haven, Conn., 1984).

The classic work on the "decline and fall" of the Roman Empire is Edward Gibbon, *The Decline and Fall of the Roman Empire*, J. B. Bury edition (London, 1909–14). An excellent survey is P. Brown, *The World of Late Antiquity* (London, 1971). Also valuable are A. Cameron, *The Later Roman Empire* (Cambridge, Mass., 1993); and R. MacMullen, *Corruption and the Decline of Rome* (New Haven, Conn., 1988). On the fourth century, see M. Grant, *Constantine the Great: The Man and His Times* (New York, 1993); and S. Williams, *Diocletian and the Roman Recovery* (London, 1985). On economic and social history, including the bureaucracy, see A. H. M. Jones, *The Later Roman Empire* (Oxford, 1964). Recent studies analyzing the aristocratic circles, the barbarian invasions, and the military problem include E. A. Thompson, *Romans and Barbarians* (Madison, 1982); A. Ferrill, *The Fall of the Roman Empire: The Military Explanation* (London, 1986); and J. M. O'Flynn, *Generalissimos of the Western Roman Empire* (Edmonton, 1983).

7

The Passing of the Roman World and the Emergence of Medieval Civilization

The period that saw the disintegration of the western part of the Roman Empire also witnessed the emergence of medieval European civilization. Scholars know that major historical transitions are never tidy; chaos is often the ground out of which new civilizations are born. The early medieval civilization that arose out of the dissolution of the Western Roman Empire was formed by the coalescence of three major elements: the Germanic peoples who moved into the western empire and established new kingdoms, the continuing attraction of the Greco-Roman cultural legacy, and the Christian church. Christianity was the most distinctive and powerful component of the new medieval civilization. The church assimilated the classical tradition and through its clergy, especially the monks, brought Christianized civilization to the Germanic tribes.

The conversion to Christianity of the pagan leaders of German tribes was sometimes dramatic, at least as it is reported by the sixth-century historian, Gregory of Tours. Clovis, leader of the Franks, married Clotilde, daughter of the king of the Burgundians. She was a Christian, but Clovis refused her pleas to become a Christian, telling her, "Your god can do nothing." But during a battle with the Alemanni, when Clovis's army was close to utter destruction, "He saw the danger; his heart was stirred; and he raised his eyes to heaven, saying, 'Jesus Christ, I beseech the glory of your aid. If you shall grant me victory over these enemies, I will believe in you and be baptized in your name.' " When he had uttered these words, the Alemanni began to flee. Clovis soon became a Christian.

During the time when the Germanic kingdoms were establishing their roots in the west, the eastern part of the old Roman Empire, increasingly Greek in culture, continued to survive as the Byzantine Empire. While serving as a buffer between Europe and the peoples to the east, the Byzantine or Eastern Roman Empire also preserved the intellectual and legal accomplishments of Greek and Roman antiquity. At the same time, a new world of Islam emerged in the east; it occupied large parts of the old Roman Empire, preserved much of

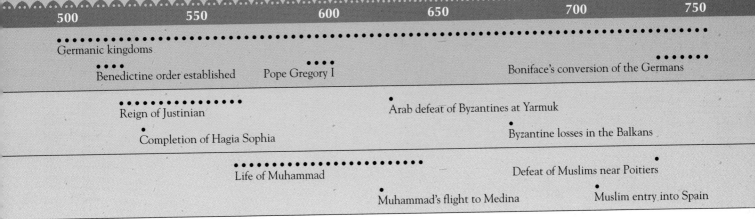

500   550   600   650   700   750

Germanic kingdoms

Benedictine order established   Pope Gregory I   Boniface's conversion of the Germans

Reign of Justinian   Arab defeat of Byzantines at Yarmuk

Completion of Hagia Sophia   Byzantine losses in the Balkans

Life of Muhammad   Defeat of Muslims near Poitiers

Muhammad's flight to Medina   Muslim entry into Spain

Greek culture, and created its own flourishing civilization. This chapter, then, largely concerns the heirs of Rome and the new world they created.

The Transformation of the Roman World: The Role of the Germanic Peoples

The Germanic peoples were an important element of the new medieval civilization. Around 500 B.C., the Germans began to migrate from their northern Scandinavian homeland south into the Baltic states and Germany and east into the fertile lands of the Ukraine. Although the Romans had established a series of political frontiers in the western empire, Romans and Germans often came into contact across those boundaries. For some time, the Romans had hired Germanic tribes to fight other Germanic tribes that threatened Rome's security or enlisted groups of Germans to fight for Rome.

In the late fourth century, the Germanic tribes came under new pressures when the Huns, a fierce tribe of nomads from Asia, moved into the Black Sea region and forced Germanic groups westward. One of the largest groups, the Visigoths, crossed the Danube and asked for Roman assistance. Mistreated by the Romans, however, they revolted and, in 378, crushed a Roman army and killed the emperor Valens. The new emperor quickly permitted the Visigoths to settle along the Danube, within the Roman Empire, as allies. But the Visigoths were soon on the move. Under their king Alaric, they moved into Italy and sacked Rome in 410. Then, at the urging of the emperor, they moved into Spain and southern Gaul as Roman allies.

The Roman experience with the Visigoths established a precedent. The emperors in the first half of the fifth century made alliances with whole groups of Germanic peoples, who settled peacefully in the western part of the empire. The Burgundians settled themselves in much of eastern Gaul, just south of another German tribe called the Alemanni. Only the Vandals consistently remained hostile to the Romans. They sacked parts of Gaul and crossed the Pyrenees Mountains into Spain. Defeated by incoming Visigoths, the Vandals crossed the Straits of Gibraltar, moved into Roman North Africa by 429, and conquered the whole province of Africa. In 455, the Vandals even attacked Rome, sacking it more ferociously than the Visigoths had in 410.

Increasingly, German military leaders dominated the imperial courts of the western empire. One such leader finally ended the charade of Roman imperial rule. Odoacer deposed the Roman emperor, Romulus Augustulus, in 476, and began to rule on his own. Meanwhile, the Ostrogoths, another branch of the Goths, had recovered from a defeat by the Huns in the fourth century. Under their king Theodoric (493–526), they had attacked Constantinople. To divert them, Zeno, emperor of the eastern empire, invited Theodoric to act as his deputy to defeat Odoacer and bring Italy back into the empire. Theodoric accepted the challenge, marched into Italy, killed Odoacer, and then, contrary to Zeno's wishes, established himself as ruler of Italy in 493.

The New Kingdoms

By 500, the Western Roman Empire was being replaced politically by a series of kingdoms ruled by German kings. The pattern of settlement and the fusion of the Romans

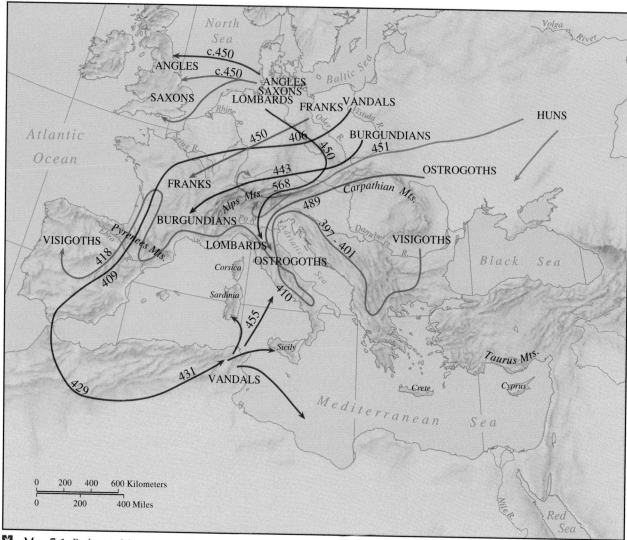

✳ **Map 7.1** Barbarian Migration and Invasion Routes.

and Germans took different forms in the various barbarian kingdoms.

THE OSTROGOTHIC KINGDOM OF ITALY

More than any other Germanic state, the Ostrogothic kingdom of Italy managed to maintain the Roman tradition of government. The Ostrogothic king Theodoric had received a Roman education while a hostage in Constantinople. After taking control of Italy, he was eager to create a synthesis of Ostrogothic and Roman practices. In addition to maintaining the entire structure of imperial Roman government, he established separate systems of rule for the Ostrogoths and Romans. The Italian population lived under Roman law administered by Roman offi-

cials. The Ostrogoths were governed by their own customs and their own officials. Nevertheless, while the Roman administrative system was kept intact, the Goths alone controlled the army.

After Theodoric's death in 526, it quickly became apparent that much of his success had been due to the force of his own personality. His successors soon found themselves face to face with opposition from the imperial forces of the Byzantine or Eastern Roman Empire. Under Emperor Justinian (527–565) (see "The Byzantine Empire" section later in this chapter), Byzantine armies reconquered Italy between 535 and 554, devastating much of the peninsula and destroying Rome as one of the great urban centers of the Mediterranean world in the process. The Byzantine reconquest proved ephemeral, however.

Another German tribe, the Lombards, invaded Italy in 568 and conquered much of northern and central Italy. Unlike the Ostrogoths, the Lombards were harsh rulers and cared little for Roman structures and traditions. The Lombards' fondness for fighting each other enabled the Byzantines to retain control of some parts of Italy.

THE VISIGOTHIC KINGDOM OF SPAIN

The Visigothic kingdom in Spain demonstrated a number of parallels to the Ostrogothic kingdom of Italy. Both favored coexistence between the Roman and German populations; both featured a warrior caste dominating a larger native population; and both continued to maintain much of the Roman structure of government while largely excluding Romans from power. There were also noticeable differences, however. Laws preventing intermarriage were dropped, and the Visigothic and Hispano-Roman peoples began to blend. A new body of law common to both peoples also developed.

The Visigothic kingdom possessed one fatal weakness. With no established procedure for choosing new rulers, powerful Visigoths fought constantly to lay claim to the kingship. Church officials tried to help develop a sense of order, as this decree illustrates: "No one of us shall dare to seize the kingdom; no one shall arouse sedition among the citizenry; no one shall think of killing the king. . . ." Church edicts failed to stop the feuds, however, and assassinations remained a way of life in Visigothic Spain. In 711, Muslim invaders destroyed the Visigothic kingdom itself (see the "Rise of Islam" section later).

THE FRANKISH KINGDOM

Only one of the German states on the European continent proved long-lasting—the kingdom of the Franks. The establishment of a Frankish kingdom was the work of Clovis (c. 482–511), a member of the Merovingian dynasty. Initially the leader of only one group of Franks, he eventually became king of them all.

Clovis became a Catholic Christian around 500. He was not the first German king to convert to Christianity, but the others had joined the Arian sect of Christianity (see later section on "Organization and Religious Disputes"). The Christian church in Rome, which had become known as the Roman Catholic church, regarded the Arians as heretics, or people who believed in teachings different from the official church doctrine. Clovis found that his conversion to Catholic Christianity gained him the support of the Roman Catholic church, which was only too eager to obtain the friendship of a major

CHRONOLOGY

The Germanic Kingdoms

Sack of Rome by Visigoths	410
Vandals in North Africa	429
Sack of Rome by Vandals	455
Odoacer deposes western emperor	476
Theodoric establishes an Ostrogothic kingdom in Italy	493
Frankish King Clovis converts to Christianity	c. 500
Reconquest of Italy by Byzantines	535–554
Lombards begin conquest of Italy	568
Muslims shatter Visigoths in Spain	711

Germanic ruler who was a Catholic Christian. The conversion of the king also paved the way for the conversion of the Frankish peoples.

By 510, Clovis had established a powerful new Frankish kingdom stretching from the Pyrenees in the west to German lands in the east (modern-day France and western Germany). Clovis was also responsible for establishing the Merovingian dynasty, a name derived from Merovech, their semilegendary ancestor. Clovis spent the last years of his life ensuring the survival of the dynasty by killing off relatives who were leaders of other groups of Franks.

After the death of Clovis, his sons divided the newly created kingdom. During the sixth and seventh centuries, the once-united Frankish kingdom came to be partitioned into three major areas: Neustria in northern Gaul; Austrasia, consisting of the ancient Frankish lands on both sides of the Rhine; and the former kingdom of Burgundy. All three were ruled by members of the Merovingian dynasty. Within the three territories, members of the Merovingian dynasty were assisted by powerful nobles. Frankish society possessed a ruling class that gradually intermarried with the old Gallo-Roman senatorial class to form a new nobility. These noble families took advantage of their position to strengthen their own lands and wealth at the expense of the monarchy. Within the royal household, the position of *major domus* or mayor of the palace, the chief officer of the king's household, began to overshadow the king. Essentially, both nobles and mayors of the palace were expanding their power at the expense of the kings.

During the sixth and seventh centuries, the Frankish kingdom witnessed a process of fusion between Gallo-Roman and Frankish cultures and peoples, a process accompanied by a significant decline in Roman standards of civilization and commercial activity. The Franks were warriors and did little to encourage either urban life or trade. By 750, Frankish Gaul was basically an agricultural society in which the old Roman villa system of the late empire had continued unimpeded. Institutionally, however, Germanic concepts of kingship and customary law replaced the Roman governmental structure.

ANGLO-SAXON ENGLAND

The barbarian pressures on the Western Roman Empire had forced the emperors to withdraw the Roman armies and abandon Britain by the beginning of the fifth century. This opened the door to the Angles and Saxons, Germanic tribes from Denmark and northern Germany. Although these same peoples had made plundering raids for the past century, the withdrawal of the Roman armies enabled them to make settlements instead. They met with resistance from the Celtic Britons, however, who still controlled the western regions of Cornwall, Wales, and Cumberland at the beginning of the seventh century. The German invaders eventually succeeded in carving out small kingdoms throughout the island, Kent in southeast England being one of them.

The Society of the Germanic Peoples

As Germans and Romans intermarried and began to create a new society, some of the social customs of the Germanic people began to play an important role. The crucial social bond among the Germanic peoples was the family, especially the extended or patriarchal family of husbands, wives, children, brothers, sisters, cousins, and grandparents. In addition to working the land together and passing it down to succeeding generations, the extended family provided protection, which was sorely needed in the violent atmosphere of Merovingian times.

The German conception of family affected the way Germanic law treated the problem of crime and punishment. In the Roman system, as in our own, a crime such as murder was considered an offense against society or the state and was handled by a court that heard evidence and arrived at a decision. Germanic law tended to be personal. An injury by one person against another could mean a blood feud in which the family of the injured party took revenge on the kin of the wrongdoer. Feuds could lead to savage acts of revenge, such as hacking off hands or feet, gouging out eyes, or slicing off ears and noses. Because this system could easily get out of control, an alternative system arose that made use of a fine called

◆ **Baptism of Clovis.** The conversion of Clovis to Catholic Christianity was an important factor in gaining papal support for his Frankish kingdom. In this illustration from a medieval manuscript, bishops and nobles look on while Clovis is baptized. One of the nobles holds a crown while a dove, symbol of the Holy Spirit, descends from heaven bringing sacred oil for the ceremony.

wergeld, which was paid by a wrongdoer to the family of the person he had injured or killed. *Wergeld*, which means "money for a man," was the value of a person in monetary terms. That value varied considerably according to social status. An offense against a nobleman, for example, cost considerably more than one against a freeman or a slave.

Under German customary law, compurgation and the ordeal were the two most commonly used procedures for determining whether an accused person was guilty and should have to pay *wergeld*. Compurgation was the swearing of an oath by the accused person, backed up by a group of "oath helpers," numbering twelve or twenty-five, who would also swear that the accused person should be believed. The ordeal functioned in a variety of ways, all of which were based on the principle of divine intervention; divine forces (whether pagan or Christian) would not allow an innocent person to be harmed (see the box on p. 136).

THE FRANKISH FAMILY AND MARRIAGE

For the Franks, like other Germanic peoples, the extended family was at the center of social organization. The Frankish family structure was quite simple. Males were dominant and made all the important decisions. A woman obeyed her father until she married and then fell under the legal domination of her husband. A widow, however, could hold property without a male guardian. In Frankish law, the *wergeld* of a wife of childbearing age—of value because she could bear children—was considerably higher than that of a man. The Salic Law stated: "If any one killed a free woman after she had begun bearing children, he shall be sentenced to 24,000 denars. . . . After she can have no more children, he who kills her shall be sentenced to 8,000 denars. . . ."[1]

Because marriage affected the extended family group, fathers or uncles could arrange marriages for the good of the family without considering their children's wishes. Most important was the engagement ceremony in which a prospective son-in-law made a payment symbolizing the purchase of paternal authority over the bride. The essential feature of the marriage itself involved placing the married couple in bed to achieve their physical union. In first marriages, it was considered important that the wife be a virgin, which ensured that any children would be the husband's. A virgin symbolized the ability of the bloodline to continue. Accordingly, adultery was viewed as pollution of the woman and her offspring, hence poisoning the future. Adulterous wives were severely punished (an adulterous woman could be strangled or even burned alive); adulterous husbands were not. Divorce was relatively simple and was initiated primarily by the husband. Divorced wives simply returned to their families.

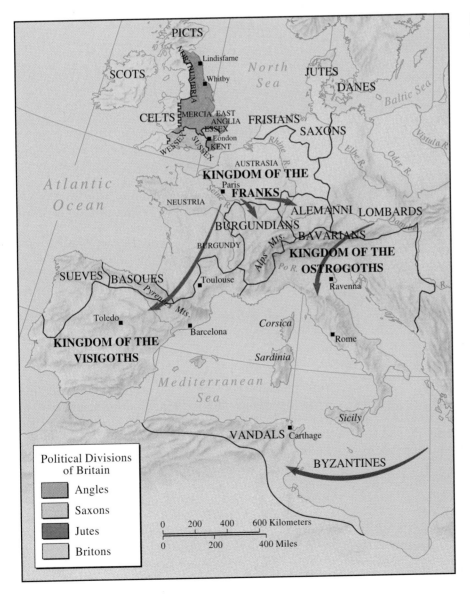

Map 7.2 The New Kingdoms of the Old Western Empire.

Germanic Customary Law: The Ordeal

In Germanic customary law, the ordeal came to be a means by which accused persons might clear themselves. Although the ordeal took different forms, all involved a physical trial of some sort, such as holding a red-hot iron. It was believed God would protect the innocent and allow them to come through the ordeal unharmed. This sixth-century account by Gregory of Tours describes an ordeal by hot water.

Gregory of Tours, An Ordeal of Hot Water (c. 580)

An Arian presbyter disputing with a deacon of our religion made venomous assertions against the Son of God and the Holy Ghost, as is the habit of that sect [the Arians]. But when the deacon had discoursed a long time concerning the reasonableness of our faith and the heretic, blinded by the fog of unbelief, continued to reject the truth, . . . the former said: "Why weary ourselves with long discussions? Let acts approve the truth; let a kettle be heated over the fire and someone's ring be thrown into the boiling water. Let him who shall take it from the heated liquid be approved as a follower of the truth, and afterward let the other party be converted to the knowledge of the truth. And do you also understand, O heretic, that this our party will fulfill the conditions with the aid of the Holy Ghost; you shall confess that there is no discordance, no dissimilarity in the Holy Trinity." The heretic consented to the proposition and they separated after appointing the next morning for the trial. But the fervor of faith in which the deacon had first made this suggestion began to cool through the instigation of the enemy. Rising with the dawn he bathed his arm in oil and smeared it with ointment. But nevertheless he made the round of the sacred places and called in prayer on the Lord. . . . About the third hour they met in the market place. The people came together to see the show. A fire was lighted, the kettle was placed upon it, and when it grew very hot the ring was thrown into the boiling water. The deacon invited the heretic to take it out of the water first. But he promptly refused, saying, "You who did propose this trial are the one to take it out." The deacon all of a tremble bared his arm. And when the heretic presbyter saw it besmeared with ointment he cried out: "With magic arts you have thought to protect yourself, that you have made use of these salves, but what you have done will not avail." While they were thus quarreling there came up a deacon from Ravenna named Iacinthus and inquired what the trouble was about. When he learned the truth he drew his arm out from under his robe at once and plunged his right hand into the kettle. Now the ring that had been thrown in was a little thing and very light so that it was thrown about by the water as chaff would be blown about by the wind; and searching for it a long time he found it after about an hour. Meanwhile the flame beneath the kettle blazed up mightily so that the greater heat might make it difficult for the ring to be followed by the hand; but the deacon extracted it at length and suffered no harm, protesting rather that at the bottom the kettle was cold while at the top it was just pleasantly warm. When the heretic beheld this he was greatly confused and audaciously thrust his hand into the kettle saying, "My faith will aid me." As soon as his hand had been thrust in all the flesh was boiled off the bones clear up to the elbow. And so the dispute ended.

The Role and Development of the Christian Church

By the end of the fourth century, Christianity had become the predominant religion of the Roman Empire. As the official Roman state disintegrated, the Christian church played an increasingly important role in the emergence and growth of the new European civilization.

Organization and Religious Disputes

During the course of the fourth century, the Christian church had undergone significant organizational and structural changes. Church government was based on a territorial plan borrowed from Roman administration. For some time, the Christian community in each city had been headed by a bishop, whose area of jurisdiction was known as a bishopric—or diocese. The bishoprics of each Roman province were clustered together under the direction of an archbishop. The bishops of four great cities, Rome, Jerusalem, Alexandria, and Antioch, held positions of special power in church affairs because the churches in these cities all asserted that they had been founded by the original apostles sent out by Christ.

One reason the church needed a more formal organization was the problem of heresy. As Christianity developed and spread, contradictory interpretations of important doctrines emerged. Heresy came to be viewed as a teaching different from the official catholic or universal beliefs of the church. In a world where people were concerned about salvation, the question of whether Christ's nature is divine or human took on great significance. These doctrinal differences also became political issues, creating political factions that actually warred with one another. It is highly unlikely that ordinary people understood what these debates meant.

One of the major heresies of the fourth century was Arianism, which was a product of the followers of Arius, a priest from Alexandria in Egypt. Arius believed that Jesus Christ had been human and thus not truly God. Arius was opposed by Athanasius, a bishop of Alexandria, who argued that Christ was human but also truly God. Emperor Constantine, disturbed by the controversy, called the first ecumenical council of the church, a meeting composed of representatives from the entire Christian community. The Council of Nicaea, held in 325, condemned Arianism and stated that Christ was of "the same substance" as God: "We believe in one God the Father All-sovereign, maker of all things visible and invisible; And in one Lord Jesus Christ, the Son of God, begotten of the Father, only-begotten, that is, of the substance of the Father, God of God, Light of Light, true God of true God, begotten not made, of one substance with the Father. . . ."[2] The Council of Nicaea did not end the controversy, however; not only did Arianism persist in some parts of the Roman Empire for many years, but more importantly, many of the Germanic Goths who established states in the west converted to Arian Christianity. As a result of these fourth-century theological controversies, the Roman emperor came to play an increasingly important role in church affairs. At the same time, such divisions also created a need for leadership within the church.

The Power of the Pope

In the early centuries of Christianity, the churches in the larger cities had great influence in the administration of the church. It was only natural, then, that the bishops of those cities would also exercise considerable power. One of the far-reaching developments in the history of the Christian church was the emergence of one bishop—that of Rome—as the recognized leader of the western Christian church.

The doctrine of Petrine supremacy, based on the belief that the bishops of Rome occupied a preeminent position in the church, was grounded in scripture. According to the gospel of Matthew, when Jesus asked his disciplines, "Who do you say I am?" Simon Peter answered:

> You are the Christ, the Son of the living God. Jesus replied, Blessed are you, Simon son of Jonah, for this was not revealed by man, but by my Father in heaven. And I tell you that you are Peter, and on this rock I will build my church, and the gates of hell will not overcome it. I will give you the keys of the kingdom of heaven; whatever you bind on earth will be bound in heaven: and whatever you loose on earth will be loosed in heaven.[3]

According to church tradition, Christ had given the keys to the kingdom of heaven to Peter, who was considered the chief apostle and the first bishop of Rome. Subsequent bishops of Rome were considered Peter's successors and later the "vicars of Christ" on earth. Though this exalted view of the bishops of Rome was by no means accepted by all early Christians, Rome's position as the traditional capital city of the Roman Empire served to buttress this claim.

Although western Christians came to accept the bishop of Rome as head of the church in the fourth and fifth centuries, there was certainly no unanimity on the extent of the powers the pope possessed as a result of this position. Nevertheless, the emergence in the sixth century of a strong pope, Gregory I, known as Gregory the Great, set the papacy and the Roman Catholic church, as the Christian church of the west came to be called, on an energetic path that enabled the church in the seventh and eighth centuries to play an increasingly prominent role in civilizing the Germans and aiding the emergence of a distinctly new European civilization.

As pope, Gregory I (590–604) assumed direction of Rome and its surrounding territories, which had suffered enormously from the Ostrogothic–Byzantine struggle and Lombard invasion of the sixth century. Gregory took charge and made Rome and its surrounding area into an administrative unit that eventually came to be known as the Papal States. While historians disagree about Gregory's motives in establishing papal temporal power, no doubt Gregory was only doing what he felt needed to be done: to provide for the defense of Rome against the Lombards, to establish a government for Rome, and to feed the people. Gregory remained loyal to the empire and continued to address the Byzantine emperor as the rightful ruler of Italy.

Gregory also pursued a policy of extending papal authority over the Christian church in the west. He intervened in ecclesiastical conflicts throughout Italy and corresponded with the Frankish rulers, urging them to reform the church in Gaul. He successfully initiated the

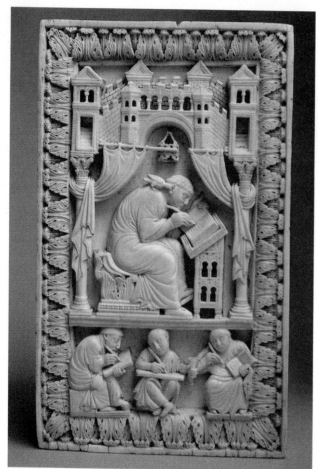

✦ **Pope Gregory I.** Pope Gregory the Great became one of the most important popes of the Early Middle Ages. This tenth-century ivory book cover shows Gregory working at his desk. On his right shoulder is a dove, symbol of the Holy Spirit, which is providing divine inspiration. The lower scene shows a monastic scriptorium or writing room with three monks busy at their work.

efforts of missionaries to convert England to Christianity and was especially active in converting the pagan peoples of Germanic Europe. His primary instrument was the monastic movement.

The Monks and Their Missions

A monk (Latin *monachus*, meaning "someone who lives alone") was a person who sought to live a life divorced from the world, cut off from ordinary human society, in order to pursue an ideal of godliness or total dedication to the will of God. Christian monasticism, which developed first in Egypt, was initially based on the model of

the solitary hermit who forsakes all civilized society to pursue spirituality. Saint Anthony (c. 250–350) was a prosperous peasant in Egypt who decided to follow Christ's injunction in the gospel of St. Mark: "Go your way, sell whatsoever you have, and give to the poor, and you shall have treasure in heaven: and come, take up the cross, and follow me." Anthony gave away his 300 acres of land to the poor and went into the desert to pursue his ideal of holiness (see the box on p. 139). Others did likewise, often to extremes. Saint Simeon the Stylite lived for three decades in a basket atop a pillar over sixty feet high. These spiritual gymnastics established a new ideal for Christianity. Whereas the early Christian model had been the martyr who died for the faith and achieved eternal life in the process, the new ideal was the monk who died to the world and achieved spiritual life through denial, asceticism, and mystical experience of God.

These early monks, however, soon found themselves unable to live in solitude. Their feats of holiness attracted followers on a wide scale, and as the monastic ideal spread throughout the east, a new form of monasticism based on the practice of communal life soon became the dominant form. Monastic communities came to be seen as the ideal Christian society that could provide a moral example to the wider society around them.

The fundamental form of monastic life in the western Christian church was established by Saint Benedict of Nursia (c. 480–c. 543), who sought hermitic solitude south of Rome but soon found himself surrounded by followers. Benedict then went to Monte Cassino where he founded a monastic house, for which he wrote his famous rule, sometime between 520 and 530. The Benedictine rule came to be used by other monastic groups and was crucial to the growth of monasticism in the western Christian world.

Benedict's rule largely rejected the ascetic ideals of eastern monasticism, which had tended to emphasize such practices as fasting and self-inflicted torments (such as living atop pillars for thirty years), in favor of an ideal of moderation. In chapter 40 of the rule, on the amount a monk should drink, this sense of moderation becomes apparent:

> 'Every man has his proper gift from God, one after this manner, another after that.' And therefore it is with some misgiving that we determine the amount of food for someone else. Still, having regard for the weakness of some brothers, we believe that a hemina of wine [a quarter liter] per day will suffice for all. Let those, however, to whom God gives the gift of abstinence, know that they shall have

The Life of Saint Anthony

In the third and early fourth centuries, the lives of martyrs had provided important models for early Christianity. But in the course of the fourth century, monks or desert fathers, who attempted to achieve spiritual perfection through asceticism, the denial of earthly life, and the struggle with demons became the new spiritual ideal for Christians. Consequently, spiritual biographies of early monks became a significant new form of Christian literature. Especially noteworthy was The Life of Saint Anthony by Saint Athanasius, the defender of Catholic orthodoxy against the Arians. His work had been translated into Latin before 386. This excerpt describes how Anthony fought off the temptations of Satan.

Athanasius, *The Life of Saint Anthony*

Now when the Enemy [Satan] saw that his craftiness in this matter was without profit, and that the more he brought temptation into Saint Anthony, the more strenuous the saint was in protecting himself against him with the armor of righteousness, he attacked him by means of the vigor of early manhood which is bound up in the nature of our humanity. With the goadings of passion he sued to trouble him by night, and in the daytime also he would vex him and pain him with the same to such an extent that even those who saw him knew from his appearance that he was waging war against the Adversary. But the more the Evil One brought unto him filthy and maddening thoughts, the more Saint Anthony took refuge in prayer and in abundant supplication, and amid them all he remained wholly chaste. And the Evil One was working upon him every shameful deed according to his wont, and at length he even appeared unto Saint Anthony in the form of a woman; and other things which resembled this he performed with ease, for such things are a subject for boasting to him.

But the blessed Anthony knelt down upon his knees on the ground, and prayed before Him who said, "Before you criest unto Me, I will answer you," and said, "O my Lord, this I entreat you. Let not Your love be blotted out from my mind, and behold, I am, by your grace, innocent before You." And again the Enemy multiplied in him the thoughts of lust, until Saint Anthony became as one who was being burned up, not through the Evil One, but through his own lusts; but he girded himself about with the threat of the thought of the Judgment, and of the torture of Gehenna, and of the worm which does not die. And while meditating on the thoughts which could be directed against the Evil One, he prayed for thoughts which would be hostile to him. Thus, to the reproach and shame of the Enemy, these things could not be performed; for he who imagined that he could be God was made a mock of by a young man, and he who boasted over flesh and blood was vanquished by a man who was clothed with flesh. . . .

their proper reward. But if either the circumstances of the place, the work, or the heat of summer necessitates more, let it lie in the discretion of the abbot to grant it. But let him take care in all things lest satiety or drunkenness supervene.

At the same time, moderation did not preclude a hard and disciplined existence based on the ideals of poverty, chastity, and obedience.

According to Benedict's rule, each day was divided into a series of activities with primary emphasis on prayer and manual labor. Physical work of some kind was required of all monks for several hours a day because idleness was "the enemy of the soul." Peasants, however, were hired to do heavy farm work. At the very heart of community practice was prayer, the proper "Work of God." While this included private meditation and reading, all monks gathered together seven times during the day for common prayer and chanting of psalms. A Benedictine life was a communal one; monks ate, worked, slept, and worshiped together.

Each Benedictine monastery was strictly ruled by an abbot, or "father" of the monastery. Although chosen by his fellow monks, the abbot possessed complete authority over them; unquestioning obedience to the will of the abbot was expected of each monk. However, Benedict cautioned the abbot to be moderate: "He should be prudent and considerate in all his commands; and whether the task he enjoins concerns God or the world, let him be discreet and temperate. . . ." Each Benedictine monastery possessed lands that enabled it to be a self-sustaining community, isolated from and independent of the world surrounding it. Within the monastery, however, monks were to fulfill their vow of poverty: "Let all things be common to all, as it is written, lest anyone should say that anything is his own or arrogate it to himself."[4] By the

♦ **Life of Saint Benedict.** This illustration with its six scenes is from an eleventh-century manuscript of Pope Gregory the Great's *Life of Saint Benedict,* written in 593 or 594. *Top left,* Benedict writes his rule; *top right,* the death of Benedict; *middle left,* his burial; *middle right and bottom left,* scenes of miracles attributed to Saint Benedict's intercession; *bottom right,* Gregory finishes his *Life of Saint Benedict.*

eighth century, Benedictine monasticism had spread throughout the west.

Although the original monks were men, women soon followed suit in withdrawing from the world to dedicate themselves to God. The first monastic rule for western women was produced by Caesarius of Arles for his sister in the fifth century. It strongly emphasized a rigid cloistering of female religious to preserve them from dangers.

Monasticism played an indispensible role in early medieval civilization. Monks became the new heroes of Christian civilization. Their dedication to God became the highest ideal of Christian life. Monks copied Latin works and passed on the legacy of the ancient world to Western civilization in its European stage. Moreover, the monks played an increasingly significant role in spreading Christianity to the entire European world.

The British Isles, in particular, became an important center of Christian culture and missionary fervor. After their conversion, the Celts of Ireland and Anglo-Saxons of England created new centers of Christian learning and, in turn, themselves became enthusiastic missionaries. Through these efforts, the monks of Ireland and England made important contributions to the development of Christianity in the Middle Ages.

By the sixth century, Irish monasticism was a flourishing institution with its own unique characteristics. Unlike Benedictine monasticism, it was strongly ascetic. Monks performed strenuous fasts, prayed and meditated frequently under extreme privations, and confessed their sins on a regular basis to their superiors. In fact, Irish monasticism gave rise to the use of penitentials or manuals that provided a guide for examining one's life to see what sins, or offenses against the will of God, one had committed (see the box on p. 141).

A great love of learning also characterized Irish monasticism. The Irish eagerly absorbed both Latin and Greek culture and fostered education as a major part of their monastic life. Irish monks were preserving classical Latin at the same time spoken Latin was being corrupted on the continent into new dialects that eventually became the Romance languages, such as Italian, French, and Spanish.

Their emphasis on asceticism led many Irish monks to go into voluntary exile. This "exile for the love of God" was not into isolation, however, but into missionary activity. Irish monks became fervid missionaries. Saint Columba (521–597) left Ireland in 565 as a "pilgrim for Christ" and founded a highly influential monastic community off the coast of Scotland on the island of Iona. From there Irish missionaries went to northern England to begin the process of converting the Angles and Saxons. Meanwhile, other Irish monks traveled to the European continent. New monasteries founded by the Irish became centers of learning wherever they were located.

At the same time the Irish monks were busy bringing their version of Christianity to the Anglo-Saxons of Britain, Pope Gregory the Great had also set into motion his own effort to convert England to Roman Christianity. His most important agent was Augustine, a monk from Rome, who arrived in England in 597. England at that time had a number of Germanic kingdoms. Augustine

⇒ Irish Monasticism and the Penitential ⇐

*I*rish monasticism became well known for its ascetic practices. Much emphasis was placed on careful examination of conscience to determine if one had committed a sin against God. To facilitate this examination, penitentials were developed that listed possible sins with appropriate penances. Penance usually meant fasting a number of days each week on bread and water. Although these penitentials were eventually used throughout Christendom, they were especially important in Irish Christianity. This excerpt from the Penitential of Cummean, an Irish abbot, was written about 650 and demonstrates a distinctive feature of the penitentials, an acute preoccupation with sexual sins.

The Penitential of Cummean

A bishop who commits fornication shall be degraded and shall do penance for twelve years.

A presbyter or a deacon who commits natural fornication, having previously taken the vow of a monk, shall do penance for seven years. He shall ask pardon every hour; he shall perform a special fast during every week except in the days between Easter and Pentecost.

He who defiles his mother shall do penance for three years, with perpetual pilgrimage.

So shall those who commit sodomy do penance every seven years.

He who merely desires in his mind to commit fornication, but is not able, shall do penance for one year, especially in the three forty-day periods.

He who is willingly polluted during sleep shall arise and sing nine psalms in order, kneeling. On the following day, he shall live on bread and water.

A cleric who commits fornication once shall do penance for one year on bread and water; if he begets a son he shall do penance for seven years as an exile; so also a virgin.

He who loves any woman, but is unaware of any evil beyond a few conversations, shall do penance for forty days.

He who is in a state of matrimony ought to be continent during the three forty-day periods and on Saturday and on Sunday, night and day, and in the two appointed week days [Wednesday and Friday], and after conception, and during the entire menstrual period.

After a birth he shall abstain, if it is a son, for thirty-three [days]; of a daughter, for sixty-six [days].

Boys talking alone and transgressing the regulations of the elders [in the monastery], shall be corrected by three special fasts.

Children who imitate acts of fornication, twenty days; if frequently, forty.

But boys of twenty years who practice masturbation together and confess [shall do penance] twenty or forty days before they take communion.

went first to Kent where he converted King Ethelbert; most of the king's subjects then followed suit. Pope Gregory's conversion techniques emphasized persuasion rather than force and, as seen in this excerpt from one of his letters, he was willing to assimilate old pagan practices in order to coax the pagans into the new faith:

We wish you [Abbot Mellitus] to inform him [Augustine] that we have been giving careful thought to the affairs of the English, and have come to the conclusion that the temples of the idols among that people should on no account be destroyed. The idols are to be destroyed, but the temples themselves are to be aspersed with holy water, altars set up in them, and relics deposited there. For if these temples are well-built, they must be purified from the worship of demons and dedicated to the service of the true God. In this way, we hope that the people, seeing that their temples are not destroyed, may abandon their error and, flocking more readily to their accustomed resorts, may come to know and adore the true God.[5]

Likewise, old pagan feasts were to be given new names and incorporated into the Christian calendar. No doubt, Gregory was aware that early Christians had done likewise. The Christian feast of Christmas, for example, was held on December 25, the day of the pagan celebration of the winter solstice.

As Roman Christianity spread northward in Britain, it encountered Irish Christianity moving southward. Roman Christianity prevailed, although the English church, despite its newfound unity and loyalty to Rome, retained some Irish features. Most important was the concentration on monastic culture with special emphasis on learning and missionary work. By 700, the English church had become the best trained and most learned in western Europe.

Following the Irish example, English monks spread to the European continent to carry on the work of conversion. Most important was Boniface (c. 680–755), who undertook the conversion of pagan Germans in Frisia, Bavaria, and Saxony. By 740, Saint Boniface, the "Apostle of the Germans," had become the most famous churchman in Europe. Fourteen years later he was killed while trying to convert the pagan Frisians. Boniface was a brilliant example of the numerous Irish and English monks whose tireless efforts made Europe the bastion of the Roman Catholic faith.

Women, too, played an important role in the monastic missionary movement and the conversion of the Germanic kingdoms. So-called double monasteries in which both monks and nuns lived in separate houses but attended church services together were found in both the English and Frankish kingdoms. The monks and nuns followed a common rule under a common head. Frequently, this leader was an abbess rather than an abbot. Many of these abbesses belonged to royal houses, especially in Anglo-Saxon England. In the kingdom of Northumbria, for example, Saint Hilda founded the monastery of Whitby in 657. As abbess, she was responsible for giving learning an important role in the life of the monastery; five future bishops were educated under her tutelage. For female intellectuals, monasteries offered opportunities for learning not found elsewhere in the society of their day.

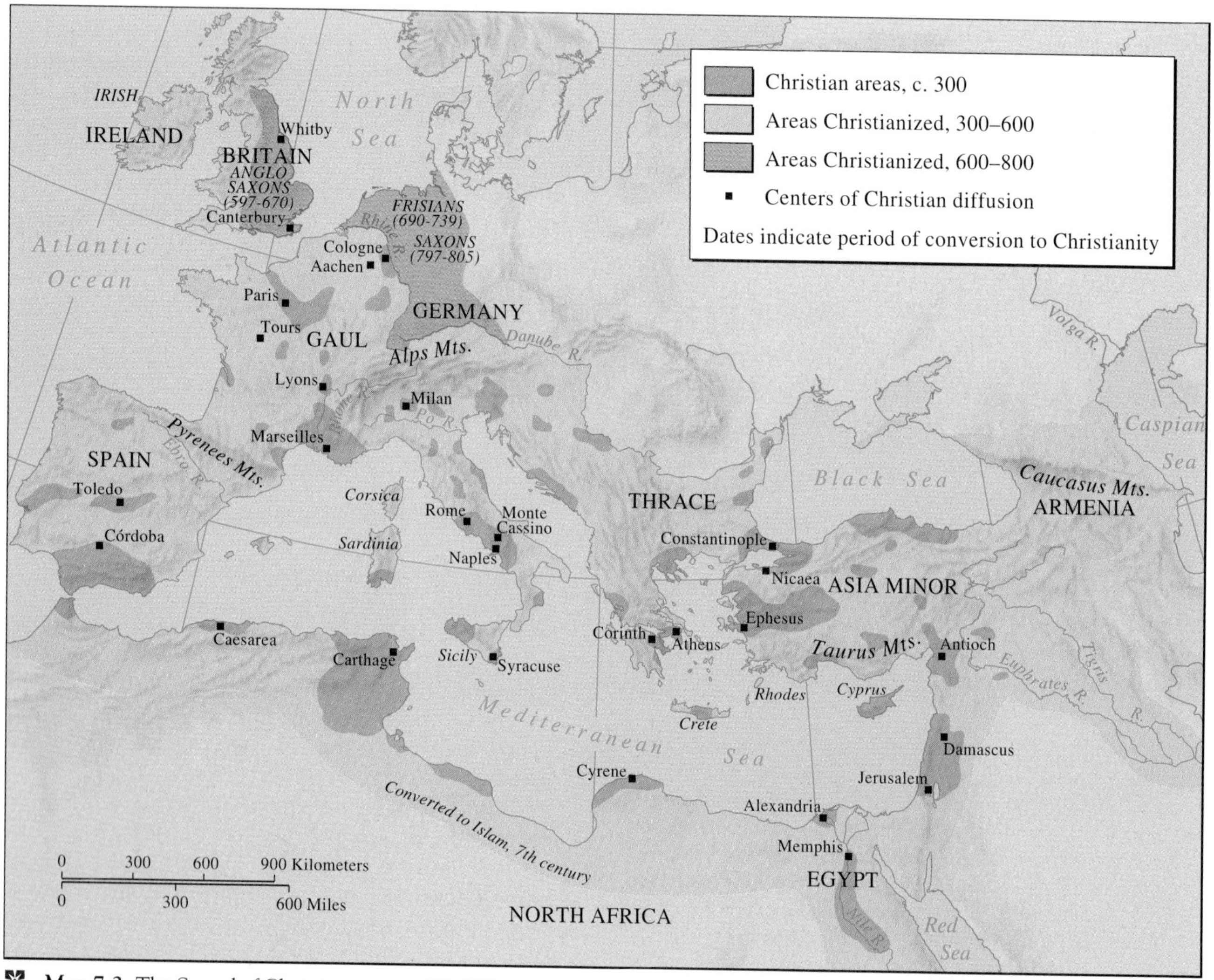

Map 7.3 The Spread of Christianity, A.D. 400–750.

Nuns of the seventh and eighth centuries also played an important role in the spread of Christianity. The great English missionary Boniface relied on nuns in England for books and money. He also asked the abbess of Wimborne to send groups of nuns to establish convents in newly converted German lands. A nun named Leoba established the first convent in Germany at Bischofsheim.

It is difficult to assess what Christianity meant to the converted pagans, especially the peasants on whom the Irish and English monks had expended their greatest efforts. As Pope Gregory had recommended, Christian beliefs and values were usually superimposed on older pagan customs. Though effective in producing quick conversions, it is an open question how much people actually understood of Christian teachings. Popular belief tended to focus on God as a judge who needed to be appeased to avert disasters in daily life and gain salvation. Except for the promise of salvation, this image of God was not all that different from Roman religious practices.

Christianity and Intellectual Life

Many early Christians expressed considerable hostility toward the pagan culture of the classical world. Tertullian (c. 160–c. 225), a Christian writer from Carthage, had proclaimed: "What has Jerusalem to do with Athens, the Church with the Academy, the Christian with the heretic? . . . After Jesus Christ we have no need of speculation, after the Gospel no need of research."[6] To many early Christians, the Bible contained all the knowledge anyone needed. Others, however, thought it was not possible to separate Christian theological thought from classical traditions and education and encouraged Christianity to absorb the classical heritage. As it spread in the eastern Roman world, Christianity adopted Greek as its language; the New Testament was written in Greek. Christians also turned to Greek thought for help in expressing complicated theological concepts. In many ways, then, Christianity served to preserve Greco-Roman culture.

The work of Augustine (354–430) provides one of the best examples of how Christianity absorbed pagan culture in the service of Christianity. Born in North Africa, he was reared by his mother, an ardent Christian. Augustine eventually became a professor of rhetoric at Milan in 384. His success opened the door to a lucrative career in the imperial bureaucracy if he had wished to pursue it. Throughout his rapid ascent, however, although he had rejected Christianity, he had continued to explore spiritual alternatives. While in Milan, he came under the influence of the popular bishop Ambrose who encouraged Augustine to return to Christianity. After experiencing a profound and moving religious experience, he gave up his teaching position and went back to North Africa, where he became bishop of Hippo from 396 until his death in 430.

As bishop of Hippo, Augustine produced an enormous outpouring of Christian literature. In his sermons, letters, treatises, and commentaries on Scripture, he gave reasoned opinions on virtually every aspect of Christian thought. He stressed that while philosophy could bring some understanding, divine revelation was a necessity for perceiving complete truth, an approach to knowledge that became standard in the education of the Middle Ages.

Augustine's most famous work, *The City of God*, was a profound expression of a Christian philosophy of government and history. It was written in response to a line of argument that arose soon after the sack of Rome in 410. Some pagan philosophers maintained that Rome's problems stemmed from the Roman state's recognition of Christianity and abandonment of the old, traditional gods. Augustine argued that Rome's troubles began long before Christianity arose in the empire. In *The City of God*, he theorized on the ideal relations between two kinds of societies existing throughout time—the City of God and the City of the World. Those who loved God would be loyal to the City of God, whose ultimate location was the kingdom of heaven. Earthly society would always be uncertain because of human beings' fallen nature and inclination to sin. And yet, the City of the World was still necessary for it was the duty of rulers to curb the depraved instincts of sinful humans and maintain the peace necessary for Christians to live in the world. Hence, Augustine posited that secular government and authority were necessary for the pursuit of the true Christian life on earth; in doing so, he provided a justification for secular political authority that would play an important role in medieval thought.

Another important intellectual of the early church was Jerome (345–420), who pursued literary studies in Rome and became a master of Latin prose. Jerome had mixed feelings about his love for classical studies, however, and like Augustine, experienced a spiritual conversion after which he tried to dedicate himself more fully to Christ. He had a dream in which Christ appeared as his judge: "Asked who and what I was, I replied: 'I am a Christian.' But He who presided said: 'You lie, you are a follower of Cicero, not of Christ. For where your treasure is, there will your heart be also.' Instantly, I became dumb, . . . Accordingly I made oath and called upon His name, saying: 'Lord, if ever again I possess worldly books [the classics], or if ever again I read such, I have denied You.'"

After this dream, Jerome determined to "read the books of God with a zeal greater than I had previously given to the books of men."[7]

Ultimately, Jerome found a compromise by purifying the literature of the pagan world and then using it to further the Christian faith. Jerome was a great scholar, and his extensive knowledge of both Hebrew and Greek enabled him to translate the Old and New Testaments into Latin. In the process, he created the so-called Latin Vulgate, or common text, of the Scriptures that became the standard edition for the Catholic church in the Middle Ages.

Although the Christian church came to accept classical culture, it was not easy to do so in the world of the new German kingdoms. Nevertheless, a number of Christian scholars managed to keep learning alive, even if it meant only preserving a heritage rather than creating new bodies of knowledge.

Cassiodorus (c. 490–c. 585) came from an aristocratic Roman family and served as an official of the Ostrogothic king Theodoric. Cassiodorus had a strong interest in history, which he used to reconcile the Romans and Goths by demonstrating how the Goths were attempting to preserve Roman tradition. His letters, written while he was secretary to Theodoric, provide us with a major source of information about this period.

The conflicts that erupted after the death of Theodoric led Cassiodorus to withdraw from public life and retire to his landed estates in southern Italy, where he wrote his final work, *Divine and Human Readings*. This was a compendium of the literature of both Christian and pagan antiquity. Cassiodorus accepted the advice of earlier Christian intellectuals to make use of classical works while treasuring the Scriptures above all else: "And therefore, as the blessed Augustine and other very learned Fathers say, secular writings should not be spurned. It is proper, however, . . . to 'meditate in the (divine) law day and night,' for, though a worthy knowledge of some matters is occasionally obtained from secular writings, this law is the source of eternal life."[8]

Cassiodorus continued the tradition of late antiquity of classifying knowledge according to certain subjects. In assembling his compendium of authors, he followed the works of late ancient authors in placing all secular knowledge into the categories of the seven liberal arts, which were divided into two major groups: the *trivium*, consisting of grammar, rhetoric, and dialectic or logic; and the *quadrivium*, consisting of the mathematical subjects of arithmetic, geometry, astronomy, and music. The seven liberal arts would become the cornerstone of education until the seventeenth century.

The Byzantine Empire

In the fourth century, a noticeable separation between the western and eastern parts of the Roman Empire began to develop. In the course of the fifth century, the Germanic tribes moved into the western part of the empire and established their states while the Roman Empire in the east, centered on Constantinople, continued to exist.

The Reign of Justinian (527–565)

When he became emperor of the Eastern Roman Empire, Justinian was determined to reestablish the Roman Empire in the entire Mediterranean world. His army, commanded by Belisarius, probably the best general of the late Roman world, sailed to North Africa and quickly destroyed the Vandals in two major battles. From North Africa Belisarius led his forces onto the Italian peninsula and defeated the Ostrogoths. By 552, Justinian appeared to have achieved his goals. He had restored the Roman Empire in the Mediterranean. His empire included Italy, part of Spain, North Africa, Asia Minor, Palestine, and Syria. But the reconquest of the western empire proved fleeting. Only three years after Justinian's death, the Lombards conquered much of Italy. Although the eastern empire maintained the fiction of Italy as a province, its forces were limited to southern and central Italy, Sicily, and some coastal areas.

Justinian's most important contribution was his codification of Roman law. The eastern empire had inherited a vast quantity of legal materials connected to the development of Roman law, which Justinian wished to simplify. The result was the Code of Law, the first part of the *Corpus Iuris Civilis* (*The Body of Civil Law*), completed in 529. Four years later, two other parts of the *Corpus* appeared: the *Digest*, a compendium of writings of Roman jurists, and the *Institutes*, a brief summary of the chief principles of Roman law. The fourth part of the *Corpus* was the *Novels*, a compilation of the most important new edicts issued during Justinian's reign.

Justinian's codification of Roman law remained the basis of imperial law in the Eastern Roman Empire until its end in 1453. More importantly, however, because it was written in Latin (it was, in fact, the last product of eastern Roman culture to be written in Latin, which was soon replaced by Greek), it was also eventually used in the west and, in fact, became the basis of the legal system of all of continental Europe.

♦ **The Emperor Justinian Surrounded by His Court.** The church of San Vitale at Ravenna contains some of the finest examples of sixth-century Byzantine mosaics. This mosaic depicts the Byzantine emperor Justinian and his court dressed in their elaborate court robes.

INTELLECTUAL LIFE UNDER JUSTINIAN

The intellectual life of the Eastern Roman Empire was highly influenced by the traditions of classical civilization. Scholars actively strived to preserve the works of the ancient Greeks while basing a great deal of their own literature on classical models. Initially, however, the most outstanding literary achievements of the eastern empire were historical and religious works.

The best known of the early Byzantine historians was Procopius (c. 500–c. 562), court historian during the reign of Justinian. Procopius served as legal assistant and secretary to the great general Belisarius and accompanied him on his wars on behalf of Justinian. Procopius's best historical work, the *Wars*, is a firsthand account of Justinian's wars of reconquest in the western Mediterranean and his wars against the Persians in the east. Deliberately modeled after the work of his hero, the Greek historian Thucydides, Procopius's narrative features vivid descriptions of battle scenes, clear judgment, and noteworthy objectivity. Procopius also wrote a work that many historians consider mostly scandalous gossip, his infamous *Secret History*, which was a scathing attack on Justinian and his wife Theodora for their alleged misdeeds.

LIFE IN CONSTANTINOPLE: THE EMPEROR'S
BUILDING PROGRAM

After riots destroyed much of Constantinople in 532, Emperor Justinian rebuilt the city and gave it the appearance it would keep for almost a thousand years. With a population estimated in the hundreds of thousands, Constantinople was the largest city in Europe during the Middle Ages. It viewed itself as center of an empire and a special Christian city.

Until the twelfth century, Constantinople was Europe's greatest commercial center, the chief marketplace where western and eastern products were exchanged. Highly desired in Europe were the products of the east: silk from China, spices from southeast Asia and India, jewelry and ivory from India (the latter used by artisans for church items), wheat and furs from southern Russia, and flax and honey from the Balkans. Many of these eastern goods were then shipped to the Mediterranean area

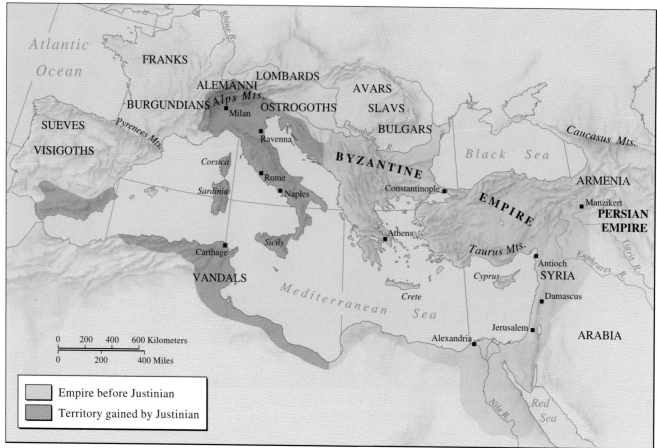

Map 7.4 The Byzantine Empire in the Time of Justinian.

and northern Europe. Moreover, imported raw materials were used in Constantinople for local industries. During Justinian's reign, two Christian monks smuggled silkworms from China to begin a Byzantine silk industry. The state controlled the production of silk cloth, and the workshops themselves were housed in Constantinople's royal palace complex. European demand for silk cloth made it the city's most lucrative product.

Much of Constantinople's appearance in the Middle Ages was due to Justinian's program of rebuilding in the sixth century. Earlier, in the mid-fifth century, Emperor Theodosius II (408–450) had constructed an enormous defensive wall to protect the city on its land side. The city was dominated by an immense palace complex, hundreds of churches, and a huge arena known as the Hippodrome. No residential district was particularly fashionable; palaces, tenements, and slums ranged alongside one another. Justinian added many new buildings. His public works projects included roads, bridges, walls, public baths, law courts, and colossal underground reservoirs to hold the city's water supply. He also built hospitals, schools, monas-

teries, and churches. The latter was his special passion, and in Constantinople alone he built or rebuilt thirty-four of them. His greatest achievement was the famous Hagia Sophia—the Church of the Holy Wisdom.

Completed in 537, Hagia Sophia was designed by a Greek architect who did not use the simple, flat-roofed basilica of western architecture. The center of Hagia Sophia consisted of four large piers crowned by an enormous dome, which seemed to be floating in space. In part, this impression was created by ringing the base of the dome with forty-two windows, which allowed an incredible play of light within the cathedral. Light served to remind the worshippers of God. As invisible light illuminates darkness, so too was it believed that invisible spirit illuminates the world.

The Hippodrome was a huge amphitheater, constructed of brick covered by marble, holding between 40,000 and 60,000 spectators. Although gladiator fights were held there, the main events were the chariot races; twenty-four would usually be presented in one day. The citizens of Constantinople were passionate fans of chariot racing.

Successful charioteers were acclaimed as heroes and honored with public statues. Crowds in the Hippodrome also took on political significance. Being a member of the two chief factions of charioteers—the Blues or Greens—was the only real outlet for political expression. Even emperors had to be aware of their demands and attitudes since rioting could threaten their power. The loss of a race in the Hippodrome frequently resulted in bloody riots.

From East Roman to Byzantine Empire

Justinian's accomplishments had been spectacular, but when he died he left the Eastern Roman Empire with serious problems: too much territory to protect far from Constantinople, an empty treasury, a decline in population after a plague, and renewed threats to its frontiers. In the first half of the seventh century, the empire faced attacks from the Persians to the east and the Slavs to the north.

The most serious challenge to the Eastern Roman Empire came from the rise of Islam, which unified the Arab tribes and created a powerful new force that swept through the east (see the next section, "The Rise of Islam"). The defeat of an eastern Roman army at Yarmuk in 636 meant the loss of the provinces of Syria and Palestine. The Arabs also moved into the old Persian empire and conquered it. Arabs and eastern Roman forces now faced each other along a frontier in southern Asia Minor. An Arab attempt to besiege Constantinople failed, in large part due to the use of Greek fire against the Arab fleets. Greek fire was a petroleum-based compound containing quicklime and sulfur. Because it would burn under water, the Byzantines created the equivalent of modern flame-throwers by blowing Greek fire from tubes onto wooden ships with frightening effect.

Problems arose along the northern frontier as well, especially in the Balkans, where an Asiatic people known as the Bulgars had arrived earlier in the sixth century. In 679, the Bulgars defeated the eastern Roman forces and took possession of the lower Danube valley, creating a strong Bulgarian kingdom.

By the beginning of the eighth century, the Eastern Roman Empire was greatly diminished in size. Consisting only of the eastern Balkans and Asia Minor, it was no longer an eastern Mediterranean state. The external challenges had important internal repercussions as well. By the eighth century, the Eastern Roman Empire had been transformed into what historians call the Byzantine Empire, a civilization with its own unique character that would last until 1453 (Constantinople was built on the site of an older city named Byzantium—hence the term *Byzantine*).

✦ **Interior View of Hagia Sophia.** Pictured here is the interior of the Church of the Holy Wisdom, constructed under Justinian by Anthemius of Tralles and Isidore of Milan. The pulpits and the great plaques bearing inscriptions from the Quran were introduced when the Turks converted this church into a mosque in the fifteenth century.

The Byzantine Empire was both a Greek and Christian state. Increasingly, Latin fell into disuse as Greek became both the common and official language of the Byzantine Empire. The Byzantine Empire was also a Christian state. Christianity, in fact, had become the fundamental foundation stone of the Byzantine state. The empire was built on a faith in Christ that was shared in a profound way by almost all of its citizens. An enormous amount of artistic talent was poured into the construction of churches, church ceremonies, and church decoration. Spiritual principles deeply permeated Byzantine art.

The Byzantine empire was characterized by what might be called a permanent war economy. Byzantine emperors maintained the late Roman policy of state regulation of economic affairs. Of course, it was easy to justify; the survival of the empire depended on careful shepherding of economic resources and the maintenance of the army. Thus, the state encouraged agricultural production, regulated the guilds or corporations responsible for industrial production and the various stages of manufacturing, and controlled commerce by making trade in grain and silk—the two most valuable products—government monopolies.

The emperor occupied a crucial position in the Byzantine state. Portrayed as chosen by God, the emperor was crowned in sacred ceremonies, and his subjects were expected to prostrate themselves in his presence. His power was considered absolute and was limited in practice only by deposition or assassination. Because the emperor appointed the head of the church (known as the patriarch), he also exercised control over both church and state. The Byzantines believed that God had commanded their state to preserve the true Christian faith. Emperor, clergy, and state officials were all bound together in service to this ideal. It can be said that spiritual values truly held the Byzantine state together.

By 750, it was apparent that two of Rome's heirs, the Germanic kingdoms and the Byzantine Empire, were moving in different directions. Nevertheless, Byzantine influence on the medieval western world was significant. The images of a Roman imperial state that continued to haunt the west had a living reality in the Byzantine state. The legal system of the west owed much to Justinian's codification of Roman law. In addition, the Byzantine Empire served in part as a buffer state, protecting the west for a long time from incursions from the east. Although the Byzantine Empire would continue to influence the west until its demise in 1453, it went its own unique way. One of its most bitter enemies was the new power of Islam that erupted out of Arabia in the name of the holy man Muhammad. This third heir of Rome soon controlled large areas of the old Roman Mediterranean area.

The Rise of Islam

Like the Hebrews and Assyrians, the Arabs were a Semitic-speaking people of the Near East with a long history. In Roman times, the Arabian peninsula was dominated by Bedouins, tribes of nomads who moved constantly to find water and food for themselves and their animals. Although some Arabs prospered from trading activities, especially in the north, most Arabs were poor Bedouins, whose tribes were known for their independence, their warlike qualities, and their dislike of urban-dwelling Arabs.

Although these early Arabs were polytheistic, there was a supreme God named Allah (Allah is Arabic for God) that ruled over the other gods. There was no priesthood; all members of the tribe were involved in the practice of the faith. Allah was symbolized by a sacred stone, and each tribe had its own stone. All tribes, however, worshiped a massive black meteorite—the Black Stone, which had been placed in a central shrine called the Ka'ba in the city of Mecca.

In the fifth and sixth centuries A.D., the Arabian peninsula took on new importance. As a result of political disorder in Mesopotamia and Egypt, the usual trade routes in the region began to change. A new trade route—from the Mediterranean through Mecca to Yemen and then by ship across the Indian Ocean—became more popular and communities in that part of the Arabian peninsula, such as Mecca, began to prosper from this caravan trade. As a result, tensions arose between the Bedouins in the desert and the increasingly wealthy merchant classes in the towns. Into this intense world stepped Muhammad.

Born in Mecca to a merchant family, Muhammad (c. 570–632) was orphaned at the age of five. Muhammad grew up to become a caravan manager and eventually married a rich widow who was also his employer. In his middle years, he began to experience visions that he believed were inspired by Allah. Muhammad believed that while Allah had already revealed himself in part through Moses and Jesus—and thus through the Hebrew and Christian traditions—the final revelations were now being given to him. Out of his revelations, which were eventually written down, came the Quran (or Koran), which contained the guidelines by which followers of Allah were to live. Muhammad's teachings formed the basis for the religion known as Islam, which means "submission to the will of Allah." Allah was the all-powerful being

☙ The Quran and the Spread of the Muslim Faith ☙

The Quran is the sacred book of the Muslims, comparable to the Bible in Christianity. In this selection from Chapter 47, entitled "Muhammad, Revealed at Medina," it is apparent that Islam encourages the spreading of the faith. Believers who died for Allah were promised a garden of paradise quite unlike the arid desert homeland of the Arab warriors.

The Quran Chapter 47, "Muhammad, Revealed at Medina"

Allah will bring to nothing the deeds of those who disbelieve and debar others from His path. As for the faithful who do good works and believe in what is revealed to Muhammad—which is the truth from their Lord—He will forgive them their sins and ennoble their state.

This, because the unbelievers follow falsehood, while the faithful follow the truth from their Lord. Thus Allah coins their sayings for mankind.

When you meet the unbelievers in the battlefield strike off their heads and, when you have laid them low, bind your captives firmly. Then grant them their freedom or take ransom from them, until War shall lay down her armor.

Thus shall you do. Had Allah willed, He could Himself have punished them; but He has ordained it thus that He might test you, the one by the other.

As for those who are slain in the cause of Allah, he will not allow their works to perish. He will vouchsafe them guidance and ennoble their state; He will admit them to the Paradise He has made known to them.

Believers, if you help Allah, Allah will help you and make you strong. But the unbelievers shall be consigned to perdition. He will bring their deeds to nothing. Because they have opposed His revelations, he will frustrate their works.

Have they never journeyed through the land and seen what was the end of those who have gone before them? Allah destroyed them utterly. A similar fate awaits the unbelievers, because Allah is the protector of the faithful; because the unbelievers have no protector.

Allah will admit those who embrace the true faith and do good works to gardens watered by running streams. The unbelievers take their full of pleasure and eat as the beasts eat: but Hell shall be their home. . . .

This is the Paradise which the righteous have been promised. There shall flow in it rivers of unpolluted water, and rivers of milk forever fresh; rivers of delectable wine and rivers of clearest honey. They shall eat therein of every fruit and receive forgiveness from their Lord. Is this like the lot of those who shall abide in Hell for ever and drink scalding water which will tear their bowels? . . .

Know that there is no god but Allah. Implore Him to forgive your sins and to forgive the true believers, men and women. Allah knows your busy haunts and resting-places.

who had created the universe and everything in it. Humans must subject themselves to Allah if they wished to achieve everlasting life. Those who became his followers were called Muslims, meaning those who practiced Islam.

After receiving the revelations, Muhammad set out to convince the people of Mecca of the truth of his revelations. At first, many thought he was insane and others feared that his attacks on the corrupt society around him would upset the established social and political order. Discouraged by the failure of the Meccans to accept his message, in 622 Muhammad and some of his closest supporters left the city and moved north to the rival city of Yathrib, a city later renamed Medina ("city of the prophet"). The year of the journey to Medina, known in history as the *Hegira*, became year one in the official calendar of Islam.

Muhammad, who had been invited to the town by a number of prominent residents, soon began to win support from people in Medina as well as from members of Bedouin tribes in the surrounding countryside. From these groups, he formed the first Muslim community. Muslims saw no separation between political and religious authority; submission to the will of Allah meant submission to his Prophet, Muhammad. Muhammad soon became both a religious and political leader. His political and military skills enabled him to put together a reliable military force, with which he returned to Mecca in 630, conquering the city and converting the townspeople to the new faith. From Mecca, Muhammad's ideas spread quickly across the Arabian peninsula and within a relatively short time had resulted in both the religious and political union of Arab society.

At the heart of Islam was the Quran with the basic message that there is no God but Allah and Muhammad is his Prophet (see the box above). Essentially, the Quran contains Muhammad's revelations of a heavenly book written down by secretaries. Consisting of 114 chapters, the Quran is the sacred book of Islam, which recorded the beliefs of the Muslims and served as their code of ethics and law.

Islam was a direct and simple faith, emphasizing the need to obey the will of Allah. This meant following a basic ethical code consisting of the "five pillars" of Islam: belief in Allah and Muhammad as his Prophet; standard prayer five times a day and public prayer on Friday at midday to worship Allah; observance of the holy month of Ramadan (the ninth month in the Muslim calendar) with fasting from dawn to sunset; making a pilgrimage (known as the *hajj*), if possible, to Mecca in one's lifetime; and giving alms to the poor and unfortunate. The faithful who observed the law were guaranteed a place in an eternal paradise.

Islam was not just a set of religious beliefs, but a way of life as well. After the death of Muhammad, Muslim scholars drew up a law code, called the *Shari'ah* to provide believers with a set of prescriptions to regulate their daily lives. Much of the *Shari'ah* was drawn from the Quran. Believers were subject to strict guidelines for their behavior. In addition to the "five pillars," Muslims were forbidden to gamble, to eat pork, to drink alcoholic beverages, and to engage in dishonest behavior. Sexual practices were also strict. Marriages were to be arranged by parents and contact between unmarried men and women was discouraged. In accordance with Bedouin custom, males were permitted to have more than one wife, but Muhammad attempted to limit the practice by restricting the number of wives to four.

The Expansion of Islam

The death of Muhammad in 632 presented his followers with a dilemma. Although Muhammad had not claimed to be divine, Muslims saw no separation between religious and political authority. Submission to the will of Allah was the same thing as submission to his Prophet, Muhammad. According to the Quran: "Whoever obeys the messenger obeys Allah." But Muhammad had never named a successor, and although he had several daughters, he left no sons. In a male-oriented society, who would lead the community of the faithful? Shortly after Muhammad's death, some of his closest followers selected Abu Bakr, a wealthy merchant who was Muhammad's father-in-law, as caliph, or temporal leader, of the Islamic community.

Muhammad and the early caliphs who succeeded him took up the Arabic tribal custom of making raids against one's enemies. The Quran called this activity "striving in the way of Lord," or a *jihad*. Although misleadingly

✦ **Muslims Celebrate the End of Ramadan.** Ramadan is the holy month of Islam during which all Muslims must fast from dawn to sunset. Observance of this holy month is regarded as one of the "five pillars" of the faith. Muhammad instituted the fast during his stay at Medina. It was designed to replace the single Jewish Day of Atonement. This Persian miniature depicts Muslims on horseback celebrating the end of Ramadan.

called a Holy War, the *jihad* grew out of the Arabic tradition of tribal raids, which were permitted as a way to channel the warlike energies of the Bedouin tribes. Such aggression was not carried out to convert others since conversion to Islam was purely voluntary. Those who did not convert were required only to submit to Muslim rule and pay taxes.

Once the Arabs had become unified under Abu Bakr, they began to direct the energy they had once expended against each other outward against neighboring peoples. The Byzantines and the Persians were the first to feel the strength of the newly united Arabs. At Yarmuk in 636, the Muslims defeated the Byzantine army, and by 640 they had taken possession of the province of Syria. To the east, the Arabs defeated the Persian forces in 637 and then went on to conquer the entire Persian Empire by 650. In the meantime, by 642, Egypt and other areas of northern Africa had been added to the new Muslim empire. Led by a series of brilliant generals, the Arabs had put together a large and highly motivated army, whose valor was enhanced by the belief that Muslim warriors were guaranteed a place in paradise if they died in battle.

CHRONOLOGY

The Rise of Islam

Birth of Muhammad	c. 570
Muhammad's flight from Mecca (Hegira)	622
Death of Muhammad	632
Defeat of Byzantines at Yarmuk	636
Seizure of Byzantine provinces of Syria and Egypt	640–642
Defeat of Persians	637–650
Invasion of Spain	710
Arab failure to capture Constantinople	717–718

Early caliphs, ruling from Medina, organized their newly conquered territories into taxpaying provinces. By the mid-seventh century, problems arose again over the succession to the Prophet until Ali, Muhammad's son-in-law, was assassinated and the general Muawiyah, the

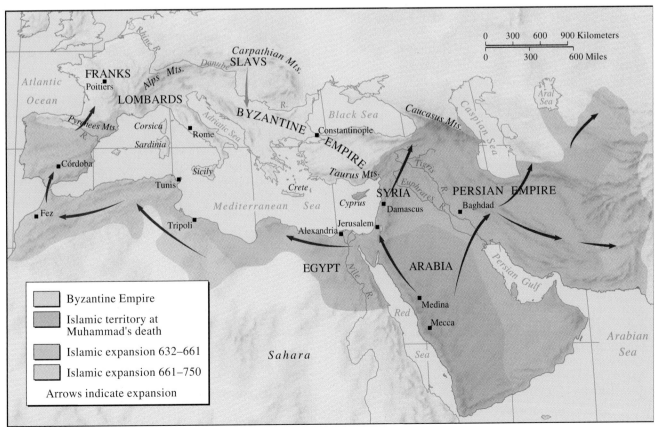

Map 7.5 The Expansion of Islam.

governor of Syria and one of Ali's chief rivals, became caliph in 661. He was known for one outstanding—virtue; he used force only when necessary. As he said, "I never use my sword when my whip will do, nor my whip when my tongue will do." Muawiyah moved quickly to make the caliphate hereditary in his own family, thus establishing the Umayyad dynasty. As one of its first actions, the Umayyad dynasty moved the capital of the Muslim empire from Medina to Damascus in Syria. This internal dissension over the caliphate created a split in Islam between the Shiites, or those who accepted only the descendants of Ali, Muhammad's son-in-law, as the true rulers, and the Sunnites, who claimed that the descendants of the Umayyads were the true caliphs. This seventh-century split in Islam has lasted until the present day.

The internal dissension, however, did not stop the expansion of Islam. At the beginning of the eighth century, new attacks were made at both the western and eastern ends of the Mediterranean world. After sweeping across North Africa, the Muslims crossed the Strait of Gibraltar and moved into Spain around 710. The Visigothic kingdom collapsed, and by 725, most of Spain had become a Muslim state with its center at Córdoba. In 732, a Muslim army, making a foray into southern France, was defeated at the Battle of Tours in 732. Muslim expansion in Europe came to a halt.

Meanwhile, in 717, another Muslim force had launched a naval attack on Constantinople with the hope of destroying the Byzantine Empire. In the spring of 718, the Byzantines destroyed the Muslim fleet and saved the Byzantine Empire and indirectly Christian Europe, because the fall of Constantinople would no doubt have opened the door to Muslim invasion of eastern Europe. The Byzantine Empire and Islam now established an uneasy frontier in southern Asia Minor.

The Arab advance had finally come to an end, but not before the southern and eastern Mediterranean parts of the old Roman Empire had been conquered. Islam had truly become heir to much of the old Roman Empire. The Umayyad dynasty at Damascus now ruled an enormous empire. While expansion had conveyed untold wealth and new ethnic groups into the fold of Islam, it also brought contact with Byzantine and Persian civilization. As a result, the new Arab empire would be influenced by Greek culture as well as the older civilizations of the ancient Near East. The children of the conquerors would be educated in new ways and produce a brilliant culture that would eventually influence western Europe intellectually.

Conclusion

The period from 400 to 750 was both chaotic and creative. Three new entities fell heir to Roman civilization: the German kingdoms, the Byzantine Empire, and the world of Islam. In the west, Roman elements combined with German and Celtic influences; in the east, Greek and eastern elements of late antiquity were of more consequence. Although the Germanic kingdoms of the west and the Byzantine civilization of the east came to share a common bond in Christianity, it proved incapable of keeping them in harmony politically, and the two civilizations continued to move apart. Christianity, however, remained a dominant influence in both civilizations and in the west was especially important as a civilizing agent that brought pagan peoples into a new European civilization that was slowly being born. The rise of Islam, Rome's third heir, resulted in the loss of the southern and eastern Mediterranean worlds of the old Roman Empire to a religious power that was neither Roman nor Christian. The new Islamic empire forced Europe proper back on itself and, slowly, a new civilization emerged that became the heart of what we know as Western civilization.

NOTES

1. Ernest F. Henderson, *Select Historical Documents of the Middle Ages* (London, 1892), p. 181.
2. The Creed of Nicaea, in Henry Bettenson, ed., *Documents of the Christian Church* (London, 1963), p. 35.
3. St. Matthew, 16: 15–19.
4. Norman F. Cantor, ed., *The Medieval World: 300–1300* (New York, 1963), pp. (in order of quotations) 104, 101, 108, 103.
5. Bede, *A History of the English Church and People*, trans. Leo Sherley-Price (Harmondsworth, 1968), pp. 86–87.
6. Tertullian, "The Prescriptions Against the Heretics," in *The Library of Christian Classics*, vol. 5, *Early Latin Theology*, ed. and trans. S. L. Greenslade (Philadelphia, 1956), p. 36.
7. Anne Fremantle, ed., *A Treasury of Early Christianity* (New York, 1953), p. 91.

8. Cassiodorus, *An Introduction to Divine and Human Readings*, trans. Leslie Jones (New York, 1969), p. 205.

9. Quoted in Arthur Goldschmidt, Jr., *A Concise History of the Middle East,* 4th ed. (Boulder, Colo., 1991), p. 56.

SUGGESTIONS FOR FURTHER READING

Good general histories of the entire medieval period can be found in S. Painter and B. Tierney, *Western Europe in the Middle Ages, 300–1475* (New York, 1983); E. Peters, *Europe and the Middle Ages*, 2d ed. (Englewood Cliffs, N.J., 1989): and G. Holmes, ed., *The Oxford Illustrated History of Medieval Europe* (Oxford, 1988). For a good general survey of the social history of the Middle Ages, see C. B. Bouchard, *Life and Society in the West: Antiquity and the Middle Ages* (San Diego, 1988). For excellent reference works on medieval history, see H. R. Loyn, *The Middle Ages: A Concise Encyclopedia* (New York, 1989); and J. R. Strayer, ed., *Dictionary of the Middle Ages*, 13 vols. (New York, 1982–1989).

Brief histories of the period covered in this chapter include R. Collins, *Early Medieval Europe, 300–1000* (New York, 1991); M. Grant, *Dawn of the Middle Ages* (New York, 1981), which contains a lively text and excellent illustrations; and J. M. Wallace-Hadrill, *The Barbarian West*, rev. ed. (Oxford, 1985).

For surveys on the German tribes and their migrations, see L. Musset, *The German Invasions* (University Park, Pa., 1975); T. S. Burns, *A History of the Ostrogoths* (Bloomington, Ind., 1984); P. Heather, *Goths and Romans* (Oxford, 1991); E. James, *The Franks* (Oxford, 1988); and especially H. Wolfram, *The Goths*, trans. T. J. Dunlop (Berkeley, 1988). Also valuable are the revisionist works of W. Goffart, *Barbarians and Romans, A.D. 418–554. The Techniques of Accommodation* (Princeton, N.J., 1980); and P. Geary, *Before France and Germany* (Oxford, 1988).

On the relationship of Christian thought to the classical tradition, see H. Chadwick, *Early Christian Thought and the Classical Tradition* (Oxford, 1966); and R. A. Markus, *Christianity in the Roman World* (London, 1974). On Augustine and Jerome, see P. Brown, *Augustine of Hippo* (Berkeley and Los Angeles, 1969); and J. N. D. Kelly, *Saint Jerome* (London, 1975). A brief, illustrated history of monasticism is G. Zarnecki, *The Monastic Achievement* (New York, 1972). For a more detailed account, see C. H. Lawrence, *Medieval Monasticism* (London, 1984). On Saint Benedict and the Benedictine ideal, see L. von Matt, *Saint Benedict* (London, 1961); and O. Chadwick, *The Making of the Benedictine Ideal* (London, 1981). For women in monastic life, see S. F. Wemple, *Women in Frankish Society: Marriage and the Cloister, 500–900* (Philadelphia, 1981).

A brief survey of the development of the papacy can be found in G. Barraclough, *The Medieval Papacy* (New York, 1968). J. Richards, *The Popes and the Papacy in the Early Middle Ages, 476–752* (Boston, 1979) is a more detailed study of the early papacy. On Pope Gregory the Great, see the biography by J. Richards, *Consul of God: The Life and Times of Gregory the Great* (Boston, 1980). On Irish monasticism, see L. M. Bitel, *Isle of the Saints: Monastic Settlement and Christian Community in Early Ireland* (Ithaca, N.Y., 1990). On Christianity and intellectual life, see J. J. O'Donnell, *Cassiodorus* (Berkeley and Los Angeles, 1979). An important aspect of Christian culture is discussed in P. Brown, *The Cult of Saints* (Chicago, 1981).

Brief but good introductions to Byzantine history can be found in H. W. Haussig, *A History of Byzantine Civilization* (New York, 1971); and C. Mango, *Byzantium: The Empire of New Rome* (London, 1980). The best single political history is G. Ostrogorsky, *A History of the Byzantine State*, 2d ed. (New Brunswick, N.J., 1968). On Justinian, see J. Moorhead, *Justinian*, (London, 1995). The role of the Christian church is discussed in J. Hussey, *The Orthodox Church in the Byzantine Empire* (Oxford, 1986).

Good brief surveys of the Islamic Middle East include A. Goldschmidt, Jr., *A Concise History of the Middle East*, 5th ed. (Boulder, Colo., 1995); and S. N. Fisher, *The Middle East: A History*, rev. ed. (New York, 1978). On the rise of Islam, see M. Lings, *Muhammad: His Life Based on the Earliest Sources* (New York, 1983); P. Crone and M. Hinds, *God's Caliph: Religious Authority in the First Centuries of Islam* (New York, 1986); and F. Donner, *The Early Islamic Conquests* (Princeton, N.J., 1980).

CHAPTER
8

European Civilization in the Early Middle Ages, 750–1000

In 800, Charlemagne, the king of the Franks, journeyed to Rome to help Pope Leo III, who was barely clinging to power in the face of rebellious Romans. On Christmas Day, Charlemagne and his family, attended by Romans, Franks, and even visitors from the Byzantine Empire, crowded into St. Peter's Basilica to hear mass. Quite unexpectedly, according to a Frankish writer, "as the king rose from praying before the tomb of the blessed apostle Peter, Pope Leo placed a golden crown on his head." In keeping with ancient tradition, the people in the church shouted, "Long life and victory to Charles Augustus, crowned by God the great and pacific Emperor of the Romans." Seemingly, the Roman Empire in the West had been reborn, and Charles had become the first western emperor since 476. But this "Roman emperor" was actually a German king, and he had been crowned by the head of the Western Christian church. In truth, the coronation of Charlemagne was a sign not of the rebirth of the Roman Empire, but of the emergence of a new European civilization.

By the year of Charlemagne's coronation, the contours of this new European civilization were beginning to emerge in western Europe. Increasingly, Europe would become the focus and center of Western civilization. Building on a fusion of Germanic, classical, and Christian elements, the medieval European world first became visible in the Carolingian Empire of Charlemagne. The agrarian foundations of the eighth and ninth centuries proved inadequate to maintain a large monarchical system, however, and a new political and military order based on the decentralization of political power subsequently evolved to become an integral part of the political world of the Middle Ages.

European civilization began on a shaky and uncertain foundation, however. In the ninth century, Vikings, Magyars, and Muslims posed threats that could easily have stifled the new society. But a vibrant civilization can absorb such challenges, and European civilization did just that. The Vikings and Magyars

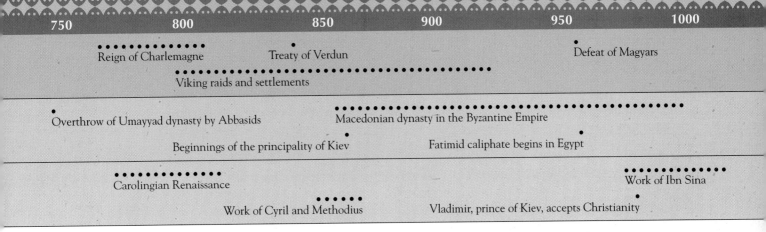

Reign of Charlemagne • • • • • • • • • • • • • • • •

Treaty of Verdun

Defeat of Magyars

Viking raids and settlements

Overthrow of Umayyad dynasty by Abbasids

Macedonian dynasty in the Byzantine Empire

Beginnings of the principality of Kiev

Fatimid caliphate begins in Egypt

Carolingian Renaissance

Work of Ibn Sina

Work of Cyril and Methodius

Vladimir, prince of Kiev, accepts Christianity

were assimilated, and recovery slowly began. By 1000, European civilization was ready to embark on a period of dazzling vitality and expansion.

The World of the Carolingians

During the seventh and eighth centuries, within the Frankish kingdom of western Europe, the Carolingian mayors of the palace of Neustria and Austrasia had expanded their power at the expense of the Merovingian dynasty (see Chapter 7). One of these mayors, Pepin, finally took the logical step of deposing the decadent Merovingians and assuming the kingship of the Frankish state for himself and his family. Pepin's actions, which were approved by the pope, created a new form of Frankish kingship. Pepin (751–768) was crowned king and formally anointed by a representative of the pope with holy oil in imitation of an Old Testament practice. Only priests had been anointed before, but now so were Frankish kings; the anointing not only symbolized that the kings had been entrusted with a sacred office but also provides yet another example of how a Germanic institution fused with a Christian practice in the Early Middle Ages.

Charlemagne and the Carolingian Empire (768–814)

Pepin's death in 768 brought to the throne of the Frankish kingdom his son, a dynamic and powerful ruler known to history as Charles the Great or Charlemagne (from *Carolus magnus* in Latin). Charlemagne was a determined and decisive man, highly intelligent and inquisitive. A fierce warrior, he was also a wise patron of learning and a

resolute statesman (see the box on p. 156). He greatly expanded the territory of the Carolingian empire during his lengthy rule.

EXPANSION OF THE CAROLINGIAN EMPIRE

In the tradition of the Germanic kings, Charlemagne was a determined warrior who undertook fifty-four military campaigns. Even though the Frankish army was relatively small—only 8,000 men gathered each spring for campaigning—supplying it and transporting it to distant areas could still present serious problems. The Frankish army comprised mostly infantry with some cavalry armed with swords and spears.

Charlemagne's campaigns took him to many areas of Europe. In 773, Charlemagne led his army into Italy, crushed the Lombards, and took control of the Lombard state. Although his son was crowned as king of Italy, Charlemagne was its real ruler. Four years after his invasion of Italy, Charlemagne moved his forces into northern Spain. This campaign proved to be disappointing; not only did the Basques harass his army as it crossed the Pyrenees on the way home, but they also ambushed and annihilated his rear guard.

Charlemagne was considerably more successful with his eastern campaigns into Germany, especially against the Saxons located between the Elbe River and the North Sea. As Einhard, Charlemagne's biographer, recounted it:

> No war ever undertaken by the Frank nation was carried on with such persistence and bitterness, or cost so much labor, because the Saxons, like almost all the tribes of Germany, were a fierce people, given to the worship of devils, and hostile to our religion, and did not consider it dishonorable to transgress and violate all law, human and divine.[1]

⋟ The Achievements of Charlemagne ⋞

Einhard, the biographer of Charlemagne, was born in the valley of the Main River in Germany about 775. Raised and educated in the monastery of Fulda, an important center of learning, he arrived at the court of Charlemagne in 791 or 792. Although he did not achieve high office under Charlemagne, he served as private secretary to Louis the Pious, Charlemagne's son and successor. Einhard's Life of Charlemagne *was modeled on Suetonius's* Lives of the Caesars, *especially his biography of Augustus. Einhard's work, written between 817 and 830, was the "first medieval biography of a lay figure." In this selection, he discusses some of Charlemagne's accomplishments.*

Einhard, *Life of Charlemagne*

Such are the wars, most skillfully planned and successfully fought, which this most powerful king waged during the forty-seven years of his reign. He so largely increased the Frank kingdom, which was already great and strong when he received it at his father's hands, that more than double its former territory was added to it. . . . He subdued all the wild and barbarous tribes dwelling in Germany between the Rhine and the Vistula, the Ocean and the Danube, all of which speak very much the same language, but differ widely from one another in customs and dress. . . .

He added to the glory of his reign by gaining the good will of several kings and nations; so close, indeed, was the alliance that he contracted with Alfonso, King of Galicia and Asturias, that the latter, when sending letters or ambassadors to Charles, invariably styled himself his man. . . . The Emperors of Constantinople [the Byzantine emperors] sought friendship and alliance with Charles by several embassies; and even when the Greeks [the Byzantines] suspected him of designing to take the empire from them, because of his assumption of the title Emperor, they made a close alliance with him, that he might have no cause of offense. In fact, the power of the Franks was always viewed with a jealous eye, whence the Greek proverb, "Have the Frank for your friend, but not for your neighbor."

This King, who showed himself so great in extending his empire and subduing foreign nations, and was constantly occupied with plans to that end, undertook also very many works calculated to adorn and benefit his kingdom, and brought several of them to completion. Among these, the most deserving of mention are the basilica of the Holy Mother of God at Aix-la-Chapelle, built in the most admirable manner, and a bridge over the Rhine River at Mainz, half a mile long, the breadth of the river at this point. . . . Above all, sacred buildings were the object of his care throughout his whole kingdom; and whenever he found them falling to ruin from age, he commanded the priests and fathers who had charge of them to repair them, and made sure by commissioners that his instructions were obeyed. . . . Thus did Charles defend and increase as well as beautify his kingdom. . . .

He cherished with the greatest fervor and devotion the principles of the Christian religion, which had been instilled into him from infancy. Hence it was that he built the beautiful church at Aix-la-Chapelle, which he adorned with gold and silver and lamps, and with rails and doors of solid brass. He had the columns and marbles for this structure brought from Rome and Ravenna, for he could not find such as were suitable elsewhere. He was a constant worshiper at this church as long as his health permitted, going morning and evening, even after nightfall, besides attending mass. . . .

He was very forward in caring for the poor, so much so that he not only made a point of giving in his own country and his own kingdom, but when he discovered that there were Christians living in poverty in Syria, Egypt, and Africa, at Jerusalem, Alexandria, and Carthage, he had compassion on their wants, and used to send money over the seas to them. . . . He sent great and countless gifts to the popes, and throughout his whole reign the wish that he had nearest at heart was to reestablish the ancient authority of the city of Rome under his care and by his influence, and to defend and protect the Church of St. Peter, and to beautify and enrich it out of his own store above all other churches.

⋟⋟⋟⋟⋟⋟⋟⋟⋟⋟⋟⋟⋟⋟⋟⋟⋟⋟ ⋞⋞⋞⋞⋞⋞⋞⋞⋞⋞⋞⋞⋞⋞⋞⋞⋞⋞⋞⋞

Charlemagne's insistence that the Saxons convert to Christianity simply fueled their resistance. Not until 804, after eighteen campaigns, was Saxony finally pacified and added to the Carolingian domain.

In southeastern Germany, Charlemagne invaded the land of the Bavarians in 787 and brought them into his empire by the following year, an expansion that then brought him into contact with the southern Slavs and the

The Carolingian Empire

Pepin crowned king of the Franks	751
Reign of Charlemagne	768–814
Campaign in Italy	773–774
Campaign in Spain	778
Charlemagne crowned emperor	800
Final conquest of Saxons	804
Reign of Louis the Pious	814–840
Treaty of Verdun divides Carolingian Empire	843

Avars. The latter disappeared from history after their utter devastation at the hands of Charlemagne's army. Now at its height, Charlemagne's empire covered much of western and central Europe; not until the time of Napoleon in the nineteenth and Hitler in the twentieth century would an empire its size be seen again in Europe.

GOVERNING THE EMPIRE

Charlemagne continued the efforts of his father in organizing the Carolingian kingdom. Because there was no system of public taxation, Charlemagne was highly dependent on the royal estates for the resources he needed to govern his empire. Food and goods derived from these lands provided support for the king, his household staff, and officials. To keep the nobles in his service, Charlemagne granted part of the royal lands as lifetime holdings to nobles who assisted him.

Besides the household staff, the administration of the empire was accomplished by counts, who were the king's chief representatives in local areas, although in dangerous border districts officials known as margraves (literally, *mark graf*, count of the border district) were used. Counts were members of the nobility who had already existed under the Merovingians. They had come to control public services in their own lands and thus acted as judges, military leaders, and agents of the king. Gradually, as the rule of the Merovingian kings weakened, many counts had simply attached the royal lands and services performed on behalf of the king to their own family possessions.

In an effort to gain greater control over his kingdom, Charlemagne attempted to limit the power of the counts. They were required to serve outside their own family lands and were moved about periodically rather than being permitted to remain in a county for life. By making the offices appointive, Charlemagne tried to prevent the counts' children from automatically inheriting their offices. Moreover, as another check on the counts, Charlemagne instituted the *missi dominici* ("messengers of the lord king"), two men, one lay lord, and one church official, who were sent out to local districts to ensure that the counts were executing the king's wishes. The counts also had assistants, but they were members of their households, not part of a bureaucratic office.

The last point is an important reminder that we should not think of Carolingian government in the modern sense of government offices run by officials committed to an impersonal ideal of state service. The Carolingian system was glaringly inefficient. Great distances had to be covered on horseback, making it impossible for Charlemagne and his household staff to exercise much supervision over local affairs. What held the system together was personal loyalty to a king who was strong enough to ensure loyalty by force when necessary.

Charlemagne also realized that the Catholic church could provide invaluable assistance in governing his kingdom. By the late seventh century, the system of ecclesiastical government within the Christian church that had been created in the late Roman Empire had largely disintegrated. Church offices were not filled or were often held by grossly unqualified relatives of the royal family. Both Pepin and his son Charlemagne took up the cause of church reform by creating new bishoprics and archbishoprics, restoring old ones, and seeing to it that the clergy accepted the orders of their superiors and executed their duties.

CHARLEMAGNE AS EMPEROR

As Charlemagne's power grew, so too did his prestige as the most powerful Christian ruler; one monk even wrote of his empire as the "kingdom of Europe." In 800, Charlemagne acquired a new title—emperor of the Romans—largely as a result of the ever closer relationship between the papacy and the Frankish monarchs.

Already during the reign of Pepin, a growing alliance emerged between the kingdom of the Franks and the papacy. The popes welcomed this support, and in the course of the second half of the eighth century, increasingly severed their ties with the Byzantine Empire and drew closer to the Frankish kingdom. Charlemagne encouraged this development. In 799, after a rebellion against his authority, Pope Leo III (795–816) managed to escape from Rome and flee to safety at Charlemagne's court. Charlemagne offered assistance, and when he went to Rome in

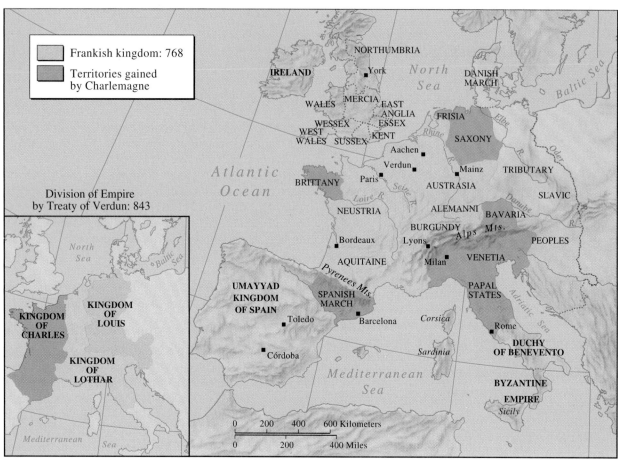

⚜ Map 8.1 The Carolingian Empire.

November 800 to settle affairs, he was received by the pope like an emperor. On Christmas Day 800, Pope Leo placed a crown on Charlemagne's head and declared him emperor of the Romans.

The significance of this imperial coronation has been much debated. Charlemagne's biographer Einhard claimed that "at first [he] had such an aversion that he declared that he would not have set foot in the Church the day that they were conferred, although it was a great feastday, if he could have foreseen the design of the Pope."[2] But Charlemagne also perceived the usefulness of the imperial title; after all, he was now on a level of equality with the Byzantine emperor, a status he did not reject. Moreover, the papacy now had a defender of great stature, although later popes in the Middle Ages would become involved in fierce struggles with emperors over who possessed the higher power.

In any case, Charlemagne's coronation as Roman emperor certainly demonstrated the strength, even after 300 years, of the concept of an enduring Roman Empire. More importantly, it symbolized the fusion of the Roman, Christian, and Germanic elements that constituted the foundation of European civilization. A Germanic king had been crowned emperor of the Romans by the spiritual leader of Western Christendom. A new civilization had emerged.

The Carolingian Intellectual Renewal

Charlemagne had a strong desire to revive learning in his kingdom, an attitude that stemmed from his own intellectual curiosity as well as the need to provide educated clergy for the church and literate officials for the government. His efforts led to a revival of learning and culture that some historians have labeled a Carolingian Renaissance or "rebirth" of learning.

The term is only partly appropriate, since the Carolingian era is hardly known for outstanding creativity and originality of ideas. Nevertheless, a true revival of classical studies and an attempt to assimilate and preserve Latin and early Christian culture did occur. This goal became a major task of the monasteries, many of which had been established by the Irish and English missionaries of the seventh and eighth centuries. By the ninth century, the "work" required of Benedictine monks was the copying of manuscripts. Monasteries established *scriptoria* or writing rooms, where monks copied not only the works of early Christianity, such as the Bible, but also the works of Latin classical authors. The production of manuscripts in Carolingian monastic *scriptoria* was a crucial factor in the preservation of the ancient legacy. About 8,000 manuscripts survive from Carolingian times. Virtually 90 percent of the ancient Roman works that we have today exist because they were copied by Carolingian monks.

Life in the Carolingian World

In daily life as well as intellectual life, the newly emerging European world of the Carolingian era witnessed a fusion of Roman, Germanic, and Christian practices. The latter in particular seems to have exercised an ever-increasing influence.

THE FAMILY, MARRIAGE, AND SEXUALITY

By Carolingian times, the Catholic church had begun to make a significant impact on Frankish family life and marital and sexual attitudes. As we have seen, marriages in Frankish society were arranged by fathers or uncles to meet the needs of the extended family. Although wives were expected to be faithful to their husbands, Frankish aristocrats often kept concubines, either slave girls or free

♦ **The Coronation of Charlemagne.** After a rebellion in 799 forced Pope Leo III to seek refuge at Charlemagne's court, Charlemagne went to Rome to settle the affair. There, on Christmas Day 800, he was crowned emperor of the Romans by the pope. This manuscript illustration shows Leo III placing a crown on Charlemagne's head.

♦ **Monk as Copyist.** Charlemagne's efforts to revive learning led to what has been called the Carolingian Renaissance. Through their copying of ancient manuscripts, Benedictine monks added an important element to this revival. Shown here at work in this medieval miniature is a monk who is meant to represent Saint Luke, one of the four apostles.

women from their estates. Even the "most Christian king" Charlemagne kept a number of concubines.

To limit such sexual license, the church increasingly emphasized its role in marriage and attempted to Christianize it. Although marriage was a civil arrangement, priests tried to add their blessings and strengthen the concept of a special marriage ceremony. Moreover, the church tried to serve as the caretaker of marriage by stipulating that a girl over fifteen must give her consent to her guardian's choice of a husband or her marriage was not valid in the eyes of the church. To stabilize marriages, the church also began to emphasize monogamy and permanence. A Frankish church council in 789 stipulated that marriage was "indissoluble" and condemned the practice of concubinage and easy divorce, and during the reign of Emperor Louis the Pious (814–840), the church finally established the right to prohibit divorce. Now a man who married was expected to remain with his wife "even though she were sterile, deformed, old, dirty, drunken, a frequenter of bad company, lascivious, vain, greedy, unfaithful, quarrelsome, abusive . . . , for when that man was free, he freely engaged himself."[3]

The acceptance and spread of the Catholic church's views on the indissolubility of marriage encouraged the development of the nuclear family at the expense of the extended family. Although the kin was still an influential social and political force, the conjugal unit came to be seen as the basic unit of society. The new practice of young couples establishing their own households brought a dynamic element to European society. It also had a significant impact on women (see the box on p. 161). In the extended family, the eldest woman controlled all the other female members; in the nuclear family, the wife was still dominated by her husband, but at least she now had control of her own household and children.

The early church fathers had stressed that celibacy and complete abstinence from sexual activity constituted an ideal state superior to marriage. Subsequently, the early church gradually developed a case for clerical celibacy, although it proved impossible to enforce in the Early Middle Ages. The early fathers had also emphasized, however, that not all people had the self-discipline to remain celibate. It was thus permissible to marry, as Paul had indicated in his first epistle to the Corinthians: "It is good for a man not to touch a woman. Nevertheless, to avoid fornication, let every man have his own wife, and let every woman have her own husband. . . . I say therefore to the unmarried and widows, it is good for them if they abide even as I. But if they cannot contain, let them marry: for it is better to marry than to burn."[4] The church thus viewed marriage as the lesser of two evils; it was a concession to human weakness and fulfilled the need for companionship, sex, and children. In the church of the Early Middle Ages, it was generally agreed that marriage gave the right to indulge in sexual intercourse. Sex, then, was permissible within marriage, but only so long as it was used for the sole purpose of procreation, not for pleasure.

Because the church developed the tradition that sexual relations between man and wife were only legitimate if done for purposes of procreation, it condemned all forms of contraception. The church also strongly condemned abortion, although its prohibition failed to stop the practice. Various herbal potions were available to prohibit conception or cause abortion. The Catholic church accepted only one way to limit children, by either periodic or total abstinence from intercourse.

The Catholic church's condemnation of sexual activity outside marriage also included homosexuality. Neither Roman religion nor Roman law had recognized any real difference between homosexual and heterosexual eroticism, and the Roman Empire had taken no legal measures against the practice of homosexuality between adults. Later, in the Byzantine Empire, the Emperor Justinian in 538 condemned homosexuality, emphasizing that such practices brought down the wrath of God ("we have provoked Him to anger") and endangered the wel-

⇒ Advice from a Carolingian Mother ⇐

The wife of a Carolingian aristocrat bore numerous responsibilities. She was entrusted with the management of the household and even the administration of extensive landed estates while her husband was absent in the royal service or on a military campaign. A wife was also expected to bear larger numbers of children and to supervise their upbringing. This selection by Dhouda, wife of Bernard, marquis of Septimania (in southern France), is taken from a manual she wrote to instruct her son on his duties to his new lord, King Charles the Bald (840–877).

Dhouda, *Handbook for William*

Direction on your comportment toward your lord.

You have Charles as your lord; you have him as lord because, as I believe, God and your father, Bernard, have chosen him for you to serve at the beginning of your career, in the flower of your youth. Remember that he comes from a great and noble lineage on both sides of his family. Serve him not only so that you please him in obvious ways, but also as one clearheaded in matters of both body and soul. Be steadfastly and completely loyal to him in all things. . . .

This is why, my son, I urge you to keep this loyalty as long as you live, in your body and in your mind. For the advancement that it brings you will be of great value both to you and to those who in turn serve you. May the madness of treachery never, not once, make you offer an angry insult. May it never give rise in your heart to

the idea of being disloyal to your lord. There is harsh and shameful talk about men who act in this fashion. I do not think that such will befall you or those who fight alongside you because such an attitude has never shown itself among your ancestors. It has not been seen among them, it is not seen now, and it will not be seen in the future.

Be truthful to your lord, my son William, child of their lineage. Be vigilant, energetic, and offer him ready assistance as I have said here. In every matter of importance to royal power take care to show yourself a man of good judgment—in your own thoughts and in public—to the extent that God gives you strength. Read the sayings and the lives of the holy Fathers who have gone before us. You will there discover how you may serve your lord and be faithful to him in all things. When you understand this, devote yourself to the faithful execution of your lord's commands. Look around as well and observe those who fight for him loyally and constantly. Learn from them how you may serve him. Then, informed by their example, with the help and support of God, you will easily reach the celestial goal I have mentioned above. And may your heavenly Lord God be generous and benevolent toward you. May he keep you safe, be your kind leader and your protector. May he deign to assist you in all your actions and be your constant defender.

fare of the state. Justinian recommended that the guilty parties be punished by castration. Although the church in the Early Middle Ages similarly condemned homosexuality, it also pursued a flexible policy in its treatment of homosexuals. In the Early Middle Ages, homosexuals were treated less harshly than married couples who practiced contraception.

DIET AND HEALTH

For both rich and poor, the fundamental staple of the Carolingian diet was bread. The aristocratic classes, as well as the monks, consumed it in large quantities. Ovens at the monastery of Saint Gall were able to bake a thousand loaves of bread. Sometimes, a gruel made of barley and oats was substituted for bread in the peasant diet.

The upper classes in Carolingian society enjoyed a much more varied diet than the peasants. Pork was the major red meat. Domestic pigs, allowed to run wild in the forests to find their own food, were collected and slaughtered in the fall, then smoked and salted to be eaten during the winter months. Because Carolingian aristocrats were especially fond of roasted meat, hunting wild game became one of their favorite activities. They ate little beef and mutton, however, because cattle were kept as dairy cows and oxen to draw plows while sheep were raised for wool.

Dairy products became prevalent in the Carolingian diet. Milk, which spoiled rapidly, was made into cheese and butter. Chickens were raised for their eggs. Vegetables also formed a crucial part of the diet of both the rich and the poor. These included legumes, such as beans, peas, and lentils, and roots, such as garlic, onions, and carrots.

Both gluttony and drunkenness were vices shared by many people in Carolingian society. Monastic rations were greatly enlarged in the eighth century to include a daily allotment of 3.7 pounds of bread (nuns were only permitted 3 pounds), one and one-half quarts of wine or ale, two or three ounces of cheese, and eight ounces of vegetables (four for nuns). These rations totaled 6,000 calories a day, and since only heavy and fatty foods—bread, milk, and cheese—were considered nourishing, we begin to understand why some Carolingians were known for their potbellies. Malnutrition, however, remained a widespread problem for common people in this period.

Everyone in Carolingian society, including abbots and monks, drank heavily and often to excess. Taverns became a regular feature of life and were found everywhere: in marketplaces, pilgrimage centers, and on royal, episcopal, and monastic estates. Drinking contests were not unusual; one penitential stated: "Does drunken bravado encourage you to attempt to out-drink your friends? If so, thirty days fast."

The aristocrats and monks favored wine above all other beverages, and much care was lavished on its production, especially by monasteries. Ale was especially popular in the northern and eastern parts of the Carolingian world. Water was also drunk as a beverage, but much care had to be taken to obtain pure sources from wells or clear streams. Monasteries were particularly active in going to the sources of water and building conduits to bring it to the cloister or kitchen fountains.

Medical practice in Carolingian times stressed the use of medicinal herbs and bleeding. Although the latter was practiced regularly, moderation was frequently recommended. Some advised carefulness as well: "Who dares to undertake a bleeding should see to it that his hand does not tremble." Physicians were also available when people faced serious illnesses. Many were clerics, and monasteries trained their own. Monasteries kept medical manuscripts copied from ancient works and grew herbs to provide stocks of medicinal plants. Carolingian medical manuscripts contained descriptions of illnesses, recipes for medical potions, and even gynecological advice, although monks in particular expended little effort on female medical needs. Some manuals even included instructions for operations, especially for soldiers injured in battle.

Physicians of the Early Middle Ages supplemented their medicines and natural practices with appeals for other worldly help. Magical rites and influences were carried over from pagan times since Germanic tribes had used magical medicine for centuries. Physicians recommended that patients wear amulets and charms around their bodies to ward off diseases:

> Procure a little bit of the dung of a wolf, preferably some which contains small bits of bone, and pack it in a tube which the patient may easily wear as an amulet.
> For epilepsy take a nail of a wrecked ship, make it into a bracelet and set therein the bone of a stag's heart taken from its body while alive; put it on the left arm; you will be astonished at the result.[5]

But as pagans were converted to Christianity, miraculous healing through the intervention of God, Christ, or the saints soon replaced pagan practices. Medieval chronicles abound with accounts of people healed by touching a saint's body. The use of Christian prayers, written down and used as amulets, however, reminds us that for centuries Christian and pagan medical practices survived side by side.

The Disintegration of the Carolingian Empire

The Carolingian Empire began to disintegrate soon after Charlemagne's death. Charlemagne was survived by his son Louis the Pious (814–840), who was unable to control either the Frankish aristocracy or his own four sons who fought continually. In 843, after their father's death, the three surviving brothers signed the Treaty of Verdun. This agreement divided the Carolingian Empire among them into three major sections: Charles the Bald (843–877) obtained the west Frankish lands, which formed the core of the eventual kingdom of France; Louis the German (843–876) took the eastern lands, which became Germany; and Lothair (840–855) received the title of emperor and a "Middle Kingdom" extending from the North Sea to Italy, including the Netherlands, the Rhineland, and northern Italy. The territories of the Middle Kingdom became a source of incessant struggle between the other two Frankish rulers and their heirs. Indeed, France and Germany would fight over the territories of the Middle Kingdom for centuries.

Although this division of the Carolingian empire was made for political reasons (dividing a kingdom among the male heirs was a traditional Frankish custom), two different cultures began to emerge. By the ninth century, inhabitants of the west Frankish area were speaking a Romance language derived from Latin that became French. Eastern Franks spoke a Germanic dialect. The later kingdoms of France and Germany did not yet exist, however.

In the ninth century, the frequent struggles among the numerous heirs of the sons of Louis the Pious led to further disintegration of the Carolingian Empire. In the meantime, while powerful aristocrats acquired even more power in their own local territories at the expense of the squabbling Carolingian rulers, the process of disintegration was abetted by external attacks on different parts of the old Carolingian world.

Invasions of the Ninth and Tenth Centuries

In the ninth and tenth centuries, western Europe was beset by a wave of invasions of several non-Christian peoples—one old enemy, the Muslims, and two new ones, the Magyars and Vikings. The Muslims began a new series of attacks in the Mediterranean in the ninth century. They raided the southern coasts of Europe, especially Italy, occupied Sicily, destroyed the Carolingian defenses in northern Spain, and conducted forays into southern France. The Magyars were a people from western Asia who moved west into eastern and central Europe at the end of the ninth century. They established themselves on

the plains of Hungary and from there made raids into western Europe. The Magyars were finally crushed at the Battle of Lechfeld in Germany in 955. At the end of the tenth century, they were converted to Christianity and settled down to establish the Kingdom of Hungary.

THE VIKINGS

By far, the most devastating and far-reaching attacks of the time came from the Northmen or Norsemen of Scandinavia, also known to us as the Vikings. The Vikings were a Germanic people based in Scandinavia. Why they invaded other areas of Europe is uncertain. Perhaps overpopulation and the emergence of more effective monarchs in Denmark, Norway, and Sweden caused some of the freedom-loving Scandinavians to seek escape from the growing order. Then, too, the Vikings' great love of adventure and their search for booty and new avenues of trade may have been important factors.

Two features of Viking society help to explain what the Vikings accomplished. First of all, they were warriors. Secondly, they were superb shipbuilders and sailors. Their

Map 8.2 Invasions of the Ninth and Tenth Centuries.

✦ **The Vikings Attack England.** This illustration from an eleventh-century English manuscript depicts a group of armed Vikings invading England. Two ships have already reached the shore, and a few Vikings are shown walking down a long gangplank onto English soil.

Novgorod and Kiev and established fortified ports throughout these territories.

Early Viking raids had been carried out largely in the summer; by the mid-ninth century, however, the Northmen had begun to establish winter settlements in Europe from which they could make expeditions to conquer and settle new lands. By 850, groups of Norsemen had settled in Ireland, while the Danes occupied an area known as the Danelaw in northeast England by 878. Beginning in 911, the ruler of the western Frankish lands gave one band of Vikings land at the mouth of the Seine River, forming a section of France that ultimately became known as Normandy. This policy of settling the Vikings and converting them to Christianity was a deliberate one, since the new inhabitants served as protectors against additional Norsemen attacks.

By the tenth century, Viking expansion was drawing to a close, but not before Viking settlements had been made throughout many parts of Europe. Like the Magyars, the Vikings were also assimilated into European civilization. Once again, Christianity proved a decisive civilizing force in Western civilization in its European form. Europe and Christianity were becoming virtually synonymous.

The Viking raids and settlements also had important political repercussions. The inability of royal authorities to protect their peoples against these incursions caused local populations to turn instead to the local aristocrats who provided security for them. In the process, the landed aristocrats not only increased their strength and prestige but also assumed even more of the functions of local governments that had previously belonged to kings; over time these developments led to a new political and military order.

The Emerging World of Feudalism

The renewed invasions and the disintegration of the Carolingian world led to the emergence of a new type of relationship between free individuals. When governments ceased to be able to defend their subjects, it became important to find some powerful lord who could offer protection in exchange for service. This practice led to a new system of rule known by later generations of historians as feudalism.

At the heart of feudalism was the idea of vassalage. In Germanic society, warriors swore an oath of loyalty to their leader. They fought for their chief, and he in turn took care of their needs. By the eighth century, an individual who served a lord in a military capacity was known as a vassal.

ships were the best of the period. Long and narrow with beautifully carved arched prows, the Viking dragon ships carried about fifty men. Their shallow draft enabled them to sail up European rivers and attack places at some distance inland. Vikings sacked villages and towns, destroyed churches, and easily defeated small local armies.

Because there were different groups of Scandinavians, Viking expansion varied a great deal. Norwegian Vikings moved into Ireland and western England, while the Danes attacked eastern England, Frisia, and the Rhineland and navigated rivers to enter western Frankish lands. Swedish Vikings dominated the Baltic Sea and progressed into the Slavic areas to the east. Moving into northwest Russia, they went down the rivers of Russia to

With the breakdown of governments, powerful nobles took control of large areas of land. They needed men to fight for them, so the practice arose of giving grants of land to vassals who in return would fight for their lord. The Frankish army had originally consisted of foot soldiers, dressed in coats of mail and armed with swords. But in the eighth century, when larger horses and the stirrup were introduced, a military change began to occur. Earlier, horsemen had been throwers of spears. Now they wore armored coats of mail (the larger horse could carry the weight) and wielded long lances that enabled them to act as battering rams (the stirrups kept them on their horses). For almost 500 years, warfare in Europe was dominated by heavily armored cavalry or knights as they came to be called. The knights came to have the greatest social prestige and formed the backbone of the European aristocracy.

Of course, a horse, armor, and weapons were expensive to purchase and maintain, and learning to wield these instruments skillfully from a horse took much time and practice. Consequently, lords who wanted men to fight for them had to grant each vassal a piece of land that provided for the support of the vassal and his family. In return for the land, the vassal provided his lord with one major service, his fighting skills. Each needed the other. In the society of the Early Middle Ages, where there was little trade and wealth was based primarily on land, land became the most important gift a lord could give to a vassal in return for military service.

The relationship between lord and vassal was made official by a public ceremony. To become a vassal, a man performed an act of homage to his lord, as described in this passage from a medieval treatise on feudal practice:

> The man should put his hands together as a sign of humility, and place them between the two hands of his lord as a token that he vows everything to him and promises faith to him; and the lord should receive him and promise to keep faith with him. Then the man should say: "Sir, I enter your homage and faith and become your man by mouth and hands [i.e., by taking the oath and placing his hands between those of the lord], and I swear and promise to keep faith and loyalty to you against all others, and to guard your rights with all my strength."[6]

As in the earlier Germanic band, loyalty to one's lord was the chief virtue.

By the ninth century, the land granted to a vassal in return for military service had come to be known as a fief. In time, many vassals who held such grants of land came to exercise rights of jurisdiction or political and legal authority within their fiefs. As the Carolingian world disintegrated politically under the impact of internal dissen-

sion and invasions, an increasing number of powerful lords arose. Instead of a single government, many people were now responsible for keeping order.

Fief-holding also became increasingly complicated with the development of subinfeudation. The vassals of a king, who were themselves great lords, might also have vassals who would owe them military service in return for a grant of land from their estates. Those vassals, in turn, might likewise have vassals, who at this low level would be simple knights with barely enough land to provide their equipment. The lord–vassal relationship, then, bound together both greater and lesser landowners. At all levels, the lord–vassal relationship was always an honorable relationship between free men and did not imply any sense of servitude. Because kings could no longer provide security in the midst of the breakdown created by the invasions of the ninth century, the system of feudalism became ever more widespread.

Feudalism was basically a product of the Carolingian world, but it also spread to England, Germany, central Europe, and in some form to Italy. Feudalism came to be characterized by a set of practices—known as the feudal contract—that determined the relationship between a lord and his vassal. The major obligation of a vassal to his lord was to perform military service, usually about forty

✦ **A Knight's Equipment Showing Saddle and Stirrups.** In return for his fighting skills, a knight received a piece of land from his lord that provided for his economic support. Pictured here is a charging knight with his equipment. The introduction of the high saddle, stirrup, and larger horses allowed horsemen to wear heavier armor and to wield long lances, thereby increasing the importance of the cavalry.

days a year. A vassal was also required to appear at his lord's court when summoned to give advice to the lord. He might also be asked to sit in judgment in a legal case because the important vassals of a lord were peers and only they could judge each other. Finally, vassals were also responsible for aids, or financial payments to the lord on a number of occasions, including the knighting of the lord's eldest son, the marriage of his eldest daughter, and the ransom of the lord's person in the event he was captured.

In turn, a lord had responsibilities toward his vassals. His major obligation was to protect his vassal, either by defending him militarily or by taking his side in a court of law if necessary. The lord was also responsible for the maintenance of the vassal, usually by granting him a fief.

The Manorial System

Feudalism was closely dependent on the economic system of manorialism. The landholding class of nobles and knights comprised a military elite whose ability to function as warriors depended on having the leisure time to pursue the arts of war. Landed estates, located on the fiefs given to a vassal by his lord and worked by a dependent peasant class, provided the economic sustenance that made this way of life possible. A manor was simply an agricultural estate operated by a lord and worked by peasants. The manor became the fundamental unit of rural organization in the Middle Ages.

Manorialism grew out of the unsettled circumstances of the Early Middle Ages, when small farmers often needed protection or food in a time of bad harvests. Free peasants gave up their freedom to the lords of large landed estates in return for protection and use of the lord's land. Although a large class of free peasants continued to exist, increasing numbers of free peasants became serfs—peasants bound to the land and required to provide labor services, pay rents, and be subject to the lord's jurisdiction. By the ninth century, probably 60 percent of the population of western Europe had become serfs.

Labor services consisted of working the lord's demesne, the land retained by the lord, which might consist of one-third to one-half of the cultivated lands scattered throughout the manor. The rest would be used by the peasants for themselves. Building barns and digging ditches were also part of the labor services. Serfs usually worked about three days a week for their lord.

The serfs paid rents by giving the lord a share of every product they raised. Moreover, serfs paid the lord for the use of the manor's common pasturelands, streams, ponds, and surrounding woodlands. For example, if a serf fished in the pond or stream on a manor, he turned over part of the catch to his lord. Peasants were also obliged to pay a tithe (a tenth of their produce) to their local village church.

Lords possessed a variety of legal rights over their serfs as a result of their unfree status. Serfs were legally bound to the lord's lands and could not leave without his permission. Although free to marry, serfs could not marry anyone outside their manor without the lord's approval. Moreover, lords sometimes exercised public rights or po-

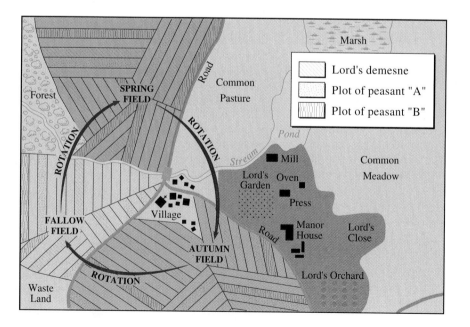

Map 8.3 A Manor.

◆ **Peasants in the Manorial System.** In the manorial system, peasants were required to provide labor services for their lord. This thirteenth-century illustration shows a group of English peasants harvesting grain. Overseeing their work is a bailiff, or manager, who supervised the work of the peasants.

litical authority on their lands, which gave them the right to try peasants in their own court. In fact, the lord's manorial court provided the only law that most peasants knew. Peasants also had to pay the lord for certain services; for example, they might be required to bring their grain to the lord's mill and pay a fee to have it ground into flour. Thus, the rights a lord possessed on his manor gave him virtual control over both the lives and property of his serfs.

In the Early Middle Ages, whether free or unfree, a vast majority of men and women, possibly as high as 90 percent, worked the land. Although trade declined precipitously in this period, it never entirely disappeared. Overall, however, compared to the Byzantine Empire or Muslim caliphates, western Europe in the Early Middle Ages was an underdeveloped, predominantly agricultural society and could not begin to match the splendor of either of the other heirs of the Roman Empire.

The Zenith of Byzantine Civilization

In the seventh and eighth centuries, the Byzantine Empire had lost much of its territory to Slavs, Bulgars, and Muslims. By 750, the empire consisted only of Asia Minor, some lands in the Balkans, and the southern coast of Italy. Although Byzantium was beset with internal dissension and invasions in the ninth century, it was able to deal with them and not only endured, but even expanded, reaching its high point in the tenth century, which some historians have called "the golden age of Byzantine civilization."

During the reign of Michael III (842–867), the Byzantine Empire continued to be plagued by problems. The Bulgars mounted new attacks, and the Arabs continued to harass the empire. Moreover, a new church problem with political repercussions erupted over differences between the pope as leader of the western Christian church and the patriarch of Constantinople as leader of the eastern (or Orthodox) Christian church. Patriarch Photius condemned the pope as a heretic for accepting a revised form of the Nicene Creed stating that the Holy Spirit proceeded from the Father and the Son instead of "The Holy Spirit, who proceeds from the Father." A council of eastern bishops followed Photius's wishes and excommunicated the pope, creating the so-called Photian schism. Although the differences were later papered over, this controversy served to further the division between the eastern and western Christian churches.

A Western View of the Byzantine Empire

Bishop Liudprand of Cremona undertook diplomatic missions to Constantinople on behalf of two western kings, Berengar of Italy and Otto I of Germany. This selection is taken from his description of his mission to the Byzantine emperor Constantine VII in 949 as an envoy for Berengar, king of Italy from 950 until his overthrow by Otto I of Germany in 964. Liudprand had mixed feelings about Byzantium: admiration, yet also envy and hostility because of its superior wealth.

Liudprand of Cremona, Antapodosis

Next to the imperial residence at Constantinople there is a palace of remarkable size and beauty which the Greeks called Magnavra . . . the name being equivalent to "fresh breeze." In order to receive some Spanish envoys, who had recently arrived, as well as myself . . . , Constantine gave orders that his palace should be got ready. . . .

Before the emperor's seat stood a tree, made of bronze gilded over, whose branches were filled with birds, also made of gilded bronze, which uttered different cries, each according to its varying species. The throne itself was so marvelously fashioned that at one moment it seemed a low structure, and at another it rose high into the air. It was of immense size and was guarded by lions, made either of bronze or of wood covered over with gold, who beat the ground with their tails and gave a dreadful roar with open mouth and quivering tongue. Leaning upon the shoulders of two eunuchs I was brought into the emperor's presence. At my approach the lions began to roar and the birds to cry out, each according to its kind; but I was neither terrified nor surprised, for I had previously made enquiry about all these things from people who were well acquainted with them. So after I had three times made obeisance to the emperor with my face upon the ground, I lifted my head, and behold! The man whom just before I had seen sitting on a moderately elevated seat had now changed his raiment and was sitting on the level of the ceiling. How it was done I could not imagine, unless perhaps he was lifted up by some such sort of device as we use for raising the timbers of a wine press. On that occasion he did not address me personally . . . but by the intermediary of a secretary he inquired about Berengar's doings and asked after his health. I made a fitting reply and then, at a nod from the interpreter, left his presence and retired to my lodging.

It would give me some pleasure also to record here what I did then for Berengar. . . . The Spanish envoys . . . had brought handsome gifts from their masters to the emperor Constantine. I for my part had brought nothing from Berengar except a letter and that was full of lies. I was very greatly disturbed and shamed at this and began to consider anxiously what I had better do. In my doubt and perplexity it finally occurred to me that I might offer the gifts, which on my account I had brought for the emperor, as coming from Berengar, and trick out my humble present with fine words. I therefore presented him with nine excellent curaisses, seven excellent shields with gilded bosses, two silver gift cauldrons, some swords, spears and spits, and what was more precious to the emperor than anything, four carzimasia; that being the Greek name for young eunuchs who have had both their testicles and their penis removed. This operation is performed by traders at Verdun, who take the boys into Spain and make a huge profit.

The problems that arose during Michael's reign were effectively dealt with by the efforts of a new dynasty of Byzantine emperors, known as the Macedonians (867–1081). In general, this dynastic line managed to repel the external enemies, go over to the offensive, and reestablish domestic order. Supported by the church, the emperors continued to think of the Byzantine Empire as a continuation of the Christian Roman Empire of late antiquity. Although for diplomatic reasons they occasionally recognized the imperial title of western emperors, such as Charlemagne, they still regarded them as little more than barbarian parvenus.

The Macedonian emperors could boast of a remarkable number of achievements in the late ninth and tenth centuries. They worked to strengthen the position of free farmers, who felt threatened by the attempts of landed aristocrats to expand their estates at the expense of the farmers. The emperors were well aware that the free farmers made up the rank and file of the Byzantine cavalry and provided the military strength of the empire. The Macedonian emperors also fostered a burst of economic prosperity by expanding trade relations with western Europe, especially by selling silks and metalworks. Thanks to this prosperity, the city of Constantinople flourished. Foreign visitors continued to be astounded by its size, wealth, and physical surroundings. To western Europeans, it was the stuff of legends and fables (see the box on p. 168).

In the midst of this prosperity, Byzantine cultural influence expanded due to the active missionary efforts of eastern Byzantine Christians. Eastern Orthodox Christianity was spread to eastern European peoples, such as the Bulgars and Serbs. Perhaps the greatest missionary success occurred when the prince of Kiev in Russia converted to Christianity in 987 (see "The Slavic Peoples of Central and Eastern Europe," the next section).

Under the Macedonian rulers, Byzantium enjoyed a strong civil service, talented emperors, and military advances. In the tenth century, these competent emperors combined with a number of talented generals to mobilize the empire's military resources and take the offensive. The Bulgars were defeated, and both the eastern and western parts of Bulgaria were annexed to the empire. The Byzantines went on to add the islands of Crete and Cyprus to the empire and defeat the Muslim forces in Syria, expanding the empire to the upper Euphrates. By the end of the reign of Basil II (976–1025), the Byzantine Empire was the largest it had been since the beginning of the seventh century.

The Slavic Peoples of Central and Eastern Europe

North of Byzantium and east of the Carolingian Empire lay a spacious plain through which a number of Asiatic nomads, such as the Huns, Bulgars, Avars, and Magyars, had pushed their way westward, terrorizing and plundering the settled peasant communities. Eastern Europe was ravaged by these successive waves of invaders who found it relatively easy to create large empires that, in turn, were overthrown by the next invaders. Over a period of time, the invaders themselves were largely assimilated with the native Slavic peoples of the area.

The Slavic peoples were originally a single people in central Europe who, through mass migrations and nomadic invaders, were gradually divided into three major groups: the western, southern, and eastern Slavs. In the region east of the eastern Frankish or Germanic kingdom emerged the Polish and Bohemian kingdoms of the western Slavs. The Germans assumed responsibility for the conversion of these Slavic peoples since some German emperors considered it their duty to spread Christianity to the barbarians. Of course, it also gave them the opportunity to

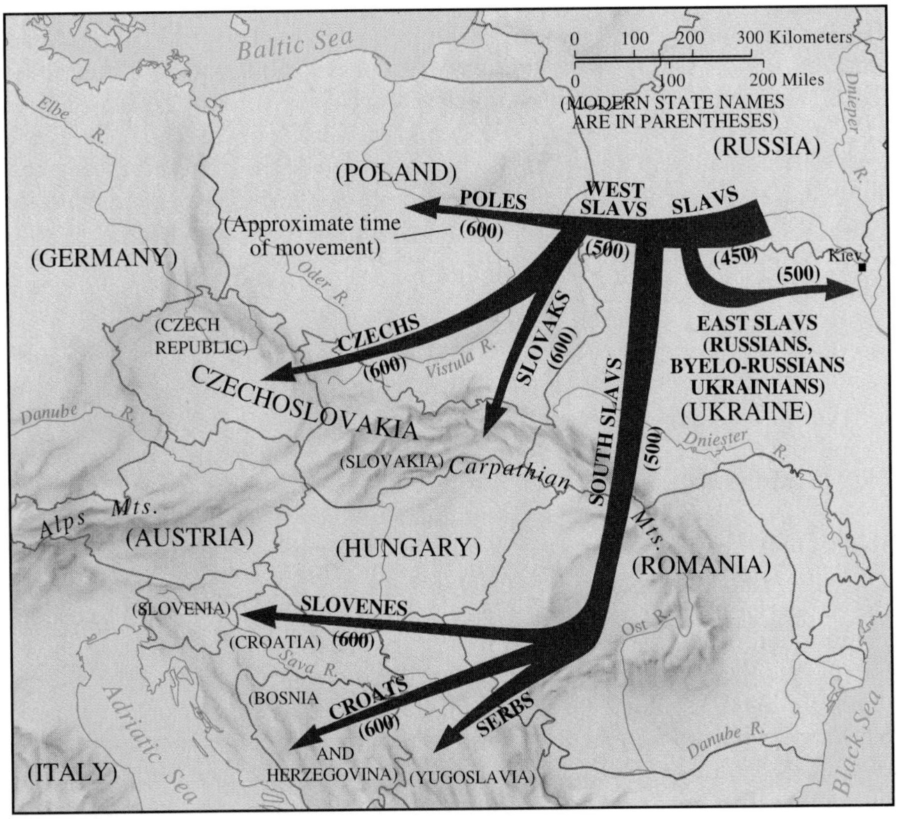

Map 8.4 The World of the Slavs.

extend their political authority as well. German missionaries had converted the Czechs in Bohemia by the end of the ninth century, and a bishopric eventually occupied by a Czech bishop was established at Prague in the tenth century. The Slavs in Poland were not converted until the reign of Prince Mieszko (c. 960–992). In 1000, an independent Polish archbishopric was set up at Gniezno by the pope. The non-Slavic kingdom of Hungary, which emerged after the Magyars settled down after their defeat at Lechfeld in 955, was also converted to Christianity by German missionaries. Saint Stephen, king of Hungary from 997 to 1038, facilitated the acceptance of Christianity by his people. The Poles, Czechs, and Hungarians all accepted Catholic or western Christianity and became closely tied to the Roman Catholic church and its Latin culture.

The southern and eastern Slavic populations largely took a different path because of their proximity to the Byzantine Empire. The Slavic peoples of Moravia were converted to the Eastern Orthodox Christianity of the Byzantine Empire by two Byzantine missionary brothers, Cyril and Methodius, who began their activities in 863. They created a Slavonic (Cyrillic) alphabet, translated the Bible into Slavonic, and created Slavonic church services. While the southern Slavic peoples accepted Christianity, a split eventually developed between the Croats who accepted the Roman church and the Serbs who remained loyal to eastern Christianity.

Although the Bulgars were originally an Asiatic people who conquered much of the Balkan peninsula, they were eventually absorbed by the larger native south Slavic population. Together, by the ninth century, they formed a largely Slavic Bulgarian kingdom. Although the conversion to Christianity of this state was complicated by the rivalry between the Roman Catholic and Eastern Orthodox churches, the Bulgarians eventually accepted the latter. By the end of the ninth century, they embraced the Slavonic church services earlier developed by Cyril and Methodius. The acceptance of Eastern Orthodoxy by the southern Slavic peoples, the Serbs and Bulgarians, meant that their cultural life was also linked to the Byzantine state.

The eastern Slavic peoples, from whom the modern Russians, White (or Byelo-) Russians, and Ukrainians are descended, had settled in the territory of present-day Ukraine and European Russia. There, beginning in the late eighth century, they began to encounter Viking invaders. Swedish Vikings, known to the eastern Slavs as Varangians, moved down the extensive network of rivers into the lands of the eastern Slavs in search of booty and new trade routes. After establishing trading links with the Byzantine state, the Varangians built trading settlements, became involved in the civil wars among the Slavic peoples, and eventually came to dominate the native peoples, just as their fellow Vikings were doing in parts of western Europe. According to the traditional version of the story, the semilegendary Rurik secured his ruling dynasty in the Slavic settlement of Novgorod in 862. Rurik and his fellow Vikings were called "the Rus," from which the name Russia is derived; eventually, that name became attached to the state they founded (see the box on p. 171). Although much about Rurik is unclear, it is certain that his follower Oleg (c. 873–913) took up residence in Kiev and created the Rus state or union of east Slavic territories known as the Principality of Kiev. Oleg's successors extended their control over the eastern Slavs and expanded the territory of Kiev until it encompassed the lands between the Baltic and Black Seas and the Danube and Volga Rivers. By marrying Slavic wives, the Viking ruling class was gradually assimilated into the Slavic population, a process confirmed by their assumption of Slavic names.

The growth of the principality of Kiev attracted religious missionaries, especially from the Byzantine Empire. One Rus ruler, Vladimir (c. 980–1015), married the Byzantine emperor's sister and officially accepted Christianity for himself and his people in 987. His primary motive was probably not a spiritual one. By all accounts, Vladimir was a cruel and vicious man who believed an established church would be helpful in the development of an organized state. From the end of the tenth century on, Byzantine Christianity became the model for Russian religious life, just as Byzantine imperial ideals came to influence the outward forms of Russian political life.

The World of Islam

The Umayyad dynasty of caliphs had established Damascus as the center of an Islamic empire created by Arab expansion in the seventh and eighth centuries. But Umayyad rule created resentment, and the Umayyads also helped bring about their own end by their corrupt behavior. One caliph, for example, supposedly swam in a pool of wine and drank enough of it to lower the wine level considerably. Finally, in 750, Abu al-Abbas, a descendant of the uncle of Muhammad, brought an end to the Umayyad dynasty and established the Abbasid dynasty, which lasted until 1258.

The Abbasid rulers brought much change to the world of Islam. They tried to break down the distinctions between Arab and non-Arab Muslims. All Muslims, regard-

⚜ A Muslim's Description of the Rus ⚜

Despite the difficulties that travel presented, early medieval civilization did witness some contact among the various cultures. This might occur through trade, diplomacy, or the conquest and migration of peoples. This document is a description of the Swedish Rus who eventually merged with the native Slavic peoples to form the Principality of Kiev, commonly regarded as the first Russian state. This account was written by Ibn Fadlan, a Muslim diplomat sent from Baghdad in 921 to a settlement on the Volga River. His comments on the filthiness of the Rus reflect the Muslim preoccupation with cleanliness.

Ibn Fadlan, Description of the Rus

I saw the Rus folk when they arrived on their trading-mission and settled at the river Atul (Volga). Never had I seen people of more perfect physique. They are tall as date-palms, and reddish in color. They wear neither coat not kaftan, but each man carried a cape which covers one half of his body, leaving one hand free. No one is ever parted from his axe, sword, and knife. Their swords are Frankish in design, broad, flat, and fluted. Each man has a number of trees, figures, and the like from the fingernails to the neck. Each woman carried on her bosom a container made of iron, silver, copper or gold—its size and substance depending on her man's wealth. . . .

The [the Rus] are the filthiest of God's creatures. They do not wash after discharging their natural functions, neither do they wash their hands after meals. They are as lousy as donkeys. They arrive from their distant river, and there they build big houses on its shores. Ten or twenty of them may live together in one house, and each of them has a couch of his own where he sits and diverts himself with the pretty slave girls whom he had brought along for sale. He will make love with one of them while a comrade looks on; sometimes they indulge in a communal orgy, and, if a customer should turn up to buy a girl, the Rus man will not let her go till he has finished with her.

They wash their hands and faces every day in incredibly filthy water. Every morning the girl brings her master a large bowl of water in which he washes his hands and face and hair, then blows his nose into it and spits into it. When he has finished the girl takes the bowl to his neighbor—who repeats the performance. Thus the bowl goes the rounds of the entire household. . . .

If one of the Rus folk falls sick they put him in a tent by himself and leave bread and water for him. They do not visit him, however, or speak to him, especially if he is a serf. Should he recover he rejoins the others; if he dies they burn him. But if he happens to be a serf they leave him for the dogs and vultures to devour. If they catch a robber they hang him to a tree until he is torn to threads by wind and weather. . . .

less of their ethnic background, could now hold both civil and military offices. This helped to open Islamic life to the influences of the civilizations they had conquered. Many Arabs now began to intermarry with the peoples they had conquered.

In 762, the Abbasids built a new capital city, Baghdad, on the Tigris River far to the east of Damascus. The new capital was well placed. It took advantage of river traffic to the Persian Gulf, and at the same time was located on the caravan route from the Mediterranean to Central Asia. The move eastward allowed Persian influence to come to the fore, encouraging a new cultural orientation. Under the Abbasids, judges, merchants, and government officials, rather than warriors, were viewed as the ideal citizens.

The new Abbasid dynasty experienced a period of splendid rule well into the ninth century. Best known of the caliphs of the time was Harun al-Rashed (786–809), whose reign is often described as the golden age of the Abbasid caliphate. His son al-Ma'mun (813–833) was a great patron of learning. He founded an astronomical observatory and created a foundation for translating classical Greek works. This was also a period of growing economic prosperity. After all, the Arabs had conquered many of the richest provinces of the old Roman Empire, and they now controlled the trade routes to the east. Baghdad became the center of an enormous trade empire that extended into Europe, Asia, and Africa, greatly adding to the wealth of the Islamic world.

Despite the prosperity, all was not quite well in the empire of the Abbasids. There was much fighting over the succession to the caliphate. When Harun al-Rashed died, his two sons fought to succeed him in a struggle that almost destroyed the city of Baghdad. As the tenth-century Muslim historian al-Mas'udi wrote: "Mansions were destroyed, most remarkable monuments obliterated; prices soared. . . . Brother turned his sword against brother, son against father, as some fought for Amin, others for Ma'mun. Houses and palaces fuelled the flames; property was put to the sack."[7]

Vast wealth also gave rise to financial corruption. By awarding important positions to court favorites, the Abbasid caliphs began to undermine the foundations of their own power and become figureheads. Rulers of the provinces of the empire broke away from the control of the caliphs and established their own independent dynasties. Even earlier, in the eighth century, Spain had already established its own caliphate when Abd-al-Rahman of the Umayyad dynasty had fled there. In 756, he seized control of southern Spain and then expanded his power into the center of the peninsula. He took the title of emir, or commander, and set up the emirate of al-Andalus with its center at Córdoba. Under Abd-al-Rahman's successors,

a unique society developed in which all religions were tolerated. The court also supported writers and artists, creating a brilliant and flourishing culture.

The breakup of the Islamic empire accelerated in the tenth century. A caliphate of the Fatimid family was established in Egypt in 973, and an independent dynasty also operated in North Africa. Despite the political disunity of the Islamic world, however, there was an underlying Islamic civilization based on two common bonds, the Quran and the spread of the Arabic language.

Islamic Civilization

From the beginning of their empire, Muslim Arabs had demonstrated a willingness to absorb the culture of their conquered territories. The Arabs were truly heirs to the remaining Greco-Roman culture of the Roman Empire. Just as readily, they assimilated Byzantine and Persian culture. In the eighth and ninth centuries, numerous Greek, Syrian, and Persian scientific and philosophical works were translated into Arabic. As the chief language in the southern Mediterranean and the Near East and the required language of Muslims, Arabic became a truly international tongue.

The Muslims created a brilliant urban culture at a time when western Europe was predominantly a rural world of petty villages. This can be seen in such new cities as Baghdad and Cairo, but also in Córdoba, the capital of the Umayyad caliphate in Spain. With a population of possibly 100,000, Córdoba was Europe's largest city after Constantinople. Its library was also the largest in Europe.

During the first few centuries of the Arab empire, it was the Islamic world that saved and spread the scientific and philosophical works of ancient civilizations. At a time when the ancient Greek philosophers were largely unknown in Europe, key works by Plato and Aristotle were translated into Arabic. They were put in a library called the "House of Wisdom" in Baghdad where they were read and studied by Muslim scholars. Texts on mathematics were brought from India. This process was aided by the use of paper. The making of paper was introduced from China in the eighth century, and by the end of the century, paper factories had been established in Baghdad. Book sellers and libraries soon followed. European universities later benefited from this scholarship when these works were translated from Arabic into Latin.

Although Islamic scholars are rightly praised for preserving much of classical knowledge for the west, they also made considerable advances of their own. Nowhere is this more evident than in their contributions to mathematics and the natural sciences. The list of Muslim achievements in mathematics and astronomy alone is impressive. They adopted and passed on the numerical system of India, including the use of the zero. In Europe, it became known as the "Arabic" system. A ninth-century Iranian mathematician created the mathematical discipline of algebra. In astronomy, Muslims set up an observatory at Baghdad to study the position of the stars. They were aware that the earth was round and named many stars. They also perfected the astrolabe, an instrument used by sailors to determine their location by observing the positions of heavenly bodies. It was the astrolabe that made it possible for Europeans to sail to the Americas.

Muslims scholars also made many new discoveries in chemistry and developed medicine as a field of scientific study. Especially well known was Ibn Sina (Avicenna to the west, 980–1037) who authored a medical encyclopedia that, among other things, stressed the contagious nature of certain diseases and showed how they could be spread by contaminated water supplies. After its translation into Latin, Avicenna's work became a basic medical textbook for medieval European university students. Avicenna was but one of many Arabic scholars whose work was translated into Latin and helped the development of intellectual life in Europe in the twelfth and thirteenth centuries.

✦ **Mosque at Córdoba.** The first Great Mosque of Córdoba was built by Abd-al-Rahman, founder of the Umayyad dynasty of Spain, in the eighth century. The mosque was later enlarged in the tenth century. Shown here is the interior of the sanctuary with its two levels of arches. Although the Umayyad caliphs of Damascus were overthrown and replaced by the Abbasid dynasty in the eighth century, the independent Umayyad dynasty in Spain lasted until the eleventh century.

Conclusion

After the turmoil of the disintegration of the Roman Empire and the establishment of the Germanic states, a new European civilization began to emerge slowly in the Early Middle Ages. The coronation of Charlemagne, descendent of a Germanic tribe converted to Christianity, as Roman emperor in 800 symbolized the fusion of the three chief components of the new European civilization: the German tribes, the classical tradition, and Christianity. In the long run, the creation of a western empire fostered the idea of a distinct European identity and marked the shift of power from the south to north. Italy and the Mediterranean had been the center of the Roman Empire. The lands north of the Alps now became the political center of Europe.

With the disintegration of the Carolingian Empire, new forms of political institutions began to develop in Europe. These were characterized by a decentralization of political power, in which lords exercised legal, administrative, and military power. The practice of feudalism transferred public power into many private hands and seemed to provide the security sorely lacking in a time of weak central government and new invasions by Muslims, Magyars, and Vikings. While Europe struggled, the Byzantine and Islamic worlds continued to prosper and flourish, the brilliance of their urban cultures standing in marked contrast to the underdeveloped rural world of Europe. By 1000, however, that rural world had not only recovered, but was beginning to expand in ways undreamed of by previous generations. Europe stood poised for a giant leap.

NOTES

1. Einhard, *The Life of Charlemagne*, trans. Samuel Turner (Ann Arbor, Mich., 1960), 30.
2. Ibid., p. 57.
3. Quoted in Pierre Riché, *Daily Life in the World of Charlemagne*, trans. Jo Ann McNamara (Philadelphia, 1978), p. 56.
4. 1 Corinthians 7: 1–2, 8–9.
5. Quoted in Brian Inglis, *A History of Medicine* (New York, 1965), p. 51.
6. Quoted in Oliver Thatcher and Edgar McNeal, eds., *A Source Book for Medieval History* (New York, 1905), p. 363.
7. Mas'udi, *The Meadows of Gold: The Abbasids*, ed. Paul Lunde and Caroline Stone (London, 1989), p. 151.

SUGGESTIONS FOR FURTHER READING

Surveys of Carolingian Europe include H. Fichtenau, *The Carolingian Empire* (Oxford 1957); P. Riché, *The Carolingians, A Family who Forged Europe* (Philadelphia, 1993); J. Boussard, *The Civilization of Charlemagne*, trans. F. Partridge (New York, 1971); and R. McKitterick, *The Frankish Kingdoms under the Carolingians, 751–987* (London, 1983). On Charlemagne, see H. R. Loyn and J. Percival, *The Reign of Charlemagne* (New York, 1976); the popular biography by R. Winston, *Charlemagne: From the Hammer to the Cross* (Indianapolis, 1954); and R. Folz, *The Coronation of Charlemagne: 25 December 800* (London, 1974). Carolingian political institutions are examined in F. L. Ganshof, *Frankish Institutions under Charlemagne* (Providence, R.I., 1968). On Carolingian culture see M. L. W. Laistner, *Thought and Letters in Western Europe, 500–900*, rev. ed. (London, 1957).

Various aspects of social life in the Carolingian world are examined in P. Riché, *Daily Life in the World of Charlemagne*, trans. J. A. McNamara (Philadelphia, 1978); M. Rouche, "The Early Middle Ages in the West," in P. Veyne, ed., *A History of Private Life* (Cambridge, Mass., 1987), 1: 411–549; C. C. Bouchard, *Life and Society in the West: Antiquity and the Middle Ages* (San Diego, 1988), Ch. 5; S. F. Wemple, *Women in Frankish Society: Marriage and the Cloister* (Philadelphia, 1981); and S. Rubin, *Medieval English Medicine* (New York, 1974). On children, see S. Shamar, *Childhood in the Middle Ages*, trans. C. Galai (London, 1992); and J. Boswell, *The Kindness of*

Strangers (New York, 1988). On the attitudes toward sexuality in the early Christian church, see the important works by P. Brown, *The Body and Society* (New York, 1988); and E. Pagels, *Adam, Eve, and the Serpent* (New York, 1988).

A good introduction to the problems of the late ninth and tenth centuries can be found in G. Barraclough, *The Crucible of Europe* (Berkeley and Los Angeles, 1976). The Vikings are examined in P. Sawyer, *Kings and Vikings* (London, 1982); F. D. Logan, *The Vikings in History*, 2d ed. (London, 1991); G. Jones, *A History of the Vikings*, rev. ed. (Oxford, 1984); and P. Sawyer, ed., *The Oxford Illustrated History of the Vikings* (New York, 1997).

Two important introductory works on feudalism are F. L. Ganshof, *Feudalism*, trans. P. Grierson (London, 1952); and the classic work by M. Bloch, *Feudal Society*, trans. L. A. Manyon (London, 1961). Military aspects of feudalism are examined in J. Beeler, *Warfare in Feudal Europe* (Ithaca, N.Y., 1954). There are good studies on early feudalism in the collection by R. F. Cheyette, ed., *Lordship and Community in Medieval Europe* (New York, 1968).

For the economic history of the Early Middle Ages, see G. Duby, *The Early Growth of the European Economy: Warriors and Peasants from the Seventh to the Twelfth Century* (Ithaca, N.Y., 1974). An important work on medieval agriculture is G. Duby, *Rural Economy and Country Life in the Medieval West*, trans. C. Postan (London, 1968). Also worthwhile is B. H. Slicher Van Bath, *The Agrarian History of Western Europe: A.D. 500–1850*, trans. O. Ordish (London, 1963).

Byzantine civilization in this period is examined in R. Jenkins, *Byzantium: The Imperial Centuries, 610–1071* (New York, 1969); and W. Treadgold, *The Byzantine Revival, 780–842* (Stanford, 1988), D. Obolensky, *The Byzantine Commonwealth* (New York, 1971) examines the impact of the Byzantine Empire on its neighbors. On the Slavic peoples of central and eastern Europe, see F. Dvornik, *The Making of Central and Eastern Europe* (London, 1949) and *The Slavs in European History and Civilization* (New Brunswick, N.J., 1962); A. P. Vlasto, *The Entry of the Slavs into Christendom* (Cambridge, 1970); and Z. Vana, *The World of the Ancient Slavs* (London, 1983). The world of Islam in this period is discussed in H. Kennedy, *The Prophet and the Age of the Caliphates: The Islamic Near East from the Sixth to the Eleventh Century* (London, 1986); J. Lassner, *The Shaping of Abbasid Rule* (Princeton, N.J. 1980); G. Wiet, *Baghdad: Metropolis of the Abbasid Caliphate*, trans. S. Feiler (Norman, Okla., 1971); and O. Grabar, *The Formation of Islamic Art* (New Haven, Conn., 1971).

The Recovery and Growth of European Society in the High Middle Ages

The new European civilization that had emerged in the ninth and tenth centuries began to come into its own in the eleventh and twelfth centuries as Europeans established new patterns that reached their zenith in the thirteenth century. The High Middle Ages (1000–1300) was a period of recovery and growth for Western civilization, characterized by a greater sense of security and a burst of energy and enthusiasm. Both the Catholic church and the feudal states recovered from the invasions and internal dissension of the Early Middle Ages. New agricultural practices that increased the food supply helped give rise to a commercial and urban revival that, accompanied by a rising population, created new dynamic elements in a formerly static society.

The recovery of the church produced a reform movement that led to exalted claims of papal authority and subsequent conflict with state authorities. At the same time, vigorous papal leadership combined with new dimensions of religious life to make the Catholic church a forceful presence in every area of life. The role of the church in the new European civilization was quite evident in the career of a man named Samson, who became abbot or head of the great English abbey of Bury St. Edmonds in 1182. According to Jocelyn of Brakeland, a monk who assisted him, Abbot Samson was a devout man who wore "undergarments of horsehair and a horsehair shirt." He loved virtue and "abhorred liars, drunkards and talkative folk." His primary concern was the spiritual well-being of his monastery, but he spent much of his time working on problems in the world beyond the abbey walls. Because the monastery had fallen into debt under his predecessors, Abbot Samson toiled tirelessly to recoup the abbey's fortunes by carefully supervising its manors. He also rounded up murderers to stand trial in St. Edmunds and provided knights for the king's army. But his actions were not always tolerant or beneficial. He was instrumental in driving the Jews from the town of St. Edmunds and was not above improving the abbey's possessions at the expense of his neighbors: "He built up

1000	1050	1100	1150	1200	1250	1300

The Investiture Controversy

Concordat of Worms

Innocent III and papal power

Emergence of Franciscans

Election of pope by cardinals

Founding of Cistercians

Crusade against the Albigensians

Expulsion of the Jews from England

Reign of Pope Gregory VII

Development of papal curia under Pope Urban II

Emergence of Dominicans

Fourth Lateran Council

the bank of the fish-pond at Babwell so high, for the service of a new mill, that by the keeping back the water there is not a man, rich or poor, but has lost his garden and his orchards." The abbot's worldly cares weighed heavily on him, but he had little choice if his abbey were to flourish and fulfill its spiritual and secular functions. But he did have regrets; as he remarked to Jocelyn: "if he could have returned to the circumstances he had enjoyed before he became a monk, he would never have become a monk or an abbot."

People and Land in the High Middle Ages

In the Early Middle Ages, Europe was a sparsely populated landscape dotted with villages of farmers and warriors. Villages were still separated from one another by swamps, mountain ridges, and forests, which provided building and heating materials as well as game and continued to dominate the European landscape. Although European weather began to improve around 700 after a centuries-long period of wetter and colder conditions, natural disasters were still a threat. Drought or too much rain could mean bad harvests, famine, and dietary deficiencies that made people particularly susceptible to a wide range of diseases. This was a period of low life expectancy. Overall, the picture of early medieval Europe is one of a relatively small population subsisting on the basis of a limited agricultural economy and leading, in most cases, a precarious existence. In the High Middle Ages, this situation changed dramatically.

The period from 1000 to 1300 witnessed an improvement in climate as a small but nevertheless significant rise in temperature made for longer and better growing seasons. At the same time, Europe experienced a dramatic increase in population after 1000: The European population virtually doubled between 1000 and 1300, from 38 to 74 million people. As Table 9.1 indicates, the rate of growth tended to vary from region to region. This rise in population was physically evident in the growth of agricultural villages, towns, and cities and in the increase in arable land.

Why this dramatic increase in population? Obviously, fertility rates increased enough to gradually outstrip the relatively high mortality rates of medieval society, which were especially acute in infancy and the childhood years. Traditionally, historians have cited a number of factors to explain the population increase. For one, they attribute it to increased security stemming from more settled and peaceful conditions after the invasions of the Early Middle Ages had stopped. The decline of slavery may also have been a factor. As it became economically more sound to have people as tenants rather than as slaves, former slaves could then marry, have families, and increase the population. Finally, agricultural production increased dramatically after 1000. Although historians are not sure whether this increase was a cause or effect of the population increase, there is no question about its importance. Without such a significant rise in food supplies, the expansion in population could never have been sustained.

The New Agriculture

During the High Middle Ages, significant changes occurred in the way Europeans farmed. Although the

❖ **Table 9.1** *Population Estimates (in millions):*
1000 and 1340

Area	1000	1340
Mediterranean		
Greece and Balkans	5	6
Italy	5	10
Iberia	7	9
Total	17	25
Western and Central Europe		
France and Low Countries	6	19
British Isles	2	5
Germany and Scandinavia	4	11.5
Total	12	35.5
Eastern Europe		
Russia	6	8
Poland	2	3
Hungary	1.5	2
Total	9.5	13
Total	38.5	73.5

Source: J. C. Russell, *The Control of Late Ancient and Medieval Population* (Philadelphia: The American Philosophical Society, 1985) p. 36. Demographic specialists admit that these are merely estimates. Some figures, especially those for eastern Europe, could be radically revised by new research.

improvement in climate played an underlying role by producing better growing conditions, another important factor in increasing the production of food was the expansion of cultivated or arable land. This was done primarily by clearing forested areas for cultivation. Millions of acres of forests were also cut down to provide timber for fuel, houses, mills, bridges, fortresses, ships, and charcoal for the iron industry (see the box on p. 179). Eager for land, peasants cut down trees, drained swamps, and, in the area of the Netherlands, even began to reclaim land from the sea. By the thirteenth century, Europeans had available a total acreage for farming greater than any used before or since.

Technological changes also furthered the development of agriculture. The Middle Ages witnessed an explosion of labor-saving devices, many of which depended on the use of iron, which was mined in various areas of Europe and traded to places where it was not found. Iron was in demand to make swords and armor as well as scythes, axeheads, new types of farming implements, such as hoes, and saws, hammers, and nails for building purposes. It was crucial to the development of the heavy-wheeled plow, the *carruca*, which had an enormous impact on medieval agriculture north of the Alps.

The plow of the Mediterranean and Near Eastern worlds had been the *aratum*, a nonwheeled light scratch plow made mostly of wood that was sufficient to break the top layer of the light soils of those areas. It could be pulled by a donkey or single animal. But such a light plow was totally ineffective in the heavy clay soils north of the Alps. The *carruca*, a new heavy-wheeled plow with an iron ploughshare, came into widespread use by the tenth century. It could turn over heavy soils and allow for their drainage. Because of its weight, six or eight oxen were needed to pull it. Oxen were slow, however, and two new inventions for the horse made greater productivity possible. A new horse collar appeared in the tenth century

◆ **The Heavy-Wheeled Plow.** The heavy-wheeled plow was an important invention that enabled peasants to turn over the heavy clay soil of northern Europe. This sixteenth-century illumination shows the heavy-wheeled plow pulled by draft horses with collars.

➤ The Elimination of Medieval Forests ⫷

One of the interesting environmental changes of the Middle Ages was the elimination of millions of acres of forest to create new areas of arable land and to meet the demand for timber, the chief raw material of the High Middle Ages. Timber was used as fuel and to build houses, mills of all kinds, bridges, fortresses, and ships. Incredible quantities of wood were burned to make charcoal for the iron forges. The clearing of the forests not only resulted in environmental damage but caused the price of wood to skyrocket by the thirteenth century. This document from 1140 illustrates the process. Suger, the abbot of Saint-Denis, needed thirty-five-foot beams for the construction of a new church. His master carpenters told him that there were no longer any trees big enough in the area around Paris and he would have to go far afield to find such tall trees. This selection recounts his efforts.

Suger's Search for Wooden Beams

On a certain night, when I had returned from celebrating Matins, I began to think in bed that I myself should go through all the forests of these parts. . . . Quickly disposing of all duties and hurrying up in the early morning, we hastened with our carpenters, and with the measurements of the beams, to the forest called Iveline. When we traversed our possession in the Valley of Chevreuse we summoned . . . the keepers of our own forests as well as men who know about the other woods, and questioned them under oath whether we would find there, no matter with how much trouble, any timbers of that measure. At this they smiled, or rather would have laughed at us if they had dared; they wondered whether we were quite ignorant of the fact that nothing of the kind could be found in the entire region, especially since Milon, the Castellan of Chevreuse . . . had left nothing unimpaired or untouched that could be used for palisades and bulwarks while he was long subjected to wars both by our Lord the King and Amaury de Montfort. We however—scorning whatever they might say—began, with the courage of our faith as it were, to search through the woods; and toward the first hour we found one timber adequate to the measure. Why say more? By the ninth hour or sooner, we had, through the thickets, the depths of the forest and the dense, thorny tangles, marked down twelve timbers (for so many were necessary) to the astonishment of all. . . .

---

that distributed the weight around the shoulders and chest rather than the throat and could be used to hitch up a series of horses, enabling them to pull the new heavy plow faster and cultivate more land. The use of the horseshoe, an iron shoe nailed to the horses's hooves, produced greater traction and better protection against the rocky and heavy clay soil of northern Europe.

The use of the heavy-wheeled plow also led to cooperative agricultural villages. Because iron was expensive, a heavy-wheeled plow had to be purchased by the entire community. Likewise, an individual family could not afford a team of animals so villagers shared their beasts. Moreover, the size and weight of the plow determined that land would be cultivated in long strips to minimize the amount of turning that would have to be done.

Besides using horsepower, the High Middle Ages harnessed the power of water and wind to do jobs formerly done by human or animal power. Although the watermill had been invented as early as the second century B.C., its use did not become widespread until the High Middle Ages. Located along streams, watermills were used to grind grains and produce flour. Even dams were constructed to increase waterpower. The development of the cam en-

abled millwrights to mechanize entire industries; waterpower was used in certain phases of cloth production and to power trip-hammers for the working of metals.

Where rivers were unavailable or not easily dammed, Europeans developed windmills to yoke the power of the wind. By the end of the twelfth century, they were beginning to dot the European landscape. The watermill and windmill were the most important devices for the harnessing of power before the invention of the steam engine in the eighteenth century; their spread had the revolutionary consequence of enabling Europeans to produce more food.

The shift from a two-field to a three-field system also contributed to the increase in agricultural production. In the Early Middle Ages, it was common to plant one field while allowing another of equal size to lie fallow to regain its fertility. Now estates were divided into three parts. One field was planted in the fall with winter grains, such as rye and wheat, while spring grains, such as oats and barley, and vegetables, such as peas, beans, or lentils, were planted in the second field. The third was allowed to lie fallow. By rotating their use, only one-third rather than one-half of the land lay fallow at any time. The rotation of crops also prevented the soil from being exhausted so quickly. Grain yields increased to heights that would not be exceeded until the agricultural revolution of the eighteenth century. The three-field system was not adopted everywhere, however. It was not used in Mediterranean lands, and even in northern Europe, two-field systems existed side by side with three-field systems for centuries.

By the thirteenth century, the growing demand for agricultural produce in the towns and cities led to higher food prices. This led lords to try to grow more food for profit. One way to do so was to lease their demesne land

♦ **Peasant Activities.** The life of the European peasant was largely determined by the seasons of the year. The peasants' primary function was labor, and the kind of work they did was determined by the month and the season. In the foreground of this illustration, a herd of sheep is being led out to pasture past a woman milking a cow. Another woman is churning butter in the background.

to their serfs. Labor services were then transformed into money payments or fixed rents, thereby converting many unfree serfs into free peasants. Although many peasants still remained economically dependent on their lords, they were no longer legally tied to the land. Lords, in turn, became collectors of rents, rather than operators of a manor with both political and legal privileges. The political and legal powers formally exercised by lords were increasingly reclaimed by the monarchical states.

Daily Life of the Peasantry

Peasant activities were largely determined by the seasons of the year. Each season brought a new round of tasks appropriate for the time, although some periods were considerably more hectic than others, especially August and September. The basic staple of the peasant diet was bread, so an adequate harvest of grains was crucial to survival in the winter months. A new cycle began in October when peasants prepared the ground for the planting of winter crops. In November came the slaughter of excess livestock because there was usually insufficient fodder to keep animals all winter. The meat would be salted to preserve it for winter use. In February and March, the land was plowed for spring crops. Early summer was a comparatively relaxed time, although there was still weeding and sheepshearing to be done. In every season, the serfs worked not only their own land, but also the lord's demesne. They also tended the small gardens attached to their dwellings where they grew the vegetables that made up part of their diet.

But peasants did not face a life of constant labor thanks to the feast days or holidays of the Catholic church, which commemorated the great events of the Christian faith or the lives of Christian saints or holy persons. The three great feasts of the Catholic church were Christmas (celebrating the birth of Christ), Easter (celebrating the resurrection of Christ), and Pentecost (celebrating the descent of the Holy Spirit on Christ's disciples fifty days after his resurrection). Numerous other feasts dedicated to saints or the Virgin Mary, the mother of Christ, were also celebrated, making a total of more than fifty days that were essentially holidays.

Religious feast days, Sunday mass, baptisms, marriages, and funerals all brought peasants into contact with the village church, a crucial part of manorial life. In the village church, the peasant was baptized as an infant, confirmed in his or her faith, sometimes married, and given the sacrament of Holy Communion as well as the last rites of the church before death. The village priest instructed the peasants in the basic elements of Christianity so that they would gain the Christian's ultimate goal—

salvation. But village priests were often barely literate peasants themselves, and it is hard to know how much church doctrine the peasants actually understood. Very likely, they regarded God as an all-powerful force who needed to be appeased by prayer to bring good harvests.

The lifestyle of the peasants was quite simple. Their cottages had wood frames surrounded by sticks with the space between them filled with straw and rubble and then plastered over with clay. Roofs were simply thatched. By the thirteenth century, richer peasants began building their houses out of stone. The houses of poorer peasants consisted of a single room, but others had at least two rooms—a main room for cooking, eating, and other activities and another room for sleeping. There was little privacy in a medieval peasant household. A hearth in the main room was used for heating and cooking, but because there were few or no windows and no chimney, the smoke created by fires in the hearth went out through cracks in the walls or more likely the thatched roof.

Peasant women occupied both an important and a difficult position in manorial society. They were expected to carry and bear their children and at the same time fulfill their obligation to labor in the fields. Their ability to manage the household might determine whether a peasant family would starve or survive in difficult times.

Though simple, a peasant's daily diet was potentially nutritious when food was available. The basic staple of the peasant diet, and the medieval diet in general, was bread. Although individual women made the dough for the bread, the loaves were usually baked in community ovens, which were a monopoly of the lord of the manor. Peasant bread was highly nutritious because it contained not only wheat and rye, but also barley, millet, and oats, giving it its dark appearance and very heavy, hard texture. Bread was supplemented by numerous vegetables from the household gardens, cheese from cow's or goat's milk, nuts and berries from woodlands, and fruits, such as apples, pears, and cherries. Chickens provided eggs and sometimes meat. Peasants usually ate meat only on the great feast days, such as Christmas, Easter, and Pentecost.

Grains were important not only for bread, but also for making ale. In northern European countries, ale was the most common drink of the poor. If records are accurate, enormous quantities of ale were consumed. A monastery in the twelfth century records a daily allotment to the monks of three gallons a day, far above the weekend consumption of many present-day college students. Peasants in the field undoubtedly consumed even more. This high consumption of alcohol might help to explain the large number of accidental deaths recorded in medieval court records.

The Recovery and Reform of the Catholic Church

In the Early Middle Ages, the Catholic church had played a leading role in converting and civilizing first the Germanic invaders and later the Vikings and Magyars. Although highly successful, this had not been accomplished without challenges that undermined the spiritual life of the church itself.

The Problems of Decline

Since the fourth century, the popes of the Catholic church had operated on the basis of their supremacy over the affairs of the church. The popes had also come to exercise more control over the territories in central Italy that came to be known as the Papal States. From the eighth through the tenth century, the papacy was faced with serious problems resulting from Italy's political fragmentation. Byzantine possessions, threats from the Muslims, and the attempts of German emperors to rule northern and central Italy menaced the papacy's own interests in the Papal States and kept popes involved in political matters, often at the expense of their spiritual obligations.

The monastic ideal had also suffered during the Early Middle Ages. Benedictine monasteries had sometimes been exemplary centers of Christian living and learning, but the invasions of Vikings, Magyars, and Muslims wreaked havoc with many monastic establishments. Discipline declined, as did the monastic reputation for learning and holiness. At the same time, a growing number of monasteries fell under the control of local lords, as did much of the church.

The domination of laypeople over the clergy was perhaps inevitable given the chaotic conditions of the Early Middle Ages. The church became increasingly entangled in the evolving feudal system. High officials of the church, such as bishops and abbots, came to hold their offices as fiefs from nobles. As vassals, they were obliged to carry out the usual duties, including military service. For some, this meant taking up arms, even though a prelate of the church was forbidden to kill; for others, it involved providing a contingent of knights to fight for the lord. Of course, lords assumed the right to choose their own vassals, even when those vassals included bishops and abbots. Because lords often selected their vassals from other noble families for political reasons, these bishops and abbots were often worldly figures who cared little about their spiritual responsibilities.

It should come as no surprise then that the standards of clerical behavior declined precipitously. Two problems were especially troublesome: clerical marriage and simony. From early on, the Catholic church had encouraged celibacy as the norms for its clergy. In the Early Middle Ages, however, this policy had become virtually impossible to enforce and was largely ignored. Simony, the sale of church offices, was a logical outcome of a system that had come to view church offices as secular positions and important sources of revenue. Both simony and clerical marriage were increasingly singled out as symbols of the church's decline. A number of people believed that the time had come to change this situation.

The Cluniac Reform Movement

Reform of the Catholic church began in Burgundy in eastern France in 910 when Duke William of Aquitaine founded the abbey of Cluny. The monastery began with a renewed dedication to the highest spiritual ideals of the Benedictine rule and was fortunate in possessing a series of abbots in the tenth century who maintained these ideals. Cluny was deliberately kept independent from any secular control. As Duke William stipulated in his original charter: "It has pleased us also to insert in this document that, from this day, those same monks there congregated shall be subject neither to our yoke, nor to that of our relatives, nor to the sway of the royal might, nor to that of any earthly power."[1] Finally, the new monastery at Cluny tried to eliminate some of the abuses that had crept into religious communities by stressing the need for work, replacing manual labor with the copying of manuscripts, and demanding more community worship and less private prayer.

The Cluniac reform movement sparked an enthusiastic response, first in France and eventually in all of western and central Europe. New monasteries were founded based on Cluniac ideals, and previously existing monasteries rededicated themselves by adopting the Cluniac program. The movement also began to reach beyond monasticism and into the papacy itself, which was in dire need of help.

The Reform of the Papacy

By the eleventh century, a movement for change, led by a series of reforming popes, was sweeping through the Catholic church. One of the reformers' primary goals was to free the church from the interference of lords in the appointment of church officials. This issue of lay investiture, or the practice by which secular rulers both chose and invested their nominees to church offices with the symbols of their office, was dramatically taken up by the greatest of the reform popes of the eleventh century, Gregory VII (1073–1085).

Elected pope in 1073, Gregory was absolutely certain that he had been chosen by God to reform the church. In pursuit of those aims, Gregory claimed that he—the pope—was truly God's "vicar on earth," and that the pope's authority extended over all of Christendom, including rulers. Gregory sought nothing less than the elimination of lay investiture. Only in this way could the church regain its freedom, by which Gregory meant the right of the church to appoint clergy and run its own affairs. If rulers did not accept these "divine" commands, then they could be deposed by the pope acting in his capacity as the vicar of Christ. Gregory VII soon found himself in conflict with the king of Germany over these claims. (The king of Germany was also the emperor-designate since it had been accepted by this time that only kings of Germany could be emperors, but they did not officially use the title "emperor" until they were crowned by the pope.)

King Henry IV (1056–1106) of Germany was just as determined as the pope. For many years, German kings had appointed high-ranking clerics, especially bishops, as their vassals in order to use them as administrators. Without them, the king could not hope to maintain his own power vis-à-vis the powerful German nobles. In 1075, Pope Gregory issued a decree forbidding important clerics from receiving their investiture from lay leaders: "We decree that no one of the clergy shall receive the investiture with a bishopric or abbey or church from the hand of an emperor or king or of any lay person, . . ."[2] Henry had no intention of obeying a decree that challenged the very heart of his administration.

The struggle between Henry IV and Gregory VII, which is known as the Investiture Controversy (see the box on p. 183), was one of the great conflicts between church and state in the High Middle Ages. It dragged on until 1122 when a new German king and a new pope achieved a compromise in 1122 called the Concordat of Worms. Under this agreement, a bishop in Germany was first elected by church officials. After election, the nominee paid homage to the king as his feudal lord, who in turn invested him with the symbols of temporal office. A representative of the pope then invested the new bishop with the symbols of his spiritual office.

This struggle between church and state was an important element in the history of Europe in the High Middle Ages. In the Early Middle Ages, popes had been dependent on emperors and had allowed them to exercise considerable authority over church affairs. But a set of new ideals championed by activist cardinals and popes in the eleventh century now supported the "freedom of the

⇒ The Investiture Controversy: The Encounter at Canossa ⇐

Perhaps no event in the Investiture Controversy is more dramatic than the encounter between Pope Gregory VII and King Henry IV at Canossa in January 1077. To forestall Gregory's meeting with the German prelates and nobles in Germany, Henry traveled to northern Italy and begged the pope for absolution. The pope granted it since he was bound not to refuse absolution to a penitent sinner. This description is from Gregory's own account.

The Correspondence of Pope Gregory VII: To the German Princes

Meanwhile we received certain information that the king was on the way to us. Before he entered Italy he sent us word that he would make satisfaction to God and St. Peter and offered to amend his way of life and to continue obedient to us, provided only that he should obtain from us absolution and the apostolic blessing. For a long time we delayed our reply and held long consultations, reproaching him bitterly through messengers back and forth for his outrageous conduct, until finally, of his own accord and without any show of hostility or defiance, he came with a few followers to the fortress of Canossa where we were staying. There, on three successive days, standing before the castle gate, laying aside all royal insignia, barefooted and in coarse attire, he ceased not with many tears to beseech the apostolic help and comfort until all who were present or who had heard the story were so moved by pity and compassion that they pleaded his cause with prayers and tears. All marveled at our unwonted severity, and some even cried out that we were showing, not the seriousness of apostolic authority, but rather the cruelty of a savage tyrant.

At last, overcome by his persistent show of penitence and the urgency of all present, we released him from the bonds of anathema and received him into the grace of Holy Mother Church, accepting from him the guarantees described below, confirmed by the signatures of the abbot of Cluny, of our daughters, the Countess Matilda [countess of Tuscany], and the Countess Adelaide [marchioness of Turin], and other princes, bishops and laymen who seemed to be of service to us.

church," which meant not only the freedom of the church to control its own affairs, but also extreme claims of papal authority. Not only was the pope superior to all other bishops, but popes now claimed the right to depose kings under certain circumstances. Such papal claims ensured further church–state confrontations.

Christianity and Medieval Civilization

Christianity was an integral part of the fabric of medieval European society and the consciousness of Europe. Papal directives affected the actions of kings and princes alike, and Christian teaching and practices touched the economic, social, intellectual, cultural, and daily lives of all Europeans.

Growth of the Papal Monarchy

The popes of the twelfth century did not abandon the reform ideals of Gregory VII, but they were less dogmatic and more inclined to consolidate their power and build a strong administrative system. What made the papal centralization of power possible was the maturation of a highly efficient papal curia or papal court, largely the work of Pope Urban II (1088–1099). The papal curia was divided into a number of specialized divisions, such as a chancery or writing office for documents, a papal chapel, and a treasury. The curia also functioned as a high court of law formulating canon (or church) law and serving as a court of final appeal for all cases touching the church's vast ecclesiastical court system, especially matters dealing with church property, marriages, and oaths. During the twelfth century, the church began to take an active interest in systematizing canon law, a crucial step in establishing a centralized administrative system. It is no accident that many of the popes in the twelfth and thirteenth century had backgrounds in canon law.

By the twelfth century, the Catholic church possessed a clearly organized hierarchical structure. The pope and papal curia (staffed by high church officials known as cardinals, the pope's major advisers and administrators) were at the center of the administrative structure. Below them were the bishops since all of Christendom was divided into dioceses under their direction. To be sure, archbishops were in principle more powerful than the bishops, but at this time were unable to exercise any real control over the internal affairs of the bishops' dioceses.

**The Catholic Church
in the High Middle Ages**

Duke William founds abbey of Cluny	910
Pope Gregory VII	1073–1085
Decree against lay investiture	1075
Absolutism of Henry IV at Canossa	1077
Pope Urban II	1088–1099
Founding of Cistercians	1098
Pope Innocent III	1198–1216
Crusade against Albigensians begins	1209
Fourth Lateran Council	1215

In the thirteenth century, the Catholic church reached the height of its political, intellectual, and secular power. The papal monarchy extended its sway over both ecclesiastical and temporal affairs, as was especially evident during the papacy of Pope Innocent III (1198–1216). At the beginning of his pontificate, in a letter to a Tuscan cleric, Innocent made a clear statement of his views on papal supremacy:

> As God, the creator of the universe, set two great lights in the firmament of heaven, the greater light to rule the day, and the lesser light to rule the night so He set two great dignities in the firmament of the universal church, . . . the greater to rule the day, that is, souls, and the lesser to rule the night, that is, bodies. These dignities are the papal authority and the royal power. And just as the moon gets her light from the sun, and is inferior to the sun . . . so the royal power gets the splendor of its dignity from the papal authority.[3]

Innocent's actions were those of a man who believed that he, the pope, was the supreme judge of European affairs. He forced King Philip Augustus of France to take back his wife and queen. The pope intervened in German affairs and established his candidate as emperor. He compelled King John of England to accept the papal choice for the position of archbishop of Canterbury. To achieve his political ends, Innocent did not hesitate to use the spiritual weapons at his command, especially the interdict, which forbade priests to dispense the sacraments of the church in the hope that the people, deprived of the comforts of religion, would exert pressure against their ruler. Pope Innocent's interdict was so effective that it caused King Philip Augustus to restore his wife to her rightful place as queen of France after he had tried to have the marriage annulled.

New Religious Orders and New Spiritual Ideals

In the second half of the eleventh century and the first half of the twelfth century, a wave of religious enthusiasm seized Europe. One of its manifestations was the crusades, but another was the spectacular growth of monastic institutions and the development of new monastic orders. Most important was the emergence of the Cistercian order, founded in 1098 by a group of monks dissatisfied with the lack of strict discipline at their Benedictine monastery. Cistercian monasticism spread rapidly from southern France into Italy, Spain, England, Germany, and eastern Europe. In 1115, there were 5 Cistercian houses; by 1150, there were more than 300.

The Cistercians were strict. They ate a simple diet and possessed only a single robe apiece. All decorations were eliminated from their churches and monastic buildings. More time for private prayer and manual labor was provided by shortening the number of hours spent at religious services. To escape from the world, many Cistercians established their monasteries on uninhabited lands, usually wastelands or virgin forests. Because their own manual labor was insufficient to meet the demands of these lands, the Cistercians initiated a separate monastic track for lay brothers from the peasant class. They took monastic vows and spent more of their time working in the fields and in the industries established by the monks. The Cistercians' attempt to live independently of the world had an ironic result. The hundreds of thousands of acres they opened for agriculture became highly productive. Adopting the technology of their age, including machines powered by water, Cistercians were soon exporting wool and wine from their farms and vineyards. As a result, the Cistercians were incredibly successful in creating a widespread "economic empire," and in the process, many of their monasteries became very wealthy.

The Cistercians played a major role in developing a new, activist spiritual model for twelfth-century Europe. A Benedictine monk often spent hours in prayer to honor God. The Cistercian ideal had a different emphasis: "Arise, soldier of Christ, arise! Get up off the ground and return to the battle from which you have fled! Fight more boldly after your flight, and triumph in glory!"[4] These were the words of Saint Bernard of Clairvaux (1090–1153), who more than any other person embodied the new spiritual ideal of Cistercian monasticism (see the box on p. 185).

Although well known for his complete dedication to the ascetic ideals of the Cistercians, Bernard of Clairvaux

A Miracle of Saint Bernard

Saint Bernard of Clairvaux has been called "the most widely respected holy man of the twelfth century." He was an outstanding preacher, wholly dedicated to the service of God. His reputation reportedly influenced many young men to join the Cistercian order. He also inspired a myriad of stories dealing with his miracles.

A Miracle of Saint Bernard

A certain monk, departing from his monastery . . . threw off his habit, and returned to the world at the persuasion of the Devil. And he took a certain parish living; for he was a priest. Because sin is punished with sin, the deserter from his Order lapsed into the vice of lechery. He took a concubine to live with him, as in fact is done by many, and by her he had children.

But as God is merciful and does not wish anyone to perish, it happened that many years after, the blessed abbot [Saint Bernard] was passing through the village in which this same monk was living, and went to stay at his house. The renegade monk recognized him, and received him very reverently, and waited on him devoutly . . . but as yet the abbot did not recognize him.

On the morrow, the holy man said Matins and prepared to be off. But as he could not speak to the priest, since he had got up and gone to the church for Matins, he said to the priest's son "Go, give this message to your master." Now the boy had been born dumb. He obeyed the command and feeling in himself the power of him who had given it, he ran to his father and uttered the words of the Holy Father clearly and exactly. His fa-

ther, on hearing his son's voice for the first time, wept for joy, and made him repeat the same words . . . and he asked what the abbot had done to him. "He did nothing to me," said the boy, "except to say 'Go and say this to your father.'"

At so evident a miracle the priest repented, and hastened after the holy man and fell at his feet saying "My Lord and Father, I was your monk so-and-so, and at such-and-such a time I ran away from your monastery. I ask your Paternity to allow me to return with you to the monastery, for in your coming God has visited my heart." The saint replied unto him, "Wait for me here, and I will come back quickly when I have done my business, and I will take you with me." But the priest, fearing death (which he had not done before), answered, "Lord, I am afraid of dying before then." But the saint replied, "Know this for certain, that if you die in this condition, and in this resolve, you will find yourself a monk before God."

The saint [eventually] returned and heard that the priest had recently died and been buried. He ordered the tomb to be opened. And when they asked him what he wanted to do, he said, "I want to see if he is lying as a monk or a clerk in his tomb." "As a clerk," they said; "we buried him in his secular habit." But when they had dug up the earth, they found that he was not in the clothes in which they had buried him; but he appeared in all points, tonsure and habit, as a monk. And they all praised God.

also became an active voice outside the monastery. He helped to settle a disputed papal election, preached the need for a new crusade (the Second Crusade), and even went to Germany to persuade the emperor to join it. At the same time, Bernard gave religious piety a more personal touch when he portrayed Christ, the Virgin Mary, and the saints in more human fashion. In the Early Middle Ages, these holy figures were most often presented in a majestic, triumphant manner and viewed as remote from people's lives. In his sermons and writings, Bernard pictured these sacred figures as living human beings to whom people could relate directly. He encouraged an emotional love for Jesus and for the mother of Christ, the

Virgin Mary, whom he portrayed as a gentle, loving, kindly intercessor with her Son.

Men were not the only ones susceptible to the religious fervor of the twelfth century; women were also active participants in the spiritual movements of the age. The number of women joining religious houses increased perceptibly with the spread of the new orders of the twelfth century, although medieval monasticism always remained an overwhelmingly male phenomenon. Even in 1200, there were only about 3,000 nuns in England compared to 14,000 monks. Moreover, male monasteries were larger and better supported financially. The nuns' secondary role stemmed from the church's view of women as subordinate

♦ **Saint Bernard.** One of the most important religious figures of the twelfth century was Saint Bernard of Clairvaux, who advocated a militant expression of Christian ideas while favoring a more personalized understanding of the relationship between humans and God. Here Saint Bernard is shown preaching a sermon to his fellow Cistercians.

to men. Not allowed to exercise priestly powers, women were dependent on male priests for the sacraments and liturgical services of the church.

In the High Middle Ages, most nuns were from the ranks of the landed aristocracy. Convents were convenient for families unable or unwilling to find husbands for their daughters and for aristocratic women who did not wish to marry. Female intellectuals found them a haven for their activities. Most of the learned women of the Middle Ages, especially in Germany, were nuns. One of the most distinguished was Hildegard of Bingen (1098–1179), who became abbess of a convent at Disibodenberg in western Germany.

Hildegard shared in the religious enthusiasm of the twelfth century. Soon after becoming abbess, she began to write down an account of the mystical visions she had experienced for years. "A great flash of light from heaven pierced my brain and . . . in that instant my mind was imbued with the meaning of the sacred books," she wrote in a description typical of the world's mystical literature. Eventually she produced three books based on her visions. Hildegard gained considerable renown as a mystic and prophet, and popes, emperors, kings, dukes, bishops, abbots, and abbesses eagerly sought her advice. She wrote to them all as an equal and did not hesitate to be critical. To

Henry II of England, she warned, "Look then with fervent zeal at the God who created you. For your heart is full of goodwill to do gladly what is good, except when the filthy habits of humankind rush at you and for a time you became entangled in them. Be resolute and flee those entanglements, beloved son of God, and call out to God!"[5] Hildegard of Bingen was also one of the first important women composers and an important contributor to the body of music known as Gregorian chant or plainsong. Gregorian chant was basically monophonic—a single line of unaccompanied vocal music—set to Latin texts and chanted by groups of monks or nuns during church services. Her work is especially remarkable because she succeeded at a time when music in general, and sacred music in particular, was almost exclusively the domain of men.

LIVING THE GOSPEL LIFE

In the thirteenth century, two religious leaders, Saint Francis and Saint Dominic, founded two new religious orders whose members did not remain in the cloister like the monks of the contemplative orders, such as the Benedictines and Cistercians, but rather went out into the secular arena of the towns and countryside to preach the word of God. By their example, the new orders strove to provide a more personal religious experience for ordinary people.

Saint Francis of Assisi (1182–1226) was born to a wealthy Italian merchant family but as a young man abandoned all worldly goods and began to live and preach in poverty. His simplicity, joyful nature, and love for others soon attracted a band of followers, all of whom took vows of absolute poverty, agreeing to reject all property and live by working and begging for their food. Francis drew up a simple rule for his followers that consisted merely of biblical precepts focusing on the need to preach and the importance of poverty. He sought approval for his new rule from Pope Innocent III, who confirmed the new order as the Order of Friars Minor, more commonly known as the Franciscans. The Franciscans struck a responsive chord in the thirteenth century and became very popular. The Franciscans lived among the people, preaching repentance and aiding the poor. Their calls for a return to the simplicity and poverty of the early church, reinforced by their own example, were especially effective.

The second new religious order of the thirteenth century—the Dominicans—arose out of the desire of a Spanish priest, Dominic de Guzmán (1170–1221), to defend church teachings from heresy. The spiritual revival of the High Middle Ages also led to the emergence of heretical movements, which became especially widespread in southern France. Unlike Francis, Dominic was an intellectual who was appalled by the growth of heresy within the church. He believed that a new religious order of men who lived lives of poverty but were learned and capable of preaching effectively would best be able to attack heresy.

Popular Religion in the High Middle Ages

We have witnessed the actions of popes, cardinals, bishops, and monks. We have seen how the church created a papal monarchy in which the pope, assisted by his curia, ran and directed the hierarchical organization of the Catholic church. But what of ordinary clergy and laypeople? What were their religious hopes and fears? What were their spiritual aspirations?

The sacramental system of the Catholic church ensured that the church was an integral part of people's lives, from birth to death. Not until the twelfth century did the church finally define the seven sacraments administered by the clergy. Sacraments were viewed as outward symbols of an inward grace (grace was God's freely given gift that enabled humans to be saved) and were considered imperative for a Christian's salvation. Five sacraments most directly affected the lives of medieval Christians. Baptism removed original sin and signified membership in the church proper. The sacrament of marriage dignified the union of two people and made valid the practice of sexual intercourse for the begetting of children. In the Eucharist or Lord's Supper, bread and wine were believed to be transformed miraculously into the body and blood of Christ. Through the sacrament of penance, Christians received forgiveness for their sins. Finally, the church had a sacrament for death as well. If possible, a priest administered extreme unction, or the last rites of the church for the dying. Of the remaining two sacraments, holy orders was reserved for the clergy, and confirmation of older children by a bishop did not become a regular practice until the thirteenth century.

Other church practices also played a significant role in the development of medieval Christianity. Saints were men and women who, through their holiness, had achieved a special position in heaven enabling them to act as intercessors before the throne of God. The saint's ability to protect poor souls enabled them to take on great importance at the popular level. Christ's apostles were, of course, recognized throughout Europe as saints, but there were also numerous local saints that were of special significance to a single area. New cults rapidly developed, particularly in the intense religious atmosphere of the eleventh and twelfth centuries. The English introduced

Saint Nicholas, the patron saint of children, who remains instantly recognizable today through his identification with Santa Claus.

Of all the saints, the Virgin Mary, the mother of Christ, occupied the foremost position in the High Middle Ages. The cult of Mary took on two important aspects. Mary was viewed as the most important mediator with her son Christ, the judge of all sinners. Moreover, from the eleventh century on, with the heightened interest in Jesus as infant, boy, and man, a fascination with Mary as Jesus's human mother became more evident. A sign of Mary's importance is the growing number of churches all over Europe that were dedicated to her in the twelfth and thirteenth centuries. (These churches were known in France as Notre Dame, or "our lady.") As Mary became more popular, the number of stories about miracles occurring through her intercession also increased dramatically.

Emphasis on the role of the saints was closely tied to the use of relics, which also increased noticeably in the High Middle Ages. Relics were usually the bones of saints or objects intimately connected to saints that were considered worthy of veneration by the faithful. A twelfth-century English monk began his description of the abbey's relics by saying that "There is kept there a thing more precious than gold, . . . the right arm of St. Oswald. . . . This we have seen with our own eyes and have kissed, and

◆ **A Group of Nuns.** Although still viewed by the medieval church as inferior to men, women were as susceptible to the spiritual fervor of the twelfth century as men, and female monasticism grew accordingly. This miniature shows a group of Flemish nuns listening to the preaching of an abbot, Gilles li Muisis. The nun at the far left wearing a white robe is a novice.

♦ **Mass of the Holy Relics.** It was customary for churches that possessed relics of saints to hold a special mass honoring those saints. At that time, the reliquaries would be brought out for the faithful to venerate. The large picture shows the celebration of this special mass of the holy relics. The reliquary is shown on a table to the left. The small pictures illustrate various stages of the mass.

have handled with our own hands, . . . There are kept here also part of his ribs and of the soil on which he fell."[6] The monk went on to list additional relics possessed by the abbey, which included two pieces of Christ's swaddling clothes, pieces of Christ's manger, and part of the five loaves of bread with which Christ fed 5,000 people. Because the holiness of the saint was considered to be inherent in his relics, these objects were believed to be capable of healing people or producing other miracles.

In the High Middle Ages, it became a regular practice of the church to attach indulgences to these relics. An in-

dulgence brought a remission of the punishment due to sin after the sinner had been absolved by a priest. Indulgences were, in turn, closely connected to the church's doctrine of purgatory, which was first clearly defined in the eleventh and twelfth centuries. Purgatory was believed to be a place of punishment in which the soul of the departed could be purified before ascending into heaven. The living could ease that suffering by masses and prayers offered on behalf of the deceased and, of course, by indulgences. Indulgences were granted for charitable contributions and viewing the relics of saints. Although it was not to be taken literally, the church attached a number of years and days to each indulgence, enabling the soul to spend less time in purgatory.

Medieval Christians believed a pilgrimage to a holy shrine was of particular spiritual benefit. The greatest shrine but the most difficult to reach was the Holy City of Jerusalem. On the continent two pilgrim centers were especially popular in the High Middle Ages. Rome, which contained the relics of Saints Peter and Paul, and the town of Santiago de Compostela, supposedly the site of the tomb of the Apostle James. Local attractions, such as shrines dedicated to the Virgin Mary, also became pilgrimage centers.

Voices of Protest and Intolerance

The desire for a more personal and deeper religious experience, which characterized the spiritual revival of the High Middle Ages, also led people in directions hostile to the institutional church. From the twelfth century on, religious dissent became a problem for the Catholic church. Most serious was heresy, or the holding of religious doctrines different from the orthodox teachings of the church. Because even contemporaries observed that heresies seemed to expand as cities grew in number and size, it may be that the concentration of people in urban areas encouraged the spread of heresy.

The best known heresy of the twelfth and thirteenth century was Catharism. The Cathars (the word *Cathar* means "pure") were often called Albigensians after the city of Albi, one of their strongholds in southern France. They believed in a dualist system in which good and evil were separate and distinct. The things of the spirit were good because they were created by a God of light; the things of the world were evil because they were created by Satan, the prince of darkness. Humans, too, were enmeshed in dualism. Their souls, which were good, were trapped in material bodies, which were evil. Jesus was not divine because he had possessed an evil human body. He was merely an emissary of God who was sent to show people the way out of the soul's entrapment. According to the Cathars, the Catholic church, itself a materialistic institution, had nothing to do with God and was essentially evil. There was no need to follow its teachings or recognize its authority. The Cathar movement gained valuable support from important nobles in southern France and northern Italy, especially Raymond IV, count of Toulouse, the chief lord of southern France.

The spread of heresy in southern France alarmed the church authorities. Pope Innocent III determined to use force to solve the problem. His appeal to the nobles of northern France for a crusade against the heretics fell on receptive ears, especially by nobles eager for adventure, plunder, and gain. The crusade against the Albigensians, which began in the summer of 1209 and lasted for almost two decades, was a bloody one. Thousands of heretics (and the innocent) were slaughtered, including entire populations of some towns. In Béziers, for example, 7,000 men, women, and children were massacred when they took refuge in the local church. The count of Toulouse and other lords were stripped of their lands.

Southern France was devastated, but Catharism remained, which caused the Catholic church to devise a regular method for discovering and dealing with heretics.

This led to the emergence of the Holy Office, as the papal inquisition was called, a formal court whose job it was to ferret out and try heretics. The Dominicans became especially known for their roles as inquisitor-generals.

Gradually, the Holy Office developed its inquisitorial procedure. Anyone could be accused of heresy because the identity of the accuser was not revealed to the indicted heretic. If the accused heretic confessed, he or she was forced to perform public penance and was subjected to punishment, such as flogging; the heretic's property was then confiscated and divided between the secular authorities and the church. Beginning in 1252, those not confessing voluntarily were subjected to torture. Those who refused to confess and were still considered guilty were turned over to the secular authorities for execution. So also were relapsed heretics—those who confessed, did penance, and then reverted to heresy again. The underlying rationale of the inquisition was quite simple: If possible, save the heretic's soul; if not, stop the heretic from endangering the souls of others. To the Christians of the thirteenth century who believed that there was only one path to salvation, heresy was a crime against God and against humanity, and force was justified to save souls from damnation. The fanaticism and fear unleashed in

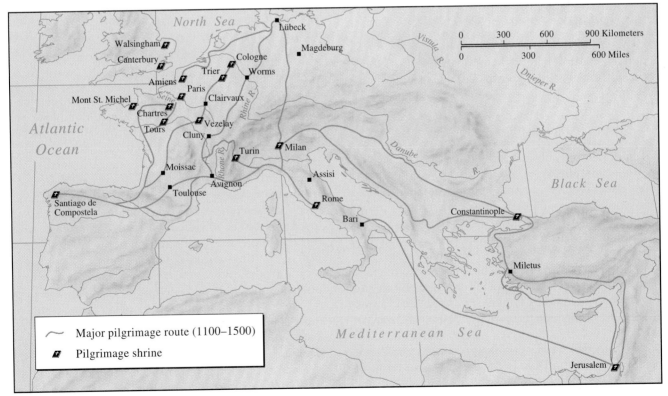

Map 9.1 Pilgrimage Routes in the Middle Ages.

✦ **Expulsion of Albigensian Heretics.** In 1209, Pope Innocent III authorized a crusade against the heretical Albigensians. In this medieval illustration, French knights are shown expelling Albigensian heretics from the town of Carcassonne near Albi, an Albigensian stronghold in southern France.

the struggle against heretics were also used against others, especially the most well-known outgroup of Western society, the Jews.

PERSECUTION OF THE JEWS

The Jews were the only religious minority in medieval Europe that was allowed to practice a non-Christian religion. But the religious enthusiasm of the High Middle Ages produced an outburst of intolerance against the supposed enemies of Christianity. Although this was evident in the crusades against the Muslims (see Chapter 11), Christians also took up the search for enemies at home, persecuting Jews in France and the Rhineland at the time of the first crusades at the end of the eleventh century and beginning of the twelfth century. Jews in Speyer, Worms, Mainz, and Cologne were all set on by bands of Christian crusaders. A contemporary chronicler described how a band of English crusaders who stopped at Lisbon, Portugal, en route to the Holy Land "drove away the pagans and Jews, servants of the king, who dwelt in the city and plundered their property and possessions, and burned

their houses; and they then stripped their vineyards, not leaving them so much as a grape or a cluster."[7]

In the thirteenth century, in the supercharged atmosphere of fear created by the struggle with the heretics, Jews were persecuted more and more often (see the box on p. 191). Friars urged action against these "murderers of Christ," referring to the traditional Christian view of the Jews as responsible for the death of Christ, and organized public burnings of Jewish books. The Fourth Lateran Council in 1215 decreed that Jews must wear distinguishing marks, such as ribbons, yellow badges, and special veils and cloaks to separate themselves from Christians. The same council encouraged the development of Jewish ghettos, or walled enclosures, not to protect the Jews, but to isolate them from Christians. The persecutions and the new image of the hated Jew stimulated a tradition of anti-Semitism that proved to be one of Christian Europe's most insidious contributions to the Western heritage.

European kings, who had portrayed themselves as protectors of the Jews, had so fleeced the Jewish communities of their money by the end of the thirteenth century that they too gave in to the mob fury. Edward I expelled all Jews from England in 1290. The French followed suit in 1306, readmitted them in 1315, and expelled them again in 1322. As this policy spread into central Europe, most northern European Jews were forced to move into Poland as a last refuge.

INTOLERANCE AND HOMOSEXUALITY

The climate of intolerance that characterized thirteenth-century attitudes toward Muslims, heretics, and Jews was also evident toward another minority group, homosexuals. Although the church had condemned homosexuality in the Early Middle Ages, it had not been overly concerned with homosexual behavior, an attitude also prevalent in the secular world. By the thirteenth century, however, these tolerant attitudes had altered drastically. Some historians connect this change to the century's climate of fear and intolerance against any minority group that deviated from the standards of the majority. A favorite approach of the critics was to identify homosexuals with other detested groups. Homosexuality was portrayed as a regular practice of Muslims and such notorious heretics as the Albigensians. Between 1250 and 1300, what had been tolerated in most of Europe became a criminal act deserving of death.

The legislation against homosexuality commonly referred to it as a "sin against nature." This is precisely the argument developed by Thomas Aquinas (see Chapter 11)

⇒ Treatment of the Jews ⇐

The development of new religious sensibilities in the High Middle Ages also had a negative side—the turning of Christians against their supposed enemies. Although the Crusades provide the most obvious example, Christians also turned on their supposed enemies, the "murderers of Christ," the Jews. As a result, Jews suffered increased persecution. These three documents show different sides of the picture. The first is Canon 68 of the decrees of the Fourth Lateran Council called by Pope Innocent III in 1215. The decree specifies the need for special dress, one of the ways Christians tried to separate Jews from their community. The second excerpt is a chronicler's account of the most absurd charge levied against the Jews—that they were guilty of the ritual murder of Christian children to obtain Christian blood for the passover service. This charge led to the murder of many Jews. The third document, taken from a list of regulations issued by the city of Avignon, France, illustrates the contempt Christian society held for the Jews.

Canon 68

In some provinces a difference in dress distinguishes the Jews or Saracens from the Christians, but in certain others such a confusion has grown up that they cannot be distinguished by any difference. Thus it happens at times that through error Christians have relations with the women of Jews or Saracens, and Jews or Saracens with Christian women. Therefore, that they may not, under pretext of error of this sort, excuse themselves in the future for the excesses of such prohibited intercourse, we decree that such Jews and Saracens of both sexes in every Christian province and at all times shall be marked off in the eyes of the public from other peoples through the character of their dress. . . .

Moreover, during the last three days before Easter and especially on Good Friday, they shall not go forth in public at all, for the reason that some of them on these very days, as we hear, do not blush to go forth better dressed and are not afraid to mock the Christians who maintain the memory of the most holy Passion by wearing signs of mourning.

The Jews and Ritual Murder of Christian Children

[. . . The eight-year-old boy] Harold, who is buried in the Church of St. Peter the Apostle, at Gloucester . . . is said to have been carried away secretly by Jews, in the opinion of many, on Feb. 21, and by them hidden till March 16. On that night, on the sixth of the preceding feast, the Jews of all England coming together as if to circumcise a certain boy, pretend deceitfully that they are about to celebrate the feast [Passover] appointed by law in such case, and deceiving the citizens of Gloucester with the fraud, they tortured the lad placed before them with immense tortures. It is true no Christian was present, or saw or heard the deed, nor have we found that anything was betrayed by any Jew. But a little while after when the whole convent of monks of Gloucester and almost all the citizens of that city, and innumerable persons coming to the spectacle, saw the wounds of the dead body, scars of fire, the thorns fixed on his head, and liquid wax poured into the eyes and face, and touched it with the diligent examination of their hands, those tortures were believed or guessed to have been inflicted on him in that manner. It was clear that they had made him a glorious martyr to Christ, being slain without sin, and having bound his feet and his own girdle, threw him into the river Severn.

The Regulations of Avignon, 1243

Likewise, we declare that Jews or whores shall not dare to touch with their hands either bread or fruit put out for sale, and that if they should do this they must buy what they have touched.

who formed Catholic opinion on the subject for centuries to come. In his *Summa Theologica*, Aquinas argued that because the purpose of sex was procreation, it could only be used legitimately in ways that did not exclude this possibility. Hence, homosexuality was "contrary to nature" and a deviation from the natural order established by God. This argument and laws prohibiting homosexual activity on pain of death remained the norm in Europe until the twentieth century.

Conclusion

The new European civilization that had emerged in the Early Middle Ages began to flourish in the High Middle Ages. Climatic improvements that produced better growing conditions, an expansion of cultivated land, and technological changes combined to enable Europe's food supply to increase significantly after 1000. This increase in agricultural production helped sustain a dramatic rise in population that was physically apparent in the expansion of towns and cities.

The Catholic church shared in the challenge of new growth by reforming itself and striking out on a path toward greater papal power, both within the church and over European society. The High Middle Ages witnessed a spiritual renewal that led to numerous and even divergent paths: revived papal leadership, the development of centralized administrative machinery that buttressed papal authority, and new dimensions to the religious life of the clergy and laity. The theology of Saint Bernard, new forms of monasticism, the doctrine of purgatory, and the emergence of a clearly defined sacramental system all seemed to reflect a greater concern for salvation and a greater possibility of achieving it.

The religious enthusiasm of the twelfth century continued well into the thirteenth as new orders of friars gave witness to spiritual growth and passion, but underneath the calm exterior lay seeds of discontent and change. Dissent from church teaching and practices grew, leading to a climate of fear and intolerance as the church responded with inquisitorial procedures to enforce conformity to its teachings. As the same time, papal claims of supremacy over secular authorities were increasingly challenged by the rising power of a new breed of monarchical authorities, who, because of the growth of cities, the revival of trade, and the emergence of a money economy, were now able to hire soldiers and officials to carry out their wishes. It is to this new world of cities and kingdoms that we must now turn.

NOTES

1. Ernest F. Henderson, ed., *Select Historical Documents of the Middle Ages* (London, 1892), p. 332.
2. Ibid., p. 365.
3. Oliver J. Thatcher and Edgar H. McNeal, eds., *A Source Book for Medieval History* (New York, 1905), p. 208.
4. Quoted in R. H. C. Davis, *A History of Medieval Europe from Constantine to Saint Louis*, 2d ed. (London and New York, 1988), p. 252.
5. Matthew Fox, ed., *Hildegard of Bingen's Book of Divine Works with Letters and Songs* (Santa Fe, New Mexico, 1987), p. 293.
6. Quoted in Rosalind and Christopher Brooke, *Popular Religion in the Middle Ages* (London, 1984), p. 19.
7. Henry T. Riley, ed. and trans., *Memorials of London and London Life in the Thirteenth, Fourteenth, and Fifteenth Centuries* (London, 1868), 2:148–49.

SUGGESTIONS FOR FURTHER READING

For a good introduction to this period, see C. N. L. Brooke, *Europe in the Central Middle Ages, 962–1154*, rev. ed. (New York, 1988); and M. Barber, *The Two Cities: Medieval Europe 1050–1320* (London, 1992). On economic conditions, see N. J. G. Pounds, *An Economic History of Medieval Europe* (New York, 1974); and *The Fontana Economic History of Europe*, vol. 1, *The Middle Ages*, ed. C. M. Cipolla (London, 1972). A good short introduction to medieval society is C. Brooke, *The Structure of Medieval Society* (London, 1971). On peasant life, see R. Fossier, *Peasant Life in the Medieval West* (New York, 1988). Technological changes are discussed in L. White, *Medieval Technology and Social Change* (Oxford, 1962); J. Gimpel, *The Medieval Machine* (Harmondsworth, 1976); and

J. Langdon, *Horses, Oxen and Technological Innovation* (New York, 1986).

For a good survey of religion in medieval Europe, see B. Hamilton, *Religion in the Medieval West* (London, 1986). On the Cluniac reform movement, see H. E. J. Cowdrey, *The Cluniacs and the Gregorian Reform* (Oxford, 1970); and G. Constable, *Cluniac Studies* (London, 1980). On the Investiture Controversy, see U. R. Blumenthal, *The Investiture Controversy* (Philadelphia, 1988). Also valuable are K. F. Morrison, *Tradition and Authority in the Western Church, 300–1140* (Princeton, N.J., 1969); and B. Tierney, *The Crisis of Church and State: 1050–1300* (Englewood Cliffs, N.J., 1964). On the evolution of papal ideology, see W. Ullmann, *A Short History* of the Papacy in the Middle Ages (London, 1974). For a general survey of church life, see R. W. Southern, Western Society and the Church in the Middle Ages (Baltimore, 1970). For a sociohistorical account of the Catholic clergy, see A. Barstow, Married Priests and the Reforming Papacy (New York, 1982).

On the papacy in the High Middle Ages, see the general survey by G. Barraclough, The Medieval Papacy (New York, 1968); C. Morris, The Papal Monarchy (Oxford, 1989); and I. S. Robinson, The Papacy (Cambridge, 1990). The papacy of Innocent III is covered in J. E. Sayers, Innocent III, Leader of Europe, 1198–1216 (New York, 1994). On the church, see P. Partner, The Lands of St. Peter (Berkeley, 1972); and D. P. Waley, The Papal State in the Thirteenth Century (London, 1961).

Good works on monasticism include B. Bolton, The Medieval Reformation (London, 1983); C. H. Lawrence, Medieval Monasticism (London, 1984), a good general account; and H. Leyser, Hermits and the New Monasticism (London, 1984). On the Cistercians, see L. J. Lekai, The Cistercians (Kent, Ohio, 1977). S. Flanagan, Hildegard of Bingen (London, 1989) is a good account of the twelfth-century mystic. The new religious orders of the thirteenth century are examined in R. B. Brooke, The Coming of the Friars (New York, 1975). L. K. Little, Religious Poverty and the Profit Economy in Medieval Europe (London, 1979) stresses the social context of the development of the mendicant orders. For a good introduction to popular religion in the eleventh and twelfth centuries, see R. and C. N. L. Brooke, Popular Religion in the Middle Ages (London, 1984). On miracles, see B. Ward, Miracles and the Medieval Mind (London, 1982). The image of women in the secular and religious realms is discussed in P. S. Gold, The Lady and the Virgin: Image, Attitude and Experience in Twelfth-Century France (Chicago, 1985).

On dissent and heresy, see M. Lambert, Medieval Heresy (New York, 1977); W. L. Wakefield, Heresy, Crusade and Inquisition in Southern France, 1100–1250 (Berkeley, 1974); J. Sumption, The Albigensian Crusade (London, 1978); and J. Strayer, The Albigensian Crusades (New York, 1971). On the Inquisition, see B. Hamilton, The Medieval Inquisition (New York, 1981). The persecution of Jews in the thirteenth century can be examined in E. A. Synan, The Popes and the Jews in the Middle Ages (New York, 1965); J. Marcus, The Jew in the Medieval World (New York, 1972); and J. Cohen, The Friars and the Jews (Oxford, 1985); The basic study on intolerance and homosexuality is J. Boswell, Christianity, Social Tolerance, and Homosexuality (Chicago, 1980).

CHAPTER
10

A New World of Cities and Kingdoms

By the fifth century A.D., the towns and cities that had been such an integral part of the Roman world began to decline, and the world of the Early Middle Ages became predominantly agricultural. Beginning in the late tenth and early eleventh centuries, however, a renewal of commercial life led to a revival of cities. Old Roman sites came back to life while new towns arose at major crossroads or natural harbors favorable to trading activities. Townspeople themselves were often great enthusiasts for their new way of life. In the twelfth century, William Fitz-Stephen spoke of London as one of the noble cities of the world: "It is happy in the healthiness of its air, in the Christian religion, in the strength of its defences, the nature of its site, the honor of its citizens, the modesty of its women; pleasant in sports; fruitful of noble men." To Fitz-Stephen, London offered a myriad of opportunities and pleasures. Fairs and markets were held regularly, and "practically anything that man may need is brought daily not only into special places but even into the open squares, and all that can be sold is loudly advertised for sale." Any man, according to Fitz-Stephen, "if he is healthy and and not a good-for-nothing, may earn his living expenses and esteem according to his station." Then, too, there are the happy inhabitants of the city: where else has one "ever met such a wonderful show of people this side or the other side of the sea?" Sporting events and leisure activities are available in every season of the year: "In Easter holidays they fight battles on water." In summer, "the youths are exercised in leaping, dancing, shooting, wrestling, casting the stone; the maidens dance as long as they can well see." In winter, "when the great fen, or moor, which waters the walls of the city on the north side, is frozen, many young men play upon the ice; some, striding as wide as they may, do slide swiftly." To Fitz-Stephen, "every convenience for human pleasure is known to be at hand" in London. One would hardly know from his cheerful description that medieval cities faced overcrowded conditions, terrible smells from rotten sanitation, and the constant challenge of epidemics and fires.

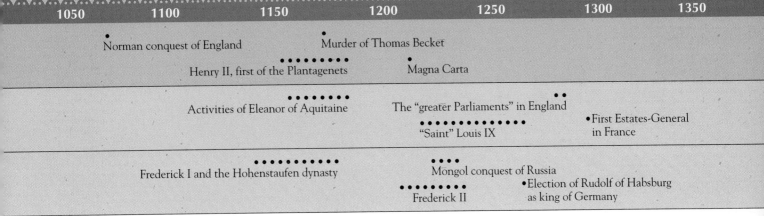

Norman conquest of England

Murder of Thomas Becket

Henry II, first of the Plantagenets

Magna Carta

Activities of Eleanor of Aquitaine

The "greater Parliaments" in England

"Saint" Louis IX

First Estates-General in France

Frederick I and the Hohenstaufen dynasty

Mongol conquest of Russia

Election of Rudolf of Habsburg as king of Germany

Frederick II

By the twelfth and thirteenth centuries, both the urban centers and the urban population of Europe were experiencing a dramatic expansion. Although European society in the High Middle Ages remained overwhelmingly agricultural, the growth of trade and cities along with the development of a money economy and new commercial practices and institutions constituted a veritable commercial revolution that affected most of Europe, including its political structures. Commerce, cities, and a money economy helped to undermine feudal institutions while strengthening monarchical authority.

During the High Middle Ages, nobles built innumerable castles that gave a distinctive look to the countryside. Although lords and vassals seemed forever mired in endless petty conflicts, some medieval kings began to exert a centralizing authority and inaugurated the process of developing new kinds of monarchical states. By the thirteenth century, European monarchs were solidifying their governmental institutions in pursuit of greater power.

The New World of Trade and Cities

Medieval Europe was an overwhelmingly agrarian society with most people living in small villages. In the eleventh and twelfth centuries, however, new elements were introduced that began to transform the economic foundation of Western civilization: a revival of trade, considerable expansion in the circulation of money, a restoration of specialized craftspeople and artisans, and the growth and development of towns. These changes were made possible by the new agricultural practices and subsequent increase in food production, which freed part of the European population from the need to produce their own food and allowed diversification in economic functions. Merchants and craftspeople could now buy their necessities.

The Revival of Trade

The revival of commercial activity was a gradual process. The uncertainties and chaotic conditions of the Early Middle Ages caused large-scale trade to decline in western Europe except for Byzantine contacts with Italy and the Jewish traders who moved back and forth between the Muslim and Christian worlds. By the end of the tenth century, however, people with both the skills and the products for commercial activity were emerging in Europe.

Cities in Italy assumed a leading role in the revival of trade. By the end of the eighth century, Venice, on the northeastern coast, had forged close commercial connections with the Byzantine Empire. Venice developed a trading fleet and by the end of the tenth century had become the chief western trading center for Byzantine and Islamic commerce. Venice sent wine, grain, and timber to Constantinople in exchange for silk cloth, which was then peddled to other communities. Other coastal communities in western Italy, such as Genoa and Pisa, also opened new trade routes. By 1100, Italian merchants began to benefit from the crusades (see Chapter 11) and were able to establish new trading centers in eastern ports. There the merchants obtained silks, sugar, and spices, which they subsequently carried back to Italy and the west. At the same time, northern Italy began to experience rapid

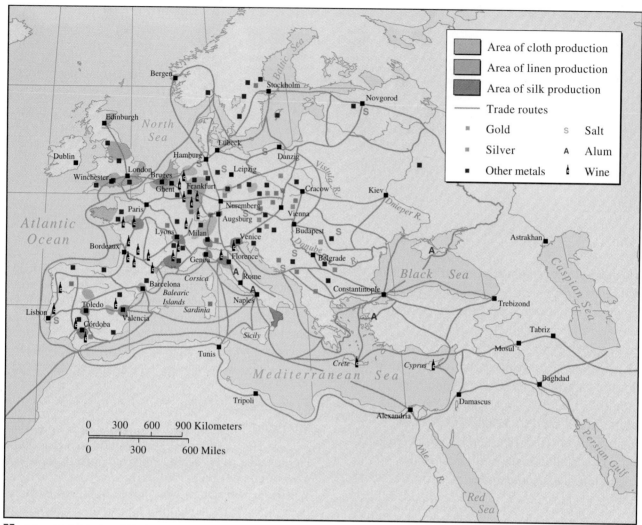

Map 10.1 Medieval Trade Routes.

economic growth from the production of high-quality cloth, which was also in demand.

While the north Italian cities were busy enlarging the scope of commercial activity in the Mediterranean, the towns of Flanders were doing likewise in northern Europe. Flanders, the area along the coast of present-day Belgium and northern France, was known for the production of a much desired high-quality woolen cloth. Flanders's location made it a logical entrepôt for the traders of northern Europe. Merchants from England, Scandinavia, France, and Germany converged there to trade their wares for woolen cloth. Flanders prospered in the eleventh and twelfth centuries, and such Flemish towns as Bruges and Ghent became centers for the trade and manufacture of woolen cloth.

By the twelfth century, both Italy and Flanders had become centers of a revived trade, making it almost inevitable that a regular exchange of goods would eventually develop between these two major centers of northern and southern European trade. To encourage this trade, the Counts of Champagne in northern France devised a series of six fairs held annually in the chief towns of their territory. They guaranteed the safety of visiting merchants, supervised the trading activities, and, of course, collected a sales tax on all goods exchanged at the fairs. The fairs of Champagne became the largest commercial marketplace in western Europe where the goods of northern Europe could be exchanged for the goods of southern Europe and the east. Northern merchants brought the furs, woolen cloth, tin, hemp, and honey of northern Europe and exchanged them for the cloth and swords of northern Italy and the silks, sugar, and spices of the East. The prosperity of the Champagne fairs caused lords everywhere to follow their example and establish trading fairs.

During the thirteenth century, trade continued to expand to the point that historians speak of a commercial revolution, a term that reflects not only the increased volume of goods traded, but also the development of new commercial practices and institutions. The cities of Venice, Genoa, and Pisa, in particular, prospered in the trade of the Mediterranean area.

The Growth of Cities

The revival of commerce also fostered the development of urban life. Merchants needed places where they could build warehouses to store their goods for trans-shipment and dwelling places that could serve as permanent bases. Medieval cities did not develop just anywhere. To meet merchants' needs, cities were located near sources of protection and alongside rivers or major arteries of some kind that provided favorable routes of transportation.

Towns in the economic sense, as centers of population where merchants and artisans practiced their trades and purchased their food from surrounding territories, had greatly declined in the Early Middle Ages, especially in Europe north of the Alps. Old Roman cities continued to exist but experienced great declines in size and population. Many had become the *sees* or seats of bishops and

archbishops or the strongholds of counts and functioned as administrative centers for both church and state. With the revival of trade, merchants began to settle in these old cities, followed by craftspeople or artisans—people who on manors or elsewhere had developed skills and now perceived the opportunity to ply their trade and produce objects that could be sold by the merchants. In the course of the eleventh and twelfth centuries, the old Roman cities came alive with new populations and growth. By 1100, the old areas of these cities had been repopulated; after 1100, the population outgrew the old walls, necessitating the construction of new city walls outside the old.

Beginning in the late tenth century, many new cities or towns were founded, particularly in northern Europe. Usually, a group of merchants established a settlement near some fortified stronghold, such as a castle or monastery. The original meaning of the English "borough" or "burgh" and the German "burg" as a fortress or walled enclosure is still evident in the name of many cities, such as Edinburgh and Nuremberg. Castles were particularly favored because they were usually located along major routes of transportation or at the intersection of two such trade routes; the lords of the castle also offered protection. If the settlement prospered and expanded, new walls were built to protect it.

Most towns were closely tied to their surrounding territories because they were dependent on the countryside for their food supplies. In addition, they were often part of the territory belonging to a lord and were subject to his

◆ **The Fortified Town of Carcassonne.** The expansion of commerce and industry led to an ongoing growth of towns and cities in the High Middle Ages. As seen in this picture of the French town of Carcassonne, medieval towns were surrounded by walls strengthened by defensive towers and punctuated by gates. As is evident here, medieval urban skylines were dominated by towers of all kinds.

jurisdiction. Although lords wanted to treat towns and townspeople as they would their vassals and serfs, cities had totally different needs and a different perspective. Townspeople needed mobility to trade. Consequently, these townspeople (the merchants and artisans who came to be called burghers or bourgeoisie from the word *burgus*, a Latinized version of the German word *burg* meaning a walled enclosure) constituted a revolutionary group who needed their own unique laws to meet their requirements. Because the townspeople were profiting from the growth of trade and sale of their products, they were willing to pay for the right to make their own laws and govern themselves. In many instances, lords and kings saw the potential for vast new sources of revenues and were willing to grant (or, more accurately, sell) to the townspeople the liberties they were beginning to demand.

By 1100, townspeople were obtaining charters of liberties from their territorial lords, either lay or ecclesiastical, that granted them the privileges they wanted, including the right to bequeath goods and sell property; freedom from any military obligation to the lord; written urban law that guaranteed them their freedom; and the right to become a free person after residing a year and a day in the town. The last provision made it possible for a runaway serf who could avoid capture to become a free person in a city. Almost all new urban communities gained these elementary liberties, but only some towns obtained the right to govern themselves by choosing their own officials and administering their own courts of law.

Medieval cities, then, possessed varying degrees of self-government depending on the amount of control retained over them by the lord or king in whose territory they were located. In Italy, for example, the decline of the emperor's authority ensured that the northern Italian cities could function as self-governing republics. In contrast, in France and England towns did not become independent city-states, but remained ultimately subject to royal authority. Nevertheless, all towns, regardless of the degree of outside control, evolved institutions of government for running the affairs of the community.

Medieval cities defined citizenship narrowly and accorded it only to males who had been born in the city or who had lived there for some time. In many cities, citizens elected members of a city council that bore primary responsibility for running the affairs of the city. City councillors (known as consuls in Italy and southern France) not only enacted legislation but also served as judges and city magistrates. The electoral process was carefully engineered to ensure that only members of the wealthiest and most powerful families, who came to be called the patricians, were elected. They kept the reins of government in their hands despite periodic protests from lesser merchants and artisans. In the twelfth and thirteenth centuries, cities added some kind of sole executive leader, even if he was only a figurehead. Although the title varied from town to town, this executive officer was frequently called a mayor.

City governments kept close watch over the activities of their community. To care for the welfare and safety of the community, a government might regulate air and water pollution; provide water barrels and delegate responsibility to people in every section of the town to fight fires, which were an ever-present danger; construct warehouses to stockpile grain in the event of food emergencies; and establish and supervise the standards of weights and measures used in the various local goods and industries. Urban crime was not a major problem in the towns of the High Middle Ages because the relatively small size of communities made it difficult for criminals to operate openly. Nevertheless, medieval urban governments did organize town guards to patrol the streets by night and the city walls by day. People caught committing criminal acts were quickly tried for their offenses. Serious offenses, such as murder, were punished by execution, usually by hanging. Lesser crimes were punished by fines, flogging, or branding.

Medieval cities remained relatively small in comparison to either ancient or modern cities. A large trading city would number about 5,000 inhabitants. By 1300, London was the largest city in England with almost 40,000 people. Otherwise, north of the Alps, only a few great urban centers of commerce, such as Bruges and Ghent, had a population close to 40,000. Italian cities tended to be larger, with Venice, Florence, Genoa, Milan, and Naples numbering almost 100,000 each. Even the largest European city, however, seemed insignificant alongside the Byzantine capital of Constantinople or the Arab cities of Damascus, Baghdad, and Cairo. For a long time to come, Europe remained predominantly rural. However, the wealth of the cities guaranteed that they would have a significantly disproportionate influence on the political and economic life of Europe. In the long run, the rise of towns and the development of commerce laid the foundations for the eventual transformation of Europe from a rural agricultural society into an urban industrial one.

Life in Medieval Cities

Medieval towns were surrounded by stone walls that were expensive to build, so the space within was precious and tightly filled. This gave medieval cities their characteristic appearance of narrow, winding streets with houses crowded against each other and the second and third stories of the dwellings built out over the streets. Because dwellings were constructed mostly of wood before the fourteenth century and candles and wood fires were used for light and heat, the danger of fire was great. Medieval cities burned rapidly once a fire started.

A medieval urban skyline was dominated by the towers of castles and town halls, but especially of churches, whose number was often staggering. At the beginning of the thirteenth century, London had 120 churches. If a city was the center of a bishop's see, a large cathedral would dominate the other buildings and be visible for miles outside the city. Monastic and parish churches added to the number of churches.

Most of the people who lived in cities were merchants involved in trade and artisans engaged in manufacturing of some kind. Generally, merchants and artisans had their own sections within a city. The merchant area included warehouses, inns, and taverns. Artisan sections were usually divided along craft lines; each craft had its own street where its activity was pursued.

The physical environment of medieval cities was not pleasant. They were often dirty and rife with smells from animal and human waste deposited in backyard privies or on the streets (see the box on p. 200). In some places, city governments required citizens to make periodic collections of garbage and waste and cart it outside of town. Atmospheric pollution was also a fact of life, not only from the ubiquitous wood fires, but also from the use of a cheaper fuel, coal, used industrially by lime-burners, brewers, and dyers, as well as by poor people who could not afford to purchase wood.

Cities were also unable to stop water pollution, especially from the tanning and animal-slaughtering industries. Both industries were forced, however, to locate downstream to avoid polluting the water used by the city upstream. Butchers dumped blood and all remaining waste products from their butchered animals into the river while tanners unloaded the tannic acids, dried blood, fat, hair, and the other waste products of their operations. Because tanneries and slaughterhouses existed in virtually every medieval town, rivers rapidly became polluted.

Because of the pollution, cities were not inclined to use the rivers for drinking water but relied instead on wells. Occasionally, communities repaired the system of aqueducts left over from Roman times and sometimes even constructed new ones. Private and public baths also existed in medieval towns. Paris, for example, had thirty-two public baths for men and women. City laws did not allow lepers and people with "bad reputations" to use them, but such measures did not prevent the public baths

◆ **Shops in a Medieval Town.** Most urban residents were merchants involved in trade and artisans who manufactured a wide variety of products. Master craftsmen had their workshops in the ground-level rooms of their houses. In this illustration, two well-dressed burghers are touring the shopping districts of a French town. Tailors, furriers, a barber, and a grocer (from left to right) are visible at work in their shops.

from being known for permissiveness due to public nudity. One contemporary commented on what occurred in public bathhouses: "Shameful things. Men make a point of staying all night in the public baths and women at the break of day come in and through 'ignorance' find themselves in the men's rooms."[1] Authorities came under increasing pressure to close the baths down, and the great plague of the fourteenth century sealed their fate. The standards of medieval hygiene broke down, and late medieval and early modern European society would prove to be remarkably dirty.

There were considerably more men than women in medieval cities. Women, in addition to supervising the household, purchasing food and preparing meals, raising the children, and managing the family finances, were also often expected to help their husbands in their trades. Some women also developed their own trades to earn extra money. Margery Kempe, for example, although the daughter of a mayor and the wife of a wealthy merchant, pursued the trade of brewing ale. When some master craftsmen died, their widows even carried on their trades. Some women in medieval towns were thus able to lead lives of considerable independence.

❧ Medieval City ❧

Environmental pollution is not new to the twentieth century. Medieval cities and towns had their own problems with filthy living conditions. This excerpt is taken from an order sent by the king of England to the town of Boutham. It demands rectification of the town's pitiful physical conditions. There is little evidence to indicate that the king's order changed the situation dramatically.

The King's Command to Boutham

To the bailiffs of the abbot of St. Mary's, York, at Boutham. Whereas it is sufficiently evident that the pavement of the said town of Boutham is so very greatly broke up that all and singular passing and going through that town sustain immoderate damages and grievances, and in addition the air is so corrupted and infected by the pigsties situated in the king's highways and in the lanes of that town and by the swine feeding and frequently wandering about in the streets and lanes and by dung and dunghills and many other foul things placed in the streets and lanes, that great repugnance overtakes the king's ministers staying in that town and also others there dwelling and passing through, the advantage of more wholesome air is impeded; the state of men is grievously injured, and other unbearable inconveniences and many other injuries are known to proceed from such corruption, to the nuisance of the king's ministers aforesaid and of others there dwelling and passing through, and to the peril of their lives . . . the king, being unwilling longer to tolerate such great and unbearable defects there, orders the bailiffs to cause the pavement to be suitably repaired within their liberty before All Saints next, and to cause the pigsties, aforesaid streets and lanes to be cleansed from all dung and dunghills, and to cause proclamation to be made throughout their bailiwick forbidding any one, under pain of grievous forfeiture, to cause or permit their swine to feed or wander outside his house in the king's streets or the lanes aforesaid.

Industry in Medieval Cities

The revival of trade enabled cities and towns to become important centers for manufacturing a wide range of goods, such as cloth, metalwork, shoes, and leather goods. A host of crafts were carried on in houses along the narrow streets of the medieval cities. From the twelfth century on, artisans began to organize themselves into guilds, which came to play a leading role in the economic life of the cities.

By the thirteenth century, virtually every group of craftspeople, such as tanners, carpenters, and bakers, had their own guild, while specialized groups of merchants, such as dealers in silk, spices, wool, or banking, had their separate guilds as well. Craft guilds directed almost every aspect of the production process. They established standards for the articles produced, specified the actual methods of production to be used, and even fixed the price at which the finished goods could be sold. Guilds also determined the number of men who could enter a specific trade and the procedure they must follow to do so.

A person who wanted to learn a trade first became an apprentice to a master craftsman, usually at around the age of ten. Apprentices were not paid, but did receive room and board from their masters. After five to seven years of service, in which they learned their craft, apprentices became journeymen (or journeywomen, although most were male) who then worked for wages for other masters. Journeymen aspired to become masters as well. To do so, they were expected to produce a "masterpiece," a finished piece in their craft that allowed the master craftsmen of the guild to judge whether the journeymen were qualified to become masters and join the guild.

Craft guilds continued to dominate manufacturing in those industries where raw materials could be acquired locally and the products sold locally. But in those industries that required raw materials from outside the local area to produce high-quality products for growing markets abroad, a new form of industry dependent on large concentrations of capital and unskilled labor began to emerge. Viewed by some observers as the beginning of commercial capitalism, it was particularly evident in the domestic system used in the production of woolen cloth in both Flanders and northern Italy. An entrepreneur, whose initial capital outlay probably came from commercial activities, bought raw wool and distributed it to workers who carried out the various stages of carding, spinning, weaving, and dyeing to produce a finished piece of woolen cloth. These laborers worked in their own homes and were paid wages. As wage earners, they were dependent on their employers and the fluctuations in prices that occurred periodically in the international market for the finished goods. The entrepreneur collected the final products and sold the finished cloth, earning a profit that could then be invested in more production.

The Aristocracy of the High Middle Ages

In the High Middle Ages, European society was dominated by a group of men whose primary preoccupation was warfare. King Alfred of England had said that a "well-peopled land" must have "men of prayer, men of war, and men of work," and medieval ideals held to a tripartite division of society into these three basic groups. The "men of war" were the aristocracy who came to form a distinct social group, albeit one with considerable variation in wealth among its members. Nevertheless, they, along with their wives and children, shared a common ethos and a distinctive lifestyle.

The Significance of the Aristocracy

King Alfred's "men of war" were the lords and vassals of medieval society. The lords were the kings, dukes, counts, barons, and viscounts (and even bishops and archbishops) who held extensive lands and considerable political power. They formed an aristocracy or nobility that consisted of people who held real political, economic, and social power. Nobles relied for military help on knights, mounted warriors who fought for them in return for weapons and daily sustenance. Knights were by no means the social equals of nobles; many knights in fact possessed little more than peasants. But in the course of the twelfth and thirteenth centuries, knights improved their social status and joined the ranks of the nobility. In the process, noble and knight came to mean much the same thing, and warfare likewise tended to become a distinguishing characteristic of a nobleman. The great lords and knights came to form a common caste; they were warriors and the institution of knighthood united them. Nevertheless, there were also social divisions among them based on extremes of wealth and landholdings.

The Daily Life of the European Nobility

Medieval theory maintained that the warlike qualities of the nobility were justified by their role as defenders of society, and the growth of the European nobility in the High Middle Ages was made visible by an increasing

♦ **Castle and Aristocrats.** This illustration from the *Trés Riches Heures* of Jean, duke of Berry, depicts the Chateau of Dourdan, France, and its surrounding lands. In the foreground, elaborately dressed aristocratic men and women are seen amusing themselves.

number of castles scattered across the landscape. Although castle architecture varied considerably, castles did possess two common features: They were permanent residences for the noble family, its retainers, and servants, and they were defensible fortifications. For defensive purposes, castles were surrounded by open areas and large stone walls. At the heart of the castle was the *keep*, a large, multistored building that housed kitchens, stables, storerooms, a great hall for visitors, dining, and administrative business, and numerous rooms for sleeping and living. The growing wealth of the High Middle Ages made it possible for the European nobility to build more elaborate castles with thicker walls and better furnished and decorated interiors. As castles became more elaborate and securely built, they proved to be more easily defended and harder to seize by force.

ARISTOCRATIC WOMEN

Although women could legally hold and inherit property, most women remained under the control of men—of their fathers until they married (usually at the age of fifteen or sixteen) and of their husbands after they married. Nevertheless, aristocratic women had numerous opportunities for playing important roles. Because the lord was often away at war, on crusade, or at court, the lady of the castle had to manage the estate, a considerable responsibility in view of the fact that households, even of lesser aristocrats, could include large numbers of officials and servants. The lady of the castle was also responsible on a regular basis for overseeing the food supply and maintaining all other supplies for the smooth operation of the household.

Although women were expected to be subservient to their husbands (see the box on p. 203), there were many strong women who advised and sometimes even dominated their husbands. Perhaps the most famous was Eleanor of Aquitaine (c. 1122–1204), heiress to the duchy of Aquitaine in southwestern France. Married to King Louis VII of France (1137–1180), Eleanor accompanied her husband on a crusade, but her alleged affair with her uncle during the crusade led Louis to have their marriage annulled. Eleanor then married Henry, duke of Normandy and count of Anjou, who became King Henry II of England (1154–1189). She took an active role in politics, even assisting her sons in rebelling against Henry in 1173–1174. Imprisoned for her activities, after Henry's death she again assumed an active political life, providing both military and political support for her sons.

THE WAY OF THE WARRIOR

At the age of seven or eight, the sons of the nobility were sent either to a clerical school to pursue a religious career or to another nobleman's castle where they prepared for the life of a noble. Their chief lessons were military; they learned how to joust, hunt, ride, and handle weapons properly. Occasionally, aristocrats' sons might also learn the basic fundamentals of reading and writing. After his apprenticeship in knighthood, at about the age of twenty-one, a young man formally entered the adult world in a ceremony of "knighting." A sponsor girded a sword on the young candidate and struck him on the cheek or neck with an open hand (or later touched him three times on the shoulder with the blade of a sword), possibly signifying the passing of the sponsor's military valor to the new knight.

In the eleventh and twelfth centuries, under the influence of the church, an ideal of civilized behavior called *chivalry* gradually evolved among the nobility. Chivalry represented a code of ethics that knights were supposed to uphold. In addition to their oath to defend the church and the defenseless, knights were expected to treat captives as honored guests instead of putting them in dungeons. Chivalry also implied that knights should fight only for glory, but this account of a group of English knights by a medieval writer reveals another motive for battle: "The whole city was plundered to the last farthing, and then they proceeded to rob all the churches throughout the city, . . . and seizing gold and silver, cloth of all colors, women's ornaments, gold rings, goblets, and precious stones. . . . they all returned to their own lords rich men."[2] Apparently not all the ideals of chivalry were taken seriously.

After his formal initiation into the world of warriors, a young man returned home to find himself once again subject to his parents' authority. Young men were discouraged from marrying until their fathers died, at which time they could marry and become lords of the castle. Trained to be warriors, but with no adult responsibilities, young knights naturally gravitated toward military activities and often furthered the private warfare endemic to the noble class. In the twelfth century, tournaments began to appear as an alternative to the socially destructive fighting that the church was increasingly trying to curb. Initially, tournaments consisted of the "melee," in which warriors on horseback fought with blunted weapons in free-for-all combat. The goal was to take prisoners who would then be ransomed, making success in tournaments a path to considerable gain. Within an eight-month span, the English knight William Marshall made a tour of the tournament circuit, defeated 203 knights, and made so much money that he had to hire two clerks to take care of it. By the late twelfth century, the "melee" was preceded by the joust or individual combat between two knights. Gradually, the joust became the main part of the tournament. No matter how much the church condemned tournaments, knights themselves continued to see them as an excellent way to train for war. As one knight explained: "a knight cannot distinguish himself in that [war] if he has not trained for it in tourneys. He must have seen his blood flow, heard his teeth crack under fist blows, felt his opponent's weight bear down upon him as

≈ Women in Medieval Thought ≈

Whether a nun or the wife of an aristocrat, townsman, or peasant, a woman in the Middle Ages was considered inferior to a man and by nature subject to a man's authority. Although there are a number of examples of strong women who flew in the face of such attitudes, church teachings also reinforced these notions. The first selection from Gratian, the twelfth-century jurist who wrote the first systematic work on canon law, supports this view. The second selection was written by a wealthy fifty-year-old merchant in Paris who wanted to instruct his fifteen-year-old bride on how to be a good wife.

Gratian, Decretum

Women should be subject to their men. The natural order for mankind is that women should serve men and children their parents, for it is just that the lesser serve the greater.

The image of God is in man and it is one. Women were drawn from man, who has God's jurisdiction as if he were God's vicar, because he has the image of the one God. Therefore woman is not made in God's image.

Woman's authority is nil; let her in all things be subject to the rule of man. . . . And neither can she teach, nor be a witness, nor give a guarantee, nor sit in judgment.

Adam was beguiled by Eve, not she by him. It is right that he whom woman led into wrongdoing should have her under his direction, so that he may not fail a second time through female-levity.

A Merchant of Paris, On Marriage

I entreat you to keep his linen clean, for this is up to you. Because the care of outside affairs is men's work, a husband must look after these things, and go and come, run here and there in rain, wind, snow, and hail—sometimes wet, sometimes dry, sometimes sweating, other times shivering, badly fed, badly housed, badly shod, badly bedded—and nothing harms him because he is cheered by the anticipation of the care his wife will take of him on his return—of the pleasures, joys, and comforts she will provide, or have provided for him in her presence: to have his shoes off before a good fire, to have his feet washed, to have clean shoes and hose, to be well fed, provided with good drink, well served, well honored, well bedded in white sheets and white nightcaps, well covered with good furs, and comforted with other joys and amusements, intimacies, affections, and secrets about which I am silent. And on the next day fresh linen and garments. . . .

Also keep peace with him. Remember the country proverb that says there are three things that drive a good man from his home: a house with a bad roof, a smoking chimney, and a quarrelsome woman. I beg you, in order to preserve your husband's love and good will, be loving, amiable, and sweet with him. . . . Thus protect and shield your husband from all troubles, give him all the comfort you can think of, wait on him, and have him waited on in your home. . . . If you do what is said here, he will always have his affection and his heart turned toward you and your service, and he will forsake all other homes, all other women, all other help, and all other households.

he lay on the ground and, after being twenty times unhorsed, have risen twenty times to fight."[3]

The Emergence and Growth of European Kingdoms, 1000–1300

The political organization of Europe had been severely tested by the internal disintegration of the Carolingian Empire and the invasions of the ninth and tenth centuries. The feudal institutions that emerged during that period persisted and, indeed, reached their high point in the eleventh and twelfth centuries. Similarly, the domination of society by the nobility reached its apex in the High Middles Ages. At the same time, kings began, however slowly, the process of extending their power in more effective ways. Out of this growth in the monarchies would eventually come the European kingdoms that dominated much of later European history.

In theory, kings were regarded as the heads of their kingdoms and were expected to lead their vassals and subjects into battle. The king's power, however, was strictly limited. He had to honor the rights and privileges of his vassals and in the case of disputes had to resolve them by principles of established law. If he failed to observe his vassals' rights, they could and did rebel. However, kings did possess some sources of power that other influential lords did not. Kings were anointed by holy oil in ceremonies reminiscent of Old Testament precedents; thus, their positions seemed sanctioned by divine favor. War and

◆ **The Tournament.** The tournament arose as a socially acceptable alternative to the private warfare that plagued the nobility. This illustration from *The Book of Tourneys* by King René of Anjou shows knights lined up for a mock battle. At the top red-robed judges and female supporters, seated in boxes, look on.

marriage alliances enabled them to increase their power, and their conquests enabled them to reward their followers with grants of land and bind powerful nobles to them. In the High Middle Ages, kings found ways to strengthen governmental institutions and consequently to extend their powers. The revival of commerce, the growth of cities, and the emergence of a money economy eventually undermined feudalism by enabling monarchs to hire soldiers and officials and to rely less on their vassals.

England in the High Middle Ages

In 1066, an army of heavily armed knights under William of Normany landed on the coast of England and soundly defeated King Harold and the Anglo-Saxon foot soldiers at the Battle of Hastings on October 14. William (1066–1087) was crowned king of England at Christmas

time in London and then began the process of combining Anglo-Saxon and Norman institutions to create a new England. Many of the Norman knights were given parcels of land by the new English king that they held as fiefs; each of these vassals in turn was responsible for supplying a quota of knights for the royal army. The great landed nobles were allowed to divide their lands among their subvassals however they wished. In 1086, however, by the Oath of Salisbury Plain, William required all subvassals to swear loyalty to him as their king. Henceforth, all subvassals owed their primary loyalty to the king rather than to their immediate feudal lords.

Thus, the Norman conquest of England brought about dramatic change. In Anglo-Saxon England, the king had held limited lands while great families controlled large stretches of land and acted rather independently of the king. In contrast, the Normans established a hierarchy of nobles holding land as fiefs from the king. William of Normany had manipulated the feudal system to create a strong, centralized monarchy. Gradually, a process of fusion between the victorious Normans and the defeated Anglo-Saxons created a new England. While the Norman ruling class spoke French, the intermarriage of the Norman-French with Anglo-Saxon nobility gradually merged Anglo-Saxon and French into a new English language. Political amalgamation also occurred as the Normans adapted existing Anglo-Saxon institutions, such as the office of sheriff. William also more fully developed the system of taxation and royal courts begun by the Anglo-Saxon kings of the tenth and eleventh centuries.

The Norman conquest of England had other repercussions as well. Because the new king of England was still the duke of Normandy, he was both a king (of England) and at the same time a vassal to a king (of France), but a vassal who was now far more powerful than his lord. This connection with France kept England heavily involved in continental affairs throughout the High Middle Ages.

In the twelfth century, the power of the English monarchy was greatly enlarged during the reign of Henry II (1154–1189), the founder of the Plantagenet dynasty. The new king was particularly successful in strengthening the power of the royal courts. Henry expanded the number of criminal cases to be tried in the king's court and also devised ways of taking property cases from feudal and county courts to the royal courts. Henry's goals were clear: expanding the jurisdiction of royal courts extended the king's power and, of course, brought revenues into his coffers. Moreover, because the royal courts were now administering law throughout England, a body of common law (law that was common to the whole kingdom) began to develop to replace the customary law used in county and feudal courts, which often varied from place to place. Thus, Henry's systematic approach to law played an important role in developing royal institutions common to the entire kingdom.

Henry was less successful at imposing royal control over the church and became involved in a famous struggle between church and state in medieval England. Henry claimed the right to punish clergymen in church courts, but Thomas Becket, archbishop of Canterbury, the highest ranking English cleric, claimed that only church courts could try clerics. Attempts at compromise failed, and the angry king publicly expressed the desire to be rid of Becket: "Who will free me of this priest?" he screamed. Four knights took the challenge, went to Canterbury, and murdered the archbishop in the cathedral. Faced with public outrage, Henry was forced to allow the right of appeal from English church courts to the papal court. Despite the compromise, Henry had succeeded overall in building a strong English monarchy.

Many English nobles came to resent the ongoing growth of the king's power and rose in rebellion during the reign of Henry's son, King John (1199–1216). At Runnymeade in 1215, John was forced to seal the Magna Carta (the Great Charter) of feudal liberties. The Magna Carta was, above all, a feudal document (see the box on p. 206). Feudal custom had always recognized that the relationship between king and vassals was based on mutual rights and obligations. Magna Carta gave written recognition to that fact and was used in subsequent years to

◆ **Norman Conquest of England from the Bayeux Tapestry.** The Bayeux tapestry, which consists of woolen embroidery on a linen backing, was made by English needlewomen before 1082 for Bayeux Cathedral. It depicts scenes from the Norman invasion of England. In this segment, the Normans are shown charging the shield wall of the Saxon infantry during the Battle of Hastings.

❧ *Magna Carta* ❧

After the dismal failure of King John to reconquer Normandy from the French king, some of the English barons rebelled against their king. At Runnymeade in 1215, King John agreed to seal the Magna Carta, the Great Charter of liberties regulating the relationship between the king and his vassals. What made Magna Carta an important historical document was its more general clauses defining rights and liberties. These were later interpreted in broader terms to make them applicable to all the English people.

Magna Carta

John, by the Grace of God, king of England, lord of Ireland, duke of Normandy and Aquitaine, count of Anjou, to the archbishops, bishops, abbots, earls, barons, justiciars, foresters, sheriffs, reeves, servants, and all bailiffs and his faithful people greeting.

1. In the first place we have granted to God, and by this our present charter confirmed, for us and our heirs forever, that the English church shall be free, and shall hold its rights entire and its liberties uninjured. . . . We have granted moreover to all free men of our kingdom for us and our heirs forever all the liberties written below, to be had and holden by themselves and their heirs from us and our heirs.

2. If any of our earls or barons, or others holding from us in chief by military service shall have died, and when he had died his heir shall be of full age and owe relief, he shall have his inheritance by the ancient relief; that is to say, the heir or heirs of an earl for the whole barony of an earl a hundred pounds; the heir or heirs of a baron for a whole barony a hundred pounds; the heir or heirs of a knight, for a whole knight's fee, a hundred shillings at most; and who owes less let him give less according to the ancient custom of fiefs.

3. If moreover the heir of any one of such shall be under age, and shall be in wardship, when he comes of age he shall have his inheritance without relief and without a fine. . . .

12. No scutage or aid shall be imposed in our kingdom except by the common council of our kingdom, except for the ransoming of our body, for the making of our oldest son a knight, and for once marrying our oldest daughter, and for these purposes it shall be only a reasonable aid. . . .

13. And the city of London shall have all its ancient liberties and free customs, as well by land as by water. Moreover, we will and grant that all other cities and boroughs and villages and ports shall have all their liberties and free customs.

14. And for holding a common council of the kingdom concerning the assessment of an aid otherwise than in the three cases mentioned above, or concerning the assessment of a scutage we shall cause to be summoned the archbishops, bishops, abbots, earls, and greater barons by our letters under seal; and besides we shall cause to be summoned generally, by our sheriffs and bailiffs all those who hold from us in chief, for a certain day, that is at the end of forty days at least, and for a certain place; and in all the letters of that summons, we will express the cause of the summons, and when the summons has thus been given the business shall proceed on the appointed day, on the advice of those who shall be present, even if not all of those who were summoned have come. . . .

39. No free man shall be taken or imprisoned or dispossessed, or outlawed, or banished, or in any way destroyed, nor will we go upon him, nor send upon him, except by the legal judgment of his peers or by the law of the land. . . .

60. Moreover, all those customs and franchises mentioned above which we have conceded in our kingdom, and which are to be fulfilled, as far as pertains to us, in respect to our men; all men of our kingdom as well as clergy as laymen, shall observe as far as pertains to them, in respect to their men.

---

strengthen the idea that the monarch's power was limited, not absolute.

During the reign of Edward I (1272–1307), an institution of great importance in the development of representative government—the English Parliament—emerged.

Originally the word *parliament* was applied to meetings of the king's Great Council in which the greater barons and chief prelates of the church met with the king's judges and principal advisers to deal with judicial affairs. But in his need for money, Edward I in 1295 invited two knights from every county and two residents from each town to meet with the Great Parliament to give their consent to new taxes. This was the first Parliament.

The English Parliament, then, came to be composed of two knights from every county and two burgesses from every borough as well as the barons and ecclesiastical lords. Eventually, barons and church lords formed the House of Lords; knights and burgesses, the House of Commons. The Parliaments of Edward I granted taxes, discussed politics, passed laws, and handled judicial business. Although not as yet the important body it would eventually become, the English Parliament had clearly emerged as an institution by the end of the thirteenth century. The law of the realm was beginning to be determined not by the king alone, but by the king in consultation with representatives of various groups that constituted the community.

The Growth of the French Kingdom

In 843, the Carolingian Empire had been divided into three major sections. The west Frankish lands formed the core of the eventual kingdom of France. In 987, after the death of the last Carolingian king, the west Frankish nobles chose Hugh Capet as the new king, thus establishing the Capetian dynasty of French kings. Although they carried the title of kings, the Capetians had little real power. They controlled as the royal domain (the lands of the king) only the lands around Paris known as the Ile-de-France. As kings of France, the Capetians were formally the overlords of the great lords of France, such as the dukes of Normandy, Brittany, Burgundy, and Aquitaine. In reality, however, many of the dukes were considerably more powerful than the Capetian kings. All in all, in the

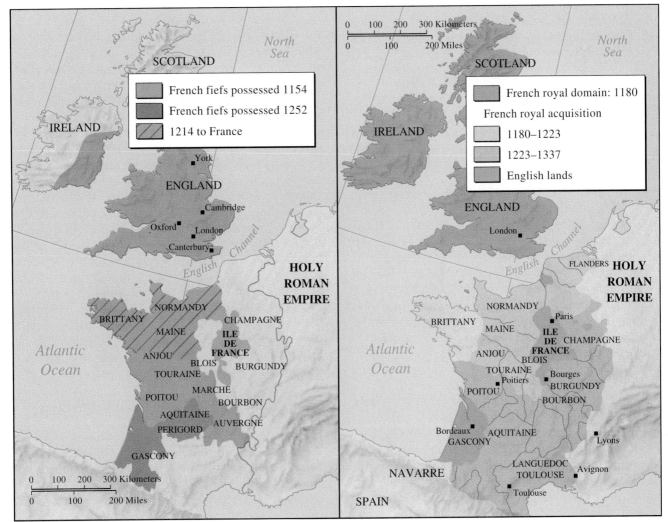

Map 10.2 England and France in the High Middle Ages: (*left*) England and its French Holdings; (*right*) Growth of the French State.

♦ **Louis IX Departs for Tunis.** The pious French king Louis IX organized the last two major crusades of the thirteenth century. Both failed miserably. This illustration shows a robust Louis IX setting out for Tunis in 1270. In truth, the king was so weak that he had to be carried to the ship.

eleventh and most of the twelfth centuries, the Capetians did little beyond consolidating their territory in the Ile-de-France. In the thirteenth century, however, this dynasty greatly enlarged its royal domain and its power, truly creating a centralized monarchical authority in France.

The reign of King Philip II Augustus (1180–1223) was an important turning point. He perceived that the power of the French monarch would never be extended until the Plantagenet power was defeated. After all, Henry II and his sons were not only kings of England, but rulers of the French territories of Normandy, Maine, Anjou, and Aquitaine. Accordingly, Philip II waged war against the Plantagenet rulers of England, but not until he defeated King John was he successful in wresting control of Normandy, Maine, Anjou, and Touraine. Through these conquests, Philip II quadrupled the income of the French monarchy and greatly enlarged its power. To administer justice and collect royal revenues in his new territories, Philip appointed new royal officials, thus inaugurating a French royal bureaucracy in the thirteenth century.

Capetian rulers after Philip II continued to add lands to the royal domain. Although Philip had used military force, other kings used both purchase and marriage to achieve the same end. Much of the thirteenth century was dominated by Louis IX (1226–1270), whom many consider the greatest of the medieval French kings. A deeply religious man, he was later canonized as a saint by the church, an unusual action regardless of the century. Louis was known for his attempts to bring justice to his people and ensure their rights. He sent out royal agents to check on the activities of royal officials after hearing complaints that they were abusing their power. Louis was also responsible for establishing a permanent royal court of justice in Paris whose work was carried on by a regular staff of professional jurists. This court came to be known as the *Parlement* of Paris. Sharing in the religious sentiments of of his age, Louis played a major role in two of the later crusades (see Chapter 11). Both were failures, and he met his death during an invasion of North Africa.

One of Louis's successors, Philip IV the Fair (1285–1314), was particularly effective in strengthening the French monarchy. The machinery of government became even more specialized. French kings going back to the early Capetians had possessed a household staff for running their affairs. In effect, it was the division and enlargement of this household staff that produced the three major branches of royal administration: a council for advice; a *chambre des comptes* or chamber of accounts for finances; and a *parlement* or royal court. By the beginning of the fourteenth century, the Capetians had created the firm foundations for a royal bureaucracy.

Philip IV was also responsible for bringing the French parliament into being. When the king became involved in a struggle with the pope, Philip summoned representatives of the church, nobility, and towns to meet with him in 1302, inaugurating the Estates-General, the first parliament. The Estates-General proved invaluable to the king because feudal custom had limited the power of kings to make changes contrary to that custom. The Estates-General came to function as an instrument to bolster the king's power because he could ask representatives of the major French social classes to change the laws or grant new taxes. By the end of the thirteenth century, France was the largest, wealthiest, and best governed monarchical state in Europe.

Christian Reconquest: The Spanish Kingdoms

Much of Spain had been part of the Islamic world since the eighth century. Muslim Spain had flourished in the Early Middle Ages. Córdoba became a major urban center with a population exceeding 300,000 people. Agriculture prospered, and Spain became known as well for excellent leather, wool, silk, and paper. Beginning in the tenth century, however, the most noticeable feature of Spanish history was the weakening of Muslim power and the beginning of a Christian reconquest that lasted until the final expulsion of the Muslims at the end of the fifteenth century.

By the beginning of the eleventh century, a number of small Christian kingdoms in northern Spain took the offensive against the Muslims. By the end of the twelfth century, the northern half of Spain had been consolidated into the Christian kingdoms of Castile, Navarre, Aragon, and Portugal, which had first emerged as a separate kingdom in 1139. The southern half of Spain remained under the control of the Muslims. But in the thirteenth century, Aragon, Castile, and Portugal made significant conquests of Muslim territory. Castile subdued most of Andalusia in the south, down to the Atlantic and Mediterranean; at the same time, Aragon conquered Valencia. The Muslims remained ensconced only in the kingdom of Granada in the southeast of the Iberian peninsula, which remained an independent Muslim state.

The Spanish kingdoms followed no consistent policy in the treatment of the conquered Muslim population. Muslim farmers continued to work the land but were forced to pay very high rents in Aragon. In Castile King Alfonso X (1252–1284), who called himself the "King of Three Religions," encouraged the continued development of a cosmopolitan culture shared by Christians, Jews, and Muslims. Toledo still flourished as an important center of intellectual life.

The Lands of the Holy Roman Empire: Germany and Italy

In the tenth century, the powerful dukes of the Saxons became kings of the lands of the eastern Frankish kingdom (or Germany, as it came to be known). The best known of the Saxon kings of Germany was Otto I (936–973), who intervened in Italian politics and for his efforts was crowned by the pope in 962, reviving a title that had not been used since the time of Charlemagne. Otto's creation of a new "Roman Empire" in the hands of the eastern Franks (or Germans, as they came to be called) added a tremendous burden to the kings of Germany who now took on the onerous task of ruling Italy as well.

In the eleventh century, German kings managed to create a strong monarchy and a powerful empire by leading armies into Italy. But they also experienced the frustrating difficulties inherent in the position of the German kings. The elective nature of the German monarchy posed a problem for the German kings. While some dynasties were strong enough for their members to be elected regularly, the great lords who were the electors did at times deliberately choose otherwise. It was to their advantage to select a weak king.

To compensate for their weaknesses, German kings had come to rely on their ability to control the church and select bishops and abbots whom they could then use as royal administrators. But the struggle between church and state during the reign of Henry IV (1056–1106)

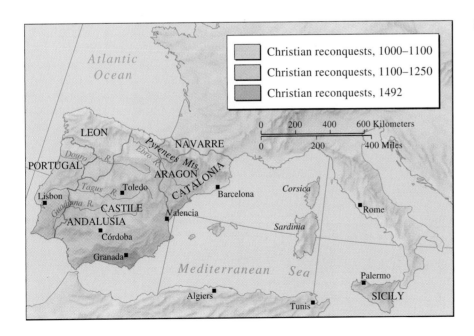

Map 10.3 Christian Reconquests in the Western Mediterranean.

weakened the king's ability to use church officials in this way (see Chapter 9). The German kings also tried to bolster their power by using their position as emperors to exploit the resources of Italy. But this tended to backfire; many a German king lost armies in Italy in pursuit of a dream of empire, and no German dynasty demonstrates this better than the Hohenstaufens.

Both Frederick I (1152–1190) and Frederick II (1212–1250) tried to create a foundation for a new kind of empire. Frederick I, known as Barbarossa or Redbeard to the Italians, was a powerful lord from the Swabian house of Hohenstaufen when he was elected king. Previous German kings had focused on building a strong German kingdom, to which Italy might be added as an appendage. To Frederick I, however, Germany was simply a feudal monarchy; he planned to get his chief revenues from Italy as the center of a "holy empire," as he called it (hence the term Holy Roman Empire). But his attempt to conquer northern Italy ran into severe difficulties. The pope opposed him, fearful that the emperor wanted to include Rome and the Papal States as part of his empire.

The cities of northern Italy, which had become virtually independent entities after overthrowing the rule of their bishops, were also not willing to be Frederick's subjects. An alliance of these northern Italian cities, called the Lombard League, with the support of the papacy, defeated the forces of Emperor Frederick at Legnano in 1176.

Frederick II was the most brilliant of the Hohenstaufen rulers. King of Sicily in 1198, king of Germany in 1212, and crowned emperor in 1220, Frederick II was a truly remarkable man who awed his contemporaries. Frederick had been raised in Sicily with its diverse peoples, languages, and religions. His court brought together a brilliant array of lawyers, poets, artists, and scientists, and he himself took a deep interest in their work. He was by no means a devout Christian by contemporary standards and had no fear of papal threats. He was not adverse to using Muslim mercenaries, and it was said that he kept a harem of Muslim women for his enjoyment.

Until 1220, Frederick spent much time in Germany; once he left in 1220, he rarely returned. He gave the German princes full control of their territories, voluntarily

Map 10.4 The Holy Roman Empire.

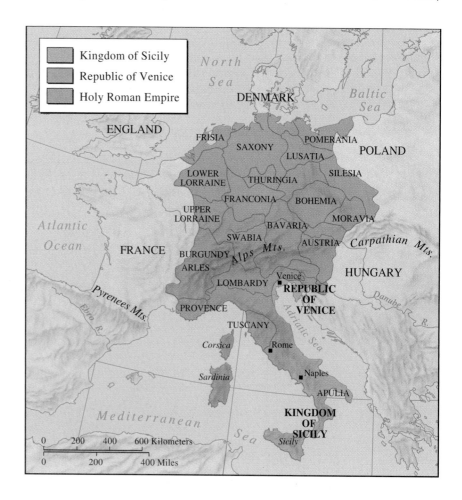

surrendering any real power over Germany to keep it quiet while he pursued his main goal, the establishment of a strong centralized state in Italy dominated by his kingdom in Sicily. Frederick's major task was to gain control of northern Italy. In trying to extend his power in Italy, he became involved in a deadly struggle with the popes, who realized that a single ruler of northern and southern Italy meant the end of papal secular power in central Italy. The northern Italian cities were also unwilling to give up their freedom. Frederick waged a bitter struggle in northern Italy, winning many battles but ultimately losing the war. After his death in 1250, the remaining Hohenstaufens were obliterated, and the papacy stood supreme over the ashes of a failed Hohenstaufen empire.

Frederick's preoccupation with the creation of an empire in Italy left Germany in confusion and chaos until 1273 when the major German princes, serving as electors, chose an insignificant German noble, Rudolf of Habsburg, as the new German king. In choosing a weak king, the princes were ensuring that the German monarchy would remain impotent and incapable of reestablishing a centralized monarchical state. The failure of the Hohenstaufens had led to a situation where his exalted majesty, the German king and Holy Roman Emperor, had no real power over either Germany or Italy. Unlike France, England, and even Spain, neither Germany nor Italy created a unified national monarchy in the Middle Ages. Both became geographical designations for loose confederations of hundreds of petty, independent states under the vague direction of king or emperor. In fact, neither Germany nor Italy would become united until the nineteenth century.

Following the death of Frederick II, Italy fell into considerable political confusion. While the papacy remained in control of much of central Italy, the defeat of imperial power left the cities and towns of northern Italy independent of any other authority. Gradually, the larger ones began to emerge as strong city-states. After defeating Pisa in 1284, Genoa came to dominate its immediate region. Florence assumed the leadership of Tuscany while Milan, under the guidance of the Visconti family, took control of the Lombard region. With its great commercial wealth, the republic of Venice dominated the northeastern part of the peninsula.

New Kingdoms in Eastern Europe

In eastern Europe, Hungary, which had been a Christian state since 1000, remained relatively stable throughout the High Middle Ages, but the history of Poland and Russia was far more turbulent. In the thirteenth century, eastern Europe was beset by two groups of invaders, the

CHRONOLOGY

The Growth of the European Kingdoms

England	
Battle of Hastings	1066
William the Conqueror	1066–1087
Henry II, first of the Plantagenet dynasty	1154–1189
Murder of Thomas Becket	1170
John	1199–1216
Magna Carta	1215
Edward I	1272–1307
The "greater Parliaments"	1295 and 1297
France	
Hugh Capet chosen as French king	987
Philip II Augustus	1180–1223
Louis IX	1226–1270
Philip IV	1285–1314
First Estates-General	1302
Spain	
Establishment of Portugal	1139
Alfonso X of Castile	1252–1284
Germany, the Empire, and Italy	
Otto I	936–973
Henry IV	1056–1106
Frederick I Barbarossa	1152–1190
Lombard League defeats Frederick at Legnano	1176
Frederick II	1212–1250
Election of Rudolf of Habsburg as king of Germany	1273
Eastern Europe	
East Prussia given to the Teutonic Knights	1226
Mongol conquest of Russia	1230s
Alexander Nevsky, Prince of Novgorod	c. 1220–1263
Defeat of Germans	1242

Teutonic Knights from the west and the Mongols from the east.

In the eleventh century, a Polish kingdom existed as a separate state, but with no natural frontiers. Consequently, German settlers encroached on its territory on a

regular basis, leading to considerable intermarriage between Slavs and Germans. During the thirteenth century,
relations between the Germans and the Slavs of eastern
Europe worsened due to the aggression of the Teutonic
Knights. The Teutonic Knights had been founded near
the end of the twelfth century to protect the Christian
Holy Land. In the early thirteenth century, however,
these Christian knights found greater opportunity to the
east of Germany where they attacked the pagan Slavs.

East Prussia was given to the military order in 1226, and
five years later, the knights moved beyond the Vistula
where they waged war against the Slavs for another thirty
years. By the end of the thirteenth century, Prussia had
become German and Christian as the pagan Slavs were
forced to convert (see the box on p. 213).

Central and eastern Europe had periodically been subject to invasions from fierce Asiatic nomads, such as the
Huns, Avars, Bulgars, and Magyars. In the thirteenth

Map 10.5 Eastern Europe.

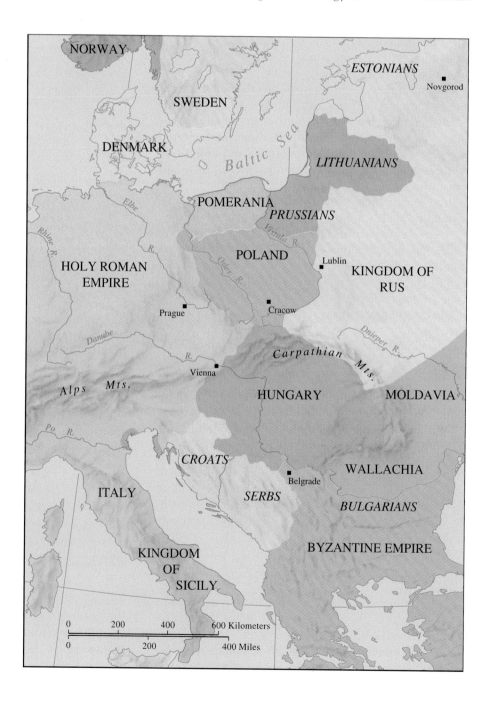

Ethnic Cleansing in Eastern Europe

One of the most important migrations in the High Middle Ages was the movement of Germans and people from the Low Countries—all of them Christians—into central and eastern Europe. This push to the east was often accompanied by a considerable slaughter of the native Slavs, who were not Christian. One of the leaders in this effort was Albert the Bear, ruler of the lands that came to be known as Brandenburg. This description of Albert's activities is taken from an account of the German expansion to the east by Helmold, a priest from Bosau.

Helmold, *The Chronicle of the Slavs*

At that time Albert, the margrave whose by-name is the Bear, held eastern Slavia. By the favor of God he also prospered splendidly in the portion of his lot; for he brought under his sway all the country of the Brizani, the Stoderani, and the many tribes dwelling along the Havel and the Elbe, and he curbed the rebellious ones among them. In the end, as the Slavs gradually decreased in number, he sent to Utrecht and to places lying on the Rhine, to those, moreover, who live by the ocean and suffer the violence of the sea—namely, Hollanders, Zeelanders, Flemings—and he brought large numbers of them and had them live in the strongholds and villages of the Slavs. The bishopric of Brandenburg, and likewise that of Havelberg, was greatly strengthened by the coming of the foreigners, because the churches multiplied and the income from the tithes grew enormously. At the same time foreigners from Holland also began to settle on the southern bank of the Elbe; the Hollanders received all the swamp and open country together with many cities and villages from the city Salzwedel clear to the Bohemian woodland. These lands, indeed, the Saxons are said to have occupied of old—namely in the time of the Ottos—as can be seen from the ancient levees that had been constructed along the banks of the Elbe. But afterward, when the Slavs got the upper hand, the Saxons were killed and the land has been held by the Slavs down to our own times. Now, however, because God gave plentiful aid and victory to our duke and to the other princes, the Slavs have been everywhere crushed and driven out. A people strong and without number have come from the bounds of the ocean, and taken possession of the territories of the Slavs. They have built cities and churches and have grown in riches beyond all estimation.

---

century, the Mongols exploded on the scene, causing far more disruption than earlier invaders. Beginning in the 1230s, the Mongols moved into Europe. They conquered Russia, advanced into Poland and Hungary, and destroyed a force of Poles and Teutonic Knights in Silesia in 1241. Europe then seemingly got lucky when the Mongol hordes turned back because of internal fighting; western and southern Europe escaped the wrath of the Mongols. Over the long run, the Mongols left little of any real importance, although their occupation of Russia certainly had some effect on that land.

THE DEVELOPMENT OF RUSSIA

The Kiev Rus state, which had formally become Christian in 987, prospered considerably afterward, reaching its high point in the first half of the eleventh century. Kievan society was dominated by a noble class of landowners known as the boyars, who represented a mixture of Scandinavian (Rus) descendents and chiefs of the old Slavic tribes. Kievan merchants maintained regular trade with Scandinavia to the north and the Islamic and Byzantine worlds to the south. But destructive civil wars and new invasions by Asiatic nomads caused the Principality of Kiev to disintegrate into a number of constituent parts. The sack of Kiev by north Russian princes in 1169 brought an inglorious end to the first Russian state.

The fundamental civilizing and unifying force of early Russia was the Christian church. The Russian church imitated the liturgy and organization of the Byzantine Empire, whose Eastern Orthodox priests had converted the Kievan Rus to Christianity at the end of the tenth century. The Russian church became known for its rigid religious orthodoxy. Although Christianity provided a common bond between Russian and European civilization, Russia's religious development guaranteed an even closer affinity between Russian and Byzantine civilization.

In the thirteenth century, the Mongols conquered Russia and cut it off even more from western Europe. The Mongols were not numerous enough to settle the vast Russian lands, but were content to rule directly an area along the lower Volga and north of the Caspian and Black

Seas to Kiev and rule indirectly elsewhere. In the latter territories, Russian princes were required to pay tribute to the Mongol overlords.

One Russian prince soon emerged as more visible and powerful than the others. Alexander Nevsky (c. 1220–1263), prince of Novgorod, defeated a German invading army at Lake Peipus in northwestern Russia in 1242. His cooperation with the Mongols, which included denouncing his own brother and crushing native tax revolts, won him their favor. The khan, the acknowledged leader of the western part of the Mongol empire, rewarded Alexander Nevsky with the title of grand-prince, enabling his descendants to become the princes of Moscow and eventually leaders of all Russia.

Conclusion

The period from 1000 to 1300 was a very dynamic one in the development of Western civilization. It witnessed economic, social, and political changes that some historians believe set European civilization on a path that lasted until the eighteenth century when the Industrial Revolution created a new pattern. The revival of trade, the expansion of towns and cities, and the development of a money economy did not mean the end of a predominantly rural European society, but they did open the door to new ways to make a living and new opportunities for people to expand and enrich their lives. Eventually, they created the foundations for the development of a predominantly urban industrial society.

The nobles, whose warlike attitudes were rationalized by labeling them as the defenders of Christian society, continued to dominate the medieval world politically, economically, and socially. But quietly and surely, within this world of castles and private power, kings gradually began to extend their public powers. Although the popes sometimes treated rulers as if they were their servants, by the thirteenth century, monarchs themselves were developing the machinery of government that would enable them to challenge these exalted claims of papal power and become the centers of political authority in Europe. Although they could not know it then, the actions of these medieval monarchs laid the foundation for the European kingdoms that in one form or another have dominated the European political scene ever since.

NOTES

1. Quoted in Jean Gimpel, *The Medieval Machine* (Harmondsworth, 1977), p. 92.
2. Quoted in Joseph and Frances Gies, *Life in a Medieval Castle* (New York, 1974), p. 175.

3. Quoted in Robert Delort, *Life in the Middle Ages*, trans. Robert Allen (New York, 1972), p. 218.

SUGGESTIONS FOR FURTHER READING

On the revival of trade, see R. S. Lopez, *The Commercial Revolution of the Middle Ages: 950–1350* (Englewood Cliffs, N.J., 1971); and A. Sapori, *The Italian Merchant in the Middle Ages* (New York, 1970). Urban history is covered in E. Ennen, *The Medieval Town* (Amsterdam, 1978); H. A. Miskimin, D. Herlihy, and A. L. Udovich, eds., *The Medieval City* (New Haven, Conn., 1977); and the classic work of H. Pirenne, *Medieval Cities* (Princeton, N.J., 1925). There is an extensive section on medieval cities in M. Girouard, *Cities and People: A Social and Architectural History* (New Haven, Conn., 1985). A popular, readable study is J. and F. Gies, *Life in a Medieval City* (New York, 1969).

Works on the function and activities of the nobility in the High Middle Ages include S. Reynolds, *Kingdoms and Communities in Western Europe 900–1300* (Oxford, 1984); T. A. Reuter, ed., *The Medieval Nobility* (Amsterdam and Oxford, 1978); M. Keen, *Chivalry* (London, 1984); P. Contamine, *War in the Middle Ages* (Oxford, 1984); G. Duby, *The Chivalrous Society* (Berkeley, 1977);

and the classic work by M. Bloch, *Feudal Society* (London, 1961). G. Duby discusses the theory of medieval social order in *The Three Orders* (Chicago, 1980). Various aspects of the social history of the nobility can be found in G. Duby, *The Knight, the Lady, and the Priest* (London, 1984), on noble marriages; R. Barber and J. Barker, *Tournaments: Jousts, Chivalry and Pageants in the Middle Ages* (New York, 1989), on tournaments; W. Anderson, *Castles of Europe* (London, 1970); C. B. Bouchard, *Life and Society in the West: Antiquity and the Middle Ages* (San Diego, 1988), Ch. 6; N. J. G. Pounds, *The Medieval Castle in England and Wales, A Social and Political History* (New York, 1990); and Robert Delort, *Life in the Middle Ages*, trans. Robert Allen (New York, 1972). Also enjoyable is the popular study by J. and F. Gies, *Life in a Medieval Castle* (New York, 1974). On women, see R. T. Morewedge, ed., *The Role of Women in the Middle Ages* (Albany, N.Y., 1975); and S. M. Stuard, ed., *Women in Medieval Society* (Philadelphia, 1976).

There are numerous works on the different feudal principalities: On England, see R. R. Davies, *Domination and Conquest: The Experience of Scotland and Wales, 1100–1300* (Cambridge, 1990); F. Barlow, *The Feudal Kingdom of England, 1042–1216*, 3d ed. (New York, 1972); D. C. Douglas, *William the Conqueror: The Norman Impact upon England* (Berkeley, 1964); R. Frame, *The Political Development of the British Isles, 1100–1400* (Oxford, 1990); and W. L. Warren, *Henry II* (Berkeley, 1973). On Germany, see A. Haverkamp, *Medieval Germany* (Oxford, 1988); B. Arnold, *German Knighthood 1050–1300* (Ox-

ford, 1985); H. Fuhrmann, *Germany in the High Middle Ages c. 1050–1250* (Cambridge, 1986), an excellent account; B. Arnold, *Princes and Territories in Medieval Germany* (Cambridge, 1991); and P. Munz's biography, *Frederick Barbarossa* (London, 1969). On France, see J. Dunbabin, *France in the Making 843–1180* (Oxford, 1985); and E. M. Hallam, *Capetian France 987–1328* (London, 1980), a well-done general account. On the Normans, see J. le Patourel, *The Norman Empire* (Oxford, 1976); and D. C. Douglas, *The Norman Achievement* (London, 1969), and *The Norman Fate* (Berkeley, 1977). On Spain, see G. Jackson, *The Making of Medieval Spain* (London, 1972); A. Mackay, *Spain in the Middle Ages* (London, 1977); J. F. Powers, *A Society Organized for War* (Berkeley, 1988); and H. Dillard, *Daughters of the Reconquest* (Cambridge, 1984). On Italy, see D. J. Herlihy, *Cities and Society in Medieval Italy* (London, 1980); J. K. Hyde, *Society and Politics in Medieval Italy* (London, 1973); and G. Tabacco, *The Struggle for Power in Medieval Italy* (New York, 1989). On eastern Europe, see N. Davies, *God's Playground: A History of Poland*, vol. 1 (Oxford, 1981); J. Fennell, *The Crisis of Medieval Russia, 1200–1304* (New York, 1983); and the books listed for Chapter 8.

For specialized studies in the political history of the thirteenth century, see J. C. Holt, *Magna Carta* (Cambridge, 1965); D. Abulafia, *Frederick II. A Medieval Emperor* (London, 1987); M. W. Labarge, *St. Louis: The Life of Louis IX of France* (London, 1968); J. R. Strayer, *The Reign of Philip the Fair* (Princeton, 1980); and J. F. O'Callaghan, *A History of Medieval Spain* (Ithaca, N.Y., 1975).

Crusades and Culture in the High Middle Ages

The economic, religious, and political growth of the High Middle Ages gave European society a new confidence that enabled it to look beyond its borders to the lands and empires of the east. Only a confident Europe could have undertaken the crusades, the military effort to recover the Holy Land of the Near East from the Muslims. The crusades gave the revived papacy of the High Middle Ages yet another opportunity to demonstrate its influence over European society. The crusades were a curious mix of God and warfare, two of the chief concerns of the Middle Ages. In the first crusade, a group of French knights under Bohemund managed to capture the city of Antioch in 1098, but a Muslim relief force counterattacked, surrounding the French knights in their newly conquered city. Bohemund's forces seemed doomed until a "miraculous discovery" was made in an Antioch church—the Holy Lance, the spear allegedly used to pierce Christ's body at the crucifixion. To prove the authenticity and power of the lance, its discoverer, Peter Bartholomew, agreed to a test. According to the chronicler Raymond of Aguilers, the crusaders set two piles of dry olive branches on fire. When the bonfires were burning fiercely, Peter Bartholomew, dressed only in his tunic but armed with the Holy Lance, stepped into the flames. He emerged a few minutes later unscathed, with no injuries, a sure sign to the onlookers of the special qualities of the lance. Inspired, the French troops marched out, defeated the Muslim forces, and lifted the siege of Antioch. The leaders of the army wrote to the pope, saying: "After firmly ordering our battle-lines, of both foot and horse, we boldly sought the place where their valor and bravery were greatest. The Holy Lance was with us, and from the very first engagement of the battle we forced the enemy to flee." The crusading knights then went on to capture the Holy City of Jerusalem.

Western assurance and energy, so crucial to the crusades, were also evident in a burst of intellectual and artistic activity. A rebirth of classical learning, new educational institutions known as universities, a

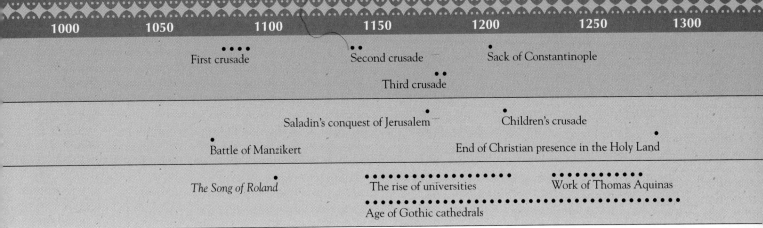

1000	1050	1100	1150	1200	1250	1300

First crusade • • • •
Second crusade • •
Sack of Constantinople •
Third crusade • •

Saladin's conquest of Jerusalem •
Children's crusade •
Battle of Manzikert •
End of Christian presence in the Holy Land •

The Song of Roland •
The rise of universities • • • • • • • • • • • • • • • •
Work of Thomas Aquinas • • • • • • • • • • • •
Age of Gothic cathedrals •

systematic approach to the study of theology and law, the development of science and technology, and a growing and diverse vernacular literature all gave witness to a vibrant intellectual life. At the same time, a religious building spree—especially evident in the great Romanesque and Gothic cathedrals of the age— left the landscape bedecked with churches that were the visible symbols of Christian Europe's vitality.

Background to the Crusades

Although European civilization developed in relative isolation, it had never entirely lost contact with the lands and empires of the east. At the end of the eleventh century, that contact increased, in part because developments in the Islamic and Byzantine worlds prompted the first major attempt of the new European civilization to expand beyond Europe proper.

The Islamic Empire

By the mid-tenth century, the Islamic empire led by the Abbasid caliphate in Baghdad was in the process of disintegration. An attempt was made in the tenth century to unify the Islamic world under the direction of a Shi'ite dynasty known as the Fatimids. Their origins lay in North Africa, but they managed to conquer Egypt and establish the new city of Cairo as their capital. In establishing a Shi'ite caliphate, they became rivals to the Sunni caliphate of Bagdad. Although the Fatimids did move into Syria and Arabia, they were unable to overcome the Abbasids in Mesopotamia, and the Islamic world remained divided.

Nevertheless, the Fatimid dynasty prospered and surpassed the Abbasid caliphate as the dynamic center of the Islamic world. Benefiting from their position in the heart of the Nile delta, the Fatimids played a major role in the regional trade passing from the Mediterranean to the Red Sea and beyond. They were tolerant in matters of religion and created a strong army by using nonnative peoples as mercenaries. One of these peoples, the Seljuk Turks, soon posed a threat to the Fatimids themselves.

The Seljuk Turks were a nomadic people from central Asia who had been converted to Islam and flourished as military mercenaries for the Abbasid caliphate. Moving gradually into Iran and Armenia, they grew in number until by the eleventh century they were able to take over the eastern provinces of the Abbasid empire. In 1055, a Turkish leader captured Baghdad and assumed command of the Abbasid empire with the title of sultan (the word means "holder of power"). While the Abbasid caliph remained as the chief Sunni religious authority, the real military and political power of the state was in the hands of the Seljuk Turks. By the last quarter of the eleventh century, the Seljuk Turks were exerting military pressure on Egypt and the Byzantine Empire. When the Byzantine emperor foolishly challenged the Turks, the latter routed the Byzantine army at Manzikert in 1071. In dire straits, the Byzantines turned to the west for help, setting in motion the papal pleas that led to the crusades. To understand the complexities of the situation, however, we need to look first at the Byzantine Empire.

The Byzantine Empire

The Macedonian dynasty of the tenth and eleventh centuries had restored much of the power of the Byzantine Empire; its incompetent successors, however, reversed most of the gains. After the Macedonian dynasty was extinguished in 1056, the empire was beset by internal struggles for power between ambitious military leaders and aristocratic families who attempted to buy the support of the great landowners of Anatolia by allowing them greater control over their peasants. This policy was self-destructive, however, because the peasant-warrior was the traditional backbone of the Byzantine state.

The growing division between the Catholic church of the west and the Eastern Orthodox church of the Byzantine Empire also weakened the Byzantine state. The Eastern Orthodox church was unwilling to accept the pope's claim that he was the sole head of the church. This issue reached a climax when Pope Leo IX and the Patriarch Michael Cerularius, head of the Byzantine church, formally excommunicated each other in 1054, initiating a schism between the two great branches of Christianity that has not been completely healed to this day.

The Byzantine Empire faced external threats to its security as well. The greatest challenge came from the Seljuk Turks who had moved into Asia Minor—the heartland of the empire and its main source of food and manpower. In 1071, the Byzantine forces were disastrously defeated at Manzikert by a Turkish army. The Turks then advanced into Anatolia where many peasants, already disgusted by their exploitation at the hands of Byzantine landowners, readily accepted Turkish control.

A new dynasty, however, soon breathed new life into the Byzantine Empire. The Comneni, under Alexius I Comnenus (1081–1118), were victorious on the Greek Adriatic coast against the Normans, defeated the Pechenegs in the Balkans, and stopped the Turks in Anatolia. Lacking the resources to undertake additional campaigns against the Turks, Emperor Alexius I turned to the west for military assistance. It was the positive response of the west to the emperor's request that led to the crusades. The Byzantine Empire lived to regret it.

The Crusades

The crusades were based on the idea of a holy war against the infidel or unbeliever. Although the concept of unbeliever was eventually broadened to include other groups, Christendom's wrath was initially directed against the Muslims. At the end of the eleventh century, Christian Europe found itself with a glorious opportunity to attack the Muslims.

The immediate impetus for the crusades came when the Byzantine emperor Alexius I asked Pope Urban II (1088–1099) for help against the Seljuk Turks. The pope saw a golden opportunity to provide papal leadership for a great cause: to rally the warriors of Europe for the liberation of Jerusalem and the Holy Land from the infidel. At the Council of Clermont in southern France near the end of 1095, Urban challenged Christians to take up their weapons against the infidel and participate in a holy war to recover the Holy Land (see the box on p. 219). The pope promised remission of sins: "All who die by the way, whether by land or by sea, or in battle against the pagans, shall have immediate remission of sins. This I grant them through the power of God with which I am invested."[1]

The initial response to Urban's speech reveals how appealing many people found this combined call to military arms and religious fervor. A self-appointed leader, Peter the Hermit, who preached of his visions of the Holy City of Jerusalem, convinced a large mob, most of them poor and many of them peasants, to undertake a crusade to the east. This "Peasants' Crusade" or "Crusade of the Poor" comprised a ragtag rabble that moved through the Balkans, terrorizing natives and looting them for their food and supplies. Their misplaced religious enthusiasm led also to the persecution of Jews, long branded by the church as the murderers of Christ. As a contemporary

◆ **Peasants' Crusade.** Before the aristocracy could organize a crusade in response to the call of Pope Urban II, a large group of peasants joined the fanatical Peter the Hermit and Walter the Penniless in an attempt to free the Holy Land. When they could not buy food, the poorly armed peasants ravaged the countryside and looted towns. This illustration shows a group of Hungarians attacking the peasants and reclaiming their goods.

≈ Pope Urban II Proclaims a Crusade ≈

Toward the end of the eleventh century, the Byzantine emperor Alexius I sent Pope Urban II a request for aid against the Seljuk Turks. At the Council of Clermont, Urban II appealed to a large crowd to take up weapons and recover Palestine from the Muslims. This description of Urban's appeal is taken from an account by Fulcher of Chartres.

Pope Urban II

Pope Urban II . . . addressed them [the French] in a very persuasive speech, as follows: "O race of the Franks, O people who live beyond the mountains [that is, reckoned from Rome], O people loved and chosen of God, as is clear from your many deeds, distinguished over all other nations by the situation of your land, your catholic faith, and your regard for the holy church, we have a special message and exhortation for you. For we wish you to know what a grave matter has brought us to your country. The sad news has come from Jerusalem and Constantinople that the people of Persia, an accursed and foreign race [the Seljuk Turks], enemies of God, . . . have invaded the lands of those Christians and devastated them with the sword, rapine, and fire. Some of the Christians they have carried away as slaves, others they have put to death. The churches they have either destroyed or turned into mosques. They desecrate and overthrow the altars. They circumcise the Christians and pour the blood from the circumcision on the altars or in the baptismal fonts. Some they kill in a horrible way by cutting open the abdomen, taking out a part of the entrails and tying them to a stake; they then beat them and compel them to walk until all their entrails are drawn out and they fall to the ground. Some they use as targets for their arrows. They compel some to stretch out their necks and then they try to see whether they can cut off their heads with one strike of the sword. It is better to say nothing of their horrible treatment of the women. They have taken from the Greek empire a tract of land so large that it takes more than two months to walk through it. Whose duty is to avenge this and recover that land, if not yours? For to you more than to any other nations the Lord has given the military spirit, courage, agile bodies, and the bravery to strike down those who resist you. Let your minds be stirred to bravery by the deeds of your forefathers, and by the efficiency and greatness of Karl the Great [Charlemagne], . . . and of the other kings who have destroyed Turkish kingdoms, and established Christianity in their lands. You should be moved especially by the holy grave of our Lord and Savior which is now held by unclean peoples, and by the holy places which are treated with dishonor and irreverently befouled with their uncleanness. . . .

"O bravest of knights, descendants of unconquered ancestors, do not be weaker than they, but remember their courage. . . . Set out on the road to the holy sepulchre, take the land from that wicked people, and make it your own. . . . Jerusalem is the best of all lands, more fruitful than all others. . . . This land our Savior made illustrious by his birth, beautiful with his life, and sacred with his suffering. . . . This royal city is now held captive by her enemies, and made pagan by those who know not God. She asks and longs to be liberated and does not cease to beg you to come to her aid. . . . Set out on this journey and you will obtain the remission of your sins and be sure of the incorruptible glory of the kingdom of heaven."

When Pope Urban had said this and much more of the same sort, all who were present were moved to cry out with one accord, "It is the will of God, it is the will of God." When the pope heard this he raised his eyes to heaven and gave thanks to God, and commanding silence with a gesture of his hand, he said: "My dear brethren, today there is fulfilled in you that which the Lord says in the Gospel, 'Where two or three are gathered together in my name, there am I in the midst.' For unless the Lord God had been in your minds you would not all have said the same thing. . . . So I say unto you, God, who put those words into your hearts, has caused you to utter them. Therefore let these words be your battle cry, because God caused you to speak them. Whenever you meet the enemy in battle, you shall all cry out, 'It is the will of God, it is the will of God. . . .' Whoever therefore shall determine to make this journey and shall make a vow to God and shall offer himself as a living sacrifice, holy, acceptable to God, shall wear a cross on his brow or on his breast. And when he returns after having fulfilled his vow he shall wear the cross on his back."

CHRONOLOGY

◆◆◆◆◆◆◆◆◆◆◆◆◆◆◆◆◆◆◆◆◆◆◆◆◆◆◆◆◆◆◆◆

The Early Crusades

Pope Urban II's call for a crusade at Clermont	1095
Peasants' crusade	1096
First crusade	1096–1099
Fall of Edessa	1144
Second crusade	1147–1149
Saladin's conquest of Jerusalem	1187
Third crusade	1189–1192

chronicler described it, " . . . while passing through the cities along the Rhine, Main, and Danube, led by their zeal for Christianity, they persecuted the hated race of the Jews wherever they were found, and strove either to destroy them completely or to compel them to become Christians."[2] Two bands of peasant crusaders led by Peter the Hermit and Walter the Penniless managed to reach Constantinople. Emperor Alexius I wisely shipped them over to Asia Minor where the undisciplined and poorly armed rabble was massacred by the Turks.

The Early Crusades

Pope Urban II did not share the wishful thinking of the peasant crusaders but was more inclined to trust knights who had been well trained in the art of war. The first crusading armies were recruited from the warrior class of western Europe, particularly France. Although the knights who made up this first serious crusading host were motivated by religious fervor, there were other attractions as well. Some sought adventure and welcomed a legitimate opportunity to pursue their favorite pastime—fighting. Others saw an opportunity to gain territory, riches, status, possibly a title, and even salvation—had the pope not offered a full remission of sins for those who participated in these "armed pilgrimages"? From the perspective of the pope and European monarchs, the crusades offered a way to rid Europe of contentious young nobles who disturbed the peace and wasted lives and energy fighting each other.

Three organized crusading bands of noble warriors, most of them French, made their way to Constantinople by 1097. Emperor Alexis was not pleased with their arrival and greatly distrusted their motives. Instead of a band of mercenaries that he could pay to fight on his be-

half, Alexius got a group of French nobles who wanted to conquer the Holy Land for their own purposes. The emperor entered into negotiations with the crusaders who eventually agreed to take an oath of allegiance to him.

The crusading army probably numbered several thousand cavalry and as many as 10,000 foot soldiers. After the capture of Antioch in 1098, much of the crusading host proceeded down the coast of Palestine, evading the garrisoned coastal cities, and reached Jerusalem in June 1099. After a five-week siege, the Holy City was taken amidst a horrible massacre of the inhabitants, men, women, and children. As executed by the crusaders, "God's judgment" on the infidels was indeed a frightful one (see the box on p. 221).

After further conquest of Palestinian lands, the crusaders largely ignored their promises to the Byzantine emperor and proceeded to organize four crusader states: the principality of Antioch, the county of Edessa, the county of Tripoli, and the kingdom of Jerusalem. In keeping with their own traditional practices, the crusading leaders created organized feudal states. Antioch, Edessa, and Tripoli were all held as fiefs under the ruler of the kingdom of Jerusalem. Because the crusader states existed in a world surrounded by Muslim enemies, they grew increasingly dependent on the Italian commercial cities for supplies from Europe. Some Italian cities, such as Genoa, Pisa, and above all, Venice, waxed rich and powerful in the process.

THE SECOND CRUSADE

It was not easy for the crusader states to maintain themselves in the east. Already by the 1120s, the Muslims had begun to strike back. In 1144, Edessa became the first of the four Latin states to be recaptured. Its fall led to renewed calls for another crusade, especially from the monastic firebrand Saint Bernard of Clairvaux (see Chapter 9), who exclaimed: "now, on account of our sins, the sacrilegious enemies of the cross have begun to show their faces. . . . What are you doing, you servants of the cross? Will you throw to the dogs that which is most holy? Will you cast pearls before swine?"[3] Bernard aimed his message at knights and even managed to enlist two powerful rulers, King Louis VII of France and Emperor Conrad III of Germany.

The second crusade seemed destined for failure. The two crusading armies of king and emperor were not well organized and failed to cooperate in coordinating their efforts against the Muslims. The new crusading hosts also found little cooperation from the crusader lords of the kingdom of Jerusalem. These local lords had found ways to live

The Christian Capture of Jerusalem

The first crusade was the most successful of the Christian world's numerous efforts to seize the Holy Land from the Muslims. The crusading host of Christian knights laid siege to Jerusalem in June 1099. After five weeks, the city capitulated, whereupon the crusaders enacted a horrible vengeance upon the city's inhabitants. This excerpt is taken from an account by Fulcher of Chartres who accompanied the crusaders to the Holy Land.

Fulcher of Chartres, *Chronicle of the First Crusade*

Then the Franks entered the city magnificently at the noonday hour on Friday, the day of the week when Christ redeemed the whole world on the cross. With trumpets sounding and with everything in an uproar, exclaiming: "Help, God!" they vigorously pushed into the city, and straightway raised the banner on the top of the wall. All the heathen, completely terrified, changed their boldness to swift flight through the narrow streets of the quarters. The more quickly they fled, the more quickly were they put to flight.

Count Raymond and his men, who were bravely assailing the city in another section, did not perceive this until they saw the Saracens jumping from the top of the wall. Seeing this, they joyfully ran to the city as quickly as they could, and helped the others pursue and kill the wicked enemy.

Then some, both Arabs and Ethiopians, fled into the Tower of David; others shut themselves in the Temple of the Lord and of Solomon, where in the halls a very great attack was made on them. Nowhere was there a place where the Saracens could escape the swordsmen.

On the top of Solomon's Temple, to which they had climbed in fleeing, many were shot to death with arrows and cast down headlong from the roof. Within this Temple, about ten thousand were beheaded. If you had been there, your feet would have been stained up to the ankles with the blood of the slain. What more shall I tell? Not one of them was allowed to live.

They did not spare the women and children.

with local Muslim leaders and were quite unwilling to destroy the symbiotic relationship they had developed. They, too, undermined the efforts of the two crusading monarchs. The second crusade proved to be a total failure. Saint Bernard attributed its lack of success to the loss of God's favor due to human sinfulness; the French king simply blamed the wickedness of the people involved.

THE THIRD CRUSADE

The Third Crusade was a reaction to the fall of the Holy City of Jerusalem. In 1169, the Sunni Muslims of Syria invaded Egypt and, under the leadership of the warrior known to the west as Saladin, demolished the Fatimid caliphate. Saladin's forces invaded the kingdom of Jerusalem and at the Battle of Hattin in 1187 destroyed the Latin forces gathered there. Saladin now began the reconquest of Palestine, and while Tripoli, Antioch, and Tyre were able to resist, Jerusalem fell in October 1187.

Now all of Christendom was ablaze with calls for a new crusade in the east. Three major monarchs agreed to lead new crusading forces in person: Emperor Frederick Barbarossa of Germany (1152–1190), Richard I the Lionhearted of England (1189–1199), and Philip II Augustus, king of France (1180–1223). This overwhelming re-

sponse seemed auspicious for the successful recovery of the Holy Land.

Some of the crusaders finally arrived in the east by 1189 only to encounter problems. Frederick Barbarossa experienced stunning successes in Asia Minor, but then drowned accidentally while swimming in a local river. Without his strong leadership, his army quickly disintegrated. The English and French arrived by sea and met with success against the coastal cities where they had the support of their fleets. When they moved inland, they failed miserably. Eventually, after Philip went home, Richard the Lionhearted negotiated a settlement whereby Saladin agreed to allow Christian pilgrims free access to Jerusalem.

The Crusades of the Thirteenth Century

It was the great pope Innocent III who inaugurated the fourth crusade. The death of Saladin in 1193 and the subsequent disintegration of his empire had created new opportunities. Innocent encouraged the nobility of Europe to put on the crusader's mantle. The nobles of France and the Netherlands responded in great numbers. The Venetians agreed to transport the crusading army to the east, but subverted it from its goal by using it first to capture Zara, a port on the Dalmatian coast and a Christian city.

◆ Richard the Lionhearted Executes Muslims at Acre.
The third crusade was organized in response to the capture of the
kingdom of Jerusalem by the Sunni Muslims under the leadership
in Saladin. Though Saladin forbade the massacre of Christians,
his Christian foes were more harsh. Here Richard the
Lionhearted (at right with crown) watches the execution of 2,700
Muslims at Acre.

The crusading army next became entangled in Byzantine
politics.

At the beginning of the thirteenth century, the Byzantine Empire was experiencing yet another struggle for the
imperial throne. One contender, Alexius, appealed to the
crusaders in Zara for assistance. Diverted to Constantinople, the crusading army sacked the great capital city of
Byzantium in 1204. Christian crusaders took gold, silver,
jewelry, and precious furs, and the Catholic clergy accompanying the crusaders stole as many relics as they
could find.

The Byzantine Empire now disintegrated into a series
of petty states ruled by crusading barons and Byzantine
princes. The chief state was the new Latin Empire of Constantinople led by Count Baldwin of Flanders as emperor.
However, the west was unable to maintain its Latin Empire—the western rulers of the newly created principalities were soon fighting each other. In 1259, Michael Paleologus, a Greek military leader, took control of the
kingdom of Nicaea in western Asia Minor, recaptured
Constantinople two years later with a Byzantine army, and
then established a new Byzantine dynasty, the Paleologi.
The Byzantine Empire had been saved, but it was no
longer a great Mediterranean power. The restored empire
was a badly truncated one comprising the city of Con-

stantinople and its surrounding territory as well as some
lands in Asia Minor. Even in its reduced size, however, the
empire limped along for another 190 years until the Ottoman Turks brought about its final capitulation in 1453.

Despite the cynical diversion of the fourth crusade to
Constantinople, the crusading ideal and the religious enthusiasm that inspired it were not completely lost. In Germany in 1212, a youth known as Nicholas of Cologne announced that God had inspired him to lead a "children's
crusade" to the Holy Land. Thousands of young people
joined Nicholas and made their way down the Rhine and
across the Alps to Italy where the pope told them to go
home. Most tried to do so. At about the same time, a group
of about 20,000 French children, also inspired by the desire to free the Holy Land from the Muslims, made their
way to Marseilles where two shipowners agreed to transport them to the Holy Land. Seven ships packed with
hymn-singing youths soon left the port. Two of the ships
perished in a storm near Sardinia; the other five sailed to
North Africa where the children were sold into slavery.
The next crusade of adult warriors was hardly more successful. The fifth crusade (1219–1221) attempted to recover the Holy Land by way of the powerful Muslim state
of Egypt. The crusade achieved some early successes, but
its ultimate failure marked an end to papal leadership of
the western crusaders.

The sixth crusade, which was led by the German emperor Frederick II, took place without papal support because the emperor had been excommunicated by the
pope for starting late. In 1228, Frederick marched into
Jerusalem and accepted the crown as king of Jerusalem after he had made an agreement with the sultan of Egypt.
The Holy City had been taken without a fight and without papal support. Once Frederick left, however, the city
fell once again, this time to a group of Turks allied with
the sultan of Egypt. The last two major crusades, poorly
organized by the saintly king of France, Louis IX, were
complete failures. Slowly, the Christian possessions in the
east were retaken. Acre, the last foothold of the crusaders,
surrendered in 1291. All in all, the crusades had failed to
accomplish their primary goal of holding the Holy Land
for the Christian west.

Effects of the Crusades

Whether the crusades had much effect on European civilization is debatable. The crusaders had little long-term
impact on the east where the only visible remnants of
their conquests were their castles. There may have been
some broadening of perspective that comes from the
exchange between two cultures, but the interaction of

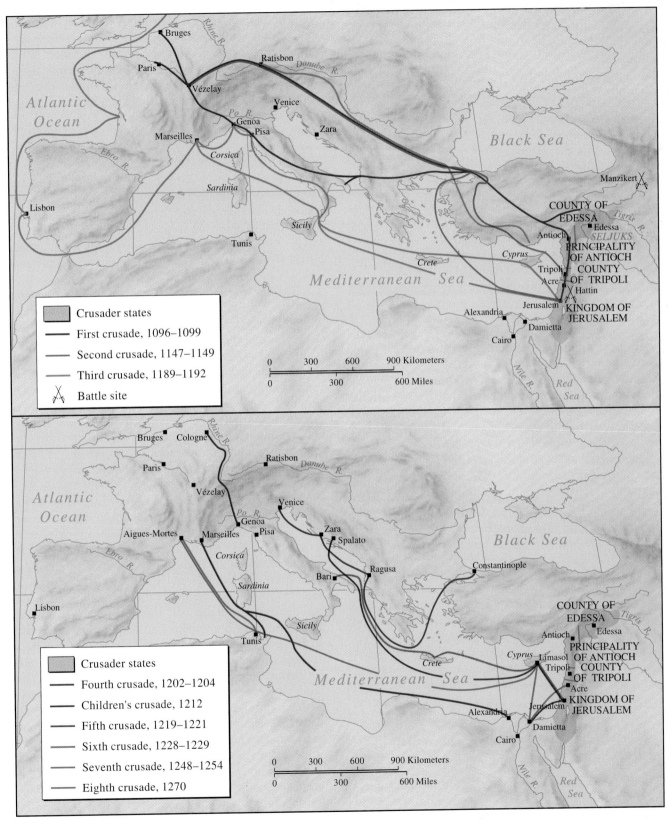

Map 11.1 The Crusades.

Christian Europe with the Muslim world was actually both more intense and more meaningful in Spain and Sicily than in the Holy Land.

Did the crusades help to stabilize European society by removing large numbers of young warriors who would have fought each other in Europe? Some historians think so and believe that western monarchs established their control more easily as a result. There is no doubt that the crusades did contribute to the economic growth of the Italian port cities, especially Genoa, Pisa, and Venice. But it is important to remember that the growing wealth and population of twelfth-century Europe had made the crusades possible in the first place. The crusades may have enhanced the revival of trade, but they certainly did not cause it. Even without the crusades, Italian merchants would have pursued new trade contacts with the eastern world.

The crusades did have unfortunate side effects that would haunt European society for generations. The first widespread attacks on the Jews began with the crusades. As some Christians argued, to undertake holy wars against infidel Muslims while the "murderers of Christ" ran free at home was unthinkable. The massacre of Jews became a regular feature of medieval European life.

The Intellectual and Artistic World of the High Middle Ages

The High Middle Ages was a time of tremendous intellectual and artistic vitality. The period witnessed the growth of educational institutions, a rebirth of interest in ancient culture, a quickening of theological thought, the revival of law, the development of a vernacular literature, and a burst of activity in art and architecture. While monks continued to play an important role in intellectual activity, increasingly the secular clergy, cities, and courts, whether of kings, princes, or high church officials, began to exert a newfound influence.

The Rise of Universities

The university as we know it with faculty, students, and degrees was a product of the High Middle Ages. The word *university* is derived from the Latin word *universitas*, meaning a corporation or guild, and referred to either a guild of teachers or a guild of students. Medieval universities were educational guilds or corporations that produced educated and trained individuals.

The first European university appeared in Bologna, Italy (unless one accords this distinction to the first medical school established earlier at Salerno, Italy). The emergence of the University of Bologna coincided with the revival of interest in Roman law, especially the rediscovery of Justinian's *Body of Civil Law* (see the section titled "The Revival of Roman Law" later in the chapter). In the twelfth century, a great teacher, such as Irnerius (1088–1125), attracted students from all over Europe. Most of them were laymen, usually older individuals who served as administrators to kings and princes and were particularly eager to learn more about law so they could apply it in their jobs. To protect themselves, students at Bologna formed a guild or *universitas*, which was recognized by Emperor Frederick Barbarossa and given a charter in 1158. Although the faculty also organized itself as a group, the *universitas* of students at Bologna was far more influential. It obtained a promise of freedom for students from local authorities, regulated the price of books and lodging, and determined the curriculum, fees, and standards for their masters. Teachers were fined if they missed a class or began their lectures late. The University of Bologna remained the greatest law school in Europe throughout the Middle Ages.

In northern Europe, the University of Paris became the first recognized university. A number of teachers or masters who had received licenses to teach from the cathedral school of Notre Dame in Paris began to take on extra students for a fee. By the end of the twelfth century, these masters teaching at Paris had formed a *universitas* or guild of masters. By 1200, the king of France, Philip Augustus, officially acknowledged the existence of the University of Paris. The University of Oxford in England, organized on the Paris model, first appeared in 1208.

A migration of scholars from Oxford in 1209 led to the establishment of Cambridge University. In the Late Middle Ages, kings, popes, and princes vied to found new universities. By the end of the Middle Ages, there were eighty universities in Europe, most of them located in England, France, Italy, and Germany.

A student's initial studies at a medieval university centered around the traditional liberal arts curriculum. The trivium consisted of grammar, rhetoric, and logic, and the quadrivium was comprised of arithmetic, geometry, astronomy, and music. All classes were conducted in Latin, which provided a common means of communication for students, regardless of their country of origin. Basically, medieval university instruction was done by a lecture method. The word *lecture* is derived from the Latin and means "to read." Before the development of the printing press in the fifteenth century, books were expensive, and few students could afford them, so masters read from a text (such as a collection of law if the subject were law) and then added commentaries, which came to be known as glosses. No exams were given after a series of lectures, but when a student applied for a degree, he (women did not attend universities in the Middle Ages) was given a comprehensive oral examination by a committee of teachers. These were taken after a four- or six-year period of study. The first degree a student could earn was an A.B., the *artium baccalarius*, or bachelor of arts; later, he might receive an A.M., *artium magister*, a master of arts. All degrees were technically licenses to teach, although most students receiving them did not become teachers.

After completing the liberal arts curriculum, a student could go on to study law, medicine, or theology, which was the most highly regarded subject of the medieval curriculum. The study of law, medicine, or theology was a long process that could take a decade or more. A student who passed his final oral examinations was granted a doctor's degree, which officially enabled him to teach his subject. Most students who pursued advanced degrees received their master's degrees first and taught the arts curriculum while continuing to pursue their advanced degrees. Students who received degrees from medieval universities could pursue other careers besides teaching that proved to be much more lucrative. A law degree was deemed essential for those who wished to serve as advisors to kings and princes. The growing administrative bureaucracies of popes and kings also demanded a supply of clerks with a university education who could keep records and draw up official documents.

Medieval universities shared in the violent atmosphere of the age. Records from courts of law reveal numerous instances of disturbances in European universi-

♦ **University Classroom.** This illustration shows a university classroom in fourteenth-century Germany. As was customary in medieval classrooms, the master is reading from a text. The students obviously vary considerably in age and in the amount of attention they are willing to give the lecturer.

ties. One German professor was finally dismissed for stabbing one too many of his colleagues in faculty meetings. A student in Bologna was attacked in the classroom by another student armed with a sword. Oxford regulations attempted to dampen the violence by forbidding students to bring weapons to class. Not uncommonly, town and gown struggles (gown refers to the academic robe worn by teachers and students) escalated into bloody riots between townspeople and students (see the box on p. 226).

Despite the violence, universities proved important to medieval civilization, not only for the growth of learning, which, after all, is the main task of the university, but also by providing a mechanism for training the personnel who served as teachers, administrators, lawyers, and doctors in an increasingly specialized society.

The Renaissance of the Twelfth Century

Another aspect of the intellectual revival of the High Middle Ages was a resurgence of interest in the works of classical antiquity—the works of the Greeks and Romans. The renaissance (or rebirth) of classical antiquity in the twelfth century has been compared to the more famous Renaissance in Italy in the fifteenth century. While the renaissance of the twelfth century was not as deep or far-reaching as the latter, it was a significant step forward in the European recovery and understanding of the classical heritage, and it generated tremendous intellectual optimism. The

✹ University Students and Violence at Oxford ✹

Medieval universities shared in the violent atmosphere of their age. Town and gown quarrels often resulted in bloody conflicts, especially during the universities' formative period. This selection is taken from an anonymous description of a student riot at Oxford at the end of the thirteenth century.

A Student Riot at Oxford

They [the townsmen] seized and imprisoned all scholars on whom they could lay hands, invaded their inns, made havoc of their goods and trampled their books under foot. In the face of such provocation the Proctors [university officials] sent their assistants about the town, forbidding the students to leave their inns. But all commands and exhortations were in vain. By nine o'clock next morning, bands of scholars were parading the streets in martial array. If the Proctors failed to restrain them, the mayor was equally powerless to restrain his townsmen. The great bell of St. Martin's rang out an alarm; oxhorns were sounded in the streets; messengers were sent into the country to collect rustic allies. The clerks [students and teachers], who numbered three thousand in all, began their attack simultaneously in various quarters. They broke open warehouses in the Spicery, the Cutlery and elsewhere. Armed with bows and arrows, swords and bucklers, slings and stones, they fell upon their opponents. Three they slew, and wounded fifty or more. One band . . . took up a position in High Street between the Churches of St. Mary and All Saints', and attacked the house of a certain Edward Hales. This Hales was a longstanding enemy of the clerks. There were no half measures with him. He seized his crossbow, and from an upper chamber sent an unerring shaft into the eye of the pugnacious rector. The death of their valiant leader caused the clerks to lose heart. They fled, closely pursued by the townsmen and country-folk. Some were struck down in the streets, and others who had taken refuge in the churches were dragged out and driven mercilessly to prison, lashed with thongs and goaded with iron spikes.

Complaints of murder, violence and robbery were lodged straightway with the King by both parties. The townsmen claimed three thousand pounds' damage. The commissioners, however, appointed to decide the matter, condemned them to pay two hundred marks, removed the bailiffs, and banished twelve of the most turbulent citizens from Oxford.

Latin language served as an international language for both speaking and writing.

In the twelfth century, western Europe was introduced to a large number of Greek scientific and philosophical works, including those of Galen and Hippocrates on medicine, Ptolemy on geography and astronomy, and Euclid on mathematics. Above all, the west now had available the complete works of Aristotle. (Greek drama and poetry, however, would not be recovered until the Italian Renaissance of the fifteenth century). During the second half of the twelfth century, all of Aristotle's scientific works were translated into Latin. This great influx of Aristotle's works had an overwhelming impact on the west. He came to be viewed as the "master of those who know," the man who seemed to have understood every field of knowledge.

The recovery of Greek scientific and philosophical works was not a simple process, however. Little knowledge of Greek had survived in Europe. It was through the Muslim world that the west recovered Aristotle's work and that of other Greeks. The translation of Greek works into Arabic had formed but one aspect of a brilliant Muslim civilization. In the twelfth century, these writings were now translated from Arabic into Latin, making them available to the west. No doubt, much became garbled in this roundabout recovery of the Greek works (Greek to Arabic to Latin). Wherever Muslim and Christian cultures met—in the Norman kingdom of Sicily, southern Italy, and above all Spain—the work of translation was carried on by both Arabic and Jewish scholars.

The Islamic world had more to contribute intellectually to the west than translations, however. Scientific work in the ninth and tenth centuries had enabled it to forge far ahead of the western world, and in the twelfth and thirteenth centuries, Arabic works on physics, mathematics, medicine, and optics became available to the west in Latin translations. In addition, when Aristotle's works were brought into the west in the second half of the twelfth century, they were accompanied by commentaries written by outstanding Arabic and Jewish philosophers. One example was Ibn-Rushd or Averroës (1126–1198), who lived in Córdoba and composed a systematic commentary on virtually all of Aristotle's surviving works.

The Development of Scholasticism

Medieval intellectuals were strongly influenced by a propensity for order. Their desire to introduce a systematic approach to knowledge greatly affected the formal study of religion that we call theology. Christianity's importance in medieval society probably made inevitable theology's central role in the European intellectual world. Whether in monastic or cathedral schools or the new universities, theology reigned as "queen of the sciences."

Beginning in the eleventh century, the effort to apply reason or logical analysis to the church's basic theological doctrines had a significant impact on the study of theology. The word *scholasticism* is used to refer to the philosophical and theological system of the medieval schools. A primary preoccupation of scholasticism was the attempt to reconcile faith and reason, to demonstrate that what was accepted on faith was in harmony with what could be learned by reason. The scholastic method came to be the basic instructional mode of the universities. In essence, this method consisted of posing a question, presenting contradictory authorities on that question, and then arriving at conclusions. It was a system that demanded rigorous analytical thought.

Scholasticism had its beginnings in the theological world of the eleventh and twelfth centuries. During that time, a major controversy—the problem of universals—occupied the work of many theologians. The basic issue involved the nature of reality itself: What constitutes what is real? Theologians were divided into two major schools of thought reflecting the earlier traditions of Greek thought, especially the divergent schools of Plato and Aristotle.

Following Plato, the scholastic realists took the position that the individual objects that we perceive with our senses, such as trees, are not real but merely manifestations of universal ideas (hence, treeness) that exist in the

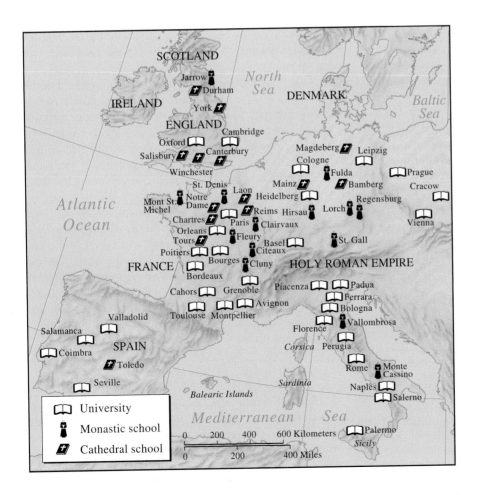

Map 11.2 Intellectual Centers of Medieval Europe.

mind of God. All knowledge, then, is based on the ideas implanted in human reason by the Creator. To the realists, truth can only be discovered by contemplating universals. The other school, the nominalists, were adherents of Aristotle's ideas and believed that only individual objects are real. In their view, universal ideas or concepts were simply names (Latin *nomina*—hence nominalism). Truth could be discovered only by examining individual objects.

By the thirteenth century, the scholastics were confronted by a new challenge—how to harmonize Christian revelation with the work of Aristotle. The great influx of Aristotle's works into the west in the High Middle Ages threw many theologians into consternation. Aristotle was so highly regarded that he was called "the philosopher," yet he had arrived at his conclusions by rational thought—not revelation—and some of his doctrines, such as the mortality of the individual soul, contradicted the teachings of the church. The most famous attempt to reconcile Aristotle and the doctrines of Christianity was that of Saint Thomas Aquinas.

Thomas Aquinas (1225–1274) studied theology at Cologne and Paris and taught at both Naples and Paris, and it was at the latter that he finished his famous *Summa Theologica* (*A Summa of Theology*—a *summa* was a compendium of knowledge that attempted to bring together all the received learning of the preceding centuries on a given subject into a single whole). Aquinas's masterpiece was organized according to the dialectical method of the scholastics. Aquinas first posed a question, cited sources that offered opposing opinions on the question, and then resolved them by arriving at his own conclusions. In this fashion, Aquinas raised and discussed some 600 articles or issues (see the box on p. 229).

Aquinas's reputation derives from his masterful attempt to reconcile faith and reason. He took it for granted that there were truths derived by reason and truths derived by faith. He was certain, however, that the two truths could not be in conflict with each other:

> The light of faith that is freely infused into us does not destroy the light of natural knowledge [reason] implanted in us naturally. For although the natural light of the human mind is insufficient to show us these things made manifest by faith, it is nevertheless impossible that these things which the divine principle gives us by faith are contrary to these implanted in us by nature [reason]. Indeed, were that the case, one or the other would have to be false, and, since both are given to us by God, God would have to the author of untruth, which is impossible . . . it is impossible that those things which are of philosophy can be contrary to those things which are of faith.[4]

The natural mind, unaided by faith, could arrive at truths concerning the physical universe. Without the help of God's grace, however, unaided reason alone could not grasp spiritual truths, such as the Trinity or the Incarnation.

The Revival of Roman Law

The development of a systematic approach to knowledge was also expressed in the area of law. Of special importance was the rediscovery of the great legal work of Justinian, the *Corpus Iuris Civilis* (*Body of Civil Law*), known to the medieval west before 1100 only in second-hand fashion. At first famous teachers of law, such as Irnerius of Bologna, were content simply to explain the meaning of Roman legal terms to their students. Gradually, they became more sophisticated so that by the mid-twelfth century, "doctors of law" had developed commentaries and systematic treatises on the legal texts. Italian cities, above all Pavia and Bologna, became prominent centers for the study of Roman law. By the thirteenth century, Italian jurists were systematizing the various professional commentaries on Roman law into a single commentary known as the ordinary gloss. Study of Roman law at the universities came to consist of learning the text of the law along with this gloss.

This revival of Roman law occurred in a world dominated by a body of law quite different from that of the Romans. European law comprised a hodgepodge of Germanic law codes, feudal customs, and urban regulations. The desire to exist in a more orderly world, already evident in the study of theology, perhaps made it inevitable that Europeans would enthusiastically welcome the more systematic approach of Roman law.

The training of students in Roman law at medieval universities led to further application of its principles as these students became judges, lawyers, scribes, and councilors for the towns and monarchies of western Europe. By the beginning of the thirteenth century, the old system of ordeal was being replaced by a rational, decision-making process based on the systematic collection and analysis of evidence, a clear indication of the impact of Roman law on the European legal system.

Literature in the High Middle Ages

Latin was the universal language of medieval civilization. Used in the church and schools, it enabled learned people to communicate anywhere in Europe. The intellectual revival of the High Middle Ages included an outpouring of Latin literature. While Latin continued to be

The Dialectical Method of Thomas Aquinas

In his masterpiece of scholastic theology, the Summa Theologica, Thomas Aquinas attempted to resolve some 600 theological issues by the dialectical method. This method consisted of posing a question, stating the objections to it, and then replying to the objections. This selection from the Summa Theologica focuses on Article 4 of Question 92, "The Production of the Woman."

Aquinas, *Summa Theologica*
Question 92: The Production of the Woman
(In Four Articles)

We must next consider the production of the woman. Under this head there are four points of inquiry: (1) Whether the woman should have been made in that first production of things? (2) Whether the woman should have been made from man? (3) Whether of man's rib? (4) Whether the woman was made immediately by God? . . .

Fourth Article: Whether the Woman Was Formed Immediately by God?

We proceed thus to the Fourth Article:—

Objection 1. It would seem that the woman was not formed immediately by God. For no individual is produced immediately by God from another individual alike in species. But the woman was made from a man who is of the same species. Therefore she was not made immediately by God.

Objection 2. Further, Augustine says that corporeal things are governed by God through the angels. But the woman's body was formed from corporeal matter. Therefore it was made through the ministry of the angels, and not immediately by God.

Objection 3. Further, those things which preexist in creatures as to their causal virtues are produced by the power of some creature, and not immediately by God. But the woman's body was produced in its causal virtues among the first created works, as Augustine says. Therefore it was not produced immediately by God.

On the contrary, Augustine says, in the same work: God alone, to Whom all nature owes its existence, could form or build up the woman from the man's rib.

I answer that, as was said above, the natural generation of every species is from some determinate matter. Now the matter whence man is naturally begotten is the human semen of man or woman. Wherefore from any other matter an individual of the human species cannot naturally be generated. Now God alone, the Author of nature, can produce an effect into existence outside the ordinary course of nature. Therefore God alone could produce either a man from the slime of the earth, or woman from the rib of man.

Reply Objection 1. This argument is verified when an individual is begotten, by natural generation, from that which is like it in the same species.

Reply Objection 2. As Augustine says, we do not know whether the angels were employed by God in the formation of the woman; but it is certain that, as the body of man was not formed by the angels from the slime of the earth, so neither was the body of the woman formed by them from the man's rib.

Reply Objection 3. As Augustine says, the first creation of things did not demand that women should be made thus; it made it possible for her to be thus made. Therefore the body of the woman did indeed preexist in these causal virtues, in the things first created; not as regards active potentiality, but as regards a potentiality passive in relation to the active potentiality of the Creator.

used for literary purposes, by the twelfth century much of the creative literature was being written in the vernacular tongues. Throughout the Middle Ages, there had been a popular vernacular literature, especially manifest in the Germanic, Celtic, Old Icelandic, and Slavonic sagas. But a new market for vernacular literature appeared in the twelfth century when educated laypeople at courts and in the new urban society sought fresh avenues of entertainment.

Perhaps the most popular vernacular literature of the twelfth century was troubadour poetry, chiefly the product of nobles and knights. This poetry focused on themes of courtly love, the love of a knight for a lady, generally a married noble lady, who inspires him to become a braver knight and a better poet. A good example is found in the laments of the crusading nobel Jaufré Rudel, who cherished a dream lady from afar whom he said he would always love, but feared he would never meet:

> Most sad, most joyous shall I go away,
> Let me have seen her for a single day,
>   My love afar,
> I shall not see her, for her land and mine
> Are sundered, and the ways are hard to find,
> So many ways, and I shall lose my way,
>   So wills it God.
>
> Yet shall I know no other love but hers,
> And if not hers, no other love at all.
>   She has surpassed all.
> So fair she is, so noble, I would be
> A captive with the hosts of paynimrie [the Muslims]
> In a far land, if so be upon me
>   Her eyes might fall.[5]

Though it originated in southern France, troubadour poetry also spread to northern France, Italy, and Germany.

Another type of vernacular literature was the *chanson de geste*, or the heroic epic. The earliest and finest example is the *Chanson de Roland (The Song of Roland)*, which appeared around 1100 and was written in a dialect of French, a Romance language derived from Latin (see the box on p. 231). The *chansons de geste* were written for a male-dominated society. The chief events described in these poems, as in *The Song of Roland*, are battles and political contests. Their world is one of combat in which knights fight courageously for their kings and lords. Women play little or no role in this literary genre.

Although *chansons de geste* were still written in the twelfth century, a different kind of long poem, the courtly romance, also became popular. It was composed in rhymed couplets and dwelt on a romantic subject matter: brave knights, virtuous ladies, evil magicians, bewitched palaces, fairies, talking animals, and strange forests. The story of King Arthur, the legendary king of the fifth-century Britons, became a popular subject matter for the courtly romance. The best versions of the Arthurian legends survive in the works of Chrétien de Troyes, whose courtly romances in the second half of the twelfth century were viewed by contemporaries as the works of a master storyteller.

Romanesque Architecture: "A White Mantle of Churches"

The eleventh and twelfth centuries witnessed an explosion of building, both private and public. The construction of castles and churches absorbed most of the surplus resources of medieval society and at the same time reflected its basic preoccupations, God and warfare. The churches were by far the most conspicuous of the public buildings. As a chronicler of the eleventh century commented,

> As the year 1003 approached, people all over the world, but especially in Italy and France began to rebuild their churches. Although most of them were well built and in little need of alterations, Christian nations were rivalling each other to have the most beautiful edifices. One might say the world was shaking herself, throwing off her old garments, and robing herself with a white mantle of churches. Then nearly all the cathedrals, the monasteries dedicated to different saints, and even the small village chapels were reconstructed more beautifully by the faithful.[6]

Hundreds of new cathedrals and abbey and pilgrimage churches, as well as thousands of parish churches in rural villages, were built in the eleventh and twelfth centuries. This building spree reflected a revived religious culture and the increased wealth of the period produced by agriculture, trade, and the growth of cities.

The cathedrals of the eleventh and twelfth centuries were built in a truly international style—the Romanesque. The construction of churches required the services of professional master builders, whose employment throughout Europe guaranteed an international unity in basic features. Prominent examples of Romanesque churches can be found in Germany, France, and Spain.

Romanesque churches were normally built in the basilica shape utilized in the construction of churches in the late Roman Empire. Basilicas were simply rectangular

⇒ The Song of Roland ⇐

The Song of Roland is one of the best examples of the medieval chanson de geste or heroic epic. Inspired by a historical event, it recounts the ambush of the rear guard of Charlemagne's Frankish army in the Pyrenees Mountains. It was written 300 years after the event it supposedly describes, however, and reveals more about the eleventh century than about the age of Charlemagne. The Basques who ambushed Charlemagne's army have been transformed into Muslims; the Frankish soldiers into French knights. This selection describes the death of Roland, Charlemagne's nephew, who was the commander of the decimated rear guard.

The Song of Roland

Now Roland feels that he is at death's door;
Out of his ears the brain is running forth.
Now for his peers he prays God call them all,
And for himself St. Gabriel's aid implores;
Then in each hand he takes, lest shame befal,
His Olifant and Durendal his sword.
Far as a quarrel flies from a cross-bow drawn,
Toward land of Spain he goes, to a wide lawn,
And climbs a mound where grows a fair tree tall,
And marble stones beneath it stand by four.

Face downward there on the green grass he falls,
And swoons away, for he is at death's door. . . .
Now Roland feels death press upon him hard;
It's creeping down from his head to his heart.
Under a pine-tree he hastens him apart,
There stretches him face down on the green grass,
And lays beneath him his sword and Olifant.
He's turned his head to where the Paynims ([Muslims] are,
And this he does for the French and for Charles,
Since fain is he that they should say, brave heart,
That he has died a conqueror at the last.
He beats his breast full many a time and fast,
Gives, with his glove, his sins into God's charge.
Now Roland feels his time is at an end;
On the steep hill-side, toward Spain he's turned his head,
And with one hand he beats upon his breast;
Saying: "Mea culpa; Thy mercy, Lord, I beg
For all the sins, both the great and the less,
That e'er I did since first I drew my breath
Unto this day when I'm struck down by death."
His right-hand glove he unto God extends;
Angels from Heaven now to his side descend.

buildings with flat wooden roofs. While using this basic plan, Romanesque builders made a significant innovation by replacing the flat wooden roof with a long, round stone vault called a barrel vault or a cross vault where two barrel vaults intersected (a vault is simply a curved roof made of masonry). The latter was used when a transept was added to create a church plan in the shape of a cross. Although barrel and cross vaults were technically difficult to construct, they were considered aesthetically more pleasing and technically more proficient and were also less apt to catch fire.

Because stone roofs were extremely heavy, Romanesque churches required massive pillars and walls to hold them up. This left little space for windows, and Romanesque churches were correspondingly dark on the inside. Their massive walls and pillars gave Romanesque churches a sense of solidity and almost the impression of a fortress. Indeed, massive walls and slit windows were also characteristic of the castle architecture of the same period.

The Gothic Cathedral

Begun in the twelfth century and brought to perfection in the thirteenth, the Gothic cathedral remains one of the greatest artistic triumphs of the High Middle Ages. Soaring skyward, almost as if to reach heaven, it was a fitting symbol for medieval people's preoccupation with God.

Two fundamental innovations of the twelfth century made Gothic cathedrals possible. The combination of ribbed vaults and pointed arches replaced the barrel vault of Romanesque churches and enabled builders to make Gothic churches higher than their Romanesque counterparts. The use of pointed arches and ribbed vaults created an impression of upward movement, a sense of weightless upward thrust that implied the energy of God. Another technical innovation, the flying buttress, basically a heavy arched pier of stone built onto the outside of the walls, made it possible to distribute the weight of the church's vaulted ceilings outward and down and thus eliminate the heavy walls used in Romanesque churches to hold the weight of the massive barrel vaults. Gothic cathedrals were built, then, with thin walls that were filled with magnificent stained glass windows, which created a play of light inside that varied with the sun at different times of the day.

Medieval craftspeople of the twelfth and thirteenth centuries perfected the art of stained glass. Small pieces of glass were stained in glowing colors that craftspeople to this day have been unable to duplicate. This preoccupation with colored light in Gothic cathedrals was not accidental, but was executed by people inspired by the belief that natural light was a symbol of the divine light of God. Light is invisible but enables people to see; so too is God invisible, but the existence of God allows the world of matter to be. Those impressed by the mystical significance of light were also impressed by the mystical signif-

◆ **Barrel Vaulting.** The eleventh and twelfth centuries witnessed an enormous amount of church construction. Utilizing the basilica shape, master builders replaced flat wooden roofs with long, round stone vaults, known as barrel vaults. As this illustration of a Romanesque church in Vienne, France, indicates, the barrel vault limited the size of a church and left little room for windows.

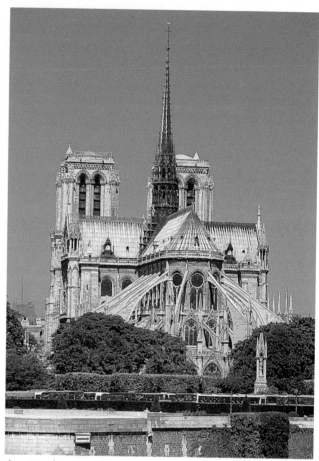

◆ **The Gothic Cathedral.** The Gothic cathedral was one of the great artistic triumphs of the High Middle Ages. Shown here is the cathedral of Notre Dame in Paris. Begun in 1163, it was not completed until the beginning of the fourteenth century.

icance of number. The proportions of Gothic cathedrals were based on mathematical ratios that their builders believed were derived from the ancient Greek school of Pythagoras and expressed the intrinsic harmony of the world as established by its Creator.

The first fully Gothic church was the abbey church of St. Denis near Paris, inspired by Suger, the famous abbot of the monastery from 1122 to 1151, and built between 1140 and 1150. Although the Gothic style was a product of northern France, by the mid-thirteenth century, French Gothic architecture had spread to England, Spain, Germany—indeed, to virtually all Europe. By the mid-thirteenth century, French Gothic architecture was seen most brilliantly in cathedrals in Paris (Notre Dame), Reims, Amiens, and Chartres.

A Gothic cathdral was the work of an entire community. Although the bishop and cathedral clergy initiated the plans to build a new cathedral, all classes contributed to its construction. Money was raised from wealthy townspeople who had profited from the new trade and industries as well as kings and nobles. Master masons who were both architects and engineers designed the cathedrals. They drew up the plans and supervised the work of construction. Stonemasons and other craftsmen were paid a daily wage and provided the skilled labor to build the cathedrals. Indeed, these buildings were the first monumental structures of consequence built by free, salaried labor.

The building of cathedrals often became highly competitive as communities vied with one another to build the highest tower, a rivalry that sometimes ended in disaster. The cathedral of Beauvais in northern France collapsed in 1284 after reaching the height of 157 feet. Gothic cathedrals also depended on a community's faith. After all, it often took two or more generations to complete a cathedral, and the first generation of builders must have begun with the knowledge that they would not live to see the completed project. Most importantly, a Gothic cathedral symbolized the chief preoccupation of a medieval Christian community, its dedication to a spiritual ideal. As we have observed before, the largest buildings of an era reflect the values of its society. The Gothic cathedral with its towers soaring toward heaven gave witness to an age when a spiritual impulse still underlay most of existence.

◆ **Interior of a Gothic Cathedral.** The use of ribbed vaults and pointed arches gave the Gothic cathedral a feeling of upward movement. Moreover, due to the flying buttress, the cathedral could have thin walls with stained glass windows that filled the interior with light. The flying buttress was a heavy pier of stone built onto the outside of the walls to bear the brunt of the weight of the church's vaulted ceiling

Conclusion

The High Middles Ages gave birth to an intellectual and spiritual revival that transformed European society. The intellectual revival led to a rediscovery of important aspects of the classical heritage, to new centers of learning in the universities, and to the use of reason to systematize the study of theology and law and develop whole new ways of thought. Spiritual renewal in the High Middle Ages led to numerous and even divergent paths. While it produced a dramatic increase in the number and size of churches and added new dimensions to the religious life of the clergy and laity, it also gave rise to the crusading "holy warrior" who killed for God.

Growth and optimism seemed to characterize the High Middle Ages, but underneath the calm exterior lay seeds of discontent and change. Dissent from church teaching and practices grew in the thirteenth century, leading to a climate of fear and intolerance as the church responded with inquisitorial instruments to enforce conformity to its teachings. Minorities of all kinds suffered intolerance, and worse still, persecution at the hands of people who worked to maintain the image of an ideal Christian society. The breakdown of the old manorial system and the creation of new relationships between lords and peasants led to local peasant uprisings in the late thirteenth century. The crusades ended ignominiously with the fall of the last crusading foothold in the east in 1291. By that time, more and more signs of ominous troubles were appearing. The fourteenth century would prove to be a time of crisis for European civilization.

NOTES

1. Oliver J. Thatcher and Edgar H. McNeal, eds., *A Source Book for Medieval History* (New York, 1905), p. 517.
2. Ibid., p. 523.
3. Quoted in Hans E. Mayer, *The Crusades*, trans. John Gillingham (New York, 1972), pp. 99–100.
4. Quoted in John Mundy, *Europe in the High Middle Ages, 1150–1309* (New York, 1973), pp. 474–475.
5. Helen Waddell, *The Wandering Scholars* (New York, 1961), p. 222.
6. Quoted in John W. Baldwin, *The Scholastic Culture of the Middle Ages 1000–1300* (Lexington, Mass., 1971), p. 15.

SUGGESTIONS FOR FURTHER READING

Two good general surveys of the crusades are H. E. Mayer, *The Crusades*, 2d ed. (New York, 1988); and J. Riley-Smith, *The Crusades: A Short History* (New Haven, Conn., 1987). Other works of value are J. Riley-Smith, ed., *The Oxford Illustrated History of the Crusades* (New York, 1995); J. Riley-Smith, *The First Crusade and the Idea of Crusading* (London, 1986); and J. Prawer, *The Latin Kingdom of Jerusalem* (London, 1972). On the background to the crusades, see B. Z. Kedar, *Crusade and Mission: European Approaches towards the Muslim* (Princeton, N.J., 1984). For a different perspective, see A. Maalouf, *The Crusades through Arab Eyes* (New York, 1985). For works on the Byzantine and Islamic Empires, see the bibliography at the end of Chapter 8 and M. Angold, *The Byzantine Empire: 1025–1204* (London, 1984); and P. M. Holt, *The Age of the Crusades* (London, 1986). An excellent, beautifully illustrated collection of firsthand accounts can be found in E. Hallam, ed., *Chronicles of the Crusades* (New York, 1989). The disastrous fourth crusade is examined in J. Godfrey, *1204: The Unholy Crusade* (Oxford, 1980); and D. Queller, *The Fourth Crusade* (Philadelphia, 1977). On the later crusades, see N. Housley, *The Later Crusades, 1274–1580* (New York, 1992).

General works on medieval intellectual life are A. Murray, *Reason and Society in the Middle Ages* (Oxford, 1978); and D. Knowles, *The Evolution of Medieval Thought* (New York, 1962). For a good general introduction to the intellectual and artistic renewal of the eleventh and twelfth centuries, see C. N. L. Brooke, *The Twelfth Cen-*tury Renaissance* (London, 1969); see also the classic work by C. H. Haskins, *The Renaissance of the Twelfth Century* (Cleveland, 1957). The development of universities is covered in the classic work by H. Rashdall, *The Universities of Europe in the Middle Ages*, 3 vols. (Oxford, 1936); S. Ferruolo, *The Origin of the University* (Standford, 1985); A. B. Cobban, *The Medieval Universities* (London, 1975); and the brief, older work by C. H. Haskins, *The Rise of Universities* (Ithaca, N.Y., 1957). Various aspects of the intellectual and literary developments of the High Middle Ages are examined in J. W. Baldwin, *The Scholastic Culture of the Middle Ages, 1000–1300* (Lexington, Mass., 1971); C. Morris, *The Discovery of the Individual, 1060–1200* (London, 1972); and H. Waddell, *The Wandering Scholars* (London, 1934). A good biography of Thomas Aquinas is J. Weisheipl, *Friar Thomas d'Aquino: His Life, His Thought and Work* (New York, 1974). See also T. O'Meara, *Thomas Aquinas Theologian* (Notre Dame, Ind., 1997).

For a good introduction to the art and architecture of the Middle Ages, see A. Shaver-Crandell, *The Middle Ages*, in the Cambridge Introduction to Art Series (Cambridge, 1982). For a good introduction to Romanesque style, see G. Künstler, *Romanesque Art in Europe* (New York, 1973); and A. Petzold, *Romanesque Art* (New York, 1995). On the Gothic movement, see M. Camille, *Gothic Art: Glorious Visions* (New York, 1996); C. Wilson, *The Gothic Cathedral* (London, 1990); O. von Simson, *The Gothic Cathedral* (New York, 1964); E. Panofsky, *Gothic Architec-*

ture and Scholasticism (New York, 1957); C. Wilson, *The Gothic Cathedral* (London, 1990); and J. Bony, *French Gothic Architecture of the Twelfth and Thirteenth Centuries* (Berkeley, 1983). Good books on the construction of Gothic cathedrals are J. Gimpel, *The Cathedral Builders* (New York, 1961); and A. Erlande-Brandenburg, *Cathedral and Castles: Building in the Middle Ages* (New York, 1995).

CHAPTER 12

The Late Middle Ages: Crisis and Disintegration in the Fourteenth Century

The High Middle Ages of the eleventh, twelfth, and thirteenth centuries had been a period of great innovation, as evidenced by significant economic, social, political, religious, intellectual, and cultural changes. And yet, by the end of the thirteenth century, certain tensions had begun to creep into European society. In the course of the next century, these tensions became a torrent of troubles. At mid-century, one of the most destructive natural disasters in history erupted—the Black Death. One contemporary observer named Henry Knighton, a canon of Saint Mary-of-the-Meadow Abbey in Leicester, England, was simply overwhelmed by the magnitude of the catastrophe. Knighton began his account of the great plague with these words, "In this year [1348] and in the following one there was a general mortality of people throughout the whole world." Few were left untouched; the plague struck even isolated monasteries: "At Montpellier, there remained out of a hundred and forty friars only seven." Animals, too, were devastated: "During this same year, there was a great mortality of sheep everywhere in the kingdom; in one place and in one pasture, more than five thousand sheep died and became so putrefied that neither beast nor bird wanted to touch them." Knighton was also stunned by the economic and social consequences of the Black Death. Prices dropped: "And the price of everything was cheap, because of the fear of death; there were very few who took any care for their wealth, or for anything else." Meanwhile laborers were scarce, so their wages increased: "In the following autumn, one could not hire a reaper at a lower wage than eight pence with food, or a mower at less than twelve pence with food. Because of this, much grain rotted in the fields for lack of harvesting." So many people died that some towns were deserted and some villages disappeared altogether: "Many small villages and hamlets were completely deserted; there was not one house left in them, but all those who had lived in them were dead." Some people thought the end of the world was at hand.

Outbreak of Hundred Years' War

Battle of Agincourt

Golden Bull in Germany

Joan of Arc inspires the French

The popes at Avignon

Peasant revolts in France •

• The Great Schism

Outbreak of the Black Death

Peasant revolt in England

Work of Giotto

Giovanni di Dondi's clock

Dante, *The Divine Comedy*

Chaucer, *The Canterbury Tales*

Plague was not the only disaster in the fourteenth century, however. Signs of disintegration were everywhere: famine, economic depression, war, social upheaval, a rise in crime and violence, and a decline in the power of the universal Catholic church. Periods of disintegration, however, are often fertile grounds for change and new developments. Out of the dissolution of medieval civilization came a rebirth of culture that many historians have labeled the Renaissance.

$\mathcal{A}$ Time of Troubles: Black Death and Social Crisis

Well into the thirteenth century, Europe had experienced good harvests and an expanding population. By the end of the thirteenth century, however, a period of disastrous changes had begun.

Famine and the Black Death

By the end of the thirteenth and beginning of the fourteenth centuries, Europe entered a period that has been called a "little ice age." A small shift in overall temperature patterns resulted in shortened growing seasons and disastrous weather conditions, including heavy storms and constant rain. Between 1315 and 1317, northern Europe experienced heavy rains that destroyed harvests and caused serious food shortages, resulting in extreme hunger and starvation. The great famine of 1315–1317 in northern Europe became an all-too-familiar pattern. Southern Europe, for example, seems to have been struck by similar conditions, especially in the 1330s and 1340s. Hunger

became widespread, and the scene described by this chronicler became common:

> We saw a larger number of both sexes, not only from nearby places but from as much as five leagues away, barefooted and maybe even, except for women, in a completely nude state, together with their priests coming in procession at the Church of the Holy Martyrs, their bones bulging out, devoutly carrying bodies of saints and other relics to be adorned hoping to get relief.[1]

Some historians have pointed out that famine could have led to chronic malnutrition, which in turn contributed to increased infant mortality, lower birth rates, and higher susceptibility to disease because malnourished people are less able to resist infection. This, they argue, helps to explain the virulence of the great plague known as the Black Death.

The Black Death of the mid-fourteenth century was the most devastating natural disaster in European history, ravaging Europe's population and causing economic, social, political, and cultural upheaval. A chronicler wrote that "father abandoned child, wife husband, one brother another, for the plague seemed to strike through breath and sight. And so they died. And no one could be found to bury the dead, for money or friendship."[2] People were horrified by an evil force they could not understand and by the subsequent breakdown of all normal human relations.

The Black Death was all the more horrible because it was the first major epidemic disease to strike Europe since the seventh century, an absence that helps explain medieval Europe's remarkable population growth. This great plague originated in Central Asia. It was spread, it is believed, both by the Mongols as they expanded across Asia and by ecological changes that caused Central Asian rodents to move westward.

Bubonic plague, which was the most common and most important form of plague in the diffusion of the Black Death, was spread by black rats infested with fleas who were host to the deadly bacterium *Yersinia pestis*. Symptoms of bubonic plague include high fever, aching joints, swelling of the lymph nodes, and dark blotches caused by bleeding beneath the skin. Bubonic plague was actually the least toxic form of plague, but nevertheless killed 50 to 60 percent of its victims. In pneumonic plague, the bacterial infection spread to the lungs, resulting in severe coughing, bloody sputum, and the relatively easy spread of the bacillus from human to human by coughing. Fortunately, because it was more deadly, this form of the plague occurred less frequently than bubonic plague.

The plague reached Europe in October 1347 when Genoese merchants brought it from the Middle East to the island of Sicily off the coast of southern Italy. It quickly spread to southern Italy and southern France and Spain by the end of 1347. Usually, the diffusion of the Black Death followed commercial trade routes. In 1348, the plague spread through France, the Low Countries, and into Germany. By the end of that year, it had moved to England, ravaging it in 1349. By the end of 1349, the plague had reached northern Europe and Scandinavia. Eastern Europe and Russia were affected by 1351, although mortality rates were never as high in eastern Europe as they were in western and central Europe.

Mortality figures for the Black Death were incredibly high. Italy was especially hard hit. Its crowded cities suffered losses of 50 to 60 percent (see the box on p. 240). In northern France, farming villages suffered mortality rates of 30 percent, and cities such as Rouen were more severely affected and experienced losses of 30 to 40 percent. In England and Germany, entire villages simply disappeared from history. In Germany, of approximately 170,000 inhabited locations, only 130,000 were left by the end of the fourteenth century.

It has been estimated that the European population declined by 25 to 50 percent between 1347 and 1351. If we accept the recent scholarly assessment of a European population of 75 million in the early fourteenth century, this means a death toll of 19 to 38 million people in four years. And the plague did not end in 1351. There were major outbreaks again in 1361–1362 and 1369 and then regular recurrences during the remainder of the fourteenth century and all of the fifteenth century. The European population did not start to recover until the end of the fifteenth century; not until the mid-sixteenth century did Europe begin to regain its thirteenth-century population levels. Even then, recurrences of the plague did not end until the beginning of the eighteenth century when a new species of brown rat began to replace the black rat.

LIFE AND DEATH: REACTIONS TO THE PLAGUE

The attempt of contemporaries to explain the Black Death and mitigate its harshness led to extreme sorts of behavior. To many, the plague had either been sent by God as a punishment for humans' sins or caused by the evil one, the devil. Some resorted to extreme asceticism to cleanse themselves of sin and gain God's forgiveness. Such was the flagellant movement, which became

◆ **Mass Burial of Plague Victims.** The Black Death spread to northern Europe by the end of 1348. Shown here is a mass burial of victims of the plague in Tournai, located in modern Belgium. As is evident in the illustration, at this stage of the plague, there was still time to make coffins for the victims' burial. Later, as the plague intensified, the dead were thrown into open pits.

popular in 1348, especially in Germany. Groups of flagellants, both men and women, wandered from town to town, flogging each other with whips to win the forgiveness of a God whom they felt had sent the plague to punish humans for their sinful ways. One contemporary chronicler described a flagellant procession:

> The penitents went about, coming first out of Germany. They were men who did public penance and scourged themselves with whips of hard knotted leather with little iron spikes. Some made themselves bleed very badly between the shoulder blades and some foolish women had cloths ready to catch the blood and smear it on their eyes, saying it was miraculous blood. While they were doing penance, they sang very mournful songs about the nativity and the passion of Our Lord. The object of this penance was to put a stop to the mortality, for in that time . . . at least a third of all the people in the world died.[3]

The flagellants attracted attention and created mass hysteria wherever they went. The Catholic church, however, became alarmed when flagellant groups began to kill Jews and attack the clergy who opposed them. Pope Clement VI condemned the flagellants in October 1349 and urged the public authorities to crush them. By the end of 1350, most of the flagellant movements had been destroyed.

An outbreak of virulent anti-Semitism also accompanied the Black Death. Jews were accused of causing the plague by poisoning town wells. Although Jews were persecuted in Spain, the worst pogroms against this helpless

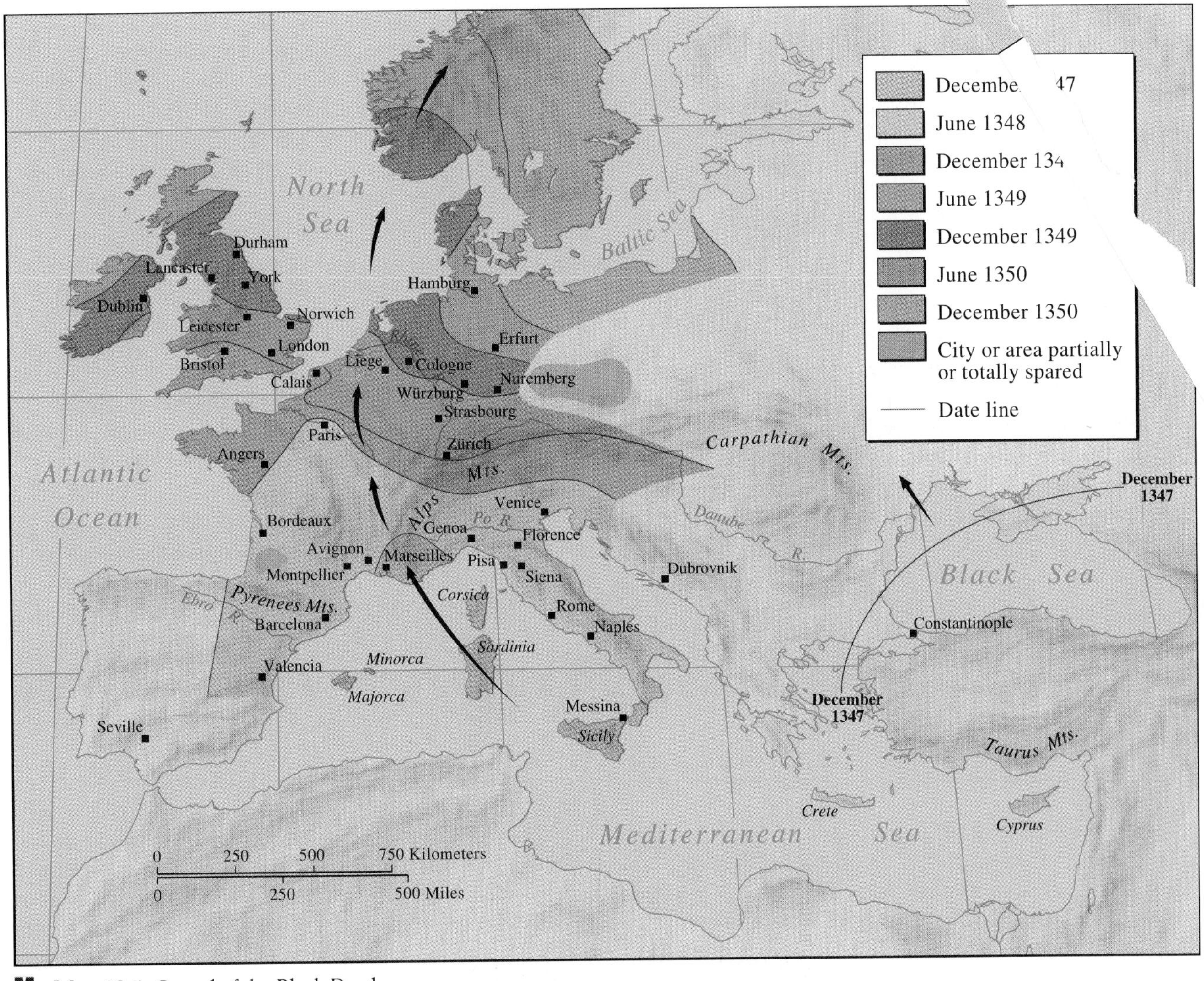

Map 12.1 Spread of the Black Death.

⇉ The Black Death ⇇

The Black Death was the most terrifying natural calamity of the entire Middle Ages. It has been estimated that 25 to 50 percent of the population died as the plague spread throughout Europe between 1347 and 1351. This contemporary description of the great plague is taken from the preface to The Decameron *by the fourteenth-century Italian writer Giovanni Boccaccio.*

Giovanni Boccaccio, *The Decameron*

In the year of Our Lord 1348 the deadly plague broke out in the great city of Florence, most beautiful of Italian cities. Whether through the operation of the heavenly bodies or because of our own iniquities which the just wrath of God sought to correct, the plague had arisen in the East some years before, causing the death of countless human beings. It spread without stop from one place to another, until, unfortunately, it swept over the West. Neither knowledge nor human foresight availed against it, though the city was cleansed of much filth by chosen officers in charge and sick persons were forbidden to enter it, while advice was broadcast for the preservation of health. Nor did humble supplications serve. Not once but many times they were ordained in the form of processions and other ways for the propitiation of God by the faithful, but, in spite of everything, toward the spring of the year the plague began to show its ravages. . . .

It did not manifest itself as in the East, where if a man bled at the nose he had certain warning of inevitable death. At the onset of the disease both men and women were afflicted by a sort of swelling in the groin or under the armpits which sometimes attained the size of a common apple or egg. Some of these swellings were larger and some smaller, and were commonly called boils. From these two starting points the boils began in a little while to spread and appear generally all over the body. Afterwards, the manifestation of the disease changed into black or livid spots on the arms, thighs, and the whole person. In many these blotches were large and far apart, in others small and closely clustered. Like the boils, which had been and continued to be a certain indication of coming death, these blotches had the same meaning for everyone on whom they appeared.

Neither the advice of physicians nor the virtue of any medicine seemed to help or avail in the cure of these diseases. Indeed, . . . not only did few recover, but on the contrary almost everyone died within three days of the appearance of the signs—some sooner, some later. . . . The virulence of the plague was all the greater in that it was communicated by the sick to the well by contact, not unlike fire when dry or fatty things are brought near it. But the evil was still worse. Not only did conversation and familiarity with the diseased spread the malady and even cause death, but the mere touch of the clothes or any other object the sick had touched or used, seemed to spread the pestilence. . . .

More wretched still were the circumstances of the common people and, for a great part, of the middle class, for, confined to their homes either by hope of safety or by poverty, and restricted to their own sections, they fell sick daily by thousands. There, devoid of help or care, they died almost without redemption. A great many breathed their last in the public streets, day and night; a large number perished in their homes, and it was only by the stench of their decaying bodies that they proclaimed their death to their neighbors. Everywhere the city was teeming with corpses. . . .

So many bodies were brought to the churches every day that the consecrated ground did not suffice to hold them, particularly according to the ancient custom of giving each corpse its individual place. Huge trenches were dug in the crowded churchyards and the new dead were piled in them, layer upon layer, like merchandise in the hold of a ship. A little earth covered the corpses of each row, and the procedure continued until the trench was filled to the top.

minority were carried out in Germany; more than sixty major Jewish communities in Germany had been exterminated by 1351 (see the box on p. 241). Many Jews fled eastward to Russia and especially to Poland where the king offered them protection. Eastern Europe became home to large Jewish communities.

The prevalence of death because of the plague and its recurrences affected people in profound ways. Some survivors apparently came to treat life as something cheap and passing. Violence and violent death appeared to be more common after the plague than before. Postplague Europe also demonstrated a morbid preoccupation with

A Medieval Holocaust: The Cremation of the Strasbourg Jews

In their attempt to explain the widespread horrors of the Black Death, medieval Christian communities looked for scapegoats. As at the time of the crusades, the Jews were blamed for poisoning wells and hence spreading the plague. This selection by a contemporary chronicler, written in 1349, gives an account of how Christians in the town of Strasbourg in the Holy Roman Empire dealt with their Jewish community. It is apparent that financial gain was also an important motive in killing the Jews.

Jacob von Königshofen, "The Cremation of the Strasbourg Jews"

In the year 1349 there occurred the greatest epidemic that ever happened. Death went from one end of the earth to the other. . . . And from what this epidemic came, all wise teachers and physicians could only say that it was God's will. . . . This epidemic also came to Strasbourg in the summer of the above-mentioned year, and it is estimated that about sixteen thousand people died.

In the matter of this plague the Jews throughout the world were reviled and accused in all lands of having caused it through the poison which they are said to have put into the water and the wells—that is what they were accused of—and for this reason the Jews were burnt all the way from the Mediterranean into Germany. . . .

[The account then goes on to discuss the situation of the Jews in the city of Strasbourg.]

On Saturday . . . they burnt the Jews on a wooden platform in their cemetery. There were about two thousand people of them. Those who wanted to baptize themselves were spared. [Some say that about a thousand accepted baptism.] Many small children were taken out of the fire and baptized against the will of their fathers and mothers. And everything that was owed to the Jews was canceled, and the Jews had to surrender all pledges and notes that they had taken for debts. The council, however, took the cash that the Jews possessed and divided it among the working-men proportionately. The money was indeed the thing that killed the Jews. If they had been poor and if the feudal lords had not been in debt to them, they would not have been burnt. . . .

Thus were the Jews burnt at Strasbourg, and in the same year in all the cities of the Rhine, whether Free Cities or Imperial Cities or cities belonging to the lords. In some towns they burnt the Jews after a trial, in others, without a trial. In some cities the Jews themselves set fire to their houses and cremated themselves.

It was decided in Strasbourg that no Jew should enter the city for a hundred years, but before twenty years had passed, the council and magistrates agreed that they ought to admit the Jews again into the city for twenty years. And so the Jews came back again to Strasbourg in the year 1368 after the birth of our Lord.

death. In their sermons, priests reminded parishioners that each night's sleep might be their last. Tombstones were decorated with macabre scenes of naked corpses in various stages of decomposition with snakes entwined in their bones and their innards filled with worms.

Economic Dislocation and Social Upheaval

The population collapse of the fourteenth century had dire economic and social consequences. Economic dislocation was accompanied by social upheaval. Both peasants and noble landlords were affected by the demographic crisis of the fourteenth century. Most noticeably, Europe experienced a serious labor shortage, which caused a dramatic rise in the price of labor. At Cuxham manor in England, for example, a farm laborer who had received two shillings a week in 1347 was paid seven in 1349 and almost eleven by 1350. At the same time, the decline in population depressed the demand for agricultural produce, resulting in falling prices for output. Because landlords were having to pay more for labor at the same time that their income from rents was declining, they began to experience considerable adversity and lower standards of living. In England, aristocratic incomes dropped more than 20 percent between 1347 and 1353.

Landed aristocrats responded to adversity by seeking to lower the wage rate. The English Parliament passed the Statute of Laborers (1351), which attempted to limit wages to preplague levels and forbid the mobility of peasants as well. Although such laws proved largely unworkable, they did keep wages from rising as high as they might have in a free market. Overall, the position of noble landlords continued to deteriorate during the late fourteenth and early fifteenth centuries. At the same time, the position of peasants improved, though not uniformly throughout Europe.

♦ **Peasant Rebellion.** The fourteenth century witnessed a number of revolts of the peasantry against noble landowners. Although the revolts were initially successful, they were soon crushed. This illustration shows nobles massacring the rebels in the French *Jacquerie*.

The decline in the number of peasants after the Black Death accelerated the process of converting labor services to rents, freeing peasants from the obligations of servile tenure and weakening the system of manorialism. But there were limits to how much the peasants could advance. They faced the same economic hurdles as the lords while the latter also attempted to impose wage restrictions and reinstate old forms of labor service. New governmental taxes also hurt. Peasant complaints became widespread and soon gave rise to rural revolts.

PEASANT REVOLTS

In 1358, a peasant revolt, known as the *Jacquerie*, broke out in northern France. The destruction of normal order by the Black Death and the subsequent economic dislocation were important factors in causing the revolt, but the ravages created by the Hundred Years' War (see the section on "War and Political Instability" later in the chapter) also affected the French peasantry. Both the French and English forces followed a deliberate policy of laying waste to peasants' lands while bands of mercenaries lived off the land by taking peasants' produce as well. Thus, the *Jacquerie* was a revolt of desperation; it was linked to the political ambitions of townspeople in Paris who were also upset with the conduct of the war and wished to limit monarchical power.

Peasant anger was also exacerbated by growing class tensions. Landed nobles were eager to hold onto their political privileged positions and felt increasingly threatened in the new postplague world of higher wages and lower prices. Many aristocrats looked on peasants with utter contempt. One French aristocrat said, "Should peasants eat meat? Rather should they chew grass on the heath with the horned cattle and go naked on all fours." The peasants reciprocated this contempt for their so-called social superiors.

The outburst of peasant anger led to savage confrontations. Castles were burned and nobles murdered. Such atrocities did not go unanswered, however. The *Jacquerie* soon failed as the privileged classes closed ranks, savagely massacred the rebels, and ended the revolt.

The English Peasants' Revolt of 1381 was the most famous of all. It was a product not of desperation but of rising expectations. After the Black Death, the condition of the English peasants had improved as they enjoyed greater freedom and higher wages or lower rents. Aristocratic landlords had fought back with legislation to depress wages and an attempt to reimpose old feudal dues. The most immediate cause of the revolt, however, was the monarchy's attempt to raise revenues by imposing a poll tax or a flat charge on each adult member of the population. Peasants in eastern England, the wealthiest part of the country, refused to pay the tax and expelled the collectors forcibly from their villages.

This action produced a widespread rebellion of both peasants and townspeople led by a well-to-do peasant called Wat Tyler and a preacher named John Ball. The latter preached an effective message against the noble class, as recounted by the chronicler Froissart:

> Good people, things cannot go right in England and never will, until goods are held in common and there are no more peasants and gentlefolk, but we are all one and the same. In what way are those whom we call lords greater masters than ourselves? How have they deserved it? Why do they hold us in bondage? If we all spring from a single father and mother, Adam and Eve, how can they claim or prove that they are lords more than us, except by making us produce and grow the wealth which they spend.[4]

The movement developed a famous jingle based on Ball's preaching: "When Adam delved and Eve span, who was then a gentleman?"

The revolt was initially successful as the rebels burned down the manor houses of aristocrats, lawyers, and government officials and murdered several important officials, including the Archbishop of Canterbury. After the peasants marched on London, the young king Richard II

(1377–1399) promised to accept the rebels' demands if they returned to their homes. They accepted the king's word and began to disperse, but the king reneged and with the assistance of the aristocrats brutally crushed the rebels. The poll tax was eliminated, however.

REVOLTS IN THE CITIES

Revolts also erupted in the cities. Commercial and industrial activity suffered almost immediately from the Black Death. An oversupply of goods and an immediate drop in demand led to a decline in trade after 1350. Some industries suffered greatly. Florence's woolen industry, one of the giants, produced 70,000 to 80,000 pieces of cloth in 1338; in 1378, it was yielding only 24,000 pieces. Bourgeois merchants and manufacturers responded to a decline in trade and production by attempts to restrict competition and resist the demands of the lower classes.

In urban areas where capitalist industrialists paid low wages and managed to prevent workers from forming organizations to help themselves, industrial revolts broke out throughout Europe. Ghent experienced one in 1381, Rouen in 1382. Most famous, however, was the revolt of the *ciompi* in Florence in 1378. The *ciompi* were wool workers in Florence's most prominent industry. In the 1370s, the woolen industry was depressed, and wool workers saw their real wages decline when the coinage in which they were paid was debased. Their revolt won them some concessions from the municipal government, including the right to form guilds and be represented in the government. But their newly won rights were short lived. A counterrevolution by government authorities brought an end to *ciompi* participation in the government by 1382.

Although the peasant and urban revolts sometimes resulted in short-term gains for the participants, the uprisings were relatively easily crushed and their gains quickly lost. Geographically dispersed, rural and urban revolters were not united and had no long-range goals. Immediate gains were uppermost in their minds. Accustomed to ruling, the established classes easily combined and crushed dissent when faced with social uprising. Nevertheless, the rural and urban revolts of the fourteenth century ushered in an age of social conflict that characterized much of later European history.

War and Political Instability

Famine, plague, economic turmoil, social upheaval, and violence were not the only problems of the fourteenth century. War and political instability must also be added

to the list. Of all the struggles that ensued in the fourteenth century, the Hundred Years' War was the most famous and the most violent.

The Hundred Years' War

In 1259, the English king, Henry III, had relinquished his claims to all the French territories previously held by the English monarchy in France except for one relatively small possession known as the duchy of Gascony. As duke of Gascony, the English king pledged loyalty as a vassal to the French king. But this territory gave rise to numerous disputes between the kings of England and France. By the thirteenth century, the Capetian monarchs had greatly increased their power over their more important vassals, the great lords of France. Royal officials interfered regularly in the affairs of the vassals' fiefs, and although this policy irritated all the vassals, it especially annoyed the king of England who considered himself the peer of the French king. When King Philip VI of France (1328–1350) seized Gascony in 1337, the duke of Gascony—King Edward III of England (1327–1377)—declared war on Philip. The attack on Gascony was a convenient excuse; Edward III had already laid claim to the throne of France after the senior branch of the Capetian dynasty had become extinct in 1328 and a cousin of the Capetians, Philip, duke of Valois, had become king as Philip VI.

The Hundred Years' War began in a burst of knightly enthusiasm. Trained to be warriors, knights viewed the clash of battle as the ultimate opportunity to demonstrate their chivalric qualities. The Hundred Years' War proved to be an important watershed, however, because the feudal way of life was on the decline. This would become most evident when peasant foot soldiers instead of knights determined the outcomes of the chief battles of the Hundred Years' War.

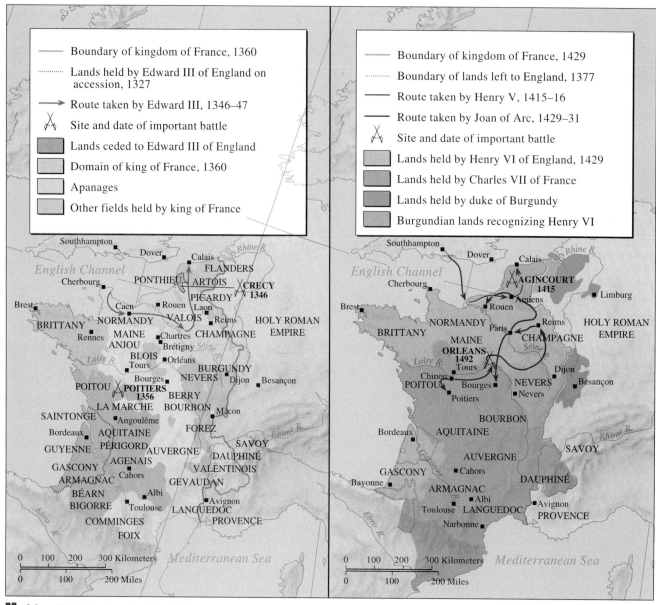

Map 12.2 The Hundred Years' War.

It was the English, more than the French, who moved beyond the traditional feudal levy. The French army of 1337 with its heavily armed noble cavalry resembled its twelfth- and thirteenth-century forebears. The noble cavalry considered themselves the fighting elite and looked with contempt on foot soldiers and crossbowmen because they were peasants or other social inferiors. The English army, however, had evolved differently and had included peasants as paid foot soldiers. Armed with pikes, many of these foot soldiers had also adopted the longbow, invented by the Welsh. The longbow had greater striking power, longer range, and more rapid speed of fire than the crossbow. Although the English made use of heavily armed cavalry, they relied even more on large numbers of foot soldiers.

Edward III's early campaigns in France were indecisive and achieved little. In 1346, Edward was forced to fight at Crécy just south of Flanders. The larger French army followed no battle plan but simply attacked the English lines in a disorderly fashion. The arrows of the English archers decimated the French cavalry. As the chronicler Froissart described it, "[with their longbows] the English continued to shoot into the thickest part of the crowd, wasting none of their arrows. They impaled or wounded horses and riders, who fell to the ground in great distress, unable to get up again without the help of several men."[5] It was a stunning victory for the English.

The Battle of Crécy was not decisive, however. The English simply did not possess the resources to subjugate all France, and hostilities continued intermittently for another fifty years until a twenty-year truce was negotiated in 1396, seemingly bringing an end to this protracted series of struggles between the French and English. However, the English king, Henry V (1413–1422), renewed the war in 1415. At the Battle of Agincourt (1415), the attempt of the heavy, armor-plated French knights to attack across a field turned to mud by heavy rain led to a disastrous French defeat and the death of 1,500 French nobles. Henry went on to reconquer Normandy and forge an alliance with the duke of Burgundy, making the English masters of northern France.

The seemingly hopeless French cause fell into the hands of Charles the dauphin (the title given to the heir to the throne), who governed the southern two-thirds of French lands from Bourges. Charles was weak and timid and was unable to rally the French against the English, who, in 1428, had turned south and were besieging the city of Orléans to gain access to the valley of the Loire. The French monarch was saved, quite unexpectedly, by a French peasant woman.

Joan of Arc was born in 1412, the daughter of well-to-do peasants from the village of Domrémy in Champagne. Deeply religious, Joan experienced visions and came to believe that her favorite saints had commanded her to free France and have the dauphin crowned king. In February 1429, Joan made her way to the dauphin's court, where her sincerity and simplicity persuaded Charles to allow her to accompany a French army to Orléans. Apparently inspired by the faith of the peasant woman who called herself "the Maid," the French armies found new confidence in themselves and liberated Orléans, changing the course of the war. Within a few weeks, the entire Loire valley had been freed of the English. In July 1429, fulfilling Joan's other task, the dauphin was crowned king of France and became Charles VII (1422–1461). In accomplishing the two commands of her angelic voices, Joan had brought the war to a decisive turning point.

Joan, however, did not live to see the war concluded. She was captured by the Burgundian allies of the English in 1430. Wishing to eliminate the "Maid" for obvious political reasons, the English turned Joan over to the Inquisition on charges of witchcraft (see the box on p. 246). In the fifteenth century, spiritual visions were thought to be inspired either by God or the devil. Because Joan dressed

◆ **Joan of Arc.** Pictured here in a suit of armor, Joan of Arc is holding aloft a banner that shows Christ and two angels. This miniature portrait is believed to be a good likeness of Joan.

in men's clothing, it was relatively easy to convince others that she was in league with the "prince of darkness." She was condemned to death as a heretic and burned at the stake in 1431. To the end, as the flames rose up around her, she declared "that her voices came from God and had not deceived her." Twenty-five years later, a new ecclesiastical court exonerated her of these charges, and five centuries later, in 1920, she was made a saint of the Roman Catholic church. Joan of Arc's accomplishments proved decisive. Although the war dragged on for another two decades, defeats of English armies in Normandy and Aquitaine led to French victory by 1453.

Political Instability

The fourteenth century was a period of adversity for the internal political stability of European governments. Although government bureaucracies grew ever larger, at the same time the question of who should control the bureaucracies led to internal conflict and instability. This instability was part of a general breakdown of customary

⇒ *The Trial of Joan of Arc* ⇐

Feared by the English and Burgundians, Joan of Arc was put on trial on charges of witchcraft and heresy after her capture. She was condemned for heresy and burned at the stake on May 30, 1431. This excerpt is taken from the records of Joan's trial, which presented a dramatic confrontation between the judges, trained in the complexities of legal questioning, and a nineteen-year-old woman who relied only on the "voices" of saints who gave her advice. In this selection, Joan describes what these voices told her to do.

The Trial of Joan of Arc

Afterward, she declared that at the age of thirteen she had a voice from God to help her and guide her. And the first time she was much afraid. And this voice came toward noon, in summer, in her father's garden. . . . She heard the voice on her right, in the direction of the church; and she seldom heard it without a light. This light came from the same side as the voice, and generally there was a great light. . . .

Asked what instruction this voice gave her for the salvation of her soul: she said it taught her to be good and to go to church often. . . . She said that the voice told her to come, and she could no longer stay where she was; and the voice told her again that she should raise the siege of the city of Orléans. She said moreover that the voice told her that she, Joan, should go to Robert de Baudricourt, in the town of Vaucouleurs of which he was captain, and he would provide an escort for her. And the said Joan answered that she was a poor maid, knowing nothing of riding or fighting. She said she went to an uncle of hers, and told him she wanted to stay with him for some time; and she stayed there about eight days. And she told her uncle she must go to the said town of Vaucouleurs, and so her uncle took her.

Then she said that when she reached Vaucouleurs she easily recognized Robert de Baudricourt, although she had never seen him before; and she knew him through her voice, for the voice had told her it was he. . . . The said Robert twice refused to hear her and repulsed her; the third time he listened to her and gave her an escort. And the voice had told her that it would be so.

feudal institutions. Traditional feudal loyalties were disintegrating rapidly and had not yet been replaced by the national loyalties of the future. Like the lord and serf relationship, the lord and vassal relationship based on land and military service was being replaced by a contract based on money. Especially after the Black Death, money payments called scutage were increasingly substituted for military service. Monarchs welcomed this development because they could now hire professional soldiers who tended to be more reliable anyway. As lord and vassal relationships became less personal and less important, new relationships based on political advantage began to be formed, creating new avenues for political influence—and for corruption as well. Especially noticeable, as the landed aristocrats suffered declining rents and social uncertainties with the new relationships, was the formation of factions of nobles who looked for opportunities to advance their power and wealth at the expense of other noble factions and of their monarchs. At the same time, two other developments, related to the rise of factions, added to the instability of governments in the fourteenth century.

First, dynasties of the fourteenth century seemed unable to produce direct male heirs. By the mid-fifteenth century, reigning monarchs in many European countries were not actually the direct male descendants of those ruling in 1300. The founders of these new dynasties had to struggle for their positions as factions of nobles vied to gain material advantages for themselves. At the end of the fourteenth century and beginning of the fifteenth, there were two claimants to the throne of France, and two aristocratic factions fought for control of England; in Germany, three princes struggled to be recognized as emperor.

Fourteenth-century monarchs, whether of old or new dynasties, found themselves with financial problems as well. The shift to the use of mercenary soldiers left monarchs perennially short on cash. Traditional revenues, especially rents from property, increasingly proved insufficient to meet their needs. Monarchs attempted to generate new sources of revenues, especially through taxes, which often meant going through parliaments. This opened the door for parliamentary bodies to gain more power by asking for favors first. Although unsuccessful in most cases, the role of parliaments simply added another element of uncertainty and confusion to fourteenth-century politics. By turning now to a survey of western and central European states (eastern Europe will be examined in Chapter 13), we can see how these disruptive factors worked in each country.

Western Europe: England and France

In the fourteenth century, the lengthy reign of Edward III (1327–1377) was an important one for the evolution of English political institutions. Parliament increased in prominence and developed its basic structure and functions during Edward's reign. Due to his constant need for money to fight the Hundred Years' War, Edward came to rely on Parliament to levy new taxes. In return for regular grants, Edward made several concessions, including a commitment to levy no direct tax without Parliament's consent and to allow committees of Parliament to examine the government accounts to ensure that the money was being spent properly. By the end of Edward's reign, Parliament had become an important component of the English governmental system.

During this same period, Parliament began to assume the organizational structure it has retained to this day. The Great Council of barons became the House of Lords and evolved into a body composed of the chief bishops and abbots of the realm and aristocratic peers whose position in Parliament was hereditary. The representatives of the shires and boroughs, who were considered less important than the lay and ecclesiastical lords, held collective meetings to decide policy and soon came to be regarded as the House of Commons. Together, the House of Lords and the House of Commons constituted Parliament. Although the House of Commons did little beyond approving measures proposed by the Lords, during Edward's reign, the Commons did begin the practice of drawing up petitions, which, if accepted by the Lords and king, became law.

After Edward III's death, England began to experience the internal instability of aristocratic factionalism that was wracking other European countries. After Richard II was deposed in 1399 and soon killed, the leader of the revolt of the barons, Henry of Lancaster, was made king. Although Henry IV (1399–1413) proved to be a competent ruler, factions of nobles soon rose to take advantage of the new situation. England would soon be embroiled in a devastating series of civil wars known as the War of the Roses.

The Hundred Years' War left France prostrate. Depopulation, desolate farmlands, ruined commerce, and independent and unruly nobles made it difficult for the kings to assert their authority throughout the fourteenth century. The insanity of King Charles VI (1380–1422) especially opened the door to rival factions of French nobles aspiring to power and wealth. The dukes of Burgundy and Orléans competed to control Charles and the French monarchy. Their struggles created chaos for the French government and the French people. Many nobles supported the Orléanist faction while Paris and other towns favored the Burgundians. By the beginning of the fifteenth century, France seemed hopelessly mired in a civil war. When the English renewed the Hundred Years' War in 1415, the Burgundians supported the English cause and the English monarch's claim to the throne of France.

✦ **Richard II.** By aspiring to absolute power, Richard II caused a baronial revolt that led to his deposition as king of England. Richard commissioned this life-size portrait of himself in the early 1390s to be placed in Westminster Abbey. The artist's use of realistic details in the portrayal of the face ensured a genuine likeness of the king.

The German Monarchy

England and France had developed strong national monarchies in the High Middle Ages. By the end of the fourteenth century, they seemed in danger of disintegrating due to dynastic problems and the pressures generated by the Hundred Years' War. In contrast, the Holy Roman Empire, whose core consisted of the lands of Germany, had already begun to fall apart in the High Middle Ages. Northern Italy, which the German emperors had tried to include in their medieval empire, had been free from any real imperial control since the end of the Hohenstaufen dynasty in the thirteenth century. In Germany itself, the failure of the Hohenstaufens ended any chance of centralized monarchical authority, and Germany became a land of hundreds of virtually independent states. These varied in size and power and included princely states, such as the duchies of Bavaria and Saxony; free imperial city-states (self-governing cities directly under the control of the Holy Roman Emperor rather than a German territorial prince), such as Nuremberg; modest territories of petty imperial knights; and ecclesiastical states, such as the archbishopric of Cologne. In the latter states, a high church official, such as a bishop, archbishop, or abbot, served in a dual capacity as an administrative official of the Catholic church and secular lord over the territories of his ecclesiastical state. Although all of the rulers of these different states had some obligations to the German king and Holy Roman emperor, increasingly they acted independently of the German ruler.

Because of its unique pattern of development in the High Middle Ages, the German monarchy had become established on an elective rather than hereditary basis. This principle of election was standardized in 1356 by the Golden Bull issued by Emperor Charles IV (1346–1378). This document stated that four lay princes and three ecclesiastical rulers would serve as electors with the legal power to elect the "king of the Romans and future emperor, to be ruler of the world and of the Christian people." "King of the Romans" was the official title of the German king; after his imperial coronation, he would also have the title emperor.

In the fourteenth century, the electoral principle further ensured that kings of Germany were generally weak. Their ability to exercise effective power depended on the extent of their own family possessions. At the beginning of the fifteenth century, three emperors claimed the throne. Although the dispute was quickly settled, Germany entered the fifteenth century in a condition that verged on anarchy. Princes fought princes and leagues of cities. The emperors were virtually powerless to control any of them.

The States of Italy

By the fourteenth century Italy, too, had failed to develop a centralized monarchical state. Papal opposition to the rule of the Hohenstaufen emperors in the thirteenth century had virtually guaranteed that. Moreover, southern Italy was divided into the kingdom of Naples, ruled by the house of Anjou, and Sicily, whose kings came from the Spanish house of Aragon. The center of the peninsula remained under the rather shaky control of the papacy (the Papal States). Lack of centralized authority had enabled numerous city-states in northern and central Italy to remain independent of any political authority.

In the course of the fourteenth century, two general tendencies can be discerned: the replacement of republican governments by tyrants and the expansion of the larger city-states at the expense of the less powerful ones. Nearly all the cities of northern Italy began their existence as free communes with republican governments. But in the fourteenth century, intense internal strife led city-states to resort to temporary expedients, allowing rule by one man with dictatorial powers. Limited rule, however, soon became long-term despotism, as tyrants proved willing to use force to maintain power. Eventually, such tyrants tried to legitimize their power by purchasing titles from the emperor (still nominally ruler of northern Italy as Holy Roman Emperor). In this fashion, the Visconti became the dukes of Milan and the d'Este the dukes of Ferrara.

The other change of great significance was the development of larger, regional states as the larger states expanded at the expense of the smaller ones. By the end of the fourteenth century and the beginning of the fifteenth century, three major states came to dominate northern Italy. Located in the rich land of the Po valley where the chief trade routes from Italian coastal cities to the Alpine passes crossed, Milan was one of the richest city-states in Italy. Politically, it was also one of the most agitated until members of the Visconti family established themselves as hereditary dukes of Milan and extended their power over all of Lombardy. The republic of Florence dominated the region of Tuscany. In the course of the fourteenth century, a small, but wealthy merchant oligarchy established control of the Florentine government, led the Florentines in a series of successful wars against their neighbors, and established Florence as a major territorial state in northern Italy. The other major northern Italian state was the maritime republic of Venice, which had grown rich from commercial activity throughout the eastern Mediterranean and into northern Europe. Venice remained an extremely stable political entity governed by a small oligarchy of merchant-aristocrats who had become extremely wealthy through their trading activities. Venice's commercial empire brought in enormous revenues and gave it the status of an international power. At the end of the fourteenth century, Venice embarked on the conquest of a territorial state in northern Italy to protect its food supply and its overland trade routes.

The Decline of the Church

The papacy of the Roman Catholic church reached the height of its power in the thirteenth century. Theories of papal supremacy included a doctrine of "fullness of power" as the spiritual head of Christendom and claims to universal temporal authority over all secular rulers. But the growing secular monarchies of Europe presented a challenge to papal claims of temporal supremacy that led the papacy into a conflict with these territorial states that it was unable to win. Papal defeat, in turn, led to other crises that brought into question and undermined not only the pope's temporal authority over all Christendom, but his spiritual authority as well.

Boniface VIII and the Conflict with the State

The struggle between the papacy and the secular monarchies began during the pontificate of Pope Boniface VIII (1294–1303). One major issue appeared to be at stake between the pope and King Philip IV (1285–1314) of France. In his desire to acquire new revenues, Philip expressed the right to tax the French clergy. Boniface VIII claimed that the clergy of any state could not pay taxes to their secular ruler without the pope's consent. Underlying this issue, however, was a basic conflict between the claims of the papacy to universal authority over both church and state, which necessitated complete control over the clergy, and the claims of the king that all subjects, including the clergy, were under the jurisdiction of the crown and subject to the king's authority on matters of taxation and justice. In short, the fundamental issue was the universal sovereignty of the papacy versus the royal sovereignty of the monarch.

Boniface VIII attempted to assert his position by issuing a series of papal bulls or letters, the most important of which was *Unam Sanctam*, issued in 1302. It was the strongest statement ever made by a pope on the supremacy of the spiritual authority over the temporal authority (see the box on p. 250). When it became apparent that the pope had decided to act on his principles by excommunicating Philip IV of France, the latter sent a small contingent of French forces to capture Boniface and bring him back to France for trial. The pope was captured in Anagni, although Italian nobles from the surrounding countryside soon rescued him. The shock of this experience, however, soon led to the pope's death. Philip's strong-arm tactics had produced a clear victory for the national monarchy over the papacy since no later pope dared renew the extravagant claims of Boniface VIII. To ensure his position and avoid any future papal threat, Philip IV brought enough pressure on the college of cardinals to achieve the election of a Frenchman, Clement V (1305–1314), as pope. Using the excuse of turbulence in the city of Rome, the new pope took up residence in Avignon on the east bank of the Rhone River. Although Avignon was located in the Holy Roman Empire and was not a French possession, it lay just across the river from the possessions of King Philip IV. Clement may have intended to return to Rome, but he and his successors remained in Avignon for the next seventy-three years.

The Papacy at Avignon (1305–1378)

The residency of the popes in Avignon for almost three-quarters of the fourteenth century led to a decline in papal prestige and a growing antipapal sentiment. The city of Rome was the traditional capital of the universal church. The pope was the bishop of Rome, and his position was based on being the successor to the apostle Peter, the first bishop of Rome. It was quite unseemly that the head of the Catholic church should reside in Avignon instead of Rome. Although the Avignonese popes frequently announced their intention to return to Rome,

♦ **Pope Boniface VIII.** The conflict between church and state in the Middle Ages reached its height in the struggle between Pope Boniface VIII and King Philip IV of France. This fourteenth-century miniature depicts Boniface VIII presiding over a gathering of cardinals.

Boniface VIII's Defense of Papal Supremacy

One of the more remarkable documents of the fourteenth century was the exaggerated statement of papal supremacy issued by Pope Boniface VIII in 1302 in the heat of his conflict with the French king Philip IV. Ironically, this strongest statement ever made of papal supremacy was issued at a time when the rising power of the secular monarchies made it increasingly difficult for the premises to be accepted. Not long after issuing it, Boniface was taken prisoner by the French. Although freed by his fellow Italians, the humiliation of his defeat led to his death a short time later.

Pope Boniface VIII, *Unam Sanctam*

We are compelled, our faith urging us, to believe and to hold—and we do firmly believe and simply confess—that there is one holy catholic and apostolic church, outside of which there is neither salvation nor remission of sins. . . . In this church there is one Lord, one faith and one baptism. . . . Therefore, of this one and only church there is one body and one head . . . Christ, namely, and the vicar of Christ, St. Peter, and the successor of Peter. For the Lord himself said to Peter, feed my sheep. . . .

We are told by the word of the gospel that in this His fold there are two swords—a spiritual, namely, and a temporal. . . . Both swords, the spiritual and the material, therefore, are in the power of the church; the one, indeed, to be wielded for the church, the other by the church; the one by the hand of the priest, the other by the hand of kings and knights, but at the will and sufferance of the priest. One sword, moreover, ought to be under the other, and the temporal authority to be subjected to the spiritual. . . .

Therefore if the earthly power err it shall be judged by the spiritual power; but if the lesser spiritual power err, by the greater. But if the greatest, it can be judged by God alone, not by man, the apostle bearing witness. A spiritual man judges all things, but he himself is judged by no one. This authority, moreover, even though it is given to man and exercised through man, is not human but rather divine, being given by divine lips to Peter and founded on a rock for him and his successors through Christ himself whom he has confessed; the Lord himself saying to Peter: "Whatsoever you shall bind, etc." Whoever, therefore, resists this power thus ordained by God, resists the ordination of God. . . .

Indeed, we declare, announce and define, that it is altogether necessary to salvation for every human creature to be subject to the Roman pontiff.

the political turmoil in the Papal States in central Italy always gave them an excuse to postpone their departure. In the decade of the 1330s, the popes began to construct a stately palace in Avignon, a clear indication that they intended to stay for some time.

Other factors also led to a decline in papal prestige during the Avignonese residency. It was widely believed that the popes at Avignon were captives of the French monarchy. Although questionable, since Avignon did not belong to the French monarchy, it was easy to believe in view of Avignon's proximity to French lands. Moreover, during the seventy-three years of the Avignonese papacy, of the 134 new cardinals created by the popes, 113 of them were French. At the same time, the popes attempted to find new sources of revenue to compensate for their loss of revenue from the Papal States. Their creation of new taxes on the clergy, frequently enforced by the threat of excommunication if they were not paid, did not improve people's opinion of the pope's use of his spiritual authority. Furthermore, the splendor in which the pope and cardinals were living in Avignon led to a highly vo-

cal criticism of both clergy and papacy in the fourteenth century. Avignon had become a powerful symbol of abuses within the church. At last, Pope Gregory XI, perceiving the disastrous decline in papal prestige, returned to Rome in 1377. His untimely death shortly afterward, however, soon gave rise to an even greater crisis for the Catholic church.

The Great Schism

Gregory XI (1370–1378) died in Rome in the spring of 1378. When the college of cardinals met in conclave to elect a new pope, the citizens of Rome, fearful that the French majority would choose another Frenchman who would return the papacy to Avignon, threatened that the cardinals would not leave Rome alive unless a Roman or Italian were elected pope. Indeed, the guards of the conclave warned the cardinals that they "ran the risk of being torn in pieces" if they did not choose an Italian. Wisely, the terrified cardinals duly elected the Italian archbishop of Bari as Pope Urban VI (1378–1389). Five months later, a group of dissenting cardinals—the French ones—declared Urban's election null and void and chose one of their number, a Frenchman, who took the title of Clement VII and promptly returned to Avignon. Because Urban remained in Rome, there were now two popes, initiating what has been called the Great Schism of the church. Europe's loyalties became divided: France, Spain, Scotland, and southern Italy supported Clement, while England, Germany, Scandinavia, and most of Italy supported Urban. These divisions generally followed political lines. Because the French supported the Avignonese, so did their allies; their enemies, particularly England and its allies, supported the Roman pope. The need for political support caused both popes to subordinate their policies to the policies of these states.

The Great Schism badly damaged the faith of Christian believers. The pope was widely believed to be the leader of Christendom and, as Boniface VIII had pointed out, held the keys to the kingdom of heaven. Since both lines of popes denounced the other as the Antichrist, such a spectacle could not help but undermine the institution that had become the very foundation of the church. The Great Schism introduced uncertainty into the daily lives of ordinary Christians.

As dissatisfaction with the papacy grew, so also did the calls for a revolutionary approach to solving the church's institutional problems. Final authority in spiritual matters must reside not with the popes, reformers claimed, but with a general church council representing all members. The Great Schism led large numbers of serious churchmen to take up the theory of conciliarism in the belief that only a general council of the church could end the schism and bring reform to the church in its "head and members." In desperation, a group of cardinals from both lines of popes finally heeded these theoretical formulations and convened a general council. This Council of Pisa, which met in 1409, deposed the two popes and elected a new one. The council's action proved disastrous when the two deposed popes refused to step down. There were now three popes and the church seemed more hopelessly divided than ever.

Leadership in convening a new council now passed to the Holy Roman emperor Sigismund. As a result of his efforts, a new ecumenical church council met at Constance from 1414 to 1418. It had three major objectives: to end the schism, to eradicate heresy, and to reform the church in "head and members." The ending of the schism proved to be the Council of Constance's easiest task. After the three competing popes either resigned or were deposed, a new conclave elected a Roman cardinal, a member of a prominent Roman family, as Pope Martin V (1417–1431).

CHRONOLOGY

The Decline of the Church

Pope Boniface VIII	1294–1303
Unam Sanctam	1302
The papacy at Avignon	1305–1378
Pope Gregory XI returns to Rome	1377
The Great Schism begins	1378
Pope Urban VI	1378–1389
Failure of Council of Pisa to end schism	1409
Council of Constance	1414–1418
End of schism; election of Martin V	1417

The council was much less successful in dealing with the problems of heresy and reform.

Culture and Society in an Age of Adversity

In the midst of disaster, the fourteenth century proved creative in its own way. The rapid growth of vernacular literature and new inventions made an impact on European life at the same time that the effects of plague were felt in many areas of medieval towns and cities.

The Development of Vernacular Literature

Although Latin remained the language of the church liturgy and the official documents of both church and state, the fourteenth century witnessed the rapid growth of vernacular languages, especially in Italy. Spoken vernacular tongues had been used in Europe for centuries, and some notable literature in French and German had appeared during the High Middle Ages. In the fourteenth century, the works of Dante and Chaucer were instrumental in transforming regional dialects into national languages, and in the late fifteenth and early sixteenth centuries, vernacular languages became broad enough in scope to create national literary forms that could compete with and eventually replace Latin.

Dante (1265–1321) came from an old Florentine noble family that had fallen on hard times. His masterpiece in the Italian vernacular was the *Divine Comedy*, written between 1313 and 1321. Cast in a typical medieval

❧ Dante's Vision of Hell ❧

The Divine Comedy of Dante Alighieri is regarded as one of the greatest literary works of all time. Many consider it the supreme summary of medieval thought. It combines allegory with a remarkable amount of contemporary history. Indeed, forty-three of the seventy-nine people consigned to hell in the "Inferno" were Florentines. This excerpt is taken from Canto XVIII of the "Inferno," in which Dante and Virgil visit the eighth circle of hell, which is divided into ten trenches containing those who had committed malicious frauds upon their fellow human beings.

Dante, "Inferno," *The Divine Comedy*

*We had already come to where the walk
crosses the second bank, from which it lifts
another arch, spanning from rock to rock.*

*Here we heard people whine in the next chasm,
and knock and thump themselves with open palms,
and blubber through their snouts as if in a spasm.*

*Steaming from that pit, a vapor rose
over the banks, crusting them with a slime
that sickened my eyes and hammered at my nose.*

*That chasm sinks so deep we could not sight
its bottom anywhere until we climbed
along the rock arch to its greatest height.*

*Once there, I peered down; and I saw long lines
of people in a river of excrement
that seemed the overflow of the world's latrines.*

*I saw among the felons of that pit
one wraith who might or might not have been tonsured—
one could not tell, he was so smeared with shit.*

*He bellowed: "You there, why do you stare at me
more than at all the others in this stew?"
And I to him: "Because if memory*

*serves me, I knew you when your hair was dry.
You are Alessio Interminelli da Lucca.
That's why I pick you from this filthy fry."*

*And he then, beating himself on his clown's head:
"Down to this have the flatteries I sold
the living sunk me here among the dead."*

*And my Guide prompted then: "Lean forward a bit
and look beyond him, there—do you see that one
scratching herself with dungy nails, the strumpet*

*who fidgets to her feet, then to a crouch?
It is the whore Thäis who told her lover
when he sent to ask her, 'Do you thank me much?'*

*'Much? Nay, past all believing?' And with this
Let us turn from the sight of this abyss."*

framework, the *Divine Comedy* is basically the story of the soul's progression to salvation, a fundamental medieval preoccupation. The lengthy poem was divided into three major sections corresponding to the realms of the afterworld: hell, purgatory, and heaven or paradise. In the "Inferno" (see the box above), Dante is led by his guide, the classical author Virgil, who is a symbol of human reason. But Virgil (or reason) can only lead the poet so far on his journey. At the end of "Purgatory," Beatrice (the true love of Dante's life), who represents revelation—which alone can explain the mysteries of heaven—becomes his guide into "Paradise." Here, Beatrice presents Dante to Saint Bernard, a symbol of mystical contemplation. The saint turns Dante over to the Virgin Mary since grace is necessary to achieve the final step of entering the presence of God, where one beholds "The love that moves the sun and the other stars."[6]

Geoffrey Chaucer (c. 1340–1400), brought a new level of sophistication to the English vernacular language in his famous work *The Canterbury Tales*. His beauty of expression and clear, forceful language were important in transforming his East Midland dialect into the chief ancestor of the modern English language. *The Canterbury Tales* constitutes a group of stories told by a group of twenty-nine pilgrims journeying from Southwark to the tomb of Saint Thomas at Canterbury. This format gave Chaucer the chance to portray an entire range of English society, both high and low born. Among others, he presented the Knight, the Squire, the Yeoman, the Prioress, the Monk, the Merchant, the Student, the Lawyer, the Carpenter, the Cook, the Doctor, the Plowman, and, of course, "A Good Wife was there from beside the city of Bath—a little deaf, which was a pity." The stories these pilgrims told to while away the time on the journey were just as varied as the storytellers themselves: knightly romances, fairy tales, saints' lives, sophisticated satires, and crude anecdotes.

Art and the Black Death

The fourteenth century produced an artistic outburst in new directions as well as a large body of morbid work influenced by the Black Death and the recurrence of the plague. The city of Florence witnessed the first dramatic break with medieval tradition in the work of Giotto (1266–1337), often considered a forerunner of Italian Renaissance painting. Although he worked throughout Italy, Giotto's most famous works were done in Padua and Florence. Coming out of the formal Byzantine school, Giotto transcended it with a new kind of realism, a desire to imitate nature that Renaissance artists later identified as the basic component of classical art. Giotto's figures were solid and rounded and—placed realistically in relationship to each other and their background—provided a sense of three-dimensional depth. The expressive faces and physically realistic bodies gave his sacred figures human qualities with which spectators could identify.

The Black Death had a visible impact on art. For one thing, it wiped out entire guilds of artists. At the same time, survivors, including the newly rich who patronized artists, were no longer so optimistic. Some were more guilty about enjoying life and more concerned about gaining salvation. Postplague art began to concentrate on pain and death. A fairly large number of artistic works came to be based on the *ars moriendi,* the art of dying.

Changes in Urban Life

One immediate by-product of the Black Death was a greater regulation of urban activities. Authorities tried to keep cities cleaner by enacting new ordinances against waste products in the streets. Viewed as unhealthy places, bathhouses were closed down, leading to a noticeable decline in cleanliness.

The effects of plague were also felt in other areas of medieval urban life. The basic unit of the late medieval urban environment was the nuclear family of husband, wife, and children. Especially in wealthier families, there might also be servants, apprentices, and other relatives, including widowed mothers and the husband's illegitimate children.

Before the Black Death, late marriages were common for urban couples. It was not unusual for husbands to be in their late thirties or forties and wives in their early twenties. The expense of beginning a household probably

◆ **Giotto, *Pietà*.** The work of Giotto marked the first clear innovation in fourteenth-century painting, making him a forerunner of the Early Renaissance. In this fresco, which was part of an elaborate series in the Arena chapel in Padua begun in 1305, the solidity of Giotto's human figures gives them a three-dimensional sense.

necessitated the delay in marriage. But the situation changed dramatically after the plague, reflecting new economic opportunities for the survivors and a reluctance to postpone living in the presence of so much death. The economic difficulties of the fourteenth century also had a tendency to strengthen the development of gender roles and to set new limits on employment opportunities for women. Based on the authority of Aristotle, Thomas Aquinas and other thirteenth-century scholastic theologians had advanced the belief that according to the natural order, men were active and domineering while women were passive and submissive. As more and more lawyers, doctors, and priests, who had been trained in universities where these notions were taught, entered society, these ideas of man's and woman's different natures became widely acceptable. Increasingly, women were expected to forego any active functions in society and remain subject to direction from males. A fourteenth-century Parisian provost commented on glass cutters that "no master's widow who keeps working at his craft after her husband's death may take on apprentices, for the men of the craft do not believe that a woman can master it well enough to teach a child to master it, for the craft is a very delicate one."[7] Although this statement suggests that some women were in fact running businesses, it also reveals that they were viewed as incapable of undertaking all of men's activities. Based on a pattern of gender, Europeans created a division of labor roles between men and women that continued until the Industrial Revolution of the eighteenth and nineteenth centuries.

Inventions and New Patterns

Despite its problems, the fourteenth century witnessed a continuation of the technological innovations that had characterized the High Middle Ages. The most extraordinary of these inventions, and one that had a visible impact on European cities, was the clock. The mechanical clock was invented at the end of the thirteenth century, but not perfected until the fourteenth. The time-telling clock was actually a by-product of a larger astronomical clock. The best-designed one was constructed by Giovanni di Dondi in the mid-fourteenth century. Dondi's clock contained the signs of the zodiac, but also struck on the hour. Because clocks were expensive, they were usually installed only in the towers of churches or municipal buildings. The first clock striking equal hours was in a church in Milan; in 1335, a chronicler described it as "a wonderful clock, with a very large clapper which strikes a bell twenty-four hours of the day and night and thus at the first hour of the night gives one sound, at the second two strikes . . . and so distinguishes one hour from another, which is of greatest use to men of every degree."[8]

Clocks introduced a wholly new conception of time into the lives of Europeans; they revolutionized how people thought about and used time. Throughout most of the Middle Ages, time was determined by natural rhythms (daybreak and nightfall) or church bells that were rung at more or less regular three-hour intervals, corresponding to the ecclesiastical offices of the church. Clocks made it possible to plan one's day and organize one's activities around the regular striking of bells. This brought a new regularity into the lives of workers and merchants, defining urban existence and enabling merchants and bankers to see the value of time in a new way.

Invented earlier by the Chinese, gunpowder also made its appearance in the west in the fourteenth century. The use of gunpowder eventually brought drastic changes to European warfare. Its primary use was in cannons, although early cannons were prone to blow up, making them as dangerous to those firing them as to the enemy. Even as late as 1460, an attack on a castle using the "Lion," an enormous Flemish cannon, proved disastrous for the Scottish king James II when the "Lion" blew up, killing the king and a number of his retainers. Continued improvement in the construction of cannons, however, soon made them extremely valuable in reducing both castles and city walls.

Conclusion

In the eleventh, twelfth, and thirteenth centuries, European civilization developed many of its fundamental features. Territorial states, parliaments, capitalist trade and industry, banks, cities, and vernacular literatures were all products of that fertile period. During the same time, the Catholic church under the direction of the papacy reached its apogee. Fourteenth-century European society, however, was challenged by an overwhelming number of crises. Devastating plague, decline in trade and industry, bank failures, peasant revolts pitting lower classes against the upper classes, seemingly constant warfare, aristocratic factional conflict that undermined political stability, the absence of the popes from Rome, and even the spectacle of two popes condemning each other as the Antichrist all seemed to overpower Europeans in this "calamitous century." Not surprisingly, much of the art of the period depicted the Four Horsemen of the Apocalypse described in the New Testament book of Revelation: Death, Famine, Pestilence, and War. No doubt, to some people the last days of the world appeared to be at hand.

The new European society, however, proved remarkably resilient. Periods of crisis are usually paralleled by the emergence of new ideas and new practices. Intellectuals of the period saw themselves as standing on the threshold of a new age or rebirth of the best features of classical civilization. It is their perspective that led historians to speak of a Renaissance in the fifteenth century.

NOTES

1. Quoted in H. S. Lucas, "The Great European Famine of 1315, 1316, and 1317." *Speculum* 5 (1930) 359.
2. Quoted in Robert Gottfried, *The Black Death* (New York, 1983), p. xiii.
3. Jean Froissart, *Chronicles*, ed. and trans. Geoffrey Brereton (Harmondsworth, 1968), p. 111.
4. Ibid., p. 212.
5. Ibid., p. 89.
6. Dante Alighieri, *The Divine Comedy*, trans. Dorothy Sayers (New York, 1962), "Paradise," Canto XXXIII, line 145.
7. Quoted in Susan Stuard, "Dominion of Gender: Women's Fortunes in the High Middle Ages," in Renate Bridenthal, Claudia Koonz, and Susan Stuard, eds., *Becoming Visible: Women in European History*, 2d ed. (Boston, 1987), p. 169.
8. Quoted in Jean Gimpel, *The Medieval Machine* (New York, 1976), p. 168.

SUGGESTIONS FOR FURTHER READING

For a general introduction to the fourteenth century, see D. Hay, *Europe in the Fourteenth and Fifteenth Centuries* (New York, 1966); G. Holmes, *Europe: Hierarchy and Revolt, 1320–1450* (New York, 1975); and the well-written popular history by B. Tuchman, *A Distant Mirror* (New York, 1978).

On the Black Death, see R. S. Gottfried, *The Black Death: Natural and Human Disaster in Medieval Europe* (New York, 1983); P. Ziegler, *The Black Death* (New York, 1969); and W. H. McNeill, *Plagues and People* (New York, 1976). On the peasant and urban revolts of the fourteenth century, see M. Mollat and P. Wolff, *The Popular Revolutions of the Late Middle Ages* (Winchester, Mass., 1973).

The classic work on the Hundred Years' War is E. Perroy, *The Hundred Years War* (New York, 1951). A more recent account is R. H. Neillands, *The Hundred Years War* (New York, 1990). On Joan of Arc, see M. Warner, *Joan of Arc: The Image of Female Heroism* (New York, 1981). On the political history of the period, see B. Guenée, *States and Rulers in Later Medieval Europe*, trans. J. Vale (Oxford, 1985); and D. Waley, *Later Medieval Europe* (New York, 1964). Works on individual countries include P. S. Lewis, *Later Medieval France: The Polity* (London, 1968); A. R. Myers, *England in the Late Middle Ages* (Harmondsworth, 1952); and F. R. H. Du Boulay, *Germany in the Later Middle Ages* (London, 1983). On the Italian political scene, see D. P. Waley, *The Italian City-Republics* (London, 1978); J. Larner, *Italy in the Age of Dante and Petrarch, 1216–1380* (London, 1980); and F. C. Lane, *Venice: A Maritime Republic* (Baltimore, 1973).

Good general studies of the church in the fourteenth century can be found in F. P. Oakley, *The Western Church in the Later Middle Ages* (Ithaca, N.Y., 1980); and S. Ozment, *The Age of Reform, 1250–1550: An Intellectual and Religious History of Late Medieval and Reformation Europe* (New Haven, Conn., 1980). On the Avignonese papacy, see Y. Renouard, *The Avignon Papacy, 1305–1403* (London, 1970); and G. Mollat, *The Popes at Avignon* (New York, 1965).

A classic work on the life and thought of the Later Middle Ages is J. Huizinga, *The Waning of the Middle Ages* (New York, 1949). On the impact of the plague on culture, see the brilliant study by M. Meiss, *Painting in Florence and Siena after the Black Death* (New York, 1964).

A wealth of material on everyday life is provided in the second volume of *A History of Private Life* edited by G. Duby, *Revelations of the Medieval World* (Cambridge, Mass., 1988). On women in the Late Middle Ages, see S. Shahar, *The Fourth Estate: A History of Women in the Middle Ages*, trans. C. Galai (London, 1983). For late medieval townspeople, see J. F. C. Harrison, *The Common People of Great Britain* (Bloomington, Ind., 1985). Poor people are discussed in M. Mollat, *The Poor in the Middle Ages* (New Haven, Conn., 1986). The importance of inventions is discussed in J. Gimpel, *The Medieval Machine* (New York, 1976). Another valuable discussion of medieval technology can be found in J. Le Goff, *Time, Work and Culture in the Middle Ages* (Chicago, 1980).

CHAPTER 13

Recovery and Rebirth: The Age of the Renaissance

Medieval and Renaissance historians have argued interminably over the significance of the fourteenth and fifteenth centuries. Did they witness a continuation of the Middle Ages or the beginning of a new era? Obviously, both positions contain a modicum of truth. Although the disintegrative patterns of the fourteenth century continued into the fifteenth, at the same time there were elements of recovery that made the fifteenth century a period of significant political, economic, artistic, and intellectual change. The humanists or intellectuals of the age called their period (from the mid-fourteenth to the mid-sixteenth century) an age of rebirth, believing that they had restored arts and letters to new glory after they had been "neglected" or "dead" for centuries. The humanists also saw their age as one of great individuals who dominated the landscape of their time. Michelangelo, the great Italian artist of the early sixteenth century, and Pope Julius II, the "warrior pope," were two such titans. The artist's temperament and the pope's temper led to many lengthy and often loud quarrels between the two. Among other commissions, the pope had hired Michelangelo to paint the ceiling of the Sistine Chapel in Rome, a difficult task for a man long accustomed to being a sculptor. Michelangelo undertook the project but refused for a long time to allow anyone, including the pope, to see his work. Julius grew anxious, pestering Michelangelo on a regular basis about when the ceiling would be finished. Exasperated by the pope's requests, Michelangelo once replied, according to Giorgio Vasari, his contemporary biographer, that the ceiling would be completed "when it satisfies me as an artist." The pope responded, "and we want you to satisfy us and finish it soon," and then threatened that if Michelangelo did not "finish the ceiling quickly he would have him thrown down from the scaffolding." Fearing the pope's anger, Michelangelo "lost no time in doing all that was wanted" and quickly completed the ceiling, one of the great masterpieces in the history of Western art.

1400	1426	1452	1478	1504	1530

Rule of Cosimo de' Medici in Florence   Marriage of Ferdinand and Isabella

Fall of Constantinople   War of the Roses   Sack of Rome

Civic humanism in Florence   Machiavelli's *The Prince*

Invention of printing   Castiglione's *Book of the Courtier*

Masaccio's frescoes in Florence   Leonardo da Vinci's *The Last Supper*

Donatello's *David*   Michelangelo's Sistine Chapel ceiling

The humanists' view of their age as a rebirth of the classical civilization of the Greeks and Romans ultimately led historians to use the word Renaissance *to identify this age. Although recent historians have emphasized the many elements of continuity between the Middle Ages and the Renaissance, the latter age was also distinguished by its own unique characteristics.*

Meaning and Characteristics of the Italian Renaissance

The word *Renaissance* means "rebirth." A number of people who lived in Italy between c. 1350 and c. 1550 believed that they had witnessed a rebirth of antiquity or Greco-Roman civilization, which marked a new age. To them, the approximately 1000 years between the end of the Roman Empire and their own era was a middle period (hence the "Middle Ages"), characterized by darkness because of its lack of classical culture. Historians of the nineteenth century later used similar terminology to describe this period in Italy. The Swiss historian and art critic Jacob Burckhardt created the modern concept of the Renaissance in his celebrated work, *Civilization of the Renaissance in Italy*, published in 1860. He portrayed Italy in the fourteenth and fifteenth centuries as the birthplace of the modern world and saw the revival of antiquity, the "perfecting of the individual," and secularism ("worldliness of the Italians") as its distinguishing features. No doubt, Burckhardt exaggerated the individuality and secularism of the Renaissance and failed to recognize the depths of its religious sentiment. Nevertheless, he established the framework for all modern interpretations of the Renaissance. Although contemporary scholars do not believe that the Renaissance represents a sudden or dramatic cultural break with the Middle Ages (as Burckhardt argued)—there was after all much continuity between the two periods in economic, political, and social life—the Renaissance can still be viewed as a distinct period of European history that manifested itself first in Italy and then spread to the rest of Europe. What, then, are the characteristics of the Italian Renaissance?

Renaissance Italy was largely an urban society. The city-states, especially those of northern Italy, became the centers of Italian political, economic, and social life. Within this new urban society, a secular spirit emerged as increasing wealth created new possibilities for the enjoyment of worldly things.

Above all, the Renaissance was an age of recovery from the "calamitous fourteenth century." Italy and Europe began a slow process of recuperation from the effects of the Black Death, political disorder, and economic recession. By the end of the fourteenth and beginning of the fifteenth centuries, Italians were using the words "recovery" and "revival" and were actively involved in a rebuilding process.

Recovery was accompanied by rebirth, specifically, a rebirth of the culture of classical antiquity. Increasingly aware of their own historical past, Italian intellectuals became intensely interested in the Greco-Roman culture of the ancient Mediterranean world. This new revival of classical antiquity (the Middle Ages, after all, had preserved much of ancient Latin culture) affected activities as diverse as politics and art and led to new attempts to reconcile the pagan philosophy of antiquity with Christian thought, as well as new ways of viewing human beings.

Though not entirely new, a revived emphasis on individual ability became characteristic of the Italian

Renaissance. As the fifteenth-century Florentine architect Leon Battista Alberti expressed it, "Men can do all things if they will."[1] A high regard for human dignity and worth and a realization of individual potentiality created a new social ideal of the well-rounded personality or universal person (*l'uomo universale*) who was capable of achievements in many areas of life.

These general features of the Italian Renaissance were not characteristic of all Italians, but were primarily the preserve of the wealthy upper classes who constituted a small percentage of the total population. The achievements of the Italian Renaissance were the product of an elite, rather than a mass, movement. Nevertheless, indirectly it did have some impact on ordinary people, especially in the cities where so many of the intellectual and artistic accomplishments of the period were most apparent and visible.

The Making of Renaissance Society

After three centuries of economic expansion, in the second half of the fourteenth century, Europeans experienced severe economic reversals and social upheavals (see Chapter 12). By the middle of the fifteenth century, a gradual economic recovery had begun with an increase in the volume of manufacturing and trade. Economic growth varied from area to area, however, and despite the recovery Europe did not experience the economic boom of the High Middle Ages.

Economic Recovery

By the fourteenth century, Italian merchants were carrying on a flourishing commerce throughout the Mediterranean and had also expanded their lines of trade north along the Atlantic seaboard. The great galleys of the Venetian Flanders Fleet maintained a direct sea route from Venice to England and the Netherlands, where Italian merchants came into contact with the increasingly powerful Hanseatic League of merchants. Hard hit by the plague, the Italians lost their commercial preeminence while the Hanseatic League continued to prosper.

As early as the thirteenth century, to protect themselves from pirates and competition from Scandinavian merchants, a number of north German coastal towns had formed a commercial and military league known as the Hansa or Hanseatic League. By 1500, more than eighty cities belonged to the League, which established settlements and commercial bases in northern Europe and England. For almost 200 years, the Hansa had a monopoly on northern European trade in timber, fish, grain, metals, honey, and wines. Its southern outlet in Flanders, the city of Bruges, became the economic crossroads of Europe in the fourteenth century because it served as the meeting place between Hanseatic merchants and the Flanders Fleet of Venice. In the fifteenth century, however, Bruges slowly began to decline. So, too, did the Hanseatic League as it proved increasingly unable to compete with the developing larger territorial states.

Overall, trade recovered dramatically from the economic contraction of the fourteenth century. The Italians and especially the Venetians continued to maintain a wealthy commercial empire. Not until the sixteenth century, when overseas discoveries gave new importance to the states facing the Atlantic, did the petty Italian city-states begin to suffer from the competitive advantages of the ever-growing and more powerful national territorial states.

The economic depression of the fourteenth century also affected patterns of manufacturing. The woolen industries of Flanders and the northern Italian cities had been particularly devastated. By the beginning of the fifteenth century, however, the Florentine woolen industry began to experience a recovery. At the same time, luxury industries in the Italian cities began to develop and expand, especially industries dealing in lace and silk, glassware, and handworked items in metal and precious stones. Unfortunately, these luxury industries employed fewer people than the woolen industry and contributed less to overall prosperity.

Other new industries, especially printing, mining, and metallurgy, began to rival the textile industry in importance in the fifteenth century. New machinery and techniques for digging deeper mines and for separating metals from ore and purifying them were developed. When rulers began to transfer their titles to underground mineral rights to financiers as collateral for loans, these entrepreneurs quickly developed large mining operations to produce copper, iron, and silver. Especially valuable were the rich mineral deposits in central Europe, Hungary, the Tyrol, Bohemia, and Saxony. Expanding iron production and new skills in metalworking, in turn, contributed to the development of firearms that were more effective than the crude weapons of the fourteenth century.

The city of Florence regained its preeminence in banking in the fifteenth century, primarily due to the Medici family. In its best days (in the fifteenth century), the House of Medici was the greatest banking house in Europe, with branches in Venice, Milan, Rome, Avignon, Bruges, London, and Lyons. Moreover, the family had controlling interests in industrial enterprises for wool, silk, and the mining of alum, which was used in the dyeing of textiles. The Medici were also the principal bankers for the papacy, a position that produced big profits and influence at the papal court. Despite its great success in the early and middle part of the fifteenth century, the Medici bank suffered a rather sudden decline at the end of the century due to poor leadership and a series of bad loans, especially uncollectible loans to rulers. In 1494, when the French expelled the Medici from Florence and confiscated their property, the Medicean financial edifice collapsed.

Social Changes in the Renaissance

The Renaissance inherited a tripartite division of society from the Middle Ages. Society was fundamentally divided into three estates: the clergy, whose preeminence was grounded in the belief that people should be guided to spiritual ends; the nobility, whose privileges were based on the principle that the nobles provided security and justice for society; and the third estate, which consisted of the peasants and inhabitants of the towns and cities. This social order experienced certain adaptations in the Renaissance, which we can see by examining the second and third estates (the clergy will be examined in Chapter 14).

THE SOCIAL CLASSES: THE NOBILITY

Throughout much of Europe, the landholding nobles were faced with declining real incomes during the greater part of the fourteenth and fifteenth centuries, while the expense of maintaining noble status rose. But members of the old nobility survived and new blood infused its ranks. A reconstruction of the aristocracy was well underway by 1500. As a result of this reconstruction, the nobles, old and new, who constituted between 2 and 3 percent of the population in most countries, managed to dominate society as they had done in the Middle Ages, serving as military officers and holding important political posts as well as advising the king.

By 1500, the noble or aristocrat was expected to evince certain ideals. These ideals were best expressed in *The Book of the Courtier* by the Italian Baldassare Castiglione (1478–1529). First published in 1528, Castiglione's work soon became popular throughout Europe, and it remained a fundamental handbook for European aristocrats well into the twentieth century.

In *The Book of the Courtier*, Castiglione described the three basic attributes of the perfect courtier. First, nobles should possess fundamental native endowments, such as impeccable character, grace, talents, and noble birth. The perfect courtier must also cultivate certain achievements. Primarily, he should participate in military and bodily exercises because the principal profession of a courtier was arms. But unlike the medieval knight who had only been required to have military skill, the Renaissance courtier was also expected to have a classical education and adorn his life with the arts by playing a musical instrument, drawing, and painting. In Castiglione's hands, the Renaissance ideal of the well-developed personality became a social ideal of the aristocracy. Finally, the aristocrat was expected to follow a certain standard of conduct. Nobles were supposed to make good impressions; while being modest, they should not hide their accomplishments, but show them with grace (see the box on p. 260).

But what was the purpose of these courtly standards? Castiglione said:

> Therefore, I think that the aim of the perfect Courtier, which we have not spoken of up to now, is so to win for himself, by means of the accomplishments ascribed to him by these gentlemen, the favor and mind of the prince whom he serves that he may be able to tell him, and always will tell him, the truth about everything he needs to know, without fear or risk of displeasing him; and that when he sees the mind of his prince inclined to a wrong action, he may dare to oppose him . . . so as to dissuade him of every evil intent and bring him to the path of virtue.[2]

This ideal of service to the prince reflected the secular ethic of the active life espoused by the earlier civic humanists (see "Italian Renaissance Humanism" later in this chapter). Castiglione put the new moral values of the Renaissance into a courtly, aristocratic form that was now acceptable to the nobility throughout Europe. Nobles would adhere to his principles for hundreds of years while they continued to dominate European life socially and politically.

THE SOCIAL CLASSES: THE THIRD ESTATE OF PEASANTS AND TOWNSPEOPLE

Traditionally, peasants made up the overwhelming mass of the third estate and indeed continued to constitute as much as 85 to 90 percent of the total European population, except in the highly urbanized areas of northern Italy and Flanders. The most noticeable trend produced by the economic crisis of the fourteenth century was the decline of the manorial system and the continuing elimination of serfdom. The contraction of the peasantry after the Black Death simply accelerated the process of converting servile

A Renaissance Banquet

As in Greek and Roman society, the Renaissance banquet was an occasion for good food, interesting conversation, music, and dancing. In Renaissance society, it was also a symbol of status and an opportunity to impress people with the power and wealth of one's family. Banquets were held to celebrate public and religious festivals, official visits, anniversaries, and weddings. The following menu lists the foods served at a grand banquet given by Pope Pius V in the sixteenth century.

A Sixteenth-Century Banquet

First Course: Cold Delicacies from the Sideboard
Pieces of marzipan and marzipan balls
Neapolitan spice cakes
Malaga wine and Pisan biscuits
Fresh grapes
Prosciutto cooked in wine, served with capers
and grape pulp
Salted pork tongues cooked in wine, sliced
Spit-roasted songbirds, cold, with their tongues
sliced over them
Sweet mustard

Second Course: Hot Foods from the Kitchen, Roasts
Fried veal sweetbreads and liver
Spit-roasted skylarks with lemon sauce
Spit-roasted quails with sliced aubergines
Stuffed spit-roasted pigeons with capers
sprinkled over them
Spit-roasted rabbits, with sauce and crushed pine nuts
Partridges larded and spit-roasted, served with lemon
Heavily seasoned poultry with lemon slices

Slices of veal, spit-roasted, with a sauce made
from the juices
Leg of goat, spit-roasted with a sauce made
from the juices
Soup of almond paste, with the flesh of three
pigeons to each serving

Third Course: Hot Foods from the Kitchen, Boiled Meats and Stews
Stuffed fat geese, boiled Lombard style and covered
with sliced almonds
Stuffed breast of veal, boiled, garnished with flowers
Very young calf, boiled, garnished with parsley
Almonds in garlic sauce
Turkish-style rice with milk, sprinkled with cinnamon
Stewed pigeons with mortadella sausage and
whole onions
Cabbage soup with sausages
Poultry pie, two chickens to each pie
Fricasseed breast of goat dressed with fried onions
Pies filled with custard cream
Boiled calves' feet with cheese and egg

Fourth Course: Delicacies from the Sideboard
Bean tarts
Quince pastries
Pear tarts, the pears wrapped in marzipan
Parmesan cheese and Riviera cheese
Fresh almonds on vine leaves
Chestnuts roasted over the coals and served
with salt and pepper
Milk curds
Ring-shaped cakes
Wafers made from ground corn

labor dues into rents paid in money. By the end of the fifteenth century, primarily in western Europe, serfdom was declining, and more and more peasants were becoming legally free.

The remainder of the third estate centered around the inhabitants of towns and cities, originally the merchants and artisans who formed the burghers. The Renaissance town or city of the fifteenth century actually possessed a multitude of townspeople widely separated socially and economically.

At the top of urban society were the patricians, whose wealth from capitalistic enterprises in trade, industry, and banking enabled them to dominate their urban communities economically, socially, and politically. Below them were the petty burghers, the shopkeepers, artisans, guildmasters, and guildsmen who were largely concerned with providing goods and services for local consumption. Below these two groups were the propertyless workers earning pitiful wages and the unemployed, living squalid and miserable lives. These people constituted as much as 30 or 40 percent of the urban population. Everywhere in Europe in the late fourteenth and fifteenth centuries, urban poverty had increased dramatically. One rich merchant of Florence wrote:

> Those that are lazy and indolent in a way that does harm to the city, and who can offer no just reason for their condition, should either be forced to work or expelled from the Commune. The city would thus rid itself of that most harmful part of the poorest class. . . . If the lowest order of society earn enough food to keep them going from day to day, then they have enough.[3]

But even this large group was not at the bottom of the social scale; beneath them stood a significantly large group of slaves, especially in the cities of Italy.

The Family in Renaissance Italy

The family played an important role in Renaissance Italy. Family meant, first of all, the extended household of parents, children, and servants (if the family was wealthy) and could also include grandparents, widowed mothers, and even unmarried sisters. The family bond was a source of great security in the dangerous urban world of Renaissance Italy. To maintain the family, careful attention was given to marriages that were arranged by parents, often to strengthen business or family ties. Details were worked out well in advance, sometimes when children were only two or three, and reinforced by a legally binding marriage contract (see the box on p. 262). The important aspect of

the contract was the size of the dowry, a sum of money presented by the wife's family to the husband upon marriage. The dowry could involve large sums of money and was expected of all families. Because poor families often had difficulty providing a dowry, wealthy families established societies to provide dowries for poor girls.

The father-husband was the center of the Italian family. He gave it his name, was responsible for it in all legal matters, managed all finances (his wife had no share in his wealth), and made the crucial decisions that determined his children's lives. A father's authority over his children was absolute until he died or formally freed his children. In Renaissance Italy, children did not become adults on reaching a certain age; instead adulthood came only when the father went before a judge and formally emancipated them. The age of emancipation varied from early teens to late twenties.

The mother managed the household, a position that gave women a certain degree of autonomy in their daily lives. Considering that marriages had been arranged, marital relationships ran the gamut from deep emotional attachments to purely formal ties. The lack of emotional attachment resulting from arranged marriages did encourage extramarital relationships, especially for those groups whose lifestyle offered special temptations. Although sexual license for males was the norm for princes and their courts, women were supposed to follow different guidelines. The first wife of Duke Filippo Maria Visconti of Milan had an affair with the court musician and was executed for it.

✦ **Wedding Banquet.** Parents arranged marriages in Renaissance Italy to strengthen business or family ties. A legally binding marriage contract was considered a necessary part of the marital arrangements. So, too, was a wedding feast. This painting by Botticelli shows the wedding banquet in Florence that celebrated the marriage of Nastagio degli Onesti and the daughter of Paulo Traversaro.

⇒ Marriage Negotiations ⇐

Marriages were so important in maintaining families in Renaissance Italy that much energy was put into arranging them. Parents made the choices for their children, most often for considerations that had little to do with the modern notion of love. This selection is taken from the letters of a Florentine matron of the illustrious Strozzi family to her son Filippo in Naples. The family's considerations were complicated by the fact that the son was in exile.

Alessandra Strozzi to Her Son Filippo in Naples

[April 20, 1464] . . . Concerning the matter of a wife [for Filippo], it appears to me that if Francesco di Messer Tanagli wishes to give his daughter, that it would be a fine marriage. . . . Now I will speak with Marco [Parenti, Alessandra's son-in-law], to see if there are other prospects that would be better, and if there are none, then we will learn if he wishes to give her [in marriage]. . . . Francesco Tanagli has a good reputation, and he has held office, not the highest, but still he has been in office. You may ask: "Why should he give her to someone in exile?" There are three reasons. First, there aren't many young men of good family who have both virtue and property. Secondly, she has only a small dowry, 1,000 florins, which is the dowry of an artisan [although not a small sum, either—senior officials in the government bureaucracy earned 300 florins a year]. . . . Third, I believe that he will give her away, because he has a large family and he will need help to settle them. . . .

[July 26, 1465] . . . Francesco is a good friend of Marco and he trusts him. On S. Jacopo's day, he spoke to him discreetly and persuasively, saying that for several months he had heard that we were interested in the girl and . . . that when we had made up our minds, she will come to us willingly. [He said that] you were a

worthy man, and that his family had always made good marriages, but that he had only a small dowry to give her, and so he would prefer to send her outside of Florence to someone of worth, rather than to give her to someone here, from among those who were available, with little money. . . . We have information that she is affable and competent. She is responsible for a large family (there are twelve children, six boys and six girls), and the mother is always pregnant and isn't very competent. . . .

[August 31, 1465] . . . I have recently received some very favorable information [about the Tanagli girl] from two individuals. . . . They are in agreement that whoever gets her will be content. . . . Concerning her beauty, they told me what I had already seen, that she is attractive and well-proportioned. Her face is long, but I couldn't look directly into her face, since she appeared to be aware that I was examining her . . . and so she turned away from me like the wind. . . . She reads quite well . . . and she can dance and sing. . . .

So yesterday I sent for Marco and told him what I had learned. And we talked about the matter for a while, and decided that he should say something to the father and give him a little hope, but not so much that we couldn't withdraw, and find out from him the amount of the dowry. . . . May God help us to choose what will contribute to our tranquility and to the consolation of us all.

[September 13, 1465] . . . Marco came to me and said that the had met with Francesco Tanagli, who had spoken very coldly, so that I understand that he had changed his mind. . . .

[Filippo Strozzi eventually married Fiametta di Donato Adimari in 1466.]

The Italian States in the Renaissance

By the fifteenth century, five major powers dominated the Italian peninsula—the duchy of Milan, Venice, Florence, the Papal States and the kingdom of Naples. Northern Italy was divided between the duchy of Milan and Venice. After the death of the last Visconti ruler of Milan in 1447, Francesco Sforza, one of the leading *condottieri* (a *condottiere* was a leader of a mercenary band) of the time, turned on his Milanese employers, conquered the city, and became its new duke. Both the Visconti and

Sforza rulers worked to create a highly centralized territorial state. They were especially successful in devising systems of taxation that generated enormous revenues for the government. The maritime republic of Venice remained an extremely stable political entity governed by a small oligarchy of merchant-aristocrats. Its commercial empire brought in enormous revenues and gave it the status of an international power.

The republic of Florence dominated the region of Tuscany. In 1434, Cosimo de' Medici (1434–1464) took control of the ruling oligarchy. Although the wealthy Medici family maintained republican forms of government for appearance's sake, it ran the government from behind the scenes. Through their lavish patronage and careful courting of political allies, Cosimo and later his grandson Lorenzo the Magnificent (1469–1492) were successful in dominating the city at a time when Florence was the center of the cultural Renaissance.

The Papal States lay in central Italy. Nominally under the control of the popes, papal residence in Avignon and the Great Schism had enabled individual cities and territories, such as Urbino and Ferrara, to become independent of papal authority. The popes of the fifteenth century directed much of their energy toward reestablishing their control over the Papal States. The kingdom of Naples, which encompassed most of Southern Italy and usually the island of Sicily, remained a largely feudal monarchy that shared little in the cultural glories of the Renaissance.

A number of independent city-states under the control of powerful ruling families also became brilliant centers of Renaissance culture in the fifteenth century. Perhaps most famous was Urbino, ruled by the Montefeltro dynasty. Federigo da Montefeltro, who ruled Urbino from 1444 to 1482, received a classical education. He had also learned the skills of fighting, since the Montefeltro family compensated for the poverty of Urbino by hiring themselves out as *condottieri*. Federigo was not only a good ruler, but a rather unusual *condottiere* by fifteenth-century standards. Although not a brilliant general, he was reliable and honest. He did not break his promises, even when urged to do so by a papal legate. At the same time, Duke Federigo was one of the greatest patrons of Renaissance culture. Under his direction, Urbino became a well-known cultural and intellectual center.

A noticeable feature of these smaller Italian courts was the important role played by women. The most famous of the Italian ruling women was Isabella d'Este (1474–1539), daughter of the duke of Ferrara, who married Francesco Gonzaga, marquis of Mantua. Their court was another important center of art and learning in the Renaissance. Educated at the brilliant court of Ferrara, Isabella was known for her intelligence and political wisdom. Called the "first

Map 13.1 Renaissance Italy.

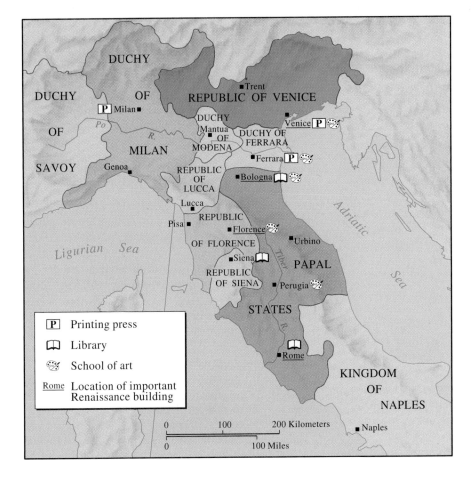

P	Printing press
📖	Library
🎨	School of art
Rome	Location of important Renaissance building

CHRONOLOGY

The Italian States in the Renaissance

Duchy of Milan	
Viscontis	1311–1447
Sforzas	1450–1494
Florence	
Cosimo de' Medici	1434–1464
Lorenzo de' Medici	1469–1492
Beginning of Italian wars—French invasion of Italy	1494
Sack of Rome	1527

lady of the world," she attracted artists and intellectuals to the Mantuan court and was responsible for amassing one of the finest libraries in all of Italy. Her numerous letters to friends, family, princes, and artists all over Europe disclose her political acumen as well as a good sense of humor. Both before and after the death of her husband Francesco, she effectively ruled Mantua and won a reputation as a clever negotiator.

The growth of powerful monarchical states led to trouble for the Italians and brought an end to the independence of the Italian states. Attracted by the riches of Italy, the French king Charles VIII (1483–1498) led an army of 30,000 men into Italy in 1494 and occupied the kingdom of Naples. Other Italian states turned for help to the Spanish, who gladly complied. For the next thirty years, the French and Spanish competed to dominate Italy, which was merely a pawn for the two great powers, a convenient arena for fighting battles. The terrible sack of Rome in 1527 by the armies of the Spanish king Charles I brought a temporary end to the Italian wars. Hereafter, the Spaniards dominated Italy; the Renaissance in Italy was at an end.

Machiavelli and the New Statecraft

No one gave better expression to the Renaissance preoccupation with political power than Niccolò Machiavelli (1469–1527). He entered the service of the Florentine republic in 1498, four years after the Medici family had been expelled from the city. As a secretary to the Florentine Council of Ten, he completed numerous diplomatic missions, including trips to France and Germany, and saw the workings of statecraft firsthand. Since Italy had been invaded in 1494, Machiavelli was active during a period

of Italian tribulation and devastation. In 1512, French defeat and Spanish victory led to the reestablishment of Medici power in Florence. Staunch republicans, including Machiavelli, were sent into exile. Forced to give up politics, the great love of his life, Machiavelli instead reflected on political power and wrote books, including *The Prince* (1513), one of the most famous treatises on political power in the Western world.

Machiavelli's ideas on politics stemmed from two major sources, his preoccupation with Italy's political problems and his knowledge of ancient Rome. His major concerns in *The Prince* were the acquisition and expansion of political power as the means to restore and maintain order in his time. Machiavelli was aware that his own approach to political power was different from previous political theorists. Late medieval political theorists believed that a ruler was justified in exercising political power only if it contributed to the common good of the people he served. The ethical side of a prince's activity—how a ruler ought to behave based on Christian moral principles—was the focus of many late medieval treatises on politics. Machiavelli bluntly contradicted this approach:

> But my hope is to write a book that will be useful, at least to those who read it intelligently, and so I thought it sensible to go straight to a discussion of how things are in real life and not waste time with a discussion of an imaginary world . . . for the gap between how people actually behave and how they ought to behave is so great that anyone who ignores everyday reality in order to live up to an ideal will soon discover he had been taught how to destroy himself, not how to preserve himself.[4]

Machiavelli considered his approach far more realistic than that of his medieval forebears.

From Machiavelli's point of view, a prince's attitude toward power must be based on an understanding of human nature, which he perceived as basically self-centered. He said, "For of men one can, in general, say this: They are ungrateful, fickle, deceptive and deceiving, avoiders of danger, eager to gain." Political activity, therefore, could not be restricted by moral considerations. The prince acts on behalf of the state and for the sake of the state must be willing to let his conscience sleep. As Machiavelli put it:

> You need to understand this: A ruler, and particularly a ruler who is new to power, cannot conform to all those rules that men who are thought good are expected to respect, for he is often obliged, in order to hold on to power, to break his word, to be uncharitable, inhumane, and irreligious. So he must be mentally prepared to act as circumstances and changes in fortune require. As I have said, he

should do what is right if he can; but he must be prepared to do wrong if necessary.[5]

In Cesare Borgia, the son of Pope Alexander VI, who used ruthless measures to achieve his goal of carving out a new state in central Italy, Machiavelli found a good example of the new Italian ruler. As he said, "So anyone who decides that the policy to follow when one has newly acquired power is to destroy one's enemies, to secure some allies, to win wars, whether by force or by fraud, to make oneself both loved and feared by one's subjects, . . . cannot hope to find, in the recent past, a better model to imitate than Cesare Borgia."[6] Machiavelli was among the first to abandon morality as the basis for the analysis of political activity (see the box on p. 266).

The Intellectual Renaissance in Italy

The emergence and growth of individualism and secularism as characteristics of the Italian Renaissance are most noticeable in the intellectual and artistic realms. Italian culture had matured by the fourteenth century. For the next two centuries, Italy was the cultural leader of Europe. This new Italian culture was primarily the product of a relatively wealthy, urban lay society. The most important literary movement associated with the Renaissance is humanism.

Italian Renaissance Humanism

Renaissance humanism was a form of education and culture based on the study of the classics. Humanism was not so much a philosophy of life as it was an educational program that revolved around a clearly defined group of intellectual disciplines or "liberal arts"—grammar, rhetoric, poetry, moral philosophy or ethics, and history—all based on an examination of classical authors.

The central importance of literary preoccupations in Renaissance humanism is evident in the professional status or occupations of the humanists. Some of them were teachers of the humanities in secondary schools and universities, where they either gave occasional lectures or held permanent positions, often as professors of rhetoric. Others served as secretaries in the chancelleries of Italian city-states or at the courts of princes or popes. All of these occupations were largely secular, and many humanists were laymen rather than members of the clergy.

Petrarch (1304–1374), who has often been called the father of Italian Renaissance humanism, did more than any other individual in the fourteenth century to foster its

◆ **Machiavelli.** In *The Prince*, Machiavelli gave concrete expression to the Renaissance preoccupation with political power. This slender volume remains one of the most famous Western treatises on politics. Machiavelli is seen here in a portrait by Santi di Tito.

development. Petrarch sought to find forgotten Latin manuscripts and set in motion a search of monastic libraries throughout Europe. In his preoccupation with the classics and their secular content, Petrarch doubted at times whether he was sufficiently attentive to spiritual ideals. His qualms, however, did not prevent him from inaugurating the humanist emphasis on the use of pure classical Latin, making it fashionable for humanists to use Cicero as a model for prose and Virgil for poetry. As Petrarch said, "Christ is my God; Cicero is the prince of the language."

In Florence, the humanist movement took a new direction at the beginning of the fifteenth century when it became closely tied to Florentine civic spirit and pride, giving rise to what one modern scholar has labeled "civic humanism." Fourteenth-century humanists such as Petrarch had described the intellectual life as one of solitude. They rejected family and a life of action in the community. In the busy civic world of Florence, however, intellectuals began to take a new view of their role as intellectuals. The classical Roman statesman and intellectual Cicero

⇒ Machiavelli: "Is It Better to Be Loved Than Feared?" ⇐

In 1513, Niccolò Machiavelli wrote a short treatise on political power that, justly or unjustly, has given him a reputation as a political opportunist. In this passage from Chapter 17 of The Prince, *Machiavelli analyzes whether it is better for a ruler to be loved than feared.*

Machiavelli, *The Prince*

This leads us to a question that is in dispute: Is it better to be loved than feared, or vice versa? My reply is one ought to be both loved and feared; but, since it is difficult to accomplish both at the same time, I maintain it is much safer to be feared than loved, if you have to do without one of the two. For of men one can, in general, say this: They are ungrateful, fickle, deceptive and deceiving, avoiders of danger, eager to gain. As long as you serve their interests, they are devoted to you. They promise you their blood, their possessions, their lives, and their children, as I said before, so long as you seem to have no need of them. But as soon as you need help, they turn against you. Any ruler who relies simply on their promises and makes no other preparations, will be destroyed. For you will find that those whose support you buy, who do not rally to you because they admire your strength of character and nobility of soul, these are people you pay for, but they are never yours, and in the end you cannot get the benefit of your investment.

Men are less nervous of offending someone who makes himself lovable, than someone who makes himself frightening. For love attaches men by ties of obligation, which, since men are wicked, they break whenever their interests are at stake. But fear restrains men because they are afraid of punishment, and this fear never leaves them. Still, a ruler should make himself feared in such a way that, if he does not inspire love, at least he does not provoke hatred. For it is perfectly possible to be feared and not hated. You will only be hated if you seize the property or the women of your subjects and citizens. Whenever you have to kill someone, make sure you have a suitable excuse and an obvious reason; but, above all else, keep your hands off other people's property; for men are quicker to forget the death of their father than the loss of their inheritance. Moreover, there are always reasons why you might want to seize people's property; and he who begins to live by plundering others will always find an excuse for seizing other people's possessions; but there are fewer reasons for killing people, and one killing need not lead to another.

When a ruler is at the head of his army and has a vast number of soldiers under his command, then it is absolutely essential to be prepared to be thought cruel; for it is impossible to keep an army united and ready for action without acquiring a reputation for cruelty.

---

became their model. Leonardo Bruni (1370–1444), a humanist, Florentine patriot, and chancellor of the city, wrote a biography of Cicero entitled the *New Cicero*, in which he waxed enthusiastically about the fusion of political action and literary creation in Cicero's life. From Bruni's time on, Cicero served as the inspiration for the Renaissance ideal that it was the duty of an intellectual to live an active life for one's state. An individual only "grows to maturity—both intellectually and morally—through participation" in the life of the state. Civic humanism reflected the values of the urban society of the Italian Renaissance. Humanists came to believe that their study of the humanities should be put to the service of the state. It is no accident that humanists served the state as chancellors, councilors, and advisors.

Also evident in the humanism of the first half of the fifteenth century was a growing interest in classical Greek civilization. Bruni was one of the first Italian humanists to gain a thorough knowledge of Greek. He became an enthusiastic pupil of the Byzantine scholar Manuel Chrysoloras, who taught in Florence from 1396 to 1400. Humanists eagerly perused the works of Plato as well as Greek poets, dramatists, historians, and orators, such as Thucydides, Euripides, and Sophocles, all of whom had been neglected by the scholastics of the High Middle Ages.

HUMANISM AND PHILOSOPHY

In the second half of the fifteenth century, a dramatic upsurge of interest in the works of Plato occurred. Cosimo de' Medici, the *de facto* ruler of Florence, encouraged this development by commissioning a translation of Plato's dialogues by Marsilio Ficino (1433–1499), who dedicated his life to the translation of Plato and the exposition of the Platonic philosophy known as Neoplatonism.

In two major works, Ficino undertook the synthesis of Christianity and Platonism into a single system. His Neo-platonism was based on two primary ideas, the Neopla-tonic hierarchy of substances and a theory of spiritual love. The former postulated a hierarchy of substances, or great chain of being, from the lowest form of physical matter (plants) to the purest spirit (God), in which humans occupied a central or middle position. They were the link between the material world (through the body) and the spiritual world (through the soul), and their highest duty was to ascend toward that union with God that was the true end of human existence. Ficino's theory of spiritual or Platonic love maintained that just as all people are bound together in their common humanity by love, so too are all parts of the universe held together by bonds of sympathetic love.

Renaissance Hermeticism was another product of the Florentine intellectual environment of the late fifteenth century. At the request of Cosimo de' Medici, Ficino translated into Latin a Greek work entitled the *Corpus Hermeticum*. The Hermetic manuscripts contained two kinds of writings. One type stressed the occult sciences with emphasis on astrology, alchemy, and magic. The other focused on theological and philosophical beliefs and speculations. For Renaissance intellectuals, the Hermetic revival offered a new view of humankind. They believed that human beings had been created as divine beings endowed with divine creative power, but had freely chosen to enter the material world (nature). Humans could recover their divinity, however, through a regenerative experience or purification of the soul. Thus regenerated, they became true sages or magi, as the Renaissance called them, who had knowledge of God and of truth. In regaining their original divinity, they reacquired an intimate knowledge of nature and the ability to employ the powers of nature for beneficial purposes.

In Italy, the most prominent magi in the late fifteenth century were Ficino and his friend and pupil, Giovanni Pico della Mirandola (1463–1494). Pico produced one of the most famous writings of the Renaissance, *Oration on the Dignity of Man*. Pico combed diligently through the writings of many philosophers of different backgrounds for the common "nuggets of universal truth" that he believed were all part of God's revelation to humanity. In the *Oration* (see the box on p. 268), Pico offered a ringing statement of unlimited human potential: "To him it is granted to have whatever he chooses, to be whatever he wills."[7] Like Ficino, Pico took an avid interest in Hermetic philosophy, accepting it as the "science of the Divine," which "embraces the deepest contemplation of the most secret things, and at last the knowledge of all nature."[8]

Education in the Renaissance

The humanist movement had a profound effect on education. Renaissance humanists believed that human beings could be dramatically changed by education. They wrote books on education and developed secondary schools based on their ideas. Most famous was the one founded in 1423 by Vittorino da Feltre (1378–1446) at Mantua, where the ruler of that small Italian state, Gian Francesco I Gonzaga, wished to provide a humanist school for his children. Vittorino based much of his educational system on the ideas of classical authors, particularly Cicero and Quintilian.

At the core of the academic training offered by Vittorino were the "liberal studies." The Renaissance view of the value of the liberal arts was most strongly influenced by a treatise on education called *Concerning Character* by Pietro Paolo Vergerio (1370–1444). This work stressed the importance of the liberal arts as the key to true freedom, enabling individuals to reach their full potential. According to Vergerio, "we call those studies liberal which are worthy of a free man; those studies by which we attain and practice virtue and wisdom; that education which calls forth, trains, and develops those highest gifts of body and mind which ennoble men, and which are rightly judged to rank next in dignity to virtue only. . . ."[9] What, then, are the "Liberal Studies"?:

> Amongst these I accord the first place to History, on grounds both of its attractiveness and of its utility, qualities which appeal equally to the scholar and to the statesman. Next in importance ranks Moral Philosophy, which indeed is, in a peculiar sense, a "Liberal Art," in that its purpose is to teach men the secret of true freedom. History, then, gives us the concrete examples of the precepts inculcated by Philosophy. The one shows what men should do, the other what men have said and done in the past, and what practical lessons we may draw therefrom for the present day. I would indicate as the third main branch of study, Eloquence. . . . By philosophy we learn the essential truth of things, which by eloquence we so exhibit in orderly adornment as to bring conviction to differing minds.[10]

The remaining liberal studies included letters (grammar and logic), poetry, mathematics, astronomy, and music. Crucial to all liberal studies was the mastery of Greek and Latin because it enabled students to read the great classical authors who were the foundation stones of the liberal arts. In short, the purpose of a liberal education (and thus the purpose of the study of the liberal arts) was to produce individuals who followed a path of virtue and wisdom and possessed the rhetorical skills to persuade others to take the same path.

Pico della Mirandola and the Dignity of Man

Giovanni Pico della Mirandola was one of the foremost intellects of the Italian Renaissance. Pico boasted that he had studied all schools of philosophy, which he tried to demonstrate by drawing up 900 theses for public disputation at the age of twenty-four. As a preface to his theses, he wrote his famous oration, On the Dignity of Man, *in which he proclaimed the unlimited potentiality of human beings.*

Pico della Mirandola, Oration on the Dignity of Man

At last the best of artisans [God] ordained that that creature to whom He had been able to give nothing proper to himself should have joint possession of whatever had been peculiar to each of the different kinds of being. He therefore took man as a creature of indeterminate nature, and assigning him a place in the middle of the world, addressed him thus: "Neither a fixed abode nor a form that is yours alone nor any function peculiar to yourself have we given you, Adam, to the end that according to your longing and according to your judgment you may have and possess what abode, what form, and what functions you yourself desire. The nature of all other beings is limited and constrained within the bounds of laws prescribed by Us. You, constrained by no limits, in accordance with your own free will, in whose hand We have placed you, shall ordain for yourself the limits of your nature. We have set you at the world's center that you may from there more easily observe whatever is in the world. We have made you neither of heaven nor of earth, neither mortal nor immortal, so that with freedom of choice and with honor, as though the maker and molder of yourself, you may fashion yourself in whatever shape you shall prefer. You shall have the power to degenerate into the lower forms of life, which are brutish. You shall have the power, out of your soul's judgment, to be reborn into the higher forms, which are divine."

O supreme generosity of God the Father, O highest and most marvelous felicity of man! To him it is granted to have whatever he chooses, to be whatever he wills. Beasts as soon as they are born bring with them from their mother's womb all they will ever possess. Spiritual beings, either from the beginning or soon thereafter, become what they are to be for ever and ever. On man when he came into life the Father conferred the seeds of all kinds and the germs of every way of life. Whatever seeds each man cultivates will grow to maturity and bear to him their own fruit. If they be vegetative, he will be like a plant. If sensitive, he will become brutish. If rational, he will grow into a heavenly being. If intellectual, he will be an angel and the son of God.

Following the Greek precept of a sound mind in a sound body, Vittorino's school at Mantua stressed the need for physical education. Pupils were taught the skills of javelin throwing, archery, and dancing and were frequently encouraged to run, wrestle, hunt, and swim. Nor was Christianity excluded from Vittorino's school. His students were taught the Scriptures and the works of the church fathers, especially Saint Augustine.

The purpose of the humanist schools was to educate an elite, the ruling classes of their communities. Largely absent from such schools were females. Vittorino's only female pupils were the two daughters of the Gonzaga ruler of Mantua. While these few female students studied the classics and were encouraged to know some history and to ride, dance, sing, play the lute, and appreciate poetry, they were discouraged from learning mathematics and rhetoric. In the educational treatises of the time, religion and morals were thought to "hold the first place in the education of a Christian lady."

Vittorino and other humanist educators considered a humanist education to be a practical preparation for life. The aim of humanist education was not to create great scholars but rather to produce complete citizens who could participate in the civic life of their communities. As Vittorino said, "Not everyone is obliged to excel in philosophy, medicine, or the law, nor are all equally favored by nature; but all are destined to live in society and to practice virtue."[11] Humanist schools, combining the classics and Christianity, provided the model for the basic education of the European ruling classes until the twentieth century.

The Impact of Printing

The period of the Renaissance witnessed the development of printing, one of the most important technological innovations of Western civilization. The art of printing had an immediate impact on European intellectual life and thought. Printing from hand-carved wooden blocks had been present in the West since the twelfth century and in China even before that. What was new in the fifteenth century was the skill of multiple printing with movable metal type. The development of printing from movable type was a gradual process that culminated some time between 1445 and 1450; Johannes Gutenberg of Mainz played an important role in bringing the process to completion. Gutenberg's Bible, completed in 1455 or 1456, was the first real book in the West produced from movable type.

The new printing capability spread rapidly throughout Europe in the last half of the fifteenth century. Printing presses were established throughout the Holy Roman Empire in the 1460s and within ten years had spread to Italy, France, the Low Countries, Spain, and eastern Europe. Especially well known as a printing center was Venice, home by 1500 to almost 100 printers who had produced almost two million volumes.

By 1500, there were more than 1000 printers in Europe who had published almost 40,000 titles (between eight and ten million copies). Probably 50 percent of these books were religious in character—Bibles, books of devotion, and sermons. Next in importance were the Latin and Greek classics, medieval grammars, legal handbooks,

works on philosophy, and an ever-growing number of popular romances.

Printing became one of the largest industries in Europe, and its effects were soon felt in many areas of European life. The printing of books encouraged the development of scholarly research and the desire to attain knowledge. Moreover, printing facilitated cooperation among scholars and helped produce standardized and definitive texts. Printing also stimulated the development of an ever-expanding lay reading public, a development that had an enormous impact on European society. Indeed, the new religious ideas of the Reformation would never have spread as rapidly as they did in the sixteenth century without the printing press.

The Artistic Renaissance

Leonardo da Vinci, one of the great Italian Renaissance artists, once explained: "Hence the painter will produce pictures of small merit if he takes for his standard the pictures of others, but if he will study from natural objects he will bear good fruit . . . those who take for their standard any one but nature . . . weary themselves in vain."[12] Renaissance artists considered the imitation of nature to be

◆ **Masaccio, *Tribute Money*.** With the frescoes of Masaccio, regarded by many as the first great works of Early Renaissance art, a new realistic style of painting was born. The *Tribute Money* was one of a series of frescoes that Masaccio painted in the Brancacci chapel in the church of Santa Maria del Carmine in Florence. In illustrating a story from the Bible, Masaccio used a rational system of perspective to create a realistic relationship between the figures and their background.

their primary goal. Their search for naturalism became an end in itself: to persuade onlookers of the reality of the object or event they were portraying. At the same time, the new artistic standards reflected a new attitude of mind as well, one in which human beings became the focus of attention, the "center and measure of all things," as one artist proclaimed.

The frescoes by Masaccio (1401–1428) in the Brancacci chapel in Florence have long been regarded as the first masterpieces of Early Renaissance art. With his use of monumental figures, the demonstration of a more realis-

◆ **Donatello, *David*.** Donatello's *David* first stood in the courtyard of the Medici Palace. On its base was an inscription praising Florentine heroism and virtue, leading art historians to assume that the statue was meant to commemorate the victory of Florence over Milan in 1428.

tic relationship between figures and landscape, and the visual representation of the laws of perspective, a new realistic style of painting was born. Onlookers became aware of a world of reality that appeared to be a continuation of their own world. Masaccio's massive, three-dimensional human figures provided a model for later generations of Florentine artists.

This new or Renaissance style was absorbed and modified by other Florentine painters in the fifteenth century. Especially important was the development of an experimental trend that took two directions. One emphasized the mathematical side of painting, the working out of the laws of perspective and the organization of outdoor space and light by geometry and perspective. The other aspect of the experimental trend involved the investigation of movement and anatomic structure. Indeed, the realistic portrayal of the human nude became one of the foremost preoccupations of Italian Renaissance art. The fifteenth century, then, was a period of experimentation and technical mastery.

The revolutionary achievements of Florentine painters in the fifteenth century were matched by equally stunning advances in sculpture and architecture. Donato di Donatello (1386–1466) spent time in Rome, studying and copying the statues of antiquity. His subsequent work in Florence reveals how well he had mastered the essence of what he saw. Among his numerous works was a statue of David, which is the first known "lifesize freestanding bronze nude in European art since antiquity." Like Donatello's other statues, *David* radiated a simplicity and strength that reflected the dignity of humanity.

Filippo Brunelleschi (1377–1446) was a friend of Donatello and accompanied him to Rome. Brunelleschi drew much inspiration from the architectural monuments of Roman antiquity, and when he returned to Florence, the Medici commissioned him to design the church of San Lorenzo. Brunelleschi, inspired by Roman models, created a church interior very different from that of the great medieval cathedrals. San Lorenzo's classical columns, rounded arches, and coffered ceiling created an environment that did not overwhelm the worshiper, materially and psychologically, as Gothic cathedrals did; instead, it comforted in that it was a space created to fit human, not divine, measurements. Like painters and sculptors, Renaissance architects sought to reflect a human-centered world.

By the end of the fifteenth century, Italian painters, sculptors, and architects had created a new artistic environment. Many artists had mastered the new techniques for a scientific observation of the world around them and were now ready to move into individualistic forms of cre-

✦ **Filippo Brunelleschi, Interior of San Lorenzo.** Cosimo de' Medici contributed massive amounts of money to the rebuilding of the church of San Lorenzo. As seen in this view of the nave and choir of the church, Brunelleschi's architectural designs were based on the basilica plan borrowed by early Christians from pagan Rome. San Lorenzo's simplicity, evident in its rows of slender Corinthian columns, created a human-centered space.

ative expression. This final stage of Renaissance art, which flourished between 1480 and 1520, is called the High Renaissance. The shift to the High Renaissance was marked by the increasing importance of Rome as a new cultural center of the Italian Renaissance.

✦ **Leonardo da Vinci, *The Last Supper.*** Leonardo da Vinci was the impetus behind the High Renaissance concern for the idealization of nature, moving from a realistic portrayal of the human figure to an idealized form. Evident in Leonardo's *The Last*

The High Renaissance was dominated by the work of three artistic giants, Leonardo da Vinci (1452–1519), Raphael (1483–1520), and Michelangelo (1475–1564). Leonardo represents a transitional figure in the shift to High Renaissance principles. He carried on the fifteenth-century experimental tradition by studying everything and even dissecting human bodies in order to better see how nature worked. But Leonardo stressed the need to advance beyond such realism and initiated the High Renaissance's preoccupation with the idealization of nature, or the attempt to generalize from realistic portrayal to an ideal form. Leonardo's *The Last Supper*, painted in Milan, is a brilliant summary of fifteenth-century trends in its organization of space and use of perspective to depict subjects three dimensionally. But it is also more. The figure of Philip is idealized, and there are profound psychological dimensions to the work. The words of Christ that "one of you shall betray me" are experienced directly as each of the apostles reveals his personality and his relationship to the Savior. Through gestures and movement, Leonardo hoped to reveal a person's inner life.

Raphael blossomed as a painter at an early age; at twenty-five, he was already regarded as one of Italy's best painters. Well-known for his frescoes in the Vatican Palace, Raphael was especially acclaimed for his numerous madonnas, in which he attempted to achieve an ideal of beauty far surpassing human standards. His *Alba Madonna* reveals a world of balance, harmony, and

Supper is his effort to depict a person's character and inner nature by the use of gesture and movement. Unfortunately, Leonardo used an experimental technique in this fresco, which soon led to its physical deterioration.

◆ Raphael, *The Alba Madonna*. Although he died at the age of thirty-seven, Raphael achieved in his own lifetime a fame comparable to that of Michelangelo and Leonardo do Vinci. In his madonnas, Raphael sought an idealized beauty that was typical of the High Renaissance. His serene *Alba Madonna* illustrates his mastery of the classical principles of balance, harmony, clarity, and rational composition.

order—basically, the underlying principles of the art of the classical world of Greece and Rome.

Michelangelo, an accomplished painter, sculptor, and architect, was another giant of the High Renaissance. Fiercely driven by his desire to create, he worked with great passion and energy on a remarkable number of projects. Michelangelo was influenced by Neoplatonism, especially evident in his figures on the ceiling of the Sistine Chapel. These muscular figures reveal an ideal type of human being with perfect proportions. In good Neoplatonic fashion, their beauty is meant to be a reflection of divine beauty; the more beautiful the body, the more God-like the figure.

The Northern Artistic Renaissance

In trying to provide an exact portrayal of their world, the artists of the north (especially the Low Countries) and Italy took different approaches. In Italy, the human form became the primary vehicle of expression as Italian artists sought to master the technical skills that allowed them to portray humans in realistic settings. The large wall spaces of Italian churches had given rise to the art of fresco painting, but in the north, the prevalence of Gothic cathedrals with their stained glass windows resulted in more emphasis on illuminated manuscripts and wooden

◆ Michelangelo, *Creation of Adam*. In 1508, Pope Julius II recalled Michelangelo to Rome and commissioned him to decorate the ceiling of the Sistine Chapel. This colossal project was not completed until 1512. Michelangelo attempted to tell the story of the Fall of Man by depicting nine scenes from the biblical book of Genesis. In this scene, the well-proportioned figure of Adam, meant by Michelangelo to be a reflection of divine beauty, awaits the divine spark.

panel painting for altarpieces. The space available in these works was limited, and great care was required to depict each object, leading northern painters to become masters at rendering details.

The most influential northern school of art in the fifteenth century was centered in Flanders. Jan van Eyck (1380?–1441) was among the first to use oil paint, a medium that enabled the artist to use a varied range of colors and make changes to create fine details. In the famous *Giovanni Arnolfini and His Bride*, van Eyck's attention to detail is staggering: precise portraits, a glittering chandelier, and a mirror reflecting the objects in the room. Although each detail was rendered as observed, it is evident that van Eyck's comprehension of perspective

◆ **Albrecht Dürer, *Adoration of the Magi*.** By the end of the fifteenth century, northern artists began studying in Italy and adopting many of the techniques used by Italian painters. As is evident in this painting, which was the central panel for an altarpiece done for Frederick the Wise in 1504, Albrecht Dürer masterfully incorporated the laws of perspective and the ideals of proportion into his works. At the same time, he did not abandon the preoccupation with detail typical of northern artists.

◆ **Jan van Eyck, *Giovanni Arnolfini and His Bride*.** Northern painters took great care in depicting each object and became masters in rendering details. This emphasis on a realistic portrayal is clearly evident in this oil painting, supposedly a portrait of Giovanni Arnolfini, an Italian merchant who had settled in Bruges, and his wife, Giovanna Cenami.

was still uncertain. His work is truly indicative of northern Renaissance painters, who, in their effort to imitate nature, did so not by mastery of the laws of perspective and proportion, but by empirical observation of visual reality and the accurate portrayal of details. Moreover, northern painters placed great emphasis on the emotional intensity of religious feeling and created great works of devotional art, especially in their altarpieces. By the end of the fifteenth century, however, artists from the north began to study in Italy and were visually influenced by what artists were doing there.

One northern artist of this later period who was greatly influenced by the Italians was Albrecht Dürer (1471–1528) from Nuremberg. Dürer made two trips to Italy and absorbed most of what the Italians could teach, as is evident in his mastery of the laws of perspective and Renaissance theories of proportion. He wrote detailed treatises on both subjects. At the same time, as in his famous *Adoration of the Magi*, Dürer did not reject the use of minute details characteristic of northern artists. He did try, however, to integrate those details more harmoniously into his works and, like the Italian artists of the High Renaissance, tried to achieve a standard of ideal beauty by a careful examination of the human form.

⚜ **Map 13.2** Europe in the Renaissance.

The European State in the Renaissance

In the first half of the fifteenth century, European states continued the disintegrative patterns of the previous century. In the second half of the fifteenth century, however, recovery set in, and attempts were made to reestablish the centralized power of monarchical governments. To characterize the results, some historians have used the label "Renaissance states"; others have spoken of the "new monarchies," especially those of France, England, and Spain at the end of the fifteenth century. Although appropriate, the term "new monarch" can also be misleading. These Renaissance monarchs were new in their concentration of royal authority, their attempts to suppress the nobility, their efforts to control the church in their lands, and their insistence on having the loyalty of people living within definite territorial boundaries. Like the

rulers of fifteenth-century Italian states, the "new monarchs" were often crafty men obsessed with the acquisition and expansion of political power. Of course, none of these characteristics was entirely new in that a number of medieval monarchs had also exhibited them. Nevertheless, the Renaissance period does mark the further extension of royal centralized authority. Of course, the degree to which rulers were successful in extending their political authority varied from area to area. In central and eastern Europe, decentralization rather than centralization of political authority remained the rule.

The "New Monarchies" in Western Europe

Although the Hundred Years' War had made it difficult for French kings to assert their authority, the war had also developed a strong degree of French national feeling toward a common enemy that the kings could use to reestablish monarchical power. The process of developing a French territorial state was greatly advanced by King Louis XI (1461–1483), known as the Spider because of his wily and devious ways. Some historians have called this "new monarch" the founder of the French national state. Louis strengthened the use of the *taille*—an annual direct tax usually on land or property—as a permanent tax imposed by royal authority, giving him a sound, regular source of income. Louis was not completely successful in repressing the French nobility whose independence posed a threat to his own state building. A major problem was his supposed vassal, Charles the Bold, duke of Burgundy (1467–1477), who tried to create a middle kingdom between France and Germany, stretching from the Low Countries in the north to Switzerland. Louis opposed his action, and when Charles was killed in 1477 fighting the Swiss, Louis added part of Charles's possessions, the duchy of Burgundy, to his own lands. Three years later, the provinces of Anjou, Maine, Bar, and Provence were brought under royal control. Many historians believe that Louis created a base for the later development of a strong French monarchy.

The Hundred Years' War also strongly affected the other protagonist in that conflict—the English. The cost of the war in its final years and the losses in manpower strained the English economy. Moreover, the end of the war brought even greater domestic turmoil to England when the War of the Roses broke out in the 1450s. This civil war pitted the ducal house of Lancaster, whose symbol was a red rose, against the ducal house of York, whose symbol was a white rose. Many aristocratic families of England were drawn into the conflict. Finally, in 1485, Henry Tudor, duke of Richmond, defeated the last Yorkist king, Richard III (1483–1485), at Bosworth Field and established a new dynasty.

As the first Tudor king, Henry VII (1485–1509) worked to reduce internal dissension and establish a strong monarchical government. Henry eliminated the private wars of the nobility by abolishing their private armies. The new king was particularly successful in obtaining sufficient income from the traditional financial resources of the English monarch, such as the crown lands, judicial fees and fines, and customs duties. By using diplomacy to avoid wars, which are always expensive, the king avoided having to call Parliament on any regular basis to grant him funds. By not overburdening the landed gentry and middle class with taxes, Henry won their favor and they provided much support for his monarchy. Henry's policies enabled him to leave England with a

stable and prosperous government and an enhanced status for the monarchy itself.

Spain, too, experienced the growth of a strong national monarchy by the end of the fifteenth century. During the Middle Ages, several independent Christian kingdoms had emerged in the course of the long reconquest of the Iberian peninsula from the Muslims. Aragon and Castile were the strongest Spanish kingdoms; in the west was the independent monarchy of Portugal; in the north the small kingdom of Navarre; and in the south the Muslim kingdom of Granada. Few people at the beginning of the fifteenth century could have predicted the unification of Spain.

A major step in that direction was taken with the marriage of Isabella of Castile (1474–1504) and Ferdinand of Aragon (1479–1516) in 1469. This marriage was a dynastic union of two rulers, not a political union. Both kingdoms maintained their own parliaments (Cortes), courts, laws, coinage, speech, customs, and political organs.

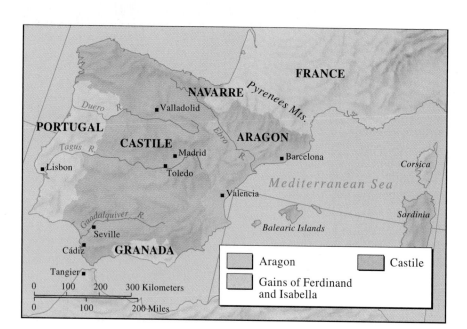

Map 13.3 Iberian Peninsula.

Nevertheless, the two rulers worked to strengthen royal control of government, especially in Castile. The royal council, which was supposed to supervise local administration and oversee the implementation of government policies, was stripped of aristocrats and filled primarily with middle-class lawyers. Trained in the principles of Roman law, these officials operated on the belief that the monarchy embodied the power of the state.

Ferdinand and Isabella reorganized the military forces of Spain, seeking to replace the undisciplined feudal levies they had inherited with a more professional royal army. The development of a strong infantry force as the heart of the new Spanish army made it the best in Europe by the sixteenth century, and Spain emerged as an important power in European affairs.

Because of its vast power and wealth, Ferdinand and Isabella recognized the importance of controlling the Catholic church. They secured from the pope the right to select the most important church officials in Spain, virtually making the clergy an instrument for the extension of royal power. Ferdinand and Isabella also pursued a policy of strict religious uniformity. Spain possessed two large religious minorities, the Jews and Muslims, both of whom had been largely tolerated in medieval Spain. Increased persecution in the fourteenth century, however, led the majority of Spanish Jews to convert to Christianity. But complaints about the faithfulness of these Jewish converts to Christianity prompted Ferdinand and Isabella to ask the pope to introduce the Inquisition into Spain in 1478.

Under royal control, the Inquisition worked with cruel efficiency to guarantee the orthodoxy of the converts, but had no authority over practicing Jews. Consequently, in 1492, flush with the success of the conquest of Muslim Granada, Ferdinand and Isabella took the drastic step of expelling all professed Jews from Spain. It is estimated that 150,000 out of possibly 200,000 Jews fled. Muslims, too, were then "encouraged" to convert to Christianity, and in 1502, Isabella issued a decree expelling all professed Muslims from her kingdom. To a very large degree, the "Most Catholic" monarchs had achieved their goal of absolute religious orthodoxy as a basic ingredient of the Spanish state. To be Spanish was to be Catholic, a policy of uniformity enforced by the Inquisition.

Central Europe: The Holy Roman Empire

After 1438, the position of Holy Roman emperor was held in the hands of the Habsburg dynasty. Having gradually acquired a number of possessions along the Danube, known collectively as Austria, the house of Habsburg had become one of the wealthiest landholders in the empire and by the mid-fifteenth century began to play an important role in European affairs. Much of the Habsburg success in the fifteenth century was due not to military victories, but to a well-executed policy of dynastic marriages.

Much was expected of the flamboyant Maximilian I (1493–1519) when he became emperor. Through the Reichstag, the imperial diet or parliament, Maximilian

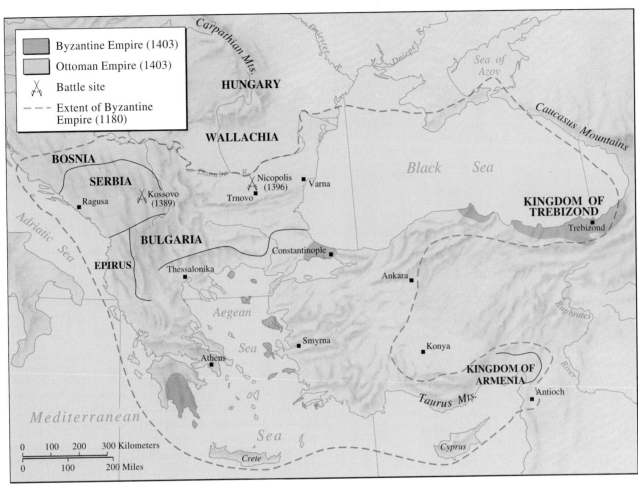

Map 13.4 Southeastern Europe.

attempted to centralize the administration by creating new institutions common to the entire empire. Opposition from the German princes doomed these efforts, however. Maximilian's only real success lay in his marriage alliances, which led to a grandson, Charles, inheriting the traditional lands of the Habsburg, Burgundian, and Spanish monarchical lines at the beginning of the sixteenth century, making him the leading monarch of his age (see Chapter 14).

The Struggle for Strong Monarchy in Eastern Europe

In eastern Europe, rulers struggled to achieve the centralization of their territorial states but faced serious obstacles. Although the population was mostly Slavic, there were islands of other ethnic groups that caused untold difficulties. Religious differences also troubled the area, as Roman Catholics, Greek Orthodox Christians, and pagans confronted each other.

Much of Polish history revolved around a bitter struggle between the crown and the landed nobility until the end of the fifteenth century when the preoccupation of the Polish monarchy with problems in Bohemia and Hungary as well as war with the Russians and Turks enabled the aristocrats to reestablish their power. Through their control of the *Sejm* or national diet, the magnates reduced the peasantry to serfdom by 1511 and established the right to elect their kings. The Polish kings proved unable to establish a strong royal authority.

Since the conversion of Hungary to Roman Catholicism by German missionaries, its history had been closely tied to that of central and western Europe. The church became a large and prosperous institution. Wealthy bishops, along with great territorial lords, became powerful, independent political figures. For a brief while, however,

Hungary developed into an important European state, the dominant power in eastern Europe. King Matthias Corvinus (1458–1490) broke the power of the wealthy lords and created a well-organized central administration. After his death, Hungary returned to weak rule, however, and the work of Corvinus was largely undone.

Since the thirteenth century, Russia had been under the domination of the Mongols. Gradually, the princes of Moscow rose to prominence by using their close relationship to the Mongol khans to increase their wealth and expand their possessions. In the reign of the great prince Ivan III (1462–1505), a new Russian state was born. Ivan III annexed other Russian principalities and took advantage of dissension among the Mongols to throw off their yoke by 1480.

The Ottoman Turks and the End of the Byzantine Empire

Eastern Europe was increasingly threatened by the steadily advancing Ottoman Turks. The Byzantine Empire had served as a buffer between the Muslim Middle East and the Latin West for centuries, but it was severely weakened by the sack of Constantinople in 1204 and its occupation by the West. Although the Paleologus dynasty (1260–1453) had tried to reestablish Byzantine power in the Balkans after the overthrow of the Latin Empire, the threat from the Turks finally doomed the long-lasting empire.

Beginning in northeastern Asia Minor in the thirteenth century, the Ottoman Turks spread rapidly, seizing the lands of the Seljuk Turks and the Byzantine Empire. In 1345, they bypassed Constantinople and moved into the Balkans, which they conquered by the end of the century. Finally in 1453, the great city of Constantinople fell to the Turks after a siege of several months. After consolidating their power, the Turks prepared to exert renewed pressure on the West, both in the Mediterranean and up the Danube Valley toward Vienna. By the end of the fifteenth century, they were threatening Hungary, Austria, Bohemia, and Poland.

The Church in the Renaissance

As a result of the efforts of the Council of Constance, the Great Schism of the Catholic church had finally been brought to an end in 1417. The council had had three major objectives: to end the schism, to eradicate heresy, and to reform the church. The ending of the schism proved to be the council's easiest task; it was much less successful in dealing with the problems of heresy and reform.

The Problems of Heresy and Reform

Heresy was, of course, not a new problem, and in the thirteenth century, the church had developed the Inquisition to deal with it. But widespread movements in the early fifteenth century—especially Hussitism—posed new threats to the church. A group of Czech reformers led by the chancellor of the university at Prague, John Hus (1374–1415), urged the elimination of the worldliness and corruption of the clergy and attacked the excessive power of the papacy within the Catholic church. Hus's objections fell on receptive ears. Widespread criticism of the Catholic church already existed because it was one of the largest landowners in Bohemia. Moreover, many clergymen were German, and the native Czechs' strong resentment of the Germans who dominated Bohemia also contributed to Hus's movement.

The Council of Constance attempted to deal with the growing problem of heresy by summoning John Hus to the council. Granted a safe conduct by Emperor Sigismund, Hus went in the hope of a free hearing of his ideas. Instead he was arrested, condemned as a heretic, and burned at the stake in 1415. This action turned the unrest in Bohemia into revolutionary upheaval, and the resulting Hussite wars wracked the Holy Roman Empire until a truce was arranged in 1436.

The reform of the church was even less successful than the attempt to eradicate heresy. Two reform decrees were passed by the Council of Constance. *Sacrosancta* stated that a general council of the church received its authority from God; hence, every Christian, including the pope, was subject to its authority. The decree *Frequens* provided for the regular holding of general councils to ensure that church reform would continue. Decrees alone, however, proved insufficient to reform the church. Councils could issue decrees, but popes had to execute them and popes would not cooperate with councils that diminished their absolute authority. Beginning already in 1417, successive popes worked steadfastly for the next thirty years to defeat the conciliar movement. The victory of the popes and the final blow to the conciliar movement came when Pope Pius II issued the papal bull *Execrabilis* in 1460, condemning appeals to a council over the head of a pope as heretical.

By the mid-fifteenth century, the popes had reasserted their supremacy over the Catholic church. No longer, however, did they have any possibility of asserting supremacy over temporal governments as the medieval papacy had. Although the papal monarchy had been maintained, it had lost much moral prestige. In the fifteenth century, the Renaissance papacy contributed to an even further decline in the moral leadership of the popes.

The Renaissance Papacy

The term *Renaissance papacy* refers to the line of popes from the end of the Great Schism (1417) to the beginnings of the Reformation in the early sixteenth century. The primary concern of the papacy is governing the Catholic church as its spiritual leader. But as heads of the church, popes had temporal preoccupations as well, and the story of the Renaissance papacy is really an account of how the latter came to overshadow the popes' spiritual functions.

The preoccupation of the popes with the territory of the Papal States and Italian politics was not new in the fifteenth century. Popes had been temporal as well as spiritual rulers for centuries. But the manner in which Renaissance popes pursued their temporal interests, especially their use of intrigue and even bloodshed, seemed shocking. Of all the Renaissance popes, Julius II (1503–1513) was most involved in war and politics. The fiery "warrior-pope" personally led armies against his enemies, much to the disgust of pious Christians who viewed the pope as a spiritual leader. As one intellectual wrote at the beginning of the sixteenth century: "How, O bishop standing in the room of the Apostles, dare you teach the people the things that pertain to war?"

To further their territorial aims in the Papal States, the popes needed loyal servants. Because they were not

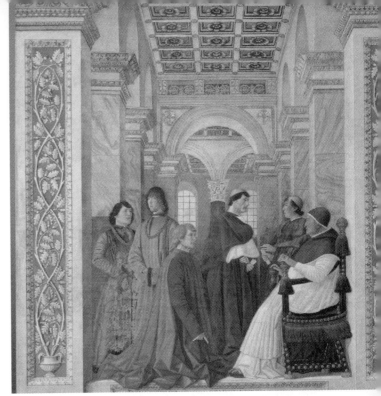

◆ **A Renaissance Pope: Sixtus IV.** The Renaissance popes allowed secular concerns to overshadow their spiritual duties. They became concerned with territorial expansion, finances, and Renaissance culture. Pope Sixtus IV built the Sistine Chapel and later had it decorated by some of the leading artists of his day. This fresco by Melozzo da Forlì shows the pope on his throne receiving the humanist Platina (kneeling), who was the keeper of the Vatican Library.

hereditary monarchs, popes could not build dynasties over several generations and came to rely on the practice of nepotism to promote their families' interests. Pope Sixtus IV (1471–1484), for example, made five of his nephews (the word *nepotism* is, in fact, derived from *nepos*, meaning nephew) cardinals and gave them an abundance of church offices to build up their finances. The infamous Borgia pope, Alexander VI (1492–1503), known for his debauchery and sensuality, raised one son, one nephew, and the brother of one mistress to the cardinalate. Alexander scandalized the church by encouraging his son Cesare to carve a territorial state out of the territories of the Papal States in central Italy.

The Renaissance popes were great patrons of Renaissance culture, and their efforts made Rome a cultural leader at the beginning of the sixteenth century. For the warrior-pope Julius II, the patronage of Renaissance culture was mostly a matter of policy as he endeavored to add to the splendor of his pontificate by tearing down the old basilica of Saint Peter and beginning construction of what was to be the greatest building in Christendom, Saint Peter's basilica. Julius's successor, Leo X (1513–1521), was also a patron of Renaissance culture, not as a matter of policy, but as a deeply involved participant. A member of the Medici family, he was made a cardinal at the age of thirteen and acquired a refined taste in art, manners, and social life among the Florentine elite. He became pope at the age of thirty-seven, supposedly remarking to the Venetian ambassador, "Let us enjoy the papacy, since God has given it to us." Raphael was commissioned to do paintings, and the construction of St. Peter's was accelerated as Rome became the literary and artistic center of the Renaissance.

Conclusion

The Renaissance was a period of transition that witnessed a continuation of the economic, political, and social trends that had begun in the High Middle Ages. It was also a movement in which intellectuals and artists proclaimed a new vision of humankind and raised funda-

mental questions about the value and importance of the individual. Of course, intellectuals and artists wrote and painted for the upper classes, and the brilliant intellectual, cultural, and artistic accomplishments of the Renaissance were really products of and for the elite. The ideas of the Renaissance did not have a broad base among the masses of the people. As Lorenzo the Magnificent, ruler of Florence, once commented, "Only men of noble birth can obtain perfection. The poor, who work with their hands and have no time to cultivate their minds, are incapable of it."

The Renaissance did, however, raise new questions about medieval traditions. In advocating a return to the early sources of Christianity and criticizing current religious practices, the humanists raised fundamental issues about the Catholic church, which was still an important institution. In the sixteenth century, the intellectual revolution of the fifteenth century gave way to a religious renaissance that touched the lives of people, including the masses, in new and profound ways. After the Reformation, Europe would never again be the unified Christian commonwealth it once believed it was.

NOTES

1. Quoted in Jacob Burckhardt, *The Civilization of the Renaissance in Italy*, trans. S. G. C. Middlemore (London, 1960), p. 81.
2. Baldassare Castiglione, *The Book of the Courtier*, trans. Charles S. Singleton (Garden City, N.Y., 1959), pp. 288–89.
3. Quoted in De Lamar Jensen, *Renaissance Europe* (Lexington, Mass., 1981), p. 94.
4. Niccolo Machiavelli, *The Prince*, trans. David Wootton (Indianapolis, 1995), p. 48.
5. Ibid., p. 55.
6. Ibid., p. 27.
7. Giovanni Pico della Mirandola, *Oration on the Dignity of Man*, in E. Cassirer, P. O. Kristeller, J. H. Randall, Jr., eds., *The Renaissance Philosophy of Man* (Chicago, 1948), p. 225.
8. Ibid., pp. 247–49.
9. W. H. Woodward, *Vittorino da Feltre and Other Humanist Educators* (Cambridge, 1897), p. 102.
10. Ibid., pp. 106–07.
11. Quoted in Iris Origo, "The Education of Renaissance Man," *The Light of the Past* (New York, 1959), p. 136.
12. Quoted in Elizabeth G. Holt, ed., *A Documentary History of Art* (Garden City, N.Y., 1959), 1:286.

SUGGESTIONS FOR FURTHER READING

The classic study of the Italian Renaissance is J. Burckhardt, *The Civilization of the Renaissance in Italy*, trans. S. G. C. Middlemore (London, 1960), first published in 1860. General works on the Renaissance in Europe include De Lamar Jensen, *Renaissance Europe* (Lexington, Mass., 1981); E. Breisach, *Renaissance Europe, 1300–1517*

(New York, 1973); J. Hale, *The Civilization of Europe in the Renaissance* (New York, 1994); and the classic work by M. P. Gilmore, *The World of Humanism, 1453–1517* (New York, 1962). Although many of its interpretations are outdated, W. Ferguson's *Europe in Transition, 1300–1520* (Boston, 1962), contains a wealth of information. The brief study by P. Burke, *The Renaissance*, 2d ed. (New York, 1997), is a good summary of recent literature on the Renaissance.

Brief, but basic works on Renaissance economic matters are H. A. Miskimin, *The Economy of Early Renaissance Europe, 1300–1460* (New York, 1975) and *The Economy of Later Renaissance Europe, 1460–1600* (New York, 1978). Numerous facets of social life in the Renaissance are examined in J. R. Hale, *Renaissance Europe: The Individual and Society* (London, 1971); J. Gage, *Life in Italy at the Time of the Medici* (New York, 1968). On family and marriage, see D. Herlihy, *The Family in Renaissance Italy* (St. Louis, 1974); and the valuable C. Klapisch-Zuber, *Women, Family, and Ritual in Renaissance Italy* (Chicago, 1985). On women, see M. L. King, *Women of the Renaissance* (Chicago, 1991).

The best overall study of the Italian city-states is L. Martines, *Power and Imagination: City-States in Renaissance Italy* (New York, 1979), although D. Hay and J. Law, *Italy in the Age of the Renaissance* (London, 1989), is also a good survey. A new approach to the culture of Renaissance Italy can be found in P. Burke, *The Italian Renaissance* (Princeton, N.J., 1986). There is an enormous literature on Renaissance Florence. The best introduction is G. A. Brucker, *Renaissance Florence*, rev. ed. (Berkeley and Los Angeles, 1983). On the Medici period, see J. R. Hale, *Florence and the Medici: The Pattern of Control* (London, 1977). Works on other Italian states and rulers include D. S. Chambers, *The Imperial Age of Venice, 1380–1580* (New York, 1970); and W. L. Gundersheimer, *Ferrara: The Style of a Renaissance Despotism* (Princeton, N.J., 1973). A popular biography of Isabella d'Este is G. Marek, *The Bed and the Throne* (New York, 1976). Machiavelli's life can be examined in J. R. Hale, *Machiavelli and Renaissance Italy* (New York, 1960); and his thought in F. Gilbert, *Machiavelli and Guicciardini: Politics and History in Sixteenth-Century Florence* (Princeton, N.J., 1965).

Brief introductions to Renaissance humanism can be found in D. R. Kelley, *Renaissance Humanism* (Boston, 1991); C. G. Nauert, Jr., *Humanism and the Culture of Renaissance Europe* (Cambridge, 1995); and F. B. Artz, *Renaissance Humanism, 1300–1550* (Oberlin, Ohio, 1966). The fundamental work on fifteenth-century civic humanism is H. Baron, *The Crisis of the Early Italian Renaissance*, 2d ed. (Princeton, N.J., 1966). The classic work on humanist education is W. H. Woodward, *Vittorino da Feltre and Other Humanist Educators* (New York, 1963), first published in 1897. The impact of printing is exhaustively examined in E. Eisenstein, *The Printing Press as an Agent of Change*, 2 vols. (New York, 1978).

For brief introductions to Renaissance art, see R. M. Letts, *The Cambridge Introduction to Art: The Renaissance* (Cambridge, 1981); and B. Cole and A. Gealt, *Art of the Western World* (New York, 1989), Chapters 6–8. Good surveys of Renaissance art include M. Levy, *Early Renaissance* (Harmondsworth, 1967); A. Smith, *The Renaissance and Mannerism in Italy* (New York, 1971); R. Turner, *Renaissance Florence: The Invention of a New Art* (New York, 1997); and L. Murray, *The High Renaissance* (New York, 1967). For studies of individual artists, see R. Jones and N. Penny, *Raphael* (New Haven, Conn., 1983); M. Kemp, *Leonardo da Vinci: The Marvellous Works of Nature and of Man* (London, 1981); and D. Summers, *Michelangelo and the Language of Art* (Princeton, N.J., 1981).

For a general work on the political development of Europe in the Renaissance, see J. H. Shennan, *The Origins of the Modern European State, 1450–1725* (London, 1974). On France, see P. M. Kendall's biography, *Louis XI: The Universal Spider* (New York, 1971). Early Renaissance England is examined in J. R. Lander, *Crown and Nobility, 1450–1509* (London, 1976). On the first Tudor king, see S. B. Chrimes, *Henry VII* (Berkeley, 1972). Good coverage of Renaissance Spain can be found in J. N. Hillgarth, *The Spanish Kingdoms, 1250–1516*, vol. 2, *Castilian Hegemony, 1410–1516* (New York, 1978). Some good works on eastern Europe include P. W. Knoll, *The Rise of the Polish Monarchy* (Chicago, 1972); and C. A. Macartney, *Hungary: A Short History* (Edinburgh, 1962). On the Ottomans and their expansion, see H. Inalcik, *The Ottoman Empire: The Classical Age, 1300–1600* (London, 1973); and the classic work by S. Runciman, *The Fall of Constantinople, 1453* (Cambridge, 1965).

On problems of heresy and reform, see C. Crowder, *Unity, Heresy and Reform, 1378–1460* (London, 1977). Aspects of the Renaissance papacy can be examined in E. Lee, *Sixtus IV and Men of Letters* (Rome, 1978); and M. Mallett, *The Borgias* (New York, 1969).

The Age of Reformation

On April 18, 1520, a lowly monk stood before the emperor and princes of Germany in the city of Worms. He had been called before this august gathering to answer charges of heresy, charges that could threaten his very life. The monk was confronted with a pile of his books and asked if he wished to defend them all or reject a part. Courageously, Martin Luther defended them all and asked to be shown where any part was in error on the basis of "Scripture and plain reason." The emperor was outraged by Luther's response and made his own position clear the next day: "Not only I, but you of this noble German nation, would be forever disgraced if by our negligence not only heresy but the very suspicion of heresy were to survive. After having heard yesterday the obstinate defense of Luther, I regret that I have so long delayed in proceeding against him and his false teaching. I will have no more to do with him." Luther's appearance at Worms set the stage for a serious challenge to the authority of the Catholic church. This was by no means the first crisis in the church's 1,500-year history, but its consequences were more far reaching than anyone at Worms in 1520 could have imagined.

Throughout the Middle Ages, the Catholic church continued to assert its primacy of position. It had overcome defiance of its temporal authority by emperors while challenges to its doctrines had been crushed by the Inquisition and combated by new religious orders that carried its message of salvation to all the towns and villages of medieval Europe. The growth of the papacy had paralleled the growth of the church, but by the end of the Middle Ages challenges to papal authority from the rising power of monarchical states had resulted in a loss of papal temporal authority. An even greater threat to papal authority and church unity arose in the sixteenth century when the unity of Christendom was shattered by the Reformation.

The movement begun by Martin Luther when he made his dramatic stand quickly spread across Europe, a clear indication of dissatisfaction with Catholic practices. Within a short time, new forms of religious

Martin Luther and the • • • •
indulgence controversy

John Calvin's church at Geneva •
Pontificate of Paul III • • •
Council of Trent • • • • • • • • • • • • • •

Reign of Charles V •
Habsburg-Valois Wars • • • • • • • • • • • • • • • •
Peasants' War • •   • Peace of Augsburg

Erasmus, *The Praise of Folly*   Calvin's *Institutes of the Christian Religion*
    • Luther's Ninety-Five Theses
    • • Ignatius Loyola, *Spiritual Exercises*

practices, doctrines, and organizations, including Zwinglianism, Calvinism, Anabaptism, and Anglicanism, were attracting adherents all over Europe. Although seemingly helpless to stop the new Protestant churches, the Catholic church also underwent a religious renaissance and managed by the mid-sixteenth century to revive its fortunes. Those historians who speak of the Reformation as the beginning of the modern world exaggerate its importance, but there is no doubt that the splintering of Christendom had consequences that ushered in new ways of thinking and at least prepared the ground for modern avenues of growth.

Prelude to Reformation

Martin Luther's reform movement was not the first in sixteenth-century Europe. Christian or northern Renaissance humanism, which evolved as Italian Renaissance humanism spread to northern Europe, had as one of its major goals the reform of Christendom. The new classical learning of the Italian Renaissance did not spread to the European countries north of the Alps until the second half of the fifteenth century. Gradually, a number of intellectuals and artists from the cities north of the Alps went to Italy and returned home enthusiastic about the new education and the recovery of ancient thought and literature that we associate with Italian Renaissance humanism.

Christian or Northern Renaissance Humanism

The most important characteristic of northern Renaissance humanism was its reform program. With their belief in the ability of human beings to reason and improve themselves, the northern humanists thought that through education in the sources of classical, and especially Christian, antiquity, they could instill a true inner piety or an inward religious feeling that would bring about a reform of the church and society. For this reason, Christian humanists supported schools, brought out new editions of the classics, and prepared new editions of the Bible and writings of such Church Fathers as Augustine, Ambrose, and Jerome. In the preface to his edition of the Greek New Testament, the famous humanist Erasmus wrote:

> Indeed, I disagree very much with those who are unwilling that Holy Scripture, translated into the vulgar tongue, be read by the uneducated, as if Christ taught such intricate doctrines that they could scarcely be understood by very few theologians, or as if the strength of the Christian religion consisted in men's ignorance of it . . . I would that even the lowliest women read the Gospels and the Pauline Epistles. And I would that they were translated into all languages so that they could be read and understood not only by Scots and Irish but also by Turks and Saracens. . . . Would that, as a result, the farmer sing some portion of them at the plow, the weaver hum some parts of them to the movement of his shuttle, the traveler lighten the weariness of the journey with stories of this kind![1]

This belief in the power of education would remain an important characteristic of European civilization. Like later intellectuals, Christian humanists believed that to

♦ **Erasmus.** Desiderius Erasmus was the most influential of the northern Renaissance humanists. He sought to restore Christianity to the early simplicity found in the teachings of Christ. This portrait of Erasmus was painted in 1523 by Hans Holbein the Younger, who had formed a friendship with the great humanist while they were both in Basel.

change society they must first change the human beings who compose it.

The most influential of all the Christian humanists was Desiderius Erasmus (1466–1536), who formulated and popularized the reform program of Christian humanism. After withdrawing from a monastery, he wandered to France, England, Italy, Germany, and Switzerland, conversing everywhere in the classical Latin that might be called his mother tongue. The *Handbook of the Christian Knight*, published in 1503, reflected his preoccupation with religion. He called his conception of religion "the philosophy of Christ," by which he meant that Christianity should be a guiding philosophy for the direction of daily life rather than the system of dogmatic beliefs and practices that the medieval church seemed to stress. In

other words, he emphasized inner piety and deemphasized the external forms of religion (such as the sacraments, pilgrimages, fasts, veneration of saints, and relics). To return to the simplicity of the early church, people needed to understand the original meaning of the Scriptures and early Church Fathers. Because Erasmus thought that the standard Latin edition of the Bible, known as the Vulgate, contained errors, he edited the Greek text of the New Testament from the earliest available manuscripts and published it, along with a new Latin translation, in 1516.

To Erasmus, the reform of the church meant spreading an understanding of the philosophy of Christ, providing enlightened education in the sources of early Christianity, and making commonsense criticism of the abuses in the church. The latter is especially evident in one of his works, *The Praise of Folly*, written in 1511, in which Erasmus was able to engage in a humorous, yet effective criticism of the most corrupt practices of his own society. He was especially harsh on the abuses within the ranks of the clergy:

> Many of them [the monks] work so hard at protocol and at traditional fastidiousness that they think one heaven hardly a suitable reward for their labors; never recalling, however, that the time will come when Christ will demand a reckoning of that which he had prescribed, namely charity, and that he will hold their deeds of little account. One monk will then exhibit his belly filled with every kind of fish; another will profess a knowledge of over a hundred hymns. Still another will reveal a countless number of fasts that he has made, and will account for his large belly by explaining that his fasts have always been broken by a single large meal.[2]

Erasmus's reform program was not destined to effect the reform of the church that he so desired. His moderation and his emphasis on education were quickly overwhelmed by the violence unleashed by the passions of the Reformation. Undoubtedly, though, his work helped to prepare the way for the Reformation; as contemporaries proclaimed, "Erasmus laid the egg that Luther hatched." Yet Erasmus eventually disapproved of Luther and the Protestant reformers. He had no intention of destroying the unity of the medieval Christian church; instead, his whole program was based on reform within the church.

Church and Religion on the Eve of the Reformation

The institutional problems of the Catholic church in the fourteenth and fifteenth centuries, especially the failure of the Renaissance popes to provide spiritual leadership, were bound to affect the spiritual life of all Christendom. The general impression of the tenor of religious life on the eve of the Reformation was one of much deterioration, coupled with evidence of a continuing desire for meaningful religious experience from millions of devout lay people.

The economic changes of the Late Middle Ages and Renaissance and the continuing preoccupation of the papal court with finances had an especially strong impact on the clergy. The highest positions of the clergy were increasingly held by either the nobility or the wealthier members of the bourgeoisie. At the same time, to enhance their revenues, high church officials accumulated church offices in ever-larger numbers. This practice of pluralism (the holding of many church offices) led, in turn, to the problem of absenteeism, as church officeholders neglected their episcopal duties and delegated the entire administration of their dioceses to priests, who were often underpaid and little interested in performing their duties.

At the same time, the atmosphere of the fourteenth and fifteenth centuries, with its uncertainty of life and immediacy of death, created a craving for meaningful religious expression and certainty of salvation. This impulse, especially strong in Germany, expressed itself in two ways that often seemed contradictory.

One manifestation of religious piety in the fifteenth century was the almost mechanical view of the process of salvation. Collections of relics grew as more and more people sought certainty of salvation through their veneration. By 1509, Frederick the Wise, elector of Saxony and Martin Luther's prince, had amassed more than 5,000 relics to which were attached indulgences that could reduce one's time in purgatory by 1,443 years (an indulgence is a remission of all or part of the temporal punishment due to sin). Despite the physical dangers, increasing numbers of Christians made pilgrimages to such holy centers as Rome and Jerusalem to gain spiritual benefits.

Another form of religious piety, the quest for a tranquil spirituality, was evident in the popular mystical movement known as the Modern Devotion. The Modern Devotion featured a disregard for religious dogma and a need to follow a life of inner piety based on the precepts of Christ. Thomas à Kempis (1380–1471), in the great mystical classic of the Modern Devotion, *The Imitation of Christ*, wrote that "Truly, at the day of judgment we shall not be examined by what we have read, but what we have done; not how well we have spoken, but how religiously we have lived."

What is striking about the revival of religious piety in the fifteenth century—whether expressed through such external forces such as the veneration of relics and the buying of indulgences or through the mystical path—was its adherence to the orthodox beliefs and practices of the Catholic church. The agitation for certainty of salvation and spiritual peace was done within the framework of the "holy mother Church." But disillusionment grew as the devout experienced the clergy's inability to live up to their expectations. The deepening of religious life, especially in the second half of the fifteenth century, found little echo among the worldly wise clergy, and it is this environment that helps to explain the tremendous and immediate impact of Luther's ideas.

Martin Luther and the Reformation in Germany

The Protestant Reformation had its beginning in a typical medieval question—what must I do to be saved? Martin Luther, a deeply religious man, found an answer that did not fit within the traditional teachings of the late medieval church. Ultimately, he split with that church, destroying the religious unity of western Christendom. That other people were concerned with the same question is evident in the rapid spread of the Reformation. But religion was so entangled in the social, economic, and political forces of the period that Protestant reformers' hope of transforming the church quickly proved illusory.

The Early Luther

Martin Luther was born in Germany on November 10, 1483. His father wanted him to become a lawyer, so Luther enrolled at the University of Erfurt where he received his bachelor's degree in 1502. In 1505, after becoming a master in the liberal arts, the young Martin began to study law. Luther was not content with the study of law and all along had shown religious inclinations. In the summer of 1505, en route back to Erfurt after a brief visit home, he was caught in a ferocious thunderstorm and vowed that, if he were spared, he would become a monk. He then entered the monastic order of the Augustinian Hermits in Erfurt, much to his father's disgust. While in the monastery, Luther focused on his major concern, the assurance of salvation. The traditional beliefs and practices of the church seemed unable to relieve his obsession with this question. Luther threw himself into his monastic routine with a vengeance:

I was indeed a good monk and kept my order so strictly that I could say that if ever a monk could get to heaven through monastic discipline, I was that monk. . . . And yet my conscience would not give me certainty, but I always doubted and said, "You didn't do that right. You weren't contrite enough. You left that out of your confession." The more I tried to remedy an uncertain, weak and troubled conscience with human traditions, the more I daily found it more uncertain, weaker and more troubled.[3]

Despite his herculean efforts, Luther achieved no certainty of salvation.

To help overcome his difficulties, his superiors recommended that the intelligent, yet disturbed monk study theology. He received his doctorate in 1512 and then became a professor in the theological faculty at the University of Wittenberg, lecturing on the Bible. Probably sometime between 1513 and 1516, through his study of the Bible, he arrived at an answer to his problem.

Catholic doctrine had emphasized that both faith and good works were required of a Christian to achieve personal salvation. In Luther's eyes, human beings, weak and powerless in the sight of an almighty God, could never do enough good works to merit salvation. Through his study of the Bible, especially his work on Paul's Epistle to the Romans, Luther rediscovered another way of viewing this problem. To Luther, humans are not saved through their good works, but through faith in the promises of God, made possible by the sacrifice of Christ on the cross. The doctrine of salvation or justification by grace through faith alone became the primary doctrine of the Protestant Reformation (justification is the act by which a person is made deserving of salvation). Because Luther had arrived at this doctrine from his study of the Bible, the Bible became for Luther as for all other Protestants the chief guide to religious truth. Justification by faith and the Bible as the sole authority in religious affairs were the twin pillars of the Protestant Reformation.

Luther did not see himself as either an innovator or heretic, but his involvement in the indulgence controversy propelled him into an open confrontation with church officials and forced him to see the theological implications of justification by faith alone. Luther was greatly distressed by the widespread selling of indulgences, certain that people were simply guaranteeing their eternal damnation by relying on these pieces of paper to assure themselves of salvation. Johann Tetzel, a rambunctious Dominican, hawked the indulgences with the slogan, "As soon as the coin in the coffer rings, the soul from purgatory springs."

In response, Luther issued his Ninety-Five Theses, which were a stunning indictment of the abuses in the sale of indulgences (see the box on p. 287). It is doubtful if Luther intended any break with the church over the issue of indulgences. If the pope had clarified the use of indulgences, as Luther wished, then he would probably have been satisfied and the controversy closed. But the Renaissance pope Leo X did not take the issue seriously and is even reported to have said that Luther was simply "some drunken German who will amend his ways when he sobers up." A German translation of the Ninety-Five Theses was quickly printed in thousands of copies and received sympathetically in a Germany that had a long tradition of dissatisfaction with papal policies and power.

In three pamphlets published in 1520, Luther moved toward a more definite break with the Catholic church. The *Address to the Nobility of the German Nation* was a political tract written in German in which Luther called on the German princes to overthrow the papacy in Germany and establish a reformed German church. *The Babylonian Captivity of the Church* attacked the sacramental system as the means by which the pope and church had held the real meaning of the Gospel in captivity for 1,000 years. He called for the reform of monasticism and for the clergy to marry. While virginity is good, Luther argued, marriage is better, and freedom of choice is best. *On the Freedom of a Christian Man* was a short treatise on the doctrine of salvation. It is faith alone, not good works, which justifies, frees, and brings salvation through Christ. Being saved and freed by his faith in Christ, however, does not free the Christian from doing good works. Rather he performs good works out of gratitude to God: "Good works do not make a good man, but a good man does good works."[4]

Unable to accept Luther's forcefully worded dissent from traditional Catholic teachings, the church excommunicated him in January 1521. He was also summoned to appear before the imperial diet or Reichstag of the Holy Roman Empire in Worms, convened by the newly elected Emperor Charles V (1519–1556). Expected to recant the heretical doctrines he had espoused, Luther refused and made the famous reply that became the battle cry of the Reformation:

Since then Your Majesty and your lordships desire a simple reply, I will answer without horns and without teeth. Unless I am convicted by Scripture and plain reason—I do not accept the authority of popes and councils, for they have contradicted each other—my conscience is captive to the Word of God. I cannot and I will not recant anything, for to go against conscience is neither right nor safe. Here I stand, I cannot do otherwise. God help me. Amen.[5]

Luther and the Ninety-Five Theses

To most historians, the publication of Luther's Ninety-Five Theses marks the beginning of the Reformation. To Luther, they were simply a response to what he considered to be the blatant abuses of Johann Tetzel's selling of indulgences. Although written in Latin, the theses were soon translated into German and disseminated widely across Germany. They made an immense impression on Germans already dissatisfied with the ecclesiastical and financial policies of the papacy.

Martin Luther, Selections from the Ninety-Five Theses

5. The Pope has neither the will nor the power to remit any penalties beyond those he has imposed either at his own discretion or by canon law.

20. Therefore the Pope, by his plenary remission of all penalties, does not mean "all" in the absolute sense, but only those imposed by himself.

21. Hence those preachers of Indulgences are wrong when they say that a man is absolved and saved from every penalty by the Pope's Indulgences.

27. It is mere human talk to preach that the soul flies out [of purgatory] immediately the money clinks in the collection-box.

28. It is certainly possible that when the money clinks in the collection-box greed and avarice can increase; but the intercession of the Church depends on the will of God alone.

45. Christians should be taught that he who sees a needy person and passes him by, although he gives money for pardons, wins for himself not Papal Indulgences but the wrath of God.

50. Christians should be taught that, if the Pope knew the exactions of the preachers of Indulgences, he would rather have the basilica of St. Peter reduced to ashes than built with the skin, flesh and bones of his sheep.

81. This wanton preaching of pardons makes it difficult even for learned men to redeem respect due to the Pope from the slanders or at least the shrewd questionings of the laity.

82. For example: "Why does not the Pope empty purgatory for the sake of most holy love and the supreme need of souls? This would be the most righteous of reasons, if he can redeem innumerable souls for sordid money with which to build a basilica, the most trivial of reason."

86. Again: "Since the Pope's wealth is larger than that of the crassest Crassi of our time, why does he not build this one basilica of St. Peter with his own money, rather than with that of the faithful poor?"

88. Again: "What greater good would be done to the Church if the Pope were to bestow these remissions and dispensations, not once, as now, but a hundred times a day, on any believer whatever."

90. To suppress these most conscientious questionings of the laity by authority only, instead of refuting them by reason, is to expose the Church and the Pope to the ridicule of their enemies, and to make Christian people unhappy.

91. If, therefore, pardons were preached in accordance with the spirit and mind of the Pope, all these difficulties would be easily overcome, or rather would never have arisen.

94. Christians should be exhorted to seek earnestly to follow Christ, their Head, through penalties, deaths, and hells.

95. And let them thus be more confident of entering heaven through many tribulations rather than through a false assurance of peace.

The young emperor Charles was outraged at Luther's audacity and gave his opinion that "a single friar who goes counter to all Christianity for a thousand years must be wrong." By the Edict of Worms, Martin Luther was made an outlaw within the empire. His works were to be burned and Luther himself captured and delivered to the emperor.

The Development of Lutheranism

Between 1521 and 1525, Luther's religious movement became a revolution. In the decade of the 1520s, Lutheranism had much appeal and spread rapidly. The preaching of evangelical sermons, based on a return to the original message of the Bible, found favor throughout Germany. In city after city, the arrival of preachers

♦ **Woodcut: Luther versus the Pope.** In the 1520s, after Luther's return to Wittenberg, his teachings began to spread rapidly, ending ultimately in a reform movement supported by state authorities. Pamphlets containing picturesque woodcuts were important in the spread of Luther's ideas. In the woodcut shown here, the crucified Jesus attends Luther's service on the left, while on the right the pope is at a table selling indulgences.

presenting Luther's teachings was soon followed by a public debate in which the new preachers proved victorious. A reform of the church was then instituted by church authorities. Also useful to the spread of the Reformation were pamphlets illustrated with vivid woodcuts portraying the pope as a hideous Antichrist and titled with catchy phrases, such as "I Wonder Why There is No Money in the Land" (which, of course, was an attack on papal greed).

Luther was able to gain the support of his prince, the elector of Saxony, as well as other German rulers among the 300-odd states that made up the Holy Roman Empire. Lutheranism spread to both princely and ecclesiastical states in northern and central Germany as well as to two-thirds of the free imperial cities, especially those of southern Germany, where prosperous burghers, for both religious and secular reasons, became committed to Luther's cause. At its outset, the Reformation in Germany was largely an urban phenomenon.

A series of crises in the mid-1520s made it apparent, however, that spreading the word of God was not as easy as Luther had originally envisioned, the usual plight of most reformers. Luther experienced dissent within his own ranks in Wittenberg as well as defection from many Christian humanists who feared that Luther's movement threatened the unity of Christendom. The Peasants' War constituted Luther's greatest challenge, however. In June 1524, peasants in Germany rose in revolt against their lords and looked to Luther for support. But Luther, who knew how much his reformation of the church depended on the full support of the German princes and magistrates, supported the rulers. To Luther, the state and its rulers were ordained by God and given the authority to maintain the peace and order necessary for the spread of the Gospel. It was the duty of princes to suppress all revolt. By May 1525, the German princes had ruthlessly suppressed the peasant hordes. By this time, Luther found himself ever more dependent on state authorities for the growth and maintenance of his reformed church.

The Lutheran churches in Germany (and later in Scandinavia) quickly became territorial or state churches in which the state supervised and disciplined church members. As part of the development of these state-dominated churches, Luther also instituted new religious services to replace the Mass. These featured a worship service consisting of a German liturgy that focused on Bible reading, preaching the word of God, and song. Following his own denunciation of clerical celibacy, Luther married a former nun, Katherina von Bora, in 1525. His union provided a model of married and family life for the new Protestant minister.

Germany and the Reformation: Religion and Politics

From its very beginning, the fate of Luther's movement was closely tied to political affairs. In 1519, Charles I, king of Spain and the grandson of the Emperor Maximilian, was elected Holy Roman emperor as Charles V (1519–1556). Charles V ruled over an immense empire, consisting of Spain and its overseas possessions, the traditional Austrian Habsburg lands, Bohemia, Hungary, the Low Countries, and the Kingdom of Naples in southern Italy. The extent of his possessions was reflected in the languages he used: "I speak Spanish to God, Italian to women, French to men, and German to

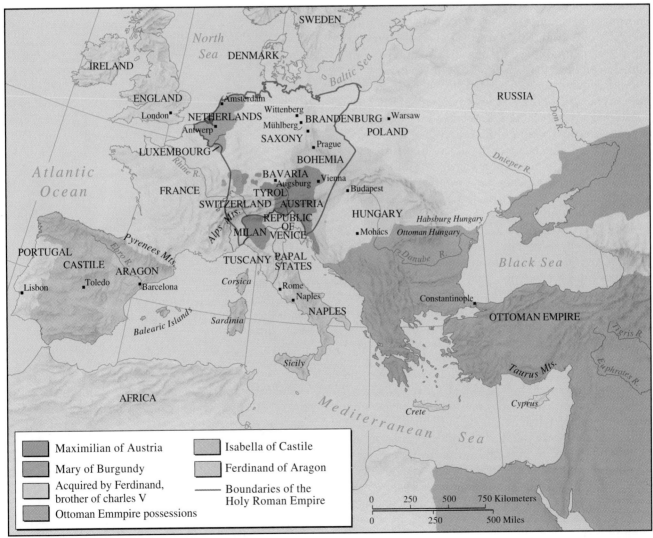

Map 14.1 The Empire of Charles V.

my horse." Politically, Charles wanted to maintain his dynasty's control over his enormous empire; religiously, he hoped to preserve the unity of the Catholic faith throughout his empire. Despite his strengths, Charles spent a lifetime in futile pursuit of his goals. Four major problems—the French, the papacy, the Turks, and Germany's internal situation—cost him both his dream and his health. At the same time, the emperor's problems gave Luther's movement time to organize before facing the concerted onslaught of the Catholic forces.

The chief political concern of Charles V was his rivalry with the Valois king of France, Francis I (1515–1547), who proved a worthy adversary. Encircled by the possessions of the Habsburg empire, Francis became embroiled in conflict with Charles over disputed territories in southern France, the Netherlands, the Rhineland, northern Spain, and Italy. These conflicts, known as the Habsburg–Valois Wars, were fought intermittently over twenty-four years (1521–1544), preventing Charles from concentrating his attention on the Lutheran problem in Germany.

At the same time, Charles faced opposition from Pope Clement VII (1523–1534), who, guided by political considerations, joined the side of Francis I. The advance of the Ottoman Turks into the eastern part of Charles's empire forced the emperor to divert forces there as well. Under the competent Suleiman the Magnificent (1520–1566), the Ottoman Turks overran most of Hungary, moved into Austria, and advanced as far as Vienna, where they were finally repulsed in 1529.

Finally, the internal political situation in the Holy Roman Empire was also not in Charles's favor. Germany was a land of several hundred territorial states: princely states, ecclesiastical principalities, and free imperial cities. While all owed loyalty to the emperor, Germany's medieval development had enabled these states to become quite independent of imperial authority. They had no desire to have a strong emperor. By the time Charles V was able to bring military forces to Germany—in 1546—Lutheranism had become well established and the Lutheran princes were well organized. Unable to impose his will on Germany, Charles was forced to negotiate a truce. An end to religious warfare in Germany came in 1555 with the Peace of Augsburg, which marks an important turning point in the history of the Reformation. The division of Christianity was formally acknowledged, with Lutheranism being granted the same legal rights as Catholicism. Moreover, the peace settlement accepted the right of each German ruler to determine the religion of his subjects.

✦ **Charles V.** Charles V sought to create religious unity throughout his vast empire by keeping all his subjects within the bounds of the Catholic church. Due to his conflict with Francis I as well as difficulties with the Turks, the papacy, and the German princes, Charles was never able to check the spread of Lutheranism. This is a portrait of Charles V by the Venetian painter Titian.

The Peace of Augsburg was a victory for the German princes. The independence of the numerous German territorial states guaranteed the weakness of the Holy Roman Empire and the continued decentralization of Germany. Charles's hope for a united empire had been completely dashed. At the same time, what had at first been merely feared was now confirmed: the ideal of medieval Christian unity was irretrievably lost. The rapid proliferation of new Protestant groups served to underscore the new reality.

The Spread of the Protestant Reformation

To Catholic critics, Luther's heresy had opened the door to more extreme forms of religious and social upheaval. For both Catholics and Protestant reformers, it also raised the question of how to determine what constituted the correct interpretation of the Bible. The inability to agree on this issue led not only to theological confrontations but also to bloody warfare because each Christian group was unwilling to admit that it could be wrong.

The Zwinglian Reformation

Switzerland, which has played little role in our history to date, was home to two major Reformation movements, Zwinglianism and Calvinism. In the sixteenth century, the Swiss Confederation was a loose association of thirteen self-governing states called cantons. Theoretically part of the Holy Roman Empire, they had become virtually independent after the Swiss defeated the forces of Emperor Maximilian in 1499. The six forest cantons were democratic republics while the seven urban cantons, which included Zürich, Bern, and Basel, were governed primarily by city councils controlled by narrow oligarchies of wealthy citizens.

Ulrich Zwingli (1484–1531) was ordained a priest in 1506 and accepted an appointment as a cathedral priest in the Great Minster of Zürich in 1518. Zwingli's preaching of the Gospel caused such unrest that the city council in 1523 held a public disputation or debate in the town hall. Zwingli's party was accorded the victory and the council declared that "Mayor, Council and Great Council of Zürich, in order to do away with disturbance and discord, have upon due deliberation and consultation decided and resolved that Master Zwingli should continue as heretofore to proclaim the Gospel and the pure sacred Scriptures."[6] During the next two years, evangelical reforms were promulgated in Zürich by a city council strongly influenced by Zwingli. Zwingli looked to the state to supervise the church. Relics and images were abolished; all paintings and decorations were removed from the churches and replaced by whitewashed walls. The mass was replaced by a new liturgy consisting of scripture reading, prayer, and sermons. Monasticism, pilgrimages, the veneration of saints, clerical celibacy, and the pope's authority were all abolished as remnants of papal Christianity.

As his movement began to spread to other cities in Switzerland, Zwingli sought an alliance with Martin Luther and the German reformers. Although both the German and Swiss reformers realized the need for unity to defend against the opposition of Catholic authorities, they were unable to agree on the interpretation of the Lord's Supper (see the box on p. 292). Zwingli believed that the scriptural words "This is my Body, This is my blood" should be taken figuratively, not literally, and refused to accept Luther's insistence on the real presence of the body and blood of Christ "in, with, and under the bread and wine."

In October 1531, war erupted between the Swiss Protestant and Catholic cantons. Zürich's army was routed, and Zwingli was found wounded on the battlefield. His enemies killed him, cut up his body, and burned the pieces, scattering the ashes. This Swiss civil war of 1531 provided an early indication of what religious passions would lead to in the sixteenth century. Unable to find peaceful ways to agree on the meaning of the Gospel, the disciples of Christianity resorted to violence and decision by force.

The Radical Reformation: The Anabaptists

Although many reformers were ready to allow the state to play an important, if not dominant, role in church affairs, some people rejected this kind of magisterial reformation and favored a far more radical reform movement. Collectively called the Anabaptists, these radicals actually formed a large variety of different groups who, nevertheless, shared some common characteristics. Anabaptism was especially attractive to those peasants, weavers, miners, and artisans who had been adversely affected by the economic changes of the age.

Anabaptists everywhere shared some common ideas. To them, the true Christian church was a voluntary association of believers who had undergone spiritual rebirth and had then been baptized into the church. Anabaptists advocated adult rather than infant baptism. They also tried to return literally to the practices and spirit of early Christianity. Adhering to the accounts of early Christian communities in the New Testament, they followed a strict sort of democracy in which all believers were considered equal. Each church chose its own minister, who might be any member of the community because all Christians were considered priests (though women were often excluded). Those chosen as ministers had the duty to lead services, which were very simple and contained nothing not found in the early church. Anabaptists rejected theological speculation in favor of simple Christian living according to what they believed was the pure

A Reformation Debate: The Marburg Colloquy

Debates played a crucial role in the Reformation period. They were a primary instrument in introducing the Reformation into innumerable cities as well as a means of resolving differences among the like-minded Protestant groups. This selection contains an excerpt from the vivacious and often brutal debate between Luther and Zwingli over the sacrament of the Lord's Supper at Marburg in 1529. The two protagonists failed to reach agreement.

The Marburg Colloquy, 1529

THE HESSIAN CHANCELLOR FEIGE: My gracious prince and lord [Landgrave Philip of Hesse] has summoned you for the express and urgent purpose of settling the dispute over the sacrament of the Lord's Supper. . . . And let everyone on both sides present his arguments in a spirit of moderation, as becomes such matters. . . . Now then, Doctor Luther, you may proceed.

LUTHER: Noble prince, gracious lord! Undoubtedly the colloquy is well intentioned. . . . Although I have no intention of changing my mind, which is firmly made up, I will nevertheless present the grounds of my belief and show where the others are in error. . . . Your basic contentions are these: In the last analysis you wish to prove that a body cannot be in two places at once, and you produce arguments about the unlimited body which are based on natural reason. I do not question how Christ can be God and man and how the two natures can be joined. For God is more powerful than all our ideas, and we must submit to his word.

Prove that Christ's body is not there where the Scripture says, "This is my body!" Rational proofs I will not listen to. . . . God is beyond all mathematics and the words of God are to be revered and carried out in awe. It is God who commands, "Take, eat, this is my body." I request, therefore, valid scriptural proof to the contrary.

Luther writes on the table in chalk, "This is my body," and covers the words with a velvet cloth.

OECOLAMPADIUS [leader of the reform movement in Basel and a Zwinglian partisan]: The sixth chapter of John clarifies the other scriptural passages. Christ is not speaking there about a local presence. "The flesh is of no avail," he says [John 6:63]. It is not my intention to employ rational, or geometrical, arguments—neither am I denying the power of God—but as long as I have the complete faith I will speak from that. For Christ is risen; he sits at the right hand of God; and so he cannot be present in the bread. Our view is neither new nor sacrilegious, but is based on faith and Scripture. . . .

ZWINGLI: I insist that the words of the Lord's Supper must be figurative. This is ever apparent, and even required by the article of faith: "taken up into heaven, seated at the right hand of the Father." Otherwise, it would be absurd to look for him in the Lord's Supper at the same time that Christ is telling us that he is in heaven. One and the same body cannot possibly be in different places. . . .

LUTHER: I call upon you as before: your basic contentions are shaky. Give way, and give glory to God!

ZWINGLI: And we call upon you to give glory to God and to quit begging the question! The issue at stake is this: Where is the proof of your position? I am willing to consider your words carefully—no harm meant! You're trying to outwit me. I stand by this passage in the sixth chapter of John, verse 63 and shall not be shaken from it. You'll have to sing another tune.

LUTHER: You're being obnoxious.

ZWINGLI: (*excitedly*): Don't you believe that Christ was attempting in John 6 to help those who did not understand?

LUTHER: You're trying to dominate things! You insist on passing judgment! Leave that to someone else! . . . It is your point that must be proved, not mine. But let us stop this sort of thing. It serves no purpose.

ZWINGLI: It certainly does! It is for you to prove that the passage in John 6 speaks of a physical repast.

LUTHER: You express yourself poorly and make about as much progress as a cane standing in a corner. You're going nowhere.

ZWINGLI: No, no, no! This is the passage that will break your neck!

LUTHER: Don't be so sure of yourself. Necks don't break this way. You're in Hesse, not Switzerland. . . .

Word of God. The Lord's Supper was interpreted as a remembrance, a meal of fellowship celebrated in the evening in private houses according to Christ's example. Finally, unlike the Catholics and other Protestants, most Anabaptists believed in the complete separation of church and state. Not only was government to be excluded from the realm of religion, it was not even supposed to exercise political jurisdiction over real Christians. Anabaptists refused to hold political office or bear arms because many took literally the commandment "Thou shall not kill," although some Anabaptist groups did become quite violent. Their political beliefs as much as their religious beliefs caused the Anabaptists to be regarded as dangerous radicals who threatened the very fabric of sixteenth-century society. Indeed, the chief thing Protestants and Catholics could agree on was the need to persecute Anabaptists.

One early group of Anabaptists known as the Swiss Brethren arose in Zürich. Their ideas frightened Zwingli, and they were soon expelled from the city. As their teachings spread through southern Germany, the Austrian Habsburg lands, and Switzerland, Anabaptists suffered ruthless persecution, especially after the Peasants' War of 1524–1525, when the upper classes resorted to repression. Virtually stamped out in Germany, Anabaptist survivors emerged in Moravia, Poland, and the Netherlands.

Menno Simons (1496–1561) was the most responsible for rejuvenating Dutch Anabaptism. A popular leader, Menno dedicated his life to the spread of a peaceful, evangelical Anabaptism that stressed separation from the world in order to live a truly Christlike life. The Mennonites, as his followers were called, spread from the Netherlands into northwestern Germany and eventually into Poland and Lithuania as well as the New World. Both the Mennonites and the Amish, who are also descended from the Anabaptists, can be found in United States and Canada today.

The Reformation in England

The English Reformation was initiated by an act of state. King Henry VIII (1509–1547) had a strong desire to divorce his first wife, Catherine of Aragon. Henry VIII's reasons were twofold. Catherine had produced no male heir, an absolute essential if his Tudor dynasty were to flourish. At the same time, Henry had fallen in love with

✦ **An Anabaptist Execution in the Netherlands.** The Anabaptists were the radicals of the Reformation. They advocated adult baptism and believed that the true Christian should not actively participate in or be governed by the secular state. Due to their radical ideas, the Anabaptists were persecuted and put to death by Catholics and Protestants alike. This sixteenth-century woodcut depicts the execution of Anabaptist reformers.

Anne Boleyn, a lady-in-waiting to Queen Catherine. Her unwillingness to be only the king's mistress, as well as the king's desire to have a legitimate male heir, made a new marriage imperative. The king's first marriage stood in the way, however.

Normally, church authorities might have been willing to grant the king an annulment of his marriage, but Pope Clement VII was dependent on the Holy Roman emperor Charles V, who happened to be the nephew of Queen Catherine. Impatient with the pope's inaction, Henry sought to obtain an annulment of his marriage in England's own ecclesiastical courts. As Archbishop of Canterbury and head of the highest ecclesiastical court in England, Thomas Cranmer held official hearings on the king's case and ruled in May 1533 that the king's marriage to Catherine was "null and absolutely void." He then validated Henry's secret marriage to Anne, who had become pregnant. At the beginning of June, Anne was crowned queen. Three months later a child was born. Much to the king's disappointment, the baby was a girl, the future Queen Elizabeth.

In 1534, upon Henry's request, Parliament moved to finalize the break of the Church of England with Rome. An Act of Supremacy of 1534 declared that the king was "taken, accepted, and reputed the only supreme head on earth of the Church of England," a position that gave him control of doctrine, clerical appointments, and discipline. Using his new powers, Henry dissolved the monasteries. About 400 religious houses were closed in 1536, and their land and possessions confiscated by the king. Many were sold to nobles, gentry, and some merchants. The king received a great boost to his treasury, as well as creating a group of supporters who now had a stake in the new Tudor order.

Although Henry VIII had broken with the papacy, little change occurred in matters of doctrine, theology, and ceremony. Some of his supporters, such as Archbishop Thomas Cranmer, wished to have a religious reformation as well as an administrative one, but Henry was unyielding. But he died in 1547 and was succeeded by his son, the underage and sickly Edward VI (1547–1553). During Edward's reign, Archbishop Cranmer and others inclined toward Protestant doctrines were able to move the Church of England (or Anglican church) in more of a Protestant direction. New acts of Parliament instituted the right of the clergy to marry, the elimination of images, and the creation of a revised Protestant liturgy that was elaborated in a new prayer book and liturgical guide known as the Book of Common Prayer. These rapid changes in doctrine and liturgy aroused much opposition and prepared the way for the reaction that occurred when Mary, Henry's first daughter by Catherine of Aragon, came to the throne.

There was no doubt that Mary (1553–1558) was a Catholic who intended to restore England to Roman Catholicism. But her restoration of Catholicism aroused much opposition. There was widespread antipathy to Mary's unfortunate marriage to Philip II, the son of Charles V and future king of Spain. Philip was strongly disliked in England, and Mary's foreign policy of alliance with Spain simply aroused further hostility. The burning of more than 300 Protestant heretics roused further ire against "bloody Mary." As a result of her policies, Mary managed to achieve the opposite of what she had intended: England was more Protestant by the end of her reign than it had been at the beginning.

John Calvin and the Development of Calvinism

Of the second generation of Protestant reformers, one stands out as the premier systematic theologian and organizer of the Protestant movement—John Calvin (1509–1564). John Calvin was educated in his native France, but after his conversion to Protestantism was forced to flee France for the safety of Switzerland. In 1536, he published the first edition of the *Institutes of the Christian Religion*, a masterful synthesis of Protestant thought, a manual for ecclesiastical organization, and a work that immediately secured Calvin's reputation as one of the new leaders of Protestantism. Although the Institutes were originally written in Latin, Calvin published a French edition in 1541, facilitating the spread of his ideas in French-speaking lands.

On most important doctrines, Calvin stood very close to Luther. He adhered to the doctrine of justification by faith alone to explain how humans achieved salvation. But Calvin also placed much emphasis on the absolute sovereignty of God or the "power, grace, and glory of God." Thus, "God asserts his possession of omnipotence, and claims our acknowledgment of this attribute; not such as is imagined by sophists, vain, idle, and almost asleep, but vigilant, efficacious, operative, and engaged in continual action."[7]

One of the ideas derived from his emphasis on the absolute sovereignty of God—predestination—gave a unique cast to Calvin's teachings. Although it was but one aspect of his doctrine of salvation, predestination became the central focus of succeeding generations of Calvinists. This "eternal decree," as Calvin called it, meant that God had predestined some people to be saved (the elect) and others to be damned (the reprobate). According to Calvin, "He has once for all determined, both whom he would admit to salvation, and whom he would condemn to destruction."[8] Calvin identified three tests that might indicate possible salvation: an open profession of faith, a "decent and godly life," and participation in the sacraments of baptism and communion. Although Calvin stressed that there could be no absolute certainty of salvation, some of his followers did not always make this distinction. The practical psychological effect of predestination was to give some later Calvinists an unshakable conviction that they were doing God's work on earth. Thus, Calvinism became a dynamic and activist faith. It is no accident that Calvinism became the militant international form of Protestantism.

To Calvin, the church was a divine institution responsible for preaching the word of God and administering the sacraments. Calvin kept only two sacraments, baptism and the Lord's Supper. Calvin believed in the real presence of Christ in the sacrament of the Lord's Supper, but only in a spiritual sense. Christ's body is at the right hand of God and thus cannot be in the sacrament, but to the believer, Christ is spiritually present in the Lord's Supper. Finally, Calvin agreed with other reformers that the church had the power to discipline its members. This element of his thought was apparent when Calvin finally had the opportunity to establish his church in Geneva.

In 1536, Calvin began working to reform the city of Geneva. He was able to fashion a tightly organized church order that employed both clergy and laymen in the service of the church. The Consistory, a special body for enforcing moral discipline, was also created and functioned as a court to oversee the moral life, daily behavior, and doctrinal orthodoxy of Genevans and to admonish and correct deviants. As its power increased, the Consistory went from "fraternal corrections" to the use of public penance and excommunication. More serious cases could be turned over to the city councils for punishments greater than excommunication. Calvin separated church and state and expected the church, as a divine institution, to function largely independently of state power.

Calvin's success in Geneva enabled the city to become a vibrant center of Protestantism. John Knox, the Calvinist reformer of Scotland, called Geneva "the most perfect school of Christ on earth." Following Calvin's lead, missionaries trained in Geneva were sent to all parts of Europe. Calvinism became established in France, the Netherlands, Scotland, and central and eastern Europe. By the mid-sixteenth century, Calvinism had replaced Lutheranism as the militant international form of Protes-

✦ **John Calvin.** After a conversion experience, John Calvin abandoned his life as a humanist and became a reformer. In 1536, Calvin began working to reform the city of Geneva, where he remained until his death in 1564. This sixteenth-century portrait of Calvin pictures him near the end of his life.

tantism, and Calvin's Geneva stood as the fortress of the Reformation.

The Social Impact of the Protestant Reformation

Because Christianity was such an integral part of European life, it was inevitable that the Reformation would have an impact on the family and popular religious practices.

In the initial zeal of the Protestant Reformation, women were frequently allowed to play unusual roles. Catherine Zell of Germany (c. 1497–1562) first preached beside her husband in 1527. After the death of her two children, she devoted the rest of her life to helping her husband and their Anabaptist faith. This selection is taken from one of her letters to a young Lutheran minister who had criticized her activities.

Catherine Zell to Ludwig Rabus of Memmingen

I, Catherine Zell, wife of the late lamented Mathew Zell, who served in Strasbourg, where I was born and reared and still live, wish you peace and enhancement in God's grace. . . .

From my earliest years I turned to the Lord, who taught and guided me, and I have at all times, in accordance with my understanding and His grace, embraced the interests of His church and earnestly sought Jesus. Even in youth this brought me the regard and affection of clergymen and others much concerned with the church, which is why the pious Mathew Zell wanted me as a companion in marriage; and I, in turn, to serve the glory of Christ, gave devotion and help to my hus-band, both in his ministry and in keeping his house. . . . Ever since I was ten years old I have been a student and a sort of church mother, much given to attending sermons. I have loved and frequented the company of learned men, and I conversed much with them, not about dancing, masquerades, and worldly pleasures but about the kingdom of God. . . .

Consider the poor Anabaptists, who are so furiously and ferociously persecuted. Must the authorities everywhere be incited against them, as the hunter drives his dog against wild animals? Against those who acknowledge Christ the Lord in very much the same way we do and over which we broke with the papacy? Just because they cannot agree with us on lesser things, is this any reason to persecute them and in them Christ, in whom they fervently believe and have often professed in misery, in prison, and under the torments of fire and water?

Governments may punish criminals, but they should not force and govern belief, which is a matter for the heart and conscience not for the temporal authorities. . . . When the authorities pursue one, they soon bring forth tears, and towns and villages are emptied.

The Family

For centuries, Catholicism had praised the family and sanctified its existence by making marriage a sacrament. But the Catholic church's high regard for abstinence from sex as the surest way to holiness made the celibate state of the clergy preferable to marriage. Nevertheless, because not all men could remain chaste, marriage offered the best means to control sexual intercourse and give it a purpose, the procreation of children. To some extent, this attitude persisted among the Protestant reformers; Luther, for example, argued that sex in marriage allowed one to "make use of this sex in order to avoid sin," and Calvin advised that every man should "abstain from marriage only so long as he is fit to observe celibacy." If "his power to tame lust fails him," then he must marry.

But the Reformation did bring some change to the conception of the family. Both Catholic and Protestant clergy preached sermons advocating a more positive side to family relationships. The Protestants were especially important in developing this new view of the family. Be-cause Protestantism had eliminated any idea of special holiness for celibacy, abolishing both monasticism and a celibate clergy, the family could be placed at the center of human life, and a new stress on "mutual love between man and wife" could be extolled. But were doctrine and reality the same? For more radical religious groups, at times they were (see the box above). One Anabaptist wrote to his wife before his execution: "My faithful helper, my loyal friend. I praise God that he gave you to me, you who have sustained me in all my trial."[9] But more often reality reflected the traditional roles of husband as the ruler and wife as the obedient servant whose chief duty was to please her husband. Luther stated it clearly:

> The rule remains with the husband, and the wife is compelled to obey him by God's command. He rules the home and the state, wages war, defends his possessions, tills the soil, builds, plants, etc. The woman on the other hand is like a nail driven into the wall . . . so the wife should stay at home and look after the affairs of the household, as one who has been deprived of the ability of administering those

affairs that are outside and that concern the state. She does not go beyond her most personal duties.[10]

But obedience to her husband was not a woman's only role; her other important duty was to bear children. To Calvin and Luther, this function of women was part of the divine plan. God punishes women for the sins of Eve by the burdens of procreation and feeding and nurturing their children, but "it is a gladsome punishment if you consider the hope of eternal life and the honor of motherhood which had been left to her."[11] Although the Protestant reformers sanctified this role of woman as mother and wife, viewing it as a holy vocation, Protestantism also left few alternatives for women. Because monasticism had been destroyed, that career avenue was no longer available; for most Protestant women, family life was their only destiny. At the same time, by emphasizing the father as "ruler" and hence the center of household religion, Protestantism even removed the woman from her traditional role as controller of religion in the home. Overall, the Protestant Reformation did not noticeably transform women's subordinate place in society.

Religious Practices and Popular Culture

Although Protestant reformers were conservative in their political and social attitudes, their attacks on the Catholic church led to radical changes in religious practices. The Protestant Reformation abolished or severely curtailed such customary practices as indulgences, the veneration of relics and saints, pilgrimages, monasticism, and clerical celibacy. The elimination of saints put an end to the numerous celebrations of religious holy days and changed a community's sense of time. Thus, in Protestant communities, religious ceremonies and imagery, such as processions and statues, tended to be replaced with individual private prayer, family worship, and collective prayer and worship at the same time each week on Sunday.

Many religious practices that had played an important role in popular culture were criticized by Protestant reformers as superstitious or remnants of pagan culture. In addition to abolishing saints' days and religious carnivals, some Protestant reformers even tried to eliminate customary forms of entertainment. English Puritans (as English Calvinists were known), for example, attempted to ban drinking in taverns, dramatic performances, and dancing. Dutch Calvinists denounced the tradition of giving small presents to children on the feast of Saint Nicholas, near Christmas. Many of these Protestant attacks on popular culture were unsuccessful, however. The importance of taverns in English social life made it impossible to eradicate them and celebrations at Christmastime persisted in the Dutch Netherlands.

The Catholic Reformation

By the mid-sixteenth century, Lutheranism had become established in Germany and Scandinavia, and Calvinism in parts of Switzerland, France, the Netherlands, and eastern Europe. In England, the split from Rome had resulted in the creation of a national church. The situation in Europe did not look particularly favorable for the Roman Catholic church. But even at the beginning of the sixteenth century, constructive, positive forces were at work for reform within the Catholic church, and by the mid-sixteenth century, these efforts were being directed by a revived and reformed papacy, giving the Catholic church new strength. By the second half of the sixteenth century, Catholicism had regained much that it had lost, especially in Germany and eastern Europe, and was able to make new conversions as well, particularly in the New World. We call the story of the revival of Roman Catholicism the Catholic Reformation, although some historians prefer to use the term Counter-Reformation, especially for those elements of the Catholic Reformation that were directly aimed at stopping the spread of the Protestant Reformation. Historians focus on three chief pillars of the Catholic Reformation: the development of the Jesuits, the creation of a reformed and revived papacy, and the Council of Trent.

The Society of Jesus

The Society of Jesus, known as the Jesuits, was founded by a Spanish nobleman, Ignatius of Loyola (1491–1556), whose injuries in battle cut short his military career. Loyola experienced a spiritual torment similar to Luther's but, unlike Luther, resolved his problems not by a new doctrine, but by a decision to submit his will to the will of the church. Unable to be a real soldier, he vowed to be a soldier of God. Over a period of twelve years, Loyola prepared for his life work by mortification, prayer, pilgrimages, going to school, and working out a spiritual program in his brief, but powerful book, *The Spiritual Exercises*. This was a training manual for spiritual development emphasizing exercises by which the human will could be strengthened and made to follow the will of God as manifested through his instrument, the Catholic church (see the box on p. 298).

❧ Loyola and Obedience to "Our Holy Mother, the Hierarchical Church" ❧

In his Spiritual Exercises, Ignatius Loyola developed a systematic program for "the conquest of self and the regulation of one's life" for service to the hierarchical Catholic church. Ignatius's supreme goal was the commitment of the Christian to active service under Christ's banner in the Church of Christ (the Catholic church). In the final section of the Spiritual Exercises, Loyola explained the nature of that commitment in a series of "Rules for Thinking with the Church."

Ignatius Loyola, "Rules for Thinking with the Church"

The following rules should be observed to foster the true attitude of mind we ought to have in the Church militant.

1. We must put aside all judgment of our own, and keep the mind ever ready and prompt to obey in all things the true Spouse of Jesus Christ, our holy Mother, the hierarchical Church.
2. We should praise sacramental confession, the yearly reception of the Most Blessed Sacrament [the Lord's Supper], and praise more highly monthly reception, and still more weekly Communion. . . .
3. We ought to praise the frequent hearing of Mass, the singing of hymns, psalmody, and long prayers whether in the church or outside. . . .
4. We must praise highly religious life, virginity, and continency; and matrimony ought not be praised as much as any of these.
5. We should praise vows of religion, obedience, poverty, chastity, and vows to perform other works of supererogation conducive to perfection. . . .
6. We should show our esteem for the relics of the saints by venerating them and praying to the saints. We should praise visits to the Station

Churches, pilgrimages, indulgences, jubilees, the lighting of candles in churches.

7. We must praise the regulations of the Church, with regard to fast and abstinence, for example, in Lent, on Ember Days, Vigils, Fridays, and Saturdays.
8. We ought to praise not only the building and adornment of churches, but also images and veneration of them according to the subject they represent.
9. Finally, we must praise all the commandments of the Church, and be on the alert to find reasons to defend them, and by no means in order to criticize them.
10. We should be more ready to approve and praise the orders, recommendations, and way of acting of our superiors than to find fault with them. Though some of the orders, etc., may not have been praise-worthy, yet to speak against them, either when preaching in public or in speaking before the people, would rather be the cause of murmuring and scandal than of profit. As a consequence, the people would become angry with their superiors, whether secular or spiritual. But while it does harm in the absence of our superiors to speak evil of them before the people, it may be profitable to discuss their bad conduct with those who can apply a remedy.
13. If we wish to proceed securely in all things, we must hold fast to the following principle: What seems to me white, I will believe black if the hierarchical Church so defines. For I must be convinced that in Christ our Lord, the bridegroom, and in His spouse the Church, only one Spirit holds sway, which governs and rules for the salvation of souls.

Loyola gathered together a small group of individuals who were recognized as a religious order by a papal bull in 1540. The new order was grounded on the principles of absolute obedience to the papacy, a strict hierarchical order for the society, the use of education to achieve its goals, and a dedication to engage in "conflict for God." The Jesuit organization came to resemble the structure of a military command. Executive leadership was put in the hands of a general, who nominated all important posi-

tions in the order and was to be revered as the absolute head of the order. Loyola served as the first general of the order until his death in 1556. A special vow of absolute obedience to the pope made the Jesuits an important instrument for papal policy.

The Jesuits pursued three major activities. They established highly disciplined schools, believing that the thorough education of young people was crucial to combat the advance of Protestantism. Another prominent Jesuit activity was the propagation of the Catholic faith among non-Christians. Jesuit activity in China, especially that of the Italian Matteo Ricci, led to a number of conversions to Catholicism. Finally, the Jesuits were determined to carry the Catholic banner and fight Protestantism. Jesuit missionaries proved singularly successful in restoring Catholicism to parts of Germany and eastern Europe.

A Revived Papacy

A reformed papacy was another important factor in the development of the Catholic Reformation. The involvement of the Renaissance papacy in dubious finances and Italian political and military affairs had created numerous sources of corruption. It took the jolt of the Protestant Reformation to bring about serious reform. The pontificate of Pope Paul III (1534–1549) proved to be a turning point. Raised in the lap of Renaissance luxury, Paul III continued Renaissance papal practices by appointing his nephews as cardinals, involving himself in politics, and patronizing arts and letters on a lavish scale. Nevertheless, he perceived the need for change and expressed it decisively. Advocates of reform, such as Gasparo Contarini and Gian Pietro Caraffa, were made cardinals. In 1535, Paul took the audacious step of appointing a Reform Commission to study the church's condition. The commission's report in 1537 blamed the church's problems on the corrupt policies of popes and cardinals. It was also Paul III who formally recognized the Jesuits and began the Council of Trent.

A decisive turning point in the direction of the Catholic Reformation and the nature of papal reform came in the 1540s, when the Catholic moderates, such as Cardinal Contarini, who favored concessions to Protestants in the hope of restoring Christian unity, were overshadowed by hardliners who regarded all compromise with Protestant innovations as heresy. It soon became apparent that the conservative reformers were in the ascendancy when Cardinal Caraffa, one of the hardliners, was able to get Paul III to establish a Roman Inquisition or Holy Office in 1542 to ferret out doctrinal errors. There was to be no compromise with Protestantism.

When Cardinal Caraffa was chosen pope as Paul IV (1555–1559), he so increased the power of the Inquisition that even liberal cardinals were silenced. This "first true pope of the Catholic Counter-Reformation," as he has been called, also created an Index of Forbidden Books, a list of books that Catholics were not allowed to read. It included all the works of Protestant theologians as well as authors considered "unwholesome." Any hope

♦ **Ignatius Loyola.** The Jesuits became the most important new religious order of the Catholic Reformation. Shown here in a sixteenth-century painting by an unknown artist is Ignatius Loyola, founder of the Society of Jesus. Loyola is seen kneeling before Pope Paul III, who officially recognized the Jesuits in 1540.

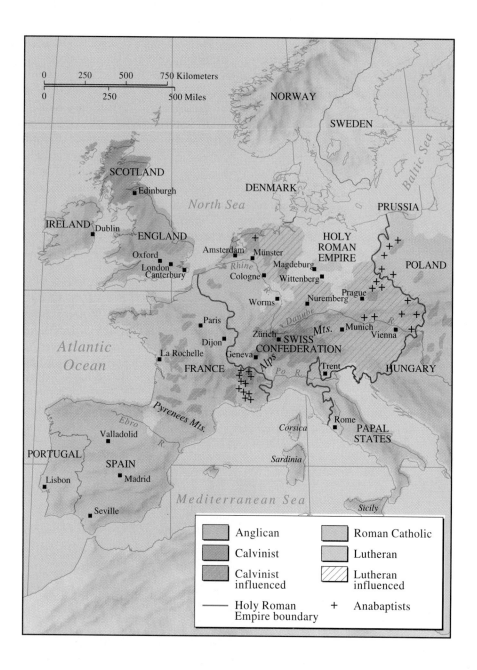

✳ **Map 14.2** Catholics and Protestants in Europe by 1560.

Legend:
- Anglican
- Calvinist
- Calvinist influenced
- Roman Catholic
- Lutheran
- Lutheran influenced
- —— Holy Roman Empire boundary
- + Anabaptists

of restoring Christian unity by compromise was fading fast. The activities of the Council of Trent, the third major pillar of the Catholic Reformation, made compromise virtually impossible.

The Council of Trent

In March 1545, a group of cardinals, archbishops, bishops, abbots, and theologians met in the city of Trent on the border between Germany and Italy and initiated the Council of Trent, which met intermittently from 1545 to 1563 in three major sessions. Moderate Catholic reformers hoped that compromises would be made in formulating doctrinal definitions that would encourage Protestants to return to the church. Conservatives, however, favored an uncompromising restatement of Catholic doctrines in strict opposition to Protestant positions. The latter group won, although not without a struggle.

The final doctrinal decrees of the Council of Trent reaffirmed traditional Catholic teachings in opposition to Protestant beliefs. Scripture and tradition were affirmed as equal authorities in religious matters; only the church could interpret Scripture. Both faith and good works were declared necessary for salvation. The seven sacraments, the Catholic doctrine of transubstantiation, and clerical celibacy were all upheld. Belief in purgatory and in the efficacy of indulgences was strengthened, although hawking of indulgences was prohibited.

After the Council of Trent, the Roman Catholic church possessed a clear body of doctrine and a unified church under the acknowledged supremacy of the popes who had triumphed over bishops and councils. The Roman Catholic church had become one Christian denomination among many with an organizational framework and doctrinal pattern that would not be significantly altered until Vatican Council II 400 years later. With a new spirit of confidence, the Catholic church entered a militant phase, as well prepared as the Calvinists to do battle for the Lord. An era of religious warfare was about to unfold.

Conclusion

When the Augustinian monk Martin Luther entered the public scene with a series of theses on indulgences, few people in Europe, or Germany for that matter, suspected that they would eventually produce a division of Europe along religious lines. But the yearning for reform of the church and meaningful religious experience caused a seemingly simple dispute to escalate into a powerful movement. Clearly, the papacy and other elements in the Catholic church underestimated the strength of Martin Luther and the desire for religious change.

Although Luther felt that his revival of Christianity based on his interpretation of the Bible would be acceptable to all, others soon appeared who interpreted the Bible in yet other different ways. Protestantism split into different sects, which, though united in their dislike of Catholicism, were themselves divided over the interpretation of the sacraments and religious practices. As reform ideas spread, religion and politics became ever more intertwined. Political support played a crucial role in the spread of the Reformation.

Although Lutheranism was legally acknowledged in the Holy Roman Empire by the Peace of Augsburg in 1555, it had lost much of its momentum and outside of Scandinavia had scant ability to attract new supporters. Its energy was largely replaced by the new Protestant form of Calvinism, which had a clarity of doctrine and a fervor that made it attractive to a whole new generation of Europeans. But while Calvinism's militancy enabled it to expand across Europe, Catholicism was also experiencing its own revival and emerged as a militant faith, prepared to do combat for the souls of the faithful. An age of religious passion would tragically be followed by an age of religious warfare.

NOTES

1. Erasmus, *The Paraclesis*, in John Olin, ed., *Christian Humanism and the Reformation: Selected Writings of Erasmus*, 3rd ed. (New York, 1987), p. 101.
2. John P. Dolan, ed., *The Essential Erasmus* (New York, 1964), p. 149.
3. Quoted in Alister E. McGrath, *Reformation Thought: An Introduction* (Oxford, 1988), p. 72.
4. *On the Freedom of a Christian Man*, quoted in E. G. Rupp and Benjamin Drewery, eds., *Martin Luther* (New York, 1970), p. 50.
5. Quoted in Roland Bainton, *Here I Stand, A Life of Martin Luther* (New York, 1950), p. 144.
6. Quoted in De Lamar Jensen, *Reformation Europe* (Lexington, Mass., 1981), p. 83.
7. John Calvin, *Institutes of the Christian Religion*, trans. John Allen (Philadelphia, 1936), 1:220.
8. Ibid., 1:228; 2:181.
9. Quoted in Roland Bainton, *Women of the Reformation in Germany and Italy* (Boston, 1971), p. 154.
10. Quoted in Bonnie S. Anderson and Judith P. Zinsser, *A History of Their Own: Women in Europe from Prehistory to the Present* (New York, 1988), 1:259.
11. Quoted in John A. Phillips, *Eve: The History of an Idea* (New York, 1984), p. 105.

SUGGESTIONS FOR FURTHER READING

Basic surveys of the Reformation period include H. J. Grimm, *The Reformation Era, 1500–1650*, 2d ed. (New York, 1973); D. L. Jensen, *Reformation Europe* (Lexington, Mass., 1981); G. R. Elton, *Reformation Europe, 1517–1559* (Cleveland, 1963); and E. Cameron, *The European Reformation* (New York, 1991). L. W. Spitz, *The Protestant Reformation, 1517–1559* (New York, 1985), is a sound and up-to-date history. The significance of the Protestant Reformation is examined in S. Ozment, *Protestants: The Birth of a Revolution* (New York, 1992). A brief but very useful introduction to the theology of the Reformation can be found in A. McGrath, *Reformation Thought: An Introduction*, 2d ed. (Oxford, 1993).

The development of humanism outside Italy is examined in C. G. Nauert, Jr., *Humanism and the Culture of Renaissance Europe* (Cambridge, 1995). The best general biography of Erasmus is still R. Bainton, *Erasmus of Christendom* (New York, 1969), although the shorter works by J. K. Sowards, *Desiderius Erasmus* (Boston, 1975); and J. McConica, *Erasmus* (Oxford, 1991), are also good. On religious conditions in Europe on the eve of the Reformation, see T. N. Tentler, *Sin and Confession on the Eve of the Reformation* (Princeton, N.J., 1977).

The Reformation in Germany can be examined in H. Holborn, *A History of Modern Germany: The Reformation* (New York, 1959), still an outstanding survey of the entire Reformation period in Germany; and J. Lortz, *The Reformation in Germany*, trans. R. Walls, 2 vols. (New York, 1968), a detailed Catholic account. The classic account of Martin Luther's life is R. Bainton, *Here I Stand: A Life of Martin Luther* (New York and Nashville, 1950). More recent works include H. A. Oberman, *Luther* (New York, 1992); W. von Loewenich, *Martin Luther: The Man and His Work* (Minneapolis, 1986); J. M. Kittelson, *Luther the Reformer: The Story of the Man and His Career* (Minneapolis, 1986); and H. G. Haile, *Luther: An Experiment in Biography* (Garden City, N.Y., 1980). An interesting psychoanalytical approach to Luther can be found in E. H. Erikson, *Young Man Luther: A Study in Psychoanalysis and History* (New York,

1962). On the Peasants' War, see especially P. Blickle, *The Revolution of 1525: The German Peasants' War from a New Perspective* (Baltimore, Md., 1981). The spread of Luther's ideas in Germany can be examined in M. Hannemann, *The Diffusion of the Reformation in Southwestern Germany, 1518–1534* (Chicago, 1975); B. Moeller, *Imperial Cities and the Reformation* (Durham, N.C., 1982); S. Ozment, *The Reformation in the Cities* (New Haven, Conn., 1975); and G. Strauss, *Nuremberg in the Sixteenth Century* (Bloomington, Ind., 1978).

The best account of Ulrich Zwingli is G. T. Potter, *Zwingli* (Cambridge, 1976). The most comprehensive account of the various groups and individuals who are called Anabaptists is G. H. Williams, *The Radical Reformation* (Philadelphia, 1962). Other valuable studies include C. P. Clasen, *Anabaptism: A Social History, 1525–1618* (Ithaca, N.Y., 1972); and M. Mullett, *Radical Religious Movements in Early Modern Europe* (London, 1980).

Two worthwhile surveys of the English Reformation are A. G. Dickens, *The English Reformation* (New York, 1964); and G. R. Elton, *Reform and Reformation: England, 1509–1558* (Cambridge, Mass., 1977). Other specialized works on the period include the controversial classic by G. R. Elton, *The Tudor Revolution in Government*, 2d ed. (Cambridge, 1973); and D. Knowles, *Bare Ruined Choirs: The Dissolution of the English Monasteries* (New York, 1976). For a good biography of Calvin, see the recent work by W. J. Bouwsma, *John Calvin* (New York, 1988). The best account of Calvin's work in the city of Geneva is W. Monter, *Calvin's Geneva* (New York, 1967).

The best overall account of the impact of the Reformation on the family is S. Ozment, *When Fathers Ruled: Family Life in Reformation Europe* (Cambridge, Mass., 1983). M. E. Wiesner's *Working Women in Renaissance Germany* (New Brunswick, N.J., 1986), covers primarily the sixteenth century. Also of value is R. Bainton, *Women of the Reformation in Germany and Italy* (Minneapolis, 1971).

A good introduction to the Catholic Reformation can be found in the beautifully illustrated brief study by

A. G. Dickens, *The Counter Reformation* (New York, 1969). Also valuable is M. R. O'Connell, *The Counter Reformation, 1559–1610* (New York, 1974). The work by J. Brodrick, *The Origin of the Jesuits* (Garden City, N.Y., 1960) offers a clear discussion of the founding of the Je-

suits. On Loyola, see P. Caravan, *Ignatius Loyola, A Biography of the Founder of the Jesuits* (San Francisco, 1990). The most detailed study of the Council of Trent is H. Jedin, *History of the Council of Trent*, trans. E. Graf, 2 vols. (London, 1957–61).

CHAPTER
15

Discovery and Crisis in the Sixteenth and Seventeenth Centuries

By the middle of the sixteenth century, it was apparent that the religious passions of the Reformation era had brought an end to the religious unity of medieval Europe. The religious division between Catholics and Protestants was instrumental in beginning a series of wars that dominated much of European history between 1560 and 1650. The struggles fought in Germany at the beginning of the seventeenth century (known as the Thirty Years' War) were especially brutal and devastating. When the Catholic general Johann Tilly captured Neubrandenburg, his forces massacred the 3,000 defenders. A month later, the army of the Protestant leader Gustavus Adolphus retaliated by slaughtering the entire garrison of 2,000 men at Frankfurt-an-der-Oder. Noncombatants suffered as well, as is evident from the contemporary description by Otto von Guericke of the sack of Magdeburg. Once the city had been captured, Tilly's forces were let loose: "Then there was nothing but beating and burning, plundering, torture, and murder." All the buildings were looted of anything valuable, and then the city was "given over to the flames, and thousands of innocent men, women, and children, in the midst of a horrible noise of heartrending shrieks and cries, were tortured and put to death in so cruel and shameful a manner that no words would suffice to describe." Thus, "in a single day this noble and famous city, the pride of the whole country, went up in fire and smoke, and the remnant of its citizens, with their wives and children, were taken prisoners and driven away by the enemy."

The wars, in turn, worsened the economic and social crises that were besetting Europe. Wars, rebellions and constitutional crises, economic depression, social disintegration, a witchcraft craze, and demographic crisis all afflicted Europe and have led some historians to speak of the ninety years between 1560 and 1650 as an age of crisis in European life.

Periods of crisis, however, are frequently ages of opportunities, and nowhere is that more apparent than in the geographical discoveries that made this an era of European expansion into new worlds. Although the dis-

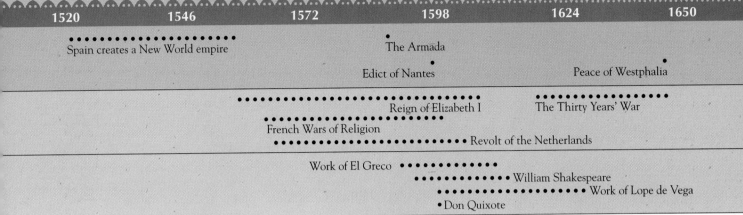

1520   1546   1572   1598   1624   1650

Spain creates a New World empire

The Armada

Edict of Nantes

Peace of Westphalia

Reign of Elizabeth I

The Thirty Years' War

French Wars of Religion

Revolt of the Netherlands

Work of El Greco

William Shakespeare

Work of Lope de Vega

Don Quixote

covery of new territories began before the sixteenth century, it was not until the sixteenth and seventeenth centuries that Europeans began to comprehend the significance of their discoveries and to exploit them for their material gain.

An Age of Discovery and Expansion

Nowhere has the dynamic and even ruthless energy of Western civilization been more apparent than in its expansion into the rest of the world. By the sixteenth century, the Atlantic seaboard had become the center of a commercial activity that raised Portugal and Spain and later the Dutch Republic, England, and France to prominence. The age of expansion was a crucial factor in the European transition from the agrarian economy of the Middle Ages to a commercial and industrial capitalistic system.

The Motives

Europeans had long been attracted to the Far East. In the Middle Ages, myths and legends of an exotic Far East of great riches and magic were widespread. The most famous medieval travelers to the east were the Polos of Venice. Niccolo and Maffeo, merchants from Venice, accompanied by Niccolo's son Marco, undertook the lengthy journey to the court of the great Mongol ruler Kublai Khan (1259–1294) in 1271. Marco traveled to Japan as well and did not return to Italy until 1295. An account of his experiences, the *Travels*, proved to be the most informa-

tive of all the descriptions of Asia by medieval European travelers. Others followed the Polos, but in the fourteenth century, the conquests of the Ottoman Turks and then the overthrow of the Mongols by the first of the Ming Chinese emperors halted Western traffic to the east. With the closing of the overland routes to the Far East, a number of people became interested in the possibility of reaching Asia by sea to gain access to eastern spices and other precious items.

An economic motive thus loomed large in Renaissance European expansion. There were high hopes of finding precious metals and new areas of trade, in particular, more direct sources for the spices of the east. Many European explorers and conquerors did not hesitate to express their desire for material gain. One Spanish conquistador explained that he and his kind went to the New World to "serve God and His Majesty, to give light to those who were in darkness, and to grow rich, as all men desire to do."[1]

This statement expresses another major reason for the overseas voyages—religious zeal. Hernan Cortés, the conqueror of Mexico, asked his Spanish rulers if it was not their duty to ensure that the native Mexicans "are introduced into and instructed in their holy Catholic faith."[2] Spiritual and secular affairs were closely intertwined in the sixteenth century. No doubt, grandeur and glory as well as plain intellectual curiosity and spirit of adventure also played some role in European expansion.

If "God, glory, and gold" were the motives, what made the voyages possible? First of all, the expansion of Europe was connected to the growth of centralized monarchies during the Renaissance. By the second half of the fifteenth century, European monarchies had increased both their authority and their resources and were in a position to turn their energies beyond their borders. At the same

♦ **Two-Masted Ocean-Going Ship.** Numerous overseas voyages to both North and South America were made in the first two decades of the sixteenth century. This detail from Pieter Brueghel's *Landscape with the Fall of Icarus* depicts a two-masted ocean-going ship of the type used in the voyages of the mid-sixteenth century.

time, by the end of the fifteenth century, European states had achieved a level of wealth and technology that enabled them to undertake a regular series of voyages beyond Europe. Cartography had developed to the point that Europeans possessed fairly accurate maps of the known world. Moreover, Europeans had developed remarkably seaworthy ships as well as navigational aids, such as the compass and astrolabe (an instrument used to determine the position of heavenly bodies).

The Development of a Portuguese Maritime Empire

Portugal took the lead in exploring the coast of Africa under the leadership of Prince Henry the Navigator (1394–1460), whose motives were a blend of seeking a Christian kingdom as an ally against the Muslims, ac-

quiring trade opportunities for Portugal, and extending Christianity. Beginning in 1419, Portuguese fleets began probing southward along the western coast of Africa. After Henry's death in 1460, there was a hiatus in Portuguese exploration until the 1470s and 1480s. Through regular expeditions, the Portuguese gradually crept down the African coast until Bartholomew Diaz finally rounded the Cape of Good Hope on the southern tip of Africa in 1487. Vasco da Gama surpassed that accomplishment by rounding the cape, skirting the eastern coast of Africa, and cutting across the Indian Ocean to the southwestern coast of India. At the port of Calicut, he took on a cargo of pepper and precious stones and then returned to Portugal, where he made a handsome profit on his valuable goods. Da Gama's successful voyage marked the beginning of an all-water route to India. By 1501, annual Portuguese fleets to India were making serious inroads into the Mediterranean trade of the Venetians and Turks.

Under the direction of officials known as viceroys, Portugal now created an overseas empire. Most important of the viceroys was Alfonso d'Albuquerque (c. 1462–1515), a tough nobleman who took the lead in establishing a ring of commercial-military bases centered at Goa, an island off the Malabar Coast of India. The Portuguese also reached beyond India by taking the island of Macao at the mouth of the Pearl River in China. The Portuguese empire remained a limited empire of enclaves or trading posts on the coasts of India and China. The Portuguese possessed neither the power nor the desire to colonize the Asian regions.

Why were the Portuguese so successful? Basically their success was a matter of guns and seamanship. Portuguese fleets, which began to arrive in Indian waters with regularity by the end of the sixteenth century, were heavily armed and were able not only to intimidate but also to inflict severe defeats if necessary on local naval and land forces. By no means did the Portuguese possess a monopoly on the use of firearms and explosives, but their effective use of naval technology, heavy guns, and tactics gave them a military superiority over lightly armed rivals that they were able to exploit until the arrival of other European forces—the English, Dutch, and French—in the seventeenth century.

Voyages to the New World

While the Portuguese sought access to the spice trade of the Indies by sailing eastward through the Indian Ocean, the Spanish attempted to reach the same destination by sailing westward across the Atlantic. Although the Spanish came to overseas discovery and exploration after the initial efforts of Henry the Navigator, their resources enabled them to establish an overseas empire that was far grander and quite different from the Portuguese enclaves.

An important figure in the history of Spanish exploration was an Italian, Cristoforo Colombo, more commonly known as Christopher Columbus (1451–1506). Knowledgeable Europeans were aware that the world was round, but had little understanding of its circumference or the extent of the continent of Asia. Convinced that the circumference of the earth was less than contemporaries believed and that Asia was larger than people thought, Columbus felt that Asia could be reached by sailing west instead of around Africa. Queen Isabella of Spain was finally persuaded to finance Columbus's exploratory expedition, which reached the Americas in October 1429, exploring the Bahamas, the coastline of Cuba, and the northern shores of Hispaniola (present-day Haiti and the Dominican Republic). Columbus believed that he had reached Asia, and in three subsequent voyages (1493, 1498, 1502), he sought in vain to find a route through the outer lands to the Asian mainland. In his four voyages, Columbus reached all the major islands of the Caribbean and the mainland of Central America.

Although Columbus clung to his belief until his death, other explorers soon realized that he had discovered a new frontier altogether. State-sponsored explorers joined the race to the New World. A Venetian seaman, John Cabot, explored the New England coastline of the Americas under a license from King Henry VII of England. The continent of South America was discovered accidentally by the Portuguese sea captain Pedro Cabral in 1500. Amerigo Vespucci, a Florentine, accompanied several voyages and wrote a series of letters describing the geography of the New World. The publication of these letters led to the use of the name "America" (after Amerigo) for the new lands.

The first two decades of the sixteenth century witnessed numerous overseas voyages that explored the eastern coasts of both North and South America. Perhaps the most dramatic of these expeditions was the journey of Ferdinand Magellan (1480–1521) in 1519. After passing through the Straits named after him at the bottom of South America, he sailed across the Pacific Ocean and reached the Philippines (named after King Philip of Spain by Magellan's crew) where he met his death at the hands of the natives. Although only one of his original fleet of five ships survived and returned to Spain, Magellan's name is still associated with the first known circumnavigation of the earth.

The newly discovered territories were called the New World, although they possessed flourishing civilizations populated by millions of people when the Europeans arrived. The Americas were, of course, new to the Europeans who quickly saw opportunities for conquest and exploitation. The Spanish, in particular, were interested because in 1494 the Treaty of Tordesillas had divided up the newly discovered world into separate Portuguese and Spanish spheres of influence. Hereafter the route east around the Cape of Good Hope was to be reserved for the Portuguese while the route across the Atlantic (except for the eastern hump of South America) was assigned to Spain.

◆ **Christopher Columbus.** Columbus was an Italian explorer who worked for the queen of Spain. He has become a symbol for two entirely different perspectives. To some, he was a great and heroic explorer who discovered the New World; to others, especially in Latin America, he was responsible for beginning a process of invasion that led to the destruction of an entire way of life. This painting by the Italian Sebastiano del Piombo in 1519 is the earliest known portrait of Columbus, but it was done thirteen years after his death and reveals as much about the painter's conception of Columbus as it does about the explorer himself.

The Spanish Empire

The Spanish conquistadors were hardy individuals motivated by a typical sixteenth-century blend of glory, greed, and religious crusading zeal. Although sanctioned by the Castilian crown, these groups were financed and outfitted privately, not by the government. Their superior weapons, organizational skills, and determination brought the conquistadors incredible success. They also benefitted from rivalries among the native peoples.

In 1519, a Spanish expedition under the command of Hernan Cortés landed at Veracruz, on the Gulf of Mexico. Marching to the city of Tenochtitlan at the head of a small contingent of troops (see the box on p. 309), Cortés received a friendly welcome from the Aztec monarch Moctezuma Xocoyotzin (often called simply Montezuma), who initially believed his visitor was a representative of Quetzacoatl, a godlike being who had departed from his homeland centuries before. But tensions soon erupted between the Spaniards and the Aztecs, provoked in part by demands by Cortés that the Aztecs denounce their native beliefs and accept Christianity. When the Spanish took Moctezuma hostage and began to destroy Aztec religious shrines, the local population revolted and drove the invaders from the city. With the assistance of other Indians, Cortés managed to fight his way back into the city. Meanwhile the Aztecs were beginning to suffer the first effects of the diseases brought by the Europeans,

Map 15.1 Discoveries and Possessions in the Fifteenth and Sixteenth Centuries.

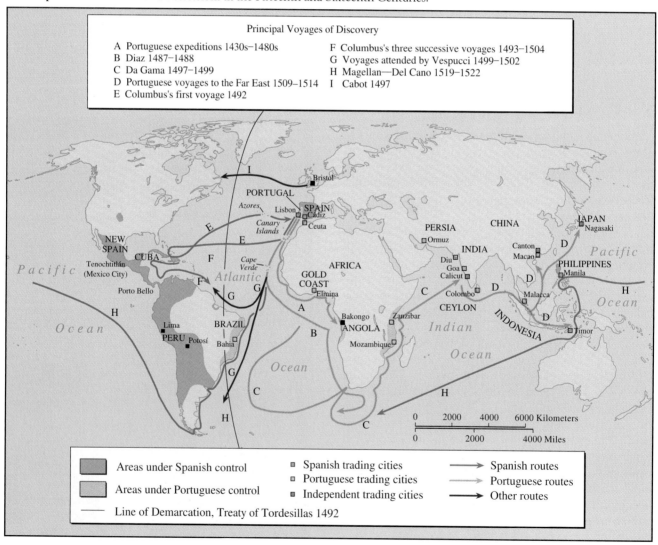

The Spanish Conquistador: Cortés and the Conquest of Mexico

Hernan Cortés was a minor Spanish nobleman who came to the New World in 1504 to seek his fortune. Contrary to his superior's orders, Cortés waged an independent campaign of conquest and overthrew the Aztec empire of Mexico (1519–1521). Cortés wrote a series of five reports to Emperor Charles V to justify his action. The second report includes a description of Tenochtitlán, the capital of the Aztec empire. The Spanish conquistador and his men were obviously impressed by this city, awesome in its architecture yet built by people who lacked European technology, such as wheeled vehicles and tools of hard metal.

Cortés's Description of an Aztec City

The great city Tenochtitlán is built in the midst of this salt lake, and it is two leagues from the heart of the city to any point on the mainland. Four causeways lead to it, all made by hand and some twelve feet wide. The city itself is as large as Seville or Córdoba. The principal streets are very broad and straight, the majority of them being of beaten earth, but a few and at least half the smaller thoroughfares are waterways along which they pass in their canoes. Moreover, even the principal streets have openings at regular distances so that the water can freely pass from one to another, and these openings which are very broad are spanned by great bridges of huge beams, very stoutly put together, so firm indeed that over many of them ten horsemen can ride at once. Seeing that if the natives intended any treachery against us they would have every opportunity from the way in which the city is built, for by removing the bridges from the entrances and exits they could leave us to die of hunger with no possibility of getting to the mainland, I immediately set to work as soon as we entered the city on the building of four brigs, and in a short space of time had them finished, so that we could ship three hundred men and the horses to the mainland whenever we so desired.

The city has many open squares in which markets are continuously held and the general business of buying and selling proceeds. One square in particular is twice as big as that of Salamanca and completely surrounded by arcades where there are daily more than sixty thousand folk buying and selling. Every kind of merchandise such as may be met with in every land is for sale there, whether of food and victuals, or ornaments of gold and silver, or lead, brass, copper, tin, precious stones, bones, shells, snails and feathers; limestone for building is likewise sold there, stone both rough and polished, bricks burnt and unburnt, wood of all kinds and in all stages of preparation. . . . There is a street of herb-sellers where there are all manner of roots and medicinal plants that are found in the land. There are houses as it were of apothecaries where they sell medicines made from these herbs, both for drinking and for use as ointments and salves. There are barbers' shops where you may have your hair washed and cut. There are other shops where you may obtain food and drink. . . .

Finally, to avoid prolixity in telling all the wonders of this city, I will simply say that the manner of living among the people is very similar to that in Spain, and considering that this is a barbarous nation shut off from a knowledge of the true God or communication with enlightened nations, one may well marvel at the orderliness and good government which is everywhere maintained.

The actual service of Moctezuma and those things which call for admiration by the greatness and state would take so long to describe that I assure your Majesty I do not know where to begin with any hope of ending. For as I have already said, what could there be more astonishing than that a barbarous monarch such as he should have reproductions made in gold, silver, precious stones, and feathers of all things to be found in his land, and so perfectly reproduced that there is no goldsmith or silversmith in the world who could better them, nor can one understand what instrument could have been used for fashioning the jewels; as for the featherwork its like is not to be seen in either wax or embroidery; it is so marvelously delicate.

which would eventually wipe out the majority of the local population. In a climactic battle, the Aztecs were finally vanquished. Within months, their magnificent city and its temples, believed by the conquerors to be the work of Satan, had been destroyed, and within three years, the mighty Aztec empire on mainland Mexico was no more.

Between 1531 and 1550, the Spanish gained control of northern Mexico.

The Inca empire high in the Peruvian Andes was still in existence when the first Spanish expeditions arrived in the area. The leader of the Spanish invaders, Francisco Pizarro, was accompanied by only a few hundred companions, but like Cortés he possessed steel weapons, gunpowder, and horses, none of which were familiar to his hosts. In the meantime, internal factionalism, combined with the onset of contagious diseases spread unknowingly by the Europeans, had weakened the ruling elite, and the empire fell rapidly to the Spanish forces in 1532. The last Inca ruler was tried by the Spaniards and executed. Although it took another three decades before the western part of Latin America was brought under Spanish control (the Portuguese took over Brazil), already by 1535, the Spanish had created a system of colonial administration that made the New World an extension of the old.

THE ADMINISTRATION OF THE SPANISH EMPIRE IN THE NEW WORLD

Spanish policy toward the Indians of the New World was a combination of confusion, misguided paternalism, and cruel exploitation. While the conquistadors made decisions based on expediency and their own interests, Queen Isabella declared the Indians (literally, "Indios") to be subjects of Castile and instituted the Spanish *encomienda*, a system that permitted the conquering Spaniards to collect tribute from the natives and use them as laborers. In return, the holders of an encomienda were supposed to protect the Indians, pay them wages, and supervise their spiritual needs. Three thousand miles from Spain, Spanish settlers largely ignored their government and brutally used the Indians to pursue their own economic interests. Indians were put to work on plantations and in the lucrative gold and silver mines. Forced labor, starvation, and especially disease took a fearful toll of Indian lives. With little or no natural resistance to European diseases, the Indians of America were ravaged by smallpox, measles, and typhus. These diseases came with the explorers and conquistadors. A reasonable guess is that at least half of the natives died of European diseases. On Hispaniola alone, out of an initial population of 100,000 natives when Columbus arrived in 1493, only 300 Indians survived by 1570.

In the New World, the Spanish developed an administrative system based on viceroys. Spanish possessions were initially divided into two major administrative units: New Spain (Mexico, Central America, and the Caribbean islands) with its center in Mexico City, and Peru (western South America), governed by a viceroy in Lima. Each viceroy served as the king's chief civil and military officer and was aided by advisory groups called *audiencias*, which also functioned as supreme judicial bodies.

By papal agreement, the Catholic monarchs of Spain were given extensive rights over ecclesiastical affairs in the New World. They could nominate church officials, build churches, collect fees, and supervise the affairs of the various religious orders who sought to Christianize the heathen. Catholic monks had remarkable success in converting and baptizing hundreds of thousands of Indians in the early years of the conquests. Soon after the missionaries came the establishment of dioceses, parishes, schools, and hospitals—all the trappings of a European society.

The Impact of European Expansion

The arrival of the Europeans had an enormous impact on both the conquerors and the conquered. The native American civilizations, which had their own unique qualities and a degree of sophistication rarely appreciated by the conquerors, were virtually destroyed, while the native populations were ravaged by diseases inadvertently introduced by the Europeans. Ancient social and political structures were ripped up and replaced by European institutions, religion, language, and culture.

European expansion also affected the conquerors, perhaps most notably in the economic arena. Wherever they went in the New World, Europeans sought to find sources of gold and silver. One Aztec commented that the Spanish conquerors "longed and lusted for gold. Their bodies swelled with greed, and their hunger was ravenous; they hungered like pigs for that gold."[3] Rich silver deposits were found and exploited in Mexico and southern Peru (modern Bolivia). When the mines at Potosí in Peru were opened in 1545, the value of precious metals imported into Europe quadrupled. It has been estimated that between 1503 and 1650 sixteen million kilograms (over thirty-five million pounds) of silver and 185,000 kilograms (407,000 pounds) of gold entered the port of Seville and helped to create a price revolution that affected the Spanish economy.

But gold and silver were only two of the products sent to Europe from the New World. Into Seville flowed sugar, dyes, cotton, vanilla, and hides from livestock raised on the grass-covered plains of South America. New agricultural products such as potatoes, coffee, corn, and tobacco were also imported. Because of its trading posts in Asia, Portugal soon challenged the Italian states as the chief entry point of the eastern trade in spices, jewels, silks, carpets, ivory, leather, and perfumes, although the Venetians clung tenaciously to the spice trade until they lost out to the Dutch in the seventeenth century. Economic historians believe that the increase in the volume and area of European trade as well as the rise in fluid capital due to this expansion were crucial factors in producing a new era of commercial capitalism that represented the first step toward the world economy that has characterized the modern historical era.

European expansion, which was in part a product of European rivalries, also deepened those rivalries and increased the tensions among European states. Bitter conflicts arose over the cargoes coming from the New World and Asia. Although the Spanish and Portuguese entered the competition first, the Dutch, French, and English soon became involved on a large scale and by the seventeenth century were challenging the Portuguese and Spanish monopolies.

*P*olitics and the Wars of Religion in the Sixteenth Century

The so-called wars of religion were a product of Reformation ideologies that allowed little room for compromise or toleration of differing opinions. By the middle of the sixteenth century, Calvinism and Catholicism had become highly militant religions dedicated to spreading the word of God as they interpreted it. Although this religious struggle for the minds and hearts of Europeans is at the heart of the religious wars of the sixteenth century, economic, social, and political forces also played an important role in these conflicts. Of the sixteenth-century religious wars, none were more momentous or shattering than the French civil wars known as the French Wars of Religion.

The French Wars of Religion (1562–1598)

Religion was at the heart of the French civil wars of the sixteenth century. The growth of Calvinism led to persecution by the French kings but did little to stop the spread of Calvinism. Huguenots (as the French Calvinists were called) came from all layers of society: artisans and shopkeepers hurt by rising prices and a rigid guild system; merchants and lawyers in provincial towns whose local privileges were tenuous; and members of the nobility. Possibly 40 to 50 percent of the French nobility became Huguenots, including the house of Bourbon, which stood next to the Valois dynasty in the royal line of succession and ruled the southern French kingdom of Navarre. The conversion of so many nobles made the Huguenots a potentially dangerous political threat to monarchical power. Though the Calvinists constituted only about 7 percent of the population, they were a dedicated, determined, and well-organized minority.

The Calvinist minority was greatly outnumbered by the Catholic majority. The Valois monarchy was staunchly

Catholic, and its control of the Catholic church gave it little incentive to look favorably on Protestantism. At the same time, an extreme Catholic party—known as the ultra-Catholics—favored strict opposition to the Huguenots and were led by the Guise family. Possessing the loyalty of Paris and large sections of northern and northwestern France, they could recruit and pay for large armies and received support abroad from the papacy and Jesuits who favored their uncompromising Catholic position.

The religious issue was not the only factor that contributed to the French civil wars. Towns and provinces, which had long resisted the growing power of monarchical centralization, were only too willing to join a revolt against the monarchy. This was also true of the nobility, and the fact that so many of them were Calvinists created an important base of opposition to the crown. The French Wars of Religion, then, constituted a major constitutional crisis for France and temporarily halted the development of the French centralized territorial state. The claim of the ruling dynasty of the state to a person's loyalties was temporarily superseded by loyalty to one's religious belief.

The wars erupted in 1562 when the powerful duke of Guise massacred a peaceful congregation of Huguenots at Vassy. For thirty years, battles raged in France between Catholic and Calvinist parties, who obviously considered the unity of France less important than religious truth. But there also emerged in France a group of politiques who placed politics before religion and believed that no religious truth was worth the ravages of civil war. The politiques ultimately prevailed, but not until both sides were exhausted by bloodshed.

Finally, in 1589, Henry of Navarre, the political leader of the Huguenots and a member of the Bourbon dynasty, succeeded to the throne as Henry IV (1589–1610). Realizing however, that he would never be accepted by Catholic France, Henry took the logical way out and converted to Catholicism. With his coronation in 1594, the Wars of Religion finally came to an end. It remained only to solve the religious problem, which was accomplished by the Edict of Nantes in 1598. Although Catholicism was acknowledged as the official religion of France, the Huguenots were guaranteed the right to worship in selected places in every district and were allowed to retain a number of fortified towns for their protection. In addition, the Huguenots were allowed to enjoy all political privileges, including the holding of public offices.

Philip II and the Cause of Militant Catholicism

The greatest advocate of militant Catholicism in the second half of the sixteenth century was King Philip II of Spain (1556–1598), the son and heir of Charles V.

Philip's reign ushered in an age of Spanish greatness, both politically and culturally. The first major goal of Philip II was to consolidate and secure the lands he had inherited from his father. These included Spain, the Netherlands, and the possessions in Italy and the New World. For Philip this meant a strict conformity to Catholicism, enforced by aggressive use of the Spanish Inquisition, and the establishment of strong, monarchical authority. The latter was not an easy task because Philip had inherited a governmental structure in which each of the various states and territories of his empire stood in an individual relationship to the king. Philip did manage, however, to expand royal power by making the monarchy less dependent on the traditional landed aristocracy, especially in the higher echelons of government.

Crucial to an understanding of Philip II is the importance of Catholicism to the Spanish people and their ruler. Driven by a heritage of crusading fervor, the Spanish had little difficulty seeing themselves as a nation of people divinely chosen to save Catholic Christianity from the Protestant heretics. Philip II, the "Most Catholic King," became the champion of Catholicism

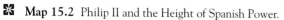 **Map 15.2** Philip II and the Height of Spanish Power.

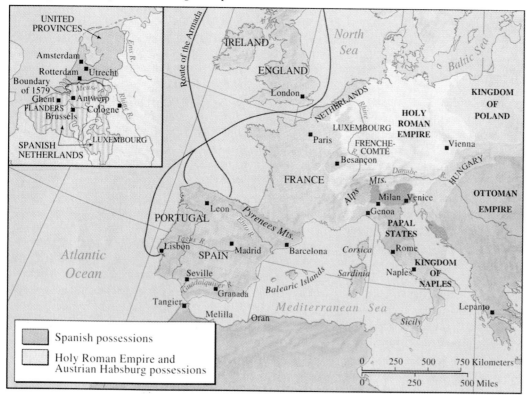

throughout Europe, a role that led to spectacular victories and equally spectacular defeats for the Spanish king. Spain's leadership of a Holy League against Turkish encroachments in the Mediterranean resulted in a stunning victory over the Turkish fleet in the Battle of Lepanto in 1571. But Philip's attempt to crush the revolt in the Netherlands and his tortured policy with the English Queen Elizabeth led to his greatest misfortunes.

The Revolt of the Netherlands

One of the richest parts of Philip's empire, the Spanish Netherlands was of great importance to the "Most Catholic King." Philip's attempt to strengthen his control in the Netherlands, which consisted of seventeen provinces (modern Netherlands, Belgium, and Luxembourg), soon led to a revolt. The nobles, who stood to lose the most politically if their jealously guarded privileges and freedoms were weakened, strongly opposed Philip's efforts. Resentment against Philip was also aroused by the collection of taxes when the residents of the Netherlands realized that these revenues were being used for Spanish interests. Finally, religion became a major catalyst for rebellion when Philip attempted to crush Calvinism. Violence erupted in 1566, when Calvinists—especially nobles—began to destroy statues and stained glass windows in Catholic churches. Philip responded by sending the duke of Alva with 10,000 veteran Spanish and Italian troops to crush the rebellion.

But the revolt became organized, especially in the seven northern provinces where the Dutch, under the leadership of William of Nassau, the prince of Orange, offered growing resistance. The struggle dragged on for decades until 1609, when a twelve-year truce ended the war, virtually recognizing the independence of the northern provinces. These seven northern provinces, which began to call themselves the United Provinces of the Netherlands in 1581, soon emerged as the Dutch Republic, although the Spanish did not formally recognize them as independent until 1648. The ten southern provinces remained a Spanish possession.

The England of Elizabeth

After the death of Queen Mary in 1558, her half-sister Elizabeth, the daughter of Henry VIII and Anne Boleyn, ascended the throne of England. During Elizabeth's reign, England rose to prominence as the relatively small island

✦ **Procession of Queen Elizabeth I.** Intelligent and learned, Elizabeth Tudor was familiar with Latin and Greek and spoke several European languages. Served by able administrators, Elizabeth ruled for nearly forty-five years and generally avoided open military action against any major power. Her participation in the revolt of the Netherlands, however, brought England into conflict with Spain. This picture painted near the end of her reign shows the queen on a ceremonial procession.

kingdom became the leader of the Protestant nations of Europe, laid the foundations for a world empire, and experienced a cultural renaissance.

Intelligent and self-confident, Elizabeth moved quickly to solve the difficult religious problem she inherited from her half-sister, Queen Mary, who had become extremely unpopular when she tried to return England to the Catholic fold. Elizabeth's religious policy was based on moderation and compromise. The Catholic legislation of Mary's reign was repealed, and a new Act of Supremacy designated Elizabeth as "the only supreme governor of this realm, as well in all spiritual or ecclesiastical things or causes, as temporal." An Act of Uniformity restored the church service of the Book of Common Prayer from the reign of Edward VI with some revisions to make it more acceptable to Catholics. Elizabeth's religious settlement was basically Protestant but a moderate Protestantism that avoided subtle distinctions and extremes. The new religious settlement worked, at least to the extent that it smothered religious differences in England in the second half of the sixteenth century.

Elizabeth's foreign policy was also dictated by caution, moderation, and expediency. Fearful of other countries' motives, Elizabeth realized that war could be disastrous for her island kingdom and her own rule. Unofficially, however, she encouraged English seamen to raid Spanish ships and colonies. Francis Drake was especially adept at plundering Spanish fleets loaded with gold and silver from Spain's New World empire. While encouraging English piracy and providing clandestine aid to French Huguenots and Dutch Calvinists to weaken France and Spain, Elizabeth pretended complete aloofness and avoided alliances that would force her into war with any major power.

Gradually, however, Elizabeth was drawn into conflict with Spain. After years of resisting the idea of invading England as too impractical, Philip II of Spain was finally persuaded to do so by advisors who assured him that the people of England would rise against their queen when the Spaniards arrived. Moreover, Philip was easily convinced that the revolt in the Netherlands would never be crushed as long as England provided support for it. In any case, a successful invasion of England would mean the overthrow of heresy and the return of England to Catholicism, surely an act in accordance with the will of God. Accordingly Philip ordered preparations for an Armada to spearhead the invasion of England in 1588.

The Armada proved to be a disaster. The Spanish fleet that finally set sail had neither the ships nor the manpower that Philip had planned to send. A conversation between a papal emissary and an officer of the Spanish fleet before the Armada departed reveals the fundamental flaw:

"And if you meet the English armada in the Channel, do you expect to win the battle?"
"Of course," replied the Spaniard.
"How can you be so sure?" [asked the emissary]
"It's very simple. It is well known that we fight in God's cause. So, when we meet the English, God will surely arrange matters so that we can grapple and board them, either by sending some strange streak of weather, or, more likely, just by depriving the English of their wits. If we can come to close quarters, Spanish valor and Spanish steel (and the great masses of soldiers we shall have on board) will make our victory certain. But unless God helps us by a miracle the English, who have faster and handier ships than ours, and many more long-range guns, and who know their advantage just as well as we do, will never close with us at all, but stand aloof and knock us to pieces with their culverins, without our being able to do them any serious hurt. So," concluded the captain, and one fancies a grim smile, "we are sailing against England in the confident hope of a miracle."[4]

The hoped-for miracle never materialized. The Spanish fleet, battered by a number of encounters with the English, sailed back to Spain by a northward route around Scotland and Ireland where it was further battered by storms. Although the English and Spanish would continue their war for another sixteen years, the defeat of the Armada guaranteed for the time being that England would remain a Protestant country. Although Spain made up for its losses within a year and a half, the defeat was a psychological blow to the Spaniards.

Economic and Social Crises

The period of European history from 1560 to 1650 witnessed severe economic and social crises as well as political upheaval. An inflation-fueled prosperity of the sixteenth century showed signs of slackening by the beginning of the seventeenth century. Economic contraction began to be evident in some parts of Europe by the 1620s. In the 1630s and 1640s, as imports of silver from the Americas declined, economic recession intensified, especially in the Mediterranean area. Once the industrial and financial center of Europe in the age of the Renaissance, Italy was now becoming an economic backwater. Spain's economy was also seriously failing by the decade of the 1640s.

Population trends of the sixteenth and seventeenth centuries also reveal Europe's worsening conditions. The sixteenth century was a period of expanding population, possibly related to a warmer climate and increased food supplies. It has been estimated that the population of Europe increased from 60 million in 1500 to 85 million by 1600, the first major recovery of European population since the devastation of the Black Death in the mid-fourteenth century. However, records also indicate a leveling off of the population by 1620 and even a decline by 1650, especially in central and southern Europe. Only the Dutch, English, and to a lesser degree, the French grew in number in the first half of the seventeenth century. Europe's longtime adversaries—war, famine, and plague—continued to affect population levels. Europe's entry into another "little ice age" after the middle of the sixteenth century, when average temperatures fell and glaciers even engulfed small Alpine villages, affected harvests and gave rise to famines. Europe's problems created social tensions that were also evident in the witchcraft craze.

The Witchcraft Craze

In the midst of the turmoil created by wars, rebellions, and economic and social uncertainties, yet another source of disorder arose as hysteria over witchcraft affected the lives of many Europeans in the sixteenth and seventeenth centuries. Witchcraft trials were prevalent in England, Scotland, Switzerland, Germany, some parts of France and the Low Countries, and even New England in America. As is evident from this list, the witchcraft craze affected both Catholic and Protestant countries.

Witchcraft was not a new phenomenon in the sixteenth and seventeenth centuries. Its practice had been part of traditional village culture for centuries, but it came to be viewed as both sinister and dangerous when the medieval church began to connect witches to the activities of the devil, thereby transforming witchcraft into a heresy that had to be extirpated. After the creation of the Inquisition in the thirteenth century, people were accused of a variety of witchcraft practices and, following the Biblical injunction, "Thou shalt not suffer a witch to live," were turned over to secular authorities for burning at the stake or hanging (in England).

What distinguished witchcraft in the sixteenth and seventeenth centuries from these previous developments was the increased number of trials and executions of presumed witches. Perhaps more than 100,000 people were prosecuted throughout Europe on charges of witchcraft. As more and more people were brought to trial, the fear of witches as well as the fear of being accused of witchcraft escalated to frightening proportions. Approximately 25 percent of the villages in the English county of Essex,

for example, had at least one witchcraft trial in the sixteenth and seventeenth centuries. Although larger cities were affected first, the trials also spread to smaller towns and rural areas as the hysteria persisted well into the seventeenth century (see the box on p. 316).

Although even city officeholders were not immune to persecution, in most witchcraft trials women of the lower classes were more likely to be accused of witchcraft. Indeed, where lists are given, those mentioned most often are milkmaids, peasant women, and servant girls. In the witchcraft trials of the sixteenth and seventeenth centuries, 80 percent of those accused were women, many of them over fifty years old. Moreover, almost all victims belonged to the lower classes, the poor and propertyless.

The accused witches usually confessed to a number of practices. Many of their confessions were extracted by torture, greatly adding to the number and intensity of activities mentioned. But even when people confessed voluntarily, certain practices stand out. Many said that they had sworn allegiance to the devil and attended sabbats or nocturnal gatherings where they feasted, danced, and even copulated with the devil in sexual orgies. More common, however, were admissions of using evil incantations and special ointments and powders to wreak havoc on neighbors by killing their livestock, injuring their children, or raising storms to destroy their crops.

A number of contributing factors have been suggested to explain why the witchcraft craze became so widespread in the sixteenth and seventeenth centuries. Religious uncertainties clearly played some part. Many witchcraft trials occurred in areas where Protestantism had been recently victorious or in regions, such as southwestern Germany, where Protestant–Catholic controversies still raged. As religious passions became inflamed, accusations of being in league with the devil became common on both sides. Recently, however, historians have emphasized the importance of social conditions, especially the problems of a society in turmoil, in explaining the witchcraft hysteria. At a time when the old communal values that stressed working together for the good of the community were disintegrating, property owners became more fearful of the growing numbers of poor among them and transformed them psychologically into agents of the devil. Old women were particularly susceptible to suspicion. Many of them, no longer the recipients of the local charity found in traditional society, may even have tried to survive by selling herbs, potions, or secret remedies for healing. When problems arose—and there were many in this crisis-laden period—these same people were the most likely scapegoats at hand.

❧ A Witchcraft Trial in France ❧

Persecutions for witchcraft reached their high point in the sixteenth and seventeenth centuries when tens of thousands of people were brought to trial. In this excerpt from the minutes of a trial in France in 1652, we can see why the accused witch stood little chance of exonerating herself.

The Trial of Suzanne Gaudry

28 May, 1652. . . . Interrogation of Suzanne Gaudry, prisoner at the court of Rieux. . . . [During interrogations on May 28 and May 29, the prisoner confessed to a number of activities involving the devil.]

Deliberation of the Court—June 3, 1652

The undersigned advocates of the Court have seen these interrogations and answers. They say that the aformentioned Suzanne Gaudry confesses that she is a witch, that she had given herself to the devil, that she had renounced God, Lent, and baptism, that she has been marked on the shoulder, that she has cohabited with the devil and that she has been to the dances, confessing only to have cast a spell upon and caused to die a beast of Philippe Cornié. . . .

Third Interrogation, June 27

The prisoner being led into the chamber, she was examined to know if things were not as she had said and confessed at the beginning of her imprisonment.

—Answers no, and that what she has said was done so by force.

Pressed to say the truth, that otherwise she would be subjected to torture, having pointed out to her that her aunt was burned for this same subject.

—Answers that she is not a witch. . . .

She was placed in the hands of the officer in charge of torture, throwing herself on her knees, struggling to cry, uttering several exclamations, without being able, nevertheless, to shed a tear. Saying at every moment that she is not a witch.

The Torture

On this same day, being at the place of torture.

This prisoner, before being strapped down, was admonished to maintain herself in her first confessions and to renounce her lover.

—Says that she denies everything she has said, and that she has no lover. Feeling herself being strapped down, says that she is not a witch, while struggling to cry. . . . and upon being asked why she confessed to being one, said that she was forced to say it.

Told that she was not forced, that on the contrary she declared herself to be a witch without any threat.

—Says that she confessed it and that she is not a witch, and being a little stretched [on the rack] screams ceaselessly that she is not a witch. . . .

Asked if she did not confess that she had been a witch for twenty-six years.

—Says that she said it, that she retracts it, crying that she is not a witch.

Asked if she did not make Philippe Cornié's horse die, as she confessed.

—Answers no, crying Jesus-Maria, that she is not a witch.

The mark having been probed by the officer, in the presence of Doctor Bouchain, it was adjudged by the aforesaid doctor and officer truly to be the mark of the devil.

Being more tightly stretched upon the torture-rack, urged to maintain her confessions.

—Said that it was true that she is a witch and that she would maintain what she had said.

Asked how long she has been in subjugation to the devil.

—Answers that it was twenty years ago that the devil appeared to her, being in her lodgings in the form of a man dressed in a little cow-hide and black breeches. . . .

Verdict

July 9, 1652. In the light of the interrogations, answers and investigations made into the charge against Suzanne Gaudry, . . . seeing by her own confessions that she is said to have made a pact with the devil, received the mark from him, . . . and that following this, she had renounced God, Lent, and baptism and had let herself be known carnally by him, in which she received satisfaction. Also, seeing that she is said to have been a part of nocturnal carols and dances.

For expiation of which the advice of the undersigned is that the office of Rieux can legitimately condemn the aforesaid Suzanne Gaudry to death, tying her to a gallows, and strangling her to death, then burning her body and burying it here in the environs of the woods.

✦ **The Persecution of Witches.** Hysteria over witchcraft affected the daily lives of many Europeans in the sixteenth and seventeenth centuries. This picture by Frans Francken the Young, painted in 1607, shows a number of activities commonly attributed to witches. In the center, several witches are casting spells with their magic books and instruments while at the top, a witch on a post prepares to fly off on her broomstick.

That women should be the chief victims of witchcraft trials was hardly accidental. Virtually all of the new witchcraft treatises written in the sixteenth and seventeenth centuries argued that there was a direct link between witchcraft and women. Nicholas Rémy, a witchcraft judge in France in the 1590s, found it "not unreasonable that this scum of humanity, i.e., witches, should be drawn chiefly from the feminine sex." To another judge, it came as no surprise that witches would confess to sexual experiences with Satan because: "The Devil uses them so, because he knows that women love carnal pleasures, and he means to bind them to his allegiance by such agreeable provocations."[5] Of course, not only witch hunters held such low estimates of women. Most theologians, lawyers, and philosophers in early modern Europe maintained a belief in the natural inferiority of women, making it plausible to them that they would be more susceptible to witchcraft.

By the mid-seventeenth century, the witchcraft hysteria began to subside. The destruction of the religious wars had at least forced people to accept a grudging toleration, causing religious passions to subside. Moreover, as governments began to stabilize after the period of crisis, fewer magistrates were willing to accept the unsettling and divisive conditions generated by the trials of witches. Finally, by the end of the seventeenth and beginning of the eighteenth centuries, more and more people were questioning altogether their old attitudes toward religion and found it especially contrary to reason to believe in the old view of a world haunted by evil spirits.

Seventeenth-Century Crises: War and Rebellions

Although many Europeans responded to the upheavals of the second half of the sixteenth century with a desire for peace and order, the first fifty years of the seventeenth century continued to be a period of crisis. A devastating war that affected much of Europe and rebellions seemingly everywhere protracted an atmosphere of disorder and violence.

The Thirty Years' War (1618–1648)

Religion, especially the struggle between a militant Catholicism and a militant Calvinism, certainly played an important role in the outbreak of the Thirty Years' War, often called the "last of the religious wars." As the war progressed, however, it became increasingly clear that secular, dynastic-nationalist considerations were far more important.

The Thirty Years' War began in 1618 in the Germanic lands of the Holy Roman Empire as a struggle between Catholic forces, led by the Habsburg Holy Roman Emperors and Protestant—primarily Calvinist—nobles in Bohemia who rebelled against Habsburg authority. What began as a struggle over religious issues soon became a wider conflict determined by political motivations as both minor and major European powers—Denmark, Sweden, France, and Spain—made the war a European-wide struggle. The conflict between the Bourbon dynasty of France and the Habsburg dynasties of Spain and the Holy Roman Empire for European leadership was an especially important factor. Nevertheless, most of the battles were fought on German soil, with devastating results for the German people (see the box on p. 319).

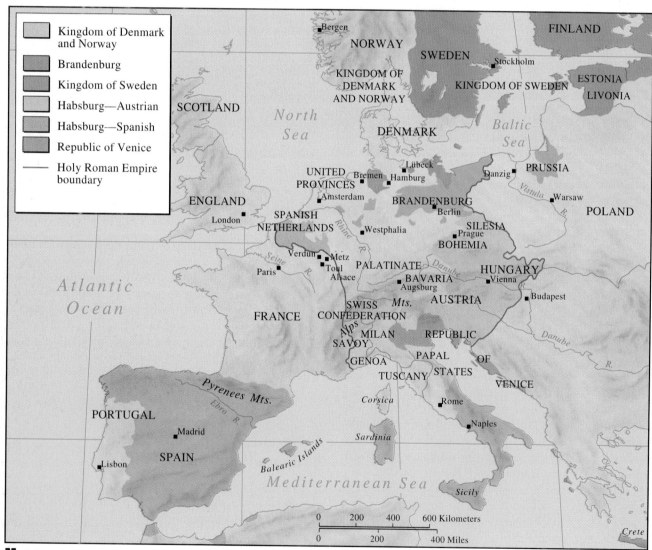

Map 15.3 The Thirty Years' War.

The Face of War in the Seventeenth Century

The Thirty Years' War was the most devastating war Europeans had experienced since the Hundred Year's War. Destruction was especially severe in Germany. We have a firsthand account of the face of war in Germany from a picaresque novel called Simplicius Simplicissimus, written by Jakob von Grimmelshausen. The author's experiences as a soldier in the Thirty Years' War gave his descriptions of the effect of the war on ordinary people a certain vividness and reality. This selection describes the fate of a peasant farm, an experience all too familiar to thousands of German peasants between 1618 and 1648.

Jakob von Grimmelshausen, Simplicius Simplicissimus

The first thing these horsemen did in the nice back rooms of the house was to put in their horses. Then everyone took up a special job, one having to do with death and destruction. Although some began butchering, heating water, and rendering lard, as if to prepare for a banquet, others raced through the house, ransacking upstairs and down; not even the privy chamber was safe, as if the golden fleece of Jason might be hidden there. Still others bundled up big packs of cloth, household goods, and clothes, as if they wanted to hold a rummage sale somewhere. What they did not intend to take along they broke and spoiled. Some ran their swords into the hay and straw, as if there hadn't' been hogs enough to stick. Some shook the feathers out of beds and put bacon slabs, hams, and other stuff in the ticking, as if they might sleep better on these. Others knocked down the hearth and broke the windows, as if announcing an everlasting summer. They flattened out copper and pewter dishes and baled the ruined goods. They burned up bedsteads, tables, chairs, and benches, though there were yards and yards of dry firewood outside the kitchen. Jars and crocks, pots and casseroles all were broken, either because they preferred their meat broiled or because they thought they'd eat only one meal with us. In the barn, the hired girl was handled so roughly that she was unable to walk away, I am ashamed to report. They stretched the hired man out flat on the ground, stuck a wooden wedge in his mouth to keep it open, and emptied a milk bucket full of stinking manure drippings down his throat; they called it a Swedish cocktail. He didn't relish it and made a very wry face. By this means they forced him to take a raiding party to some other place where they carried off men and cattle and brought them to our farm. Among these were my father, mother, and Ursula [sister].

Then they used thumbscrews, which they cleverly made out of their pistols, to torture the peasants, as if they wanted to burn witches. Though he had confessed to nothing as yet, they put one of the captured hayseeds in the bake-oven and lighted a fire in it. They put a rope around someone else's head and tightened it like a tourniquet until blood came out of his mouth, nose, and ears. In short, every soldier had his favorite method of making life miserable for peasants, and every peasant had his own misery. My father was, as I thought, particularly lucky because he confessed with a laugh what others were forced to say in pain and martyrdom. No doubt because he was the head of the household, he was shown special consideration; they put him close to a fire, tied him by his hands and legs, and rubbed damp salt on the bottoms of his feet. Our old nanny goat had to lick it off and this so tickled my knan [father] that he could have burst laughing. This seemed so clever and entertaining to me—I had never seen or heard my knan laugh so long—that I joined him in laughter, to keep him company or perhaps to cover up my ignorance. In the midst of such glee he told them the whereabouts of hidden treasure much richer in gold, pearls, and jewelry than might have been expected on a farm.

I can't say much about the captured wives, hired girls, and daughters because the soldiers didn't let me watch their doings. But I do remember hearing pitiful screams from various dark corners and I guess that my mother and our Ursula had it no better than the rest.

The war in Germany was officially ended by the Peace of Westphalia in 1648. What were the results of this "basically meaningless conflict," as one historian has called it? The Peace of Westphalia ensured that all German states, including the Calvinist ones, were free to determine their own religion. The major contenders gained new territories, and one of them, France, emerged as the dominant nation in Europe. The more than 300 states that made up the Holy Roman Empire were virtually recognized as independent states, because each received the power to conduct its own foreign policy; this brought an end to the Holy Roman Empire as a political entity and ensured German disunity for another 200 years. The Peace of Westphalia also made it clear that religion and politics were now separate worlds. The pope was completely ignored in all decisions at Westphalia, and political motives became the guiding forces in public affairs as religion moved closer to becoming primarily a matter of personal conviction and individual choice.

The economic and social effects of the Thirty Years' War on Germany are still debated. An older view pictured a ruined German economy and a decline in German population from 21 to 13 million between 1600 and 1650, but more recent opinions have estimated that Germany's population grew from 16 to 17 million while a redistribution of economic activity rather than an overall decline took place. Both views contain some truth. Some areas of Germany were completely devastated while others remained relatively untouched and even experienced economic growth. In any case, the Thirty Year's War was undoubtedly the most destructive conflict Europeans had yet experienced. Unfortunately, it was not the last.

Rebellions

Before, during, and after the Thirty Years' War, a series of rebellions and civil wars stemming from the discontent of both nobles and commoners rocked the domestic stability of many European governments. To strengthen their power, monarchs attempted to extend their authority at the expense of traditional powerful elements who resisted the rulers' efforts. At the same time, to fight their battles, governments increased taxes and created such hardships that common people also rose in opposition.

Between 1590 and 1640, peasant and lower-class revolts occurred in central and southern France, Austria, and Hungary. In the decades of the 1640s and 1650s, even greater unrest occurred. Portugal and Catalonia rebelled against the Spanish government in 1640. The common people in Naples and Sicily revolted against both the government and the landed nobility in 1647. Russia, too, was rocked by urban uprisings in 1641, 1645, and 1648. Nobles rebelled in France from 1648 to 1652 to halt the growth of royal power (see Chapter 16). The northern states of Sweden, Denmark, and Holland also were not immune from upheavals involving clergy, nobles, and mercantile groups. Even relatively stable Switzerland had a peasant rebellion in 1656. By far the most famous and wide-ranging struggle, however, was the civil war and rebellion in England, commonly known as the English Revolution (see Chapter 16).

Culture in a Turbulent World

Art and literature passed through two major stylistic stages between the Renaissance and 1650. These changes were closely linked to the religious, political, and intellectual developments of the period.

Art: Mannerism and the Baroque

The artistic Renaissance came to an end when a new movement called Mannerism emerged in Italy in the decades of the 1520s and 1530s. The age of the Reformation had brought a revival of religious values accompanied by much political turmoil. Especially in Italy, the worldly enthusiasm of the Renaissance gave way to anxiety, uncertainty, suffering, and a yearning for spiritual experience. Mannerism reflected this environment in its deliberate attempt to break down the High Renaissance principles of balance, harmony, and moderation. Italian Mannerist painters deliberately distorted the rules of proportion by portraying elongated figures that conveyed a sense of suffering and a strong emotional atmosphere filled with anxiety and confusion.

Mannerism spread from Italy to other parts of Europe and perhaps reached its apogee in the work of El Greco (1541–1614). Doménikos Theotocópoulos (called "the Greek"—El Greco) was from Crete, but after studying in Venice and Rome, he moved to Spain in the 1570s where he became a church painter in Toledo. El Greco's elongated figures, portrayed in unusual shades of yellow and green against an eerie background of turbulent grays, reflect well the artist's desire to create a world of intense emotion.

Mannerism was eventually replaced by a new movement—the Baroque—that dominated the artistic world for another century and a half. The Baroque began in Italy in the last quarter of the sixteenth century and spread to the rest of Europe. Baroque artists sought to harmonize the classical traditions of Renaissance art with the intense religious feelings fostered by the revival of religion in the Reformation. Although Protestants were also affected, the Baroque was most wholeheartedly embraced by the Catholic reform movement, as is evident at the Catholic courts, especially those of the Habsburgs in Madrid, Prague, Vienna, and Brussels. Eventually the Baroque style spread to all of Europe and Latin America.

In large part, Baroque art and architecture reflected the search for power that was characteristic of much of the seventeenth century. Baroque churches and palaces featured richly ornamented facades, sweeping staircases,

◆ **El Greco,** *Laocöon.* Mannerism reached one of its highest expressions in the work of El Greco. Born in Crete, trained in Venice and Rome, and settling finally in Spain, El Greco worked as a church painter in Toledo. Pictured here is his version of the *Laocöon,* a famous piece of Hellenistic sculpture that had been discovered in Rome in 1506. The elongated, contorted bodies project a world of suffering while the somber background scene of the city of Toledo adds a sense of terror and doom.

and an overall splendor that were meant to impress people. Kings and princes wanted other kings and princes as well as their subjects to be in awe of their power. The Catholic church, which commissioned many new churches, wanted people to see the triumphant power of the Catholic faith.

Baroque painting was known for its use of dramatic effects to heighten emotional intensity. This style was especially evident in the works of Peter Paul Rubens (1577–1640), a prolific artist and an important figure in the spread of the Baroque from Italy to other parts of Europe. In his artistic masterpieces, bodies in violent motion, heavily fleshed nudes, a dramatic use of light and shadow, and rich sensuous pigments converge to show intense emotions. The restless forms and constant movement blend together into a dynamic unity.

Perhaps the greatest figure of the Baroque was the Italian architect and sculptor Gian Lorenzo Bernini (1598–1680), who completed Saint Peter's basilica and designed the vast colonnade enclosing the piazza in front of it. Action, exuberance, profusion, and dramatic effects mark the work of Bernini in the interior of Saint Peter's,

◆   **Peter Paul Rubens, *The Landing of Marie de' Medici at Marseilles*.** Peter Paul Rubens played a key role in spreading the Baroque style from Italy to other parts of Europe. In *The Landing of Marie de' Medici at Marseilles*, Rubens made a dramatic use of light and color, bodies in motion, and luxurious nudes to heighten the emotional intensity of the scene. This was one of a cycle of twenty-one paintings dedicated to the queen mother of France.

where Bernini's *Throne of St. Peter* hovers in mid-air, held by the hands of the four great doctors of the Catholic church. Above the chair, rays of golden light drive a mass of clouds and angels toward the spectator.

A Golden Age of Literature: England and Spain

Periods of crisis often produce great writing, and so it was of this age, which was characterized by a golden age of theater. In both England and Spain, writing for the stage reached new heights between 1580 and 1640. The golden age of English literature is often called the Elizabethan Era because much of the English cultural flowering of the late sixteenth and early seventeenth centuries occurred during her reign. Elizabethan literature exhibits the exu-

berance and pride associated with English exploits under Queen Elizabeth (see the box on p. 323). Of all the forms of Elizabethan literature, none expressed the energy and intellectual versatility of the era better than drama. Of all the dramatists, none is more famous than William Shakespeare (1564–1614).

Shakespeare was the son of a prosperous glovemaker from Stratford-upon-Avon. When he appeared in London in 1592, Elizabethans were already addicted to the stage. By 1576, two professional theaters run by actors' companies were in existence. Elizabethan theater became a tremendously successful business. In or near London, at least four to six theaters were open six afternoons a week. London theaters ranged from the Globe, which was a circular unroofed structure holding 3,000, to the Blackfriars, which was roofed and held only 500. In the former, an admission charge of one or two pennies enabled even the lower classes to attend, while the higher prices in the latter ensured an audience of the well-to-do. Elizabethan audiences varied greatly, putting pressure on playwrights to write works that pleased nobles, lawyers, merchants, and even vagabonds.

William Shakespeare was a "complete man of the theater." Although best known for writing plays, he was also an actor and shareholder in the chief company of the time, the Lord Chamberlains' Company, which played in theaters as diverse as the Globe and the Blackfriars. Shakespeare has long been recognized as a universal genius. A master of the English language, he was instrumental in transforming a language that was still in a period of transition. His technical proficiency, however, was matched by an incredible insight into human psychology. Whether in his tragedies or comedies, Shakespeare exhibited a remarkable understanding of the human condition.

The theater was one of the most creative forms of expression during Spain's golden century. The first professional theaters created in Seville and Madrid in the 1570s were run by actors' companies as in England. Soon, a public playhouse could be found in every large town, including Mexico City in the New World. Touring companies brought the latest Spanish plays to all parts of the Spanish empire.

Beginning in the 1580s, the agenda for playwrights was set by Lope de Vega (1562–1635). Like Shakespeare, he was from a middle-class background. He was an incredibly prolific writer; almost 500 of his 1,500 plays survive. They have been characterized as witty, charming, action-packed, and realistic. Lope de Vega made no apologies for the fact that he wrote his plays to please his audiences. In a treatise on drama written in 1609, he stated that the foremost duty of the playwright was to satisfy public de-

➤ William Shakespeare: In Praise of England ➤

William Shakespeare is one of the most famous play-wrights of the Western world. He was a universal genius, outclassing all others in his psychological insights, depth of characterization, imaginative skills, and versatility. His historical plays reflected the patriotic enthusiasm of the English in the Elizabethan era, as this excerpt from Richard II illustrates.

William Shakespeare, Richard II

This royal throne of kings, this sceptered isle,
This earth of majesty, this seat of Mars,
This other Eden, demi-Paradise,
This fortress built by Nature for herself
Against infection and the hand of war,
This happy breed of men, this little world,
This precious stone set in the silver sea,
Which serves it in the office of a wall
Or as a moat defensive to a house
Against the envy of less happier lands—

This blessed plot, this earth, this realm, this England,
This nurse, this teeming womb of royal kings,
Feared by their breed and famous by their birth,
Renowned for their deeds as far from home,
For Christian service and true chivalry,
As is the sepulcher in stubborn Jewry [the Holy Sepulcher
    in Jerusalem]
Of the world's ransom, blessed Mary's Son—
This land of such dear souls, this dear dear land,
Dear for her reputation through the world,
Is now leased out, I die pronouncing it,
Like a tenement or pelting farm.
England, bound in with the triumphant sea,
Whose rocky shore beats back the envious siege
Of watery Neptune, is now bound in with shame,
With inky blots and rotten parchment bonds.
That England, what was wont to conquer others,
Hath made a shameful conquest of itself.
Ah, would the scandal vanish with my life,
How happy then were my ensuing death!

mand. He remarked that if anyone thought he had written his plays for fame, "undeceive him and tell him that I wrote them for money."

One of the crowning achievements of the golden age of Spanish literature was the work of Miguel de Cervantes (1547–1616), whose *Don Quixote* has been acclaimed as one of the greatest literary works of all time. While satirizing medieval chivalric literature, Cervantes also perfected the chivalric novel and reconciled it with literary realism. The two main figures of his famous work represented the dual nature of the Spanish character. The knight Don Quixote from La Mancha is the visionary who is so involved in his lofty ideals that he is oblivious to the hard realities around him. To him, for example, windmills appear as four-armed giants. In contrast, the knight's fat and earthy squire, Sancho Panza, is the realist who cannot get his master to see the realities in front of him. But after adventures that take them to all parts of Spain, each comes to see the value of the other's perspective. We are left with Cervantes's conviction that idealism and realism, visionary dreams and the hard work of reality, are both necessary to the human condition.

Conclusion

The period from 1560 to 1650 witnessed Europe's attempt to adjust to a whole range of change-laden forces. Populations contracted as economic expansion gave way to economic recession. The discovery of new trade routes to the Far East and the "accidental" discovery of the Americas led Europeans to plunge outside the medieval world in which they had been enclosed for virtually 1,000 years. The conquest of the Americas brought out the worst and some of the best of European civilization. The greedy plundering of resources and the brutal enslavement and virtual annihilation of millions of Indians were hardly balanced by attempts to create new institutions, convert the natives to Christianity, and foster the rights of the indigenous peoples.

In the sixteenth century, the discoveries made little impact on Europeans preoccupied with the problems of dynastic expansion and, above all, religious division. It took 100 years of religious warfare complicated by serious political, economic, and social issues—the worst series of wars and civil wars since the collapse of the Roman Empire in the west—before Europeans finally admitted that they would have to tolerate different ways of worshiping God. That men who were disciples of the Apostle of Peace would kill each other—often in brutal and painful fashion—aroused skepticism about Christianity itself. As one German writer put it in 1650: "Lutheran, popish, and Calvinistic, we've got all these beliefs here; but there is some doubt about where Christianity has got to." It is surely no accident that the search for a stable, secular order of politics and for order in the universe through natural laws played such important roles in the seventeenth century. The religious wars of the sixteenth and seventeenth centuries opened the door to the secular perspectives that have characterized modern Western civilization.

NOTES

1. Quoted in J. H. Parry, *The Age of Reconnaissance: Discovery, Exploration and Settlement, 1450 to 1640* (New York, 1963), p. 33.
2. Quoted in Richard B. Reed, "The Expansion of Europe," in Richard DeMolen, ed., *The Meaning of the Renaissance and Reformation* (Boston, 1974), p. 308.
3. Miguel Leon-Portilla, ed., *The Broken Spears: The Aztec Account of the Conquest of Mexico* (Boston, 1969), p. 51.
4. Quoted in Garrett Mattingly, *The Armada* (Boston, 1959), pp. 216–17.
5. Quoted in Joseph Klaits, *Servants of Satan: The Age of the Witch Hunts* (Bloomington, Ind., 1985), p. 68.

SUGGESTIONS FOR FURTHER READING

General works on the period from 1560 to 1650 include C. Wilson, *The Transformation of Europe, 1558–1648* (Berkeley, 1976); and H. Kamen, *The Iron Century: Social Change in Europe, 1550–1660* (New York, 1971). For an extremely detailed account of all aspects of life in the Mediterranean basin in the second half of the sixteenth century, see F. Braudel, *The Mediterranean and the Mediterranean World in the Age of Philip II*, trans. S. Reynolds, 2 vols (New York, 1972–73).

The best general accounts of European discovery and expansion are G. V. Scammell, *The First Imperial Age* (London, 1989); J. H. Parry, *The Age of Reconnaissance: Discovery, Exploration and Settlement, 1450 to 1650* (New York, 1963); and B. Penrose, *Travel and Discovery in the Renaissance, 1420–1620* (New York, 1962). On the Portuguese expansion, the fundamental work is C. R. Boxer, *The Portuguese Seaborne Empire: 1415–1825* (New York, 1969); but see also W. B. Diffie and G. D. Winius, *Foundations of the Portuguese Empire, 1415–1580* (Minneapolis, 1979). On Columbus, see the brief biography by J. S. Collis, *Christopher Columbus* (London, 1976); and F. Fernandez-Armesto, *Columbus* (New York, 1991). For a fundamental work on Spanish colonization, see J. H. Parry, *The Spanish Seaborne Empire* (New York, 1966). The standard work on the conquistadors is F. A. Kirkpatrick, *The Spanish Conquistadores* (Cleveland, 1968). Cortés is examined in W. W. Johnson, *Cortés* (Boston, 1975). The impact of expansion on European consciousness is explored in J. H. Elliott, *The Old World and the New, 1492–1650* (Cambridge, 1970). The human and ecological effects of the interaction of New World and Old World cultures are examined thoughtfully in A. W. Crosby, *The Columbian Exchange, Biological and Cultural Consequences of 1492* (Westport, Conn., 1972).

Two works by J. H. M. Salmon provide good background on the French Wars of Religion. They are *Society in Crisis: France in the Sixteenth Century* (New York, 1975) and *French Government and Society in the Wars of Religion* (St. Louis, 1976). For a recent view, see M. P. Holt, *The French Wars of Religion* (New York, 1995). An adequate popular biography of Henry of Navarre can be found in D. Seward, *The First Bourbon: Henry IV, King of France and Navarre* (Boston, 1971).

Two good histories of Spain in the sixteenth century are J. H. Elliott, *Imperial Spain, 1469–1716* (New York, 1964); and J. Lynch, *Spain under the Habsburgs*, vol. 1,

Empire and Absolutism, 1516–1598 (New York, 1964). The best biographies of Philip II are P. Pierson, *Philip II of Spain* (London, 1975); and G. Parker, *Philip II* (Boston and London, 1978). On the revolt of the Netherlands, see the classic work by P. Geyl, *The Revolt of the Netherlands, 1555–1609* (London, 1962); and the more recent work of G. Parker, *The Dutch Revolt* (London, 1977).

Elizabeth's reign can be examined in three good biographies, J. Ridley, *Elizabeth I* (New York, 1988); W. T. MacCaffrey, *Elizabeth I* (London, 1993); and L. B. Smith, *Elizabeth Tudor, Portrait of a Queen* (London, 1976). The classic work on the Armada is the beautifully written *The Armada* by G. Mattingly (Boston, 1959).

The classic study on the Thirty Years' War is C. V. Wedgwood, *The Thirty Years War* (Garden City, N.Y., 1961), but it needs to be supplemented by the more recent works by S. H. Steinberg, *The Thirty Years' War and the Conflict for European Hegemony, 1600–1660* (New York, 1966), which emphasizes the wider context of the struggle; G. Parker, *The Thirty Years War*, 2d ed. (London,

1997); and the brief study by S. J. Lee, *The Thirty Years War* (London, 1991).

The story of the witchcraft craze can be examined in three recent works, J. Klaits, *Servants of Satan: The Age of the Witch Hunts* (Bloomington, Ind., 1985); J. B. Russell, *A History of Witchcraft* (London, 1980); and B. P. Levack, *The Witch-Hunt in Early Modern Europe* (London, 1987).

For a brief, readable guide to Mannerism, see L. Murray, *The Late Renaissance and Mannerism* (New York, 1967). For a general survey of Baroque culture, see M. and L. Mainstone, *The Cambridge Introduction to Art: The Seventeenth Century* (Cambridge, 1981); and J. S. Held, *Seventeenth and Eighteenth Century Art: Baroque Painting, Sculpture, Architecture* (New York, 1971). On the Spanish golden century of literature, see R. O. Jones, *The Golden Age: Prose and Poetry*, which is volume 2 of *The Literary History of Spain* (London, 1971). The literature on Shakespeare is enormous. For a biography, see A. L Rowse, *The Life of Shakespeare* (New York, 1963).

Response to Crisis: State Building and the Search for Order in the Seventeenth Century

The age of crisis from 1560 to 1650 was accompanied by a decline in religious orientation and a growing secularization that affected both the political and the intellectual worlds of Europe (on the intellectual effect, see discussions of the Scientific Revolution in Chapter 17). Some historians like to speak of the seventeenth century as a turning point in the evolution of a modern state system in Europe. The idea of a united Christian Europe (the practice of a united Christendom had actually been moribund for some time) gave way to the practical realities of a system of secular states in which reason of state took precedence over the salvation of subjects' souls. Of course, these states had emerged and begun their development during the Middle Ages, but medieval ideas about statehood had still been couched in religious terms. By the seventeenth century, the credibility of Christianity had been so weakened in the religious wars that more and more Europeans could think of politics in secular terms.

One of the responses to the crises of the seventeenth century was a search for order. As the internal social and political rebellions and revolts died down, it became apparent that the privileged classes of society—the aristocrats—remained in control, although the various states exhibited important differences in political forms. The most general trend saw an extension of monarchical power as a stabilizing force. This development, which historians have called absolutism or absolute monarchy, was most evident in France during the flamboyant reign of Louis XIV, regarded by some as the perfect embodiment of an absolute monarch. In his memoirs, the duc de Saint-Simon, who had firsthand experience of French court life, said that Louis was "the very figure of a hero, so imbued with a natural but most imposing majesty that it appeared even in his most insignificant gestures and movements." The king's natural grace gave him a special charm as well: "He was as dignified and majestic in his dressing gown as when dressed in robes of state, or on horseback at the head of his troops." He spoke well and learned quickly. He was naturally kind and "he loved truth, justice,

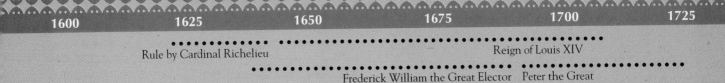

| 1600 | 1625 | 1650 | 1675 | 1700 | 1725 |

Rule by Cardinal Richelieu   Reign of Louis XIV

Frederick William the Great Elector   Peter the Great

English, French, Dutch settle North America   The Glorious Revolution

• Official recognition of the Dutch Republic

• • • English Civil War

Paintings of Rembrandt   John Locke, *Two Treatises of Government*

• Thomas Hobbes, *Leviathan*   Plays of Molière

order, and reason." His life was orderly: "nothing could be regulated with greater exactitude than were his days and hours." His self-control was impeccable: "He did not lose control of himself ten times in his whole life, and then only with inferior persons." But even absolute monarchs had imperfections, and Saint-Simon had the courage to point them out: "Louis XIV's vanity was without limit or restraint," which led to his "distaste for all merit, intelligence, education, and, most of all, for all independence of character and sentiment in others," as well as his "mistakes of judgment in matters of importance."

But absolutism was not the only response to crisis in the seventeenth century. Other states, such as England, reacted differently to domestic crisis, and another very different system emerged where monarchs were limited by the power of their representative assemblies. Absolute and limited monarchy were the two poles of seventeenth-century state building.

The Practice of Absolutism: Western Europe

Absolute monarchy or absolutism meant that the sovereign power or ultimate authority in the state rested in the hands of a king who claimed to rule by divine right—that kings received their power from God and were responsible to no one (including parliaments) except God. But what did sovereignty mean? The late sixteenth-century political theorist Jean Bodin believed that sovereign power consisted of the authority to make laws, tax, administer justice, control the state's administrative system, and determine foreign policy. These powers made a ruler sovereign.

France and Absolute Monarchy

France during the reign of Louis XIV (1661–1715) has traditionally been regarded as the best example of the practice of absolute monarchy in the seventeenth century. By the end of the seventeenth century, France had come to play a dominant role in European affairs. French culture, language, and manners reached into all levels of European society. French diplomacy and wars shaped the political affairs of western and central Europe. The court of Louis XIV seemed to be imitated everywhere in Europe. Of course, the stability of Louis's reign was magnified by the instability that had preceded it.

The history of France before the reign of Louis XIV was hardly a story of steady, unbroken progress toward an ideal of absolute monarchy. During the fifty years or so before Louis, royal and ministerial governments had to struggle to avoid the breakdown of the state. The line between order and anarchy was often a narrow one. The situation was especially complicated by the fact that, both in 1610 and 1643, when Louis XIII and Louis XIV succeeded to the throne, they were only boys, leaving the government dependent on royal ministers. Two especially competent ministers played crucial roles in maintaining monarchical authority.

Cardinal Richelieu, Louis XIII's chief minister from 1624 to 1642, initiated policies that eventually strengthened the power of the monarchy. By eliminating the political and military rights of the Huguenots while preserving their religious ones, Richelieu transformed the

♦ **Louis XIV.** Louis XIV was determined to be the sole ruler of France. Louis eliminated the threat of the high nobility by removing them from the royal council and replacing them with relatively new aristocrats whom he could dominate. This portrait by Hyacinth Rigaud captures the king's sense of royal dignity and grandeur.

Huguenots into more reliable subjects. Richelieu acted more cautiously in "humbling the pride of the great men," the important French nobility. He understood the influential role played by the nobles in the French state. The dangerous ones were those who asserted their territorial independence when they were excluded from participating in the central government. Proceeding slowly but determinedly, Richelieu developed an efficient network of spies to uncover noble plots and then crushed the conspiracies and executed the conspirators, thereby eliminating a major threat to royal authority.

When Louis XIV succeeded to the throne in 1643 at the age of four, Cardinal Mazarin, the trained successor of Cardinal Richelieu, dominated the government. An Italian who had come to France as a papal legate and then become naturalized, Mazarin attempted to carry on Richelieu's policies until his death in 1661. The most important event during Mazarin's rule was the Fronde, a revolt led primarily by nobles who wished to curb the centralized administrative power being built up at the expense of the provincial nobility. The Fronde was crushed by 1652, and with its end, a vast number of Frenchmen concluded that the best hope for stability in France lay in the crown. When Mazarin died in 1661, the greatest of the seventeenth-century monarchs, Louis XIV (1661–1715), took over supreme power.

THE REIGN OF LOUIS XIV (1643–1715)

The day after Cardinal Mazarin's death, Louis XIV, at the age of twenty-three, expressed his determination to be a real king and the sole ruler of France:

> Up to this moment I have been pleased to entrust the government of my affairs to the late Cardinal. It is now time that I govern them myself. You [secretaries and ministers of state] will assist me with your counsels when I ask for them. I request and order you to seal no orders except by my command, . . . I order you not to sign anything, not even a passport . . . without my command; to render account to me personally each day and to favor no one.[1]

His mother, who was well aware of Louis's proclivity for fun and games and getting into the beds of the maids in the royal palace, laughed aloud at these words. But Louis was quite serious.

Louis proved willing to pay the price of being a strong ruler (see the box on p. 329). He established a conscientious routine from which he seldom deviated, but he did not look on his duties as drudgery because he judged his royal profession to be "grand, noble, and delightful." Eager for glory (in the French sense of achieving what was expected of one in an important position), Louis created a grand and majestic spectacle at the court of Versailles. Consequently, Louis and his court came to set the standard for monarchies and aristocracies all over Europe. Less than fifty years after his death, the great French writer Voltaire selected the "Age of Louis XIV" for his history of Europe from 1661 to 1715. Historians have tended to use it ever since.

Although Louis may have believed in the theory of absolute monarchy and consciously fostered the myth of himself as the Sun King, the source of light for all of his people, historians are quick to point out that the realities fell far short of the aspirations. Despite the centralizing

≋ Louis XIV: Kingly Advice ≋

Throughout his reign, Louis XIV was always on stage, acting the role of the wise, "Grand Monarch." In 1661, after he became a father, Louis began his Memoirs for the Dauphin, *a frank collection of precepts for the education of his oldest son and heir to the throne. He continued to add to these* Memoirs *over the next twenty years.*

Louis XIV, *Memoirs for the Dauphin*

Kings are often obliged to do things which go against their inclinations and offend their natural goodness. They should love to give pleasure and yet they must often punish and destroy persons on whom by nature they wish to confer benefits. The interest of the state must come first. One must constrain one's inclinations and not put oneself in the position of berating oneself because one could have done better in some important affair but did not because of some private interest, because one was distracted from the attention one should have for the greatness, the good and the power of the state. Often there are troublesome places where it is difficult to make out what one should do. One's ideas are confused. As long as this lasts, one can refrain from making a decision. But as soon as one has fixed one's mind upon something which seems best to do, it must be acted upon. This is what enabled me to succeed so often in what I have done. The mistakes which I made, and which gave me infinite trouble, were the result of the desire to please or of allowing myself to accept too carelessly the opinions of others. Nothing is more dangerous than weakness of any kind whatsoever. In order to command others, one must raise oneself above them and once one has heard the reports from every side one must come to a decision upon the basis of one's own judgment, without anxiety but always with the concern not to command anything which is of itself unworthy either of one's place in the world or of the greatness of the state. Princes with good intentions and some knowledge of their affairs, either from experience or from study and great diligence in making themselves capable, find numerous cases which instruct them that they must give special care and total application to everything. One must be on guard against oneself, resist one's own tendencies, and always be on guard against one's own natural bent. The craft of a king is great, noble and delightful when one feels worthy of doing well whatever one promises to do. But it is not exempt from troubles, weariness and worries. Sometimes uncertainty causes despair, and when one has spent a reasonable time in examining an affair, one must make a decision and take the step which one believes to be best. When one has the state in view, one works for one's self. The good of the one constitutes the glory of the other. When the former is fortunate, eminent and powerful, he who is the cause thereof becomes glorious and consequently should find more enjoyment than his subjects in all the pleasant things of life for himself and for them. When one has made a mistake, it must be corrected as soon as possible, and no other consideration must stand in the way, not even kindness.

---

efforts of Cardinals Richelieu and Mazarin, France still possessed a bewildering system of overlapping authorities in the seventeenth century. Provinces had their own regional courts, their own local Estates, their own sets of laws. Members of the high nobility with their huge estates and clients among the lesser nobility still exercised much authority. Both towns and provinces possessed privileges and powers seemingly from time immemorial that they would not easily relinquish. Much of Louis's success rested less on the modernization of administrative machinery, as is frequently claimed, than on his clever and adroit manipulation of the traditional priorities and values of French society.

One of the keys to Louis's power was that he was able to restructure the central policy-making machinery of government because it was part of his own court and household. The royal court located at Versailles was an elaborate structure that served three purposes simultaneously: It was the personal household of the king, the location of central governmental machinery, and the place where powerful subjects came to find favors and offices for themselves and their clients as well as the main arena where rival aristocratic factions jostled for power. The greatest danger to Louis's personal rule came from the very high nobles and princes of the blood (the royal princes) who considered it their natural function to assert the policy-making role of royal ministers. Louis eliminated this threat by removing them from the royal council, the chief administrative body of the king and overseer of the central machinery of government, and enticing them to his court where he could keep them preoccupied with court life and out of politics. Instead of the high nobility and royal princes, Louis relied for his ministers on nobles who came from relatively new aristocratic families. His ministers were expected to be subservient; said Louis, "I had no intention of sharing my authority with them."

Louis's domination of his ministers and secretaries gave him control of the central policy-making machinery of government and thus authority over the traditional areas of monarchical power: the formulation of foreign policy, the making of war and peace, the assertion of the secular power of crown against any religious authority, and the ability to levy taxes to fulfill these functions. However, Louis had considerably less success with the internal administration of the kingdom. The traditional groups and institutions of French society—the nobles, officials, town councils, guilds, and representative Estates in some provinces—were simply too powerful for the king to have direct control over the lives of his subjects. As a result, the control of the central government over the provinces and the people was carried out largely by careful bribery of the important people to see that the king's policies were executed.

The maintenance of religious harmony had long been considered an area of monarchical power. The desire to keep it led Louis to pursue an anti-Protestant policy, aimed at converting the Huguenots to Catholicism. In October 1685, Louis issued the Edict of Fontainebleau. In addition to revoking the Edict of Nantes, the new edict provided for the destruction of Huguenot churches and the closing of their schools. Although they were forbid-

CHRONOLOGY

Absolutism in Western Europe

France	
Louis XIII	1610–1643
Cardinal Richelieu as chief minister	1624–1642
Ministry of Cardinal Mazarin	1642–1661
Fronde	1648–1652
Louis XIV	1643–1715
Edict of Fontainebleau	1685
Spain	
Philip III	1598–1621
Philip IV	1621–1665

den to leave France, it is estimated that 200,000 Huguenots left for shelter in England, the United Provinces, and the German states.

The cost of building palaces, maintaining his court, and pursuing his wars made finances a crucial issue for Louis XIV. He was most fortunate in having the services of Jean-Baptiste Colbert (1619–1683) as controller-general of finances. Colbert sought to increase the wealth and power of France by general adherence to mercantilism, a name historians use to identify a set of economic principles that dominated economic thought in the seventeenth century. According to the mercantilists, the prosperity of a nation depended on a plentiful supply of bullion or gold and silver. For this reason, it was desirable to achieve a favorable balance of trade in which goods exported were of greater value than those imported, promoting an influx of gold and silver payments that would increase the quantity of bullion. To encourage exports, governments should stimulate and protect export industries and trade by granting trade monopolies, encouraging investment in new industries through subsidies, and improving transportation systems by building roads, bridges, and canals. By placing high tariffs on foreign goods, they could be kept out of the country and prevented from competing with domestic industries. Colonies were also deemed valuable sources of raw materials and markets for finished goods. As a system of economic principles, mercantilism focused on the role of the state, believing that state intervention in some aspects of the economy was desirable for the sake of the national good.

Colbert was an avid practitioner of mercantilism. To decrease the need for imports and increase exports, he

◆ **Palace of Versailles.** Louis XIV spent untold sums of money in the construction of a new royal residence at Versailles. The enormous palace of Versailles also housed the members of the king's government and served as home for thousands of French nobles. As the largest royal residence in Europe, Versailles impressed foreigners and became a source of envy for other rulers.

founded new luxury industries; drew up instructions regulating the quality of goods produced; oversaw the training of workers; and granted special privileges, including tax exemptions, loans, and subsidies to those who established new industries. To improve communications and the transportation of goods internally, he built roads and canals. To decrease imports directly, Colbert raised tariffs on foreign manufactured goods and created a merchant marine to facilitate the conveyance of French goods.

The increase in royal power that Louis pursued as well as his desire for military glory led the king to develop a professional army numbering 100,000 men in peacetime and 400,000 in time of war. Louis made war an almost incessant activity of his reign. To achieve the prestige and military glory befitting a Sun King as well as to ensure the domination of his Bourbon dynasty over European affairs,

Louis waged four wars between 1667 and 1713. His ambitions roused much of Europe to form coalitions that were determined to prevent the certain destruction of the European balance of power by a Bourbon hegemony. Although Louis added some territory to France's northeastern frontier and established a member of his own Bourbon dynasty on the throne of Spain, he also left France impoverished and surrounded by enemies.

The Decline of Spain

At the beginning of the seventeenth century, Spain possessed the most populous empire in the world, controlling almost all of South America and a number of settlements in Asia and Africa. To most Europeans, Spain still seemed the greatest power of the age, but the reality was quite

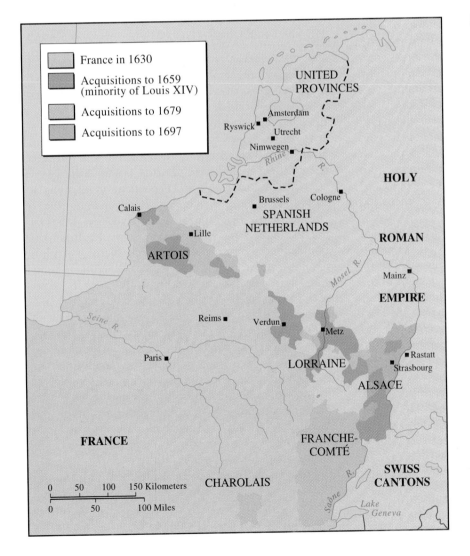

�֍ **Map 16.1** The Wars of Louis XIV.

France in 1630

Acquisitions to 1659 (minority of Louis XIV)

Acquisitions to 1679

Acquisitions to 1697

different. The treasury was empty; Philip II went bankrupt in 1596 from excessive expenditures on war while his successor did the same in 1607 by spending a fortune on his court. The armed forces were out-of-date; the government inefficient; and the commercial class weak in the midst of a suppressed peasantry, a luxury-loving class of nobles, and an oversupply of priests and monks. Spain continued to play the role of a great power, but appearances were deceiving.

During the reign of Philip III (1598–1621), many of Spain's weaknesses became only too apparent. Interested only in court luxury or miracle-working relics, Philip III allowed his first minister, the greedy Duke of Lerma, to run the country. The aristocratic Lerma's primary interest was accumulating power and wealth for himself and his family. While important offices were filled with his relatives, crucial problems went unsolved.

At first, the reign of Philip IV (1621–1665) seemed to offer hope for a revival of Spain's energies, especially in the capable hands of his chief minister, Gaspar de Guzman, the count of Olivares. This clever, hard-working, and power-hungry statesman dominated the king's every move and worked to revive the interests of the monarchy. A flurry of domestic reform decrees, aimed at curtailing the power of the church and the landed aristocracy, was soon followed by a political reform program whose purpose was to further centralize the government of all Spain and its possessions in monarchical hands. All of these efforts met with little real success, however, because both the number (estimated at one-fifth of the population) and power of the Spanish aristocrats made them too strong to curtail in any significant fashion.

At the same time, most of the efforts of Olivares and Philip were undermined by their desire to pursue Spain's imperial glory and by a series of internal revolts. During the 1620s, 1630s, and 1640s, Spain's involvement in the Thirty Years' War led to a series of frightfully expensive military campaigns that led to internal revolts and years of civil war. Unfortunately for Spain, the campaigns also failed to produce victory. As Olivares wrote to King Philip IV, "God wants us to make peace; for He is depriving us visibly and absolutely of all the means of war."[2] The defeats in Europe and the internal revolts of the 1640s ended any illusions about Spain's greatness. The actual extent of Spain's economic difficulties is still debated, but there is no question about Spain's foreign losses. Dutch independence was formally recognized by the Peace of Westphalia in 1648, and the Peace of the Pyrenees with France in 1659 meant the surrender of certain border regions, such as the Catalan province of Roussillon, to France.

Absolutism in Central and Eastern Europe

During the seventeenth century, a development of great importance for the modern Western world took place in central and eastern Europe, the appearance of three new powers: Prussia, Austria, and Russia.

The German States

The Peace of Westphalia, which officially ended the Thirty Years' War in 1648, left each of the 300 or more German states comprising the Holy Roman Empire virtually autonomous and sovereign. Properly speaking, there was no German state, but over 300 "Germanies." Of these states, two emerged in the seventeenth and eighteenth centuries as great European powers.

THE RISE OF BRANDENBURG-PRUSSIA

The development of Brandenburg as a state was largely the story of the Hohenzollern dynasty. By the seventeenth century, the dominions of the house of Hohenzollern, now called Brandenburg-Prussia, consisted of three disconnected masses in western, central, and eastern Germany. Each had its own privileges, customs, and loyalties; only the person of the Hohenzollern ruler connected them. Brandenburg-Prussia was an artificial creation, highly vulnerable and dependent on its ruling dynasty to create a state where one simply did not exist.

Frederick William the Great Elector (1640–1688) laid the foundation for the Prussian state. Realizing that Brandenburg-Prussia was a small, open territory with no natural frontiers for defense, Frederick William built a competent and efficient standing army. By 1678, he possessed a force of 40,000 men that absorbed more than 50 percent of the state's revenues. To sustain the army and his own power, Frederick William established the General War Commissariat to levy taxes for the army and oversee its growth and training. The Commissariat soon evolved into an agency for civil government as well. Directly responsible to the elector, the new bureaucractic machine became his chief instrument to govern the state. Many of its officials were members of the Prussian landed aristocracy, the Junkers, who also served as officers in the all-important army.

Frederick William the Great Elector laid the foundations for the Prussian state. He was succeeded by his son Frederick III (1688–1713), who made one significant contribution to the development of Prussia. In return for aiding the Holy Roman Emperor in the War of the Spanish Succession, he received officially the title of king in Prussia in 1701. Elector Frederick III was transformed into King Frederick I, and Brandenburg-Prussia became simply Prussia. In the eighteenth century, Prussia emerged as a great power on the European stage.

The Emergence of Austria

The Austrian Habsburgs had long played a significant role in European politics as Holy Roman Emperors. By the end of the Thirty Years' War, the Habsburg hopes of creating an empire in Germany had been dashed. In the seventeenth century, the House of Austria made a difficult transition; the German Empire was lost, but a new empire was created in eastern and southeastern Europe.

The nucleus of the new Austrian Empire remained the traditional Austrian hereditary possessions: Lower and Upper Austria, Carinthia, Carniola, Styria, and Tyrol. To these had been added the kingdom of Bohemia and parts of northwest Hungary in the sixteenth century. In the seventeenth century, Leopold I (1658–1705) encouraged the eastward movement of the Austrian Empire, but he was sorely challenged by the revival of Turkish power. Having moved into Transylvania, the Turks eventually pushed westward and laid seige to Vienna in 1683. A European army, led by the Austrians, counterattacked and decisively defeated the Turks in 1687. Austria took control of Hungary, Transylvania, Croatia, and Slovenia, thus establishing an Austrian Empire in southeastern Eu-

rope. At the end of the War of Spanish Succession in 1713, Austria gained possession of the Spanish Netherlands and received formal recognition of its occupation of the Spanish possessions in Italy, namely, Milan, Mantua, Sardinia, and Naples, thus making Austria the dominant power in divided Italy. By the beginning of the eighteenth century, the house of Austria had acquired a new empire of considerable size.

The Austrian monarchy, however, never became a highly centralized, absolutist state, primarily because it contained so many different national groups. The Austrian Empire remained a collection of territories held together by a personal union. The Habsburg emperor was archduke of Austria, king of Bohemia, and king of Hungary. Each of these areas, however, had its own laws, Estates-General, and political life. The landed aristocrats throughout the empire were connected by a common bond of service to the house of Habsburg, whether as military officers or government bureaucrats, but there was no common sentiment to tie the regions together. The nobles in the Austrian Empire remained quite strong and were also allowed to impose serfdom on their peasants. By the beginning of the eighteenth century, Austria was a populous empire in central Europe of great potential military strength.

From Muscovy to Russia

A new Russian state had emerged in the fifteenth century under the leadership of the principality of Muscovy and

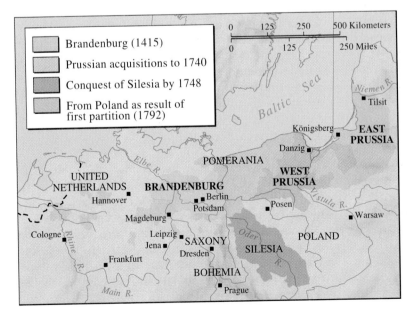

✖ **Map 16.2** The Growth of Brandenburg-Prussia.

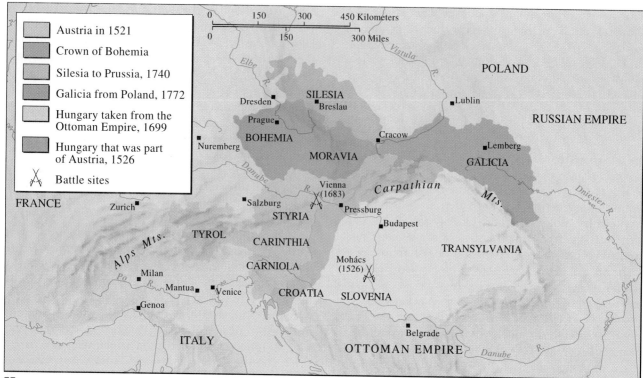

Map 16.3 The Growth of the Austrian Empire.

its grand dukes. In the sixteenth century, Ivan IV the Terrible (1533–1584), who was the first ruler to take the title of tsar, expanded the territories of Russia eastward, after finding westward expansion blocked by the powerful Swedish and Polish states. Ivan also extended the autocracy of the tsar by crushing the power of the Russian nobility, known as the boyars. Ivan's dynasty came to an end in 1598 and was followed by a resurgence of aristocratic power in a period of anarchy known as the Time of Troubles. It did not end until the Zemsky Sobor, or national assembly, chose Michael Romanov in 1613 as the new tsar, beginning a dynasty that lasted until 1917.

In the seventeenth century, Muscovite society was highly stratified. At the top was the tsar, who claimed to be a divinely ordained autocratic ruler, assisted by two consultative bodies, a Duma, or council of boyars, and the Zemsky Sobor, a landed assembly begun in 1550 by Ivan IV to facilitate support for his programs. Russian society was dominated by an upper class of landed aristocrats who, in the course of the seventeenth century, managed to bind their peasants to the land. An abundance of land and a shortage of peasants made serfdom desirable to the landowners, who sustained a highly oppressive system. Townspeople were also stratified and controlled. Artisans

were sharply separated from merchants, and many of the latter were not allowed to move from their cities without government permission or to sell their businesses to anyone outside their class. In the seventeenth century, merchant and peasant revolts as well as a schism in the Russian Orthodox church created very unsettled conditions. In the midst of these political and religious upheavals, seventeenth-century Muscovy was experiencing more frequent contacts with the West while Western ideas also began to penetrate a few Russian circles. At the end of the seventeenth century, Peter the Great noticeably accelerated this westernizing process.

THE REIGN OF PETER THE GREAT (1689–1725)

Peter the Great was an unusual character. A strong man, towering six feet, nine inches tall, Peter was coarse in his tastes and rude in his behavior. He enjoyed a low kind of humor—belching contests and crude jokes—and vicious punishments—flogging, impalings, and roastings (see the box on p. 337). Peter received a firsthand view of the West when he made a trip there in 1697–1698 and returned to Russia with a firm determination to westernize or Europeanize Russia. Perhaps too much has been made of Peter's desire to westernize a "backward country." Peter's policy of Europeanization was largely technical. He admired European technology and gadgets and desired to transplant these to Russia. Only this kind of modernization could give him the army and navy he needed to make Russia a great power.

As could be expected, one of his first priorities was the reorganization of the army and the creation of a navy. Employing both Russians and Europeans as officers, he conscripted peasants for twenty-five year stints of service to build a standing army of 210,000 men. Peter has also been given credit for forming the first Russian navy.

Peter reorganized the central government, partly along Western lines. What remained of the consultative bodies disappeared; neither the Duma of boyars nor the Zemsky Sobor was ever summoned. In 1711, Peter created a Senate to supervise the administrative machinery of state while he was away on military campaigns. In time the Senate became something like a ruling council, but its ineffectiveness caused Peter to borrow the Western institution of "colleges," or boards of administrators entrusted with specific functions, such as foreign affairs, war, and justice. To impose the rule of the central government more effectively throughout the land, Peter divided Russia into eight provinces and later, in 1719, into fifty. Although he hoped to create a "police state," by which he meant a well-ordered community governed in accordance with law, few of his bureaucrats shared his concept of honest service and duty to the state. Peter hoped for a sense of civic duty, but his own forceful personality created an atmosphere of fear that prevented it.

To satisfy his insatiable need of money for an army and navy that absorbed as much as four-fifths of the state revenue, Peter adopted Western mercantilistic policies to stimulate economic growth. He tried to increase exports and develop new industries while exploiting domestic resources like the iron mines in the Urals. But his military needs were endless, and he came to rely on the old expedient of simply raising taxes, imposing additional burdens on the hapless peasants who were becoming ever more oppressed in Peter's Russia.

Peter also sought to gain state control of the Russian Orthodox church. In 1721, he abolished the position of patriarch and created a body called the Holy Synod to make decisions for the church. At its head stood a Procurator, a layman who represented the interests of the tsar and assured Peter of effective domination of the church.

Already after his first trip to the West in 1697–1698, Peter began to introduce Western customs, practices, and manners into Russia. He ordered the preparation of the first Russian book of etiquette to teach Western manners. Among other things, it pointed out that it was not polite

Map 16.4 From Muscovy to Russia.

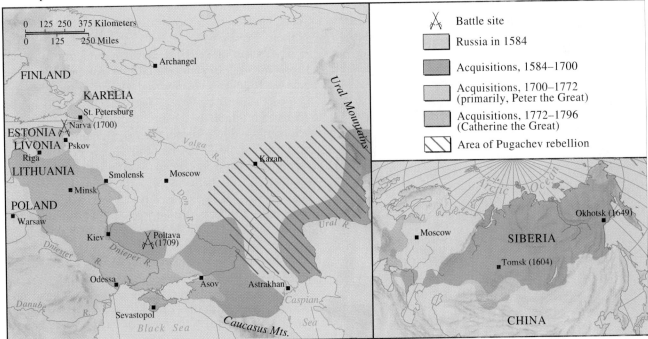

to spit on the floor or scratch oneself at dinner. Because westerners did not wear beards or the traditional long-skirted coat, Russian beards had to be shaved and coats shortened, a reform Peter personally enforced at court by shaving off his nobles' beards and cutting their coats at the knees with his own hands. Outside the court, the edicts were enforced by barbers and tailors planted at town gates with orders to cut the beards and cloaks of those who entered or left. Anyone who failed to conform was to be "beaten without mercy."

One group of Russians benefited greatly from Peter's cultural reforms—women. Having watched women mixing freely with men in Western courts, Peter shattered the seclusion of upper-class Russian women and demanded that they remove the traditional veils that covered their faces. Peter also decreed that social gatherings be held three times a week in the large houses of St. Petersburg

◆ **Peter the Great.** Peter the Great wished to westernize Russia, especially in the realm of technical skills. His foremost goal was the creation of a strong army and navy in order to make Russia a great power. A Dutch painter created this portrait of the armored tsar during his visit to the West in 1697.

CHRONOLOGY

Absolutism in Central and Eastern Europe

Brandenburg-Prussia	
Frederick William the Great Elector	1640–1688
Elector Frederick III (King Frederick I)	1688–1713
The Austrian Empire	
Leopold I	1658–1705
Turkish siege of Vienna	1683
Russia	
Ivan IV the Terrible	1533–1584
Time of Troubles	1598–1613
Michael Romanov	1613–1645
Peter the Great	1689–1725
First trip to the West	1697–1698
Great Northern War	1701–1721
Construction of St. Petersburg begins	1703
Battle of Poltava	1709
Holy Synod	1721

where men and women could mix for conversation, card games, and dancing, which Peter had learned in the West. The tsar also now insisted that women could marry of their own free will.

The object of Peter's domestic reforms was to make Russia into a great state and military power. His primary goal was to "open a window to the west," meaning an ice-free port easily accessible to Europe. This could only be achieved on the Baltic, but at that time the Baltic coast was controlled by Sweden, the most important power in northern Europe. Desirous of these lands, Peter, with the support of Poland and Denmark, attacked Sweden in the summer of 1700, believing that the young king of Sweden, Charles XII, could easily be defeated. Charles, however, proved to be a brilliant general. He smashed the Danes, flattened the Poles, and, with a well-disciplined force of only 8,000 men, routed the Russian army of 40,000 at the Battle of Narva (1700). The Great Northern War (1701–1721) had begun.

But Peter fought back. He reorganized his army along Western lines and at the Battle of Poltava in July 1709 decisively defeated Charles's army. Although the war dragged on for another twelve years, the Peace of Nystadt

Peter the Great Deals with a Rebellion

During his first visit to the West in 1697–1698, Peter received word that the streltsy, an elite military unit stationed in Moscow, had revolted against his authority. Peter hurried home and crushed the revolt in a very savage fashion. This selection is taken from an Austrian account of how Peter dealt with the rebels.

Peter and the Streltsy

How sharp was the pain, how great the indignation, to which the tsar's Majesty was mightily moved, when he knew of the rebellion of the Streltsy, betraying openly a mind panting for vengeance! He was still tarrying at Vienna, quite full of the desire of setting out for Italy; but, fervid as was his curiosity of rambling abroad, it was, nevertheless, speedily extinguished on the announcement of the troubles that had broken out in the bowels of his realm. Going immediately to Lefort. . . , he thus indignantly broke out: "Tell me, Francis, how I can teach Moscow by the shortest way, in a brief space, so that I may wreak vengeance on this great perfidy of my people, with punishments worthy of their abominable crime. Not one of them shall escape with impunity. Around my royal city, which, with their impious efforts, they planned to destroy, I will have gibbets and gallows set upon the walls and ramparts, and each and every one of them will I put to a direful death." Nor did he long delay the plan for his justly excited wrath; he took the quick post, as his ambassador suggested, and in four weeks' time he had got over about three hundred miles without accident, and arrived the 4th of September, 1698,—a monarch for the well deposed, but an avenger for the wicked.

His first anxiety after his arrival was about the rebellion—in what it consisted, what the insurgents meant, who dared to instigate such a crime. And as nobody could answer accurately upon all points, and some pleaded their own ignorance, others the obstinacy of the Streltsy, he began to have suspicions of everybody's loyalty. . . . No day, holy or profane, were the inquisitors idle; every day was deemed fit and lawful for torturing. There was as many scourges as there were accused, and every inquisitor was a butcher. . . . The whole month of October was spent on lacerating the backs of culprits with the knout and with flames; no day were those that were left alive exempt from scourging or scorching; or else they were broken upon the wheel, or driven to the gibbet, or slain with the ax. . . .

To prove to all people how holy and inviolable are those walls of the city which the Streltsy rashly meditated scaling in a sudden assault, beams were run out from all the embrasures in the walls near the gates, in each of which two rebels were hanged. This day beheld about two hundred and fifty die that death. There are few cities fortified with as many palisades as Moscow has given gibbets to her guardian Streltsy.

---

in 1721 gave formal recognition to what Peter had already achieved: the acquisition of Estonia, Livonia, and Karelia. Sweden became a second-rate power while Russia was now the great European state Peter had wanted. Already in 1703, in these northern lands on the Baltic, Peter had begun the construction of a new city, St. Petersburg, his window on the west and a symbol that Russia was looking westward to Europe. Built on marshland, the lives of thousands of peasants were lost during its construction. Finished during Peter's lifetime, St. Petersburg remained the Russian capital until 1917.

Peter modernized and westernized Russia to the extent that it became a great military power and, by his death in 1725, an important member of the European state system. But his policies were also detrimental to Russia. Westernization was a bit of a sham, because Western culture reached only the upper classes while the real object of the reforms, the creation of a strong military, only added more burdens to the masses of the Russian people. The forceful way in which Peter the Great brought westernization led to a distrust of Europe and Western civilization.

Limited Monarchy: The Examples of the Dutch Republic and England

Almost everywhere in Europe in the seventeenth century, kings and their ministers were in control of central governments. But not all European states followed the pattern of absolute monarchy. In western Europe, two great states—the Dutch Republic and England—successfully resisted the power of hereditary monarchs.

Limited Monarchy and Republics

The United Provinces	
Official recognition of United Provinces	1648
House of Orange	
William III	1672–1702
England	
James I	1603–1625
Charles I	1625–1649
Petition of Right	1628
Civil Wars	1642–1648
Execution of Charles I	1649
Commonwealth	1649–1653
Death of Cromwell	1658
Restoration of monarchy—Charles II	1660
Charles II	1660–1685
Declaration of Indulgence	1672
Test Act	1673
James II	1685–1688
Declaration of Indulgence	1687
Glorious Revolution	1688
Bill of Rights	1689

The "Golden Age" of the Dutch Republic

The seventeenth century has often been called the "golden age" of the Dutch Republic as the United Provinces held center stage as one of Europe's great powers. Like France and England, the United Provinces was an Atlantic power, underlining the importance of that shift of political and economic power in the seventeenth century from the Mediterranean Sea to the countries on the Atlantic seaboard. As a result of the sixteenth-century revolt of the Netherlands, the seven northern provinces, which began to call themselves the United Provinces of the Netherlands in 1581, became the core of the modern Dutch state. The new state was officially recognized by the Peace of Westphalia in 1648.

With independence came internal dissension. There were two chief centers of political power in the new state. Each province had an official known as a stadholder who was responsible for leading the army and maintaining order. Beginning with William of Orange and his heirs, the

House of Orange occupied the stadholderate in most of the seven provinces and favored the development of a centralized government with themselves as hereditary monarchs. The States General, an assembly of representatives from every province, opposed the Orangist ambitions and advocated a decentralized or republican form of government. For much of the seventeenth century, the republican forces were in control. But in 1672, burdened with war against both France and England, the United Provinces allowed William III (1672–1702) of the house of Orange to establish a monarchical regime. However, his death in 1702, without direct heirs, enabled the republican forces to gain control once more. The Dutch Republic would not be seriously threatened again by the monarchical forces.

Underlying Dutch prominence in the seventeenth century was its economic prosperity, fueled by the Dutch role as carriers of Europe trade. But war proved disastrous to the Dutch Republic. Wars with France and England placed heavy burdens on Dutch finances and manpower. English shipping began to challenge what had been Dutch commercial supremacy, and by 1715, the Dutch were experiencing a serious economic decline.

England and the Emergence of Constitutional Monarchy

One of the most prominent examples of resistance to absolute monarchy came in seventeenth-century England where king and Parliament struggled to determine the role each should play in governing England. But the struggle over this political issue was complicated by a deep and profound religious controversy. Along with the victory of Parliament came the foundation for constitutional monarchy by the end of the seventeenth century.

REVOLUTION AND CIVIL WAR

With the death of Queen Elizabeth in 1603, the Tudor dynasty became extinct, and the Stuart line of rulers was inaugurated with the accession to the throne of Elizabeth's cousin, King James VI of Scotland, who became James I (1603–1625) of England. Although used to royal power as king of Scotland, James understood little about the laws, institutions, and customs of the English. He espoused the divine right of kings: the belief that kings receive their power directly from God and are responsible to no one except God. This viewpoint alienated Parliament, which had grown accustomed under the Tudors to act on the premise that monarch and Parliament together ruled England as a "balanced polity." Parliament expressed its displeasure with James's claims by refusing his requests for additional monies needed by the king to meet the increased cost of government. Parliament's power of the purse proved to be its trump card in its relationship with the king.

Some members of Parliament were also alienated by James's religious policy. The Puritans—those Protestants within the Anglican church inspired by Calvinist theology—wanted James to eliminate the episcopal system of church organization used in the Church of England (in which the bishop or *episcopos* played the major administrative role) in favor of a Presbyterian model (used in Scotland and patterned after Calvin's church organization in Geneva, where ministers and elders—also called presbyters—played an important governing role). James refused because he realized that the Anglican church, with its bishops appointed by the crown, was a major support of monarchical authority. But the Puritans were not easily cowed and added to the rising chorus of opposition to the king. Many of England's gentry, mostly well-to-do landowners below the level of the nobility, had become Puritans, and these Puritan gentry not only formed an important and substantial part of the House of Commons, the lower house of Parliament, but also held important positions locally as justices of the peace and sheriffs. It was not wise to alienate them.

The conflict that began during the reign of James came to a head during the reign of his son Charles I (1625–1649). In 1628, Parliament passed a Petition of Right that the king was supposed to accept before being granted any taxes. This petition prohibited taxes without Parliament's consent, arbitrary imprisonment, the quartering of soldiers in private houses, and the declaration of martial law in peacetime. Although he initially accepted it, Charles later reneged on the agreement because of its limitations on royal power. In 1629, Charles decided that because he could not work with Parliament, he would not summon it to meet. From 1629 to 1640, Charles pursued a course of "personal rule," which forced him to find ways to collect taxes without Parliament's cooperation. These expedients aroused opposition from middle-class merchants and landed gentry who believed the king was attempting to tax without Parliament's consent.

The king's religious policy also proved disastrous. The attempt of Charles to impose more ritual on the Anglican church struck the Puritans as a return to Catholic popery. Charles's efforts to force them to conform to his religious policies infuriated the Puritans, thousands of whom went to the "howling wildernesses" of America rather than be forced to conform their consciences to the king's supposed pro-popery nonsense.

◆ **Oliver Cromwell.** Oliver Cromwell was a dedicated Puritan who formed the New Model Army and defeated the forces supporting King Charles I. Unable to work with Parliament, he came to rely on military force to rule England. Cromwell is pictured here in 1649, on the eve of his military campaign in Ireland.

Grievances mounted until England finally slipped into a civil war (1642–1648) that was won by the parliamentary forces. Most important to Parliament's success was the creation of the New Model Army by Oliver Cromwell, the only real military genius of the war. The New Model Army was composed primarily of more extreme Puritans known as the Independents, who, in typical Calvinist fashion, believed they were doing battle for the Lord. It is striking to read in Cromwell's military reports such statements as "Sir, this is none other but the hand of God; and to Him alone belongs the glory."

Between 1648 and 1660, England faced a trying situation. After the execution of Charles I on January 30, 1649, Parliament abolished the monarchy and the House of Lords and proclaimed England a republic or Commonwealth. But Cromwell and his army, unable to work effectively with Parliament, dispersed it by force. As the members of Parliament departed (April 1653),

Cromwell shouted after them: "It's you that have forced me to do this, for I have sought the Lord night and day that He would slay me rather than put upon me the doing of this work." With the certainty of one who is convinced he is right, Cromwell had destroyed both king and Parliament.

After another disastrous period of working with a new Parliament, Cromwell dissolved Parliament and divided the country into eleven regions, each ruled by a major general who served virtually as a military governor. Unable to establish a constitutional basis for a working government, Cromwell had resorted to military force to maintain the rule of the Independents, ironically using even more arbitrary policies than those of Charles I.

Oliver Cromwell died in 1658. After floundering for eighteen months, the military establishment decided that arbitrary rule by the army was no longer feasible and reestablished the monarchy in the person of Charles II, the son of Charles I. The restoration of the Stuart monarchy ended England's time of troubles, but it was not long before England experienced yet another constitutional crisis.

Restoration and a Glorious Revolution

After eleven years of exile, Charles II (1660–1685) returned to England. As he entered London amid the acclaim of the people, he remarked sardonically: "I never knew that I was so popular in England." The restoration of the monarchy and the House of Lords did not mean, however, that the work of the English Revolution was undone. Parliament kept much of the power it had won; arbitrary courts were still abolished; Parliament's role in government was acknowledged; and the necessity for its consent to taxation was accepted. Yet Charles continued to push his own ideas, some of which were clearly out of step with many of the English people.

A serious religious problem disturbed the tranquillity of Charles II's reign. After the restoration of the monarchy, a new Parliament met in 1661 and restored the Anglican church as the official church of England. In addition, laws were passed to force everyone, particularly Catholics and Puritan Dissenters, to conform to the Anglican church. Charles, however, was sympathetic to and perhaps even inclined to Catholicism. Moreover, Charles's brother James, heir to the throne, did not hide the fact that he was a Catholic. Parliament's suspicions were therefore aroused in 1672 when Charles took the audacious step of issuing a Declaration of Indulgence that suspended the laws that Parliament had passed against Catholics and Puritans after the restoration of the

monarchy. Parliament would have none of it and induced the king to suspend the declaration. Propelled by a strong anti-Catholic sentiment, Parliament then passed a Test Act in 1673, specifying that only Anglicans could hold military and civil offices.

The accession of James II (1685–1688) to the crown virtually guaranteed a new constitutional crisis for England. An open and devout Catholic, his attempt to further Catholic interests made religion once more a primary cause of conflict between king and Parliament. Contrary to the Test Act, James named Catholics to high positions in the government, army, navy, and universities. In 1687, he issued a Declaration of Indulgence, which suspended all laws that excluded Catholics and Puritans from office. Parliamentary outcries against James's policies stopped short of rebellion because members knew that he was an old man and his successors were his Protestant daughters Mary and Anne, born to his first wife. But on June 10, 1688, a son was born to James II's second wife, also a Catholic. Suddenly the spector of a Catholic hereditary monarchy loomed large. A group of seven prominent English noblemen invited the Dutch chief executive, William of Orange, husband of James's daughter Mary, to invade England. William and Mary raised an army and invaded England while James, his wife, and infant son fled to France. With almost no bloodshed, England had undergone a "Glorious Revolution," not over the issue of whether there would be monarchy, but rather over who would be monarch.

The events of late 1688 constituted only the initial stage of the Glorious Revolution. The second, and far more important part, was the Revolution Settlement that confirmed William and Mary as monarchs. In January 1689, Parliament offered the throne to William and Mary, who accepted it along with the provisions of a Bill of Rights (see the box on p. 341). The Bill of Rights affirmed Parliament's right to make laws and levy taxes and made it impossible for kings to oppose or do without Parliament by stipulating that standing armies could be raised only with the consent of Parliament. The rights of citizens to petition the sovereign, keep arms, have a jury trial, and not be subject to excessive bail were also confirmed. The Bill of Rights helped to fashion a system of government based on the rule of law and a freely elected Parliament, thus laying the foundation for a constitutional monarchy.

The Bill of Rights did not settle the religious questions that had played such a large role in England's troubles in the seventeenth century. The Toleration Act of 1689 granted Puritan Dissenters the right of free public worship (Catholics were still excluded). Although the Toleration

⇛ *The Bill of Rights* ⇚

In 1688, the English experienced yet another revolution, a rather bloodless one in which the Stuart king James II was replaced by Mary, James's daughter, and her husband, William of Orange. After William and Mary had assumed power, Parliament passed a Bill of Rights that specified the rights of Parliament and laid the foundation for a constitutional monarchy.

The Bill of Rights

Whereas the said late King James II having abdicated the government, and the throne being thereby vacant, his Highness the prince of Orange (whom it has pleased Almighty God to make the glorious instrument of delivering this kingdom from popery and arbitrary power) did (by the device of the lords spiritual and temporal, and diverse principal persons of the Commons) cause letters to be written to the lords spiritual and temporal, being Protestants, and other letters to the several counties, cities, universities, boroughs, and Cinque Ports, for the choosing of such persons to represent them, as were of right to be sent to parliament, to meet and sit at Westminster upon the two and twentieth day of January, in this year 1689, in order to such an establishment as that their religion, laws, and liberties might not again be in danger of being subverted; upon which letters elections have been accordingly made.

And thereupon the said lords spiritual and temporal and Commons, pursuant to their respective letters and elections, being now assembled in a full and free representation of this nation, taking into their most serious consideration the best means for attaining the ends aforesaid, do in the first place (as their ancestors in like case have usually done), for the vindication and assertion of their ancient rights and liberties, declare:

1. That the pretended power of suspending laws, or the execution of laws, by regal authority, without consent of parliament is illegal.

2. That the pretended power of dispensing with the laws, or the execution of law by regal authority, as it has been assumed and exercised of late, is illegal.

3. That the commission for erecting the late court of commissioners for ecclesiastical causes, and all other commissions and courts of like nature, are illegal and pernicious.

4. That levying money for or to the use of the crown by pretense of prerogative, without grant of parliament, for longer time or in other manner than the same is or shall be granted, is illegal.

5. That it is the right of the subjects to petition the king, and all commitments and prosecutions for such petitioning are illegal.

6. That the raising or keeping a standing army within the kingdom in time of peace, unless it be with consent of parliament, is against law.

7. That the subjects which are Protestants may have arms for their defense suitable to their conditions, and as allowed by law.

8. That election of members of parliament ought to be free.

9. That the freedom of speech, and debates or proceedings in parliament, ought not to be impeached or questioned in any court or place out of parliament.

10. That excessive bail ought not to be required, nor excessive fines imposed, nor cruel and unusual punishments inflicted.

11. That jurors ought to be duly impaneled and returned, and jurors which pass upon men in trials for high treason ought to be freeholders.

12. That all grants and promises of fines and forfeitures of particular persons before conviction are illegal and void.

13. And that for redress of all grievances, and for the amending, strengthening, and preserving of the laws, parliament ought to be held frequently.

Act did not mean complete religious freedom and equality, it marked a departure in English history because few people would ever again be persecuted for religious reasons.

Many historians have viewed the Glorious Revolution as the end of the seventeenth-century struggle between king and Parliament. By deposing one king and establishing another, Parliament had destroyed the divine-right theory of kingship (William was, after all, king by grace of Parliament, not God) and confirmed its right to participate in the government. Parliament did not have complete control of the government, but it now had an unquestioned right to participate in affairs of state. During the next century, it would gradually prove to be the real authority in the English system of constitutional monarchy.

Responses to Revolution

The English revolutions of the seventeenth century prompted very different responses from two English political thinkers—Thomas Hobbes and John Locke. Thomas Hobbes, who lived during the English Civil War, was alarmed by the revolutionary upheavals in his contemporary England. Hobbes's name has since been associated with the state's claim to absolute authority over its subjects, which he elaborated in his major treatise on political thought known as the *Leviathan*, published in 1651.

Hobbes claimed that in the state of nature, before society was organized, human life was "solitary, poor, nasty, brutish, and short." Humans were guided not by reason and moral ideals, but by animalistic instincts and a ruthless struggle for self-preservation. To save themselves from destroying each other (the "war of every man against every man"), people contracted to form a commonwealth, which Hobbes called "that great Leviathan (or rather, to speak more reverently, that mortal god) to which we owe our peace and defense." This commonwealth placed its collective power into the hands of a sovereign authority, preferably a single ruler, who served as executor, legislator, and judge. This absolute ruler possessed unlimited power. In Hobbes's view, subjects may not rebel; if they do, they must be suppressed.

John Locke (1632–1704) viewed the exercise of political power quite differently from Hobbes and argued against the absolute rule of one man. Locke's experience of English politics during the Glorious Revolution was incorporated into a political work called *Two Treatises of Government*. Like Hobbes, Locke began with the state of nature before human existence became organized socially. But, unlike Hobbes, Locke believed humans lived then in a state of equality and freedom rather than a state of war. In this state of nature, humans had certain inalienable natural rights—to life, liberty, and property. Like Hobbes, Locke did not believe all was well in the state of nature. Since there was no impartial judge in the state of nature, people found it difficult to protect these natural rights. So they mutually agreed to establish a government to ensure the protection of their rights. This agreement established mutual obligations: Government would protect the rights of people while the people would act reasonably toward government. But if a government broke this agreement—if a monarch, for example, failed to live up to his obligation to protect the natural rights or claimed absolute authority and made laws without the consent of the community—the people might form a new government. For Locke, however, the community of people was primarily the landholding aristocracy who were represented in Parliament, not the landless masses. Locke was hardly an advocate of political democracy, but his ideas proved important to both Americans and French in the eighteenth century and were used to support demands for constitutional government, the rule of law, and the protection of rights.

Economic Trends in the Seventeenth Century

The seventeenth century was marked by economic contraction, although variations existed depending on the country or region. Trade, industry, and agriculture all felt the pinch of a depression, which some historians believe bottomed out between 1640 and 1680. Translated into everyday life, for many people the economic contraction of the seventeenth century meant scarce food, uncertain population, and high rates of taxation.

Population was also affected. Based on the birthrate of the seventeenth century, demographers would expect the European population to have doubled every twenty-five years. In reality, the population either declined or increased only intermittently as a result of a variety of factors. Infant mortality rates were high, 30 percent in the first year of life and 50 percent before the age of ten. Epidemics and famines were again common experiences in European life. The last great epidemic of bubonic plague spread across Europe in the middle and late years of the seventeenth century. The Mediterranean region suffered from 1646 to 1657, when the plague killed off 130,000 persons in Naples alone. In 1665, it struck England and devastated London, killing 20 percent of its population.

Mercantilism and Colonies

As we saw in our discussion of Colbert's policies in France, one of the principles of mercantilism was a high regard for colonies as sources of raw materials and markets for finished goods. Mercantilist theory on the role of colonies was matched in practice by Europe's overseas expansion. With the development of colonies and trading posts in the Americas and Far East, Europeans entered into an age of international commerce in the seventeenth century. We should remember, however, that local, regional, and intra-European trade still dominated the scene. About one-tenth of English and Dutch exports were shipped across the Atlantic; slightly more went to the Far East. What made the transoceanic trade rewarding, however, was not the volume, but the value of its goods. Dutch, English, and French merchants were bringing back products that were still consumed largely by the wealthy, but were beginning to make their way into the lives of artisans and merchants. Pepper and spice from the Indies, West Indian and Brazilian sugar, and Asian coffee and tea were becoming more readily available to European consumers. The first coffee and tea houses opened in London in the 1650s and spread rapidly to other parts of Europe.

In 1600, much overseas trade was still carried by the Spanish and Portuguese, who alone possessed colonies of any significant size. But war and steady pressure from their Dutch and English rivals eroded Portuguese trade in both the west and the east. The Spanish also maintained an enormous South American empire, but Spain's importance as a commercial power declined rapidly in the seventeenth century.

The Dutch became a major economic power in the seventeenth century. The Dutch East India Company, formed in 1602 to exploit the riches of the Far East, gradually took control of most of the Portuguese bases in the Far East and opened trade with China and Japan. Its profits were spectacular in the first ten years. The Dutch West India Company, created in 1621, was less successful. One of its projects was the mainland colony of New Netherlands, which stretched from the mouth of the Hudson as far north as Albany. In 1664, the English seized the colony of New Netherlands and renamed it New York while the Dutch West India Company soon went bankrupt.

The Dutch overseas trade and commercial empire faced two major rivals in the seventeenth century—the English and French. The English had founded their own East India Company in 1601 and proceeded to create a colonial empire in the New World along the Atlantic seaboard of North America. French commercial companies in the Far East experienced much difficulty. The East Indian companies set up by Henry IV and Richelieu all failed. The French had greater success in North America where in 1663 Canada was made the property of the crown and administered like a French province. But the French failed to provide adequate men or money, allowing their continental wars to take precedence over the conquest of the North American continent. Already in 1713, by the Treaty of Utrecht, the French began to cede some of their American possessions to their English rival.

The World of European Culture

The seventeenth century was a remarkably talented one. In addition to the intellectuals responsible for the Scientific Revolution (see Chapter 17), the era was blessed with a number of prominent thinkers, artists, and writers.

Art: French Classicism and Dutch Realism

In the second half of the seventeenth century, France replaced Italy as the cultural leader of Europe. Rejecting the Baroque style as overly showy and passionate, the French remained committed to the classical values of the High Renaissance. French late classicism, with its emphasis on clarity, simplicity, balance, and harmony of design was,

◆ **Nicholas Poussin, *Landscape with the Burial of Phocian.*** France became the new cultural leader of Europe in the second half of the seventeenth century. French classicism upheld the values of High Renaissance style, but in a more static version. In Nicholas Poussin's work, we see the emphasis of French classicism on the use of scenes from classical sources and the creation of a sense of grandeur and noble strength in both human figures and landscape.

however, a rather austere version of the High Renaissance style. Its triumph reflected the shift in seventeenth-century French society from chaos to order. While rejecting the emotionalism and high drama of the Baroque, French classicism continued the Baroque's conception of grandeur in the portrayal of noble subjects, especially those from classical antiquity. Nicholas Poussin (1594–1665) exemplified these principles in his paintings. His choice of scenes from classical mythology, the orderliness of his landscapes, the postures of his figures copied from the sculptures of antiquity, and his use of brown tones all reflect the classical principles of the French Academy.

The supremacy of Dutch commerce in the seventeenth century was paralleled by a brilliant flowering of Dutch painting. Wealthy patricians and burghers of Dutch urban society commissioned works of art for their guild halls, town halls, and private dwellings. Following the wishes of these patrons, Dutch painters became primarily interested in the realistic portrayal of secular, everyday life.

The finest example of the golden age of Dutch painting was Rembrandt van Rijn (1606-1669). Although Rembrandt shared the Dutch predilection for realistic portraits, he became more introspective as he grew older. He refused to follow his contemporaries whose pictures were largely secular in subject matter; half of his paintings focused on scenes from biblical tales. Since the Protestant tradition of hostility to religious pictures had discouraged artistic expression, Rembrandt stands out as the one great Protestant painter of the seventeenth century.

◆   **Rembrandt van Rijn, *Syndics of the Cloth Guild.***   The Dutch experienced a Golden Age of painting during the seventeenth century. The burghers and patricians of Dutch urban society commissioned works of art, and these quite naturally reflected the burghers' interests, as this painting by Rembrandt illustrates.

French Comedy: The Would-Be Gentleman

The comedy writer Jean-Baptiste Molière has long been regarded as one of the best playwrights of the age of Louis XIV. Molière's comedy, The Would-Be Gentleman, focuses on Monsieur Jourdain, a vain and pretentious Parisian merchant who aspires to become a gentleman (at that time, a term for a member of the nobility who possessed, among other things, a title, fine clothes, and good taste). Jourdain foolishly believes that he can buy these things and hires a number of teachers to instruct him. In this scene from Act II, Jourdain learns from his philosophy teacher that he has been speaking prose all his life.

Jean-Baptiste Moliére, *The Would-Be Gentleman*

PHILOSOPHY MASTER: I will explain to you all these curiosities to the bottom.

M. JOURDAIN: Pray do. But now, I must commit a secret to you. I'm in love with a person of great quality, and I should be glad you would help me to write something to her in a short *billet-doux* [love letter], which I'll drop at her feet.

PHILOSOPHY MASTER: Very well.

M. JOURDAIN: That will be very gallant, won't it?

PHILOSOPHY MASTER: Without doubt. Is it verse that you would write to her?

M. JOURDAIN: No, no, none of your verse.

PHILOSOPHY MASTER: You would only have prose?

M. JOURDAIN: No, I would neither have verse nor prose.

PHILOSOPHY MASTER: It must be one or the other.

M. JOURDAIN: Why so?

PHILOSOPHY MASTER: Because , sir, there's nothing to express one's self by, but prose, or verse.

M. JOURDAIN: Is there nothing then but prose, or verse?

PHILOSOPHY MASTER: No, sir, whatever is not prose, is verse; and whatever is not verse, is prose.

M. JOURDAIN: And when one talks, what may that be then?

PHILOSOPHY MASTER: Prose.

M. JOURDAIN: How? When I say, Nicole, bring me my slippers, and give me my nightcap, is that prose?

PHILOSOPHY MASTER: Yes, sir.

M. JOURDAIN: On my conscience, I have spoken prose above these forty years without knowing anything of the matter; and I have all the obligations in the world to you for informing me of this. I would therefore put into a letter to her: Beautiful marchioness, your fair eyes make me die with love; but I would have this placed in a gallant manner; and have a gentle turn.

PHILOSOPHY MASTER: Why, add that the fire of her eyes has reduced your heart to ashes: that you suffer for her night and day all the torments—

M. JOURDAIN: No, no, no, I won't have all that—I'll have nothing but what I told you. Beautiful marchioness, your fair eyes make me die with love.

PHILOSOPHY MASTER: You must by all means lengthen the thing out a little.

M. JOURDAIN: No, I tell you. I'll have none but those very words in the letter: but turned in a modish way, ranged handsomely as they should be. I desire you'd show me a little, that I may see the different manners in which one may place them.

PHILOSOPHY MASTER: One may place them first of all as you said: Beautiful marchioness, your fair eyes make me die for love. Or suppose: For love die me make, beautiful marchioness, your fair eyes. Or perhaps: Your eyes fair, for love me make, beautiful marchioness, die. Or suppose: Die your fair eyes, beautiful marchioness, for love me make. Or however: Me make your eyes fair die, beautiful marchioness, for love.

M. JOURDAIN: But of all these ways, which is the best?

PHILOSOPHY MASTER: That which you said: Beautiful marchioness, your fair eyes make me die for love.

M. JOURDAIN: Yet at the same time, I never studied it, and I made the whole of it at the first touch. I thank you with all my heart, and desire you would come in good time tomorrow.

PHILOSOPHY MASTER: I shall not fail.

The Theater: The Triumph of French Neoclassicism

As the great age of theater in England and Spain was drawing to a close around 1630, a new dramatic era began to dawn in France that lasted into the 1680s. Unlike Shakespeare in England and Lope de Vega in Spain, French playwrights wrote more for an elite audience and were forced to depend on royal patronage. Louis XIV used theater as he did art and architecture—to attract attention to his monarchy.

French dramatists cultivated a classical style in which the Aristotelian rules of dramatic composition, observing the three unities of time, place, and action, were closely followed. French neoclassicism emphasized the clever, polished, and correct over the emotional and imaginative. Many of the French works of this period derived both their themes and plots from Greek and Roman sources.

Jean-Baptiste Molière (1622–1673) enjoyed the favor of the French court and benefited from the patronage of the Sun King. He wrote, produced, and acted in a series of comedies that often satirized the religious and social world of his time (see the box on p. 345). In *The Misanthrope*, he mocked the corruption of court society, while in *Tartuffe*, he ridiculed religious hypocrisy. Molière's satires, however, sometimes got him into trouble. The Paris clergy did not find *Tartuffe* funny and had it banned for five years. Only the protection of Louis XIV saved Molière from more severe harassment.

Conclusion

To many historians, the seventeenth century has assumed extraordinary proportions. The divisive effects of the Reformation had been assimilated and the concept of a united Christendom, held as an ideal since the Middle Ages, had been irrevocably destroyed by the religious wars, making possible the emergence of a system of nation-states in which power politics took on an increasing significance. The growth of political thought focusing on the secular origins of state power reflected the changes that were going on in seventeenth-century society.

Within those states, there slowly emerged some of the machinery that made possible a growing centralization of power. In those states called absolutist, strong monarchs with the assistance of their aristocracies took the lead in providing the leadership for greater centralization. But in England, where the landed aristocracy gained power at the expense of the monarchs, the foundations were laid for a constitutional government in which Parliament provided the focus for the institutions of centralized power. In all the major European states, a growing concern for power and dynastic expansion led to larger armies and greater conflict. War remained an endemic feature of Western civilization.

But the search for order and harmony continued, evident in art and literature. At the same time, while it would be misleading to state that Europe had become a secular world, we would have to say that religious preoccupations and values were losing ground to secular considerations. The seventeenth century was a transitional period to a more secular spirit that has characterized modern Western civilization until the present time. No stronger foundation for this spirit could be found than in the new view of the universe that was created by the Scientific Revolution of the seventeenth century, and it is to that story that we must now turn.

NOTES

1. Quoted in John B. Wolf, *Louis XIV* (New York, 1968), p. 134.

2. Quoted in J. H. Elliott, *Imperial Spain, 1469–1716* (New York, 1963), p. 338.

SUGGESTIONS FOR FURTHER READIING

In addition to the general works listed in Chapter 15, see also D. H. Pennington, *Europe in the Seventeenth Century*, 2d ed. (London and New York, 1989); T. Munck, *Seventeenth Century Europe 1598–1700* (London, 1990); and R. S. Dunn, *The Age of Religious Wars, 1559–1715*, 2d ed. (New York, 1979).

For a brief account of seventeenth-century French history, see R. Briggs, *Early Modern France, 1560–1715* (Oxford, 1977). A solid and very readable biography of Louis XIV is J. B. Wolf, *Louis XIV* (New York, 1968). Also of value are the works by O. Bernier, *Louis XIV* (New York, 1988); and P. Goubert, *Louis XIV and Twenty Million*

Frenchmen, trans. A Carter (New York, 1970). A now classic work on life in Louis XIV's France is W. H. Lewis, *The Splendid Century* (Garden City, N.Y., 1953). Well-presented summaries of revisionist views on Louis's monarchical power are R. Mettam, *Power and Faction in Louis XIV's France* (Oxford, 1988); and W. Beik, *Absolutism and Society in Seventeenth Century France* (Cambridge, 1985).

Good general works on seventeenth-century Spanish history include the relevant sections of J. Lynch, *Spain Under Habsburgs*, 2d ed. (New York, 1981); H. Kamen, *Spain 1469–1716: A Society of Conflict* (London, 1983); and R. A. Stradling, *Europe and the Decline of Spain, 1580–1720* (London, 1981). On the last half of the seventeenth century, see the more detailed work by H. Kamen, *Spain in the Later Seventeenth Century, 1665–1700* (London, 1980).

An older, but still valuable survey of the German states in the seventeenth century can be found in H. Holborn, *A History of Modern Germany, 1648–1840* (London, 1965). An important recent work is M. Hughes, *Early Modern Germany, 1477–1806* (Philadelphia, 1992). On the creation of an Austrian state, see R. J. W. Evans, *The Making of the Habsburg Monarchy, 1550–1700* (Oxford, 1979). The older work by F. L. Carsten, *The Origins of Prussia* (Oxford, 1954), remains an outstanding study of early Prussian history.

On Russian history before Peter the Great, see the classic work by V. O. Klyuchevsky, *A Course in Russian History: The Seventeenth Century* (Chicago, 1968). Works on Peter the Great include V. O. Klyuchevsky, *Peter the Great*, trans. L. Archibald (New York, 1958); M. S. Anderson, *Peter the Great* (London, 1978); B. H. Sumner, *Peter the Great and the Emergence of Russia* (New York, 1962); and the massive popular biography by R. K. Massie, *Peter the Great* (New York, 1980).

Good general works on the period of the English Revolution include G. E. Aylmer, *Rebellion or Revolution? England, 1640–1660* (New York, 1986); and the brief study by R. Howell, Jr., *The Origins of the English Revolution* (St. Louis, 1975). On the war itself, see R. Ashton, *The English Civil War: Conservatism and Revolution, 1604–1649* (London, 1976). On Oliver Cromwell, see P. Gaunt, *Oliver Cromwell* (Cambridge, Mass., 1996); R. Howell, Jr., *Cromwell* (Boston, 1977); and the beautifully written popular account by A. Fraser, *Cromwell: The Lord Protector* (New York, 1974). For a general survey of the post-Cromwellian era, see J. R. Jones, *Country and Court: England, 1658–1714* (London, 1978). On Charles II, see the scholarly biography by R. Hutton, *Charles II* (Oxford, 1989). Locke's political ideas are examined in J. H. Franklin, *John Locke and the Theory of Sovereignty* (London, 1978). On Thomas Hobbes, see D. D. Raphael, *Hobbes* (London, 1977).

On the United Provinces, see two short, but sound introductions, K. H. D. Haley, *The Dutch in the Seventeenth Century* (London, 1972); and C. Wilson, *The Dutch Republic and the Civilization of the Seventeenth Century* (London, 1968). There is also a valuable but very lengthy study by J. Israel, *The Dutch Republic: Its Rise, Greatness, and Fall* (New York, 1995).

On the economic side of the seventeenth century, there are the three volumes by F. Braudel, *Civilization and Capitalism in the 15th to 18th Century*, which obviously cover much more than just the seventeenth century: *The Structures of Everyday Life* (London, 1981); *The Wheels of Commerce* (London, 1982); and *The Perpsective of the World* (London, 1984). A single-volume comprehensive survey is J. de Vries, *The Economy of Europe in an Age of Crisis* (Cambridge, 1976). On overseas trade and colonial empires, see C. R. Boxer, *The Dutch Seaborne Empire, 1600–1800* (New York, 1965); and R. Davis, *English Overseas Trade, 1500–1700* (London, 1973).

French theater and literature are examined in A. Adam, *Grandeur and Illusion: French Literature and Society, 1600–1715*, trans. J. Tint (New York, 1972). For an examination of French and Dutch art, see A. Blunt, *Art and Architecture in France, 1500–1700* (London, 1953); J. Rosenberg, S. Silve, and E. H. ter Kuele, *Dutch Art and Architecture, 1600–1800* (London, 1966); and C. White, *Rembrandt and His World* (London, 1964).

Toward a New Heaven and a New Earth: The Scientific Revolution and the Emergence of Modern Science

In addition to the political, economic, social, and intellectual crises of the seventeenth century, we need to add an intellectual one. The Scientific Revolution questioned and ultimately challenged conceptions and beliefs about the nature of the external world and reality that had crystallized into a rather strict orthodoxy by the Late Middle Ages. Derived from the works of ancient Greeks and Romans and grounded in Christian thought, the medieval worldview had become a formidable one. No doubt, the breakdown of Christian unity during the Reformation and the subsequent religious wars had created an environment in which Europeans became accustomed to challenging both the ecclesiastical and political realms. Should it surprise us that a challenge to intellectual authority soon followed?

The Scientific Revolution taught Europeans to view the universe and their place in it in a new way. The shift from an earth-centered to a sun-centered cosmos had an emotional as well as an intellectual effect on those who understood it. Thus, the Scientific Revolution, popularized in the eighteenth-century Enlightenment, stands as the major force in the transition to the largely secular, rational, and materialistic perspective that has defined the modern Western mentality since its full acceptance in the nineteenth and twentieth centuries.

The transition to a new worldview, however, was not an easy one. In the seventeenth century, the Italian scientist Galileo, an outspoken advocate of the new worldview, found that his ideas were strongly opposed by the authorities of the Catholic church. Galileo's position was clear: "I hold the sun to be situated motionless in the center of the revolution of the celestial bodies, while the earth rotates on its axis and revolves about the sun." Moreover, "nothing physical that sense-experience sets before our eyes . . . ought to be called in question (much less condemned)

- Copernicus, *On the Revolutions of the Heavenly Spheres*

• • • Kepler's laws

Galileo, *The Starry Messenger*

Newton, Law of universal gravitation

- Vesalius, *On the Fabric of the Human Body*

Harvey's theory of circulation

- Cavendish, *Grounds of Natural Philosophy*

Descartes, *Discourse on Method*

- Pascal, *Pensées*

Bacon, *The Great Instauration*

• • • Establishment of French Royal Academy of Sciences

Beginnings of English Royal Society

upon the testimony of Biblical passages." But the church had a different view, and in 1633, Galileo, now sixty-eight and in ill health, was called before the dreaded Inquisition in Rome. He was kept waiting for two months before he was tried and found guilty of heresy and disobedience. Completely shattered by the experience, he denounced his errors: "With a sincere heart and unfeigned faith I curse and detest the said errors and heresies contrary to the Holy Church, and I swear that I will nevermore in future say or assert anything that may give rise to a similar suspicion of me." Legend holds that when he left the trial rooms, Galileo muttered to himself: "And yet it does move!" In any case, Galileo had been silenced, but his writings remained, and they began to spread through Europe. The actions of the Inquisition had failed to stop the spread of the new ideas of the Scientific Revolution.

In one sense, the Scientific Revolution was not a revolution. It was not characterized by the explosive change and rapid overthrow of traditional authority that we normally associate with the word revolution. The Scientific Revolution did overturn centuries of authority, but only in a gradual and piecemeal fashion. Nevertheless, its results were truly revolutionary. The Scientific Revolution was a key factor in setting Western civilization along its modern secular and material path.

Background to the Scientific Revolution

To say that the Scientific Revolution brought about a dissolution of the medieval worldview is not to say that the Middles Ages was a period of scientific ignorance. Many educated Europeans took an intense interest in the world around them since it was, after all, "God's handiwork" and therefore an appropriate subject for study. Late medieval scholastic philosophers had advanced mathematical and physical thinking in many ways, but the subjection of these thinkers to a strict theological framework and their unquestioning reliance on a few ancient authorities, especially Aristotle and Galen, limited where they could go. Many "natural philosophers," as medieval scientists were known, preferred refined logical analysis to systematic observations of the natural world. A number of changes and advances in the fifteenth and sixteenth centuries may have played a major role in helping "natural philosophers" abandon their old views and develop new ones.

The Renaissance humanists mastered Greek as well as Latin and made available new works of Ptolemy and Archimedes as well as Plato. These writings made it apparent that even the unquestioned authorities of the Middle Ages, Aristotle and Galen, had been contradicted by other thinkers. The desire to discover which school of thought was correct stimulated new scientific work that sometimes led to a complete rejection of the classical authorities.

Renaissance artists have also been credited with making an impact on scientific study. Their desire to imitate nature led them to rely on a close observation of nature.

Their accurate renderings of rocks, plants, animals, and human anatomy established new standards for the study of natural phenomena. At the same time, the "scientific" study of the problems of perspective and correct anatomical proportions led to new insights. "No painter," one Renaissance artist declared, "can paint well without a thorough knowledge of geometry."[1]

Technical problems, such as calculating the tonnage of ships accurately, also served to stimulate scientific activity because they required careful observation and accurate measurements. Then, too, the invention of new instruments and machines, such as the telescope and microscope, often made new scientific discoveries possible. Above all, the printing press had an indirect, but crucial role in spreading innovative ideas quickly and easily.

Mathematics, which played such a fundamental role in the scientific achievements of the sixteenth and seventeenth centuries, was promoted in the Renaissance by the rediscovery of the works of ancient mathematicians and the influence of Plato, who had emphasized the importance of mathematics in explaining the universe. While mathematics was applauded as the key to navigation, military science, and geography, the Renaissance also held the widespread belief that mathematics was the key to understanding the nature of things. According to Leonardo da Vinci, since God eternally geometrizes, nature is inherently mathematical: "Proportion is not only found in numbers and measurements but also in sounds, weights, times, positions, and in whatsoever power there may."[2] Copernicus, Kepler, Galileo, and Newton were all great mathematicians who believed that the secrets of nature were written in the language of mathematics.

Another factor in the origins of the Scientific Revolution was possibly the role of magic. Renaissance magic was the preserve of an intellectual elite from all of Europe. By the end of the sixteenth century, Hermetic magic had become fused with alchemical thought into a single intellectual framework. This tradition believed that the world was a living embodiment of divinity. Humans, who it was believed also had that spark of divinity within, could use magic, especially mathematical magic, to understand and dominate the world of nature or employ the powers of nature for beneficial purposes. Was it Hermeticism, then, that inaugurated the shift in consciousness that made the Scientific Revolution possible, since the desire to control and dominate the natural world was a crucial motivating force in the Scientific Revolution? Scholars debate the issue, but histories of the Scientific Revolution frequently overlook the fact that the great names we associate with the revolution in cosmology—Copernicus, Kepler, Galileo, and Newton—all had a seri-

ous interest in Hermetic ideas and the fields of astrology and alchemy. The mention of these names also reminds us of one final consideration in the origins of the Scientific Revolution: It resulted largely from the work of a handful of great intellectuals.

Toward a New Heaven: A Revolution in Astronomy

The greatest achievements in the Scientific Revolution of the sixteenth and seventeenth centuries came in those fields most dominated by the ideas of the Greeks—astronomy, mechanics, and medicine. The cosmological views of the Late Middle Ages had been built on a synthesis of the ideas of Aristotle, Claudius Ptolemy (the greatest astronomer of antiquity who lived in the second century A.D.), and Christian theology. In the resulting Ptolemaic or geocentric conception, the universe was seen as a series of concentric spheres with a fixed or motionless earth as its center. Composed of material substance, the earth was imperfect and constantly changing. The spheres that surrounded the earth were made of a crystalline, transparent substance and moved in circular orbits around the earth. Circular movement, according to Aristotle, was the most "perfect" kind of motion and hence appropriate for the "perfect" heavenly bodies thought to consist of a nonmaterial, incorruptible "quintessence." These heavenly bodies, pure orbs of light, were embedded in the moving, concentric spheres, and in 1500 the number of known spheres was ten. Working outward from the earth, eight spheres contained the moon, Mercury, Venus, the sun, Mars, Jupiter, Saturn, and the fixed stars. The ninth sphere imparted to the eighth sphere of the fixed stars its motion while the tenth sphere was frequently described as the prime mover that moved itself and imparted motion to the other spheres. Beyond the tenth sphere was the Empyrean Heaven—the location of God and all the saved souls. This Christianized Ptolemaic universe, then, was a finite one. It had a fixed end in harmony with Christian thought and expectations. God and the saved souls were at one end of the universe while humans were at the center. They had been given power over the earth, but their real purpose was to achieve salvation.

Copernicus

In May 1543, shortly before his death, Nicholas Copernicus (1473–1543), who had studied mathematics and astronomy first at Cracow in his native Poland and later at

On the Revolutions of the Heavenly Spheres

Nicolaus Copernicus began a revolution in astronomy when he argued that it was the sun and not the earth that was at the center of the universe. Expecting controversy and scorn, Copernicus hesitated to publish the work in which he put forth his heliocentric theory. He finally relented, however, and managed to see a copy of it just before he died.

Nicolaus Copernicus, *On the Revolutions of the Heavenly Spheres*

For a long time, then, I reflected on this confusion in the astronomical traditions concerning the derivation of the motions of the universe's spheres. I began to be annoyed that the movements of the world machine, created for our sake by the best and most systematic Artisan of all, were not understood with greater certainty by the philosophers, who otherwise examined so precisely the most insignificant trifles of this world. For this reason I undertook the task of rereading the works of all the philosophers which I could obtain to learn whether anyone had ever proposed other motions of the universe's spheres than those expounded by the teachers of astronomy in the schools. And in fact first I found in Cicero that Hicetas supposed the earth to move. Later I also discovered in Plutarch that certain others were of this opinion. I have decided to set his words down here, so that they may be available to everybody:

> Some think that the earth remains at rest. But Philolaus the Pythagorean believes that, like the sun and moon, it revolves around the fire in an oblique circle. Heraclides of Pontus and Ecphantus the Pythagorean make the earth move, not in a progressive motion, but like a wheel in a rotation from the west to east about its own center.

Therefore, having obtained the opportunity from these sources, I too began to consider the mobility of the earth. And even though the idea seemed absurd, nevertheless I know that others before me had been granted the freedom to imagine any circles whatever for the purpose of explaining the heavenly phenomena. Hence I thought that I too would be readily permitted to ascertain whether explanations sounder than those of my predecessors could be found for the revolution of the celestial spheres on the assumption of some motion of the earth.

Having thus assumed the motions which I ascribe to the earth later on in the volume, by long and intense study I finally found that if the motions of the other planets are correlated with the orbiting of the earth, and are computed for the revolution of each planet, not only do their phenomena follow therefrom but also the order and size of all the planets and spheres, and heaven itself is so linked together that in no portion of it can anything be shifted without disrupting the remaining parts and the universe as a whole. . . .

Hence I feel no shame in asserting that this whole region engirdled by the moon, and the center of the earth, traverse this grand circle amid the rest of the planets in an annual revolution around the sun. Near the sun is the center of the universe. Moreover, since the sun remains stationary, whatever appears as a motion of the sun is really due rather to the motion of the earth.

the Italian universities of Bologna and Padua, published his famous book, *On the Revolutions of the Heavenly Spheres*. Copernicus was not an accomplished observational astronomer and relied for his data on the records of his predecessors. But he was a mathematician who felt that Ptolemy's geocentric system was too complicated and failed to accord with the observed motions of the heavenly bodies (see the box above). Copernicus hoped that his heliocentric or sun-centered conception would offer a more accurate explanation.

Copernicus argued that the universe consisted of eight spheres with the sun motionless at the center and the sphere of the fixed stars at rest in the eighth sphere. The planets revolved around the sun in the order of Mercury, Venus, the earth, Mars, Jupiter, and Saturn. The moon, however, revolved around the earth. Moreover, according to Copernicus, what appeared to be the movement of the sun and the fixed stars around the earth was really explained by the daily rotation of the earth on its axis and the journey of the earth around the sun each year. Copernicus, however, was basically conservative. He did not reject Aristotle's principle of the existence of heavenly spheres moving in circular orbits.

The immediate impact of Copernicus was not momentous—no revolution occurred overnight. Nevertheless, although most people were not yet ready to accept the theory of Copernicus, there were growing doubts about the Ptolemaic system. The next step in destroying the geocentric conception and supporting the Copernican system was taken by Johannes Kepler.

Kepler

The work of Johannes Kepler (1571–1630) illustrates well the narrow line that often separated magic and science in the early Scientific Revolution. An avid astrologer, Kepler possessed a keen interest in Hermetic thought and mathematical magic. In a book written in 1596, he elaborated on his theory that the universe was constructed on the basis of geometric figures, such as the pyramid and the cube. Believing that the harmony of the human soul (a divine attribute) was mirrored in the numerical relationships existing between the planets, he focused much of his attention on discovering the "music of the spheres." Kepler was also a brilliant mathematician and astronomer who took a post as imperial mathematician to Emperor Rudolf II. Using the detailed astronomical data of his predecessor, Kepler arrived at his laws of planetary motion that confirmed Copernicus's heliocentric theory. In his first law he contradicted Copernicus by showing that the orbits of the planets around the sun were not circular but elliptical in shape with the sun at one focus of the ellipse rather than at the center.

Kepler's work effectively eliminated the idea of uniform circular motion as well as the idea of crystalline spheres revolving in circular orbits. The basic structure of the traditional Ptolemaic system had been destroyed, and people had been freed to think in new terms of the actual paths of planets revolving around the sun in elliptical orbits. By the end of Kepler's life, the Ptolemaic system was rapidly losing ground to the new ideas. Important questions remained unanswered, however. What were the planets made of? And how does one explain motion in the universe? It was an Italian scientist who achieved the next important breakthrough to a new cosmology by answering the first question.

Galileo

Galileo Galilei (1564–1642) taught mathematics, first at Pisa and later at Padua, one of the most prestigious universities in Europe. Galileo was the first European to

◆ **Medieval Conception of the Universe.** As this sixteenth-century illustration shows, the medieval cosmological view placed the earth at the center of the universe, surrounded by a series of concentric spheres. The earth was imperfect and constantly changing while the heavenly bodies that surrounded it were perfect and incorruptible. Beyond the tenth and final sphere was heaven where God and all the saved souls were located.

make systematic observations of the heavens by means of a telescope, thereby inaugurating a new age in astronomy. He had heard of a Flemish lens grinder who had created a "spyglass" that magnified objects seen at a distance and soon constructed his own after reading about it. Instead of peering at terrestrial objects, Galileo turned his telescope to the skies and made a remarkable series of discoveries: mountains on the moon, four moons revolving around Jupiter, the phases of Venus, and sun spots. Galileo's observations seemed to destroy yet another aspect of the traditional cosmology in that the universe seemed to be composed of a material substance similar to that of earth rather than an ethereal or perfect and unchanging substance.

Galileo's revelations, published in the *The Starry Messenger* in 1610, stunned his contemporaries and probably did more to make Europeans aware of the new picture of the universe than the mathematical theories of Copernicus and Kepler (see the box on p. 354). But even in the midst of his newfound acclaim, Galileo found himself increasingly suspect by the authorities of the Catholic church. The Roman Inquisition (or Holy Office) of the Catholic church condemned Copernicanism and ordered Galileo to abandon the Copernican thesis. The report of the Inquisition ran: "That the doctrine that the sun was the center of the world and immovable was false and absurd, formally heretical and contrary to Scripture, whereas the doctrine that the earth was not the center of the world but moved, and has further a daily motion, was philosophically false and absurd and theologically at least erroneous."[3] It is apparent from the Inquisition's response that the church attacked the Copernican system because it threatened not only Scripture, but also an entire conception of the universe. The heavens were no longer a spiritual world, but a world of matter. Humans were no longer at the center and God was no longer in a specific place. The new system raised such uncertainties that it seemed prudent simply to condemn it. In 1633, Galileo was found guilty of teaching the condemned Copernician system and was forced to recant his errors. Placed under house arrest on his estate near Florence, he spent the remaining eight years of his life studying mechanics, a field in which he made significant contributions.

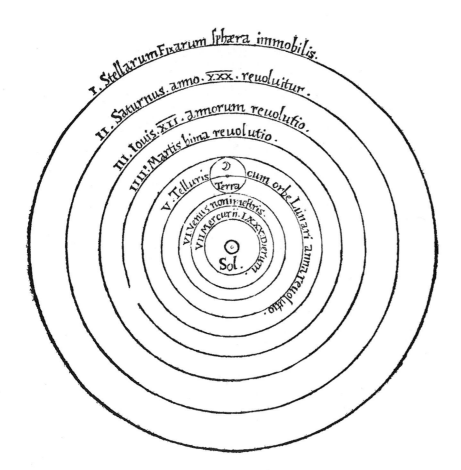

◆ **The Copernican System.** The Copernican system was presented in *On the Revolutions of the Heavenly Spheres*, published shortly before Copernicus's death. As shown in this illustration from the first edition of the book, Copernicus maintained that the sun was the center of the universe while the planets, including the earth, revolved around it. Moreover, the earth rotated daily on its axis.

❧ The Starry Messenger ❧

The Italian Galileo Galilei was the first European to use a telescope to make systematic observations of the heavens. His observations, as reported in The Starry Messenger *in 1610, stunned European intellectuals by revealing that the celestial bodies were not perfect and immutable, as had been believed, but were apparently composed of a material substance similar to the earth. In this selection, Galileo describes how he devised a telescope and what he saw with it.*

Galileo Galilei, The Starry Messenger

About ten months ago a report reached my ears that a certain Fleming had constructed a spyglass by means of which visible objects, though very distant from the eye of the observer, were distinctly seen as if nearby. Of this truly remarkable effect several experiences were related, to which some persons gave credence while others denied them. A few days later the report was confirmed to me in a letter from a noble Frenchman at Paris, Jacques Badovere, which caused me to apply myself wholeheartedly to inquire into the means by which I might arrive at the invention of a similar instrument. This I did shortly afterwards, my basis being the theory of refraction. First I prepared a tube of lead, at the ends of which I fitted two glass lenses, both plane on one side while on the other side one was spherically convex and the other concave. Then placing my eye near the concave lens I perceived objects satisfactorily large and near, for they appeared three times closer and nine times larger than when seen with the naked eye alone. Next I constructed another one, more accurate, which represented objects as enlarged more than sixty times. Finally, sparing neither labor nor expense, I succeeded in constructing for myself so excellent an instrument that objects seen by means of it appeared nearly one thousand times larger and over thirty times closer than when regarded without natural vision.

It would be superfluous to enumerate the number and importance of the advantages of such an instrument at sea as well as on land. But forsaking terrestrial observations, I turned to celestial ones, and first I saw the moon from as near at hand as if it were scarcely two terrestrial radii. After that I observed often with wondering delight both the planets and the fixed stars, and since I saw these latter to be very crowded, I began to see (and eventually found) a method by which I might measure their distances apart. . . .

Now let us review the observations made during the past two months, once more inviting the attention of all who are eager for true philosophy to the first steps of such important contemplations. Let us speak first of that surface of the moon which faces us. For greater clarity I distinguish two parts of this surface, a lighter and a darker; the lighter part seems to surround and to pervade the whole hemisphere, while the darker part discolors the moon's surface like a kind of cloud, and makes it appear covered with spots. . . . From observation of these spots repeated many times I have been led to the opinion and conviction that the surface of the moon is not smooth, uniform, and precisely spherical as a great number of philosophers believe it (and the other heavenly bodies) to be, but is uneven, rough, and full of cavities and prominences, being not unlike the face of the earth, relieved by chains of mountains and deep valleys.

The condemnation of Galileo by the Inquisition seriously hampered further scientific work in Italy, which had been at the forefront of scientific innovation. Leadership in science now passed to the northern countries, especially England, France, and the Dutch Netherlands. By the 1630s and 1640s, no reasonable astronomer could overlook that Galileo's discoveries combined with Kepler's mathematical laws had made nonsense of the Ptolemaic–Aristotelian world system and clearly established the reasonableness of the Copernican model. Nevertheless, the problem of explaining motion in the universe and tying together the ideas of Copernicus, Galileo, and Kepler had not yet been solved. This would be the work of an Englishman who has long been considered the greatest genius of the Scientific Revolution.

Newton

Born in the little English village of Woolsthorpe in 1642, the young Isaac Newton showed little brilliance until he attended Cambridge University. In 1669, he accepted a chair of mathematics at the university. During an intense period of creativity from 1684 to 1686, he wrote his major work, *Mathematical Principles of Natural Philosophy*, known simply as the *Principia* by the first word of its Latin title. In this work, Newton spelled out the mathematical

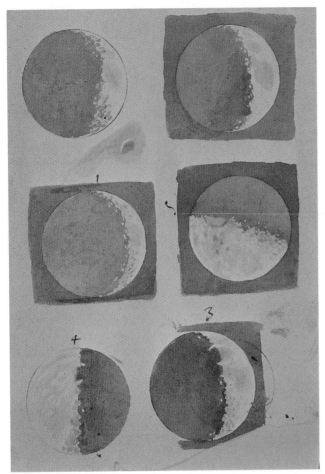

✦ **Galileo's Sketch of the Phases of the Moon.** Galileo Galilei was the first European scientist to use a telescope in making systematic observations of the heavens. Galileo discovered mountains on the moon, sunspots, and the phases of Venus. Shown here are drawings of the moon from Galileo's notes for one of his books.

proofs demonstrating his universal law of gravitation. Newton's work was the culmination of the theories of Copernicus, Kepler, and Galileo. While each had undermined some part of the Ptolemaic–Aristotelian cosmology, no one until Newton had pieced together a coherent synthesis for a new cosmology.

In the first book of the *Principia*, Newton defined the basic concepts of mechanics by elaborating the three laws of motion: the law of inertia that every object continues in a state of rest or uniform motion in a straight line unless deflected by a force; the rate of change of motion of an object is proportional to the force acting on it; and to every action there is always an equal and opposite reaction. In Book Three, Newton applied his theories of mechanics to the problems of astronomy by demonstrating that these three laws of motion govern the planetary bod-

ies as well as terrestrial objects. Integral to his whole argument was the universal law of gravitation to explain why the planetary bodies did not go off in straight lines but continued in elliptical orbits about the sun. In mathematical terms, Newton explained that every object in the universe was attracted to every other object with a force (that is, gravity) that is directly proportional to the product of their masses and inversely proportional to the square of the distances between them.

The implications of Newton's universal law of gravitation were enormous, even if it took another century before they were widely recognized. Newton had demonstrated that one universal law mathematically proved could explain all motion in the universe. The secrets of the natural world could be known by human investigations. At the same time, the Newtonian synthesis created a new cosmology in which the world was seen largely in mechanistic terms. The universe was one huge, regulated,

✦ **Isaac Newton.** Pictured here is a portrait of Isaac Newton by Sir Godfrey Kneller. With a single law, that of universal gravitation, Newton was able to explain all motion in the universe. His great synthesis of the work of his predecessors created a new picture of the universe, one in which the universe was viewed as a great machine operating according to natural laws.

and uniform machine that operated according to natural laws in absolute time, space, and motion. Although Newton believed that God was "everywhere present" and acted as the force that moved all bodies on the basis of the laws he had discovered, later generations dropped his spiritual assumptions. Newton's world-machine, conceived as operating absolutely in space, time, and motion, dominated the modern worldview until the twentieth century, when the Einsteinian revolution based on a concept of relativity superseded the Newtonian mechanistic concept.

Newton's ideas were soon accepted in England, possibly out of national pride, conviction, and, as has been argued recently, for political reasons. Natural philosophers on the continent resisted Newton's ideas, and it took much of the eighteenth century before they were generally accepted everywhere in Europe. They were also reinforced by developments in other fields, especially medicine.

Advances in Medicine

Although the Scientific Revolution of the sixteenth and seventeenth centuries is associated primarily with the dramatic changes in astronomy and mechanics that precipitated a new perception of the universe, a third field that had been dominated by Greek thought in the Late Middle Ages, that of medicine, also experienced a transformation. Late medieval medicine was dominated by the teachings of the Greek physician Galen who had lived in the second century A.D.

Galen's influence on the medieval medical world was pervasive in anatomy, physiology, and disease. Galen had relied on animal, rather than human, dissection to arrive at a picture of human anatomy that was quite inaccurate in many instances. Even when Europeans began to practice human dissection in the Late Middle Ages, instruction in anatomy still relied on Galen. While a professor read a text of Galen, an assistant dissected a cadaver for illustrative purposes. Physiology or the functioning of the body was also dominated by Galenic hypotheses, including the belief that there were two separate blood systems. One controlled muscular activities and contained bright red blood moving upward and downward through the arteries; the other governed the digestive functions and contained dark red blood that ebbed and flowed in the veins.

Two major figures are associated with the changes in medicine in the sixteenth and seventeenth centuries: Andreas Vesalius and William Harvey. The new anatomy of the sixteenth century was the work of Andreas Vesalius (1514–1564). His study of medicine at Paris involved him in the works of Galen, the great ancient authority. Especially important to him was a recently discovered text of Galen, *On Anatomical Procedures*, that led Vesalius to emphasize practical research as the principal avenue for understanding human anatomy.

After receiving a doctorate in medicine at the University of Padua in 1536, he accepted a position there as professor of surgery. In 1543, he published his masterpiece, *On the Fabric of the Human Body*. This book was based on his Paduan lectures, in which he deviated from traditional practice by personally dissecting a body to illustrate what he was discussing. Vesalius's anatomical treatise presented a careful examination of the individual organs and general structure of the human body. The book would not have been feasible without the artistic advances of the Renaissance and the technical developments in the art of printing. Together, these advances made possible the creation of illustrations superior to any hitherto produced.

Vesalius's "hands-on" approach to teaching anatomy enabled him to overthrow some of Galen's most glaring errors. He did not hesitate, for example, to correct Galen's assertion that the great blood vessels originated from the liver since his own observations made it apparent that they came from the heart. Nevertheless, Vesalius still clung to a number of Galen's erroneous assertions, including the Greek physician's ideas on the ebb and flow of two kinds of blood in the veins and arteries. It was not until William Harvey's work on the circulation of the blood that this Galenic misperception was corrected.

William Harvey (1578–1657) attended Cambridge University and later Padua where he received a doctorate of medicine in 1602. His reputation rests on his book *On the Motion of the Heart and Blood*, published in 1628. Although questions had been raised in the sixteenth century about Galen's physiological principles, no major break from his system had occurred. Harvey's work, which was based on meticulous observations and experiments, led him to demolish the ancient Greek's work. Harvey demonstrated that the heart and not the liver was the beginning point of the circulation of blood in the body, that the same blood flows in both veins and arteries, and, most importantly, that the blood makes a complete circuit as it passes through the body. Although Harvey's work dealt a severe blow to Galen's theories, his ideas did not begin to achieve general recognition until the 1660s, when the capillaries, which explained the passing of the body's blood from the arteries to veins, were discovered. Harvey's theory of the circulation of the blood laid the foundation for modern physiology.

Women in the Origins of Modern Science

During the Middle Ages, except for members of religious orders, women who sought a life of learning were severely hampered by the traditional attitude that a woman's proper role was as a daughter, wife, and mother. But in the late fourteenth and early fifteenth centuries, new opportunities for elite women emerged as enthusiasm for the new secular learning called humanism encouraged Europe's privileged and learned men to encourage women to read and study classical and Christian texts. The ideal of a humanist education for some of the daughters of Europe's elite persisted into the seventeenth century.

In the same fashion as they were drawn to humanism, women were also attracted to the Scientific Revolution. Unlike females educated formally in humanist schools, women attracted to science had to obtain a largely informal education. European nobles had the leisure and resources that gave them easy access to the world of learning. This door was also open to noblewomen who could participate in the informal scientific networks of their fathers and brothers. One of the most prominent female scientists of the seventeenth century, Margaret Cavendish (1623–1673), came from an aristocratic background. Cavendish was not a popularizer of science for women but a participant in the crucial scientific debates of her time. Despite her achievement, however, she was excluded from membership in the Royal Society (see "The Spread of Scientific Knowledge" later in the chapter), although she was once allowed to attend a meeting.

She wrote a number of works on scientific matters including *Observations upon Experimental Philosophy* and *Grounds of Natural Philosophy*. In these works she did not hesitate to attack what she considered the defects of the rationalist and empiricist approaches to scientific knowledge and was especially critical of the growing belief that humans through science were the masters of nature: "We have no power at all over natural causes and effects . . . for man is but a small part, . . . his powers are but particular actions of Nature, and he cannot have a supreme and absolute power."[4]

As an aristocrat, the Duchess of Cavendish was a good example of the women in France and England who worked in science. Women interested in science who lived in Germany came from a different background. There the tradition of female participation in craft production enabled some women to become involved in observational science, especially astronomy. Between 1650 and 1710, women constituted 14 percent of all German astronomers.

The most famous of the female astronomers in Germany was Maria Winkelmann (1670–1720). She was educated by her father and uncle and received advanced training in astronomy from a nearby self-taught astronomer. Her opportunity to be a practicing astronomer came when she married Gottfried Kirch, Germany's foremost astronomer. She became his assistant at the astronomical observatory operated in Berlin by the Academy of Science. She made some original contributions, including a hitherto undiscovered comet, as her husband related:

> Early in the morning (about 2:00 A.M.) the sky was clear and starry. Some nights before, I had observed a variable star, and my wife (as I slept) wanted to find and see it for herself. In so doing, she found a comet in the sky. At which time she woke me, and I found that it was indeed a comet . . . I was surprised that I had not seen it the night before.[5]

When her husband died in 1710, she applied for a position as assistant astronomer for which she was highly qualified. As a woman—with no university degree—she was denied the post by the Berlin Academy, which feared that it would establish a precedent if it hired a woman ("mouths would gape").

Winkelmann's difficulties with the Berlin Academy reflect the obstacles women faced in being accepted in scientific work, which was considered a male preserve. Although there were no formal statutes excluding women from membership in the new scientific societies, no woman was invited to join either the Royal Society of

England or the French Academy of Sciences until the twentieth century. All of these women scientists were exceptional women because a life devoted to any kind of scholarship was still viewed as at odds with the domestic duties women were expected to perform.

The nature and value of women had been the subject of an ongoing, centuries-long debate. Male opinions in the debate were largely a carryover from medieval times and were not favorable. Women were portrayed as inherently base, prone to vice, easily swayed, and "sexually insatiable." Hence, men needed to control them. Learned women were viewed as having overcome female liabilities to become like men. One man in praise of a woman scholar remarked that her writings were so good that you "would hardly believe they were done by a woman at all."

In the seventeenth century, women joined this debate by arguing against the distorted images of women held by men. They argued that women also had rational minds and could grow from education. Further, since most women were pious, chaste, and temperate, there was no need for male authority over them. These female defenders of women emphasized education as the key to women's ability to move into the world. How, then, did the era of the Scientific Revolution affect this debate over the nature of women? As an era of intellectual revolution in which traditional authorities were being overthrown, we might expect significant change in men's views of women. But by and large, instead of becoming an instrument for liberation, science was used to find new support for the old, traditional views about a woman's true place in the scheme of things. New views on anatomy appeared, for example, but interestingly enough were used to perpetuate old stereotypes about women.

An important project in the new anatomy of the sixteenth and seventeenth centuries was the attempt to illustrate the human body and skeleton. For Vesalius, the portrayal of physical differences between males and females was limited to external bodily form (the outlines of the body) and the sexual organs. Vesalius saw no difference in skeletons and portrayed them as the same for men or women. It was not until the eighteenth century, in fact, that a new anatomy finally prevailed. Drawings of female skeletons between 1730 and 1790 varied, but females tended to have a larger pelvic area, and, in some instances, female skulls were portrayed as smaller than those of males. Eighteenth-century studies on the anatomy and physiology of sexual differences provided "scientific evidence" to reaffirm the traditional inferiority of women. The larger pelvic area "proved" that women were meant to be childbearers while the larger skull "demonstrated" the superiority of the male mind. Male-dominated science had been used to "prove" male social dominance.

Overall the Scientific Revolution reaffirmed traditional ideas about women's nature. Male scientists used the new science to spread the view that women were inferior by nature, subordinate to men, and suited by nature to play a domestic role as nurturing mothers. The widespread distribution of books ensured the continuation of these ideas (see the box on p. 359). Jean de La Bruyère, the seventeenth-century French moralist, was typical when he remarked that an educated woman was like a gun that was a collector's item "which one shows to the curious, but which has no use at all, any more than a carousel horse."[6]

Toward a New Earth: Descartes, Rationalism, and a New View of Humankind

The fundamentally new conception of the universe contained in the cosmological revolution of the sixteenth and seventeenth centuries inevitably had an impact on the Western view of humankind. Nowhere is this more evident than in the work of René Descartes (1596–1650), an extremely important figure in Western history. Descartes began by reflecting the doubt and uncertainty that seemed pervasive in the confusion of the seventeenth century and ended with a philosophy that dominated Western thought until the twentieth century.

The starting point for Descartes's new system was doubt, as he explained at the beginning of his most famous work, *Discourse on Method*, written in 1637:

> From my childhood I have been familiar with letters; and as I was given to believe that by their means a clear and assured knowledge can be acquired of all that is useful in life, I was extremely eager for instruction in them. As soon, however, as I had completed the course of study, at the close of which it is customary to be admitted into the order of the learned, I entirely changed my opinion. For I found myself entangled in so many doubts and errors that, as it seemed to me, the endeavor to instruct myself had served only to disclose to me more and more of my ignorance.[7]

Descartes decided to set aside all that he had learned and begin again. One fact seemed to Descartes beyond doubt—his own existence:

> But I immediately became aware that while I was thus disposed to think that all was false, it was absolutely necessary

The "Natural" Inferiority of Women

Despite the shattering of old views and the emergence of a new worldview in the Scientific Revolution of the seventeenth century, attitudes toward women remained tied to traditional perspectives. In this selection, the philosopher Benedict de Spinoza argues for the "natural" inferiority of women to men.

Benedict de Spinoza, A Political Treatise

But, perhaps, someone will ask, whether women are under men's authority by nature or institution. For if it has been by mere institution, then we had no reason compelling us to exclude women from government. But if we consult experience itself, we shall find that the origin of it is in their weakness. For there has never been a case of men and women reigning together, but wherever on the earth men are found, there we see that men rule, and women are ruled, and that on this plan, both sexes live in harmony. But on the other hand, the Amazons, who are reported to have held rule of old, did not suffer men to stop in their country, but reared only their female children, killing the males to whom they gave birth. But if by nature women were equal to men, and were equally distinguished by force of character and ability, in which human power and therefore human right chiefly consist; surely among nations so many and different some would be found, where both sexes rule alike, and others, where men are ruled by women, and so brought up, that they can make less use of their abilities. And since this is nowhere the case, one may assert with perfect propriety, that women have not by nature equal right with men: but that they necessarily give way to men, and that thus it cannot happen, that both sexes should rule alike, much less that men should be ruled by women. But if we further reflect upon human passions, how men, in fact, generally love women merely from the passion of lust, and esteem their cleverness and wisdom in proportion to the excellence of their beauty, and also how very ill-disposed men are to suffer the women they love to show any sort of favor to others, and other facts of this kind, we shall easily see that men and women cannot rule alike without greater hurt to peace.

---

that I who thus thought should be something; and noting that this truth *I think, therefore I am*, was so steadfast and so assured that the suppositions of the skeptics, to whatever extreme they might all be carried, could not avail to shake it, I concluded that I might without scruple accept it as being the first principle of the philosophy I was seeking.[8]

With this emphasis on the mind, Descartes asserted that he would accept only those things that his reason said were true.

From his first postulate, Descartes deduced an additional principle, the separation of mind and matter. Descartes argued that since "the mind cannot be doubted but the body and material world can, the two must be radically different." From this came an absolute dualism between mind and matter, or what has also been called Cartesian dualism. Using mind or human reason, the path to certain knowledge, and its best instrument, mathematics, humans can understand the material world because it is pure mechanism, a machine that is governed by its own physical laws because it was created by God—the great geometrician.

Descartes's conclusions about the nature of the universe and human beings had important implications. His separation of mind and matter allowed scientists to view matter as dead or inert, as something that was totally separate from themselves and could be investigated independently by reason. The split between mind and body led Westerners to equate their identity with mind and reason rather than with the whole organism. Descartes has rightly been called the father of modern rationalism. His books were placed on the papal Index of Forbidden Books and condemned by many Protestant theologians. The radical Cartesian split between mind and matter, and between mind and body, had devastating implications not only for traditional religious views of the universe, but for how Westerners viewed themselves.

Science and Religion in the Seventeenth Century

In Galileo's struggle with the inquisitorial Holy Office of the Catholic church, we see the beginning of the conflict between science and religion that has marked the history of modern Western civilization. Since time immemorial, theology had seemed to be the queen of the sciences. It

✦ **Descartes with Queen Christina of Sweden.** René Descartes was one of the primary figures in the Scientific Revolution. Claiming to use reason as his sole guide to truth, Descartes posited a sharp distinction between mind and matter. He is shown here, standing to the right of Queen Christina of Sweden. The queen had a deep interest in philosophy and invited Descartes to her court.

was natural that the churches would continue to believe that religion was the final measure of everything. To the emerging scientists, however, it often seemed that theologians knew not of what they spoke. These "natural philosophers" then tried to draw lines between the knowledge of religion and the knowledge of "natural philosophy" or nature. Galileo had clearly felt that it was unnecessary to pit science against religion when he wrote that:

> in discussions of physical problems we ought to begin not from the authority of scriptural passages, but from sense-experiences and necessary demonstrations; for the holy Bible and the phenomena of nature proceed alike from the divine word, the former as the dictate of the Holy Ghost and the latter as the observant executrix of God's commands. It is necessary for the Bible, in order to be accommodated to the understanding of every man, to speak many things which appear to differ from the absolute truth so far as the bare meaning of the words is concerned. But Nature,

on the other hand, is inexorable and immutable; she never transgresses the laws imposed upon her, or cares a whit whether her abstruse reasons and methods of operation are understandable to men.[9]

To Galileo it made little sense for the church to determine the nature of physical reality on the basis of biblical texts that were subject to radically divergent interpretations. The church, however, decided otherwise in Galileo's case and lent its great authority to one scientific theory, the Ptolemaic–Aristotelian cosmology, no doubt because it fit so well with its own philosophical views of reality. But the church's decision had tremendous consequences, just as the rejection of Darwin's ideas did in the nineteenth century. For educated individuals, it established a dichotomy between scientific investigations and religious beliefs. As the scientific beliefs triumphed, it became almost inevitable that religious beliefs would suffer, leading to a growing secularization in European intellectual life, precisely what the church had hoped to combat by opposing Copernicanism. Many seventeenth-century intellectuals were both religious and scientific and believed that the implications of this split would be tragic. Some believed that the split was largely unnecessary while others felt the need to combine God, humans, and a mechanistic universe into a new philosophical synthesis. One individual—Pascal—illustrates how one European intellectual responded to the implications of the cosmological revolution of the seventeenth century.

Blaise Pascal (1623–1662) was a French scientist who sought to keep science and religion united. Pascal had a brief, but checkered career. He was an accomplished scientist and brilliant mathematician, who excelled at both the practical, by inventing a calculating machine, and the abstract, by devising a theory of chance or probability and doing work on conic sections. After a profound mystical vision on the night of November 23, 1654, which assured him that God cared for the human soul, he devoted the rest of his life to religious matters. He planned to write an "Apology for the Christian Religion" but died before he could do so. He did leave a set of notes for the larger work, however, which in published form became known as *Pensées* or *The Thoughts*.

In the *Pensées*, Pascal tried to convert rationalists to Christianity by appealing both to their reason and their emotions. Humans were, he argued, frail creatures, often deceived by their senses, misled by reason, and battered by their emotions. And yet they were beings whose very nature involved thinking: "Man is but a reed, the weakest in nature; but he is a thinking reed. . . . Our whole dignity consists, therefore, in thought. By thought we must raise ourselves. . . . Let us endeavour, then, to think well; this is the beginning of morality."[10]

Pascal was determined to show that the Christian religion was not contrary to reason: "If we violate the principles of reason, our religion will be absurd, and it will be laughed at." Christianity, he felt, was the only religion that recognized people's true state of being as both vulnerable and great. To a Christian, a human being was both fallen and at the same time God's special creation. But it was not necessary to emphasize one at the expense of the other—to view humans as only rational or only hopeless. Thus, "Knowledge of God without knowledge of man's wretchedness leads to pride. Knowledge of man's wretchedness without knowledge of God leads to despair. Knowledge of Jesus Christ is the middle course, because by it we discover both God and our wretched state." Pascal even had an answer for skeptics in his famous wager. God is a reasonable bet; it is worthwhile to assume that God exists. If he does, then we win all; if he does not, we lose nothing.

Despite his own background as a scientist and mathematician, Pascal refused to rely on the scientist's world of order and rationality to attract people to God: "If we submit everything to reason, there will be no mystery and no supernatural element in our religion." In the new cosmology of the seventeenth century, "finite man," Pascal believed, was lost in the new infinite world, a realization that frightened him: "The eternal silence of those infinite spaces strikes me with terror" (see the box on p. 362). The world of nature, then, could never reveal God: "Because they have failed to contemplate these infinites, men have rashly plunged into the examination of nature, as though they bore some proportion to her. . . . Their assumption is as infinite as their object." A Christian could only rely on a God who through Jesus cared for human beings. In the final analysis, after providing reasonable arguments for Christianity, Pascal came to rest on faith. Reason, he believed, could take people only so far: "The heart has its reasons of which the reason knows nothing." As a Christian, faith was the final step: "The heart feels God, not the reason. This is what constitutes faith: God experienced by the heart, not by the reason."[11]

In retrospect, it is obvious that Pascal failed to achieve his goal. Increasingly, the gap between science and traditional religion grew wider as Europe continued along its path of secularization. Of course, traditional religions were not eliminated, nor is there any evidence that churches had yet lost their numbers. That would happen later. Nevertheless, more and more of the intellectual, social, and political elites began to act on the basis of secular rather than religious assumptions.

The Spread of Scientific Knowledge

During the seventeenth century, scientific learning and investigation began to increase dramatically. Major universities in Europe established new chairs of science, especially in medicine. Royal and princely patronage of individual scientists became an international phenomenon. Of great importance to the work of science, however, was the creation of a scientific method and new learned societies that enabled the new scientists to communicate their ideas to each other and to disseminate them to a wider, literate public.

The Scientific Method

In the course of the Scientific Revolution, attention was paid to the problem of establishing the proper means to examine and understand the physical realm. This creation of a scientific method was crucial to the evolution of science in the modern world. Curiously enough, it was an Englishman with few scientific credentials who attempted to put forth a new method of acquiring knowledge that made an impact on English scientists in the seventeenth century and other European scientists in the eighteenth century. Francis Bacon (1561–1626), a lawyer and lord chancellor, rejected Copernicus and Kepler and misunderstood Galileo. And yet in his unfinished work, *The Great Instauration* (*The Great Restoration*), he called for his contemporaries "to commence a total reconstruction of sciences, arts, and all human knowledge, raised upon the proper foundations." Bacon did not doubt humans' ability to know the natural world, but believed that they had proceeded incorrectly: "The entire fabric of human reason which we employ in the inquisition of nature is badly put together and built up, and like some magnificent structure without foundation."

Bacon's new foundation—a correct scientific method—was to be built on inductive principles. Rather than beginning with assumed first principles from which logical conclusions could be deduced, he urged scientists to proceed from the particular to the general. From carefully organized experiments and systematic, thorough observations, correct generalizations could be developed. Bacon was clear about what he believed his method could accomplish. His concern was more for practical than for pure science. He stated that "the true and lawful goal of the sciences is none other than this: that human life be endowed with new discoveries and power." He wanted science to contribute to the "mechanical arts," by creating devices that would benefit industry, agriculture, and trade. Bacon was prophetic when he said that "I am

Pascal: "What Is a Man in the Infinite?"

Perhaps no intellectual in the seventeenth century gave greater expression to the uncertainties generated by the cosmological revolution than Blaise Pascal. Himself a scientist, Pascal's mystical vision of God's presence caused him to pursue religious truths with a passion. His work, the Pensées, consisted of notes for a larger, unfinished work justifying the Christian religion. In this selection, Pascal presents his musings on the human place in an infinite world.

Blaise Pascal, *Pensées*

Let man then contemplate the whole of nature in her full and exalted majesty. Let him turn his eyes from the lowly objects which surround him. Let him gaze on that brilliant light set like an eternal lamp to illumine the Universe; let the earth seem to him a dot compared with the vast orbit described by the sun, and let him wonder at the fact that this vast orbit itself is no more than a very small dot compared with that described by the stars in their revolutions around the firmament. But if our vision stops here, let the imagination pass on; it will exhaust its powers of thinking long before nature ceases to supply it with material for thought. All this visible world is no more than an imperceptible speck in nature's ample bosom. No idea approaches it. We may extend our conceptions beyond all imaginable space; yet produce only atoms in comparison with the reality of things. It is an infinite sphere, the center of which is everywhere, the circumference nowhere. In short, it is the greatest perceptible mark of God's almighty power that our imagination should lose itself in that thought.

Returning to himself, let man consider what he is compared with all existence; let him think of himself as lost in his remote corner of nature; and from this little dungeon in which he finds himself lodged—I mean the Universe—let him learn to set a true value on the earth, its kingdoms, and cities, and upon himself. What is a man in the infinite? . . .

For, after all, what is a man in nature? A nothing in comparison with the infinite, an absolute in comparison with nothing, a central point between nothing and all. Infinitely far from understanding these extremes, the end of things and their beginning are hopelessly hidden from him in an impenetrable secret. He is equally incapable of seeing the nothingness from which he came, and the infinite in which he is engulfed. What else then will he perceive but some appearance of the middle of things, in an eternal despair of knowing either their principle or their purpose? All things emerge from nothing and are borne onward to infinity. Who can follow this marvelous process? The Author of these wonders understands them. None but He can.

---

laboring to lay the foundation, not of any sect or doctrine, but of human utility and power." And how would this "human power" be used? To "conquer nature in action."[12] The control and domination of nature became a central proposition of modern science and the technology that accompanied it. Only in the twentieth century have some scientists asked whether this assumption might not be at the heart of the twentieth-century ecological crisis.

René Descartes proposed a different approach to scientific methodology by emphasizing deduction and mathematical logic. Descartes believed that one could start with self-evident truths, comparable to geometrical axioms, and deduce more complex conclusions. His emphasis on deduction and mathematical order complemented Bacon's stress on experiment and induction. It was Sir Isaac Newton who synthesized them into a single scientific methodology by uniting Bacon's empiricism with Descartes's rationalism. This scientific method began with systematic observations and experiments, which were used to arrive at general concepts. New deductions derived from these general concepts could then be tested and verified by precise experiments.

The Scientific Societies

The first of the scientific societies appeared in Italy but those of England and France were ultimately of more significance. The English Royal Society evolved out of informal gatherings of scientists at London and Oxford in the 1640s, although it did not receive a formal charter from King Charles II until 1662. The French Royal Academy of Sciences also arose out of informal scientific meetings in Paris during the 1650s. In 1666, Louis XIV bestowed on the group a formal recognition. The French Academy received abundant state support and remained under government control; its members were appointed and paid salaries by the state. In contrast, the Royal Society of England received little government encouragement, and its fellows simply co-opted new members.

Early on, both the English and French scientific societies formally emphasized the practical value of scientific research. The Royal Society created a committee to investigate technological improvements for industry while the French Academy collected tools and machines. This concern with the practical benefits of science proved short lived, however, as both societies came to focus their primary interest on theoretical work in mechanics and astronomy. The construction of observatories at Paris in 1667 and at Greenwich, England, in 1675 greatly facilitated research in astronomy by both groups. While both the English and French societies made useful contributions to scientific knowledge in the second half of the seventeenth century, their true significance arose from their example that science should proceed along the lines of a cooperative venture.

Science and Society

The importance of science in the history of modern Western civilization is usually taken for granted. But how did science become such an integral part of Western culture in the seventeenth and early eighteenth centuries? Recent research has stressed that one cannot simply assert that people perceived that science was a rationally superior system. An important social factor, however, might help to explain the relatively rapid acceptance of the new science.

It has been argued that the literate mercantile and propertied elites of Europe were attracted to new science because it offered new ways to exploit resources for profit. Some of the early scientists made it easier for these groups to accept the new ideas when they showed how they could be applied directly to specific industrial and technological needs. Galileo, for example, consciously sought an alliance between science and the material interests of the educated elite when he assured his listeners that the science of mechanics would be quite useful "when it becomes necessary to build bridges or other structures over water, something occurring mainly in affairs of great importance." At the same time, Galileo stressed that science was fit for the "minds of the wise" and not for "the shallow minds of the common people." This made science part of the high culture of Europe's wealthy elites at a time when that culture was being increasingly separated from the popular culture of the lower classes.

Conclusion

The Scientific Revolution represents a major turning point in modern Western civilization. In the Scientific Revolution, the Western world overthrew the medieval, Ptolemaic–Aristotelian worldview and arrived at a new conception of the universe: the sun at the center, the planets as material bodies revolving around the sun in elliptical orbits, and an infinite rather than finite world. With the changes in the conception of "heaven" came changes in the conception of "earth." The work of Bacon and Descartes left Europeans with the separation of mind and matter and the belief that by using only reason they could, in fact, understand and dominate the world of nature. The development of a scientific method furthered the work of scientists while the creation of scientific societies and learned journals spread its results. Although traditional churches stubbornly resisted the new ideas and a few intellectuals pointed to some inherent flaws, nothing was able to halt the replacement of the traditional ways of thinking by new ways that created a more fundamental break with the past than that represented by the breakup of Christian unity in the Reformation.

The Scientific Revolution forced Europeans to change their conception of themselves. At first, some were appalled and even frightened by its implications. Formerly,

◆ **Louis XIV and Colbert Visit the Academy of Sciences.** In the seventeenth century, individual scientists received royal and princely patronage, and a number of learned societies were established. In France, Louis XIV, urged on by his minister Colbert, gave formal recognition to the French Academy in 1666. In this painting by Henri Testelin, Louis XIV is shown seated, surrounded by Colbert and members of the French Royal Academy of Sciences.

humans on earth had been at the center of the universe. Now the earth was only a tiny planet revolving around a sun that was itself only a speck in a boundless universe. Most people remained optimistic despite the apparent blow to human dignity. After all, had Newton not demonstrated that the universe was a great machine governed by natural laws? Newton had found one—the uni-

versal law of gravitation. Could others not find other laws? Were there not natural laws governing every aspect of human endeavor that could be found by the new scientific method? Thus, the Scientific Revolution leads us logically to the age of the Enlightenment of the eighteenth century.

NOTES

1. Quoted in Alan G. R. Smith, *Science and Society in the Sixteenth and Seventeenth Centuries* (London, 1972), p. 59.
2. Edward MacCurdy, *The Notebooks of Leonardo da Vinci* (London, 1948), 1:634.
3. Quoted in John H. Randall, *The Making of the Modern Mind* (Boston, 1926), p. 234.
4. Quoted in Londa Schiebinger, *The Mind Has No Sex? Women in the Origins of Modern Science* (Cambridge, Mass., 1989), pp. 52–53.
5. Ibid., p 85.
6. Quoted in Phyllis Stock, *Better Than Rubies: A History of Women's Education* (New York, 1978), p. 16.
7. René Descartes, *Philosophical Writings,* ed. and trans. Norman K. Smith (New York, 1958), p. 95.
8. Ibid., pp. 118–119.
9. Stillman Drake, ed. and trans., *Discoveries and Opinions of Galileo* (New York, 1957), p. 182.
10. Pascal, *The Pensées,* trans. J. M. Cohen (Harmondsworth, 1961), p. 100.
11. Ibid. (in order of appearance), pp. 31, 45, 52–53, 164, 165.
12. Francis Bacon, *The Great Instauration,* trans. Jerry Weinberger (Arlington Heights, Ill., 1989), pp. (in order of appearance) 2, 8, 2, 16, 21.

SUGGESTIONS FOR FURTHER READING

Three general surveys of the entire Scientific Revolution are A. G. R. Smith, *Science and Society in the Sixteenth and Seventeenth Centuries* (London, 1972); M. Boas, *The Scientific Renaissance: 1450–1630* (London, 1962); and H. Butterfield, *The Origins of Modern Science* (New York, 1962). A more detailed and technical introduction can be found in A. R. Hall, *The Revolution in Science, 1500–1750* (London, 1983). Also of much value are A. G. Debus, *Man and Nature in the Renaissance* (Cambridge, 1978), which covers the period from the mid-fifteenth through the mid-seventeenth century; and the recent work by J. R. Jacob, *The Scientific Revolution: Aspirations and Achievements, 1500–1700* (Atlantic Highlands, N. J., 1998). The importance of mathematics to the Scientific Revolution is brought out in P. L. Rose, *The Italian Renaissance of Mathematics: Studies on Humanists and Mathematicians from Petrarch to Galileo* (Geneva, 1975). On the relationship of magic to the beginnings of the Scientific Revolution, see the pioneering

works by F. Yates, *Giordano Bruno and the Hermetic Tradition* (New York, 1964), and *The Rosicrucian Enlightenment* (London, 1975). Some criticism of this approach is provided in R. S. Westman and J. E. McGuire, eds., *Hermeticism and the Scientific Revolution* (Los Angeles, 1977). An important book on magic in the early modern period is K. Thomas, *Religion and the Decline of Magic* (London, 1971).

A good introduction to the transformation from the late medieval to the early modern worldview is A. Koyré, *From the Closed World to the Infinite Universe* (New York, 1958). Also still of value are A. Koestler, *The Sleepwalkers: A History of Man's Changing Vision of the Universe* (New York, 1959); and E. A. Burtt, *The Metaphysical Foundations of Modern Physical Science* (London, 1942). On the important figures of the revolution in astronomy, see E. Rosen, *Copernicus and the Scientific Revolution* (New York, 1984); M. Sharratt, *Galileo: Decisive Innovator* (Oxford, 1994); S. Drake, *Galileo, Pioneer Scientist* (Toronto,

1990); M. Casper, *Johannes Kepler*, trans. C. D. Hellman (London, 1959), the standard biography; and R. S. Westfall, *The Life of Isaac Newton* (New York, 1993). On Newton's relationship to alchemy, see the invaluable study by B. J. Dobbs, *The Foundations of Newton's Alchemy* (Cambridge, 1975).

The standard biography of Vesalius is C. D. O'Malley, *Andreas Vesalius of Brussels, 1514–1564* (Berkeley, 1964). The work of Harvey is discussed in G. Whitteridge, *William Harvey and the Circulation of the Blood* (London, 1971). A good general account of the development of medicine can be found in W. P. D. Wightman, *The Emergence of Scientific Medicine* (Edinburgh, 1971).

The importance of Francis Bacon in the early development of science is underscored in P. Rossi, *Francis Bacon: From Magic to Science* (Chicago, 1968); C. Webster, *The Great Instauration: Science, Medicine, and Reform,* 1620–1660 (London, 1975); and P. Zagorin, *Francis Bacon* (Princeton, N. J., 1998). A good introduction to the work of Descartes can be found in G. Radis-Lewis, *Descartes: A Biography* (Ithaca, N. Y., 1998).

For histories of the scientific academies, see R. Hahn, *The Anatomy of a Scientific Institution: The Paris Academy of Sciences, 1666–1803* (Berkeley, 1971); and M. Purver, *The Royal Society, Concept and Creation* (London, 1967).

On the subject of women and early modern science, see the comprehensive and highly informative work by L. Schiebinger, *The Mind Has No Sex? Women in the Origins of Modern Science* (Cambridge, Mass., 1989). The social and political context for the triumph of science in the seventeenth and eighteenth centuries is examined in M. Jacobs, *The Cultural Meaning of the Scientific Revolution* (New York, 1988), and *The Newtonians and the English Revolution, 1689–1720* (Ithaca, N.Y., 1976).

CHAPTER

18

The Eighteenth Century: An Age of Enlightenment

The earth-shattering work of the "natural philosophers" in the Scientific Revolution had affected only a relatively small number of Europe's educated elite. In the eighteenth century, this changed dramatically as a group of intellectuals known as the philosophes popularized the ideas of the Scientific Revolution and used them to undertake a dramatic examination of all aspects of life. In Paris, the cultural capital of Europe, women took the lead in bringing together groups of men and women to discuss the new ideas of the philosophes. At her fashionable home in the Rue St. Honoré, Marie-Thérèse de Geoffrin, wife of a wealthy merchant, held sway over gatherings that became the talk of France and even Europe. Distinguished foreigners, including a future king of Sweden and a future king of Poland, competed to receive invitations. When Madame Geoffrin made a visit to Vienna, she was so well received that she exclaimed, "I am better known here than a couple of yards from my own house." Madame Geoffrin was an amiable but firm hostess who allowed wide-ranging discussions as long as they remained in good taste. When she found that artists and philosophers did not mix particularly well (the artists were high-strung and the philosophers talked too much), she set up separate meetings. Artists were invited only on Mondays; philosophers on Wednesdays. These gatherings were but one of many avenues for the spread of the ideas of the philosophes. And those ideas had such a widespread impact on their society that historians ever since have called the eighteenth century an age of Enlightenment.

For most of the philosophes, "enlightenment" included the rejection of traditional Christianity. The religious wars and intolerance of the sixteenth and seventeenth centuries had created an environment in which intellectuals had become so disgusted with religious fanaticism that they were open to the new ideas of the Scientific Revolution. While the great scientists of the seventeenth century believed that their work exalted God, the intellectuals of the eighteenth century read their conclusions a different way and

Montesquieu, *The Spirit of the Laws* •   • Voltaire, *Candide*

Rousseau, *The Social Contract, Emile* •

Wollstonecraft, *Vindication of* •
the Rights of Woman

• • • • • • • • • • • • •
Work of Watteau

• • • • • • • • • • •
Diderot, *The Encyclopedia*

• Smith, *The Wealth of Nations*

• Bach, Mass in B Minor   • Handel, *Messiah*   Haydn, *The Creation* •

Mozart, *The Marriage of Figaro* •

increasingly turned their backs on Christian orthodoxy. Consequently, European intellectual life in the eighteenth century was marked by the emergence of the secularization that has characterized the modern Western mentality. While some historians have argued that this secularism first arose in the Renaissance, it never developed then to the same extent that it did in the eighteenth century. Ironically, at the same time that reason and materialism were beginning to replace faith and worship, a great outburst of religious sensibility manifested itself in music and art. Merely to mention the name of Johann Sebastian Bach is to remind us that the growing secularization of the eighteenth century had not yet captured the hearts and minds of all European intellectuals and artists.

The Enlightenment

In 1784, the German philosopher Immanuel Kant defined the Enlightenment as "man's leaving his self-caused immaturity." Whereas earlier periods had been handicapped by the inability to "use one's intelligence without the guidance of another," Kant proclaimed as the motto of the Enlightenment: "Dare to Know!: Have the courage to use your own intelligence!" The eighteenth-century Enlightenment was a movement of intellectuals who dared to know. They were greatly impressed with the accomplishments of the Scientific Revolution, and when they used the word *reason*—one of their favorite words— they were advocating the application of the scientific method to an understanding of all life. All institutions

and all systems of thought were subject to the rational, scientific way of thinking if people would only free themselves from the shackles of past, worthless traditions, especially religious ones. If Isaac Newton could discover the natural laws regulating the world of nature, they too by using reason could find the laws that governed human society. This belief in turn led them to hope that they could make progress toward a better society than the one they had inherited. Reason, natural law, hope, progress—these were common words in the heady atmosphere of the eighteenth century.

The Paths to Enlightenment

Although the intellectuals of the eighteenth century were much influenced by the scientific ideas of the seventeenth century, they did not always acquire this knowledge directly from the original sources. After all, Newton's *Principia* was not an easy book to read or comprehend. Scientific ideas were spread to ever-widening circles of educated Europeans not so much by scientists themselves as by popularizers. Especially important as the direct link between the Scientific Revolution of the seventeenth century and the intellectuals of the eighteenth was Bernard de Fontenelle (1657–1757). In his *Plurality of Worlds*, he used the form of an intimate conversation between a lady aristocrat and her lover to present a detailed account of the new mechanistic universe. Scores of the educated elite of Europe learned the new cosmology in this lighthearted fashion.

Thanks to Fontenelle, science was no longer the monopoly of experts, but part of literature. He was especially fond of downplaying the religious backgrounds of the seventeenth-century scientists. Himself a skeptic, Fontenelle contributed to the growing skepticism toward religion at the end of the seventeenth century by portraying the churches as enemies of scientific progress.

Although the Reformation had attempted to restore religion as the central focus of people's lives, it was perhaps inevitable that the dogmatic controversies, religious intolerance, and religious warfare engendered by it would open the door to the questioning of religious truths and values. The overthrow of medieval cosmology and the advent of scientific ideas and rational explanations in the seventeenth century likewise affected the belief of edu-

♦ **The Popularization of Science: Fontenelle and the *Plurality of Worlds*.** The most important of the popularizers of the ideas of the Scientific Revolution was Bernard de Fontenelle who, while not a scientist himself, had much knowledge of scientific matters. In this frontispiece illustration to his *Plurality of Worlds*, an aristocratic lady listens while her astronomer-friend explains the details of the new cosmology.

cated men and women in the traditional teachings of Christianity. Skepticism about religion and a growing secularization of thought were important factors in the emergence of the Enlightenment.

Skepticism about Christianity as well as European culture itself was nourished by travel reports. In the course of the seventeenth century, traders, missionaries, medical men, and navigators began to publish an increasing number of travel books that gave accounts of many different cultures. By the end of the seventeenth century, this travel literature began to have an impact on the minds of educated Europeans. The realization that there were highly developed civilizations with different customs in other parts of the world forced Europeans to evaluate their own civilization relative to others. What had seemed to be practices grounded in reason now appeared to be matters of custom. This development of cultural relativism was a healthy antidote to European parochialism.

A final source of inspiration for the Enlightenment came primarily from two Englishmen, Isaac Newton and John Locke. Newton was frequently singled out for praise as the "greatest and rarest genius that ever rose for the ornament and instruction of the species." One English poet declared: "Nature and Nature's Laws lay hid in Night; God said, 'Let Newton be,' and all was Light." Enchanted by the grand design of the Newtonian world-machine, the intellectuals of the Enlightenment were convinced that by following Newton's rules of reasoning they could discover the natural laws that governed politics, economics, justice, religion, and the arts. The world and everything in it were like a giant machine.

John Locke's theory of knowledge had a great impact on eighteenth-century intellectuals. In his *Essay Concerning Human Understanding*, written in 1690, Locke denied Descartes's belief in innate ideas. Instead, argued Locke, every person was born with a *tabula rasa*, a blank mind:

> Let us then suppose the mind to be, as we say, white paper, void of all characters, without any ideas. How comes it to be furnished? Whence comes it by that vast store which the busy and boundless fancy of man has painted on it with an almost endless variety? Whence has it all the materials of reason and knowledge? To this I answer, in one word, from experience. . . . Our observation, employed either about external sensible objects or about the internal operations of our minds perceived and reflected on by ourselves, is that which supplies our understanding with all the materials of thinking.[1]

Our knowledge, then, is derived from our environment, not from heredity; from reason, not from faith. Locke's philosophy implied that people were molded by their environment, by the experiences that they received through their senses from their surrounding world. By changing the environment and subjecting people to proper influences, they could be changed and a new society created. Evil was not innate in human beings, but a product of bad education, rotten institutions, and inherited prejudices. And how should the environment be changed? Newton had already paved the way by showing how reason enabled enlightened people to discover the natural laws to which all institutions should conform. No wonder the philosophes were enamored of Newton and Locke. Taken together, their ideas seemed to offer the hope of a "brave new world" built on reason.

The Philosophes and Their Ideas

The intellectuals of the Enlightenment were known by the French name of philosophes although not all of them were French and few were philosophers in the strict sense of the term. They were literary people, professors, journalists, statesmen, economists, political scientists, and, above all, social reformers. They came from both the nobility and middle class, and a few even stemmed from lower-middle-class origins. Although it was a truly international and cosmopolitan movement, the Enlightenment also enhanced the dominant role already being played by French culture; Paris was its recognized capital. Most of the leaders of the Enlightenment were French. The French philosophes, in turn, affected intellectuals elsewhere and created a movement that touched the entire Western world, including the British and Spanish colonies in America.

Although the philosophes faced different political circumstances depending on the country in which they lived, they shared common bonds as part of a truly international movement. Although they were called philosophers, what did philosophy mean to them? The role of philosophy was to change the world, not just to discuss it. As one writer said, the philosophe is one who "applies himself to the study of society with the purpose of making his kind better and happier." To the philosophes, rationalism did not mean the creation of a grandiose system of thought to explain all things. Reason was scientific method, and it meant an appeal to facts and experience. A spirit of rational criticism was to be applied to everything, including religion and politics.

Although the philosophes constituted a kind of "family circle" bound together by common intellectual bonds, they often disagreed. Spanning almost an entire century, the Enlightenment evolved over time, with each succeeding generation becoming more radical as it built on the contributions of the previous one. A few people, however, dominated the landscape completely, and we might best begin our survey of the ideas of the philosophes by looking at the three French giants—Montesquieu, Voltaire, and Diderot.

MONTESQUIEU AND POLITICAL THOUGHT

Charles de Secondat, the baron de Montesquieu (1689–1755), came from the French nobility. He received a classical education and then studied law. In his first work published in 1721, the *Persian Letters*, he used the format of two Persians supposedly traveling in Western Europe and sending their impressions back home to enable him to criticize French institutions, especially the Catholic church and the French monarchy. Much of the program of the French Enlightenment is contained in this work: the attack on traditional religion, the advocacy of religious toleration, the denunciation of slavery, and the use of reason to liberate human beings from their prejudices.

His most famous work, *The Spirit of the Laws*, was published in 1748. This treatise was a comparative study of governments in which Montesquieu attempted to apply the scientific method to the social and political arena to ascertain the "natural laws" governing the social relationships of human beings. Montesquieu distinguished three basic kinds of governments: republics, suitable for small states and based on citizen involvement; monarchy, appropriate for middle-sized states and grounded in the ruling class's adherence to law; and despotism, apt for large empires and dependent on fear to inspire obedience. Montesquieu used England as an example of the second category, and it was his praise and analysis of England's constitution that led to his most far-reaching and lasting contribution to political thought—the importance of checks and balances created by means of a separation of powers. He believed that England's system, with its separate executive, legislative, and judicial powers that served to limit and control each other, provided the greatest freedom and security for a state. The translation of his work into English two years after publication ensured its being read by American philosophes who incorporated its principles into the American constitution (see Chapter 20).

VOLTAIRE AND THE ENLIGHTENMENT

The greatest figure of the Enlightenment was François-Marie Arouet, known simply as Voltaire (1694–1778). Son of a prosperous middle-class family from Paris, Voltaire received a classical education typical of Jesuit

◆ **Voltaire.** François-Marie Arouet, better known as Voltaire, achieved his first success as a playwright. A philosophe, Voltaire was well known for his criticism of traditional religion and his support of religious toleration.

schools. Although he studied law, he wished to be a writer and achieved his first success as a playwright. Voltaire was a prolific author and wrote an almost endless stream of pamphlets, novels, plays, letters, philosophical essays, and histories. His writings brought him both fame and wealth.

Although he touched on all of the themes of importance to the philosophes, Voltaire was especially well known for his criticism of traditional religion and his strong attachment to the ideal of religious toleration (see the box on p. 371). He lent his prestige and skills as a polemicist to fight cases of intolerance in France. In 1763, he penned his *Treatise on Toleration* in which he argued that religious toleration had created no problems for England and Holland and reminded governments that "all men are brothers under God." As he grew older, Voltaire became ever more strident in his denunciations. "Crush the infamous thing," he thundered repeatedly—the infamous thing being religious fanaticism, intolerance, and superstition.

Throughout his life, Voltaire championed not only religious tolerance, but also deism, a religious outlook shared by most other philosophes. Deism was built on the Newtonian world-machine, which implied the existence of a mechanic (God) who had created the universe. To Voltaire and most other philosophes, God had no direct involvement in the world he had created and allowed to run according to its own natural laws. Jesus might be a "good fellow," as Voltaire called him, but he was not divine as Christianity claimed.

DIDEROT AND THE ENCYCLOPEDIA

Denis Diderot (1713–1784) was the son of a skilled craftsman from eastern France. He received a Jesuit education and went on to the University of Paris to fulfill his father's hopes that he would be a lawyer or pursue a career in the church. Diderot did neither. Instead he became a freelance writer so that he could be free to study and read in many subjects and languages. For the rest of his life, Diderot remained dedicated to his independence and was always in love with new ideas.

Diderot's numerous writings reflected typical Enlightened interests. One of his favorite topics was Christianity, which he condemned as fanatical and unreasonable. As he grew older, his literary attacks on Christianity grew more vicious. Of all religions, Christianity, he maintained, was the worst, "the most absurd and the most atrocious in its dogma." This progression reflected his own movement from deism to atheism, ending with a basic materialistic conception of life: "This world is only a mass of molecules."

Diderot's most famous contribution to the Enlightenment was the twenty-eight-volume *Encyclopedia, or Classified Dictionary of the Sciences, Arts, and Trades,* that he edited and referred to as the "great work of his life." Its purpose, according to Diderot, was to "change the general way of thinking." It did precisely that in becoming a major weapon of the philosophes' crusade against the old French society. The contributors included many philosophes who expressed their major concerns. They attacked religious superstition and advocated toleration as well as a program for social, legal, and political improvements that would lead to a society that was more cosmopolitan, more tolerant, more humane, and more reasonable. In later editions, the price of the *Encyclopedia* was drastically reduced, dramatically increasing its sale and making it available to doctors, clergymen, teachers, lawyers, and even military officers. The ideas of the Enlightenment were spread even further as a result.

➢ *The Attack on Religious Intolerance* ➢

Although Voltaire's attacks on religion were in no way original, his lucid prose, biting satire, and clever wit caused his works to be widely read and all the more influential. These two selections present different sides of Voltaire's attack on religious intolerance. The first is from his straightforward treatise, The Ignorant Philosopher, while the second is from his only real literary masterpiece, the novel Candide, where he uses humor to make the same fundamental point about religious intolerance.

Voltaire, *The Ignorant Philosopher*

The contagion of fanaticism then still subsists. . . . The author of the Treatise upon Toleration has not mentioned the shocking executions wherein so many unhappy victims perished in the valleys of Piedmont. He has passed over in silence the massacre of six hundred inhabitants of Valtelina, men, women, and children, who were murdered by the Catholics in the month of September, 1620. I will not say it was with the consent and assistance of the archbishop of Milan, Charles Borome, who was made a saint. Some passionate writers have averred this fact, which I am very far from believing; but I say, there is scarce any city or borough in Europe, where blood has not been spilt for religious quarrels; I say, that the human species has been perceptibly diminished, because women and girls were massacred as well as men; I say, that Europe would have had a third larger population, if there had been no theological disputes. In fine, I say, that so far from forgetting these abominable times, we should frequently take a view of them, to inspire an eternal horror for them; and that it is for our age to make reparation by toleration, for this long collection of crimes, which has taken place through the want of toleration, during sixteen barbarous centuries.

Let it not then be said, that there are no traces left of that shocking fanaticism, of the want of toleration; they are still everywhere to be met with, even in those countries that are esteemed the most humane. The Lutheran and Calvinist preachers, were they masters, would, perhaps, be as little inclined to pity, as obdurate, as insolent as they upbraid their antagonists with being.

Voltaire, *Candide*

At last he [Candide] approached a man who had just been addressing a big audience for a whole hour on the subject of charity. The orator peered at him and said:

"What is your business here? Do you support the Good Old Cause?"

"There is no effect without a cause," replied Candide modestly. "All things are necessarily connected and arranged for the best. It was my fate to be driven from Lady Cunégone's presence and made to run the gauntlet, and now I have to beg my bread until I can earn it. Things should not have happened otherwise."

"Do you believe that the Pope is Antichrist, my friend?" said the minister.

"I have never heard anyone say so," replied Candide; "but whether he is or he isn't, I want some food."

"You don't deserve to eat," said the other. "Be off with you, you villain, you wretch! Don't come near me again or you'll suffer for it."

The minister's wife looked out of the window at that moment, and seeing a man who was not sure that the Pope was Antichrist, emptied over his head a pot full of urine, which shows to what lengths ladies are driven by religious zeal.

TOWARD A NEW "SCIENCE OF MAN"

The Enlightenment belief that Newton's scientific methods could be used to discover the natural laws underlying all areas of human life led to the emergence in the eighteenth century of what the philosophes called a "science of man" or what we would call the social sciences. In a number of areas, philosophes arrived at natural laws that they believed governed human actions. If these "natural laws" seem less than universal to us, it reminds us how much the philosophes were people of their times reacting to the conditions they faced. Nevertheless, their efforts did at least lay the foundations for the modern social sciences.

The Physiocrats and Adam Smith have been viewed as founders of the modern discipline of economics. The leader of the Physiocrats was François Quesnay (1694–1774), a highly successful French court physician. Quesnay and the Physiocrats claimed they would discover the natural

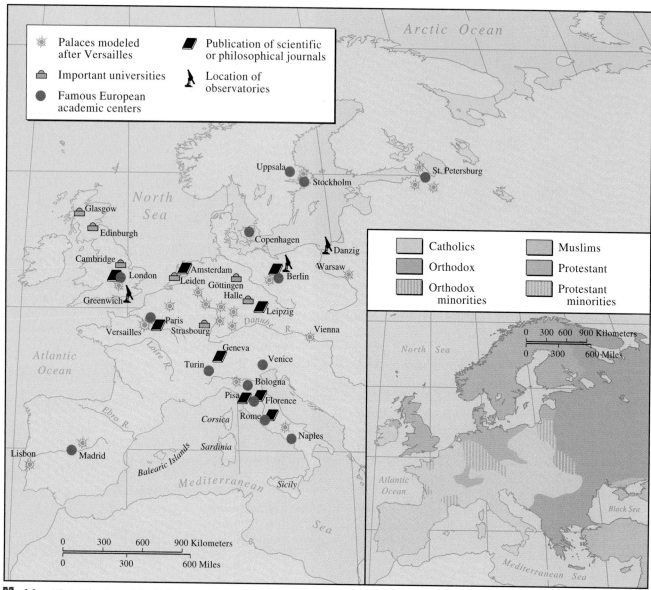

Map 18.1 The Age of the Enlightenment in Europe.

economic laws that governed human society. Their major "natural law" of economics represented a repudiation of mercantilism, specifically, its emphasis on a controlled economy for the benefit of the state. Instead the Physiocrats stressed that the existence of the natural economic forces of supply and demand made it imperative that individuals should be left free to pursue their own economic self-interest. In doing so, all of society would ultimately benefit. Consequently, they argued that the state should in no way interrupt the free play of natural economic forces by government regulation of the economy, but leave it alone, a doctrine that subsequently became known by its French title, *laissez-faire* (to let alone).

The best statement of *laissez-faire* was made in 1776 by a Scottish philosopher, Adam Smith (1723–1790), when he published his famous work *Inquiry into the Nature and Causes of the Wealth of Nations*, known simply as *The Wealth of Nations*. Like the Physiocrats, Smith believed that the state should not interfere in economic matters; indeed, he gave to government only three basic functions: it should protect society from invasion (army); defend individuals from injustice and oppression (police); and keep up certain public works, such as roads and canals that private individuals could not afford. Thus, in Smith's view the state should be a kind of "passive policeman" that remains out of the lives of individuals. In emphasizing the economic liberty of the individual, the Physiocrats and Adam Smith laid the foundation for what became known in the nineteenth century as economic liberalism.

THE LATER ENLIGHTENMENT

By the late 1760s, a new generation of philosophes who had grown up with the worldview of the Enlightenment began to move beyond their predecessors' beliefs. Most famous was Jean-Jacques Rousseau (1712–1778). He was born in the city of Geneva, the son of a watchmaker. Almost entirely self-educated, he spent a wandering existence as a youth holding various jobs in France and Italy. Eventually he made his way to Paris where he was introduced into the circles of the philosophes. He never really liked the social life of the cities, however, and frequently withdrew into long periods of solitude.

Rousseau's political beliefs were presented in two major works. In his *Discourse on the Origins of the Inequality of Mankind*, Rousseau argued that people had adopted laws and governors in order to preserve their private property. In the process, they had become enslaved by government. In his celebrated treatise *The Social Contract*, published in 1762, Rousseau tried to harmonize individual liberty with governmental authority (see the box on p. 374). The social contract was basically an agreement on the part of an entire society to be governed by its general will. If any individual wished to follow his own self-interest, then he should be forced to abide by the general will. "This means nothing less than that he will be forced to be free," said Rousseau, because the general will represented a community's highest aspirations, that which was best for the entire community. Thus liberty was achieved through being forced to follow what was best for all people because, he believed, what was best for all was best for each individual. True freedom is adherence to laws that one has imposed on one's self. To Rousseau, because everybody was responsible for framing the general will, the creation of laws could never be delegated to a parliamentary body:

> Thus the people's deputies are not and could not be its representatives; they are merely its agents; and they cannot decide anything finally. Any law which the people has not

CHRONOLOGY

Works of the Philosophes

Montesquieu, *Persian Letters*	1721
Montesquieu, *The Spirit of the Laws*	1748
Diderot, *The Encyclopedia*	1751–1765
Rousseau, *The Social Contract, Emile*	1762
Voltaire, *Treatise on Toleration*	1763
Beccaria, *On Crimes and Punishments*	1764
Smith, *The Wealth of Nations*	1776
Wollstonecraft, *Vindication of the Rights of Woman*	1792

ratified in person is void; it is not law at all. The English people believes itself to be free; it is gravely mistaken; it is free only during the election of Members of Parliament; as soon as the Members are elected, the people is enslaved; it is nothing.[2]

This is an extreme, idealistic statement, but it is the ultimate statement of participatory democracy.

Another influential treatise by Rousseau also appeared in 1762. Entitled *Emile*, it is one of the Enlightenment's most important works on education. Written in the form of a novel, the work was really a general treatise "on the education of the natural man." His fundamental concern was that education should encourage rather than restrict children's natural instincts. Life's experiences had shown Rousseau the importance of the promptings of the heart, and what he sought was a balance between heart and mind, between sentiment and reason. This emphasis on heart and sentiment made him a precursor of the intellectual movement called Romanticism that dominated Europe at the beginning of the nineteenth century.

But Rousseau did not necessarily practice what he preached. His own children were sent to foundling homes, where many children died at a young age. Rousseau also viewed women as "naturally" different from men: "to fulfill [a woman's] functions, an appropriate physical constitution is necessary to her . . . she needs a soft sedentary life to suckle her babies. How much care and tenderness does she need to hold her family together." In Rousseau's *Emile*, Sophie, who was Emile's intended wife, was educated for her role as wife and mother by learning obedience and the nurturing skills that would enable her to provide loving care for her husband and

A Social Contract

Although Jean-Jacques Rousseau was one of the French *philosophes*, he has also been called "the father of Romanticism." His political ideas have proved extremely controversial. While some have hailed him as the prophet of democracy, others have labeled him an apologist for totalitarianism. This selection is taken from one of his most famous books, The Social Contract.

Jean-Jacques Rousseau, *The Social Contract*
Book 1, Chapter 6: The Social Pact

"How to find a form of association which will defend the person and goods of each member with the collective force of all, and under which each individual, while uniting himself with the others, obeys no one but himself, and remains as free as before." This is the fundamental problem to which the social contract holds the solution. . . .

Chapter 7: The Sovereign

Despite their common interest, subjects will not be bound by their commitment unless means are found to guarantee their fidelity.

For every individual as a man may have a private will contrary to, or different from, the general will that he has as a citizen. His private interest may he speak with a very different voice from that of the public interest; his absolute and naturally independent existence may make him regard what he owes to the common cause as a gratuitous contribution, the loss of which would be less painful for others than the payment is onerous for him; and fancying that the artificial person which constitutes the state is a mere rational entity, he might seek to enjoy the rights of a citizen without doing the duties of a subject. The growth of this kind of injustice would bring about the ruin of the body politic.

Hence, in order that the social pact shall not be an empty formula, it is tacitly implied in that commitment—which alone can give force to all others—that whoever refused to obey the general will shall be constrained to do so by the whole body, which means nothing other than that he shall be forced to be free; for this is the condition which, by giving each citizen to the nation, secures him against all personal dependence, it is the condition which shapes both the design and the working of the political machine, and which alone bestows justice on civil contracts—without it, such contracts would be absurd, tyrannical and liable to the grossest abuse.

children. Not everyone in the eighteenth century, however, agreed with Rousseau, making ideas of gender an important issue in the Enlightenment.

THE "WOMAN QUESTION" IN THE ENLIGHTENMENT

For centuries, men had dominated the debate about the nature and value of women. In general, many male intellectuals had argued that the base nature of women made them inferior to men and made male domination of women necessary (see Chapter 17). In the seventeenth and eighteenth centuries, many male thinkers reinforced this view by arguing that it was based on "natural" biological differences between men and women. Like Rousseau, they argued that the female constitution made women mothers. Male writers, in particular, were critical of the attempts of some women in the Enlightenment to write on intellectual issues, arguing that women by nature were intellectually inferior to men. Nevertheless, there were some Enlightenment thinkers who offered more positive views of women. Diderot, for example, maintained that men and women were not all that different while Voltaire asserted that "women are capable of all that men are" with regard to intellectual activity.

It was women thinkers, however, who added new perspectives to the "woman question" by making specific suggestions for improving the conditions of women. Mary Astell (1666–1731), daughter of a wealthy English coal merchant, argued in 1697 in *A Serious Proposal to the Ladies* that women needed to become better educated. Men, she believed, would resent her proposal, "but they must excuse me, if I be as partial to my own sex as they are to theirs, and think women as capable of learning as men are, and that it becomes them as well."[3]

The strongest statement for the rights of women in the eighteenth century was advanced by the English writer Mary Wollstonecraft (1759–1797), viewed by many as the founder of modern European feminism. In *Vindication of the Rights of Women*, written in 1792, Wollstonecraft pointed out two contradictions in the views of women held by such Enlightenment thinkers as Rousseau. To argue that women must obey men, she said, was contrary to the beliefs of the same individuals that a system based on the arbitrary power of monarchs over their subjects or slave owners over their slaves was wrong. The subjection of women to men was equally wrong. In addition, she argued that the Enlightenment was based on an ideal of reason innate in all human beings. If women have reason, then they too are entitled to the same rights that men have. Women, Wollstonecraft declared, should have equal rights with men in education and in economic and political life as well (see the box on p. 376).

The Social Environment of the Philosophes

The social backgrounds of the philosophes varied considerably, from the aristocratic Montesquieu to the lower-middle-class Diderot and Rousseau. The Enlightenment was not the preserve of any one class, although obviously its greatest appeal was to the aristocracy and upper middle classes of the major cities. The common people, especially the peasants, were little affected by the Enlightenment.

Of great importance to the Enlightenment was the spread of its ideas to the literate elite of European society. Although the publication and sale of books and treatises were crucial to this process, the salon was also a factor. Salons came into being in the seventeenth century but rose to new heights in the eighteenth. The salons were the elegant drawing rooms in the urban houses of the wealthy where invited philosophes and guests gathered to engage in witty, sparkling conversations often centered on the new ideas of the philosophes. In France's rigid hierarchical society, the salons were important in bringing together writers and artists with aristocrats, government officials, and wealthy bourgeoisie.

As hostesses of the salons, women found themselves in a position to affect the decisions of kings, sway political opinion, and influence literary and artistic taste. Salons provided havens for people and views unwelcome in the royal court. When Diderot's *Encyclopedia* was suppressed by the French authorities, Marie-Thérèse de Geoffrin (1699–1777), a wealthy bourgeois widow whose father had been a valet, welcomed the encyclopedists to her salon and offered financial assistance to complete the work in secret. Mme. Geoffrin was not without rivals, however. The marquise du Deffand (1697–1780) had abandoned her husband in the provinces and established herself in Paris where her ornate drawing room attracted many of the Enlightenment's great figures, including Montesquieu and Voltaire.

Although the salons were run by women, the reputation of a salon depended on the stature of the males a hostess was able to attract. Despite this male domination, however, both French and foreign observers complained that females exerted undue influence in French political

✦ **The Salon of Madame Geoffrin.** An important factor in the development of the Enlightenment was the spread of new ideas to the literate elites of European society. Salons were an important part of this process. Madame Geoffrin, who presided over one of the best-known Parisian salons, is shown here, the third figure from the right in the front row.

≥ The Rights of Women ≤

Mary Wollstonecraft responded to an unhappy childhood in a large family by seeking to lead an independent life. Few occupations were available for middle-class women in her day, but she survived by working as a teacher, chaperone, and governess to aristocratic children. All the while, she wrote and developed her ideas on the rights of women. This excerpt is taken from her Vindication of the Rights of Woman, *written in 1792. This work led to her reputation as the foremost British feminist thinker of the eighteenth century.*

Mary Wollstonecraft, *Vindication of the Rights of Woman*

It is a melancholy truth—yet such is the blessed effect of civilization—the most respectable women are the most oppressed; and, unless they have understandings far superior to the common run of understandings, taking in both sexes, they must, from being treated like contemptible beings, become contemptible. How many women thus waste life away the prey of discontent, who might have practiced as physicians, regulated a farm, managed a shop, and stood erect, supported by their own industry, instead of hanging their heads surcharged with the dew of sensibility, that consumes the beauty to which it at first gave luster. . . .

Proud of their weakness, however, [women] must always be protected, guarded from care, and all the rough toils that dignify the mind. If this be the fiat of fate, if they will make themselves insignificant and contemptible, sweetly to waste 'life away,' let them not expect to be valued when their beauty fades, for it is the fate of the fairest flowers to be admired and pulled to pieces by the careless hand that plucked them. In how many ways do I wish, from the purest benevolence, to impress this truth on my sex; yet I fear that they will not listen to a truth that dear-bought experience has brought home to many an agitated bosom, nor willingly resign the privileges of rank and sex for the privileges of humanity, to which those have no claim who do not discharge its duties. . . .

Would men but generously snap our chains, and be content with rational fellowship instead of slavish obedience, they would find us more osbervant daughters, more affectionate sisters, more faithful wives, and more reasonable mothers—in a word, better citizens. We should then love them with true affection, because we should learn to respect ourselves; and the peace of mind of a worthy man would not be interrupted by the idle vanity of his wife. . . .

---

affairs. While exaggerated, this perception led to the decline of salons during the French Revolution.

The salon served an important role in making possible conversation and sociability between upper-class men and women as well as spreading the ideas of the Enlightenment. But other means of spreading Enlightenment ideas were also available. Coffeehouses, cafes, reading clubs, and public lending libraries established by the state were gathering places to exchange ideas. Secret societies also developed. The most famous was the Freemasons, established in London in 1717, France and Italy in 1726, and Prussia in 1744. It was no secret that the Freemasons were sympathetic to the ideas of the philosophes.

Culture and Society in an Age of Enlightenment

The intellectual adventure fostered by the philosophes was accompanied by both traditional practices and important changes in the eighteenth-century world of culture and society.

Innovations in Art, Music, and Literature

Although the Baroque and neoclassical styles that had dominated the seventeenth century continued into the eighteenth century, by the 1730s a new style known as Rococo began to affect decoration and architecture all over Europe. Though a French invention and enormously popular in Germany, Rococo became a truly international style.

Unlike the Baroque, which stressed majesty, power, and movement, Rococo emphasized grace and gentle action. Rococo rejected strict geometrical patterns and had a fondness for curves; it liked to follow the wandering lines of natural objects, such as seashells and flowers. It made much use of interlaced designs colored in gold with delicate contours and graceful curves. Highly secular, its lightness and charm spoke of the pursuit of pleasure, happiness, and love.

Some of Rococo's appeal is evident in the work of Antoine Watteau (1684–1721), whose lyrical views of aristocratic life—refined, sensual, civilized, with gentlemen and ladies in elegant dress—revealed a world of upper-class pleasure and joy. Underneath that exterior, however, was an element of sadness as the artist revealed the fragility and transitory nature of pleasure, love, and life.

Another aspect of Rococo was a sense of enchantment and exuberance, especially evident in the work of Giovanni Battista Tiepolo (1696–1770). Much of Tiepolo's painting came to adorn the walls and ceilings of churches and palaces. His masterpiece is the ceiling of the Bishop's Palace at Würzburg, a massive scene representing the four continents. Tiepolo's work reminds us that Rococo decorative work could easily be used with Baroque architecture.

The palace of Versailles had an enormous impact on Europe. "Keeping up with the Bourbons" became important as the Austrian emperor, the Swedish king, German princes, Italian princes, and even a Russian tsar built grandiose palaces. While imitating Versailles's size, they were modeled less after the French classical style of Versailles than after the seventeenth-century Italian Baroque, as modified by a series of brilliant German and Austrian sculptor-architects. This Baroque-Rococo architectural style of the eighteenth century was conceived as a total work of art in which building, sculptural figures, and wall and ceiling paintings were blended into a harmonious whole. This style was used in both palaces and churches, and often the same architects did both. This is evident in the work of one of the greatest architects of the eighteenth century, Balthasar Neumann (1687–1753).

Neumann's two masterpieces are the pilgrimage church of the Vierzehnheiligen (The Fourteen Saints) in southern Germany and the Bishop's Palace known as the Residenz, the residential palace of the Schönborn prince-bishop of Würzburg. Secular and spiritual become easily interchangeable as lavish and fanciful ornament, light, bright colors, and elaborate and rich detail greet us in both buildings.

The eighteenth century was one of the greatest in the history of European music. In the first half of the eighteenth century two composers—Handel and Bach—stand out as musical geniuses. Johann Sebastian Bach (1685–1750) came from a family of musicians. Bach held the post of organist and music director at a number of small German courts before becoming director of church music at the church of St. Thomas in Leipzig in 1723. There Bach composed his Mass in B Minor, his St. Matthew's Passion, and the cantatas and motets that have established his reputation as one of the greatest composers of all time. Above all for Bach, music was a means to worship God; in his own words, his task in life was to make "well-ordered music in the honor of God."

The other great musical giant of the early eighteenth century, George Frederick Handel (1685–1759), was, like Bach, born in Saxony in Germany and in the same year. Unlike Bach, however, he was profoundly secular in temperament. After studying in Italy, where he began his career by writing operas in the Italian manner, in 1712 he moved to England where he spent most of his adult life

✦ **Antoine Watteau, *The Pilgrimage to Cythera.*** Antoine Watteau was one of the most gifted painters in eighteenth-century France. His portrayal of aristocratic life reveals a world of elegance, wealth, and pleasure. In this painting, Watteau depicts a group of aristocratic pilgrims about to depart the island of Cythera, where they have paid homage to Venus, the goddess of love.

trying to run an operatic company. Although patronized by the English royal court, Handel wrote music for large public audiences and was not adverse to writing huge, unusual-sounding pieces. The band for his Fireworks Music, for example, was supposed to be accompanied by 101 cannon. Although he wrote much secular music, ironically the worldly Handel is probably best known for his religious music. He had no problem moving from Italian opera to religious oratorios when they proved to be more popular with his English public. An oratorio was a musical composition on a religous subject, usually taken from a Biblical story. Only one of Handel's great oratorios, the *Messiah*, is well known today. It has been called "one of those rare works that appeal immediately to everyone, and yet is indisputably a masterpiece of the highest order."[4]

◆ **Vierzehnheiligen, Interior View.** Pictured here is the interior of the Vierzehnheiligen, the pilgrimage church designed by Balthasar Neumann. As this illustration shows, the Baroque-Rococo style of architecture created lavish buildings in which secular and spiritual elements became easily interchangeable. Elaborate detail, blazing light, rich colors, and opulent decoration were blended to create a work of stunning beauty.

Bach and Handel perfected the Baroque musical style with its monumental and elaborate musical structures. Two geniuses of the second half of the eighteenth century—Haydn and Mozart—were innovators who wrote music called classical rather than Baroque. Their renown caused the musical center of Europe to shift from Italy to the Austrian Empire.

Franz Joseph Haydn (1732–1809) spent most of his adult life as musical director for the wealthy Hungarian princes, the Esterhazy brothers. Haydn was incredibly prolific, composing 104 symphonies in addition to string quartets, concerti, songs, oratorios, and masses. His visits to England in 1790 and 1794 introduced him to another world where musicians wrote for public concerts rather than princely patrons. This "liberty," as he called it, induced him to write his two great oratorios, *The Creation* and *The Seasons*, both of which were dedicated to the common people.

Wolfgang Amadeus Mozart (1756–1791) was truly a child prodigy who gave his first harpsichord concert at six and wrote his first opera at twelve. He, too, sought a patron, but his discontent with the overly demanding archbishop of Salzburg forced him to move to Vienna where his failure to find a permanent patron made his life miserable. Nevertheless, he wrote music prolifically and passionately—string quartets, sonatas, symphonies, concerti, and operas—until he died at thirty-five, a debt-ridden pauper. *The Marriage of Figaro*, *The Magic Flute*, and *Don Giovanni* are three of the world's greatest operas. Mozart composed with an ease of melody and a blend of grace, precision, and emotion that arguably no one has ever excelled. Haydn remarked to Mozart's father that "your son is the greatest composer known to me either in person or by reputation."

The eighteenth century was also decisive in the development of the novel. The novel was not a completely new literary genre but grew out of the medieval romances and the picaresque stories of the sixteenth century. The English are credited with establishing the "modern novel as the chief vehicle" for fiction writing. With no established rules, the novel was open to much experimentation. It also proved especially attractive to women readers and women writers.

Henry Fielding (1707–1754) wrote novels about people without scruples who survived by their wits. His best work was *The History of Tom Jones, A Foundling*, a lengthy novel about the numerous adventures of a young scoundrel. Fielding presented scenes of English life from the hovels of London to the country houses of the English aristocracy. In a number of hilarious episodes, he described characters akin to real types in English society. Although he emphasized action rather than inner feeling, Fielding did his own moralizing by attacking the hypocrisy of his age.

The High Culture of the Eighteenth Century

Historians and cultural anthropologists have grown accustomed to distinguishing between a civilization's high culture and popular culture. High culture usually means the literary and artistic culture of the educated and wealthy ruling classes; popular culture refers to the written and unwritten culture of the masses, most of which is passed down orally. By the eighteenth century, European high culture consisted of a learned world of theologians, scientists, philosophers, intellectuals, poets, and dramatists, for whom Latin remained a truly international language. Their work was supported by a wealthy and literate lay group, the most important of whom were the landed aristocracy and the wealthier upper classes in the cities. European high culture was noticeably cosmopolitan. In addition to Latin, French had become an international language of the cultural elites.

Especially noticeable in the eighteenth century was an expansion of both the reading public and publishing. One study of French publishing, for example, reveals that French publishers were issuing about 1,600 titles yearly in the 1780s, up from 300 titles in 1750. Though many of these titles were still aimed at small groups of the educated elite, many were also directed to the new reading public of the middle classes, which included women and even urban artisans. The growth of publishing houses made it possible for authors to make money from their works and be less dependent on wealthy patrons.

An important aspect of the growth of publishing and reading in the eighteenth century was the development of magazines for the general public. Great Britain, an important center for the new magazines, saw 25 periodicals published in 1700, 103 in 1760, and 158 in 1780. Along with magazines came daily newspapers. The first was printed in London in 1702, but by 1780, thirty-seven other English towns had their own newspapers. Filled with news and special features, they were relatively cheap and were provided free in coffeehouses.

Popular Culture

As mentioned, popular culture refers to the often unwritten and unofficial culture passed down orally that was fundamental to the lives of most people. The distinguish-

ing characteristic of popular culture is its collective and public nature. Group activity was especially evident in the festival, a broad name used to cover a variety of celebrations: family festivals, such as weddings; community festivals in Catholic Europe that celebrated the feastday of the local patron saint; annual festivals, such as Christmas and Easter that go back to medieval Christianity; and Carnival, the most spectacular form of festival, which was celebrated in the Mediterranean world of Spain, Italy, and France as well as in Germany and Austria. All of these festivals shared common characteristics. While having a spiritual function, they were celebrated in a secular fashion. They were special occasions on which people ate, drank, and celebrated to excess. In traditional societies, festival was a time to waste because much of the rest of the year was a time of unrelieved work. As the poet Thomas Gray in 1739 said of Carnival in Turin: "This Carnival lasts only from Christmas to Lent; one half of the remaining part of the year is passed in remembering the last, the other in expecting the future Carnival."[5]

"The example par excellence of the festival" was Carnival, which started in January and lasted until Lent began, traditionally the forty-day period of fasting and purification leading up to Easter. Carnival was a time of great indulgence, just the reverse of Lent when people were expected to abstain from meat, sex, and most recreations. A heavy consumption of food, especially meat and other delicacies, and heavy drinking were the norm. Carnival was a time of intense sexual activity as well. Songs with double meanings could be sung publicly at this time of year whereas otherwise they would be considered offensive to the community. A float of Florentine "key-makers," for example, sang this ditty to the ladies: "Our tools are fine, new and useful; We always carry them with us; They are good for anything, If you want to touch them, you can." Finally, it was a time of aggression, a time to release pent-up feelings. Most often this took the form of verbal aggression since people could openly insult other people and were even allowed to criticize their social superiors and authorities. But other acts of violence were also permitted. People pelted each other with apples, eggs, flour, and pig's bladders filled with water. This limited and sanctioned violence also led to unplanned violence. All contemporaries observed that Carnival was a time when the incidence of murder increased dramatically.

The same sense of community evident in festival was also present in the chief gathering places of the common people, the local taverns or cabarets. Taverns functioned as a regular gathering place for neighborhood men to talk, play games, conduct small business matters, and, of course, to drink. In some countries, the favorite drinks of poor people, such as gin in England and vodka in Russia, proved devastating as poor people regularly drank themselves into oblivion. Gin was cheap; the classic sign in English taverns, "Drunk for a penny, dead drunk for two pence," was literally true. In England, the consumption of gin rose from two to five million gallons between 1714 and 1733 and only declined when complaints finally led to strict laws to restrict sales in the 1750s.

In the eighteenth century, the separation between elite and poor grew ever wider. In 1500, popular culture was for everyone; although, a second culture for the elite, it was the only culture for the rest of society. But between 1500 and 1800, the nobility, clergy, and bourgeoisie abandoned popular culture to the lower classes. This was, of course, a gradual process, and in abandoning the popular festivals, the upper classes were also abandoning the popular worldview as well. The new scientific outlook had brought a new mental world for the upper classes, and they now viewed such things as witchcraft, faith healing, fortune telling, and prophecy as the beliefs of "such as are of the weakest judgment and reason, as women, children, and ignorant and superstitious persons."

Popular culture had always included a vast array of traditional songs and stories that were passed down from generation to generation. But popular culture was not entirely based on an oral tradition; a popular literature existed as well. So-called chapbooks, printed on cheap paper, were short brochures sold by itinerant peddlers to the lower classes. They contained both spiritual and secular material; lives of saints and inspirational stories competed with crude satires and adventure stories.

It is apparent from the chapbooks that popular culture did not have to remain primarily oral. Its ability to change was dependent on the growth of literacy. Some reasonable estimates based on studies in France indicate that literacy rates for men increased from 29 percent in the late seventeenth century to 47 percent in the late eighteenth century; for women, the increase was from 14 to 27 percent during the same period of time. Of course, certain groups were more likely to be literate than others. Upper-class elites as well as the upper middle classes in the cities were mostly all literate. However, the figures also indicate dramatic increases for lower-middle-class artisans in urban areas. In the city of Marseilles, for example, there was an increase in literacy for male artisans and workers from 28 percent in 1710 to 85 percent in 1789 while rates for women remained at 15 percent. Peasants, who consti-

tuted as much as 75 percent of France's population, remained largely illiterate.

Crime and Punishment

By the eighteenth century, most European states had developed a hierarchy of courts to deal with crimes. Except in England, judicial torture remained an important means of obtaining evidence before a trial. Courts used the rack, thumbscrews, and other instruments to obtain confessions in criminal cases. Most crimes in the eighteenth century fell into four broad categories: violent crimes such as murder; crimes against property; crimes against the government, such as smuggling; and begging or public vagrancy. The eighteenth century seems to have witnessed a decline in crimes of violence but experienced a noticeable increase in theft and other crimes against property, especially in the cities. Particularly in rural areas, the unplanned violence of desperate people that had been a prominent feature of the seventeenth century was replaced by "semiprofessional vagabonds" who were primarily interested in theft.

Punishments for crimes were often cruel and even spectacular. Public executions were a basic part of traditional punishment and were regarded as a necessary means of deterring potential offenders in an age when a state's police arm was too weak to ensure the capture of criminals. Although nobles were executed by simple beheading, lower-class criminals condemned to death were

◆ **Cruel Punishments: Breaking on the Wheel.** Judicial torture remained a means of obtaining evidence in the eighteenth century. Punishments for crimes were also often cruel. One of the harshest punishments, breaking the limbs of the criminal on a wheel with an iron bar, is pictured here. This punishment was used in France for murder, highway robbery, and arson.

tortured, broken on the wheel, or drawn and quartered. The death penalty was still commonly used in property as well as criminal cases. By 1800, more than 200 crimes were subject to the death penalty in England. In addition to executions, European states resorted to forced labor in mines, forts, and navies. England also sent criminals as indentured servants to colonies in the New World and, after the American Revolution, to Australia.

Appalled by the unjust laws and brutal punishments of their times, some philosophes had sought to create a new approach to justice. The most notable effort was made by the Italian philosophe Cesare Beccaria (1738–1794). In his essay *On Crimes and Punishments*, written in 1764, Beccaria argued that punishments should serve only as deterrents, not as exercises in brutality: "Such punishments . . . ought to be chosen as will make the strongest and most lasting impressions on the minds of others, with the least torment to the body of the criminal."[6] Beccaria was also opposed to the use of capital punishment. It was spectacular, but failed to stop others from committing crimes. Imprisonment, the deprivation of freedom, made a far more lasting impression. Moreover, capital punishment was harmful to society because it set an example of barbarism: "Is it not absurd, that the laws, which detest and punish homicide, should, in order to prevent murder, publicly commit murder themselves?"

By the end of the eighteenth century, a growing sentiment against executions and torture led to a decline in both corporal and capital punishment. A new type of prison, in which criminals were placed in cells and subjected to discipline and regular work to rehabilitate them, began to replace the public spectacle of barbarous punishments.

Religion and the Churches

The music of Bach and the pilgrimage and monastic churches of southern Germany and Austria make us aware of a curious fact. While much of the great art and music of the time was religious, the thought of the time was antireligious as life became increasingly secularized and men of reason attacked the established churches. And yet most Europeans were still Christians. Even many of those most critical of the churches accepted that society could not function without religious faith.

In the eighteenth century, the established Catholic and Protestant churches were basically conservative institutions that upheld society's hierarchical structure, privileged classes, and traditions. Although churches ex-

perienced change because of new state policies, they did not sustain any dramatic internal changes. Whether in Catholic or Protestant countries, the parish church run by priest or pastor remained the center of religious practice. In addition to providing religious services, the parish church kept records of births, deaths, and marriages, provided charity for the poor, supervised whatever primary education there was, and cared for orphans.

Toleration and Religious Minorities

One of the chief battle cries of the philosophes had been a call for religious toleration. Out of political necessity, a certain level of tolerance of different creeds had occurred in the seventeenth century in such places as Germany after the Thirty Years' War and France after the divisive religious wars. But many rulers still found it difficult to accept. Louis XIV had turned back the clock in France at the end of the seventeenth century, insisting on religious uniformity and suppressing the rights of the Huguenots. Even devout rulers continued to believe that there was only one path to salvation; it was the true duty of a ruler not to allow subjects to be condemned to hell by being heretics. Catholic minorities in Protestant countries and Protestant minorities in Catholic countries did not enjoy full civil or political rights. Persecution of heretics continued; the last burning of a heretic took place in 1781.

The Jews remained the despised religious minority of Europe. The largest number of Jews (known as the Ashkenazic Jews) lived in eastern Europe. Except in relatively tolerant Poland, Jews were restricted in their movements, forbidden to own land or hold many jobs, forced to pay burdensome special taxes, and also subject to periodic outbursts of popular wrath. The resulting pogroms in which Jewish communities were looted and massacred made Jewish existence precarious and dependent on the favor of their territorial rulers.

Another major group was the Sephardic Jews who had been expelled from Spain in the fifteenth century. Although many had migrated to Turkish lands, some of them had settled in cities, such as Amsterdam, Venice, London, and Frankfurt, where they were relatively free to participate in the banking and commercial activities that Jews had practiced since the Middle Ages. The highly successful ones came to provide valuable services to rulers, especially in central Europe where they were known as the court Jews. But even these Jews were insecure because their religion set them apart from the Christian majority and served as a catalyst to social resentment.

Some Enlightenment thinkers in the eighteenth century favored a new acceptance of Jews. They argued that Jews and Muslims were all human and deserved the full rights of citizenship despite their religion. Many philosophes denounced persecution of the Jews but made no attempt to hide their hostility and ridiculed Jewish customs. Diderot, for example, said that the Jews had "all the defects peculiar to an ignorant and superstitious nation." Many Europeans favored the assimilation of the Jews into the mainstream of society, but only by the conversion of Jews to Christianity as the basic solution to the "Jewish problem." This, of course, was not acceptable to most Jews.

The Austrian emperor Joseph II (1780–1790) attempted to adopt a new policy toward the Jews, although it too was limited. It freed Jews from nuisance taxes and allowed them more freedom of movement and job opportunities, but they were still restricted from owning land and worshiping in public. At the same time, Joseph II encouraged Jews to learn German and work toward greater assimilation into Austrian society. Joseph's policy was but a small step in the liberation of the Jews in that it took a moderate position between toleration and assimilation.

Popular Religion in the Eighteenth Century

Despite the rise of skepticism and the intellectuals' belief in deism and natural religion, it would appear that religious devotion remained active in the eighteenth century. Catholic popular piety continued to be strong while within Protestantism the desire for more direct spiritual experience actually led to religious revivalism, especially in England.

It is difficult to assess the religiosity of Europe's Catholics precisely. The Catholic parish church remained an important center of life for the entire community. How many people went to church regularly cannot be known exactly, but it has been established that 90 to 95 percent of Catholic populations did go to Mass on Easter Sunday, one of the church's most special celebrations. Confraternities, which were organizations of laypeople dedicated to good works and acts of piety, were especially popular with townspeople. Each confraternity honored its patron saint by holy processions in which members proudly wore their special robes.

After the initial century of religious fervor that created Protestantism in the sixteenth century, Protestant churches in the seventeenth century had settled down into well-established patterns controlled by state authorities and served by a well-educated clergy. Protestant churches became bureaucratized and bereft of religious

enthusiasm. In Germany and England, where rationalism and deism had become influential and moved some theologians to a more "rational" Christianity, the desire of ordinary Protestant churchgoers for greater depths of religious experience led to new and dynamic religious movements.

One of the most famous movements—Methodism—was the work of John Wesley (1703–1791). An ordained Anglican minister, John Wesley took religion very seriously, experienced a deep spiritual crisis, and underwent a mystical experience: "I felt I did trust in Christ alone for salvation; and an assurance was given me, that He had taken away my sins, even mine, and saved me from the law of sin and death. I felt my heart strangely warmed." To Wesley, "the gift of God's grace" assured him of salvation and led him to become a missionary to the English people, bringing the "glad tidings" of salvation to all people, despite opposition from the Anglican church, which criticized this emotional mysticism or religious enthusiasm as superstitious nonsense. To Wesley, all could be saved by experiencing God and opening the doors to his grace.

In taking the Gospel to the people, Wesley preached to the masses in open fields, appealing especially to the lower classes neglected by the socially elitist Anglican church. He tried, he said, "to lower religion to the level of the lowest people's capacities." Wesley's charismatic preaching often provoked highly charged and even violent conversion experiences (see the box on p. 383). Afterward, converts were organized into so-called Methodist societies or chapels in which they could aid each other in doing the good works that Wesley considered a component of salvation. A Central Methodist Conference supervised new lay preachers from Methodist circles. Controlled by Wesley, it enabled him to dominate the evangelical movement he had created. Although Wesley sought to keep Methodism within the Anglican church, after his death it became a separate and independent sect. Methodism represents an important revival of Christianity and proved that the need for spiritual experience had not been expunged by the eighteenth-century search for reason.

Conclusion

One prominent historian of the eighteenth century has appropriately characterized it as a century of change and tradition. Highly influenced by the new worldview created by the Scientific Revolution and especially the ideas

The Conversion Experience in Wesley's Methodism

After his own conversion experience, John Wesley traveled extensively to bring the "glad tidings" of Christ to other people. It has been estimated that he preached over 40,000 sermons, some of them to audiences numbering 20,000 listeners. Wesley gave his message wherever people gathered—in the streets, hospitals, private houses, and even pubs. In this selection from his journal, Wesley describes how emotional and even violent conversion experiences could be.

The Works of the Reverend John Wesley

Sunday, May 20 [1759], being with Mr. B—ll at Everton, I was much fatigued, and did not rise: but Mr. B. did, and observed several fainting and crying out, while Mr. Berridge was preaching: afterwards at Church, I heard many cry out, especially children, whose agonies were amazing: one of the eldest, a girl of ten or twelve years old, was full in my view, in violent contortions of body, and weeping aloud, I think incessantly, during the whole service. . . . The Church was equally crowded in the afternoon, the windows being filled within and without, and even the outside of the pulpit to the very top; so that Mr. B. seemed almost stifled by their breath; yet feeble and sickly as he is, he was continually strengthened, and his voice, for the most part, distinguishable; in the midst of all the outcries. I believe there were present three times more men than women, a great part of whom came from far; thirty of them having set out at two in the morning, from a place thirteen miles off. The text was, *Having a form of godliness, but denying the power thereof.* When the power of religion began to be spoken of, the presence of God really filled the place: and while poor sinners felt the sentence of death in their souls, what sounds of distress did I hear! The greatest number of them who cried or fell, were men: but some women, and several children, felt the power of the same almighty Spirit, and seemed just sinking into hell. This occasioned a mixture of several sounds; some shrieking, some roaring aloud. The most general was a loud breathing, like that of people half strangled and gasping for life: and indeed almost all the cries were like those of human creatures, dying in bitter anguish. Great numbers wept without any noise: others fell down as death: some sinking in silence; some with extreme noise and violent agitation. I stood on the pew-seat, as did a young man in the opposite pew, an able-bodied, fresh, healthy countryman: but in a moment, while he seemed to think of nothing less, down he dropped with a violence inconceivable. The adjoining pews seemed to shake with his fall: I heard afterwards the stamping of his feet; ready to break the boards, as he lay in strong convulsions, at the bottom of the pew. Among several that were struck down in the next pew, was a girl, who was as violently seized as he. . . . Among the children who felt the arrows of the Almighty, I saw a sturdy boy, about eight years old, who roared above his fellows, and seemed in his agony to struggle with the strength of a grown man. His face was as red as scarlet: and almost all on whom God laid his hand, turned either very red or almost black. . . .

The violent struggling of many in the above-mentioned churches, has broken several pews and benches. Yet it is common for people to remain unaffected there, and afterwards to drop down in their way home. Some have been found lying as dead on the road: others, in Mr. B.'s garden; not being able to walk from the Church to his house, though it is not two hundred yards. . . .

of Locke and Newton, the philosophes hoped that they could create a new society by using reason to discover the natural laws that governed it. Like the Christian humanists of the fifteenth and sixteenth centuries, they believed that education could create better human beings and a better human society. By attacking traditional religion as the enemy and creating the new "sciences of man" in economics, politics, and justice, the philosophes laid the foundation for a modern worldview based on rationalism and secularism.

But it was also an age of tradition. While secular thought and rational ideas began to pervade the mental world of the ruling elites, most people in eighteenth-century Europe still lived by seemingly eternal verities and practices—God, religious worship, and farming. The most brilliant architecture and music of the age were religious. And yet, the forces of secularization were too strong to stop. In the midst of intellectual change, economic, political, and social transformations of great purport were taking shape that by the end of the eighteenth century were to lead to both political and industrial revolutions. It is time now to examine the political, economic, and social traditions and changes of the century.

NOTES

1. John Locke, *An Essay Concerning Human Understanding* (New York, 1964), pp. 89–90.
2. Jean-Jacques Rousseau, *The Social Contract*, trans. Maurice Cranston (Harmondsworth, 1968), p. 141.
3. *A Serious Proposal to the Ladies*, in Moira Ferguson, ed., *First Feminists: British Women Writers, 1578–1799* (Bloomington, Ind., 1985), p. 190.

4. Kenneth Clark, *Civilisation* (New York, 1969), p. 231.
5. Quoted in Peter Burke, *Popular Culture in Early Modern Europe* (New York, 1978), p. 179.
6. Cesare Beccaria, *An Essay on Crimes and Punishments*, trans. E. D. Ingraham (Philadelphia, 1819), pp. 59–60.

SUGGESTIONS FOR FURTHER READING

Two sound, comprehensive surveys of eighteenth-century Europe are I. Woloch, *Eighteenth-Century Europe* (New York, 1982); and M. S. Anderson, *Europe in the Eighteenth Century* (London, 1987). See also R. Birn, *Crisis, Absolutism, Revolution: Europe 1648–1789*, 2d ed. (Fort Worth, Tex., 1992).

Good, brief introductions to the Enlightenment can be found in N. Hampson, *A Cultural History of the Enlightment* (New York, 1968); and D. Outram, *The Enlightenment* (Cambridge, 1995). A more detailed synthesis can be found in P. Gay, *The Enlightenment: An Interpretation*, 2 vols. (New York, 1966–69). Two older works still of value are by P. Hazard, *The European Mind, 1680–1715* (New York, 1963), and *European Thought in the Eighteenth Century* (New York, 1963). For a short, popular survey on the French philosophes, see F. Artz, *The Enlightenment in France* (Kent, Ohio, 1968). Studies of the major Enlightenment intellectuals include R. Schackleton, *Montesquieu, A Critical Biography* (London, 1961); H. T. Mason, *Voltaire: A Biography* (Baltimore, 1981); A. Wilson, *Diderot* (New York, 1972); P. N. Furbank, *Diderot: A Critical Biography* (New York, 1992); and M. Cranston, *Jean-Jacques: The Early Life and Work of Jean-Jacques Rousseau* (London, 1983). Specialized studies on various aspects of the Enlightenment include F. Manuel, *The Eighteenth*

Century Confronts the Gods (New York, 1967); M. W. Cranston, *Philosophers and Pamphleteers: Political Theorists of the Enlightenment* (London, 1986); M. C. Jacob, *The Radical Enlightenment: Pantheists, Freemasons and Republicans* (London, 1981); and R. Darnton, *The Business of Enlightenment: A Publishing History of the Encyclopédie, 1775–1800* (Cambridge, Mass., 1979). On women in the eighteenth century, see N. Z. Davis and A. Farge, eds., *A History of Women: Renaissance and Enlightenment Paradoxes* (Cambridge, Mass., 1993); P. Quennell, ed., *Affairs of the Mind: The Salon in Europe and America from the 18th to the 20th Century* (Washington, D.C., 1980); and B. S. Anderson and J. P. Zinsser, *A History of Their Own*, vol. 2 (New York, 1988).

A readable general survey on the arts is M. Levey, *Rococo to Revolution* (London, 1966). On the development of the novel in England, see I. Watt, *The Rise of the Novel: Studies in Defoe, Richardson, and Fielding* (Berkeley, 1957). The growth of publishing is examined in J. Black, *The English Press in the Eighteenth Century* (London, 1987). Different facets of crime and punishment are examined in the important works by M. Foucault, *Discipline and Punish: The Birth of the Prison* (New York, 1977); and J. Langbein, *Torture and the Law of Proof* (Chicago, 1977). Important studies on popular culture include P. Burke,

Popular Culture in Early Modern Europe (New York, 1978); and R. Darnton, *The Great Cat Massacre and Other Episodes in French Cultural History* (New York, 1984).

A good introduction to the religious history of the eighteenth century can be found in G. R. Cragg, *The Church and the Age of Reason, 1648–1789* (London, 1966). The problem of religious toleration is examined in C. H. O'Brien, *Ideas of Religious Toleration at the Time of Joseph II* (Philadelphia, 1969); and A. Hertzberg, *The French Enlightenment and the Jews* (New York, 1968).

CHAPTER

19

The Eighteenth Century: European States, International Wars, and Social Change

Historians have often defined the eighteenth century chronologically as spanning the years from 1715 to 1789. Politically, this makes sense because 1715 marks the end of the age of Louis XIV, and 1789 was the year in which the French Revolution erupted. This period has often been portrayed as the final phase of Europe's old order, before the violent upheaval and reordering of society associated with the French Revolution. Europe's old order, still largely agrarian, dominated by kings and landed aristocrats, and grounded in privileges for nobles, clergy, towns, and provinces, seemed to continue a basic pattern that had prevailed in Europe since medieval times. But new ideas and new practices were also beginning to emerge. Just as a new intellectual order based on rationalism and secularism was emerging in Europe from the intellectual revolution of the Scientific Revolution and Enlightenment, demographic, economic, and social patterns were beginning to change in ways that represent the emergence of a modern new order.

For some, the ideas of the Enlightenment seemed to herald the possibility of a new political age as well. Catherine the Great, who ruled Russia from 1762 to 1796, wrote to Voltaire: "Since 1746 I have been under the greatest obligations to you. Before that period I read nothing but romances, but by chance your works fell into my hands, and ever since then I have never ceased to read them, and have no desire for books less well written than yours, or less instructive." The empress of Russia also invited Diderot to Russia and, when he arrived, urged him to speak frankly "as man to man." Diderot did, offering her advice for a far-ranging program of political and financial reform. But Catherine's apparent eagerness to make enlightened reforms was tempered by skepticism. She said of Diderot: "If I had believed him everything would have been turned upside down in my kingdom; legislation, administration, finance—all would have been turned topsy-turvy to make room for impractical theories." For Catherine, enlightened reform remained more a dream

Louis XV of France
Maria Theresa of Austria
Frederick the Great of Prussia
Catherine the Great of Russia

Robert Walpole as prime minister
First partition of Poland
William Pitt the Younger becomes prime minister •
Joseph II of Austria

Britain enters Spanish American markets
War of the Austrian Succession
Seven Years' War

than a reality, and in the end, the waging of wars to gain more power was more important.

In the eighteenth century, the process of centralization that had characterized the growth of states since the Middle Ages continued as most European states enlarged their bureaucratic machinery and consolidated their governments in order to collect the revenues and build the armies they needed to compete militarily with the other European states. International competition continued to be the favorite pastime of eighteenth-century rulers. Within the European state system, the nations that would dominate Europe until World War I—Britain, France, Austria, Prussia, and Russia—emerged as the five great powers of Europe. Their rivalries led to major wars. In the midst of this state building and war making, dramatic demographic, economic, and social changes heralded the emergence of a radical transformation in the way Europeans would raise food and produce goods.

The European States

Most European states in the eighteenth century were ruled by monarchs. Although the seventeenth-century justification for strong monarchy on the basis of divine right continued into the succeeding century, as the eighteenth century became increasingly secularized, divine-right assumptions were gradually superseded by influential utilitarian arguments. The Prussian king Frederick II

expressed these well when he attempted to explain the services a monarch must provide for his people:

> These services consisted in the maintenance of the laws; a strict execution of justice; an employment of his whole powers to prevent any corruption of manners; and defending the state against its enemies. It is the duty of this magistrate to pay attention to agriculture; it should be his care that provisions for the nation should be in abundance, and that commerce and industry should be encouraged. He is a perpetual sentinel, who must watch the acts and the conduct of the enemies of the state. . . . If he be the first general, the first minister of the realm, it is not that he should remain the shadow of authority, but that he should fulfill the duties of such titles. He is only the first servant of the state.[1]

This utilitarian argument was reinforced by the praises of the philosophes.

Enlightened Absolutism?

There is no doubt that Enlightenment thought had some impact on the political development of European states in the eighteenth century. Closely related to the Enlightenment idea of natural laws was the belief in natural rights, which were thought to be inalienable privileges that ought not to be withheld from any person. These natural rights included equality before the law, freedom of religious worship, freedom of speech and press, and the right to assemble, hold property, and pursue happiness. The American Declaration of Independence summarized the Enlightenment concept of natural rights in its opening paragraph: "We hold these truths to be self-evident, that all men are created equal; that they are endowed by their creator with certain unalienable rights; that among these are life, liberty and pursuit of happiness."

But how were these natural rights to be established and preserved? In the opinion of most philosophes, most people needed the direction provided by an enlightened ruler. What, however, made rulers enlightened? They must allow religious toleration, freedom of speech and press, and the rights of private property. They must foster the arts, sciences, and education. Above all, they must not be arbitrary in their rule; they must obey the laws and enforce them fairly for all subjects. Only strong monarchs seemed capable of overcoming vested interests and effecting the reforms society needed. Reforms then should come from above—from the rulers rather than from the people. Distrustful of the masses, the philosophes believed that absolute rulers, swayed by enlightened principles, were the best hope of reforming their societies.

The extent to which rulers actually did so is frequently discussed in the political history of Europe in the eighteenth century. Many historians once assumed that a new type of monarchy emerged in the later eighteenth cen-

tury, which they called "enlightened despotism" or "enlightened absolutism." Monarchs such as Frederick II of Prussia, Catherine the Great of Russia, and Joseph II of Austria supposedly followed the advice of the philosophes and ruled by enlightened principles, establishing a path to modern nationhood. Recent scholarship, however, has questioned the usefulness of the concept of "enlightened absolutism." We can best determine the extent to which it can be applied by surveying the development of the European states and then making a judgment about the "enlightened absolutism" of the later eighteenth century.

The Atlantic Seaboard States

As a result of overseas voyages in the sixteenth century, the European economic axis began to shift from the Mediterranean to the Atlantic seaboard. In the seventeenth century, the English and Dutch countries ex-

✖ **Map 19.1** Europe in 1763.

panded as Spain and Portugal declined. By the eighteenth century, Dutch power had waned, and it was left to the English and French to build the commercial empires that presaged the growth of a true global economy.

FRANCE: THE LONG RULE OF LOUIS XV

In the eighteenth century, France experienced an economic revival while the movement of the Enlightenment gained strength. The French monarchy, however, was not overly influenced by the philosophes and resisted reforms while the French aristocracy grew stronger.

Louis XIV had left France with enlarged territories, an enormous debt, an unhappy populace, and a five-year-old great-grandson as his successor. Louis XV (1715–1774) did not begin to rule in his own right until 1743. But Louis was both lazy and weak, and ministers and mistresses soon began to influence the king, control the affairs of state, and undermine the prestige of the monarchy. The loss of an empire in the Seven Years' War, accompanied by burdensome taxes, an ever-mounting public debt, more hungry people, and a frivolous court life at Versailles forced even Louis to realize the growing disgust with his monarchy. "Things will last my time at any rate," he remarked myopically and prophetically.

The new king, Louis's twenty-year-old grandson who became Louis XVI (1774–1792) knew little about the operations of the French government and lacked the energy to deal decisively with state affairs. His wife, Marie Antoinette, was a spoiled Austrian princess who devoted much of her time to court intrigues. As France's financial crises worsened, neither Louis nor his queen seemed able to fathom the depths of despair and discontent that soon led to violent revolution.

GREAT BRITAIN: KING AND PARLIAMENT

The success of the Glorious Revolution in England had prevented absolutism without clearly inaugurating constitutional monarchy. The eighteenth-century British political system was characterized by a sharing of power between king and Parliament, with Parliament gradually gaining the upper hand. (The United Kingdom of Great Britain came into existence in 1707 when the governments of England and Scotland were united; the term *British* came into use to refer to both English and Scots.) The king chose ministers responsible to himself who set policy and guided Parliament; Parliament had the power to make laws, levy taxes, pass the budget, and indirectly influence the king's ministers. The eighteenth-century British Parliament was dominated by a landed aristocracy

that historians usually divide into two groups: the peers, who sat for life in the House of Lords, and the landed gentry, who sat in the House of Commons and served as justices of the peace. The two groups had much in common; both were made up of landowners with similar economic interests, and they frequently intermarried.

The deputies to the House of Commons were chosen from the boroughs and counties but not by popular voting. Who was eligible to vote in the boroughs varied wildly, enabling wealthy landed aristocrats to gain support by patronage and bribery; the result was a number of "pocket boroughs" controlled by a single person (hence "in his pocket"). The duke of Newcastle, for example, controlled the representatives from seven boroughs. It has been estimated that out of 405 borough deputies, 293 were chose by fewer than 500 voters. This aristocratic control also extended to the county delegates, two from each of England's forty counties. Although all holders of property worth at least forty shillings a year could vote, members of the leading landed gentry families were elected over and over again.

In 1714, a new dynasty—the Hanoverians—was established when the last Stuart ruler, Queen Anne (1702–1714), died without an heir. The crown was offered to the Protestant rulers of the German state of Hanover. Because the first Hanoverian king, George I (1714–1727), did not speak English and neither George I nor George II

(1727–1760) had much familiarity with the British system, their chief ministers were allowed to handle Parliament. Many historians believe that this exercise of ministerial power was an important step in the development of the modern cabinet system in British government.

Robert Walpole served as prime minister from 1721 to 1742 and pursued a peaceful foreign policy to avoid new land taxes. But new forces were emerging in eighteenth-century England as growing trade and industry led an ever-increasing middle class to favor expansion of trade and world empire. The exponents of empire found a spokesman in William Pitt the Elder, who became prime minister in 1757 and furthered imperial ambitions by acquiring Canada and India in the Seven Years' War (see the "Seven Years' War" later in this chapter).

Despite his successes, however, Pitt the Elder was dismissed by the new king George III (1760–1820) in 1761 and replaced by the king's favorite, Lord Bute. However, discontent over the electoral system and the loss of the American colonies (see Chapter 20) brought public criticism of the king. In 1780, the House of Commons affirmed that "the influence of the crown has increased, is increasing, and ought to be diminished." King George III managed to avoid drastic change by appointing William Pitt the Younger (1759–1806), son of William Pitt the Elder, as prime minister in 1783. Supported by the merchants, industrial classes, and the king, Pitt managed to stay in power through the French revolutionary and Napoleonic eras. George III, however, remained an un-

certain supporter because of periodic bouts of insanity (he once thought a tree in Windsor Park was the King of Prussia). With Pitt's successes, however, serious reform of the corrupt parliamentary system was avoided for another generation.

Absolutism in Central and Eastern Europe

Of the five major European powers, three were located in central and eastern Europe and came to play an increasingly important role in European international politics.

PRUSSIA: THE ARMY AND THE BUREAUCRACY

Two able Prussian kings in the eighteenth century, Frederick William I and Frederick II, further developed the two major institutions—the army and the bureaucracy—that were the backbone of Prussia. Frederick William I (1713–1740) promoted the evolution of Prussia's highly efficient civil bureaucracy by establishing the General Directory. It served as the chief administrative agent of the central government, supervising military, police, economic, and financial affairs. Because Prussia's disjointed territories could hardly have been maintained without a centralized administrative machine, Frederick William strove to maintain a highly efficient bureaucracy of civil service workers. It became a special kind of organization with its own code in which the supreme values were obedience, honor, and service to the king as the highest duty.

✦   **The British House of Commons.** A sharing of power between king and Parliament characterized the British political system in the eighteenth century. Parliament was divided into a House of Lords and a House of Commons. The painting shows the House of Commons in session in 1793 during a debate over the possibility of war with France. William Pitt is addressing the House.

As Frederick William asserted: "One must serve the king with life and limb, with goods and chattels, with honor and conscience, and surrender everything except salvation. The latter is reserved for God. But everything else must be mine."[2] Close, personal supervision of the bureaucracy became a hallmark of the eighteenth-century Prussian rulers.

The nobility or landed aristocracy known as Junkers, who owned large estates with many serfs, continued to play a dominating role in the Prussian state. The Junkers held a complete monopoly over the officer corps of the Prussian army, which Frederick William passionately continued to expand. By the end of his reign, the army had grown from 45,000 to 83,000 men. Though tenth in physical size and thirteenth in population in Europe, Prussia had the fourth largest army after France, Russia, and Austria.

While nobles served as officers, rank-and-file soldiers were usually peasants who served a long number of years. By using nobles as officers, Frederick William ensured a close bond between the nobility and the army and, in turn, the loyalty of the nobility to the absolute monarch. As officers, the Junker nobility became imbued with a sense of service to the king or state. All the virtues of the Prussian nobility were, in effect, military virtues: duty, obedience, sacrifice. At the same time, because of its size and reputation as one of the best armies in Europe, the Prussian army was the most important institution in the state. "Prussian militarism" became synonymous with the extreme exaltation of military virtues. Indeed, one Prussian minister remarked around 1800 that "Prussia was not a country with an army, but an army with a country which served as headquarters and food magazine."[3]

Frederick the Great (1740–1786) was one of the best educated and most cultured monarchs in the eighteenth century. He was well versed in Enlightenment thought and even invited Voltaire to live at his court for several years. His intellectual interests were despised by his father who forced his intelligent son to prepare for a career in ruling (see the box on p. 392). A believer in the king as the "first servant of the state," Frederick the Great became a conscientious ruler who made few innovations in the administration of the state. His diligence in overseeing its operation, however, made the Prussian bureaucracy well known for both its efficiency and honesty.

For a time, Frederick seemed quite willing to follow the philosophes' suggestions for reform. He established a single code of laws for his territories that eliminated the use of torture except in treason and murder cases. He also granted a limited freedom of speech and press as well as complete religious toleration, no difficult task since he

✦ **Frederick II at Sans-Souci.** Frederick II was one of the most cultured and well-educated European monarchs. In this painting, he is shown visiting the building site of his residential retreat of Sans-Souci at Potsdam.

had no strong religious convictions anyway. Although Frederick was well aware of the philosophes' condemnation of serfdom, he was too dependent on the Prussian nobility to interfere with it or with the hierarchical structure of Prussian society. In fact, Frederick II was a social conservative who made Prussian society even more aristocratic than it had been before. Frederick II reversed his father's policy of allowing commoners to have power in the civil service and reserved the higher positions in the bureaucracy for members of the nobility. The upper ranks of the bureaucracy came close to constituting a hereditary caste over time.

Like his predecessors, Frederick the Great took a great interest in military affairs and enlarged the Prussian army (to 200,000 men). Unlike his predecessors, he had no objection to using it. Frederick did not hesitate to take advantage of a succession crisis in the Habsburg monarchy to seize the Austrian province of Silesia for Prussia. This act aroused Austria's bitter hostility to Prussia and embroiled Frederick in two major wars, the War of the Austrian Succession and the Seven Years' War. Although the latter war left his country exhausted, Frederick succeeded in keeping Silesia. After the wars, the first partition of Poland with Austria and Russia in 1772 gave him the

Frederick the Great and His Father

As a young man, the future Frederick the Great was quite different from his strict and austere father, Frederick William I. Possessing a high regard for French culture, poetry, and flute playing, Frederick resisted his father's wishes that he immerse himself in governmental and military affairs. Eventually, Frederick capitulated to his father's will and accepted the need to master affairs of state. These letters, written when Frederick was sixteen, illustrate the difficulties in their relationship.

Frederick to His Father, Frederick William I (September 11, 1728)

I have not ventured for a long time to present myself before my dear papa, partly because I was advised against it, but chiefly because I anticipated an even worse reception than usual and feared to vex my dear papa still further by the favor I have now to ask; so I have preferred to put it in writing.

I beg my dear papa that he will be kindly disposed toward me. I do assure him that after long examination of my conscience I do not find the slightest thing with which to reproach myself; but if, against my wish and will, I have vexed my dear papa, I hereby beg most humbly for forgiveness, and hope that my dear papa will give over the fearful hate which has appeared so plainly in his whole behavior and to which I cannot accustom myself. I have always thought hitherto that I had a kind father, but now I see the contrary. However, I will

take courage and hope that my dear papa will think this all over and take me again into his favor. Meantime I assure him that I will never, my life long, willingly fail him, and in spite of his disfavor I am still, with most dutiful and childlike respect, my dear papa's

Most obedient and faithful servant and son,

Frederick

Frederick William to His Son Frederick

A bad, obstinate boy, who does not love his father; for when one does one's best, and especially when one loves one's father, one does what he wishes not only when he is standing by but when he is not there to see. Moreover you know very well that I cannot stand an effeminate fellow who has no manly tastes, who cannot ride or shoot (to his shame be it said!), is untidy about his person, and wears his hair curled like a fool instead of cutting it; and that I have condemned all these things a thousand times, and yet there is no sign of improvement. For the rest, haughty, offish as a country lout, conversing with none but a favored few instead of being affable and popular, grimacing like a fool, and never following my wishes out of love for me but only when forced into it, caring for nothing but to have his own way, and thinking nothing else is of any importance.

This is my answer.

Frederick William

Polish territory between Prussia and Brandenburg and created greater unity for the scattered lands of Prussia. By the end of his reign, Prussia was recognized as a great European power.

THE AUSTRIAN EMPIRE OF THE HABSBURGS

The Austrian Empire had become one of the great European states by the beginning of the eighteenth century. The city of Vienna, center of the Habsburg monarchy, was filled with magnificent palaces and churches built in the Baroque style and became the music capital of Europe. And yet Austria, by its very nature as a sprawling empire composed of many different nationalities, languages, religions, and cultures, found it difficult to provide common laws and administrative centralization for its people. Although empress Maria Theresa (1740–1780) managed to

make administrative reforms that helped centralize the Austrian Empire, these reforms were done for practical reasons—to strengthen the power of the Habsburg state—and were accompanied by an enlargement and modernization of the armed forces. Maria Theresa remained staunchly Catholic and conservative and was not open to the wider reform calls of the philosophes. But her successor was.

Joseph II (1780–1790) was determined to make changes; at the same time, he carried on his mother's chief goal of enhancing Habsburg power within the monarchy and Europe. Joseph II was an earnest man who believed in the need to sweep away anything standing in the path of reason. He was not a practical reformer like Frederick II but a doctrinaire idealist. As Joseph expressed it: "I have made Philosophy the lawmaker of my empire, her logical applications are going to transform Austria."

Joseph's reform program was far-reaching. He abolished serfdom and tried to give the peasants hereditary rights to their holdings. An exponent of the Physiocratic ideas, he abandoned economic restraints by eliminating internal trade barriers, ending monopolies, and removing guild restrictions. A new penal code was instituted that abrogated the death penalty and established the principle of equality of all before the law. Joseph introduced drastic religious reforms as well, including complete religious toleration and restrictions on the Catholic church. Altogether, Joseph II issued 6,000 decrees and 11,000 laws in his effort to transform Austria.

Joseph's reform program proved overwhelming for Austria, however. He alienated the nobility by freeing the serfs and alienated the church by his attacks on the monastic establishment. Even the serfs were unhappy, unable to comprehend the drastic changes inherent in Joseph's policies. His attempt to rationalize the administration of the empire by imposing German as the official bureaucratic language alienated the non-German nationalities. As Joseph complained, there were not enough people for the kind of bureaucracy he needed. His deep sense of failure is revealed in the epitaph he wrote for his gravestone: "Here lies Joseph II who was unfortunate in everything that he undertook." His successors undid many of his reform efforts.

RUSSIA UNDER CATHERINE THE GREAT

Peter the Great was followed by a series of six successors who were made and unmade by the palace guard. After the last of these six, Peter III, was murdered by a faction of nobles, his German wife emerged as autocrat of all the Russians. Catherine II (1762–1796) was an intelligent woman who was familiar with the works of the philosophes. She claimed that she wished to reform Russia along the lines of Enlightenment ideas, but she was always shrewd enough to realize that her success depended on the support of the palace guard and the gentry class from which it stemmed. She could not afford to alienate the Russian nobility.

Initially, Catherine seemed eager to pursue reform. She called for the election of an assembly in 1767 to debate the details of a new law code. In her *Instruction*, written as a guide to the deliberations, Catherine questioned the institution of serfdom, torture, and capital punishment and even advocated the principle of the equality of all people in the eyes of the law. But one and one-half years of negotiation produced little real change.

In fact, Catherine's subsequent policies had the effect of strengthening the landholding class at the expense of

◆ **Catherine the Great.** Autocrat of Russia, Catherine was an intelligent ruler who favored reform. She found it expedient, however, to retain much of the old system in order to keep the support of the landed nobility. In this portrait by Dmitry Levitsky, she is shown in legislative regalia in the Temple of Justice in 1783.

all others, especially the Russian serfs. To reorganize local government, Catherine divided Russia into fifty provinces, each of which in turn was subdivided into districts ruled by officials chosen by the nobles. In this way, the local nobility became responsible for the day-to-day governing of Russia. Moreover, the gentry were now formed into corporate groups with special legal privileges, including the right to trial by peers and exemption from personal taxation and corporal punishment. A Charter of the Nobility formalized these rights in 1785.

Catherine's policy of favoring the landed nobility led to even worse conditions for the Russian peasantry. In 1767, serfs were forbidden to appeal to the state against their masters. The attempt of the Russian government to impose restrictions on free peasants in the border districts of the Russian empire soon led to a full-scale revolt that spread to the Volga valley. It was intensified by the support of the Cossacks, independent tribes of fierce warriors

The European States: Absolutism in Central and Eastern Europe

Prussia	
Frederick William I	1713–1740
Frederick II the Great	1740–1786
The Austrian Empire	
Maria Theresa	1740–1780
Joseph II	1780–1790
Russia	
Peter III	1762
Catherine II the Great	1762–1796
Pugachev's rebellion	1773–1775
Charter of the Nobility	1785
Poland	
First partition	1772
Second partition	1793
Third partition	1795

who had at times fought for the Russians against the Turks but who now resisted the government's attempt to absorb them into the empire.

An illiterate Cossack, Emelyan Pugachev, succeeded in welding the elements of discontent into a mass revolt. Beginning in 1773, Pugachev's rebellion spread across southern Russia from the Urals to the Volga River. Initially successful, Pugachev won the support of many peasants when he issued a manifesto in July 1774, freeing all peasants from oppressive taxes and military service. The rebellion soon faltered, however, as government forces became more effective. Betrayed by his own subordinates, Pugachev was captured, tortured, and executed. The rebellion collapsed completely, and Catherine responded with even greater repression of the peasantry. All rural reform was halted; serfdom was expanded into newer parts of the empire and peasants on crown land were also reduced to serfdom.

Above all, Catherine proved a worthy successor to Peter the Great by expanding Russia's territory westward (into Poland) and southward (to the Black Sea). Russia spread southward by defeating the Turks. In the Treaty of Kuchuk-Kainarji in 1774, the Russians gained some land and the privilege of protecting Greek Orthodox Christians in the Ottoman Empire. Russian expansion west-

ward occurred at the expense of neighboring Poland. In the three partitions of Poland in 1772, 1793, and 1795, Russia gained about 50 percent of Polish territory; Austria and Prussia took the rest.

Enlightened Absolutism Revisited

Of the three major rulers most closely associated traditionally with enlightened absolutism—Joseph II, Frederick II, and Catherine the Great—only Joseph II sought truly radical changes based on Enlightenment ideas. Both Frederick and Catherine liked to be cast as disciples of the Enlightenment, expressed interest in enlightened reforms, and even attempted some. But the policies of neither seemed seriously affected by Enlightenment thought. Necessities of state and maintenance of the existing system took precedence over reform. Indeed, many historians maintain that Joseph, Frederick, and Catherine were all primarily guided by a concern for the power and well-being of their states and that their policies were not all that different from those of their predecessors. In the final analysis, heightened state power was used to create armies and wage wars to gain more power. Nevertheless, in their desire to build stronger state systems, these rulers did pursue such enlightened reforms as legal reform, religious toleration, and the extension of education since these served to create more satisfied subjects and strengthened the state in significant ways.

It would be foolish, however, to overlook the fact that political and social realities limited the ability of enlightened rulers to make reforms. Everywhere in Europe the hereditary aristocracy was still the most powerful class in society. Enlightened reforms were often limited to changes in the administrative and judicial systems that did not seriously undermine the powerful interests of the European nobility. Although aristocrats might join the populace in opposing monarchical extension of centralizing power, as the chief beneficiaries of a system based on traditional rights and privileges for their class, they were certainly not willing to support a political ideology that trumpeted the principle of equal rights for all.

Wars and Diplomacy

The philosophes had denounced war as a foolish waste of life and resources in stupid quarrels of no value to humankind. Rulers, however, paid little attention to these comments and continued their costly struggles. By the eighteenth century, the European system of self-governing, individual states was grounded largely in the principle of self-interest. Because international relations were based on considerations of power, the eighteenth-century concept of a "balance of power" was predicated on how to counterbalance the power of one state by another to prevent any one power from dominating the others. This balance of power, however, did not imply a desire for peace. Large armies created to defend a state's security were often used for offensive purposes as well. As Frederick the Great of Prussia remarked, "the fundamental rule of governments is the principle of extending their territories." Nevertheless, the regular use of diplomacy served at times to lead to compromise.

The diplomacy of the eighteenth century still focused primarily on dynastic interests or the desire of ruling families to provide for their dependents and extend their dynastic holdings. But the eighteenth century also saw the emergence of the concept of "reason of state," on the basis of which rulers looked beyond dynastic interests to the long-term future of their states.

International rivalry and the continuing centralization of the European states were closely related. The need for taxes to support large armies and navies created its own imperative for more efficient and effective control of power in the hands of bureaucrats who could collect taxes and organize states for the task of winning wars. At the same time, the development of large standing armies ensured that political disputes would periodically be resolved by armed conflict rather than diplomacy. Between 1715 and 1740, it had seemed that Europe preferred peace. But in 1740, a major conflict erupted over the succession to the Austrian throne.

After the death of the Habsburg emperor Charles VI (1711–1740), King Frederick II of Prussia took advantage of the succession of a woman, Maria Theresa, to the throne of Austria by invading Austrian Silesia. The vulnerability of Maria Theresa encouraged France to enter the war against its traditional enemy, Austria; in turn, Maria Theresa made an alliance with Great Britain who feared French hegemony over continental affairs. All too quickly, the Austrian succession had produced a worldwide conflagration. The War of the Austrian Succession (1740–1748) was fought not only in Europe where Prussia seized Silesia and France occupied the Austrian Netherlands, but in the Far East where France took Madras in India from the British and in North America where the British captured the French fortress of Louisbourg at the entrance to the St. Lawrence River. By 1748, all parties were exhausted and agreed to stop. The peace treaty of Aix-la-Chapelle promised the return of all occupied territories to their original owners except for Silesia. Prussia's refusal to return Silesia guaranteed another

CHRONOLOGY

The Mid-Century Wars

War of the Austrian Succession	1740–1748
Peace of Aix-la-Chapelle	1748
The Seven Years' War	1756–1763
Diplomatic revolution	1756
Battle of Quebec	1759
Peace of Hubertusburg	1763
Peace of Paris	1763

war, at least between the two hostile central European powers of Prussia and Austria.

The Seven Years' War (1756–1763)

Maria Theresa refused to accept the loss of Silesia and prepared for its return by rebuilding her army while working diplomatically to separate Prussia from its chief ally, France. In 1756, Austria achieved what was soon labeled a diplomatic revolution. French–Austrian rivalry had been a fact of European diplomacy since the late sixteenth century. But two new rivalries made this old one seem superfluous: Britain and France over colonial empires, and Austria and Prussia over Silesia. France now abandoned Prussia and allied with Austria. Russia, who saw Prussia as a major hindrance to Russian goals in central Europe, joined the new alliance. In turn, Great Britain allied with Prussia. This diplomatic revolution of 1756 now led to another worldwide war.

There were three major areas of conflict: Europe, India, and North America. Europe witnessed the clash of the two major alliances: the British and Prussians against the Austrians, Russians, and French. With his superb army and military prowess, Frederick the Great of Prussia was able for some time to defeat the Austrian, French, and Russian armies. Under attack from three different directions, however, the forces of Frederick II were gradually worn down and faced utter defeat when they were saved by the death of Tsarina Elizabeth of Russia, which brought her nephew Peter III to power. A great admirer of Frederick the Great, Peter withdrew the Russian troops from the conflict and from the Prussian lands that they had occupied. His withdrawal guaranteed a stalemate and led to the desire for peace. The European conflict was ended by the Peace of Hubertusburg in 1763. All

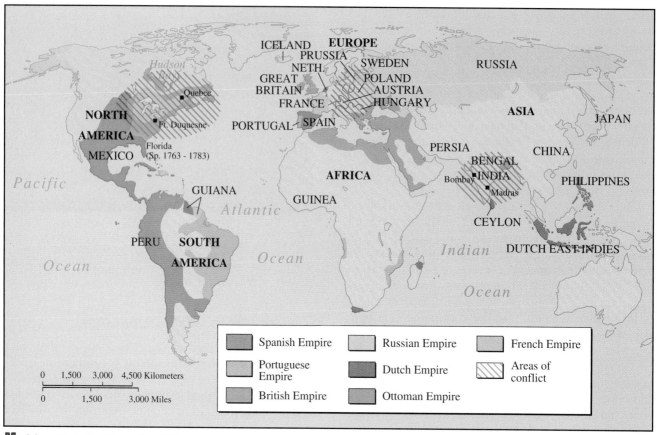

■ **Map 19.2** The Seven Years' War.

occupied territories were returned while Austria officially recognized Prussia's permanent control of Silesia.

The Anglo-French struggle in the rest of the world had more decisive results. Known as the Great War for Empire, it was fought in India and North America. The French had returned Madras to Britain after the War of the Austrian Succession, but jockeying for power continued as the French and British supported opposing native Indian princes. The British under Robert Clive (1725–1774) ultimately won out, not because they had better forces but because they were more persistent. By the Treaty of Paris in 1763, the French withdrew and left India to the British.

By far, the greatest conflicts of the Seven Years' War took place in North America (where the war was known as the French and Indian War). There were two primary areas of contention. One consisted of the waterways of the Gulf of St. Lawrence, protected by the fortress of Louisbourg and by forts near the Great Lakes and Lake Champlain that protected French Quebec and French traders. The other was the unsettled Ohio River valley. As the French moved south from the Great Lakes and

north from their forts on the Mississippi, they began to establish forts from the Appalachians to the Mississippi River. To British settlers in the thirteen colonies to the east, this French activity threatened to cut off a vast area from British exploitation. The French found allies among the Indians, who considered the French traders less threatening than the British settlers.

Despite initial French successes, British fortunes were revived by the efforts of William Pitt the Elder who was convinced that the destruction of the French colonial empire was a necessary prerequisite for the creation of Britain's own colonial empire. Accordingly, Pitt decided to make a minimal effort in Europe while concentrating resources, especially the British navy, on the colonial war. Although French troops were greater in number, the ability of the French to use them in the New World was contingent on naval support. The defeat of French fleets in major naval battles in 1759 gave the British an advantage because the French could no longer easily reinforce their garrisons. A series of British victories soon followed. On the night of September 13, 1759, British forces led by General James

Wolfe scaled the heights outside Quebec and defeated the French under General Louis-Joseph Montcalm on the Plains of Abraham (see the box on p. 398). Both generals died in the battle. The British went on to seize Montreal, the Great Lakes Area, and the Ohio Valley. The French were forced to make peace. By the Treaty of Paris, they ceded Canada and the lands east of the Mississippi to England. Their ally Spain transferred Spanish Florida to British control; in return, the French gave their Louisiana territory to the Spanish. By 1763, Great Britain had become the world's greatest colonial power.

Armies and Warfare in the Eighteenth Century

The professional standing army, initiated in the seventeenth century, became a standard feature of eighteenth-century Europe. Especially noticeable was the increase in the size of armies, which paralleled the development of absolutist states. Between 1740 and 1780, the French army grew from 190,000 to 300,000 men; the Prussian from 83,000 to 200,000; the Austrian from 108,000 to 282,000; and the Russian from 130,000 to 290,000.

The composition of these armies reflected the hierarchical structure of European society and the great chasm that separated the upper and lower classes. Officers were primarily from the landed aristocracy, which had for centuries regarded military activity as one of its major functions. Middle-class individuals were largely kept out of the higher ranks of the officer corps while being admitted to the middle ranks. A prejudice against commoners in the officer corps remained a regular feature of military life in the eighteenth century.

Rank-and-file soldiers came mostly from the lower classes of society. Some states, such as Prussia and Russia, conscripted able-bodied peasants. But many states realized that this was counterproductive since they could not afford to waste farmers. For that reason, eighteenth-century armies were partially composed of foreign troops, many from Switzerland or the petty German states. Of the great powers, Britain alone had no regular standing army and relied on mercenaries, evident in its use of German troops in America. Most troops in European armies, especially the French and Austrians, were natives who enlisted voluntarily for six-year terms. Some were not exactly volunteers; often vagabonds and the unemployed were pressed into service. Most, however, came from the lower classes—peasants and also artisans from the cities—who saw the military as an opportunity to escape from hard times or personal problems.

The maritime powers, such as Britain and the Dutch Republic, regarded navies as more important than armies. In the second half of the eighteenth century, the British possessed 174 warships manned by 80,000 sailors. Conditions on these ships were often poor. Diseases such as scurvy and yellow fever were rampant, and crews were frequently gang pressed into duty.

◆ **The Death of Wolfe.** The great powers of Europe fought the Seven Years' War in Europe, India, and North America. Despite initial French successes in North America, the British went on to win the war. This painting by Benjamin West presents a heroic rendering of the death of General James Wolfe, the British commander who defeated the French forces at the Battle of Quebec.

⇒ British Victory at Quebec ⇐

One of the major battles of the French and Indian War occurred in Canada in 1759 when British forces under General James Wolfe defeated the French under General Louis-Joseph Montcalm outside Quebec. This description of the important battle is taken from a detailed account of the British campaign in North America by Captain John Knox, an experienced soldier.

John Knox, *Historical Journal of the Campaign in North America*

Before daybreak this morning [September 13, 1759] we made a descent upon the north shore, about half a quarter of a mile to the eastward of Sillery. . . . We had in this debarkation thirty flat-bottomed boats, containing about sixteen hundred men. This was a great surprise on the enemy, who from the natural strength of the place did not suspect, and consequently were not prepared against so bold an attempt. The chain of sentries which they had posted along the summit of the heights galled us a little, and picked off several men and some officers before our light infantry got up to dislodge them. This great enterprise was conducted and executed with great good order and discretion.

As fast as we landed the boats put off for reenforcements, and the troops formed with much regularity, General Wolfe. . . . was ashore with the first division. We lost no time here, but clambered up one of the steepest precipices that can be conceived, being almost a perpendicular, and of an incredible height. As soon as we gained the summit all was quiet, and not a shot was heard, owing to the excellent conduct of the light infantry under Colonel Howe: It was by this time clear daylight. Here we formed again . . . and halted a few minutes. . . . We then faced to the right, and marched toward the town by files till we came to the Plains of Abraham, an even piece of ground which Mr. Wolfe had made choice of, while we stood forming upon the hill. Weather showery. About six

o'clock the enemy first made their appearance upon the heights between us and the town, whereupon we halted and wheeled to the right, thereby forming the line of battle. . . .

About ten o'clock the enemy began to advance briskly in three columns, with loud shots and recovered arms . . . from the distance of one hundred and thirty, until they came within forty yards, which our troops withstood with the greatest firmness, still reserving their fire and paying the strictest obedience to their officers. This uncommon steadiness, together with the havoc which the grape-shot from our field-pieces made among them, threw them into some disorder and was most critically maintained by a well-timed, regular, and heavy discharge of our small arms, such as they could no longer oppose. Hereupon they gave way, and fled, so that by the time the cloud of smoke was vanished our men were again over them, pursued them almost to the gates of the town and the bridge over the little river, making many officers and men prisoners. . . .

Our joy at this success is inexpressibly damped by the loss we sustained of one of the greatest heroes which this or any other age can boast of—General James Wolfe. . . . After [he] was carried off wounded to the rear of the front line, he desired those who were about him to lay him down. Being asked if he would have a surgeon, he replied, "It is needless: it is all over with me." One of them cried out, "They run, see how they run!" "Who runs?" demanded our hero with great earnestness, like a person roused from sleep. The officer answered: "The enemy, sir. Egad, they give way everywhere." Thereupon the general rejoined: "Go, one of you, my lads, to Colonel Burton; tell him to march Webb's regiment with all speed down to Charles River, to cut off the retreat of the fugitives from the bridge." Then, turning on his side, he added, "Now, God be praised, I will die in peace!" and thus expired.

Economic Expansion and Social Change

The economic depression that had characterized the seventeenth century began to end in the early eighteenth century. Rapid population growth, an agricultural revolu-

tion (at least in Britain), the beginnings of a new pattern of industrialization, and an increase in worldwide trade characterized the economic patterns of the eighteenth century.

Population and Food

Despite regional variations, Europe's population began to grow around 1750 and continued a slow upward movement. It has been estimated that the total European population was around 120 million in 1700, expanded to 140 million by 1750, and then grew to 190 million by 1790; thus, the growth rate in the second half of the century was double that of the first half. These increases occurred during the same time that several million Europeans were going abroad as colonists. A falling death rate was perhaps the most important cause of population growth. But why the decline in the death rate? More plentiful food and better transportation of available food supplies led to some improvement in diet and relief from devastating famines. Also of great significance was the lowering of death rates brought by the ending of bubonic plague.

More food was in part a result of improvements in agricultural practices and methods in the eighteenth century, especially in Britain, parts of France, and the Low Countries. Eighteenth-century agriculture was characterized by increases in food production that can be attributed to four interrelated factors: more farmland, healthier and more abundant livestock, increased yields per acre, and an improved climate.

Climatologists believe that the "little ice age" of the seventeenth century declined in the eighteenth, especially evident in the moderate summers that provided more ideal growing conditions. The amount of land under cultivation was increased by abandoning the old open field system in which part of the land was left to lie fallow to renew it. New crops, such as alfalfa and clover, which stored nitrogen in their roots, restored the soil's fertility and also provided winter fodder for livestock, enabling landlords to maintain an ever-larger number of animals. The more numerous livestock made available more animal manure, which was used to fertilize fields and produce better yields per acre. Also important to the increased yields was the spread of new vegetables, including two important American crops, the potato and maize (Indian corn). Both had been brought to Europe from America in the sixteenth century although they were not grown in quantity until after 1700. The potato became a staple in Germany, the Low Countries, and especially Ireland, where repression by British landlords forced large numbers of poor peasants to survive on small pieces of marginal land. The potato took relatively little effort to produce in large quantities. High in carbohydrates and calories, rich in vitamins A and C, it could be easily stored for winter use.

In the eighteenth century, the English were the leaders in adopting the new techniques that have been characterized as an agricultural revolution. This early modernization of English agriculture with its noticeable increase in productivity made possible the feeding of an expanding population about to enter a new world of industrialization and urbanization.

New Methods of Finance and Industry

The decline in the available supply of gold and silver in the seventeenth century had created a chronic shortage of money that undermined the efforts of governments to meet their needs. The creation of new public and private banks and the acceptance of paper notes made possible an expansion of credit in the eighteenth century.

Perhaps the best example of this process can be observed in England where the Bank of England was founded in 1694. Unlike other banks accustomed to receiving deposits and exchanging foreign currencies, the Bank of England also made loans. In return for lending money to the government, the bank was allowed to issue paper "bank notes" backed by its credit. These soon became negotiable and provided a paper substitute for gold and silver currency.

The most important product of European industry in the eighteenth century was textiles, most of which were still produced by traditional methods. In cities that were textile centers, master artisans used timeworn methods to turn out finished goods in their guild workshops. But a shift in textile production to the countryside was spreading to parts of Europe by the eighteenth century. Industrial production in the countryside was done by the "putting-out" or "domestic" system in which a merchant-capitalist entrepreneur bought the raw materials, mostly wool and flax, and "put them out" to rural workers who spun the raw material into yarn and then wove it into cloth on simple looms. Capitalist-entrepreneurs sold the finished product, made a profit, and used it to manufacture more. This system became known as the "cottage industry," because spinners and weavers did their work on spinning wheels and looms in their own cottages. Cottage industry was truly a family enterprise since women and children could spin while men wove on the looms, enabling rural people to earn incomes that supplemented their pitiful wages as agricultural laborers.

The cottage system utilized traditional methods of manufacturing and spread to many areas of rural Europe in the eighteenth century. But significant changes in industrial production also began to occur in the second half of the century, pushed along by the introduction of cotton, originally imported from India. The importation of raw cotton from slave plantations encouraged the production of cotton cloth in Europe where a profitable market developed because of the growing demand for light-weight cotton clothes that were less expensive than linens and woolens. But the traditional methods of the cottage industry proved incapable of keeping up with the growing demand, leading British cloth entrepreneurs to develop new methods and new machines. The flying shuttle sped up the process of weaving on a loom, thereby increasing the need for large quantities of yarn. In response, Richard Arkwright (1732–1792) invented a "water frame," powered by horse or water, which turned out yarn much faster than cottage spinning wheels. This abundance of yarn, in turn, led to the development of mechanized looms, invented in the 1780s but not widely adopted until the early nineteenth century. By that time Britain was in the throes of an industrial revolution.

Toward a Global Economy: Mercantile Empires and Worldwide Trade

While bankers and industrialists came to dominate the economic life of the nineteenth century, in the eighteenth century merchants and traders still reigned supreme. Intra-European trade still dominated total trade figures as wheat, timber, and naval stores from the Baltic, wines from France, wool and fruit from Spain, and silk from Italy were exchanged along with a host of other products. But the eighteenth century witnessed only a slight increase in this trade while overseas trade boomed. From 1716 to 1789, total French exports quadrupled while intra-European trade, which constituted 75 percent of these exports in 1716, constituted only 50 percent of the total in 1789. This increase in overseas trade has led some historians to speak of the emergence of a truly global economy in the eighteenth century. By the beginning of the century, Spain, Portugal, and the Dutch Republic, which had earlier monopolized overseas trade, found themselves increasingly overshadowed by France and Britain. The rivalry between these two great western European powers was especially evident in the Americas and the Far East.

COLONIAL EMPIRES

Both the French and British colonial empires in the New World included large parts of the West Indies and the North American continent. In the former, the British held Barbados, Jamaica, and Bermuda while the French possessed Martinique, Saint Dominique, and Guadeloupe. On these tropical islands both the British and the French had developed plantation economies, worked by African slaves, which produced tobacco, cotton, coffee, and sugar, all products increasingly in demand in Europe.

The French and British colonies on the North American continent were structured in different ways. French North America (Canada and Louisiana) was run autocratically as a vast trading area, where valuable fur, leather, fish, and timber were acquired. However, the inability of the French state to get its people to emigrate to these North American possessions left them thinly populated.

British North America had come to consist of thirteen colonies on the eastern coast of the present United States. They were thickly populated, containing about 1.5 million people by 1750, and were also prosperous. Supposedly run by the British Board of Trade, the Royal Council, and Parliament, these thirteen colonies had legislatures that tended to act independently. Merchants in such port cities as Boston, Philadelphia, New York, and Charleston resented and resisted regulation from the British government.

Both the North American and West Indian colonies of Britain and France were assigned roles in keeping with mercantilist theory. They provided raw materials for the mother country while buying the latter's manufactured goods. Navigation acts regulated what could be taken from and sold to the colonies. Theoretically, the system was supposed to provide a balance of trade favorable to the mother country.

British and French rivalry was also evident in the Spanish and Portuguese colonial empires in Latin America, where both countries sought successfully to break into the Portuguese and Spanish Latin American market. Their rivalry also extended to the Far East where Britain and France competed for the tea, spices, cotton, hardwoods, and luxury goods of India and the East Indies. In the course of the eighteenth century, the British defeated the French, and by the mid-nineteenth century, they had assumed control of the entire Indian subcontinent.

GLOBAL TRADE

To justify the term global economy, historians have usually pointed to the patterns of trade that interlocked Europe, Africa, the Far East, and the American continents. In an example of triangular trade, British merchant ships carried manufactured goods to Africa, where they were traded for a cargo of slaves, which were then shipped to Virginia and paid for by tobacco, which in turn was shipped back to England where it was processed and then sold in Germany for cash.

Of all the goods traded in the eighteenth century, perhaps the most profitable and certainly the most infamous were African slaves. The need for slaves on the plantations in the Americas where they produced the lucrative sugar, tobacco, rice, and cotton crops made the eighteenth century the high point of the Atlantic slave trade. It has been estimated that of the total 9,300,000 slaves transported from Africa, almost two-thirds were taken in the eighteenth century.

Slaving ships sailed from a European port to the African coast where Europeans had established bases. There, merchants could trade manufactured goods, rum, and brandy for blacks captured by African middlemen. The captives were then closely packed into cargo ships, 300 to 450 per ship, and chained in holds without sanitary facilities or enough space to stand up; there they remained during the voyage to America, which took at least 100 days (see the box on p. 402). As soon as the human cargo arrived in the New World, they entered the plantation economy. Here the "sugar factories," as the sugar plantations in the Caribbean were called, played an especially prominent role. The French colony of Saint Dominique (later Haiti) had 500,000 slaves working on 3,000 plantations by the last two decades of the eighteenth century. This colony produced 100,000 tons of sugar a year but at the expense of a high death rate from the brutal treatment of the slaves. It was not until the 1790s that the French abolished slavery. The British followed suit in 1808.

◆ **The Sale of Slaves.** In the eighteenth century, the slave trade was one of the more profitable commercial enterprises. This painting shows a Western slave merchant negotiating with a local African leader over slaves at Goree, Senegal, in West Africa in the late eighteenth century.

The Social Order of the Eighteenth Century

The pattern of Europe's social organization, first established in the Middle Ages, continued well into the eighteenth century. Social status was still largely determined not by wealth and economic standing but by the division into the traditional "orders" or "estates" determined by heredity and quality. This divinely sanctioned division of society into traditional orders was supported by Christian teaching, which emphasized the need to fulfill the responsibilities of one's estate. Although Enlightenment intellectuals attacked these traditional distinctions, they did not die easily. In the Prussian law code of 1794, marriage between noble males and middle-class females was forbidden without a government dispensation. Even without government regulation, however, different social groups remained easily distinguished everywhere in Europe by the distinctive, traditional clothes they wore.

Nevertheless, some forces of change were at work in this traditional society. The ideas of the Enlightenment made headway as reformers argued that the idea of an unchanging social order based on privilege was hostile to the progress of society. Moreover, especially in some cities, the old structures were more difficult to maintain as new economic patterns, especially the growth of larger industries, brought new social contrasts that destroyed the old order. Despite these forces of change, however, not until the revolutionary upheavals at the end of the eighteenth century did the old order finally begin to disintegrate.

❧ The Atlantic Slave Trade ❧

One of the most odious practices of early modern Western society was the Atlantic slave trade, which reached its height in the eighteenth century. Blacks were transported in densely packed cargo ships from the western coast of Africa to the Americas to work as slaves in the plantation economy. Not until late in the eighteenth century did a rising chorus of voices raise serious objections to this trade in human beings. This excerpt presents a criticism of the slave trade from an anonymous French writer.

Diary of a Citizen

As soon as the ships have lowered their anchors off the coast of Guinea, the price at which the captains have decided to buy the captives is announced to the Negroes who buy prisoners from various princes and sell them to the Europeans. Presents are sent to the sovereign who rules over that particular part of the coast, and permission to trade is given. Immediately the slaves are brought by inhuman brokers like so many victims dragged to a sacrifice. White men who covet that portion of the human race receive them in a little house they have erected on the shore, where they have entrenched themselves with two pieces of cannon and twenty guards. As soon as the bargain is concluded, the Negro is put in chains and led aboard the vessel, where he meets his fellow sufferers. Here sinister reflections come to his mind; everything shocks and frightens him and his uncertain destiny gives rise to the greatest anxiety. . . .

The vessel sets sail for the Antilles, and the Negroes are chained in a hold of the ship, a kind of lugubrious prison where the light of day does not penetrate, but into which air is introduced by means of a pump. Twice a day some disgusting food is distributed to them. Their consuming sorrow and the sad state to which they are reduced would make them commit suicide if they were not deprived of all the means for an attempt upon their lives. Without any kind of clothing it would be difficult to conceal from the watchful eyes of the sailors in charge any instrument apt to alleviate their despair. The fear of a revolt, such as sometimes happens on the voyage from Guinea, is the basis of a common concern and produces as many guards as there are men in the crew. The slightest noise or a secret conversation among two Negroes is punished with utmost severity. All in all, the voyage is made in a continuous state of alarm on the part of the white men, who fear a revolt, and in a cruel state of uncertainty on the part of the Negroes, who do not know the fate awaiting them.

When the vessel arrives at a port in the Antilles, they are taken to a warehouse where they are displayed, like any merchandise, to the eyes of buyers. The plantation owner pays according to the age, strength, and health of the Negro he is buying. He has him taken to his plantation, and there he is delivered to an overseer who then and there becomes his tormentor. In order to domesticate him, the Negro is granted a few days of rest in his new place, but soon he is given a hoe and a sickle and made to join a work gang. Then he ceases to wonder about his fate; he understands that only labor is demanded of him. But he does not know yet how excessive this labor will be. As a matter of fact, his work begins at dawn and does not end before nightfall; it is interrupted for only two hours at dinnertime. The food a full-grown Negro is given each week consists of two pounds of salt beef or cod and two pots of tapioca meal. . . . A Negro of twelve or thirteen years or under is given only one pot of meal and one pound of beef or cod. In place of food some planters give their Negroes the liberty of working for themselves every Saturday; others are even less generous and grant them this liberty only on Sundays and holidays.

The Peasants

Because society was still mostly rural in the eighteenth century, the peasantry constituted the largest social group, making up as much as 85 percent of Europe's population. There were rather wide differences, however, between peasants from area to area. The most important distinction—at least legally—was between the free peasant and the serf. Peasants in Britain, northern Italy, the Low Countries, Spain, most of France, and some areas of western Germany shared freedom despite numerous regional and local differences. Legally free peasants, however, were not exempt from burdens. Some free peasants in Andalusia in Spain, southern Italy, Sicily, and Portugal lived in a poverty more desperate than that of many serfs in Russia and eastern Germany. In France, 40 percent of free peasants owned little or no land whatever by 1789.

Small peasant proprietors or tenant farmers in western Europe were also not free from compulsory services. Most owed tithes, often one-third of their crops. Although tithes were intended for parish priests, in France only 10 percent of the priests received them. Instead they wound up in the hands of towns and aristocratic landowners. Moreover, in addition to giving up their crops, some peasants also owed a variety of dues and fees. Local aristocrats claimed hunting rights on peasant land and had monopolies over the flour mills, community ovens, and wine and oil presses needed by the peasants. Hunting rights, dues, fees, and tithes were all deeply resented.

The local villages in which they dwelt remained the centers of peasants' social lives. Villages, especially in western Europe, maintained public order; provided poor relief, a village church, and sometimes a schoolmaster; collected taxes for the central government; maintained roads and bridges; and established common procedures for sowing, ploughing, and harvesting crops. But villages were often dominated by richer peasants and proved highly resistant to innovations, such as new agricultural practices.

The Nobility

The nobles, who constituted about 2 or 3 percent of the European population, played a dominating role in society. Being born a noble automatically guaranteed a place at the top of the social order with all of its attendant special privileges and rights. The legal privileges of the nobility included judgment by their peers, immunity from severe punishment, and exemption from many forms of taxation. Especially in central and eastern Europe, the rights of landlords over their serfs were overwhelming.

Nobles also played important roles in military and government affairs. Since medieval times, landed aristocrats had functioned as military officers. While monarchs found it impossible to exclude commoners from the ranks of officers, the tradition remained that nobles made the most natural and hence best officers. Moreover, the eighteenth-century nobility played a significant role in the administrative machinery of state. In some countries, such as Prussia, the entire bureaucracy reflected aristocratic values. Moreover, in most of Europe, the landholding nobility controlled much of the life of their local districts.

✦ **A Market in Turin.** Below the wealthy patrician elites who dominated the towns and cities were a number of social groups with a wide range of incomes and occupations. This remarkable diversity is evident in this view of a market square in the Italian city of Turin.

Although the nobles clung to their privileged status and struggled to keep others out, almost everywhere the possession of money made it possible to enter the ranks of the nobility. Rights of nobility were frequently attached to certain lands so purchasing the lands made one a noble; the acquisition of government offices also often conferred noble status.

The Inhabitants of Towns and Cities

Townspeople were still a distinct minority of the total population except in the Dutch Republic, Britain, and parts of Italy. At the end of the eighteenth century, about one-sixth of the French population lived in towns of 2,000 or more. The biggest city in Europe was London with its 1,000,000 inhabitants; Paris numbered between 550,000 and 600,000. Altogether, Europe had at least twenty cities in twelve countries with populations over 100,000, including Naples, Lisbon, Moscow, St. Petersburg, Vienna, Amsterdam, Berlin, Rome, and Madrid.

Although urban dwellers were vastly outnumbered by rural inhabitants, towns played an important role in Western culture. The contrasts between a large city with its education, culture, and material consumption and the surrounding, often poverty-stricken countryside were striking, as evidenced by this British traveler's account of Russia's St. Petersburg in 1741:

> The country about Petersbourg has full as wild and desert a look as any in the Indies; you need not go above 200 paces out of the town to find yourself in a wild wood of firs, and such a low, marshy, boggy country that you would think God when he created the rest of the world for the use of mankind had created this for an inaccessible retreat for all sorts of wild beasts.[4]

Peasants often resented the prosperity of towns and their exploitation of the countryside to serve urban interests. Palermo in Sicily used one-third of the island's food production while paying only one-tenth of the taxes. Towns lived off the countryside not by buying their goods and crops, but by using tithes, rents, and feudal dues to acquire peasant produce.

Many cities in western and even central Europe had a long tradition of patrician oligarchies that continued to control their communities by dominating town and city councils. Despite their domination, patricians constituted only a small minority of the urban population. Just below the patricians stood an upper crust of the middle classes: nonnoble officeholders, financiers and bankers, merchants, wealthy rentiers who lived off their investments, and important professionals, including lawyers. Another large urban group was the petty bourgeoisie or lower middle class made up of master artisans, shopkeepers, and small traders. Below them were the laborers or working classes. Much urban industry was still done in small guild workshops by masters, journeymen, and apprentices. Urban communities also had a large group of unskilled workers who served as servants, maids, and cooks at pitifully low wages.

Despite an end to the ravages of plague, eighteenth-century cities still experienced high death rates, especially among children, because of unsanitary living conditions, polluted water, and a lack of sewage facilities. One observer compared the stench of Hamburg to an open sewer that could be smelled for miles around. Overcrowding also exacerbated urban problems as cities continued to grow from an influx of rural immigrants. But cities proved no paradise for them as unskilled workers found few employment opportunities. The result was a serious problem of poverty in the eighteenth century (see the box on p. 405).

Conclusion

Everywhere in Europe at the beginning of the eighteenth century, the old order remained strong. Nobles, clerics, towns, provinces all had privileges, some medieval in origin, others the result of the attempt of monarchies in the sixteenth and seventeenth centuries to gain financial support from their subjects. Everywhere in the eighteenth century, monarchs sought to enlarge their bureaucracies to raise taxes to support the new large standing armies that had originated in the seventeenth century. The existence of these armies made wars more likely. The existence of five great powers, with two of them (France and Britain) in conflict in the Far East and the New World, initiated a new scale of conflict; the Seven Years' War could legitimately be viewed as the first world war. The wars altered some boundaries on the European continent, but were perhaps more significant for the British victories that marked the emergence of Great Britain as the world's greatest naval and colonial power. Everywhere in Europe, increased demands for taxes to support these conflicts led to attacks on the privileged orders and a desire for change not met by the ruling monarchs.

❧ Poverty in France ❧

Unlike the British, who had a system of public-supported poor relief, the French responded to poverty with ad hoc policies when conditions became acute. This selection is taken from an intendant's report to the controller-general at Paris describing his suggestions for a program to relieve the grain shortages expected for the winter months.

M. de la Bourdonnaye, Intendant of Bordeaux, to the Controller-General, September 30, 1708

Having searched for the means of helping the people of Agen in this cruel situation and having conferred with His Eminence, the Bishop, it seems to us that three things are absolutely necessary if the people are not to starve during the winter.

Most of the inhabitants do not have seed to plant their fields. However, we decided that we would be going too far if we furnished it, because those who have seed would also apply [for more]. Moreover, we are persuaded that all the inhabitants will make strenuous efforts to find some seed, since they have every reason to expect prices to remain high next year. . . .

But this project will come to nothing if the collectors of the taille continue to be as strict in the exercise of their functions as they have been of late and continue to employ troops [to force collection]. Those inhabitants who have seed grain would sell it to be freed from an oppressive garrison, while those who must buy seed, since they had none left from their harvest and have scraped together a little money for this purchase, would prefer to give up that money [for taxes] when put under police constraint. To avoid this, I feel it is absolutely necessary that you order the receivers-general to reduce their operations during this winter, at least with respect to the poor. . . .

We are planning to import wheat for this region from Languedoc and Quercy, and we are confident that there will be enough. But there are two things to be feared: one is the greed of the merchants. When they see that general misery has put them in control of prices, they will raise them to the point where the calamity is almost as great as if there were no provisions at all. The other fear is that the artisans and the lowest classes, when they find themselves at the mercy of the merchants, will cause disorders and riots. As a protective measure, it would seem wise to establish two small storehouses. . . . Ten thousand ecus [30,000 livres] would be sufficient for each. . . .

A third point demanding our attention is the support of beggars among the poor, as well as of those who have no other resources than their wages. Since there will be very little work, these people will soon be reduced to starvation. We should establish public workshops to provide work as was done in 1693 and 1694. I should choose the most useful kind of work, located where there are the greatest number of poor. In this manner, we should rid ourselves of those who do not want to work and assure the others of a moderate subsistence. For these workshops, we would need about 40,000 livres, or altogether 100,000 livres. The receiver-general of the taille of Agen could advance this sum. The 60,000 livres for the storehouses he would get back very soon. I shall await your orders on all of the above.

Marginal Comments by the Controller-General

Operations for the collection of the taille are to be suspended. The two storehouses are to be established; great care must be taken to put them to good use. The interest on the advances will be paid by the king. His Majesty has agreed to the establishment of the public workshops for the able-bodied poor and is willing to spend up to 40,000 livres on them this winter.

At the same time, sustained population growth, dramatic changes in finance, trade, and industry, and the growth of poverty created tensions that undermined the traditional foundations of the old order. The inability of that old order to deal meaningfully with these changes led to a revolutionary outburst at the end of the eighteenth century that brought the beginning of the end for that old order.

NOTES

1. Frederick II, *Forms of Government*, in Eugen Weber, *The Western Tradition* (Lexington, Mass., 1972), pp. 538, 544.
2. Quoted in Reinhold A. Dorwart, *The Administrative Reforms of Frederick William I of Prussia* (Cambridge, Mass., 1953), p. 36.
3. Quoted in Hans Rosenberg, *Bureaucracy, Aristocracy, and Autocracy: The Prussian Experience, 1660–1815* (Cambridge, Mass., 1958), p. 40.
4. Igor Vinogradoff, "Russian Missions to London, 1711–1789: Further Extracts from the Cottrell Papers," *Oxford Slavonic Papers*, New Series (1982), 15:76.

SUGGESTIONS FOR FURTHER READING

For a good introduction to the political history of the eighteenth century, see the relevant chapters in the general works by Woloch, Anderson, and Birn listed in Chapter 18. See also G. Treasure, *The Making of Modern Europe, 1648–1780* (London, 1985); W. Doyle, *The Old European Order, 1660–1800* (Oxford, 1978); and O. Hufton, *Europe: Privilege and Protest, 1730–1789* (London, 1980). On the theory of enlightened absolutism, see L. Krieger, *An Essay on the Theory of Enlightened Depotism* (Chicago, 1970); and H. M. Scott, ed., *Enlightened Absolutism: Reform and Reformers in Later Eighteenth-Century Europe* (Ann Arbor, Mich., 1990). For a brief study of its practice, see J. Gagliardo, *Enlightened Despotism* (New York, 1967). Good studies of individual states include J. B. Owen, *The Eighteenth Century, 1714–1815* (London, 1975), on England; P. R. Campbell, *The Ancient Régime in France* (Oxford, 1988); E. Wangermann, *The Austrian Achievement, 1700–1800* (London, 1973); R. Vierhaus, *Germany in the Age of Absolutism* (Cambridge, 1988); S. B. Fay, *The Rise of Brandenburg-Prussia to 1786* (New York, 1964); and P. Dukes, *The Making of Russian Absolutism, 1613–1801* (London, 1982). Good biographies of some of Europe's monarchs include R. Asprey, *Frederick the Great, The Magnificent Enigma* (New York, 1986); I. de Madariaga, *Catherine the Great, A Short History* (New Haven, Conn., 1990); J. T. Alexander, *Catherine the Great: Life and Legend* (New York, 1989); the first volume of a major new work on Joseph II by D. Deales, *Joseph II* (Cambridge, 1987); T. C. W. Blanning, *Joseph II* (New York, 1994); and J. Brooke, *King George III* (London, 1972).

The warfare of this period is examined in J. Childs, *Armies and Warfare in Europe, 1648–1789* (Manchester, 1982). On the social composition of European armies, see A. Corvisier, *Armies and Society in Europe, 1494–1789* (Bloomington, Ind., 1978).

A good introduction to European population can be found in M. W. Flinn, *The European Demographic System, 1500–1820* (Brighton, 1981). See also J. C. Riley, *Population Thought in the Age of Demographic Revolution* (Durham, N. C., 1985).

A different perspective on economic history can be found in F. Braudel's *Capitalism and Material Life, 1400–1800* (New York, 1973). The subject of mercantile empires and worldwide trade is covered in J. H. Parry, *Trade and Dominion: European Overseas Empires in the Eighteenth Century* (London, 1971); D. K. Fieldhouse, *The Colonial Empires* (New York, 1971); P. K. Liss, *Atlantic Empires: The Network of Trade and Revolution, 1713–1826* (Baltimore, 1983); and R. Davis, *The Rise of the Atlantic Economies* (Ithaca, N. Y., 1973). On the problem of slavery, see H. Thomas, *The Slave Trade: The Story of the Atlantic Slave Trade, 1440–1870* (New York, 1997); and M. Craton, *Sinews of Empire: A Short History of British Slavery* (New York, 1974). On England's agricultural revolution, see J. D. Chambers and G. E. Mingay, *The Agricultural Revolution, 1750–1880* (London, 1966). Eighteenth-century cottage industry and the beginnings of industrialization are examined in the early chapters of D. Landes, *The Unbound Prometheus: Technological Change and Industrial Development in Western Europe from*

1750 to the Present (New York, 1969); and M. Berg, *The Age of Manufactures: Industry, Innovation, and Work in Britain, 1700–1820* (Oxford, 1985).

For an introduction to the social order of the eighteenth century, see P. Goubert, *The Ancien Régime* (New York, 1973); and P. Laslett, *The World We Have Lost*, 3d ed. (New York, 1984). On the peasantry, see J. Blum, *The End of the Old Order in Rural Europe* (Princeton, N.J., 1978). Also of much interest is E. Le Roy Ladurie, *The Peasants of Languedoc* (Urbana, Ill., 1974). On the European nobility, see the specialized studies of R. E. Jones, *The Emancipation of the Russian Nobility, 1762–1785* (Princeton, N.J., 1973); J. Cameron, *Aristocratic Century: The Peerage of Eighteenth-Century England* (Cambridge,

1984); and G. E. Mingay, *The Gentry: The Rise and Fall of a Ruling Class* (London, 1976). Studies of urban communities include M. Walker, *German Home Towns: Community, State, and General Estate, 1648–1871* (Ithaca, N.Y., 1971); G. Rudé, *Hanoverian London, 1714–1808* (Berkeley, 1971); and G. L. Soliday, *A Community in Conflict: Frankfurt Society in the Seventeenth and Early Eighteenth Centuries* (Hanover, N.H., 1974). On the lower urban classes, see J. Kaplow, *The Names of Kings: The Parisian Laboring Poor in the Eighteenth Century* (New York, 1972); and R. M. Schwartz, *Policing the Poor in Eighteenth-Century France* (Chapel Hill, N.C., 1988). There is no better work on the problem of poverty than O. Hufton, *The Poor of Eighteenth-Century France* (Oxford, 1974).

A Revolution in Politics: The Era of the French Revolution and Napoleon

On the morning of July 14, 1789, a Parisian mob of some 8,000 people in search of weapons streamed toward the Bastille, a royal armory filled with arms and ammunition. The Bastille was also a state prison and, although it now contained only seven prisoners, in the eyes of these angry Parisians it was a glaring symbol of the government's despotic policies. The armory was defended by the Marquis de Launay and a small garrison of 114 men. The attack began in earnest in the early afternoon, and, after three hours of fighting, de Launay and the garrison surrendered. Angered by the loss of ninety-eight of their members, the victorious mob beat de Launay to death, cut off his head, and carried it aloft in triumph through the streets of Paris. When King Louis XVI was told the news of the fall of the Bastille by the Duc de La Rochefoucauld-Liancourt, he exclaimed, "Why, this is a revolt." "No, Sire," replied the duke, "It is a revolution."

Historians have long assumed that the modern history of Europe began with two major transformations—the French Revolution and the Industrial Revolution (on the latter, see Chapter 21). Accordingly, the French Revolution has been portrayed as the major turning point in European political and social history when the institutions of the "old regime" were destroyed and a new order was created based on individual rights, representative institutions, and a concept of loyalty to the nation rather than the monarch. This perspective does have certain limitations, however.

France was only one of a number of areas in the Western world where the assumptions of the old order were challenged. Although some historians have used the phrase "democratic revolution" to refer to the upheavals of the late eighteenth and nineteenth centuries, it is probably more appropriate to speak not of a "democratic movement," but of a liberal movement to extend political rights and power to the bourgeoisie "possessing capital," namely, those besides the aristocracy who were literate and had become wealthy through capitalist enterprises in trade, industry,

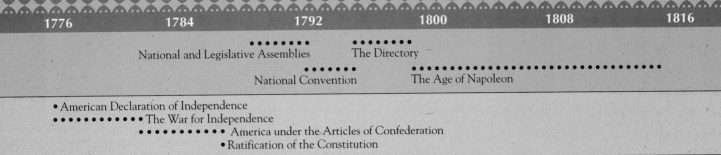

National and Legislative Assemblies   The Directory

National Convention   The Age of Napoleon

• American Declaration of Independence
• • • • • • • • • • The War for Independence
• • • • • • • • • • America under the Articles of Confederation
• Ratification of the Constitution

Fall of the Bastille   Reign of Terror

Napoleon becomes emperor of France   Battle of Waterloo

and finance. *The years preceding and accompanying the French Revolution included attempts at reform and revolt in the North American colonies, Britain, the Dutch Republic, some Swiss cities, and the Austrian Netherlands. The success of the American and French Revolutions makes them the center of attention for this chapter.*

Not all of the decadent privileges that characterized the old European regime were destroyed in 1789, however. The revolutionary upheaval of the era, especially in France, did create new liberal and national political ideals, summarized in the French revolutionary slogan, "Liberty, Equality, and Fraternity," that transformed France and were then spread to other European countries through the conquests of Napoleon. After Napoleon's defeat, however, the forces of reaction did their best to restore the old order and resist pressures for reform.

The Beginnings of the Revolutionary Era: The American Revolution

The revolutionary era began in North America when the thirteen British colonies along the eastern seaboard revolted against their mother country. Despite their differences, the colonists found ways to create a new government based on liberal principles that made an impact on the "old world" European states.

Reorganization, Resistance, and Rebellion

The immediate causes of the American Revolution stemmed from Britain's response to its victory over France in the Seven Years' War (1756–1763), known as the French and Indian War in America. The colonists were not pleased when British policymakers asked them to contribute new revenues to pay the expenses the British army incurred in defending the colonies. In 1765, the British Parliament enacted the Stamp Act, which attempted to levy new taxes on the colonies, but riots quickly led to the statute's repeal.

The immediate crisis had ended, but the fundamental cause of the dispute had not been resolved. In the course of the eighteenth century, significant differences had arisen between the American and British political worlds. The property requirement for voting—voters had to possess property that could be rented for at least 40 shillings a year—was the same in both areas, but the number of voters differed markedly. In Britain fewer than one in five adult males had the right to vote. In the colonies, where a radically different economic structure led to an enormous group of independent farmers, the property requirement allowed over 50 percent of adult males to vote.

While both the British and Americans had representative governments, different systems had evolved. Representation in Britain was indirect; the members of Parliament did not speak for local interests but their entire kingdom. In the colonies representation was direct; representatives were not only expected to reside in and own property in the communities electing them, but also to represent the interests of their local districts.

This divergence in political systems was paralleled by conflicting conceptions of the British Empire. The British envisioned the empire as a single unit with Parliament as the supreme authority throughout. All the people in the empire, including the American colonists, were represented indirectly by members of Parliament, whether they were from the colonies or not. Colonial assemblies in the British perspective were only committees that made "temporary by-laws"; the real authority to make laws for the empire resided in London.

The Americans had developed their own peculiar view of the British Empire. To them, the British Empire was composed of self-regulating parts. While they conceded that as British subjects they owed allegiance to the king and that Parliament had the right to make laws for the peace and prosperity of the whole realm, they argued, nevertheless, that neither king nor Parliament had any right to interfere in the internal affairs of the colonies since they had their own representative assemblies. American colonists were especially defensive about property and believed strongly that no tax could be levied without the consent of an assembly whose members actually represented the people.

By the 1760s, the American colonists had developed a sense of a common national identity. It was not unusual for American travelers to Britain in the eighteenth century to see British society as old and decadent in sharp contrast to the youthfulness and vitality of their own. This sense of superiority made Americans resentful of British actions that seemed to treat them like children. Resentment eventually led to a desire for independence.

Crisis followed crisis in the 1770s. The colonies' desire to take collective action against what was perceived as Britain's repressive actions led to the First Continental Congress, which met at Philadelphia in September 1774. The more militant members refused to compromise and urged colonists to "take up arms and organize militias." When the British army under General Gage attempted to stop rebel mobilization in Massachusetts, fighting erupted at Lexington and Concord between colonists and redcoats in April 1775.

The War for Independence

Despite the outbreak of hostilities, the colonists did not rush headlong into rebellion and war. More than a year passed after Lexington and Concord before the colonists

◆ **The Declaration of Independence.** John Trumbull's famous painting, *The Signing of the Declaration*, shows members of the committee responsible for the Declaration of Independence (from left to right, John Adams, Roger Sherman, Robert Livingston, Thomas Jefferson, and Benjamin Franklin) standing before John Hancock, president of the Second Continental Congress.

⋙ The Argument for Independence ⋘

On July 2, 1776, the Second Continental Congress adopted a resolution declaring the independence of the American colonies. Two days later the delegates approved the Declaration of Independence, which gave the reasons for their action. Its principal author was Thomas Jefferson who basically restated John Locke's theory of revolution (see Chapter 16).

The Declaration of Independence

When in the course of human events it becomes necessary for one people to dissolve the political bands which have connected them with another, and to assume among the Powers of the earth, the separate and equal station to which the Laws of Nature and of Nature's God entitle them, a decent respect to the opinions of mankind requires that they should declare the causes which impel them to the separation.

We hold these truths to be self-evident, that all men are created equal, that they are endowed by their Creator with certain unalienable Rights, that among these are Life, Liberty and the pursuit of Happiness. That to secure these rights, Governments are instituted among Men, deriving their just powers from the consent of the governed, That whenever any Form of Government becomes destructive of these ends, it is the Right of the People to alter or to abolish it and to institute new Government, laying its foundation on such principles and organizing its powers in such form, as to them shall seem most likely to effect their Safety and Happiness. Prudence, indeed, will dictate that Governments long established should not be changed for light and transient causes; and accordingly all experience has shown, that mankind are more disposed to suffer, while evils are sufferable, than to right themselves by abolishing the forms to which they are accustomed. But when a long train of abuses and usurpations, pursuing invariably the same Object evinces a design to reduce them under absolute Despotism, it is their right, it is their duty, to throw off such Government, and to provide new Guards for their future security.—Such has been the patient sufferance of these Colonies; and such is now the necessity which constrains them to alter their former Systems of government. The history of the present King of Great Britain is a history of repeated injuries and usurpations, all having in direct object the establishment of an absolute Tyranny over these States.

---

decided to declare their independence from the British Empire. On July 4, 1776, the Second Continental Congress approved a Declaration of Independence written by Thomas Jefferson (see the box above). A stirring political document, the Declaration of Independence affirmed the Enlightenment's natural rights of "life, liberty, and the pursuit of happiness" and declared the colonies to be "free and independent states absolved from all allegiance to the British crown." The war for American independence had formally begun.

The war against Great Britain was a huge gamble. Britain was a strong European military power with enormous financial resources; by 1778, Britain had sent 50,000 regular British troops and 30,000 German mercenaries to America. The Second Continental Congress had authorized the formation of a Continental Army under George Washington as commander-in-chief. As a southerner, Washington brought balance to an effort that up to now had been led by New Englanders. Nevertheless, compared to the British forces, the Continental Army consisted of undisciplined amateurs whose terms of service were usually very brief. The colonies also had militia units, but they likewise tended to be unreliable. Although 400,000 men served in the Continental Army and the militias during the course of the war, Washington never had more than 20,000 troops available for any single battle.

Of great importance to the colonies' cause was the assistance provided by foreign countries who were eager to gain revenge for their defeats in earlier wars at the hands of the British. The French were particularly generous in supplying arms and money to the rebels from the beginning of the war. French officers also served in Washington's army. The defeat of the British at Saratoga in October 1777 finally led the French to grant diplomatic recognition to the American state. When Spain and the Dutch Republic entered the war against Great Britain in 1779 and 1780, respectively, and Russia formed the League of Armed Neutrality in 1780 to protect neutral shipping from British attacks, the British were faced with war against much of Europe as well as the Americans. Despite having won most of the battles, the British were in danger of losing the war. When the army of General

Cornwallis was forced to surrender to a combined American and French army and French fleet under Washington at Yorktown in 1781, the British decided to call it quits. After extensive negotiations, the Treaty of Paris was signed in 1783. It recognized the independence of the American colonies and granted the Americans control of the western territory from the Appalachians to the Mississippi River. The Americans were off to a good start but soon showed signs of political disintegration.

Toward a New Nation

Although the thirteen American colonies agreed to "hang together" to gain their independence from the British, a fear of concentrated power and concern for their own interests caused them to have little enthusiasm for establishing a united nation with a strong central government. The Articles of Confederation, ratified in 1781, did little to provide for a strong central government. A series of economic, international, and political problems soon led to a movement for a different form of national government. In the summer of 1787, fifty-five delegates attended a convention in Philadelphia that was authorized by the Confederation Congress "for the sole and express purpose of revising the Articles of Confederation." The convention's delegates—wealthy, politically experienced, well educated and nationalistically inclined—rejected revision and decided to devise a new Constitution.

The proposed Constitution created a central government distinct from and superior to the governments of the individual states. The national government was given the power to levy taxes, raise a national army, regulate domestic and foreign trade, and establish a national currency. Following Montesquieu's principle of a "separation of powers" to provide a system of "checks and balances," the central or federal government was divided into three branches, each with some power to check the functioning of the others. A president would serve as the chief executive with the power to execute laws, veto the legislature's acts, make judicial and executive appointments, supervise foreign affairs, and direct military forces. Legislative power was vested in the second branch of government, a bicameral legislature composed of a Senate elected by the state legislatures and a House of Representatives elected directly by the people. The federal judiciary embodied in a Supreme Court and other courts "as deemed necessary" by Congress, provided the third branch of government. With judges nominated by the executive and approved by the legislative branch, the federal judiciary would enforce the Constitution as the "supreme law of the land."

The Constitutional Convention had stipulated that the new Constitution would have to be ratified by popularly chosen conventions in nine of the thirteen states before it would take effect. After fierce contests, the Federalists, who favored the new Constitution, won, although the margin of victory had been quite slim. Important to their success had been a promise to add a Bill of Rights to the Constitution as the new government's first piece of business. Accordingly, in March 1789, the new Congress enacted the first ten amendments to the Constitution, ever since known as the Bill of Rights. These guaranteed freedom of religion, speech, press, petition, and assembly, as well as the right to bear arms, protection against unreasonable searches and arrests, trial by jury, due process of law, and the protection of property rights. Although many of these guarantees had their origins in English law, others were derived from the natural rights philosophy of the eighteenth-century philosophes and American experience. Is it any wonder that many European intellectuals saw the American Revolution as the embodiment of the Enlightenment's political dreams?

The French Revolution

Although we associate events like the French Revolution with sudden changes, the causes of such events involve long-range problems as well as immediate, precipitating forces. The causes of the French Revolution must be found in a multifaceted examination of French society and its problems in the late eighteenth century.

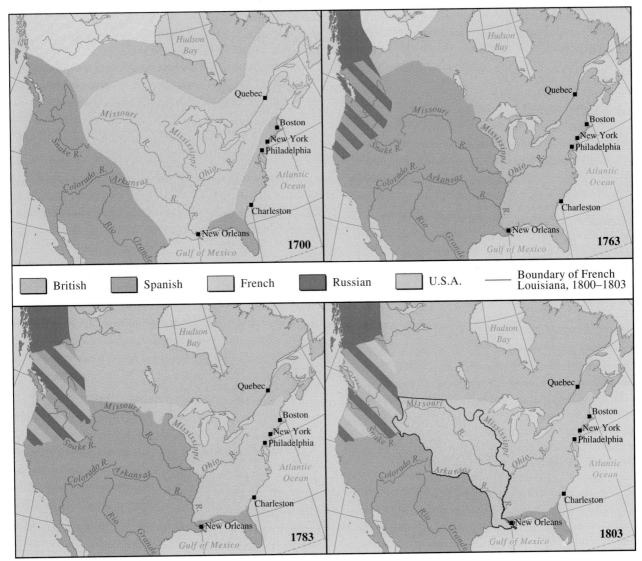

Map 20.1 North America, 1700–1803.

Legend: British | Spanish | French | Russian | U.S.A. | —— Boundary of French Louisiana, 1800–1803

Background to the French Revolution

Although France experienced an increase in economic growth in the eighteenth century, the wealth was not evenly distributed. The long-range or indirect causes of the French Revolution must first be sought in the condition of French society. Before the Revolution, French society was grounded in the inequality of rights or the idea of privilege. The population of 27 million was divided, as it had been since the Middle Ages, into legal categories known as the three orders or estates.

The first estate consisted of the clergy and numbered about 130,000 people. The church owned approximately 10 percent of the land. Clergy were exempt from the *taille*, France's chief tax, although the church had agreed to pay a "voluntary" contribution every five years to the state. Clergy were also radically divided, since the higher clergy, stemming from aristocratic families, shared the interests of the nobility while the parish priests were often poor commoners.

The second estate was the nobility, composed of no more than 350,000 people who nevertheless owned about 25 to 30 percent of the land. Under Louis XV and Louis XVI, the nobility had continued to play an important and even crucial role in French society, holding many of the leading positions in the government, the military, the law courts, and the higher church offices. The French nobility was also divided. The nobility of the robe derived their status from officeholding, a pathway that had often enabled commoners to attain noble rank. These nobles now dominated the royal law courts and important administrative offices. The nobility of the sword claimed to be descendants of the original medieval nobility. As a group, the nobles sought to expand their privileges at the expense of the monarchy—to defend liberty by resisting the arbitrary actions of monarchy, as some nobles asserted—and to maintain their monopolistic control over positions in the military, church, and government. Moreover, the possession of privileges remained a hallmark of the nobility. Common to all were tax exemptions, especially from the *taille*.

The third estate, or the commoners of society, constituted the overwhelming majority of the French population. They were divided by vast differences in occupation, level of education, and wealth. The peasants who alone constituted 75 to 80 percent of the total population were by far the largest segment of the third estate. They owned about 35 to 40 percent of the land, although their landholdings varied from area to area and over half had no or little land on which to survive. Serfdom no longer existed on any large scale in France, but French peasants still had obligations to their local landlords that they deeply resented. These "relics of feudalism," survivals from an earlier age, included the payment of fees for the use of village facilities, such as the flour mill, community oven, and winepress, as well as tithes to the clergy.

Another part of the third estate consisted of skilled artisans, shopkeepers, and other wage earners in the cities. Although the eighteenth century had been a period of rapid urban growth, 90 percent of French towns had fewer than 10,000 inhabitants while only nine cities had more than 50,000. In the eighteenth century, consumer prices rose faster than wages, with the result that these urban groups experienced a noticeable decline in purchasing power. In Paris, for example, income lagged behind food prices and especially behind a 140 percent rise in rents for working people in skilled and unskilled trades. The economic discontent of this segment of the third estate—and often simply their struggle for survival—led them to play an important role in the Revolution, especially in the city of Paris.

About 8 percent or 2.3 million people constituted the bourgeoisie or middle class who owned about 20 to 25 percent of the land. This group included merchants, bankers, and industrialists who controlled the resources of trade, finance, and manufacturing and benefited from the economic prosperity after 1730. The bourgeoisie also included professional people—lawyers, holders of public offices, doctors, and writers. Many members of the bourgeoisie sought security and status through the purchase of land. They had their own set of grievances because they were often excluded from the social and political privileges monopolized by nobles. At the same time, remarkable similarities existed at the upper levels of society between the wealthier bourgeoisie and the nobility. It was still possible for wealthy middle-class individuals to enter the ranks of the nobility by obtaining public offices and entering the nobility of the robe. Over the century as a whole, 6,500 new noble families were created. Moreover, the new and critical ideas of the Enlightenment proved attractive to both aristocrats and bourgeoisie. Members of both groups shared a common world of liberal political thought. Both aristocratic and bourgeois elites, long accustomed to a new socioeconomic reality based on wealth and economic achievement, were increasingly frustrated by a monarchical system resting on privileges and on an old and rigid social order based on the concept of estates. The opposition of these elites to the old order ultimately led them to take drastic action against the monarchical regime, although they soon split over the problem of how far to proceed in eliminating traditional privileges. In a real sense, the Revolution had its origins in political grievances.

The inability of the French monarchy to deal with new social realities and problems was exacerbated by specific problems in the 1780s. Although the country had enjoyed fifty years of growth overall, periodic economic crises still occurred. Bad harvests in 1787 and 1788 and the beginnings of a manufacturing depression resulted in food shortages, rising prices for food and other necessities, and unemployment in the cities. The number of poor, estimated by some at almost one-third of the population, reached crisis proportions on the eve of the Revolution.

The immediate cause of the French Revolution was the near collapse of government finances. French governmental expenditures continued to grow due to costly wars and royal extravagance. On the verge of a complete financial collapse, the government of Louis XVI was finally forced to call a meeting of the Estates-General, the French parliamentary body that had not met since 1614.

The Estates-General consisted of representatives from the three orders of French society. In the elections for the Estates-General, the government had ruled that the Third Estate should get double representation (it did, after all, constitute 97 percent of the population). Consequently, while both the first estate (the clergy) and the second (the nobility) had about 300 delegates each, the commoners had almost 600 representatives. Two-thirds of the latter were people with legal training while three-fourths were from towns with over 2,000 inhabitants, giving the Third Estate a particularly strong legal and urban representation. Most members of the Third Estate advocated a regular constitutional government that would abolish the fiscal privileges of the church and nobility as the major way to regenerate France.

The Estates-General opened at Versailles on May 5, 1789. It was divided from the start over the question of whether voting should be by order or by head (each delegate having one vote). Traditionally, each order would vote separately; each would have veto power over the other two, thus guaranteeing aristocratic control over reforms. But the Third Estate was opposed to this approach and pushed its demands for voting by head. Since it had double representation, with the assistance of liberal nobles and clerics, it could turn the three estates into a single-chamber legislature that would reform France in its own way. Most delegates still desired to make changes within a framework of respect for the authority of the king; revival or reform did not mean the overthrow of traditional institutions. When the First Estate declared in favor of voting by order, the Third Estate felt compelled to respond in a significant fashion. On June 17, 1789, the Third Estate voted to constitute itself a "National Assembly" and decided to draw up a constitution. Three days later, on June 20, the deputies of the Third Estate arrived at their meeting place, only to find the door locked; thereupon they moved to a nearby indoor tennis court and swore (hence, the Tennis Court Oath) that they would continue to meet until they had produced a French constitution. These actions of June 17 and June 20 constitute the first step in the French Revolution since the Third Estate had no legal right to act as the National Assembly. This revolution, largely the work of the lawyers of the Third Estate, was soon in jeopardy, however, as the king sided with the first estate and threatened to dissolve the Estates-General. Louis XVI now prepared to use force.

The intervention of the common people, however, in a series of urban and rural uprisings in July and August of 1789 saved the Third Estate from the king's attempt to stop the revolution. The most famous of the urban risings was the fall of the Bastille (see the box on p. 416). Parisians organized a popular force and on July 14 attacked the Bastille, a royal armory. But the Bastille had also been a state prison, and though it now contained only seven prisoners (five forgers and two insane people), its fall quickly became a popular symbol of triumph over despotism. Paris was abandoned to the insurgents, and Louis XVI was soon informed that the royal troops were unreliable. Louis's acceptance of that reality signaled the collapse of royal authority; the king could no longer enforce his will. The fall of the Bastille had saved the National Assembly.

At the same time, independently of what was going on in Paris, popular revolutions broke out in numerous cities.

◆ **The Tennis Court Oath.**
Finding themselves locked out of their regular meeting place on June 20, 1789, the deputies of the Third Estate met instead in the nearby tennis courts of the Jeu de Paume and committed themselves to continue to meet until they established a new constitution for France. In this painting, the neoclassicist Jacques-Louis David presents a dramatic rendering of the Tennis Court Oath.

≈ The Fall of the Bastille ≈

On July 14, 1789, Parisian crowds in search of weapons attacked and captured the royal armory known as the Bastille. It had also been a state prison, and its fall marked the triumph of "liberty" over despotism. This intervention of the Parisian populace saved the Third Estate from Louis XVI's attempted counterrevolution.

A Parisian Newspaper Account
of the Fall of the Bastille

First, the people tried to enter this fortress by the Rue St.—Antoine, this fortress, which no one has ever penetrated against the wishes of this frightful despotism and where the monster still resided. The treacherous governor had put out a flag of peace. So a confident advance was made; a detachment of French Guards, with perhaps five to six thousand armed bourgeois, penetrated the Bastille's outer courtyards, but as soon as some six hundred persons had passed over the first drawbridge, the bridge was raised and artillery fire mowed down several French Guards and some soldiers; the cannon fired on the town, and the people took fright; a large number of individuals were killed or wounded; but then they rallied and took shelter from the fire . . . meanwhile, they tried to locate some cannon; they attacked from the water's edge through the gardens of the arsenal, and from there made an orderly siege; they advanced from various directions, beneath a ceaseless round of fire. It was a terrible scene. . . . The fighting grew steadily more intense; the citizens had become hardened to the fire; from all directions they clambered onto the roofs or broke into the rooms; as soon as an enemy appeared among the turrets on the tower, he was fixed in the sights of a hundred guns and mown down in an instant; meanwhile cannon fire was hurriedly directed against the second drawbridge, which it pierced, breaking the chains; in vain did the cannon on the tower reply, for most people were sheltered from it; the fury was at its height; people bravely faced death and every danger; women, in their eagerness, helped us to the utmost; even the children, after the discharge of fire from the fortress, ran here and there picking up the bullets and shot; [and so the Bastille fell and the governor, De Launey, was captured]. . . . Serene and blessed liberty, for the first time, has at last been introduced into this abode of horrors, this frightful refuge of monstrous despotism and its crimes.

Meanwhile, they get ready to march; they leave amidst an enormous crowd; the applause, the outbursts of joy, the insults, the oaths hurled at the treacherous prisoners of war; everything is confused; cries of vengeance and of pleasure issue from every heart; the conquerors, glorious and covered in honor, carry their arms and the spoils of the conquered, the flags of victory, the militia mingling with the soldiers of the fatherland, the victory laurels offered them from every side, all this created a frightening and splendid spectacle. On arriving at the square, the people, anxious to avenge themselves, allowed neither De Launey nor the other officers to reach the place of trial; they seized them from the hands of their conquerors, and trampled them underfoot one after the other. De Launey was struck by a thousand blows, his head was cut off and hoisted on the end of a pike with blood streaming down all sides . . . This glorious day must amaze our enemies, and finally usher in for us the triumph of justice and liberty. In the evening, there were celebrations.

The collapse of royal authority in the cities was paralleled by peasant revolutions in the countryside. A growing resentment of the entire landholding system with its fees and obligations created the conditions for a popular uprising. The fall of the Bastille and the king's apparent capitulation to the demands of the Third Estate now encouraged peasants to take matters into their own hands. From July 19 to August 3, peasant rebellions occurred throughout France. The agrarian revolts served as a backdrop to the Great Fear, a vast panic that spread like wildfire through France between July 20 and August 6. Fear of invasion by foreign troops, aided by a supposed aristocratic plot, encouraged the formation of more citizens' militias and permanent committees. The greatest impact of the agrarian revolts and Great Fear was on the National Assembly meeting in Versailles. We will now examine its attempt to reform France.

The Destruction of the Old Regime

One of the first acts of the National Assembly was to destroy the relics of feudalism or aristocratic privileges. On

◆ **Storming of the Bastille.** Louis XVI planned to use force to dissolve the Estates-General, but a number of rural and urban uprisings by the common people prevented this action. The fall of the Bastille, pictured here in an anonymous painting, is perhaps the most famous of the urban risings.

the "night of 4 August," 1789, the National Assembly in an astonishing session voted to abolish seigneurial rights as well as the fiscal privileges of nobles, clergy, towns, and provinces. On August 26, the assembly provided the ideological foundation for its actions and an educational device for the nation by adopting the Declaration of the Rights of Man and the Citizen. This charter of basic liberties began with a ringing affirmation of "the natural and imprescriptible rights of man" to "liberty, property, security and resistance to oppression." It went on to affirm the destruction of aristocratic privileges by proclaiming an end to exemptions from taxation, freedom and equal rights for all men, and access to public office based on talent. The monarchy was restricted, and all citizens were to have the right to take part in the legislative process. Freedom of speech and press were coupled with the outlawing of arbitrary arrests.

The Declaration also raised another important issue. Did the proclamation's ideal of equal rights for all men also include women? Many deputies insisted that it did, at least in terms of civil liberties, provided that, as one said, "women do not aspire to exercise political rights and functions." Olympe de Gouges, a playwright and pamphleteer, refused to accept this exclusion of women from

The French Revolution

The National Assembly	
(Constituent Assembly)	**1789–1791**
Meeting of Estates-General	May 5, 1789
Formation of National Assembly	June 17, 1789
Tennis Court Oath	June 20, 1789
Fall of the Bastille	July 14, 1789
Great Fear	Summer 1789
Abolition of feudalism	August 4, 1789
Declaration of the Rights of Man and the Citizen	August 26, 1789
Women's march to Versailles; the king's return to Paris	October 5–6, 1789
Civil Constitution of the Clergy	July 12, 1790
Flight of the king	June 1791
The Legislative Assembly	**1791–1792**
France declares war on Austria	April 20, 1792
Attack on the royal palace	August 1792
The National Convention	**1792–1795**
Abolition of the monarchy	September 21, 1792
Execution of the king	January 21, 1793
Universal mobilization of the nation	August 23, 1793
Execution of Robespierre	July 28, 1794
The Directory	**1795–1799**
Constitution of 1795 is adopted	August 22, 1795

political rights. Echoing the words of the official declaration, she penned a Declaration of the Rights of Woman and the Female Citizen, in which she insisted that women should have all the same rights as men. The National Assembly ignored her demands.

In the meantime, Louis XVI had remained inactive at Versailles. He did refuse, however, to promulgate the decrees on the abolition of feudalism and the Declaration of Rights, but an unexpected turn of events soon forced the king to change his mind. On October 5, after marching to the Hôtel de Ville, the city hall, to demand bread, crowds of Parisian women numbering in the thousands set off for Versailles, twelve miles away, to confront the king and the National Assembly. One eyewitness was amazed at the sight of "detachments of women coming up from every direction, armed with broomsticks, lances, pitchforks, swords, pistols and muskets." The crowd now insisted that the royal family return to Paris. On October 6, the king complied. As a goodwill gesture, he brought along wagonloads of flour from the palace stores. All were escorted by women armed with pikes (some of which held the severed heads of the king's guards) singing, "We are bringing back the baker, the baker's wife, and the baker's boy" (the king, queen, and their son). The king now accepted the National Assembly's decrees and was virtually a prisoner in Paris.

The Catholic church was viewed as an important pillar of the old order, and it soon also felt the impact of reform. Most of the lands of the church were confiscated, and the church was also secularized. In July 1790, a new Civil Constitution of the Clergy was put into effect. Both bishops and priests of the Catholic church were to be elected by the people and paid by the state. All clergy were also required to swear an oath of allegiance to the Civil Constitution. Only 54 percent of the French parish clergy took the oath while the majority of bishops refused. The Catholic church, still an important institution in the life of the French people, now became an enemy of the Revolution.

By 1791, the National Assembly had finally completed a new constitution that established a limited, constitutional monarchy. There was still a monarch (now called king of the French), but he enjoyed few powers not subject to review by the new Legislative Assembly. The Legislative Assembly, in which sovereign power was vested, was to sit for two years and consist of 745 representatives chosen by an indirect system of election that preserved power in the hands of the more affluent members of society. Only active citizens (those men over the age of twenty-five paying taxes equivalent in value to three days' unskilled labor) could vote for electors (those men paying taxes equal in value to ten days' labor). This relatively small group of 50,000 electors then chose the deputies. To qualify as a deputy, one had to pay taxes equal in value to fifty-four days' labor.

By 1791, a revolutionary consensus that was largely the work of the wealthier bourgeoisie had moved France into a drastic reordering of the old regime. By mid-1791, however, this consensus faced growing opposition from clerics angered by the Civil Constitution of the Clergy, lower classes hurt by a rise in the cost of living, peasants who remained opposed to dues that had still not been abandoned, and political clubs like the Jacobins who offered more radical solutions to France's problems. In addition, by mid-1791, the government was still facing several financial difficulties due to massive tax evasion. Despite all of their problems, however, the bourgeois politicians in charge remained relatively unified on the basis of their trust in the king. But Louis XVI disastrously undercut them. Quite upset with the whole turn of revolutionary events, he sought to flee France in June 1791 and almost succeeded before being recognized, captured, and brought back to Paris. In this unsettled situation, with a discredited and seemingly disloyal monarch, the new Legislative Assembly held its first session in October 1791. France's relations with the rest of Europe soon led to Louis's downfall.

Over a period of time, some European countries had become concerned about the French example and feared that revolution would spread to their countries. On August 27, 1791, Emperor Leopold II of Austria and King Frederick William II of Prussia invited other European monarchs to use force to reestablish monarchical authority in France. Insulted by this threat, the Legislative Assembly declared war on Austria on April 20, 1792.

The French fared badly in the initial fighting, and loud recriminations were soon heard in Paris. A frantic search for scapegoats began; as one observer noted, "Everywhere you hear the cry that the king is betraying us, the generals are betraying us, that nobody is to be trusted; . . . that Paris will be taken in six weeks by the Austrians . . . we are on a volcano ready to spout flames."[1] Defeats in war coupled with economic shortages in the spring reinvigorated popular groups that had been dormant since the previous summer and led to renewed political demonstrations, especially against the king. Radical Parisian political groups, declaring themselves an insurrectionary commune, organized a mob attack on the royal palace and Legislative Assembly in August 1792, took the king captive, and forced the Legislative Assembly to suspend the monarchy and call for a National Convention, chosen on the basis of universal male suffrage, to decide on the future form of government. The French Revolution was about to enter a more radical stage as power passed from the assembly to the new Paris Commune, composed of many who proudly called themselves the sans-culottes, ordinary patriots without fine clothes. Although it has become customary to equate the more radical sans-culottes with working people or the poor, many were merchants and better-off artisans who were often the elite of their neighborhoods.

The Radical Revolution

Before the National Convention met, the Paris Commune dominated the political scene. Led by the newly ap-

pointed minister of justice, Georges Danton, the sans-culottes sought revenge on those who had aided the king and resisted the popular will. Thousands of presumed traitors were arrested and then massacred as ordinary Parisian tradespeople and artisans solved the problem of overcrowded prisons by mass executions of their inmates. In September 1792, the newly elected National Convention began its sessions. Although it was called to draft a new constitution, it also acted as the sovereign ruling body of France.

Socially, the composition of the National Convention was similar to its predecessors. Dominated by lawyers, professionals, and property owners, two-thirds of its deputies were under forty-five, and almost all had had political experience as a result of the Revolution. Almost all were also intensely distrustful of the king and his activities. It was therefore no surprise that the Convention's first major step on September 21 was to abolish the monarchy and establish a republic. But that was about as far as members of the convention could agree, and the National Convention soon split into factions over the fate of the king. The two most important were the Girondins, who represented the provinces and feared the radical mobs in Paris, and the Mountain, who represented the interests of the city of Paris and owed much of its strength to the radical and popular elements in the city. The Mountain won out at the beginning of 1793 when they passed a decree condemning Louis XVI to death. On January 21, 1793, the king was executed and the destruction of the old regime was complete. Now there could be no turning back. But the execution of the king produced new challenges by creating new enemies for the Revolution both at home and abroad while strengthening those who were already its enemies.

Factional disputes between Girondins and the Mountain were only one aspect of France's domestic crisis in 1792 and 1793. Within Paris the local government known as the Commune favored radical change and put constant pressure on the Convention, pushing it to ever more radical positions. Moreover, the National Convention itself still did not rule all France. Peasants in western France as well as inhabitants of France's major provincial cities refused to accept the authority of the Convention.

Domestic turmoil was paralleled by a foreign crisis. By the beginning of 1793, after the king had been executed, much of Europe—an informal coalition of Austria, Prussia, Spain, Portugal, Britain, and the Dutch Republic—was pitted against France. Grossly overextended, the French armies began to experience reverses, and by late spring some members of the anti-French coalition were poised for an invasion of France. If successful, both the

Revolution and the revolutionaries would be destroyed and the old regime reestablished. The Revolution had reached a decisive moment.

To meet these crises, the Convention gave broad powers to an executive committee of twelve known as the Committee of Public Safety, which came to be dominated by Maximilien Robespierre, the leader of the Jacobins. For a twelve-month period, from 1793 to 1794, virtually the same twelve members were reelected and gave the country the leadership it needed to weather the domestic and foreign crises of 1793.

A NATION IN ARMS

To meet the foreign crisis and save the republic from its foreign enemies, the Committee of Public Safety decreed a universal mobilization of the nation on August 23, 1793:

> Young men will fight, young men are called to conquer. Married men will forge arms, transport military baggage and guns and will prepare food supplies. Women, who at long last are to take their rightful place in the revolution and follow their true destiny, will forget their futile tasks: their delicate hands will work at making clothes for sol-

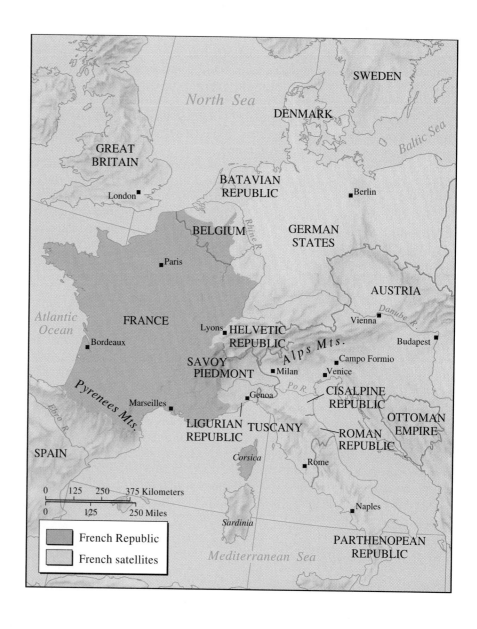

Map 20.2 French Conquests during the Revolutionary Wars.

diers; they will make tents and they will extend their tender care to shelters where the defenders of the Patrie will receive the help that their wounds require. Children will make lint of old cloth. It is for them that we are fighting: children, those beings destined to gather all the fruits of the revolution, will raise their pure hands toward the skies. And old men, performing their missions again, as of yore, will be guided to the public squares of the cities where they will kindle the courage of young warriors and preach the doctrines of hate for kings and the unity of the Republic.[2]

In less than a year, the French revolutionary government had raised an army of 650,000; by September 1794, it numbered 1,169,000. The Republic's army was the largest ever seen in European history. It now pushed the allies back across the Rhine and even conquered the Austrian Netherlands.

Historians have focused on the importance of the French revolutionary army as an important step in the creation of modern nationalism. Previously, wars had been fought between governments or ruling dynasties by relatively small armies of professional soldiers. The new French army, however, was the creation of a "people's" government; its wars were now "people's" wars. The entire nation was to be involved in the war. But when dynastic wars became people's wars, warfare increased in ferocity and lack of restraint. Although innocent civilians had suffered in the earlier struggles, now the carnage became appalling at times. The wars of the French revolutionary era opened the door to the total war of the modern world.

THE COMMITTEE OF PUBLIC SAFETY
AND THE REIGN OF TERROR

To meet the domestic crisis, the National Convention and the Committee of Public Safety established the "Reign of Terror." Revolutionary courts were organized to protect the revolutionary Republic from its internal enemies (see the box on p. 422). In the course of nine months, 16,000 people were officially killed under the blade of the guillotine, the latter a revolutionary device for the quick and efficient separation of heads from bodies. But the true number of the Terror's victims was probably closer to 50,000. The bulk of the Terror's executions took place in places that had been in open rebellion against the authority of the National Convention. The Terror demonstrated no class prejudice. Estimates are that the nobles constituted 8 percent of its victims, the middle classes, 25, the clergy, 6, and the peasant and laboring classes, 60. To the Committee of Public Safety, this

♦ **Citizens Enlist in the New French Army.** To save the Republic from its foreign enemies, the National Convention created a new revolutionary army of unprecedented size. In this painting, citizens joyfully hasten to sign up at the recruitment tables set up in the streets. On this occasion, officials are distributing coins to those who have enrolled.

bloodletting was only a temporary expedient. Once the war and domestic emergency were over, then would follow "the republic of virtue" in which the Declaration of Rights of the Man and Citizen would be fully established.

Military force in the form of Revolutionary Armies was used to bring recalcitrant cities and districts back under the control of the National Convention. Because Lyons was France's second city after Paris and had defied the National Convention during a time when the Republic was in peril, the Committee of Public Safety decided to make an example of it. By April 1794, 1,880 citizens of Lyons had been executed. When guillotining proved too slow, cannon fire and grape shot were used to blow condemned men into open graves. A German observed:

> . . . whole ranges of houses, always the most handsome, burnt. The churches, convents, and all the dwellings of the former patricians were in ruins. When I came to the guillotine, the blood of those who had been executed a few hours beforehand was still running in the street . . . I said to a group of sansculottes that it would be decent to clear away all this human blood. Why should it be cleared? one of them said to me. It's the blood of aristocrats and rebels. The dogs should lick it up.[3]

In western France, Revolutionary Armies were also brutal in defeating the rebel armies. The commander of the

⇒ A Victim of the Reign of Terror ⇐

The Reign of Terror created a repressive environment in which even quite innocent people could be accused of crimes against the Republic. As seen in this letter by Anne-Félicité Guinée, wife of a wig maker, merely insulting an official could lead to an arrest and imprisonment.

Letter of Anne-Félicité Guinée

Citizen Anne-Félicité Guinée, twenty-four years old . . . informs you that she was arrested at the Place des Droits de l'Homme, where I had gone to get butter. I point out to you that for a long time I have had to feed the members in my household on bread and cheese and that, tired of complaints from my husband and my boys, I was compelled to go wait in line to get something to eat. For three days I had been going to the same market without being able to get anything, despite the fact that I had waited from 7 or 8 A.M. until 5 or 6 P.M. After the distribution of butter on the twenty-second, . . . a citizen came over to me and said that I was in very delicate condition. To that I answered, "You can't be delicate and be on your legs for so long. I wouldn't have come if there were any other food." He replied that I needed to drink milk. I answered that I had men in my house who worked and that I couldn't nourish them with milk, that I was convinced that if he, the speaker, was sensitive to the difficulty of obtaining food, he would not vex me so, and that he was an imbecile and wanted to play despot, and no one had that right. Here, on the spot, I was arrested and brought to the guard house. I wanted to explain myself. I was silenced and dragged off to prison. . . . About 7 P.M., I was led to the Revolution-

ary Committee [of the section], where I was called a counterrevolutionary and was told I was asking for the guillotine because I told them I preferred death to being treated ignominiously the way he was treating me. . . . I was asked if I knew whom I had called a despot. I answered, "I didn't know him," and I was told that he was the commander of the post. I said that he was more [a commander] beneath his own roof than anyone, given that he was there to maintain order and not to provoke bad feelings. . . . I was told that I had done three times more than was needed to get the guillotine and that I would be explaining myself before the Revolutionary Tribunal. The next day, I was taken to the Revolutionary Committee, which, without waiting to hear me, had me taken to the Mairie, where I stayed for nine days without a bed or a chair with vermin and with women addicted to all sorts of crimes. . . .

On the ninth day I was transferred to the prison of La Force. . . . In the end I can give you only the very slightest idea of all the horrors that are committed in these terrible prisons. . . . I was thrown together not with women but with monsters who gloried in all their crimes and who gave themselves over to all the most horrible excesses. One day, two of them fought each other with knives. Day and night I lived in mortal fear. The food that was sent in to me was grabbed away immediately. That was my cruel situation for seventeen days. My whole body was swollen from . . . the poor treatment I had endured. . . . [Anne-Félicité Guinée was discharged provisionally after the authorities realized that she was pregnant.]

Revolutionary Army ordered that no quarter be given: "The road to Laval is strewn with corpses. Women, priests, monks, children, all have been put to death. I have spared nobody." Perhaps the most notorious act of violence occurred in Nantes where victims were executed by sinking them in barges in the Loire River.

THE "REPUBLIC OF VIRTUE"

Along with the terror, the Committee of Public Safety took other steps both to control France and to create a new republican order and new republican citizens. By spring 1793, they were sending "representatives on mission" as agents of the central government to all parts of

France to implement the laws dealing with the wartime emergency. The committee also attempted to provide some economic controls by establishing price limits on goods declared of first necessity ranging from food and drink to fuel and clothing. The controls failed to work very well since the government lacked the machinery to enforce it.

In its attempts to create a new order, the National Convention also pursued a policy of dechristianization. A new calendar was instituted in which years would no longer be numbered from the birth of Christ but from September 22, 1792, the first day of the French Republic. The new calendar also eliminated Sundays and church holidays. The word "saint" was removed from street names, churches were pillaged and closed by Revolutionary Armies, and priests were encouraged to marry. In Paris, the cathedral of Notre Dame was designated a Temple of Reason; in November 1793, a public ceremony dedicated to the worship of reason was held in the former cathedral in which patriotic maidens adorned in white dresses paraded before a temple of reason where the high altar once stood. As Robespierre came to realize, dechristianization backfired because France was still overwhelmingly Catholic.

By the summer of 1794, the French had been successful on the battlefield against their foreign foes. The military successes meant that the Terror no longer served much purpose. But the Terror continued because Robespierre, now its dominant figure, had become obsessed with purifying the body politic of all the corrupt. Only then could the Republic of Virtue follow. Many deputies in the National Convention feared, however, that they were not safe while Robespierre was free to act. An anti-Robespierre coalition in the National Convention gathered enough votes to condemn him. Robespierre was guillotined on July 28, 1794.

Reaction and the Directory

After the death of Robespierre, revolutionary fervor began to give way to the Thermidorean Reaction, named after the month of Thermidor on the new French calendar. The Terror began to abate. The National Convention curtailed the power of the Committee of Public Safety, shut down the Jacobin club, and attempted to provide better protection for its deputies against the Parisian mobs. Churches were allowed to reopen for public worship. Economic regulation was dropped in favor of laissez-faire policies, another clear indication that moderate forces were again gaining control of the Revolution. In addition, a new constitution was created in August 1795 that reflected this more conservative republicanism or a desire for a stability that did not sacrifice the ideals of 1789.

To avoid the dangers of another single legislative assembly, the Constitution of 1795 established a national legislative assembly consisting of two chambers: a lower house, known as the Council of 500, which initiated legislation, and an upper house, the Council of Elders, which accepted or rejected the proposed laws. The 750 members of the two legislative bodies were chosen by electors who had to be owners or renters of property worth between 100 and 200 days' labor, a requirement that limited their number to 30,000. The Council of Elders elected five directors from a list presented by the Council of 500 to act as the executive committee or Directory.

The period of the Directory was an era of stagnation, corruption, and graft, a materialistic reaction to the sufferings and sacrifices that had been demanded in the Reign of Terror and the Republic of Virtue. Speculators made fortunes in property by taking advantage of the republic's severe monetary problems. At the same time, the government of the Directory was faced with political enemies from both the left and the right of the political spectrum. On the right, royalists who dreamed of restoring the monarchy continued their agitation. On the left, Jacobin hopes of power were revived by continuing economic problems. Battered by the left and right, unable to find a definitive solution to the country's economic problems, and still carrying on the wars left from the Committee of Public Safety, the Directory increasingly relied on the military to maintain its power. This led to a coup d'etat in 1799 in which the successful and popular military general Napoleon Bonaparte was able to seize power.

The Age of Napoleon

Napoleon dominated both French and European history from 1799 to 1815. In a sense, Napoleon brought the Revolution to an end in 1799, but Napoleon was also a child of the Revolution; he called himself the son of the Revolution. The French Revolution had made possible his rise first in the military and then to supreme power in France. Even beyond this, Napoleon had once said, "I am the revolution," and he never ceased to remind the

◆ **Women Patriots.** Women played a variety of roles in the events of the French Revolution. This picture shows a women's patriotic club discussing the decrees of the National Convention, an indication that some women had become highly politicized by the upheavals of the Revolution.

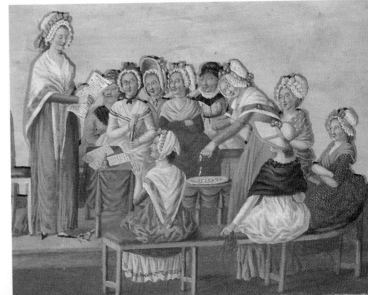

⇒ Napoleon and Psychological Warfare ⇐

In 1796, at the age of twenty-seven, Napoleon Bonaparte was given command of the French army in Italy where he won a series of stunning victories. His use of speed, deception, and surprise to overwhelm his opponents is well known. In this selection from a proclamation to his troops in Italy, Napoleon also appears as a master of psychological warfare.

Napoleon Bonaparte, Proclamation to the French Troops in Italy (April 26, 1796)

Soldiers:

In a fortnight you have won six victories, taken twenty-one standards, fifty-five pieces of artillery, several strong positions, and conquered the richest part of Piedmont [in northern Italy]; you have captured 15,000 prisoners and killed or wounded more than 10,000 men. . . . You have won battles without cannon, crossed rivers without bridges, made forced marches without shoes, camped without brandy and often without bread. Soldiers of liberty, only republican troops could have endured what you have endured. Soldiers, you have our

thanks! The grateful Patrie [nation] will owe its prosperity to you. . . .

The two armies which but recently attacked you with audacity are fleeing before you in terror; the wicked men who laughed at your misery and rejoiced at the thought of the triumphs of your enemies are confounded and trembling.

But, soldiers, as yet you have done nothing compared with what remains to be done. . . . Undoubtedly the greatest obstacles have been overcome; but you still have battles to fight, cities to capture, rivers to cross. Is there one among you whose courage is abating? No. . . . All of you are consumed with a desire to extend the glory of the French people; all of you long to humiliate those arrogant kings who dare to contemplate placing us in fetters; all of you desire to dictate a glorious peace, one which will indemnify the Patrie for the immense sacrifices it has made; all of you wish to be able to say with pride as you return to your villages,"I was with the victorious army of Italy!"

French that they owed to him the preservation of all that was beneficial in the revolutionary program.

The Rise of Napoleon

Napoleon was born in 1769 in Corsica, only a few months after France had annexed the island. The son of a lawyer whose family stemmed from the Florentine nobility, the young Napoleon obtained a royal scholarship to study at a military school in France. When the revolution broke out in 1789, Napoleon was a lieutenant, but the Revolution and the European war that followed broadened his sights and presented him with new opportunities.

Napoleon rose quickly through the ranks. In 1794, when he was only twenty-five, the Committee of Public Safety promoted him to the rank of brigadier general. Two years later, he was made commander of the French armies in Italy (see the box above) where he won a series of stunning victories and dictated peace to the Austrians in 1797. Throughout his Italian campaigns, Napoleon won the confidence of his men by his energy, charm, and ability to comprehend complex issues quickly and make decisions rapidly. These qualities, combined with his keen intelligence, ease with words, and supreme confidence in himself, enabled him throughout the rest of his

life to influence people and win their firm support. He returned to France as a conquering hero. After a disastrous expedition to Egypt in 1799, Napoleon returned to Paris where he participated in the coup d'etat that ultimately led to his virtual dictatorship of France. He was only thirty years old at the time.

With the coup d'etat of 1799, a new form of the republic was proclaimed in which, as first consul, Napoleon directly controlled the entire executive authority of government. He had overwhelming influence over the legislature, appointed members of the administrative bureaucracy, controlled the army, and conducted foreign affairs. In 1802, Napoleon was made consul for life and in 1804 returned France to monarchy when he crowned himself as Emperor Napoleon I. The revolutionary era that had begun with an attempt to limit arbitrary government had ended with a government far more autocratic than the monarchy of the old regime.

The Domestic Policies of Emperor Napoleon

Napoleon once claimed that he had preserved the gains of the Revolution for the French people. The ideal of republican liberty had, of course, been destroyed by Napoleon's thinly disguised autocracy. But were revolutionary ideals maintained in other ways? An examination of his domestic policies will enable us to judge the truth or falsehood of Napoleon's assertion.

In 1801, Napoleon established peace with the oldest and most implacable enemy of the Revolution, the Catholic church. Both sides gained from the Concordat that Napoleon arranged with the pope. Napoleon agreed to recognize Catholicism as the religion of a majority of the French people. Although the Catholic church was permitted to hold processions again and reopen the seminaries, the pope agreed not to raise the question of the church lands confiscated in the Revolution. As a result of the Concordat, the Catholic church was no longer an enemy of the French government. At the same time the agreement reassured those who had acquired church lands during the Revolution that they would not be stripped of them, an assurance that obviously made them supporters of the Napoleonic regime.

Napoleon's most famous domestic achievement was his codification of the laws. Before the Revolution, France did not have a single set of laws, but rather virtually 300 different legal systems. During the Revolution, efforts were made to prepare a codification of the laws for the entire nation, but it remained for Napoleon to bring the work to completion in seven codes of law, of which the most important was the Civil Code (or Code Napoléon). This preserved most of the revolutionary gains by recognizing the principle of the equality of all citizens before the law, the right of the individual to choose his profession, religious toleration, and the abolition of serfdom and feudalism. Property rights continued to be carefully protected, and the interests of employers were safeguarded by outlawing trade unions and strikes. The Civil Code clearly reflected the revolutionary aspirations for a uniform legal system, legal equality, and protection of property and individuals.

Napoleon also worked on rationalizing the bureaucratic structure of France by developing a powerful, centralized administrative machine. Administrative centralization required a bureaucracy of capable officials, and Napoleon worked hard to develop one. Early on, the regime showed its preference for experts and cared little whether that expertise had been acquired in royal or revolutionary bureaucracies. Promotion, whether in civil or military offices, was to be based not on rank or birth but only on demonstrated abilities. This was, of course, what many bourgeoisie had wanted before the Revolution. Napoleon, however, also created a new aristocracy based on merit in the state service. Napoleon created 3,263 nobles between 1808 and 1814; nearly 60 percent were mil-

♦ **The Coronation of Napoleon.** In 1804, Napoleon restored monarchy to France when he had himself crowned as emperor. In the coronation scene painted by Jacques-Louis David, Napoleon is shown crowning the empress Josephine while the pope looks on. Shown seated in the box in the background is Napoleon's mother, even though she was not at the ceremony.

itary officers; the remainder came from the upper ranks of the civil service and other state and local officials. Socially, only 22 percent of Napoleon's aristocracy came from the nobility of the old regime; almost 60 percent were bourgeois in origin.

In his domestic policies, then, Napoleon both destroyed and preserved aspects of the Revolution. Liberty had been replaced by an initially benevolent despotism that grew increasingly arbitrary as the demands of war overwhelmed Napoleon and the French. While equality was preserved in the law code and the opening of careers to talent, the creation of a new aristocracy and the strong protection accorded to property rights make it clear that a loss of equality accompanied the loss of liberty.

Napoleon's Empire and the European Response

When Napoleon became consul in 1799, France was at war with a second European coalition of Russia, Great Britain, and Austria. Napoleon realized the need for a pause and achieved a peace treaty in 1802 that left France with new frontiers and a number of client territories from the North Sea to the Adriatic. But the peace did not last, and war was renewed in 1803 with Britain, who was soon joined by Austria, Russia, and Prussia in the Third Coalition. In a series of battles at Ulm, Austerlitz, Jena, and Eylau from 1805 to 1807, Napoleon's Grand Army defeated the continental members of the coalition, giving him the opportunity to create a new European order.

Map 20.3 Napoleon's Grand Empire.

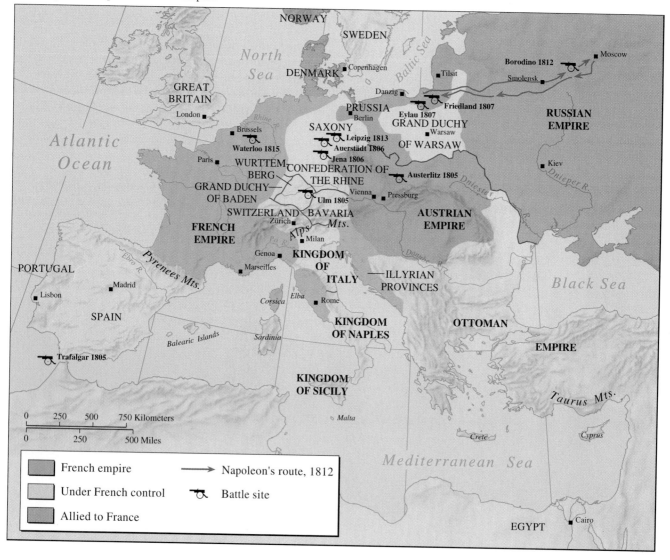

The Grand Empire was composed of three major parts: the French empire, dependent states, and allied states. The French empire, the inner core of the Grand Empire, consisted of an enlarged France extending to the Rhine in the east and including the western half of Italy north of Rome. Dependent states were kingdoms under the rule of Napoleon's relatives; these included Spain, Holland, the kingdom of Italy, the Swiss Republic, the Grand Duchy of Warsaw, and the Confederation of the Rhine, the latter a union of all German states except Austria and Prussia. Allied states were those defeated by Napoleon and forced to join his struggle against Britain; they included Prussia, Austria, and Russia. Although the internal structure of the Grand Empire varied outside its inner core, Napoleon considered himself leader of the whole.

Within his empire, Napoleon sought acceptance everywhere of certain revolutionary principles, including legal equality, religious toleration, and economic freedom. As he explained to his brother Jerome after he had made him king of the new German state of Westphalia:

> What the peoples of Germany desire most impatiently is that talented commoners should have the same right to your esteem and to public employments as the nobles, that any trace of serfdom and of an intermediate hierarchy between the sovereign and the lowest class of the people should be completely abolished. The benefits of the Code Napoléon, the publicity of judicial procedure, the creation of juries must be so many distinguishing marks of your monarchy. . . . What nation would wish to return under the arbitrary Prussian government once it had tasted the benefits of a wise and liberal administration? The peoples of Germany, the peoples of France, of Italy, of Spain all desire equality and liberal ideas. I have guided the affairs of Europe for many years now, and I have had occasion to convince myself that the buzzing of the privileged classes is contrary to the general opinion. Be a constitutional king.[4]

In the inner core and dependent states of his Grand Empire, Napoleon tried to destroy the old order. Nobility and clergy everywhere in these states lost their special privileges. He decreed equality of opportunity with offices open to talent, equality before the law, and religious toleration. This spread of French revolutionary principles was an important factor in the development of liberal traditions in these countries.

Like Hitler 130 years later, Napoleon hoped that his Grand Empire would last for centuries; like Hitler's empire, it collapsed almost as rapidly as it had been formed. Two major reasons help to explain this: the survival of Great Britain and the force of nationalism. Britain's survival was primarily due to its sea power. As long as Britain

CHRONOLOGY

The Napoleonic Era, 1799–1815

Napoleon as first consul	1799–1804
Concordat with Catholic church	1801
Emperor Napoleon I	1804–1815
Battles of Austerlitz; Trafalgar; Ulm	1805
Battle of Jena	1806
Continental System established	1806
Battle of Eylau	1807
Invasion of Russia	1812
War of liberation	1813–1814
Exile to Elba	1814
Battle of Waterloo; exile to Saint Helena	1815

ruled the waves, it was almost invulnerable to military attack. Although Napoleon contemplated an invasion of Britain and even collected ships for it, he could not overcome the British navy's decisive defeat of a combined French–Spanish fleet at Trafalgar in 1805. Napoleon then turned to his Continental System to defeat Britain. Put into effect between 1806 and 1808, it attempted to prevent British goods from reaching the European continent in order to weaken Britain economically and destroy its capacity to wage war. But the Continental System failed. Allied states resented the ever-tightening French economic hegemony; some began to cheat and others to resist, thereby opening the door to British collaboration. New markets in the Levant and in Latin America also provided compensation for the British. Indeed, by 1809–1810 British overseas exports were at near-record highs.

A second important factor in the defeat of Napoleon was nationalism. This political creed had arisen during the French Revolution in the French people's emphasis on brotherhood (fraternité) and solidarity against other peoples. Nationalism involved the unique cultural identity of a people based on common language, religion, and national symbols. The spirit of French nationalism had made possible the mass armies of the revolutionary and Napoleonic eras. But Napoleon's spread of the principles of the French Revolution beyond France inadvertently brought a spread of nationalism as well. The French aroused nationalism in two ways: by making themselves hated oppressors and thus arousing the patriotism of others in opposition to French nationalism, and by showing the people of Europe what nationalism was and what a nation in arms could do. The lesson was not lost on other peoples and rulers. A Spanish uprising against Napoleon's rule, aided by British support, kept a French force of 200,000 pinned down for years.

The beginning of Napoleon's downfall came in 1812 with the invasion of Russia. The latter's defection from the Continental System left Napoleon with little choice. Although aware of the risks of invading such a large country, he also knew that if the Russians were allowed to challenge the Continental System unopposed, others would soon follow suit. In June 1812, a Grand Army of more than 600,000 men entered Russia. Napoleon's hopes for victory depended on quickly meeting and defeating the Russian armies, but the Russian forces refused to give battle and retreated for hundreds of miles while torching their own villages and countryside to prevent Napoleon's army from finding food and forage. When the Russians did stop to fight at Borodino, Napoleon's forces won an indecisive and costly victory. When the remaining troops of the Grand Army arrived in Moscow, they found the city ablaze. Lacking food and supplies, Napoleon abandoned Moscow late in October and made the "Great Retreat" across Russia in terrible winter conditions. Only 40,000 out of the original army managed to straggle back to Poland in January 1813. This military disaster then led to a war of liberation all over Europe, culminating in Napoleon's defeat in April 1814.

The defeated emperor of the French was allowed to play ruler on the island of Elba, off the coast of Tuscany, while the Bourbon monarchy was restored to France in the person of Louis XVIII, brother of the executed king. But the new king had little support, and Napoleon, bored on the island of Elba, slipped back into France. The troops sent to capture him went over to his side, and Napoleon entered Paris in triumph on March 20, 1815. The powers who had defeated him pledged once more to fight this person they called the "Enemy and Disturber of the Tranquility of the World." Having decided to strike first at his enemies, Napoleon raised yet another army and moved to attack the nearest allied forces stationed in Belgium. At Waterloo on June 18, Napoleon met a combined English and Prussian army under the Duke of Wellington and suffered a bloody defeat. This time the victorious Allies exiled him to St. Helena, a small and forsaken island in the south Atlantic. Only Napoleon's memory would continue to haunt French political life.

Conclusion

The revolutionary era of the late eighteenth century witnessed a dramatic political transformation. Revolutionary upheavals, beginning in North America and continuing in France, produced movements for political liberty and equality. The documents created by these revolutions, the Declaration of Independence and the Declaration of the Rights of Man and Citizen, embodied the fundamental ideas of the Enlightenment and set forth a liberal political agenda based on a belief in popular sovereignty—the people are the source of political power—and the principles of liberty and equality. Liberty, frequently limited in practice, meant, in theory, freedom from arbitrary power as well as the freedom to think, write, and worship as one chose. Equality meant equality in rights and the equality of opportunity based on talent rather than birth. In practice, equality remained limited; those who owned property had greater opportunities for voting and office holding, and there was certainly no equality between men and women.

The French Revolution created a modern revolutionary concept. No one had foreseen or consciously planned the upheaval that began in 1789, but after 1789 "revolutionaries" knew that the proper use of mass uprisings could succeed in overthrowing unwanted governments. The French Revolution became the classical political and social model for revolution. At the same time, the liberal and national political ideals created by the Revolution and spread through Europe by Napoleon dominated the political landscape of the nineteenth and early twentieth centuries. A new European era had begun and Europe would never again be the same.

NOTES

1. Quoted in William Doyle, *The Oxford History of the French Revolution* (Oxford, 1989), p. 184.
2. Quoted in Leo Gershoy, *The Era of the French Revolution* (Princeton, 1957), p. 157.
3. Quoted in Doyle, *The Oxford History of the French Revolution*, p. 254.
4. Quoted in J. Christopher Herold, ed., *The Mind of Napoleon* (New York, 1955), pp. 74–75.

SUGGESTIONS FOR FURTHER READING

A well-written, up-to-date introduction to the French Revolution can be found in W. Doyle, *The Oxford History of the French Revolution* (Oxford, 1989). For the entire revolutionary and Napoleonic eras, see O. Connelly, *The French Revolution and Napoleonic Era*, 2d ed. (Fort Worth, 1991); and D. M. G. Sutherland, *France 1789–1815: Revolution and Counter-Revolution* (New York, 1986). Although controversial, the massive and beautifully written work by S. Schama, *Citizens* (New York, 1989), makes exciting reading. A different approach to the French Revolution can be found in E. Kennedy, *A Cultural History of the French Revolution* (New Haven, Conn., 1989). Three comprehensive reference works are S. F. Scott and B. Rothaus, eds., *Historical Dictionary of the French Revolution*, 2 vols. (Westport, Conn., 1985); F. Furet and M. Ozouf, *A Critical Dictionary of the French Revolution*, trans. A. Goldhammer (Cambridge, Mass., 1989); and O. Connelly, et al., *Historical Dictionary of Napoleonic France, 1799–1815* (Westport, Conn., 1985).

The origins of the French Revolution are examined in the classic work by G. Lefebvre, *The Coming of the French Revolution* (Princeton, N.J., 1947), although his interpretive framework has been superseded by new work. On the latter, see especially W. Doyle, *Origins of the French Revolution* (Oxford, 1988). See also R. Chartier, *The Cultural Origins of the French Revolution* (Durham, N.C., 1991). On the early years of the Revolution, see M. Kennedy, *The Jacobin Clubs in the French Revolution: The First Years* (Princeton, N.J., 1982); and N. Hampson, *Prelude to Terror* (Oxford, 1988). Important works on the radical stage of the French Revolution include N. Hampson, *The Terror in the French Revolution* (London, 1981); R. R. Palmer, *Twelve Who Ruled* (New York, 1965); and R. Cobb, *The People's Armies* (London, 1987). For a biography of Robespierre, one of the leading figures of this period, see N. Hampson, *The Life and Opinions of Maximilien Robespierre* (London, 1974). The importance of the popular revolutionary crowds is examined in the classic work by G. Rudé, *The Crowd in the French Revolution* (Oxford, 1959); and D. Roche, *The People of Paris: An Essay in Popular Culture* (Berkeley, 1987). On the Directory, see M. Lyons, *France under the Directory* (Cambridge, 1975); and R. B. Rose, *Gracchus Babeuf* (Stanford, 1978).

The religious history of the French Revolution is covered in J. McManners, *The French Revolution and the Church* (London, 1969). On the Great Fear, there is the classic work by G. Lefebvre, *The Great Fear of 1789: Rural Panic in Revolutionary France* (London, 1973). Two recent works that take rather different approaches to the French Revolution are W. H. Sewell, *Work and Revolution in France* (Cambridge, 1980); and P. Higonnet, *Class, Ideology and the Rights of Nobles during the French Revolution* (Oxford, 1981). On the role of women in revolutionary Paris, there is much to be found in the collection of documents edited by D. G. Levy, H. B. Applewhite, and M. D. Johnson, *Women in Revolutionary Paris, 1789–1795* (Urbana, Ill., 1979); and the essays in G. Fraisse and M. Perrot, eds., *A History of Women in the West*, vol. 4 (Cambridge, Mass., 1993).

The best, brief biography of Napoleon is F. Markham, *Napoleon* (New York, 1963). Also valuable are P. Geyl, *Napoleon, For and Against* (New Haven, Conn., 1963), a study of biographical writings on the French leader; and the recent massive biographies by F. J. McLynn, *Napoleon: A Biography* (London, 1997); and A. Schom, *Napoleon Bonaparte* (New York, 1997). A good, recent treatment is L. Bergeron, *France under Napoleon* (Princeton, N.J., 1981). On Napoleon's military campaigns, see D. Chandler, *The Campaigns of Napoleon* (London, 1966).

A good, brief survey of the revolutionary era in America can be found in the relevant chapters of S. Thernstrom, *A History of the American People*, 2d ed. (San Diego, 1989); and E. S. Morgan, *Birth of the Republic, 1763–1789*, rev. ed. (New York, 1977). The importance of ideology is treated in G. Wood, *The Radicalism of the American Revolution* (New York, 1992). A comparative study that puts the American Revolution into a larger context is R. R. Palmer, *The Age of the Democratic Revolutions: A Political History of Europe and America, 1760–1800*, 2 vols. (Princeton, N.J., 1959–64). A more recent comparative study is the stimulating work by P. Higonnet, *Sister Republics: Origins of the French and American Revolutions* (Cambridge, Mass., 1988).

The Industrial Revolution and Its Impact on European Society

The French Revolution dramatically and quickly altered the political structure of France while the Napoleonic conquests spread many of the revolutionary principles in an equally rapid and stunning fashion to other parts of Europe. During the late eighteenth and early nineteenth centuries, another revolution—an industrial one—was transforming the economic and social structure of Europe, although in a less dramatic and rapid fashion.

The period of the Industrial Revolution led to a quantum leap in industrial production. New sources of energy and power, especially coal and steam, replaced wind and water to create labor-saving machines that dramatically decreased the use of human and animal labor and, at the same time, increased the level of productivity. In turn, power machinery called for new ways of organizing human labor to maximize the benefits and profits from the new machines; factories replaced shop and home workrooms. Many early factories were dreadful places with difficult working conditions. Reformers, appalled at these conditions, were especially critical of the treatment of married women. One reported: "We have repeatedly seen married females, in the last stage of pregnancy, slaving from morning to night beside these never-tiring machines, and when . . they were obliged to sit down to take a moment's ease, and being seen by the manager, were fined for the offense." But there were other examples of well-run factories. William Cobbett described one in Manchester in 1830: "In this room, which is lighted in the most convenient and beautiful manner, there were five hundred pairs of looms at work, and five hundred persons attending those looms; and, owing to the goodness of the masters, the whole looking healthy and well-dressed."

During the Industrial Revolution, Europe experienced a shift from a traditional, labor-intensive economy based on farming and handicrafts to a more capital-intensive economy based on manufacturing by machines, specialized labor, and industrial factories. Although the Industrial Revolution took decades to

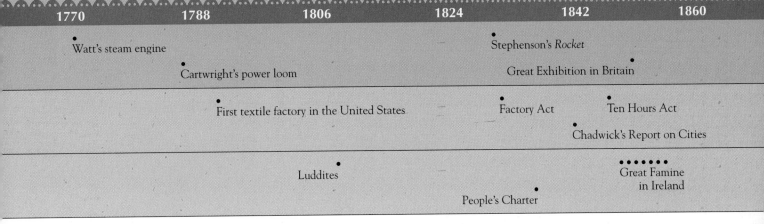

1770	1788	1806	1824	1842	1860

Watt's steam engine

Cartwright's power loom

First textile factory in the United States

Luddites

Stephenson's *Rocket*

Great Exhibition in Britain

Factory Act

Ten Hours Act

Chadwick's Report on Cities

People's Charter

Great Famine in Ireland

spread, it was truly revolutionary in the way it fundamentally changed Europeans, their society, and their relationship to other peoples. The development of large factories encouraged mass movements of people from the countryside to urban areas where impersonal coexistence replaced the traditional intimacy of rural life. Higher levels of productivity led to a search for new sources of raw materials, new consumption patterns, and a revolution in transportation that allowed raw materials and finished products to be moved quickly around the world. The creation of a wealthy industrial middle class and a huge industrial working class (or proletariat) substantially transformed traditional social relationships.

The Industrial Revolution in Great Britain

Historians generally agree that the Industrial Revolution had its beginnings in Britain in the second half of the eighteenth century. By 1850, the Industrial Revolution had made Great Britain the wealthiest country in the world; by that time it had also spread to the European continent and the New World.

Origins

A number of factors or conditions coalesced in Britain to produce the first Industrial Revolution. One of these was the agricultural revolution of the eighteenth century, which led to a significant increase in food produc-

tion. British agriculture could now feed more people at lower prices with less labor; even ordinary British families did not have to use most of their income to buy food, giving them the potential to purchase manufactured goods. At the same time, a rapid growth of population in the second half of the eighteenth century provided a pool of surplus labor for the new factories of the emerging British industry.

Britain had a ready supply of capital for investment in the new industrial machines and the factories that were needed to house them. In addition to profits from trade and the cottage industry, Britain possessed an effective central bank and well-developed, flexible credit facilities. Many early factory owners were merchants and entrepreneurs who had profited from the eighteenth-century cottage industry. But capital alone is only part of the story. Britain had a fair number of individuals who were interested in making profits if the opportunity presented itself (see the box on p. 432). The British were a people, as one historian has said, "fascinated by wealth and commerce, collectively and individually."

Britain was richly supplied with the important mineral resources, such as coal and iron ore, needed in the manufacturing process. Britain was also a small country, and the relatively short distances made transportation readily accessible. In addition to nature's provision of abundant rivers, from the mid-seventeenth century onward, both private and public investment poured into the construction of new roads, bridges, and canals. By 1780, roads, rivers, and canals linked the major industrial centers of the North, the Midlands, London, and the Atlantic.

Finally, a supply of markets gave British industrialists a ready outlet for their manufactured goods. British exports quadrupled from 1660 to 1760. In the course of its eighteenth-century wars and conquests, Great Britain

The Traits of the British Industrial Entrepreneur

Richard Arkwright (1732–1792), inventor of a spinning frame and founder of cotton factories, was a good example of the successful entrepreneur in the early Industrial Revolution in Britain. In this selection, Edward Baines, who wrote The History of the Cotton Manufacture in Great Britain *in 1835, discusses the traits that explain the success of Arkwright and presumably other British entrepreneurs.*

Edward Baines, The History of the Cotton Manufacture in Great Britain

Richard Arkwright rose by the force of his natural talents from a very humble condition in society. He was born at Preston on the 23rd of December, 1732, of poor parents: being the youngest of thirteen children, his parents could only afford to give him an education of the humblest kind, and he was scarcely able to write. He was brought up to the trade of a barber at Kirkham and Preston, and established himself in that business at Bolton in the year 1760. Having become possessed of a chemical process for dyeing human hair, which in that day (when wigs were universal) was of considerable value, he travelled about collecting hair, and again disposing of it when dyed. In 1761, he married a wife from Leigh, and the connexions he thus formed in that town are supposed to have afterwards brought him acquainted with Highs's experiments in making spinning machines. He himself manifested a strong bent for experiments in mathematics, which he is stated to have followed with so much devotedness as to have neglected his business and injured his circumstances.

His natural disposition was ardent, enterprising, and stubbornly persevering: his mind was as coarse as it was bold and active, and his manners were rough and unpleasing. . . .

The most marked traits in the character of Arkwright were his wonderful ardour, energy, and perseverance. He commonly laboured in his multifarious concerns from five o'clock in the morning till nine at night; and when considerably more than fifty years of age,—feeling that the defects of his education placed him under great difficulty and inconvenience in conducting his correspondence, and in the general management of his business,—he encroached upon his sleep, in order to gain an hour each day to learn English grammar, and another hour to improve his writing and orthography [spelling]! He was impatient of whatever interfered with his favorite pursuits; and the fact is too strikingly characteristic not to be mentioned, that he separated from his wife not many years after their marriage, because she, convinced that he would starve his family [because of the impractical nature of his schemes], broke some of his experimental models of machinery. Arkwright was a severe economist of time; and, that he might not waste a moment, he generally travelled with four horses, and at a very rapid speed. His concerns in Derbyshire, Lancashire, and Scotland were so extensive and numerous, as to [show] at once his astonishing power of transacting business and his all grasping spirit. In many of these he had partners, but he generally managed in such a way, that, whoever lost, he himself was a gainer.

---

had developed a vast colonial empire at the expense of its leading continental rivals, the Dutch Republic and France. Britain also possessed a well-developed merchant marine that was able to transport goods to any place in the world. A crucial factor in Britain's successful industrialization was the ability to produce cheaply those articles most in demand abroad. And the best markets abroad were not in Europe, where countries protected their own incipient industries, but in the Americas, Africa, and the Far East, where people wanted sturdy, inexpensive clothes rather than costly, highly finished, luxury items. Britain's machine-produced textile industry fulfilled that demand. Nor should we overlook the British domestic market. Britain had the highest standard of living in Europe and a rapidly growing population. This demand from both domestic and foreign markets and the inability of the old system to fulfill it led entrepreneurs to seek and accept the new methods of manufacturing that a series of inventions provided. In so doing, these individuals produced the Industrial Revolution.

Technological Changes and New Forms of Industrial Organization

In the 1770s and 1780s, the cotton textile industry took the first major step toward the Industrial Revolution with the creation of the modern factory.

THE COTTON INDUSTRY

Already in the eighteenth century, Great Britain had surged ahead in the production of cheap cotton goods using the traditional methods of cottage industry. The development of the flying shuttle had sped the process of weaving on a loom and enabled weavers to double their output. This created shortages of yarn, however, until James Hargreaves's spinning jenny, perfected by 1768, allowed spinners to produce yarn in greater quantities. Edmund Cartwright's power loom, invented in 1787, allowed the weaving of cloth to catch up with the spinning of yarn and presented new opportunities to entrepreneurs. It was much more efficient to bring workers to the machines and organize their labor collectively in factories located next to rivers and streams, the sources of power for many of these early machines, than to leave the workers dispersed in their cottages. The concentration of labor in the new factories also brought the laborers and their families to live in the new towns that rapidly grew up around the factories.

Map 21.1 Britain in the Industrial Revolution.

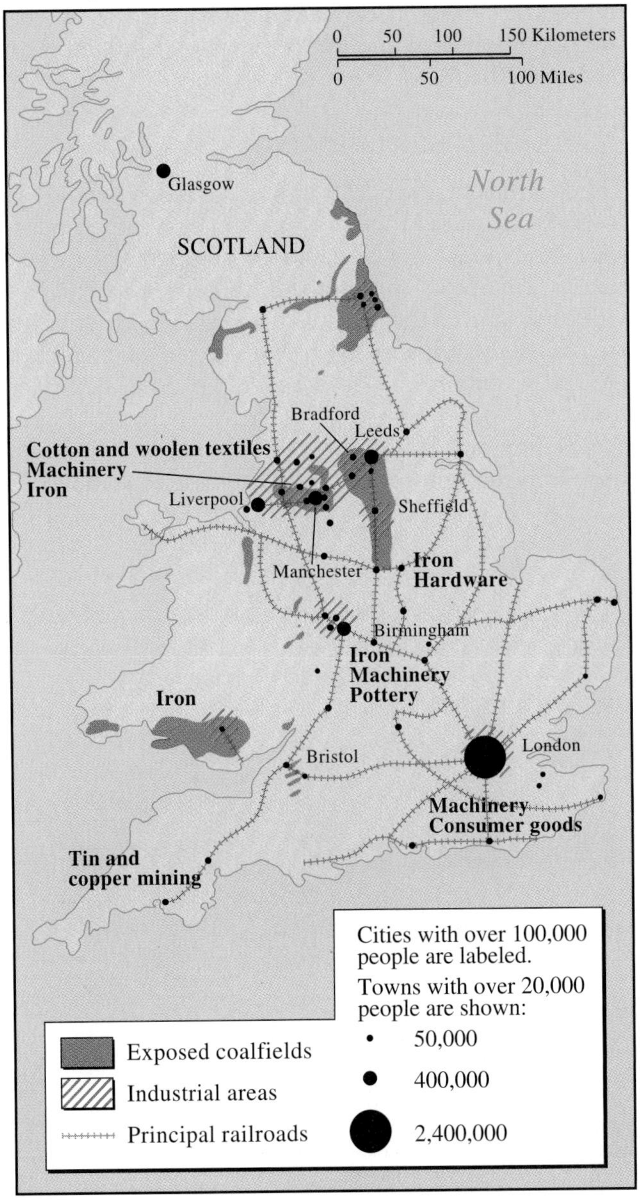
0 50 100 150 Kilometers
0 50 100 Miles
Glasgow
North Sea
SCOTLAND
Bradford
Leeds
Cotton and woolen textiles
Machinery
Iron
Liverpool
Sheffield
Manchester
Iron
Hardware
Birmingham
Iron
Machinery
Pottery
Iron
Bristol
London
Machinery
Consumer goods
Tin and
copper mining
Cities with over 100,000 people are labeled.
Towns with over 20,000 people are shown:
50,000
400,000
2,400,000
Exposed coalfields
Industrial areas
Principal railroads

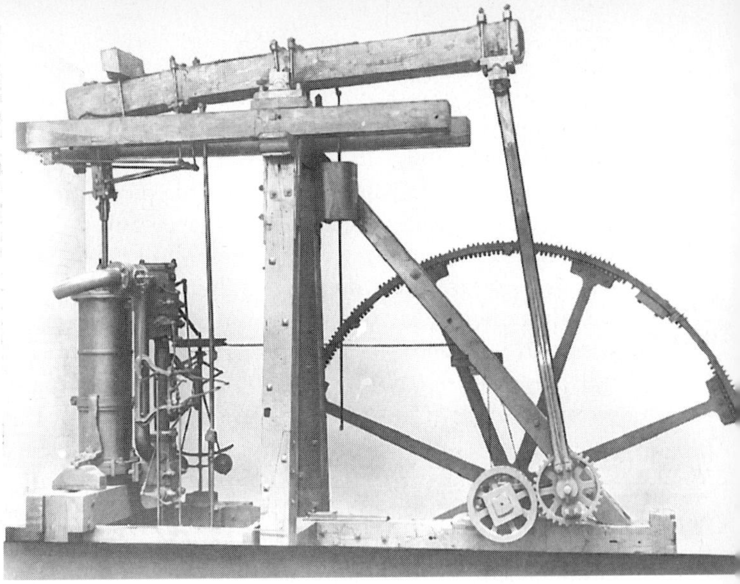

✦ **A Boulton and Watt Steam Engine.** Encouraged by his business partner, Matthew Boulton, James Watt developed the first genuine steam engine. Pictured here is a typical Boulton and Watt engine. Steam pressure in the cylinder on the left drives the beam upward and sets the flywheel in motion.

THE STEAM ENGINE

What pushed the cotton industry to even greater heights of productivity was the invention of the steam engine, which played a major role in the Industrial Revolution. It revolutionized the production of cotton goods and caused the factory system to spread to other areas of production, thereby creating whole new industries. The steam engine secured the triumph of the Industrial Revolution.

In the 1760s, a Scottish engineer, James Watt (1736–1819), created an engine powered by steam that could pump water from mines three times as quickly as previous engines. In 1782, Watt enlarged the possibilities of the steam engine when he developed a rotary engine that could turn a shaft and thus drive machinery. Steam power could now be applied to spinning and weaving cotton, and before long cotton mills using steam engines were multiplying across Britain. Because steam engines were fired by coal, they did not need to be located near rivers; entrepreneurs now had greater flexibility in their choice of location.

The new boost given to cotton textile production by technological changes became readily apparent. In 1760, Britain had imported 2.5 million pounds of raw cotton, which was farmed out to cottage industries. In 1787, the British imported 22 million pounds of cotton; most of it was spun on machines, some powered by water in large mills. By 1840, 366 million tons of cotton—now Britain's most important product in value—were imported. By this time, most cotton industry employees worked in factories. The cheapest labor in India could not compete in quality or quantity with Britain. British cotton goods sold everywhere in the world. And in Britain itself, cheap cotton cloth made it possible for millions of poor people to wear undergarments, long a preserve of the rich who alone could afford underwear made with expensive linen cloth. New work clothing that was tough, comfortable to the skin, and yet cheap and easily washable became common.

The steam engine proved invaluable to Britain's Industrial Revolution. Unlike horses, the steam engine was a tireless source of power and depended for fuel on a substance—namely, coal—that seemed then to be unlimited in quantity. The popular saying that "Steam is an Englishman" had real significance by 1850. The success of the steam engine led to a need for more coal and an expansion in coal production; between 1815 and 1850, the output of coal quadrupled. In turn, new processes using coal furthered the development of an iron industry.

THE IRON INDUSTRY

The British iron industry was radically transformed during the Industrial Revolution. Britain had large resources of iron ore, but at the beginning of the eighteenth century, the basic process of producing iron had altered little since the Middle Ages and still depended heavily on charcoal. In the early eighteenth century, new methods of smelting iron ore to produce cast iron were devised based on the use of coke derived from coal. Still, a better quality of iron was not possible until the 1780s when Henry Cort developed a system called puddling, in which coke was used to burn away impurities in pig iron and produce an iron of high quality. A boom then ensued in the British iron industry. In 1740, Britain produced 17,000 tons of iron; by the 1840s, over 2 million tons; and by 1852, almost 3 million tons, more than the rest of the world combined.

A REVOLUTION IN TRANSPORTATION

The high-quality wrought iron produced by the Cort process encouraged the use of machinery in other industries, most noticeably in such new means of transportation as steamboats and railroads. In 1804, Richard Trevithick pioneered the first steam-powered locomotive on an industrial rail-line in south Wales. It pulled ten tons of ore and seventy people at five miles per hour. Better locomotives soon followed. The engines built by George Stephenson and his son proved superior, and it was in their workshops in Newcastle upon Tyne that the loco-

✦ **Railroad Line from Liverpool to Manchester.** The railroad line from Liverpool to Manchester, first opened in 1830, relied on steam locomotives. As is evident in this illustration, carrying passengers was the railroad's main business. First-class passengers rode in covered cars; second- and third-class passengers in open cars.

motives for the first modern railways in Britain were built. George Stephenson's *Rocket* was used on the first public railway line, which opened in 1830, extending thirty-two miles from Liverpool to Manchester. *Rocket* sped along at sixteen miles per hour. Within twenty years, locomotives had reached fifty miles per hour, an incredible speed to contemporary passengers. During the same time period, new companies were formed to build additional railroads as the infant industry proved to be not only technically but financially successful. In 1840, Britain had almost 2,000 miles of railroads; by 1850, 6,000 miles of railroad track crisscrossed much of the country.

The railroad contributed significantly to the success and maturing of the Industrial Revolution. The railroad's demands for coal and iron furthered the growth of those industries. Railway construction created new job opportunities, especially for farm laborers and peasants who had long been accustomed to finding work outside their local villages. Perhaps most importantly, a cheaper and faster means of transportation had a rippling effect on the growth of an industrial economy. By reducing the price of goods, larger markets were created; increased sales necessitated more factories and more machinery, thereby reinforcing the self-sustaining nature of the Industrial Revolution, which marked a fundamental break with the traditional European economy. The great productivity of the Industrial Revolution enabled entrepreneurs to reinvest their profits in new capital equipment, further expanding the productive capacity of the economy. Continuous, even rapid, self-sustaining economic growth came to be seen as a fundamental characteristic of the new industrial economy.

The railroad was the perfect symbol of this aspect of the Industrial Revolution. The ability to transport goods and people at dramatic speeds also provided visible confirmation of a new sense of power. When railway engineers pierced mountains with tunnels and spanned chasms with breathtaking bridges, contemporaries experienced a sense of power over nature not felt before in Western civilization.

THE INDUSTRIAL FACTORY

Another visible symbol of the Industrial Revolution was the factory, which became the chief means of organizing labor for the new machines. From its beginning, the factory system demanded a new type of discipline from its employees. Factory owners could not afford to let their expensive machinery stand idle. Workers were forced to work regular hours and in shifts to keep the machines pro-ducing at a steady pace for maximum output. This represented a massive adjustment for early factory laborers.

Preindustrial workers were not accustomed to a "timed" format. Agricultural laborers had always kept irregular hours; hectic work at harvest time might be followed by periods of inactivity. Even in the burgeoning cottage industry of the eighteenth century, weavers and spinners who worked at home might fulfill their weekly quotas by working around the clock for two or three days, followed by a leisurely pace until the next week's demands forced another work spurt.

Factory owners, therefore, faced a formidable task. They had to create a system of time–work discipline in which employees became accustomed to working regular, unvarying hours during which they performed a set number of tasks over and over again as efficiently as possible. One early industrialist said that his aim was "to make such machines of the men as cannot err." Such work, of course, tended to be repetitive and boring, and factory owners resorted to tough methods to accomplish their goals. Factory regulations were minute and detailed (see the box on p. 436). Adult workers were fined for a wide variety of minor infractions, such as being a few minutes late for work, and dismissed for more serious misdoings, especially drunkenness. The latter was viewed as particularly offensive because it set a bad example for younger workers and also courted disaster in the midst of dangerous machinery. Employers found that dismissals and fines worked well for adult employees; in a time when great population growth had produced large masses of unskilled labor, dismissal could be disastrous. Children were less likely to understand the implications of dismissal so they were sometimes disciplined more directly—by beating. In one crucial sense, the early industrialists proved successful in their efforts. As the nineteenth century progressed, the second and third generations of workers came to view a regular working week as a natural way of life. It was, of course, an attitude that made possible Britain's incredible economic growth in that century.

The Great Exhibition: Britain in 1851

In 1851, the British organized the world's first industrial fair. It was housed at Kensington in London in the Crystal Palace, an enormous structure made entirely of glass and iron, a tribute to British engineering skills. Covering nineteen acres, the Crystal Palace contained 100,000 exhibits that showed the wide variety of products created by the Industrial Revolution. Six million people visited the fair in six months. The Great Exhibition displayed

➤ Discipline in the New Factories ➤

Workers in the new factories of the Industrial Revolution had been accustomed to a lifestyle free of overseers. Unlike the cottages, where workers spun thread and wove cloth in their own rhythm and time, the factories demanded a new, rigorous discipline geared to the requirements of the machines. This selection is taken from a set of rules for a factory in Berlin in 1844. They were typical of company rules everywhere the factory system had been established.

The Foundry and Engineering Works of the Royal Overseas Trading Company, Factory Rules

In every large works, and in the co-ordination of any large number of workmen, good order and harmony must be looked upon as the fundamentals of success, and therefore the following rules shall be strictly observed.

1. The normal working day begins at all seasons at 6 A.M. precisely and ends, after the usual break of half an hour for breakfast, an hour for dinner and half an hour for tea, at 7 P.M., and it shall be strictly observed. . . .

   Workers arriving 2 minutes late shall lose half an hour's wages; whoever is more than 2 minutes late may not start work until after the next break; or at least shall lose his wages until then. Any disputes about the correct time shall be settled by the clock mounted above the gatekeeper's lodge. . . .

3. No workman, whether employed by time or piece, may leave before the end of the working day, without having first received permission from the overseer and having given his name to the gatekeeper. Omission of these two actions shall lead to a fine of ten silver groschen [pennies] payable to the sick fund.

4. Repeated irregular arrival at work shall lead to dismissal. This shall also apply to those who are found idling by an official or overseer, and refused to obey their order to resume work. . . .

6. No worker may leave his place of work otherwise than for reasons connected with his work.

7. All conversation with fellow-workers is prohibited; if any worker requires information about his work, he must turn to the overseer, or to the particular fellow-worker designated for the purpose.

8. Smoking in the workshops or in the yard is prohibited during working hours; anyone caught smoking shall be fined five silver groschen for the sick fund for every such offense. . . .

10. Natural functions must be performed at the appropriate places, and whoever is found soiling walls, fences, squares, etc., and similarly, whoever is found washing his face and hands in the workshop and not in the places assigned for the purpose, shall be fined five silver groschen for the sick fund. . . .

12. It goes without saying that all overseers and officials of the firm shall be obeyed without question, and shall be treated with due deference. Disobedience will be punished by dismissal.

13. Immediate dismissal shall also be the fate of anyone found drunk in any of the workshops. . . .

14. Every workman is obliged to report to his superiors any acts of dishonesty or embezzlement on the part of his fellow workmen. If he omits to do so, and it is shown after subsequent discovery of a misdemeanor that he knew about it at the time, he shall be liable to be taken to court as an accessory after the fact and the wage due to him shall be retained as punishment.

Britain's wealth to the world; it was a gigantic symbol of British success. Even trees were brought inside the Crystal Palace as a visible symbol of how the Industrial Revolution had achieved human domination over nature.

By the year of the Great Exhibition, Great Britain had become the world's first and richest industrial nation. Britain was the "workshop, banker, and trader of the world." It produced one-half of the world's coal and manufactured goods; its cotton industry alone in 1851 was equal in size to the industries of all other European coun-

tries combined. No doubt, Britain's certainty about its mission in the world in the nineteenth century was grounded in its incredible material success story.

The Spread of Industrialization

Beginning first in Great Britain, industrialization spread to the continental countries of Europe and the United States at different times and speeds during the nineteenth century. First to be industrialized on the Continent were Belgium, France, and the German states and in North America, the new nation of the United States. Not until after 1850 did the Industrial Revolution spread to the rest of Europe and other parts of the world.

Industrialization on the Continent

Industrialization on the Continent faced numerous hurdles, and as it proceeded in earnest after 1815, it did so along lines that were somewhat different from Britain's. Lack of technical knowledge was initially a major obstacle to industrialization. But the continental countries possessed an advantage here; they could simply borrow British techniques and practices. Of course, the British tried to prevent that. Until 1825, British artisans were prohibited from leaving the country; until 1842, the export of important machinery and machine parts was forbidden. Nevertheless, the British were not able to control this situation by legislation. Already by 1825, there were at least 2,000 skilled British mechanics on the Continent, and British equipment was also being sold abroad, whether legally or illegally.

Gradually, the Continent achieved technological independence as local people learned all the skills their British teachers had to offer. By the 1840s, a new generation of skilled mechanics from Belgium and France was spreading their knowledge east and south. More importantly, however, continental countries, especially France and the German states, began to establish a wide range of technical schools to train engineers and mechanics.

That government played an important role in this regard brings us to a second difference between British and continental industrialization. Governments in most of the continental countries were accustomed to playing a significant role in economic affairs. Furthering the development of industrialization was a logical extension of that attitude. Hence, governments provided for the costs of technical education; awarded grants to inventors and foreign entrepreneurs; exempted foreign industrial equipment from import duties; and in some places, even financed factories. Of equal, if not greater importance in the long run, governments actively bore much of the cost of building roads and canals, deepening and widening river channels, and constructing railroads. By 1850, a network of iron rails had spread across Europe, although only Germany and Belgium had completed major parts of their systems by that time.

The Industrial Revolution on the Continent occurred in three major centers between 1815 and 1850—Belgium, France, and the German states. Here, too, cotton played an important role, although it was not as significant as the iron and coal of heavy industry. As traditional methods persisted alongside the new methods in cotton manufacturing, the new steam engine came to be used primarily in mining and metallurgy on the Continent rather than in textile manufacturing.

The Industrial Revolution in the United States

In 1800, the United States was an agrarian society. There were no cities with populations of more than 100,000,

◆ **The Crystal Palace.** The Great Exhibition, organized in 1851, was a symbol of the success of Great Britain, which had become the world's first and richest industrial nation. Over 100,000 exhibits were housed in the Crystal Palace, a giant structure of cast iron and glass. This illustration shows the front of the palace and some of its numerous visitors.

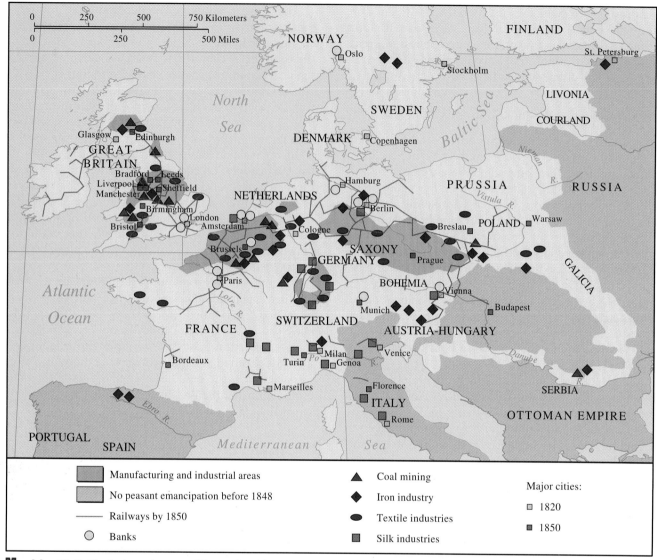

Map 21.2 The Industrialization of Europe by 1850.

and six out of every seven American workers were farmers. By 1860, however, the population had grown from 5 to 30 million people, larger than Great Britain. Almost half of them lived west of the Appalachian mountains. The number of states had more than doubled, from sixteen to thirty-four, and nine American cities had populations of more than 100,000. Only 50 percent of American workers were farmers. From 1800 to the eve of the Civil War, the United States had experienced an Industrial Revolution and the urbanization that accompanied it.

The initial application of machinery to production was accomplished—as in continental Europe—by borrowing from Great Britain. A British immigrant, Samuel

Slater, established the first textile factory using water-powered spinning machines in Rhode Island in 1790. By 1813, factories with power looms copied from British versions were being established. Soon thereafter, however, Americans began to equal or surpass British technical inventions. The Harpers Ferry arsenal, for example, built muskets with interchangeable parts. Because all the individual parts of a musket were identical (e.g., all triggers were the same), the final product could be put together quickly and easily; this enabled Americans to avoid the more costly system in which skilled craftsmen fitted together individual parts made separately. The so-called "American system" reduced costs and revolutionized pro-

"S-t-e-a-m-boat a-coming!"

Steamboats and railroads were crucial elements in a transportation revolution that enabled industrialists to expand markets by shipping goods cheaply and efficiently. At the same time, these marvels of technology aroused a sense of power and excitement that was an important aspect of the triumph of industrialization. The American novelist Mark Twain captured this sense of excitement in this selection from Life on the Mississippi.

Mark Twain, *Life on the Mississippi*

After all these years I can picture that old time to myself now, just as it was then: the white town drowsing in the sunshine of a summer's morning; the streets empty, or pretty nearly so; one or two clerks sitting in front of the Water street stores, with their splint-bottomed chairs tilted back against the walls, chins on breasts, hats slouched over their faces, asleep; . . . two or three lonely little freight piles scattered about the "levee"; a pile of "skids" on the slope of the stone-paved wharf, and the fragrant town drunkard asleep in the shadow of them; . . . the great Mississippi, the majestic, the magnificent Mississippi, rolling its mile-wide along, shining in the sun; the dense forest away on the other side; the "point" above the town, and the "point" below, bounding the river glimpse and turning it into a sort of sea, and withal a very still and brilliant and lonely one. Presently a film of dark smoke appears above on those remote "points"; instantly a negro drayman, famous for his quick eye and prodigious voice, lifts up to cry, "S-t-e-a-m-boat a-coming'!" and the scene changes! The town drunkard stirs, the clerks wake up, a furious clatter of drays follows, every house and store pours out a human contribution, and all in a twinkling the dead town [Hannibal, Missouri] is alive and moving. Drays, carts, men, boys, all go hurrying from many quarters to a common center, the wharf. Assembled there, the people fasten their eyes upon the coming boat as upon a wonder they are seeing for the first time. And the boat is rather a handsome sight, too. She is long and sharp and trim and pretty; she has two tall, fancy-topped chimneys, with a gilded device of some kind swung between them; a fanciful pilot-house, all glass and "ginger bread," perched on top of the "texas" deck behind them; the paddle-boxes are gorgeous with a picture or with gilded rays above the boat's name; the boiler deck, the hurricane deck, and the texas deck are fenced and ornamented with clean white railings; there is a flag gallantly flying from the jack-staff; the furnace doors are open and the fires glaring bravely; the upper decks are black with passengers; the captain stands by the big bell, calm, imposing, the envy of all; great volumes of the blackest smoke are rolling and tumbling out of the chimneys—a husbanded grandeur created with a bit of pitch pine just before arriving at a town; the crew are grouped on the forecastle; the broad stage is run far out over the port bow, and an envied deck-hand stands picturesquely on the end of it with a coil of rope in his hand; the pent steam is screaming through the gauge-cocks; the captain lifts his hand, a bell rings, the wheels stop; then they turn back, churning the water to foam, and the steam is at rest. Then such a scramble as there is to get aboard, and to get ashore, and to take in freight and to discharge freight, all at one and the same time; and such a yelling and cursing as the mates facilitate it all with! Ten minutes later the steamer is under way again, with no flag on the jack-staff and no black smoke issuing from the chimneys. After ten more minutes the town is dead again, and the town drunkard asleep by the skids once more.

---

duction by saving labor, important to a society that had few skilled artisans.

Unlike Britain, the United States was a large country. The lack of a good system of internal transportation seemed to limit American economic development by making the transport of goods prohibitively expensive. This was gradually remedied, however. Thousands of miles of roads and canals were built linking east and west. The steamboat facilitated transportation on the Great Lakes, Atlantic coastal waters, and rivers. It was especially important to the Mississippi Valley; by 1860, 1,000 steamboats plied that river (see the box above). Most important of all in the development of an American transportation system was the railroad. Beginning with 100 miles in 1830, by 1860 there were more than 27,000 miles of railroad track covering the United States. This transportation revolution turned the United States into a single massive market for the manufactured goods of the Northeast, the early center of American industrialization.

Labor for the growing number of factories in this area came primarily from rural New England. The United States did not possess a large number of craftsmen, but it did have a rapidly expanding farm population; its size in the Northeast soon outstripped the available farmland. While some of this excess population, especially men, went West, others, mostly women, found work in the new textile and shoe factories of New England. Indeed, women made up more than 80 percent of the laboring force in the large textile factories. In Massachusetts mill towns, company boarding houses provided rooms for large numbers of young women who worked for several years before marriage. Outside Massachusetts, factory owners sought entire families including children to work in their mills; one mill owner ran this advertisement in a newspaper in Utica, New York: "Wanted: A few sober and industrious families of at least five children each, over the age of eight years, are wanted at the Cotton Factory in Whitestown. Widows with large families would do well to attend this notice." When a decline in rural births threatened to dry up this labor pool in the 1830s and 1840s, European immigrants, especially poor and unskilled Irish, English, Scottish, and Welsh, appeared in large numbers to replace American women and children in the factories.

By 1860, the United States was well on its way to being an industrial nation. In the Northeast, the most industrialized section of the country, per capita income was 40 percent higher than the national average. Diets, it has been argued, were better and more varied; machine-made clothing was more abundant. Nevertheless, despite a growing belief in a myth of social mobility based on equality of economic opportunity, the reality was that the richest 10 percent of the population in the cities held 70 to 80 percent of the wealth compared to 50 percent in 1800. Nevertheless, American historians generally argue that while the rich got richer, the poor, as a result of experiencing an increase in their purchasing power, did not get poorer.

The Social Impact of the Industrial Revolution

Eventually, the Industrial Revolution revolutionized the social life of Europe and the world. Although much of Europe remained bound by its traditional ways, already in the first half of the nineteenth century, the social impact of the Industrial Revolution was being felt, and future avenues of growth were becoming apparent. Vast changes in the number of people and where they lived were already dramatically evident.

Population Growth

Population increases had already begun in the eighteenth century, but they became dramatic in the nineteenth century. In 1750, the total European population stood at an estimated 140 million; by 1800, it had increased to 187 million and by 1850 to 266 million, almost twice its 1750 level. The key to the expansion of population was the decline in death rates evident throughout Europe. Two major causes explain this decline. There was a drop in the number of deaths from famines, epidemics, and war. Major epidemic diseases, in particular, such as plague and smallpox, declined noticeably, although small-scale epidemics continued. The ordinary death rate also declined as a general increase in the food supply, already evident in the agricultural revolution of Britain in the late eighteenth century, spread to more areas. More food enabled a greater number of people to be better fed and therefore more resistant to disease. Famine largely disappeared from western Europe, although there were dramatic exceptions in isolated areas where overpopulation magnified the already existing problem of rural poverty. In Ireland, it produced the century's great catastrophe.

Ireland was one of the most oppressed areas in western Europe. The predominantly Catholic peasant population rented land from mostly absentee British Protestant landlords whose primary concern was collecting their rents. Irish peasants lived in mud hovels in desperate poverty. The cultivation of the potato, a nutritious and relatively easy food to grow that produced three times as much food per acre as grain, gave Irish peasants a basic staple that enabled them to survive and even expand in numbers. Between 1781 and 1845, the Irish population doubled from 4 to 8 million. Probably half of this population depended on the potato for survival. In the summer of 1845, the potato crop in Ireland was struck by blight due to a fungus that turned the potato black. Between 1845 and 1851, the Great Famine decimated the Irish population. More than 1 million died of starvation and disease while almost 2 million emigrated to the United States and Britain. Of all the European nations, only Ireland had a declining population in the nineteenth century.

The flight of so many Irish to America reminds us that the traditional safety valve for overpopulation has always been emigration. Between 1821 and 1850, the number of emigrants from Europe averaged about 110,000 a year. Most of these emigrants came from places like Ireland and southern Germany, where peasant life had been reduced to marginal existence. More often than emigration, however, the rural masses sought a solution to their poverty by moving to towns and cities within their own countries to find work. It should not astonish us then that the first half of the nineteenth century was a period of rapid urbanization.

The Growth of Cities

Cities and towns grew dramatically in the first half of the nineteenth century, a phenomenon related to industrialization. Cities had traditionally been centers for princely courts, government and military offices, churches, and commerce. By 1850, especially in Great Britain and Belgium, they were rapidly becoming places for manufacturing and industry. With the steam engine, entrepreneurs could locate their manufacturing plants in urban centers where they had ready access to transportation facilities and unemployed people from the country looking for work.

In 1800, Great Britain had one major city, London, with a population of 1 million, and six cities between 50,000 and 100,000. Fifty years later, London's population had swelled to 2,363,000, and there were nine cities over 100,000 and eighteen cities with populations between 50,000 and 100,000. When the population of cities under 50,000 are added to these, we realize that more than 50 percent of the British population lived in towns and cities by 1850. Urban populations also grew on the Continent, but less dramatically.

URBAN LIVING CONDITIONS IN THE EARLY INDUSTRIAL REVOLUTION

The dramatic growth of cities in the first half of the nineteenth century produced miserable living conditions for many of the inhabitants. Of course, this had been true for centuries in European cities, but the rapid urbanization associated with the Industrial Revolution intensified the problems in the first half of the nineteenth century and made these wretched conditions all the more apparent. Wealthy, middle-class inhabitants, as usual, insulated themselves as best they could, often living in suburbs or the outer ring of the city where they could have individual houses and gardens. In the inner ring of the city stood the small row houses, some with gardens, of the artisans and lower middle class. Finally, located in the center of most industrial towns were the row houses of the industrial workers. This report on working-class housing in the British city of Birmingham in 1843 gives an idea of the general conditions they faced:

> The courts [of working class row houses] are extremely numerous; . . . a very large portion of the poorer classes of the inhabitants reside in them. . . . The courts vary in the num-

ber of the houses which they contain, from four to twenty, and most of these houses are three stories high, and built, as it is termed, back to back. There is a wash-house, an ash-pit, and a privy at the end, or on one side of the court, and not unfrequently one or more pigsties and heaps of manure. Generally speaking, the privies in the old courts are in a most filthy condition. Many which we have inspected were in a state which renders it impossible for us to conceive how they could be used; they were without doors and overflowing with filth.

Rooms were not large and were frequently overcrowded, as this government report of 1838 revealed: "I entered several of the tenements. In one of them, on the ground floor, I found six persons occupying a very small room, two in bed, ill with fever. In the room above this were two more persons in one bed, ill with fever." Another report said: "There were 63 families where there were at least five persons to one bed; and there were some in which even six were packed in one bed, lying at the top and bottom—children and adults."[1]

Sanitary conditions in these towns were appalling. Due to the lack of municipal direction, city streets were often used as sewers and open drains: "In the centre of this street is a gutter, into which potato parings, the refuse of animal and vegetable matters of all kinds, the dirty water from the washing of clothes and of the houses, are all poured, and there they stagnate and putrefy."[2] Unable to deal with human excrement, cities in the new industrial

◆ **A New Industrial Town.** Cities and towns grew dramatically in Britain in the first half of the nineteenth century, largely as a result of industrialization. Pictured here is Saltaire, a model textile factory and town founded near Bradford by Titus Salt in 1851. To facilitate the transportation of goods, the town was built on the Leeds and Liverpool canals.

era smelled horrible and were extraordinarily unhealthy. Towns and cities were fundamentally death traps. As deaths outnumbered births in most large cities in the first half of the nineteenth century, only a constant influx of people from the country kept them alive and growing.

To many of the well-to-do middle classes, this situation presented a clear danger to society. Were not these masses of workers, sunk in crime, disease, and immorality, a potential threat to their own well-being? Might not the masses be organized and used by unscrupulous demagogues to overthrow the established order? Some observers, however, wondered if the workers could be held responsible for their fate. One of the best of a new breed of urban reformers was Edwin Chadwick (1800–1890). Chadwick became obsessed with eliminating the poverty and squalor of the metropolitan areas. As secretary of the Poor Law Commission, he initiated a passionate search for detailed facts about the living conditions of the working classes. After three years of investigation, Chadwick summarized the results in his *Report on the Condition of the Labouring Population of Great Britain*, published in 1842. In it he concluded that "the various forms of epidemic, endemic, and other disease" were directly caused by the "atmospheric impurities produced by decomposing animal and vegetable substances, by damp and filth, and close overcrowded dwellings [prevailing] amongst the population in every part of the kingdom." Such conditions, he argued, could be eliminated. As to the means: "The primary and most important measures, and at the same time the most practicable, and within the recognized province of public administration, are drainage, the removal of all refuse of habitations, streets, and roads, and the improvement of the supplies of water."[3] In other words, Chadwick was advocating a system of modern sanitary reforms consisting of efficient sewers and a supply of piped water. Six years after his report and largely due to his efforts, Britain's first Public Health Act created a National Board of Health empowered to form local boards that would establish modern sanitary systems.

New Social Classes: The Industrial Middle Class

The rise of industrial capitalism produced a new middle-class group. The bourgeois or middle class was not new; it had existed since the emergence of cities in the Middle Ages. Originally, the bourgeois was the burgher or town dweller, whether active as a merchant, official, artisan, lawyer, or man of letters, who enjoyed a special set of rights from the charter of his town. As wealthy townspeople bought land, the original meaning of the word *bourgeois* became lost, and the term came to include peo-

ple involved in commerce, industry, and banking as well as professionals, such as lawyers, teachers, and physicians, and government officials at varying levels. At the lower end of the economic scale were master craftsmen and shopkeepers.

Lest we make the industrial middle class too much of an abstraction, we need to look at who the new industrial entrepreneurs actually were. These were the people who constructed the factories, purchased the machines, and figured out where the markets were. Their qualities included resourcefulness, single-mindedness, resolution, initiative, vision, ambition, and often, of course, greed. As Jedediah Strutt, a cotton manufacturer said, "Getting of money . . . is the main business of the life of men." But this was not an easy task. The early industrial entrepreneurs were called on to superintend an enormous array of functions that are handled today by teams of managers; they raised capital, determined markets, set company objectives, organized the factory and its labor, and trained supervisors who could act for them. The opportunities for making money were great, but the risks were also tremendous.

By 1850, in Britain at least, the kind of traditional entrepreneurship that had created the Industrial Revolution was declining and being replaced by a new business aristocracy. This new generation of entrepreneurs stemmed from the professional and industrial middle classes, especially as sons inherited the successful businesses established by their fathers. Increasingly, the new industrial entrepreneurs—the bankers and owners of factories and mines—came to amass much wealth and play an important role alongside the traditional landed elites of their societies. The Industrial Revolution began at a time when the preindustrial agrarian world was still largely dominated by landed elites. As the new bourgeoisie bought great estates and acquired social respectability, they also sought political power, and in the course of the nineteenth century, their wealthiest members would merge with those old elites.

New Social Classes: Workers in the Industrial Age

At the same time the members of the industrial middle class were seeking to reduce the barriers between themselves and the landed elite, they were also trying to separate themselves from the laboring classes below them. The working class was actually a mixture of different groups in the first half of the nineteenth century. In the course of the nineteenth century, factory workers would form an industrial proletariat, but in the first half of that century, they by no means constituted a majority of the working class in any major city, even in Britain. According to the 1851 census in Britain, while there were 1.8 million agricultural laborers and 1 million domestic servants, there were only 811,000 workers in the cotton and woolen industries. Even one-third of these were still working in small workshops or in their own homes.

WORKING CONDITIONS FOR THE INDUSTRIAL WORKING CLASS

Workers in the new industrial factories faced wretched working conditions. Unquestionably, in the early decades of the Industrial Revolution, "places of work," as early factories were called, were dreadful. Work hours ranged from twelve to sixteen hours a day, six days a week, with a half hour for lunch and dinner. There was no security of employment and no minimum wage. The worst conditions were in the cotton mills where temperatures were especially debilitating. One report noted that "in the cotton-spinning work, these creatures are kept, fourteen hours in each day, locked up, summer and winter, in a heat of from eighty to eighty-four degrees." Mills were also dirty, dusty, and unhealthy:

> Not only is there not a breath of sweet air in these truly infernal scenes, but, . . . there is the abominable and pernicious stink of the gas to assist in the murderous effects of the heat. In addition to the noxious effluvia of the gas, mixed with the steam, there are the dust, and what is called cotton-flyings or fuz, which the unfortunate creatures have to inhale; and . . . the notorious fact is that well constitutioned men are rendered old and past labour at forty years of age, and that children are rendered decrepit and deformed, and thousands upon thousands of them slaughtered by consumptions, before they arrive at the age of sixteen.[4]

Thus ran a report on working conditions in the cotton industry in 1824.

Conditions in the coal mines were also harsh. The introduction of steam power in the coal mines meant only that steam-powered engines mechanically lifted coal to the top. Inside the mines, men still bore the burden of digging the coal out while horses, mules, women, and children hauled coal carts on rails to the lift. Dangers abounded in coal mines; cave-ins, explosions, and gas fumes (called "bad air") were a way of life. The cramped conditions—tunnels often did not exceed three or four feet in height—and constant dampness in the mines resulted in deformed bodies and ruined lungs.

Both children and women were employed in large numbers in early factories and mines. Children had been an important part of the family economy in preindustrial times, working in the fields or carding and spinning wool at home with the growth of cottage industry. In the Industrial Revolution, however, child labor was exploited more than ever and in a considerably more systematic fashion (see the box on p. 444). The owners of cotton factories appreciated certain features of child labor. Children had an especially delicate touch as spinners of cotton. Their smaller size made it easier for them to crawl under machines to gather loose cotton. Moreover, children were more easily broken to factory work. Above all, children represented a cheap supply of labor. In 1821, 49 percent of the British people were under twenty years of age. Hence, children made up a particularly abundant supply of labor, and they were paid only about one-sixth or one-third of what a man was paid. In the cotton factories in 1838, children under eighteen made up 29 percent of the total workforce; children as young as seven worked twelve to fifteen hours per day six days a week in cotton mills.

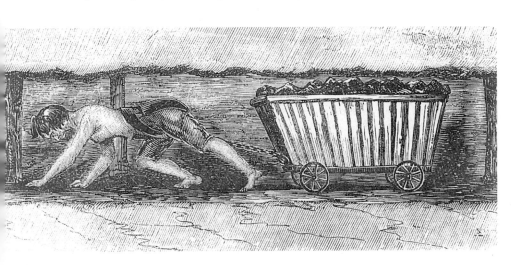

◆ **Women in the Mines.** Both women and children were often employed in the early factories and mines of the nineteenth century. As is evident in this illustration of a woman dragging a cart loaded with coal behind her, they often worked under very trying conditions.

Child Labor: Discipline in the Textile Mills

Child labor was certainly not new, but in the early Industrial Revolution it was exploited more systematically. These selections are taken from the Report of Sadler's Committee, which was commissioned in 1832 to inquire into the condition of child factory workers.

How They Kept the Children Awake

It is a very frequent thing at Mr. Marshall's [at Shrewsbury] where the least children were employed (for there were plenty working at six years of age), for Mr. Horseman to start the mill earlier in the morning than he formerly did; and provided a child should be drowsy, the overlooker walks round the room with a stick in his hand, and he touches that child on the shoulder, and says, "Come here." In a corner of the room there is an iron cistern; it is filled with water; he takes this boy, and takes him up by the legs, and dips him over head in the cistern, and sends him to work for the remainder of the day. . . .

What means were taken to keep the children to their work?—Sometimes they would tap them over the head, or nip them over the nose, or give them a pinch of snuff, or throw water in their faces, or pull them off where they were, and job them about to keep them waking.

The Sadistic Overlooker

Samuel Downe, age 29, factory worker living near Leeds; at the age of about ten began work at Mr. Marshall's mills at Shrewsbury, where the customary hours when work was brisk were generally 5 A.M. to 8 P.M., sometimes from 5:30 A.M. to 8 or 9:

What means were taken to keep the children awake and vigilant, especially at the termination of such a day's labour as you have described?—There was generally a blow or a box, or a tap with a strap, or sometimes the hand.

Have you yourself been strapped?—Yes, most severely, till I could not bear to sit upon a chair without having pillows, and through that I left. I was strapped both on my own legs, and then I was put upon a man's back, and than strapped and buckled with two straps to an iron pillar, and flogged, and all by one overlooker; after that he took a piece of tow, and twisted it in the shape of a cord, and put it in my mouth, and tied it behind my head.

He gagged you?—Yes; and then he ordered me to run round a part of the machinery where he was overlooker, and he stood at one end, and every time I came there he struck me with a stick, which I believe was an ash plant, and which he generally carried in his hand, and sometimes he hit me, and sometimes he did not; and one of the men in the room came and begged me off, and that he let me go, and not beat me any more, and consequently he did.

You have been beaten with extraordinary severity?—Yes, I was beaten so that I had not power to cry at all, or hardly speak at one time. What age were you at that time?—Between 10 and 11.

By 1830, women and children made up two-thirds of the cotton industry's labor. However, as the number of children employed declined under the Factory Act of 1833, their places were taken by women, who came to dominate the labor forces of the early factories. Women made up 50 percent of the labor force in textile (cotton and woolen) factories before 1870. They were mostly unskilled labor and were paid half or less of what men received. Excessive working hours for women were outlawed in 1844, but only in textile factories and mines; not until 1867 were they outlawed in craft workshops.

The employment of children and women in large part represents a continuation of a preindustrial kinship pattern. Cottage industry had always involved the efforts of the entire family, and it seemed perfectly natural to continue this pattern. Men migrating from the countryside to industrial towns and cities took their wives and children with them into the factory or into the mines. Of 136 employees in Robert Peel's factory at Bury in 1801, 95 belonged to twenty-six families. The impetus for this family work often came from the family itself. The factory owner Jedediah Strutt was opposed to child labor under ten but was forced by parents to take children as young as seven.

The employment of large numbers of women in factories did not produce a significant transformation in female working patterns, as was once assumed. Studies of urban households in France and Britain, for example, have revealed that throughout the nineteenth century traditional types of female labor still predominated in the women's work world. In 1851, fully 40 percent of the female workforce in Britain consisted of domestic servants. In France, the largest group of female workers, 40 percent, worked in agriculture. In addition, only 20 percent of female workers labored in Britain's factories, only 10 percent in France. Regional and local studies have also indicated that most of them were single women. Few married women worked outside their homes.

The Factory Acts that limited the work hours of children and women also began to break up the traditional kinship pattern of work and led to a new pattern based on a separation of work and home. Men were expected to be responsible for the primary work obligations while women assumed daily control of the family and performed low-paying jobs such as laundry work that could be done in the home. Domestic industry made it possible for women to continue their contributions to family survival.

Efforts at Change: The Workers

Before long, workers in Great Britain began to look to the formation of labor organizations to gain decent wages and working conditions. Despite government opposition, new associations known as trade unions were formed by skilled workers in a number of new industries, including the cotton spinners, ironworkers, coal miners, and shipwrights. These unions served two purposes. One was to preserve their own workers' positions by limiting entry into their trade; another was to gain benefits from the employers. These early trade unions had limited goals. They favored a working-class struggle against employers, but only to win improvements for the members of their own trades. The largest and most successful was the Amalgamated Society of Engineers, formed in 1850. Its provision of generous unemployment benefits in return for a small weekly payment was precisely the kind of practical gains these trade unions sought.

Trade unionism was not the only type of collective action by workers in the early decades of the Industrial Revolution. The Luddites were skilled craftsmen in the Midlands and northern England who in 1812 attacked the machines that they believed threatened their livelihoods. These attacks, however, failed to stop the industrial mechanization of Britain. Nevertheless, the inability of 12,000 troops to find the culprits provides stunning evidence of the local support they received in their area.

A more meaningful expression of the attempts of British workers to improve their condition developed in the movement known as Chartism. Its aim was to achieve political democracy. A People's Charter drawn up in 1838 demanded universal male suffrage and payment for members of Parliament. Two national petitions incorporating

◆ **A Trade Union Membership Card.** Skilled workers in a number of new industries formed trade unions in an attempt to gain higher wages, better working conditions, and special benefits. The scenes at the bottom of this membership card for the Associated Shipwright's Society illustrate some of the medical and social benefits for its members.

these points, affixed with millions of signatures, were presented to Parliament in 1839 and 1842. Although both were rejected by the members of Parliament as "fatal to all the purposes for which government exists," Chartism had not been a total failure. Its true significance stemmed from its ability to arouse and organize millions of working-class men and women, to give them a sense of working-class consciousness that they had not really possessed before. The political education of working people was important to the ultimate acceptance of all the points of the People's Charter in the future.

Efforts at Change: Reformers and Government

Efforts to improve the worst conditions of the industrial factory system also came from outside the ranks of the working classes. Reform-minded individuals, be they factory owners who felt twinges of conscience or social reformers in Parliament, campaigned against the evils of the industrial factory, especially condemning the abuse of children. Their efforts eventually met with success, especially in the reform-minded decades of the 1830s and 1840s. The Factory Act of 1833 stipulated that children between nine and thirteen could work only eight hours a day; those between thirteen and eighteen, twelve hours. Another piece of legislation in 1833 required that children between nine and thirteen have at least two hours of elementary education during the working day. In 1847, the Ten Hours Act reduced the work day for children between thirteen and eighteen to ten hours. Women were also now included in the ten-hour limitation. In 1842, a Coal Mines Act eliminated the employment of boys under ten and women in mines. Eventually, men too would benefit from the move to restrict factory hours.

*C*onclusion

The Industrial Revolution became one of the major forces of change in the nineteenth century as it led Western civilization into the industrial era that has characterized the modern world. Beginning in Britain, its spread to the Continent and the new American nation ensured its growth and domination of the Western world.

The Industrial Revolution seemed to prove to Europeans the underlying assumption of the Scientific Revolution of the seventeenth century—that human beings were capable of dominating nature. By rationally manipulating the material environment for human benefit, people could create new levels of material prosperity and produce machines not dreamed of in their wildest imaginings. Lost in the excitement of the Industrial Revolution were the voices that pointed to the dehumanization of the workforce and the alienation from one's work, one's associates, one's self, and the natural world.

The Industrial Revolution also transformed the social world of Europe. The creation of an industrial proletariat produced a whole new force for change. The development of a wealthy industrial middle class presented a challenge to the long-term hegemony of landed wealth. While that wealth had been threatened by the fortunes of commerce, it had never been overturned. But the new bourgeoisie was more demanding. How, in some places, this new industrial bourgeoisie came to play a larger role in the affairs of state will become evident in the next chapter.

NOTES

1. Quotations can be found in E. Royston Pike, *Human Documents of the Industrial Revolution in Britain* (London, 1966), pp. (in order of quotations) 320, 314, 343.

2. Ibid., p. 315.
3. Ibid., pp. 343–344.
4. Ibid., pp. 60–61.

SUGGESTIONS FOR FURTHER READING

The well-written work by D. Landes, *The Unbound Prometheus: Technological Change and Industrial Development in Western Europe from 1750 to the Present* (Cambridge, 1969) is still the best introduction to the Industrial Revolution. Although more technical, also of value are C. Trebilcock, *The Industrialization of the Continental* *Powers, 1780–1914* (London, 1981); and S. Pollard, *Peaceful Conquest: The Industrialization of Europe, 1760–1970* (Oxford, 1981). There is a good collection of essays in P. Mathias and J. A. Davis, eds., *The First Industrial Revolutions* (Oxford, 1989); and M. Teich and R. Porter, eds., *The Industrial Revolution in National Con-*

text: *Europe and the USA* (Cambridge, 1996). A volume in the Fontana Economic History of Europe edited by C. M. Cipolla, *The Industrial Revolution* (London, 1973) is also valuable. Although older and dated, T. S. Ashton, *The Industrial Revolution, 1760–1830* (New York, 1948) still provides an interesting introduction to the Industrial Revolution in Britain. Much better, however, are P. Mathias, *The First Industrial Nation: An Economic History of Britain, 1700–1914*, 2d ed. (New York, 1983); and R. Brown, *Society and Economy in Modern Britain, 1700–1850* (London, 1991). On the spread of industrialization to the Continent, see A. Milward and S. B. Saul, *The Development of the Economies of Continental Europe* (Oxford, 1977).

Given the importance of Great Britain in the Industrial Revolution, a number of books are available that place the Industrial Revolution in Britain into a broader context. See E. J. Evans, *The Forging of the Modern State: Early Industrial Britain, 1783–1870* (London, 1983); S. Checkland, *British Public Policy, 1776–1939: An Economic, Social and Political Perspective* (Cambridge, 1983); and E. J. Hobsbawn, *Industry and Empire* (London, 1968).

The early industrialization of the United States is examined in P. Temin, *Causal Factors in American Economic Growth in the Nineteenth Century* (London, 1975); and B. Hindle and S. Lubar, *Engines of Change: The American Industrial Revolution, 1790–1860* (Washington, D. C., 1986). On the economic ties between Great Britain and the United States, see D. Jeremy, *Transatlantic Industrial Revolution: The Diffusion of Textile Technology between Britain and America, 1790–1830* (Cambridge, Mass., 1981).

A general discussion of population growth in Europe can be found in T. McKeown, *The Modern Rise of Population* (London, 1976), although it has been criticized for its emphasis on nutrition and hygiene as the two major causes of that growth. For an examination of urban growth, see the older but classic work of A. F. Weber, *The Growth of Cities in the Nineteenth Century: A Study in Statistics* (Ithaca, N.Y., 1963); and the more recent work by A. R. Sutcliffe, *Towards the Planned City: Germany, Britain, the United States and France, 1780–1914* (Oxford, 1981). C. Kinealy, *A Death-Dealing Famine: The Great Hunger in Ireland* (Chicago, 1997) is a good account of the great Irish tragedy. Many of the works cited above have much information on the social impact of the Industrial Revolution, but additional material is available in C. Morazé, *The Triumph of the Middle Classes* (London, 1966); F. Crouzet, *The First Industrialists: The Problems of Origins* (Cambridge, 1985), on British entrepreneurs; E. P. Thompson, *The Making of the English Working Class* (New York, 1964); and E. Gauldie, *Cruel Habitations, A History of Working-Class Housing, 1790–1918* (London, 1974). G. Himmelfarb, *The Idea of Poverty: England in the Early Industrial Age* (New York, 1984) traces the concepts of poverty and poor from the mid-eighteenth century to the mid-nineteenth century. A valuable work on female labor patterns is L. A. Tilly and J. W. Scott, *Women, Work, and Family* (New York, 1978).

CHAPTER

22

Reaction, Revolution, and Romanticism, 1815–1850

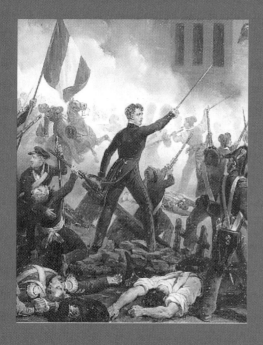

In September 1814, hundreds of foreigners began to converge on Vienna, the capital city of the Austrian Empire. Many were members of European royalty— kings, princes, archdukes, and their wives— accompanied by their diplomatic advisers and scores of servants. Their congenial host was the Austrian emperor Francis I, who never tired of providing Vienna's guests with concerts, glittering balls, sumptuous feasts, and an endless array of hunting parties. One participant remembered, "Eating, fireworks, public illuminations. For eight or ten days, I haven't been able to work at all. What a life!" Of course, not every waking hour was spent in pleasure during this gathering of notables, known to history as the Congress of Vienna. These people were also representatives of all the states that had fought Napoleon, and their real business was to arrange a final peace settlement after almost a decade of war. On June 8, 1815, they finally completed their task.

The forces of upheaval unleashed during the French revolutionary and Napoleonic wars were temporarily quieted in 1815 as rulers sought to restore stability by reestablishing much of the old order to a Europe ravaged by war. Kings, landed aristocrats, and bureaucratic elites regained their control over domestic governments while internationally the forces of conservatism tried to maintain the new status quo; some states even used military force to intervene in the internal affairs of other countries in their desire to crush revolutions.

But the Western world had been changed, and it would not readily go back to the old system. New ideologies of change, especially liberalism and nationalism, both products of the revolutionary upheaval initiated in France, had become too powerful to be contained. Not content with the status quo, the forces of change gave rise first to the revolts and revolutions that periodically shook Europe in the 1820s and 1830s and then to the widespread revolutions of 1848. Some of the revolutions and revolutionaries were successful; most were not. Although the old order usually appeared to have prevailed, by 1850, it was apparent that its days

Congress of Vienna

Revolutions in Belgium, Poland, and Italian states

July Revolution in France

Revolutions in France, German and Italian states, and Austrian Empire

Revolutions in Latin America

Germanic Confederation established

Reform Act in Britain

Frankfurt Assembly

Shelley, *Prometheus Unbound*   Beethoven's Ninth Symphony

Shelley, *Frankenstein*   Friedrich, *Man and Woman Gazing at the Moon*

were numbered. This perception was reinforced by the changes wrought by the Industrial Revolution. Together the forces unleashed by the dual revolutions—the French Revolution and the Industrial Revolution—made it impossible to return to prerevolutionary Europe. Nevertheless, although these two revolutions initiated what historians like to call the modern European world, as we study this era, it will also be apparent that much of the old still remained in the midst of the new.

The Conservative Order, 1815–1830

The immediate response to the defeat of Napoleon was the desire to contain revolution and the revolutionary forces by restoring much of the old order. But the triumphant rulers were not naive and realized that they could not return to 1789.

The Peace Settlement

The great powers—Great Britain, Austria, Prussia, and Russia—met at a congress in Vienna in September 1814 to arrange a final peace settlement after the Napoleonic wars. The congress was dominated by the Austrian foreign minister, Prince Klemens von Metternich (1773–1859), who claimed that he was guided at Vienna by the principle of legitimacy. To reestablish peace and stability in Europe, he considered it necessary to restore the legitimate monarchs who would preserve traditional institutions. This had already been done in the restoration of the Bourbons in France and Spain, as well as in the return of a number of rulers to their thrones in the Italian states. Elsewhere, however, the principle of legitimacy was largely ignored and completely overshadowed by more practical considerations of power. The great powers all grabbed lands to add to their states.

In making these territorial rearrangements, the powers at Vienna believed they were following the familiar eighteenth-century practice of maintaining a balance of power or equilibrium among the great powers. Essentially, this meant a balance of political and military forces that guaranteed the independence of the great powers by ensuring that no one country could dominate Europe. For example, to balance Russian gains, Prussia and Austria had been strengthened. According to Metternich, this arrangement had clearly avoided a great danger: "Prussia and Austria are completing their systems of defence; united, the two monarchies form an unconquerable barrier against the enterprises of any conquering prince who might perhaps once again occupy the throne of France or that of Russia."[1]

The Vienna peace settlement of 1815 has sometimes been criticized for its failure to recognize the liberal and national forces unleashed by the French revolutionary and Napoleonic eras. Containing these revolutionary forces was precisely what the diplomats at Vienna hoped to achieve. Their transfers of territories and peoples to the victors to create a new balance of power, with little or no regard for the wishes of the people themselves, was in accord with long-standing traditions of European diplomatic practices. One could hardly expect Metternich, foreign minister of the Austrian Empire, a dynastic state composed of many different peoples, to espouse a principle of self-determination for European nationalities. Whatever its weaknesses, the Congress of Vienna has received credit for establishing a European order that managed to avoid a general European conflict for almost 100 years.

The Conservative Domination: The Concert of Europe

The peace arrangements of 1815 were but the beginning of a conservative reaction determined to contain the liberal and nationalist forces unleashed by the French Revolution. Metternich and his kind were representatives of the ideology known as conservatism (see the box on p. 451). As a modern political philosophy, conservatism dates from 1790 when Edmund Burke wrote his *Reflections on the Revolution in France* in reaction to the French Revolution, especially its radical republican and democratic ideas. Burke maintained that society was a contract, but "the state ought not to be considered as nothing better than a partnership agreement in a trade of pepper and coffee, to be taken up for a temporary interest and to be dissolved by the fancy of the parties." The state was a partnership but one "not only between those who are living, but between those who are living, those who are dead and those who are to be born."[2] No one generation therefore has the right to destroy this partnership; instead each generation has the duty to preserve and transmit it to the next. Burke advised against the violent overthrow of a govern-

♦ **Metternich.** Prince Klemens von Metternich, the foreign minister of Austria, played a major role at the Congress of Vienna as the chief exponent of the principle of legitimacy. To maintain the new conservative order after 1815, Metternich espoused the principle of intervention, by which he meant that the great powers had the right to intervene militarily in other countries in order to crush revolutionary movements against legitimate rulers.

Map 22.1 Europe after the Congress of Vienna.

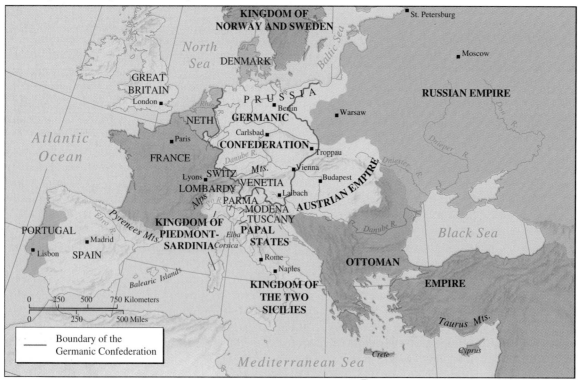

The Voice of Conservatism: Metternich of Austria

There was no greater symbol of conservatism in the first half of the nineteenth century than Prince Klemens von Metternich of Austria. Metternich played a crucial role at the Congress of Vienna and worked tirelessly for thirty years to repress the "revolutionary seed," at he called it, that had been spread to Europe by the "military despotism of Bonaparte."

Klemens von Metternich, *Memoirs*

We are convinced that society can no longer be saved without strong and vigorous resolutions on the part of the Governments still free in their opinions and actions.

We are also convinced that this may be, if the Governments face the truth, if they free themselves from all illusion, if they join their ranks and take their stand on a line of correct, unambiguous, and frankly announced principles.

By this course the monarchs will fulfill the duties imposed upon them by Him who, by entrusting them with power, has charged them to watch over the maintenance of justice, and the rights of all, to avoid the paths of error, and tread firmly in the way of truth. . . .

If the same elements of destruction which are now throwing society into convulsions have existed in all ages—for every age has seen immoral and ambitious men, hypocrites, men of heated imaginations, wrong motives, and wild projects—yet ours, by the single fact of the liberty of the press, possesses more than any preceding age the means of contact, seduction, and attraction whereby to act on these different classes of men.

We are certainly not alone in questioning if society can exist with the liberty of the press, a scourge unknown to the world before the latter half of the seventeenth century, and restrained until the end of the eighteenth, with scarcely any expectations but England—a part of Europe separated from the continent by the sea, as well as by her language and by her peculiar manners.

The first principle to be followed by the monarchs, united as they are by the coincidence of their desires and opinions, should be that of maintaining the stability of political institutions against the disorganized excitement which has taken possession of men's minds; the immutability of principles against the madness of their interpretation; and respect for laws actually in force against a desire for their destruction. . . .

The first and greatest concern for the immense majority of every nation is the stability of the laws, and their uninterrupted action—never their change. Therefore, let the Governments govern, let them maintain the groundwork of their institutions, both ancient and modern; for if it is at all times dangerous to touch them, it certainly would not now, in the general confusion, be wise to do so. . . .

Let them maintain religious principles in all their purity, and not allow the faith to be attacked and morality interpreted according to the social contract or the visions of foolish sectarians.

Let them suppress Secret Societies, that gangrene of society. . . .

To every great State determined to survive the storm there still remain many changes of salvation, and a strong union between the States on the principles we have announced will overcome the storm itself.

ment by revolution, but he did not reject the possibility of change. Sudden change was unacceptable, but that did not eliminate gradual or evolutionary improvements.

Most conservatives favored obedience to political authority, believed that organized religion was crucial to social order, hated revolutionary upheavals, and were unwilling to accept either the liberal demands for civil liberties and representative governments or the nationalistic aspirations generated by the French revolutionary era. The community took precedence over individual rights; society must be organized and ordered, and tradition remained the best guide for order. After 1815, the political philosophy of conservatism was supported by hereditary monarchs, government bureaucracies, landowning aristocracies, and revived churches, be they Protestant or Catholic. Although not unopposed, both internationally and domestically the conservative forces appeared dominant after 1815.

One method used by the great powers to maintain the new status quo they had constructed was the Concert of Europe, according to which Great Britain, Russia, Prussia, and Austria (and later France) agreed to meet periodically in conferences to discuss their common interests and examine measures that "will be judged most salutary for the repose and prosperity of peoples, and for the maintenance of peace in Europe."

Eventually, the five great powers formed a Quintuple Alliance and adopted a principle of intervention that was based on the right of the great powers to send armies into countries where there were revolutions to restore legitimate monarchs to their thrones. Britain refused to agree to the principle, arguing that it had never been the intention of the alliance to interfere in the internal affairs of other states. Ignoring the British response, Austria, Prussia, Russia, and France used military intervention to defeat revolutionary movements in Spain and Italy and to restore legitimate (and conservative) monarchs to their thrones. This success for the policy of intervention was done at a price, however. The Concert of Europe had broken down when the British rejected Metternich's principle of intervention. And although the British had failed to thwart allied intervention in Spain and Italy, they were successful in keeping the continental powers from interfering with the revolutions in Latin America.

THE REVOLT OF LATIN AMERICA

While much of North America had been freed of European domination in the eighteenth century by the American Revolution, Latin America remained in the hands of the Spanish and Portuguese. However, when the Bourbon monarchy of Spain was toppled by Napoleon Bonaparte, Spanish authority in its colonial empire was weakened. By 1810, the disintegration of royal power in Argentina had led to that nation's independence. In Venezuela a bitter struggle for independence was led by Simón Bolivar, hailed as the Liberator. His forces freed Colombia in 1819 and Venezuela in 1821. A second liberator was José de San Martin who liberated Chile in 1817 and then, in 1821, moved on to Lima, Peru, the center of Spanish authority. He was soon joined by Bolivar who assumed the task of crushing the last significant Spanish army in 1824. Mexico and the Central American provinces also achieved their freedom, and by 1825, after Portugal had recognized the independence of Brazil, almost all of Latin America had been freed of colonial domination.

THE GREEK REVOLT, 1821–1832

The principle of intervention proved to be a double-edged sword. Designed to prevent revolution, it could also be used to support revolution if the great powers found it in their interests to do so. In 1821, the Greeks revolted against their Turkish masters. Although subject to Muslim control for 400 years, they had been allowed to maintain their language and their Greek Orthodox faith. A revival of Greek national sentiment at the beginning of the nineteenth century added to the growing desire for "the liberation of the fatherland from the terrible yoke of Turkish oppression." The Greek revolt was soon transformed into a noble cause by an outpouring of European sentiment for the Greeks' struggle. In 1827, a combined British and French fleet went to Greece and defeated a large Turkish fleet. A year later, Russia declared war on the Ottoman Empire and invaded its European provinces of Moldavia and Wallachia. By the Treaty of Adrianople in 1829, which ended the Russian–Turkish war, the Russians received a protectorate over the two provinces. By the same treaty, the Turks agreed to allow Russia, France, and Britain to decide the fate of Greece. In 1830, the three powers declared Greece an independent kingdom and two years later a new royal dynasty was established. The revolution in Greece had been successful only because the great powers themselves supported it. Until 1830 the Greek revolt had been the only successful one in Europe; the conservation domination was still largely intact.

The Conservative Domination: The European States

Between 1815 and 1830, the conservative domination of Europe evident in the Concert of Europe was also apparent in domestic affairs as conservative governments throughout Europe worked to maintain the old order.

In 1815, Great Britain was governed by the aristocratic landowning classes that dominated both houses of Parliament. Within Parliament there were two political factions, the Tories and Whigs. Both of them were still dominated by members of the landed classes, although the Whigs were beginning to receive support from the new industrial middle class generated by industrialization. Tory ministers largely dominated the government until 1830 and had little desire to change the existing political and electoral system. Calls for electoral reforms were met by repression and minor reforms that enabled the Tories to maintain their conservative domination.

In 1814, the Bourbon family was restored to the throne of France in the person of Louis XVIII (1814–1824). Louis understood the need to accept some of the changes brought to France by the revolutionary and Napoleonic eras. He maintained Napoleon's Concordat with the pope and accepted Napoleon's Civil Code with its recognition of the principle of equality before the law. The property rights of those who had purchased confiscated lands during the Revolution were also preserved. In 1824, Louis died and was succeeded by his brother, who became Charles X (1824–1830). Charles's attempt to restore the old regime as far as possible led to public outrage. By 1830, France was on the brink of another revolution.

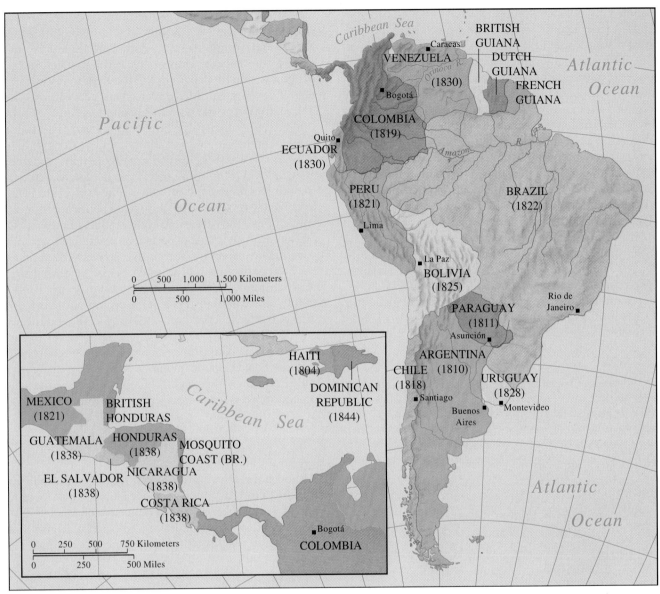

Map 22.2 Latin America in the First Half of the Nineteenth Century.

The Congress of Vienna had established nine states in Italy, including the Kingdom of Sardinia in the north ruled by the House of Savoy; the Kingdom of the Two Sicilies (Naples and Sicily); the Papal States; a handful of small duchies ruled by relatives of the Austrian emperor; and the important northern provinces of Lombardy and Venetia that were now part of the Austrian Empire. Italy was largely under Austrian domination while all the states had extremely reactionary governments eager to smother any liberal or nationalist sentiment. Attempts at change were ruthlessly crushed.

After 1815, the forces of repression were particularly successful in central Europe. The Habsburg empire and its chief agent, Prince Klemens von Metternich, played an important role. Metternich boasted, "You see in me the chief Minister of Police in Europe. I keep an eye on everything. My contacts are such that nothing escapes me."[3] Metternich's spies were everywhere, searching for evidence of liberal or nationalist plots. Metternich worried too much in 1815. Although both liberalism and nationalism emerged in the German states and the Austrian Empire, they were initially weak as central Europe tended to remain under the domination of aristocratic landowning classes and autocratic, centralized monarchies.

The Vienna settlement in 1815 had recognized the existence of thirty-eight sovereign states (called the

Germanic Confederation) in what had once been the Holy Roman Empire. Austria and Prussia were the two great powers while the other states varied considerably in size. The confederation had little real power. It had no real executive, and its only central organ was the federal diet, which needed the consent of all member states to take action. However, it also came to serve as Metternich's instrument to repress revolutionary movements within the German states. When some university professors and students began to organize societies dedicated to fostering the goal of a free, united Germany, Metternich had the diet of the Germanic Confederation place the universities under close supervision and control in 1819. Thereafter, Metternich and the cooperative German rulers maintained the conservative status quo.

The Austrian Empire was a multinational state, a collection of different peoples under the Habsburg emperor who provided a common bond. Eleven peoples of different national origin constituted the empire, including Germans, Czechs, Slovaks, Magyars (Hungarians), Romanians, Slovenes, Poles, Serbians, and Italians. The

♦ **Portrait of Nicholas I.** Tsar Nicholas I was a reactionary ruler who sought to prevent rebellion in Russia by strengthening the government bureaucracy, increasing censorship, and suppressing individual freedom by the use of political police. One of his enemies remarked about his facial characteristics: "The sharply retreating forehead and the lower jaw were expressive of iron will and feeble intelligence."

Germans, though only a quarter of the population, were economically the most advanced and played a leading role in governing Austria. Although these national groups, especially the Hungarians, began to favor the belief that each national group had the right to its own system of government, Metternich managed to repress the nationalist forces and hold the empire together.

At the beginning of the nineteenth century, Russia was overwhelmingly rural, agricultural, and autocratic. The Russian tsar was still regarded as a divine-right monarch. Alexander I (1801–1825) had been raised in the ideas of the Enlightenment and initially seemed willing to make reforms. He relaxed censorship, freed political prisoners, and reformed the educational system. But after the defeat of Napoleon, Alexander became a reactionary, and his government reverted to strict and arbitrary censorship. His brother Nicholas I (1825–1855), who succeeded him, was transformed from a conservative into a strict reactionary after a military revolt at the beginning of his reign. Nicholas strengthened both the bureaucracy and the secret police to maintain order. There would be no revolutions in Russia during the rest of his reign; if he could help it, there would be none in Europe either. Contemporaries called him the Policeman of Europe because of his willingness to use Russian troops to crush revolutions.

The Ideologies of Change

Although the conservative forces were in the ascendancy from 1815 to 1830, powerful movements for change were also at work. These depended on ideas embodied in a series of political philosophies or ideologies that came into their own in the first half of the nineteenth century.

Liberalism

One of these ideologies was liberalism, which owed much to the Enlightenment of the eighteenth century and the American and French Revolutions at the end of that century. In addition, liberalism became even more significant as the Industrial Revolution progressed since the developing industrial middle class largely adopted the doctrine as its own. There were divergences of opinion among people classified as liberals, but all began with a common denominator: the belief that people should be as free from restraint as possible. This opinion is evident in both economic and political liberalism.

Also called classical economics, economic liberalism has as its primary tenet the concept of laissez-faire, or the belief that the state should not interrupt the free play of natural economic forces, especially supply and demand.

Government should not interfere with the economic liberty of the individual and should restrict itself to only three primary functions: defense of the country, police protection of individuals, and the construction and maintenance of public works too expensive for individuals to undertake. If individuals were allowed economic liberty, ultimately they would bring about the maximum good for the maximum number and benefit the general welfare of society.

Like economic liberalism, political liberalism stressed that people should be free from restraint. Politically, liberals came to hold a common set of beliefs. Chief among them was the protection of civil liberties or the basic rights of all people, which included equality before the law, freedom of assembly, speech, and press, and freedom from arbitrary arrest. All of these freedoms should be guaranteed by a written document, such as the American Bill of Rights or the French Declaration of the Rights of Man and the Citizen. In addition to religious toleration for all, most liberals advocated separation of church and state. The right of peaceful opposition to the government in and out of parliament and the making of laws by a representative assembly (legislature) elected by qualified voters constituted two other liberal demands. Many liberals believed, then, in a constitutional monarchy or constitutional state with limits on the powers of government in order to prevent despotism, and in written constitutions that would also help to guarantee these rights.

Many liberals also advocated ministerial responsibility or a system in which ministers of the king were responsible to the legislature rather than to the king, giving the legislative branch a check on the power of the executive. Liberals in the first half of the nineteenth century also believed in a limited suffrage. While all people were entitled to equal civil rights, they should not have equal political rights. The right to vote and hold office would be open only to men who met certain property qualifications. As a political philosophy, liberalism was tied to middle-class, and especially industrial, middle-class men who favored the extension of voting rights so that they could share power with the landowning classes. They had little desire to let the lower classes share that power. Liberals were not democrats.

One of the most prominent advocates of liberalism in the nineteenth century was the English philosopher John Stuart Mill (1806–1873). *On Liberty*, his most famous work published in 1859, has long been regarded as a classic statement on the liberty of the individual (see the box on p. 456). Mill argued for an "absolute freedom of opinion and sentiment on all subjects" that needed to be protected from both government censorship and the tyranny of the majority.

Mill was also instrumental in expanding the meaning of liberalism by becoming an enthusiastic supporter of women's rights. When his attempt to include women in the voting reform bill of 1867 failed, Mill published an essay entitled *On the Subjection of Women*, which he had written earlier with his wife, Harriet Taylor. He argued that "the legal subordination of one sex to the other" was wrong. Differences between women and men, he claimed, were not due to different natures but simply to social practices. With equal education, women could achieve as much as men. *On the Subjection of Women* would become an important work in the nineteenth-century movement for women's rights.

Nationalism

Nationalism can be defined as a state of mind rising out of an awareness of being part of a community that has common institutions, traditions, language, and customs. This community is called a "nation," and it, rather than a dynasty, city-state, or other political unit, becomes the focus of the individual's primary political loyalty. Nationalism did not become a popular force for change until the French Revolution, and even then nationalism was not so much political as cultural with its emphasis on the uniqueness of a particular nationality. Cultural nationalism, however, evolved into political nationalism. The latter advocated that governments should coincide with nationalities. Thus, a divided people such as the Germans wanted national unity in a German nation-state with one central government. Subject peoples, such as the Hungarians, wanted national self-determination or the right to establish their own autonomy rather than be subject to a German minority in a multinational empire.

Nationalism was fundamentally radical in that it threatened to upset the existing political order, both internationally and nationally. A united Germany or united Italy would upset the balance of power established in 1815. By the same token, an independent Hungarian state would mean the breakup of the Austrian Empire. The conservatives tried extremely hard to repress nationalism because they were acutely aware of its potential to bring about such dramatic change.

At the same time, in the first half of the nineteenth century, nationalism and liberalism became strong allies. Most liberals believed that freedom could only be realized by peoples who ruled themselves. One British liberal said, "it is in general a necessary condition of free institutions that the boundaries of government should coincide in the main with those of nationalities." The combination of liberalism with nationalism also gave a cosmopolitan dimension to nationalism. Many nationalists believed that once each people obtained their own state, all nations could be linked into a broader community of all humanity.

The Voice of Liberalism: John Stuart Mill on Liberty

John Stuart Mill (1806–1873) was one of Britain's most famous philosophers of liberalism. Mill's On Liberty is viewed as a classic statement of the liberal belief in the unfettered freedom of the individual. In this excerpt, Mill defends freedom of opinion from both government and the coercion of the majority.

John Stuart Mill, On Liberty

The object of this Essay is to assert one very simple principle, as entitled to govern absolutely the dealings of society with the individual in the way of compulsion and control, whether the means used by physical force in the form of legal penalties, or the moral coercion of public opinion. That principle is, that the sole end for which mankind are warranted, individually or collectively, interfering with the liberty of action of any of their number, is self-protection. That the only purpose for which power can be rightfully exercised over any members of a civilized community, against his will, is to prevent harm to others. His own good, either physical or moral, is not a sufficient warrant. . . . These are good reasons for remonstrating with him, or reasoning with him, or persuading him, or entreating him, but not for compelling him, or visiting him with any evil in case he do otherwise. To justify that, the conduct from which it is desired to deter him, must be calculated to produce evil to some one else. The only part of the conduct of any one, for which he is amenable to society, is that which concerns others. In the part which merely concerns himself, his independence is, of right, absolute. Over himself, over his own body and mind, the individual is sovereign. . . .

Society can and does execute its own mandates: and if it issues wrong mandates instead of right, or any mandates at all in things with which it ought not to meddle, it practices a social tyranny more formidable than many kinds of political oppression, since, though not usually upheld by such extreme penalties, it leaves fewer means of escape, penetrating more deeply into the details of life, and enslaving the soul itself. Protection, therefore, against the tyranny of the magistrae is not enough: there needs protection also against the tyranny of prevailing opinion and feeling, against the tendency of society to impose, by other means than civil penalties, its own ideas and practices as rules of conduct on those who dissent from them. . . .

But there is a sphere of action in which society, as distinguished from the individual has, if any, only an indirect interest; comprehending all that portion of a person's life and conduct which affects only himself, or if it also affects others, only with their free, voluntary and undeceived consent and participation. . . . This then is the appropriate region of human liberty. It comprises, first, the inward domain of consciousness; demanding liberty of conscience in the most comprehensive sense; liberty of thought and feeling; absolute freedom of opinion and sentiment on all subjects, practical or speculative, scientific, moral, or theological. . . .

Let us suppose, therefore, that the government is entirely at one with the people, and never thinks of exerting any power of coercion unless in agreement with what it conceives to be their voice. But I deny the right of the people to exercise such coercion, either by themselves or by their government. The power itself is illegitimate. The best government has no more title to it than the worst. It is as noxious, or more noxious, when exerted in accordance with public opinion, than when in opposition to it. If all mankind minus one were of one opinion, and only one person were of the contrary opinion, mankind would be no more justified in silencing that one person, than he, if he had the power, would be justified in silencing mankind. . . . The peculiar evil of silencing the expression of an opinion is, that it is robbing the human race; posterity as well as the existing generation; those who dissent from the opinion, still more than those who hold it. If the opinion is right, they are deprived of the opportunity of exchanging error for truth: if wrong, they lose, what is almost as great a benefit, the clearer perception and livelier impression of truth, produced by its collision with error.

Early Socialism

In the first half of the nineteenth century, the pitiful conditions found in the slums, mines, and factories of the Industrial Revolution gave rise to another ideology for change known as socialism. The term eventually became associated with a Marxist analysis of human society (see Chapter 23), but early socialism was largely the product of political theorists or intellectuals who wanted to introduce equality into social conditions and believed

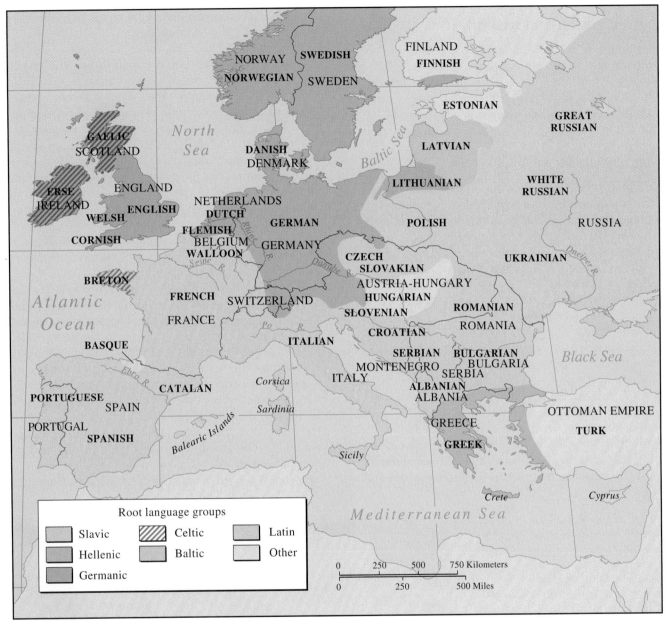

Map 22.3 Nationalism in Europe in the Nineteenth Century.

that human cooperation was superior to the competition that characterized early industrial capitalism. To later Marxists, such ideas were impractical dreams, and they contemptuously labeled the theorists utopian socialists. The term has endured to this day.

The utopian socialists were against private property and the competitive spirit of early industrial capitalism. By eliminating them and creating new systems of social organization, they thought that a better environment for humanity could be achieved. One prominent utopian

socialist was Robert Owen (1771–1858), a British cotton manufacturer, who believed that humans would reveal their true natural goodness if they lived in a cooperative environment. At New Lanark in Scotland, he was successful in transforming a squalid factory town into a flourishing, healthy community. But when he attempted to create a self-contained cooperative community at New Harmony, Indiana, in the United States in the 1820s, internal bickering within the community eventually destroyed his dream.

Revolution and Reform, 1830–1850

Beginning in 1830, the forces of change began to break through the conservative domination of Europe, more successfully in some places than in others. Finally, in 1848, a wave of revolutionary fervor moved through Europe, causing liberals and nationalists everywhere to think that they were on the verge of creating a new order.

The Revolutions of 1830

In France, the attempt of the ultraroyalists under the Bourbon monarch Charles X (1824–1830) to restore the old regime as far as possible led to a revolt by liberals in 1830 known as the July Revolution. Barricades went up in Paris as a provisional government led by a group of moderate, propertied liberals was hastily formed and appealed to Louis-Philippe, a cousin of Charles X, to become the constitutional king of France. Charles X fled to Britain; a new monarchy had been born.

Louis-Philippe (1830–1848) was soon called the bourgeois monarch because political support for his rule came from the upper middle class. Louis-Philippe even dressed like a member of the middle class in business suits and hats. Constitutional changes that favored the interests of the upper bourgeoisie were instituted. Financial qualifications for voting were reduced, yet remained sufficiently high that the number of voters only increased from 100,000 to barely 200,000 continuing to guarantee that only the wealthiest people would vote. To the upper mid-

dle class, the bourgeois monarchy represented the stopping place for political progress.

Supporters of liberalism played a primary role in the revolution in France, but nationalism was the crucial force in three other revolutionary outbursts in 1830. In an effort to create a stronger, larger state on France's northern border, the Congress of Vienna had added the area once known as the Austrian Netherlands (modern-day Belgium) to the Dutch Republic. But the Belgians rose up against the Dutch and succeeded in convincing the major European powers to accept an independent, neutral Belgium. The revolutionary scenarios in Poland and Italy were much less successful. Russian forces crushed the attempt of Poles to liberate themselves from foreign domination and established an oppressive military dictatorship over Poland. Metternich sent Austrian troops to crush revolts in three Italian states.

The successful July Revolution in France served to catalyze change in Britain. The Industrial Revolution had led to an expanding group of industrial leaders who objected to the corrupt British electoral system, which excluded them from political power. The Whigs, though also members of the landed classes, realized that concessions to reform were superior to revolution; the demands of the wealthy industrial middle class could no longer be ignored. In 1832, Parliament passed a Reform Bill that increased the numbers of male voters, primarily benefiting the upper middle class; the lower middle class, artisans, and industrial workers still had no vote. Nevertheless, a significant step had been taken. The "monied, manufacturing,

◆ **The July Revolution in Paris.** In 1830, the forces of change began to undo the conservative domination of Europe. In France, the reactionary Charles X was overthrown. In this painting, students, former soldiers of the Empire, and middle-class citizens are seen joining the rebels who are marching on city hall to demand a republic. The forces of Charles X, seen firing from a building above, failed to halt the rebels.

and educated elite" had been joined to the landed interest in ruling Britain. As a result of reforms, Britain would experience no revolutionary disturbances during 1848.

The Revolutions of 1848

Despite the successes of revolutions in France, Belgium, and Greece, the conservative order continued to dominate much of Europe. But the forces of liberalism and nationalism, first generated by the French Revolution, continued to grow as a second great revolution—the Industrial Revolution—expanded and brought new groups of people who wanted change. In 1848, these forces of change erupted once more. As usual, revolution in France provided the spark for other countries, and soon most of central and southern Europe was ablaze with revolutionary fires. Tsar Nicholas I of Russia lamented to Queen Victoria in April 1848, "What remains standing in Europe? Great Britain and Russia."

YET ANOTHER FRENCH REVOLUTION

A severe industrial and agricultural depression beginning in 1846 brought untold hardship in France to the lower middle class, workers, and peasants. Scandals, graft, and corruption were rife while the government's persistent refusal to extend the suffrage angered the disenfranchised members of the middle class. As Louis-Philippe's government continued to refuse to make changes, opposition grew and finally overthrew the monarchy on February 24, 1848. A group of moderate and radical republicans established a provisional government and called for the election by universal manhood suffrage of a Constituent Assembly that would draw up a new constitution.

The provisional government also established national workshops, which were supposed to be cooperative factories run by the workers. In fact, the workshops became unemployment compensation units or public works, except that they provided little work beyond leaf raking and ditch digging. The cost of the program became increasingly burdensome to the government.

The result was a growing split between the moderate republicans, who had the support of most of France, and the radical republicans, whose main support came from the Parisian working class. From March to June, the number of unemployed enrolled in the national workshops rose from 10,000 to almost 120,000, emptying the treasury and frightening the moderates who responded by closing the workshops on June 21. The workers refused to accept this decision and poured into the streets. Four days of bitter and bloody fighting by government forces crushed the working-class revolt. Thousands were killed,

and 11,000 prisoners were deported to the French colony of Algeria in northern Africa.

The new constitution, ratified on November 4, 1848, established a republic (Second Republic) with a one-house legislature of 750 elected by universal male suffrage for three years and a president, also elected by universal male suffrage, for four years. In the elections for the presidency held in December 1848, four republicans who had been associated with the early months of the Second Republic were resoundingly defeated by Charles Louis Napoleon Bonaparte, the nephew of the famous French ruler. Within four years President Napoleon would become Emperor Napoleon. The French had once again made a journey from republican chaos to authoritarian order, a pattern that was becoming all too common in French history.

REVOLUTION IN CENTRAL EUROPE

Like France, central Europe experienced rural and urban tensions due to an agricultural depression beginning in 1845. But the upheaval here seems to have been set off by news of the revolution in Paris in February 1848 (see the box on p. 460). Revolutionary cries for change caused many German rulers to promise constitutions, a free press, jury trials, and other liberal reforms. In Prussia concessions were also made to appease the revolutionaries. King Frederick William IV (1840–1861) agreed to abolish censorship, establish a new constitution, and work for a united Germany. The latter promise had its counterpart throughout all the German states as governments allowed elections by universal male suffrage for deputies to an all-German parliament. Its purpose was to fulfill a liberal and nationalist dream—the preparation of a constitution for a new united Germany.

But the Frankfurt Assembly (as the all-German parliament was called) disbanded in 1849. Although some members spoke of using force, they had no real means of compelling the German rulers to accept the constitution they had drawn up. The attempt of the German liberals at Frankfurt to create a German state had failed, and leadership for unification would now pass to the Prussian military monarchy.

The Austrian Empire also had its social, political, and nationalist grievances and needed only the news of the revolution in Paris to encourage it to erupt in flames in March 1848. The Hungarian liberal gentry under Louis Kossuth agitated for "commonwealth" status; they were willing to keep the Habsburg monarch, but wanted their own legislature. In March, demonstrations in Budapest, Prague, and Vienna led to Metternich's dismissal. The arch-symbol of the conservative order fled abroad. In Vienna, revolutionary forces, carefully guided by the

Revolutionary Excitement: Carl Schurz and the Revolution of 1848 in Germany

The excitement with which German liberals and nationalists received the news of the February Revolution in France and their own expectations for Germany are well captured in this selection from the Reminiscences of Carl Schurz (1829–1906). Schurz made his way to America after the failure of the German revolution and eventually became a United States senator.

Carl Schutz, Reminiscences

One morning, toward the end of February, 1848, I sat quietly in my attic-chamber, working hard at my tragedy of "Ulrich von Hutten," [a sixteenth-century German knight] when suddenly a friend rushed breathlessly into the room, exclaiming: "What, you sitting here! Do you not know that has happened?"

"No, what?"

"The French have driven away Louis Philippe and proclaimed the republic."

I threw down by pen—and that was the end of "Ulrich von Hutten." I never touched the manuscript again. We tore down the stairs, into the street, to the market-square, the accustomed meeting-place for all the student societies after their midday dinner. Although it was still forenoon, the market was already crowded with young men talking excitedly. There was no shouting, no noise, only agitated conversation. What did we want there? This probably no one knew. But since the French had driven away Louis Philippe and proclaimed the republic, something of source must happen here, too. . . . We were dominated by a vague feeling as if a great outbreak of elemental forces had begun, as if an earthquake was impending of which we had felt the first shock, and we instinctively crowded together. . . .

The next morning there were the usual lectures to be attended. But how profitless! The voice of the professor sounded like a monotonous drone coming from far away. What he had to say did not seem to concern us. The pen that should have taken notes remained idle. At last we closed with a sigh the notebook and went away, impelled by a feeling that now we had something more important to do—to devote ourselves to the affairs of the fatherland. And this we did by seeking as quickly as possible again the company of our friends, in order to discuss what had happened and what was to come. In these conversations, excited as they were, certain ideas and catchwords worked themselves to the surface, which expressed more or less the feelings of the people. Now had arrived in Germany the day for the establishment of "German Unity," and the founding of a great, powerful national German Empire, In the first line the convocation of a national parliament. Then the demands for civil rights and liberties, free speech, free press, the right of free assembly, equality before the law, a freely elected representation of the people with legislative power, responsibility of ministers, self-government of the communes, the right of the people to carry arms, the formation of a civic guard which elective officers, and so on—in short, that which was called a "constitutional form of government on a broad democratic basis." Republican ideas were at first only sparingly expressed. But the word democracy was soon on all tongues, and many, too, thought it a matter of course that if the princes should try to withhold from the people the rights and liberties demanded, force would take the place of mere petition. Of course the regeneration of the fatherland must, if possible, be accomplished by peaceable means. . . . Like many of my friends, I was dominated by the feeling that at last the great opportunity had arrived for giving to the German people the liberty which was their birthright and to the German fatherland its unity and greatness, and that it was now the first duty of every German to do and to sacrifice everything for this sacred object.

educated and propertied classes, took control of the capital and insisted that a constituent assembly be summoned to draw up a liberal constitution. Hungary was granted its wish for its own legislature, a separate national army, and control over foreign policy and budget. In Bohemia, the Czechs began to demand their own government as well.

Although Emperor Ferdinand I (1835–1848) and Austrian officials had made concessions to appease the revolutionaries, they awaited an opportunity to reestablish their firm control. As in the German states, they were increasingly encouraged by the divisions between radical and moderate revolutionaries and played on the middle-class fear of a working-class social revolution. Their first success came in June 1848 when Austrian military forces under General Alfred Windischgrätz ruthlessly suppressed the Czech rebels in Prague. By the end of October, radical rebels had been crushed in Vienna. In December the feeble-minded Ferdinand I agreed to abdicate in favor of his nephew, Francis Joseph I (1848–1916), who worked vigorously to restore the imperial government in Hungary. The Austrian armies, however, were unable to defeat Kossuth's forces, and it was only through the intervention of Nicholas I, who sent a Russian army of 140,000 men to aid the Austrians, that the Hungarian revolution was finally crushed in 1849. The revolutions in the Austrian Empire had also failed. Autocratic government was restored; emperor and propertied classes remained in control and the numerous nationalities were still subject to the Austrian government.

REVOLTS IN THE ITALIAN STATES

The failure of revolutionary uprisings in Italy in 1830–1831 had encouraged the Italian movement for unification to take a new direction. The leadership of Italy's resurgence passed into the hands of Giuseppe Mazzini (1805–1872), a dedicated Italian nationalist who founded an organization known as Young Italy in 1831. This group set as its goal the creation of a united Italian republic. In his work *The Duties of Man*, Mazzini urged Italians to dedicate their lives to the Italian nation: "O my Brother! Love your country. Our Country is our home."

Mazzini's dreams seemed on the verge of fulfillment when a number of Italian states rose in revolt in 1848. Beginning in Sicily, rebellions spread northward as ruler after ruler granted a constitution to his people. Citizens in Lombardy and Venetia also rebelled against their Austrian overlords. The Venetians declared a republic in Venice. The king of the northern Italian state of Piedmont, Charles Albert (1831–1849), took up the call and assumed the leadership for a war of liberation from Austrian domination. His invasion of Lombardy proved unsuccessful, however, and by 1849 the Austrians had reestablished complete control over Lombardy and Venetia. Counterrevolutionary forces also prevailed throughout Italy as Italian rulers managed to recover power on their own. Only Piedmont was able to keep its liberal constitution.

Throughout Europe in 1848, popular revolts had initiated revolutionary upheavals that had produced the formation of liberal constitutions and liberal governments. But the failure of the revolutionaries to stay united soon led to the reestablishment of the old regimes. In 1848, nationalities everywhere had also revolted in pursuit of self-government. But here, too, frightfully little was achieved

◆ **Austrian Students in the Revolutionary Civil Guard.** In 1848, revolutionary fervor swept through Europe and toppled governments in France, central Europe, and Italy. In the Austrian Empire, students joined the revolutionary civil guard in taking control of Vienna and forcing the Austrian emperor to call a constituent assembly to draft a liberal constitution.

CHRONOLOGY

Reaction, Reform, and Revolution: The European States, 1815–1850

Great Britain		The Austrian Empire	
Reform Act	1832	Emperor Ferdinand I	1835–1848
France		Revolt in Austrian Empire; Metternich dismissed	1848 (March)
Louis XVIII	1814–1824	Austrian forces under General Windischgrätz crush Czech rebels	1848 (June)
Charles X	1824–1830	Viennese rebels crushed	1848 (October)
July Revolution	1830	Abdication of Ferdinand I	1848 (December)
Louis-Philippe	1830–1848	Francis Joseph I	1848–1916
Abdication of Louis-Philippe; formation of provisional government	1848 (February 22–24)	Defeat of Hungarians with help of Russian troops	1849
Formation of national workshops	1848 (February 26)	The Italian States	
June days: workers' revolt in Paris	1848 (June)	King Charles Albert of Piedmont	1831–1849
Establishment of Second Republic	1848 (November)	Revolutions in Italy	1848
Election of Louis Napoleon as French president	1848 (December)	Charles Albert attacks Austrians	1848
Low Countries		Austrians reestablish control in Lombardy and Venetia	1849
Union of Netherlands and Belgium	1815	Russia	
Belgian revolt	1830	Tsar Alexander I	1801–1825
The German States		Tsar Nicholas I	1825–1855
Germanic Confederation established	1815	Polish uprising	1830
Frederick William IV of Prussia	1840–1861	Suppression of Polish revolt	1831
Revolution in Germany	1848		
Frankfurt Assembly	1848–1849		

because divisions among nationalities proved utterly disastrous. Though the Hungarians demanded autonomy from the Austrians, at the same time they refused the same to their minorities—the Slovenes, Croats, and Serbs. Instead of joining together against the old empire, minorities fought each other.

The Growth of the United States

The American Constitution, ratified in 1789, committed the United States to two of the major forces of the first half of the nineteenth century, liberalism and nationalism. Initially, this constitutional commitment to national unity was challenged by divisions over the power of the federal government vis-à-vis the individual states. Bitter conflict erupted between the Federalists and the Republicans. Led by Alexander Hamilton (1757–1804), the Federalists favored a financial program that would establish a strong central government. The Republicans, guided by Thomas Jefferson (1743–1826) and James Madison (1751–1836), feared centralization and its consequences for popular liberties. These divisions were intensified by European rivalries because the Federalists were pro-British and the Republicans pro-French. The successful conclusion of the War of 1812 brought an end to the Federalists, who had opposed the war, while the surge of national feeling generated by the war served to heal the nation's divisions.

Another strong force for national unity came from the Supreme Court while John Marshall (1755–1835) was

Chief Justice from 1801 to 1835. Marshall made the Supreme Court into an important national institution by asserting the right of the Court to overrule an act of Congress if the Court found it to be in violation of the Constitution. Under Marshall, the Supreme Court contributed further to establishing the supremacy of the national government by curbing the actions of state courts and legislatures.

The election of Andrew Jackson (1767–1845) as president in 1828 opened a new era in American politics. Jacksonian democracy introduced a mass democratic politics. The electorate was expanded by dropping traditional property qualifications; by the 1830s suffrage had been extended to almost all adult white males. During the period from 1815 to 1850, the traditional liberal belief in the improvement of human beings was also given concrete expression. Americans developed detention schools for juvenile delinquents and new penal institutions, both motivated by the liberal belief that the right kind of environment would rehabilitate those in need of it.

Culture in an Age of Reaction and Revolution: The Mood of Romanticism

At the end of the eighteenth century, a new intellectual movement known as Romanticism was developing as a reaction against the Enlightenment's preoccupation with reason in discovering truth. Although the Romantics, especially the early Romantics, by no means disparaged reason, they tried to balance its use by stressing the importance of feeling, emotion, and imagination as sources of knowing. As one German Romantic put it, "It was my heart that counseled me to do it, and my heart cannot err."

The Characteristics of Romanticism

Romantic writers emphasized emotion, sentiment, and the importance of inner feelings in their works. An important model for Romantics was the tragic figure in *The Sorrows of the Young Werther*, a novel by the great German writer Johann Wolfgang von Goethe (1749–1832), who later rejected Romanticism in favor of classicism. Werther was a Romantic figure who sought freedom in order to fulfill himself. Misunderstood and rejected by society, he continued to believe in his own worth through his inner feelings, but his deep love for a girl who did not love him finally led him to commit suicide. After Goethe's *Sorrows of Young Werther*, numerous novels and plays appeared whose plots revolved around young maidens tragically carried off at an early age (twenty-three was most

common) by disease (usually tuberculosis, at that time a protracted disease that was usually fatal) to the sorrow and sadness of their male lovers.

Another important characteristic of Romanticism was individualism or an interest in the unique traits of each person. The Romantics' desire to follow their inner drives led them to rebel against middle-class conventions. Long hair, beards, and outrageous clothes served to reinforce the individualism that young Romantics were trying to express.

Many Romantics possessed a passionate interest in the past. This historical mindedness was manifested in many ways. In Germany, the Grimm brothers collected and published local fairy tales, as did Hans Christian Andersen in Denmark. The revival of medieval Gothic architecture left European countrysides adorned with pseudo-medieval castles and cities bedecked with grandiose neo-Gothic cathedrals, city halls, parliamentary buildings, and even railway stations. Literature, too, reflected this historical consciousness. The novels of Walter Scott (1771–1832) became European best-sellers in the first half of the nineteenth century. *Ivanhoe*, in which Scott tried to evoke the clash between Saxon and Norman knights in medieval England, became one of his most popular works.

To the historical mindedness of the Romantics could be added an attraction to the bizarre and unusual. In an exaggerated form, this preoccupation gave rise to so-called Gothic literature (see the box on p. 464), chillingly evident in the short stories of horror by the American Edgar Allan Poe (1808–1849) and *Frankenstein* by Mary Shelley. Her novel was the story of a mad scientist who brings into being a humanlike monster who goes berserk. Some Romantics even sought the unusual in their own lives by pursuing extraordinary states of experience in dreams, nightmares, supernatural possession, frenzies, and suicidal depression or by experimenting with cocaine, opium, and hashish to produce drug-induced, altered states of consciousness.

Romantic Poets and the Love of Nature

To the Romantics, poetry ranked above all other literary forms because they believed it was the direct expression of one's soul. The Romantic poets were viewed as seers who could reveal the invisible world to others. Their incredible sense of drama made some of them the most colorful figures of their era, living intense but short lives. Percy Bysshe Shelley (1792–1822), expelled from school for advocating atheism, set out to reform the world. His *Prometheus Unbound*, completed in 1820, is a portrait of the revolt of human beings against the laws and customs

Gothic Literature: Edgar Allan Poe

American writers and poets made significant contributions to the movement of Romanticism. Although Edgar Allan Poe (1809–1849) was influenced by the German Romantic school of mystery and horror, many literary historians give him the credit for pioneering the modern short story. This selection from the conclusion of "The Fall of the House of Usher" gives a sense of the nature of so-called Gothic literature.

Edgar Allan Poe, "The Fall of the House of Usher"
No sooner had these syllables passed by lips, than—as if a shield of brass had indeed, at the moment, fallen heavily upon a floor of silver—I became aware of a distinct, hollow, metallic, and clangorous, yet apparently muffled, reverberation. Complete unnerved, I leaped to my feet; but the measured rocking movement of Usher was undisturbed. I rushed to the chair in which he sat. His eyes were bent fixedly before him, and throughout his whole countenance there reigned a stony rigidity. But, as I placed my hand upon his shoulder, there came a strong shudder over his whole person; a sickly smile quivered about his lips and I saw that he spoke in a low, hurried, and gibbering murmur, as if unconscious of my presence. Bending closely over him, I at length drank in the hideous import of his words.

"Not hear it?—yes, I hear it, and *have* heard it. Long-long-long-many minutes, many hours, many days, have I heard it—yet I dared not—oh, pity me, miserable wretch that I am!—I dared not—I *dared* not speak! We have put her living in the tomb! Said I not that my senses were acute? I *now* tell you that I heard her first feeble movements in the hollow coffin. I heard them—many, many days ago—yet I dared not—I *dared not speak!* And now—to-night—. . . the rending of her coffin, and the grating of the iron hinges of her prison, and her struggles within the coppered archway of the vault! Oh wither shall I fly? Will she not be here anon? Is she not hurrying to upbraid me for my haste? Have I not heard her footstep on the stair? Do I not distinguish that heavy and horrible beating of her heart? MAD MAN!"—here he sprang furiously to his feet, and shrieked out his syllables, as if in the effort he were giving up his soul—"MADMAN! I TELL YOU THAT SHE NOW STANDS WITHOUT THE DOOR!"

As if in the superhuman energy of his utterance there had been found the potency of a spell, the huge antique panels to which the speaker pointed threw slowly back, upon the instant, their ponderous and ebony jaws. It was the work of the rushing gust—but then without those doors there DID stand the lofty and enshrouded figure of the lady Madeline of Usher. There was blood upon her white robes, and the evidence of some bitter struggle upon every portion of her emaciated frame. For a moment she remained trembling and reeling to and fro upon the threshold, then, with a low moaning cry, fell heavily inward upon the person of her brother, and in her violent and now final death-agonies, bore him to the floor a corpse, and a victim to the terrors he had anticipated.

---

that oppress them. He drowned in a storm in the Mediterranean. Lord Byron (1788–1824) dramatized himself as the melancholy romantic hero that he had described in his own work, *Childe Harold's Pilgrimage*. He participated in the movement for Greek independence and died in Greece fighting the Turks.

Romantic poetry gave full expression to one of the most important characteristics of Romanticism: love of nature, especially evident in William Wordsworth (1770–1850). His experience of nature was almost mystical as he claimed to receive "authentic tidings of invisible things":

> One impulse from a vernal wood
> May teach you more of man,
> Of Moral Evil and of good,
> Than all the sages can.[4]

To Wordsworth, nature contained a mysterious force that the poet could perceive and learn from. Nature served as a mirror into which humans could look to learn about themselves. Nature was, in fact, alive and sacred:

> To every natural form, rock, fruit or flower,
> Even the loose stones that cover the high-way,
> I gave a moral life, I saw them feel,
> Or link'd them to some feeling: the great mass
> Lay bedded in a quickening soul, and all
> That I beheld, respired with inward meaning.[5]

Other Romantics carried this worship of nature further into pantheism by identifying the great force in nature with God. As the German Romantic poet Friedrich Novalis said, "Anyone seeking God will find him anywhere."

Romanticism in Art and Music

Like the literary arts, the visual arts were also deeply affected by Romanticism. Although their works varied widely, Romantic artists shared at least two fundamental characteristics. All artistic expression to them was a reflection of the artist's inner feelings; a painting should mirror the artist's vision of the world and be the instrument of his own imagination. Moreover, Romantic artists deliberately rejected the principles of classicism. Beauty was not a timeless thing; its expression depended on one's culture and one's age. The Romantics abandoned classical restraint for warmth, emotion, and movement.

The early life experiences of Caspar David Friedrich (1774–1840) left him with a lifelong preoccupation with God and nature. Friedrich painted many landscapes but with an interest that transcended the mere presentation of natural details. His portrayal of mountains shrouded in mist, gnarled trees bathed in moonlight, and the stark ruins of monasteries surrounded by withered trees all conveyed a feeling of mystery and mysticism. For Friedrich, nature was a manifestation of divine life. As in *Man and Woman Gazing at the Moon*, he liked to depict one or two solitary figures gazing on the grandeur of a natural scene with their backs to the viewer. Not only were his human figures dwarfed by the overwhelming presence of nature, but they expressed the human yearning for infinity, the desire to lose oneself in the universe. To Friedrich, the artistic process depended on the use of an unrestricted imagination that could only be achieved through inner vision. He advised artists: "Shut your physical eye and look first at your picture with your spiritual eye, then bring to the light of day what you have seen in the darkness."

Eugène Delacroix (1798–1863) was the most famous French Romantic artist. Largely self-taught, he was fascinated by the exotic and had a passion for color. Both characteristics are visible in his *Women of Algiers*. Significant for its use of light and its patches of interrelated color, this portrayal of the world of harem concubines in exotic north Africa was actually somewhat scandalous to the early nineteenth century. Delacroix combined theatricality and movement with a daring use of color. Many of his works reflect his own belief that "a painting should be a feast to the eye."

To many Romantics, music was the most Romantic of the arts because it enabled the composer to probe deeply into human emotions. One Romantic writer noted: "It has been rightly said that the object of music is the awakening of emotion. No other art can so sublimely arouse human sentiments in the innermost heart of man."[6] Although music historians have called the eighteenth century an age of classicism and the nineteenth the era of Romanticism, there was much carryover of classical forms from one century to the next. One of the greatest composers of all time, Ludwig van Beethoven, served as a bridge between classicism and Romanticism.

Beethoven (1770–1827) was born in Bonn (Germany) but soon made his way to Vienna, then the musical capital of Europe, where he studied briefly under Mozart.

✦ **Caspar David Friedrich, *Man and Woman Gazing at the Moon*.** The German artist Caspar David Friedrich sought to express in painting his own mystical view of nature. "The divine is everywhere," he once wrote, "even in a grain of sand." In this painting, two solitary wanderers are shown from the back gazing at the moon. Overwhelmed by the all-pervasive presence of nature, the two figures express the human longing for infinity.

Beginning in 1792, this city became his permanent residence although his unruly manner and offensive appearance made him barely tolerable to Viennese society. During his first major period of composing, which extended from 1792 to 1802, his work was still largely within the classical framework of the eighteenth century, and the influences of Mozart and Haydn are paramount. During the next period of his creative life, which began in 1800, Beethoven declared, "I am making a fresh start." With the composition of the Third Symphony (1804), also called the *Eroica*, which was originally intended for Napoleon, Beethoven broke through to the elements of Romanticism in his use of uncontrolled rhythms to create dramatic struggle and uplifted resolutions. E. T. A. Hoffman, a contemporary composer and writer, said, "Beethoven's music opens the flood gates of fear, of terror, of horror, of pain, and arouses that longing for the eternal which is the essence of Romanticism. He is thus a pure Romantic composer."[7] Beethoven went on to write a vast quantity of works including symphonies, piano and violin sonatas, concerti, masses, an opera, and a cycle of songs. In the midst of this productivity and growing fame, Beethoven was more and more burdened by his growing deafness, which intensified noticeably after 1800. One of the most moving pieces of music of all time, the chorale finale of his Ninth Symphony, was composed when Beethoven was totally deaf.

♦ **Eugène Delacroix, *Women of Algiers*.** Also characteristic of Romanticism was its love of the exotic and unfamiliar. In his *Women of Algiers*, Delacroix reflected this fascination with the exotic in his portrayal of harem concubines from Morocco. At the same time, Delacroix's painting reflects his preoccupation with light and color.

Conclusion

In 1815, a conservative order was reestablished throughout Europe, and the cooperation of the great powers, embodied in the Concert of Europe, tried to ensure its durability. But the revolutionary waves of the early 1820s and the early 1830s made it clear that the ideologies of liberalism and nationalism, unleashed by the French Revolution and now reinforced by the spread of the Industrial Revolution, were still alive and active. They faced enormous difficulties, however, as failed revolutions in Poland, Russia, Italy, and Germany all testify. At the same time, reform legislation in Britain and successful revolutions in Greece, France, and Belgium demonstrated the continuing strength of these forces of change. In 1848, they erupted once more all across Europe. And once more they failed. But all was not lost. Both liberalism and nationalism would succeed in the second half of the nineteenth century but in ways not foreseen by the idealistic liberals and nationalists who were utterly convinced that their time had come when they manned the barricades in 1848.

NOTES

1. Quoted in M. S. Anderson, *The Ascendancy of Europe 1815–1914*, 2d ed. (London, 1985), p. 1.
2. Quotations from Burke can be found in Peter Viereck, *Conservatism* (Princeton, N.J., 1956), p. 27.
3. Quoted in G. de Berthier de Sauvigny, *Metternich and His Times* (London, 1962), p. 105.
4. William Wordsworth, "The Tables Turned," *Poems of Wordsworth*, ed. Matthew Arnold (London, 1963), p. 138.
5. William Wordsworth, *The Prelude* (Harmondsworth, 1971), p. 109.
6. Quoted in H. G. Schenk, *The Mind of the European Romantics* (Garden City, N.Y., 1969), p. 205.
7. Quoted in Siegbert Prawer, ed., *The Romantic Period in Germany* (London, 1970), p. 285.

SUGGESTIONS FOR FURTHER READING

For a good survey of the entire nineteenth century, see R. Gildea, *Barricades and Borders: Europe 1800–1914* (Oxford, 1987) in the Short Oxford History of the Modern World series. Also valuable is M. S. Anderson, *The Ascendancy of Europe, 1815–1914*, 2d ed. (London, 1985). For surveys of the period covered in this chapter, see M. Broers, *Europe after Napoleon: Revolution, Reaction, and Romanticism, 1814–1848* (New York, 1996); C. Breunig, *The Age of Revolution and Recreation, 1789–1850*, 2d ed. (New York, 1979); and J. Droz, *Europe between Revolutions, 1815–1848* (London, 1967). There are also some useful books on individual countries that cover more than the subject of this chapter. These include R. Magraw, *France, 1815–1914: The Bourgeois Century* (London, 1983); H. Seton-Watson, *The Russian Empire, 1801–1917* (Oxford, 1967); H. Holborn, *A History of Modern Germany*, vol. 2, *1648–1840* (New York, 1964); C. A. Macartney, *The Habsburg Empire, 1790–1918* (London, 1971); S. J. Woolf, *A History of Italy, 1700–1860* (London, 1979); and N. Gash, *Aristocracy and People: Britain 1815–1865* (London, 1979).

On the peace settlement of 1814–1815, there is the older work by H. Nicolson, *The Congress of Vienna, 1814–15* (New York, 1946). A concise summary of the international events of the entire nineteenth century can be found in R. Bullen and F. R. Bridge, *The Great Powers and the European States System, 1815–1914* (London, 1980). For the period covered in this chapter, see A. Sked, ed., *Europe's Balance of Power, 1815–1848* (London, 1979). On the man whose conservative policies dominated this era, see the brief but good biography by A. Palmer, *Metternich* (New York, 1972). On the revolutions in Europe in 1830, see C. Church, *Europe in 1830: Revolution and Political Change* (Chapel Hill, N.C., 1983). On Great Britain's reform legislation, see M. Brock, *Great Reform Act* (London, 1973). The Greek revolt is examined in detail in D. Dakin, *The Greek Struggle for Independence, 1821–33* (Berkeley, 1973).

The best introduction to the revolutions of 1848 is J. Sperber, *The European Revolutions, 1848–1851* (New York, 1994). See also P. Stearns, *1848: The Revolutionary Tide in Europe* (New York, 1974). Good accounts of the revolutions in individual countries include G. Duveau, *1848: The Making of a Revolution* (New York, 1967); R. J. Rath, *The Viennese Revolution of 1848* (Austin, Tex., 1957); I. Déak, *The Lawful Revolution: Louis Kossuth and the Hungarians, 1848–49* (New York, 1979); P. Brock, *The Slovak National Awakening* (Toronto, 1976); R. Stadelmann, *Social and Political History of the German 1848 Revolution* (Athens, Ohio, 1975); and P. Ginsborg, *Daniele Manin and the Venetian Revolution of 1848–9* (New York, 1979).

Good introductions to the major ideologies of the first half of the nineteenth century including both analysis and readings from the major figures can be found in H. Kohn, *Nationalism* (Princeton, N.J., 1955); J. S. Schapiro, *Liberalism: Its Meaning and History* (Princeton, N.J., 1958); and P. Viereck, *Conservatism* (Princeton, N.J., 1956). On liberalism, see J. Gray, *Liberalism* (Minneapolis, Minn., 1995). For a general survey, see R. Stromberg, *An Intellectual History of Modern Europe*, 5th ed. (Englewood Cliffs, N.J., 1990). An excellent work on French utopian socialism is F. Manuel, *The Prophets of Paris* (New York, 1962).

G. L. Mosse, *The Culture of Western Europe: The Nineteenth and Twentieth Centuries* (Chicago, 1961), remains a good introduction to the cultural history of Europe. On the ideas of the Romantics, see H. G. Schenk, *The Mind of the European Romantics* (Garden City, N.Y., 1969); and M. Cranston, *The Romantic Movement* (Oxford, 1994). There is an excellent collection of writings by Romantics in J. B. Halsted, ed., *Romanticism* (New York, 1969). On Wordsworth and English Romanticism, see J. Wordsworth, *William Wordsworth and the Age of English Romanticism* (New Brunswick, N.J., 1987). A beautifully illustrated introduction to the arts can be found in H. Honour, *Romanticism* (New York, 1979). Briefer surveys (with illustrations) can be found in D. M. Reynolds, *Cambridge Introduction to the History of Art: The Nineteenth Century* (Cambridge, 1985); and B. Cole and A. Gealt, *Art of the Western World* (New York, 1989).

An Age of Nationalism and Realism, 1850–1871

Across the Continent, the revolutions of 1848 had failed. The forces of liberalism and nationalism appeared to have been decisively defeated as authoritarian governments reestablished their control almost everywhere in Europe by 1850. And yet within twenty-five years, many of the goals sought by the liberals and nationalists during the first half of the nineteenth century seemed to have been achieved. National unity became a reality in Italy and Germany while many European states were governed by constitutional monarchies, even though the constitutional-parliamentary features were frequently facades.

All the same, these goals were not achieved by liberal and nationalist leaders but by a new generation of conservative leaders who were proud of being practitioners of Realpolitik, the "politics of reality." One reaction to the failure of the revolutions of 1848 had been a new toughness of mind in which people prided themselves on being realistic in their handling of power. The new conservative leaders used armies and power politics to achieve their foreign policy goals. And they did not hesitate to manipulate liberal means to achieve conservative ends at home. Nationalism had failed as a revolutionary movement in 1848–1849, but between 1850 and 1871, these new leaders found a variety of ways to pursue nation building. One of the most successful was the Prussian Otto von Bismarck who used both astute diplomacy and war to achieve the unification of Germany. On January 18, 1871, Bismarck and 600 German princes, nobles, and generals filled the Hall of Mirrors in the palace of Versailles, twelve miles outside the city of Paris. The Prussian army had defeated the French, and the assembled notables were gathered for the proclamation of the Prussian king as the new emperor of a united German state. When the words, "Long live His Imperial Majesty, the Emperor William!" rang out, the assembled guests took up the cry. One participant wrote, "A thundering cheer, repeated at least six times,

Louis Napoleon becomes emperor

Creation of Austro-Hungarian dual monarchy

Unification of Italy

Unification of Germany

• Emancipation of the Russian serfs

• American Civil War

• British Reform Act

• Creation of Canada as a nation

Marx and Engels, *The Communist Manifesto*

Flaubert, *Madame Bovary*

Darwin, *On the Origin of Species*

Pasteur and pasteurization

thrilled through the room while the flags and standards waved over the head of the new emperor of Germany." European rulers who feared the power of the new German state were not so cheerful. "The balance of power has been entirely destroyed," declared the British prime minister.

The France of Napoleon III

After 1850, a new generation of conservative leaders came to power in Europe. Foremost among them was Napoleon III (1852–1870) of France who taught his contemporaries how authoritarian governments could use liberal and nationalistic forces to bolster their own power. It was a lesson others quickly learned.

Louis Napoleon and the Second Napoleonic Empire

Even after his election as the president of the French Republic, many of his contemporaries dismissed Napoleon "the Small" as a nonentity whose success was due only to his name. But Louis Napoleon was a clever politician who was especially astute at understanding the popular forces of his day. When the National Assembly rejected his proposal to revise the constitution and allow him to stand for reelection, Louis used troops loyal to the president to seize control of the government on December 1, 1851. After restoring universal male suffrage, Napoleon asked the French people to restructure the government by electing him president for ten years. They agreed by an overwhelming majority. A year later, on November 21,

1852, Louis Napoleon returned to the people to ask for the restoration of the Empire. This time 97 percent responded affirmatively, and on December 2, 1852, Louis Napoleon assumed the title of Napoleon III (the first Napoleon had abdicated in favor of his son, Napoleon II, on April 6, 1814). The Second Empire had begun.

The government of Napoleon III was clearly authoritarian in a Bonapartist sense. As chief of state, Napoleon III controlled the armed forces, police, and civil service. Only he could introduce legislation and declare war. The Legislative Corps gave an appearance of representative government since its members were elected by universal male suffrage for six-year terms. But they could neither initiate legislation nor affect the budget.

The first five years of Napoleon III's reign were a spectacular success as he reaped the benefits of worldwide economic prosperity as well as some of his own economic policies. Napoleon believed in using the resources of government to stimulate the national economy and took many steps to expand industrial growth. Government subsidies were used to foster the rapid construction of railroads as well as harbors, roads, and canals. The major French railway lines were completed during Napoleon's reign while industrial expansion was evident in the tripling of iron production. In the midst of this economic expansion, Napoleon III also undertook a vast reconstruction of the city of Paris. The medieval Paris of narrow streets and old city walls was destroyed and replaced by a modern Paris of broad boulevards, spacious buildings, circular plazas, public squares, an underground sewage system, a new public water supply, and gaslights. The new Paris served a military as well as an aesthetic purpose. Broad streets made it more difficult for would-be insurrectionists to throw up barricades and easier for troops to move rapidly through the city in the event of revolts.

✦ Emperor Napoleon III. On December 2, 1852, Louis Napoleon took the title of Napoleon III and then proceeded to create an authoritarian monarchy. As opposition to his policies intensified in the 1860s, Napoleon III began to liberalize his government. However, a disastrous military defeat at the hands of Prussia in 1870–1871 brought the collapse of his regime.

In the 1860s, as opposition to some of Napoleon's policies began to mount, his sensitivity to the change in the public mood led him to undertake new policies liberalizing his regime. Napoleon III reached out to the working class by legalizing trade unions and granting them the right to strike. He also began to liberalize the political process. The Legislative Corps was permitted more say in affairs of state, including debate over the budget. Liberalization policies did serve initially to strengthen the hands of the government. In a plebiscite in May 1870, on whether to accept a new constitution

that might have inaugurated a parliamentary regime, the French people gave Napoleon another resounding victory. This triumph was short-lived, however. Foreign policy failures led to growing criticism, and war with Prussia in 1870 turned out to be the death blow for Napoleon III's regime. Napoleon was ousted, and a republic proclaimed.

Foreign Policy: The Crimean War

As heir to the Napoleonic Empire, Napoleon III was motivated by a desire to make France the chief arbiter of Europe. Although his foreign policy ultimately led to disaster and his own undoing, Napoleon had an initial success in the Crimean War (1854–1856).

The Crimean War was yet another chapter in the story of the Eastern Question, or who would be the chief beneficiaries of the disintegration of the Turkish or Ottoman Empire. The Ottoman Empire had long been in control of much of southeastern Europe, but by the beginning of the nineteenth century, it had begun to decline. As Ottoman authority over the outlying territories in southeastern Europe waned, European governments began to take an active interest in the empire's apparent demise. Russia's proximity to the Ottoman Empire naturally gave it special opportunities to enlarge its sphere of influence. War erupted between the Russians and Turks in 1853 when the Russians demanded the right to protect Christian shrines in Palestine, a privilege that had already been extended to the French. When the Turks refused, the Russians invaded Turkish Moldavia and Walachia. Failure to resolve the dispute by negotiations led the Turks to declare war on Russia on October 4, 1853. In the following year, on March 28, Great Britain and France, fearful of Russian gains at the expense of the disintegrating Ottoman Empire, declared war on Russia.

The Crimean War was poorly planned and poorly fought. Britain and France decided to attack Russia's Crimean peninsula in the Black Sea. After a long siege and at a terrible cost in manpower for both sides, the main Russian fortress of Sevastopol fell in September 1855, and the Russians soon sued for peace. By the Treaty of Paris, signed in March 1856, Russia was forced to give up Bessarabia at the mouth of the Danube and accept the neutrality of the Black Sea. In addition, the Danubian principalities of Moldavia and Walachia were placed under the protection of all the great powers.

The Crimean War broke up long-standing European power relationships and effectively destroyed the Concert of Europe. Austria and Russia, the two chief powers maintaining the status quo in the first half of the nineteenth century, were now enemies because of Austria's unwillingness to support Russia in the war. Russia, defeated, humiliated, and weakened by the obvious failure of its armies, withdrew from European affairs for the next two decades to set its house in order. Great Britain, disillusioned by its role in the war, also pulled back from continental affairs. Austria, paying the price for its neutrality, was now without friends among the great powers. Not until the 1870s were new combinations formed to replace those that had disappeared, and in the meantime the European international situation remained fluid. Those willing to pursue the "politics of reality" found themselves in a situation rife with opportunity. It was this new international situation that made possible the unification of Italy and Germany.

National Unification: Italy and Germany

The breakdown of the Concert of Europe opened the way for the Italians and the Germans to establish national states. Their successful unifications transformed the power structure of the Continent. Well into the twentieth century, Europe and the world would still be dealing with the consequences.

The Unification of Italy

The Italians were the first people to benefit from the breakdown of the Concert of Europe. In 1850, Austria was still the dominant power on the Italian peninsula. After the failure of the revolution of 1848–1849, a growing number of advocates for Italian unification focused on the northern Italian state of Piedmont as their best hope to achieve their goal. The royal house of Savoy ruled the kingdom of Piedmont, which also included the island of Sardinia. The little state seemed unlikely to supply the needed leadership to unify Italy, however, until King Victor Emmanuel II (1849–1878) named Count Camillo di Cavour (1810–1861) as his prime minister in 1852.

Cavour was a consummate politician with the ability to persuade others of the rightness of his own convictions. After becoming prime minister in 1852, he pursued a policy of economic expansion that increased government revenues and enabled Cavour to pour money into equipping a large army. Cavour, however, had no illusions about Piedmont's military strength and was only too well aware that he could not challenge Austria directly. Consequently, he made an alliance in 1858 with the French emperor Louis Napoleon and then provoked the Austrians into invading Piedmont in 1859. In the initial stages of fighting, it was the French who were largely responsi-

CHRONOLOGY

The Unification of Italy

Victor Emmanuel II	1849–1878
Count Cavour becomes prime minister of Piedmont	1852
Agreement with Napoleon III	1858
The Austrian War	1859
Plebiscites in the northern Italian states	1860
Garibaldi's invasion of the Kingdom of the Two Sicilies	1860
Kingdom of Italy is proclaimed	1861
Italy's annexation of Venetia	1866
Italy's annexation of Rome	1870

ble for defeating the Austrians in two major battles at Magenta and Solferino. A peace settlement gave the French Nice and Savoy, which they had been promised for making the alliance, and Lombardy to Cavour and the Piedmontese. More importantly, however, Cavour's success caused nationalists in some northern Italian states (Parma, Modena, and Tuscany) to overthrow their governments and join their states to Piedmont.

Italian unification might have stopped here since there is little indication that Cavour envisioned uniting all of Italy in the spring of 1860. But the forces of romantic republican nationalism forced Cavour to act. Giuseppe Garibaldi (1807–1882), a dedicated Italian patriot who had supported the republican cause of Young Italy, raised an army of a thousand Red Shirts, as his volunteers were called because of their distinctive dress, and landed in Sicily where a revolt had broken out against the Bourbon king of the Two Sicilies. By the end of July 1860, most of Sicily had been pacified under Garibaldi's control. In August Garibaldi and his forces crossed over to the mainland and began a victorious march up the Italian peninsula. Naples and the kingdom of the Two Sicilies fell in early September. Ever the patriot, Garibaldi chose to turn over his conquests to Cavour's Piedmontese forces. On March 17, 1861, a new Kingdom of Italy was proclaimed under a centralized government subordinated to the control of Piedmont and King Victor Emmanuel II of the house of Savoy. Worn out by his efforts, Cavour died three months later.

Despite the proclamation of a new kingdom, the task of unification was not yet complete because Venetia in the north was still held by Austria and Rome was under papal control, supported by French troops. To attack either one meant war with a major European state, which the Italian army was not prepared to handle. It was the Prussian army that indirectly completed the task of Italian unification. In the Austro-Prussian War of 1866, the new Italian state became an ally of Prussia. Although the Italian army was defeated by the Austrians, Prussia's victory left the Italians with Venetia. In 1870, the Franco-Prussian War resulted in the withdrawal of French troops from Rome. The Italian army then annexed the city on September 20, 1870, and Rome became the new capital of the united Italian state.

The Unification of Germany

After the failure of the Frankfurt Assembly to achieve German unification in 1848–1849, German nationalists focused on Austria and Prussia as the only two states powerful enough to dominate German affairs. Austria had long controlled the existing Germanic Confedera-

tion, but Prussian power had grown, strongly reinforced by economic expansion in the 1850s. Prussia had formed the *Zollverein*, a German customs union, in 1834. By eliminating tolls on rivers and roads among member states, the *Zollverein* had stimulated trade and added to the prosperity of its member states. By 1853, all the German states except Austria had joined the Prussian-dominated customs union. A number of middle-class liberals now began to see Prussia in a new light; some even looked openly to Prussia to bring about the unification of Germany.

In the 1860s, King William I (1861–1888) attempted to enlarge and strengthen the Prussian army. When the Prussian legislature refused to levy new taxes for the proposed military changes in March 1862, William I appointed a new prime minister, Count Otto von Bismarck (1815–1898). Bismarck went on to determine the course of modern German history. Until 1890, he dominated both German and European politics.

Bismarck ignored the legislative opposition to the military reforms, arguing that, "Germany does not look to

Map 23.1 The Unification of Italy.

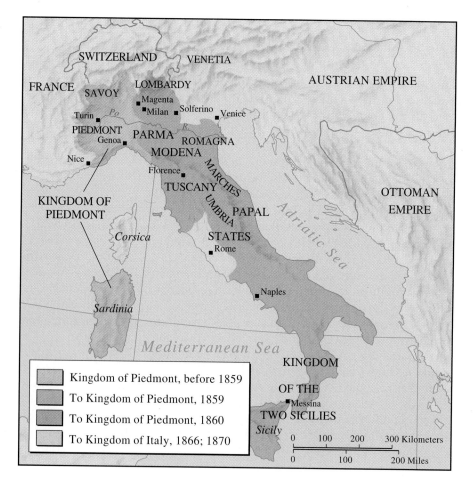

Prussia's liberalism but to her power. . . . Not by speeches and majorities will the great questions of the day be decided—that was the mistake of 1848–1849—but by iron and blood."[1] Bismarck went ahead, collected the taxes, and reorganized the army anyway, blaming the liberals for causing the breakdown of constitutional government. From 1862 to 1866, Bismarck governed Prussia by simply ignoring parliament. Unwilling to revolt, parliament did nothing. In the meantime, opposition to his domestic policy determined Bismarck on an active foreign policy, which led to war and German unification.

Because Bismarck succeeded in guiding Prussia's unification of Germany, it is often assumed that he had determined on a course of action that led precisely to that goal. That is hardly the case. Bismarck was a consummate politician and opportunist. He was not a political gambler, but a moderate who waged war only when all other diplomatic alternatives had been exhausted and when he was reasonably sure that all the military and diplomatic advantages were on his side. Bismarck has often been portrayed as the ultimate realist, the foremost nineteenth-century practitioner of *realpolitik*. His ability to manipulate people and power makes that claim justified, but unlike Hitler in the twentieth century, Bismarck also recognized the limitations of power. When he perceived that the advantages to be won from war "no longer justified the risks involved," he became an ardent defender of peace.

Bismarck's first war was against Denmark and was fought over the duchies of Schleswig and Holstein. Bismarck persuaded the Austrians to join Prussia in declaring war on Denmark on February 1, 1864. The Danes were quickly defeated and surrendered Schleswig

✛ Map 23.2 The Unification of Germany.

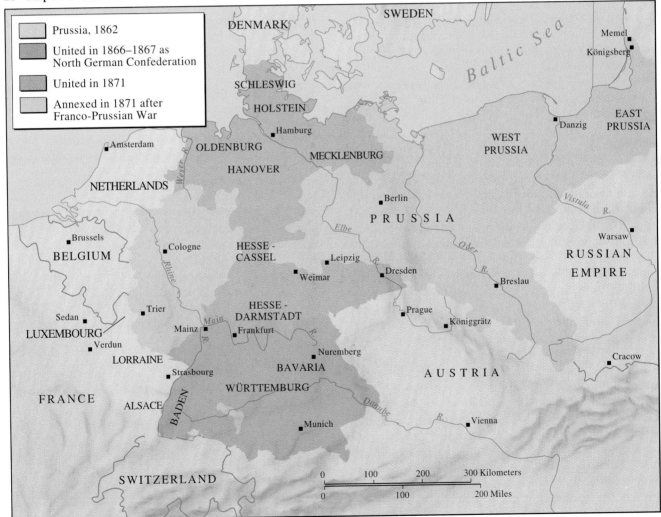

and Holstein to the victors. Austria and Prussia then agreed to divide the administration of the two duchies; Prussia took Schleswig while Austria administered Holstein. But Bismarck used the joint administration of the two duchies to create friction with the Austrians and goad them into a war on June 14, 1866.

Many Europeans expected a quick Austrian victory but they overlooked the effectiveness of the Prussian military reforms of the 1860s. The Prussian breech-loading needle gun had a much faster rate of fire than the Austrian muzzle-loader, and a superior network of railroads enabled the Prussians to mass troops quickly. At Königgrätz (or Sadowa) on July 3, the Austrian army was decisively defeated. Austria was now excluded from German affairs, and the German states north of the Main River were organized into a North German Confederation controlled by Prussia. Each German state kept its own local government, but the king of Prussia was head of the Confederation while the chancellor (Bismarck) was responsible directly to the king. Both army and foreign policy remained in the hands of the king and his chancellor. The south German states, largely Catholic, remained independent but were coerced into signing military agreements with Prussia.

THE FRANCO–PRUSSIAN WAR, 1870–1871

Bismarck and William I had achieved a major goal by 1866. Prussia now dominated all of northern Germany, and Austria had been excluded from any significant role in German affairs. Nevertheless, unsettled business led to new international complications and further change. Bismarck realized that France would never be content with a strong German state to its east because of the potential threat to French security. At the same time, after a series of setbacks, Napoleon III, the French ruler, needed a diplomatic triumph to offset his serious domestic problems. The French were not happy with the turn of events in Germany and looked for opportunities to humiliate the Prussians.

In 1870, Prussia and France became embroiled in a dispute over the candidacy of a relative of the Prussian king for the throne of Spain. Bismarck manipulated the misunderstandings between the French and Prussians to goad the French into declaring war on Prussia on July 15, 1870 (see the box on p. 475). The French proved no match for the better led and organized Prussian forces. The south German states honored their military alliances with Prussia and joined the war effort against the French. The Prussian armies advanced into France, and at Sedan, on September 2, 1870, an entire French army and Napoleon III himself were captured. Paris finally capitulated on January 28, 1871, and an official peace treaty was signed in May. France had to pay an indemnity of five billion francs (about one billion dollars) and give up the provinces of Alsace and Lorraine to the new German state, a loss that angered the French and left them burning for revenge.

◆ **The Unification of Germany.** Under Prussian leadership, a new German empire was proclaimed on January 18, 1871, in the Hall of Mirrors in the palace at Versailles. King William of Prussia became Emperor William I of the Second German Empire. In this painting by Anton von Werner, Otto von Bismarck, the man who had been so instrumental in creating the new German state, is shown, resplendently attired in his white uniform, standing at the foot of the throne.

⋙ Bismarck "Goads" France into War ⋘

After his meeting with the French ambassador at Ems, King William I of Prussia sent a telegraph to Bismarck with a report of their discussions. By editing the telegraph from King William I before he released it to the press, Bismarck made it sound as if the Prussian king had treated the ambassador in a demeaning fashion. Six days later, France declared war on Prussia.

The Abeken [Privy Councillor] Text, Ems, July 13, 1870

To the Federal Chancellor, Count Bismarck. His Majesty the King writes to me:

"M. Benedetti intercepted me on the Promenade in order to demand of me most insistently that I should authorize him to telegraph immediately to Paris that I shall obligate myself for all future time never again to give my approval to the candidacy of the Hohenzollerns should it be renewed. I refused to agree to this, the last time somewhat severely, informing him that one dare not and cannot assume such obligations *à tout jamais* [forever]. Naturally, I informed him that I had received no news as yet, and since he had been informed earlier than I by way of Paris and Madrid, he could easily understand why my government was once again out of the matter."

Since then His Majesty has received a dispatch from the Prince [father of the Hohenzollern candidate for the Spanish throne]. As His Majesty has informed Count Benedetti that he was expecting news from the Prince, His Majesty himself, in view of the above-mentioned demand and in consonance with the advice of Count Eulenburg and myself, decided not to receive the French envoy again but to inform him through an adjutant that His Majesty had now received from the Prince confirmation of the news which Benedetti had already received from Paris, and that he had nothing further to say to the Ambassador. His Majesty leaves it to the judgment of Your Excellency whether or not to communicate at once the new demand by Benedetti and its rejection to our ambassadors and to the press.

Bismarck's Edited Version

After the reports of the renunciation by the hereditary Prince of Hohenzollern had been officially transmitted by the Royal Government of Spain to the Imperial Government of France, the French Ambassador presented to His Majesty the King at Ems the demand to authorize him to telegraph to Paris that His Majesty the King would obligate himself for all future time never again to give his approval to the candidacy of the Hohenzollerns should it be renewed.

His Majesty the King thereupon refused to receive the French envoy again and informed him through an adjutant that His Majesty had nothing further to say to the Ambassador.

Even before the war had ended, the south German states had agreed to enter the North German Confederation. On January 18, 1871, in the Hall of Mirrors in Louis XIV's palace at Versailles, William I was proclaimed kaiser or emperor of the Second German Empire (the first was the medieval Holy Roman Empire). German unity had been achieved by the Prussian monarchy and the Prussian army. In a real sense, Germany had been merged into Prussia, not Prussia into Germany. German liberals also rejoiced. They had dreamed of unity and freedom, but the achievement of unity now seemed much more important. One old liberal proclaimed:

> I cannot shake off the impression of this hour. I am no devotee of Mars; I feel more attached to the goddess of beauty and the mother of graces than to the powerful god of war, but the trophies of war exercise a magic charm even upon the child of peace. One's view is involuntarily chained and one's spirit goes along with the boundless row of men who acclaim the god of the moment—success.[2]

The Prussian leadership of German unification meant the triumph of authoritarian, militaristic values over liberal, constitutional sentiments in the development of the new German state. With its industrial resources and military might, the new state had become the strongest power on the Continent. A new European balance of power was at hand.

Nation Building and Reform: The National State in Mid-Century

While European affairs were dominated by the unification of Italy and Germany, other states in the Western world were also undergoing transformations. War, civil war, and changing political alignments served as catalysts for domestic reforms.

The Austrian Empire: Toward a Dual Monarchy

After the Habsburgs had crushed the revolutions of 1848–1849, they restored centralized, autocratic government to the empire. But failure in war led to severe internal consequences for Austria. Austria's defeat at the hands of the Prussians in 1866 forced the Austrians to deal with the fiercely nationalistic Hungarians. The result was the negotiated *Ausgleich*, or Compromise, of 1867, which created the dual monarchy of Austria-Hungary. Each part of the empire now had its constitution, its own bicameral legislature, its own governmental machinery for domestic affairs, and its own capital (Vienna for Austria and Budapest for Hungary). Holding the two states together were a single monarch (Francis Joseph was Emperor of Austria and King of Hungary) and a common army, foreign policy, and system of finances. In domestic affairs, the Hungarians had become an independent nation. The *Ausgleich* did not, however, satisfy the other nationalities that made up the multinational Austro-Hungarian Empire. The dual monarchy simply enabled the German-speaking Austrians and Hungarian

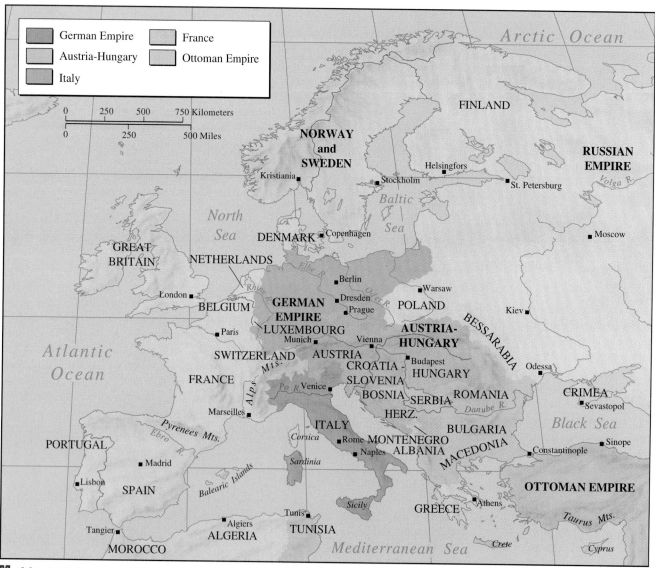

Map 23.3 Europe in 1871.

Magyars to dominate the minorities, especially the Slavs, in their respective states. As the Hungarian nationalist Louis Kossuth remarked, "Dualism is the alliance of the conservative, reactionary and any apparently liberal elements in Hungary with those of the Austrian Germans who despise liberty, for the oppression of the other nationalities and races."[3]

Imperial Russia

The defeat in the Crimean War in 1856 at the hands of the British and French revealed the blatant deficiencies behind the facade of absolute power and made it clear even to staunch conservatives that Russia was falling hopelessly behind the western European powers. Tsar

Alexander II (1855–1881), who came to power in the midst of the Crimean War, turned his energies to a serious overhaul of the Russian system. Following the autocratic procedures of his predecessors, he attempted to impose reforms on the Russian people.

Serfdom was the most burdensome problem in tsarist Russia. The continuing subjugation of millions of peasants to the land and their landlords was an obviously corrupt and failing system. On March 3, 1861, Alexander issued his emancipation edict (see the box on p. 478). Peasants could now own property, marry as they chose, and bring suits in the law courts. Nevertheless, the benefits of emancipation were limited. The government provided land for the peasants by purchasing it from the landlords, but the landowners often chose to keep the

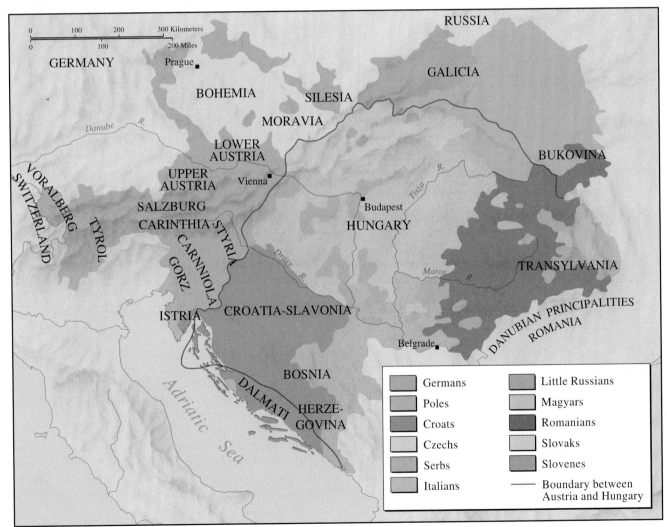

Map 23.4 Ethnic Groups in the Dual Monarchy, 1867.

Emancipation: Serfs and Slaves

Although overall their histories have been quite different, Russia and the United States shared a common feature in the 1860s. They were the only states in the Western world that still had large enslaved populations (the Russian serfs were virtually slaves). The leaders of both countries issued emancipation proclamations within two years of each other. The first excerpt is taken from the Imperial Decree of March 3, 1861, which freed the Russian serfs. The second excerpt is from Abraham Lincoln's Emancipation Proclamation, issued on January 1, 1863.

The Imperial Decree, March 3, 1861

By the grace of God, we, Alexander II, Emperor and Autocrat of all the Russias, King of Poland, Grand Duke of Finland, etc., to all our faithful subjects, make known:

Called by Divine Providence and by the sacred right of inheritance to the throne of our ancestors, we took a vow in our innermost heart to respond to the mission which is intrusted to us as to surround with our affection and our Imperial solicitude all our faithful subjects of every rank and of every condition, from the warrior, who nobly bears arms for the defense of the country to the humble artisan devoted to the works of industry; from the official in the career of the high offices of the State to the laborer whose plough furrows the soil. . . .

We thus came to the conviction that the work of a serious improvement of the condition of the peasants was a sacred inheritance bequeathed to us by our ancestors, a mission which, in the course of events, Divine providence called upon us to fulfill. . . .

In virtue of the new dispositions above mentioned, the peasants attached to the soil will be invested within a term fixed by the law with all the rights of free cultivators. . . .

At the same time, they are granted the right of purchasing their close, and, with the consent of the proprietors, they may acquire in full property the arable lands and other appurtenances which are allotted to them as a permanent holding. By the acquisition in full property of the quantity of land fixed, the peasants are free from their obligations toward the proprietors for land thus purchased, and they enter definitely into the condition of free peasants—landholders.

The Emancipation Proclamation, January 1, 1863

Now therefore, I, Abraham Lincoln, President of the United States, by virtue of the power in me vested as Commander-in-Chief of the Army and Navy of the United States in time of actual armed rebellion against the authority and government of the United States, and as a fit and necessary war measure for suppressing such rebellion, do, on this 1st day of January, A.D. 1863, and in accordance with my purpose to do so, . . . order and designate as the States and parts of States wherein the people thereof, respectively, are this day in rebellion against the United States the following, to wit:

Arkansas, Texas, Louisiana, . . . Mississippi, Alabama, Florida, Georgia, South Carolina, North Carolina, and Virginia . . .

And by virtue of the power for the purpose aforesaid, I do order and declare that all persons held as slaves within said designated States and parts of States are, and henceforeward shall be free; and that the Executive Government of the United States, including the military and naval authorities thereof, will recognize and maintain the freedom of said persons.

best lands. The Russian peasants soon found that they had inadequate amounts of good arable land to support themselves, a situation that worsened as the peasant population increased rapidly in the second half of the nineteenth century.

Nor were the peasants completely free. The state compensated the landowners for the land given to the peasants, but the peasants, in turn, were expected to repay the state in long-term installments. To ensure that the payments were made, peasants were subjected to the authority of their *mir* or village commune, which was collec-

tively responsible for the land payments to the government. In a very real sense, then, the village commune, not the individual peasants, owned the land the peasants were purchasing. And since the village communes were responsible for the payments, they were reluctant to allow peasants to leave their land. Emancipation, then, led not to a free, landowning peasantry along the Western model, but to an unhappy, land-starved peasantry that largely followed the old ways of farming.

Alexander II also attempted other reforms. In 1864, he instituted a system of zemstvos, or local assemblies, that provided a moderate degree of self-government. Representatives to the zemstvos were to be elected from the noble landowners, townspeople, and peasants, but the property-based system of voting gave a distinct advantage to the nobles. Zemstvos were given a limited power to provide public services, such as education, famine relief, and road and bridge maintenance. They could levy taxes for these services, but their efforts were frequently disrupted by bureaucrats who feared any hint of self-government. The legal reforms of 1864, which created a regular system of local and provincial courts and a judicial code that accepted the principle of equality before the law, proved successful, however.

Even the autocratic tsar was unable to control the forces he unleashed by his reform program. Reformers wanted more and rapid change; conservatives opposed what they perceived as the tsar's attempts to undermine the basic institutions of Russian society. By 1870, Russia was witnessing increasing levels of dissatisfaction. When one group of radicals assassinated Alexander II in 1881, his son and successor, Alexander III (1881–1894), turned against reform and returned to the traditional methods of repression.

Great Britain: The Victorian Age

Like Russia, Britain was not troubled by revolutionary disturbances during 1848, although for quite different reasons. The Reform Act of 1832 had opened the door to political representation for the industrial middle class, and in the 1860s Britain's liberal parliamentary system demonstrated once more its ability to make both social and political reforms that enabled the country to remain stable and prosperous.

One of the reasons for Britain's stability was its continuing economic growth. After 1850, middle-class prosperity was at last coupled with some improvements for the working classes as well. Real wages for laborers increased more than 25 percent between 1850 and 1870. The British sense of national pride was well reflected in Queen Victoria (1837–1901), whose self-contentment and sense of moral respectability mirrored the attitudes of her age. The Victorian Age, as Britain during the reign of Queen Victoria has ever since been known, was characterized by a pious complacency.

Politically, this was an era of uneasy stability as the aristocratic and upper-middle-class representatives who dominated Parliament blurred party lines by their internal strife and shifting positions. One important issue was the extension of voting rights. The Tory leader in Parliament, Benjamin Disraeli (1804–1881), became a supporter of voting reform, primarily because he thought he could win over the newly enfranchised groups to the Conservative Party. The Reform Act of 1867 was an important step toward the democratization of Britain. By lowering the monetary requirements for voting (taxes paid or income

✦ **Queen Victoria and Her Family.** Queen Victoria, who ruled Britain from 1837 to 1901, married Prince Albert of Saxe-Coburg and Gotha in 1840 and subsequently gave birth to four sons and five daughters, who were married into a number of European royal families. Queen Victoria is seated at the center of this 1881 photograph, surrounded by members of her family.

earned), it by and large enfranchised many male urban workers. The number of voters increased from about 1 million to slightly over 2 million. Although Disraeli believed this would benefit the Conservatives, industrial workers helped to produce a huge Liberal victory in 1868.

The United States: Civil War and Reunion

By the mid-nineteenth century, American national unity was increasingly threatened by the issue of slavery. Like the North, the South had grown dramatically in population during the first half of the nineteenth century. But its development was quite different. Its cotton economy and social structure were based on the exploitation of enslaved black Africans and their descendants. The importance of cotton is evident from production figures. In 1810, the South produced a raw cotton crop of 178,000 bales worth $10 million. By 1860, it was generating 4.5 million bales of cotton with a value of $249 million. Ninety-three percent of southern cotton in 1850 was produced by a slave population that had grown dramatically in fifty years. Although new slave imports had been barred in 1808, there were 4 million Afro-American slaves in the South by 1860 compared to 1 million in 1800. The cotton economy and a plantation-based slavery were intimately related, and the attempt to maintain them in the course of the first half of the nineteenth century led the South to become increasingly defensive, monolithic, and isolated. At the same time, the growth of an abolitionist movement in the North challenged the southern order and created an "emotional chain reaction" that led to civil war.

The push of Americans westward was a major factor in bringing the issue of slavery to the forefront of American politics. A debate arose over whether to admit new states to the union as free or slave states. The issue had already arisen in the 1810s as new states were being created by the rush of settlers beyond the Mississippi. The free states of the North feared the creation of a slave-state majority in the national government. Attempts at compromise over this issue had merely postponed, not solved, this divisive issue. By the 1850s, slavery had caused the Whig party to become defunct and the Democrats to split along North–South lines while angry northerners created a new one-issue party. The Republicans were united by antislavery and were especially driven by the fear that the "slave power" of the South would attempt to spread the slave system throughout the country.

As polarization over the issue of slavery intensified, compromise became less feasible. When Abraham Lincoln, the man who had said in a speech in Illinois in 1858 that "this government cannot endure permanently half slave and half free," was elected president in November 1860, the die was cast. Lincoln carried only 2 of the 1,109 counties in the South; the Republicans were not even on the ballot in ten southern states. On December 20, 1860, a South Carolina convention voted to repeal ratification of the Constitution of the United States. In February 1861, six more southern states did the same, and a rival nation—the Confederate States of America—was formed. In March fighting erupted between North and South.

The American Civil War (1861–1865) was an extraordinarily bloody struggle, a clear foretaste of the total war to come in the twentieth century. More than 360,000 soldiers died, either in battle or from deadly infectious diseases spawned by filthy camp conditions. Over a period of four years, the Union states mobilized their superior assets and gradually wore down the South. As the war dragged on, it had the effect of radicalizing public opinion in the North. What began as a war to save the Union became a war against slavery. On January 1, 1863, Lincoln's Emancipation Proclamation made most of the nation's slaves "forever free" (see the box on p. 478). The increasingly effective Union blockade of the South combined with a shortage of fighting men made the Confederate cause desperate by the end of 1864. The final push of Union troops under General Ulysses S. Grant forced General Robert E. Lee's army to surrender on April 9, 1865. Although the problems of reconstruction were ahead, the Union victory confirmed that the United States would be "one nation, indivisible."

The Emergence of a Canadian Nation

To the north of the United States, the process of nation building was also making progress. By the Treaty of Paris in 1763, Canada—or New France as it was called—passed into the hands of the British. By 1800, most Canadians favored more autonomy, although the colonists disagreed on the form this autonomy should take. Upper Canada (now Ontario) was predominantly English-speaking while Lower Canada (now Quebec) was dominated by French Canadians. Increased immigration to Canada after 1815 also fueled the desire for self-government.

The head of Upper Canada's Conservative Party, John Macdonald, became an avid apostle for union and self-government. Fearful of American desires on Canada during the American Civil War, the British government finally capitulated to Macdonald's demands, and in 1867, Parliament established a Canadian nation—the Dominion of Canada—with its own constitution. John Macdonald became the first prime minister of the Dominion. Canada now possessed a parliamentary system and ruled itself, although foreign affairs still remained under the control of the British government.

Industrialization and the Marxist Response

Between 1850 and 1871, continental industrialization came of age. The innovations of the British Industrial Revolution—mechanized factory production, the use of coal, the steam engine, and the transportation revolution—all became regular features of economic expansion. Although marred periodically by economic depression (1857–1858) or recession (1866–1867), this was an age of considerable economic prosperity, particularly evident in the growth of domestic and foreign markets.

Before 1870, capitalist factory owners remained largely free to hire labor on their own terms based on market forces. Although workers formed trade unions as organizations that would fight for improved working conditions and reasonable wages, they tended to represent only a small part of the industrial working class and proved largely ineffective. Real change for the industrial proletariat would only come with the development of socialist parties and socialist trade unions. These emerged after 1870, but the theory that made them possible had already been developed by mid-century in the work of Karl Marx.

Marx and Marxism

The beginnings of Marxism can be found in 1848 with the publication of a short treatise entitled *The Communist Manifesto*, written by two Germans, Karl Marx (1818–1883) and Friedrich Engels (1820–1895). Although the work was known to only a few of Marx's friends at the time, it eventually became one of the most influential political treatises in modern European history.

What, then, was the basic picture of historical development that Marx and Engels offered in *The Communist Manifesto*? They began their treatise with the statement that "the history of all hitherto existing society is the history of class struggles." Throughout history, oppressed and oppressor have "stood in constant opposition to one another." In an earlier struggle, the feudal classes of the Middle Ages were forced to accede to the emerging middle class or bourgeoisie. As the bourgeoisie took control in turn, their ideas became the dominant views of the era, and government became their instrument. Marx and En-

The National State

France	
Louis Napoleon is elected president	1848
Coup d'etat by Louis Napoleon	1851
Creation of the Second Empire	1852
Emperor Napoleon III	1852–1870
The "authoritarian empire"	1852–1860
Crimean War	1854–1856
The "liberal empire"	1860–1870
The Austrian Empire	
Ausgleich: the dual monarchy	1867
Russia	
Tsar Alexander II	1855–1881
Emancipation edict	1861 (March 3)
Creation of zemstvos and legal reforms	1864
Great Britian	
Queen Victoria	1837–1901
Reform Act	1867
The United States	
Election of Lincoln and secession of South Carolina	1860
Outbreak of Civil War	1861
Surrender of Lee	1865 (April 9)
Canada	
Formation of the Dominion of Canada	1867

gels declared: "The executive of the modern State is but a committee for managing the common affairs of the whole bourgeoisie."[4] In other words, the government of the state reflected and defended the interests of the industrial middle class and its allies.

Although bourgeois society had emerged victorious out of the ruins of feudal society, Marx and Engels insisted that it had not triumphed completely. Now once again the bourgeoisie were antagonists in an emerging class struggle, but this time they faced the proletariat, or the industrial working class. The struggle would be fierce; in fact, Marx and Engels predicted that the workers would eventually overthrow their bourgeois masters. After their victory, the

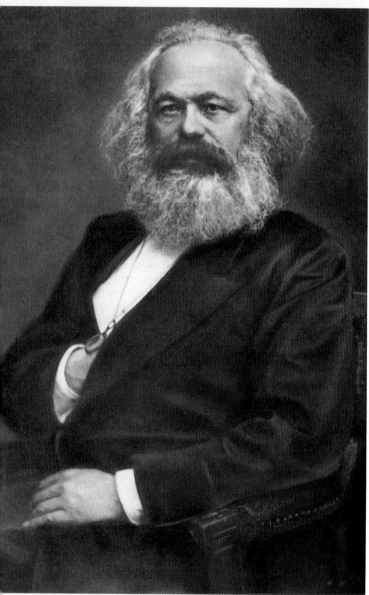

◆ **Karl Marx.** Karl Marx was a radical journalist who joined with Friedrich Engels to write *The Communist Manifesto*, which proclaimed the ideas of a revolutionary socialism. After the failure of the 1848 revolution in Germany, Marx fled to Britain, where he continued to write and became involved in the work of the first International Working Men's Association.

proletariat would form a dictatorship to reorganize the means of production. Then, a classless society would emerge, and the state—itself an instrument of the bourgeoisie—would wither away since it no longer represented the interests of a particular class. Class struggles would then be over (see the box on p. 483). Marx believed that the emergence of a classless society would lead to

progress in science, technology, and industry and to greater wealth for all.

After the failure of the revolutions of 1848, Marx went to Britain, where he spent the rest of his life in exile. Marx continued his writing on political economy, especially his famous work, *Das Kapital* (*Capital*), but his own preoccupation with organizing the working-class movement kept Marx from ever finishing *Capital*. In *The Communist Manifesto*, Marx had defined the communists as "the most advanced and resolute section of the working-class parties of every country." Their advantage was their ability to understand "the line of march, the conditions, and the ultimate general results of the proletarian movement." Marx saw his role in this light and participated enthusiastically in the activities of the International Working Men's Association. Formed in 1864 by British and French trade unionists, this "First International" served as an umbrella organization for working-class interests. Marx was the dominant personality on the organization's General Council and devoted much time to its activities. Internal dissension, however, soon damaged the organization, and it failed in 1872. Although it would be revived in 1889, the fate of socialism by that time was in the hands of national socialist parties.

Science and Culture in an Age of Realism

Between 1850 and 1870, two major intellectual developments were evident: the growth of scientific knowledge with its rapidly increasing impact on the Western worldview; and the shift from Romanticism with its emphasis on the inner world of reality to Realism with its focus on the outer, material world.

A New Age of Science

By the mid-nineteenth century, science was having a greater and greater impact on European life. The Scientific Revolution of the sixteenth and seventeenth centuries had fundamentally transformed the Western worldview and created a modern, rational approach to the study of the natural world. Even in the eighteenth century, however, these intellectual developments had remained the preserve of an educated elite and resulted in few practical benefits. Moreover, the technical advances of the early Industrial Revolution had depended little on pure science and much more on the practical experiments of technologically oriented amateur inventors. Advances in industrial technology, however, fed an interest in basic

The Classless Society

In The Communist Manifesto, *Karl Marx and Friedrich Engels projected the creation of a classless society as the final end product of the struggle between the bourgeoisie and the proletariat. In this selection, they discuss the steps by which that classless society would be reached. Although Marx had criticized the utopian socialists for their failure to approach the labor problem scientifically, his solution sounds equally utopian.*

Karl Marx and Friedrich Engels,
The Communist Manifesto

We have seen above, that the first step in the revolution by the working class, is to raise the proletariat to the position of ruling class. . . . The proletariat will use its political supremacy to wrest, by degrees, all capital from the bourgeoisie, to centralize all instruments of production in the hands of the State, i.e., of the proletariat organized as the ruling class; and to increase the total of productive forces as rapidly as possible.

Of course, in the beginning, this cannot be effected except by means of despotic inroads on the rights of property, and on the conditions of bourgeois production; by means of measures, therefore, which appear economically insufficient and untenable, but which, in the course of the movement, outstrip themselves, necessitate further inroads upon the old social order, and are unavoidable as a means of entirely revolutionizing the mode of production.

These measures will of course be different in different countries.

Nevertheless, in the most advanced countries, the following will be pretty generally applicable:

1. Abolition of property in land and application of all rents of land to public purposes.
2. A heavy progressive or graduated income tax.
3. Abolition of all right of inheritance. . . .
5. Centralization of credit in the hands of the State, by means of a national bank with State capital and an exclusive monopoly.
6. Centralization of the means of communication and transport in the hands of the State.
7. Extension of factories and instruments of production owned by the State. . . .
8. Equal liability of all to labor. Establishment of industrial armies, especially for agriculture.
9. Combination of agriculture with manufacturing industries; gradual abolition of the distinction between town and country, by a more equable distribution of the population over the country.
10. Free education for all children in public schools. Abolition of children's factory labor in its present form. . . .

When, in the course of development, class distinctions have disappeared, and all production has been concentrated in the whole nation, the public power will lose its political character. Political power, properly so called, is merely the organized power of one class for oppressing another. If the proletariat during its contest with the bourgeoisie is compelled, by the force of circumstances, to organize itself as a class, if, by means of a revolution, it makes itself the ruling class, and, as such, sweeps away by force the old conditions of production, then it will, along with these conditions, have swept away the conditions for the existence of class antagonisms and of classes generally, and will thereby have abolished its own supremacy as a class.

In place of the old bourgeois society, with its classes and class antagonisms, we shall have an association, in which the free development of each is the condition for the free development of all.

scientific research, which, in turn, in the 1830s and afterward resulted in a rash of basic scientific discoveries that were soon transformed into technological improvements that affected all Europeans.

The development of the steam engine was important in encouraging scientists to work out its theoretical foundations, a preoccupation that led to the study of thermodynamics, the science of the relationship between heat and mechanical energy. The laws of thermodynamics were at the core of nineteenth-century physics. In chemistry, the Russian Dmitri Mendeleev in the 1860s classified all the material elements then known on the basis of their atomic weights and provided the systematic foundation for the periodic law. The Englishman Michael Faraday discovered the phenomenon of electromagnetic induction and put together a primitive generator that laid the foundation for the use of electricity, although economically efficient generators were not built until the 1870s.

In biology, the Frenchman Louis Pasteur formulated the germ theory of disease. The work of Pasteur and the many others who followed him in isolating the specific bacteriological causes of numerous diseases had a far-reaching impact. By providing a rational means of treating and preventing infectious diseases, they transformed the medical world. The practice of surgery, in particular, experienced dramatic change. Following the work of Pasteur, Joseph Lister (1827–1912) perceived that bacteria might enter a wound and cause infection. His use of carbolic acid, a newly discovered disinfectant, proved remarkably effective in eliminating infections during surgery. Lister's discoveries dramatically transformed surgery wards in that patients no longer succumbed regularly to what was called "hospital gangrene." Then, too, the discovery of sulfuric ether and chloroform as anesthetics enabled doctors to reduce the pain of the patient during surgery.

The steadily increasing and often dramatic material benefits generated by science and technology led Europeans to a growing faith in the benefits of science. The popularity of scientific and technological achievements produced a widespread acceptance of the scientific method, based on observation, experiment, and logical analysis, as the only path to objective truth and objective reality. This, in turn, undermined the faith of many people in religious revelation and truth. It is no accident that the nineteenth century was an age of increasing secularization, particularly evident in the growth of materialism or the belief that everything mental, spiritual, or ideal was simply an outgrowth of physical forces. Truth was to be found in the concrete material existence of human beings, not as Romanticists imagined in revelations gained by feeling or intuitive flashes. The importance of materialism was strikingly evident in the most important scientific event of the nineteenth century, the development of the theory of organic evolution according to natural selection. On the theories of Charles Darwin could be built a picture of humans as material beings that were simply part of the natural world.

Charles Darwin and the Theory of Organic Evolution

In 1859, Charles Darwin (1809–1882) published his celebrated book, *On the Origin of Species by Means of Natural Selection*. The basic idea of this book was that all plants and animals had evolved over a long period of time from earlier and simpler forms of life, a principle known as organic evolution. Darwin's work was important in that it explained how this natural process worked. In every species, he argued, "many more individuals of each species

are born than can possibly survive." This results in a "struggle for existence." Darwin believed that "As more individuals are produced than can possibly survive, there must in every case be a struggle for existence, either one individual with another of the same species, or with the individuals of distinct species, or with the physical conditions of life." Those who succeeded in this struggle for existence had adapted better to their environment, a process made possible by the appearance of "variants." Chance variations that occurred in the process of inheritance enabled some organisms to be more adaptable to the environment than others, a process that Darwin called natural selection:

> Owing to this struggle [for existence], variations, however slight . . . , if they be in any degree profitable to the individuals of a species, in their infinitely complex relations to other organic beings and to their physical conditions of life, will tend to the preservation of such individuals, and will generally be inherited by the offspring.[5]

Those that were naturally selected for survival ("survival of the fit") survived. The unfit did not and became extinct. The fit who survived, in turn, propagated and passed on the variations that enabled them to survive until, from Darwin's point of view, a new separate species emerged.

In *On the Origin of Species*, Darwin discussed plant and animal species only. He was not concerned with humans themselves and only later applied his theory of natural selection to humans. In *The Descent of Man*, published in 1871, he argued for the animal origins of human beings: "man is the co-descendant with other mammals of a common progenitor." Humans were not an exception to the rule governing other species.

Although Darwin's ideas were eventually accepted, initially they were highly controversial. Some people objected to what they considered Darwin's debasement of humans; his theory, they claimed, made human beings ordinary products of nature rather than unique beings. Others were disturbed by the implications of life as a struggle for survival, of "nature red in tooth and claw." Was there a place in the Darwinian world for moral values? For those who believed in a rational order in the world, Darwin's theory seemed to eliminate purpose and design from the universe. Gradually, however, Darwin's theory was accepted by scientists and other intellectuals although Darwin was somewhat overly optimistic when he wrote in 1872 that "almost every scientist admits the principle of evolution." In the process of accepting Darwin's ideas, some people even tried to apply them to society, yet another example of science's increasing prestige.

Realism in Literature and Art

The belief that the world should be viewed realistically, frequently expressed after 1850, was closely related to the materialistic outlook. The word *Realism* was first employed in 1850 to describe a new style of painting and soon spread to literature.

THE REALISTIC NOVEL

The literary Realists of the mid-nineteenth century were distinguished by their deliberate rejection of Romanticism. The literary Realists wanted to deal with ordinary characters from actual life rather than Romantic heroes in unusual settings. They also sought to avoid flowery and sentimental language by using careful observation and accurate description, an approach that led them to eschew poetry in favor of prose and the novel. Realists often combined their interest in everyday life with a searching examination of social questions. Even then they tried not to preach but to allow their characters to speak for themselves. Although the French were preeminent in literary Realism, it proved to be international in scope.

The leading novelist of the 1850s and 1860s, the Frenchman Gustave Flaubert (1821–1880), perfected the Realist novel. His *Madame Bovary* (1857) was a straightforward description of barren and sordid provincial life in France. Emma Bovary, a woman of some vitality, is trapped in a marriage to a drab provincial doctor. Impelled by the images of romantic love she has read about in novels, she seeks the same thing for herself in adulterous love affairs. Unfulfilled, she is ultimately driven to suicide, unrepentant to the end for her lifestyle. Flaubert's hatred of bourgeois society was evident in his portrayal of middle-class hypocrisy and smugness.

William Thackeray (1811–1863) wrote the opening manifesto of the Realist novel in Britain with his *Vanity Fair* in 1848. Subtitled *A Novel Without a Hero*, Thackeray deliberately flaunted the Romantic conventions. A novel, Thackeray said, should "convey as strongly as possible the sentiment of reality as opposed to a tragedy or poem, which may be heroical." Perhaps the greatest of the Victorian novelists was Charles Dickens (1812–1870), whose realistic novels focusing on the lower and middle classes in Britain's early industrial age became extraordinarily successful. His descriptions of the urban poor and the brutalization of human life were vividly realistic (see the box on p. 486).

REALISM IN ART

In art, too, Realism became dominant after 1850, although Romanticism was by no means dead. Among the most important characteristics of Realism are a desire to depict the everyday life of ordinary people, whether peasants, workers, or prostitutes; an attempt at photographic realism; and an interest in the natural environment. The French became leaders in realist painting.

Gustave Courbet (1819–1877) was the most famous artist of the realist school. In fact, the word *Realism* was first coined in 1850 to describe one of his paintings. Courbet reveled in a realistic portrayal of everyday life. His subjects were factory workers, peasants, and the wives of saloon keepers. "I have never seen either angels

◆ **Gustave Courbet, *The Stonebreakers*.** Realism, largely developed by French painters, aimed at a lifelike portrayal of the daily activities of ordinary people. Gustave Courbet was the most famous of the Realist artists. As is evident in *The Stonebreakers*, he sought to portray things as they really appear. He shows an old road builder and his young assistant in their tattered clothes, engrossed in their dreary work of breaking stones to construct a road.

Realism: Charles Dickens and an Image of Hell on Earth

Charles Dickens was one of Britain's greatest novelists. While he realistically portrayed the material, social, and psychological milieu of his time, an element of Romanticism still pervaded his novels. This is evident in this selection from The Old Curiosity Shop *in which his description of the English mill town of Birmingham takes on the imagery of Dante's Hell.*

Charles Dickens, *The Old Curiosity Shop*

A long suburb of red brick houses,—some with patches of garden ground, where coal-dust and factory smoke darkened the shrinking leaves, and coarse rank flowers; and where the struggling vegetation sickened and sank under the hot breath of kiln and furnace, making them by its presence seem yet more blighting and unwholesome than in the town itself,—a long, flat, straggling suburb passed, they came by slow degrees upon a cheerless region, where not a blade of grass was seen to grow; where not a bud put forth its promise in the spring; where nothing green could live but on the surface of the stagnant pools, which here and there lay idly sweltering by the black roadside.

Advancing more and more into the shadow of this mournful place, its dark depressing influence stole upon their spirits, and filled them with a dismal gloom. On every side, and as far as the eye could see into the heavy distance, tall chimneys, crowding on each other, and presenting that endless repetition of the same dull, ugly form, which is the horror of oppressive dreams, poured out their plague of smoke, obscured the light, and made foul the melancholy air. On mounds of ashes by the wayside, sheltered only by a few rough boards, or rotten pent-house roofs, strange engines spun and writhed like tortured creatures; clanking their iron chains, shrieking in their rapid whirl from time to time as though in torment unendurable, and making the ground tremble with their agonies. Dismantled houses here and there appeared, tottering to the earth, propped up by fragments of others that had fallen down, unroofed, windowless, blackened, desolate, but yet inhabited. Men, women, children, wan in their looks and ragged in attire, tended the engines, fed their tributary fires, begged upon the road, or scowled half-naked from the doorless houses. Then came more of the wrathful monsters, whose like they almost seemed to be in their wildness and their untamed air, screeching and turning to the right and left, with the same interminable perspective of brick towers, never ceasing in their black vomit, blasting all things living or inanimate, shutting out the face of day, and closing in on all these horrors with a dense dark cloud.

But night-time in this dreadful spot!—night, when the smoke was changed to fire; when every chimney spurted up its flame; and places, that had been dark vaults all day, now shone red-hot, with figures moving to and fro within their blazing jaws, and calling to one another with hoarse cries—night, when the noise of every strange machine was aggravated by the darkness; when the people near them looked wilder and more savage; when bands of unemployed labourers paraded in the roads, or clustered by torchlight round their leaders, who told them in stern language of their wrongs, and urged them on by frightful cries and threats; when maddened men, armed with sword and firebrand, spurning the tears and prayers of women who would restrain them, rushed forth on errands of terror and destruction, to work no ruin half so surely as their own—night, when carts came rumbling by, filled with rude coffins (for contagious disease and death had been busy with the living crops); or when orphans cried, and distracted women shrieked and followed in their wake—night, when some called for bread, and some for drink to drown their cares; and some with tears, and some with staggering feet, and so with bloodshot eyes, went brooding home—night, which, unlike the night that Heaven sends on earth, brought with it no peace, nor quiet, nor signs of blessed sleep—who shall tell the terrors of the night to that young wandering child!

or goddesses, so I am not interested in painting them," he exclaimed. One of his famous works, *The Stonebreakers*, painted in 1849, shows two road workers engaged in the deadening work of breaking stones to build a road. This representation of human misery was a scandal to those who objected to his "cult of ugliness." To Courbet, no subject was too ordinary, too harsh, or too ugly to interest him.

Jean-François Millet (1814–1875) was preoccupied with scenes from rural life, especially peasants laboring in the fields, although his Realism still contained an element of romantic sentimentality. In *The Sower*, a peasant, energetically scattering seeds in a field, becomes a symbol of new life and the symbiotic relationship between humans and nature. Millet made landscape and country life an important subject matter for French artists, but he, too, was criticized by his contemporaries for crude subject matter and unorthodox technique.

Conclusion

Between 1850 and 1871, the national state became the focus of people's loyalty. Wars, both foreign and civil, were fought to create unified nation-states. Political nationalism had emerged during the French revolutionary era and had become a powerful force of change during the first half of the nineteenth century, but its triumph came only after 1850. Tied initially to middle-class liberals, by the end of the nineteenth century it would have great appeal to the broad masses as well. In 1871, however, the political transformations stimulated by the force for nationalism were by no means complete. Significantly large minorities, especially in the polyglot empires controlled by the Austrians, Ottoman Turks, and Russians, had not achieved the goal of their own national states. Moreover, the nationalism that had triumphed by 1871 was no longer the nationalism that had been closely identified with liberalism. Liberal nationalists had believed that unified nation-states would preserve individual rights and lead to a greater community of peoples. Rather than unifying people, however, the loud and chauvinistic nationalism of the late nineteenth century divided them

✦ **Jean-François Millet, *The Sower*.** Jean-François Millet, another prominent French Realist painter, took a special interest in the daily activities of French peasants, although he tended to transform his peasants into heroic figures who dominated their environment. In *The Sower*, for example, despite his rough clothes, the peasant scattering seed into the newly plowed fields appears as a powerful figure, symbolizing the union of humans with the earth.

as the new national states became embroiled in bitter competition after 1871.

Europeans, however, were hardly aware of nationalism's dangers in 1871. The spread of industrialization and the wealth of scientific and technological achievements were sources of optimism, not pessimism. After the revolutionary and military upheavals of the mid-century decades, many Europeans undoubtedly believed that they stood on the verge of a new age of progress.

NOTES

1. Louis L. Snyder, ed., *Documents of Germany History* (New Brunswick, N.J., 1958), p. 202.
2. Quoted in Otto Pflanze, *Bismarck and the Development of Germany, The Period of Unification, 1815–1871* (Princeton, N.J., 1963), p. 327.
3. Quoted in György Szabad, *Hungarian Political Trends Between the Revolution and the Compromise, 1849–1867* (Budapest, 1977), p. 163.
4. Karl Marx and Friedrich Engels, *The Communist Manifesto* (Harmondsworth, 1967), pp. (in order of quotations) 79, 81, 82.
5. Charles Darwin, *On the Origins of Species* (New York, 1872), 1:77, 79.

SUGGESTIONS FOR FURTHER READING

Three general surveys of the mid-century decades are N. Rich, *The Age of Nationalism and Reform, 1850–1890*, 2d ed. (New York, 1979); E. Hobsbawm, *The Age of Capital, 1845–1875* (London, 1975); and J. A. S. Grenville, *Europe Reshaped, 1848–1878* (London, 1976). In addition to the books listed for individual countries in Chapter 22 that also cover the material of this chapter, see H. Holborn, *A History of Modern Germany*, vol. 3, *1840–1945* (New York, 1969); G. Craig, *Germany, 1866–1945* (Oxford, 1981); the two detailed volumes of T. Zeldin, *France, 1848–1945* (Oxford, 1973–77); A. J. May, *The Habsburg Monarchy, 1867–1914* (Cambridge, Mass., 1951); and D. Read, *England, 1868–1914* (London, 1979).

For a good introduction to the French Second Empire, see A. Plessis, *The Rise and Fall of the Second Empire, 1852–1871*, trans. J. Mandelbaum (New York, 1985). Napoleon's role can be examined in W. H. C. Smith, *Napoleon III* (New York, 1972); and J. F. McMillan, *Napoleon III* (New York, 1991). On life in France during the reign of Napoleon III, see R. L. Williams, *Gaslight and Shadow: The World of Napoleon III* (New York, 1957). The Crimean War and its impact are examined in P. W. Schroeder, *Austria, Great Britain and the Crimean War: The Destruction of the European Concert* (Ithaca, N.Y., 1972).

The unification of Italy can best be examined in the works of D. M. Smith, *Victor Emmanuel, Cavour and the Risorgimento* (London, 1971); and *Cavour* (London, 1985). See also H. Hearder, *Cavour* (New York, 1994). The unification of Germany can be pursued first in two good biographies of Bismarck, E. Crankshaw, *Bismarck*

(New York, 1981); and G. O. Kent, *Bismarck and His Times* (Carbondale, Ill., 1978). T. S. Hamerow, *The Social Foundations of German Unification, 1858–1871* (Princeton, N.J., 1969) is good on the political implications of social changes in Germany. Also valuable is O. Pflanze, *Bismarck and the Development of Germany: The Period of Unification, 1815–1871* (Princeton, N.J., 1963).

On the emancipation of the Russian serfs, see D. Field, *The End of Serfdom: Nobility and Bureaucracy in Russia, 1855–1861* (Cambridge, 1976); and T. Emmons, ed., *Emancipation of the Russian Serfs* (New York, 1970). On the 1867 Reform Act in Britain, see M. Cowling, *1867: Disraeli, Gladstone and Revolution* (London, 1967), while the evolution of British political parties in mid-century is examined in H. J. Hanham, *Elections and Party Management: Politics in the Time of Disraeli and Gladstone*, 2d ed. (London, 1978). On the background to the American Civil War, see D. Potter, *The Impending Crisis, 1845–1861* (New York, 1976); and M. Holt, *The Political Crisis of the 1850's* (New York, 1978). A good, brief biography of Lincoln is O. and L. Handlin, *Abraham Lincoln and the Union* (Boston, 1980). A good one-volume survey of the Civil War can be found in P. J. Parish, *The American Civil War* (New York, 1975).

In addition to the general works on economic development listed in Chapters 21 and 22, some specialized works on this period are worthwhile. These include P. O'Brien, *The New Economic History of the Railways* (New York, 1977); and F. Crouzet, *The Victorian Economy* (London, 1982). On Marx there is the standard work by

D. McLellan, *Karl Marx: His Life and Thought* (New York, 1974), but it can be supplemented by the interesting and comprehensive work by L. Kolakowski, *Main Currents of Marxism*, 3 vols. (Oxford, 1978).

For an introduction to the intellectual changes of the nineteenth century, see O. Chadwick, *The Secularization of the European Mind in the Nineteenth Century* (Cambridge, 1975). A good biography of Darwin can be found in J. Bowlby, *Charles Darwin, A Biography* (London, 1990). On the popularization of Darwinism, see A. Kelly, *The Descent of Darwin* (Chapel Hill, N.C., 1981). On Realism, L. Nochlin, *Realism* (Harmondsworth, 1971) is a good introduction.

CHAPTER

24

Mass Society in an "Age of Progress," 1871–1894

In the late nineteenth century, Europe witnessed a dynamic age of material prosperity. With new industries, new sources of energy, and new goods, a Second Industrial Revolution transformed the human environment, dazzled Europeans, and led them to believe that their material progress meant human progress. Scientific and technological achievements, many naively believed, would improve humanity's condition and solve all human problems. The doctrine of progress became an article of great faith.

The new urban and industrial world created by the rapid economic changes of the nineteenth century led to the emergence of a mass society by the late nineteenth century. A mass society meant improvements for the lower classes who benefited from the extension of voting rights, a better standard of living, and mass education. It also brought mass leisure. New work patterns established the "weekend" as a distinct time of recreation and fun while new forms of mass transportation—railroads and streetcars—enabled even workers to make brief excursions to amusement parks. Coney Island was only eight miles from central New York City; Blackpool in England was a short train ride from nearby industrial towns. With their Ferris wheels and other daring rides that threw young men and women together, amusement parks offered a whole new world of entertainment. Thanks to the railroad, seaside resorts, once the preserve of the wealthy, also became accessible to more people for weekend visits, much to the disgust of one upper-class regular who described the new "day-trippers": "They swarm upon the beach, wandering listlessly about with apparently no other aim than to get a mouthful of fresh air." Enterprising entrepreneurs in resorts like Blackpool, however, welcomed the masses of new visitors and built piers laden with food, drink, and entertainment to serve them.

The coming of mass society also created new roles for the governments of European nation-states, which now fostered national loyalty, created mass armies by conscription, and took more responsibility for public health and housing measures in their cities. By 1871,

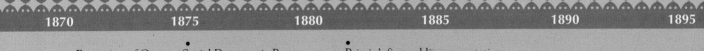

Formation of German Social Democratic Party   Britain's first public power station

First birth control clinic   Germany's social welfare legislation

Bell's invention of the telephone   First internal combustion engine

Emergence of mass newspapers   Compulsory primary education in France

The Paris Commune   Second ministry of Gladstone   Bismarck as German chancellor

Reign of Tsar Alexander III

the national state had become the focus of Europeans' lives. Within many of these nation-states, the growth of the middle class had led to the triumph of liberal practices: constitutional governments, parliaments, and principles of equality. The period after 1871 also witnessed the growth of political democracy as the right to vote was extended to all adult males; women, though, would still have to fight for the same political rights. With political democracy came a new mass politics and a new mass press. Both would become regular features of the twentieth century.

The Growth of Industrial Prosperity

At the heart of Europeans' belief in progress after 1871 was the stunning material growth produced by what historians have called the Second Industrial Revolution. The first Industrial Revolution had given rise to textiles, railroads, iron, and coal. In the second revolution, steel, chemicals, electricity, and petroleum led the way to new industrial frontiers.

New Products and New Patterns

The first major change in industrial development after 1870 was the substitution of steel for iron. New methods of rolling and shaping steel made it useful in the construction of lighter, smaller, and faster machines and engines, as well as railways, ships, and armaments. In 1860, Great Britain, France, Germany, and Belgium produced 125,000 tons of steel; by 1913, the total was 32 million

tons. By 1910, German steel production was double that of Great Britain, and both had been surpassed by the United States in 1890.

Electricity was a major new form of energy that proved to be of great value because it could be easily converted into other forms of energy, such as heat, light, and motion, and moved relatively effortlessly through space by means of transmitting wires. In the 1870s, the first commercially practical generators of electrical current were developed. By 1881, Britain had its first public power station. By 1910, hydroelectric power stations and coal-fired steam-generating plants enabled entire districts to be tied into a single power distribution system that provided a common source of power for homes, shops, and industrial enterprises.

Electricity spawned a whole new series of inventions. The invention of the lightbulb by the American Thomas Edison and the Briton Joseph Swan opened homes and cities to illumination by electric lights. A revolution in communications was fostered when Alexander Graham Bell invented the telephone in 1876 and Guglielmo Marconi sent the first radio waves across the Atlantic in 1901. Although most electricity was initially used for lighting, it was eventually put to use in transportation. By the 1880s, streetcars and subways had appeared in major European cities. Electricity also transformed the factory. Conveyor belts, cranes, machines, and machine tools could all be powered by electricity and located anywhere. Thanks to electricity, all countries could now enter the industrial age.

The development of the internal combustion engine had a similar effect. The first internal combustion engine, fired by gas and air, was produced in 1878. It proved unsuitable for widespread use as a source of power in transportation until the development of liquid fuels, namely,

The development of the internal combustion engine gave rise to the automobile and airplane. In 1900, world production stood at 9,000 cars; by 1906, Americans had overtaken the initial lead of the French. It was an American, Henry Ford, who revolutionized the car industry with the mass production of the Model T. By 1916, Ford's factories were producing 735,000 cars a year. In the meantime an age of air transportation began with the Zeppelin airship in 1900. In 1903, at Kitty Hawk, North Carolina, the Wright brothers made the first flight in a fixed-wing plane powered by a gasoline engine. It took World War I to stimulate the aircraft industry, however, and the first regular passenger air service was not established until 1919.

The growth of industrial production depended on the development of markets for the sale of manufactured goods. After 1870, the best foreign markets were already heavily saturated, forcing Europeans to take a renewed look at their domestic markets. Between 1850 and 1900, real wages increased by two-thirds in Britain and by one-third in Germany. As the prices of both food and manufactured goods declined due to lower transportation costs, Europeans could spend more on consumer products. Businesses soon perceived the value of using new techniques of mass marketing to sell the consumer goods made possible by the development of the steel and electrical industries. By bringing together a vast array of new products in one place, they created the department store (see the box on p. 493). The desire to own sewing machines, clocks, bicycles, electric lights, and typewriters rapidly created a new consumer ethic that became a crucial part of the modern economy.

Meanwhile, increased competition for foreign markets and the growing importance of domestic demand led to a reaction against the free trade that had characterized much of the European economy between 1820 and 1870. To many industrial and political leaders, protective tariffs guaranteed domestic markets for the products of their own industries. By the 1870s, Europeans returned to tariff protection. At the same time, cartels were being formed to decrease competition internally. In a cartel, independent enterprises worked together to control prices and fix production quotas, thereby restraining the kind of competition that led to reduced prices. Cartels were especially strong in Germany, where banks moved to protect their investments by eliminating the "anarchy of competition." Founded in 1893, the Rhenish-Westphalian Coal Syndicate controlled 98 percent of Germany's coal production by 1904.

The formation of cartels was paralleled by a move toward ever-larger factories, especially in the iron and steel, machine, heavy electrical equipment, and chemical in-

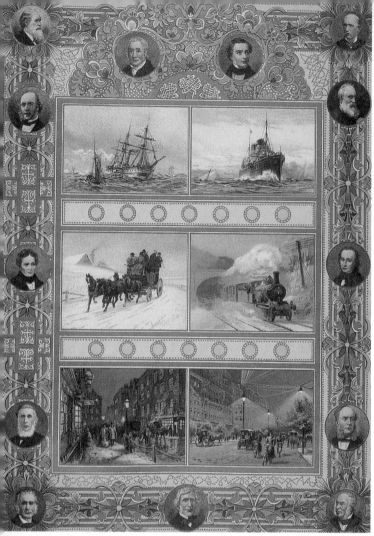

◆ **An Age of Progress.** Between 1871 and 1914, a Second Industrial Revolution led many Europeans to believe that they were living in an age of progress when most human problems would be solved by scientific achievements. This illustration is taken from a special issue of *The Illustrated London News* celebrating the Diamond Jubilee of Queen Victoria in 1897. On the left are scenes from 1837, when Victoria came to the British throne; on the right are scenes from 1897. The vivid contrast underscored the magazine's conclusion: "The most striking . . . evidence of progress during the reign is the ever increasing speed which the discoveries of physical science have forced into everyday life. Steam and electricity have conquered time and space to a greater extent during the last sixty years than all the preceding six hundred years witnessed."

petroleum and its distilled derivatives, made possible the widespread use of the internal combustion engine as a source of power in transportation. An oil-fired engine was made in 1897, and by 1902, the Hamburg-Amerika Line had switched from coal to oil on its new ocean liners. By the end of the nineteenth century, some naval fleets had been converted to oil burners as well.

The Department Store and the Beginnings of Mass Consumerism

Domestic markets were especially important for the sale of the goods being turned out by Europe's increasing number of industrial plants. New techniques of mass marketing arose to encourage people to purchase the new consumer goods. The Parisians pioneered in the development of the department store, and this selection is taken from a contemporary's account of the growth of these stores in the French capital city.

E. Lavasseur, On Parisian Department Stores, 1907

It was in the reign of Louis-Philippe that department stores for fashion goods and dresses, extending to material and other clothing began to be distinguished. The type was already one of the notable developments of the Second Empire; it became one of the most important ones of the Third Republic. These stores have increased in number and several of them have become extremely large. Combining in their different departments all articles of clothing, toilet articles, furniture and many other ranges of goods, it is their special object so to combine all commodities as to attract and satisfy customers who will find conveniently together an assortment of a mass of articles corresponding to all their various needs. They attract customers by permanent display, by free entry into the shops, by periodic exhibitions, by special sales, by fixed prices, and by their ability to deliver the goods purchased to customers' homes, in Paris and to the provinces. Turning themselves into direct intermediaries between the producer and the consumer, even producing sometimes some of their articles in their own workshops, buying at lowest prices because of their large orders and because they are in a position to profit from bargains, working with large sums, and selling to most of their customers for cash only, they can transmit these benefits in lowered selling prices. They can even decide to sell at a loss, as an advertisement or to get rid of out-of-date fashions. Taking 5–6 percent on 100 million brings them in more than 20 percent would bring to a firm doing a turnover of 50,000 francs.

The success of these department stores is only possible thanks to the volume of their business and this volume needs considerable capital and a very large turnover. Now capital, having become abundant, is freely combined nowadays in large enterprises, although French capital has the reputation of being more wary of the risks of industry than of State or railway securities. On the other hand, the large urban agglomerations, the ease with which goods can be transported by the railways, the diffusion of some comforts to strata below the middle classes, have all favored these developments.

As example we may cite some figures relating to these stores, since they were brought to the notice of the public in the *Revue des Deux-Mondes*. . . .

Le Louvre, dating to the time of the extension of the rue de Rivoli under the Second Empire, did in 1893 a business of 120 million at a profit of 6.4 percent. *Le Bon-Marché*, which was a small shop when Mr. Boucicaut entered it in 1852, already did a business of 20 million at the end of the Empire. During the republic its new buildings were erected; Mme. Boucicaut turned it by her will into a kind of cooperative society, with shares and an ingenious organization; turnover reached 150 million in 1893, leaving a profit of 5 percent. . . .

According to the tax records of 1891, these stores in Paris, numbering 12, employed 1,708 persons and were rated on their site values at 2,159,000 francs; the largest had then 542 employees. These same stores had, in 1901, 9,784 employees; one of them over 2,000 and another over 1,600; their site value has doubled (4,089,000 francs).

---

dustries. This growth in the size of industrial plants led to pressure for greater efficiency in factory production at the same time that competition led to demands for greater economy. The result was a desire to streamline or rationalize production as much as possible. The development of precision tools enabled manufacturers to produce interchangeable parts, which, in turn, led to the creation of the assembly line for production. First used in the United States for small arms and clocks, the assembly line had moved to Europe by 1850. In the last half of the nineteenth century, it was primarily used in manufacturing nonmilitary goods, such as sewing machines, typewriters, bicycles, and finally the automobile.

The emergence of protective tariffs and cartels was clearly a response to the growth of the multinational industrial system. Economic competition intensified the political rivalries of the age. The growth of the national state, which had seemed to be the answer to old problems in the mid-nineteenth century, now seemed to be creating new ones.

New Patterns in an Industrial Economy

The Second Industrial Revolution played a role in the emergence of basic economic patterns that have characterized much of modern European economic life. Although we have described the period after 1871 as an age of material prosperity, recessions and crises were still very much a part of economic life. From 1873 to 1895, Europeans experienced a series of economic crises. Prices, especially those of agricultural products, fell dramatically. After 1895, however, until World War I, Europe overall experienced an economic boom and achieved a level of prosperity that encouraged people later to look back to that era as *la belle époque*—a golden age in European civilization.

After 1870, Germany replaced Great Britain as the industrial leader of Europe. Already in the 1890s, Germany's superiority was evident in new areas of manufacturing, such as organic chemicals and electrical equipment, and increasingly apparent in its ever-greater share of worldwide trade. But the struggle for economic (and political) supremacy between Great Britain and Germany should not cause us to overlook the other great

Map 24.1 The Industrial Regions of Europe by 1914.

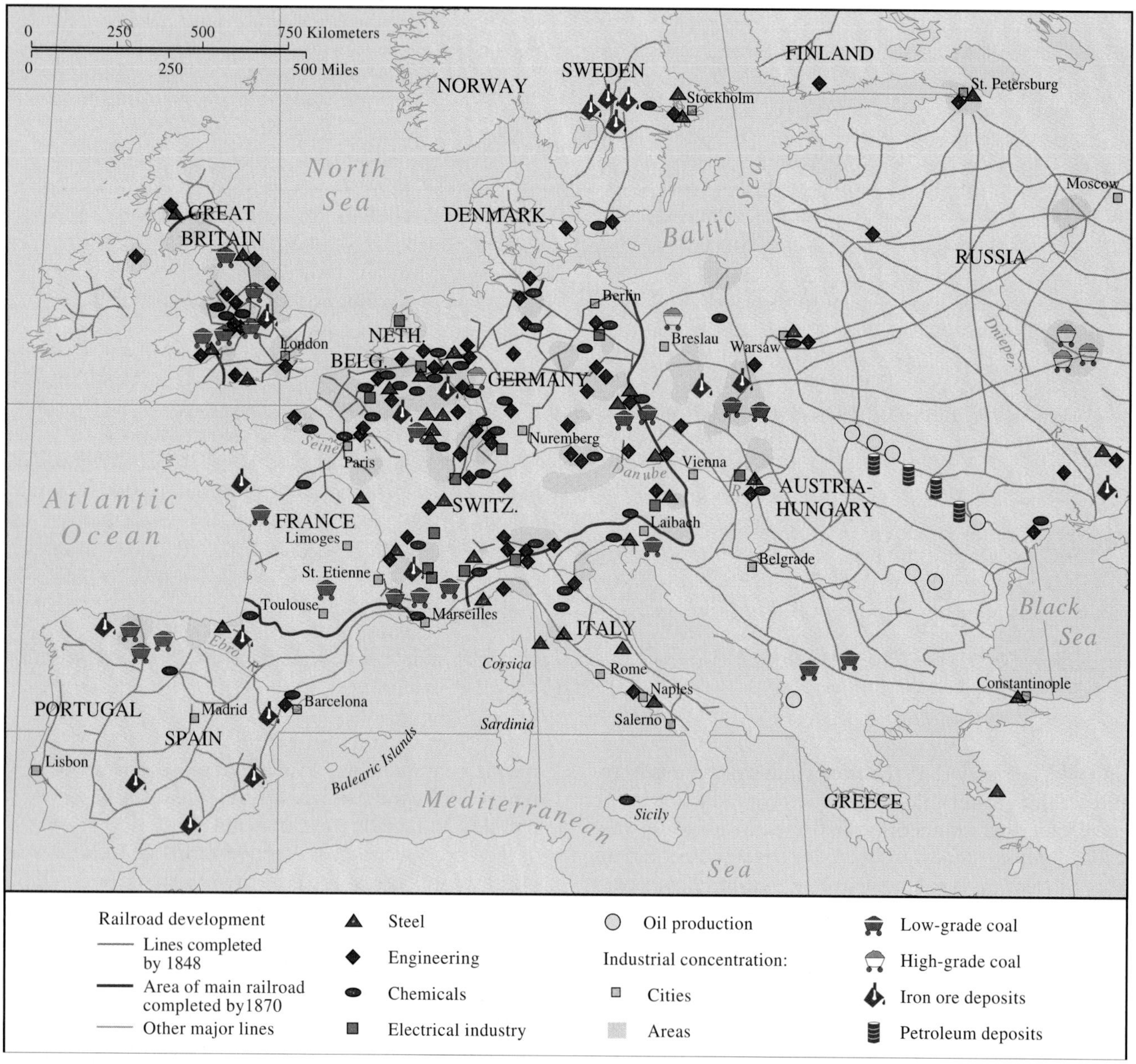

polarization of the age. By 1900, Europe was divided into two economic zones. Great Britain, Belgium, France, the Netherlands, Germany, the western part of the Austro-Hungarian empire, and northern Italy constituted an advanced industrialized core that had a high standard of living, decent systems of transportation, and relatively healthy and educated peoples. Another part of Europe, the backward and little industrialized area to the south and east, consisting of southern Italy, most of Austria-Hungary, Spain, Portugal, the Balkan kingdoms, and Russia was still largely agricultural and relegated by the industrial countries to the function of providing food and raw materials. The presence of Romanian oil, Greek olive oil, and Serbian pigs and prunes in western Europe served as reminders of an economic division of Europe that continued well into the twentieth century.

The economic developments of the late nineteenth century, combined with the transportation revolution that saw the growth of marine transport and railroads, also fostered a true world economy. By 1900, Europeans were importing beef and wool from Argentina and Australia, coffee from Brazil, nitrates from Chile, iron ore from Algeria, and sugar from Java. European capital was also invested abroad to develop railways, mines, electrical power plants, and banks. High rates of return, such as 11.3 percent on Latin American banking shares that were floated in London, provided plenty of incentive. Of course, foreign countries also provided markets for the surplus manufactured goods of Europe. With its capital, industries, and military might, Europe dominated the world economy by the end of the nineteenth century.

Women and Work: New Job Opportunities

The Second Industrial Revolution had an enormous impact on the position of women in the labor market. During the course of the nineteenth century, considerable controversy erupted over a woman's "right to work." Working-class organizations tended to reinforce the underlying ideal of domesticity; women should remain at home to bear and nurture children and should not be allowed in the industrial workforce. Working-class men argued that keeping women out of industrial work would ensure the moral and physical well-being of families. In reality, keeping women out of the industrial workforce simply made it easier to exploit them when they needed income to supplement their husbands' wages or to support their families when their husbands were unemployed. The desperate need to work at times forced women to do marginal work at home or labor as pieceworkers in sweatshops.

After 1870, however, new job opportunities for women became available. The development of larger in-dustrial plants and the expansion of government services created a large number of service or white-collar jobs. The increased demand for white-collar workers at relatively low wages coupled with a shortage of male workers led employers to hire women. Big businesses and retail shops needed clerks, typists, secretaries, file clerks, and sales clerks. The expansion of government services created opportunities for women to be secretaries and telephone operators and to take jobs in health and social services. Compulsory education necessitated more teachers, and the development of modern hospital services opened the way for an increase in nurses.

Many of the new white-collar jobs were by no means exciting. Their work was routine and, except for teaching and nursing, required few skills beyond basic literacy. Although there was little hope for advancement, these jobs had distinct advantages for the daughters of the middle classes and especially the upward-aspiring working classes. For some middle-class women, the new jobs offered freedom from the domestic patterns expected of them. Most of them, however, were filled by working-class females who saw their opportunity to escape from the "dirty" work of the lower-class world.

Organizing the Working Classes

The desire to improve their working and living conditions led many industrial workers to form political parties and labor unions. One of the most important of the working-class or socialist parties was formed in Germany in 1875. Under the direction of its two Marxist leaders, Wilhelm Liebknecht and August Bebel, the German Social Democratic Party (SPD) espoused revolutionary Marxist rhetoric while organizing itself as a mass political party competing in elections for the Reichstag (the German parliament). Once in the Reichstag, SPD delegates worked to enact legislation to improve the condition of the working class. As August Bebel explained, "Pure negation would not be accepted by the voters. The masses demand that something should be done for today irrespective of what will happen on the morrow."[1] Despite government efforts to destroy it, the German Social Democratic Party continued to grow. In 1890, it received 1.5 million votes and thirty-five seats in the Reichstag. When it received 4 million votes in the 1912 elections, it became the largest single party in Germany.

Socialist parties also emerged in other European states, although none proved as successful as the German Social Democrats. As the socialist parties grew, agitation for an international organization that would strengthen their position against international capitalism grew. In 1889, leaders of the various socialist parties formed the Second

International, which was organized as a loose association of national groups. While the Second International took some coordinated actions—May Day (May 1), for example, was made an international labor day to be marked by strikes and mass labor demonstrations—differences often wreaked havoc at the congresses of the organization. Two issues proved particularly divisive: nationalism and revisionism.

One divisive issue for international socialism was nationalism. Despite the belief of Karl Marx and Friedrich Engels that "the working men have no country," in truth, socialist parties varied from country to country and remained tied to national concerns and issues. Nationalism had proved a much more powerful force than socialism.

♦ **"Proletarians of the World, Unite."** To improve their working and living conditions, many industrial workers, inspired by the ideas of Karl Marx, joined working-class or socialist parties. Pictured here is a socialist-sponsored poster that proclaims in German the closing words of *The Communist Manifesto:* "Proletarians of the World, Unite!"

Marxist parties also divided over the issue of revisionism. Some Marxists believed in a pure Marxism that accepted the imminent collapse of capitalism and the need for socialist ownership of the means of production. But others rejected the revolutionary approach and argued in a revisionist direction that the workers must continue to organize in mass political parties and even work together with the other progressive elements in a nation to gain reform. With the extension of the right to vote, workers were in a better position than ever to achieve their aims by democratic channels. As the most prominent revisionist Eduard Bernstein (1850–1932) argued in his book *Evolutionary Socialism,* evolution by democratic means, not revolution, would achieve the desired goal of socialism. The Second International condemned revisionism as heresy, but many socialist parties, including the German Social Democrats, while spouting revolutionary slogans, continued to practice Bernstein's gradualist approach.

Workers also formed trade unions to improve their working conditions. Attempts to organize the workers did not come until the last two decades of the nineteenth century after unions had won the right to strike in the 1870s. Strikes proved necessary to achieve the workers' goals. A walkout by female workers in the match industry in 1888 and by dock workers in London the following year led to the establishment of trade union organizations for both groups. By 1900, 2 million workers were enrolled in British trade unions, and by the outbreak of World War I, this number had risen to between 3 and 4 million, although this was still less than one-fifth of the total workforce. By 1914, its three million members made the German trade union movement the second largest in Europe after Great Britain's.

The Emergence of Mass Society

The new patterns of industrial production, mass consumption, and working-class organization that we identify with the Second Industrial Revolution were only one aspect of the new mass society that emerged in Europe after 1870. A larger and vastly improved urban environment, new patterns of social structure, gender issues, mass education, and mass leisure were also important features of Europe's mass society.

Population Growth

The European population increased dramatically between 1850 and 1910, rising from 270 million to more than 460 million by 1910 (see Table 24.1). After 1880, a noticeable decline in death rates largely explains the in-

Table 24.1   *European Populations, 1851–1911*

	1851	1881	1911
England and Wales	17,928,000	25,974,000	36,070,000
Scotland	2,889,000	3,736,000	4,761,000
Ireland	6,552,000	5,175,000	4,390,000
France	35,783,000	37,406,000	39,192,000
Germany	33,413,000	45,234,000	64,926,000
Belgium	4,530,000	5,520,000	7,424,000
Netherlands	3,309,000	4,013,000	5,858,000
Denmark	1,415,000	1,969,000	2,757,000
Norway	1,490,000	1,819,000	2,392,000
Sweden	3,471,000	4,169,000	5,522,000
Spain	15,455,000	16,622,000	19,927,000
Portugal	3,844,000	4,551,000	5,958,000
Italy	24,351,000	28,460,000	34,671,000
Switzerland	2,393,000	2,846,000	3,753,000
Austria	17,535,000	22,144,000	28,572,000
Hungary	18,192,000	15,739,000	20,886,000
Russia	68,500,000	97,700,000	160,700,000
Romania		4,600,000	7,000,000
Bulgaria		2,800,000	4,338,000
Greece		1,679,000	2,632,000
Serbia		1,700,000	2,912,000

Source: B. R. Mitchell, *European Historical Statistics, 1750–1970* (1975).

crease in population. Although the causes of this decline have been debated, two major factors—medical discoveries and environmental conditions—stand out. Some historians have stressed the importance of developments in medical science. Smallpox vaccinations, for example, were compulsory in many European countries by the mid-1850s. More important were improvements in the urban environment in the last half of the nineteenth century that greatly decreased fatalities from such infectious diseases as diarrhea, dysentery, typhoid fever, and cholera, which had been spread through contaminated water supplies and improper elimination of sewage. Improved nutrition also made a significant difference in the health of the population. The increase in agricultural productivity combined with improvements in transportation facilitated the shipment of food supplies from areas of surplus to regions with poor harvests.

Although growing agricultural and industrial prosperity supported an increase in European population, it could not do so indefinitely, especially in areas that had little industrialization and a severe problem of rural overpopulation. Some of the excess labor from underdeveloped areas migrated to the industrial regions of Europe. By 1913, more than 400,000 Poles were working in the heavily industrialized Ruhr region of western Germany. But a booming American economy and cheap shipping fares after 1898 led to mass emigration from southern and eastern Europe to America at the beginning of the twentieth century. In 1880, about 500,000 people left Europe each year on average; between 1906 and 1910, annual departures increased to 1,300,000, many of them from southern and eastern Europe.

Transformation of the Urban Environment

One of the most important consequences of industrialization and the population explosion of the nineteenth century was urbanization. In the course of the nineteenth century, urban dwellers came to make up an ever-increasing percentage of the European population. In 1800, they constituted 40 percent of the population in Britain, 25 percent in France and Germany, and only 10 percent in eastern Europe. By 1914, urban inhabitants had increased to 80 percent of the population in Britain, 45 percent in France, 60 percent in Germany, and 30 percent in eastern Europe. The size of cities also expanded dramatically, especially in industrialized countries. Between 1800 and 1900, London's population grew from 960,000 to 6,500,000 and Berlin's from 172,000 to 2,700,000.

Urban populations grew faster than the general population primarily because of the vast migration from rural areas to cities. People were driven from the countryside to the city by sheer economic necessity—unemployment, land hunger, and physical want. Urban centers offered something positive as well, usually mass employment in factories and later in service trades and professions. But cities also grew faster in the second half of the nineteenth century because health and living conditions in them were improving.

In the 1840s, a number of urban reformers, such as Edwin Chadwick in England and Rudolf Virchow and Solomon Neumann in Germany, had pointed to filthy living conditions as the primary cause of epidemic diseases and urged sanitary reforms to correct the problem. Soon, legislative acts created boards of health that brought governmental action to bear on public health issues. Urban medical officers and building inspectors were authorized to inspect dwellings for public health hazards. New building regulations made it more difficult for private contractors to build shoddy housing. The Public Health Act of 1875 in Britain, for example, prohibited the construction of new buildings without running water and an internal drainage system. For the first time in Western history, the role of municipal governments had been expanded to include detailed regulations for the improvement of the living conditions of urban dwellers.

Essential to the public health of the modern European city was the ability to bring clean water into the city and

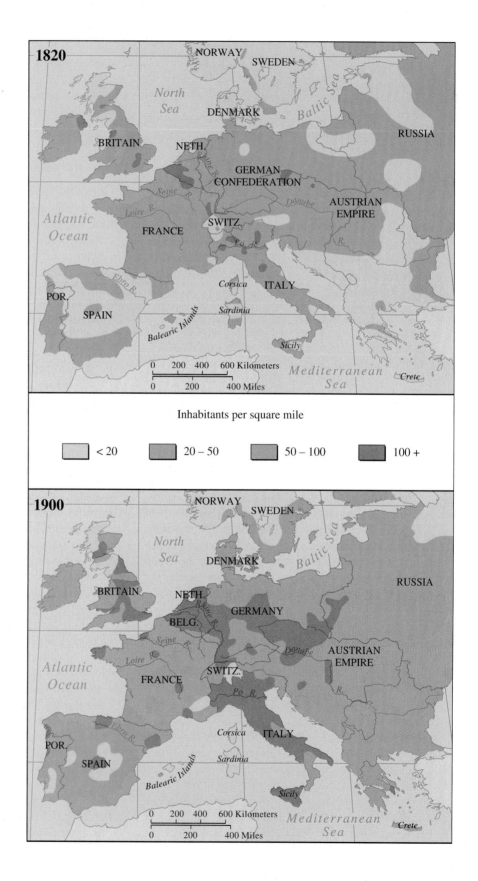

Map 24.2 Population Growth in Europe, 1820–1900.

to expel sewage from it. The accomplishment of those two tasks was a major engineering feat in the last half of the nineteenth century. The problem of freshwater was solved by a system of dams and reservoirs that stored the water and aqueducts and tunnels that carried it from the countryside to the city and into individual dwellings. By the second half of the nineteenth century, regular private baths became accessible to many people as gas heaters in the 1860s and later electric heaters made hot baths possible. The treatment of sewage was also improved by building mammoth underground pipes that carried raw sewage far from the city for disposal. Unfortunately, in many places new underground sewers simply continued to discharge their raw sewage into what soon became highly polluted lakes and rivers. Nevertheless, the development of pure water and sewerage systems dramatically improved the public health of European cities by 1914.

Middle-class reformers who denounced the unsanitary living conditions of the working class also focused on their housing needs. Overcrowded, disease-ridden slums were viewed as dangerous not only to physical health, but to the political and moral health of the entire nation. V. A. Huber, the foremost early German housing reformer, wrote in 1861: "Certainly it would not be too much to say that the home is the communal embodiment of family life. Thus the purity of the dwelling is almost as important for the family as is the cleanliness of the body for the individual."[2] To Huber, good housing was a prerequisite for stable family life, and without stable family life one of the "stabilising elements of society" would be dissolved, much to society's detriment.

Early efforts to attack the housing problem emphasized the middle-class, liberal belief in the efficacy of private enterprise. Reformers such as Huber believed that the

◆ **The City at Night.** Industrialization and the population explosion of the nineteenth century fostered the growth of cities. At the same time, technological innovations dramatically improved living conditions in European cities. Gas lighting and later electricity also transformed the nighttime environment of Europe's cities, as is evident in this painting of Liverpool.

The Housing Venture of Octavia Hill

Octavia Hill was a practical-minded British housing reformer who believed that workers and their families were entitled to happy homes. At the same time, she was convinced that the poor needed guidance and encouragement, not charity. In this selection, she describes her housing venture.

Octavia Hill, *Homes of the London Poor*

About four years ago I was put in possession of three houses in one of the worst courts of Marylebone. Six other houses were bought subsequently. All were crowded with inmates.

The first thing to be done was to put them in decent tenantable order. The set last purchased was a row of cottages facing a bit of desolate ground, occupied with wretched, dilapidated cow-sheds, manure heaps, old timber, and rubbish of every description. The houses were in a most deplorable condition—the plaster was dropping from the walls; on one staircase a pail was placed to catch the rain that fell through the roof. All the staircases were perfectly dark; the banisters were gone, having been burnt as firewood by tenants. The grates, with large holes in them, were falling forward into the rooms. The washhouse, full of lumber belonging to the landlord, was locked up; thus the inhabitants had to wash clothes, as well as to cook, eat and sleep in their small rooms. The dustbin, standing in the front part of the houses, was accessible to the whole neighbourhood, and boys often dragged from it quantities of unseemly objects and spread them over the court. The state of the drainage was in keeping with everything else. The pavement of the backyard was all broken up, and great puddles stood in it, so that the damp crept up the outer walls. . . .

As soon as I entered into possession, each family had an opportunity of doing better: those who would not pay, or who led clearly immoral lives, were ejected. The rooms they vacated were cleansed; the tenants who showed signs of improvement moved into them, and thus, in turn, an opportunity was obtained for having each room distempered and papered. The drains were put in order, a large slate cistern was fixed, the washhouse was cleared of its lumber, and thrown open on stated days to each tenant in turn. The roof, the plaster, the woodwork were repaired; the staircase walls were distempered; new grates were fixed; the layers of paper and rag (black with age) were torn from the windows, and glass put in; out of 192 panes only eight were found unbroken. The yard and footpath were paved.

The rooms, as a rule, were re-let at the same prices at which they had been let before; but tenants with large families were counselled to take two rooms, and for these much less was charged than if let singly: this plan I continue to pursue. In-coming tenants are not allowed to take a decidedly insufficient quantity of room, and no sub-letting is permitted. . . .

The pecuniary result has been very satisfactory. Five percent has been paid on all the capital invested. A fund for the repayment of capital is accumulating. A liberal allowance has been made for repairs. . . .

My tenants are mostly of a class far below that of mechanics. They are, indeed, of the very poor. And yet, although the gifts they have received have been next to nothing, none of the families who have passed under my care during the whole four years have continued in what is called "distress," except such as have been unwilling to exert themselves. Those who will not exert the necessary self-control cannot avail themselves of the means of livelihood held out to them. But, for those who are willing, some small assistance in the form of work has, from time to time, been provided—not much, but sufficient to keep them from want or despair.

---

construction of model dwellings renting at a reasonable price would force other private landlords to elevate their housing standards. A fine example of this approach was the work of Octavia Hill (see the box above). With the financial assistance of a friend, she rehabilitated some old dwellings and constructed new ones to create housing for 3,500 tenants.

As the number and size of cities continued to mushroom, governments by the 1880s came to the conclusion—although reluctantly—that private enterprise could not solve the housing crisis. In 1890, a British Housing Act empowered local town councils to construct cheap housing for the working classes. London and Liverpool were the first communities to take advantage of their new powers. Similar activity had been set in motion in Germany by 1900. Everywhere, however, these lukewarm measures failed to do much to meet the real housing needs of the working classes. Nevertheless, by the start of World

War I, the need for planning had been recognized, and after the war municipal governments moved into housing construction on a large scale. In housing, as in so many other areas of life in the late nineteenth and early twentieth centuries, the liberal principle that the government that governs least governs best had simply proven untrue. More and more, governments were stepping into areas of activity that they would have never touched earlier.

The Social Structure of Mass Society

At the top of European society stood a wealthy elite, constituting only 5 percent of the population but controlling between 30 and 40 percent of its wealth. This nineteenth-century elite was an amalgamation of the traditional landed aristocracy that had dominated European society for centuries and the wealthy upper middle class. In the course of the nineteenth century, aristocrats coalesced with the most successful industrialists, bankers, and merchants to form a new elite. The growth of big business had created this group of wealthy plutocrats while aristocrats, whose income from landed estates declined, invested in railway shares, public utilities, government bonds, and even businesses. Gradually, the greatest fortunes shifted into the hands of the upper middle class. In Great Britain, for example, landed aristocrats constituted 73 percent of the country's millionaires in mid-century while the commercial and financial magnates made up 14 percent. By the period 1900–1914, landowners had declined to 27 percent.

Increasingly, aristocrats and plutocrats fused as the wealthy upper middle class purchased landed estates to join the aristocrats in the pleasures of country living while the aristocrats bought lavish town houses for part-time urban life. Common bonds were also forged when the sons of wealthy middle-class families were admitted to the elite schools dominated by the children of the aristocracy. This educated elite, whether aristocratic or middle class in background, assumed leadership roles in government bureaucracies and military hierarchies. Marriage also served to unite the two groups. Daughters of tycoons acquired titles while aristocratic heirs gained new sources of cash. Wealthy American heiresses were in special demand. When Consuelo Vanderbilt married the duke of Marlborough, the new duchess brought £2 million (approximately $10 million) to her husband.

The middle classes consisted of a variety of groups. Below the upper middle class was a middle level that included such traditional groups as professionals in law, medicine, and the civil service as well as moderately well-

to-do industrialists and merchants. The industrial expansion of the nineteenth century also added new groups to this segment of the middle class. These included business managers and new professionals, such as the engineers, architects, accountants, and chemists who formed professional associations as the symbols of their newfound importance. A lower middle class of small shopkeepers, traders, manufacturers, and prosperous peasants provided goods and services for the classes above them.

Standing between the lower middle class and the lower classes were new groups of white-collar workers who were the product of the Second Industrial Revolution. They were the traveling salesmen, bookkeepers, bank tellers, telephone operators, department store salespeople, and secretaries. Although largely propertyless and often little better paid than skilled laborers, these white-collar workers were often committed to middle-class ideals and optimistic about improving their status.

The moderately prosperous and successful middle classes shared a common lifestyle, one whose values tended to dominate much of nineteenth-century society. The members of the middle class were especially active in preaching their worldview to their children and to the upper and lower classes of their society. This was especially evident in Victorian Britain, often considered a model of middle-class society. It was the European middle classes who accepted and promulgated the importance of progress and science. They believed in hard work, which they viewed as the primary human good, open to everyone and guaranteed to have positive results. They were also regular churchgoers who believed in the good conduct associated with traditional Christian morality. The middle class was concerned with propriety, the right way of doing things. This concern gave rise to an incessant number of books aimed at the middle-class market with such titles as *The Habits of Good Society* or *Don't: A Manual of Mistakes and Improprieties More or Less Prevalent in Conduct and Speech*.

The lower classes of European society constituted almost 80 percent of the European population. Many of them were landholding peasants, agricultural laborers, and sharecroppers, especially in eastern Europe. This was less true, however, in western and central Europe. About 10 percent of the British population worked in agriculture, while in Germany the figure was 25 percent.

There was no such thing as a single urban working class. The elite of the working class included, first of all, skilled artisans in such traditional handicraft trades as cabinetmaking, printing, and jewelry making. As the production of more items was mechanized in the course of the nineteenth century, these highly skilled workers found their economic security threatened. The Second Industrial Revolution, however, also brought new entrants into the group of highly skilled workers, such as shipbuilders and metal workers. Many of the skilled workers attempted to pattern themselves after the middle class by seeking good housing and educating their children.

Semiskilled laborers, who included carpenters, bricklayers, and many factory workers, earned wages that were about two-thirds of those of highly skilled workers. At the bottom of the working-class hierarchy stood the largest group of workers, the unskilled laborers. This group included day laborers, who worked irregularly for very low wages, and large numbers of domestic servants. One out of every seven employed persons in Great Britain in 1900 was a domestic servant. Most of them were women.

Urban workers did experience a real betterment in the material conditions of their lives after 1871. For one thing, urban improvements meant better living conditions. A rise in real wages, accompanied by a decline in many consumer costs, especially in the 1880s and 1890s, made it possible for workers to buy more than just food and housing. Workers' budgets now provided money for more clothes and even leisure at the same time that strikes and labor agitation were providing ten-hour days and Saturday afternoons off.

The "Woman Question": The Role of Women

The "woman question" was the term used to identify the debate over the role of women in society. In the nineteenth century, women remained legally inferior, economically dependent, and largely defined by family and household roles. Many women still aspired to the ideal of femininity popularized by writers and poets. Alfred Lord Tennyson's *The Princess* expressed it well:

> Man for the field and woman for the hearth:
> Man for the sword and for the needle she:
> Man with the head and woman with the heart:
> Man to command and woman to obey;
> All else confusion.

This traditional characterization of the sexes, based on gender-defined social roles, was virtually elevated to the status of universal male and female attributes in the nineteenth century, largely due to the impact of the Industrial Revolution on the family. As the chief family wage earners, men worked outside the home while women were left with the care of the family for which they were paid nothing. Of course, the ideal did not always match reality, es-

pecially for the lower classes, where the need for supplemental income drove women to do "sweated" work.

Throughout most of the nineteenth century, marriage was viewed as the only honorable and available career for most women. While the middle class glorified the ideal of domesticity (see the box on p. 503), for most women marriage was a matter of economic necessity. The lack of meaningful work and the lower wages paid to women made it difficult for single women to earn a living. Most women chose to marry, which was reflected in the increase in marriage rates and a decline in illegitimacy rates in the course of the nineteenth century.

Birthrates also dropped significantly at this time. A very important factor in the evolution of the modern family was the decline in the number of offspring born to the average woman. The change was not necessarily due to new technological products. Although the invention of vulcanized rubber in the 1840s made possible the production of condoms and diaphragms, they were not widely used as effective contraceptive devices until the era of World War I. Some historians maintain that the change in attitude that led parents to deliberately limit the number of offspring was more important than the method used. While some historians attribute increased birth control to more widespread use of coitus interruptus, or male withdrawal before ejaculation, others have emphasized the ability of women to restrict family size through abortion and even infanticide or abandonment. That a change in attitude occurred was apparent in the emergence of a movement to increase awareness of birth control methods. Europe's first birth control clinic opened in Amsterdam in 1882.

THE MIDDLE-CLASS AND WORKING-CLASS FAMILY

The family was the central institution of middle-class life. Men provided the family income while women focused on household and child care. The use of domestic servants in many middle-class homes, made possible by an abundant supply of cheap labor, reduced the amount of time middle-class women had to spend on household labor. At the same time, by reducing the number of children in the family, mothers could devote more time to child care and domestic leisure.

The middle-class family fostered an ideal of togetherness. The Victorians created the family Christmas with its yule log, Christmas tree, songs, and exchange of gifts. In the United States, Fourth of July celebrations changed from drunken revels to family picnics by the 1850s. The education of middle-class females in domes-

Advice to Women: Be Dependent

Industrialization had a strong impact on middle-class women as gender-based social roles became the norm. Men worked outside the home to support the family while women provided for the needs of their children and husband at home. In this selection, one woman gives advice to middle-class women on their proper role and behavior.

Elizabeth Poole Sanford, Woman in Her Social and Domestic Character

The changes wrought by Time are many. It influences the opinions of men as familiarity does their feelings; it has a tendency to do away with superstition, and to reduce every thing to its real worth.

It is thus that the sentiment for woman has undergone a change. The romantic passion which once almost deified her is on the decline; and it is by intrinsic qualities that she must now inspire respect. She is no longer the queen of song and the star of chivalry. But if there is less of enthusiasm entertained for her, the sentiment is more rational, and, perhaps, equally sincere; for it is in relation to happiness that she is chiefly appreciated.

And in this respect it is, we must confess, that she is most useful and most important. Domestic life is the chief source of her influence; and the greatest debt society can owe to her is domestic comfort; for happiness is almost an element of virtue; and nothing conduces more to improve the character of men than domestic peace. A woman may make a man's home delightful, and may thus increase his motives for virtuous exertion. She may refine and tranquilize his mind,—may turn away his anger or allay his grief. Her smile may be the happy influence to gladden his heart, and to disperse the cloud that gathers on his brow. And in proportion to her endeavors to make those around her happy, she will be esteemed and loved. She will secure by her excellence that interest and that regard which she might formerly claim as the privilege of her sex, and will really merit the deference which was then conceded to her as a matter of course. . . .

Perhaps one of the first secrets of her influence is adaptation to the tastes, and sympathy in the feelings, of those around her. This holds true in lesser as well as in graver points. It is in the former, indeed, that the absence of interest in a companion is frequently most disappointing. Where want of congeniality impairs domestic comfort, the fault is generally chargeable on the female side. It is for woman, not for man, to make the sacrifice, especially in indifferent matters. She must, in a certain degree, be plastic herself if she would mould others. . . .

Nothing is so likely to conciliate the affections of the other sex as a feeling that woman looks to them for support and guidance. In proportion as men are themselves superior, they are accessible to this appeal. On the contrary, they never feel interested in one who seems disposed rather to offer than to ask assistance. There is, indeed, something unfeminine in independence. It is contrary to nature, and therefore it offends. We do not like to see a woman affecting tremors, but still less do we like to see her acting the amazon. A really sensible woman feels her dependence. She does what she can; but she is conscious of inferiority, and therefore grateful for support. She knows that she is the weaker vessel, and that as such she should receive honor. In this view, her weakness is an attraction, not a blemish.

In everything, therefore, that women attempt, they should show their consciousness of dependence. If they are learners, let them evince a teachable spirit; if they give an opinion, let them do it in an unassuming manner. There is something so unpleasant in female self-sufficiency that it not unfrequently deters instead of persuading, and prevents the adoption of advice which the judgment even approves.

tic crafts, singing, and piano playing prepared them for their function of providing a proper environment for home recreation.

Women in working-class families were more accustomed to hard work. Daughters in working-class families were expected to work until they married; even after marriage, they often did piecework at home to support the family. For the children of the working classes, childhood was over by age of nine or ten when they became apprentices or were employed in odd jobs.

Between 1890 and 1914, however, family patterns among the working class began to change. High-paying jobs in heavy industry and improvements in the standard of living made it possible for working-class families to depend on the income of husbands and the wages of grown children. By the early twentieth century, some working-class mothers could afford to stay at home, following the pattern of middle-class women. At the same time, new consumer products, such as sewing machines, clocks, bicycles, and cast-iron stoves, created a new mass consumer society whose focus was on higher levels of consumption.

These working-class families also followed the middle classes in limiting the size of their families. Children began to be viewed as dependents rather than wage earners as child labor laws and compulsory education took children out of the workforce and into schools. Improvements in public health as well as advances in medicine and a better diet resulted in a decline in infant mortality rates for the lower classes and made it easier for working-class families to choose to have fewer children. At the same time, strikes and labor agitation led to laws that reduced work hours to ten per day by 1900 and eliminated work on Saturday afternoons, which enabled working-class parents to devote more attention to their children and develop more emotional ties with them.

Education and Leisure in an Age of Mass Society

Mass education was a product of the "mass society" of the late nineteenth century. Being "educated" in the early nineteenth century meant attending a secondary school or possibly even a university. Secondary schools mostly emphasized a classical education based on the study of Greek and Latin. Secondary and university education were primarily for the elite, the sons of government officials, nobles, or the wealthier middle class. After 1850, secondary education was expanded as more middle-class families sought employment in public service and the professions or entry into elite scientific and technical schools. Existing secondary schools also placed more emphasis on practical and scientific education by adding foreign languages and natural sciences to their curriculum.

In the decades after 1870, the functions of the state were extended to include the development of mass education in state-run systems. Between 1870 and 1914, most Western governments began to offer at least primary education to both boys and girls between the ages of six and twelve. States also assumed responsibility for the quality of teachers by establishing teacher-training schools. By 1900, many European states, especially in northern and western Europe, were providing state-financed primary schools, salaried and trained teachers, and free, compulsory mass elementary education.

Why did European states make this commitment to mass education? Liberals believed that education was important to personal and social improvement and sought in Catholic countries to supplant Catholic education with moral and civic training based on secular values. Even conservatives were attracted to mass education as a means of improving the quality of military recruits and

♦ **A Middle-Class Family.** Nineteenth-century middle-class moralists considered the family the fundamental pillar of a healthy society. The family was a crucial institution in middle-class life, and togetherness constituted one of the important ideals of the middle-class family. This painting by William P. Frith, entitled *Many Happy Returns of the Day*, shows a family birthday celebration for a little girl in which grandparents, parents, and children take part. The servant at the left holds the presents for the little girl.

training people in social discipline. In 1875, a German military journal stated: "We in Germany consider education to be one of the principal ways of promoting the strength of the nation and above all military strength."[3]

Another incentive for mass education came from industrialization. In the early Industrial Revolution, unskilled labor was sufficient to meet factory needs, but the new firms of the Second Industrial Revolution demanded skilled labor. Both boys and girls with an elementary education had new possibilities of jobs beyond their villages or small towns, including white-collar jobs in railways, new metro stations, post offices, banking and shipping firms, teaching, and nursing. To industrialists, then, mass education furnished the trained workers they needed.

Nevertheless, the chief motive for mass education was political. On the one hand, the expansion of voting rights necessitated a more educated electorate. Even more important, however, mass compulsory education instilled patriotism and nationalized the masses, providing an opportunity for even greater national integration. As people lost their ties to local regions and even to religion, nationalism supplied a new faith. The use of a single national language created greater national unity than did loyalty to a ruler.

A nation's motives for universal elementary education largely determined what was taught in the elementary schools. Obviously, indoctrination in national values took on great importance. At the core of the academic curriculum were reading, writing, arithmetic, national history, especially geared to a patriotic view, geography, literature, and some singing and drawing. The education of boys and girls varied, however. Where possible, the sexes were separated. Girls did less math and no science but concentrated on such domestic skills as sewing, washing, ironing, and cooking, all prerequisites for providing a good home for husband and children. Boys were taught some practical skills, such as carpentry, and even some military drill. Most of the elementary schools also inculcated the middle-class virtues of hard work, thrift, sobriety, cleanliness, and respect for the family. For most students, elementary education led to apprenticeship and a job.

The development of compulsory elementary education created a demand for teachers, and most of them were female. In the United States, for example, females constituted two-thirds of all teachers by the 1880s. Many men viewed the teaching of children as an extension of women's "natural role" as nurturers of children. Moreover, females were paid lower salaries, in itself a considerable incentive for governments to encourage the establishment of teacher-training institutes for women. The first female colleges were really teacher-training schools. It was not until the beginning of the twentieth century that women were permitted to enter the male-dominated universities. In France, 3 percent of university students in 1902 were women; by 1914, their number had increased to 10 percent of the total.

The most immediate result of mass education was an increase in literacy. In Germany, Great Britain, France, and the Scandinavian countries, adult illiteracy was virtually eliminated by 1900. Where there was less schooling, the story is very different. Adult illiteracy rates were 79 percent in Serbia, 78 percent in Romania, and 79 percent in Russia. All of these countries had made only a minimal investment in mass education.

With the dramatic increase in literacy after 1871 came the rise of mass newspapers, such as the *Evening News* (1881) and *Daily Mail* (1896) in London, which sold millions of copies a day. Known as the "yellow press" in the United States, these newspapers shared some common characteristics. They were written in an easily understood style and tended to be extremely sensational, providing lurid details of crimes, jingoistic diatribes, gossip, and sports news. Mass newspapers were but one feature of a new mass culture; another was the emergence of new forms of mass leisure.

MASS LEISURE

In the preindustrial centuries, play or leisure activities had been closely connected to work patterns based on the seasonal or daily cycles typical of the life of peasants and artisans. Fairs and festivals, which might last for days, were an important part of traditional village culture. The process of industrialization in the nineteenth century had an enormous impact on those traditional patterns. The factory imposed new work patterns that were determined by the rhythms of machines and clocks and removed work time completely from the family environment of farms and workshops. Work and leisure became opposites as leisure was viewed as what people do for fun after work. In fact, the new leisure hours created by the industrial system—evening hours after work, weekends, and later a week or two in the summer—largely determined the contours of the new mass leisure.

New technology and business practices also determined the forms of the new mass leisure. The new technology created novel experiences for leisure, such as the Ferris wheel at amusement parks, while the mechanized urban transportation systems of the 1880s meant that even the working classes were no longer dependent on neighborhood bars, but could make their way to athletic games, amusement parks, and dance halls. Likewise, railroads could take people to the beaches on weekends.

Music and dance halls appeared in the last half of the nineteenth century. By the 1880s, London boasted 500 music halls. Promoters gradually made them more respectable and broadened their fare to entice both women and children to attend the programs. The new dance halls, which were all the rage by 1900, were more strictly oriented toward adults. Contemporaries were often shocked by the sight of young people engaged in sexually suggestive dancing.

The upper and middle classes had created the first market for tourism, but as wages increased and workers were given paid vacations, tourism, too, became another form of mass leisure. Thomas Cook (1808–1892) was a British pioneer of mass tourism. Secretary to a British temperance group, Cook had been responsible for organizing a railroad trip to temperance gatherings in 1841. This experience led him to offer trips on a regular basis after he found that he could make substantial profits by renting special trains, lowering prices, and increasing the number of passengers.

By the late nineteenth century, team sports had also developed into yet another form of mass leisure. Unlike the old rural games, however, they were no longer chaotic and spontaneous activities, but became strictly organized with sets of rules and officials to enforce them. These rules were the products of organized athletic groups, such as the English Football Association (1863) and the American Bowling Congress (1895).

The new team sports rapidly became professionalized. In Britain, soccer had its Football Association in 1863 and rugby its Rugby Football Union in 1871. In the United States, the first national association to recognize professional baseball players was formed in 1863. By 1900, the National League and American League had a complete monopoly over professional baseball. The development of urban transportation systems made possible the construction of stadiums where thousands could attend, making mass spectator sports a big business. Professional teams became objects of mass adulation by crowds of urbanites who compensated for their lost sense of identity in mass urban areas by developing these new loyalties.

The new forms of popular leisure were standardized forms of amusement that drew mass audiences. Although some argued that the new amusements were important for improving people, in truth, they served primarily to provide entertainment and distract people from the realities of their work lives. Much of mass leisure was secular. Churches found that they had to compete with popular amusements for people's attention on Sundays. The new mass leisure also represented a significant change from earlier forms of popular culture. Festivals and fairs had been based on active community participation, whereas the new forms of mass leisure were standardized for largely passive mass audiences. Amusement parks and professional sports teams were, after all, big businesses organized to make profits.

The National State

Within the major European states, considerable progress was made in achieving liberal practices (constitutions, parliaments, and individual liberties) and reforms that encouraged the expansion of political democracy through voting rights for men and the creation of mass political parties. At the same time, however, these developments were strongly resisted in parts of Europe where the old political forces remained strong.

Western Europe: The Growth of Political Democracy

In general, parliamentary government was most firmly rooted in the western European states. The growth of political democracy was one of the preoccupations of British politics after 1871, and its cause was pushed along by the expansion of suffrage. Much advanced by the Reform Act of 1867 (see Chapter 23), the right to vote was further extended during the second ministry of William Gladstone (1880–1885) with the passage of the Reform Act of 1884. It gave the vote to all men who paid regular rents or taxes,

◆ **Middle Classes at the Beach.** By the beginning of the twentieth century, changing work and leisure patterns had created a new mass leisure. The upper and middle classes created the first market for tourism, although it too became another form of mass leisure as wages increased and workers received paid vacations. This photograph shows middle-class Britons enjoying a beach at the beginning of the twentieth century.

thus largely enfranchising the agricultural workers, a group previously excluded. The following year, a Redistribution Act eliminated historic boroughs and counties and established constituencies with approximately equal populations and one representative each. The payment of salaries to members of the House of Commons beginning in 1911 further democratized that institution by at least opening the door to people other than the wealthy. The British system of gradual reform through parliamentary institutions had become the way of British political life.

The defeat of France by the Prussian army in 1870 brought the downfall of Louis Napoleon's Second Empire. In new elections based on universal male suffrage, the French people rejected the republicans and overwhelmingly favored the monarchists, who won two-thirds of the seats in the new National Assembly. In response, on March 26, 1871, radical republicans formed an independent republican government in Paris known as the Commune (see the box on p. 508).

But the National Assembly refused to give up its power and decided to crush the revolutionary Commune. Vicious fighting in April and May finally ended in a government victory when government troops massacred thousands of the Commune's defenders in the last week of May. Estimates are that 20,000 were shot; another 10,000 were shipped overseas to the French penal colony of New Caledonia. The brutal repression of the Commune bequeathed a legacy of hatred that continued to plague French politics for decades.

Although a majority of the members of the monarchist-dominated National Assembly wished to restore a monarchy in France, inability to agree on who should be king caused the monarchists to miss their opportunity and led in 1875 to an improvised constitution that established a republican form of government as the least divisive compromise. This constitution established a bicameral legislature with an upper house or Senate elected indirectly and a lower house or Chamber of Deputies chosen by universal male suffrage; a president, selected by the legislature for a term of seven years, served as executive of the government. The Constitution of 1875, intended only as a stopgap measure, solidified the republic—the Third Republic—which lasted sixty-five years. New elections in 1876 and 1877 strengthened the hands of the republicans who managed by 1879 to institute ministerial responsibility and establish the power of the Chamber of Deputies. The prime minister or premier and his ministers were now responsible not to the president, but to the Chamber of Deputies.

By 1870, Italy had emerged as a geographically united state with pretensions to great power status. Its internal

weaknesses, however, gave that claim a particularly hollow ring. Sectional differences—a poverty-stricken south and an industrializing north—weakened any sense of community. Chronic turmoil between workers and industrialists undermined the social fabric. The Italian government was unable to deal effectively with these problems because of the extensive corruption among government officials and the lack of stability created by ever-changing government coalitions. The granting of universal male suffrage in 1912 did little to correct the extensive corruption and weak government. Even Italy's pretensions to great power status proved hollow when Italy became the first European power to lose to an African state—Ethiopia.

Central and Eastern Europe: Persistence of the Old Order

Germany, Austria-Hungary, and Russia pursued political policies that were quite different from those of the western European nations. The central European states (Germany and Austria-Hungary) had the trappings of parliamentary government including legislative bodies and elections by universal male suffrage, but authoritarian forces, especially powerful monarchies and conservative

⇒ *Parisian Violence* ⇐

In March 1871, an insurrection erupted in Paris when the National Assembly attempted to disarm the Parisian National Guard. When troops were sent to seize guns that had been moved earlier to the hills of Montmartre, fighting broke out. Georges Clemenceau, the mayor of Montmartre, wrote a description of the day's events. Two generals had been taken prisoner by the National Guard and shot before Clemenceau could arrive to prevent it. This excerpt describes what happened next. Eight days after the events described here, the Parisians established the Commune.

Georges Clemenceau, How the Uprising Began, March 18, 1871

We had hardly turned the corner of the wall when a man ran up and said that the Generals had just been shot. We did not stop to answer him but ran even faster. He did not seem very sure of his facts, anyhow, and seemed to repeating a rumor rather than something he had seen for himself.

The *Buttes* [hills of Montmartre] were covered with armed National Guards. We made our way into this crowd. My sash called everybody's attention to me, and I at once became the object of the most hostile demonstrations. They reproached me for having conspired with the Government to have the guns taken away, they accused me of betraying the National Guard, they insulted me.

Keeping between Mayer and Sabourdy, who were both fairly well-known in the *arrondissement* [district] and were my only safeguard, I continued on my way without answering.

As we went on, I heard people saying, "It's all over! Justice has been done! The traitors are punished! If anybody doesn't like it, we'll do the same to him! It's too late!" . . . It was no longer possible to doubt the assassination of the Generals, for everyone was repeating the news with somber enthusiasm. . . .

Suddenly there was a great noise, and the mob which filled the courtyard of no. 6 burst into the street, in the grip of a kind of frenzy.

There were chasseurs, soldiers of the line, National Guards, women and children. They were all shrieking like wild beasts, without realizing what they were doing. I observed then that pathological phenomenon which could be called blood lust. A breath of madness seemed to have passed over this mob. From the top of a wall children were waving indescribable trophies, women with streaming hair and all disheveled twisted their bare arms and uttered raucous cries, bereft of any sense. I saw some of them weeping and shouting louder than the others. Men were dancing about and jostling one another in a kind of frenzied fury. It was one of those nervous phenomena so frequent in the Middle Ages, and occasionally occurring still among masses of human beings under the stress of some powerful emotion.

Suddenly a piece of artillery, drawn by four horses, arrived in front of the house. The confusion increased, if that was possible. Men clad in ill-matched uniforms, riding on the horses, swore and shouted. I saw one woman jump onto one of the horses. She was waving her bonnet and yelling, "Down with the traitors!"—a cry the crowd repeated and repeated.

The situation was becoming more and more dangerous for me. The mob looked at me in crazed defiance, shouting its cry of "Down with the traitors!" Several fists were raised.

I could do nothing more in this place. I had not been able to prevent the crime. It remained for me to look after the fate of the prisoners whom I had just seen go by, and to stop any misfortune befalling my prisoners at the Mairie, against whom there was very great hostility.

social groups, remained strong. In eastern Europe, especially Russia, the old system of autocracy was barely touched by the winds of change.

The constitution of the new imperial Germany begun by Bismarck in 1871 provided for a federal system with a bicameral legislature. The lower house of the German parliament, known as the Reichstag, was elected on the basis of universal male suffrage, but it did not have ministerial responsibility. Ministers of government, the most important of which was the chancellor, were responsible not to the parliament, but to the emperor. The emperor also commanded the armed forces and controlled foreign policy and internal administration. While the creation of a parliament elected by universal male suffrage presented opportunities for the growth of a real political democracy, it failed to develop in Germany before World War I. The army and Bismarck were two major reasons why it did not.

The German (largely Prussian) army viewed itself as the defender of monarchy and aristocracy and sought to escape any control by the Reichstag by operating under a general staff responsible only to the emperor. Prussian military tradition was strong, and military officers took steps to ensure the loyalty of their subordinates to the emperor.

The policies of Bismarck, who served as chancellor of the new German state until 1890, often served to prevent the growth of more democratic institutions. At first, Bismarck worked with the liberals, especially in launching an attack on the Catholic church, the so-called *Kulturkampf* or "struggle for civilization." Like Bismarck, middle-class liberals distrusted Catholic loyalty to the new Germany. But Bismarck's tactics proved counterproductive, and Bismarck soon abandoned the attack on Catholicism by making an abrupt shift in policy.

In 1878, Bismarck abandoned the liberals and began to persecute the socialists. Bismarck became alarmed by the growth of the Social Democratic Party. He genuinely believed that the socialists' antinationalistic, anticapitalistic, and antimonarchical stance represented a danger to the empire. In 1878, Bismarck got the parliament to pass a law that limited socialist meetings and publications while still allowing socialist candidates to run for the Reichstag. Bismarck also attempted to woo workers away from socialism by enacting social welfare legislation. Between 1883 and 1889, the Reichstag passed laws that created sickness, accident, and disability benefits as well as old age pensions, financed by compulsory contributions from workers, employers, and the state. Bismarck's social security system was the most progressive the world had yet seen. Nevertheless, both the repressive and the social welfare measures failed to stop the growth of socialism. In his frustration, Bismarck planned still more antisocialist measures in 1890, but before he could carry them out, the new emperor, William II (1888–1918), eager to pursue his own policies, cashiered the aged chancellor.

After the creation of the dual monarchy of Austria-Hungary in 1867, the Austrian part received a constitution that established a parliamentary system with the principle of ministerial responsibility. But Emperor Francis Joseph (1848–1916) largely ignored ministerial responsibility and proceeded to personally appoint and dismiss his ministers and rule by decree when parliament was not in session.

The problem of the minorities continued to trouble the empire. The ethnic Germans, who made up only one-third of Austria's population, governed Austria but felt increasingly threatened by the Czechs, Poles, and other Slavic groups within the empire. The granting of univer-

♦ **Bismarck and William II.** In 1890, Bismarck sought to undertake new repressive measures against the Social Democrats. Disagreeing with this policy, Emperor William II forced him to resign. This political cartoon shows William II reclining on a throne made of artillery and cannonballs and holding a doll labeled "socialism." Bismarck bids farewell while Germany, personified as a woman, looks on with grave concern.

sal male suffrage in 1907 served only to make the problem worse as nationalities that had played no role in the government now agitated in the parliament for autonomy. This led prime ministers after 1900 to ignore the parliament and rely increasingly on imperial emergency decrees to govern.

In Russia, the assassination of Alexander II in 1881 convinced his son and successor, Alexander III (1881–1894), that reform had been a mistake, and he quickly returned to the repressive measures of earlier tsars. Advocates of constitutional monarchy and social reform, along with revolutionary groups, were persecuted. Entire districts of Russia were placed under martial law if the government suspected the inhabitants of treason. The powers of the zemstvos, created by the reforms of Alexander II, were sharply curtailed. When Alexander III died, his weak son and successor, Nicholas II (1894–1917), began his rule with his father's conviction that the absolute power of the tsars should be preserved: "I shall maintain the principle of autocracy just as firmly and unflinchingly as did my unforgettable father."[4] But conditions were changing, especially with the growth of industrialization, and the tsar's approach was not realistic in view of the new circumstances he faced.

Conclusion

The Second Industrial Revolution helped create a new material prosperity that led Europeans to believe they had ushered in a new "age of progress." A major feature of this age was the emergence of a mass society. The lower classes in particular benefited from the right to vote, a higher standard of living, and new schools that provided them with a modicum of education. New forms of mass transportation, combined with new work patterns, enabled large numbers of people to enjoy weekend excursions to amusement parks and seaside resorts and to participate in new mass leisure activities.

By 1871, the national state had become the focus of people's lives. Liberal and democratic reforms brought new possibilities for greater participation in the political process, although women were still largely excluded from political rights. After 1871, the national state also began to expand its functions beyond all previous limits. Fearful

of the growth of socialism and trade unions, governments attempted to appease the working masses by adopting such social insurance measures as protection against accidents, illness, and old age. These social welfare measures were narrow in scope and limited in benefits, but they signaled a new direction for state action to benefit the mass of its citizens. The enactment of public health and housing measures, designed to curb the worst ills of urban living, was yet another indication of how state power could be used to benefit the people.

This extension of state functions took place in an atmosphere of increased national loyalty. After 1871, nation-states increasingly sought to solidify the social order and win the active loyalty and support of their citizens by deliberately cultivating national feelings. Yet this policy contained potentially great dangers. As we shall see in the next chapter, nations had discovered once again that imperialistic adventures and military successes could arouse nationalistic passions and smother domestic political unrest. But they also found that nationalistic feelings could also lead to intense international rivalries that made war almost inevitable.

NOTES

1. Quoted in W. L. Guttsman, *The German Social Democratic Party, 1875–1933* (London, 1981), p. 63.
2. Quoted in Nicholas Bullock and James Read, *The Movement for Housing Reform in Germany and France 1840–1914* (Cambridge, 1985), p. 42.
3. Quoted in Robert Gildea, *Barricades and Borders, Europe, 1800–1914* (Oxford, 1987), p. 249.
4. Quoted in Shmuel Galai, *The Liberation Movement in Russia, 1900–1905* (Cambridge, 1973), p. 26.

SUGGESTIONS FOR FURTHER READING

In addition to the general works on the nineteenth century and individual European countries cited in Chapters 22 and 23, two more specialized works on the subject matter of this chapter are available in N. Stone, *Europe Transformed, 1878–1919* (London, 1983); and F. Gilbert, *The End of the European Era, 1890 to the Present*, 4th ed. (New York, 1991).

The subject of the Second Industrial Revolution is well covered in D. Landes, *The Unbound Prometheus*, cited in Chapter 21. For a fundamental survey of European industrialization, see A. S. Milward and S. B. Saul, *The Development of the Economies of Continental Europe, 1850–1914* (Cambridge, Mass., 1977). For an introduction to the development of mass consumerism in Britain, see W. H. Fraser, *The Coming of the Mass Market, 1850–1914* (Hamden, Conn., 1981). The impact of the new technology on European thought is imaginatively discussed in S. Kern, *The Culture of Time and Space, 1880–1918* (Cambridge, Mass., 1983).

For an introduction to international socialism, see J. Joll, *The Second International, 1889–1914*, 2d ed. (New York, 1975); and L. Derfler, *Socialism since Marx: A Century of the European Left* (New York, 1973). On the emergence of German social democracy, see W. L. Guttsman, *The German Social Democratic Party, 1875–1933* (London, 1981); and V. Lidtke, *The Outlawed Party: Social Democracy in Germany, 1878–1890* (Princeton, N.J., 1966).

Demographic problems are examined in T. McKeown, *The Modern Rise of Population* (New York, 1976). On European emigration, see C. Erickson, *Emigration from Europe, 1815–1914* (Cambridge, 1976); and L. P. Moch, *Moving Europeans: Migration in Western Europe since 1650* (Bloomington, Ind., 1993).

For a good introduction to housing reform on the Continent, see N. Bullock and J. Read, *The Movement for Housing Reform in Germany and France, 1840–1914* (Cambridge, 1985). E. Gauldie, *Cruel Habitations* (London, 1974) is a good account of working-class housing in Britain. The reconstruction of Paris is discussed in D. Pinkney, *Napoleon III and the Rebuilding of Paris* (Princeton, N.J., 1958).

An interesting work on aristocratic life is G. D. Philips, *The Diehards: Aristocratic Society and Politics in Edwardian England* (Cambridge, 1979). The argument for the continuing importance of the aristocracy is presented in the provocative book by A. Mayer, *Persistence of the Old Regime: Europe to the Great War* (New York, 1981). On the working classes, see L. Berlanstein, *The Working People of Paris, 1871–1914* (Baltimore, 1984).

There are good overviews of women's experiences in the nineteenth century in B. S. Anderson and J. P. Zinsser, *A History of Their Own*, vol. 2 (New York, 1988); and M. J. Boxer and J. H. Quataert, eds., *Connecting Spheres: Women in the Western World, 1500 to the Present* (New York, 1987). The world of women's work is examined in L. A. Tilly and J. W. Scott, *Women, Work, and Family* (New York, 1978). Important studies of middle-class women include P. Branca, *Silent Sisterhood: Middle Class Women in the Victorian Home* (London, 1975); and B. G. Smith, *Ladies of the Leisure Class: The Bourgeoises of Northern France in the Nineteenth Century* (Princeton, N.J., 1981). On the family and children, see M. Mitterauer and R. Sieder, *The European Family* (Chicago, 1982); and the controversial E. Shorter, *The Making of the Modern Family* (New York, 1975).

On various aspects of education, see M. J. Maynes, *Schooling in Western Europe: A Social History* (Albany, N.Y., 1985); and J. S. Hurt, *Elementary Schooling and the Working Classes, 1860–1918* (London, 1979). A concise and well-presented survey of leisure patterns is G. Cross, *A Social History of Leisure since 1600* (State College, Pa., 1990). On the expansion of reading material, see A. J. Lee, *The Origins of the Popular Press in Britain, 1855–1914* (London, 1978).

The domestic politics of the period can be examined in the general works on individual countries listed in the bibliographies for Chapters 22 and 23. There are also specialized works on aspects of each country's history. For a detailed examination of French history from 1871 to 1914, see J. M. Mayeur and M. Reberioux, *The Third Republic from Its Origins to the Great War, 1871–1914* (Cambridge, 1984). On the Paris Commune, see R. Tombs, *The War against Paris, 1871* (Cambridge, 1981). On the nationalities problem in the Austro-Hungarian Empire, see R. Kann, *The Multinational Empire, Nationalism and National Reform in the Habsburg Monarchy, 1848–1918*, 2 vols. (New York, 1950). On aspects of Russian history, see H. Rogger, *Russia in the Age of Modernization and Revolution, 1881–1917* (London, 1983).

CHAPTER
25

An Age of Modernity and Anxiety, 1894–1914

Many Europeans after 1894 continued to believe they lived in an era of material and human progress. For some, however, progress entailed much struggle. Emmeline Pankhurst, who became the leader of the women's suffrage movement in Britain, said that her determination to fight for women's rights stemmed from a childhood memory: "My father bent over me, shielding the candle flame with his big hand and I heard him say, somewhat sadly, 'What a pity she wasn't born a lad.' " Eventually, Emmeline Pankhurst and her daughters marched and fought for women's right to vote. The struggle was often violent: "They came in bruised, hatless, faces scratched, eyes swollen, noses bleeding," one of the Pankhurst daughters recalled. Arrested and jailed in 1908, Pankhurst informed her judges: "If you had the power to send us to prison, not for six months, but for six years, or for our lives, the Government must not think they could stop this agitation. It would go on!" It did go on, and women in Britain did eventually receive the right to vote; to some, this was yet another confirmation of Europe's progress.

But the period after 1894 was not just a time of progress; it was also a time of great tension as imperialist adventures, international rivalries, and cultural uncertainties disturbed the apparent calm. After 1880, Europeans engaged in a great race for colonies around the world. This competition for lands abroad greatly intensified existing antagonisms among European states.

Ultimately, Europeans proved incapable of finding constructive ways to cope with their international rivalries. The development of two large alliance systems—the Triple Alliance and the Triple Entente—may have helped preserve peace for a time, but eventually the alliances made it easier for the European nations to be drawn into World War I. The alliances helped maintain a balance of power, but also led to the creation of large armies, enormous military establishments, and immense arsenals. The alliances also helped create tensions that were unleashed when Europeans rushed into the catastrophic carnage of World War I.

Freud, *The Interpretation of Dreams*

Einstein's special theory of relativity

Picasso, first Cubist painting

Stravinsky, *The Rite of Spring*

Dreyfus affair in France

Women's Social and Political Union in Britain

Social Democratic Party • as largest party in Germany

Revolution in Russia

U.S. annexation of Hawaii

Russo-Japanese War

Triple Entente: France, Britain, and Russia

First Balkan War

The cultural life of Europe in the decades before 1914 reflects similar dynamic tensions. The advent of mass education produced more well-informed citizens, but also made it easier for governments to stir up the masses by nationalistic appeals through the new mass journalism. At the same time, despite the appearance of progress, European philosophers, writers, and artists were creating modern cultural expressions that questioned traditional ideas and values and increasingly provoked a crisis of confidence. Before 1914, many intellectuals had a sense of unease about the direction society was heading, accompanied by a feeling of imminent catastrophe. They proved remarkably prophetic.

Toward the Modern Consciousness: Intellectual and Cultural Developments

Before 1914, most Westerners continued to believe in the values and ideals that had been generated by the Scientific Revolution and the Enlightenment. Reason, science, and progress were still important words in the European vocabulary. The ability of human beings to improve themselves and achieve a better society seemed to be well demonstrated by a rising standard of living, urban improvements, and mass education. Such products of modern technology as electric lights, phonographs, and automobiles reinforced the popular prestige of science and the belief in the ability of the human mind to comprehend the universe. Near the end of the nineteenth century, however, a dramatic transformation in the realm of ideas and culture challenged many of these assumptions.

A new view of the physical universe, alternative views of human nature, and radically innovative forms of literary and artistic expression shattered old beliefs and opened the way to a modern consciousness. Although the real impact of many of these ideas was not felt until after World War I, they served to provoke a sense of confusion and anxiety before 1914 that would become even more pronounced after the war.

Developments in the Sciences: The Emergence of a New Physics

Science was one of the chief pillars underlying the optimistic and rationalistic view of the world that many Westerners shared in the nineteenth century. Supposedly based on hard facts and cold reason, science offered a certainty of belief in the orderliness of nature that was comforting to many people for whom traditional religious beliefs no longer had much meaning. Many naively believed that the application of already known scientific laws would give humanity a complete understanding of the physical world and an accurate picture of reality. The new physics dramatically altered that perspective.

Throughout much of the nineteenth century, Westerners adhered to the mechanical conception of the universe postulated by the classical physics of Isaac Newton. In this perspective, the universe was viewed as a giant machine in which time, space, and matter were objective realities that existed independently of those observing them. Matter was thought to be composed of indivisible and solid material bodies called atoms.

These views were first seriously questioned at the end of the nineteenth century. Some scientists had discovered that certain elements such as radium and polonium spontaneously gave off rays or radiation that apparently came from within the atom itself. Atoms were not simply hard, material bodies but small worlds containing such subatomic particles as electrons and protons that behaved in a seemingly random and inexplicable fashion. Inquiry into the disintegrative process within atoms became a central theme of the new physics.

Building on this work, in 1900 a Berlin physicist, Max Planck (1858–1947), rejected the belief that a heated body radiates energy in a steady stream but maintained instead that energy is radiated discontinuously, in irregular packets of energy that he called "quanta." The quantum theory raised fundamental questions about the subatomic realm of the atom. By 1900, the old view of atoms as the basic building blocks of the material world was be-

◆   **Sigmund Freud.** Freud was one of the intellectual giants of the nineteenth century. His belief that unconscious forces strongly determine human behavior formed the foundation for twentieth-century psychoanalysis.

ing seriously questioned, and the world of Newtonian physics was in trouble.

Albert Einstein (1879–1955), a German-born patent officer working in Switzerland, pushed these new theories of thermodynamics into new terrain. In 1905, Einstein published a paper titled "The Electro-dynamics of Moving Bodies" that contained his special theory of relativity. According to relativity theory, space and time are not absolute, but relative to the observer, and both are interwoven into what Einstein called a four-dimensional space–time continuum. Neither space nor time had an existence independent of human experience. As Einstein later explained simply to a journalist: "It was formerly believed that if all material things disappeared out of the universe, time and space would be left. According to the relativity theory, however, time and space disappear together with the things."[1] Moreover, matter and energy reflected the relativity of time and space. Einstein concluded that matter was nothing but another form of energy. His epochal formula $E = mc^2$—that each particle of matter is equivalent to its mass times the square of the velocity of light—was the key theory explaining the vast energies contained within the atom. It led to the atomic age.

Sigmund Freud and the Emergence of Psychoanalysis

Although poets and mystics had revealed a world of unconscious and irrational behavior, many scientifically oriented intellectuals under the impact of Enlightenment thought continued to believe that human beings responded to conscious motives in a rational fashion. At the end of the nineteenth and beginning of the twentieth centuries, the Viennese doctor Sigmund Freud (1856–1939) put forth a series of theories that undermined optimism about the rational nature of the human mind. Freud's thought, like the new physics, added to the uncertainties of the age. His major ideas were published in 1900 in his *The Interpretation of Dreams*, which contained the basic foundation of what came to be known as psychoanalysis.

According to Freud, human behavior was strongly determined by the unconscious, by former experiences and inner forces of which people were largely oblivious. To explore the contents of the unconscious, Freud relied not only on hypnosis but also on dreams, but the latter were dressed in an elaborate code that had to be deciphered if the contents were to be properly understood.

But why did some experiences whose influence persisted in controlling an individual's life remain unconscious? According to Freud, the answer was repression (see the box on p. 515), a process by which unsettling ex-

≋ *Freud and the Concept of Repression* ≋

Freud's psychoanalytical theories resulted from his attempt to understand the world of the unconscious. This excerpt is taken from a lecture given in 1909 in which Freud describes how he arrived at his theory of the role of repression. Although Freud valued science and reason, his theories of the unconscious produced a new image of the human being as governed less by reason than by irrational forces.

Sigmund Freud, *Five Lectures on Psychoanalysis*

I did not abandon it [his technique of encouraging patients to reveal forgotten experiences], however, before the observations I made during my use of it afforded me decisive evidence. I found confirmation of the fact that the forgotten memories were not lost. They were in the patient's possession and were ready to emerge in association to what was still known by him; but there was some force that prevented them from becoming conscious and compelled them to remain unconscious. The existence of this force could be assumed with certainty, since one became aware of an effort corresponding to it if, in opposition to it, one tried to introduce the unconscious memories into the patient's consciousness. The force which was maintaining the pathological condition became apparent in the form of resistance on the part of the patient.

It was on this idea of resistance, then, that I based my view of the course of physical events in hysteria. In order to effect a recovery, it had proved necessary to remove these resistances. Starting out from the mechanism of cure, it now became possible to construct quite definite ideas of the origin of the illness. The same forces which, in the form of resistance, were now offering opposition to the forgotten material's being made conscious, must formerly have brought about the forgetting and must have pushed the pathogenic experiences in question out of consciousness. I gave the name of "repression" to this hypothetical process, and I considered that it was proved by the undeniable existence of resistance.

The further question could then be raised as to what these forces were and what the determinants were of the repression in which we now recognized the pathogenic mechanism of hysteria. A comparative study of the pathogenic situations which we had come to know through the cathartic procedure made it possible to answer this question. All these experiences had involved the emergence of a wishful impulse which was in sharp contrast to the subject's other wishes and which proved incompatible with the ethical and aesthetic standards of his personality. There had been a short conflict, and the end of this internal struggle was that the idea which had appeared before consciousness as the vehicle of this irreconcilable wish fell a victim to repression, was pushed out of consciousness with all its attached memories, and was forgotten. Thus the incompatibility of the wish in question with the patient's ego was the motive for the repression; the subject's ethical and other standards were the repressing forces. An acceptance of the incompatible wishful impulse or a prolongation of the conflict would have produced a high degree of unpleasure; this unpleasure was avoided by means of repression, which was thus revealed as one of the devices serving to protect the mental personality.

---

periences were blotted from conscious awareness but still continued to influence behavior because they had become part of the unconscious. To explain how repression worked, Freud elaborated an intricate theory of the inner life of human beings.

According to Freud, a human being's inner life was a battleground of three contending forces: the id, the ego, and the superego. The id was the center of unconscious drives and was ruled by what Freud termed the pleasure principle. As creatures of desire, human beings directed their energy toward pleasure and away from pain. The id contained all kinds of lustful drives and desires and crude appetites and impulses. The ego was the seat of reason and hence the coordinator of the inner life. It was governed by the reality principle. Although humans were dominated by the pleasure principle, a true pursuit of pleasure was not feasible. The reality principle meant that people rejected pleasure so that they might live together in society. The superego was the locus of conscience and represented the inhibitions and moral values that society in general and parents in particular imposed on people. The superego served to force the ego to curb the unsatisfactory drives of the id.

The human being was thus a battleground between id, ego, and superego. Ego and superego exerted restraining influences on the unconscious id and repressed or kept out of consciousness what they wanted to. Repression began in childhood, and psychoanalysis was accomplished through a dialogue between psychotherapist and patient in which the therapist probed deeply into memory in order to retrace the chain of repression all the way back to its childhood origins. By making the conscious mind aware of the unconscious and its repressed contents, the patient's psychic conflict was resolved.

The Impact of Darwin: Social Darwinism and Racism

In the second half of the nineteenth century, scientific theories were sometimes wrongly applied to achieve other ends. The application of Darwin's principle of organic evolution to the social order came to be known as Social Darwinism. Using Darwin's terminology, Social Darwinists argued that societies were organisms that evolved through time from a struggle with their environment. Progress came from the "struggle for survival," as the "fit"—the strong—advanced while the weak declined.

Darwin's ideas were also applied to human society in an even more radical way by rabid nationalists and racists. In their pursuit of national greatness, extreme nationalists argued that nations, too, were engaged in a "struggle for existence" in which only the fittest survived. The German general Friedrich von Bernhardi gave war a Darwinist interpretation in his book, *Germany and the Next War,* published in 1907. He argued that:

> War is a biological necessity of the first importance, a regulative element in the life of mankind which cannot be dispensed with, since without it an unhealthy development will follow, which excludes every advancement of the race, and therefore all real civilization. 'War is the father of all things.' The sages of antiquity long before Darwin recognized this.[2]

Numerous nationalist organizations preached the same doctrine as Bernhardi.

Although certainly not new to Western society, racism, too, was dramatically revived and strengthened by new biological arguments. Perhaps nowhere was the combination of extreme nationalism and racism more evident and more dangerous than in Germany where racist nationalism was expressed in volkish thought. The concept of the *Volk* (nation, people, or race) had been an underlying idea in German history since the beginning of the nineteenth century. One of the chief propagandists for German volkish ideology at the turn of the century was Houston Stewart Chamberlain (1855–1927), an Englishman who became a German citizen. His book, *The Foundations of the Nineteenth Century,* published in 1899,

made a special impact on Germany. Modern-day Germans, according to Chamberlain, were the only pure successors of the Aryans who were portrayed as the true and original creators of Western culture. The Aryan race, under German leadership, must be prepared to fight for Western civilization and save it from the destructive assaults of such lower races as Jews, Negroes, and Orientals. Increasingly, Jews were singled out by German volkish nationalists as the racial enemy in biological terms and as parasites who wanted to destroy the Aryan race.

The Attack on Christianity and the Response of the Churches

The growth of scientific thinking as well as the forces of modernization presented new challenges to the Christian churches. Industrialization and urbanization had an adverse effect on religious institutions. The mass migration of people from the countryside to the city meant a change from the close-knit, traditional ties of the village in which the church had been a key force to new urban patterns of social life from which the churches were often excluded. The established Christian churches had a weak hold on workers. Although workers were not atheists, as is sometimes claimed, they tended to develop their own culture in which organized religion played little role.

Science became one of the chief threats to all the Christian churches and even to religion itself in the nineteenth century. Darwin's theory of evolution, accepted by ever-larger numbers of educated Europeans, seemed to contradict the doctrine of divine creation. By suppressing Darwin's books and forbidding the teaching of evolution, the churches often caused even more educated people to reject established religions.

One response of the Christian churches to these attacks was the outright rejection of modern ideas and forces. Protestant fundamentalist sects were especially important in maintaining a literal interpretation of the Bible. Some sought compromise, an approach especially evident in the Catholic church during the pontificate of Leo XIII (1878–1903). Pope Leo permitted the teaching of evolution as a hypothesis in Catholic schools and also responded to the challenges of modernization in the economic and social spheres. In his encyclical *De Rerum Novarum,* issued in 1891, he upheld the individual's right to private property but at the same time criticized "naked" capitalism for the poverty and degradation in which it had left the working classes. Much in socialism, he declared, was Christian in principle, but he condemned Marxian socialism for its materialistic and antireligious foundations. The pope recommended that Catholics form socialist parties and labor unions of their own to help the workers.

The Culture of Modernity

The revolution in physics and psychology was paralleled by a revolution in literature and the arts. Before 1914, writers and artists were rebelling against the traditional literary and artistic styles that had dominated European cultural life since the Renaissance. The changes that they produced have since been called Modernism.

NATURALISM AND SYMBOLISM IN LITERATURE

Throughout much of the late nineteenth century, literature was dominated by Naturalism. Naturalists accepted the material world as real and felt that literature should be realistic. By addressing social problems, writers could contribute to an objective understanding of the world. Although Naturalism was a continuation of Realism, it lacked the underlying note of liberal optimism about people and society that had still been prevalent in the 1850s. The Naturalists were pessimistic about Europe's future. They doubted the existence of free will and often portrayed characters caught in the grip of forces beyond their control.

The novels of the French writer Émile Zola (1840–1902) provide a good example of Naturalism. Against a backdrop of the urban slums and coal fields of northern France, Zola showed how alcoholism and different environments affected people's lives. The materialistic science of his age had an important influence on Zola. He had read Darwin's *Origin of Species* and had been impressed by its emphasis on the struggle for survival and the importance of environment and heredity. These themes were central to his *Rougon-Macquart*, a twenty-volume series of novels on the "natural and social history of a family." Zola maintained that the artist must analyze and dissect life as a biologist would a living organism. He said, "I have simply done on living bodies the work of analysis which surgeons perform on corpses."

At the turn of the century, a new group of writers, known as the Symbolists, reacted against Realism. Primarily interested in writing poetry, the Symbolists believed that an objective knowledge of the world was impossible. The external world was not real but only a collection of symbols that reflected the true reality of the individual human mind. Art, they believed, should function for its own sake instead of serving, criticizing, or seeking to understand society. In the works of two of the symbolist poets, W. B. Yeats and Rainer Maria Rilke, po-

etry ceased to be part of popular culture because only through a knowledge of the poet's personal language could one hope to understand what the poet was saying.

MODERNISM IN THE ARTS

Since the Renaissance, artists had tried to represent reality as accurately as possible. By the late nineteenth century, however, artists were seeking new forms of expression. The preamble to modern painting can be found in Impressionism, a movement that originated in France in the 1870s when a group of artists rejected the studios and museums and went out into the countryside to paint nature directly. Camille Pissarro (1830–1903), one of Impressionism's founders, expressed what they sought:

> Precise drawing is dry and hampers the impression of the whole, it destroys all sensations. Do not define too closely the outlines of things; it is the brush stroke of the right value and color which should produce the drawing. . . . The eye should not be fixed on one point, but should take in everything, while observing the reflections which the colors produce on their surroundings. Work at the same time upon sky, water, branches, ground, keeping everything going on an equal basis and unceasingly rework until you have got it. . . . Don't proceed according to rules and principles, but paint what you observe and feel. Paint generously and unhesitatingly, for it is best not to lose the first impression.[3]

Impressionists like Pissarro sought to put into painting their impressions of the changing effects of light on objects in nature. Capturing the untold variety of ways in which light reflected off different kinds of surfaces proved especially challenging to them.

Pisarro's suggestions are visibly portrayed in the work of Claude Monet (1840–1926). He was especially enchanted with water and painted many pictures in which he sought to capture the interplay of light, water, and atmosphere, especially evident in *Impression, Sunrise*. But the Impressionists did not just paint scenes from nature. Streets and cabarets, rivers, and busy boulevards—wherever people congregated for work and leisure—formed their subject matter.

By the 1880s, a new movement known as Post-Impressionism arose in France but soon spread to other European countries. Post-Impressionism retained the Impressionist emphasis on light and color but revolutionized it even further by paying more attention to structure and form. Post-Impressionists sought to use both color and line to express inner feelings and produce a personal statement of reality rather than an imitation of objects. Impressionist paintings had retained a sense of realism,

✦ **Claude Monet, *Impression, Sunrise.*** Impressionists rejected "rules and principles" and sought to paint what they observed and felt in order "not to lose the first impression." As is evident in *Impression, Sunrise*, Monet sought to capture his impression of the fleeting moments of sunrise through the simple interplay of light, water, and atmosphere.

but the Post-Impressionists shifted from objective reality to subjective reality and, in so doing, began to withdraw from the artist's traditional task of depicting the external world. Post-Impressionists were the real forerunners of modern art.

A famous Post-Impressionist was the tortured and tragic figure Vincent van Gogh (1853–1890). For van Gogh, art was a spiritual experience. He was especially interested in color and believed that it could act as its own form of language. Van Gogh maintained that artists should paint what they feel. In his *Starry Night*, he painted a sky alive with whirling stars that overwhelmed the huddled buildings in the village below.

By the beginning of the twentieth century, the belief that the task of art was to represent "reality" had lost much of its meaning. By that time, the new psychology and the new physics had made it evident that many people were not sure what constituted reality anyway. Then, too, the development of photography gave artists another reason to reject visual realism. First invented in the 1830s, photography became popular and widespread after George Eastman created the first Kodak camera for the mass market in 1888. What was the point of an artist doing what the camera did better? Unlike the camera, which could only mirror reality, artists could create reality. As in literature, so also in modern art, individual consciousness became the source of meaning. Between 1905 and 1914, this search for individual expression produced

a great variety of painting schools, all of which had their greatest impact after World War I.

By 1905, one of the most important figures in modern art was just beginning his career. Pablo Picasso (1881–1973) was from Spain but settled in Paris in 1904. Picasso was extremely flexible and painted in a remarkable variety of styles. He was instrumental in the development of a new style called Cubism that used geometric designs as visual stimuli to recreate reality in the viewer's mind. Picasso's 1907 work *Les Demoiselles d'Avignon* has been called the first cubist painting.

The modern artist's flight from "visual reality" reached a high point in 1910 with the beginning of abstract painting. A Russian who worked in Germany, Vasily Kandinsky (1866–1944), was one of the founders of abstract expressionism. As is evident in his *Painting with White Border*, Kandinsky sought to avoid representation altogether. He believed that art should speak directly to the soul. To do so, it must avoid any reference to visual reality and concentrate on color.

At the beginning of the twentieth century, developments in music paralleled those in painting. Expressionism in music was a Russian creation, the product of the composer Igor Stravinsky (1882–1971) and the Ballet Russe, the dancing company of Sergei Diaghilev (1872–1929). Together they revolutionized the world of music with Stravinsky's ballet *The Rites of Spring*. At the premiere on May 29, 1913, the pulsating rhythms, sharp dissonances, and unusual dancing overwhelmed the Paris audience and caused a riot at the theater.

*P*olitics: New Directions and New Uncertainties

The uncertainties in European intellectual and cultural life were paralleled by growing anxieties in European political life. The seemingly steady progress in the growth of liberal principles and political democracy after 1871 soon slowed or possibly even halted altogether after 1894. The new mass politics had opened the door to changes that many nineteenth-century liberals found unacceptable, and liberals themselves were forced to move in new directions. The appearance of a new right-wing politics based on racism added an ugly note to the already existing anxieties. With their newfound voting rights, workers elected socialists who demanded new reforms when they took their places in legislative bodies. Women, too, made new demands, insisting on the right to vote and using new tactics to gain it. In central and eastern Europe, tensions grew as authoritarian governments refused to meet the de-

✦ **Vincent van Gogh, *The Starry Night*, 1889.** The Dutch painter Vincent van Gogh was a major figure among the Post-Impressionists. His originality and power of expression made a strong impact on his artistic successors. In *The Starry Night*, van Gogh's subjective vision was given full play as the dynamic swirling forms of the heavens above overwhelmed the village below. The heavens seem alive with a mysterious spiritual force.

mands of reformers. And outside Europe, a new giant appeared in the Western world as the United States emerged as a great industrial power with immense potential.

The Movement for Women's Rights

In the 1830s, a number of women in the United States and Europe, who worked together in several reform movements, became frustrated by the apparent prejudice against females. They sought improvements for women by focusing on specific goals. Family and marriage laws were especially singled out because it was difficult for women to secure divorces and property laws gave husbands almost complete control over the property of their wives. These early efforts, however, were not overly successful. For example, women did not gain the right to their own property until 1870 in Britain, 1900 in Germany, and 1907 in France.

Custody and property rights were only a beginning for the women's movement, however. Some middle- and upper-middle-class women gained access to higher education while others sought entry into occupations dominated by men. The first to fall was teaching. Because medical training was largely closed to women, they sought

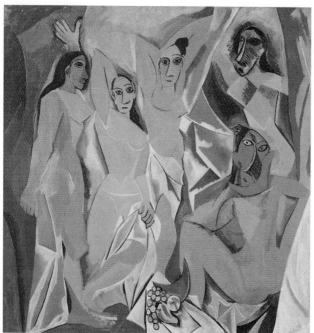

◆ **Pablo Picasso, *Les Demoiselles d'Avignon*, 1907.**
Pablo Picasso, a major pioneer and activist of modern art,
experimented with a remarkable variety of modern styles. His *Les
Demoiselles d'Avignon* was the first great example of Cubism,
which one art historian has called "the first style of this century
to break radically with the past." Geometric shapes replace
traditional forms, forcing the viewer to recreate reality in his or
her own mind.

alternatives in the development of nursing. One nursing
pioneer was Amalie Sieveking (1794–1859), who founded
the Female Association for the Care of the Poor and Sick
in Hamburg, Germany. As she explained: "To me, at least
as important were the benefits which [work with the poor]
seemed to promise for those of my sisters who would join
me in such a work of charity. The higher interests of my
sex were close to my heart."[4] Sieveking's work was followed by the more famous British nurse Florence Nightin-
gale (1820–1910), whose efforts during the Crimean War,
combined with those of Clara Barton (1821–1912) in the
American Civil War, transformed nursing into a profession of trained, middle-class "women in white."

By the 1840s and 1850s, the movement for women's
rights had entered the political arena with the call for
equal political rights. Many feminists believed that the
right to vote was the key to all other reforms to improve
the position of women. The British women's movement
was the most vocal and active in Europe, but divided over
tactics. Moderates believed that women must demonstrate that they would use political power responsibly if
they wanted Parliament to grant them the right to vote.
Another group, however, favored a more radical approach. Emmeline Pankhurst (1858–1928) and her
daughters, Christabel and Sylvia, founded the Women's
Social and Political Union in 1903, which enrolled
mostly middle- and upper-class women. Pankhurst's organization realized the value of the media and used un-

◆ **Vasily Kandinsky, *Composition
VIII, No. 2 (Painting with White
Border)*.** One of the founders of
Abstract Expressionism was the Russian
Vasily Kandinsky, who sought to
eliminate representation altogether by
focusing on color and avoiding any
resemblance to visual reality. In *Painting
with White Border*, Kandinsky used color
"to send light into the darkness of men's
hearts." He believed that color, like
music, could fulfill a spiritual goal of
appealing directly to the human being.

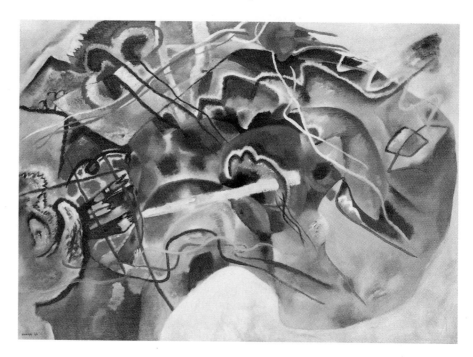

usual publicity stunts to call attention to its demands. Derisively labeled suffragettes by male politicians, they pelted government officials with eggs, chained themselves to lampposts, smashed the windows of department stores on fashionable shopping streets, burned railroad cars, and went on hunger strikes in jail. Suffragists had one fundamental aim, the right of women to full citizenship in the nation-state (see the box on p. 522).

Although demands for women's rights were heard throughout Europe and the United States before World War I, only in Finland, Norway, and some American states did women actually receive the right to vote before 1914. It would take the dramatic upheaval of World War I before male-dominated governments capitulated on this basic issue.

Jews within the European Nation-State

Near the end of the nineteenth century, a revival of racism combined with extreme nationalism to produce a new right-wing politics aimed primarily against the Jews. Of course, anti-Semitism was not new to European civilization. Since the Middle Ages, Jews had been portrayed as the murderers of Christ and subjected to mob violence; their rights had been restricted, and they had been physically separated from Christians in quarters known as ghettos.

In the nineteenth century, as a result of the ideals of the Enlightenment and the French Revolution, Jews were increasingly granted legal equality in many European countries. Nevertheless, Jews were not completely accepted, and this ambivalence toward the Jews was apparent throughout Europe. In Prussia, for example, Jews were emancipated in 1812 but still restricted. They could not hold government offices or take advanced degrees in universities. After the revolutions of 1848, emancipation became a fact of life for Jews throughout western and central Europe. For many Jews, emancipation enabled them to leave the ghetto and become assimilated as hundreds of thousands of Jews entered what had been the closed worlds of parliaments and universities. Many Jews became eminently successful as bankers, lawyers, scientists, scholars, journalists, and stage performers. In 1880, for example, Jews made up 10 percent of the population of the city of Vienna, Austria, but 39 percent of its medical students and 23 percent of its law students.

These achievements represent only one side of the picture, however, as is evident from the Dreyfus affair in France. Alfred Dreyfus, a Jew, was a captain in the French general staff. Early in 1895, a secret military court found him guilty of selling army secrets and condemned him to life imprisonment on Devil's Island. During his trial, right-wing mobs yelled "Death to the Jews." Soon after the trial, however, evidence emerged that pointed to Dreyfus's innocence. The government pardoned Dreyfus in 1899, and in 1906, he was finally fully exonerated.

In Germany and Austria during the 1880s and 1890s, conservatives founded right-wing anti-Semitic parties that used anti-Semitism to win the votes of traditional lower-middle-class groups who felt threatened by the new economic forces of the times. These German and Austrian anti-Semitic parties were based on race. To modern racial anti-Semites, Jews were racially stained; this could not be altered by conversion. One could not be both German and Jew.

The worst treatment of Jews in the last two decades of the nineteenth century and the first decade of the twentieth occurred in eastern Europe where 72 percent of the entire world Jewish population lived. Russian Jews were admitted to secondary schools and universities only under a quota system and were forced to live in certain regions of the country. Persecutions and pogroms were widespread. Hundreds of thousands of Jews decided to emigrate to escape the persecution. Between 1881 and 1899, an average of 23,000 Jews left Russia each year. Many of them went to the United States, although some (probably about 25,000) moved to Palestine, which soon became the focus for a Jewish nationalist movement called Zionism.

The emancipation of the nineteenth century had presented vast opportunities for some Jews, but dilemmas for others. What was the price of citizenship? Did emancipation mean full assimilation and did assimilation mean the disruption of traditional Jewish life? Many paid the price willingly, but others questioned its value and advocated a different answer, a return to Palestine. For many Jews, Palestine, the land of ancient Israel, had long been the land of their dreams. During the nineteenth century, as nationalist ideas spread and Italians, Poles, Irish, Greeks, and others sought national emancipation, so too did the idea of national independence capture the imagination of some Jews. A key figure in the growth of political Zionism was Theodor Herzl (1860–1904). In 1896, he published a book called *The Jewish State* in which he advocated that "The Jews who wish it will have their state." Financial support for the development of yishuvs or settlements in Palestine came from wealthy Jewish banking families who wanted a refuge in Palestine for persecuted Jews, not a political Jewish state. Even settlements were difficult because Palestine was then part of the Ottoman Empire and Turkish authorities were opposed to Jewish immigration. Despite the problems, however, the First Zionist

Advice to Women: Be Independent

Although a majority of women probably followed the nine-teenth-century middle-class ideal of women as keepers of the household and nurturers of husband and children, an increasing number of women fought for the rights of women. This selection is taken from Act III of Henrik Ibsen's A Doll's House (1879), in which the character of Nora Helmer declares her independence from her husband's control.

Henrik Ibsen, *A Doll's House*

NORA: (*Pause*) Does anything strike you as we sit here?

HELMER: What should strike me?

NORA: We've been married eight years; does it not strike you that this is the first time we two, you and I, man and wife, have talked together seriously?

HELMER: Seriously? What do you mean, *seriously?*

NORA: For eight whole years, and more—ever since the day we first met—we have never exchanged one serious word about serious things. . . .

HELMER: Why, my dearest Nora, what have you to do with serious things?

NORA: There we have it! You have never understood me. I've had great injustice done to me, Torvald; first by father, then by you.

HELMER: What! Your father *and* me? We, who have loved you more than all the world!

NORA: (*Shaking her head*): You have never loved me. You just found it amusing to think you were in love with me.

HELMER: Nora! What a thing to say!

NORA: Yes, it's true, Torvald. When I was living at home with father, he told me his opinions and mine were the same. If I had different opinions, I said nothing about them, because he would not have liked it. He used to call me his doll-child and played with me as I played with my dolls. Then I came to live in your house.

HELMER: What a way to speak of our marriage!

NORA (*Undisturbed*): I mean that I passed from father's hands into yours. You arranged everything to your taste and I got the same tastes as you; or pretended to—I don't know which—both, perhaps; sometimes one, sometimes the other. When I look back on it now, I seem to have been living here like a beggar, on handouts. I lived by performing tricks for you, Torvald. But that was how you wanted it. You and father have done me a great wrong. It is your fault that my life has come to naught.

HELMER: Why, Nora, how unreasonable and ungrateful! Haven't you been happy here?

NORA: No, never. I thought I was, but I never was.

HELMER: Not—not happy!. . .

NORA: I must stand quite alone if I am ever to know myself and my surroundings; so I cannot stay with you.

HELMER: Nora! Nora!

NORA: I am going at once. I daresay [my friend] Christina will take me in for tonight.

HELMER: You are mad! I shall not allow it! I forbid it!

NORA: It's no use your forbidding me anything now. I shall take with me only what belongs to me; from you I will accept nothing, either now or later.

HELMER: This is madness!

NORA: Tomorrow I shall go home—I mean to what was my home. It will be easier for me to find a job there.

HELMER: On, in your blind inexperience—

NORA: I must try to gain experience, Torvald.

HELMER: Forsake your home, your husband, your children! And you don't consider what the world will say.

NORA: I can't pay attention to that. I only know that I must do it.

HELMER: This is monstrous! Can you forsake your holiest duties?

NORA: What do you consider my holiest duties?

HELMER: Need I tell you that? Your duties to your husband and children.

NORA: I have other duties equally sacred.

HELMER: Impossible! What do you mean?

NORA: My duties toward myself.

HELMER: Before all else you are a wife and a mother.

NORA: That I no longer believe. Before all else I believe I am a human being just as much as you are—or at least that I should try to become one. I know that most people agree with you, Torvald, and that they say so in books. But I can no longer be satisfied with what most people say and what is in books. I must think things out for myself and try to get clear about them.

Congress, which met in Switzerland in 1897, proclaimed as its aim the creation of a "home in Palestine secured by public law" for the Jewish people. In 1900, 1,000 Jews migrated to Palestine. And although 3,000 Jews went annually to Palestine between 1904 and 1914, the Zionist dream remained just that on the eve of World War I.

The Transformation of Liberalism: Great Britain

In dealing with the problems created by the new mass politics, liberal governments often followed policies that undermined the basic tenets of liberalism. This was certainly true in Great Britain, where the demands of the working-class movement caused Liberals to move away from their ideals. Liberals were forced to adopt significant social reforms due to the pressure of two new working-class organizations: trade unions and the Labour Party.

Trade unions began to advocate more radical change of the economic system, calling for "collective ownership and control over production, distribution and exchange." At the same time, a movement for laborers emerged among a group of intellectuals known as the Fabian Socialists. Neither the Fabian Socialists nor the British trade unions were Marxist oriented. They did not advocate class struggle and revolution but evolution toward a socialist state by democratic means. In 1900, representatives of the trade unions and Fabian Socialists coalesced to form the Labour Party. By 1906 they had managed to elect twenty-nine members to the House of Commons.

The Liberals, who held the government from 1906 to 1914, perceived that they would have to enact a program of social welfare or lose the support of the workers. Under the leadership of David Lloyd George (1863–1945), the Liberals abandoned the classical principles of laissez-faire and voted for a series of social reforms. The National Insurance Act of 1911 provided benefits for workers in case of sickness and unemployment; the act was financed by compulsory contributions from workers, employers, and the state. Additional legislation provided a small pension for those over seventy and compensation for those injured in accidents while at work. Though the benefits of the program and tax increases were both modest, they were the first hesitant steps toward the future British welfare state. Liberalism, which had been based on the principle that the government that governs least governs best, had been transformed.

Growing Tensions in Germany

The new imperial Germany begun by Bismarck continued as an "authoritarian, conservative, military-

bureaucratic power state" during the reign of Emperor William II (1888–1918). By 1914, Germany had become the strongest military and industrial power on the Continent. More than 50 percent of German workers had jobs in industry while only 30 percent of the workforce was still in agriculture. Urban centers had mushroomed in number and size. The rapid changes in William's Germany helped to produce a society torn between modernization and traditionalism.

The growth of industrialization led to even greater expansion of the Social Democratic Party. By 1912, it had become the largest single party in the Reichstag. At the same time, the party became less revolutionary and more revisionist in its outlook. Nevertheless, its growth frightened the middle and upper classes who blamed labor for their own problems.

With the expansion of industry and cities came demands for more political participation and growing sentiment for reforms that would produce greater democratization. Conservative forces, especially the landowning nobility and representatives of heavy industry, two of the powerful ruling groups in Germany, tried to block it by supporting William II's activist foreign policy of finding Germany's "place in the sun." Expansionism would divert people from further democratization.

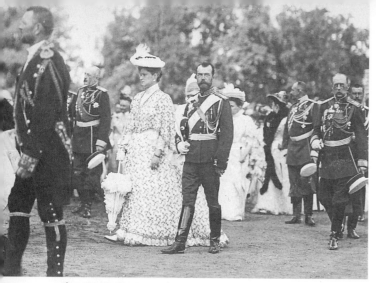

♦ Nicholas II. The last tsar of Russia hoped to preserve the traditional autocratic ways of his predecessors. In this photograph, Nicholas II and his wife Alexandra are shown returning from a church at Tsarskoe-Selo.

The tensions in German society created by the conflict between modernization and traditionalism were also manifested in a new, radicalized, right-wing politics. A number of nationalist pressure groups arose to support nationalistic goals. Such groups as the Pan-German League stressed strong German nationalism and advocated imperialism as a tool to overcome social divisions and unite all classes. They were also anti-Semitic and denounced Jews as the destroyers of national community.

Industrialization and Revolution in Imperial Russia

Although industrialization came late to Russia, it progressed rapidly after 1890, especially with the assistance of foreign investment capital. By 1900, Russia had become the fourth largest producer of steel behind the United States, Germany, and Great Britain. With industrialization came factories, an industrial working class, and the development of socialist parties, although repression in Russia soon forced them to go underground and become revolutionary. The Marxist Social Democratic Party, for example, held its first congress in Minsk in 1898, but the arrest of its leaders caused the next one to be held in Brussels in 1903, attended by Russian emigres. The Social Revolutionaries worked to overthrow the tsarist autocracy and establish peasant socialism. Having no other outlet for opposition to the regime, they advocated political terrorism, attempting to assassinate government officials and members of the ruling dynasty. The growing opposition to the tsarist regime finally exploded into revolution in 1905.

The defeat of the Russians by the Japanese in 1904–1905 encouraged antigovernment groups to rebel against the tsarist regime. After a general strike in October 1905, the government capitulated. Nicholas II (1894–1917) issued the October Manifesto, in which he granted civil liberties and agreed to create a Duma, or legislative assembly, elected directly by a broad franchise. But real constitutional monarchy proved short-lived. Already by 1907, the tsar had curtailed the power of the Duma, and he fell back on the army and bureaucracy to rule Russia.

The Rise of the United States

Between 1860 and World War I, the United States made the shift from an agrarian to a mighty industrial nation. American heavy industry stood unchallenged in 1900. In that year, the Carnegie Steel Company alone produced more steel than Great Britain's entire steel industry. Industrialization also led to urbanization. While established cities, such as New York, Philadelphia, and Boston, grew even larger, other moderate-size cities, such as Pittsburgh, grew by leaps and bounds because of industrialization. Whereas 20 percent of Americans lived in cities in 1860, more than 40 percent did in 1900.

By 1900, the United States had become the world's richest nation and greatest industrial power. Yet serious questions remained about the quality of American life. In 1890, the richest 9 percent of Americans owned an incredible 71 percent of all the wealth. Labor unrest over unsafe working conditions, strict work discipline, and periodical cycles of devastating unemployment led workers to organize. By the turn of the century, one national organization, the American Federation of Labor, emerged as labor's dominant voice. Its lack of real power, however, is reflected in its membership figures. In 1900, it included only 8.4 percent of the American industrial labor force.

During the so-called "Progressive Era" after 1900, an age of reform swept through the United States. At the state level, reforming governors sought to achieve clean government by introducing elements of direct democracy, such as direct primaries for selecting nominees for public office. State governments also enacted economic and social legislation, such as laws that governed hours, wages, and working conditions, especially for women and children. The realization that state laws were ineffective in dealing with nationwide problems, however, led to a Progressive movement at the national level. The Meat Inspection Act and Pure Food and Drug Act provided for a limited degree of federal regulation of corrupt industrial practices. The presidency of Woodrow Wilson

(1913–1921) witnessed the creation of a graduated federal income tax and the establishment of the Federal Reserve System, which permitted the federal government to play a role in important economic decisions formerly made by bankers. Like European states, the United States was moving slowly into policies that extended the functions of the state.

The Growth of Canada

Canada faced problems of national unity at the end of the nineteenth century. At the beginning of 1870, the Dominion of Canada had four provinces: Quebec, Ontario, Nova Scotia, and New Brunswick. With the addition of two more provinces in 1871—Manitoba and British Columbia—the Dominion of Canada extended from the Atlantic to the Pacific.

Real unity was difficult to achieve, however, because of the distrust between the English-speaking and French-speaking peoples of Canada. Wilfred Laurier, who became the first French-Canadian prime minister in 1896, was able to reconcile Canada's two major groups. During his administration, industrialization boomed and immigrants from Europe helped to populate Canada's vast territories.

The New Imperialism

Beginning in the 1880s, European states engaged in an intense scramble for overseas territory. This revival of imperialism, or the "new imperialism" as some have called it, led Europeans to carve up Asia and Africa. But why did Europeans begin their mad scramble for colonies after 1880?

The existence of competitive nation-states after 1870 was undoubtedly a major determinant in the growth of this new imperialism. As European affairs grew tense, heightened competition led European states to acquire colonies abroad that provided ports and coaling stations for their navies. Colonies were also a source of international prestige. Once the scramble for colonies began, failure to enter the race was perceived as a sign of weakness, totally unacceptable to an aspiring great power.

Then, too, imperialism was tied to Social Darwinism and racism. Social Darwinists believed that in the struggle between nations, the fit are victorious and survive. Superior races must dominate inferior races by military force to show how strong and virile they are. As one Englishman wrote: "To the development of the White Man, the Black Man and the Yellow must ever remain inferior, and as the former raised itself higher and yet higher, so did

these latter seem to shrink out of humanity and appear nearer and nearer to the brutes."[5]

Some Europeans took a more religious-humanitarian approach to imperialism when they argued that Europeans had moral responsibility to civilize ignorant peoples. This notion of the "white man's burden" (see the box on p. 526) helped at least the more idealistic individuals to rationalize imperialism in their own minds. Nevertheless, the belief that the superiority of their civilization obligated them to impose modern industry, cities, and new medicines on supposedly primitive nonwhites, even if they had to be killed to do so, was yet another form of racism.

Some historians have emphasized an economic motivation for imperialism. There was a great demand for natural resources and products not found in Western countries, such as rubber, oil, and tin. Instead of just trading for these products, European investors advocated direct control of the raw material-producing areas. The large surpluses of capital that were being accumulated by bankers and industrialists often encouraged them to seek higher rates of profit in underdeveloped areas. All of these factors combined to create an economic imperialism whereby European finance dominated the economic activity of a large part of the world.

The Creation of Empires

Whatever the reasons for the new imperialism, it had a dramatic effect on Africa and Asia as European powers competed for control of these two continents.

THE SCRAMBLE FOR AFRICA

Europeans controlled relatively little of the African continent before 1880. During the Napoleonic wars, the British had established themselves in south Africa by taking control of Capetown, originally founded by the Dutch. After the wars, the British encouraged settlers to come to what they called Cape Colony. British policies disgusted the Boers or Afrikaners, as the descendants of the Dutch colonists were called, and led them in 1835 to migrate north on the Great Trek to the region between the Orange and Vaal Rivers (later known as the Orange Free State) and north of the Vaal River (the Transvaal). Hostilities between the British and the Boers continued.

In the 1880s British policy in south Africa was largely determined by Cecil Rhodes (1853–1902). Rhodes founded both diamond and gold companies that monopolized production of these precious commodities and enabled him to gain control of a territory north of Transvaal that he named Rhodesia after himself. His imperialist

≽ The White Man's Burden ≼

One of the justifications for European imperialism was the notion that superior white peoples had the moral responsibility to raise ignorant native peoples to a higher level of civilization. The British poet Rudyard Kipling (1865–1936) captured this notion in his poem, The White Man's Burden.

Rudyard Kipling, *The White Man's Burden*

Take up the White Man's burden—
Send forth the best ye breed—
Go bind your sons to exile
To serve your captives' needs;
To wait in heavy harness,
On fluttered folk and wild—
Your new-caught sullen peoples,
Half-devil and half-child.

Take up the White Man's burden—
In patience to abide,
To veil the threat of terror
And check the show of pride;
By open speech and simple,
An hundred times made plain
To seek another's profit,
And work another's gain.

Take up the White Man's burden—
The savage wars of peace—
Fill full the mouth of Famine
And bid the sickness cease;
And when your goal is nearest
The end for others sought,
Watch sloth and heathen Folly
Bring all your hopes to nought.

Take up the White Man's burden—
No tawdry rule of kings,
But toil of serf and sweeper—
The tale of common things.
The ports ye shall not enter,
The roads ye shall not read,
Go mark them with your living,
And mark them with your dead.

Take up the White Man's burden—
And reap his old reward:
The blame of those ye better,
The hate of those ye guard—
The cry of hosts ye humour
(Ah, slowly; 1) toward the light:—
'Why brought he us from bondage,
Our loved Egyptian night?'

Take up the White Man's burden—
Ye dare not stoop to less—
Nor call too loud on Freedom
To cloke your weariness;
By all ye cry or whisper,
By all you leave or do,
The silent, sullen peoples
Shall weigh your gods and you.

Take up the White Man's burden—
Have done with childish days—
The lightly proferred laurel,
The easy, ungrudged praise.
Comes now, to search your manhood
Through all the thankless years,
Cold, edged with dear-bought wisdom,
The judgment of your peers!

ambitions led to his downfall in 1896, however, when the British government forced him to resign as prime minister of Rhodesia after he conspired to overthrow the neighboring Boer government without British approval. Although the British government had hoped to avoid war with the Boers, it could not stop extremists on both sides from precipitating such action. The Boer War dragged on from 1899 to 1902 when the Boers were overwhelmed by the larger British army. British policy toward the defeated Boers was remarkably conciliatory. Transvaal and the Orange Free State had representative governments by 1907 and in 1910 a Union of South Africa was created. Like Canada, Australia, and New Zealand, it became a fully self-governing dominion within the British Empire.

Before 1880, the only other European settlements in Africa had been made by the French and Portuguese. The Portuguese had held on to their settlements in Angola on the west coast and Mozambique on the east coast. The French had started the conquest of Algeria in Muslim North Africa in 1830, although it was not until 1879 that French civilian rule was established there. The next year, 1880, the European scramble for possession of Africa began in earnest. Before 1900, the French had added the huge area of French West Africa and Tunisia to their African empire. In 1912 they created a protectorate over much of Morocco; the rest was left to Spain.

The British took an active interest in Egypt after the Suez Canal was opened by the French in 1869. Believing that the canal was essential to their lifeline to India, the British sought to control the canal area. The British landed an expeditionary force in 1882 and soon established a protectorate over Egypt. From Egypt, the British moved south into Sudan and seized it after narrowly averting a war with France. Not to be outdone, Italy joined in the imperialist scramble. Their humiliating defeat by the Ethiopians in 1896 only led the Italians to try again in 1911 by invading and seizing Ottoman Tripoli, which they renamed Libya.

Central Africa was also added to the list of European colonies. Popular interest in the forbiddingly dense tropical jungles of central Africa was first aroused in the 1860s and 1870s by explorers such as the Scottish missionary David Livingstone and the British-American journalist Henry M. Stanley. But the real driving force for the colonization of central Africa was King Leopold II (1865–1909) of Belgium, who had rushed enthusiastically into pursuit of empire in Africa: "To open to civilization," he said, "the only part of our globe where it has not yet

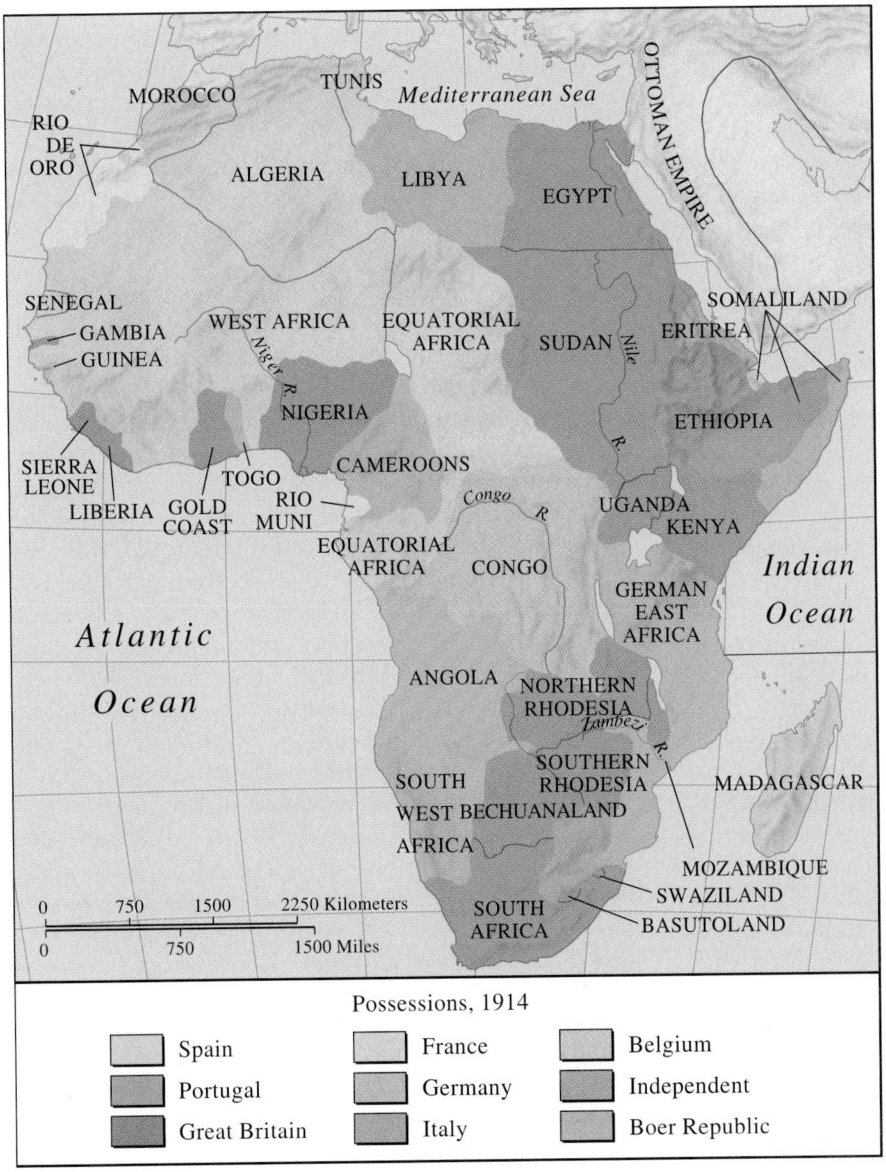

Map 25.1 Africa in 1914.

Possessions, 1914

- Spain
- Portugal
- Great Britain
- France
- Germany
- Italy
- Belgium
- Independent
- Boer Republic

CHRONOLOGY

The New Imperialism: Africa

Opening of the Suez Canal	1869
Leopold of Belgium establishes settlements in the Congo	1876
French complete conquest of Algeria	1879
British expeditionary force in Egypt	1882
Ethiopians defeat the Italians	1896
Boer War	1899–1902
Union of South Africa	1910
Italians seize Tripoli	1911
French protectorate over Morocco	1912

penetrated, to pierce the darkness which envelops whole populations, is a crusade, if I may say so, a crusade worthy of this century of progess." Profit, however, was far more important to Leopold than progress. In 1876, Leopold created the International Association for the Exploration and Civilization of Central Africa and engaged Henry Stanley to establish Belgian settlements in the Congo. Alarmed by Leopold's actions, the French also moved into the territory north of the Congo River.

Between 1884 and 1900, most of the rest of Africa was carved up by the European powers. Germany also entered the ranks of the imperialist powers at this time. Initially, Bismarck had downplayed the significance of colonies, but as domestic political pressures for a German empire increased, Bismarck became a political convert to colonialism. As he expressed it, "All this colonial business is a sham, but we need it for the elections." The Germans established colonies in Southwest Africa, the Cameroons, Togoland, and East Africa.

By 1914, Britain, France, Germany, Belgium, Spain, and Portugal had divided Africa. Only Liberia, founded by emancipated American slaves, and Ethiopia, remained free states. Despite the humanitarian rationalizations about the "white man's burden," Africa had been conquered by European states determined to create colonial empires. Any peoples who dared to resist (with the exception of the Ethiopians, who defeated the Italians) were simply devastated by the superior military force of the Europeans.

ASIA IN AN AGE OF IMPERIALISM

Although Asia had been open to Western influence since the sixteenth century, not much of its immense territory had fallen under direct European control. The Dutch were established in the East Indies and the Spanish in the Philippines while the French and Portuguese had trading posts on the Indian coast. China, Japan, Korea, and Southeast Asia had largely managed to exclude westerners. The British and the Russians had acquired the most Asian territory.

It was not until the explorations of Australia by Captain James Cook between 1768 and 1771 that Britain took an active interest in the Far East. The availability of land for grazing sheep and the discovery of gold led to an influx of free settlers who slaughtered many of the indigenous inhabitants. In 1850 the British government granted the various Australian colonies virtually complete self-government, and fifty years later, on January 1, 1901, all the colonies were unified into a Commonwealth of Australia. Nearby New Zealand, which the British had declared a colony in 1840, was also granted dominion status in 1907.

A private trading company known as the British East India Company had been responsible for subjugating much of India. In 1858, however, after a revolt of the sepoys, or Indian troops, of the East India Company's army had been crushed, the British Parliament transferred the company's powers directly to the government in London. In 1876 the title Empress of India was bestowed on Queen Victoria; Indians were now her colonial subjects.

Russian expansion in Asia was a logical outgrowth of its traditional territorial aggrandizement. Gradually Russian settlers moved into cold and forbidding Siberia. Altogether seven million Russians settled in Siberia between 1800 and 1914. The Russians also moved south, attracted by the crumbling Ottoman Empire. By 1830, the Russians had established control over the entire northern coast of the Black Sea and then pressed on into central Asia, securing the trans-Caspian area by 1881 and Turkestan in 1885. These advances brought the Russians to the borders of Persia and Afghanistan where the British also had interests because of their desire to protect their holdings in India. In 1907, the Russians and British agreed to make Afghanistan a buffer state between Russian Turkestan and British India and divide Persia into two spheres of influence. Halted by the British in their expansion to the south, the Russians moved east in Asia. The Russian occupation of Manchuria and their attempt to move into Korea brought war with Japan. After losing the Russo-Japanese War in 1905, the Russians agreed to a Japanese protectorate in Korea; their Asian expansion was brought to a temporary halt.

The thrust of imperialism after 1880 led Westerners to move into new areas of Asia hitherto largely free of Western influence. By the nineteenth century the ruling

Manchu dynasty of the Chinese empire was showing signs of decline. In 1842 the British had obtained (through war) the island of Hong Kong and rights of trade in a number of Chinese cities. Other Western nations soon rushed in to gain similar trading privileges. Britain, France, Germany, Russia, the United States, and Japan established spheres of influence and long-term leases of Chinese territory.

Japan avoided Western intrusion until 1853–1854 when American naval forces under Commodore Matthew Perry forced the Japanese to grant the United States trading and diplomatic privileges. Japan, however, managed

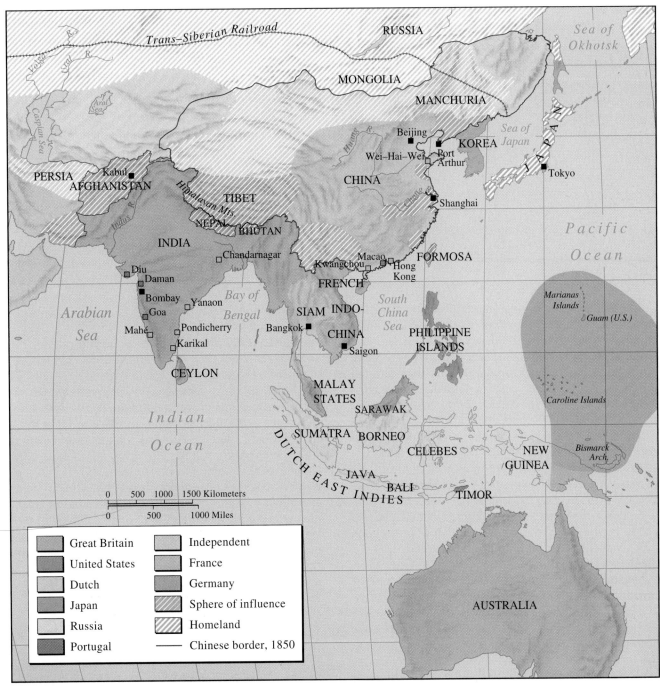

🔆 **Map 25.2** Asia in 1914.

CHRONOLOGY

❖◆❖◆❖◆❖◆❖◆❖◆❖◆❖◆❖◆❖

The New Imperialism: Asia

Britain obtains Hong Kong and trading rights from Chinese government	1842
Australian colonies receive self-government	1850
Mission of Commodore Perry to Japan	1853–1854
Great Rebellion in India	1857–1858
French occupy Saigon	1858
Queen Victoria is made Empress of India	1876
Russians in central Asia (trans-Caspian area)	1881
Russians in Turkestan	1885
Spanish-American War; United States annexes Philippines	1898
Commonwealth of Australia	1901
Commonwealth of New Zealand	1907
Russian-British agreement over Afghanistan and Persia	1907
Japan annexes Korea	1910

to avoid China's fate. By absorbing and adopting Western military and industrial methods, the Japanese developed a modern commercial and industrial system as well as a powerful military state. They established their own sphere of influence in China and five years after they defeated the Russians in 1905, the Japanese formally annexed Korea. The Japanese had proved that an Eastern power could play the "white man's" imperialistic game and provided a potent example to peoples in other regions of Asia and Africa.

In Southeast Asia, Britain established control over Burma and the Malay States while France played an active role in subjugating Indochina. The city of Saigon was occupied in 1858, and four years later Cochin China was taken. In the 1880s the French extended "protection" over Cambodia, Annam, Tonkin, and Laos and organized them into a Union of French Indochina. Only Siam (Thailand) remained free as a buffer state because of British-French rivalry.

The Pacific Islands were also the scene of great power struggles and witnessed the entry of the United States onto the imperialist stage. The Samoan Islands became the first important American colony; the Hawaiian Islands were the next to fall. Soon after Americans had made Pearl Harbor into a naval station in 1887, Ameri-

can settlers gained control of the sugar industry on the islands. When Hawaiian natives tried to reassert their authority, the United States Marines were brought in to "protect" American lives. Hawaii was annexed by the United States in 1898 during the era of American nationalistic fervor generated by the Spanish-American war. The American defeat of Spain encouraged Americans to extend their empire by acquiring Cuba, Puerto Rico, Guam, and the Philippine Islands. Although the Filipinos hoped for independence, the Americans refused to grant it. As President McKinley said, the United States had the duty "to educate the Filipinos and uplift and Christianize them," a remarkable statement in view of the fact that most of them had been Roman Catholics for centuries. It took three years and 60,000 troops to pacify the Philippines and establish American control.

International Rivalry and the Coming of War

Before 1914, Europeans had experienced almost fifty years of peace. There had been wars (including wars of conquest in the non-Western world), but none had involved the great powers. A series of crises occurred, however, that might easily have led to general war. One reason they did not is that until 1890, Bismarck of Germany exercised a restraining influence on the Europeans.

Bismarck knew that the emergence of a unified Germany in 1871 had upset the balance of power established at Vienna in 1815. Fearing a possible anti-German alliance between France, Russia, and possibly even Austria, Bismarck made a defensive alliance with Austria in 1879. In 1882, this German-Austrian alliance was enlarged with the entrance of Italy. The Triple Alliance of 1882 committed Germany, Austria-Hungary, and Italy to support the existing political order while providing a defensive alliance against France. At the same time, Bismarck maintained a separate treaty with Russia, hoping to prevent a French-Russian alliance that would threaten Germany with the possibility of a two-front war. The Bismarckian system of alliances, geared to preserving peace and the status quo, had worked, but in 1890 Emperor William II dismissed Bismarck and began to chart a new direction for Germany's foreign policy.

New Directions and New Crises

Emperor William II embarked on an activist foreign policy dedicated to enhancing German power by finding, as he put it, Germany's rightful "place in the sun." One of his changes in Bismarck's foreign policy was to drop the treaty with Russia, which he viewed as being at odds with Germany's alliance with Austria. The ending of the alliance achieved what Bismarck had feared; it brought France and Russia together. Republican France leapt at the chance to draw closer to tsarist Russia, and in 1894 the two powers concluded a military alliance.

During the next ten years, German policies abroad caused the British to draw closer to France (see the box on p. 532). By 1907, a loose confederation of Great Britain, France, and Russia—known as the Triple Entente—stood opposed to the Triple Alliance of Germany, Austria-Hungary, and Italy. Europe became divided into two opposing camps that became more and more inflexible and unwilling to compromise. When the members of the two alliances became involved in a new series of crises between 1908 and 1913 over the struggle for the control of the remnants of the Ottoman Empire in the Balkans, the stage was set for World War I.

(see the box on p. 532)

CHRONOLOGY

European Diplomacy

Defensive alliance: Germany and Austria	1879
Triple Alliance: Germany, Austria, and Italy	1882
Reinsurance Treaty: Germany and Russia	1887
Triple Entente: France, Britain, and Russia	1907
First Balkan War	1912
Second Balkan War	1913

Crises in the Balkans, 1908–1913

The Bosnian Crisis of 1908–1909 initiated a chain of events that eventually became out of control. Since 1878, Bosnia and Herzegovina had been under the protection of Austria, but in 1908 Austria took the drastic step of

◆ **Ottoman Army in Retreat.** In 1912, a coalition of Serbia, Bulgaria, Montenegro, and Greece defeated the Ottomans and took possession of the Ottoman provinces of Macedonia and Albania. This picture shows the Ottoman army in retreat, pursued by Bulgarian forces.

The Emperor's "Big Mouth"

Emperor William II's world policy, which was aimed at finding Germany's "place in the sun," created considerable ill will and unrest among other European states, especially Britain. Moreover, the emperor had the unfortunate tendency to stir up trouble by his often tactless public remarks. In this 1908 interview, for example, William II intended to strengthen Germany's ties with Britain. His words had just the opposite effect and raised a storm of protest in both Britain and Germany.

Daily Telegraph Interview, October 28, 1908

As I have said, his Majesty honoured me with a long conversation, and spoke with impulsive and unusual frankness. "You English," he said, "are mad, mad, mad as March hares. What has come over you that you are so completely given over to suspicions quite unworthy of a great nation? What more can I do than I have done? I declared with all the emphasis at my command, in my speech at Guildhall, that my heart is set upon peace, and that it is one of my dearest wishes to live on the best of terms with England. Have I ever been false to my word? Falsehood and prevarication are alien to my nature. My actions ought to speak for themselves, but you listen not to them but to those who misinterpret and distort them. That is a personal insult which I feel and resent. To be forever misjudged, to have my repeated offers of friendship weighed and scrutinized with jealous, mistrustful eyes, taxes my patience severely. I have said time after time that I am a friend of England, and your Press—or, at least, a considerable section of it—bids the people of England to refuse my proffered hand, and insinuates that the other holds a dagger. How can I convince a nation against its will?"

"I repeat," continued his Majesty, "that I am a friend of England, but you make things difficult for me. My task is not of the easiest. The prevailing sentiment among large sections of the middle and lower classes of my own people is not friendly to England. I am, therefore, so to speak, in a minority in my own land, but it is a minority of the best elements as it is in England with respect to Germany. That is another reason why I resent your refusal to accept my pledged word that I am the friend of England. I strive without ceasing to improve relations, and you retort that I am your arch-enemy. You make it hard for me. Why is it?. . . ."

"But, you will say, what of the German Navy? Surely, that is a menace to England! Against whom but England are my squadrons being prepared? If England is not in the minds of those Germans who are bent on creating a powerful fleet, why is Germany asked to consent to such new and heavy burdens of taxation? My answer is clear. Germany is a young and growing Empire. She has a world-wide commerce, which is rapidly expanding, and to which the legitimate ambition of patriotic Germans refuses to assign any bounds. Germany must have a powerful fleet to protect that commerce, and her manifold interests in even the most distant seas. She expects those interests to go on growing, and she must be able to champion them manfully in any quarter of the globe. Germany looks ahead. Her horizons stretch far away. She must be prepared for any eventualities in the Far East. Who can foresee what may take place in the Pacific in the days to come, days not so distant as some believe, but days, at any rate, for which all European Powers with Far Eastern interests ought steadily to prepare? Look at the accomplished rise of Japan; think of the possible national awakening of China; and then judge of the vast problems of the Pacific. Only those Powers which have great navies will be listened to with respect, when the future of the Pacific comes to be solved; and, if for that reason only, Germany must have a powerful fleet. It may even be that England herself will be glad that Germany has a fleet when they speak together on the same side in the great debates of the future."

annexing these two Slavic-speaking territories. Serbia became outraged at this action because it dashed the Serbians' hopes of creating a large Serbian kingdom that would include most of the south Slavs. This was why the Austrians had annexed Bosnia and Herzegovina. To the Austrians, a large Serbia would be a threat to the unity of the Austro-Hungarian Empire with its large Slavic population. The Russians, as protectors of their fellow Slavs and with their own desire to increase their authority in the Balkans, supported the Serbs and opposed the Austrian action. Backed by the Russians, the Serbs prepared for war against Austria. At this point William II intervened and demanded that the Russians accept Austria's annexation of Bosnia and Herzegovina or face war with

Germany. Weakened from their defeat in the Russo-Japanese War in 1904–1905, the Russians were afraid to risk war and backed down. Humiliated, the Russians vowed revenge.

European attention returned to the Balkans in 1912 when Serbia, Bulgaria, Montenegro, and Greece organized a Balkan League and defeated the Ottomans in the First Balkan War. When the victorious allies were unable to agree on how to divide the conquered Ottoman provinces of Macedonia and Albania, a second Balkan War erupted in 1913. Greece, Serbia, Romania, and the Ottoman Empire attacked and defeated Bulgaria. As a result, Bulgaria obtained only a small part of Macedonia and most of the rest was divided between Serbia and Greece. Yet Serbia's aspirations remained unfulfilled. The two Balkan wars left the inhabitants embittered and created more tensions among the great powers.

One of Serbia's major ambitions had been to acquire Albanian territory that would give it a port on the Adriatic. At the London Conference arranged by Austria at the end of the two Balkan wars, the Austrians had blocked Serbia's wishes by creating an independent Albania. The Germans, as Austrian allies, had supported this move. In their frustration, Serbian nationalists increasingly portrayed the Austrians as evil monsters who were keeping the Serbs from becoming a great nation. As Serbia's chief supporters, the Russians were also upset by the turn of events in the Balkans. A feeling had grown

✻ **Map 25.3** The Balkans in 1913.

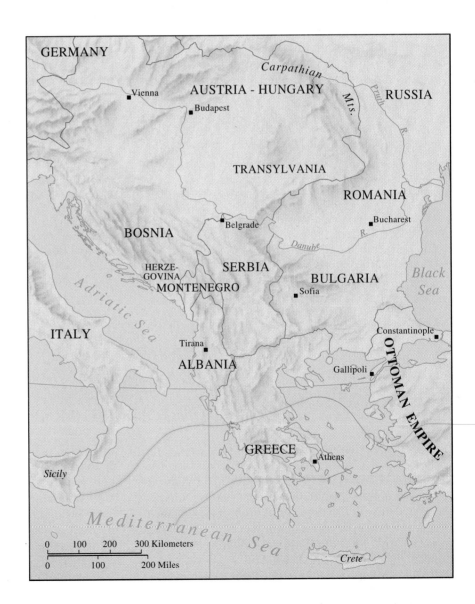

among Russian leaders that they could not back down again in the event of a confrontation with Austria or Germany in the Balkans.

Austria-Hungary had achieved another of its aims, but it was still convinced that Serbia was a mortal threat to its empire and must at some point be crushed. Meanwhile, the French and Russian governments renewed their alliance and promised each other that they would not back down at the next crisis. Britain drew closer to France. By the beginning of 1914 two armed camps viewed each other with suspicion. The European "age of progress" was about to come to an inglorious and bloody end.

Conclusion

What many Europeans liked to call their "age of progress" in the decades before 1914 was also an era of anxiety. Frenzied imperialist expansion had created vast European empires and spheres of influence around the globe. This feverish competition for colonies, however,

had markedly increased the existing antagonisms among the European states. At the same time, the Western treatment of non-Western peoples as racial inferiors caused educated, non-Western elites in these colonies to initiate movements for national independence. Before these movements could be successful, however, the power that Europeans had achieved through their mass armies and technological superiority had to be weakened. The Europeans inadvertently accomplished this task for their colonial subjects by demolishing their own civilization on the battlegrounds of Europe in World War I and World War II.

The cultural revolutions before 1914 had also produced anxiety and a crisis of confidence in European civilization. A brilliant minority of intellectuals had created a modern consciousness that questioned most Europeans' optimistic faith in reason, the rational structure of nature, and the certainty of progress. The devastating experiences of World War I turned this culture of uncertainty into a way of life after 1918.

NOTES

1. Quoted in Arthur E. E. McKenzie, *The Major Achievements of Science* (New York, 1960), 1:310.
2. Friedrich von Bernhardi, *Germany and the Next War*, trans. Allen H. Powles (New York, 1914), pp. 18–19.
3. Quoted in John Rewald, *History of Impressionism* (New York, 1961), pp. 456–458.
4. Quoted in Catherine M. Prelinger, "Prelude to Consciousness: Amalie Sieveking and the Female Association for the Care of the Poor and the Sick," in John C. Fout, ed., *German Women in the Nineteenth Century: A Social History* (New York, 1984), p. 119.
5. Quoted in John Ellis, *The Social History of the Machine Gun* (New York, 1975), p. 80.

SUGGESTIONS FOR FURTHER READING

A well-regarded study of Freud is P. Gay, *Freud: A Life for Our Time* (New York, 1988). Also see R. Clark, *Freud: The Man and the Cause* (New York, 1980). A useful study on the impact of Darwinian thought on religion is J. Moore, *The Post-Darwinian Controversies: A Study of the Protestant Struggle to Come to Terms with Darwin in Great Britain and America, 1870–1900* (Cambridge, 1979). Studies of the popular religion of the period include T. A. Kselman, *Miracles and Prophesies in Nineteenth-Century France* (New Brunswick, N.J., 1983); and J. Sperber, *Popular Catholicism in Nineteenth-Century Germany* (Princeton, N.J., 1984). Very valuable on modern art are J. Rewald, *The History of Impressionism*, 4th ed. (New York, 1973), and *Post-Impressionism*, 3d ed. (New York, 1962). See also B. Denvir, *Post-impressionism* (New York, 1992); and D. M. Reynolds, *The Cambridge Introduction to the History of Art: The Nineteenth Century* (Cambridge, 1985). On literature, see R. Pascal, *From Naturalism to Expressionism:*

German *Literature and Society, 1880–1918.* (New York, 1973). The intellectual climate of Vienna is examined in C. E. Schorske, *Fin de Siècle Vienna: Politics and Culture* (New York, 1980).

The rise of feminism is examined in J. Rendall, *The Origins of Modern Feminism: Women in Britain, France and the United States* (London, 1985). The subject of modern anti-Semitism is covered in J. Katz, *From Prejudice to Destruction* (Cambridge, Mass., 1980) For a more general overview of anti-Semitism, see A. Eban, *Heritage: Civilization and the Jews* (New York, 1984). European racism is analyzed in G. L. Mosse, *Toward the Final Solution* (New York, 1980); while German anti-Semitism as a political force is examined in P. J. Pulzer, *The Rise of Political Anti-Semitism in Germany and Austria* (New York, 1964). Anti-Semitism in France is the subject of S. Wilson, *Ideology and Experience: Anti-Semitism in France at the Time of the Dreyfus Affair* (Rutherford, N.J. 1982). The problems of Jews in Russia are examined in J. Frankel, *Prophecy and Politics: Socialism, Nationalism and the Russian Jews, 1862–1917* (Cambridge, 1981). For a recent biography of Theodor Herzl, see J. Kornberg, *Theodor Herzl: From Assimilation to Zionism* (Bloomington, Ind., 1993). The beginnings of the Labour Party are examined in H. Pelling, *The Origins of the Labour Party*, 2d ed. (Oxford, 1965). There is a good introduction to the political world of William II's Germany in T. A. Kohut, *Wilhelm II and the Germans: A Study in Leadership* (New York, 1991). An important study on right-wing German politics is G. Eley, *Reshaping the German Right: Radical Nationalism and Political Change after Bismarck* (New Haven, Conn., 1980). The best, one-volume biography in English on Emperor William II is M. Balfour, *The Kaiser and His Times* (London, 1964). On Russia, see A. Ascher, *The Revolution of 1905: Russia in Disarray*, 2 vols. (Stanford, 1988–1992).

For broad perspectives on imperialism, see the works by T. Smith, *The Pattern of Imperialism* (Cambridge, 1981); and P. Darby, *Three Faces of Imperialism: British and American Approaches to Asia and Africa, 1870–1970* (New Haven, Conn., 1987). Different aspects of imperialism are covered in R. Robinson and J. Gallagher, *Africa and the Victorians*, 2d ed. (New York, 1981); and W. Baumgart, *Imperialism: The Ideas and Reality of British and French Colonial Expansion, 1880–1914* (London, 1982).

Two fundamental works on the diplomatic history of the period are W. L. Langer, *European Alliances and Alignments*, 2d ed. (New York, 1966), and *The Diplomacy of Imperialism*, 2d ed. (New York, 1965). Also valuable are G. Kennan, *The Decline of Bismarck's European Order: Franco-Prussian Relations, 1875–1890* (Princeton, N.J., 1979); and the masterful study by P. Kennedy, *The Rise of Anglo-German Antagonism, 1860–1914* (London, 1982).

CHAPTER
26

The Beginning of the Twentieth-Century Crisis: War and Revolution

On July 1, 1916, British and French infantry forces attacked German defensive lines along a twenty-five-mile front near the Somme River in France. Each soldier carried almost seventy pounds of equipment, making it "impossible to move much quicker than a slow walk." German machine guns soon opened fire: "We were able to see our comrades move forward in an attempt to cross No-Man's Land, only to be mown down like meadow grass," recalled one British soldier. "I felt sick at the sight of this carnage and remember weeping." In one day more than 21,000 British soldiers died. After six months of fighting, the British had advanced five miles; one million British, French, and German soldiers had been killed or wounded.

World War I (1914–1918) was the defining event of the twentieth century. It devastated the prewar economic, social, and political order of Europe, and its uncertain outcome served to prepare the way for an even more destructive war. Overwhelmed by the size of its battles, the extent of its casualties, and the effects of its impact on all facets of life, contemporaries referred to it simply as the "Great War."

The Great War was all the more disturbing to Europeans because it came after a period that many believed to have been an age of progress. There had been international crises before 1914, but somehow Europeans had managed to avoid serious and prolonged military confrontations. When smaller European states had gone to war, as in the Balkans in 1912 and 1913, the great European powers had shown the ability to keep the conflict localized. Material prosperity and a fervid belief in scientific and technological progress had convinced many people that the world stood on the verge of creating the utopia that humans had dreamed of for centuries. The historian Arnold Toynbee expressed what the pre–World War I era had meant to his generation:

> [it was expected] that life throughout the World would become more rational, more humane, and more democratic and that, slowly, but surely, political democracy would produce greater social justice. We had

Assassination of Archduke Francis Ferdinand   Battle of Verdun

United States enters the war   Surrender of Germany

First Battle of the Marne   Peace of Versailles

The Bolshevik Revolution   Civil War in Russia

Defence of the Realm Act in Britain   Complete mobilization for total war in Germany   Second Battle of the Marne
• November Revolution in Germany

also expected that the progress of science and technology would make mankind richer, and that this increasing wealth would gradually spread from a minority to a majority. We had expected that all this would happen peacefully. In fact we thought that mankind's course was set for an earthly paradise.[1]

After 1918, it was no longer possible to maintain naive illusions about the progress of Western civilization. As World War I was followed by the destructiveness of World War II and the mass murder machines of totalitarian regimes, it became all too apparent that instead of a utopia, European civilization had become a nightmare. The Great War resulted not only in great loss of life and property, but also in the annihilation of one of the basic intellectual precepts on which Western civilization had been thought to have been founded—the belief in progress. World War I and the revolutions it spawned can properly be seen as the first stage in the crisis of the twentieth century.

The Road to World War I

On June 28, 1914, the heir to the Austrian throne, the Archduke Francis Ferdinand, was assassinated in the Bosnian city of Sarajevo. Although this event precipitated the confrontation between Austria and Serbia that led to World War I, there were also long-range, underlying forces that were propelling Europeans toward armed conflict.

Nationalism and Internal Dissent

In the first half of the nineteenth century, liberals had maintained that the organization of European states along national lines would lead to a peaceful Europe based on a sense of international fraternity. They were very wrong. The system of nation-states that had emerged in Europe in the last half of the nineteenth century led not to cooperation but to competition. Rivalries over colonial and commercial interests intensified during an era of frenzied imperialist expansion while the division of Europe's great powers into two loose alliances (Germany, Austria, and Italy, and France, Great Britain, and Russia) only added to the tensions. The series of crises that tested these alliances in the 1900s and early 1910s had left European states with the belief that their allies were important and that their security depended on supporting those allies, even when they took foolish risks.

The growth of nationalism in the nineteenth century had yet another serious consequence. Not all ethnic groups had achieved the goal of nationhood. Slavic minorities in the Balkans and the polyglot Habsburg empire, for example, still dreamed of creating their own national states. So did the Irish in the British Empire and the Poles in the Russian Empire.

National aspirations, however, were not the only source of internal strife at the beginning of the twentieth century. Socialist labor movements had grown more powerful and were increasingly inclined to use strikes, even violent ones, to achieve their goals. Some conservative leaders, alarmed at the increase in labor strife and class division, even feared that European nations were on the verge of revolution. Did these statesmen opt for war in 1914 because they believed that "prosecuting an active foreign policy," as one leader expressed it, would smother "internal troubles"? Some historians have argued that the desire to suppress internal disorder may have encouraged some leaders to take the plunge into war in 1914.

Militarism

The growth of large mass armies after 1900 not only heightened the existing tensions in Europe, but made it inevitable that if war did come it would be highly destructive. Conscription had been established as a regular practice in most Western countries before 1914 (the United States and Britain were major exceptions). European military machines had doubled in size between 1890 and 1914. With its 1.3 million men, the Russian army had grown to be the largest, while the French and Germans were not far behind with 900,000 each. The British, Italian, and Austrian armies numbered between 250,000 and 500,000 soldiers each.

Militarism, however, involved more than just large armies. As armies grew, so too did the influence of military leaders who drew up vast and complex plans for quickly mobilizing millions of men and enormous quantities of supplies in the event of war. Fearful that changes in these plans would cause chaos in the armed forces, military leaders insisted that their plans could not be altered. In the crises during the summer of 1914, the generals' lack of flexibility forced European political leaders to make decisions for military instead of political reasons.

The Outbreak of War: The Summer of 1914

Militarism, nationalism, and the desire to stifle internal dissent may all have played a role in the coming of World War I, but the decisions made by European leaders in the summer of 1914 directly precipitated the conflict. It was another crisis in the Balkans that forced this predicament on European statesmen.

As we have seen, states in southeastern Europe had struggled to free themselves of Ottoman rule in the course of the nineteenth and early twentieth centuries. But the rivalry between Austria-Hungary and Russia for domination of these new states created serious tensions in the

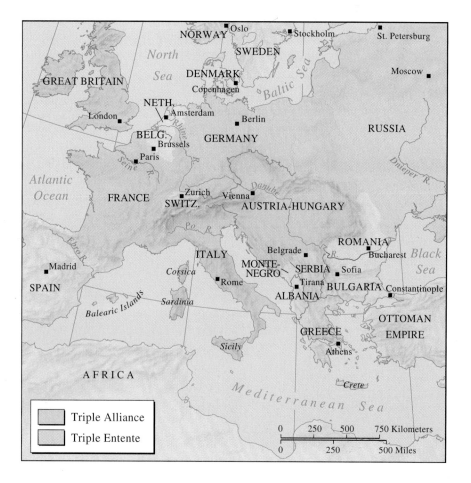

Map 26.1 Europe in 1914.

region. By 1914, Serbia, supported by Russia, was determined to create a large, independent Slavic state in the Balkans, whereas Austria, which had its own Slavic minorities to contend with, was equally set on preventing that possibility. Many Europeans perceived the inherent dangers in this combination of Serbian ambition bolstered by Russian hatred of Austria and Austrian conviction that Serbia's success would mean the end of its empire. The British ambassador to Vienna wrote in 1913:

> Serbia will some day set Europe by the ears, and bring about a universal war on the Continent. . . . I cannot tell you how exasperated people are getting here at the continual worry which that little country causes to Austria under encouragement from Russia. . . . It will be lucky if Europe succeeds in avoiding war as a result of the present crisis. The next time a Serbian crisis arises . . . , I feel sure that Austria-Hungary will refuse to admit of any Russian interference in the dispute and that she will proceed to settle her differences with her little neighbor by herself.[2]

It was against this backdrop of mutual distrust and hatred between Austria-Hungary and Russia, on the one hand, and Austria-Hungary and Serbia, on the other, that the events of the summer of 1914 were played out.

The assassination of the Austrian Archduke Francis Ferdinand and his wife Sophia on June 28, 1914, was carried out by a Bosnian activist who worked for the Black Hand, a Serbian terrorist organization dedicated to the creation of a pan-Slavic kingdom. Although the Austrian government did not know whether the Serbian government had been directly involved in the archduke's assassination, it saw an opportunity to "render Serbia innocuous once and for all by a display of force," as the Austrian foreign minister put it. Fearful of Russian intervention on Serbia's behalf, Austrian leaders sought the backing of their German allies. Emperor William II and his chancellor gave their assurance that Austria-Hungary could rely on Germany's "full support," even if "matters went to the length of a war between Austria-Hungary and Russia."

Strengthened by German support, Austrian leaders issued an ultimatum to Serbia on July 23 in which they made such extreme demands that Serbia had little choice but to reject some of them in order to preserve its sovereignty. Austria then declared war on Serbia on July 28. Still smarting from its humiliation in the Bosnian crisis of 1908, Russia was determined to support Serbia's cause. On July 28, Tsar Nicholas II ordered partial mobilization of the Russian army against Austria. At this point, the Russian General Staff informed the tsar that their mobilization plans were based on a war against both Germany and Austria simultaneously. They could not execute par-

tial mobilization without creating chaos in the army. Consequently, the Russian government ordered full mobilization of the Russian army on July 29, knowing that the Germans would consider this an act of war against them. Germany responded to Russian mobilization with its own ultimatum that the Russians must halt their mobilization within twelve hours. When the Russians ignored it, Germany declared war on Russia on August 1.

At this stage of the conflict, German war plans determined whether or not France would become involved in the war. Under the guidance of General Alfred von Schlieffen, chief of staff from 1891 to 1905, the German General Staff had devised a military plan based on the assumption of a two-front war with France and Russia, since the two powers had formed a military alliance in 1894. The Schlieffen plan called for a minimal troop deployment against Russia while most of the German army would rapidly invade western France by way of neutral Belgium. After the planned quick defeat of the French, the German army expected to redeploy to the east against Russia. Under the Schlieffen plan, Germany could not mobilize its troops solely against Russia and therefore declared war on France on August 3 after issuing an ultimatum to Belgium on August 2 demanding the right of German troops to pass through Belgian territory. On August 4, Great Britain declared war on Germany, officially over this violation of Belgian neutrality, but in fact over the British desire to maintain their world power. As one British diplomat argued, if Germany and Austria won the war, "what would be the position of a friendless England?" By August 4, all the great powers of Europe were at war.

The War

Before 1914, many political leaders had become convinced that war involved so many political and economic risks that it was not worth fighting. Others had believed that "rational" diplomats could control any situation and prevent the outbreak of war. At the beginning of August 1914, both of these prewar illusions were shattered, but the new illusions that replaced them soon proved to be equally foolish.

1914–1915: Illusions and Stalemate

Europeans went to war in 1914 with remarkable enthusiasm. Government propaganda had been successful in stirring up national antagonisms before the war. Now in August 1914, the urgent pleas of governments for defense against aggressors fell on receptive ears in every belligerent nation. Most people seemed genuinely convinced that their nation's cause was just. A new set of illusions also fed the enthusiasm for war. Almost everyone in August 1914 believed that the war would be over in a few weeks. People were reminded that all European wars since 1815 had,

◆   **The Excitement of War.** World War I was greeted with incredible enthusiasm. Each of the major belligerents was convinced of the rightness of its cause. Everywhere in Europe, jubilant civilians sent their troops off to war with joyous fervor. Their belief that the soldiers would be home by Christmas proved to be a pathetic illusion.

in fact, ended in a matter of weeks, conveniently overlooking the American Civil War (1861–1865), which was the "real prototype" for World War I. Both the soldiers who exuberantly boarded the trains for the war front in August 1914 and the jubilant citizens who bombarded them with flowers when they departed believed that the warriors would be home by Christmas.

German hopes for a quick end to the war rested on a military gamble. The Schlieffen plan had called for the German army to make a vast encircling movement through Belgium into northern France that would sweep around Paris and encircle most of the French army. But the German advance was halted only twenty miles from Paris at the first Battle of the Marne (September 6–10). The war quickly turned into a stalemate—neither the Germans nor French could dislodge each other from the trenches they had begun to dig for shelter. Two lines of trenches soon extended from the English Channel to the frontiers of Switzerland. The Western Front had become bogged down in trench warfare that kept both sides immobilized in virtually the same positions for four years.

In contrast to the West, the war in the East was marked by much more mobility, although the cost in lives was equally enormous. At the beginning of the war, the Russian army moved into eastern Germany but was decisively defeated at the Battles of Tannenberg on August 26–30 and the Masurian Lakes on September 15. The Russians were no longer a threat to German territory.

The Austrians, Germany's allies, fared less well initially. They had been defeated by the Russians in Galicia and thrown out of Serbia as well. To make matters worse, the Italians betrayed the Germans and Austrians and entered the war on the Allied side by attacking Austria in May 1915. By this time, the Germans had come to the aid of the Austrians. A German-Austrian army defeated and routed the Russian army in Galicia and pushed the Russians back 300 miles into their own territory. Russian casualties stood at 2.5 million killed, captured, or wounded; the Russians had almost been knocked out of the war. Buoyed by their success, the Germans and Austrians, joined by the Bulgarians in September 1915, attacked and eliminated Serbia from the war.

1916–1917: The Great Slaughter

The successes in the East enabled the Germans to move back to the offensive in the West. The early trenches dug in 1914 had by now become elaborate systems of defense. Both lines of trenches were protected by barbed wire entanglements three to five feet high and thirty yards wide, concrete machine-gun nests, and mortar batteries, sup-

◆ **The Horrors of War.** The slaughter of millions of men in the trenches of World War I created unimaginable horrors for the participants. For the sake of survival, many soldiers learned to harden themselves against the stench of decomposing bodies and the sight of bodies horribly dismembered by artillery barrages.

ported further back by heavy artillery. Troops lived in holes in the ground, separated from each other by a "no man's land."

The unexpected development of trench warfare baffled military leaders who had been trained to fight wars of movement and maneuver. The only plan generals could devise was to attempt a breakthrough by throwing masses of men against enemy lines that had first been battered by artillery barrages. Once the decisive breakthrough had been achieved, they thought, they could then return to the war of movement that they knew best. Periodically, the high command on either side would order an offensive that would begin with an artillery barrage to flatten the enemy's barbed wire and leave the enemy in a state of shock. After "softening up" the enemy in this fashion, a mass of soldiers would climb out of their trenches with fixed bayonets and hope to work their way toward the enemy trenches. The attacks rarely worked, since the machine gun put hordes of men advancing unprotected across open fields at a severe disadvantage. In 1916 and 1917, millions of young men were sacrificed in the search for the elusive breakthrough. In ten months at Verdun in 1916, 700,000 men lost their lives over a few miles of terrain.

Warfare in the trenches of the Western Front produced unimaginable horrors (see the box on p. 544). Battlefields were hellish landscapes of barbed wire, shell holes, mud, and injured and dying men. The introduction of poison gas in 1915 produced new forms of injuries, as one British writer described:

I wish those people who write so glibly about this being a holy war could see a case of mustard gas . . . could see the poor things burnt and blistered all over with great mustard-coloured suppurating blisters with blind eyes all sticky . . . and stuck together, and always fighting for breath, with voices a mere whisper, saying that their throats are closing and they know they will choke.[3]

Soldiers in the trenches also lived with the persistent presence of death. Because combat went on for months, soldiers had to carry on in the midst of countless bodies of dead men or the remains of men dismembered by artillery barrages. Many soldiers remembered the stench of decomposing bodies and the swarms of rats that grew fat in the trenches.

The Widening of the War

As another response to the stalemate on the Western front, both sides sought to gain new allies who might provide a winning advantage. The Ottoman Empire had already come into the war on Germany's side in August 1914. Russia, Great Britain, and France declared war on the Ottoman Empire in November. Although the Allies attempted to open a Balkan front by landing forces at Gallipoli, southwest of Constantinople, in April 1915, the entry of Bulgaria into the war on the side of the Central Powers (as Germany, Austria-Hungary, and the

◆ **Impact of the Machine Gun.** The development of trench warfare on the Western Front stymied military leaders who had expected to fight a war based on movement and maneuver. Their efforts to effect a breakthrough by sending masses of men against enemy lines was the height of folly in view of the machine gun. Masses of men advancing across open land made magnificent targets.

Ottoman Empire were called) and a disastrous campaign at Gallipoli caused them to withdraw. The Italians, as we have seen, also entered the war on the Allied side after France and Britain promised to further their acquisition of Austrian territory. In the long run, however, Italian military incompetence forced the Allies to come to the assistance of Italy.

By 1917, the war that had begun in Europe was having an increasing impact on other parts of the world. In the Middle East, a British officer who came to be known as Lawrence of Arabia incited Arab princes to revolt in 1917 against their Ottoman overlords. In 1918, British forces from Egypt destroyed the rest of the Ottoman Empire in the Middle East. For their Middle East campaigns, the British mobilized forces from India, Australia, and New Zealand. The Allies also took advantage of Germany's preoccupations in Europe and lack of naval strength to seize German colonies in the rest of the world.

Most important to the Allied cause was the entry of the United States into the war. At first, the United States tried to remain neutral in the Great War, but found it more difficult to do so as the war dragged on. The immediate cause of American involvement grew out of the naval conflict between Germany and Great Britain. Britain used its superior naval power to maximum effect by creating a naval blockade of Germany. Germany retaliated by imposing a counterblockade enforced by the use of unrestricted submarine warfare. Strong American protests over the German sinking of passenger liners, especially the British ship *Lusitania* on May 7, 1915, when more than 100 Americans lost their lives, forced the German government to suspend unrestricted submarine warfare in September 1915 to avoid further antagonizing the Americans.

In January 1917, however, eager to break the deadlock in the war, the Germans decided on another military

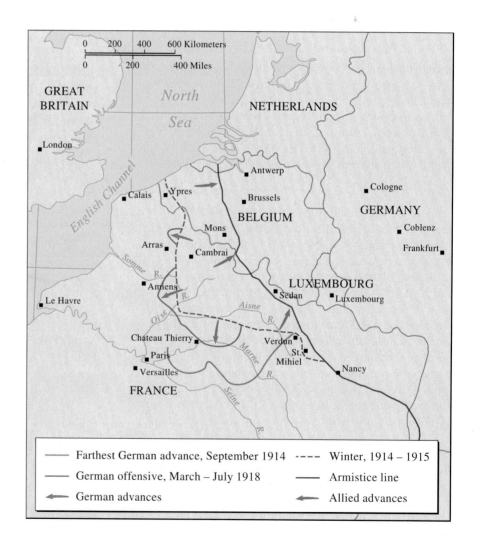

✖ **Map 26.2** The Western Front, 1914–1918.

gamble by returning to unrestricted submarine warfare. German naval officers convinced Emperor William II that the use of unrestricted submarine warfare could starve the British into submission within five months, certainly before the Americans could act. The return to unrestricted submarine warfare brought the United States into the war on April 6, 1917. Although American troops did not arrive in large numbers in Europe until 1918, the entry of the United States into the war in 1917 gave the Allied powers a psychological boost when they needed it. The year 1917 was not a good year for them. Allied offensives on the Western Front were disastrously defeated. The Italian armies were smashed in October, and in November 1917 the Bolshevik revolution in Rus-

sia (see "The Russian Revolution" later in the chapter) led to Russia's withdrawal from the war. The cause of the Central Powers looked favorable, although war weariness in the Ottoman Empire, Bulgaria, Austria-Hungary, and Germany was beginning to take its toll. The home front was rapidly becoming a cause for as much concern as the war front.

The Home Front: The Impact of Total War

The prolongation of World War I made it a total war that affected the lives of all citizens, however remote they might be from the battlefields. The need to organize masses of men and matériel for years of combat (Germany

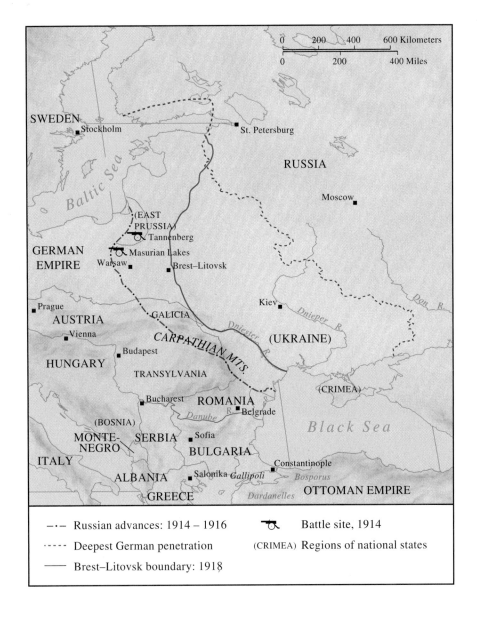

Map 26.3 The Eastern Front, 1914–1918.

The Reality of War: Trench Warfare

The romantic illusions about the excitement and adventure of war that filled the minds of so many young men who marched off to battle quickly disintegrated after a short time in the trenches on the Western Front. This description of trench warfare is taken from the most famous novel that emerged from World War I, Erich Maria Remarque's All Quiet on the Western Front, *written in 1929. Remarque had fought in the trenches in France.*

Erich Maria Remarque,
All Quiet on the Western Front

We wake up in the middle of the night. The earth booms. Heavy fire is falling on us. We crouch into corners. We distinguish shells of every calibre.

Each man lays hold of his things and looks again every minute to reassure himself that they are still there. The dug-out heaves, the night roars and flashes. We look at each other in the momentary flashes of light, and with pale faces and pressed lips shake our heads.

Every man is aware of the heavy shells tearing down the parapet, rooting up the embankment and demolishing the upper layers of concrete. . . . Already by morning a few of the recruits are green and vomiting. They are too inexperienced. . . .

The bombardment does not diminish. It is falling in the rear too. As far as one can see it spouts fountains of mud and iron. A wide belt is being raked.

The attack does not come, but the bombardment continues. Slowly we become mute. Hardly a man speaks. We cannot make ourselves understood.

Our trench is almost gone. At many places it is only eighteen inches high, it is broken by holes, and craters, and mountains of earth. A shell lands square in front of our post. At once it is dark. We are buried and must dig ourselves out. . . .

Towards morning, while it is still dark, there is some excitement. Through the entrance rushes in a swarm of fleeing rats that try to storm the walls. Torches light up the confusion. Everyone yells and curses and slaughters. The madness and despair of many hours unloads itself in this outburst. Faces are distorted, arms strike out, the beasts scream; we just stop in time to avoid attacking one another. . . .

Suddenly it howls and flashes terrifically, the dugout cracks in all its joints under a direct hit, fortunately only a light one that the concrete blocks are able to withstand. It rings metallically, the walls reel, rifles, helmets, earth, mud, and dust fly everywhere. Sulphur fumes pour in. . . . The recruit starts to rave again and two others follow suit. One jumps up and rushes out, we have trouble with the other two. I start after the one who escapes and wonder whether to shoot him in the leg—then it shrieks again, I fling myself down and when I stand up the wall of the trench is plastered with smoking splinters, lumps of flesh, and bits of uniform. I scramble back.

The first recruit seems actually to have gone insane. He butts his head against the wall like a goat. We must try tonight to take him to the rear. Meanwhile we bind him, but so that in case of attack he can be released.

Suddenly the nearer explosions cease. The shelling continues but it has lifted and falls behind us, our trench is free. We seize the hand-grenades, pitch them out in front of the dug-out and jump after them. The bombardment has stopped and a heavy barrage now falls behind us. The attack has come.

No one would believe that in this howling waste there could still be men; but steel helmets now appear on all sides out of the trench, and fifty yards from us a machine-gun is already in position and barking.

The wire-entanglements are torn to pieces. Yet they offer some obstacle. We see the storm-troops coming. Our artillery opens fire. Machine-guns rattle, rifles crack. The charge works its way across. Haie and Kropp begin with the hand-grenades. They throw as fast as they can, others pass them, the handles with the strings already pulled. Haie throws seventy-five yards, Kropp sixty, it has been measured, the distance is important. The enemy as they run cannot do much before they are within forty yards.

We recognize the distorted faces, the smooth helmets: they are French. They have already suffered heavily when they reach the remnants of the barbed-wire entanglements. A whole line has gone down before our machine-guns; then we have a lot of stoppages and they come nearer.

I see one of them, his face upturned, fall into a wire cradle. His body collapses, his hands remain suspended as though he were praying. Then his body drops clean away and only his hands with the stumps of his arms, shot off, now hang in the wire.

alone had 5.5 million men in active units in 1916) led to increased centralization of government powers, economic regimentation, and manipulation of public opinion to keep the war effort going.

Because the war was expected to be short, little thought had been given to economic problems and long-term wartime needs. Governments had to respond quickly, however, when the war machines failed to achieve their knockout blows and made ever-greater demands for men and matériel. The extension of government power was a logical outgrowth of these needs. Most European countries had already devised some system of mass conscription or military draft. It was now carried to unprecedented heights as countries mobilized tens of millions of young men for that elusive breakthrough to victory. Even countries that continued to rely on volunteers (Great Britain had the largest volunteer army in modern history—one million men—in 1914 and 1915) were forced to resort to conscription, especially to ensure that skilled laborers did not enlist but remained in factories that were important to the production of munitions. In 1916, despite widespread resistance to this extension of government power, compulsory military service was introduced in Great Britain.

Throughout Europe, wartime governments expanded their powers over their economies. Free-market capitalistic systems were temporarily shelved as governments experimented with price, wage, and rent controls, the rationing of food supplies and materials, the regulation of imports and exports, the nationalization of transportation systems and industries, and compulsory labor employment. In effect, in order to mobilize the entire resources of their nations for the war effort, European nations had moved toward planned economies directed by government agencies. Under total war mobilization, the distinction between soldiers at war and civilians at home was narrowed. In the view of political leaders, all citizens constituted a national army dedicated to victory. As the American president Woodrow Wilson expressed it, the men and women "who remain to till the soil and man the factories are no less a part of the army than the men beneath the battle flags."

As the Great War dragged on and both casualties and privations worsened, internal dissatisfaction replaced the patriotic enthusiasm that had marked the early stages of World War I. By 1916, there were numerous signs that civilian morale was beginning to crack under the pressure of total war. War governments, however, fought back against the growing opposition to the war. Authoritarian regimes, such as those of Germany, Russia, and Austria-Hungary, had always relied on force to subdue their pop-

ulations. Under the pressures of the war, however, even parliamentary regimes resorted to an expansion of police powers to stifle internal dissent. The British Parliament passed a Defence of the Realm Act (DORA) at the very beginning of the war that allowed the public authorities to arrest dissenters as traitors. The act was later extended to authorize public officials to censor newspapers by deleting objectional material and even to suspend newspaper publication. In France, government authorities had initially been lenient about public opposition to the war. But by 1917, they began to fear that open opposition to the war might weaken the French will to fight. When Georges Clemenceau became premier near the end of 1917, the lenient French policies came to an end, and basic civil liberties were suppressed for the duration of the

✦ **British Recruiting Poster.** As the conflict persisted month after month, governments resorted to active propaganda campaigns to generate enthusiasm for the war. In this British recruiting poster, the government tried to pressure men into volunteering for military service. By 1916, the British were forced to adopt compulsory military service.

war. The editor of an antiwar newspaper was even executed on a charge of treason.

Wartime governments made active use of propaganda to arouse enthusiasm for the war. At the beginning, public officials needed to do little to achieve this goal. The British and French, for example, exaggerated German atrocities in Belgium and found that their citizens were only too willing to believe these accounts. But as the war progressed and morale sagged, governments were forced to devise new techniques for stimulating declining enthusiasm. In one British recruiting poster, for example, a small daughter asked her father, "Daddy, what did YOU do in the Great War?" while her younger brother played with toy soldiers and cannon.

THE SOCIAL IMPACT OF TOTAL WAR

Total war had a significant impact on European society, most visibly by bringing an end to unemployment. The withdrawal of millions of men from the labor market to fight, combined with the heightened demand for wartime products, led to jobs for everyone able to work.

World War I also created new roles for women. With so many men off fighting at the front, women were called on to take over jobs and responsibilities that had not been available to them before. Overall, 1,345,000 women in Britain obtained new jobs or replaced men during the war. Women were also now employed in jobs that had been considered beyond the "capacity of women." These included such occupations as chimney sweeps, truck drivers, farm laborers, and above all, factory workers in heavy industry (see the box on p. 547). Thirty-eight percent of the workers in the Krupp Armaments works in Germany in 1918 were women.

While male workers expressed concern that the employment of females at lower wages would depress their own wages, women began to demand equal pay legislation. The French government passed a law in July 1915 that established a minimum wage for women homeworkers in textiles, an industry that had grown dramatically because of the need for military uniforms. Later in 1917, the government decreed that men and women should receive equal rates for piecework. Despite the noticeable increase in women's wages that resulted from government regulations, women's industrial wages still were not equal to men's wages by the end of the war.

Even worse, women had achieved little real security about their place in the workforce. Both men and women seemed to think that many of the new jobs for women were only temporary, an expectation quite evident in the British poem, "War Girls," written in 1916:

There's the girl who clips your ticket for the train,
And the girl who speeds the lift from floor to floor,
There's the girl who does a milk-round in the rain,
And the girl who calls for orders at your door.
Strong, sensible, and fit,
They're out to show their grit,
And tackle jobs with energy and knack.
No longer caged and penned up,
They're going to keep their end up
Till the khaki soldier boys come marching back.[4]

At the end of the war, governments moved quickly to remove women from the jobs they had encouraged them to take earlier. By 1919, there were 650,000 unemployed women in Britain while wages for women who were still employed were also lowered. The work benefits for women from World War I seemed to be short-lived.

Nevertheless, in some countries the role played by women in the wartime economies did have a positive impact on the women's movement for social and political emancipation. The most obvious gain was the right to vote that was given to women in Germany and Austria immediately after the war (in Britain already in January 1918). Contemporary media, however, tended to focus on the more noticeable, yet in some ways more superficial, social emancipation of upper- and middle-class women. In ever-larger numbers, these young women took jobs, had their own apartments, and showed their new independence by smoking in public and wearing shorter dresses, cosmetics, and new hair styles.

War and Revolution

By 1917, total war was creating serious domestic turmoil in all of the European belligerent states. Most countries were able to prop up their regimes and convince their peoples to continue the war for another year, but others were coming close to collapse. Russia, however, was the only belligerent that actually experienced the kind of complete collapse in 1917 that others were predicting might happen throughout Europe. Out of Russia's collapse came the Russian Revolution.

The Russian Revolution

After the Revolution of 1905 had failed to bring any substantial changes to Russia, Tsar Nicholas II fell back on the army and bureaucracy as the basic props for his autocratic regime. But World War I magnified Russia's problems and put the tsarist government to a test that it could not meet. Russia was unprepared both militarily and

⋟ Women in the Factories ⋞

During World War I, women were called on to assume new job responsibilities, including factory work. In this selection, Naomi Loughnan, a young, upper-middle-class woman, describes the experiences in a munitions plant that considerably broadened her perspective on life.

Naomi Loughnan, "Munition Work"

We little thought when we first put on our overalls and caps and enlisted in the Munition Army how much more inspiring our life was to be than we had dared to hope. Though we munition workers sacrifice our ease we gain a life worth living. Our long days are filled with interest, and with the zest of doing work for our country in the grand cause of Freedom. As we handle the weapons of war we are learning great lessons of life. In the busy, noisy workshops we come face to face with every kind of class, and each one of these classes has something to learn from the others. . . .

Engineering mankind is possessed of the unshakable opinion that no woman can have the mechanical sense. If one of us asks humbly why such and such an alteration is not made to prevent this or that drawback to a machine, she is told, with a superior smile, that a man has worked her machine before her for years, and that therefore if there were any improvement possible it would have been made. As long as we do exactly what we are told and do not attempt to use our brains, we give entire satisfaction, and are treated as nice, good children. Any swerving from the easy path prepared for us by our males arouses the most scathing contempt in their manly bosoms. . . . Women have, however, proved that their entry into the munition world has increased the output. Employers who forget things personal in their patriotic desire for large results are enthusiastic over the success of women in the shops. But their workmen have to be handled with the utmost tenderness and caution lest they should actually imagine it was being suggested that women could do their work equally well, given equal conditions of training—at least where muscle is not the driving force. . . .

The coming of the mixed classes of women into the factory is slowly but surely having an educative effect upon the men. "Language" is almost unconsciously becoming subdued. There are fiery exceptions who make our hair stand up on end under our close-fitting caps, but a sharp rebuke or a look of horror will often straighten out the most savage. . . . It is grievous to hear the girls also swearing and using disgusting language. Shoulder to shoulder with the children of the slums, the upper classes are having their eyes opened at last to the awful conditions among which their sisters have dwelt. Foul language, immorality, and many other evils are but the natural outcome of overcrowding and bitter poverty. . . . Sometimes disgust will overcome us, but we are learning with painful clarity that the fault is not theirs whose actions disgust us, but must be placed to the discredit of those other classes who have allowed the continued existence of conditions which generate the things from which we shrink appalled.

---

technologically for the total war of World War I. Competent military leadership was lacking. Even worse, the tsar, alone of all European monarchs, insisted on taking personal charge of the armed forces despite his obvious lack of ability and training for such an awesome burden. Russian industry was unable to produce the weapons needed for the army. Ill-led and ill-armed, Russian armies suffered incredible losses. Between 1914 and 1916, two million soldiers had been killed while another four to six million had been wounded or captured. By 1917, the Russian will to fight had vanished.

The tsarist government was totally inadequate for the tasks that it faced in 1914. At the same time, Tsar Nicholas II was increasingly insulated from events by his German-born wife Alexandra, a willful woman who had fallen under the influence of Rasputin, a Siberian peasant who belonged to a religious sect that indulged in sexual orgies. To the tsarina, Rasputin was a holy man for he alone seemed able to stop the bleeding of her hemophiliac son, Alexis. Rasputin's influence made him an important power behind the throne, and he did not hesitate to interfere in government affairs. As the leadership at the top stumbled its way through a series of military and economic disasters, the middle class, aristocrats, peasants, soldiers, and workers grew more and more disenchanted with the tsarist regime. Even conservative aristocrats who supported the monarchy felt the need to do something to reverse the deteriorating situation. For a start, they assassinated Rasputin in December 1916. By then it was too late to save the monarchy, and its fall came quickly.

At the beginning of March 1917, a series of strikes broke out in the capital city of Petrograd (formerly St. Petersburg). Here the actions of working-class women helped to change the course of Russian history. In February 1917, the government had introduced bread rationing in the capital city after the price of bread had skyrocketed. Many of the women who stood in the lines waiting for bread were also factory workers who had to put in twelve-hour days. The Russian government had become aware of the volatile situation in the capital from a police report:

> Mothers of families, exhausted by endless standing in line at stores, distraught over their half-starving and sick children, are today perhaps closer to revolution than [the liberal opposition leaders] and of course they are a great deal more dangerous because they are the combustible material for which only a single spark is needed to burst into flame.[5]

On March 8, about 10,000 Petrograd women marched through the city demanding "Peace and Bread" and "Down with Autocracy." Soon the women were joined by other workers, and together they called for a general strike that succeeded in shutting down all the factories in

the city on March 10. Nicholas ordered the troops to disperse the crowds by shooting them if necessary, but soon significant numbers of the soldiers joined the demonstrators. The Duma, or legislative body, which the Tsar had tried to dissolve, met anyway and on March 12 established a Provisional Government that urged the tsar to abdicate. He did so on March 15.

The Provisional Government, headed by Alexander Kerensky, decided to carry on the war to preserve Russia's honor—a major blunder because it satisfied neither the workers nor the peasants who above all wanted an end to the war. The Provisional Government was also faced with another authority, the soviets, or councils of workers' and soldiers' deputies. The soviet of Petrograd had been formed in March 1917; at the same time soviets sprang up spontaneously in army units, factory towns, and in rural areas. The soviets represented the more radical interests of the lower classes and were largely composed of socialists of different kinds. One group—the Bolsheviks—came to play a crucial role.

The Bolsheviks were a small faction of Marxist Social Democrats who had come under the leadership of Vladimir Ulianov, known to the world as V. I. Lenin (1870–1924). Arrested for his revolutionary activity, Lenin was shipped to Siberia. After his release, he chose to go into exile in Switzerland and eventually assumed the leadership of the Bolshevik wing of the Russian Social Democratic Party. Under Lenin's direction, the Bolsheviks became a party dedicated to a violent revolution that would destroy the capitalist system. He believed that a "vanguard" of activists must form a small party of well-

♦ **Lenin Addresses a Crowd.** V. I. Lenin was the driving force behind the success of the Bolsheviks in seizing power in Russia and creating the Union of Soviet Socialist Republics. Here Lenin is seen addressing a rally in Moscow in 1917.

disciplined professional revolutionaries to accomplish the task. Between 1900 and 1917, Lenin spent most of his time in Switzerland. When the Provisional Government was formed in March 1917, he believed that an opportunity for the Bolsheviks to seize power had come. In April 1917, with the connivance of the German High Command, who hoped to create disorder in Russia, Lenin was shipped to Russia in a "sealed train" by way of Finland.

Lenin's arrival in Russia on April 3 opened a new stage of the Russian Revolution. Lenin maintained that the soviets of soldiers, workers, and peasants were ready-made instruments of power. The Bolsheviks must work toward gaining control of these groups and then use them to overthrow the Provisional Government. At the same time, Bolshevik propaganda must seek mass support through promises geared to the needs of the people: an end to the war, redistribution of all land to the peasants, the transfer of factories and industries from capitalists to committees of workers, and the relegation of government power from the Provisional Government to the soviets. Three simple slogans summed up the Bolshevik program: "Peace, Land, Bread," "Worker Control of Production," and "All Power to the Soviets."

By the end of October, the Bolsheviks had achieved a slight majority in the Petrograd and Moscow soviets. The number of party members had also grown from 50,000 to 240,000. With the close cooperation of Leon Trotsky (1877–1940), a fervid revolutionary, Lenin organized a Military Revolutionary Committee within the Petrograd soviet to plot the overthrow of the government. On the night of November 6–7, Bolshevik forces seized the Winter Palace, seat of the Provisional Government. The Provisional Government quickly collapsed with little bloodshed. This coup d'etat had been timed to coincide with a meeting in Petrograd of the all-Russian Congress of Soviets representing local soviets from all over the country. Lenin nominally turned over the sovereignty of the Provisional Government to this Congress of Soviets. Real power, however, passed to a Council of People's Commissars, headed by Lenin (see the box on p. 550).

But the Bolsheviks, soon renamed the Communists, still had a long way to go. Lenin had promised peace and that, he realized, was not an easy task because of the humiliating losses of Russian territory that it would entail. There was no real choice, however. On March 3, 1918, Lenin signed the Treaty of Brest-Litovsk with Germany and gave up eastern Poland, Ukraine, Finland, and the Baltic provinces. To his critics, Lenin argued that it made no difference since the spread of socialist revolution throughout Europe would make the treaty largely irrelevant. In any case, he had promised peace to the Russian people; but real peace did not come because the country soon sank into civil war.

CIVIL WAR

There was great opposition to the new Bolshevik or Communist regime, not only from groups loyal to the tsar but also from bourgeois and aristocratic liberals and anti-Leninist socialists. In addition, thousands of Allied troops were eventually sent to different parts of Russia in the hope of bringing Russia back into the war.

Between 1918 and 1921, the Bolshevik (or Red) Army was forced to fight on many fronts. The first serious threat to the Bolsheviks came from Siberia where a White (anti-Bolshevik) force attacked westward and advanced almost to the Volga River before being stopped. Attacks also came from the Ukrainians in the southeast and from the Baltic regions. In mid-1919, White forces swept through the Ukraine and advanced almost to Moscow. At one point by late 1919, three separate White armies seemed to be closing in on the Bolsheviks, but were eventually pushed back. By 1920, the major White forces had been defeated and the Ukraine retaken. The next year, the Communist regime regained control over the independent nationalist governments in the Caucasus: Georgia, Russian Armenia, and Azerbaijan.

How had Lenin and the Bolsheviks triumphed over what seemed at one time to be overwhelming forces? For one thing, the Red Army became a well-disciplined and formidable fighting force, largely due to the organizational genius of Leon Trotsky. As commissar of war, Trotsky reinstated the draft and insisted on rigid discipline; soldiers who deserted or refused to obey orders were summarily executed.

The disunity of the anti-Communist forces seriously weakened the efforts of the Whites. Political differences created distrust among the Whites and prevented them from cooperating effectively with each other. Some Whites insisted on restoring the tsarist regime, while others understood that only a more liberal and democratic program had any chance of success. It was difficult enough to achieve military cooperation; political differences made it virtually impossible. The lack of a common goal on the part of the Whites was paralleled by a clear sense of purpose on the part of the Communists. Inspired by their vision of a new socialist order, the Communists had the advantage of possessing that determination that comes from revolutionary fervor and revolutionary convictions.

The Communists also succeeded in translating their revolutionary faith into practical instruments of power. A policy of "war communism," for example, was used to

Ten Days That Shook the World: Lenin and the Bolshevik Seizure of Power

John Reed was an American journalist who helped to found the American Communist Labor Party. Accused of sedition, he fled the United States and went to Russia. In Ten Days That Shook the World, Reed left an impassioned eyewitness account of the Russian Revolution. It is apparent from his comments that Reed considered Lenin the indispensable hero of the Bolshevik success.

John Reed, Ten Days That Shook the World

It was just 8:40 when a thundering wave of cheers announced the entrance of the presidium, with Lenin—great Lenin—among them. A short, stocky figure, with a big head set down in his shoulders, bald and bulging. Little eyes, a snubbish nose, wide, generous mouth, and heavy chin; clean-shaven now, but already beginning to bristle with the well-known beard of his past and future. Dressed in shabby clothes, his trousers much too long for him. Unimpressive, to be the idol of a mob, loved and revered as perhaps few leaders in history have been. A strange popular leader—a leader purely by virtue of intellect; colorless, humorless, uncompromising and detached; without picturesque idiosyncrasies—but with the power of explaining profound ideas in simple terms, of analyzing a concrete situation. And combined with shrewdness, the greatest intellectual audacity. . . .

Now Lenin, gripping the edge of the reading stand, letting his little winking eyes travel over the crowd as he stood there waiting, apparently oblivious to the long-rolling ovation, which lasted several minutes. When it finished, he said simply, "We shall now proceed to construct the Socialist order!" Again that overwhelming human roar.

"The first thing is the adoption of practical measures to realize peace. . . . We shall offer peace to the peoples of all the belligerent countries upon the basis of the Soviet terms—no annexations, no indemnities, and the right of self-determination of peoples. At the same time, according to our promise, we shall publish and repudiate the secret treaties. . . . The question of War and Peace is so clear that I think that I may, without preamble, read the project of a Proclamation to the Peoples of All the Belligerent Countries. . . ."

His great mouth, seeming to smile, opened wide as he spoke; his voice was hoarse—not unpleasantly so, but as if it had hardened that way after years and years of speaking—and went on monotonously, with the effect of being able to go forever. . . . For emphasis he bent forward slightly. No gestures. And before him, a thousand simple faces looking up in intent adoration.

[Reed then reproduces the full text of the Proclamation.]

When the grave thunder of applause had died away, Lenin spoke again: "We propose to the Congress to ratify this declaration. . . . This proposal of peace will meet with resistance on the part of the imperialist governments—we don't fool ourselves on that score. But we hope that revolution will soon break out in all the belligerent countries; that is why we address ourselves especially to the workers of France, England, and Germany. . . ."

"The revolution of November 6th and 7th," he ended, "has opened the era of the Social Revolution. . . . The labor movement, in the name of peace and Socialism, shall win, and fulfill its destiny. . . ."

There was something quiet and powerful in all this, which stirred the souls of men. It was understandable why people believed when Lenin spoke.

ensure regular supplies for the Red Army. "War communism" included the nationalization of banks and most industries, the forcible requisition of grain from peasants, and the centralization of state administration under Bolshevik control. Another Bolshevik instrument was "revolutionary terror." Although the old tsarist secret police had been abolished, a new Red secret police—known as the Cheka—replaced it. The Red Terror instituted by the Cheka aimed at nothing less than the destruction of all those who opposed the new regime. The Red Terror added an element of fear to the Bolshevik regime.

Finally, the intervention of foreign armies enabled the Communists to appeal to the powerful force of Russian patriotism. Although the Allied powers had intervened initially in Russia to encourage the Russians to remain in the war, the end of the war on November 11, 1918, had made that purpose inconsequential. Nevertheless, Allied troops remained, and even more were sent because Allied countries did not hide their anti-Bolshevik feelings. At one point, more than 100,000 foreign troops, mostly Japanese, British, French, and American, were stationed on Russian soil. These forces rarely engaged in pitched battles, however, nor did they pursue a common strategy, although they did give material assistance to anti-Bolshevik forces. This intervention by the Allies enabled the Communist government to appeal to patriotic Russians to fight the attempts of foreigners to control their country. Allied interference was never substantial enough to win the civil war, but it did serve indirectly to help the Bolshevik cause.

By 1921, the Communists had succeeded in retaining control of Russia. In the course of the civil war, the Bolshevik regime had also transformed Russia into a bureaucratically centralized state dominated by a single party. It was also a state that was largely hostile to the Allied powers that had sought to assist the Bolsheviks' enemies in the civil war.

The Last Year of the War

For Germany, the withdrawal of the Russians from the war in March 1918 offered renewed hope for a favorable end to the war. The victory over Russia persuaded Erich Ludendorff, who guided German military operations, and most German leaders to make one final military gamble—a grand offensive in the west to break the military stalemate. The German attack was launched in March and lasted into July, but an Allied counterattack, supported by the arrival of 140,000 fresh American troops, defeated the Germans at the Second Battle of the Marne on July 18. Ludendorff's gamble had failed. With the arrival of two million more American troops on the Continent, Allied forces began making a steady advance toward Germany.

On September 29, 1918, General Ludendorff informed German leaders that the war was lost and demanded that the government sue for peace at once. When German officials discovered that the Allies were unwilling to make peace with the autocratic imperial government, they instituted reforms to create a liberal government. But these constitutional reforms came too late for the exhausted and angry German people. On November 3, naval units in Kiel mutinied, and within days councils of workers and soldiers were forming throughout northern Germany and taking over the supervision of civilian and military administrations. William II capitulated to public pressure and abdicated on November 9, while the Socialists under Friedrich Ebert announced the establishment of a republic. Two

days later, on November 11, 1918, the new German government agreed to an armistice. The war was over.

The Peace Settlement

In January 1919, the delegations of twenty-seven victorious Allied nations gathered in Paris to conclude a final settlement of the Great War. Harold Nicolson, one of the British delegates, expressed what he believed this conference would achieve: "We were journeying to Paris not merely to liquidate the war, but to found a New Order in

Europe. We were preparing not Peace only, but Eternal Peace. There was about us the halo of some divine mission. . . . For we were bent on doing great, permanent and noble things." [6]

National expectations, however, made Nicolson's quest for "eternal peace" a difficult one. Over a period of years, the reasons for fighting World War I had been transformed from selfish national interests to idealistic principles. No one expressed the latter better than Woodrow Wilson. The American president outlined "Fourteen Points" to the American Congress that he believed justified the enormous military struggle then being waged. Later, Wilson spelled out additional steps for a truly just and lasting peace. Wilson's proposals included: "open covenants of peace, openly arrived at" instead of secret diplomacy; the reduction of national armaments to a "point consistent with domestic safety"; and the self-determination of people so that "all well-defined national aspirations shall be accorded the utmost satisfaction." Wilson characterized World War I as a people's war waged against "absolutism and militarism," two scourges of liberty that could only be eliminated by creating democratic governments and a "general association of nations" that would guarantee the "political independence and territorial integrity to great and small states alike" (see the box on p. 553). As the spokesman for a new world order based on democracy and international cooperation, Wilson was enthusiastically cheered by many Europeans when he arrived in Europe for the peace conference.

Wilson soon found, however, that other states at the Paris Peace Conference were guided by considerably more pragmatic motives. The secret treaties and agreements that had been made before the war could not be totally ignored, even if they did conflict with the principle of self-determination enunciated by Wilson. National interests also complicated the deliberations of the Paris Peace Conference. David Lloyd George, prime minister of Great Britain, had won a decisive electoral victory in December 1918 on a platform of making the Germans pay for this dreadful war.

France's approach to peace was primarily determined by considerations of national security. To Georges Clemenceau, the feisty premier of France who had led his country to victory, the French people had borne the brunt of German aggression. They deserved revenge and security against future German aggression. Clemenceau wanted a demilitarized Germany, vast German reparations to pay for the costs of the war, and a separate Rhineland as a buffer state between France and Germany, demands that Wilson viewed as vindictive and contrary to the principle of national self-determination.

Although twenty-seven nations were represented at the Paris Peace Conference, the most important decisions were made by Woodrow Wilson, Georges Clemenceau, and David Lloyd George. Italy was considered one of the so-called Big Four powers, but played a much less important role than the other three countries. Germany, of course, was not invited to attend and Russia could not because of its civil war.

In view of the many conflicting demands at Versailles, it was inevitable that the Big Three would quarrel. Wilson was determined to create a League of Nations to prevent future wars. Clemenceau and Lloyd George were equally determined to punish Germany. In the end, only compromise made it possible to achieve a peace settlement. On January 25, 1919, the conference adopted the principle of a League of Nations while Wilson agreed to make compromises on territorial arrangements. Clemenceau also compromised to obtain some guarantees for French security. He renounced France's desire for a separate Rhineland and instead accepted a defensive alliance with Great Britain and the United States. Both states pledged to help France if it were attacked by Germany.

The final peace settlement of Paris consisted of five separate treaties with the defeated nations—Germany, Austria, Hungary, Bulgaria, and Turkey. The Treaty of Versailles with Germany, signed on June 28, 1919, was by far the most important one. The Germans considered it a

◆ **The Big Four at Paris.** Shown here are the Big Four at the Paris Peace Conference: Lloyd George of Britain, Orlando of Italy, Clemenceau of France, and Wilson of the United States. Although Italy was considered one of the Big Four powers, Britain, France, and the United States (the Big Three) made the major decisions at the peace conference.

⇒ Two Voices of Peacemaking: Woodrow Wilson and Georges Clemenceau ⇐

When the Allied powers met at Paris in January 1919, it soon became apparent that the victors had different opinions on the kind of peace they expected. The first excerpt is from a speech of Woodrow Wilson in which the American president presented his idealistic goals for a peace based on justice and reconciliation. The French wanted revenge and security. In the second selection, from Georges Clemenceau's Grandeur and Misery of Victory, *the French premier revealed his fundamental dislike and distrust of Germany.*

Woodrow Wilson, May 26, 1917

We are fighting for the liberty, the self-government, and the undictated development of all peoples, and every feature of the settlement that concludes this war must be conceived and executed for that purpose. Wrongs must first be righted and then adequate safeguards must be created to prevent their being committed again. . . .

No people must be forced under sovereignty under which it does not wish to live. No territory must change hands except for the purpose of securing those who inhabit it a fair chance of life and liberty. No indemnities must be insisted on except those that constitute payment for manifest wrongs done. No readjustments of power must be made except such as will tend to secure the future peace of the world and the future welfare and happiness of its peoples.

And then the free peoples of the world must draw together in some common covenant, some genuine and practical cooperation that will in effect combine their force to secure peace and justice in the dealings of nations with one another.

Georges Clemenceau, *Grandeur and Misery of Victory*

War and peace, with their strong contrasts, alternate against a common background. For the catastrophe of 1914 the Germans are responsible. Only a professional liar would deny this. . . .

I have sometimes penetrated into the sacred cave of the Germanic cult, which is, as every one knows, the *Bierhaus* [beer hall]. A great aisle of massive humanity where there accumulate, amid the fumes of tobacco and beer, the popular rumblings of a nationalism upheld by the sonorous brasses blaring to the heavens the supreme voice of Germany, *Deutschland über alles! Germany above everything!* Men, women, and children, all petrified in reverence before the divine stoneware pot, brows furrowed with irrepressible power, eyes lost in a dream of infinity, mouths twisted by the intensity of willpower, drink in long draughts the celestial hope of vague expectations. These only remain to be realized presently when the chief marked out by Destiny shall have given the word. There you have the ultimate framework of an old but childish race.

---

harsh peace and were particularly unhappy with Article 231, the so-called War Guilt Clause, which declared Germany (and Austria) responsible for starting the war and ordered Germany to pay reparations for all the damage to which the Allied governments and their people were subjected as a result of the war "imposed upon them by the aggression of Germany and her allies."

The military and territorial provisions of the treaty also rankled Germans, although they were by no means as harsh as the Germans claimed. Germany had to reduce its army to 100,000 men, cut back its navy, and eliminate its air force. German territorial losses included the cession of Alsace and Lorraine to France and sections of Prussia to the new Polish state. German land west and as far as thirty miles east of the Rhine was established as a demilitarized zone and stripped of all armaments or fortifica-

tions to serve as a barrier to any future German military moves westward against France. Outraged by the "dictated peace," the new German government complained but accepted the treaty.

The separate peace treaties made with the other Central Powers (Austria, Hungary, Bulgaria, and the Ottoman Empire) extensively redrew the map of eastern Europe. Many of these changes merely ratified what the war had already accomplished. Both the German and Russian Empires lost considerable territory in eastern Europe while the Austro-Hungarian Empire disappeared altogether. New nation-states emerged from the lands of these three empires: Finland, Latvia, Estonia, Lithuania, Poland, Czechoslovakia, Austria, and Hungary. Territorial rearrangements were also made in the Balkans. Romania acquired additional lands from Russia, Hungary, and

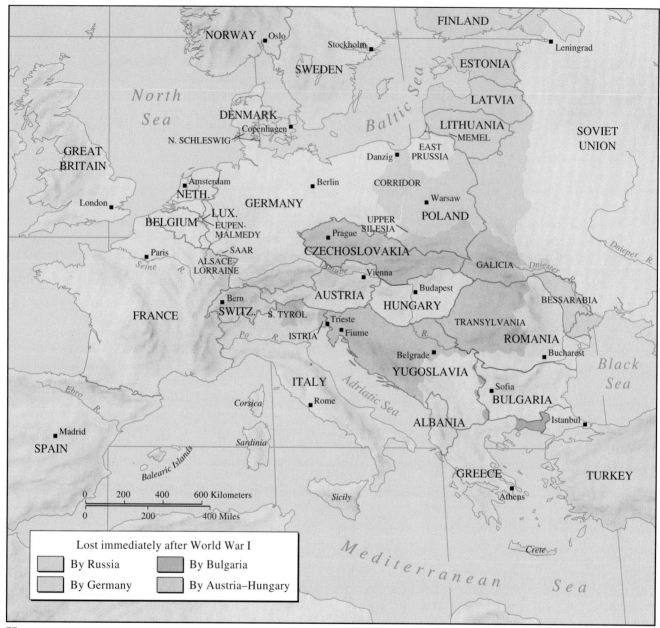

🞧 **Map 26.4** Europe in 1919.

Bulgaria. Serbia formed the nucleus of a new South Slav State, called Yugoslavia, which combined Serbs, Croats, and Slovenes.

Although the Paris Peace Conference was supposedly guided by the principle of self-determination, the mixtures of peoples in eastern Europe made it impossible to draw boundaries along neat ethnic lines. As a result of compromises, virtually every eastern European state was left with a minorities problem that could lead to future conflicts. Germans in Poland; Hungarians, Poles, and Germans in Czechoslovakia; and the combination of Serbs, Croats, Slovenes, Macedonians, and Albanians in

Yugoslavia all became sources of later conflict. Moreover, the new map of eastern Europe was based on the temporary collapse of power in both Germany and Russia. Because neither country accepted the new eastern frontiers, it seemed only a matter of time before a resurgent Germany or Russia would make changes.

Yet another centuries-old empire—the Ottoman Empire—was dismembered by the peace settlement after the war. To gain Arab support against the Ottomans during the war, the Allies had promised to recognize the independence of Arab states in the Middle Eastern lands of the Ottoman Empire. But the imperialist habits of Europeans died hard. After the war, France took control of Lebanon and Syria while Britain received Iraq and Palestine. Officially, both acquisitions were called mandates whereby a nation officially administered a territory on behalf of the League of Nations. The system of mandates could not hide the fact that the principle of national self-determination at the Paris Peace Conference was largely for Europeans.

The peace settlement negotiated at Paris soon came under attack, not only by the defeated Central Powers, but by others who felt that the peacemakers had been shortsighted. Some people, however, thought the peace settlement was the best that could be achieved under the circumstances. Self-determination, they believed, had served reasonably well as a central organizing principle while the establishment of the League of Nations gave some hope that future conflicts could be resolved peacefully. And yet, within twenty years after the signing of the peace treaties, Europe was again engaged in deadly conflict. As some historians have suggested, perhaps lack of enforcement rather than the structure of the peace may have caused the failure of the peace of 1919.

Successful enforcement of the peace necessitated the active involvement of its principal architects, especially in assisting the new German state to develop a peaceful and democratic republic. The failure of the American Senate to ratify the Treaty of Versailles, however, meant that the United States never joined the League of Nations. In addition, the American Senate also rejected Wilson's defensive alliance with Great Britain and France. Already by the end of 1919, the United States was pursuing policies intended to limit its direct involvement in future European wars.

This retreat had dire consequences. American withdrawal from the defensive alliance with Britain and France led Britain to withdraw as well. By removing itself from European affairs, the United States forced France to stand alone facing its old enemy, leading the embittered nation to take strong actions against Germany that only intensified German resentment. By the end of 1919, it appeared that the peace of 1919 was already beginning to unravel.

Conclusion

World War I shattered the liberal and rational assumptions of late nineteenth- and early twentieth-century Europe. The incredible destruction and the death of almost 10 million people undermined the whole idea of progress. New propaganda techniques had manipulated entire populations into sustaining their involvement in a meaningless slaughter.

World War I was a total war and involved a mobilization of resources and populations and increased government centralization of power over the lives of its citizens. Civil liberties, such as the freedom of press, speech, assembly, and movement, were circumscribed in the name of national security. Governments' need to plan the production and distribution of goods and to ration consumer goods restricted economic freedom. Although the late nineteenth and early twentieth centuries had witnessed the extension of government authority into such areas as mass education, social welfare legislation, and mass conscription, World War I made the practice of strong central authority a way of life.

Finally, World War I ended the age of European hegemony over world affairs. In 1917, the Russian Revolution laid the foundation for the creation of a new Soviet power, and the United States entered the war. The termination of the European age was not evident to all, however, for it was clouded by two developments—American isolationism and the withdrawal of the Soviets from world affairs while they nurtured the growth of their own socialist system. Although these developments were only temporary, they created a political vacuum in Europe that was filled all too soon by the revival of German power.

NOTES

1. Arnold Toynbee, *Surviving the Future* (New York, 1971), pp. 106–107.
2. Quoted in Joachim Remak, "1914—The Third Balkan War: Origins Reconsidered," *Journal of Modern History*, 43 (1971): 364–365.
3. Quoted in J. M. Winter, *The Experience of World War I* (New York, 1989), p. 142.
4. Quoted in Catherine W. Reilly, ed., *Scars Upon My Heart: Women's Poetry and Verse of the First World War* (London, 1981), p. 90.
5. Quoted in William M. Mandel, *Soviet Women* (Garden City, N.Y., 1975), p. 43.
6. Harold Nicolson, *Peacemaking, 1919* (Boston and New York, 1933), pp. 31–32.

SUGGESTIONS FOR FURTHER READING

The historical literature on the causes of World War I is enormous. A good starting point is the work by J. Joll, *The Origins of the First World War* (London, 1984). Also useful is J. Remak, *The Origins of World War I, 1871–1914* (New York, 1967). The belief that Germany was primarily responsible for the war was argued vigorously by the German scholar F. Fischer, *Germany's Aims in the First World War* (New York, 1967); *World Power or Decline: The Controversy over Germany's Aims in World War I* (New York, 1974); and *War of Illusions: German Policies from 1911 to 1914* (New York, 1975). The role of each great power has been reassessed in a series of books on the causes of World War I. They include V. R. Berghahn, *Germany and the Approach of War in 1914* (London, 1973); Z. S. Steiner, *Britain and the Origins of the First World War* (New York, 1977); R. Bosworth, *Italy and the Approach of the First World War* (New York, 1983); J. F. Keiger, *France and the Origins of the First World War,* (New York, 1984); and D. C. B. Lieven, *Russia and the Origins of the First World War* (New York, 1984). The domestic origins of the war are probed in A. Mayer, *The Persistence of the Old Regime* (New York, 1981).

There are two good recent accounts of World War I in M. Gilbert, *The First World War* (New York, 1994); and the lavishly illustrated book by J. M. Winter, *The Experience of World War I* (New York, 1989). See also the brief work by N. Heyman, *World War I* (Westport, Conn., 1997). For an account of the military operations of the war, see the classic work by B. H. Liddell Hart, *History of the First World War* (Boston, 1970). The nature of trench warfare is examined in T. Ashworth, *Trench Warfare, 1914–1918: The Live and Let-Live System* (London, 1980). In *The Great War and Modern Memory* (London, 1975), Paul Fussell attempted to show how British writers described their war experiences. Although scholars do not always agree with her conclusions, B. Tuchman's *The Guns of August* (New York, 1962) is a magnificently written account of the opening days of the war. For an interesting perspective on World War I and the beginnings of the modern world, see M. Eksteins, *Rites of Spring, The Great War and the Birth of the Modern Age* (Boston, 1989).

On the role of women in World War I, see G. Braybon, *Women Workers in the First World War: The British Experience* (London, 1981); and J. M. Winter and R. M. Wall, eds., *The Upheaval of War: Family, Work and Welfare in Europe, 1914–1918* (Cambridge, 1988). For a general survey of women in twentieth-century Europe, see B. Anderson and J. P. Zinsser, *A History of Their Own*, vol. 2 (New York, 1988).

A good introduction to the Russian Revolution can be found in S. Fitzpatrick, *The Russian Revolution, 1917–1932*, 2d ed. (New York, 1994); and R. V. Daniels, *Red October* (New York, 1967). On Lenin, see R. W. Clark, *Lenin* (New York, 1988); and the valuable work by A. B. Ulam, *The Bolsheviks* (New York, 1965). There is now a comprehensive study of the Russian civil war in W. B. Lincoln, *Red Victory: A History of the Russian Civil War* (New York, 1989).

The role of war aims in shaping the peace settlement is examined in V. H. Rothwell, *British War Aims and Peace Diplomacy, 1914–1918* (Oxford, 1971); and D. R. Stevenson, *French War Aims against Germany, 1914–1919* (New York, 1982).

World War I and the Russian Revolution are also well covered in two good general surveys of European history in the twentieth century, R. Paxton, *Europe in the Twentieth Century*, 2d ed. (New York, 1985); and A. Rudhart, *Twentieth Century Europe* (Englewood Cliffs, N.J., 1986).

CHAPTER

27

The Futile Search for a New Stability: Europe Between the Wars, 1919–1939

Only twenty years after the Treaty of Versailles, Europeans were again at war. And yet in the 1920s, many people assumed that Europe and the world were about to enter a new era of international peace, economic growth, and political democracy. In all of these areas, the optimistic hopes of the 1920s failed to be realized. After 1919, most people wanted peace but were unsure about how to maintain it. The League of Nations, conceived as a new instrument to provide for collective security, failed to work well. New treaties that renounced the use of war looked good on paper but had no means of enforcement. Then, too, virtually everyone favored disarmament, but few could agree on how to achieve it.

At home, Europe was faced with severe economic problems after World War I. The European economy did not begin to recover from the war until 1922, and even then it was beset by financial problems left over from the war and, most devastating of all, the Great Depression that began at the end of 1929. The Great Depression brought untold misery to millions of people. Begging for food on the streets became widespread, especially when soup kitchens were unable to keep up with the demand. Larger and larger numbers of people were homeless and moved from place to place looking for work and shelter. In the United States, the homeless set up shantytowns they named "Hoovervilles" after the American president, Herbert Hoover. In their misery, some people saw but one solution, as one unemployed person expressed it: "Today, when I am experiencing this for the first time, I think that I should prefer to do away with myself, to take gas, to jump into the river, or leap from some high place. . . . Would I really come to such a decision? I do not know. Animals die, plants wither, but men always go on living." Social unrest spread rapidly, and some unemployed staged hunger marches to get attention. In democratic countries, more and more people began to listen to and vote for radical voices calling for extreme measures.

Mussolini and Fascists come to power in Italy   Stalin gains control of Russia

Hitler and Nazis come to power in Germany   Popular Front in France

Locarno Pact   Spanish Civil War

Beginning of the Great Depression   *Kristallnacht*

Mass production of radios begins   Heisenberg's "uncertainty principle"

Hannah Höch, *Cut with the Kitchen Knife*   Dali, *The Persistence of Memory*

According to Woodrow Wilson, World War I had been fought to make the world safe for democracy, and for a while after 1919, political democracy seemed well established. But the hopes for democracy, too, soon faded as authoritarian regimes spread into Italy and Germany and across eastern Europe.

An Uncertain Peace: The Search for Security

The peace settlement at the end of World War I had tried to fulfill the nineteenth-century dream of nationalism by the creation of new boundaries and new states. From its inception, however, this peace settlement had left nations unhappy. Conflicts over disputed border regions poisoned mutual relations in eastern Europe for years. Many Germans viewed the Peace of Versailles as a dictated peace and vowed to seek its revision. The American president Woodrow Wilson had recognized that the peace treaties contained unwise provisions that could serve as new causes for conflicts and had placed many of his hopes for the future in the League of Nations. The league, however, was not particularly effective in maintaining the peace. The failure of the United States to join the league and the subsequent American retreat into isolationism undermined the effectiveness of the league from its beginning. Moreover, the league could use only economic sanctions to halt aggression.

The weakness of the League of Nations and the failure of both the United States and Great Britain to honor their promises to form defensive military alliances with

France left France embittered and alone. France's search for security between 1919 and 1924 was founded primarily on a strict enforcement of the Treaty of Versailles. This tough policy toward Germany began with the issue of reparations, or the payments that the Germans were supposed to make to compensate for the "damage done to the civilian population of the Allied and Associated Powers and to their property," as the treaty asserted. In April 1921, the Allied Reparations Commission settled on a sum of 132 billion marks ($33 billion) for German reparations, payable in annual installments of 2.5 billion (gold) marks. The new German republic made its first payment in 1921, but by the following year, faced with rising inflation, domestic turmoil, and lack of revenues due to low tax rates, announced that it was unable to pay more. Outraged by what they considered to be Germany's violation of one aspect of the peace settlement, the French government sent troops to occupy the Ruhr valley, Germany's chief industrial and mining center. Because the Germans would not pay reparations, the French would collect reparations in kind by operating and using the Ruhr mines and factories.

Both Germany and France suffered from the French occupation of the Ruhr. The German government adopted a policy of passive resistance that was largely financed by printing more paper money, but this only intensified the inflationary pressures that had already appeared in Germany by the end of the war. The German mark soon became worthless. In 1914, 4.2 marks equaled one dollar; by the end of November 1923, it had increased to an incredible 4.2 trillion. Germany faced economic disaster. The formation of new governments in both Great Britain and France opened the door to conciliatory approaches to Germany and the reparations problem. At the same time, a new German government led by Gustav Stresemann (1878–1929) ended the policy of passive resistance and committed Germany to carry out most of the provisions of the Versailles Treaty while seeking a new settlement of the reparations question.

In August 1924, an international commission produced a new plan for reparations. Named the Dawes plan after the American banker who chaired the commission, it reduced reparations and stabilized Germany's payments on the basis of its ability to pay. The Dawes plan also granted an initial $200 million loan for German recovery, which opened the door to heavy American investments in Europe that helped create a new era of European prosperity between 1924 and 1929.

A new era of European diplomacy accompanied the new economic stability. A spirit of international cooperation was fostered by the foreign ministers of Germany and France, Stresemann and Aristide Briand (1862–1932), respectively, who concluded the Treaty of Locarno in 1925. This guaranteed Germany's new western borders with France and Belgium. Although Germany's new eastern borders with Poland were conspicuously absent from the agreement, the Locarno pact was viewed by many as the beginning of a new era of European peace. On the day after the pact was concluded, the headlines in the *New York Times* ran "France and Germany Ban War Forever," while the London *Times* declared, "Peace at Last."[1]

The spirit of Locarno was based on little real substance. Germany lacked the military power to alter its western borders even if it wanted to. And the issue of disarmament soon proved that even the spirit of Locarno could not bring nations to cut back on their weapons. The League of Nations covenant had suggested the "reduction of national armaments to the lowest point consistent with national safety." Germany, of course, had been disarmed with the expectation that other states would do likewise. Numerous disarmament conferences, however, failed to achieve anything substantial as states proved unwilling to trust their security to anyone but their own military forces. When a World Disarmament Conference finally met in Geneva in 1932, the issue was already dead.

The Great Depression

Two factors played a major role in the coming of the Great Depression: a downturn in domestic economies and an international financial crisis created by the collapse of the American stock market in 1929. Already in the mid-1920s, prices for agricultural goods were beginning to decline rapidly due to overproduction of basic commodities, such as wheat. In 1925, states in central and eastern Europe began to impose tariffs to close their markets to other countries' goods. An increase in the use

✦ **The Great Depression: Bread Lines in Paris.** The Great Depression devastated the European economy and had serious political repercussions. Because of its more balanced economy, France did not feel the effects of the depression as quickly as other European countries. By 1931, however, even France was experiencing lines of unemployed people at free-food centers.

of oil and hydroelectricity led to a slump in the coal industry even before 1929.

In addition to these domestic economic troubles, much of the European prosperity between 1924 and 1929 had been built on American bank loans to Germany. Twenty-three billion marks had been invested in German municipal bonds and German industries since 1924. In 1928 and 1929, American investors began to pull money out of Germany in order to invest in the booming New York stock market. The crash of the American stock market in October 1929 led panicky American investors to withdraw even more of their funds from Germany and other European markets. The withdrawal of funds seriously weakened the banks of Germany and other central European states. The Credit-Anstalt, Vienna's most prestigious bank, collapsed on May 31, 1931. By that time, trade was slowing down, industrialists were cutting back production, and unemployment was increasing as the ripple effects of international bank failures had a devastating impact on domestic economies.

Economic depression was by no means a new phenomenon in European history. But the depth of the economic downturn after 1929 fully justifies the label Great Depression. During 1932, the worst year of the depression, one British worker in four was unemployed, while six million (40 percent) of the German labor force were out of work. Between 1929 and 1932, industrial production plummeted almost 50 percent in the United States and more than 40 percent in Germany. The unemployed and homeless filled the streets of the cities throughout the advanced industrial countries (see the box on p. 562).

Governments seemed powerless to deal with the crisis. The classical liberal remedy for depression, a deflationary policy of balanced budgets, which involved cutting costs by lowering wages and raising tariffs to exclude other countries' goods from home markets, only served to worsen the economic crisis and create even greater mass discontent. This, in turn, led to serious political repercussions. Increased government activity in the economy was one reaction, even in countries like the United States that had a strong laissez-faire tradition. Another effect was a renewed interest in Marxist doctrines since Marx had predicted that capitalism would destroy itself through overproduction. Communism took on new popularity, especially with workers and intellectuals. Finally, the Great Depression increased the attractiveness of simplistic dictatorial solutions, especially from a new movement known as fascism. Everywhere, democracy seemed on the defensive in the 1930s.

The Democratic States

According to Woodrow Wilson, World War I had been fought to make the world safe for democracy. In 1919, there seemed to be some justification for his claim. Four major European states and a host of minor ones had functioning political democracies. In a number of states, universal male suffrage had even been replaced by universal suffrage as male politicians rewarded women for their contributions to World War I by granting them the right to vote (except in Italy, France, and Spain where women had to wait until the end of World War II).

After World War I, Great Britain went through a period of painful readjustment and serious economic difficulties. During the war, Britain had lost many of the markets for its industrial products, especially to the United States and Japan. The postwar decline of such staple industries as coal, steel, and textiles led to a rise in unemployment, which reached the two-million mark in 1921. But Britain soon rebounded, and from 1925 to 1929, experienced an era of renewed prosperity.

By 1929, Britain was faced with the growing effects of the Great Depression. The Labour Party, which had now become the largest party in Britain, failed to solve the nation's economic problems and fell from power in 1931. A National Government (a coalition of Liberals, Conservatives, and Labour Party) claimed credit for bringing Britain out of the worst stages of the depression, primarily by using the traditional policies of balanced budgets and protective tariffs. British politicians largely ignored the new ideas of a Cambridge economist, John Maynard Keynes (1883–1946). In 1936, Keynes published his *General Theory of Employment, Interest, and Money*. He condemned the traditional view that in a free economy, depressions should be left to work themselves out. Instead, Keynes argued that unemployment stemmed not from overproduction but a decline in demand, and that demand could be increased by public works, financed, if necessary, through deficit spending to stimulate production. These policies, however, could only be accomplished by government intervention in the economy, and Britain's political leaders were unwilling to go that far in the 1930s.

After the defeat of Germany, France had become the strongest power on the European continent. Its greatest need was to rebuild the areas of northern and eastern France that had been devastated in World War I. But no French government seemed capable of solving France's financial problems between 1921 and 1926. Like other

The Great Depression: Unemployed and Homeless in Germany

In 1932, Germany had six million unemployed workers, many of them wandering aimlessly through the country, begging for food and seeking shelter in city lodging houses for the homeless. The Great Depression was an important factor in the rise to power of Adolf Hitler and the Nazis. This selection presents a description of unemployed homeless in 1932.

Heinrich Hauser, "With Germany's Unemployed"
An almost unbroken chain of homeless men extends the whole length of the great Hamburg-Berlin highway. . . . All the highways in Germany over which I have traveled this year presented the same aspect. . . .

Most of the hikers paid no attention to me. They walked separately or in small groups, with their eyes on the ground. And they had the queer, stumbling gait of barefooted people, for their shoes were slung over their shoulders. Some of them were guild members,—carpenters . . . milkmen . . . and bricklayers . . . but they were in a minority. Far more numerous were those whom one could assign to no special profession or craft—unskilled young people, for the most part, who had been unable to find a place for themselves in any city or town in Germany, and who had never had a job and never expected to have one. There was something else that had never been seen before—whole families that had piled all their goods into baby carriages and wheelbarrows that they were pushing along as they plodded forward in dumb despair. It was a whole nation on the march.

I saw them—and this was the strongest impression that the year 1932 left with me—I saw them, gathered into groups of fifty or a hundred men, attacking fields of potatoes. I saw them digging up the potatoes and throwing them into sacks while the farmer who owned the field watched them in despair and the local policeman looked on gloomily from the distance. I saw them staggering toward the lights of the city as night fell, with their sacks on their backs. What did it remind me of? Of the War, of the worst periods of starvation in 1917 and 1918, but even then people paid for the potatoes. . . .

I saw that the individual can know what is happening only by personal experience. I know what it is to be a tramp. I know what cold and hunger are. . . . But there are two things that I have only recently experienced—begging and spending the night in a municipal lodging house.

I entered the huge Berlin municipal lodging house in a northern quarter of the city. . . .

Distribution of spoons, distribution of enameled-ware bowls with the words "Property of the City of Berlin" written on their sides. Then the meal itself. A big kettle is carried. Men with yellow smocks have brought it in and men with yellow smocks ladle out the food. These men, too, are homeless and they have been expressly picked by the establishment and given free food and lodging and a little pocket money in exchange for their work about the house.

Where have I seen this kind of food distribution before? In a prison that I once helped to guard in the winter of 1919 during the German civil war. There was the same hunger then, the same trembling, anxious expectation of rations. Now the men are standing in a long row, dressed in their plain nightshirts that reach to the ground, and the noise of their shuffling feet is like the noise of big wild animals walking up and down the stone floor of their cages before feeding time. The men lean far over the kettle so that the warm steam from the food envelops them and they hold out their bowls as if begging and whisper to the attendant, "Give me a real helping. Give me a little more." A piece of bread is handed out with every bowl.

My next recollection is sitting at a table in another room on a crowded bench that is like a seat in a fourth-class railway carriage. Hundreds of hungry mouths make an enormous noise eating their food. The men sit bent over their food like animals who feel that someone is going to take it away from them. They hold their bowl with their left arm part way around it, so that nobody can take it away, and they also protect it with their other elbow and with their head and mouth, while they move the spoon as fast as they can between their mouth and the bowl.

European countries, though, France did experience a period of relative prosperity between 1926 and 1929. By 1932, France began to feel the full effects of the Great Depression, and economic instability soon had political repercussions. During a nineteenth-month period in 1932 and 1933, six different cabinets were formed as France faced political chaos. Finally, in 1936, fearful that rightists intended to seize power, a coalition of leftist parties—Communists, Socialists, and Radicals—formed a Popular Front government in June 1936.

The Popular Front succeeded in initiating a program for workers that some have called the French New Deal. It established the right of collective bargaining, a forty-hour work week, two-week paid vacations, and minimum wages. The Popular Front's policies failed to solve the problems of the depression, however. Although the French Popular Front survived in name until 1938, it was for all intents and purposes dead before then. By 1938, the French were experiencing a serious decline of confidence in their political system that left them unprepared to deal with their aggressive Nazi enemy to the east.

After Germany, no Western nation was more affected by the Great Depression than the United States. Between 1929 and the end of 1932, industrial production fell to 50 percent of what it had been in 1929. By 1933, there were 15 million unemployed. Under these circumstances, the Democrat Franklin Delano Roosevelt (1882–1945) won the 1932 presidential election by a landslide.

During his first 100 days in office, the new president pushed for the rapid enactment of major new legislation to combat the worst effects of the depression. This policy of active government intervention in the economy came to be known as the New Deal. The first New Deal created a variety of new agencies designed to bring relief, recovery, and reform. By 1935, when it was becoming apparent that these initial efforts had produced only a slow recovery at best, Roosevelt inaugurated new efforts that collectively became known as the Second New Deal. These included a stepped-up program of public works, such as the Works Progress Administration (WPA) established in 1935. This government organization employed between 2 and 3 million people who worked at building bridges, roads, post offices, and airports. The Roosevelt administration was also responsible for social legislation that launched the American welfare state. In 1935, the Social Security Act created a system of old age pensions and unemployment insurance. Moreover, the National Labor Relations Act of 1935 encouraged the rapid growth of labor unions.

No doubt, the New Deal provided some social reform measures that perhaps averted the possibility of social revolution in the United States. It did not, however, solve the unemployment problems of the Great Depression. In May 1937, during what was considered a period of full recovery, American unemployment still stood at seven million; by the following year it had increased to eleven million. Only World War II and the subsequent growth of armaments industries brought American workers back to full employment.

The Retreat from Democracy: The Authoritarian and Totalitarian States

The apparent triumph of liberal democracy in 1919 proved extremely short-lived. By 1939, only two major states in Europe, France and Great Britain, and a host of minor ones remained democratic. Italy and Germany had succumbed to the political movement called fascism while Soviet Russia, under Stalin, had moved toward a repressive totalitarian state. A host of other European states, especially in eastern Europe, adopted authoritarian structures of various kinds.

The dictatorial regimes between the wars assumed both old and new forms. Dictatorship was by no means a new phenomenon, but the modern totalitarian state was. The totalitarian regimes, whose best examples can be found in Stalinist Russia and Nazi Germany, extended the functions and power of the central state far beyond what they had been in the past. The immediate origins of totalitarianism can be found in the total warfare of World War I when governments, even in the democratic states, exercised controls over economic, political, and personal freedom in order to achieve victory.

The modern totalitarian state soon moved beyond the ideal of passive obedience expected in a traditional dictatorship or authoritarian monarchy. The new "total states" expected the active loyalty and commitment of citizens to the regime's goals. They used modern mass propaganda techniques and high-speed modern communications to conquer the minds and hearts of their subjects. The total state aimed to control not only the economic, political, and social aspects of life, but the intellectual and cultural as well. But that control also had a purpose: the active involvement of the masses in the achievement of the regime's goals, whether they be war or a thousand-year Reich.

The modern totalitarian state was to be led by a single leader and single party. It ruthlessly rejected the liberal ideal of limited government power and constitutional guarantees of individual freedoms. Indeed, individual freedom was to be subordinated to the collective will of the masses, organized and determined for them by a leader or leaders. Modern technology also gave total states unprecedented police controls to enforce their wishes on their subjects. The fascist states—Italy and Nazi Germany—as well as Stalin's Communist Russia have all been labeled totalitarian, although their regimes exhibited significant differences and met with varying degrees of success.

Fascist Italy

In the early 1920s, in the wake of economic turmoil, political disorder, and the general insecurity and fear stemming from World War I, Benito Mussolini burst upon the Italian scene with the first fascist movement in Europe. Mussolini (1883–1945) began his political career as a Socialist, but was expelled from the Socialist Party after supporting Italy's entry into World War I, a position contrary to the socialist position of ardent neutrality. In 1919, Mussolini established a new political group, the *Fascio di Combattimento*, or League of Combat. It received little attention in the elections of 1919, but political stalemate in Italy's parliamentary system and strong nationalist sentiment saved Mussolini and the Fascists.

The new parliament elected in November quickly proved to be incapable of governing Italy. The three major parties were unable to form an effective governmental coalition, while the Socialists, who had now become the largest party, spoke theoretically of the need for revolution and alarmed conservatives who quickly associated them with Bolsheviks or Communists. Thousands of industrial and agricultural strikes in 1919 and 1920 created a climate of class warfare and continual violence. In 1920 and 1921, bands of armed Fascists called *squadristi* were formed and turned loose in attacks on Socialist offices and newspapers. Strikes by trade unionists and socialist workers and peasant leagues were broken up by force. Mussolini's Fascist movement began to gain support from middle-class industrialists fearful of working-class agitation and large landowners who objected to the agricultural strikes. Mussolini also perceived that Italians were angry over the failure of Italy to receive more territorial acquisitions after World War I. By 1922, Mussolini's movement began to mushroom as Mussolini's nationalist rhetoric and the middle-class fear of socialism, Communist revolution, and disorder made the Fascists attractive. On October 29, 1922, after Mussolini and the Fascists threatened to march on Rome if they were not given power, King Victor Emmanuel III (1900–1946) capitulated and made Mussolini prime minister of Italy.

MUSSOLINI AND THE ITALIAN FASCIST STATE

By 1926, Mussolini had established his Fascist dictatorship. Press laws gave the government the right to suspend any publications that fostered disrespect for the Catholic church, monarchy, or the state. The prime minister was made "Head of Government" with the power to legislate by decree. A police law empowered the police to arrest and confine anybody for both nonpolitical and political crimes without due process of law. In 1926, all antifascist parties were outlawed, and a secret police, known as the OVRA, was established. By the end of 1926, Mussolini ruled Italy as *Il Duce,* the leader.

Mussolini conceived of the Fascist state as totalitarian: "Fascism is totalitarian, and the Fascist State, the synthesis and unity of all values, interprets, develops and gives strength to the whole life of the people."[2] Mussolini did try to create a totalitarian apparatus for police surveillance and for controlling mass communications, but this machinery was not all that effective. Police activities in Italy were never as repressive, efficient, or savage as those of Nazi Germany. Likewise, the Italian Fascists' attempt to exercise control over all forms of mass media, including newspapers, radio, and cinema, in order to use propaganda as an instrument to integrate the masses into the state failed to achieve its major goals. Most commonly, Fascist propaganda was disseminated through simple slo-

◆ **Mussolini—The Dynamic *Duce*.** Mussolini worked hard to portray himself as a dynamic and virile leader. He created numerous poses for photographers that were supposed to reinforce this image of himself. Here Mussolini is shown leading his officers on a jog in full uniform.

gans, such as "Mussolini is always right," plastered on walls all over Italy.

Mussolini and the Fascists also attempted to mold Italians into a single-minded community by developing Fascist organizations. Because the secondary schools maintained considerable freedom from Fascist control, the regime relied more and more on the activities of Fascist youth organizations, known as the Young Fascists, to indoctrinate the young people of the nation in Fascist ideals. By 1939, about 6,800,000 children, teenagers, and young adults of both sexes, or 66 percent of the population between eight and eighteen, were enrolled in some kind of Fascist youth group. Activities for these groups included Saturday afternoon marching drills and calisthenics, seaside and mountain summer camps, and youth contests. Beginning in the 1930s, all male groups were given some kind of premilitary exercises to develop discipline and provide training for war. Results were mixed. Italian teenagers, who liked neither military training nor routine discipline of any kind, simply refused to attend Fascist youth group meetings on a regular basis.

The Fascist organizations hoped to create a new Italian, one who would be hard-working, physically fit, disciplined, intellectually sharp, and martially inclined. In practice, the Fascists largely reinforced traditional social attitudes in Italy, as is evident in their policies regarding women. The Fascists portrayed the family as the pillar of the state and women as the basic foundation of the family. "Woman into the home" became the Fascist slogan. Women were to be homemakers and baby producers, "their natural and fundamental mission in life," according to Mussolini, who viewed population growth as an indicator of national strength. Employment outside the home distracted women from conception. "It forms an independence and consequent physical and moral habits contrary to child bearing."[3] A practical consideration also underlay the Fascist attitude toward women. Eliminating women from the job market reduced male unemployment figures in the depression economy of the 1930s.

Despite the instruments of repression, the use of propaganda, and the creation of numerous Fascist organizations, Mussolini never really achieved the degree of totalitarian control accomplished in Hitler's Germany or Stalin's Soviet Union. Mussolini and the Fascist party never really destroyed the old power structure. Some institutions, including the armed forces and monarchy, were never absorbed into the Fascist state and mostly managed to maintain their independence. Mussolini had boasted that he would help workers and peasants, but instead he generally allied himself with the interests of industrialists and large landowners at the expense of the lower classes.

Even more indicative of Mussolini's compromise with the traditional institutions of Italy was his attempt to gain the support of the Catholic church. In the Lateran Accords of February 1929, Mussolini's regime recognized the sovereign independence of a small enclave of 109 acres within Rome, known as Vatican City, which had remained in the church's possession since unification in 1870; in return, the papacy recognized the Italian state. The Lateran Accords also guaranteed the church a large grant of money and recognized Catholicism as the "sole religion of the state." In return, the Catholic church urged Italians to support the Fascist regime.

In all areas of Italian life under Mussolini and the Fascists, there was a noticeable dichotomy between Fascist ideals and practice. The Italian Fascists promised much but actually delivered considerably less, and they were soon overshadowed by a much more powerful fascist movement to the north.

Hitler and Nazi Germany

In 1923, a small, south German rightist party, known as the Nazis, led by an obscure Austrian rabble-rouser named Adolf Hitler, created a stir when it tried to seize power in southern Germany. Although the attempt failed, Adolf Hitler and the Nazis achieved sudden national prominence. Within ten years, Hitler and the Nazis had taken over complete power.

WEIMAR GERMANY AND THE RISE OF THE NAZIS

After Germany's defeat in World War I, a German democratic state known as the Weimar Republic was established. From its beginnings, the Weimar Republic was

CHRONOLOGY

Fascist Italy

Creation of *Fascio di Combattimento*	1919
Squadristi violence	1920–1921
Mussolini is made prime minister	1922 (October 29)
Establishment of Fascist dictatorship	1925–1926
Lateran Accords with Catholic church	1929

plagued by a series of problems. The republic had no truly outstanding political leaders. In 1925, Paul von Hindenburg, the World War I military hero, was elected president. Hindenburg was a traditional military man, monarchist in sentiment, who at heart was not in favor of the republic. The young republic also suffered politically from attempted uprisings and attacks from both the left and right.

The Weimar Republic also faced serious economic difficulties. Germany experienced runaway inflation in 1922 and 1923, and widows, orphans, the retired elderly, army officers, teachers, civil servants, and others who lived on fixed incomes all watched their monthly stipends become worthless or their lifetime savings disappear. Their economic losses increasingly pushed the middle class to the rightist parties that were hostile to the republic. To make matters worse, after a period of prosperity from 1924 to 1929, Germany faced the Great Depression. Unemployment increased to 4.38 million by December 1930. The depression paved the way for social discontent, fear, and extremist parties. The political, economic, and social problems of the Weimar Republic provided an environment in which Adolf Hitler and the Nazis were able to rise to power.

Born on April 20, 1889, Adolf Hitler was the son of an Austrian customs official. He was a total failure in secondary school and eventually made his way to Vienna to become an artist. In Vienna, Hitler established the basic ideas of an ideology from which he never deviated for the rest of his life. At the core of Hitler's ideas was racism, especially his anti-Semitism. His hatred of the Jews lasted to the very end of his life. Hitler had also become an extreme German nationalist who had learned from the mass politics of Vienna how political parties could effectively use propaganda and terror. Finally, in his Viennese years, Hitler also came to a firm belief in the need for struggle, which he saw as the "granite foundation of the world."

At the end of World War I, after four years of service on the Western Front, Hitler went to Munich and decided to enter politics. He joined the obscure German Workers' Party, one of a number of right-wing extreme nationalist parties in Munich. By the summer of 1921, Hitler had assumed total control over the party, which he renamed the National Socialist German Workers' Party (NSDAP), or Nazi for short. His idea was that the party's name would distinguish the Nazis from the socialist parties while gaining support from both working-class and nationalist circles. Hitler worked assiduously to develop the party into a mass political movement with flags, party badges, uniforms, its own newspaper, and its own police force or party militia known as the SA, the *Sturmabteilung*, or Storm

Troops. The SA was used to defend the party in meeting halls and break up the meetings of other parties. Hitler's own oratorical skills were largely responsible for attracting an increasing number of followers. By 1923, the party had grown from its early hundreds into a membership of 55,000 with 15,000 SA members.

Overconfident, Hitler staged an armed uprising against the government in Munich in November 1923. The so-called Beer Hall Putsch was quickly crushed, and Hitler was sentenced to prison. During his brief stay in jail, Hitler wrote *Mein Kampf* (*My Struggle*), an autobiographical account of his movement and its underlying ideology. Extreme German nationalism, virulent anti-Semitism, and vicious anticommunism are linked by a Social Darwinian theory of struggle that stresses the right of superior nations to *Lebensraum* (living space) through expansion and the right of superior individuals to secure authoritarian leadership over the masses.

During his imprisonment, Hitler also came to the realization that the Nazis would have to come to power by constitutional means, not by overthrowing the Weimar Republic. This implied the formation of a mass political party that would actively compete for votes with the other political parties. After his release from prison, Hitler worked to build such a party. He reorganized the Nazi party on a regional basis and expanded it to all parts of Germany. By 1929, the Nazi party had a national party organization. It also grew from 27,000 members in 1925 to 178,000 by the end of 1929. Especially noticeable was the youthfulness of the regional, district, and branch leaders of the Nazi organization. Many were between the ages of twenty-five and thirty and were fiercely committed to Hitler because he gave them the kind of active politics they sought. Rather than democratic debate, they wanted brawls in beer halls, enthusiastic speeches, and comradeship in the building of a new Germany. One new, young Nazi member expressed his excitement about the party:

> For me this was the start of a completely new life. There was only one thing in the world for me and that was service in the movement. All my thoughts were centred on the movement. I could talk only politics. I was no longer aware of anything else. At the time I was a promising athlete; I was very keen on sport, and it was going to be my career. But I had to give this up too. My only interest was agitation and propaganda.[4]

Such youthful enthusiasm gave the Nazi movement an aura of a "young man's movement" and a sense of dynamism that the other parties could not match.

By 1932, the Nazi party had 800,000 members and had become the largest party in the Reichstag. No doubt, Germany's economic difficulties were a crucial factor in the Nazi rise to power. Unemployment rose dramatically, from 4.35 million in 1931 to 6 million by the winter of 1932. The economic and psychological impact of the Great Depression made extremist parties more attractive. The Nazis were especially effective in developing modern electioneering techniques. In their election campaigns, party members pitched their themes to the needs and fears of different social groups. In working-class districts, for example, the Nazis attacked international high finance, but in middle-class neighborhoods, they exploited fears of a Communist revolution and its threat to private property. At the same time that the Nazis made blatant appeals to class interests, they were denouncing conflicts of interest and maintaining that they stood above classes and parties. Hitler, in particular, claimed to stand above all differences and promised to create a new Germany free of class differences and party infighting. His appeal to national pride, national honor, and traditional militarism struck chords of emotion in his listeners.

Increasingly, the right-wing elites of Germany, the industrial magnates, landed aristocrats, military establishment, and higher bureaucrats began to see Hitler as the man who had the mass support to establish a right-wing, authoritarian regime that would save Germany and their privileged positions from a Communist takeover. Under pressure, President Hindenburg agreed to allow Hitler to become chancellor (on January 30, 1933) and form a new government.

Within two months, Hitler had laid the foundations for the Nazis' complete control over Germany. On the day after a fire broke out in the Reichstag building (February 27), supposedly caused by the Communists, Hitler convinced President Hindenburg to issue a decree that gave the government emergency powers. It suspended all basic rights of the citizens for the full duration of the emergency, thus enabling the Nazis to arrest and imprison anyone without redress. The crowning step of Hitler's "legal seizure" of power came on March 23 when a two-thirds vote of the Reichstag passed the Enabling Act, which empowered the government to dispense with constitutional forms for four years while it issued laws that would deal with the country's problems. The Enabling Act provided the legal basis for Hitler's subsequent acts. He no longer needed either the Reichstag or President Hindenburg. In effect, Hitler became a dictator appointed by the parliamentary body itself.

◆ **Hitler and the Blood Flag Ritual.** In developing his mass political movement, Adolf Hitler used ritualistic ceremonies as a means of binding party members to his own person. Hitler is shown here touching the "blood flag," which had supposedly been stained with the blood of Nazis killed during the Beer Hall Putsch, to an SS banner while the SS standard-bearer made a "blood oath" of allegiance: "I vow to remain true to my Führer, Adolf Hitler. I bind myself to carry out all orders conscientiously and without reluctance. Standards and flags shall be sacred to me."

Nazi Germany

Hitler as Munich politician	1919–1923
Beer Hall Putsch	1923
Election of Hindenburg as president	1925
Hitler is made chancellor	1933 (January 30)
Reichstag fire	1933 (February 27)
Enabling Act	1933 (March 23)
Hindenburg dies; Hitler as sole ruler	1934 (August 2)
Nuremberg laws	1935
Kristallnacht	1938 (November 9–10)

With their new source of power, the Nazis acted quickly to enforce *Gleichschaltung*, or the coordination of all institutions under Nazi control. The civil service was purged of Jews and democratic elements, concentration camps were established for opponents of the new regime, the autonomy of the federal states was eliminated, trade unions were dissolved, and all political parties except the Nazis were abolished. By the end of the summer of 1933, within seven months of being appointed chancellor, Hitler and the Nazis had established the foundations for a totalitarian state. When Hindenburg died on August 2, 1934, the office of Reich president was abolished, and Hitler became sole ruler of Germany. Public officials and soldiers were all required to take a personal oath of loyalty to Hitler as the "Führer of the German Reich and people."

THE NAZI STATE, 1933–1939

Having smashed the parliamentary state, Hitler now felt the real task was at hand: to develop the "total state." Hitler's aims had not been simply power for power's sake; he had larger ideological goals. The development of an Aryan racial state that would dominate Europe and possibly the world for generations to come required a movement in which the German people would be actively involved, not passively cowed by force. Hitler stated:

> We must develop organizations in which an individual's entire life can take place. Then every activity and every need of every individual will be regulated by the collectiv-

ity represented by the party. There is no longer any arbitrary will, there are no longer any free realms in which the individual belongs to himself. . . . The time of personal happiness is over.[5]

The Nazis pursued the creation of this totalitarian state in a variety of ways.

Mass demonstrations and spectacles were employed to integrate the German nation into a collective fellowship and to mobilize it as an instrument for Hitler's policies (see the box on p. 569). These mass demonstrations, especially the Nuremberg party rallies that were held every September, combined the symbolism of a religious service with the merriment of a popular amusement. They had great appeal and usually evoked mass enthusiasm and excitement.

Some features of the state apparatus of Hitler's "total state" seem contradictory. One usually thinks of Nazi Germany as having an all-powerful government that maintained absolute control and order. In truth, Nazi Germany was the scene of almost constant personal and institutional conflict, which resulted in administrative chaos. In matters such as foreign policy, education, and economics, parallel government and party bureaucracies competed with each other over spheres of influence. Incessant struggle characterized relationships within the party, within the state, and between party and state. By fostering rivalry within the party and between party and state, Hitler became the ultimate decision maker.

In the economic sphere, Hitler and the Nazis also established control. Although the regime pursued the use of public works projects and "pump-priming" grants to private construction firms to foster employment and end the depression, there is little doubt that rearmament was a far more important contributor to solving the unemployment problem. Unemployment dropped to 2.6 million in 1934 and less than 500,000 in 1937. The regime claimed full credit for solving Germany's economic woes, an important factor that led many Germans to accept the new regime, despite its excesses.

For those who needed coercion, the Nazi total state had its instruments of terror and repression. Especially important was the SS. Originally created as Hitler's personal bodyguard, the SS, under the direction of Heinrich Himmler (1900–1945), came to control all of the regular and secret police forces. Himmler and the SS functioned on the basis of two principles: terror and ideology. Terror included the instruments of repression and murder: the secret police, criminal police, concentration camps, and later the execution squads and death camps for the extermination of the Jews. For Himmler, the primary goal of

⋟ Propaganda and Mass Meetings in Nazi Germany ⋞

Propaganda and mass rallies were two of the chief instruments that Hitler used to prepare the German people for the tasks he set before them. In the first selection, taken from Mein Kampf, Hitler explains the psychological importance of mass meetings in creating support for a political movement. In the second excerpt, taken from his speech to a crowd at Nuremberg, he describes the kind of mystical bond he hoped to create through his mass rallies.

Adolf Hitler, *Mein Kampf*

The mass meeting is also necessary for the reason that in it the individual, who at first, while becoming a supporter of a young movement, feels lonely and easily succumbs to the fear of being alone, for the first time gets the picture of a larger community, which in most people has a strengthening, encouraging effect. . . . When from his little workshop or big factory, in which he feels very small, he steps for the first time into a mass meeting and has thousands and thousands of people of the same opinions around him, when, as a seeker, he is swept away by three or four thousand others into the mighty effect of suggestive intoxication and enthusiasm, when the visible success and agreement of thousands confirm to him the rightness of the new doctrine and for the first time arouse doubt in the truth of his previous conviction—then he himself has succumbed to the magic influence of what we designate as "mass suggestion." The will, the longing, and also the power of thousands are accumulated in every individual. The man who enters such a meeting doubting and wavering leaves it inwardly reinforced: he has become a link in the community.

Adolf Hitler, Speech at the Nuremberg Party Rally, 1936

Do we not feel once again in this hour the miracle that brought us together? Once you heard the voice of a man, and it struck deep into your hearts; it awakened you, and you followed this voice. Year after year you went after it, though him who had spoken you never even saw. You heard only a voice, and you followed it. When we meet each other here, the wonder of our coming together fills us all. Not everyone of you sees me, and I do not see everyone of you. But I feel you, and you feel me. It is the belief in our people that has made us small men great, that has made us poor men rich, that has made brave and courageous men out of us wavering, spiritless, timid folk; this belief made us see our road when we were astray; it joined us together into one whole! . . . You come, that . . . you may, once in a while, gain the feeling that now we are together; we are with him and he with us, and we are now Germany!

---

the SS was to further the Aryan master race. SS members, who constituted a carefully chosen elite, were thoroughly indoctrinated in racial ideology.

Other institutions, such as the Catholic and Protestant churches, primary and secondary schools, and universities, were also brought under the control of the Nazi total state. Nazi professional organizations and leagues were formed for civil servants, teachers, women, farmers, doctors, and lawyers. Because the early indoctrination of the youth would create the foundation for a strong totalitarian state for the future, youth organizations, the *Hitler Jugend* (Hitler Youth) and its female counterpart, the *Bund deutscher Mädel* (League of German Maidens), were given special attention. The oath required of Hitler Youth members demonstrates the degree of dedication expected of youth in the Nazi state: "In the presence of this blood banner, which represents our Führer, I swear to devote all my energies and my strength to the savior of our country, Adolf Hitler. I am willing and ready to give up my life for him, so help me God."

The creation of the Nazi total state also had an impact on women. The Nazi attitude toward women was largely determined by ideological considerations. Women played a crucial role in the Aryan racial state as bearers of the children who would bring about the triumph of the Aryan race. To the Nazis, the differences between men and women were quite natural. Men were warriors and political leaders while women were destined to be wives and mothers.

Nazi ideas determined employment opportunities for women. The Nazis hoped to drive women out of heavy industry or other jobs that might hinder women from bearing healthy children, as well as certain professions, including university teaching, law, and medicine, which were considered inappropriate for women, especially married women. The Nazis encouraged women to pursue professional occupations that had direct practical application, such as social work and nursing. In addition to restrictive legislation against females, the Nazi regime pushed its campaign against working women with such poster slogans as "Get ahold of pots and pans and broom and you'll sooner find a groom!"

The Nazi total state was intended to be an Aryan racial state. From its beginning, the Nazi party reflected the strong anti-Semitic beliefs of Adolf Hitler. Once in power, the Nazis translated anti-Semitic ideas into anti-Semitic policies. In September 1935, the Nazis announced new racial laws at the annual party rally in Nuremberg. These "Nuremberg laws" excluded German Jews from German citizenship, forbade marriages and extramarital relations between Jews and German citizens, and essentially separated Jews from the Germans politically, socially, and legally. They were the natural extension of Hitler's stress on the creation of a pure Aryan race.

Another, considerably more violent phase of anti-Jewish activity took place in 1938 and 1939; it was initiated on November 9–10, 1938, the infamous *Kristallnacht*, or night of shattered glass. The assassination of a third secretary in the German embassy in Paris by a Polish Jew became the occasion for a Nazi-led destructive rampage against the Jews in which synagogues were burned, 7,000 Jewish businesses were destroyed, and at least 100 Jews were killed. Moreover, 30,000 Jewish males were rounded up and sent to concentration camps. Under the direction of the SS, Jews were now encouraged to "emigrate from Germany."

Soviet Russia

Yet another example of totalitarianism was to be found in Soviet Russia. The civil war in Russia had taken an enormous toll of life. Drought, which caused a great famine between 1920 and 1922, claimed as many as 5 million lives. Industrial collapse paralleled the agricultural disaster. By 1921, industrial output was only 20 percent of its 1913 levels. Russia was exhausted. As Leon Trotsky said, "the collapse of the productive forces surpassed anything of the kind that history had ever seen. The country, and the government with it, were at the very edge of the abyss."[6]

In March 1921, Lenin pulled Russia back from the abyss by establishing his New Economic Policy (NEP). Lenin's New Economic Policy was a modified version of the old capitalist system. Peasants were now allowed to sell their produce openly while retail stores as well as small industries that employed fewer than twenty employees could now operate under private ownership;

CHRONOLOGY

The Soviet Union

New Economic Policy begins	1921
Death of Lenin	1924
Trotsky is expelled from the Communist Party	1927
First five-year plan begins	1928
Stalin's dictatorship is established	1929
Stalin's purge	1936–1938

heavy industry, banking, and mines remained in the hands of the government. Already by 1922, a revived market and good harvest had brought an end to famine; Soviet agriculture climbed to 75 percent of its prewar level. Industry, especially state-owned heavy industry, fared less well and continued to stagnate. Overall, the NEP had saved Communist Russia from complete economic disaster even though Lenin and other leading Communists intended it to be only a temporary, tactical retreat from the goals of Communism.

Lenin's death in 1924 inaugurated a struggle for power among the seven members of the Politburo, the institution that had become the leading organ of the party. The Politburo was severely divided over the future direction of Soviet Russia. The Left, led by Leon Trotsky, wanted to end the NEP and launch Russia on the path of rapid industrialization. This same group wanted to carry the revolution on, believing that the survival of the Russian Revolution ultimately depended on the spread of communism abroad. Another group in the Politburo, called the Right, rejected the cause of world revolution and wanted instead to concentrate on constructing a socialist state in Russia.

These ideological divisions were underscored by an intense personal rivalry between Leon Trotsky and Joseph Stalin. In 1924, Trotsky held the post of commissar of war and was the leading spokesman for the Left in the Politburo. Joseph Stalin (1879–1953) was content to hold the dull bureaucratic job of party general secretary. But Stalin was a good organizer, and the other members of the Politburo soon found that the position of party secretary was really the most important in the party hierarchy. Stalin used his post as party general secretary to gain control of the Communist Party. Trotsky was expelled from the party in 1927. By 1929, Stalin had succeeded in eliminating the Old Bolsheviks of the revolutionary era from the Politburo and establishing a dictatorship so powerful that the Russian tsars of old would have been envious.

THE STALIN ERA, 1929–1939

The Stalinist era marked the beginning of an economic, social, and political revolution that was more sweeping in its results than the revolutions of 1917. Stalin made a significant shift in economic policy in 1928 when he launched his first five-year plan. Its real goal was nothing less than the transformation of Russia from an agricultural country into an industrial state virtually overnight. Instead of consumer goods, the first five-year plan emphasized maximum production of capital goods and armaments and succeeded in quadrupling the production of heavy machinery and doubling oil production. Between 1928 and 1937, during the first two five-year plans, steel production increased from four to eighteen million tons per year while hard coal output went from 36 to 128 million tons. At the same time, new industrial cities, located near iron ore and coal deposits, sprang up overnight in the Urals and Siberia.

The social and political costs of industrialization were enormous. While the industrial labor force increased by millions between 1932 and 1940, total investment in housing actually declined after 1929, with the result that millions of workers and their families lived in pitiful conditions. Real wages in industry also declined by 43 percent between 1928 and 1940 while strict laws limited workers' freedom of movement. To inspire and pacify the workers, government propaganda stressed the need for sacrifice to create the new socialist state.

Rapid industrialization was accompanied by an equally rapid collectivization of agriculture. Its goal was to eliminate private farms and push people into collective farms (see the box on p. 572). Strong resistance to his plans from peasants who hoarded crops and killed livestock only led him to step up the program. By 1930, ten million peasant households had been collectivized; by 1934, Russia's 26 million family farms had been collectivized into 250,000 units. This was done at tremendous cost, since the hoarding of food and the slaughter of livestock produced widespread famine. Stalin himself is supposed to have told Winston Churchill during World War II that 10 million peasants died in the artificially created famines of 1932 and 1933. The only concession Stalin made to the peasants was to allow each collective farm worker to have one tiny, privately owned garden plot.

Stalin's program of rapid industrialization entailed additional costs as well. To achieve his goals, Stalin strengthened the party bureaucracy under his control. Those who resisted were sent into forced labor camps in Siberia. Stalin's desire for sole control of decision making also led to purges of the Old Bolsheviks, army officers, diplomats, union officials, party members, intellectuals, and numerous ordinary citizens. Estimates are that between 1936 and 1938, eight million Russians were

✦ **Stalin Signs a Death Warrant.** Terror played an important role in the authoritarian system established by Joseph Stalin. In this photograph, Stalin is shown signing what is supposedly a death warrant in 1933. As the terror increased in the late 1930s, Stalin signed such lists everyday.

The Formation of Collective Farms

Accompanying the rapid industrialization of the Soviet Union was the collectivization of agriculture, a feat that involved nothing less than transforming Russia's 26 million family farms into 250,000 collective farms (kolkhozes). This selection provides a firsthand account of how the process worked.

Max Belov, *The History of a Collective Farm*

General collectivization in our village was brought about in the following manner: Two representatives of the [Communist] Party arrived in the village. All the inhabitants were summoned by the ringing of the church bell to a meeting at which the policy of general collectivization was announced. . . . The upshot was that although the meeting lasted two days, from the viewpoint of the Party representatives nothing was accomplished.

After this setback the Party representatives divided the village into two sections and worked each one separately. Two more officials were sent to reinforce the first two. A meeting of our section of the village was held in a stable which had previously belonged to a kulak. The meeting dragged on until dark. Suddenly someone threw a brick at the lamp, and in the dark the peasants began to beat the Party representatives who jumped out the window and escaped from the village barely alive. The following day seven people were arrested. The militia was called in and stayed in the village until the peasants, realizing their helplessness, calmed down. . . .

By the end of 1930 there were two kolkhozes in our village. Though at first these collectives embraced at most only 70 percent of the peasant households, in the months that followed they gradually absorbed more and more of them.

In these kolkhozes the great bulk of the land was held and worked communally, but each peasant household owned a house of some sort, a small plot of ground and perhaps some livestock. All the members of the kolkhoz were required to work on the kolkhoz a certain number of days each month; the rest of the time they were allowed to work on their own holdings. They derived their income partly from what they grew on their garden strips and partly from their work in the kolkhoz.

When the harvest was over, and after the farm had met its obligations to the state and to various special funds (for instance, seed, etc.) and had sold on the market whatever undesignated produce was left, the remaining produce and the farm's monetary income were divided among the kolkhoz members according to the number of "labor days" each one had contributed to the farm's work. . . . It was in 1930 that the kolkhoz members first received their portions out of the "communal kettle." After they had received their earnings, at the rate of 1 kilogram of grain and 55 kopecks per labor day, one of them remarked, "You will live, but you will be very, very thin."

In the spring of 1931 a tractor worked the fields of the kolkhoz for the first time. The tractor was "capable of plowing every kind of hard soil and virgin soil," as Party representatives told us at the meeting in celebration of its arrival. The peasants did not then know that these "steel horses" would carry away a good part of the harvest in return for their work. . . .

By late 1932 more than 80 percent of the peasant households . . . had been collectivized. . . . That year the peasants harvested a good crop and had hopes that the calculations would work out to their advantage and would help strengthen them economically. These hopes were in vain. The kolkhoz workers received only 200 grams of flour per labor day for the first half of the year; the remaining grain, including the seed fund, was taken by the government. The peasants were told that industrialization of the country, then in full swing, demanded grain and sacrifices from them.

arrested; millions were sent to Siberian forced labor camps, from which they never returned.

The Stalin era also reversed much of the permissive social legislation of the early 1920s. Advocating complete equality of rights for women, the Communists had made divorce and abortion easy to obtain while also encouraging women to work outside the home and liberate themselves sexually. After Stalin came to power, the family was praised as a miniature collective in which parents were responsible for inculcating values of duty, discipline, and hard work. Abortion was outlawed, and divorced fathers who did not support their children were fined heavily. The new divorce law of June 1936 imposed fines for repeated divorces.

Authoritarian States

There were a number of other states in Europe that were not totalitarian but did possess conservative authoritarian governments. These states adopted some of the trappings of totalitarian states, especially their wide police powers, but their greatest concern was not the creation of a mass movement aimed at the establishment of a new kind of society, but rather the defense of the existing social order. Consequently, the authoritarian states tended to limit the participation of the masses and were content with passive obedience rather than active involvement in the goals of the regime.

Nowhere had the map of Europe been more drastically altered by World War I than in eastern Europe. The new states of Austria, Poland, Czechoslovakia, and Yugoslavia (known as the kingdom of the Serbs, Croats, and Slovenes until 1929) adopted parliamentary systems while the preexisting kingdoms of Romania and Bulgaria gained new parliamentary constitutions in 1920. Greece became a republic in 1924. Hungary's government was parliamentary in form, but controlled by its landed aristocrats. At the beginning of the 1920s, political democracy seemed well established, but almost everywhere in eastern Europe, parliamentary governments soon gave way to authoritarian regimes.

Several problems helped to create this situation. Eastern European states had little tradition of liberalism or parliamentary politics and no substantial middle class to support them. Then, too, these states were largely rural and agrarian in character. Much of the land was still dominated by large landowners who feared the growth of agrarian peasant parties with their schemes for land redistribution. Ethnic conflicts also threatened to tear these countries apart. Fearful of land reform, agrarian upheaval, and ethnic conflict, powerful landowners and the churches looked to authoritarian governments to maintain the old system. Only Czechoslovakia, with its substantial middle class, liberal tradition, and strong industrial base, maintained its political democracy.

In Spain, political democracy also failed to survive. Led by General Francisco Franco (1892–1975), Spanish military forces revolted against the democratic government in 1936 and inaugurated a brutal and bloody civil war that lasted three years. Foreign intervention complicated the Spanish Civil War. Franco's forces were aided by arms, money, and men from the fascist regimes of Italy and Germany while the government was assisted by 40,000 foreign volunteers and trucks, planes, tanks, and military advisers from the Soviet Union. After Franco's forces captured Madrid on March 28, 1939, the Spanish Civil War finally came to an end. General Francisco Franco soon established a dictatorship that favored large landowners, businessmen, and the Catholic clergy, and was yet another example of a traditional, conservative, authoritarian regime.

The Expansion of Mass Culture and Mass Leisure

Technological innovations continued to have profound effects on European society. Nowhere is this more evident than in mass culture and mass leisure. The mass distribution of commercialized popular forms of entertainment had a profound effect on European society.

Radio and Movies

A series of technological inventions in the late nineteenth century had prepared the way for a revolution in mass communications. Especially important was Marconi's discovery of "wireless" radio waves. But it was not until June 16, 1920, that a radio broadcast (of a concert by soprano Nellie Melba from London) for a mass audience was attempted. Permanent broadcasting facilities were then constructed in the United States, Europe, and Japan during 1921 and 1922, while mass production of radios (receiving sets) also began. In 1926, when the British Broadcasting Corporation (BBC) was made into a public corporation, there were 2,200,000 radios in Great Britain. By the end of the 1930s there were nine million. The technical foundation for motion pictures had already been developed in the 1890s when short moving pictures were produced as novelties for music halls. Shortly before World War I, full-length features, such as the Italian film *Quo Vadis* and the American film *Birth of a Nation*, became available and made it apparent that cinema had created a new form of mass entertainment.

Mass forms of communication and entertainment were, of course, not new, but the increased size of mass audiences and the ability of radio and cinema, unlike the printed word, to provide a different kind of immediate experience, did add new dimensions to mass culture. Film, for example, had propaganda potential, a possibility not lost on Joseph Goebbels (1897–1945), the propaganda minister of Nazi Germany. Believing that film constituted one of the "most modern and scientific means of influencing the masses," Goebbels created a special film section in his Propaganda Ministry and encouraged the production of both documentaries and popular feature films that carried the Nazi message. *The Triumph of the Will*, for example, was a documentary of the 1934 Nuremberg party rally that conveyed forcefully to viewers the power of Nazism.

Mass Leisure

Mass leisure activities had developed at the turn of the century, but new work patterns after World War I expanded dramatically the amount of free time available to take advantage of them. By 1920, the eight-hour day had become the norm for many office and factory workers in northern and western Europe.

Professional sporting events for mass audiences became an important aspect of mass leisure. Attendance at association football (soccer) games increased dramatically while the inauguration of the World Cup contest in 1930 added to the nationalistic rivalries that began to surround such mass sporting events. Increased attendance also made the 1920s and 1930s a great era of stadium-building. The Germans built a stadium in Berlin for the 1936 Olympics that seated 140,000 people.

Travel opportunities also added new dimensions to mass leisure activities. The military use of aircraft during World War I helped to improve planes and make civilian air travel a reality. The first regular international mail service began in 1919, and regular passenger service soon followed. Although air travel remained the preserve of the wealthy or the adventurous, trains, buses, and private cars made excursions to beaches or holiday resorts more and more popular and possible. Beaches were increasingly mobbed by crowds of people from all social classes.

Mass leisure provided totalitarian regimes with new ways to control their populations. The Nazi regime created the *Kraft durch Freude* (Strength Through Joy) program, whose purpose was to coordinate the free time of the working class by offering a variety of leisure time activities, including concerts, operas, films, guided tours, and sporting events. Especially popular were the inexpensive vacations, essentially the modern package tour. This could be a cruise to Scandinavia or the Mediterranean or, more likely for workers, a shorter trip to various sites in Germany. Essentially, the *Kraft durch Freude* enabled the German government to provide, but also to supervise, recreational activities. By doing so, the state imposed new rules and regulations on previously spontaneous activities, thus breaking down old group solidarities and enabling these groups to be guided by the goals of the state.

Cultural and Intellectual Trends in the Interwar Years

The artistic and intellectual innovations of the pre–World War I period, which had shocked many Europeans, had been the preserve primarily of a small group of avant-garde artists and intellectuals. In the 1920s and 1930s, they became more widespread as intellectuals continued to work out the implications of the ideas developed before 1914. But what made the prewar avant-garde culture acceptable in the 1920s and the 1930s? Perhaps most important was the impact of World War I.

Four years of devastating war left many Europeans with a profound sense of despair and disillusionment. To many people, the experiences of World War I seemed to confirm the prewar avant-garde belief that human beings were really violent and irrational animals who were incapable of creating a sane and rational world. The Great Depression, as well as the growth of fascist movements based on violence and the degradation of individual rights, only added to the uncertainties generated by World War I. The crisis of confidence in Western civilization indeed ran deep. Political, economic, and social uncertainties were paralleled by intellectual uncertainties, which were quite evident in the cultural and intellectual achievements of the interwar years.

Nightmares and New Visions: Art and Music

Postwar artistic trends were largely a working out of the implications of prewar developments. Abstract expressionism, for example, became ever more popular as many pioneering artists of the early twentieth century matured between the two world wars. In addition, prewar fascination with the absurd and the unconscious contents of the mind seemed even more appropriate after the nightmare landscapes of World War I battlefronts. This gave rise to both the Dada movement and Surrealism.

Dadaism attempted to enshrine the purposelessness of life (see the box on p. 576). Revolted by the insanity of life, the Dadaists tried to give it expression by creating anti-art. The 1918 Berlin Dada Manifesto maintained that "Dada is the international expression of our times, the great rebellion of artistic movements." In the hands of Hannah Höch (1889–1978), however, Dada became an instrument to comment on women's roles in the new mass culture. In a number of works, she created positive images of the modern woman and expressed a keen interest in new freedoms for women.

Perhaps more important as an artistic movement was Surrealism, which sought a reality beyond the material, sensible world and found it in the world of the unconscious through the portrayal of fantasies, dreams, or nightmares. Employing logic to portray the illogical, the Surrealists created disturbing and evocative images. The Spaniard Salvador Dalí (1904–1989) became the high priest of Surrealism and in his mature phase became a master of representational Surrealism. In *The Persistence of Memory*, Dalí portrayed recognizable objects that have nevertheless been divorced from their normal context. By placing these objects into unrecognizable relationships, Dalí created a disturbing world in which the irrational had become tangible.

The move to functionalism in modern architecture also became more widespread in the 1920s and 1930s. First conceived near the end of the nineteenth century, functionalism meant that buildings should be "functional" or useful, fulfilling the purpose for which they were constructed. Art and engineering were to be unified, and all unnecessary ornamentation was to be stripped away. Especially important in the spread of functionalism was the Bauhaus school, founded in 1919 at Weimar, Germany, by the Berlin architect Walter Gropius. The Bauhaus teaching staff consisted of architects, artists, and designers who worked together to combine the study of fine arts (painting and sculpture) with the applied arts (printing, weaving, and furniture making).

The postwar acceptance of modern art forms was by no means universal. Many traditionalists denounced what they considered the degeneracy and decadence in the arts. This was especially evident in the totalitarian state of Nazi Germany. In the 1920s, Weimar Germany was one of the chief European centers for modern arts and sciences. Hitler and the Nazis rejected modern art as "degenerate" or "Jewish" art. In 1937, Hitler said: "The people regarded this art [modern art] as the outcome of an impudent and unashamed arrogance or of a simply shocking lack of skill; it felt that . . . these achievements which might have been produced by untalented children of from eight to ten years old could never be valued as an expression of our own times or of the German future."[7] Hitler and the Nazis believed that they had laid the foundation for a new and genuine German art, which would glorify the strong, the healthy, and the heroic—all of which were supposedly attributes of the Aryan race.

At the beginning of the twentieth century, a revolution in music parallel to the revolution in art had begun with the work of Igor Stravinsky. But Stravinksy still

◆ **Hannah Höch, *Cut with the Kitchen Knife Dada through the Last Weimar Beer Belly Cultural Epoch of Germany*.** Hannah Höch, a prominent figure in the postwar Dada movement, used photomontage to create images that reflected on women's issues. In *Cut with the Kitchen Knife*, she combined pictures of German political leaders with sports stars, Dada artists, and scenes from urban life. One major theme emerged: the confrontation between the anti-Dada world of German political leaders and the Dada world of revolutionary ideals. Höch associated women with Dada and the new world.

wrote music in a definite key. The Viennese composer Arnold Schönberg (1874–1951) began to experiment with a radically new style by creating musical pieces in which tonality is completely abandoned, a system that he called atonic music.

The Search for the Unconscious

The interest in the unconscious, evident in Surrealism, was also apparent in the development of new literary techniques that emerged in the 1920s. One of its most apparent manifestations was in a "stream of consciousness"

The Voice of Dadaism

The Dadaists attempted to give expression to what they saw as the meaninglessness and absurdity of life. In this excerpt, Tristan Tzara (1896–1945), a Romanian-French poet and one of the founders of Dadaism, expressed the Dadaist contempt for the Western tradition.

Tristan Tzara, "Lecture on Dada," 1922

I know that you have come here today to hear explanations. Well, don't expect to hear any explanations about Dada. You explain to me why you exist. You haven't the faintest idea. . . .

The acts of life have no beginning or end. Everything happens in a completely idiotic way. That is why everything is alike. Simplicity is called Dada. . . .

The beginnings of Dada were not the beginnings of an art, but of a disgust. Disgust with the magnificence of philosophers who for 3,000 years have been explaining everything to us (what for?), disgust with the pretensions of these artists—God's-representatives-on-earth, . . . disgust with a false form of domination and restriction *en masse*, that accentuates rather than appeases man's instinct of domination, disgust with . . . the false prophets who are nothing but a front for the interests of money, pride, disease.

Dada is a state of mind. . . . Dada applies itself to everything, and yet is nothing, it is the point where the yes and the no and all the opposites meet, not solemnly in the castles of human philosophies, but very simply at street corners, like dogs and grasshoppers.

Like everything in life, Dada is useless.

Dada is without pretension, as life should be.

---

technique in which the writer presented an interior monologue or a report of the innermost thoughts of each character. The most famous example of this genre was written by the Irish exile James Joyce (1882–1941). His *Ulysses*, published in 1922, told the story of one day in the life of ordinary people in Dublin by following the flow of their inner dialogue.

The German writer Hermann Hesse (1877–1962) dealt with the unconscious in a considerably different fashion. His novels reflected the influence of new psychological theories and Eastern religions and focused, among other things, on the spiritual loneliness of modern human beings in a mechanized urban society. *Demian* was a psychoanalytic study of incest while *Steppenwolf* mirrored the psychological confusion of modern existence. Hesse's novels had a large impact on German youth in the 1920s. He won the Nobel prize for literature in 1946.

The growing concern with the unconscious also led to greater popular interest in psychology. The full impact of Sigmund Freud's thought was not felt until after World War I. The 1920s witnessed a worldwide acceptance of his ideas. Freudian terms, such as *unconscious, repression, id,* and *ego,* entered the popular vocabulary. Popularization of Freud's ideas led to the widespread misconception that an uninhibited sex life was necessary for a healthy mental life. Despite such misperceptions, psychoanalysis did develop into a major profession, especially in the United States. But Freud's ideas did not go unchallenged, even by his own pupils. One of the most prominent challenges came from Carl Jung.

A disciple of Freud, Carl Jung (1856–1961) came to believe that Freud's theories were too narrow and based on Freud's own personal biases. Jung's study of dreams—his own and others—led him to diverge sharply from Freud. Whereas for Freud the unconscious was the seat of repressed desires or appetites, for Jung, it was an opening to deep spiritual needs and ever-greater vistas for humans.

Jung viewed the unconscious as twofold: a "personal unconscious" and a "collective unconscious," which existed at a deeper level of the unconscious. The collective unconscious was the repository of memories that all human beings share and consisted of archetypes, mental forms or images that appear in dreams. The archetypes are common to all people and have a special energy that creates myths, religions, and philosophies. To Jung, the archetypes proved that mind was only in part personal or individual because their origin was buried so far in the past that they seemed to have no human source. Their function was to bring the original mind of humans into a new, higher state of consciousness.

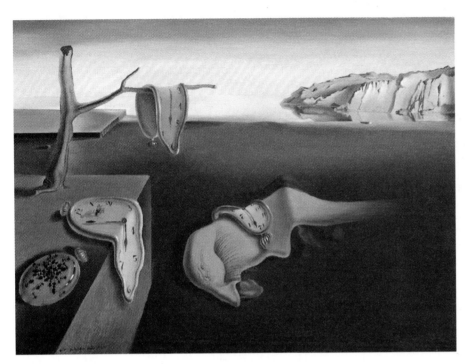

◆ **Salvador Dali, *The Persistence of Memory*, 1931.** Surrealism was another important artistic movement between the wars. Influenced by the theories of Freudian psychology, Surrealists sought to reveal the world of the unconscious, or the "greater reality" that they believed existed beyond the world of physical appearances. As is evident in this painting, Salvador Dalí sought to portray the world of dreams by painting recognizable objects in unrecognizable relationships.

The "Heroic Age of Physics"

The prewar revolution in physics initiated by Max Planck and Albert Einstein continued in the interwar period. In fact, Ernest Rutherford (1871–1937), one of the physicists responsible for demonstrating that the atom could be split, dubbed the 1920s the "heroic age of physics."

The new picture of the universe that was unfolding continued to undermine the old scientific certainties of classical physics. Classical physics had rested on the fundamental belief that all phenomena could be predicted if they could be completely understood; thus, the weather could be predicted if we only knew everything about the wind, sun, and water. In 1927, the German physicist Werner Heisenberg (1901–1976) upset this belief when he posited the "uncertainty principle." In essence, Heisenberg posited that no one could determine the path of an electron because the very act of observing the electron with light affected the electron's location. The "uncertainty principle" was more than an explanation for the path of an electron, however; it was a new worldview. Heisenberg shattered confidence in predictability and dared to propose that uncertainty was at the bottom of all the physical laws.

Conclusion

The devastation wrought by World War I destroyed the liberal optimism of the prewar era. Yet many in the 1920s still hoped that the progress of Western civilization, so seemingly evident before 1914, could somehow be restored. These hopes proved largely unfounded as plans for economic reconstruction gave way to inflation and to an even more devastating Great Depression at the end of the 1920s. Likewise, confidence in political democracy was soon shattered by the rise of authoritarian governments that not only restricted individual freedoms but, in the cases of Italy, Germany, and the Soviet Union, sought even great control over the lives of their subjects in order to manipulate and guide them to achieve the goals of their totalitarian regimes. For many people, despite the loss of personal freedom, these mass movements at least offered some sense of security in a world that seemed fraught with uncertainties.

But the seeming security of these mass movements gave rise to even greater uncertainties as Europeans, after a brief twenty-year interlude of peace, once again plunged into war, this time on a scale even more horrendous than that of World War I. The twentieth-century crisis, begun in 1914, seemed only to be worsening in 1939.

NOTES

1. Quoted in Robert Paxton, *Europe in the Twentieth Century*, 2d ed. (San Diego, 1985), p. 237.
2. Benito Mussolini, "The Doctrine of Fascism," in Adrian Lyttleton, ed., *Italian Fascisms from Pareto to Gentile* (London, 1973), p. 42.
3. Quoted in Alexander De Grand, "Women Under Italian Fascism," *Historical Journal*, 19 (1976): 958–959.
4. Quoted in Jeremy Noakes and Geoffrey Pridham, eds., *Nazism 1919–1945* (Exeter, 1983), 1:50–51.
5. Quoted in Joachim Fest, *Hitler*, trans. Richard and Clara Winston (New York, 1974), p. 418.
6. Irving Howe, ed., *The Basic Writings of Trotsky* (London, 1963), p. 162.
7. Norman H. Baynes, ed., *The Speeches of Adolf Hitler, 1922–1939* (Oxford, 1942), 1:591.

SUGGESTIONS FOR FURTHER READING

For a general introduction to the interwar period, see R. J. Sontag, *A Broken World, 1919–39* (New York, 1971); and the general survey by R. Paxton, *Europe in the Twentieth Century*, 2d ed. (New York, 1985). On European security issues after the Peace of Paris, see S. Marks, *The Illusion of Peace: Europe's International Relations, 1918–1933* (New York, 1976). The Locarno agreements have been well examined in J. Jacobson, *Locarno Diplomacy* (Princeton, N.J., 1972). The best study on the problem of reparations is now M. Trachtenberg, *Reparations in World Politics* (New York, 1980), which paints a positive view of French policies. On the Great Depression, see C. P. Kindleberger, *The World in Depression, 1929–39*, rev. ed. (Berkeley, 1986).

The best biography of Mussolini is now D. Mack Smith, *Mussolini* (New York, 1982). Two brief, but excellent surveys of Fascist Italy are A. Cassels, *Fascist Italy*, 2d ed. (Arlington Heights, Ill., 1985); and J. Whittam, *Fascist Italy* (New York, 1995). An excellent reference guide for all aspects of Fascist Italy is P. Cannistraro, ed., *Historical Dictionary of Fascist Italy* (Westport, Conn., 1982).

Two brief but sound surveys of Nazi Germany are J. Spielvogel, *Hitler and Nazi Germany: A History*, 3d ed. (Englewood Cliffs, N.J., 1996); and J. Bendersky, *A History of Nazi Germany* (Chicago, 1985). The best biographies of Hitler are A. Bullock, *Hitler: A Study in Tyranny* (New York, 1964); and J. Fest, *Hitler*, trans. R. and C. Winston (New York, 1974). Two recent works that examine the enormous literature on Hitler are J. Lukacs, *The Hitler of History* (New York, 1997; and R. Rosenbaum, *Explaining Hitler* (New York, 1998). A good regional study of the Nazi Party's rise to power is W. S. Allen's "classic" *The Nazi Seizure of Power: The Experience of a Single German Town*, rev. ed. (New York, 1984). On the SA, see P. Merkl, *The Making of a Stormtrooper* (Princeton, N.J., 1980). On the Nazi administration of the state, see M. Broszat, *The Hitler State: The Foundations and Development of the Internal Structure of the Third Reich* (New York, 1981). A brief perspective on Germany's economic recovery can be found in R. J. Overy, *The Nazi Economic Recovery, 1932–1938* (London, 1982). Basic studies of the SS include R. Koehl, *The Black Corps: The Structure and Power Struggles of the Nazi SS* (Madison, Wis., 1983); and H. Krausnick and M. Broszat, *Anatomy of the SS State* (London, 1970). On women, see J. Stephenson, *Women in Nazi Society* (London, 1975); and C. Koonz, *Mothers in the Fatherland: Women, the Family, and Nazi Politics* (New York, 1987). The Hitler Youth is examined in H. W. Koch, *The Hitler Youth* (New York, 1976). On Nazi anti-Jewish policies between 1933 and 1939 see S. Friedländer, *Nazi Germany and the Jews*, vol. 1: *The Years of Persecution, 1933–1939* (New York, 1997). The importance of racial ideology in Nazi Germany is evident in R. Proctor, *Racial Hygiene: Medicine Under the Nazis* (Cambridge, Mass., 1988).

For a general study of other fascist movements, see S. Payne, *A History of Fascism* (Madison, Wis. 1996). Starting points for the study of eastern Europe are J. Rothschild, *East Central Europe between the Two World Wars* (New York, 1974); and B. Jelavich, *History of the Balkans*, vol. 2: *The Twentieth Century* (New York, 1983). On France, see J. W. D. Trythall, *El Caudillo: A Political Biography* (New York, 1970).

The collectivization of agriculture is examined in R. W. Davies, *The Socialist Offensive: The Collectivization of Soviet Agriculture, 1929–30* (Cambridge, Mass., 1980). Industrialization is covered in H. Kuromiya, *Stalin's Industrial Revolution: Politics and Workers, 1928–1932* (New York, 1988). Stalin's purges are examined in R. Conquest, *The Great Terror: Stalin's Purge of the Thirties*, rev. ed.

(New York, 1973); and R. W. Thurston, *Life and Terror in Stalin's Russia, 1934–1941* (New Haven, 1996). For a biography of Stalin, see R. H. McNeal, *Stalin: Man and Ruler* (New York, 1988).

The use of cinema for propaganda purposes is well examined in D. Welch, *Propaganda and the German Cinema* (New York, 1985). On the cultural and intellectual environment of Weimar Germany, see W. Laqueur, *Weimar: A Cultural History* (New York, 1974); and P. Gay, *Weimar Culture: The Outsider as Insider* (New York, 1968).

The Deepening of the European Crisis: World War II

On February 3, 1933, only four days after he had been appointed chancellor of Germany, Adolf Hitler met secretly with Germany's leading generals. He revealed to them his desire to remove the "cancer of democracy," create a new authoritarian leadership, and forge a new domestic unity. All Germans would need to realize that "only a struggle can save us and that everything else must be subordinated to this idea." Youth especially must be trained and their wills strengthened "to fight with all means." Because Germany's living space was too small for its people, above all, Hitler said, Germany must rearm and prepare for "the conquest of new living space in the east and its ruthless Germanization." Even before he had consolidated his power, Adolf Hitler had a clear vision of his goals, and their implementation meant another European war. World War II was clearly Hitler's war. Although other countries may have helped to make the war possible by not resisting Hitler's Germany earlier, it was Nazi Germany's actions that made World War II inevitable.

World War II was more than just Hitler's war, however. This chapter focuses on the European theater of war, but both European and American armies were also involved in fighting around the world. World War II consisted of two conflicts: one provoked by the ambitions of Germany in Europe, the other by the ambitions of Japan in Asia. By 1941, with the involvement of the United States in both wars, the two had merged into one global conflict.

Although World War I has been described as a total war, World War II was even more so and was fought on a scale unheard of in history. Almost everyone in the warring countries was involved in one way or another: as soldiers; as workers in wartime industries; as ordinary citizens subject to invading armies, military occupation, or bombing raids; as refugees; or as victims of mass extermination. The world had never witnessed such widespread human-made death and destruction.

Hitler occupies demilitarized Rhineland

Occupation of the Sudetenland

Germany invades Poland

German surrender at Stalingrad

Munich Conference

Churchill becomes British prime minister

Teheran Conference · Surrender of Germany

Germany defeats France

Axis forces surrender in North Africa
Allied invasion of France ·
Japan surrenders ·

Prelude to War

Only twenty years after the war to end war, the world plunged back into the nightmare of total war. The efforts at collective security in the 1920s—the League of Nations, the attempts at disarmament, the pacts and treaties—all proved meaningless in view of the growth of Nazi Germany and its deliberate scrapping of the postwar settlement in the 1930s.

The "Diplomatic Revolution," 1933–1937

World War II in Europe had its beginnings in the ideas of Adolf Hitler, who believed that only the Aryans were capable of building a great civilization. But to Hitler, the Germans, in his view the leading group of Aryans, were threatened from the east by a large mass of inferior peoples, the Slavs, who had learned to use German weapons and technology. Germany needed more land to support a larger population and be a great power. Already in the 1920s, in the second volume of Mein Kampf, Hitler had indicated where a National Socialist regime would find this land: "And so we National Socialists . . . take up where we broke off six hundred years ago. We stop the endless German movement to the south and west, and turn our gaze toward the land in the east. . . . If we speak of soil in Europe today, we can primarily have in mind only Russia and her vassal border states."[1] Once it had been conquered, the land of Russia could be resettled by German peasants while the Slavic population could be used as slave labor to build the Aryan racial state that would dominate Europe for a thousand years. Hitler's conclusion was apparent: Germany must prepare for its inevitable war with the Soviet Union. Hitler's ideas were by no means secret. He had spelled them out in Mein

Kampf, a book readily available to anyone who wished to read it.

When Hitler became chancellor of Germany on January 30, 1933, Germany's situation in Europe seemed weak. The Treaty of Versailles had created a demilitarized zone on Germany's western border that would allow the French to move into the heavily industrialized parts of Germany in the event of war. To Germany's east, the smaller states, such as Poland and Czechoslovakia, had defensive treaties with France. The Versailles treaty had also limited Germany's army to 100,000 troops with no air and limited naval forces.

Posing as a man of peace in his public speeches, Hitler emphasized that Germany wished only to revise the unfair provisions of Versailles by peaceful means and achieve Germany's rightful place among the European states. On March 9, 1935, Hitler announced the creation of a new air force, and one week later, the introduction of a military draft that would expand Germany's army from 100,000 to 550,000 troops. Hitler's unilateral repudiation of the Versailles treaty brought a swift reaction as France, Great Britain, and Italy condemned Germany's action and warned against future aggressive steps. But nothing concrete was done.

On March 7, 1936, buoyed by his conviction that the Western democracies had no intention of using force to maintain the Treaty of Versailles, Hitler sent German troops into the demilitarized Rhineland. According to the Versailles treaty, the French had the right to use force against any violation of the demilitarized Rhineland. But France would not act without British support, and the British viewed the occupation of German territory by German troops as another reasonable action by a dissatisfied power. The London Times noted that the Germans were only "going into their own back garden."

Meanwhile, Hitler gained new allies. In October 1935, Benito Mussolini had committed Fascist Italy to imperial expansion by invading Ethiopia. Angered by French and British opposition to his invasion, Mussolini welcomed Hitler's support and began to draw closer to the German dictator he had once called a buffoon. In October 1936, Mussolini and Hitler concluded an agreement that recognized their common political and economic interests, and one month later, Mussolini re-ferred publicly to the new Rome-Berlin Axis. Also in November, Germany and Japan (the rising military power in the Far East), concluded the Anti-Comintern Pact and agreed to maintain a common front against communism. By the beginning of 1937, Hitler and Nazi Germany had achieved a "diplomatic revolution" in Europe. The Treaty of Versailles had been virtually scrapped and Germany was once more a "world power," as Hitler proclaimed.

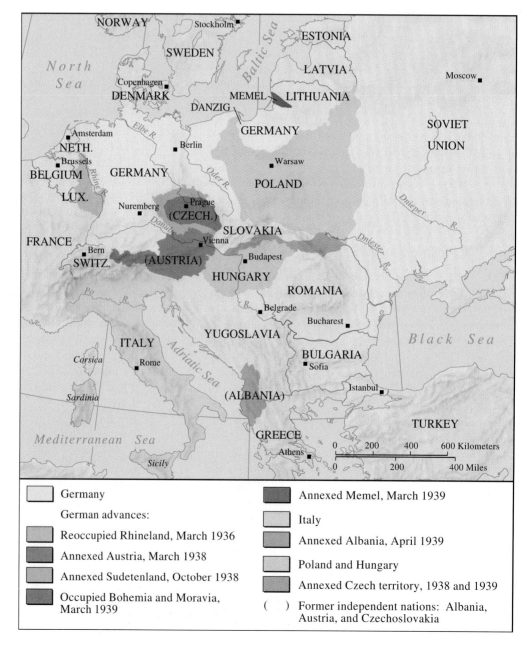

Map 28.1 Changes in Central Europe, 1936–Summer 1939.

Germany

German advances:

Reoccupied Rhineland, March 1936

Annexed Austria, March 1938

Annexed Sudetenland, October 1938

Occupied Bohemia and Moravia, March 1939

Annexed Memel, March 1939

Italy

Annexed Albania, April 1939

Poland and Hungary

Annexed Czech territory, 1938 and 1939

( ) Former independent nations: Albania, Austria, and Czechoslovakia

The Path to War, 1938–1939

By the beginning of 1938, Hitler was convinced that neither the French nor the British would provide much opposition to his plans and decided to move on Austria. By threatening Austria with invasion, Hitler coerced the Austrian chancellor into putting Austrian Nazis in charge of the government. The new government promptly invited German troops to enter Austria and assist in maintaining law and order. One day later, on March 13, 1938, after his triumphal return to his native land, Hitler formally annexed Austria to Germany. Great Britain's ready acknowledgment of Hitler's action only increased the German dictator's contempt for Western weakness.

The annexation of Austria improved Germany's strategic position in central Europe and put Germany in position for Hitler's next objective—the destruction of Czechoslovakia. This goal might have seemed unrealistic since democratic Czechoslovakia was quite prepared to defend itself and was well supported by pacts with France and Soviet Russia. Nevertheless, Hitler believed that France and Britain would not use force to defend Czechoslovakia.

He was right again. When, on September 15, 1938, Hitler demanded the cession of the Sudetenland, the mountainous northwestern border area of Czechoslovakia that was home to 3.5 million ethnic Germans, to Germany and expressed his willingness to risk "world war" to

◆ **Hitler Enters the Sudetenland.** The Sudetenland was an area of Czechoslovakia inhabited by 3.5 million Germans. The Munich Conference allowed the Germans to occupy the Sudetenland. This picture shows Hitler and his entourage arriving at Eger (now Cheb) in October 1938 to the cheers of an enthusiastic crowd.

⟫ The Munich Conference ⟪

At the Munich Conference, the leaders of France and Great Britain capitulated to Hitler's demands on Czechoslovakia. While the British prime minister, Neville Chamberlain, defended his actions at Munich as necessary for peace, another British statesman, Winston Churchill, characterized the settlement at Munich as "a disaster of the first magnitude."

Winston Churchill, Speech to the House of Commons, October 5, 1938

I will begin by saying what everybody would like to ignore or forget but which must nevertheless be stated, namely, that we have sustained a total and unmitigated defeat, and that France has suffered even more than we have. . . . The utmost my right honorable Friend the Prime Minister . . . has been able to gain for Czechoslovakia and in the matters which were in dispute has been that the German dictator, instead of snatching his victuals from the table, has been content to have them served to him course by course. . . . And I will say this, that I believe the Czechs, left to themselves and told they were going to get no help from the Western Powers, would have been able to make better terms than they have got. . . .

We are in the presence of a disaster of the first magnitude which has befallen Great Britain and France. Do not let us blind ourselves to that. . . .

And do not suppose that this is the end. This is only the beginning of the reckoning. This is only the first sip, the first foretaste of a bitter cup which will be proffered to us year by year unless by a supreme recovery of moral health and martial vigor, we arise again and take our stand for freedom as in the olden time.

Neville Chamberlain, Speech to the House of Commons, October 6, 1938

That is my answer to those who say that we should have told Germany weeks ago that, if her army crossed the border of Czechoslovakia, we should be at war with her. We had no treaty obligations and no legal obligations to Czechoslovakia. . . . When we were convinced, as we became convinced, that nothing any longer would keep the Sudetenland within the Czechoslovakian State, we urged the Czech Government as strongly as we could to agree to the cession of territory, and to agree promptly. . . . It was a hard decision for anyone who loved his country to take, but to accuse us of having by that advice betrayed the Czechoslovakian State is simply preposterous. What we did was to save her from annihilation and give her a chance of new life as a new State, which involves the loss of territory and fortifications, but may perhaps enable her to enjoy in the future and develop a national existence under a neutrality and security comparable to that which we see in Switzerland today. Therefore, I think the Government deserve the approval of this House for their conduct of affairs in this recent crisis which has saved Czechoslovakia from destruction and Europe from Armageddon.

---

achieve his objective, the British, French, Germans, and Italians—at a hastily arranged conference at Munich—reached an agreement that essentially met all of Hitler's demands. German troops were allowed to occupy the Sudetenland as the Czechs, abandoned by their Western allies, stood by helplessly. The Munich Conference was the high point of Western appeasement of Hitler. When Neville Chamberlain, the British prime minister, returned to England from Munich, he boasted that the Munich agreement meant "peace in our times." Hitler had promised Chamberlain that he had made his last demand. Like many German politicians, Chamberlain had believed Hitler's assurances (see the box above).

In fact, Munich confirmed Hitler's perception that the Western democracies were weak and would not fight. In-creasingly, Hitler was convinced of his own infallibility, and he had by no means been satisfied at Munich. In March 1939, Hitler occupied the Czech lands (Bohemia and Moravia) while the Slovaks, with Hitler's encouragement, declared their independence of the Czechs and became a puppet state (Slovakia) of Nazi Germany. On the evening of March 15, 1939, Hitler triumphantly declared in Prague that he would be known as the greatest German of them all.

At last, the Western states reacted to Hitler's threat. Hitler's naked aggression made clear that his promises were utterly worthless. When Hitler began to demand the return of Danzig (which had been made a free city by the Treaty of Versailles to serve as a seaport for Poland) to Germany, Britain recognized the danger and offered to protect Poland in the event of war. At the same time, both France and Britain realized that only the Soviet Union was powerful enough to help contain Nazi aggression, and began political and military negotiations with Joseph Stalin and the Soviets. The West's distrust of Soviet Communism, however, made an alliance unlikely.

Meanwhile, Hitler pressed on in the belief that the West would not really fight over Poland. To preclude an alliance between the West and the Soviet Union, which would create the danger of a two-front war, Hitler, ever the opportunist, negotiated his own nonaggression pact with Stalin and shocked the world with its announcement on August 23, 1939. The treaty with the Soviet Union gave Hitler the freedom to attack Poland. He told his generals: "Now Poland is in the position in which I wanted her . . . I am only afraid that at the last moment some swine or other will yet submit to me a plan for mediation."[2] He need not have worried. On September 1, German forces invaded Poland; two days later, Britain and France declared war on Germany. Europe was again at war.

The Course of World War II

Using *Blitzkrieg,* or "lightning war," Hitler stunned Europe with the speed and efficiency of the German attack. Armored columns or panzer divisions (a panzer division was a strike force of about 300 tanks and accompanying forces and supplies) supported by airplanes broke quickly through Polish lines and encircled the bewildered Polish troops. Regular infantry units then moved in to hold the newly conquered territory. Within four weeks, Poland had surrendered. On September 28, 1939, Germany and the Soviet Union officially divided Poland between them.

Victory and Stalemate

Although Hitler's hopes to avoid a war with the West were dashed when France and Britain declared war on September 3, he was confident that he could control the situation. After a winter of waiting (called the "phony war"), Hitler resumed the war on April 9, 1940, with another *Blitzkrieg,* this time against Denmark and Norway. One month later, on May 10, the Germans launched their attack on the Netherlands, Belgium, and France. The main assault through Luxembourg and the Ardennes forest was completely unexpected by the French and British forces. German panzer divisions broke through the weak French defensive positions there and raced across northern France, splitting the Allied armies and

trapping French troops and the entire British army on the beaches of Dunkirk. Only by heroic efforts did the British succeed in achieving an evacuation of 330,000 Allied (mostly British) troops. The French surrendered on June 22. German armies occupied about three-fifths of France while the French hero of World War I, Marshal Henri Pétain (1856–1951), established an authoritarian regime (known as Vichy France) over the remainder. Germany was now in control of western and central Europe, but Britain had still not been defeated.

As Hitler realized, an amphibious invasion of Britain would only be possible if Germany gained control of the air. At the beginning of August 1940, the *Luftwaffe* (the German air force) launched a major offensive against British air and naval bases, harbors, communication centers, and war industries. Led by the stubbornly determined Winston Churchill, now prime minister of Britain, the British fought back doggedly, supported by an effective radar system that gave them early warning of German attacks. Nevertheless, the British air force suffered critical losses by the end of the August and was probably saved by Hitler's change of strategy. In September, in retaliation for a British attack on Berlin, Hitler ordered a shift from military targets to massive bombing of British cities to break British morale. The British rebuilt their air strength quickly and were soon inflicting major losses on *Luftwaffe* bombers. By the end of September, Germany had lost the Battle of Britain, and the invasion of Britain had to be postponed.

At this point, Hitler pursued the possibility of a Mediterranean strategy, which would involve capturing Egypt and the Suez Canal and closing the Mediterranean to British ships, thereby shutting off Britain's supply of oil. Hitler's commitment to the Mediterranean was never wholehearted, however. His initial plan was to let the Italians defeat the British in North Africa, but this strategy failed when the British routed the Italian army. Although Hitler then sent German troops to the North African theater of war, his primary concern lay elsewhere; he had already reached the decision to fulfill his lifetime obsession with the acquisition of territory in the east.

Although he had no desire for a two-front war, Hitler became convinced that Britain was remaining in the war only because it expected Russian support. If Russia were smashed, Britain's last hope would be eliminated. Moreover, Hitler had convinced himself that the Soviet Union, with its Jewish-Bolshevik leadership and a pitiful army, could be defeated quickly and decisively. Although the invasion of the Soviet Union was scheduled for spring 1941, the attacked was delayed because of problems in the Balkans. Hitler had already obtained the political co-operation of Hungary, Bulgaria, and Romania, but Mussolini's disastrous invasion of Greece in October 1940 exposed Hitler's southern flank to British air bases in Greece. To secure his Balkan flank, German troops seized both Yugoslavia and Greece in April. Now reassured, Hitler turned to the east and invaded the Soviet Union on June 22, 1941, in the belief that the Russians could still be decisively defeated before winter arrived.

The massive attack stretched out along an 1,800-mile front. German troops advanced rapidly, capturing two million Russian soldiers. By November, one German army group had swept through Ukraine, while a second was besieging Leningrad; a third approached within 25 miles of Moscow, the Russian capital. An early Russian winter and unexpected Russian resistance, however, brought a halt to the German advance. For the first time in the war, German armies had been stopped. A Soviet counterattack in December 1941 by a Soviet army supposedly exhausted by Nazi victories came as an ominous ending to the year for the Germans. By that time, another of Hitler's decisions—the declaration of war on the United States—probably made Hitler's defeat inevitable and turned another European conflict into a global war.

The War in Asia

On December 7, 1941, Japanese carrier-based aircraft attacked the United States naval base at Pearl Harbor in the Hawaiian Islands. The same day, other units launched additional assaults on the Philippines and began advancing toward the British colony of Malaya. Shortly after, Japanese forces invaded the Dutch East Indies and occupied a number of islands in the Pacific Ocean. In some cases, as on the Bataan Peninsula and the island of Corregidor in the Philippines, resistance was fierce, but by the spring of 1942 almost all of Southeast Asia and much of the western Pacific had fallen to Japanese hands. Tokyo declared the creation of a Great East-Asia Co-prosperity Sphere of the entire region under Japanese tutelage and announced its intention to liberate the colonial areas of Southeast Asia from Western colonial rule. For the moment, however, Japan needed the resources of the region for its war machine and placed the countries under its rule on a wartime basis.

Japanese leaders had hoped that their lightning strike at American bases would destroy the United States Pacific Fleet and persuade the Roosevelt administration to accept Japanese domination of the Pacific. The American people, in the eyes of Japanese leaders, had been made soft by material indulgence. But Tokyo had miscalculated. The attack on Pearl Harbor galvanized American opinion and won broad support for Roosevelt's war policy. The United States now joined with European nations and Nationalist China in a combined effort to defeat Japan and bring to an end its hegemony in the Pacific.

The Turning Point of the War, 1942–1943

The entry of the United States into the war created a coalition (the Grand Alliance) that ultimately defeated the Axis powers (Germany, Italy, Japan). Nevertheless,

♦ **German Panzer Troops in Russia.** At first, the German attack on Russia was enormously successful, leading one German general to remark in his diary, "It is probably no overstatement to say that the Russian campaign has been won in the space of two weeks." This picture shows German panzer troops jumping from their armored troop carriers to attack Red Army snipers who had taken refuge in a farmhouse.

the three major Allies, Britain, the United States, and the Soviet Union, had to overcome mutual suspicions before they could operate as an effective alliance. Two factors aided that process. First, Hitler's declaration of war on the United States made it easier for the United States to accept the British and Russian contention that the defeat of Germany should be the first priority of the United States. For that reason, the United States increased the quantity of trucks, planes, and other arms that it sent to the British and Soviets. Also important to the alliance was the tacit agreement of the three chief Allies to stress military operations while ignoring political differences. At the beginning of 1943, the Allies agreed to fight until the Axis powers surrendered unconditionally. This principle of unconditional surrender had the effect of cementing the Grand Alliance by making it nearly impossible for Hitler to divide his foes.

Defeat was far from Hitler's mind at the beginning of 1942, however. As Japanese forces advanced into Southeast Asia and the Pacific after crippling the American naval fleet at Pearl Harbor, Hitler and his European allies continued the war in Europe against Britain and the Soviet Union. Until the fall of 1942, it appeared that the Germans might still prevail on the battlefield. Reinforcements in North Africa enabled the Afrika Korps under General Erwin Rommel to break through the British defenses in Egypt and advance toward Alexandria. In the spring of 1942, a renewed German offensive in Russia led to the capture of the entire Crimea, causing Hitler to boast in August 1942:

> As the next step, we are going to advance south of the Caucasus and then help the rebels in Iran and Iraq against the English. Another thrust will be directed along the Caspian Sea toward Afghanistan and India. Then the English will run out of oil. In two years we'll be on the borders of India. Twenty to thirty elite German divisions will do. Then the British Empire will collapse.[3]

But this would be Hitler's last optimistic outburst. By the fall of 1942, the war had turned against the Germans.

In North Africa, British forces had stopped Rommel's troops at El Alamein in the summer of 1942 and then forced them back across the desert. In November 1942, British and American forces invaded French North Africa and forced the German and Italian troops to surrender in May 1943. On the Eastern Front, the turning point of the war occurred at Stalingrad. After the capture of the Crimea, Hitler's generals wanted him to concentrate on the Caucasus and its oil fields, but Hitler decided that Stalingrad, a major industrial center on the Volga,

should be taken first. Between November 1942 and February 1943, German troops were stopped, then encircled, and finally forced to surrender on February 2, 1943 (see the box on p. 588). The entire German Sixth Army of 300,000 men was lost. By February 1943, German forces in Russia were back to their positions of June 1942. By the spring of 1943, even Hitler knew that the Germans would not defeat the Soviet Union.

The tide of battle in the Far East also turned dramatically in 1942. In the Battle of the Coral Sea on May 7–8, 1942, American naval forces stopped the Japanese advance and temporarily relieved Australia of the threat of invasion. On June 4, at the Battle of Midway Island,

❧ A German Soldier at Stalingrad ❧

The Russian victory at Stalingrad was a major turning point in World War II. This excerpt comes from the diary of a German soldier who fought and died in the Battle of Stalingrad. His dreams of victory and a return home with medals were soon dashed by the realities of Russian resistance.

Diary of a German Soldier

Today, after we'd had a bath, the company commander told us that if our future operations are as successful, we'll soon reach the Volga, take Stalingrad and then the war will inevitably soon be over. Perhaps we'll be home by Christmas.

July 29. The company commander says the Russian troops are completely broken, and cannot hold out any longer. To reach the Volga and take Stalingrad is not so difficult for us. The Führer knows where the Russians' weak point is. Victory is not far away. . . .

August 10. The Führer's orders were read out to us. He expects victory of us. We are all convinced that they can't stop us.

August 12. This morning outstanding soldiers were presented with decorations. . . . Will I really go back to Elsa without a decoration? I believe that for Stalingrad the Führer will decorate even me. . . .

September 4. We are being sent northward along the front toward Stalingrad. We marched all night and by dawn had reached Voroponovo Station. We can already see the smoking town. It's a happy thought that the end of the war is getting nearer. That's what everyone is saying. . . .

September 8. Two days of non-stop fighting. The Russians are defending themselves with insane stubbornness. Our regiment has lost many men. . . .

September 16. Our battalion, plus tanks, is attacking the [grain storage] elevator, from which smoke is pouring—the grain in it is burning, the Russians seem to have set light to it themselves. Barbarism. The battalion is suffering heavy losses. . . .

October 10. The Russians are so close to us that our planes cannot bomb them. We are preparing for a decisive attack. The Führer has ordered the whole of Stalingrad to be taken as rapidly as possible. . . .

October 22. Our regiment has failed to break into the factory. We have lost many men; every time you move you have to jump over bodies. . . .

November 10. A letter from Elsa today. Everyone expects us home for Christmas. In Germany everyone believes we already hold Stalingrad. How wrong they are. If they could only see what Stalingrad has done to our army. . . .

November 21. The Russians have gone over to the offensive along the whole front. Fierce fighting is going on. So, there it is—the Volga, victory and soon home to our families! We shall obviously be seeing them next in the other world.

November 29. We are encircled. It was announced this morning that the Führer has said: "The army can trust me to do everything necessary to ensure supplies and rapidly break the encirclement."

December 3. We are on hunger rations and waiting for the rescue that the Führer promised. . . .

December 14. Everybody is racked with hunger. Frozen potatoes are the best meal, but to get them out of the ice-covered ground under fire from Russian bullets is not so easy. . . .

December 26. The horses have already been eaten. I would eat a cat; they say its meat is also tasty. The soldiers look like corpses or lunatics, looking for something to put in their mouths. They no longer take cover from Russian shells; they haven't the strength to walk, run away and hide. A curse on this war!

American planes destroyed all four of the attacking Japanese aircraft carriers and established American naval superiority in the Pacific. After a series of bitter engagements in the waters of the Solomon Islands from August to November, Japanese fortunes began to fade.

The Last Years of the War

By the beginning of 1943, the tide of battle had turned against Germany, Italy, and Japan. After the Axis forces had surrendered in Tunisia on May 13, 1943, the Allies crossed the Mediterranean and carried the war to Italy. After taking Sicily, Allied troops began the invasion of mainland Italy in September. In the meantime, after the ouster and arrest of Benito Mussolini, a new Italian government offered to surrender to Allied forces. But Mussolini was liberated by the Germans in a daring raid and then set up as the head of a puppet German state in northern Italy while German troops moved in and occupied much of Italy. The new defensive lines established by

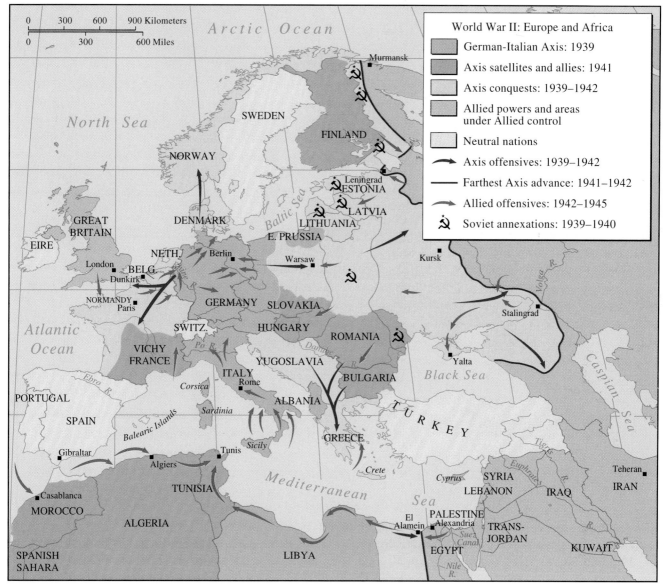

Map 28.2 World War II in Europe and North Africa.

the Germans in the hills south of Rome were so effective that the Allied advance up the Italian peninsula was a painstaking affair accompanied by heavy casualties. Rome did not fall to the Allies until June 4, 1944. By that time, the Italian war had assumed a secondary role anyway as the Allies opened their long-awaited "second front" in Western Europe.

Since the autumn of 1943, the Allies had been planning a cross-channel invasion of France from Britain. Under the direction of the American general Dwight D. Eisenhower (1890–1969), the Allies landed five assault divisions on the Normandy beaches on June 6 in history's greatest naval invasion. An initially indecisive German response enabled the Allied forces to establish a beach-head. Within three months, they had landed two million men and a half-million vehicles that pushed inland and broke through German defensive lines.

After the breakout, Allied troops moved south and east and liberated Paris by the end of August. By March 1945, they had crossed the Rhine River and advanced further into Germany. At the end of April, Allied forces in northern Germany moved toward the Elbe River

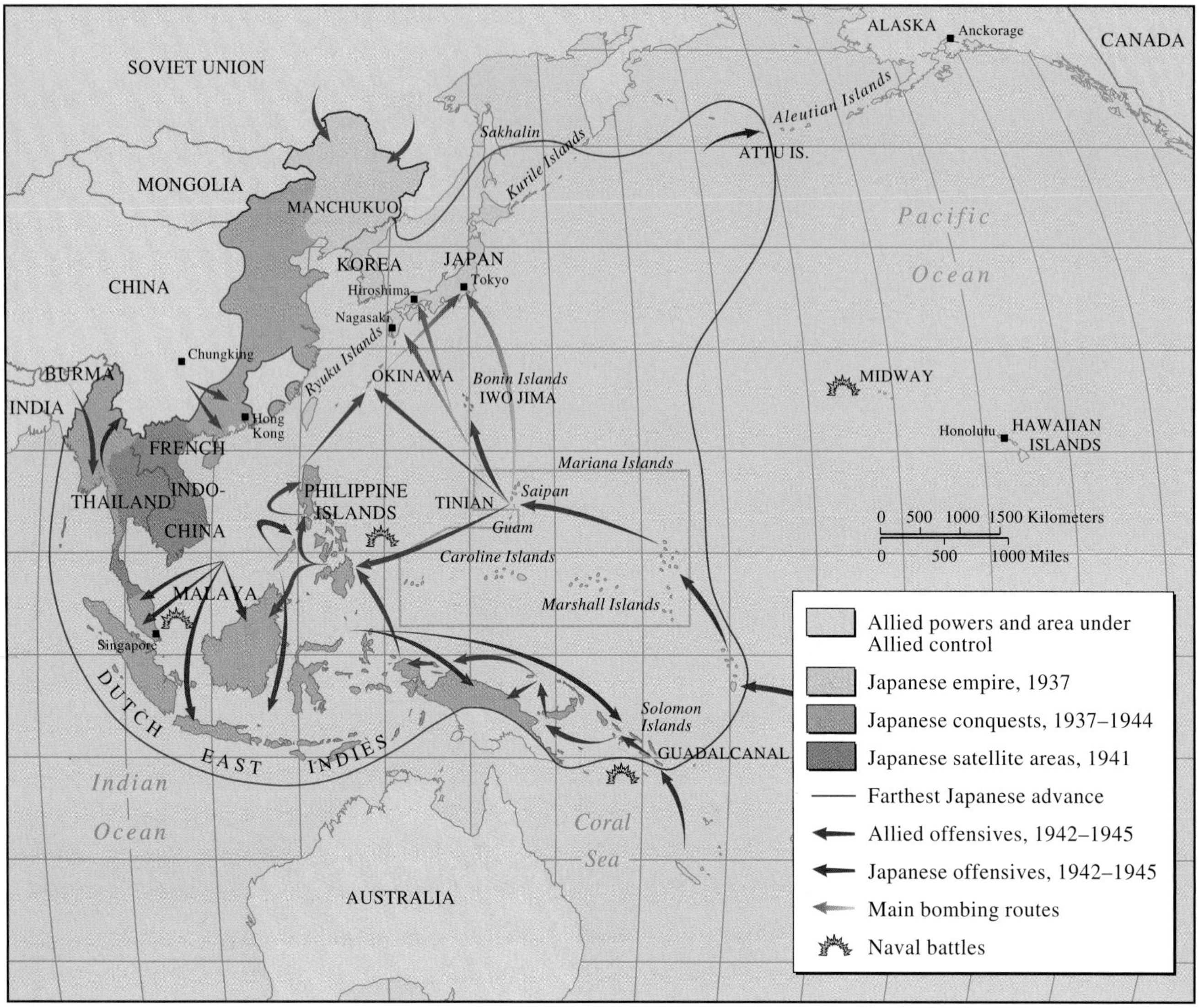

Map 28.3 World War II in Asia and the Pacific.

where they finally linked up with the Russians. The Russians had come a long way since the Battle of Stalingrad in 1943. In the summer of 1943, Hitler gambled on taking the offensive by making use of newly developed heavy tanks. German forces were soundly defeated by the Russians at the Battle of Kursk (July 5–12), the greatest tank battle of World War II. Soviet forces now began a relentless advance westward. The Soviets had reoccupied Ukraine by the end of 1943 and lifted the siege of Leningrad and moved into the Baltic States by the beginning of 1944. Advancing along a northern front, Soviet troops occupied Warsaw in January 1945 and entered Berlin in April. Meanwhile, Soviet troops swept along a southern front through Hungary, Romania, and Bulgaria.

In January 1945, Adolf Hitler had moved into a bunker fifty-five feet under Berlin to direct the final stages of the war. In his final political testament, Hitler, consistent to the end in his rabid anti-Semitism, blamed the Jews for the war: "Above all I charge the leaders of the nation and those under them to scrupulous observance of the laws of race and to merciless opposition to the universal poisoner of all peoples, international Jewry."[4] Hitler committed suicide on April 30, two days after Mussolini had been shot by partisan Italian forces. On

May 7, German commanders surrendered. The war in Europe was over.

The war in Asia continued. Beginning in 1943, American forces had gone on the offensive and advanced their way, slowly at times, across the Pacific. American forces took an increasing toll of enemy resources, especially at sea and in the air. When President Harry Truman (Roosevelt had died on April 12, 1945) and his advisers became convinced that American troops might suffer heavy casualties in the invasion of the Japanese homeland, they made the decision to drop the newly developed bomb on Hiroshima and Nagasaki. The Japanese surrendered unconditionally on August 14. World War II, in which 17 million men died in battle and perhaps 18 million civilians perished as well (some estimate total losses at 50 million), was finally over.

The Nazi New Order

After the German victories in Europe between 1939 and 1941, Nazi propagandists painted glowing images of a new European order based on "equal chances" for all nations and an integrated economic community. This was not Hitler's conception of a European New Order. He saw the Europe he had conquered simply as subject to German domination. Only the Germans, he once said, "can really organize Europe."

The Nazi Empire

The Nazi empire stretched across continental Europe from the English Channel in the west to the outskirts of Moscow in the east. In no way was this empire organized systematically or governed efficiently. Nazi-occupied Europe was largely organized in one of two ways. Some areas, such as western Poland, were directly annexed by Nazi Germany and made into German provinces. Most of occupied Europe was administered by German military or civilian officials, combined with different degrees of indirect control from collaborationist regimes.

Racial considerations played an important role in how conquered peoples were treated. German civil administrations were established in Norway, Denmark, and the Netherlands because the Nazis considered their peoples to be Aryan or racially akin to the Germans and hence worthy of more lenient treatment. "Inferior" Latin peoples, such as the occupied French, were given military administrations. By 1943, however, as Nazi losses continued to multiply, all the occupied territories of northern and

✦ **Crossing the Rhine.** After landing at Normandy, Allied forces liberated France and prepared to move into Germany. Makeshift bridges enabled the Allies to cross the Rhine in some areas and advance deeper into Germany. Units of the 7th United States Army of General Patch are shown here crossing the Rhine at Worms on a pontoon bridge constructed by battalions of engineers alongside the ruins of the old bridge.

western Europe were ruthlessly exploited for material goods and manpower for Germany's war needs.

Because the conquered lands in the east contained the living space for German expansion and were populated in Nazi eyes by racially inferior Slavic peoples, Nazi administration there was considerably more ruthless. Hitler's racial ideology and his plans for an Aryan racial empire were so important to him that he and the Nazis began to implement their racial program soon after the conquest of Poland. Heinrich Himmler, a strong believer in Nazi racial ideology and the leader of the SS, was put in charge of German resettlement plans in the east. Himmler's task was to evacuate the inferior Slavic peoples and replace them with Germans, a policy first applied to the new

◆ **The Holocaust: Activities of the *Einsatzgruppen*.** The activities of the mobile killing units known as the *Einsatzgruppen* were the first stage in the mass killings of the Holocaust. This picture shows the execution of a Jew by a member of one of these SS killing squads. Onlookers include members of the German Army, the German Labor Service, and even Hitler youth. When it became apparent that this method of killing was inefficient, it was replaced by the death camps.

German provinces created from the lands of western Poland. One million Poles were uprooted and dumped in southern Poland. Hundreds of thousands of ethnic Germans (descendants of Germans who had migrated years earlier from Germany to different parts of southern and eastern Europe) were encouraged to colonize the designated areas in Poland. By 1942, two million ethnic Germans had been settled in Poland.

The invasion of the Soviet Union inflated Nazi visions of German colonization in the east. Hitler spoke to his intimate circle of a colossal project of social engineering after the war, in which Poles, Ukrainians, and Russians would become slave labor while German peasants settled on the abandoned lands and Germanized them. Nazis involved in this kind of planning were well aware of the human costs. Himmler told a gathering of SS officers that although the destruction of 30 million Slavs was a prerequisite for German plans in the east, "Whether nations live in prosperity or starve to death interests me only insofar as we need them as slaves for our culture. Otherwise it is of no interest."[5]

Labor shortages in Germany led to a policy of ruthless mobilization of foreign labor for Germany. After the invasion of Russia, the four million Russian prisoners of war captured by the Germans became a major source of heavy labor, but it was wasted by allowing three million of them to die from neglect. In 1942, a special office was created to recruit labor for German farms and industries. By the summer of 1944, seven million foreign workers were laboring in Germany and constituted 20 percent of Germany's labor force. At the same time, another seven million workers were supplying forced labor in their own countries on farms, in industries, and even in military camps. Forced labor often proved counterproductive, however, because it created economic chaos in occupied countries and disrupted industrial production that could have helped Germany. Even worse for the Germans, the brutal character of Germany's recruitment policies often led more and more people to resist the Nazi occupation forces.

The Holocaust

There was no more terrifying aspect of the Nazi New Order than the deliberate attempt to exterminate the Jewish people of Europe. Racial struggle was a key element in Hitler's ideology and meant to him a clearly defined conflict of opposites: the Aryans, creators of human cultural development, against the Jews, parasites who were trying to destroy the Aryans. By the beginning of 1939, Nazi policy focused on promoting the "emigration" of German

Jews from Germany. Once the war began in September 1939, however, the so-called "Jewish problem" took on new dimensions. For a while there was discussion of the Madagascar plan, which aspired to the mass shipment of Jews to the African island of Madagascar. When war contingencies made this plan impractical, an even more drastic policy was conceived.

Heinrich Himmler and the SS organization closely shared Adolf Hitler's racial ideology. The SS was given responsibility for what the Nazis called their Final Solution to the Jewish problem, that is, the annihilation of the Jewish people. Reinhard Heydrich (1904–1942), head of the SS's Security Service, was given administrative responsibility for the Final Solution. After the defeat of Poland, Heydrich ordered the special strike forces (*Einsatzgruppen*) that he had created to round up all Polish Jews and concentrate them in ghettos established in a number of Polish cities.

In June 1941, the *Einsatzgruppen* were given new responsibilities as mobile killing units. These SS death squads followed the regular army's advance into Russia. Their job was to round up Jews in their villages and execute and bury them in mass graves, often giant pits dug by the victims themselves before they were shot. Such regular killing produced morale problems among the SS executioners. During a visit to Minsk in the Soviet Union, SS leader Heinrich Himmler tried to build morale by pointing out that "He would not like it if Germans did such a thing gladly. But their conscience was in no way impaired, for they were soldiers who had to carry out every order unconditionally. He alone had responsibility before God and Hitler for everything that was happening, . . . and he was acting from a deep understanding of the necessity for this operation."[6]

Although it has been estimated that as many as one million Jews were killed by the *Einsatzgruppen,* this approach to solving the Jewish problem was soon perceived as inadequate. Instead, the Nazis opted for the systematic annihilation of the European Jewish population in specially built death camps. The plan was basically simple. Jews from countries occupied by Germany (or sympathetic to Germany) would be rounded up, packed like cattle into freight trains, and shipped to Poland, where six extermination centers were built for this purpose. The largest and most infamous was Auschwitz-Birkenau. Medical technicians chose Zyklon B (the commercial name for hydrogen cyanide) as the most effective gas for quickly killing large numbers of people in gas chambers designed to look like "shower rooms" to facilitate the cooperation of the victims. After gassing, the corpses would be burned in specially built crematoria.

By the spring of 1942, the death camps were in operation. Although initial priority was given to the elimination of the ghettos in Poland, by the summer of 1942, Jews were also being shipped from France, Belgium, and Holland. Even as the Allies were making important

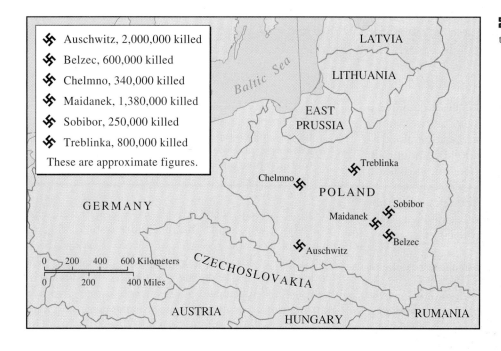

⚞ **Map 28.4** The Death Camps of the Holocaust.

The Holocaust: The Camp Commandant and the Camp Victims

The systematic annihilation of millions of men, women, and children in extermination camps makes the Holocaust one of the most horrifying events in history. The first document is taken from an account by Rudolf Höss, commandant of the extermination camp at Auschwitz-Birkenau. In the second document, a French doctor explains what happened to the victims at one of the crematoria described by Höss.

Commandant Höss Describes the Equipment

The two large crematoria, Nos. I and II, were built during the winter of 1942–43. . . . They each . . . could cremate c. 2,000 corpses within twenty-four hours. . . . Crematoria I and II both had underground undressing and gassing rooms which could be completely ventilated. The corpses were brought up to the ovens on the floor above by lift. The gas chambers could hold c. 3,000 people.

The firm of Topf had calculated that the two smaller crematoria, III and IV, would each be able to cremate 1,500 corpses within twenty-four hours. However, owing to the wartime shortage of materials, the builders were obliged to economize and so the undressing rooms and gassing rooms were built above ground and the ovens were of a less solid construction. But it soon became apparent that the flimsy construction of these two four-retort ovens was not up to the demands made on it. No. III ceased operating altogether after a short time and later was no longer used. No. IV had to be repeat-

edly shut down since after a short period in operation of 4–6 weeks, the ovens and chimneys had burnt out. The victims of the gassing were mainly burnt in pits behind crematorium IV.

The largest number of people gassed and cremated within twenty-four hours was somewhat over 9,000.

A French Doctor Describes the Victims

It is mid-day, when a long line of women, children, and old people enter the yard. The senior official in charge . . . climbs on a bench to tell them that they are going to have a bath and that afterward they will get a drink of hot coffee. They all undress in the yard. . . . The doors are opened and an indescribable jostling begins. The first people to enter the gas chamber begin to draw back. They sense the death which awaits them. The SS men put an end to this pushing and shoving with blows from their rifle butts beating the heads of the horrified women who are desperately hugging their children. The massive oak double doors are shut. For two endless minutes one can hear banging on the walls and screams which are no longer human. And then—not a sound. Five minutes later the doors are opened. The corpses, squashed together and distorted, fall out like a waterfall. . . . The bodies which are still warm pass through the hands of the hairdresser who cuts their hair and the dentist who pulls out their gold teeth. . . . One more transport has just been processed through No. IV crematorium.

---

advances in 1944, Jews were being shipped from Greece and Hungary. These shipments depended on the cooperation of Germany's Transport Ministry, and despite desperate military needs, the Final Solution had priority in using railroad cars for the transportation of Jews to death camps.

A harrowing experience awaited the Jews when they arrived at one of the six death camps. Rudolf Höss, commandant at Auschwitz-Birkenau, described it:

> We had two SS doctors on duty at Auschwitz to examine the incoming transports of prisoners. The prisoners would be marched by one of the doctors who would make spot decisions as they walked by. Those who were fit for work were sent into the camp. Others were sent immediately to the extermination plants. Children of tender years were in-

variably exterminated since by reason of their youth they were unable to work. . . . at Auschwitz we endeavored to fool the victims into thinking that they were to go through a delousing process. Of course, frequently they realized our true intentions and we sometimes had riots and difficulties due to that fact.[7]

About 30 percent of the arrivals at Auschwitz were sent to a labor camp, while the remainder went to the gas chambers (see the box above). After they had been gassed, the bodies were burned in the crematoria. The victims' goods and even their bodies were used for economic gain. Female hair was cut off, collected, and turned into mattresses or cloth. Some inmates were also subjected to cruel and painful "medical" experiments. The Germans killed between five and six million Jews, over three million of them in the death camps. Virtually 90 percent of the Jewish populations of Poland, the Baltic countries, and Germany were exterminated. Overall, the Holocaust was responsible for the death of nearly two out of every three European Jews.

The Nazis were also responsible for the deliberate death by shooting, starvation, or overwork of at least another nine to ten million people. Because the Nazis also considered the Gypsies of Europe (like the Jews) a race containing alien blood, they were systematically rounded up for extermination. About 40 percent of Europe's one million Gypsies were killed in the death camps. The leading elements of the "subhuman" Slavic peoples—the clergy, intelligentsia, civil leaders, judges, and lawyers—were arrested and deliberately killed. Probably, an additional four million Poles, Ukrainians, and Belorussians lost their lives as slave laborers for Nazi Germany while at least three to four million Soviet prisoners of war were killed in captivity. The Nazis also singled out homosexuals for persecution, and thousands lost their lives in concentration camps.

The Home Front

World War II was even more of a total war than World War I. Fighting was much more widespread and covered most of the world. Economic mobilization was more extensive; so too was the mobilization of women. The number of civilians killed was far higher; almost twenty million died as a result of bombing raids, mass extermination policies, and attacks by invading armies.

The Mobilization of Peoples: Three Examples

The home fronts of the major Western countries varied considerably, based on national circumstances. World War II had an enormous impact on the Soviet Union. Known to the Soviets as the Great Patriotic War, the German-Soviet war witnessed the greatest land battles in history as well as incredible ruthlessness. To Nazi Germany, it was a war of oppression and annihilation that called for merciless measures. Two out of every five persons killed in World War II were Soviet citizens.

The initial defeats of the Soviet Union led to drastic emergency mobilization measures that affected the civilian population. Leningrad, for example, experienced 900 days of siege, during which its inhabitants were so desperate for food that they ate dogs, cats, and mice. As the German army made its rapid advance into Soviet territory, the factories in the western part of the Soviet Union were dismantled and shipped to the interior—to the Urals, western Siberia, and the Volga regions. Machines were placed on the bare ground, and walls went up around them as workers began their work.

Stalin called this widespread military, industrial, and economic mobilization a "battle of machines," and the Soviets won, producing 78,000 tanks and 98,000 artillery pieces. Fifty-five percent of Soviet national income went for war materials compared to 15 percent in 1940. As a result of the emphasis on military goods, Soviet citizens experienced incredible shortages of both food and housing.

Soviet women played a major role in the war effort. Women and girls worked in industries, mines, and railroads. Overall, the number of women working in industry increased almost 60 percent. Soviet women were also expected to dig antitank ditches and work as air-raid wardens. In addition, the Soviet Union was the only country in World War II to use women as combatants. Soviet women functioned as snipers and also as aircrews in bomber squadrons. The female pilots who helped to defeat the Germans at Stalingrad were known as the "Night Witches."

The home front in the United States was quite different from those of the other major belligerents, largely because the United States faced no threat of war in its own territory. Although the economy and labor force were slow to mobilize, eventually the United States became the arsenal of the Allied powers, producing the military equipment they needed. During the high point of war production in the United States in November 1943, the country was constructing six ships a day and $6 billion worth of war-related goods a month.

The mobilization of the American economy produced social problems. The construction of new factories created boomtowns where thousands came to work but then faced a shortage of houses, health facilities, and schools. The dramatic expansion of small towns into large cities often brought a breakdown in traditional social mores, especially evident in the growth of teenage prostitution. Economic mobilization also led to a widespread movement of people, which in turn created new social tensions. Sixteen million men and women were enrolled in the military, while another sixteen million, mostly wives and sweethearts of the servicemen or workers looking for jobs, also relocated. More than one million blacks migrated from the rural South to the industrial cities of the North and West, looking for jobs in industry. The presence of blacks in areas where they had not lived before led to racial tensions and sometimes even racial riots. In Detroit in June 1943, white mobs roamed the streets attacking blacks.

Japanese-Americans were treated even more shabbily. On the West Coast, 110,000 Japanese-Americans, 65 percent of whom had been born in the United States, were removed to camps encircled by barbed wire and required to take loyalty oaths. Although public officials claimed this policy was necessary for security reasons, no similar treatment of German-Americans or Italian-Americans ever took place. The racism inherent in this treatment of Japanese-Americans was evident when the California governor, Culbert Olson, said: "You know, when I look out at a group of Americans of German or Italian descent, I can tell whether they're loyal or not. I can tell how they think and even perhaps what they are thinking. But it is impossible for me to do this with inscrutable orientals, and particularly the Japanese."[8]

In August 1914, Germans had enthusiastically cheered their soldiers marching off to war. In September 1939, the streets were quiet. Many Germans were apathetic or, even worse for the Nazi regime, had a foreboding of disaster. Hitler was very aware of the importance of the home front. He believed that the collapse of the home front in World War I had caused Germany's defeat, and in his determination to avoid a repetition of that experience, he adopted economic policies that may have cost Germany the war.

To maintain the morale of the home front during the first two years of the war, Hitler refused to convert production from consumer goods to armaments. Blitzkrieg allowed the Germans to win quick victories, after which they could plunder the food and raw materials of conquered countries in order to avoid diverting resources away from the civilian economy. After the German defeats on the Russian front and the American entry into the war, the economic situation changed. Early in 1942, Hitler finally ordered a massive increase in armaments production and the size of the army. Hitler's personal architect, Albert Speer, was made minister for armaments and munitions in 1942. By eliminating waste and rationalizing procedures, Speer was able to triple the production of armaments between 1942 and 1943 despite the intense Allied air raids. Speer's urgent plea for a total mobilization of resources for the war effort went unheeded, however. Hitler, fearful of civilian morale problems that would undermine the home front, refused any dramatic cuts in the production of consumer goods. A total mobilization of the economy was not implemented until July 1944, when schools, theaters, and cafes were closed and Speer was finally permitted to use all remaining resources for the production of a few basic military items. But by that time, it was too late to save Germany from defeat.

The war produced a reversal in Nazi attitudes toward women. Nazi resistance to female employment declined as the war progressed and more and more men were called up for military service. Nazi magazines now proclaimed: "We see the woman as the eternal mother of our people, but also as the working and fighting comrade of the man."[9] But the number of women working in industry, agriculture, commerce, and domestic service increased only slightly. The total number of employed women in September 1944 was 14.9 million compared to 14.6 in May 1939. Many women, especially those of the middle class, resisted regular employment, particularly in factories.

The Frontline Civilians: The Bombing of Cities

Bombing was used in World War II in a variety of ways: against nonhuman military targets, against enemy troops, and against civilian populations. The latter made World War II as devastating for civilians as for frontline soldiers (see the box on p. 597). A small number of bombing raids in the last year of World War I had given rise to the argument, expressed in 1930 by the Italian general Giulio Douhet, that the public outcry generated by the bombing of civilian populations would be an effective way to coerce governments into making peace. Consequently, European air forces began to develop long-range bombers in the 1930s.

The first sustained use of civilian bombing contradicted Douhet's theory. Beginning in early September, the German Luftwaffe subjected London and many other British cities and towns to nightly air raids, making the Blitz (as the British called the German air raids) a national experience. Londoners took the first heavy blows and set the standard for the rest of the British population by refusing to panic. But London morale was helped by the fact that German raids were widely scattered over a very large city. Smaller communities were more directly affected by the devastation. On November 14, 1940, for example, the Luftwaffe destroyed hundreds of shops and 100 acres of the city center of Coventry. The destruction of smaller cities did produce morale problems as wild rumors of heavy casualties spread quickly in these communities. Nevertheless, morale was soon restored. In any case, war production in these areas seems to have been little affected by the raids.

The British failed to learn from their own experience, however, and soon proceeded with the bombing of Germany. Churchill and his advisers believed that destroying German communities would break civilian morale and bring victory. Major bombing raids began in 1942 under the direction of Arthur Harris, the wartime leader of the

The Bombing of Civilians

The home front became a battle front when civilian populations became the targets of mass bombing raids. Many people believed that mass bombing could effectively weaken the morale of the people and shorten the war. Rarely did it achieve its goal. In these selections, British, German, and Japanese civilians relate their experiences during bombing raids.

London, 1940

Early last evening, the noise was terrible. My husband and Mr. P. were trying to play chess in the kitchen. I was playing draughts with Kenneth in the cupboard. . . . Presently I heard a stifled voice "Mummy! I don't know what's become of my glasses." "I should think they are tied up in my wool." My knitting had disappeared and wool seemed to be everywhere! We heard a whistle, a bang which shook the house, and an explosion. . . . Well, we straightened out, decided draughts and chess were no use under the circumstances, and waited for a lull so we could have a pot of tea.

Hamburg, 1943

As the many fires broke through the roofs of the burning buildings, a column of heated air rose more than two and a half miles high and one and a half miles in diameter. . . . This column was turbulent, and it was fed from its base by in-rushing cooler ground-surface air. One and one half miles from the fires this draught increased the wind velocity from eleven to thirty-three miles per hour. At the edge of the area the velocities must have been appreciably greater, as trees three feet in diameter were uprooted. In a short time the temperature reached ignition point for all combustibles, and the entire area was ablaze. In such fires complete burn-out occurred; that is, no trace of combustible material remained, and only after two days were the areas cool enough to approach.

Hiroshima, August 6, 1945

I heard the airplane; I looked up at the sky, it was a sunny day, the sky was blue. . . . Then I saw something drop—and pow!—a big explosion knocked me down. Then I was unconscious—I don't know for how long. Then I was conscious but I couldn't see anything. . . . Then I see people moving away and I just follow them. It is not light like it was before, it is more like evening. I look around; houses are all flat! . . . I follow the people to the river. I couldn't hear anything, my ears are blocked up. I am thinking a bomb has dropped! . . . I didn't know my hands were burned, nor my face. . . . My eyes were swollen and felt closed up.

British air force's Bomber Command, which was rearmed with four-engine heavy bombers capable of taking the war into the center of occupied Europe. On May 31, 1942, Cologne became the first German city to be subjected to an attack by 1,000 bombers.

With the entry of the Americans into the war, bombing strategy changed. American planes flew daytime missions aimed at the precision bombing of transportation facilities and wartime industries, while the British Bomber Command continued nighttime saturation bombing of all German cities with populations over 100,000. Bombing raids added an element of terror to circumstances already made difficult by growing shortages of food, clothing, and fuel. Germans especially feared the incendiary bombs that created firestorms that swept destructive paths through the cities. Four raids on Hamburg in August 1943 produced temperatures of 1,800 degrees Fahrenheit, obliterated half the city's buildings, and killed 50,000 civilians. The ferocious bombing of Dresden from February 13 to 15, 1945, created a firestorm that may have killed as many as 100,000 inhabitants and refugees. Even some Allied leaders began to criticize what they saw as the unnecessary terror bombing of German cities.

Germany suffered enormously from the Allied bombing raids. Millions of buildings were destroyed, and possibly half a million civilians died from the raids. Nevertheless, it is highly unlikely that Allied bombing sapped the morale of the German people. Instead, Germans, whether pro-Nazi or anti-Nazi, fought on stubbornly, often driven simply by a desire to live. Nor did the bombing destroy Germany's industrial capacity. The Allied Strategic Bombing survey revealed that the production of war materials actually increased between 1942 and 1944. Even in 1944 and 1945, Allied raids cut German production of armaments by only 7 percent. Nevertheless, the widespread destruction of transportation systems and fuel supplies made it extremely difficult for the new materials to reach the German military.

✦ **The Destruction of Clydebank.** The bombing of an enemy's cities brought the war home to civilian populations. This picture shows a street in Clydebank, near Glasgow in Scotland, the day after the city was bombed by the Germans in March 1941. Only seven of the city's 12,000 houses were left undamaged; 35,000 of the 47,000 inhabitants became homeless overnight. Clydebank was Scotland's only severe bombing experience.

The bombing of civilians eventually reached a new level with the dropping of the first atomic bomb. Japan was especially vulnerable to air raids because its air force had been virtually destroyed in the course of the war, and its crowded cities were built of flimsy materials. Attacks on Japanese cities by the new American B-29 Superfortresses, the biggest bombers of the war, had begun on November 24, 1944. By the summer of 1945, many of Japan's factories had been destroyed along with one-fourth of its dwellings. After the Japanese government decreed the mobilization of all people between the ages of thirteen and sixty into a People's Volunteer Corps, President Truman and his advisers feared that Japanese fanaticism might mean a million American casualties. This concern led them to drop the atomic bomb on Hiroshima (August 6) and Nagasaki (August 9). The destruction was incredible. Of 76,000 buildings near the hypocenter of the explosion in Hiroshima, 70,000 were flattened, while 140,000 of the city's 400,000 inhabitants died by the end of 1945. By the end of 1950, another 50,000 had perished from the effects of radiation.

The Aftermath of the War: The Emergence of the Cold War

The total victory of the Allies in World War II was not followed by a real peace, but by the beginnings of a new conflict known as the Cold War that dominated world politics until the end of the 1980s. The origins of the Cold War stemmed from the military, political, and ideological differences, especially between the Soviet Union and the United States, that became apparent at the Allied war conferences held in the last years of the war. Although Allied leaders were primarily preoccupied with how to end the war, they also were strongly motivated by differing, and often conflicting, visions of postwar Europe.

The Conferences at Teheran, Yalta, and Potsdam

Stalin, Roosevelt, and Churchill, the leaders of the Big Three of the Grand Alliance, met at Teheran (the capital of Iran) in November 1943 to decide the future course of the war. Their major tactical decision concerned the final assault on Germany. Stalin and Roosevelt argued successfully for an American-British invasion of the Continent through France, which they scheduled for the spring of 1944. The acceptance of this plan had important consequences. It meant that Soviet and British-American forces would meet in defeated Germany along a north–south dividing line and that, most likely, Eastern Europe would be liberated by Soviet forces. The Allies also agreed to a partition of postwar Germany.

By the time of the conference at Yalta in southern Russia in February 1945, the defeat of Germany was a foregone conclusion. The Western powers, which had earlier believed that the Soviets were in a weak position, were now faced with the reality of eleven million Red Army soldiers taking possession of Eastern and much of central Europe. Stalin was still operating under the notion of spheres of influence. He was deeply suspicious of the Western powers and desired a buffer to protect the Soviet Union from possible future Western aggression. At the same time, however, Stalin was eager to obtain economically important resources and strategic military positions. Roosevelt by this time was moving away from the notion of spheres of influence to the ideal of self-determination. He called for "the end of the system of unilateral action, exclusive alliances, and spheres of influence." The Grand Alliance approved a "Declaration on Liberated Europe." This was a pledge to assist liberated European nations in the creation of "democratic institutions of their own choice." Liberated countries were to hold free elections to determine their political systems.

At Yalta, Roosevelt sought Russian military help against Japan. The atomic bomb was not yet assured, and American military planners feared the possible loss of as many as one million men in amphibious assaults on the Japanese home islands. Roosevelt therefore agreed to Stalin's price for military assistance against Japan: possession of Sakhalin and the Kurile Islands, as well as two warm water ports and railroad rights in Manchuria.

The creation of the United Nations was a major American concern at Yalta. Roosevelt hoped to ensure the participation of the Big Three powers in a postwar international organization before difficult issues divided them into hostile camps. After a number of compromises, both Churchill and Stalin accepted Roosevelt's plans for a United Nations organization and set the first meeting for San Francisco in April 1945.

The issues of Germany and Eastern Europe were treated less decisively. The Big Three reaffirmed that Germany must surrender unconditionally and created four occupation zones. German reparations were set at $20 billion. A compromise was also worked out in regard to Poland. Stalin agreed to free elections in the future to determine a new government. But the issue of free elections in Eastern Europe caused a serious rift between the Soviets and the Americans. The principle was that Eastern European governments would be freely elected, but they were also supposed to be pro-Soviet. As Churchill expressed it: "The Poles will have their future in their own hands, with the single limitation that they must honestly follow in harmony with their allies, a policy friendly to Russia."[10] This attempt to reconcile two irreconcilable goals was doomed to failure, as soon became evident at the next conference of the Big Three powers.

Even before the conference at Potsdam took place in July 1945, Western relations with the Soviets were deteriorating rapidly. The Grand Alliance had been one of necessity in which disagreements had been subordinated to the pragmatic concerns of the war. The Allied powers' only common aim was the defeat of Nazism. Once this aim had all but been accomplished, the many differences that troubled East–West relations came to the surface. Each side committed acts that the other viewed as unbecoming of "allies."

From the perspective of the Soviets, the United States' termination of the Lend-Lease aid before the war was over and its failure to respond to the Soviet request for a $6 billion loan for reconstruction exposed the Western desire to keep the Soviet state weak. On the American side, the Soviet Union's failure to fulfill its Yalta pledge on the "Declaration on Liberated Europe" as applied to Eastern Europe set a dangerous precedent. This was evident in Romania as early as February 1945, when the Soviets engineered a coup and installed a new government under the Communist Petra Groza, called the "Little Stalin." One month later, the Soviets sabotaged the Polish settlement by arresting the London Poles and their sympathizers and placing the Soviet-backed Lublin Poles in power. To the Americans, the Soviets seemed to be asserting control of Eastern European countries under puppet Communist regimes.

The Potsdam conference of July 1945 consequently began under a cloud of mistrust. Roosevelt had died on April 12 and had been succeeded by Harry Truman. Dur-

◆ **The Victorious Allied Leaders at Yalta.** Even before World War II ended, the leaders of the Big Three of the Grand Alliance, Churchill, Roosevelt, and Stalin (shown from left to right), met in wartime conferences to plan the final assault on Germany and negotiate the outlines of the postwar settlement. At the Yalta meeting (February 5–11, 1945), the three leaders concentrated on postwar issues. The American president, who died two months later, was already a worn-out man at Yalta.

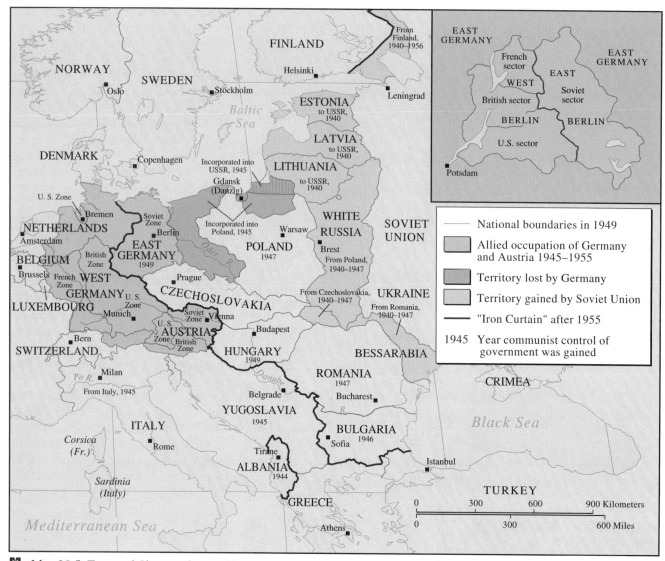

Map 28.5 Territorial Changes after World War II.

ing the conference, Truman received word that the atomic bomb had been successfully tested. Some historians have argued that this knowledge resulted in Truman's stiffened resolve against the Soviets. Whatever the reasons, there was a new coldness in the relations between the Soviets and Americans. At Potsdam, Truman demanded free elections throughout Eastern Europe. Stalin responded: "A freely elected government in any

of these East European countries would be anti-Soviet, and that we cannot allow."[11] After a bitterly fought and devastating war, Stalin sought absolute military security. To him, it could only be gained by the presence of Communist states in Eastern Europe. Free elections might result in governments hostile to the Soviets. By the middle of 1945, only an invasion by Western forces could undo developments in Eastern Europe, and after the world's most destructive conflict had ended, few people favored such a policy.

As the war slowly receded into the past, the reality of conflicting ideologies had reappeared. Many in the West interpreted Soviet policy as part of a worldwide Communist conspiracy. The Soviets, on the other hand, viewed Western, especially American, policy as nothing less than global capitalist expansionism or, in Leninist terms, as nothing less than economic imperialism. Vyacheslav Molotov, the Russian foreign minister, referred to the Americans as "insatiable imperialists" and "war-mongering groups of adventurers."[12] In March 1946, in a speech to an American audience, former British prime minister Winston Churchill declared that "an iron curtain" had "descended across the continent," dividing Germany and Europe into two hostile camps. Stalin branded Churchill's speech a "call to war with the Soviet Union." Only months after the world's most devastating conflict had ended, the world seemed once again bitterly divided.

Conclusion

Between 1933 and 1939, Europeans watched as Adolf Hitler rebuilt Germany into a great military power. For Hitler, military power was an absolute prerequisite for the creation of a German racial empire that would dominate Europe and the world for generations to come. If Hitler had been successful, the Nazi New Order, built on authoritarianism, racial extermination, and the brutal oppression of peoples, would have meant a triumph of barbarism and the end of freedom and equality, which, however imperfectly realized, had become important ideals in Western civilization.

The Nazis lost, but only after tremendous sacrifices and costs. Much of European civilization lay in ruins, and the old Europe had disappeared forever. Europeans, who had been accustomed to dominating the world at the beginning of the twentieth century, now watched helplessly at mid-century as the two new superpowers created by the two world wars took control of their destinies. Even before the last battles had been fought, the United States and the Soviet Union had arrived at different visions of the postwar world. No sooner had the war ended than their differences created a new and potentially even more devastating conflict known as the Cold War. Yet even though Europeans seemed merely pawns in the struggle between the two superpowers, they managed to stage a remarkable recovery of their own civilization.

NOTES

1. Adolf Hitler, *Mein Kampf,* trans. Ralph Manheim (Boston, 1971), p. 654.
2. *Documents on German Foreign Policy* (London, 1956), Series D, 7:204.
3. Albert Speer, *Spandau,* trans. Richard and Clara Winston (New York, 1976), p. 50.
4. *Nazi Conspiracy and Aggression* (Washington, D.C., 1946), 6:262.
5. International Military Tribunal, *Trial of the Major War Criminals* (Nuremberg, 1947–1949), 22:480.
6. Quoted in Raul Hilberg, *The Destruction of the European Jews,* rev. ed. (New York, 1985), 1:332–333.
7. *Nazi Conspiracy and Aggression,* 6:789.
8. Quoted in John Campbell, *The Experience of World War II* (New York, 1989), p. 170.
9. Quoted in Claudia Koonz, "Mothers in the Fatherland: Women in Nazi Germany," in Renate Bridenthal and Claudia Koonz, eds., *Becoming Visible: Women in European History* (Boston, 1977), p. 466.
10. Quoted in Norman Graebner, *Cold War Diplomacy, 1945–1960* (Princeton, N.J., 1962), p. 117.
11. Quoted in ibid.
12. Quoted in Wilfried Loth, *The Division of the World, 1941–1955* (New York, 1988), p. 81.

SUGGESTIONS FOR FURTHER READING

The basic study of Germany's foreign policy from 1933 to 1939 can be found in G. Weinberg, *The Foreign Policy of Hitler's Germany: Diplomatic Revolution in Europe, 1933–36* (Chicago, 1970), and *The Foreign Policy of Hitler's Germany: Starting World War II, 1937–1939* (Chicago, 1980). For a detailed account of the immediate events leading to World War II, see D. C. Watt, *How War Came: The Immediate Origins of the Second World War, 1938–1939* (New York, 1989).

Hitler's war aims and the importance of ideology to those aims are examined in N. Rich, *Hitler's War Aims*, vol. 1, *Ideology, the Nazi State and the Course of Expansion* (New York, 1973), and vol. 2, *The Establishment of the New Order* (New York, 1974). General works on World War II include the comprehensive work by G. Weinberg, *A World at Arms: A Global History of World War II* (Cambridge, 1994); M. K. Dziewanowski, *War at Any Price: World War II in Europe, 1939–1945*, 2d ed. (Englewood Cliffs, N.J., 1991); P. Calvocoressi and G. Wint, *Total War: Causes and Courses of the Second World War* (New York, 1979); J. Campbell, *The Experience of World War II* (New York, 1989); and G. Wright, *The Ordeal of Total War, 1939–1945* (New York, 1968). On Hitler as a military leader, see R. Lewin, *Hitler's Mistakes* (New York, 1986). The Eastern Front is covered in J. Erickson, *Stalin's War with Germany*, vol. 1, *The Road to Stalingrad*; vol. 2, *The Road to Berlin* (London, 1973, 1985); and O. Bartov, *The Eastern Front, 1941–45: German Troops and the Barbarisation of Warfare* (London, 1986). The second front in Europe is examined in C. D'Este, *Decision in Normandy* (London, 1983). See also S. E. Ambrose, *Eisenhower: The Soldier* (London, 1984).

A standard work on the German New Order in Russia is A. Dallin, *German Rule in Russia, 1941–1945*, rev ed. (London, 1981). On Poland, see J. T. Gross, *Polish Society under German Occupation* (Princeton, N.J., 1981). On foreign labor, see E. Homze, *Foreign Labor in Nazi Germany* (Princeton, N.J., 1967).

The best studies of the Holocaust include R. Hilberg, *The Destruction of the European Jews*, rev. ed., 3 vols. (New York, 1985); L. Dawidowicz, *The War against the Jews* (New York, 1975); L. Yahil, *The Holocaust* (Oxford, 1990); and M. Gilbert, *The Holocaust: The History of the Jews of Europe during the Second World War* (New York, 1985). See also the recent brief work by J. Fischel, *The Holocaust* (Westport, Conn., 1998). There is a good overview of the scholarship on the Holocaust in M. Marrus, *The Holocaust in History* (New York, 1987). The role of Hitler in the Holocaust has been well examined in G. Fleming, *Hitler and the Final Solution* (Berkeley, 1984). On the extermination camps, see K. G. Feig, *Hitler's Death Camps: The Sanity of Madness* (New York, 1981). Other Nazi atrocities are examined in R. C. Lukas, *Forgotten Holocaust: The Poles under German Occupation, 1939–44* (Lexington, Ky., 1986); and B. Wytwycky, *The Other Holocaust* (Washington, D.C., 1980).

General studies on the impact of total war include J. Costello, *Love, Sex and War: Changing Values, 1939–1945* (London, 1985); A. Marwick, *War, and Social Change in the Twentieth Century: A Comparative Study of Britain, France, Germany, Russia and the United States* (London, 1974); A. S. Milward, *War, Economy and Society, 1939–1945* (London, 1977); and M. R. Marrus, *The Unwanted: European Refugees in the Twentieth Century* (New York, 1985). On the home front in Germany, see E. R. Beck, *Under the Bombs: The German Home Front, 1942–1945* (Lexington, Ky., 1986); J. Stephenson, *The Nazi Organisation of Women* (London, 1981); and L. J. Rupp, *Mobilizing Women for War: German and American Propaganda, 1939–1945* (Princeton, N.J., 1978). The Soviet Union during the war is examined in M. Harrison, *Soviet Planning in Peace and War, 1938–1945* (Cambridge, 1985). On the American home front, see G. Perrett, *Days of Sadness, Years of Triumph: The American People, 1939–1945* (New York, 1973). There is also a good collection of essays in K. P.

O'Brien and L. H. Parsons, *The Home-Front War: World War II and American Society* (Westport, Conn., 1995).

On the destruction of Germany by bombing raids, see H. Rumpf, *The Bombing of Germany* (London, 1963). The German bombing of Britain is covered in T. Harrisson, *Living through the Blitz* (London, 1985). On Hiroshima, see A. Chisholm, *Faces of Hiroshima* (London, 1985).

On the emergence of the Cold War, see W. Loth, *The Division of the World, 1941–1955* (New York, 1988), and the more extensive list of references at the end of Chapter 29. On the wartime summit conferences, see H. Feis, *Churchill, Roosevelt, Stalin: The War They Waged and the Peace They Sought*, 2d ed. (Princeton, N.J., 1967).

CHAPTER
29

Cold War and a New Western World, 1945–1970

The end of World War II in Europe was met with great joy. One visitor to Moscow reported, "I looked out of the window [at 2 A.M.], almost everywhere there were lights in the window—people were staying awake. Everyone embraced everyone else, someone sobbed aloud." But after the victory parades and celebrations, Europeans awoke to a devastating realization: Their civilization was in ruins. Some wondered if Europe would ever regain its former prosperity and importance. Winston Churchill wrote: "What is Europe now? A rubble heap, a charnel house, a breeding ground of pestilence and hate." There was ample reason for his pessimism. Almost 40 million people (both soldiers and civilians) had been killed during the last six years. Massive air raids and artillery bombardments had reduced many of the great cities of Europe to heaps of rubble. The Polish capital of Warsaw had been almost completely obliterated. An American general described Berlin: "Wherever we looked we saw desolation. It was like a city of the dead. Suffering and shock were visible in every face. Dead bodies still remained in canals and lakes and were being dug out from under bomb debris." Millions of Europeans faced starvation because grain harvests were only half of what they had been in 1939. Millions were also homeless. In the parts of the Soviet Union that had been occupied by the Germans, almost 25 million people were without homes. The destruction of bridges, roads, and railroads had left transportation systems paralyzed. Untold millions of people had been uprooted by the war; now they became "displaced persons," trying to find food and then their way home. Eleven million prisoners of war had to be returned to their native countries, and 15 million Germans and East Europeans were driven out of countries where they were no longer wanted. Yet, despite the chaos, Europe was soon on the road to a remarkable recovery. Already by 1950, Europe's industrial and agricultural output was 30 percent above prewar levels.

World War II had cost Europe more than physical destruction, however. European supremacy in world affairs had also been destroyed. After 1945, the

Emergence of welfare state in Britain   Formation of European Common Market

Marshall Plan   Student revolts

Creation of NATO   Formation of Warsaw Pact   Cuban Missile Crisis

Korean War   Vietnam War

Berlin blockade   Charles de Gaulle assumes power in France

Building of Berlin Wall •   Soviets crush "Prague Spring" in Czechoslovakia

colonial empires of the European nations rapidly disintegrated and Europe's place in the world changed radically. As the Cold War conflict between the world's two superpowers—the United States and the Soviet Union—intensified, the European nations were divided into two armed camps dependent on one or the other of these two major powers. The United States and the Soviet Union, whose rivalry raised the specter of nuclear war, seemed to hold the survival of Europe and the world in their hands.

The Development of the Cold War

Even before World War II had ended, the two major Allied powers—the United States and the Soviet Union—had begun to disagree on the nature of the postwar European world. Unity had been maintained during the war because of the urgent need to defeat the Axis powers, but once they were defeated, the differences between the Americans and Soviets again surged to the front. Stalin had never overcome his fear of capitalist superiority, and Western leaders still had serious misgivings about communism.

The Confrontation of the Superpowers

Considerable historical debate has been waged about who was most responsible for the beginning of the Cold War. No doubt, both the United States and the Soviet Union took steps at the end of the war that were unwise or might

have been avoided. Both nations, however, were working within a framework conditioned by the past. Ultimately, the rivalry between the two superpowers stemmed from their different historical perspectives and their irreconcilable political ambitions. Intense competition for political and military supremacy had long been a regular feature of Western civilization. The United States and the Soviet Union were the heirs of that European tradition of power politics, and it should not surprise us that two such different systems would seek to extend their way of life to the rest of the world. Because of its need to feel secure on its western border, the Soviet Union was not prepared to give up the advantages it had gained in Eastern Europe from Germany's defeat. But neither were American leaders willing to give up the power and prestige the United States had gained throughout the world. Suspicious of each other's motives, the United States and Soviet Union soon raised their mutual fears to a level of intense competition. Between 1945 and 1949, a number of events entangled the two countries in continual conflict.

Eastern Europe was the first area of disagreement. The United States and Great Britain had championed self-determination and democratic freedom for the liberated nations of Eastern Europe. Stalin, however, fearful that the Eastern European nations would return to traditional anti-Soviet attitudes if they were permitted free elections, opposed the West's plans. Having liberated Eastern Europe from the Nazis, the Red Army proceeded to install pro-Soviet governing regimes in Poland, Romania, Bulgaria, and Hungary. These pro-Soviet governments satisfied Stalin's desire for a buffer zone against the West, but the local populations and their sympathizers in the West saw the regimes as an expansion of Stalin's empire. Only another war could change this situation, and few people advocated another armed conflict.

The Truman Doctrine

By 1947, the battlelines had been clearly drawn in the Cold War. This selection is taken from a speech by President Harry S Truman to the American Congress in which he justified his request for aid to Greece and Turkey. Truman expressed the urgent need to contain the expansion of communism.

President Harry S Truman Addresses Congress, March 12, 1947

The peoples of a number of countries of the world have recently had totalitarian regimes forced upon them against their will. The Government of the United States has made frequent protests against coercion and intimidation, in violation of the Yalta agreement, in Poland, Romania, and Bulgaria. I must also state that in a number of other countries there have been similar developments.

At the present moment in world history nearly every nation must choose between alternative ways of life. The choice is too often not a free one.

One way of life is based upon the will of the majority, and is distinguished by free institutions, representative government, free elections, guaranties of individual liberty, freedom of speech and religion, and freedom from political oppression.

The second way of life is based upon the will of a minority forcibly imposed upon the majority. It relies upon terror and oppression, a controlled press and radio, fixed elections, and the suppression of personal freedoms.

I believe that it must be the policy of the United States to support free peoples who are resisting attempted subjugation by armed minorities or by outside pressures.

I believe that we must assist free people to work out their own destinies in their own way.

I believe that our help should be primarily through economic and financial aid which is essential to economic stability and orderly political processes. . . . I therefore ask the Congress for assistance to Greece and Turkey in the amount of $400,000,000.

A civil war in Greece created another arena for confrontation between the superpowers. The Communist People's Liberation Army and the anti-Communist forces supported by the British were fighting each other for control of Greece in 1946. President Harry S Truman of the United States, alarmed by British weakness and the possibility of Soviet expansion into the eastern Mediterranean, responded with the Truman Doctrine (see the box above). Truman requested $400 million in economic and military aid for Greece and Turkey from the American Congress. The Truman Doctrine said in essence that the United States would provide money to countries that claimed they were threatened by Communist expansion. If the Soviets were not stopped in Greece, the Truman argument ran, then the United States would have to face the spread of communism throughout the free world. As Dean Acheson, the American secretary of state explained, "Like apples in a barrel infected by disease, the corruption of Greece would infect Iran and all the East . . . likewise Africa . . . Italy . . . France. . . . Not since Rome and Carthage had there been such a polarization of power on this earth."[1]

The proclamation of the Truman Doctrine was soon followed in June 1947 by the European Recovery Program, better known as the Marshall Plan. Intended to re-

build prosperity and stability, this program included $13 billion for the economic recovery of war-torn Europe. Underlying it was the belief that Communist aggression fed off economic turmoil. General George C. Marshall had noted in his commencement speech at Harvard: "Our policy is not directed against any country or doctrine but against hunger, poverty, desperation and chaos."[2] From the Soviet perspective, the Marshall Plan aimed at "the construction of a bloc of states bound by obligations to the USA," and guaranteed "the American loans in return for the relinquishing by the European states of their economic and later also their political independence." The Marshall Plan was not intended to shut out either the Soviet Union or its Eastern European satellite states, but they refused to participate.

By 1947, the split in Europe between East and West had become a fact of life. At the end of World War II, the United States had favored a quick end to its commitments in Europe. But American fears of Soviet aims caused the United States to play an increasingly important role in European affairs. In an important article in *Foreign Affairs* in July 1947, George Kennan, a well-known American diplomat with much knowledge of Soviet affairs, advocated a policy of containment against further aggression by the Soviets. Kennan favored the "adroit and vigilant application of counter-force at a series of constantly shifting geographical and political points, corresponding to the shifts and manoeuvres of Soviet policy." After the Soviet blockade of Berlin in 1948, containment of the Soviet Union became formal American policy.

The fate of Germany also became a source of heated contention between East and West. Besides the partitioning of Germany (and Berlin) into four occupied zones, the Allied powers had agreed on little else with regard to the conquered nation. The Soviets, hardest hit by the war, took reparations from Germany in the form of booty. The technology-starved Soviets dismantled and removed to Russia 380 factories from the western zones of Berlin before transferring their control to the Western powers. By the summer of 1946, 200 chemical, paper, and textile factories in the Soviets' East German zone had likewise been shipped to the Soviet Union. At the same time, the German Communist party was reestablished under the control of Walter Ulbricht (1893–1973) and was soon in charge of the political reconstruction of the Soviet zone in eastern Germany.

At the same time, the British, French, and Americans gradually began to merge their zones economically and, by February 1948, were making plans for the unification of these three Western sections of Germany and the formal creation of a West German federal government. The Soviets responded with a blockade of West Berlin that allowed neither trucks nor trains to enter the three Western zones of Berlin. The Russians hoped to secure economic control of all Berlin and force the Western powers to stop the creation of a separate West German state.

The Western powers were faced with a dilemma. Direct military confrontation seemed dangerous, and no one wished to risk World War III. Therefore, an attempt to break through the blockade with tanks and trucks was ruled out. The solution was the Berlin air lift. At its peak, 13,000 tons of supplies were flown daily to Berlin. The Soviets, also not wanting war, did not interfere and finally lifted the blockade in May 1949. The blockade of Berlin had severely increased tensions between the United States and the Soviet Union and resulted in the separation of Germany into two states. The West German Federal Republic was formally created in September 1949, and a month later, a separate German Democratic Republic was established in East Germany. Berlin remained a divided city and the source of much contention between East and West.

In that same year, the Cold War spread from Europe to the rest of the world. The victory of the Chinese Communists in 1949 in the Chinese civil war created a new

✦ **The Berlin Air Lift.** The Berlin air lift enabled the United States to fly 13,000 tons of supplies daily to Berlin and thus break the Soviet land blockade of the city. In this photograph, children in West Berlin are watching another American plane arrive with supplies for the city.

Communist regime and only intensified American fears about the spread of communism. The Soviet Union also detonated its first atomic bomb in 1949, and all too soon both powers were involved in an escalating arms race that resulted in the construction of ever more destructive nuclear weapons. Soon the search for security took the form of mutual deterrence or the belief that an arsenal of nuclear weapons prevented war by ensuring that even if one nation launched its nuclear weapons in a preemptive first strike, the other nation would still be able to respond and devastate the attacker. It was assumed that neither side would risk using the massive arsenals that had been assembled.

The search for security in the new world of the Cold War also led to the formation of military alliances. The North Atlantic Treaty Organization (NATO) was formed

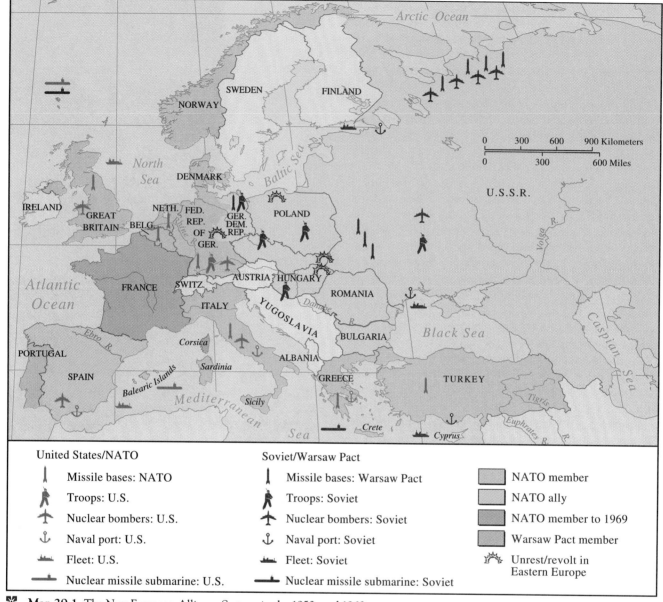

Map 29.1 The New European Alliance Systems in the 1950s and 1960s.

in April 1949 when Belgium, Luxembourg, the Netherlands, France, Britain, Italy, Denmark, Norway, Portugal, and Iceland signed a treaty with the United States and Canada. All the powers agreed to provide mutual assistance if any one of them was attacked. A few years later West Germany, Greece, and Turkey joined NATO.

The Eastern European states soon followed suit. In 1949, they had already formed the Council for Mutual Assistance (COMECON) for economic cooperation. Then in 1955, Albania, Bulgaria, Czechoslovakia, East Germany, Hungary, Poland, Romania, and the Soviet Union organized a formal military alliance in the Warsaw Pact. Once again, Europe was tragically divided into hostile alliance systems.

A system of military alliances spread to the rest of the world after the United States became involved in the Korean War in 1950. In 1950, probably with Stalin's approval, North Korean forces invaded South Korea. The Americans, seeing this as yet another example of Communist aggression and expansion, gained the support of the United Nations and intervened by sending American troops to turn back the invasion. When the American and South Korean forces pushed the North Koreans back toward the Chinese border, Chinese forces entered the fray and forced the American and South Korean troops to retreat back to South Korea. Believing that the Chinese were simply the puppets of Moscow, American policymakers created an image of communism as a monolithic force directed by the Soviet Union. After two more years of inconclusive fighting, an uneasy truce was reached in 1953 and the division of Korea reaffirmed. To many Americans, the policy of containing communism had succeeded in Asia, just as it had earlier in Europe.

The Korean experience seemed to confirm American fears about Communist expansion and reinforced American determination to contain Soviet power. In the mid-1950s, the administration of President Dwight D. Eisenhower (1890–1969) adopted a policy of massive retaliation, which advocated the full use of American nuclear bombs to counteract even a Soviet ground attack in Europe. Moreover, American military alliances were extended around the world. The Central Treaty Organization (CENTO) of Turkey, Iraq, Iran, Pakistan, Britain, and the United States was intended to prevent the Soviet Union from expanding at the expense of its southern neighbors. To stem Soviet aggression in the Far East, the United States, Britain, France, Pakistan, Thailand, the Philippines, Australia, and New Zealand formed the Southeast Asia Treaty Organization (SEATO). By the mid-1950s, the United States found itself allied militarily with forty-two states around the world.

Despite the continued escalation of the Cold War, hopes for a new era of peaceful coexistence also appeared. Certainly, the death of Stalin in 1953 caused some people in the West to think that the new Soviet leadership might be more flexible in its policies. But this optimism seemed premature. A summit conference at Geneva in 1955 between President Eisenhower and Nikolai Bulganin, then leader of the Soviet government, produced no real benefits. A year later, all talk of rapprochement between East and West temporarily ceased when the Soviet Union used its armed forces in 1956 to crush Hungary's attempt to assert its independence from Soviet control.

A crisis over Berlin also added to the tension in the late 1950s. In August 1957, the Soviet Union had launched its first intercontinental ballistic missile (ICBM) and, shortly after, *Sputnik I*, the first space satellite. Fueled by partisan political debate, fears of a missile gap between the United States and the Soviet Union seized the American public. Nikita Khrushchev (1894–1971), the new leader

CHRONOLOGY

The Cold War

Truman Doctrine	1947
European Recovery Program (Marshall Plan)	1947
Berlin blockade	1948–1949
Communists win civil war in China	1949
Soviet Union explodes first atomic bomb	1949
Formation of North Atlantic Treaty Organization	1949
Formation of COMECON	1949
Korean War	1950–1953
Formation of Warsaw Pact	1955
Berlin Crisis	1958
Vienna summit	1961
Cuban Missile Crisis	1962
Vietnam War	1964–1973

of the Soviet Union, attempted to take advantage of the American frenzy over missiles to solve the problem of West Berlin. West Berlin had remained a "Western island" of prosperity in the midst of the relatively poverty-stricken East Germany. Many East Germans also managed to escape East Germany by fleeing through West Berlin.

In November 1958, Khrushchev announced that, unless the West removed its forces from West Berlin within six months, he would turn over control of the access routes to Berlin to the East Germans. Unwilling to accept an ultimatum that would have abandoned West Berlin to the Communists, Eisenhower and the West stood firm, and Khrushchev eventually backed down. In 1961, the East German government built a wall separating West Berlin from East Berlin, and the Berlin issue faded.

It was revived when John F. Kennedy (1917–1963) became the American president. During a summit meeting in Vienna in June 1961, Khrushchev threatened Kennedy with another six-month ultimatum over West Berlin. Kennedy left Vienna convinced of the need to deal firmly with the Soviet Union, and Khrushchev was forced once again to lift his six-month ultimatum. However, determined to achieve some foreign policy success, the Soviet leader soon embarked on an even more dangerous adventure in Cuba.

The Cuban Missile Crisis and the Move Toward Détente

The Cold War confrontation between the United States and the Soviet Union reached frightening levels during the Cuban Missile Crisis. In 1959, a left-wing revolutionary named Fidel Castro (b. 1927) had overthrown the Cuban dictator Fulgencio Batista and established a Soviet-supported totalitarian regime. In 1961, an American-supported attempt (the "Bay of Pigs" incident) to overthrow Castro's regime ended in utter failure. The next year, in 1962, the Soviet Union decided to place nuclear missiles in Cuba. The United States was not prepared to allow nuclear weapons to be within such close striking distance of the American mainland, even though it had placed nuclear weapons in Turkey within easy range of the Soviet Union. Khrushchev was quick to point out that "your rockets are in Turkey. You are worried by Cuba . . . because it is 90 miles from the American coast. But Turkey is next to us."[3] When American intelligence discovered that a Soviet fleet carrying missiles was heading to Cuba, President Kennedy decided to blockade Cuba and prevent the fleet from reaching its destination. This approach to the problem had the benefit of delaying confrontation and giving each side time to find a peaceful solution (see the box on p. 611). Khrushchev agreed to turn back the fleet if Kennedy pledged not to invade Cuba.

The intense feeling that the world might have been annihilated in a few days had a profound influence on both sides. A hotline communications system between Moscow and Washington was installed in 1963 to expedite rapid communications between the two superpowers in a time of crisis. In the same year, the two powers agreed to ban nuclear tests in the atmosphere, a step that served to lessen the tensions between the two nations.

By that time, the United States had also been drawn into a new confrontation that had an important impact on the Cold War—the Vietnam War. In 1964, under President Lyndon Johnson (1908–1973), increasing numbers of American troops were sent to Vietnam to keep the Communist regime of the north from uniting the entire country under its control. Although nationalism played a powerful role in this conflict, the American policy-makers saw it in terms of a domino theory concerning the spread of communism. If the Communists succeeded in Vietnam, so the argument went, all the other countries in the Far East freeing themselves from colonial domination would fall (like dominoes) to communism.

Despite their massive superiority in equipment and firepower, American forces failed to prevail over the persistence of the North Vietnamese. The mounting destruction and increasing brutalization of the war, brought into American homes every evening on television, also turned American public opinion against the war. Finally,

◆ **John F. Kennedy and the Cuban Missile Crisis.** During the Cuban Missile Crisis, the United States and the Soviet Union came frighteningly close to a direct nuclear confrontation. This photograph shows President John F. Kennedy meeting with his cabinet and advisers during the Cuban crisis in October 1962. At Kennedy's left is Robert McNamara, the secretary of defense, and to his right is Dean Rusk, the secretary of state.

The Cuban Missile Crisis: Khrushchev's Perspective

The Cuban Missile Crisis was one of the sobering experiences of the Cold War. It led the two superpowers to seek new ways to lessen the tensions between them. This version of the events is taken from the memoirs of Nikita Khrushchev.

Khrushchev Remembers

I will explain what the Caribbean crisis of October 1962, was all about. . . . At the time that Fidel Castro led his revolution to victory and entered Havana with his troops, we had no idea what political course his regime would follow. . . . All the while the Americans had been watching Castro closely. At first they thought that the capitalist underpinnings of the Cuban economy would remain intact. So by the time Castro announced that he was going to put Cuba on the road toward Socialism, the Americans had already missed their chance to do any thing about it by simply exerting their influence: there were no longer any forces left which could be organized to fight on America's behalf in Cuba. That left only one alternative—invasion! . . .

After Castro's crushing victory over the counterrevolutionaries we intensified our military aid to Cuba . . . We were sure that the Americans would never reconcile themselves to the existence of Castro's Cuba. They feared, as much as we hoped, that a Socialist Cuba might become a magnet that would attract other Latin American countries to Socialism. . . . It was clear to me that we might very well lose Cuba if we didn't take some decisive steps in her defense. . . . We had to think up some way of confronting America with more than words. We had to establish a tangible and effective deterrent to American interference in the Caribbean. But what exactly? The logical answer was missiles. We knew that American missiles were aimed against us in Turkey and Italy, to say nothing of West Germany. . . . My thinking went like this: if we installed the missiles secretly and then if the United States discovered the missiles were there after they were already poised and ready to strike, the Americans would think twice before trying to liquidate our installations by military means. . . . I want to make one thing absolutely clear: when we put our ballistic missiles in Cuba we had no desire to start a war. On the contrary, our principal aim was only to deter America from starting a war. . . .

President Kennedy issued an ultimatum, demanding that we remove our missiles and bombers from Cuba. . . . We sent the Americans a note saying that we agreed to remove our missiles and bombers on the condition that the President give us his assurance that there would be no invasion of Cuba by the forces of the United States or anybody else. Finally Kennedy gave in and agreed to make a statement giving us such an assurance. . . . It had been, to say the least, an interesting and challenging situation. The two most powerful nations of the world had been squared off against each other, each with its finger on the button. You'd have thought that war was inevitable. But both sides showed that if the desire to avoid war is strong enough, even the most pressing dispute can be solved by compromise. And a compromise over Cuba was indeed found. The episode ended in a triumph of common sense. . . . It was a great victory for us, though, that we had been able to extract from Kennedy a promise that neither America nor any of her allies would invade Cuba. . . . The Caribbean crisis was a triumph of Soviet foreign policy and a personal triumph in my own career as a statesman and as a member of the collective leadership. We achieved, I would say, a spectacular success without having to fire a single shot!

---

in 1973 President Richard Nixon (1913–1994) reached an agreement with North Vietnam that allowed the United States to withdraw its forces. Within two years, Vietnam had been forcibly reunited by Communist armies from the North.

Despite the success of the North Vietnamese Communists, the domino theory proved unfounded. A noisy rupture between Communist China and the Soviet Union put an end to the idea of a monolithic communism directed by Moscow. Under President Nixon, American relations with China were resumed. New nations in Southeast Asia also managed to avoid Communist governments. Above all, Vietnam helped to show the limitations of American power. By the end of the Vietnam war, a new era in American–Soviet relations—known as *détente*—had begun to emerge.

Recovery and Renewal in Europe

Within a few years after the defeat of Germany and Italy, economic revival brought a renewed growth to European society, although major differences remained between Western and Eastern Europe. Moreover, many Europeans found that they could even adjust to decolonization.

The End of European Colonies

Not only did World War II leave Europe in ruins, but it also cost Europe its supremacy in world affairs. The power of the European states had been destroyed by the exhaustive struggles of World War II. The greatest colonial empire builder, Great Britain, no longer had the energy or wealth to maintain its colonial empire after the war and quickly sought to let its colonies go. A rush of decolonization swept through the world. Between 1947 and 1962, virtually every colony achieved independence and attained statehood. Although some colonial powers willingly relinquished their control, others, especially the French, had to be driven out by national wars of liberation. Decolonization was a difficult and even bitter process, but it created a new world as the non-Western states ended the long-held ascendancy of the Western nations.

In Asia, the United States initiated the process of decolonization in 1946 when it granted independence to the Philippines. Britain soon followed suit with its oldest and largest nonwhite possession—India. The conflict between India's Hindu and Muslim populations was solved by form-

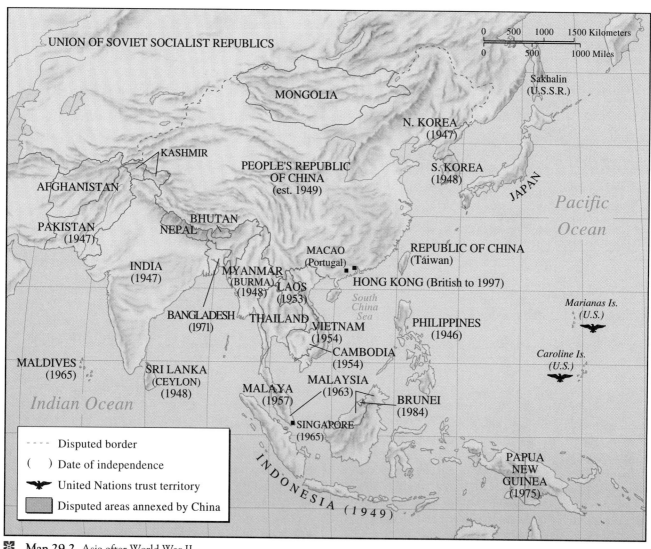

❋ **Map 29.2** Asia after World War II.

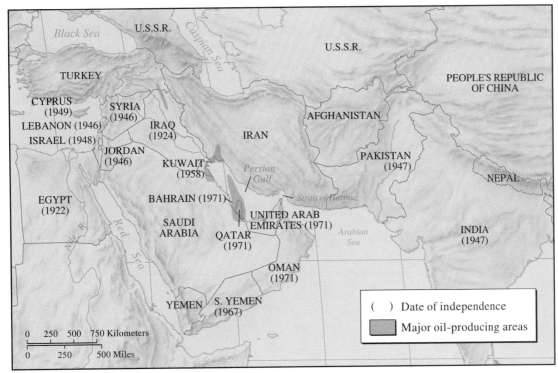

🔆 **Map 29.3** The Middle East after World War II.

ing two states, a mostly Hindu India and a predominantly Muslim Pakistan in 1947. The French efforts to remain in Indochina led to a bloody struggle with the Vietminh, Vietnamese nationalist guerrillas, led by Ho Chi Minh, the Communist and nationalist leader of the Vietnamese. The division of Vietnam by Communists and pro-Western regimes eventually led to the Vietnam War.

In the Middle East, Arab nationalism was a powerful factor in ending colonial empires, but not without considerable bloodshed and complications. When the British left Palestine in 1947, the United Nations voted to create both an Arab state and a Jewish state. When the Arabs attempted to destroy the new Israeli state, Israel's victory secured its existence. But the problem of the Palestinian refugees, supported by existing Arab states, created an Arab–Israeli conflict that has lasted to this day.

In North Africa, the French granted full independence to Morocco and Tunisia in 1956. Because Algeria was home to two million French settlers, however, France chose to retain its dominion there. But a group of Algerian nationalists organized the National Liberation Front (FLN) and in 1954 initiated a guerrilla war to liberate their homeland. The French leader, Charles de Gaulle, granted Algerian independence in 1962. Decolonization in Africa south of the Sahara took place less turbulently.

Ghana proclaimed its independence in 1957, and by 1960, almost all French and British possessions in Africa had gained their freedom.

Although expectations ran high in the new states, they soon found themselves beset with problems of extreme poverty and antagonistic tribal groups that felt little loyalty to the new nations. These states came to be known collectively as the "Third World" (the "First World" consisted of the advanced industrial countries—Japan and the states of Western Europe and North America; the "Second World" comprised the Soviet Union and its satellites). Their status as "backward" nations led many Third World countries to modernize by pursuing Western technology and industrialization. In many instances, this has meant that these peoples have had to adjust to the continuing imposition of Western institutions and values on their societies.

The Soviet Union: From Stalin to Khrushchev

World War II devastated the Soviet Union. To create a new industrial base, Stalin returned to the method that he had used in the 1930s—the acquisition of development capital from Soviet labor. Working hard for little pay, poor housing, and precious few consumer goods,

Soviet laborers were expected to produce goods for export with little in return for themselves. The incoming capital from abroad could then be used to purchase machinery and Western technology. The loss of millions of men in the war meant that much of this tremendous work load fell on Soviet women. Almost 40 percent of heavy manual labor was performed by women.

Economic recovery in the Soviet Union was nothing less than spectacular. By 1947, Russian industrial production had attained prewar levels; three years later, it had surpassed them by 40 percent. New power plants, canals, and giant factories were built, while new industrial plants and oil fields were established in Siberia and Soviet Central Asia. Stalin's newly announced five-year plan of 1946 reached its goals in less than five years.

Although Stalin's economic policy was successful in promoting growth in heavy industry, primarily for the benefit of the military, consumer goods were scarce. Although the development of thermonuclear weapons in 1953, MIG fighters from 1950 to 1953, and the first space satellite (*Sputnik*) in 1957 elevated the Soviet state's reputation as a world power abroad, domestically the Russian people were shortchanged. Heavy industry grew at a rate three times that of personal consumption. Moreover, the housing shortage was acute. A British military attaché in Moscow reported that "all houses, practically without exception, show lights from every window after dark. This seems to indicate that every room is both a living room by day and a bedroom by night. There is no place in overcrowded Moscow for the luxury of eating and sleeping in separate rooms."[4]

Map 29.4 Africa after World War II.

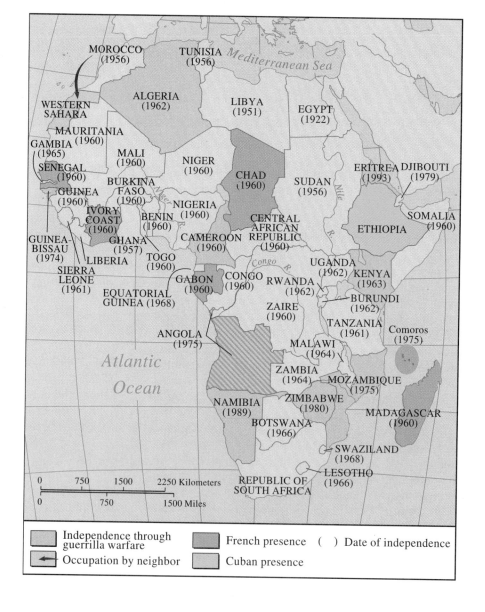

✦ **Khrushchev's Visit to Yugoslavia.** The leadership of Nikita Khrushchev appeared for a while to open the door to more flexible Soviet policies. In 1955, he visited Yugoslavia in an attempt to improve relations with a Communist state that had deviated from Soviet policies. Khrushchev is shown here making a conciliatory speech with Marshall Tito, the leader of Yugoslavia, looking on.

When World War II ended in 1945, Stalin had been in power for more than fifteen years. During that time, he had removed all opposition to his rule and remained the undisputed master of the Soviet Union. Other leading members of the Communist Party were completely obedient to his will. Increasingly distrustful of competitors, Stalin exercised sole authority and pitted his subordinates against one another.

Stalin's morbid suspicions fueled the constantly increasing repression that was a characteristic of his regime. In 1946, the government decreed that all literary and scientific works must conform to the political needs of the state. Along with this anti-intellectual campaign came political terror. A new series of purges seemed imminent in 1953 when a number of Jewish doctors were implicated in a spurious plot to kill high-level party officials. Only Stalin's death on March 5, 1953, prevented more bloodletting.

A new collective leadership succeeded Stalin until Nikita Khrushchev (1894–1971) emerged as the chief Soviet policy-maker. Khrushchev had been responsible for ending the system of forced-labor camps, a regular feature of Stalinist Russia. At the Twentieth Congress of the Communist Party in 1956, Khruschchev condemned Joseph Stalin for his "administrative violence, mass repression, and terror."

Once in power, Khrushchev took steps to undo some of the worst features of Stalin's repressive regime. A certain degree of intellectual freedom was now permitted; as Khrushchev said, "readers should be given the chance to make their own judgements" regarding the acceptability of controversial literature, and that "police measures shouldn't be used."[5] In 1962, he allowed the publication of Alexander Solzhenitsyn's *A Day in the Life of Ivan Denisovich*, a grim portrayal of the horrors of Russia's forced-labor camps. Most importantly, Khrushchev extended the process of destalinization by reducing the powers of the secret police and closing some of the Siberian prison camps. Nevertheless, when Khrushchev's revelations about Stalin at the Twentieth Congress created turmoil in Communist ranks everywhere and encouraged a spirit of rebellion in Soviet satellite countries in Eastern Europe, there was a reaction. Soviet troops crushed an uprising in Hungary in 1956, and Khrushchev and the Soviet leaders, fearful of further undermining the basic foundations of the regime, downplayed their campaign of destalinization.

Economically, Khrushchev tried to place more emphasis on light industry and consumer goods. Khrushchev's attempts to increase agricultural output by cultivating vast lands east of the Ural Mountains proved less successful and damaged his reputation within the party. These failures, combined with increased military spending, hurt the Soviet economy. The industrial growth rate, which had soared in the early 1950s, now declined dramatically from 13 percent in 1953 to 7.5 percent in 1964.

Khrushchev's personality also did not endear him to the higher Soviet officials who frowned at his tendency to crack jokes and play the clown. Nor were the higher members of the party bureaucracy pleased when Khrushchev tried to curb their privileges. Foreign policy failures caused additional damage to Khrushchev's reputation among his colleagues. His rash plan to place missiles in Cuba was the final straw. While he was away on vacation in 1964, a special meeting of the Soviet Politburo voted him out of office (because of "deteriorating health") and forced him into retirement. Although a group of leaders succeeded him, real power came into the hands of Leonid Brezhnev (1906–1982), the "trusted" supporter of Khrushchev who had engineered his downfall.

Eastern Europe: Behind the Iron Curtain

At the end of World War II, Soviet military forces had occupied all of Eastern Europe and the Balkans (except for Greece, Albania, and Yugoslavia). All of the occupied states came to be part of the Soviet sphere of influence and, after 1945, experienced similar political developments. Between 1945 and 1947, one-party Communist governments became firmly entrenched in East Germany, Bulgaria, Romania, Poland, and Hungary. In Czechoslovakia, where there was a strong tradition of democratic institutions, the Communists did not achieve their goals until 1948 when all other parties were dissolved, and Klement Gottwald, the leader of the Communists, became the new president of Czechoslovakia.

Albania and Yugoslavia were notable exceptions to this progression of Soviet dominance in Eastern Europe. Both had had strong Communist resistance movements during the war, and in both countries, the Communist Party simply took over power when the war ended. In Albania, local Communists established a rigidly Stalinist regime, but one that grew increasingly independent of the Soviet Union.

In Yugoslavia, Josip Broz, known as Tito (1892–1980), leader of the Communist resistance movement, seemed to be a loyal Stalinist. After the war, however, he moved toward the establishment of an independent Communist state in Yugoslavia. Stalin hoped to take control of Yugoslavia, just as he had done in other Eastern European countries, but Tito refused to capitulate to Stalin's demands and gained the support of the people by portraying the struggle as one of Yugoslav national freedom. In 1958, the Yugoslav party congress asserted that Yugoslav Communists did not see themselves as deviating from communism, only Stalinism. They considered their way closer to the Marxist-Leninist ideal. This included a more decentralized economic and political system in which workers could manage themselves and local communes could exercise some political power.

Between 1948 and Stalin's death in 1953, the Eastern European satellite states followed a policy of Stalinization. They instituted Soviet-type five-year plans with emphasis on heavy industry rather than consumer goods. They began to collectivize agriculture. They established the institutions of repression—secret police and military forces. But communism—a foreign product—had not developed deep roots among the peoples of Eastern Europe. Moreover, Soviet economic exploitation of Eastern Europe made living conditions harsh for most people. The Soviets demanded reparations from their defeated wartime enemies Bulgaria, Romania, and Hungary and forced all of the Eastern European states to trade with the Soviet Union to the latter's advantage.

After Stalin's death, many Eastern European states began to pursue a new, more nationalistically oriented course, while the new Soviet leaders, including Khrushchev, interfered less in the internal affairs of their satellites. But in the late 1950s and 1960s, the Soviet Union also made it clear, particularly in Poland, Hungary, and Czechoslovakia, that it would not allow its Eastern European satellites to become independent of Soviet control.

In 1956, worker protests erupted in Poland. In response, the Polish Communist Party adopted a series of reforms in October and elected Wladyslaw Gomulka (1905–1982) as first secretary. Gomulka declared that Poland had the right to follow its own socialist path. Fearful of Soviet armed response, however, the Poles compromised. Poland pledged to remain loyal to the Warsaw Pact, while the Soviets agreed to allow Poland to follow its own path to socialism.

The developments in Poland in 1956 inspired national Communists in Hungary to seek the same kinds of reforms and independence. Intense debates eventually resulted in the ouster of the ruling Stalinist and the selection of Imre Nagy (1896–1958) as the new Hungarian leader. Internal dissent, however, was not simply directed against the Soviets, but against communism in general, which was viewed as a creation of the Soviets, not the

Hungarians. The Stalinist secret police had also bred much terror and hatred. This dissatisfaction, combined with economic difficulties, created a situation ripe for revolt. To quell the rising rebellion, Nagy declared Hungary a free nation on November 1, 1956. He promised free elections, and the mood of the country made it clear that this could mean the end of Communist rule in Hungary. But Khrushchev was in no position at home to allow a member of the Communist flock to leave. Just three days after Nagy's declaration, the Red Army attacked Budapest (see the box on p. 618). The Soviets reestablished control over the country while János Kádár (1912–1989), a reform-minded cabinet minister, replaced Nagy. By collaborating with the Soviet invaders, Kádár saved many of Nagy's economic reforms.

The developments in Poland and Hungary in 1956 did not generate similar revolts in Czechoslovakia. The "Little Stalin," Antonin Novotny (1904–1975), placed in power in 1952 by Stalin himself, remained firmly in control. By the late 1960s, however, Novotny had alienated many members of his own party and was particularly resented by Czechoslovakia's writers, such as the playwright Vaclav Havel (b. 1936). A writers' rebellion late in 1967, in fact, led to Novotny's resignation. In January 1968, Alexander Dubcek (1921–1992) was elected first secretary of the Communist party and soon introduced a number of reforms, including freedom of speech and press, freedom to travel abroad, and a relaxation of secret police

CHRONOLOGY

The Soviet Union and Satellite States in Eastern Europe

Death of Stalin	1953
Khrushchev's denunciation of Stalin	1956
Attempt at reforms in Poland	1956
Hungarian revolt is crushed	1956
Berlin Wall is built	1961
Brezhnev replaces Khrushchev	1964
Soviets crush "Prague Spring" in Czechoslovakia	1968

activities. Dubcek hoped to create "communism with a human face." A period of euphoria erupted that came to be known as the "Prague Spring."

It proved to be short-lived. This euphoria had led many to call for more far-reaching reforms, including neutrality and withdrawal from the Soviet bloc. To forestall the spreading of this "spring" fever, the Red Army invaded Czechoslovakia in August 1968 and crushed the reform movement. Gustav Husák (b. 1913), a committed nonreformist, replaced Dubcek, crushed his reforms, and reestablished the old order.

Western Europe: The Revival of Democracy and the Economy

With the economic aid of the Marshall Plan, the countries of Western Europe recovered relatively rapidly from the devastation of World War II. Between 1947 and 1950, European countries received $9.4 billion to be used for new equipment and raw materials. By 1950, industrial output in Europe was 30 percent above prewar levels. And this economic recovery continued well into the 1950s and 1960s, both decades of dramatic economic growth and prosperity in Western Europe. Indeed, Western Europe experienced virtually full employment during these decades.

FRANCE: THE DOMINATION OF DE GAULLE

The history of France for nearly a quarter century after the war was dominated by one man—Charles de Gaulle (1890–1970)—who possessed an unshakable faith that he had a historical mission to reestablish the greatness of

◆ **Soviet Invasion of Czechoslovakia, 1968.** The attempt of Alexander Dubcek, the new first secretary of the Communist Party, to liberalize Communist rule in Czechoslovakia failed when Soviet troops invaded and crushed the reform movement. This photograph shows a confrontation between Soviet tanks and Czechs in Prague. The tanks won.

Soviet Repression in Eastern Europe: Hungary, 1956

Developments in Poland in 1956 inspired the Communist leaders of Hungary to begin to remove their country from Soviet control. But there were limits to Khrushchev's tolerance, and he sent Soviet troops to crush Hungary's movement for independence. The first selection is a statement by the Soviet government justifying the use of Soviet troops, while the second is a brief and tragic final statement from Imry Nagy, the Hungarian leader.

Statement of the Soviet Government, October 30, 1956

The Soviet Government regards it as indispensable to make a statement in connection with the events in Hungary.

The course of the events has shown that the working people of Hungary, who have achieved great progress on the basis of their people's democratic order, correctly raise the question of the necessity of eliminating serious shortcomings in the field of economic building, the further raising of the material well-being of the population, and the struggle against bureaucratic excesses in the state apparatus.

However, this just and progressive movement of the working people was soon joined by forces of black reaction and counterrevolution, which are trying to take advantage of the discontent of part of the working people to undermine the foundations of the people's democratic order in Hungary and to restore the old landlord and capitalist order.

The Soviet Government and all the Soviet people deeply regret that the development of events in Hungary has led to bloodshed. On the request of the Hungarian People's Government the Soviet Government consented to the entry into Budapest of the Soviet Army units to assist the Hungarian People's Army and the Hungarian authorities to establish order in the town.

The Last Message of Imry Nagy, November 4, 1956

This fight is the fight for freedom by the Hungarian people against the Russian intervention, and it is possible that I shall only be able to stay at my post for one or two hours. The whole world will see how the Russian armed forces, contrary to all treaties and conventions, are crushing the resistance of the Hungarian people. They will also see how they are kidnapping the Prime Minister of a country which is a Member of the United Nations, taking him from the capital, and therefore it cannot be doubted at all that this is the most brutal form of intervention. I should like in these last moments to ask the leaders of the revolution, if they can, to leave the country. I ask that all that I have said in my broadcast, and what we have agreed on with the revolutionary leaders during meetings in Parliament, should be put in a memorandum, and the leaders should turn to all the peoples of the world for help and explain that today it is Hungary and tomorrow, or the day after tomorrow, it will be the turn of other countries because the imperialism of Moscow does not know borders, and is only trying to play for time.

---

the French nation. During the war, de Gaulle had assumed leadership of some resistance groups and played an important role in ensuring the establishment of a French provisional government after the war. The creation of the Fourth Republic, with a return to a parliamentary system based on parties that de Gaulle considered weak, led him to withdraw from politics. Eventually, he formed the "French Popular Movement," a decidedly rightist organization. It blamed the parties for France's political mess and called for an even stronger presidency, a goal that de Gaulle finally achieved in 1958.

The fragile political stability of the Fourth Republic had been badly shaken by the Algerian crisis. The French army had suffered defeat in Indochina in 1954 and was determined to resist Algerian demands for independence. But a strong antiwar movement among French intellectuals and church leaders led to bitter divisions within France that opened the door to the possibility of civil war. The panic-stricken leaders of the Fourth Republic offered to let de Gaulle take over the government and revise the constitution.

In 1958, de Gaulle immediately drafted a new constitution for the Fifth Republic that greatly enhanced the power of the office of president, who now had the right to choose the prime minister, dissolve parliament, and supervise both defense and foreign policy. De Gaulle had always believed in strong leadership, and the new Fifth Republic was by no means a democratic system. As the new president de Gaulle sought to return France to the position of a great power. He believed that playing a pivotal role in the Cold War might enhance France's stature. For that reason, he pulled France out of the NATO high command. He increased French prestige among the Third World countries by consenting to Algerian independence despite strenuous opposition from the army. With an eye toward achieving the status of a world power, de Gaulle invested heavily in the nuclear arms race. France exploded its first nuclear bomb in 1960. Despite his successes, de Gaulle did not really achieve his ambitious goals of world power. Although his successors maintained that France was the "third nuclear power" after the United States and the Soviet Union, in truth France was too small for such global ambitions.

Although the cost of the nuclear program increased the defense budget, de Gaulle did not neglect the French economy. Economic decision making was centralized, a reflection of the overall centralization undertaken by the Gaullist government. Between 1958 and 1968, the French gross national product experienced an annual increase of 5.5 percent, faster than that of the United States. By the end of de Gaulle's era, France was a major industrial producer and exporter, particularly in such areas as automobiles and armaments. Nevertheless, problems remained. The expansion of traditional industries, such as coal, steel, and railroads, which had all been nationalized (put under government ownership), led to large government deficits. The cost of living increased faster than in the rest of Europe.

Increased dissatisfaction with the inability of de Gaulle's government to deal with these problems soon led to more violent action. In May 1968, a series of student protests, followed by a general strike by the labor unions, shook the government. Although de Gaulle managed to restore order, the events of May 1968 had seriously undermined the French people's respect for their aloof and imperious president. Tired and discouraged, de Gaulle resigned from office in April 1969 and died within a year.

WEST GERMANY: A NEW NATION?

As a result of the pressures of the Cold War, the unification of the three Western zones into the West German Federal Republic became a reality in 1949. Konrad Adenauer (1876–1967), the leader of the Christian Democratic Union (CDU) who served as chancellor from 1949 to 1963, became the "founding hero" of the Federal Republic. Adenauer sought respect for Germany by cooper-

CHRONOLOGY

Western Europe

Welfare state emerges in Great Britain	1946
Konrad Adenauer becomes chancellor of West Germany	1949
Formation of European Coal and Steel Community	1951
West Germany joins NATO	1955
Formation of EURATOM	1957
Formation of European Economic Community (Common Market)	1957
Charles de Gaulle assumes power in France	1958
Erhard becomes chancellor of Germany	1963
Student protests in France	1968

ating with the United States and the other Western European nations. He was especially desirous of reconciliation with France—Germany's longtime enemy. The beginning of the Korean War in June 1950 had unexpected repercussions for West Germany. The fear that South Korea might fall to the Communist forces of the north led many Germans and westerners to worry about the security of West Germany and led to calls for the rearmament of West Germany. Although many people, concerned about a revival of German militarism, condemned this proposal, Cold War tensions were decisive. West Germany rearmed in 1955 and became a member of NATO.

Adenauer's chancellorship is largely associated with the resurrection of the West German economy, often referred to as the "economic miracle." It was largely guided by the minister of finance, Ludwig Erhard. Although West Germany had only 75 percent of the population and 52 percent of the territory of prewar Germany, by 1955 the West German gross national product exceeded that of prewar Germany. Real wages doubled between 1950 and 1965 even though work hours were cut by 20 percent. Unemployment fell from 8 percent in 1950 to 0.4 percent in 1965. To maintain its economic expansion, West Germany even imported hundreds of thousands of guest workers, primarily from Italy, Spain, Greece, Turkey, and Yugoslavia.

Throughout its postwar existence, West Germany was troubled by its Nazi past. The surviving major Nazi leaders had been tried and condemned as war criminals at the Nuremberg war crimes trials in 1945 and 1946. As part of the denazification of Germany, the victorious Allies continued war crimes trials of lesser officials, but these diminished as the Cold War produced a shift in attitudes. By 1950, German courts had begun to take over the war crimes trials, and the German legal machine persisted in prosecuting cases. Beginning in 1953, the West German government also began to make payments to Israel and to Holocaust survivors and their relatives in order to make some restitution for the crimes of the Nazi era. The German president Richard von Weizsäcker was especially eloquent in reminding Germans of their responsibility "for the unspeakable sorrow that occurred in the name of Germany."

Adenauer resigned in 1963, after fourteen years of firmly guiding West Germany through its postwar recovery. Adenauer had wanted no grand experimentation at home or abroad; he was content to give Germany time to regain its equilibrium. Ludwig Erhard succeeded Adenauer and largely continued his policies. But an economic downturn in the mid-1960s opened the door to the rise of the Social Democrats, and in 1969, they became the leading party.

✦ **Welfare State: Free Milk at School.** The creation of the welfare state was a prominent social development in postwar Europe. The desire to improve the health of children led to welfare programs that provided free food for young people. Pictured here are boys at Manchester Grammar School in England during a milk break.

GREAT BRITAIN: THE WELFARE STATE

The end of World War II left Britain with massive economic problems. In elections held immediately after the war, the Labour Party overwhelmingly defeated Churchill's Conservative Party. The Labour Party had promised far-reaching reforms, particularly in the area of social welfare, and in a country with a tremendous shortage of consumer goods and housing, its platform was quite appealing. The new Labour government, under Clement Atlee (1883–1967), the new prime minister, proceeded to enact the reforms that created a modern welfare state.

The establishment of the British welfare state began with the nationalization of the Bank of England, the coal and steel industries, public transportation, and public utilities, such as electricity and gas. In the area of social welfare, the new government enacted the National Insurance Act and the National Health Service Act in 1946. The insurance act established a comprehensive social security program and nationalized medical insurance, thereby enabling the state to subsidize the unemployed, the sick, and the aged. The health act created a system of socialized medicine that forced doctors and dentists to work with state hospitals, although private practices could be maintained. This measure was especially costly for the state, but within a few years 90 percent of the medical profession were participating. The British welfare state became the norm for most European states after the war.

The cost of building a welfare state at home forced the British to reduce expenses abroad. This meant the dismantling of the British Empire and the reduction of military aid to such countries as Greece and Turkey. Not a belief in the morality of self-determination, but economic necessity brought an end to the British Empire.

Continuing economic problems brought the Conservatives back into power from 1951 to 1964. Although they favored private enterprise, the Conservatives accepted the welfare state and even extended it when they undertook an ambitious construction program to improve British housing. Although the British economy had recovered from the war, it had done so at a slower rate than other European countries. Moreover, the slow rate of recovery masked a long-term economic decline caused by a variety of factors. The demands of British trade unions for wages that rose faster than productivity were certainly a problem in the 1950s and 1960s. The unwillingness of the British to invest in modern industrial machinery and to adopt new methods also did not help. Underlying the immediate problems, however, was a deeper issue. As a result of World War II, Britain had lost much of its prewar revenues from abroad but was left with a burden of debt from its many international commitments. At the same time, with the rise of the United States and the Soviet Union, Britain's ability to play the role of a world power declined substantially.

Western Europe: The Move Toward Unity

As we have seen, the divisions created by the Cold War led the nations of Western Europe to form the North Atlantic Treaty Organization in 1949. But military unity was not the only kind of unity fostered in Europe after 1945. The destructiveness of two world wars caused many thoughtful Europeans to consider the need for some form of European unity. National feeling was still too powerful, however, for European nations to give up their political sovereignty. Consequently, the desire for unity was forced to focus primarily on the economic arena, not the political one.

In 1951, France, West Germany, the Benelux countries (Belgium, Netherlands, and Luxembourg), and Italy formed the European Coal and Steel Community (ECSC). Its purpose was to create a common market for coal and steel products among the six nations by eliminating tariffs and other trade barriers. The success of the ECSC encouraged its members to proceed further, and in 1957 they created the European Atomic Energy Community (EURATOM) to further European research on the peaceful uses of nuclear energy.

In the same year the same six nations signed the Rome treaty, which created the European Economic Community (EEC), also known as the Common Market. The EEC eliminated customs barriers for the six member nations and created a large free-trade area protected from the rest of the world by a common external tariff. By promoting free trade, the EEC also encouraged cooperation and standardization in many aspects of the six nations' economies. All the member nations benefited economically. With a total population of 165 million, the EEC became the world's largest exporter and purchaser of raw materials. Only the United States surpassed the EEC in steel production.

The United States and Canada: A New Era

At the end of World War II, the United States emerged as one of the world's two superpowers. As the Cold War with the Soviet Union intensified, the United States worked hard to combat the spread of communism throughout the world. American domestic political life after 1945 was played out against a background of American military power abroad.

American Politics and Society in the 1950s

Between 1945 and 1970, the ideals of Franklin Roosevelt's New Deal largely determined the patterns of American domestic politics. The New Deal had brought basic changes to American society. These included: a dramatic increase in the role and power of the federal government; the rise of organized labor as a significant force in the economy and politics; the beginning of a welfare state; and a grudging realization of the need to deal fairly with the concerns of minorities.

The New Deal tradition in American politics was bolstered by the election of Democratic presidents—Harry Truman in 1948, John F. Kennedy in 1960, and Lyndon B. Johnson in 1964. Even the election of a Republican president, Dwight D. Eisenhower, in 1952 and 1956 did not change the basic direction of the New Deal. As Eisenhower stated, "Should any political party attempt to abolish Social Security and eliminate labor laws and farm programs, you would not hear of that party again in our political history."

No doubt, the economic boom after World War II fueled confidence in the American way of life. A shortage of consumer goods during the war left Americans with both extra income and the desire to buy these goods after the war. Then, too, the growth of labor unions brought higher wages and gave more and more workers the ability to buy consumer goods. Government expenditures also indirectly helped the American private economy. Especially after the Korean War began in 1950, outlays on defense provided money for scientific research in the universities and markets for weapons industries. Between 1945 and 1973, real wages grew on an average of 3 percent a year, the most prolonged advance in American history.

A new prosperity was not the only characteristic of the early 1950s. Cold War confrontations abroad had repercussions at home. The takeover of China by Mao Zedong's Communist forces in 1949 and Communist North Korea's invasion of South Korea in 1950 led to a fear that Communists had infiltrated America. President Truman's attorney general warned that Communists "are everywhere—in factories, offices, butcher stores, on street corners, in private businesses. And each carried in himself the germ of death for society." The demagogic senator from Wisconsin, Joseph R. McCarthy, helped to intensify a massive "Red Scare" with his exposés of supposed

Communists in high government positions. McCarthy went too far when he attacked alleged "Communist conspirators" in the United States army and was censured by Congress in 1954. Very quickly, his anticommunist crusade came to an end.

An Age of Upheaval: America from 1960 to 1970

Between 1960 and 1970, the United States experienced a period of upheaval that brought to the fore problems that had been glossed over in the 1950s. The 1960s began on a youthful and optimistic note. At age forty-three, John F. Kennedy (1917–1963) became the youngest elected president in the history of the United States. His own administration, cut short by an assassin's bullet on November 22, 1963, focused primarily on foreign affairs. Kennedy's successor, Lyndon B. Johnson, who won a new term as president in a landslide in 1964, used his stunning mandate to pursue the growth of the welfare state, first begun in the New Deal. Johnson's programs included health care for the elderly; a War on Poverty to be fought with food stamps and a Job Corps; a new Department of Housing and Urban Development to deal with the problems of the cities; and federal assistance for education.

Lyndon Johnson's other domestic passion was equal rights for blacks. The civil rights movement had its beginnings in 1954 when the United States Supreme Court took the dramatic step of striking down the practice of racially segregated public schools. The eloquent-speaking Martin Luther King (1929–1968) became the leader of a growing movement for racial equality, and by the early 1960s, a number of groups, including King's Southern Christian Leadership Conference (SCLC), were organizing sit-ins and demonstrations across the South to end racial segregation. In August 1963, Martin Luther King led a March on Washington for Jobs and Freedom that dramatized the blacks' desire for freedom. This march and King's impassioned plea for racial equality had an electrifying effect on the American people. By the end of 1963, 52 percent of the American people called civil rights the most significant national issue; eight months earlier, only 4 percent had done so.

President Johnson took up the cause of civil rights. As a result of his initiative, Congress passed a Civil Rights Act in 1964, which created the machinery to end segregation and discrimination in the workplace and all public places. A Voting Rights Act the following year made it easier for blacks to vote in southern states. But laws alone could not guarantee a Great Society, and Johnson soon faced bitter social unrest, both from blacks and a burgeoning antiwar movement.

In the North and West, blacks had had voting rights for many years, but local patterns of segregation led to higher unemployment rates for blacks than for whites and left blacks segregated in huge urban ghettos. In these ghettos, the calls for action by radical black leaders, such as Malcolm X of the Black Muslims, attracted more attention than the nonviolent appeals of Martin Luther King. Malcolm X's advice was straightforward: "If someone puts a hand on you, send him to the cemetery."

In the summer of 1965, race riots broke out in the Watts district of Los Angeles. Thirty-four people died and over one thousand buildings were destroyed. Cleveland, San Francisco, Chicago, Newark, and Detroit likewise exploded in the summers of 1966 and 1967. After the assassination of Martin Luther King in 1968, more than 100 cities had riots. The combination of riots and extremist comments by radical black leaders led to a "white backlash" and a severe division of America.

Antiwar protests also divided the American people after President Johnson sent American troops to war in Vietnam. As the war progressed and a military draft ensued, protests escalated. Teach-ins, sit-ins, and the occupations of buildings at universities alternated with more radical demonstrations that led to violence. The killing of four student protestors at Kent State University in 1970 by the Ohio National Guard caused a reaction, and the antiwar movement began to decline. By that time, however, antiwar demonstrations had helped to weaken the willingness of many Americans to continue the war. But the combination of antiwar demonstrations and ghetto riots in the cities also prepared many people for "law and order," an appeal used by Richard Nixon, the Republican presidential candidate in 1968. With Nixon's election in 1968, a shift to the right in American politics had begun.

The Development of Canada

Canada experienced many of the same developments that the United States did in the postwar years. For twenty-five years after World War II, a prosperous Canada set out on a new path of industrial development. Canada had always had a strong export economy based on its abundant natural resources. Now it developed electronic, aircraft, nuclear, and chemical engineering industries as well on a large scale. Much of the Canadian growth, however, was financed by capital from the United States, which led to American ownership of Canadian businesses. Although many Canadians welcomed the economic growth, others feared American economic domination of Canada.

Canadians also worried about playing a secondary role politically and militarily to its neighboring superpower.

Canadians agreed to join the North Atlantic Treaty Organization in 1949 and even sent military forces to fight in Korea the following year. But to avoid subordination to the United States, Canada actively supported the United Nations. Nevertheless, concerns about the United States did not keep Canada from maintaining a special relationship with its southern neighbor. The North American Air Defense Command (Norad), formed in 1957, was based on close cooperation between the air forces of the two countries for the defense of North America against missile attack.

After 1945, the Liberal Party continued to dominate Canadian politics until 1957, when John Diefenbaker (1895–1979) achieved a Conservative Party victory. But major economic problems returned the Liberals to power, and under Lester Pearson (1897–1972), they created Canada's welfare state by enacting a national social security system (the Canada Pension Plan) and a national health insurance program.

The Emergence of a New Society

Rapid changes in postwar society, fueled by scientific advances and rapid economic growth, led many to view it as a new society. Called a technocratic society by some and the consumer society by others, postwar Western society was characterized by a changing social structure and new movements for change.

The Structure of European Society

The structure of European society was altered after 1945. Especially noticeable were the changes in the middle class. Such traditional middle-class groups as businesspeople and professionals in law, medicine, and the universities were greatly augmented by a new group of managers and technicians, as large companies and government agencies employed increasing numbers of white-collar supervisory and administrative personnel. Whether in Eastern or Western Europe, the new managers and experts were very much alike. Everywhere their positions depended on specialized knowledge acquired from some form of higher education. Everywhere they focused on the effective administration of their corporations. Because their positions usually depended on their skills, they took steps to ensure that their own children would be educated.

Changes also occurred among the traditional lower classes. Especially noticeable was the dramatic shift of people from rural to urban areas. The number of people in agriculture declined drastically; by the 1950s, the number

of peasants throughout most of Europe had dropped by 50 percent. Nor did the size of the industrial working class expand. In West Germany, industrial workers made up 48 percent of the labor force throughout the 1950s and 1960s. Thereafter, the number of industrial workers began to dwindle as the number of white-collar service employees increased. At the same time, a substantial increase in their real wages enabled the working classes to aspire to the consumption patterns of the middle class, leading to what some observers have called the "consumer society." Buying on the installment plan, which was introduced in the 1930s, became widespread beginning in the 1950s and gave workers a chance to imitate the middle class by buying such products as televisions, washing machines, refrigerators, vacuum cleaners, and stereos. But the most visible symbol of mass consumerism was the automobile. Before World War II, cars were reserved mostly for the European upper classes. In 1948, there were 5 million cars in all of Europe, but by 1957, the number had tripled. By the 1960s, there were almost 45 million cars.

Rising incomes, combined with shorter working hours, created an even greater market for mass leisure activities. Between 1900 and 1960, the workweek was reduced from sixty hours to almost forty hours, and the number of paid holidays increased. All aspects of popular culture—music, sports, media—became commercialized and offered opportunities for leisure activities including concerts, sporting events, and television viewing.

Another very visible symbol of mass leisure was the growth of mass tourism. Before World War II, mostly the upper and middle classes traveled for pleasure. After the war, the combination of more vacation time, increased prosperity, and the flexibility provided by package tours with their lower rates and low-budget rooms enabled millions to expand their travel possibilities. By the mid-1960s, 100 million tourists were crossing European boundaries each year.

The Permissive Society

The "permissive society" was yet another term used by critics to describe the new society of postwar Europe. World War I had seen the first significant crack in the rigid code of manners and morals of the nineteenth century. Subsequently, the 1920s had witnessed experimentation with drugs, the appearance of hard-core pornography, and a new sexual freedom (police in Berlin, for example, issued cards that permitted female and male homosexual prostitutes to practice their trade). But these indications of a new attitude appeared mostly in major cities and touched only small numbers of people. After

World War II, changes in manners and morals were far more extensive and far more noticeable.

Sweden took the lead in the propagation of the so-called sexual revolution of the 1960s, but the rest of Europe and the United States soon followed. Sex education in the schools and the decriminalization of homosexuality were but two aspects of Sweden's liberal legislation. The introduction of the birth control pill, which became widely available by the mid-1960s, gave people more freedom in sexual behavior. Meanwhile, sexually explicit movies, plays, and books broke new ground in the treatment of once-hidden subjects.

The new standards were evident in the breakdown of the traditional family. Divorce rates increased dramatically, especially in the 1960s, while premarital and extramarital sexual experiences also rose substantially. A survey in the Netherlands in 1968 revealed that 78 percent of men and 86 percent of women had participated in extramarital sex.

The decade of the 1960s also saw the emergence of a drug culture. Marijuana was widely used among college and university students as the recreational drug of choice. For young people more interested in mind expansion into higher levels of consciousness, Timothy Leary, who had done psychedelic research at Harvard on the effects of LSD (lysergic acid diethylamide), became the high priest of hallucinogenic experiences.

New attitudes toward sex and the use of drugs were only two manifestations of a growing youth movement in the 1960s that questioned authority and fostered rebellion against the older generation. Spurred on by the Vietnam War and a growing political consciousness, the youth rebellion became a youth protest movement by the second half of the 1960s (see the box on p. 625).

Education and Student Revolt

Before World War II, higher education had largely remained the preserve of Europe's wealthier classes. Even in 1950, for example, only 3 or 4 percent of West European young people were enrolled in a university. In addition, European higher education remained largely centered on the liberal arts, pure science, and preparation for the professions of law and medicine.

Much of this changed after World War II. European states began to foster greater equality of opportunity in higher education by eliminating fees, and universities experienced an influx of students from the middle and lower classes. Enrollments grew dramatically; in France, 4.5 percent of young people went to a university in 1950. By 1965, the figure had increased to 14.5 percent. Enrollments in European universities more than tripled between 1940 and 1960.

But there were problems. Classrooms with too many students, professors who paid little attention to students, administrators who acted in an authoritarian fashion, and an education that to many seemed irrelevant to the real-

◆ **The "Love-in."** In the 1960s, a number of outdoor public festivals for young people combined music, drugs, and sex. Flamboyant dress, facial painting, free-form dancing, and drugs were vital ingredients in creating an atmosphere dedicated to "love and peace." Shown here is a "love-in" that was held on the grounds of an English country estate in the Summer of Love, 1967.

⇒ "The Times They Are a-Changin' ": The Music of Youthful Protest ⇐

In the 1960s, the lyrics of rock music reflected the rebellious mood of many young people. Bob Dylan (b. 1941), a well-known recording artist, expressed the feelings of the younger generation. His song, "The Times They Are a-Changin'," released in 1964, has been called an "anthem for the protest movement."

Bob Dylan, *The Times They Are a-Changin'*

Come gather round people
Wherever you roam
And admit that the waters
Around you have grown
And accept it that soon
You'll be drenched to the bone
If your time to you
Is worth savin'
Then you better start swimmin'
Or you'll sink like a stone
For the times they are a'changin'

Come writers and critics
Who prophesize with your pen
And keep your eyes wide
The chance won't come again
And don't speak too soon
For the wheel's still in spin
And there's no tellin' who
That it's namin'
For the loser now
Will be later to win
For the times they are a'changin'

Come senators, congressmen
please heed the call

Don't stand in the doorway
Don't block up the hall
For he that gets hurt
Will be he who has stalled
There's a battle outside
And it is ragin'
It'll soon shake your windows
And rattle your walls
For the times they are a'changin'

Come mothers and fathers
Throughout the land
And don't criticize
What you can't understand
Your sons and your daughters
Are beyond your command
Your old road
Is rapidly agin'
Please get out of the new one
If you can't lend your hand
For the times they are a'changin'

The line it is drawn
The curse it is cast
The slow one now
Will later be fast
As the present now
Will later be past
The order is
Rapidly fadin'
And the first one now
Will later be last
For the times they are a'changin'

ities of the modern age led to an outburst of student revolts in the late 1960s. In part, these protests were an extension of the spontaneous disruptions in American universities in the mid-1960s, which were often sparked by student opposition to the Vietnam War. Perhaps the most famous student revolt occurred in France in 1968. It erupted at the University of Nanterre outside Paris but soon spread to the Sorbonne, the main campus of the University of Paris. French students demanded a greater voice in the administration of the university, took over buildings, and then expanded the scale of their protests by inviting workers to support them. Half of France's workforce went on strike in May 1968. After the Gaullist government instituted a hefty wage hike, the workers returned to work and the police repressed the remaining student protestors.

The student protest movement reached its high point in 1968, although scattered incidents lasted into the early 1970s. There were several reasons for the student radicalism. Some students were genuinely motivated by the desire to reform the university. Others were protesting the Vietnam War, which they viewed as a product of Western imperialism. They also attacked other aspects of Western society, such as its materialism, and expressed concern about becoming cogs in the large and impersonal bureaucratic jungles of the modern world. For many students, the calls for democratic decision making within the universities were a reflection of their deeper concerns about the direction of Western society. Although student revolts fizzled out in the 1970s, the larger issues they raised have been increasingly revived in the 1990s.

Conclusion

At the end of World War II, a new conflict erupted in the Western world as the two new superpowers, the United States and the Soviet Union, competed for political domination. Europeans, whether they wanted to or not, were forced to become supporters of one side or the other. But this ideological division also spread to the rest of the world as the United States fought in Korea and Vietnam to prevent the spread of communism, while the Soviet

Union used its armies to prop up pro-Soviet regimes in Eastern Europe.

In addition to the Cold War conflict, the postwar era was characterized by decolonization and the creation of a New Europe. After World War II, the colonial empires of the European states were largely dissolved, and the liberated territories of Africa, Asia, and the Middle East emerged as sovereign states. By the late 1980s, the approximately 160 sovereign states of the world would become an emerging global community.

Western Europe also became a new community in the 1950s and 1960s. Although Western Europeans staged a remarkable economic recovery, the Cuban Missile Crisis made it clear that their future still depended on the conflict between the two superpowers. At the same time, the student protests of the late 1960s caused many to rethink some of their basic assumptions. And yet, looking back, the student upheavals were not a "turning point in the history of postwar Europe," as some people thought at the time. In the 1970s and 1980s, student rebels would become middle-class professionals, and the vision of a revolutionary politics would remain mostly a memory.

NOTES

1. Quoted in Joseph M. Jones, *The Fifteen Weeks (February 21–June 5, 1947)*, 2d ed. (New York, 1964), pp. 140–141.
2. Quoted in Walter Lacqueur, *Europe in Our Time* (New York, 1992), p. 111.
3. Quoted in Peter Lane, *Europe Since 1945; An Introduction* (Totowa, N.J., 1985), p. 248.

4. R. Hilton, *Military Attache in Moscow* (London, 1949), p. 41.
5. Khrushchev, *Khrushchev Remembers*, trans. Strobe Talbott (Boston, 1970), p. 77.

SUGGESTIONS FOR FURTHER READING

Three introductory surveys on postwar Europe are P. Lane, *Europe since 1945: An Introduction* (Totowa, N.J., 1985); J. R. Wegs, *Europe since 1945: A Concise History*, 2d ed. (New York, 1984); and W. Laqueur, *Europe in Our Time* (New York, 1992). A convenient reference guide is J. Krieger, ed., *The Oxford Companion to Politics of the World* (Oxford, 1993). There is a detailed literature on the Cold War. Two general accounts are J. W. Langdon, *A Hard and Bitter Peace: A Global History of the Cold War*

(Englewood Cliffs, N.J., 1995); and B. A. Weisberger, *Cold War, Cold Peace: The United States and Russia since 1945* (New York, 1984). Two brief works on the entire Cold War are J. H. Mason, *The Cold War* (New York, 1996); and J. Smith, *The Cold War, 1945–1991* (Oxford, 1998). There is a brief survey of the early Cold War in M. Dockrill, *The Cold War 1945–1963* (Atlantic Highlands, N.J., 1988). The following works maintain that the Soviet Union was chiefly responsible for the Cold War: H.

Feis, *From Trust to Terror: The Onset of the Cold War, 1945–1950* (New York, 1970); and A. Ulam, *The Rivals: America and Russia since World War II* (New York, 1971). Revisionist studies on the Cold War have emphasized the responsibility of the United States for the Cold War, especially its global aspects. These works include J. and G. Kolko, *The Limits of Power: The World and United States Foreign Policy, 1945–1954* (New York, 1972); W. LaFeber, *America, Russia and the Cold War, 1945–1966*, 2d ed. (New York, 1972); and M. Sherwin, *A World Destroyed: The Atomic Bomb and the Grand Alliance* (New York, 1975). For a critique of the revisionist studies, see R. L. Maddox, *The New Left and the Origins of the Cold War* (Princeton, N.J., 1973). For important studies of Soviet foreign policy, see A. B. Ulam, *Expansion and Coexistence: Soviet Foreign Policy 1917–1973*, 2d ed. (New York, 1974), and *Dangerous Relations: The Soviet Union in World Politics, 1970–1982* (New York, 1983). On the Cuban Missile Crisis, see R. A. Chayes, *The Cuban Missile Crisis* (New York, 1974).

On decolonization after World War II, see R. F. Holland, *European Decolonization, 1918–1981: An Introductory Survey* (London, 1985). On the problems of the Third World, see P. Harrison, *Inside the Third World*, 2d ed. (New York, 1984).

For a general view of Soviet society, see D. K. Shipler, *Russia: Broken Idols, Solemn Dreams* (New York, 1983). On the Khrushchev years, see C. A. Linden, *Khrushchev and the Soviet Leadership* (Baltimore, 1990). For a general study of the Soviet satellites in Eastern Europe, see A. Brown and J. Gary, *Culture and Political Changes in Communist States* (London, 1977). On the Soviet Union's actions against Czechoslovakia in 1968, see J. Valenta, *Intervention in Czechoslovakia in 1968* (Baltimore, 1979). The unique path of Yugoslavia is examined in L. J. Cohen and P. Warwick, *Political Cohesion in a Fragile Mosaic: The Yugoslav Experience* (Boulder, Colo., 1983). On Romania, see L. S. Graham, *Rumania: A Developing Socialist State* (Boulder, Colo., 1978). On Hungary, see B. Kovrig, *The Hungarian People's Republic* (Baltimore, 1970). On East Germany, see C. B. Scharf, *Politics and Change in East Germany* (Boulder, Colo., 1984).

The rebuilding of postwar Europe is examined in A. S. Milward, *The Reconstruction of Western Europe, 1945–51* (Berkeley, 1984). For a general survey, see F. Tipton and R. Aldrich, *An Economic and Social History of Europe from 1939 to the Present* (Baltimore, 1987). On the building of common institutions in Western Europe, see J. Pinder, *European Community: The Building of a Union*, 2d ed. (New York, 1995). For a survey of West Germany, see M. Balfour, *West Germany: A Contemporary History* (London, 1983). France under de Gaulle is examined in A. Shennan, *De Gaulle* (New York, 1993); and D. J. Mahoney, *De Gaulle: Statesmanship, Grandeur, and Modern Democracy* (Westport, Conn., 1996). On Britain, see K. O. Morgan, *The People's Peace: British History 1945–1990* (Oxford, 1992).

For a survey of contemporary Western society, see A. Sampson, *The New Europeans* (New York, 1968). The student revolts of the late 1960s are put into a broader context in L. S. Feuer, *The Conflict of Generations* (New York, 1969).

CHAPTER

30

The Contemporary Western World (Since 1970)

After more than two decades of the Cold War, Europeans had become accustomed to a new division of Europe between West and East. A prosperous Western Europe still allied to the United States stood opposed to a still-struggling Eastern Europe that remained largely subject to the Soviet Union. The division of Germany symbolized the new order that seemed so well established. And yet, within two decades, a revolutionary upheaval in the Soviet Union and Eastern Europe brought an end to the Cold War and destroyed the long-standing division of postwar Europe. Even the Soviet Union ceased to exist as a single nation. On August 19, 1991, a group of Soviet leaders opposed to reform arrested Mikhail Gorbachev, the president of the Soviet Union, and tried to seize control of the government. Hundreds of thousands of Russians, led by Boris Yeltsin, poured into the streets of Moscow and Leningrad to resist the attempted coup. Some army units defected to Yeltsin's side, and within days, the rebels were forced to surrender. This failed attempt to seize power had unexpected results as Russia and a host of other Soviet states declared their independence. By the end of 1991, the Soviet Union—one of the largest empires in world history—had come to an end, and a new era of cooperation between the successor states in the old Soviet Union and the nations of the West had begun.

In the midst of the transformation from Cold War to post–Cold War, other changes also shaped a new Western world. New artistic and intellectual currents, the growth of science and technology, a religious revival, new threats from terrorists, the realization of environmental problems, and the surge of a women's liberation movement—all of these spoke of a vibrant, ever-changing, and yet challenging new world.

• Era of Brezhnev　　　　　　　　　• End of war in Bosnia
　　　　　　　　　　　　　　　　• Gorbachev comes to power in Soviet Union
　　　　　　　　　　　Revolutions in Eastern Europe •
　　　　　　　　　　　Dissolution of the Soviet Union •

　　　　　　　　　•　　　　　　　　　　　•　　　　　　　　　　　　　　　　　　•
Common Market expands (European Community)　Margaret Thatcher becomes prime minister of Britain　Election of Tony Blair
　　　　　　　　　　　　　　　　　　　　　　　　　　•
　　　　　　　　　　　　　　Reunification of Germany　　　　　　　European Union

　　　　Active terrorist groups •
　　　John Paul II becomes pope •

　Organization of Green Party in Germany

ℱrom Cold War to Post–Cold War: Toward a New World Order?

By the 1970s, American–Soviet relations had entered a new phase known as *détente,* which was marked by a reduction of tensions between the two superpowers. An appropriate symbol of détente was the antiballistic missiles (ABM) Treaty in 1972. Despite some lessening of tensions after the Cuban Missile Crisis, both the Soviet Union and the United States had continued to expand their nuclear arsenals. In the 1960s, both nations sought to extend the destructive power of their missiles by arming them with multiple warheads. By 1970, Americans had developed the capacity to arm their intercontinental ballistic missiles (ICBMs) with "multiple independently targeted reentry vehicles" (MIRVs) that enabled one missile to hit ten different targets. The Soviet Union soon followed suit. Between 1968 and 1972, both sides had also developed ABMs, whose purpose was to hit and destroy incoming missiles. In the 1972 ABM Treaty, the two nations agreed to limit their antiballistic missile systems.

In 1975, the Helsinki Agreements provided yet another example of reduced tensions between the superpowers. Signed by the United States, Canada, and all European nations, these accords recognized all borders in central and eastern Europe that had been established since the end of World War II, thereby acknowledging the Soviet sphere of influence in Eastern Europe. The Helsinki Agreements also committed the signatory powers to recognize and protect the human rights of their citizens.

This protection of human rights became one of the major foreign policy goals of the next American president, Jimmy Carter (b. 1924). Although hopes ran high for the continuation of détente, the Soviet invasion of Afghanistan in 1979, undertaken to restore a pro-Soviet regime, hardened relations between the United States and the Soviet Union. President Carter placed an embargo on the shipment of American grain to the Soviet Union.

The early administration of Ronald Reagan (b. 1911) witnessed a return to the harsh rhetoric, if not all of the harsh practices, of the Cold War. Calling the Soviet Union an "evil empire," Reagan began a military buildup that stimulated a renewed arms race. In 1982, the Reagan administration introduced the nuclear-tipped cruise missile, whose ability to fly at low altitudes made it difficult to detect. By providing military support to the Afghan insurgents, the Reagan administration helped to maintain a Vietnam-like war in Afghanistan that the Soviet Union could not win. Like the Vietnam War, the war in Afghanistan demonstrated that the power of a superpower was actually limited in the face of strong nationalist, guerrilla-type opposition.

The End of the Cold War

The accession of Mikhail Gorbachev to power in the Soviet Union in 1985 eventually brought a dramatic end to the Cold War. Gorbachev was willing to rethink many of the fundamental assumptions underlying Soviet foreign policy, and his "New Thinking," as it was called, opened the door to a series of stunning changes. For one, Gorbachev initiated a plan for arms limitation that led in 1987 to an agreement with the United States to eliminate intermediate-range nuclear weapons (the INF Treaty). Both sides had incentives to dampen the expensive arms race. Gorbachev hoped to make extensive economic and internal reforms while the United States had serious deficit

♦ **Reagan and Gorbachev.** The willingness of Mikhail Gorbachev and Ronald Reagan to dampen the arms race was a significant factor in ending the Cold War confrontation between the United States and the Soviet Union. Reagan and Gorbachev are shown here standing before St. Basil's Cathedral during Reagan's visit to Moscow in 1988.

problems. During the Reagan years, the United States had moved from being a creditor nation to the world's biggest debtor nation. By 1990, both countries were becoming aware that their large military budgets made it difficult for them to solve their serious social problems.

The years 1989 and 1990 were a crucial period in the ending of the Cold War. The postwar settlements that had become the norm in central and eastern Europe came unstuck as a mostly peaceful revolutionary upheaval swept through Eastern Europe. According to Gorbachev's new policy, the Soviet Union would no longer militarily support Communist governments that were faced with internal revolt. The unwillingness of the Soviet regime to use force to maintain the status quo, as it had in Hungary in 1956 and in Czechoslovakia in 1968, opened the door to the overthrow of the Communist regimes (see "Eastern Europe: The Collapse of the Communist Order" below). On October 3, 1990, the reunification of Germany also destroyed one of the most prominent symbols of the Cold War era.

The Persian Gulf War provided the first major opportunity for testing the new relationship between the United States and the Soviet Union in the post–Cold War era. In early August 1990, Iraqi military forces occupied the small neighboring country of Kuwait in the northeastern corner of the Arabian peninsula at the head of the Persian Gulf. The Iraqi invasion sparked an international outcry and the creation of an international force led by the United States that liberated Kuwait and destroyed a substantial part of Iraq's armed forces in the early months of 1991.

The Gulf War was the first important military conflict in the post–Cold War period. Mikhail Gorbachev and the Soviets played a minor role in the crisis and supported the American action. By the end of 1991, the Soviet Union had disintegrated, making any renewal of the global rivalry between two competing superpowers impossible. Although the United States emerged as the world's leading military power by 1992, its role in the creation of the "New World Order" that President Bush advocated at the time of the Gulf War was not clear. After some hesitation, President Bill Clinton (b. 1946) began to reassert American power in the world. In December 1995, the United States took the lead in bringing a negotiated end to the war in Bosnia. As part of the agreement signed by the warring parties, 20,000 American troops were sent to the region as part of a NATO military presence intended to enforce the peace.

Toward a New Western Order

Between 1945 and 1970, economic recovery had brought renewed growth to Europe. Nevertheless, the political divisions between Western and Eastern Europe remained; so, too, did the disparity in levels of prosperity. But in the late 1980s and early 1990s, the Soviet Union and its Eastern European satellite states underwent a revolutionary upheaval that dramatically altered the European scene and left many Europeans with both new hopes and new fears.

Map 30.1 The New Europe.

The Revolutionary Era in the Soviet Union

Between 1964 and 1982, revolutionary change in the Soviet Union appeared highly unlikely. After the overthrow of Khrushchev in 1964, Leonid Brezhnev (1906–1982) had become head of both party and state. He was always optimistic, yet reluctant to reform. The Brezhnev doctrine—the right of the Soviet Union to intervene if socialism was threatened in another "socialist state"—became an article of faith and led to the use of Soviet troops in Czechoslovakia in 1968.

Brezhnev benefited from the more relaxed atmosphere associated with détente. The Soviets had reached a rough parity with the United States in nuclear arms and enjoyed a sense of external security that seemed to allow for a relaxation of authoritarian rule. The regime permitted more access to Western styles of music, dress, and art, although dissenters were still punished. Andrei Sakharov, for example, who had played an important role in the development of the Soviet hydrogen bomb, was placed under house arrest for his defense of human rights.

In his economic policies, Brezhnev continued to emphasize heavy industry. Overall industrial growth declined, although the Soviet production of iron, steel, coal, and cement surpassed that of the United States. Two problems bedeviled the Soviet economy. The government's insistence on vigorous central planning led to a huge, complex bureaucracy that discouraged efficiency and reduced productivity. Moreover, the Soviet system, based on guaranteed employment and a lack of incentives, bred apathy, complacency, absenteeism, and drunkenness. Agricultural problems added to Soviet economic woes. Bad harvests in the mid-1970s, caused by a series of droughts, heavy rains, and early frosts, forced the Soviet government to buy grain from the West, particularly the United States. To their chagrin, the Soviets were increasingly dependent on capitalist countries.

By the 1970s, party and state leaders—as well as leaders of the army and secret police (KGB)—had come to expect numerous advantages and material privileges. Brezhnev was unwilling to tamper with the party leadership and state bureaucracy, regardless of the inefficiency and corruption that the system encouraged. By 1980, the Soviet Union was seriously ailing. A declining economy, a rise in infant mortality rates, a dramatic surge in alcoholism, and a deterioration in working conditions all gave impetus to a decline in morale and a growing perception that the system was floundering. Within the party, a small group of reformers emerged who understood the real condition of the Soviet Union, including a young reforming leader—Mikhail Gorbachev. A new era began when party leaders chose Gorbachev to lead the Soviet Union in March 1985.

THE GORBACHEV ERA

Born into a peasant family in 1931, Mikhail Gorbachev combined farm work with school and received the Order of the Red Banner for his agricultural efforts. This award and his good school record enabled him to study law at the University of Moscow. After receiving his law degree in 1955, he returned to his native southern Russia, where he eventually became first secretary of the Communist Party in the city of Stavropol (he had joined the Communist Party in 1952) and then first secretary of the regional party committee. In 1978, Gorbachev was made a member of the party's Central Committee in Moscow. Two years later, he became a full member of the ruling Politburo and secretary of the Central Committee. In March 1985, party leaders elected him general secretary of the party, and he became the new leader of the Soviet Union.

Educated during the reform years of Khrushchev, Gorbachev seemed intent on taking earlier reforms to their logical conclusions. By the 1980s, Soviet economic problems were obvious. Rigid, centralized planning led to mismanagement and stifled innovation. Although the Soviets still excelled in space exploration, they fell behind the West in high technology, especially in the development and production of computers for private and public use.

Most noticeable to the Soviet people was the actual decline in the standard of living. From the start, Gorbachev preached the need for radical reforms.

The cornerstone of Gorbachev's radical reforms was *perestroika* or "restructuring" (see the box on p. 633). At first this meant only a reordering of economic policy as Gorbachev called for the beginning of a market economy with limited free enterprise and some private property. However, Gorbachev soon perceived that in the Soviet system, the economic sphere was intimately tied to the social and political spheres. Attempting to reform the economy without political or social reform would be doomed to failure. One of the most important instruments of *perestroika* was *glasnost* or "openness." Soviet citizens and officials were encouraged to discuss openly the strengths and weaknesses of the Soviet Union. *Pravda*, the official newspaper of the Communist Party, began to include reports of official corruption, sloppy factory work, and protests against government policy. The arts also benefited from the new policy. Previously banned works were now published, and music based on Western styles, such as jazz and rock, began to be performed openly.

Political reforms were equally revolutionary. In June 1987, the principle of two-candidate elections was introduced, whereas before voters were presented with only one candidate. Most dissidents, including Andrei Sakharov, who had spent years in internal exile, were released. At the Communist Party conference in 1988, Gorbachev called for the creation of a new Soviet parliament, the Congress of People's Deputies, whose members were to be chosen in competitive elections. It convened in 1989, the first such meeting in Russia since 1918. Early in 1990, Gorbachev legalized the formation of other political parties and struck out Article 6, which had guaranteed the "leading role" of the Communist Party, from the Soviet constitution. At the same time, Gorbachev attempted to consolidate his power by the creation of a new state presidency. Hitherto, the position of first secretary of the party was the most important post in the Soviet Union, but as the Communist Party became less closely associated with the state, the powers of this office diminished correspondingly. In March 1990, Gorbachev became the Soviet Union's first president.

One of Gorbachev's most serious problems stemmed from the character of the Soviet Union. The Union of Soviet Socialist Republics was a truly multiethnic country, containing 92 nationalities and 112 recognized languages. Previously, the iron hand of the Communist Party, centered in Moscow, kept a lid on the centuries-old ethnic tensions that had periodically erupted in the history of this region. As Gorbachev released this iron grip,

⋙ Gorbachev and Perestroika ⋘

After assuming the leadership of the Soviet Union in 1985, Mikhail Gorbachev worked to liberalize and restructure the country. His policies opened the door to rapid changes in Eastern Europe and in Soviet–American relations at the end of the 1980s. In his book Perestroika, *Gorbachev explained some of his "New Thinking."*

Mikhail Gorbachev, *Perestroika*

The fundamental principle of the new political outlook is very simple: *nuclear war cannot be a means of achieving political, economic, ideological or any other goals.* This conclusion is truly revolutionary, for it means discarding the traditional notions of war and peace. It is the political function of war that has always been a justification for war, a "rational" explanation. Nuclear war is senseless; it is irrational. There would be neither winners nor losers in a global nuclear conflict: world Civilization would inevitably perish. . . .

But military technology has developed to such an extent that even a non-nuclear war would now be comparable with a nuclear war in its destructive effect. That is why it is logical to include in our category of nuclear wars this "variant" of an armed clash between major powers as well.

Thereby, an altogether different situation has emerged. A way of thinking and a way of acting, based on the use of force in world politics, have formed over centuries, even millennia. It seems they have taken root as something unshakable. Today, they have lost all reasonable grounds. . . . For the first time in history,
basing international politics on moral and ethical norms that are common to all humankind, as well as humanizing interstate relations, has become a vital requirement. . . .

There is a great thirst for mutual understanding and mutual communication in the world. It is felt among politicians, it is gaining momentum among the intelligentsia, representatives of culture, and the public at large. And if the Russian word "perestroika" has easily entered the international lexicon, this due to more than just interest in what is going on in the Soviet Union. Now the whole world needs restructuring, i.e., progressive development, a fundamental change.

People feel this and understand this. They have to find their bearings, to understand the problems besetting mankind, to realize how they should live in the future. The restructuring is a must for a world overflowing with nuclear weapons; for a world ridden with serious economic and ecological problems; for a world laden with poverty, backwardness and disease; for a human race now facing the urgent need of ensuring its own survival.

We are all students, and our teacher is life and time. I believe that more and more people will come to realize that through RESTRUCTURING in the broad sense of the word, the integrity of the world will be enhanced. Having earned good marks from our main teacher—life—we shall enter the twenty-first century well prepared and sure that there will be further progress.

tensions resurfaced, a by-product of *glasnost* that Gorbachev had not anticipated. Ethnic groups took advantage of the new openness to protest what they perceived to be ethnically motivated slights. As violence erupted, the Soviet Army, in disrepair since Afghanistan, had difficulty controlling the situation.

The period 1988 to 1990 also witnessed the appearance of nationalist movements throughout the republics of the Soviet Union. Many were motivated by ethnic concerns, with calls for sovereignty of the republics and independence from the Russian-based rule centered in Moscow. These movements first sprang up in Georgia in late 1988 and then in Latvia, Estonia, Moldavia, Uzbekistan, Azerbaijan, and most dramatically, Lithuania. On March 11, 1990, the Lithuanian Supreme Council proclaimed Lithuania an independent state. Four days later, the Soviet Congress of People's Deputies declared the Lithuanian proclamation null and void and stated that proper procedures must be established and followed before secession would be acceptable.

The End of the Soviet Union

During 1990 and 1991, Gorbachev struggled to deal with Lithuania and the other problems unleashed by his reforms. On one hand, he tried to appease conservative forces who complained about the growing disorder within the Soviet Union. On the other hand, he tried to accommodate the liberal forces, especially those in the Soviet republics, who increasingly favored a new kind of

The Soviet Bloc and Its Demise

Era of Brezhnev	1964–1982
Rule of Ceausescu in Romania	1965–1989
Honecker succeeds Ulbricht in East Germany	1971
Emergence of Solidarity in Poland	1980
Gorbachev comes to power in the Soviet Union	1985
1989	
Zhivkov loses power in Bulgaria	November 10
Collapse of Communist government in Czechoslovakia	December
East German government collapses	December
Execution of Ceausescu in Romania	December 25
1990	
Lithuania declares independence	March 11
East German elections—victory of Christian Democrats	March 18
Hungarian elections	March 25
Reunification of Germany	October 3
Walesa becomes president of Poland	December
1991	
Yeltsin becomes president of Russia	June
Slovenia and Croatia declare independence	June
Right-wing coup in the Soviet Union	August 19
Dissolution of the Soviet Union	December
1993	
Czechoslovakia splits into Czech Republic and Slovakia	January 1
Havel becomes president of Czech Republic	February 2
1995	
Aleksander Kwasniewski becomes Polish president	November
Dayton accords—end of war in Bosnia	December
1996	
Russian presidential elections	June–July

decentralized Soviet federation. In particular, Gorbachev labored to cooperate more closely with Boris Yeltsin, who had been elected president of the Russian Republic in June 1991.

By 1991, the conservative leaders of the traditional Soviet institutions—the army, government, KGB, and military industries—had grown increasingly worried about the impending dissolution of the Soviet Union and its impact on their own fortunes. On August 19, 1991, a group of these discontented rightists arrested Gorbachev and attempted to seize power. Gorbachev's unwillingness to work with the conspirators and the brave resistance in Moscow of Yeltsin and thousands of Russians who had grown accustomed to their new liberties caused the coup to disintegrate rapidly. The actions of these right-wing plotters, however, served to accelerate the very process they had hoped to stop—namely, the disintegration of the Soviet Union.

Despite desperate pleas by Gorbachev, the Soviet republics soon moved for complete independence. Ukraine voted for independence on December 1, 1991, and, a week later, the leaders of Russia, Ukraine, and Belarus announced that the Soviet Union had "ceased to exist" and would be replaced by a Commonwealth of Independent States. Gorbachev resigned on December 25, 1991, and turned over his responsibilities as commander-in-chief to Boris Yeltsin, the president of Russia. By the end of 1991, one of the largest empires in world history had come to an end, and a new era had begun in its lands.

Within Russia, a new power struggle soon ensued. Yeltsin was committed to introducing a free market economy as quickly as possible, but the transition was not easy. Economic hardships and social disarray, made worse by a dramatic rise in the activities of organized crime mobs, led increasing numbers of Russians to support both former Communists and hard-line nationalists, who criticized Russia's loss of prestige in world affairs. Yeltsin's brutal use of force against the Chechens, who wanted to secede from Russia and create their own state, also undermined his support. Despite the odds against him, however, Yeltsin won reelection as Russian president in 1996.

Eastern Europe: The Collapse of the Communist Order

Stalin's postwar order had imposed Communist regimes throughout Eastern Europe, and few people believed that the new order could be undone. But discontent with their Soviet-style regimes always simmered beneath the surface of these satellite states, and after Mikhail Gorbachev made it clear that his government would not intervene militarily, their Communist regimes fell quickly in the revolutions of 1989.

Poland had achieved a certain stability in the 1960s, but economic problems continued. Edward Gierek, who came to power in 1971, attempted to solve these problems by borrowing heavily from the West. But in 1980, when he announced huge increases in food prices in an effort to pay off part of the Western debt, workers' protests erupted and led directly to the rise of the independent labor movement called Solidarity. Led by Lech Walesa (b. 1943), Solidarity represented 10 million of Poland's 35 million people. With the support of the workers, many intellectuals, and the Catholic church, Solidarity was able to win a series of concessions, which the Polish government seemed powerless to stop until December 1981, when it arrested Walesa and other Solidarity leaders, outlawed the union, and imposed military rule under General Wojciech Jaruzelski (b. 1923).

But martial rule did not solve Poland's serious economic problems, and in 1988, new demonstrations led the Polish regime to agree to free parliamentary elections—the first free elections in Eastern Europe in forty years. Bowing to the inevitable, Jaruzelski's regime allowed the newly elected Solidarity coalition to form a new government, thus ending forty-five years of Communist rule in Poland. In December 1990, Lech Walesa was chosen as the new Polish president. But rapid free market reforms led to severe unemployment and popular discontent, and in November 1995, Alexander Kwasniewski, a former Communist, defeated Walesa and became the new Polish president.

In Hungary, too, the process of liberation from Communist rule had begun before 1989. Remaining in power for more than thirty years, the government of János Kádár enacted the most far-reaching economic reforms in Eastern Europe. In the early 1980s, he legalized small private enterprises, such as shops, restaurants, and artisan shops. Hungary moved slowly away from its strict adherence to Soviet dominance and even established fairly friendly relations with the West.

As the 1980s progressed, however, the economy sagged, and Kádár fell from power in 1988. By 1989, the Hungarian Communist government was aware of the growing dissatisfaction and began to undertake reforms. But they came too late as new political parties called for Hungary to become a democratic republic. In elections in March 1990, the Communists came in fourth, winning only 8.5 percent of the vote, a clear repudiation of communism. The Democratic Forum, a right-of-center, highly patriotic party, won the election and formed a new coalition government that committed Hungary to democratic government and the institution of a free market economy.

Communist regimes in Poland and Hungary had attempted to make some political and economic reforms in the 1970s and 1980s, but this was not the case in Czechoslovakia. After Soviet troops had crushed the reform movement in 1968, hard-line Czech Communists under Gustav Husák purged the party and instituted a policy of massive repression to maintain their power. Only writers and other intellectuals provided any real opposition to the government, but they did not have any success until the late 1980s. Government attempts to suppress mass demonstrations in Prague and other Czechoslovakian cities in 1988 and 1989 only led to more and larger demonstrations. By November 1989, crowds as large as 500,000, which included many students, were forming in Prague. In December 1989, as demonstrations continued, the Communist government, lacking any real support, collapsed. President Husák resigned and at the end of December was replaced by Vaclav Havel, the dissident playwright who had played an important role in bringing the Communist government down. In January 1990, Havel declared amnesty for some 30,000 political prisoners. He also set out on a goodwill visit to various Western countries in which he proved to be an eloquent spokesman for Czech democracy and a new order in Europe (see the box on p. 636).

Within Czechoslovakia, the shift to non-Communist rule was complicated by old problems, especially ethnic issues. Czechs and Slovaks disagreed over the makeup of the new state but were able to agree to a peaceful division of the country. On January 1, 1993, Czechoslovakia split into the Czech Republic and Slovakia. Vaclav Havel was elected the first president of the new Czech Republic.

Czechoslovakia's revolutionary path was considerably less violent than Romania's. In 1965, leadership of the Communist government in Romania passed into the hands of Nicolae Ceausescu (1918–1989), who with his wife Elena established a rigid and dictatorial regime. Ceausescu ruled Romania with an iron grip, using a secret police—the Securitate—as his personal weapon against any dissent. Nevertheless, opposition to his regime grew as Ceausescu rejected the reforms in Eastern Europe promoted by Gorbachev. A small incident became the spark that ignited heretofore suppressed flames of discontent. The ruthless crushing of a demonstration in Timisoara in December 1989 led to other mass demonstrations. After the dictator was booed at a mass rally on December 21, the army refused to support any more repression. Ceausescu and his wife were captured on December 22 and tried and executed on Christmas Day, 1989. Leadership now

Vaclav Havel: The Call for a New Politics

In attempting to deal with the world's problems, some European leaders have pointed to the need for a new perspective, especially a moral one, if people are to live in a sane world. These two excerpts are taken from speeches by Vaclav Havel, who was elected the new president of Czechoslovakia at the end of 1989. The first is from his inaugural address as president of Czechoslovakia on January 1, 1990; the second is from a speech given to the American Congress.

Vaclav Havel, Address to the People of Czechoslovakia, January 1, 1990

But all this is still not the main problem [the environmental devastation of the country by its Communist leaders]. The worst thing is that we live in a contaminated moral environment. We fell morally ill because we became used to saying something different from what we thought. We learned not to believe in anything, to ignore each other, to care only about ourselves. Concepts such as love, friendship, compassion, humility, or forgiveness lost their depth and dimensions, and for many of us they represented only psychological peculiarities, or they resembled gone astray greetings from ancients, a little ridiculous in the era of computers and spaceships. Only a few of us were able to cry out loud that the powers that be should not be all-powerful, and that special farms, which produce ecologically pure and top-quality food just for them should send their produce to schools, children's homes and hospitals if our agriculture was unable to offer them to all. The previous regime—armed with its arrogant and intolerant ideology—reduced man to a force of production and nature to a tool of production. In this it attacked both their very substance and their mutual relationship. It reduced gifted and autonomous people, skillfully working in their own country, to nuts and bolts of some monstrously huge, noisy, and stinking machine, whose real meaning is not clear to anyone.

Vaclav Havel, Speech to Congress, February 21, 1990

For this reason, the salvation of this human world lies nowhere else than in the human heart, in the human power to reflect, in human meekness and in human responsibility.

Without a global revolution in the sphere of human consciousness, nothing will change for the better in the sphere of our being as humans, and the catastrophe toward which this world is headed—be it ecological, social, demographic or a general breakdown of civilization—will be unavoidable. . . .

We are still a long way from that "family of man." In fact, we seem to be receding from the ideal rather than growing closer to it. Interests of all kinds—personal, selfish, state, nation, group, and if you like, company interests—still considerably outweigh genuinely common and global interests. We are still under the sway of the destructive and vain belief that man is the pinnacle of creation and not just a part of it and that therefore everything is permitted. . . .

In other words, we still don't know how to put morality ahead of politics, science and economics. We are still incapable of understanding that the only genuine backbone of all our actions, if they are to be moral, is responsibility.

Responsibility to something higher than my family, my country, my company, my success—responsibility to the order of being where all our actions are indelibly recorded and where and only where they will be properly judged.

The interpreter or mediator between us and this higher authority is what is traditionally referred to as human conscience.

passed into the hands of a hastily formed National Salvation Front, which won elections in the spring of 1990. Questions remained, however, about the new government's commitment to democracy.

In Bulgaria, Todor Zhivkov (b. 1911) became leader of the Bulgarian Communist Party and hence leader of the nation in 1954. Not until the late 1980s did a number of small opposition groups begin to emerge. In October 1989, antigovernment demonstrations were held in the capital city of Sofia, and a month later, Zhivkov was unexpectedly relieved of his post as general secretary of the Communist Party, a position he had held for thirty-five years. Elections in November 1991 brought about a new government coalition, led by the United Democratic

Front, to take over power. Nevertheless, the Socialist Party (the former Communists) remained a potent force in Bulgarian politics.

The Reunification of Germany

Until 1989, the existence of West Germany and East Germany remained the most powerful symbol of a divided postwar Europe. In the early 1950s, the ruling Communist government in East Germany, led by Walter Ulbricht, had consolidated its position and become a faithful Soviet satellite. Industry was nationalized and agriculture collectivized. After a workers' revolt in 1953 was crushed by Soviet tanks, a steady flight of East Germans to West Germany ensued, primarily through the city of Berlin. This exodus of mostly skilled laborers created economic problems and led the East German government in 1961 to build the infamous Berlin Wall in 1961 separating West from East Berlin. After building the wall, East Germany succeeded in developing the strongest economy among the Soviet Union's Eastern European satellites. In 1971, Walter Ulbricht was succeeded by Erich Honecker (b. 1912), a party hardliner who made use of the *Stasi*, the secret police, to rule with an iron fist for the next eighteen years.

In 1988, however, popular unrest, partly fueled by the continual economic slump of the 1980s (which affected most of Eastern Europe) as well as the ongoing oppressiveness of Honecker's regime, caused another mass exodus of East German refugees. Violent repression as well as Honecker's refusal to institute reforms only led to a larger exodus and mass demonstrations against the regime in the summer and fall of 1989. Capitulating to popular pressure on November 9, the Communist government opened the entire border with the West. Hundreds of thousands of Germans swarmed across the borders, mostly to visit and return. The Berlin Wall, long the symbol of the Cold War, became the sight of massive celebrations as thousands of people used sledgehammers to tear down the wall. By December, new political parties had emerged, and on March 18, 1990, in East Germany's first free elections ever, the Christian Democrats won almost 50 percent of the vote. The Christian Democrats supported political unification with West Germany, which was achieved on October 3, 1990. What had seemed almost impossible at the beginning of 1989 had become a reality by the end of 1990—the country of East Germany had ceased to exist.

The Disintegration of Yugoslavia

From its beginning in 1919, Yugoslavia had been an artificial creation. After World War II, the dictatorial Tito had managed to hold the six republics and two autonomous provinces that constituted Yugoslavia together. After his death in 1980, no strong leader emerged, and his responsibilities passed to a collective state presidency and the League of Communists of Yugoslavia. At the end of the 1980s, Yugoslavia was caught up in the reform movements sweeping through Eastern Europe. The League of Communists collapsed and new parties quickly emerged.

✦ **And the Wall Came Tumbling Down.** The Berlin Wall, long a symbol of Europe's Cold War divisions, became the site of massive celebrations after the East German government opened its border with the West. The activities included spontaneous acts of demolition as Germans used sledgehammers and crowbars to tear down parts of the wall.

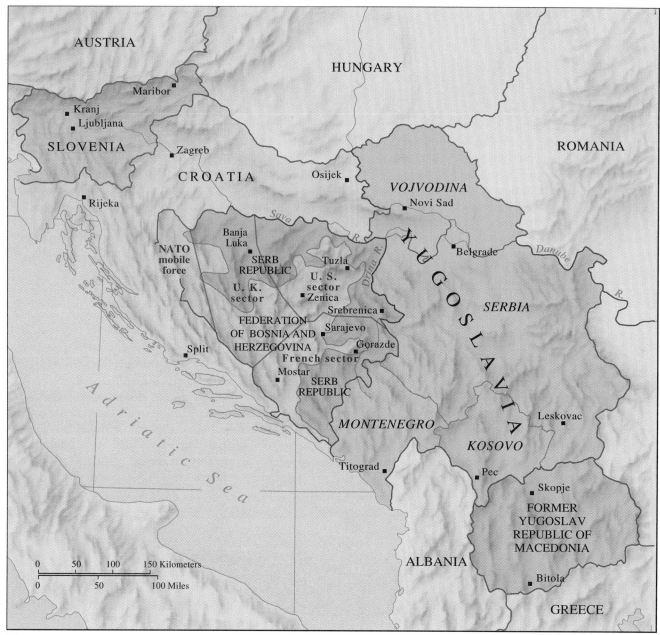

❋ **Map 30.2** The Lands of Former Yugoslavia.

The development of separatist movements complicated the Yugoslav political scene. In 1990, the republics of Slovenia, Croatia, Bosnia-Herzegovina, and the Former Yugoslav Republic of Macedonia began to lobby for a new federal structure of Yugoslavia that would fulfill their separatist desires. Slobodan Milosevic, who had become leader of the Serbian Communist party in 1987 and had managed to stay in power by emphasizing his Serbian nationalism, rejected these efforts. He asserted that these republics could only be independent if new border arrangements were made to accommodate the Serb minorities in those republics who did not want to live outside the boundaries of a Greater Serbian state. Serbs constituted 11.6 percent of Croatia's population and 32 percent of Bosnia-Herzegovina's population in 1981.

After negotiations among the six republics failed, Slovenia and Croatia declared their independence in June 1991. Milosevic's government sent the Yugoslavian army, which it controlled, into Slovenia, but without much success. In September 1991, it began a full assault against Croatia. Increasingly, the Yugoslavian army was becoming the Serbian army, while Serbian irregular forces played an important role in military operations. Before a cease-fire was arranged, the Serbian forces had captured one-third of Croatia's territory in brutal and destructive fighting. Early in 1992, the Serbs turned their guns on Bosnia-Herzegovina, and by mid-1993 had acquired 70 percent of Bosnian territory. The Serbian policy of "ethnic cleansing"—killing or forcibly removing Bosnian Muslims from their lands—revived memories of Nazi atrocities in World War II. Nevertheless, despite worldwide outrage, European governments failed to take a decisive and forceful stand against these Serbian activities. By 1995, 250,000 Bosnians had been killed and two million others were left homeless.

In that same year, a sudden turn of events occurred. New offensives by mostly Muslim Bosnian government army forces and by the Croatian army regained considerable territory that had been lost to Serbian forces. Air strikes by NATO bombers, strongly advocated by President Bill Clinton, were launched in retaliation for Serb attacks on civilians and weakened the Serb military positions. All sides were now encouraged by the United States to end the war. A formal peace treaty was signed in Paris on December 14 that split Bosnia into a loose union of a Serb republic and a Muslim-Croat federation. NATO agreed to send a force of 60,000 troops to monitor the frontier between the new political entities.

After the Fall

The fall of Communist governments in Eastern Europe during the revolutions of 1989 brought a wave of euphoria to Europe. In 1989 and 1990, new governments throughout Eastern Europe worked diligently to scrap the remnants of the old system and introduce the democratic procedures and market systems that they believed would revitalize their scarred lands. But it was neither a simple nor easy process, and the mood of euphoria had largely faded by 1992.

Most Eastern European countries had little or virtually no experience with democratic systems. Then, too, ethnic divisions that had troubled these areas before World War II and had been forcibly submerged under Communist rule, reemerged with a vengeance, making political unity almost impossible. While Czechoslovakia resolved

its differences peacefully, Yugoslavia descended into the kind of brutal warfare that had not been seen in Europe since World War II. In the lands of the former Soviet Union, ethnic and nationalist problems threatened to tear some of the new states apart.

The rapid conversion to market economies also proved painful. Unemployment climbed to over 15 percent in the former East Germany and 13 percent in Poland in 1992. Wages remained low while prices skyrocketed. Russia experienced a 2000 percent inflation rate in 1992. At the same time, in many countries former Communists were able to retain important positions of power or become the new owners of private property. For both political and economic reasons, the new non-Communist states of Eastern Europe faced dangerous and uncertain futures. Nevertheless, by 1998, some of these states, such as Poland and the Czech Republic, were making a successful transition to both free markets and democracy.

Western Europe: The Winds of Change

After two decades of incredible economic growth, Europe experienced severe economic recessions in the mid-1970s and early 1980s. Both inflation and unemployment rose dramatically. No doubt, the substantial increase in the price of oil that followed the Arab–Israeli conflict in 1973 was a major cause of the first downturn. Moreover, a worldwide recession had led to a decline in demand for European goods. The economies of the Western European states recovered in the course of the 1980s, although problems remained.

Europeans also moved toward further integration of their economies after 1970. The European Economic Community expanded in 1973 when Great Britain, Ireland, and Denmark gained membership in what its members now began to call the European Community (EC). By 1986, three additional members—Spain, Portugal, and Greece—had been added. The European Community was primarily an economic union, not a political one. By 1992, the EC comprised 344 million people and constituted the world's largest single trading entity, transacting almost one-fourth of the world's commerce. In the 1980s and 1990s, the European Community moved toward even greater economic integration. The Treaty on European Union (also called the Maastricht Treaty after the city in the Netherlands where the agreement was reached) represented an attempt to create a true economic and monetary union of all EC members. On January 1, 1994, the European Community became the European Union. One of its first goals was to introduce a common currency, called the "euro," by 2002.

CHRONOLOGY

◆◆◆◆◆◆◆◆◆◆◆◆◆◆◆◆◆◆◆◆◆◆◆◆◆◆

Western Europe

Willy Brandt becomes chancellor of West Germany	1969
Common Market expands (European Community)	1973
Helmut Schmidt becomes chancellor of West Germany	1974
Margaret Thatcher becomes prime minister of Britain	1979
Francois Mitterrand becomes president of France	1981
Falklands War	1982
Helmut Kohl becomes chancellor of West Germany	1982
European Community expands	1986
Reelection of Mitterrand	1988
First all-German federal election	1990
Conservative victory in France	1993
Creation of European Union	1994
Jacques Chirac becomes president of France	1995
Victory of Labour Party in Britain	1997

FROM WEST GERMANY TO GERMANY

After the Adenauer era, German voters moved politically from the center-right politics of the Christian Democrats to center-left politics, and in 1969, the Social Democrats became the leading party. The first Social Democratic chancellor was Willy Brandt (1913–1992). Brandt was especially successful with his "opening toward the east" (known as *Ostpolitik*), for which he received the Nobel Peace Prize in 1972. In that year, Brandt made a Basic Treaty with East Germany that called for "good neighborly" relations, which soon led to greater cultural, personal, and economic contacts between West and East Germany.

Brandt's successor, Helmut Schmidt (b. 1918), was more of a technocrat than a reform-minded socialist and concentrated primarily on the economic problems largely brought about by high oil prices between 1973 and 1975. Schmidt was successful in eliminating a deficit of 10 billion marks in three years. In 1982, when the coalition of Schmidt's Social Democrats with the Free Democrats fell apart over the reduction of social welfare expenditures, the Free Democrats joined with the Christian Democra-

tic Union of Helmut Kohl (b. 1930) to form a new government.

Helmut Kohl was a clever politician who benefited greatly from the reunification of the two Germanies, which made the new Germany with its 79 million people the leading power in Europe. In the first all-German federal election, held in 1990, Kohl's Christian Democrats won 44 percent of the vote, while their coalition partners—the Free Democrats—received 11 percent.

But the excitement over reunification soon dissipated as new problems arose. All too soon, the realization set in that the revitalization of eastern Germany would take far more money than was originally thought, and Kohl's government was soon forced to raise taxes. Moreover, the virtual collapse of the economy in eastern Germany led to extremely high levels of unemployment and severe discontent. One of the responses was an attack on foreigners. For years foreigners seeking asylum and illegal immigrants had found haven in Germany because of its extremely liberal immigration laws. In 1992, more than 440,000 immigrants came to Germany seeking asylum. Attacks against foreigners by right-wing extremists—especially young neo-Nazis—became an all-too-frequent part of German life.

GREAT BRITAIN: THATCHER AND THATCHERISM

Between 1964 and 1979, Conservatives and Labour alternated in power. Neither party could solve the problem of fighting between Catholics and Protestants in Northern Ireland. Violence increased as the Irish Republican Army (IRA) staged a series of dramatic terrorist acts in response to the suspension of Northern Ireland's parliament in 1972 and the establishment of direct rule by London. Nor was either party able to deal with Britain's ailing economy. Failure to modernize made British industry less and less competitive. Moreover, Britain was hampered by frequent labor strikes, many of them caused by conflicts between rival labor unions.

In 1979, the Conservatives returned to power under Margaret Thatcher (b. 1925), who became the first woman prime minister in British history. Thatcher pledged to lower taxes, reduce government bureaucracy, limit social welfare, restrict union power, and end inflation. The "Iron Lady," as she was called, did break the power of the labor unions. Although she did not eliminate the basic components of the social welfare system, she did use austerity measures to control inflation. "Thatcherism," as her economic policy was termed, improved the British economic situation but at a price. The south of England, for example, prospered, but the old industrial areas of the Midlands and north declined and were beset by high unemployment and poverty.

In the area of foreign policy, Thatcher, like Ronald Reagan in the United States, took a hard-line approach against communism. She oversaw a large military buildup aimed at replacing older technology and reestablishing Britain as a world policeman. In 1982, when Argentina attempted to take control of the Falkland Islands (one of Britain's few remaining colonial outposts) 300 miles off its coast, the British successfully rebuked it, although at great economic cost and the loss of 255 lives. The Falklands War, however, did generate much popular patriotic support for Thatcher.

Margaret Thatcher dominated British politics in the 1980s. Only in 1990 did Labour's fortunes seem to revive when Thatcher's government attempted to replace local property taxes with a flat-rate tax payable by every adult to his or her local authority. Many argued that this was nothing more than a poll tax that would enable the rich to pay the same rate as the poor. In 1990, after antitax riots broke out, Thatcher's once remarkable popularity fell to all-time lows. At the end of November, a revolt within her own party caused Thatcher to resign as prime minister and be replaced by John Major. His government, however, failed to capture the imagination of most Britons. In new elections on May 1, 1997, the Labour Party led by Tony Blair won a landslide victory.

UNCERTAINTIES IN FRANCE

The worsening of France's economic situation in the 1970s brought a shift to the left politically. By 1981, the Socialists had become the dominant party in the National Assembly, and the Socialist leader, François Mitterrand (1916–1995), was elected president. His first concern was with France's economic difficulties. In 1982, Mitterrand froze prices and wages in the hope of reducing the huge budget deficit and high inflation. He also passed a number of liberal measures to aid workers: an increased minimum wage, expanded social benefits, a thirty-nine-hour workweek, higher taxes for the rich, and nationalization of major banks. Mitterrand's administrative reforms included both centralization (nationalization of banks and industry) and decentralization (granting local governments greater powers).

The Socialist policies largely failed to work, however, and within three years, a decline in support for the Socialists caused the Mitterrand government to return some of the economy to private enterprise. Some economic improvements in the late 1980s enabled Mitterrand to win a second seven-year term in the 1988 presidential elec-

◆ **Margaret Thatcher.** Great Britain's first woman prime minister, Margaret Thatcher was a strong leader who dominated British politics in the 1980s. This picture of Thatcher was taken at the Chelsea Flower Show in May 1990. Six months later, a revolt within her own party caused her to resign as prime minister.

tion. But France's economic decline continued. In 1993, French unemployment stood at 10.6 percent, and, in the elections in March of that year, the Socialists won only 28 percent of the vote while a coalition of conservative parties won 80 percent of the seats in the National Assembly. The move to the right was strengthened when the conservative mayor of Paris, Jacques Chirac, was elected president in May 1995.

The United States: The American Domestic Scene

With the election of Richard Nixon as president in 1968, American politics made a shift to the right. Nixon ended American involvement in Vietnam by gradually withdrawing American troops. Politically, he pursued a "southern strategy," carefully calculating that "law and order" issues and a slowdown in racial desegregation would appeal to southern whites. The South, which had once been a stronghold for the Democrats, began to form a new allegiance to the Republican party. The Republican strategy, however, also gained support among white Democrats in northern cities, where court-mandated busing to achieve racial integration had led to a white backlash.

As president, Nixon was paranoid about conspiracies and began to use illegal methods to gain political intelligence on his political opponents. One of the president's advisers explained that their intention was to "use the available Federal machinery to screw our political enemies." Nixon's zeal led to the Watergate scandal—the attempted bugging of Democratic National Headquarters, located in the Watergate Hotel in Washington, D.C. Although Nixon repeatedly lied to the American public about his involvement in the affair, secret tapes of his own conversations in the White House revealed the truth. On August 9, 1974, Nixon resigned the presidency rather than face trial and possible impeachment by the Senate.

After Watergate, American domestic politics focused on economic issues. Vice-President Gerald Ford (b. 1913) became president when Nixon resigned, only to lose in the 1976 election to the former governor of Georgia, Jimmy Carter (b. 1924). Both Ford and Carter faced severe economic problems. The period from 1973 to the mid-1980s was one of economic stagnation, which came to be known as stagflation—a combination of high inflation and high unemployment. In part, the economic downturn stemmed from a dramatic change in oil prices. Oil was considered a cheap and abundant source of energy in the 1950s, and Americans had grown dependent on its importation from the Middle East. But an oil embargo and price increases by the Organization of Petroleum Exporting Countries (OPEC) as a result of the Arab-Israel War in 1973 quadrupled oil prices. Additional price hikes led oil prices to increase twentyfold by the end of the 1970s, no doubt encouraging inflationary tendencies throughout the entire economy.

By 1980, the Carter administration was faced with two devastating problems. High inflation and a noticeable decline in average weekly earnings were causing a drop in American living standards. At the same time, a crisis abroad had erupted when fifty-three Americans were held hostage by the Iranian government of Ayatollah Khomeini. Carter's inability to gain the release of the American hostages led to perceptions at home that he was a weak president. His overwhelming loss to Ronald Reagan (b. 1911) in the election of 1980 brought forward the chief exponent of right-wing Republican policies and a new political order.

The Reagan Revolution, as it has been called, consisted of a number of new directions. Reversing decades of changes, Reagan cut back on the welfare state by decreasing spending on food stamps, school lunch programs, and job programs. At the same time, his administration fostered the largest peacetime military buildup in American history. Total federal spending rose from $631 billion in 1981 to over a trillion dollars by 1986. But instead of raising taxes to pay for the new expenditures, which far outweighed the budget cuts in social areas, Reagan convinced Congress to support supply-side economics. Massive tax cuts would supposedly stimulate rapid economic growth and produce new revenues. Much of the tax cut went to the wealthy. Reagan's policies seemed to work in the short run as the United States experienced an economic upturn that lasted until the end of the 1980s. The spending policies of the Reagan administration, however, also produced record government deficits, which loomed as an obstacle to long-term growth. In the 1970s, the total deficit was $420 billion. Between 1981 and 1987, Reagan budget deficits were three times that amount.

The inability of George Bush (b. 1924), Reagan's successor, to deal with the deficit problem as well as an economic downturn, enabled a Democrat, William Clinton, to become president in November 1992. The new president was a southern Democrat who claimed to be a new Democrat—one who favored a number of the Republican policies of the 1980s. This was a clear indication that the rightward drift in American politics was by no means ended by this Democratic victory. In fact, Clinton's reelection in 1996 was partially due to his adoption of Republican ideas and policies.

The Development of Canada

In 1963, during a major economic recession, the Liberals had been returned to power in Canada. The most prominent Liberal government was that of Pierre Trudeau (b. 1919), who came to power in 1968. Although French in background, Trudeau was dedicated to Canada's federal union, and in 1968 his government passed the Official Languages Act that allowed both English and French to be used in the federal civil service. Although Trudeau's government vigorously pushed an industrialization program, high inflation and Trudeau's efforts to impose the will of the federal government on the powerful provincial governments alienated voters and weakened his government. Economic recession in the early 1980s brought Brian Mulroney (b. 1939), leader of the Progressive Conservative party, to power in 1984. Mulroney's government sought greater privatization of Canada's state-run corporations and negotiated a free trade agreement with the United States. Bitterly resented by many Canadians, the agreement cost Mulroney's government much of its popularity. In 1993, the ruling Conservatives were drastically defeated, and the Liberal leader, Jean Chrétien, became prime minister.

Mulroney's government was also unable to settle the ongoing crisis over the French-speaking province of Quebec. In the late 1960s, the Parti Québécois, headed by René Lévesque, ran on a platform of Quebec's secession from the Canadian union. To pursue their dream of separation, some underground separatist groups even used terrorist bombings. In 1976, the Parti Québécois won Quebec's provincial elections and in 1980 called for a referendum that would enable the provincial government to negotiate Quebec's independence from the rest of Canada. Voters in Quebec narrowly rejected the plan in 1995, however, and debate over Quebec's status continues to divide Canada in the late 1990s.

New Directions and New Problems in Western Society

Dramatic social developments have accompanied political and economic changes since the end of World War II. New opportunities for women emerged while new problems for Western society arose with the advent of terrorism and a growing awareness of environmental dangers.

New (and Old) Patterns: Women in the Postwar World

Although birthrates rose immediately after World War II, they have for the most part declined since then as contraceptive devices and abortion have become widely available. It is estimated that women need to average 2.1 children in order to ensure a natural replacement of a country's population. In many European countries, the population stopped growing in the 1960s, and the downward trend has continued since then. By the 1990s, fertility rates were down drastically; among the twelve nations of the European Union, the average number of children per mother was 1.58.

The character of women's employment in both Europe and the United States also changed after World War II as an increasing number of married women entered the workforce. At the beginning of the twentieth century, even working-class wives tended to stay at home if they could afford to do so. In the postwar period, this was no longer the case. In the United States, for example, in 1900, married women made up about 15 percent of the female labor force; by 1970, their number had increased to 62 percent. But the increased number of women in the workforce has not changed some old patterns. Working-class women in particular still earn salaries lower than those of men for equal work. Women still tend to enter traditionally female jobs. A 1980 study of twenty-five European nations re-

vealed that women still made up over 80 percent of the typists, nurses, tailors, and dressmakers in their countries. Many European women also still faced the double burden of earning income on the one hand and raising a family and maintaining the household on the other. Such inequalities led increasing numbers of women to rebel.

THE FEMINIST MOVEMENT: THE SEARCH FOR LIBERATION

The participation of women in World Wars I and II helped them achieve one of the major aims of the nineteenth-century feminist movement—the right to vote. Already after World War I, many governments acknowledged the contributions of women to the war effort by granting them the right to vote, although women in France and Italy did not obtain the right to vote until 1945. After World War II, European women tended to

✦ **Women's Liberation Movement.** In the late 1960s, as women began once again to assert their rights, a revived women's liberation movement emerged. Feminists in the movement maintained that women themselves must alter the conditions of their lives. During this women's liberation rally, some women climbed the statue of Admiral Farragut in Washington, D.C., to exhibit their signs.

fall back into the traditional roles expected of them, but by the late 1960s, women began to asset their rights again. Along with the student upheavals of the late 1960s came renewed interest in feminism, or the women's liberation movement as it was now called. Increasingly, women protested that the acquisition of political and legal equality had not brought true equality with men:

> We are economically oppressed: in jobs we do full work for half pay, in the home we do unpaid work full time. We are commercially exploited by advertisement, television and the press; legally we often have only the status of children. We are brought up to feel inadequate, educated to narrower horizons than men. This is our specific oppression as women. It is as women that we are, therefore, organizing.[1]

These were the words of a British Women's Liberation Workshop in 1969.

Of great importance to the emergence of the postwar women's liberation movement was the work of Simone de Beauvoir (1908–1986). Born into a Catholic middle-class family and educated at the Sorbonne in Paris, she supported herself as a teacher and later as a writer. She maintained a lifelong relationship (but not marriage) with Jean-Paul Sartre and became actively involved in political causes. De Beauvoir believed that she lived a "liberated" life for a twentieth-century European woman, but for all her freedom, she still came to perceive that as a woman she faced limits that men did not. In 1949, she published her highly influential work, *The Second Sex,* in which she argued that as a result of male-dominated societies, women had been defined by their differences from men and consequently received second-class status. De Beauvoir took an active role in the French women's movement of the 1970s, and her book was a major influence on both the American and European women's movements (see the box on p. 645).

Feminists in the women's liberation movement came to believe that women themselves must transform the fundamental conditions of their lives. They did so in a variety of ways. In the 1960s and 1970s, women sought and gained a measure of control over their own bodies by seeking to overturn the illegality of both contraception and abortion. Hundreds of thousands of European women worked to repeal the laws that outlawed contraception and abortion and began to meet with success. A French law in 1968 permitted the sale of contraceptive devices; another in 1979 legalized abortion. In the 1980s and 1990s, women faculty in universities concentrated on developing new cultural attitudes through the new academic field of "women's studies." Other women began to

try to affect the political and natural environment by allying with the antinuclear and ecological movements.

The Growth of Terrorism

Acts of terror by those opposed to governments became a frightening aspect of modern Western society. Bands of terrorists used assassination, indiscriminate bombing of civilians, the taking of hostages, and the hijacking of airplanes to draw attention to their demands or to destabilize governments in the hope of achieving their political goals. Terrorist acts garnered considerable media attention. When Palestinian terrorists kidnapped and killed eleven Israeli athletes at the Munich Olympic games in 1972, hundreds of millions of people watched the drama unfold on television. Indeed, some observers believe that media exposure has been an important catalyst for some terrorist groups.

Motivations for terrorist acts varied considerably. Left-wing groups, such as the Baader-Meinhof gang (also known as the Red Army Faction) in Germany and the Red Brigades in Italy, consisted chiefly of affluent middle-class young people who denounced the injustices of capitalism and supported acts of revolutionary terrorism in order to bring down the system. Right-wing terrorist groups, such as the New Order in Italy and the Charles Martel Club in France, used bombings to foment disorder and bring about authoritarian regimes. These groups received little or no public support, and authorities were able to crush them fairly quickly.

But terrorist acts also stemmed from militant nationalists who wished to create separatist states. Because they received considerable support from local populations sympathetic to their cause, these terrorist groups could maintain their activities over a long period of time. Most prominent was the Irish Republican Army (IRA), which resorted to vicious attacks against the ruling government and innocent civilians in Northern Ireland. Over a period of twenty years, IRA terrorists were responsible for the deaths of 2,000 people in Northern Ireland; three-fourths of them were civilians.

Governments fought back by creating special antiterrorist units that became extremely effective in responding to terrorist acts. In 1977, for example, the German special antiterrorist unit, known as GSG, rescued 91 hostages from a Lufthansa airplane that had been hijacked to Mogadishu in Somalia. Counterterrorism, or a calculated policy of direct retaliation against terrorists, also made states that sponsored terrorism more cautious. In 1986, the Reagan administration responded to the terrorist bombing of a West German disco club popular with

The Voice of the Women's Liberation Movement

Simone de Beauvoir was an important figure in the emergence of the postwar women's liberation movement. This excerpt is taken from her influential book, The Second Sex, *in which she argued that women have been forced into a position subordinate to men.*

Simone de Beauvoir, *The Second Sex*

Now, woman has always been man's dependent, if not his slave; the two sexes have never shared the world in equality. And even today woman is heavily handicapped, though her situation is beginning to change. Almost nowhere is her legal status the same as man's and frequently it is much to her disadvantage. Even when her rights are legally recognized in the abstract, long-standing custom prevents their full expression in the mores. In the economic sphere men and women can almost be said to make up two castes; other things being equal, the former hold the better jobs, get higher wages, and have more opportunity for success than their new competitors. In industry and politics men have a great many more positions and they monopolize the most important posts. In addition to all this they enjoy a traditional prestige that the education of children tends in every way to support, for the present enshrines the past—and in the past all history has been made by men. At the present time, when women are beginning to take part in the affairs of the world, it is still a world that belongs to men—they have no doubt of it at all and women have scarcely any. To decline to be the Other, to refuse to be a party to a deal—this would be for women to renounce all the advantages conferred upon them by their alliance with the superior caste. Man-the-sovereign will provide woman-the-liege with material protection and will undertake the moral justification of her existence; thus she can evade at once both economic risk and the metaphysical risk of a liberty in which ends and aims must be contrived without assistance. Indeed, along with the ethical urge of each individual to affirm his subjective existence, there is also the temptation to forgo liberty and become a thing. This is an inauspicious road, for he who takes it—passive, lost, ruined—becomes henceforth the creature of another's will, frustrated in his transcendence and deprived of every value. But it is an easy road; on it one avoids the strain involved in undertaking an authentic existence. When man makes of woman the *Other* he may, then, expect her to manifest deep-seated tendencies toward complicity. Thus woman may fail to lay claim to the status of subject because she lacks definite resources, because she feels the necessary bond that ties her to man regardless of reciprocity, and because she is often very well pleased with her role as the *Other*.

Now, what peculiarly signalizes the situation of woman is that she—a free and autonomous being like all human creatures—nevertheless finds herself living in a world where men compel her to assume the status of the Other.

American soldiers by an air attack on Libya, long suspected to be a major sponsor of terrorist organizations.

The Environment and the Green Movements

By the 1970s, serious ecological problems had become all too apparent. Air pollution, produced by nitrogen oxide and sulfur dioxide emissions from road vehicles, power plants, and industrial factories, was causing respiratory illnesses and having corrosive effects on buildings and monuments. Many rivers, lakes, and seas had become so polluted that they posed serious health risks. Dying forests and disappearing wildlife alarmed more and more people. The Soviet nuclear power disaster at Chernobyl in 1986 made Europeans even more aware of potential environmental hazards. The opening of Eastern Europe after the revolutions of 1989 brought to the world's attention the incredible environmental destruction of that region caused by unfettered industrial pollution. Environmental concerns forced the major political parties in Europe to advocate new regulations for the protection of the environment.

Growing ecological awareness also gave rise to Green movements and Green parties that emerged throughout Europe in the 1970s. Some of these parties came from the antinuclear movement; others from such causes as women's liberation and concerns for foreign workers. Most visible was the Green Party in Germany, which was officially organized in 1979 and, by 1987, had elected forty-two delegates to the West German parliament.

Green parties also competed successfully in Sweden, Austria, and Switzerland.

Although the Green movements and parties have played an important role in making people aware of ecological problems, they have by no means replaced the traditional political parties, as some political analysts in the mid-1980s forecast. For one thing, the coalitions that made up the Greens found it difficult to agree on all issues and tended to splinter into different cliques. Moreover, traditional political parties have co-opted the environmental issues of the Greens. By 1990, more and more Eu-

◆ **Jackson Pollock Does a Painting.** One of the best-known practitioners of Abstract Expressionism, which remained at the center of the artistic mainstream after World War II, was the American Jackson Pollock, who achieved his ideal of total abstraction in his drip paintings. He is shown here at work in his Long Island studio. Pollock found it easier to cover his large canvases with exploding patterns of color when he put them on the floor.

ropean governments were beginning to sponsor projects to safeguard the environment and clean up the worst sources of pollution.

The World of Western Culture

Intellectually and culturally, the Western world during the last half of the nineteenth century has been marked by much diversity. Although many trends represent a continuation of prewar modern developments, new directions in the last two decades have led some to speak of a postmodern cultural world.

Recent Trends in Art and Literature

For the most part, the United States dominated the art world. American art, often vibrantly colored and filled with activity, reflected the energy and exuberance of postwar America. After 1945, New York City became the artistic center of the Western world. The Guggenheim Museum, the Museum of Modern Art, and the Whitney Museum of American art, together with New York's numerous art galleries, promoted modern art and helped determine artistic tastes not only in New York and the United States, but throughout much of the world.

Abstractionism, especially Abstract Expressionism, emerged as the artistic mainstream. American exuberance in Abstract Expressionism is evident in the enormous canvases of Jackson Pollock (1912–1956). In such works as *Lavender Mist* (1950), paint seems to explode, assaulting the viewer with emotion and movement. Pollock's swirling forms and seemingly chaotic patterns broke all conventions of form and structure. His drip paintings, with their total abstraction, were extremely influential with other artists, although the public was initially quite hostile to his work.

The early 1960s saw the emergence of Pop Art, which took images of popular culture and transformed them into works of fine art. Andy Warhol (1930–1987), who began as an advertising illustrator, was the most famous of the pop artists. Warhol adapted images from commercial art, such as the Campbell soup cans, and photographs of such celebrities as Marilyn Monroe.

In the 1980s, styles emerged that some have referred to as Postmodern. Although as yet ill defined, Postmodernism tends to move away from the futurism or "cutting edge" qualities of Modernism. Instead it favors "utilizing tradition," whether that includes more styles of painting, or elevating traditional craftsmanship to the level of fine art. Weavers, potters, glassmakers, and furniture makers gained respect as artists.

The most significant new trend in postwar literature has been called the "Theater of the Absurd." Its most famous proponent was the Irishman Samuel Beckett (1906–1990), who lived in France. In Beckett's *Waiting for Godot* (1952), two men wait incessantly for the appearance of someone, with whom they may or may not have an appointment. No background information on the two men is provided. During the course of the play, nothing seems to be happening. The audience is never told if the action in front of them is real or unreal. Unlike traditional theater, suspense is maintained not by having the audience wonder "What is going to happen next?," but simply "What is happening now?"

The sense of meaninglessness that inspired the Theater of the Absurd also underscored the philosophy of existentialism of Albert Camus (1913–1960) and Jean-Paul Sartre (1905–1980). The beginning point of the existentialism of Sartre and Camus was the absence of God in the universe. While the death of God was tragic, it meant that humans had no preordained destiny and were utterly alone in the universe with no future and no hope. As Camus expressed it:

> A world that can be explained even with bad reasons is a familiar world. But, on the other hand, in a universe suddenly divested of illusions and lights, man feels an alien, a stranger. His exile is without remedy since he is deprived of the memory of a lost home or the hope of a promised land. This divorce between man and his life, the actor and his setting, is properly the feeling of absurdity.[2]

According to Camus, then, the world was absurd and without meaning; humans, too, are without meaning and purpose. Reduced to despair and depression, humans have but one ground of hope—themselves.

The Revival of Religion

Existentialism was one response to the despair generated by the apparent collapse of civilized values in the twentieth century. The revival of religion has been another. Ever since the Enlightenment of the eighteenth century, Christianity and religion had been on the defensive. But a number of religious thinkers and leaders attempted to bring new life to Christianity in the twentieth century.

One expression of this religious revival was the attempt by such theologians as the Protestant Karl Barth (1886–1968) and the Catholic Karl Rahner (1904–1984) to infuse traditional Christian teachings with new life. In his numerous writings, Barth attempted to reinterpret the religious insights of the Reformation era for the modern world. To Barth, the sinful and hence imperfect nature of human beings meant that humans could know religious truth not through reason, but only through the grace of God. Karl Rahner attempted to revitalize traditional Catholic theology by incorporating aspects of modern thought. He was careful, however, to emphasize the continuity between ancient and modern interpretations of Catholic doctrine.

In the Catholic church, attempts at religious renewal also came from two charismatic popes—John XXIII and John Paul II. Pope John XXIII (1881–1963) reigned as pope for only a short time (1958–1963), but sparked a dramatic revival of Catholicism when he summoned the twenty-first ecumenical council of the Catholic church. Known as Vatican Council II, it liberalized a number of Catholic practices. The mass was henceforth to be celebrated in the vernacular languages rather than Latin.

John Paul II (b. 1920), who had been the archbishop of Cracow in Poland before his elevation to the papacy in 1978, was the first non-Italian to be elected pope since the sixteenth century. Although he reasserted traditional Catholic teaching on such issues as birth control, women in the priesthood, and clerical celibacy, John Paul's numerous travels around the world helped strengthen the Catholic church throughout the non-Western world. A strong believer in social justice, the charismatic John Paul II has been a powerful figure in reminding Europeans of their spiritual heritage and the need to temper the pursuit of materialism with spiritual concerns.

The New World of Science and Technology

Many of the scientific and technological achievements since World War II have revolutionized people's lives. Before World War II, theoretical science and technology were largely separated. Pure science was the domain of university professors who were quite far removed from the practical technological matters of technicians and engineers. But during World War II, university scientists were recruited to work for their governments and develop new weapons and practical instruments of war. British physicists played a crucial role in the development of an improved radar system in 1940 that helped to defeat the German air force in the Battle of Britain. German scientists created self-propelled rockets as well as jet airplanes to keep Hitler's hopes alive for a miraculous turnaround in the war. The computer, too, was a wartime creation. The British mathematician Alan Turing designed a primitive computer to assist British intelligence in breaking the secret codes of German ciphering machines. The most famous product of wartime scientific research was the atomic bomb, created by a team of American and European scientists under the guidance of the physicist

J. Robert Oppenheimer. Obviously, most wartime devices were created for destructive purposes, but merely to mention computers and jet airplanes demonstrates that they could easily be adapted for peacetime uses.

The postwar alliance of science and technology led to an accelerated rate of change that became a fact of life in Western society. One product of this alliance—the computer—may yet prove to be the most revolutionary of all the technological inventions of the twentieth century. Early computers, which required thousands of vacuum tubes to function, were large and took up considerable room space. The development of the transistor and then the silicon chip produced a revolutionary new approach to computers. In 1971, the invention of the microprocessor, a machine that combines the equivalent of thousands of transitors on a single, tiny silicon chip, opened the road for the development of the personal computer.

The computer is a new kind of machine whose chief function is to store and produce information, now considered a fundamental asset of our fast-paced civilization. By the 1990s, the personal computer had become a regular fixture in businesses, schools, and homes. It not only makes a whole host of tasks much easier, but it has also become an important tool in virtually every area of modern life. Indeed, other tools and machines now depend for their functioning on computers. Many of the minute-by-minute decisions required to fly an airplane, for example, are done by a computer.

Despite the marvels that were produced by the alliance of science and technology, the underlying assumption of this alliance—that scientific knowledge gave human beings the ability to manipulate the environment for their benefit—was questioned by some in the 1960s and 1970s who believed that some technological advances had far-reaching side effects damaging to the environment. The chemical fertilizers, for example, that were touted for producing larger crops wreaked havoc with the ecological balance of streams, rivers, and woodlands. *Small Is Beautiful*, written by the British economist E. F. Schumacher (1911–1977), was a fundamental critique of the dangers of the new science and technology (see the box on p. 649). The threat of global warming and the widespread proliferation of dying forests and lakes made environmentalism one of the important issues of the 1990s.

The Explosion of Popular Culture

Since World War II, popular culture has played an increasingly important role in helping Western people define themselves. The history of popular culture is also the history of the economic system that supports it, for it is this system that manufactures, distributes, and sells the images that people consume as popular culture. As popular culture and its economic support system became increasingly intertwined, industries of leisure emerged. As one historian of popular culture has argued, "industrial societies turn the provision of leisure into a commercial activity, in which their citizens are sold entertainment, recreation, pleasure, and appearance as commodities that differ from the goods at the drugstore only in the way they are used."[3] Modern popular culture therefore is inextricably tied to the mass consumer society in which it has emerged.

POPULAR CULTURE AND THE AMERICANIZATION OF THE WORLD

The United States has been the most influential force in shaping popular culture in the West and, to a lesser degree, the entire world. Through movies, music, advertising, and television, the United States has spread its particular form of consumerism and the American Dream to millions around the world. Already in 1923 the New York *Morning Post* noted that "the film is to America what the flag was once to Britain. By its means Uncle Sam may hope some day . . . to Americanize the world."[4] In movies, television, and popular music, the impact of American popular culture on the Western world is apparent.

Motion pictures were the primary vehicle for the diffusion of American popular culture in the years immediately following the war, and they continued to dominate both European and American markets in the next decades. Although developed in the 1930s, television did not become readily available until the late 1940s. By 1954, there were 32 million sets in the United States as television became the centerpiece of middle-class life. In the 1960s, as television spread around the world, American networks unloaded their products on Europe and the Third World at extraordinarily low prices. The United States has also dominated popular music since the end of World War II. Jazz, blues, rhythm and blues, rap, and rock and roll have been by far the most popular music forms in the Western world—and much of the non-Western world—during this time. All of them originated in the United States, and all are rooted in African-American musical innovations. These forms later spread to the rest of the world, inspiring local artists who then transformed the music in their own way.

In the postwar years, sports have become a major product of both popular culture and the leisure industry. The development of satellite television and various electronic breakthroughs helped make sports a global phenomenon.

⇒ Small Is Beautiful: The Limits of Modern Technology ⇐

Although science and technology have produced an amazing array of achievements in the postwar world, some voices have been raised in criticism of their sometimes destructive aspects. In 1975, in his book Small Is Beautiful, *the British economist E. F. Schumacher examined the effects modern industrial technology has had on the earth's resources.*

E. F. Schumacher, *Small Is Beautiful*

Is it not evident that our current methods of production are already eating into the very substance of industrial man? To many people this is not at all evident. Now that we have solved the problem of production, they say, have we ever had it so good? Are we not better fed, better clothed, and better housed than ever before—and better educated? Of course we are: most, but by no means all, of us: in the rich countries. But this is not what I mean by "substance." The substance of man cannot be measured by Gross National Product. Perhaps it cannot be measured at all, except for certain symptoms of loss. However, this is not the place to go into the statistics of these symptoms, such as crime, drug addiction, vandalism, mental breakdown, rebellion, and so forth. Statistics never prove anything.

I started by saying that one of the most fateful errors of our age is the belief that the problem of production has been solved. This illusion, I suggested, is mainly due to our inability to recognize that the modern industrial system, with all its intellectual sophistication, consumes the very basis on which it has been erected. To use the language of the economist, it lives on irreplaceable capital which it cheerfully treats as income. I specified three categories of such capital: fossil fuels, the tolerance margins of nature, and the human substance. Even if some readers should refuse to accept all three parts of my argument, I suggest that any one of them suffices to make my case.

And what is my case? Simply that our most important task is to get off our present collision course. And who is there to tackle such a task? I think every one of us. . . . To talk about the future is useful only if it leads to action *now.* And what can we do *now,* while we are still in the position of "never having had it so good"? To say the least . . . we must thoroughly understand the problem and begin to see the possibility of evolving a new life-style, with new methods of production and new patterns of consumption: a life-style designed for permanence. To give only three preliminary examples: in agriculture and horticulture, we can interest ourselves in the perfection of production methods which are biologically sound, build up soil fertility, and produce health, beauty and permanence. Productivity will then look after itself. In industry, we can interest ourselves in the evolution of small-scale technology, relatively nonviolent technology, "technology with a human face," so that people have a chance to enjoy themselves while they are working, instead of working solely for their pay packet and hoping, usually forlornly, for enjoyment solely during their leisure time.

Olympic games could now be broadcast across the world from anywhere in the world. Sports became a cheap form of entertainment for the consumers as fans did not have to leave their homes to enjoy athletic competitions.

*T*oward a Global Civilization?

Increasingly, more and more people are becoming aware of the political and economic interdependence of the world's nations as well as the global nature of our contemporary problems. On the threshold of the twenty-first century, human beings are coming to understand that destructive forces unleashed in one part of the world soon affect the entire world. Nuclear proliferation makes nuclear war an ever-present possibility; nuclear war would mean radioactive fallout for the entire planet. Smokestack pollution in one nation can produce acid rain in another. Oil spills and dumping of wastes in the ocean have an impact on the shores of many nations. The consumption of drugs in the world's wealthy nations affects the stability of both wealthy and less developed nations. As food, water, energy, and natural resources crises proliferate, solutions by one nation often affect other nations. The new globalism includes the recognition that the challenges that seem to threaten human existence at the beginning of the twenty-first century are global.

As the heirs of Western civilization have become aware that the problems humans face are global—not only national—they have responded to this challenge in different ways. One approach has been to develop grass-roots social movements, including environmental, women's and men's liberation, human potential, appropriate-technology, and nonviolence movements. "Think globally, act locally" is frequently the slogan of these grass-roots groups. Related to the emergence of these social movements is the growth of nongovernmental organizations (NGOs). According to one analyst, NGOs are an important instrument in the cultivation of global perspectives: "Since NGOs by definition are identified with interests that transcend national boundaries, we expect all NGOs to define problems in global terms, to take account of human interests and needs as they are found in all parts of the planet."[5] NGOs are often represented at the United Nations and include professional, business, and cooperative organizations; foundations; religious, peace, and disarmament groups; youth and women's organizations; environmental and human rights groups; and research institutes. The number of international NGOs increased from 176 in 1910 to 18,000 in 1990.

And yet, hopes for global approaches to global problems have also been hindered by political, ethnic, and religious disputes. Pollution of the Rhine River by factories along its banks provokes angry disputes among European nations, while the United States and Canada have argued about the effects of acid rain on Canadian forests. The collapse of the Soviet Union and its satellite system between 1989 and 1991 seemed to provide an enormous boost to the potential for international cooperation on global issues. In fact, the collapse of the Soviet empire has had almost the opposite effect; its disintegration has led to the emergence of squabbling new nations and an atmosphere of conflict and tension throughout much of Eastern Europe. The bloody conflict in the lands of the former Yugoslavia clearly indicates the dangers in the rise of nationalist sentiment among various ethnic and religious groups in Eastern Europe.

Thus, even as the world becomes more global in culture and interdependent in its mutual relations, centrifugal forces are still at work attempting to redefine the political, cultural, and ethnic ways in which the world is divided. Such efforts are often disruptive and can sometimes work against measures to enhance our human destiny.

Many lessons can be learned from the history of Western civilization, but one of them is especially clear. Lack of involvement in the affairs of one's society can lead to a sense of powerlessness. In an age that is often crisis-laden and chaotic, an understanding of our Western heritage and its lessons can be instrumental in helping us create new models for the future. For we are all creators of history and upon us depends the future of Western and indeed world civilization.

◆ **The Beatles in Concert.**
Although rock and roll originated in the United States, it also inspired musical groups in Europe. This was certainly true of Britain's Beatles, who created a sensation among young people when they came to the United States in the 1960s. Here the Beatles are shown during a performance on *The Ed Sullivan Show.*

NOTES

1. Quoted in Marsha Rowe et al., *Spare Rib Reader* (Harmondsworth, 1982), p. 574.
2. Quoted in Henry Grosshans, *The Search for Modern Europe* (Boston, 1970), p. 421.
3. Richard Maltby, ed., *Passing Parade: A History of Popular Culture in the Twentieth Century* (New York, 1989), p. 8.

4. Quoted in ibid., p. 11.
5. Elise Boulding, *Women in the Twentieth Century World* (New York, 1977), p. 186.

SUGGESTIONS FOR FURTHER READING

For general surveys of contemporary European history, see the references in Chapter 29. General studies on the Cold War are also listed in Chapter 29. There is a detailed analysis of American-Soviet relations in the 1970s and 1980s in R. Garthoff, *Détente and Confrontation: American-Soviet Relations from Nixon to Reagan* (Washington, D.C., 1985). On the end of the Cold War, see B. Denitch, *The End of the Cold War* (Minneapolis, Minn., 1990) and W. G. Hyland, *The Cold War Is Over* (New York, 1990).

Recent problems in the Soviet Union are analyzed in M. Lewin, *The Gorbachev Phenomenon* (Berkeley, Calif., 1988); G. Hosking, *The Awakening of the Soviet Union* (London, 1990); and S. White, *Gorbachev and After* (Cambridge, 1991). For general studies of the Soviet satellites in Eastern Europe, see S. Fischer-Galati, *Eastern Europe in the 1980s* (London, 1981); and the references in Chapter 29. Additional studies on the recent history of these countries include T. G. Ash, *The Polish Revolution: Solidarity* (New York, 1984); B. Kovrig, *Communism in Hungary from Kun to Kadar* (Stanford, Calif., 1979); T. G. Ash, *The Magic Lantern: The Revolution of '89 Witnessed in Warsaw, Budapest, Berlin and Prague* (New York, 1990); M. Shafir, *Romania: Politics, Economics and Society* (London, 1985); and S. Ramet, *Nationalism and Federalism in Yugoslavia* (Bloomington, Ind., 1992).

For general works on Western Europe and individual countries, see the references in Chapter 29. On the recent history of these countries, see E. J. Evans, *Thatcher and Thatcherism* (New York, 1997); S. Baumann-Reynolds, *Francois Mitterrand* (Westport, Conn., 1995); R. J. Dalton, *Politics in West Germany* (Glenview, Ill., 1989); and K. Jarausch, *The Rush to German Unity* (New York, 1994).

The changing role of women is examined in A. Cherlin, *Marriage, Divorce, Remarriage* (Cambridge, Mass., 1981). On the women's liberation movement, see

D. Bouchier, *The Feminist Challenge: The Movement for Women's Liberation in Britain and the United States* (New York, 1983). More general works that include much information on the contemporary period are B. S. Anderson and J. P. Zinsser, *A History of Their Own*, vol. 2 (New York, 1988); and B. G. Smith, *Changing Lives: Women in European History since 1700* (Lexington, Mass., 1989). On terrorism, see the works by W. Laqueur, *Terrorism*, 2d ed. (New York and London, 1988); and R. Rubenstein, *Alchemists of Revolution: Terrorism in the Modern World* (London, 1987). On the development of the Green parties, see M. O'Neill, *Green Parties and Political Change in Contemporary Europe* (Aldershot, 1997).

For a general view of postwar thought, see R. N. Stromberg, *European Intellectual History since 1789*, 5th ed. (Englewood Cliffs, N.J. 1990). On contemporary art, see R. Lambert, *Cambridge Introduction to the History of Art: The Twentieth Century* (Cambridge, 1981); and the general work by B. Cole and A. Gealt, *Art of the Western World* (New York, 1989). A physicist's view of science is contained in J. Ziman, *The Force of Knowledge: The Scientific Dimension of Society* (Cambridge, 1976). A classic work on existentialism is W. Barrett, *Irrational Man* (Garden City, N.Y., 1962). There is an excellent survey of twentieth-century popular culture in R. Maltby, ed., *Passing Parade: A History of Popular Culture in the Twentieth Century* (Oxford, 1989). On film and the media, see L. May, *Screening Out the Past: The Birth of Mass Culture and the Motion Picture Industry* (New York, 1980); and F. Wheen, *Television* (London, 1985). On popular music, see P. Eberly, *Music in the Air* (New York, 1982). Sport is examined in A. Guttmann, *From Ritual to Record: The Nature of Modern Sports* (New York, 1978); and R. Mandell, *Sport: A Cultural History* (New York, 1984).

Index

A

Abbasid dynasty, 170–72
Abraham, 28
Absolutism/absolute monarchy, 326–27
  in central/eastern Europe
    in eighteenth century, 390–94
    in seventeenth century, 332–37
  enlightened, 387–88, 394
  France as example of, 327–31
  limits of, 337–42
  Spain, decline of, 331–32
Abstractionism, 646
Abstract Expressionism, 646
Abu Bakr, 150, 151
Achaemenid dynasty, 38
Acheson, Dean, 606
Achilles, 48, 49, 72
Acropolis, 49, 55, 60
Actium, battle of, 101–2, 110
Address to the Nobility of the German Nation
  (Luther), 286
Adenauer, Konrad, 619, 620
Adoration of the Magi (Dürer), 273
Adrianople, battle of, 126
Adrianople, treaty of, 452
Aegean Sea, 45, 48, 55
Aegospotami, battle of, 56
Aelius Spartianus, 106
Aeneid (Virgil), 115
Aeolian Greeks, 48
Aequi, 89
Aeschylus, 57–58
Afghanistan, 28, 528
  Soviet invasion of, 629
Africa
  decolonization of, 613
  imperialism in, 525–28
  north
    Byzantines reconquer from Vandals, 144
    Carthage, 34, 91–92, 93, 94
    Muslims, 151, 152
    Romans, 91, 92
    Vandals, 126, 131
    World War II theater, 585, 587
  slave trade and, 402
Agamemnon, 47, 48, 58
Agincourt, battle of, 245

Agricultural Revolution, 5–6
Agriculture, 2. *See also* Agricultural Revolution
  ancient Near East
    Assyrian, 36
    beginnings, 5–6
    Egyptian, 17, 18
    Mesopotamian, 10
  classical Athens, 63
  collective farms in Soviet Union, 571, 572
  Early Middle Ages, 168
    manorialism, origins of, 166–67
  Hellenistic, 75
  High Middle Ages, 177–81
  improvements in eighteenth century, 431
  in Neolithic Europe, 27
  in nineteenth century, 497
  revolutions in, 5–6, 431
  Roman, 114
Agrippina, 117
Ahriman, 42
Ahuramazda, 40, 41, 42, 120
Airplane, 492
Akhenaten, pharaoh, 21
Akhetaton (Egypt), 21
Akkad/Akkadians, 9
Alaric (Visigoth), 126, 131
Alba Madonna (Raphael), 271–72
Albania, 608, 616
Albert (husband of Queen Victoria), 479
Alberti, Leon Battista, 258
Albigensians. *See* Catharism
Alemanni, 130
Alexander II, tsar, 477–79, 509
Alexander III, tsar, 479, 509
Alexander VI, pope, 279
Alexander the Great, 21, 30, 68, 69–73
Alexandra (wife of Nicholas II), 524, 547
Alexandria (Egypt)
  Christian, 136
  Hellenistic, 70, 74, 75, 77, 78, 79, 81, 82
  Roman, 112
Alexis (son of Nicholas II), 547
Alexius I, Byzantine emperor, 218, 220, 222
Alfonso X, Spanish king, 209
Alfred the Great, king of Wessex, 201
Algeria, 526
  independence from France, 613, 618, 619

Ali (son-in-law of Muhammad), 151, 152
Allah, 148–49, 150. *See also* Islam
All Quiet on the Western Front (Remarque), 544
Alsace, 474, 553
Ambrose of Milan, 143
Amenhotep IV, 21
American Civil War, 540
American Federation of Labor, 524
American Revolution, 409–12
Amon, 18
Amon-Re, 18, 21
Amores (Ovid), 115
Amorites, 9. *See also* Old Babylonians
Amos, 32, 33
Amsterdam (Netherlands), 502
An, 12
Anabaptism, 291, 293
Anatolia, 28, 218
Anchises of Troy, 115
Andersen, Hans Christian, 463
Andromache, 49
Angles, 134, 140. *See also* England, Anglo-Saxon
Anglican church, 339
Angola, 526
Annals of Imperial Rome (Tacitus), 116
Antapodosis (Liudprand of Cremona), 168
Anthony, saint, 138
Aniballistic Missiles (ABM) Treaty, 629
Antigone (Sophocles), 58
Antigonid dynasty, 73
Antioch, 112
  Christian, 136
  crusades and, 216, 220, 221
Antiochus IV, Seleucid king, 81–82
Anti-Semitism. *See also* Jews
  Dreyfus affair, 521
  Hitler and, 566, 570, 590
  Holocaust and, 592–95
  in nineteenth and early twentieth
    centuries, 516
  in Vienna, 566
Antony, Mark, 99, 101, 102
Aphrodite, 62
Apollo, 58, 62, 63
Aquinas, Thomas, 190–91, 228, 229
Arabic language, 172
Arabs. *See also* Islam; Muslims; *specific dynasties*

Photo Credits

CHAPTER 1

1 © Will and Deni McIntyre/Photo Researchers, Inc.; **5** © Francois Ducasse/Photo Researchers, Inc.; **7** Reproduced by Courtesy of the Trustees of the British Museum; **11** Babylonian, *Stele of Hammurabi*, Musee du Louvre, © Photo R.M.N.; **13** Samuel Kramer, *The Sumerians*, Univ. of Chicago Press, 1963, © Univ. of Chicago Press; **17** Pair Statue of King Mycerinus and His Queen; From Giza, Dynasty IV, 2599-1571 BC, Slate Schist, 54 1/2 in. Harvard MFA Expedition. Courtesy Museum of Fine Arts, Boston; **20** © Will and Deni McIntyre/Photo Researchers, Inc.; **22** Erich Lessing/Art Resource, NY

CHAPTER 2

26 British Museum, London; **28** © Adam Woolfitt/Robert Harding Picture Library; **30** British Museum, London; **31** Ronald Sheridan/Ancient Art and Architecture; **37** Reproduced by Courtesy of the Trustees of the British Museum; **40** © G. Dagli Orti

CHAPTER 3

44 © Michael Holford, London; **46** © Dimitrios Harissiadis, Athens; **50** Scala/Art Resource, NY; **60** © Michael Holford, London; **61** Scala/Art Resource, NY; **65** The Metropolitan Museum of Art, Fletcher Fund, 1931 (31.11.10). Photograph © 1971 The Metropolitan Museum of Art

CHAPTER 4

68 Bust of Alexander, Musee du Louvre, © Photo R.M.N.; **70** Bust of Alexander, Musee du Louvre, © Photo R.M.N.; **71** Scala/Art Resource, NY; **75** Giraudon/Art Resource, NY; **77** The Metropolitan Museum of Art, Rogers Fund, 1920 (20.2.21). Photograph © 1986 The Metropolitan Museum of Art; **79** The Metropolitan Museum of Art, Rogers Fund, 1909 (09.39); **82** © Leonard von Matt/Photo Researchers, Inc.

CHAPTER 5

84 British Museum, Photo © Michael Holford, London; **87** Art Resource, NY; **88** Alinari/Art Resource, NY; **92** British Museum, Photo © Michael Holford, London; **95** Scala/Art Resource, NY; **96** The Metropolitan Museum of Art, Rogers Fund, 1903 (03.14.5). Photograph © 1978 The Metropolitan Museum of Art; **101** Scala/Art Resource, NY

CHAPTER 6

106 British Museum, London; **108** Photo Vatican Museums; **111** British Museum, London; **113** Photo Eberhard Thiem, Lotos-Film, Kaufbeuren, Germany; **120** © Roger Wood, London/Corbis; **121** Scala/Art Resource, NY; **124** Scala/Art Resource, NY

CHAPTER 7

130 Bibliotheque Nationale, Paris, Ms. Nouv. Acq. Fr. 1098; **134** Bibliotheque Nationale, Paris, Ms. Nouv. Acq. Fr. 1098; **138** Kunsthistorisches Museum, Vienna; **140** Vat. Lat. 1202F.80r, Foto Biblioteca Vaticana; **145** Scala/Art Resource, NY; **147** © Erich Lessing/Art Resource, NY; **150** Bibliotheque Nationale, Paris

CHAPTER 8

154 The Granger Collection; **159** The Granger Collection; **160** © J. L. Charmet. From Chroniques de Saint-Denis. XV Eme, MS2028, Bibliotheque Mazarine; **164** The Pierpont Morgan Library/ Art Resource, NY. M.736, f.9v; **165** Leiden, University Library, BPL20, f.60r; **167** E.T. Archive, London, from the Collections of the British Library, Psalter, Calendar, c1250-1260; **173** Scala/Art Resource, NY

CHAPTER 9

176 The Pierpont Morgan Library/ Art Resource, NY. MS399, f.5v, c.1515, Bruges; **178** SC12053 Add 18855 October: Ploughing and Sowing, Book of Hours, c.1540, by Simon Bening (1483-1561), Victoria & Albert Museum, London, UK/Bridgeman Art Library, London/New York; **180** The Pierpont Morgan Library/ Art Resource, NY. MS399, f.5v, c.1515, Bruges; **186** Giraudon/Art Resource, NY; **187** © Bibliotheque Royale Albert ler (Ms IV 119, fol. 72 verso); **188** Bibliotheque Nationale, Paris; **190** BL53185 Cott Nero E II pt2 f.20v, The Expulsion of the Albigensians from Carcasonne: Catherist Heretics of the 12th and 13th Centuries, from 'The Chronicles of France, from Priam King of Troy until the Crowning of Charles VI' by the Boucicaut Master and Workshop, Chronicles of France, 1388, British Library, London, UK/Bridgeman Art Library, London/New York

CHAPTER 10

194 Bibliotheque Nationale, Paris; **197** © Wysocki/Explorer/ Photo Researchers, Inc.; **199** Bibliotheque Nationale, Paris;